MW00643594

LESS THAN NOTHING

LESS THAN NOTHING

HEGEL AND THE SHADOW OF DIALECTICAL MATERIALISM

SLAVOJ ŽIŽEK

VERSO
London • New York

First published by Verso 2012

1 3 5 7 9 10 8 6 4 2

Verso
UK: 6 Meard Street, London W1F 0EG
US: 20 Jay Street, Suite 1010, Brooklyn, NY 11201
www.versobooks.com

Verso is the imprint of New Left Books

ISBN-13: 978-1-84467-897-6

British Library Cataloguing in Publication Data
A catalogue record for this book is available from the British Library

Library of Congress Cataloging-in-Publication Data
/ıek, Slavoj.
Less than nothing : Hegel and the shadow of dialectical materialism / by Slavoj /ıek.
p. cm.
Includes index.
ISBN 978-1-84467-897-6 -- ISBN 978-1-84467-889-1 (ebook)
1. Hegel, Georg Wilhelm Friedrich, 1770-1831. I. Title.
B2948.Z55 2012
193--dc23
2011050465

Typeset in Minion Pro by MJ Gavan, Cornwall, UK
Printed by in the US by Maple Vail

To Alenka and Maden—because die Partei hat immer Recht.

Contents

PART IV. THE CIGARETTE AFTER

Introduction: *Eppur Si Muove*

There are two opposed types of stupidity. The first is the (occasionally) hyper-intelligent subject who just doesn't "get it," who understands a situation logically, but simply misses its hidden contextual rules. For example, when I first visited New York, a waiter at a café asked me: "How was your day?" Mistaking the phrase for a genuine question, I answered him truthfully ("I am dead tired, jet-lagged, stressed out …"), and he looked at me as if I were a complete idiot … and he was right: this kind of stupidity is precisely that of an idiot. Alan Turing was an exemplary idiot: a man of extraordinary intelligence, but a proto-psychotic unable to process implicit contextual rules. In literature, one cannot avoid recalling Jaroslav Hašek's good soldier Švejk, who, when he saw soldiers shooting from their trenches at the enemy soldiers, ran into no-man's land and started to shout: "Stop shooting, there are people on the other side!" The arch-model of this idiocy is, however, the naïve child from Andersen's tale who publicly exclaims that the emperor is naked—thereby missing the point that, as Alphonse Allais put it, we are all naked beneath our clothes.

The second and opposite figure of stupidity is that of the moron: the stupidity of those who fully identify with common sense, who fully stand for the "big Other" of appearances. In the long series of figures beginning with the Chorus in Greek tragedy—which plays the role of canned laughter or crying, always ready to comment on the action with some common wisdom—one should mention at least the "stupid" common-sense partners of the great detectives: Sherlock Holmes's Watson, Hercule Poirot's Hastings … These figures are there not only to serve as a contrast to and thus make more visible the detective's grandeur; they are indispensable for the detective's work. In one of the novels, Poirot explains to Hastings his role: immersed in his common sense, Hastings reacts to the crime scene the way the murderer who wanted to erase the traces of his act expected the public to react, and it is only in this way, by including in his analysis the expected reaction of the common-sense "big Other," that the detective can solve the crime.

But does this opposition cover the entire field? Where, for instance, are we to put Franz Kafka, whose greatness resides (among other things) in his unique ability to present idiocy as something entirely normal and conventional? (Recall the extravagantly "idiotic" reasoning in the long debate between the priest and Josef K. which follows the parable "Before the Law.") For this third position, we need look no further than the Wikipedia entry for "imbecile": "Imbecile is a term for moderate to severe mental retardation, as well as for a type of criminal. It arises from the Latin word *imbecillus*, meaning weak, or weak-minded. 'Imbecile' was once applied to people with an IQ of 26–50, between 'moron' (IQ of 51–70) and 'idiot' (IQ 0–25)." So it is not too bad: beneath a moron, but ahead of an idiot—the situation is catastrophic, but not serious, as (who else?) an Austrian imbecile would have put it. Problems begin with the question: where does the root "becile" preceded by the negation ("im-") come from? Although the origins are murky, it is probably derived from the Latin *baculum* (stick, walking stick, staff), so an "imbecile" is someone walking around without the help of a stick. One can bring some clarity and logic into the issue if one conceives of the stick on which we all, as speaking beings, have to lean, as language, the symbolic order, that is, what Lacan calls the "big Other." In this case, the tripartite idiot-imbecile-moron makes sense: the idiot is simply alone, outside the big Other, the moron is within it (dwelling in language in a stupid way), while the imbecile is in between the two—aware of the need for the big Other, but not relying on it, distrusting it, something like the way the Slovene punk group Laibach defined their relationship towards God (and referring to the words on a dollar bill "In God we trust"): "Like Americans, we believe in God, but unlike Americans, we don't trust him." In Lacanese, an imbecile is aware that the big Other does not exist, that it is inconsistent, "barred." So if, measured by the IQ scale, the moron appears brighter than the imbecile, he is too bright for his own good (as reactionary morons, but not imbeciles, like to say about intellectuals). Among the philosophers, the late Wittgenstein is an imbecile *par excellence*, obsessively dealing with variations of the question of the big Other: is there an agency which guarantees the consistency of our speech? Can we reach certainty about the rules of our speech?

Does not Lacan aim at the same position of the (im)becile when he concludes his "Vers un signifiant nouveau" with: "I am only relatively stupid—that is to say, I am as stupid as all people—perhaps because I got a little bit enlightened"?[1] One should read this relativization of stupidity—"not totally stupid"—in the strict sense of non-All: the point is not that Lacan has some specific insights which make him not entirely stupid. There is nothing in Lacan which is not stupid, no exception to stupidity, so that what makes him not totally stupid is only *the very inconsistency of his stupidity*. The name of this stupidity in which all people participate is, of course, the big Other. In a conversation with Edgar Snow in the early 1970s, Mao Zedong characterized himself as a hairless monk with an umbrella. Holding an umbrella hints at the separation from heaven, and, in Chinese, the character for "hair" also designates law and heaven, so that what Mao is saying is that—in Lacanese—he is subtracted from the dimension of the

1 Jacques Lacan, "Vers un signifiant nouveau," *Ornicar* 17–18 (1979), p. 23.

big Other, the heavenly order which regulates the normal run of things. What makes this self-designation paradoxical is that Mao still designates himself as a monk (a monk is usually perceived as someone who, precisely, dedicates his life to heaven)—so how can one be a monk subtracted from heaven? This "imbecility" is the core of the subjective position of a radical revolutionary (and of the analyst).

The present book is thus neither *The Complete Idiot's Guide to Hegel*, nor is it yet another university textbook on Hegel (which would be for morons, of course); it is something like *The Imbecile's Guide to Hegel*—Hegel for those whose IQ is somewhere close to their bodily temperature (in Celsius), as the insult goes. But only something like it: the problem with "imbeciles" is that none of us, as ordinary speakers, knows what the "im" negates: we know what "imbecile" means, but we don't know what "becile" is—we simply suspect that it must somehow be the opposite of "imbecile."[2] But what if, here too, persists the mysterious tendency for antonyms (such as *heimlich* and *unheimlich*—about which Freud wrote a famous short text) to mean the same thing? What if "becile" is the same as "imbecile," only with an additional twist? In our daily use, "becile" does not stand on its own, it functions as a negation of "imbecile," so that, insofar as "imbecile" already is a negation of a kind, "becile" must be a negation of negation—but, and this is crucial, this double negation does not bring us back to some primordial positivity. If an "imbecile" is one who lacks a substantial basis in the big Other, a "becile" redoubles the lack, transposing it into the Other itself. The becile is a not-imbecile, aware that if he is an imbecile, God himself also has to be one.

So what does a becile know that idiots and morons don't? The legend has it that, in 1633, Galileo Galilei muttered, "*Eppur si muove*" ("And yet it moves"), after recanting before the Inquisition his theory that the Earth moves around the Sun: he was not tortured, it was enough to take him on a tour and show him the torture devices ... There is no contemporary evidence that he did in fact mutter this phrase, but today the phrase is used to indicate that, although someone who possesses true knowledge is forced to renounce it, this does not stop it from being true. But what makes this phrase so interesting is that it can also be used in the exact opposite sense, to assert a "deeper" symbolic truth about something which is literally not true—like the "*Eppur si muove*" story itself, which may well be false as a historical fact about Galileo's life, but is true as a designation of Galileo's subjective position while he was forced to renounce his views. In this sense, a materialist can say that, although he knows there is no God, the idea of a God nonetheless "moves" him. It is interesting to note that, in "Terma," an episode from the fourth season of *The X-Files*, "E pur si muove" replaces the usual "The truth is out there," meaning that, even if their existence

2 See Alain Badiou, *Le fini et l'infini*, Paris: Bayard 2010, p. 10.

is denied by official science, alien monsters nonetheless move around out there. But it can also mean that, even if there are no aliens out there, the fiction of an alien invasion (like the one in *The X-Files*) can nonetheless engage us and move us: beyond the fiction of reality, there is the reality of the fiction.[3]

Less Than Nothing endeavors to draw all the ontological consequences from this *eppur si muove*. Here is the formula at its most elementary: "moving" is the striving to reach the void, namely, "things move," there is something instead of nothing, not because reality is in excess in comparison with mere nothing, but because reality is *less than nothing*. This is why reality has to be supplemented by fiction: to conceal its emptiness. Recall the old Jewish joke, loved by Derrida, about a group of Jews in a synagogue, publicly admitting their nullity in the eyes of God. First, a rabbi stands up and says: "O, God, I know I am worthless, I am nothing!" After he has finished, a rich businessman stands up and says, beating himself on the chest: "O, God, I am also worthless, obsessed with material wealth, I am nothing!" After this spectacle, an ordinary poor Jew also stands up and proclaims: "O, God, I am nothing ..." The rich businessman kicks the rabbi and whispers in his ear with scorn: "What insolence! Who is that guy who dares to claim that he too is nothing!" Effectively, one already has to be something in order to be able to achieve pure nothingness, and *Less Than Nothing* discerns this weird logic in the most disparate ontological domains, on different levels, from quantum physics to psychoanalysis.

This weird logic, the logic of what Freud called the *drive*, is perfectly rendered in the hypothesis of the "Higgs field," widely discussed in contemporary particle physics. Left to their own devices in an environment in which they can pass on their energy, all physical systems will eventually assume a state of lowest energy; to put it another way, the more mass we take from a system, the more we lower its energy, until we reach the vacuum state of zero energy. There are, however, phenomena which compel us to posit the hypothesis that there has to be something (some substance) that we cannot take away from a given system without *raising* that system's energy. This "something" is called the Higgs field: once this field *appears* in a vessel that has been pumped empty and whose temperature has been lowered as much as possible, its energy will be further *lowered*. The "something" which thus appears is a something that contains *less* energy than nothing, a "something" that is characterized by an overall negative energy—in short, what we get here is the physical version of how "something appears out of nothing."

3 Freud's own *eppur si muove* was the saying of his teacher Charcot which Freud often repeated: "*La théorie, c'est bon, mais ça n'empêche pas d'exister*" ("Theory is good, but it doesn't prevent [facts which do not fit it] from existing"), and it goes without saying that the same ambiguity holds for this version, i.e., that it should not be reduced to simple empiricism.

Eppur si muove should thus be read in contrast to many versions of the extinction/overcoming of the drive, from the Buddhist notion of gaining a distance towards desire up to the Heideggerian "going-through" Will which forms the core of subjectivity. This book tries to demonstrate that the Freudian drive cannot be reduced to what Buddhism denounces as desire or to what Heidegger denounces as the Will: even after we reach the end of this critical overcoming of desire-will-subjectivity, something continues to move. What survives death is the Holy Spirit sustained by an obscene "partial object" that stands for the indestructible drive. One should thus (also) invert Elisabeth Kübler-Ross's five stages of how we relate to the proximity of death in the Kierkegaardian sense of the "sickness unto death," as the series of five attitudes towards the unbearable fact of immortality. One first denies it: "What immortality? After my death, I will just dissolve into dust!" Then, one explodes into anger: "What a terrible predicament I'm in! No way out!" One continues to bargain: "OK, but it is not me who is immortal, only the undead part of me, so one can live with it ..." Then one falls into depression: "What can I do with myself when I am condemned to stay here forever?" Finally, one accepts the burden of immortality.

So why do we focus on Hegel? In the history of philosophy (or Western philosophy, which amounts to the same thing), this *eppur si muove* arrived at its most consistent formulation in German Idealism, especially in Hegel's thought. Since, however, the axiom of this book is that "One divides into two," the central body of the book is split into a part on Hegel and a part on Lacan as a repetition of Hegel. In each case, the book follows the same systematic four-step approach. With Hegel, we begin with the obvious historical question: in what meaningful sense can one still be a Hegelian today, bearing in mind the radically changed historical constellation? Then comes a description of the basic mechanisms or formulae of the dialectical process, followed by the more detailed explication of Hegel's basic thesis on the Absolute as not only Substance, but also Subject; finally, we raise the difficult non-trivial question of the limitations of the Hegelian project. With Lacan, and bearing in mind that Lacan's theory is here interpreted as a repetition of Hegel, the first step is the presentation of Lacan's (explicit and implicit) references to Hegel, that is, of Lacan as a reader of Hegel. What follows is the presentation of suture as the elementary mechanism of the signifying process, the mechanism which enables us to understand Lacan's definition of the signifier as "that which represents the subject for another signifier." The next logical step is to examine the object generated by the signifying process, the Lacanian *objet a* in all its dimensions. Finally, Lacan's notion of sexual difference and his logic of non-All are submitted to a close reading which uncovers the ultimate limitation and deadlock of Lacanian theory.

It was said (in the old days before smoking became stigmatized) that the second and the third most pleasurable things in the world were the drink before and the cigarette after. Accordingly, apart from the Hegelian Thing, *Less Than Nothing* also deals with a series of befores (Plato, Christianity, Fichte) and afters (Badiou, Heidegger, quantum physics). Plato's *Parmenides* deserves a close reading as the first exercise in dialectics proper, celebrated by Hegel and Lacan. Since Hegel was *the* philosopher of Christianity, it is no wonder that a Hegelian approach to Christ's death brings out a radical emancipatory potential. Fichte's thought is enjoying a deserved comeback: although he sometimes appears to be just one step from Hegel, their universes are thoroughly different, since the way Fichte articulates the relationship between the I and its Other reaches well beyond so-called "subjective idealism." Alain Badiou's attempt to overcome Lacan's antiphilosophy confronts us with the basic question of the possibility of ontology today. Reading Heidegger against the grain, one discovers a thinker who was, at some points, strangely close to communism. The philosophical implications and consequences of quantum physics are still unexplored—what if, beyond the false alternative of pragmatism ("it works, who cares what it means philosophically") and New Age obscurantism, a Hegelian reading opens up the path for a new materialist interpretation?

On top of this, six interludes are inserted between the chapters of the two central parts, dealing with the reverberations of these philosophical topics in literature, art, science, and ideology, as well as in the work of philosophers opposed to the Hegel/Lacan axis. Three additional topics are elaborated apropos of Hegel: the ambiguities of Marx's references to Hegel; the unique status of madness in Hegel's theory of mind; the multiple points at which Hegel's system generates an excess which threatens to explode its framework (rabble, sexuality, marriage). With regard to Lacan, the first interlude deals with the retroactivity of the signifying process; the second one opposes Lacan's anti-correlationism to Quentin Meillassoux's recent critique of post-Kantian correlationism; the third one explores the limitations of the notion of the subject at work in the cognitive sciences. Finally, the conclusion elaborates the political implications of Lacan's repetition of Hegel.

But how does this reference to Hegel fit our own historical moment? There are four main positions which, together, constitute today's ideologico-philosophical field: first, the two sides of what Badiou appropriately baptized "democratic materialism": (1) scientific naturalism (brain sciences, Darwinism ...), and (2) discursive historicism (Foucault, deconstruction ...); then, the two sides of the spiritualist reaction to it: (3) New Age "Western Buddhism," and (4) the thought of transcendental finitude (culminating in Heidegger). These four positions form a kind of Greimasian square along the two axes of ahistorical versus historical thought and of materialism versus spiritualism. The thesis of the present book is double: (1) there is a dimension missed by all four, that of a pre-transcendental gap/rupture, the Freudian name for which is the drive; (2) this dimension designates the very core of modern subjectivity.

The basic premise of discursive materialism was to conceive language itself as a mode of production, and to apply to it Marx's logic of commodity fetishism. So, in the same way that, for Marx, the sphere of exchange obliterates (renders invisible) its process of production, the linguistic exchange also obliterates the textual process that engenders meaning: in a spontaneous fetishistic misperception, we experience the meaning of a word or act as something that is a direct property of the designated thing or process; that is, we overlook the complex field of discursive practices which produces this meaning. What one should focus on here is the fundamental ambiguity of this notion of linguistic fetishism: is the idea that, in the good old modern way, we should distinguish between "objective" properties of things and our projections of meanings onto things, or are we dealing with the more radical linguistic version of transcendental constitution, for which the very idea of "objective reality," of "things existing out there, independently of our mind," is a "fetishistic illusion" which is blind to how our symbolic activity ontologically constitutes the very reality to which it "refers" or which it designates? Neither of these two options is correct—what one should drop is their underlying shared premise, the (crude, abstract-universal) homology between discursive "production" and material production.[4]

Kafka was (as always) right when he wrote: "One means that Evil has is the dialogue." Consequently, this book is not a dialogue, since the underlying premise that sustains its double thesis is unashamedly Hegelian: what we refer to as the continent of "philosophy" can be considered as extending as much as one wants into the past or into the future, but there is a unique philosophical moment in which philosophy appears "as such" and which serves as a key—as the *only* key—to reading the entire preceding and following tradition as philosophy (in the same way that Marx claims that the bourgeoisie is the first class in the history of humanity which is posited as such, as a class, so that it is only with the rise of capitalism that the entirety of history hitherto becomes readable as the history of class struggle). This moment is the moment of German

4 This "discursive materialism" relies on the so-called "linguistic turn" in philosophy which emphasizes how language is not a neutral medium of designation, but a practice embedded in a life world: we do things with it, accomplish specific acts … Is it not time to turn this cliché around: who *is* it that, today, claims that language is a neutral medium of designation? So, perhaps one should emphasize how language is not a mere moment of the life world, a practice within it: the true miracle of language is that it can *also* serve as a neutral medium which just designates a conceptual/ideal content. In other words, the true task is not to locate language as a neutral medium within a life-world practice, but to show how, within this life world, a neutral medium of designation can nonetheless emerge.

Idealism delimited by two dates: 1787, the year in which Kant's *Critique of Pure Reason* appeared, and 1831, the year of Hegel's death. These few decades represent a breathtaking concentration of the intensity of thinking: in this short span of time, more happened than in centuries or even millennia of the "normal" development of human thought. All that took place before can and should be read in an unashamedly anachronistic way as the preparation for this explosion, and all that took place in its aftermath can and should be read as precisely this—the aftermath of interpretations, reversals, critical (mis)readings, of German Idealism.

In his rejection of philosophy, Freud quoted Heinrich Heine's ironic description of the Hegelian philosopher: "With his nightcap and his night-shirt tatters, he botches up the loopholes in the structure of the world." (The nightcap and night-shirt are, of course, ironic references to the well-known portrait of Hegel.) But is philosophy at its most fundamental really reducible to a desperate attempt to fill in the gaps and inconsistencies in our notion of reality and thus to provide a harmonious *Weltanschauung*? Is philosophy really a more developed form of the *sekundäre Bearbeitung* in the formation of a dream, of the effort to harmonize the elements of a dream into a consistent narrative? One can say that, at least with Kant's transcendental turn, the exact opposite happens: does Kant not fully expose a crack, a series of irreparable antinomies, which emerges the moment we want to conceive reality as All? And does not Hegel, instead of overcoming this crack, radicalize it? Hegel's reproach to Kant is that he is too gentle with things: he locates antinomies in the limitation of our reason, instead of locating them in things themselves, that is, instead of conceiving reality-in-itself as cracked and antinomic. It is true that one finds in Hegel a systematic drive to cover everything, to propose an account of all phenomena in the universe in their essential structure; but this drive does not mean that Hegel strives to locate every phenomenon within a harmonious global edifice; on the contrary, the point of dialectical analysis is to demonstrate how every phenomenon, everything that happens, fails in its own way, implies a crack, antagonism, imbalance, in its very heart. Hegel's gaze upon reality is that of a Roentgen apparatus which sees in everything that is alive the traces of its future death.

The basic coordinates of this time of the unbearable density of thought are provided by the mother of all Gangs of Four: Kant, Fichte, Schelling, Hegel.[5]

5 I, of course, fully endorse the results of the new research which demonstrated conclusively not only that there is no simple linear progression in the order of succession of these four names—Fichte and Hegel clearly "misunderstood" Kant in their critique, Schelling misunderstood Fichte, Hegel was totally blind to what is arguably Schelling's greatest achievement, his treatise of human freedom—but also that, often, one cannot even directly pass from one name to another: Dieter Henrich showed how, in order to grasp the inner logic of the passage from Kant to Fichte, one should take into account

Although each of these four names stands for a "world of its own," for a unique radical philosophical stance, one can arrange the series of the four great German Idealists precisely with reference to the four "conditions" of philosophy elaborated by Badiou: Kant relates to (Newtonian) science, his basic question being what kind of philosophy is adequate to the Newtonian breakthrough; Fichte relates to politics, to the event that is the French Revolution; Schelling relates to (Romantic) art and explicitly subordinates philosophy to art as the highest approach to the Absolute; and Hegel, finally, relates to love; his underlying problem is, from the very beginning of his thought, that of love.

It all begins with Kant, with his idea of the *transcendental constitution of reality*. In a way, one can claim that it is only with this idea of Kant's that philosophy reached its own terrain: prior to Kant, philosophy was ultimately perceived as a general science of Being as such, as a description of the universal structure of entire reality, with no qualitative difference from particular sciences. It was Kant who introduced the difference between ontic reality and its ontological horizon, the *a priori* network of categories which determines how we understand reality, what appears to us as reality. From here, previous philosophy is readable not as the most general positive knowledge of reality, but in its hermeneutic core, as the description of the historically predominant "disclosure of Being," as Heidegger would have put it. (Say, when Aristotle, in his *Physics*, struggles to define life and proposes a series of definitions—a living being is a thing which is moved by itself, which has in itself the cause of its movement—he is not really exploring the reality of living beings; he is rather describing the set of pre-existing notions which determine what we always-already understand by "living being" when we designate an object as "alive.")

The most appropriate way to grasp the radical character of the Kantian philosophical revolution is with regard to the difference between *Schein* (appearance as illusion) and *Erscheinung* (appearance as phenomenon). In pre-Kantian philosophy, appearance was conceived as the illusory (defective) mode in which things appear to us, finite mortals; our task is to reach beyond these false appearances to the way things really are (from Plato's Ideas to scientific "objective reality"). With Kant, however, appearance loses this pejorative characteristic: it designates the way things appear (are) to us in what we perceive as reality, and the task is not to denounce them as "mere illusory appearances" and to reach over them to transcendent reality, but an entirely different one, that of discerning the *conditions of possibility of this appearing of things*, of their "transcendental genesis": what does such an appearing presuppose, what must always-already have taken place for things to appear to us the way they do? If, for Plato, a table that I see in front of me is a defective/imperfect copy of the

Kant's first critical followers, Reinhold, Jacobi, and Schulze, in other words, how Fichte's early system can only be properly understood as a reaction to these early critics of Kant.

eternal Idea of the table, for Kant, it would have been meaningless to say that the table I see is a defective temporal/material copy of its transcendental conditions. Even if we take a transcendental category like that of Cause, for a Kantian it is meaningless to say that the empirical relation of causality between two phenomena participates in (is an imperfect copy of) the eternal Idea of a cause: the causes that I perceive between phenomena are the only causes that there are, and the a priori notion of Cause is not their perfect model, but, precisely, the condition of possibility of me perceiving the relationship between phenomena as causal.

Although an insurmountable abyss separates Kant's critical philosophy from his great idealist successors (Fichte, Schelling, Hegel), the basic coordinates which render possible Hegel's *Phenomenology of Spirit* are already there in Kant's *Critique of Pure Reason*. First, as Dieter Henrich put it concisely, "Kant's philosophical motivation was not identical with what he took to be the original motivation for doing philosophy"[6]: the original motivation for doing philosophy is a metaphysical one, to provide an explanation of the totality of noumenal reality; as such, this motivation is illusory, it prescribes an impossible task, while Kant's motivation is a critique of all possible metaphysics. Kant's endeavor thus comes afterwards: in order for there to be a critique of metaphysics, there first has to be an original metaphysics; in order to denounce the metaphysical "transcendental illusion," this illusion must first exist. In this precise sense Kant was "the inventor of the philosophical history of philosophy"[7]: there are necessary stages in the development of philosophy, that is, *one cannot directly get at truth*, one cannot begin with it, philosophy necessarily began with metaphysical illusions. The path from illusion to its critical denunciation is the very core of philosophy, which means that successful ("true") philosophy is no longer defined by its truthful explanation of the totality of being, but by successfully accounting for the illusions, that is, by explaining not only why illusions are illusions, but also why they are structurally necessary, unavoidable, and not just accidents. The "system" of philosophy is thus no longer a direct ontological structure of reality, but "a pure, complete system of all metaphysical statements and proofs."[8] The proof of the illusory nature of metaphysical propositions is that they necessarily engender antinomies (contradictory conclusions), and since metaphysics tries to avoid the antinomies which emerge when we think metaphysical notions to their end, the "system" of critical philosophy is the complete—and therefore self-contradictory, "antinomic"—series of metaphysical notions and propositions: "Only the one who can look through the illusion of metaphysics can develop the

6 Dieter Henrich, *Between Kant and Hegel: Lectures on German Idealism*, Cambridge, MA: Harvard University Press 2008, p. 32.

7 Ibid.

8 Ibid.

most coherent, consistent system of metaphysics, because the consistent system of metaphysics is also contradictory"—that is to say, precisely, *inconsistent*.[9] The critical "system" is the systematic *a priori* structure of all possible/thinkable "errors" in their immanent necessity: what we get at the end is not the Truth that overcomes/sublates the preceding illusions—the only truth is the inconsistent edifice of the logical interconnection of all possible illusions ... is this not what Hegel did in his *Phenomenology* (and, at a different level, in his *Logic*)? The only (but key) difference is that, for Kant, this "dialogic" process of truth emerging as the critical denunciation of the preceding illusion belongs to the sphere of our knowledge and does not concern the noumenal reality which remains external and indifferent to it, while, for Hegel, the proper *locus* of this process is the Thing itself.

Schopenhauer famously compared Kant "to a man at a ball, who all evening has been carrying on a love affair with a masked beauty in the vain hope of making a conquest, when at last she throws off her mask and reveals herself to be his wife"—the situation of Johann Strauss's *Fledermaus*. For Schopenhauer, of course, the point of the comparison is that the masked beauty is philosophy and the wife Christianity—Kant's radical critique is really just a new attempt to support religion, his transgression is a false one. What, however, if there is more truth in the mask than in the real face beneath it? What if this critical game radically changes the nature of religion, so that Kant effectively *did* undermine what it was his goal to protect? Perhaps those Catholic theologians who saw Kant's criticism as the original catastrophe of modern thought that opened up the way to liberalism and nihilism were actually right?

Fichte's "radicalization" of Kant is the most problematic link in the chain of German Idealists: he was and is dismissed, ridiculed even, as a half-crazy solipsistic "subjective idealist." (No wonder that, for the Anglo-Saxon analytic tradition, Kant is the only German Idealist to be taken seriously—with Fichte, we enter the domain of obscure speculation.) Being the least popular, it takes the greatest effort to get to the true core of his thought, his "fundamental insight" (*Fichte's Grundeinsicht*—the title of Dieter Henrich's study on Fichte). However, his work is worth the effort: as with all truly great thinkers, a proper understanding of his work reveals an unsurpassed description of the deep structure of engaged subjectivity.

Schelling's thought is to be divided into two phases, the early "philosophy of identity" and the late "philosophy of revelation"—and, as is so often the case, Schelling's true breakthrough occurs between the two, in the short period between 1805 and 1815 when he produced his two absolute masterpieces, the treatise on human freedom and the three versions of the "ages of the world"

9 Ibid.

manuscript. A whole new universe is disclosed here: the universe of pre-logical drives, the dark "ground of Being" which dwells even in the heart of God as that which is "in God more than God himself." For the first time in the history of human thought, the origin of Evil is located not in humanity's Fall from God, but in a split in the heart of God himself.

In Schelling, the ultimate figure of Evil is not Spirit as opposed to Nature, but Spirit directly materialized in Nature as un-natural, as a monstrous distortion of natural order, from evil spirits and vampires to monstrous products of technological manipulations (clones, etc.). Nature in itself is Good, in it, the evil-ground is by definition always subordinated to the Good: "at each stage of nature prior to the appearance of man the ground is subordinated to existence; in other words, the self-will of the particular is necessarily subordinated to the universal will of the whole. Hence, the self-will of each individual animal is necessarily subordinated to the will of the species, which contributes to the harmony of the whole of nature."[10] When, with the emergence of man, the ground of existence is allowed to operate on its own, egotistically asserting itself, this does not only mean that it asserts itself *against* divine love, the harmony of the whole, the universal (non-egotistic) will—it means that it asserts itself *in the very form of its opposite*: the horror of man is that, in it, Evil becomes radical: no longer simple egotistic evil, but Evil masked (appearing) as universality, as is exemplarily the case in political totalitarianism, in which a particular political agent presents itself as the direct embodiment of the universal Will and Freedom of humanity.[11]

Nowhere is the difference between Hegel's thought and Schelling's late philosophy more palpable than regarding the question of the beginning: while Hegel begins with the poorest notion of being (which, in its abstraction, its lack of determinations, equals nothing), Schelling's "negative philosophy" (which remains part of his system, but supplemented by "positive" philosophy) also begins with the affirmation of a negation, of a void, but this void is the affirmative force of the will's desire: "all beginning lies in an absence; the deepest potency, which holds fast to everything, is non-being and its hunger for being."[12] From the domain of logic and its a priori notions, we pass into the domain of actual life, whose starting point is a yearning, the "hunger" of a void to be filled in by positive actual being. Schelling's critique of Hegel is thus that, in order to really pass from being/nothingness to actual becoming which results in "something"

10 Bret W. Davis, *Heidegger and the Will: On the Way to the Gelassenheit*, Evanston: Northwestern University Press 2007, p. 107.

11 For a more detailed analysis of this reversal, see my *The Indivisible Remainder*, London: Verso Books 1996.

12 F. W. J. Schelling, *Sämmtliche Werke*, Part 2, Vol. 1, Stuttgart-Augsberg: J. G. Cotta, 1856–61, p. 294, as quoted and translated by Bruce Matthews in his introduction to Schelling's *The Grounding of Positive Philosophy*, Albany: SUNY Press 2007, p. 34.

positive, the "nothing" with which we begin should be a "living nothing," the void of a desire which expresses a will to generate or get hold of some content.

The enigma of Henrich's reading of German Idealism is why he systematically downplays the role of Schelling, especially the middle Schelling of *Freiheitschrift* and *Weltalter*. This is mysterious because it was precisely this middle Schelling who explored in the greatest depth what Henrich designates as Fichte's (and German Idealism's) central problem, that of the "Spinozism of freedom": how to think the *Ground of Freedom*, a trans-subjective Ground of subjectivity which not only does not constrain human freedom but literally grounds it? Schelling's answer in *Freiheitschrift* is literally Ground itself: human freedom is rendered possible by the distinction, in God itself, between the existing God and its own Ground, what in God is not yet fully God. This accounts for Schelling's uniqueness, also with regard to Hölderlin's "On Judgment and Being": like the late Fichte (although in a totally different mode, of course), Schelling arrives at the trans-subjective Ground of subjective freedom, but for Hölderlin (and Fichte), this trans-subjective order of Being (or divine Life) is fully One, pre-reflective, indivisible, not even self-identical (because self-identity already involves a formal distance of a term from itself)—it was only Schelling who introduced a radical gap, instability, discord, into this very pre-subjective/pre-reflexive Ground. In his most daring speculative attempt in *Weltalter*, Schelling tries to reconstruct (to "narrate") in this way the very rise of *logos*, of articulated discourse, out of the pre-logical Ground: *logos* is an attempt to resolve the debilitating deadlock of this Ground. This is why the two true highpoints of German Idealism are the middle Schelling and the mature Hegel: they did what no one else dared to do—they introduced a gap into the Ground itself.

Hölderlin's famous fragment "On Judgment and Being" deserves further mention, since it is often taken as an indication of a kind of "alternative reality," of a different path that German Idealism might have taken in order to break out of the Kantian inconsistencies. Its underlying premise is that subjective self-consciousness strives to overcome the lost unity with Being/the Absolute/God from which it has been irrevocably separated by the "primordial division [*Ur-Theilung*]," the discursive activity of "judgment [*Urteil*]":

> Being [Seyn]—expresses the joining [Verbindung] of Subject and Object. Where Subject and Object are absolutely, not just partially united [vereiniget], and hence so united that no division can be undertaken, without destroying the essence [Wesen] of the thing that is to be sundered [getrennt], there and not otherwise can we talk of an absolute Being, as is the case in intellectual intuition.
>
> But this Being must not be equated [verwechselt] with Identity. When I say: I am I, the Subject (Ego) and the Object (Ego) are not so united that absolutely no sundering can be undertaken, without destroying the essence of the thing that is to

> be sundered; on the contrary the Ego is only possible through this sundering of Ego from Ego. How can I say "I" without self-consciousness? But how is self-consciousness possible? Precisely because I oppose myself to myself; I sunder myself from myself, but in spite of this sundering I recognize myself as the same in the opposites. But how far as the same? I can raise this question and I must; for in another respect [Rüksicht] it [the Ego] is opposed to itself. So identity is not a uniting of Subject and Object that takes place absolutely, and so Identity is not equal to absolute Being.
>
> Judgment: is in the highest and strictest sense the original sundering of Subject and Object most intimately united in intellectual intuition, the very sundering which first makes Object and Subject possible, their Ur-Theilung. In the concept of division [Theilung] there lies already the concept of the reciprocal relation [Beziehung] of Object and Subject to one another, and the necessary presupposition of a whole of which Object and Subject are the parts. "I am I" is the most appropriate example for this concept of Urtheilung in its theoretical form, but in practical Urtheilung, it [the ego] posits itself as opposed to the Non-ego, not to itself.
>
> Actuality and possibility are to be distinguished as mediate and immediate consciousness. When I think of an object [Gegenstand] as possible, I merely duplicate the previous consciousness in virtue of which it is actual. There is for us no thinkable possibility, which was not an actuality. For this reason the concept of possibility has absolutely no valid application to the objects of Reason, since they come into consciousness as nothing but what they ought to be, but only the concept of necessity [applies to them]. The concept of possibility has valid application to the objects of the understanding, that of actuality to the objects of perception and intuition.[13]

Hölderlin's starting point is the gap between (the impossible return to) the traditional organic unity and the modern reflexive freedom: we are, as finite, discursive, self-conscious subjects cast out of oneness with the whole of being to which we nevertheless long to return, yet without sacrificing our independence—how are we to overcome this gap? His answer is what he calls the "eccentric path": the split between substance and subjectivity, Being and reflection, is insurmountable, and the only reconciliation possible is a *narrative* one, that of the subject telling the story of his endless oscillation between the two poles. While the content remains non-reconciled, *reconciliation occurs in the narrative form itself*—the exact inverse of the logical assertion of the subject's identity (I = I) where the very form (division, redoubling, of the I's) undermines content (identity).

---

13 Friedrich Hölderlin, "Über Urtheil und Seyn" (1795), as translated in H. S. Harris, *Hegel's Development: Toward the Sunlight* 1770–1801, Oxford: Clarendon Press 1972, pp. 515–16.

Hölderlin's solution should be put in its context and conceived as one of the three versions of how to solve the same problem—the gap between subjective autonomy and the organic Whole that characterizes modernity; the other two versions are Schiller's and Schlegel's. For Schiller, free human life within nature and culture is possible if it achieves that kind of internal organization, determination from within, or harmony of parts that is characteristic of both natural and artistic beauty. In a beautiful natural object, we find, as it were, "the person of the thing"; we have a sense of "the free consent of the thing to its technique" and of "a rule which is at once given and obeyed by the thing," and this is a model for the free consent of an individual to the worth of a social repertoire or way of life. Friedrich Schlegel, on the contrary, seeks to enact a kind of imperfect yet always energetic freedom in continuous, ironic, witty, self-revising activity that characterizes romantic poetry—a kind of commitment to eternal restlessness. It is easy to see how these three positions form a kind of triangle: Schiller-Schlegel-Hölderlin. Schiller believes in the subject's integration into the organic substantial order—free selfhood can wholly appear in beautiful nature and art; Schlegel asserts the force of subjectivity as the constant unsettling of any substantial harmony (one can claim that, in German Idealism, this opposition repeats itself in the guise of Schelling versus Fichte—the positivity of the *Ur-Grund* prior to reflection versus the "eternal restlessness" of subjectivity).

Hegel occupies here a fourth position—what he adds to Hölderlin is a purely formal shift of transposing the tragic gap that separates the reflecting subject from pre-reflexive Being into this Being itself. Once we do this, the problem becomes its own solution: it is our very division from absolute Being which unites us with it, since this division is immanent to Being. Already in Hölderlin, division is redoubled, self-relating: the ultimate division is not the Subject-Object division, but the very division between division (of Subject-Object) and unity. One should thus supplement the formula of "identity of identity and non-identity" with "division between division and non-division." Once we accomplish this step, Being as the inaccessible pre-reflexive Ground disappears; more precisely, it reveals itself as the ultimate reflexive category, as the result of the self-relating division: Being emerges when division divides itself from itself. Or, to put it in Hölderlin's terms, the narrative is not merely the subject coping with its division from Being, it is simultaneously the story Being is telling itself about itself. The loss supplemented by the narrative is inscribed into Being itself. Which means that the last distinction on which Hölderlin insists, the one between intellectual intuition (the immediate access to Being, the subject's direct one-ness with it) and the "eccentric" narrative path (that mediates access to Being through narrative reconciliation), has to fall: the narrative already does the job of intellectual intuition, of uniting us with Being. Or, in more paradoxical terms: the standard relationship between the two terms should be turned around. It is intellectual intuition which is merely a reflexive category, separating us from Being in its very enacting of the subject's immediate one-ness with Being, and it is the narrative path which directly renders the life of Being itself:

> That "the truth is the whole" means that we should not look at the process that is self-manifestation as a deprivation of the original Being. Nor should we look at it only as an ascent to the highest. The process is already the highest ... The *subject* for Hegel is ... nothing but the active relationship to itself. In the subject there is nothing underlying its self-reference, there is *only* the self-reference. For this reason, there is only the process and nothing underlying it. Philosophical and metaphorical models such as "emanation" (neo-Platonism) or "expression" (Spinozism) present the relationship between the infinite and the finite in a way that fails to characterize what the process (self-manifestation) is.[14]

It is, therefore, Hölderlin, not Hegel, who remains here metaphysical, clinging to the notion of a pre-reflexive Ground accessible through intellectual intuition—what is properly meta-physical is the very presupposition of a substantial Being beyond the process of (self-)differentiation. (This is also the reason why—as we can see in the last paragraph of the fragment—Hölderlin subordinates possibility to actuality.) This is why Hegel appropriates the solution of Hölderlin's *Hyperion* (what, in reality, cannot be reconciled is reconciled afterwards, through its narrative reconstruction) against Hölderlin himself: in a clear parallel to Hegel's *Phenomenology of Spirit*, Hölderlin sees the solution in a narrative which retroactively reconstructs the very "eccentric path" (the path of the permanent oscillation between the loss of the Center and the repeated failed attempts to regain the immediacy of the Center) as the process of maturation, of spiritual education. This solution does not imply discursive constructivism (the consistency of our reality is that of an *après-coup* narrative), but a much more radical Hegelian position: while the discursive constructivism can be read as a neo-Kantian language-transcendentalism (as Gadamer put it in his paraphrase of Heidegger's thesis on "language as a house of being," "to be is to be understood"; that is, the horizon of understanding sustained by language is the ultimate transcendental horizon of our approach to being), that is, while the discursive transcendentalism focuses on how what we experience as "reality" is always-already mediated/constructed by language, Hölderlin's solution shifts the focus to how (as Lacan put it) *the signifier itself falls into the real*, that is, how the signifying intervention (narrativization) intervenes into the real, how it brings about the resolution of a real antagonism.

14 Henrich, *Between Kant and Hegel*, pp. 289–90.

Hegel thus remains the peak of the entire movement of German Idealism: all four are not equal, they are three plus one. But why? What makes Hegel unique? One of the ways to circumscribe this uniqueness of Hegel is to use the Lacanian notion of the "lack in the Other" which, in Hegel's case, points towards the unique epistemologico-ontological mediation absent in all three other Idealists: the most elementary figure of dialectical reversal resides in transposing an epistemological obstacle into the thing itself, as its ontological failure (what appears to us as our inability to know the thing indicates a crack in the thing itself, so that our very failure to reach the full truth is the indicator of truth). It is the premise of the present book that this "fundamental insight" of Hegel has lost none of its power today; that it is far more radical (and a far greater threat to metaphysical thinking) than all the combined anti-totality topics of contingency-alterity-heterogeneity.[15]

One can well imagine a truly obscene version of the famous "The Aristocrats" joke that easily beats all the vulgarity of family members vomiting, defecating, fornicating, and humiliating each other in all possible ways: when asked to perform, they give the talent agent a short course in Hegelian thought, debating the true meaning of negativity, of sublation, of Absolute Knowledge, and so forth, and, when the bewildered agent asks them the name of the weird show, they enthusiastically reply: "The Perverts!" Indeed, to paraphrase the good old Brecht's slogan "What is the robbing of a bank against a founding of a new bank?": what is the disturbing shock of family members defecating into one another's mouths compared to the shock of a proper dialectical reversal?[16]

---

15 I am here deeply indebted to Catherine Malabou, *L'avenir de Hegel*, Paris: J. Vrin 1996 (available in English as *The Future of Hegel*, trans. Lisabeth During, London: Routledge 2005). *L'avenir de Hegel* is—together with Gérard Lebrun's *La patience du concept* and Beatrice Longuenesse's *Hegel et la critique de la métaphysique*—one of *the* books on Hegel that, in an almost regular rhythm of every decade or two, mysteriously surface in France, books which are *epochal* in the strictest meaning of the word: they redefine the entire field into which they intervene—literally, *nothing remains the same* after one immerses oneself in one of these books. One cannot but fully agree with Derrida when he wrote that "nothing will ever absolve us from following step by step, page by page, the extraordinary trajectory of *The Future of Hegel* … I once again urge all to read this book."

To this series we should add Rebecca Comay's *Mourning Sickness* (Palo Alto: Stanford University Press 2011), the latest "*the* book" on Hegel, confirming the suspicion that—over the past few decades, at least—only a woman can write a really good book on Hegel.

16 For "The Aristocrats" see the *Wikipedia* entry for "The Aristocrats (joke)." One should nonetheless insist that, instead of relying on the reversal of superficial innocence into a dirty (sexualized) message, good jokes more often practice the opposite reversal of vulgar obscenity into innocence, as in the wonderfully stupid (apolitical!) Russian joke from the time of the Soviet Union: two men, strangers to each other, sit in the same compartment on a train. After a long silence, one suddenly addresses the other: "Have

However, the aim of *Less Than Nothing* is not to simply (or not so simply) return to Hegel, but, rather, to repeat Hegel (in the radical Kierkegaardian sense). Over the last decade, the theoretical work of the Party Troika to which I belong (along with Mladen Dolar and Alenka Zupančič) had the axis of Hegel-Lacan as its "undeconstructible" point of reference: whatever we were doing, the underlying axiom was that reading Hegel through Lacan (and vice versa) was our unsurpassable horizon. Recently, however, limitations of this horizon have appeared: with Hegel, his inability to think pure repetition and to render thematic the singularity of what Lacan called the *objet a*; with Lacan, the fact that his work ended in an inconsistent opening: *Seminar XX (Encore)* stands for his ultimate achievement and deadlock—in the years after, he desperately concocted different ways out (the *sinthome*, knots …), all of which failed. So where do we stand now?

My wager was (and is) that, through their interaction (reading Hegel through Lacan and vice versa), psychoanalysis and Hegelian dialectics mutually redeem themselves, shedding their accustomed skin and emerging in a new unexpected shape. The book's motto could have been Alain Badiou's claim that "the antiphilosopher Lacan is a condition of the renaissance of philosophy. A philosophy is possible today only if it is compatible with Lacan."[17] Guy Lardreau made the same point with regard to the ethico-political space when he wrote that Lacan "is the only one thinking today, the only one who never lies, *le chasse-canaille* [the scoundrels-hunter]"—and "scoundrels" here are those who propagate the semblance of liberation which only covers up the reality of capitalist perversion, which, for Lardreau, means thinkers such as Lyotard and Deleuze, and for us many more. What Badiou shares with Lardreau is the idea that one should think through Lacan, go further than he did, but that the only way beyond Lacan is through Lacan. The stakes of this diagnosis are clearly political: Lacan unveiled the illusions on which capitalist reality as well as its false transgressions are

you ever fucked a dog?" Surprised, the other replies: "No—have you?" "Of course not. I just asked to start a conversation!"

17 Alain Badiou, *Manifesto for Philosophy*, London: Verso Books 1999, p. 84. Who is antiphilosopher to whom? Badiou somewhere speculates that Heraclitus is the antiphilosopher to Parmenides, the sophists to Plato (although they temporarily and logically precede him), Pascal to Descartes, Hume to Leibniz, Kierkegaard (and Marx?) to Hegel, and even Lacan to Heidegger. However, this picture has to be complicated: is Kant's thought—or even the entirety of German Idealism with its central motif, the primacy of practical over theoretical reason—not the antiphilosophy to classical metaphysics in its last great mode (of Spinoza and Leibniz)? Or is Sade—in the Lacanian reading—not the antiphilosopher to Kant, so that Lacan's "avec" means to read a philosopher through his antiphilosopher? And is Hegel's true antiphilosopher not already the late Schelling? Or, a step even further, is Hegel's uniqueness not that he is *his own antiphilosopher*?

based, but his final result is that we are condemned to domination—the Master is the constitutive ingredient of the very symbolic order, so the attempts to overcome domination only generate new figures of the Master. The great task of those who are ready to go through Lacan is thus to articulate the space for a revolt which will not be recaptured by one or another version of the discourse of the Master. Lardreau, together with Christian Jambet, first tried to develop this opening by focusing on the link between domination and sexuality: since there is no sexuality without a relation of domination, any project of "sexual liberation" ends up generating new forms of domination—or, as Kafka would have put it, revolt is not a cage in search of a bird, but a bird in search of a cage. Based on this insight that a revolt has to be thoroughly de-sexualized, Lardreau and Jambet outlined the ascetic-Maoist-Lacanian figure of "angel" as the agent of radical emancipation. However, confronted with the destructive violence of the Cultural Revolution and especially of the Khmer Rouge regime in Kampuchea, they abandoned any notion of a radical emancipation in social relations and ended up in a split position of affirming the lesser evil in politics and the need for an inner spiritual revolution: in politics, we should be modest and simply accept that some Masters are better than others, and that the only revolt possible is an inner spiritual one.[18] The present book rejects this spiritualization of revolt and remains faithful to Badiou's original project of a radical emancipatory project which passes through Lacan.

18 Following this path, Jambet immersed himself in the thought of Molla Sadra, the great Iranian thinker from the seventeenth century—a position which is not foreign to the Gnostic turn of European thinkers like Peter Sloterdijk. See Christian Jambet, *The Act of Being*, New York: Zone Books 2006.

Part I

THE DRINK BEFORE

CHAPTER 1

"Vacillating the Semblances"

What cannot be said must be shown

The famous last proposition of Wittgenstein's *Tractatus*—"Whereof one cannot speak, thereof one must be silent"—involves an obvious paradox: it contains a superfluous prohibition, since it prohibits something which is already in itself impossible.[1] This paradox faithfully reproduces the predominant attitude towards the aesthetic representation of the Holocaust: it shouldn't be done, because it can't be done. Jorge Semprún's Spanish-Catholic origins play a crucial role in his reversal of this prohibition: for Semprún, it is not poetic fiction but prosaic documentary which is impossible after Auschwitz. For Elie Wiesel, by contrast, there can be no novel about the Holocaust: any text claiming to be such is either not about the Holocaust or is not a novel. Rejecting this claim that literature and the Holocaust are incommensurable, Semprún argues that the Holocaust can *only* be represented by the arts: it is not the aestheticization of the Holocaust which is false, but its reduction to being the object of a documentary report. Every attempt to "reproduce the facts" in a documentary way neutralizes the traumatic impact of the events described—or as Lacan, another atheist Catholic, put it: truth has the structure of a fiction. Almost no one is able to endure, still less to enjoy, a snuff film showing real torture and killing, but we can enjoy it as a fiction: when truth is too traumatic to be confronted directly, it can only be accepted in the guise of a fiction. Claude Lanzmann was right to say that if by chance he were to stumble upon some documentary footage showing the actual murder of inmates in Auschwitz, he would destroy it immediately. Such a documentary would be obscene, disrespectful towards the victims even. When considered in this way, the pleasure of aesthetic fiction is not a simple form of escapism, but a mode of coping with traumatic memory—a survival mechanism.

But how are we to avoid the danger that the aesthetic pleasure generated by fiction will obliterate the proper trauma of the Holocaust? Only a minimal aesthetic sensitivity is needed to recognize that there would be something false about an epic novel on the Holocaust, written in the grand style of nineteenth-century

1 Ludwig Wittgenstein, *Tractatus Logico-Philosophicus*, New York: Cosimo Classics 2007.

psychological realism: the universe of such novels, the perspective from which they are written, belongs to the historical epoch that preceded the Holocaust. Anna Akhmatova encountered a similar problem when, in the Soviet Union of the 1930s, she tried to depict the atmosphere of the Stalinist terror. In her memoirs she describes what happened when, at the height of the Stalinist purges, she was waiting in a long queue outside the Leningrad prison to learn the fate of her arrested son Lev:

> One day somebody in the crowd identified me. Standing behind me was a young woman, with lips blue from the cold, who had of course never heard me called by name before. Now she started out of the torpor common to us all and asked me in a whisper (everyone whispered there), "Can you describe this?" And I said, "I can." Then something like a smile passed fleetingly over what had once been her face.[2]

What kind of description is intended here? Surely it is not a realistic description of the situation, but a description which extracts from the confused reality its own inner form, in the same way that, in his atonal music, Schoenberg extracted the inner form of totalitarian terror. At this level, truth is no longer something that depends on the faithful reproduction of facts. One should introduce here the difference between (factual) truth and truthfulness: what makes a report of a raped woman (or any other narrative of a trauma) truthful is its very factual unreliability, confusion, inconsistency. If the victim were able to report on her painful and humiliating experience in a clear way, with all the data arranged into a consistent order of exposition, this very quality would make us suspicious. The same holds for the unreliability of the verbal reports given by Holocaust survivors: a witness who was able to offer a clear narrative of his camp experience would thereby disqualify himself. In a Hegelian way, the problem is here part of the solution: the very deficiencies of the traumatized subject's report on the facts bear witness to the truthfulness of his report, since they signal that the reported content has contaminated the very form in which it is reported.[3]

What we are dealing with here is, of course, the gap between the enunciated content and the subjective position of enunciation. G. K. Chesterton wrote

---

2 Quoted from Elaine Feinstein, *Anna of All the Russians*, New York: Alfred A. Knopf 2005, p. 170.

3 Primo Levi's late book on the chemical elements (*The Periodic Table*, New York: Alfred A. Knopf 1996) should be read against this background of the difficulties—indeed the fundamental impossibility—of fully narrativizing one's condition, of telling one's life story as a consistent narrative: for Levi, the trauma of the Holocaust prevented it. So, for him, the only way to avoid the collapse of his symbolic universe was to find support in some extra-symbolic Real, the Real of the classification of chemical elements (and, of course, in his version, the classification served only as an empty frame: each element was explained in terms of its symbolic associations).

apropos of Nietzsche that he "denied egoism simply by preaching it": "To preach anything is to give it away. First, the egoist calls life a war without mercy, and then he takes the greatest possible trouble to drill his enemies in war. To preach egoism is to practice altruism."[4] The medium here is not the message, quite the opposite: the very medium that we use—the universal intersubjectivity of language—undermines the message. It is not only that we should, therefore, denounce the particular position of enunciation that sustains the universal enunciated content—the white, wealthy male subject who proclaims the universality of human rights, for example. It is far more important to unearth the universality that sustains, and potentially undermines, his particular claim. The supreme case here, as noted by Bertrand Russell, is that of the solipsist trying to convince others that he alone really exists. Could one extend this argument to the problem of tolerance or intolerance? Perhaps not altogether, although there is a similar catch involved in preaching tolerance: it (presup)poses its presupposition—that is, the subject deeply "bothered" by the Neighbor—and thus only reasserts it. Did Paul Claudel not get it right in his famous reply to Jules Renard: "*Mais la tolérance?*" "*Il y a des maisons pour ça!*" (*une maison de tolérance* is one French expression for a brothel)? And did not Chesterton, as was so often the case, also get it right with his famous quip, "Tolerance is the virtue of the man without convictions"?

The aesthetic lesson of this paradox is clear. The horror of the Holocaust cannot be represented; but this excess of represented content over its aesthetic representation has to infect the aesthetic form itself. What cannot be *described* should be *inscribed* into the artistic form as its uncanny distortion. Perhaps a reference to Wittgenstein's *Tractatus* can again be of some help here. According to the *Tractatus*, language depicts reality by virtue of sharing a logical form in common with it.

> 4.121 Propositions cannot represent logical form: it is mirrored in them. What finds its reflection in language, language cannot represent. What expresses itself in language, we cannot express by means of language. Propositions show the logical form of reality. They display it.

We know that a picture of a sunset represents a sunset because both the picture and the sunset share a similar "pictorial form." Similarly, a proposition and what it represents share a similar "logical form": a proposition depicts a fact, and just as a fact can be analyzed into independent states of affairs, a proposition can be analyzed into independent elementary propositions. Wittgenstein here draws a distinction between saying and showing: while a proposition

---

4 G. K. Chesterton, *Orthodoxy*, San Francisco: Ignatius Press 1995, p. 38.

says that such-and-such fact is the case, it shows the logical form by virtue of which this fact is the case. The upshot of this distinction is that we can only say things about facts in the world; logical form cannot be spoken about, only shown: "4.1212 What can be shown, cannot be said." If we read this proposition together with the final proposition ("Whereof one cannot speak, thereof one must be silent."), the conclusion is that what we cannot speak about can be shown, that is, directly rendered in/by the very form of speaking. In other words, Wittgenstein's "showing" should be understood not merely in a mystical sense, but as inherent to language, as the form of language. Let us return to our example of trauma: we cannot directly talk about or describe it, but the traumatic excess can nevertheless be "shown" in the distortion of our speech about the trauma, in its elliptic repetitions and other distortions. In his novel *Le grand voyage*, Semprún invented just such a new form—a "logical form" of narrative that would be adequate to the trauma of the Holocaust by way of "showing" what cannot be directly described.[5]

The narrative of Semprún's novel unfolds during a journey in a cramped and squalid boxcar carrying 120 resistance fighters from Compiègne to Buchenwald; Gérard, the first-person narrator of the story, is one of these prisoners. The narrative only fleetingly remains in the boxcar: in sudden temporal switches Gérard's narration lurches back and forth from the time before the war to the moment of liberation in 1945, to two, three, sixteen, or an unspecified number of years later. These switches are rendered as moments within Gérard's fractured stream of consciousness; as he undergoes the ordeal of the journey in the present, he remembers and "fore-members" (remembers-imagines the future), since the experience has fragmented him into a splintered self. Details of his life in the past, present, and future flow through his mind like multiple currents in an unimpeded stream: he is simultaneously a partisan in the French resistance, a deported prisoner of the Germans, and a survivor of Buchenwald. By recreating Gérard's consciousness as an intersection of three time zones, Semprún renders the fluid timeless ordeal of the camp inmate who has lost his sense of life as a chronological passage from yesterday through today into tomorrow.

The topic of the "death of the subject," of its dispersal in a pandemonium of conflicting and fragmented narrative lines, is usually seen as a result of elitist artistic reflections, divorced from the real concerns of real people; Semprún's unique achievement is to establish the link between this modernist revolution in writing and our most traumatic historical experience. The true focus of *Le grand voyage* is not what really happened on the way to Buchenwald, but how such a terrible event affects the very identity of the subject: its elementary contours of reality are shattered, the subject no longer experiences himself as part

5 Jorge Semprún, *The Long Voyage*, New York: Overlook Press 2005.

of a continuous flow of history which devolves from the past towards the future. Instead, his experience moves in a kind of eternal present in which present, past, and future, reality and fantasy, directly interact. In his theory of relativity, Einstein proposes to interpret time as a fourth dimension of space in which past and future are all "now," already here; because of our limited perception, we just cannot see them, we can only see the present. In Semprún's novel, it is as if, after going through the nightmare of the life in a camp, our perception widens and we can see all three dimensions of time simultaneously—time becomes space, giving us an uncanny freedom to move back and forth along it just as we wander around in an open space, with past and future as different paths that we can take at will. There is, however, a price to be paid for this freedom, a blind spot in this field of spatialized time: we can see everything except the present of the camp itself. This prohibited present is, of course, death—being alive after Buchenwald is not the same as having survived it intact: the shadow of death taints Gérard's memories of innocent prewar friendships—he learns later that many of his friends have been killed—and poisons his postwar life. Life in the camp is thus not so much the ultimate referent of his memories as the distorting screen which taints and spoils them all. Semprún juxtaposes Gérard's pleasure at reading the childhood memories offered in Proust with the painful and deferred memory of his arrival at the Buchenwald concentration camp—his "madeleine" is the strange smell that recalls the crematory oven:

> And suddenly, borne on the breeze, the curious odor: sweetish, cloying, with a bitter and truly nauseating edge to it. The peculiar odor that would later prove to be from the crematory oven … The strange smell would immediately invade the reality of memory. I would be reborn there; I would die if returned to life there. I would embrace and inhale the muddy, heady odor of that estuary of death.[6]

What resuscitates the trauma are not merely the immediate painful associations of the details which recall the camp, but, even more, the power of these recent memories to "color" and thus spoil the more ancient, gentle memories. Robert Antelme, in his testimony *L'espèce humaine*, evokes a similar case of overdetermination: the pleasurable memory of a lover ringing the doorbell has been indelibly colored by the painful memory of the Gestapo ringing the same bell at the moment of one's arrest.[7] Both in this instance and in Semprún's use of Proust's ringing garden bell, the survivors find that memory has been colonized by the experience of the Holocaust: there is no way to retrieve the pleasant memory of a lover waiting at the door without simultaneously triggering the corruption of that memory by the trauma.

---

6 Ibid., p. 39.

7 See Robert Antelme, *L'espèce humaine*, Paris: Gallimard 1978.

The same shift from linear narrative time to the fragmented synchronicity of different times characterizes French vanguard cinema of the late 1950s and early 1960s, most visibly in the work of Alain Resnais, whose first film, the documentary *Night and Fog*, also deals with the Holocaust. Resnais's masterpiece, *Last Year in Marienbad*, is about a couple whose affair is told in temporal slices the order of which is never clear: the time structure of the narrative exists as a synchronic mass wherein past, present, and future are all equally available, and can potentially all be present. The script for *Marienbad* was written by Alain Robbe-Grillet, the leading author of the French *nouveau roman* who also directed films. No wonder Semprún collaborated with Resnais: apart from writing two scenarios for him, he was an unacknowledged contributor to Resnais's *Je t'aime, je t'aime*. In discussing this film, Gilles Deleuze introduced the concept of the "sheet of time"—a traumatic point in time, a kind of magnetic attractor which tears moments of past, present, and future out of their proper context, combining them into a complex field of multiple, discrete, and interacting temporalities. In *Je t'aime, je t'aime*, the "sheet" is the narrator's traumatic memory of the death (murder?) of his beloved. Claude Ridder—a writer who, in despair after the death of his love, has attempted suicide—is approached to be a test-subject at a mysterious facility devoted to researching time travel. The scientists' plan is to send him back into his own past, exactly one year earlier, but for only one minute. Unfortunately, the experiment goes out of control, and Claude finds himself unstuck in time, bounced between random moments of his life, re-experiencing snippets from his past, in a mixture of moments of love, doubt, confusion, happiness, and even day-to-day routine, all in the form of tiny fragments, shuffled about or replayed like a scratched record. While the scientists running the botched experiment frantically try to retrieve Claude, he becomes more and more fixated on past moments, returning to them and repeating them endlessly. Does something similar not happen to Gérard in *Le grand voyage*? He also comes unstuck from the linear temporal flow, caught in an interactive loop between multiple traumatic sheets of time.

There is more than just a formal parallel between these procedures in cinema and literature: *Le grand voyage* is a novel which was only possible after the arrival of cinema, incorporating as it does the cinematic sensibility and techniques of montage, flashbacks, imagining the future, visual hallucinations, etc. Another distinguishing cinematic feature of the novel's narrative is the sudden rise of details (images, objects, sounds) shown in close-up, their excessive and intrusive proximity overshadowing the narrative context of which they are a part. The hermeneutic temptation to read these details as symbols and to search for their hidden meaning should be resisted: they are exposed fragments of the real which resist meaning. The meaning of their context—the terrible situation of the Shoah—is too traumatic to be assumed, so this sudden focus on material details serves the purpose of keeping meaning at a distance.

The problem the survivors encounter is not only that witnessing is impossible, that it always has an element of prosopopoeia, since the true witness is always already dead and we can only speak on his behalf. There is also a symmetric problem encountered at the opposite end: there is no proper public, no listener adequate to receive the witnessing. The most traumatic dream Primo Levi had in Auschwitz was about his survival: the war is over, he is reunited with his family, telling them about his life in the camp, but they gradually become bored, start to yawn and, one after another, leave the table, so that finally Levi is left alone. An anecdote from the Bosnian war in the early 1990s makes the same point: many of the girls who survived brutal rapes later killed themselves, having rejoined their community only to find that no one was really ready to listen to them, or accept their testimony. In Lacan's terms, what is missing here is not only another human being, the attentive listener, but the "big Other" itself, the space of the symbolic inscription or registration of my words. Levi made the same point in his direct and simple way: "What we are doing to Jews is so irrepresentable in its horror that even if someone will survive the camps, he will not be believed by those who were not there—they will simply declare him a liar or a mentally ill person!"[8] Since Levi was not an artist, he did not draw the artistic consequences of this fact—but Semprún did. During the "present" of the boxcar journey in *Le grand voyage*, Gérard conveys his memories to an unnamed companion dubbed "le gars de Semur" (the guy from Semur). Why this need for an interlocutor? What function does he have? Gérard informs us at the outset that his companion will die upon arriving at the camp, so he clearly stands for the dwindling presence of the big Other, the recipient of our speech. In the concentration camp, there is no big Other, no one on whom we can count to receive and verify our testimony. This is what makes even our survival meaningless.

This brings us again to the fate of modern art. Schoenberg still hoped that somewhere there would be at least one listener who would truly understand his atonal music. It was only his greatest pupil, Anton Webern, who accepted the fact that there is no listener, no big Other to receive the work and properly recognize its value. In literature, James Joyce still counted on future generations of literary critics as his ideal public, claiming that he wrote *Finnegans Wake* to keep them occupied for the next 400 years. In the aftermath of the Holocaust, we, writers and readers, have to accept that we are alone, reading and writing at our own risk, with no guarantee from the big Other. (It was Beckett who drew this conclusion in his break with Joyce.)

---

8 Primo Levi, *If This Is a Man*, New York: Alfred A. Knopf 2000, p. 63.

This lack of the big Other does not, however, mean that we are irrevocably trapped in the misery of our finitude, deprived of any redemptive moments. In Semprún's novel, Gérard witnesses the arrival of a truckload of Polish Jews at Buchenwald; they had been stacked into a freight train almost 200 to a car, traveling for days without food and water in the coldest winter of the war. On arrival, all had frozen to death except for fifteen children, kept warm in the middle of a bundle of bodies. When the children were removed from the car the Nazis let their dogs loose on them. Soon only two fleeing children were left:

> The little one began to fall behind, the SS were howling behind them and then the dogs began to howl too, the smell of blood was driving them mad, and then the bigger of the two children slowed his pace to take the hand of the smaller … together they covered a few more yards … till the blows of the clubs felled them and, together they dropped, their faces to the ground, their hands clasped for all eternity.[9]

What should not escape our attention is that the freeze of eternity is (again) embodied in the hand as partial object: while the bodies of the two boys perish, the clasped hands persist for all eternity like the smile of the Cheshire cat … It is not hard to imagine how this scene might appear on screen: as the soundtrack records what is happening in reality (the two children being clubbed to death), the image of their clasped hands freezes, immobilized for eternity—while the sound renders temporary reality, the image renders the eternal Real. (Exactly such a procedure was used by Manuel de Oliveira in the last scene of his *A Talking Picture*.)[10] It is the pure surface of such fixed images of eternity, not any deeper Meaning, which allows for redemptive moments in the bleak story of the Shoah. One should read this imagined scene together with two variations. Recall the final shot of *Thelma and Louise*: the frozen image of the two women in the car "flying" over the precipice. Is this a vision of positive utopia (the triumph of feminine subjectivity over death), or a masking of the miserable reality about to come? From my youth, I remember an old Croatian avant-garde short film about a man chasing a woman around a large table, the two of them madly giggling. The chase goes on, and the giggling gets louder and louder, even when the couple disappear behind the table and we see only the man's hands being raised. In the final shot, we see the dead woman's mutilated body, but the giggling goes on …

The weakness of the final shot from *Thelma and Louise* is that the frozen image is not accompanied by a soundtrack recording what is "really" happening (the car crashing, the screams of the women)—strangely, this lack of reality undermines the utopian dimension of the frozen image. In the Croat film, the

9 Semprún, *The Long Voyage*, p. 172.
10 I owe this information to Dalmar Abdulmejid, Chicago.

relations are inverted: it is the soundtrack which continues the fantasy of the erotic play, while the frozen image of the dead body confronts us with reality. The image thereby radically changes our perception of the soundtrack: the same laughter loses its erotic innocence, turning into the obscene giggling of haunting undead voices. The lesson is clear: in the scene imagined by Semprún, the frozen image accompanying the reality registered in sound stands for a positive eternal-ethical utopia, while in the Croat film, the laughter which persists even after its bearer has been murdered stands for the evil-obscene undead.

Eternity is to be taken here in the strictest Platonic sense. In one of the Agatha Christie stories, Hercule Poirot discovers that an ugly nurse is the same person as the beautiful woman he had previously met on a trans-Atlantic voyage, she has merely disguised herself to hide her natural beauty. Hastings, Poirot's Watson-like companion, remarks sadly that if a beauty can make herself appear ugly, then the same can also be done vice versa. What then remains in man's infatuation beyond deception? Does this insight into the unreliability of the beautiful woman not signal the end of love? "No, my friend," replies Poirot, "it announces the beginning of wisdom." In other words, such skepticism, such awareness of the deceptive nature of feminine beauty, misses the point, which is that feminine beauty is nonetheless absolute, an absolute which appears: no matter how fragile and deceptive it may be at the level of substantial reality, what transpires in/through the moment of Beauty is an Absolute—there is more truth in the appearance than in what may be hidden beneath it. Therein resides Plato's deep insight: Ideas are not the hidden reality beneath appearances (Plato was well aware that this hidden reality is that of ever-changing corrupting and corrupted matter); Ideas are nothing but the very form of appearance, this form as such—or, as Lacan succinctly rendered Plato's point, the supra-sensible is appearance as appearance. For this reason, neither Plato nor Christianity are forms of Wisdom—they are both anti-Wisdom embodied.

What this means is that, in conceiving of art, we can return to Plato without shame. Plato's reputation has suffered on account of his claim that poets should be thrown out of the city. (Rather sensible advice, judging from my own post-Yugoslav experience, where the path to ethnic cleansing was prepared by the dangerous dreams of poets—the Bosnian Serb leader Radovan Karadžić being only one among them. If the West has its military-industrial complex, we in the ex-Yugoslavia had a poetic-military complex: the post-Yugoslav war was triggered by an explosive mixture of poetic and military components.) From a Platonic standpoint, what does a poem about the Holocaust do? It provides a "description without place": it renders the Idea of Holocaust.

Recall the old Catholic strategy for guarding men against the sins of the flesh: when tempted by a voluptuous female body, imagine how it will look in a couple of decades—the wrinkled skin and sagging breasts ... (better still, imagine what lurks even now beneath the skin: the raw flesh and bones, bodily fluids, half-digested food and excrement ...). The same advice had already been given by Marcus Aurelius in his *Meditations*:

> Like seeing roasted meat and other dishes in front of you and suddenly realizing: This is a dead fish. A dead bird. A dead pig. Or that this noble vintage is grape juice, and the purple robes are sheep wool dyed with shellfish blood. Or making love—something rubbing against your penis, a brief seizure and a little cloudy liquid.
>
> Perceptions like that—latching onto things and piercing through them, so we see what they really are. That's what we need to do all the time—all through our lives when things lay claim to our trust—to lay them bare and see how pointless they are, to strip away the legend that encrusts them.[11]

Far from enacting a return to the Real destined to break the imaginary spell of the body, such procedures amount to an *escape from the Real*, the Real which announces itself in the seductive appearance of the naked body. That is to say, in the opposition between the spectral appearance of the sexualized body and the repulsive body in decay, it is the spectral appearance which is the Real, while the decaying body is merely reality—that to which we take recourse in order to avoid the deadly fascination of the Real as it threatens to draw us into its vortex of *jouissance*. A "raw" Platonism would claim here that only the beautiful body fully materializes the Idea, and that a body in material decay simply falls away from its Idea, is no longer its faithful copy. From a Deleuzian (and, here, Lacanian) perspective, on the contrary, the specter that attracts us is the Idea of the body as Real. This body is not the body in reality, but the virtual body in Deleuze's sense of the term: the incorporeal/immaterial body of pure intensities. (One should thus invert the usual opposition within which true art is "deep" and commercial kitsch superficial: the problem with kitsch is that it is all too "profound," manipulating deep libidinal and ideological forces, while genuine art knows how to remain at the surface, how to subtract its subject from the "deeper" context of historical reality.)

The same goes for contemporary art, where we encounter often brutal attempts to "return to the real," to remind the spectator (or reader) that she is perceiving a fiction, to awaken her from the sweet dream. This gesture has two main forms which, although opposed, amount to the same thing. In literature or cinema, there are (especially in postmodern texts) self-reflexive reminders that what we are watching is a mere fiction, such as when the actor on screen addresses us directly as spectators, thus ruining the illusion of the autonomous

---

11 Marcus Aurelius, *Meditations*, trans. Gregory Hays, New York: Modern Library 2002, pp. 70–1.

space of the narrative, or the writer directly intervenes in the story to add an ironic comment; in theatre, there are occasional brutal acts (like slaughtering a chicken onstage) which awaken us to the reality of the stage. Instead of conferring on these gestures a kind of Brechtian dignity, perceiving them as versions of extraneation, one should rather denounce them for what they are: *escapes from the Real*, the exact opposite of what they claim to be, desperate attempts to avoid the real of the illusion itself, the Real that emerges in the guise of an illusory spectacle.

IDEA'S APPEARING

And the same goes for love—that is to say, what is it to find oneself passionately in love? Is it not a kind of permanent state of exception? All the proper balances of our daily life are disturbed, everything we do is colored by the underlying thought of "that." The situation is properly "beyond Good and Evil": we feel a weird indifference towards our moral obligations with regard to our parents, children, friends—even if we continue to meet them, we do so in a mechanical way, in a mode of "as if"; everything pales into insignificance compared to our passionate attachment. In this sense, falling in love is like the blinding light that hit Saul/Paul on the road to Damascus: a kind of religious suspension of the Ethical, to use Kierkegaard's terms. An Absolute intervenes and derails the normal run of our affairs: it is not so much that the standard hierarchy of values is inverted, but, more radically, that another dimension enters the scene, a different level of being. And, of course, the same holds for an authentic political engagement. In his *Conflict of the Faculties*, written in the mid-1790s, Immanuel Kant addresses a simple but difficult question: is there true progress in history? (He meant ethical progress in regard to freedom, not just material development.) Kant conceded that actual history is confused and offers no clear proof: we might think of how the twentieth century brought unprecedented democracy and welfare, but also the Holocaust and the Gulag. But Kant nonetheless concluded that, although progress cannot be proven, we can discern signs which indicate that it is possible. Kant interpreted the French Revolution as such a sign which pointed towards the possibility of freedom: the hitherto unthinkable happened, a whole people fearlessly asserted their freedom and equality. For Kant, even more important than the often bloody reality of what occurred on the streets of Paris was the enthusiasm that the events in France gave rise to in the eyes of sympathetic observers all around Europe (and also in Haiti!):

> The recent Revolution of a people which is rich in spirit, may well either fail or succeed, accumulate misery and atrocity, it nevertheless arouses in the heart of all spectators (who are not themselves caught up in it) a taking of sides according to desires which borders on enthusiasm and which, since its very expression was not without danger, can only have been caused by a moral disposition within the human race.[12]

Do not these words also fit perfectly the Egyptian uprising of February 2011 that toppled President Mubarak? The French Revolution was for Kant a sign of history in the triple sense of *signum rememorativum*, *demonstrativum*, *prognosticum*. The Egyptian uprising was also a sign in which the memory of the long *past* of authoritarian oppression and the struggle for its abolition reverberates; an event which *now* demonstrates the possibility of a change; and a hope for *future* achievements. Whatever our doubts, fears, and compromises, for that instant of enthusiasm, each of us was free and participating in the universal freedom of humanity. All the skepticism expressed behind closed doors even by many worried progressives was proven wrong.

First, one could not help but note the "miraculous" nature of the events in Egypt: something happened that few had predicted, violating the experts' opinions, as if the uprising was the result not simply of social causes but of the intervention of a foreign agency into history, an agency that we can call, in a Platonic fashion, the eternal Idea of freedom, justice, and dignity.

Second, the uprising was universal: it was immediately possible for all of us around the world to identify with it, to know what it was about, without any need for a cultural analysis of the specific features of Egyptian society. In contrast to the Khomeinist revolution in Iran—where leftists had to smuggle their message into a predominantly Islamist frame—here, the frame was clearly that of a universal and secular call for freedom and justice, so that even the Muslim Brotherhood had to adopt this language of secular demand. The most sublime moment occurred when Muslims and Copts joined in a common prayer on the Tahrir square, chanting "We are One!" thus providing the best answer to the sectarian religious violence. Those neoconservatives who criticized multiculturalism in the name of the universal values of freedom and democracy were confronted with a moment of truth: You want universal freedom and democracy? This is what people are demanding in Egypt, so why are you uneasy? Is it because the Egyptian protesters also want social and economic justice, not just market freedom?

Third, the violence of the protesters was purely symbolic, an act of radical and collective civil disobedience: they suspended the authority of the state—it

12 Immanuel Kant, "The Conflict of Faculties," in *Political Writings*, Cambridge: Cambridge University Press 1991, p. 182.

How can universal appear in history? Must be universal, miraculous

was not just an inner liberation, but a social act of breaking the chains of *servitude volontaire*. The physical violence was perpetrated by Mubarak's hired thugs, who entered Tahrir Square on horses and camels to knock the protesters around; the most the protesters did was defend themselves.

Fourth, although combative, the protesters' message was not one of killing. The demand was for Mubarak to go, to leave his post and the country, and thus open up a space for freedom in Egypt, a freedom that excluded no one—the protesters' call to the army and even the hated police was not "Death to you!" but "We are brothers! Join us!" This last feature clearly distinguishes emancipatory from rightist-populist demonstrations: although the rightist mobilization proclaims the organic unity of the People, this unity is sustained by a call to annihilate a designated enemy (Jews, traitors ...).

When President Obama welcomed the uprising as a legitimate expression of opinion that needed to be acknowledged by the government, the confusion was total: the crowds in Cairo and Alexandria did not want their demands to be acknowledged by the government; they denied the very legitimacy of the government. They did not want the Mubarak regime as a partner in dialogue; they wanted Mubarak to go. They not only wanted a new government that would listen to their opinions, they wanted to reshape the entire state. They did not have "opinions"; they were the truth of the situation in Egypt. Mubarak understood this much better than Obama. There was no room for compromise here: either the entire Mubarak power edifice fell, or the uprising would be co-opted and betrayed. The protracted struggle which dragged on in Egypt was not a conflict of visions, but the conflict between a vision of freedom, the "eternal" Platonic Idea of freedom, and a blind clinging to power ready to use all means possible—terror, food deprivation, exhaustion, bribery—to crush the will to freedom.

This "truth of Plato" received its clearest formulation in one of the great anti-Platonic works, Gilles Deleuze's *The Logic of Sense*, where Deleuze begins by "inverting" Plato's dualism of eternal Ideas and their imitations in sensuous reality into the dualism of substantial (material) bodies and the pure impassive surface of Sense, the flux of Becoming which is to be located on the very borderline of Being and non-Being. Senses are surfaces which do not exist, but merely subsist: "They are not things or facts, but events. We cannot say that they exist, but rather that they subsist or inhere (having this minimum of being which is appropriate to that which is not a thing, a nonexisting entity)."[13] The Stoics, who developed this notion of "incorporeals," were

13 Gilles Deleuze, *The Logic of Sense*, trans. Mark Lester with Charles Stivale, New York: Columbia University Press 1990, p. 5.

> the first to reverse Platonism and to bring about a radical inversion. For if bodies with their states, qualities, and quantities, assume all the characteristics of substance and cause, conversely, the characteristics of the Idea are relegated to the other side, that is to this impassive extra-Being which is sterile, inefficacious, and on the surface of things: the ideational or the incorporeal can no longer be anything other than an "effect."[14]

This dualism is the "materialist truth" of the dualism of Ideas and material things, and it is against this background that one should envisage a return to Plato. Let us take an unexpected example: *A Woman Throwing a Stone*, a lesser known painting by Picasso from his surrealist period in the 1920s, offers itself easily to a Platonist reading: the distorted fragments of a woman on a beach throwing a stone are, of course, a grotesque misrepresentation, if measured by the standard of realist reproduction; however, in their very plastic distortion, they immediately/intuitively render the Idea of a "woman throwing a stone," the "inner form" of such a figure. This painting makes clear the true dimension of Plato's philosophical revolution, so radical that it was misinterpreted by Plato himself: the assertion of the gap between the spatio-temporal order of reality in its eternal movement of generation and corruption, and the "eternal" order of Ideas—the notion that empirical reality can "participate" in an eternal Idea, that an eternal Idea can shine through it, appear in it. Where Plato got it wrong is in his ontologization of Ideas (strictly homologous to Descartes's ontologization of the *cogito*), as if Ideas form another, even more substantial and stable order of "true" reality. What Plato was not ready (or, rather, able) to accept was the thoroughly virtual, "immaterial" (or, rather, "insubstantial") status of Ideas: like sense-events in Deleuze's ontology, Ideas have no causality of their own; they are virtual entities generated by spatio-temporal material processes. Take an attractor in mathematics: all positive lines or points in its sphere of attraction only endlessly approach it, without ever reaching its form—the existence of this form is purely virtual; it is nothing more than the form towards which the lines and points tend. However, precisely as such, the virtual is the Real of this field: the immovable focal point around which all elements circulate—the term "form" here should be given its full Platonic weight, since we are dealing with an "eternal" Idea in which reality imperfectly "participates." One should thus fully accept that spatio-temporal material reality is "all there is," that there is no other "more true" reality: the ontological status of Ideas is that of *pure appearing*. The ontological problem of Ideas is the same as the fundamental problem addressed by Hegel: how is meta-physics possible, how can temporal reality *participate* in the eternal Order, how can this order *appear*, transpire, in it? It is not "how can we reach the true reality beyond appearances?" but "how can *appearance* emerge

14 Ibid, p. 7.

in reality?" The conclusion Plato avoids is implied in his own line of thought: *the supersensible Idea* does not dwell *beyond* appearances, in a separate ontological sphere of fully constituted Being; it *is appearance as appearance*. No wonder that the two great admirers of Plato's *Parmenides*, Hegel and Lacan, both provide exactly the same formula of the "truth" of the Platonic supersensible Idea: the supersensible

> *comes from* the world of appearance which has mediated it; in other words, appearance is its essence and, in fact, its filling. The supersensible is the sensuous and the perceived posited as it is *in truth*; but the *truth* of the sensuous and the perceived is to be *appearance*. The supersensible is therefore *appearance qua appearance*. . . It is often said that the supersensible world is *not* appearance; but what is here understood by appearance is not appearance, but rather the *sensuous* world as itself the really actual.[15]

When Lacan describes how Parrhasius painted the curtain in order to prompt Zeuxis to ask him, "OK, now please draw aside the veil and show me what you have painted!" his interpretation of the story reads as an explication of the above-quoted passage from Hegel. Parrhasius's painting

> appears as something else (as another thing) than that as what it gives/presents itself, or, rather, it gives/presents itself now as being this (an)other thing. The painting does not rival appearance, it rivals what Plato designated as the Idea which is beyond appearance. It is because the painting is this appearance which says that it is what gives appearance, that Plato raises himself against painting as an activity which rivals his own.[16]

The implicit lesson of Plato is *not* that everything is appearance, that it is not possible to draw a clear line of separation between appearance and reality (that would have meant the victory of sophism), but that essence is "appearance as appearance," that essence appears in contrast to appearance within appearance; that *the distinction between appearance and essence has to be inscribed into appearance itself*. Insofar as the gap between essence and appearance is inherent to appearance, in other words, insofar as essence is nothing but appearance reflected into itself, appearance is appearance against the background of nothing—everything that appears ultimately appears out of nothing (or, to put it in terms of quantum physics, all entities arise out of the quantum vacillations

15 G. W. F. Hegel, *Phenomenology of Spirit*, trans. A. V. Miller, Oxford: Oxford University Press 1977, p. 89.

16 Jacques Lacan, *The Four Fundamental Concepts of Psycho-Analysis*, New York: W. W. Norton & Company 1978, p. 103.

of the void). Appearance is nothing in itself; it is just an illusory being, but this illusory being is the only being of essence, so that the reflective movement of essence

> is the movement nothing to nothing, and so back to itself. The transition, or becoming, sublates itself in its passage; the other that in this transition comes to be, is not the non-being of a being, but the nothingness of a nothing, and this, to be the negation of a nothing, constitutes being. Being only *is* as the movement of nothing to nothing, and as such it is essence; and the latter does not *have* this movement *within* it, but is this movement as a being that is itself absolutely illusory, pure negativity, outside of which there is nothing for it to negate but which negates only its own negative, and this negative, which latter is only in this negating.[17]

The answer to "Why is there Something rather than Nothing?" is thus that there *is* only Nothing, and all processes take place "from Nothing through Nothing to Nothing." However, this nothing is not the Oriental or mystical Void of eternal peace, but the nothingness of a pure gap (antagonism, tension, "contradiction"), the pure form of dislocation ontologically preceding any dislocated content. Such a radical ontological claim is not only dismissed by common sense as a meaningless play with words, it was also problematized by many followers and critics of Hegel from Schelling to Dieter Henrich, whose diagnosis is that the Hegelian negation of negation only works if we confuse two meanings of immediacy: immediacy as the immediate starting point of a process and immediacy as the result of mediation (self-relating negation). Henrich's critical conclusion is that Hegel's attempt to provide a circular foundation for the dialectical process by way of demonstrating how the process itself retroactively posits/grounds its own presuppositions fails, and that what is needed is an immediate absolute starting point provided by the subject's *Selbst-Vertrautheit* (self-acquaintance), preceding any reflexive movement of self-consciousness.

One can nonetheless defend Hegel here: as a model of what he has in mind, let us take the notion of the *clinamen* in all its radicality: it is not that there are first atoms, which then deviate from their straight path (or not)—atoms are nothing but their *clinamen*. There is no substantial "something" prior to the *clinamen* which gets caught up in it; this "something" which deviates is created, emerges, through the *clinamen itself*. The *clinamen* is thus like the photon with no mass: for an ordinary particle (if there is such a thing), we imagine it as an object with a mass, such that when its movement is accelerated its mass grows; a photon, however, has no mass in itself, its entire mass is the result of its acceleration. The paradox is here the paradox of a thing which is always (and nothing

17 G. W. F. Hegel, *The Science of Logic*, trans. A. V. Miller, Atlantic Highlands: Humanities Press 1969, p. 400.

but) an excess with regard to itself: in its "normal" state, it is nothing. This brings us back to Lacan's notion of the *objet a* as surplus-enjoyment: there is no "basic enjoyment" to which one adds the surplus-enjoyment; enjoyment is always a surplus, in excess. The object-in-itself (photon, atom) is here not negated/mediated, it *emerges as the (retroactive) result of its mediation.*

This result brings us back unexpectedly to Plato's *Parmenides*, which uncannily ends up evoking a hypothesis that points forward towards the thesis that *there is only Nothing*, that all processes take place "from Nothing through Nothing to Nothing": "If one is not, then nothing is."[18] Is not *Parmenides*, even more than Plato's *Sophist*, *the* dialogue on the corrosive all-pervasive force of nothingness? It begins already in *Parmenides* 130c-d, when Parmenides raises a question that perplexes Socrates and forces him to admit his limitation: are there also Ideas of the lowest material things, Ideas of excrement, dust …? Is there an *eidos* for "things that might seem absurd, like hair and mud and dirt, or anything else totally undignified and worthless?" (130c). What lurks behind this question is not only the embarrassing fact that the noble notion of Form could also apply to excremental objects, but a much more precise paradox that Plato approaches in his *Statesman* (262a–263a), in which he makes a crucial claim: divisions (of a genus into species) should be made at the proper joints. For example, it is a mistake to divide the genus of all human beings into Greeks and barbarians: "barbarian" is not a proper form because it does not designate a positively defined group (species), but merely all persons who are not Greeks. The positivity of the term "barbarian" thus conceals the fact that it serves as the container for all those who do not fit the form "Greek." Hegel's (and Lacan's) hypothesis is that this holds for all divisions of a genus into species: every genus, in order to be fully divided into species, has to include such a negative pseudo-species, a "part of no-part" of the genus, all those who belong to the genus but are not covered by any of its species. This "contradiction" between a genus and its species, embodied in an excessive group whose consistency is purely "negative," is what sets a dialectical process in motion.

In the domain of art as the "sensible appearing of the Idea" (a notion which should be fully rehabilitated—on condition that we conceive of the Idea as the surface of an Event that shines through a unique physical constellation), we confront a strictly homologous question: what object-content can be made into a topic of art? The history of art is a history of the gradual disclosure of new domains: with Romanticism, chaotic ruins and mountains become sublime; in high-quality detective novels, corrupted megalopolises and decaying suburbs, not to mention murder, are included; in *fin de siècle* modernism, feminine hysteria becomes a topic, and so on. Mladen Dolar is right to link this problem

18 Plato, *The Dialogues of Plato*, Vol. 4, trans. B. Jowett, Oxford: Oxford University Press 1892.

to that of the *agalma*, the ineffable *x*, the secret treasure that (also) eludes predication:

> we have here the necessary counterpart, the Platonian missing half, as it were, for a theory of the object a. There are two very different, sharply opposed, views of the object in Plato—agalma and junk (shall we say "agalma and shit" to make for a better slogan?)—which should ultimately be made to converge in the concept of object a, and the theory of the object has to account for both from the same pivot.[19]

The *objet a* is thus the name for the ultimate unity of the opposites in Plato … In the early 1920s, Lenin proposed that Marxist philosophers should form a "society of the materialist friends of Hegel"—today, perhaps, the time has come for radical philosophers to form a "society of the materialist friends of Plato." Plato is the first in a series of philosophers (Descartes and Hegel being the two main others) who fell out of favor in the twentieth century, being blamed for all our misfortunes. Badiou has enumerated six main (and partially intertwined) forms of twentieth-century anti-Platonism:

1. *Vitalist* anti-Platonism (Nietzsche, Bergson, Deleuze): the assertion of the real of life-becoming against the intellectualist sterility of Platonic Forms—as Nietzsche put it, "Plato" is the name for a disease …

2. *Empiricist-analytic* anti-Platonism: Plato believed in the independent existence of Ideas; but, as Aristotle already knew, Ideas do not exist independently of sensuous things whose forms they are. The main counter-Platonic thesis of analytic empiricists is that all truths are either analytic or empirical.

3. *Marxist* anti-Platonism (for which Lenin is not blameless): the dismissal of Plato as the first Idealist, opposed to pre-Socratic materialists as well as to the more "progressive" and empirically oriented Aristotle. In this view (which conveniently forgets that, in contrast to Aristotle's notion of the slave as a "talking tool," there is no place for slaves in Plato's *Republic*), Plato was the main ideologist of the class of slave owners …[20]

4. *Existentialist* anti-Platonism: Plato denies the uniqueness of singular existence and subordinates the singular to the universal. This anti-Platonism has

---

19 Mladen Dolar, "In Parmenidem Parvi Commentarii," *Helios* 31:1–2 (2004), p. 65.

20 Does the parallel between the passage from Plato to Aristotle and the passage from Kant to Hegel really hold? Is Hegel really, as Bukharin put it, "the Aristotle of the bourgeoisie"? Not so fast …

a Christian version (Kierkegaard: Socrates versus Christ) and an atheist one (Sartre: "existence precedes essence").

5. *Heideggerian* anti-Platonism: Plato as the founding figure of "Western metaphysics, " the key moment in the historical process of the "forgetting of Being," the starting point of the process which culminates in today's technological nihilism ("from Plato to NATO …").

6. *"Democratic"* anti-Platonism in political philosophy, from Popper to Arendt: Plato as the originator of the "closed society," as the first thinker who elaborated in detail the project of totalitarianism. (For Arendt, at a more refined level, Plato's original sin was to have subordinated politics to Truth, not seeing that politics is a domain of phronesis, of judgments and decisions made in unique, unpredictable situations.)

Plato's position is thus similar to that of Descartes: "Plato" is the negative point of reference which unites otherwise irreconcilable enemies: Marxists and anti-Communist liberals, existentialists and analytic empiricists, Heideggerians and vitalists …

So why a return to Plato? Why do we need a *repetition* of Plato's founding gesture? In his *Logiques des mondes*, Badiou provides a succinct definition of "democratic materialism" and its opposite, "materialist dialectics": the axiom which condenses the first is "*There is nothing but bodies and languages …*," to which materialist dialectics adds "*… with the exception of truths.*"[21] One should bear in mind the Platonic, properly meta-physical, thrust of this distinction: *prima facie*, it cannot but appear as a proto-idealist gesture to assert that material reality is not all that there is, that there is also another level of incorporeal truths. Badiou here makes the paradoxical philosophical gesture of defending, *as a materialist*, the autonomy of the "immaterial" order of Truth. As a materialist, and in order to be thoroughly materialist, Badiou focuses on the *idealist topos par excellence*: how can a human animal forsake its animality and put its life in the service of a transcendent Truth? How can the "transubstantiation" from the pleasure-oriented life of an *individual* to the life of a *subject* dedicated to a Cause occur? In other words, how is a free act possible? How can one break (out of) the network of the causal connections of positive reality and conceive an act that begins by and in itself? Again, Badiou repeats, within the materialist frame, the elementary gesture of idealist anti-reductionism: human Reason cannot be reduced to the result of evolutionary adaptation; art is not just a heightened procedure for producing sensual pleasure but a medium of Truth; and so on.

21 *Author's translation:* Alain Badiou, *Logiques des mondes*, Paris: Seuil 2006, p. 9.

This, then, is our basic philosophico-political choice (decision) today: either repeat in a materialist vein Plato's assertion of the meta-physical dimension of "eternal Ideas," or continue to dwell in the postmodern universe of "democratic-materialist" historicist relativism, caught in the vicious cycle of the eternal struggle with "premodern" fundamentalisms. How is this gesture possible, thinkable even? Let us begin with the surprising fact that Badiou identifies the "principal contradiction," the predominant antagonism, of today's ideological situation not as the struggle between idealism and materialism, but as the struggle between two forms of materialism (democratic and dialectical). Plus, to add insult to injury, "democratic materialism" stands for the reduction of all there is to the historical reality of bodies and languages (the twins of Darwinism, brain science, etc., and of discursive historicism), while "materialist dialectics" adds the "Platonic" ("idealist") dimension of "eternal" Truths. To anyone acquainted with the dialectics of history, however, there should be no surprise here.

From fictions to semblances

In order to discern the emancipatory potential of Plato's thought, it must be placed against the background of the sophist revolution. In breaking with the "closed" mythic universe, the Ancient Greek sophists like the ill-famed Gorgias asserted and played upon the self-referential abyss of language, which turns in its circle, lacking any external support. Plato's main task was to deal with this predicament which he experienced as a true *horror vacui*: aware that there could be no return to mythic closure, he tried to control the damage by re-anchoring language in the meta-physical reality of Ideas.

This is why his *Parmenides*, in which Plato himself enacts a self-critical collapse of his teaching on Ideas, is the closest he comes to being a sophist—the conclusion of the eight sophistic logical exercises covering the matrix of all logically possible relations between Being and the One is a Gorgias one: nothing exists, etc. Is not *Parmenides* the ultimate treatise on the signifier (One) and the real (Being), deploying the full matrix of their possible relations? The result is a version of the beautiful neopagan ("wicca") notion that after death everybody gets what they believed in: Valhalla for the Vikings, Hell or Paradise for the Christians, nothing at all for the materialists, and so on—all variations, even if they are contradictory (self-contradictory and contradictory with regard to each other), are in some sense true. That is to say, each of the hypotheses in the second part of *Parmenides* is to be read as pointing towards a specific ontological sphere within a "crazy" pluralistic ontology, and the task is to provide a precise description of each of these spheres, notwithstanding eventual logical mistakes in Plato's reasoning.

In all his later dialogues, Plato endeavors to control the damage by trying to draw a clear line of separation between self-referential sophistic language games and a speech which refers to substantial truths external to it. What Plato cannot accept is the Hegelian solution: all such exercises are true, they all have ontological relevance.

The crucial dialogue in this series is the *Sophist*, in which Plato deals with the problem of non-being, trying to outline a third way between two opposite extremes: Parmenides's assertion of the unconditional One and Gorgias's sophistic playing with the multiplicity of non-being. Plato classifies sophistry as the *appearance-making art*: imitating true wisdom, sophists produce appearances that deceive; in their empty ratiocinations and search for rhetorical effects, they obviously talk about something that does not exist. But how can one talk about non-being, making it appear as something that is? To answer this question, Plato is compelled to counter Parmenides's thesis that "it is impossible that things that are not are": things which are not (but only appear to be) also somehow are—how? Plato defines Not-Being not as the opposite of Being (i.e., not as excluded from the domain of Being), but as a Difference within the domain of Being: negative predication indicates something different from the predicate (when I say "this is not black," I thereby imply that it is a color other than black). Plato's basic strategy is thus to relativize non-being, that is, to treat it not as an absolute negation of being but as a relational negation of a predicate. This is how the sophist brings about a (relative) non-being and thus produces a false appearance: not by talking about absolute Nothing, but by attributing false predicates to entities.

At the origin of Plato's troubles is thus the undecidable ontological status of semblances. What is a semblance? As a key to understanding the notion of *semblant*, Lacan proposes Bentham's theory of fictions, which fascinates him for a very precise reason: the axis on which Lacan focuses is not "fiction versus reality" but "fiction versus (the real of) *jouissance*." As Jelica Sumic explains:

> semblance, as conceived by Lacan, is intended to designate that which, coming from the symbolic, is directed towards the real. This is precisely what characterizes Bentham's fictions. Indeed, as a fact of language, made of nothing but the signifier, Bentham's legal fictions are nonetheless capable of distributing and modifying pleasures and pains, thereby affecting the body. What held Lacan's attention in reading Bentham's *Theory of Fictions* was precisely that something which is ultimately an apparatus of language—Bentham defines fictions as owing their existence to language alone—is capable of inflicting pain or provoking satisfaction that can only be experienced in the body. . . . Hence by openly stating that fictions are nothing but an artificial device, "a contrivance," to use Bentham's proper term, designed to provoke either pain or pleasure, Bentham brings into question all human institutions insofar as they are an apparatus destined to regulate the modes of jouissance by dressing

them up in the virtues of the useful and the good. Bentham's concept of fictions can be seen as an effective manner of denouncing the moral and social ideals of the epoch, of exposing them as being nothing but a semblance, a make-believe.[22]

So, when Lacan claims that every discourse generates a semblance of *jouissance*, one should read this as involving *genitivus objectivus* as well as *subjectivus*: the semblance of *jouissance* (not a fully real one) and a *jouissance* in (the fact that what we are dealing with is a mere) semblance.[23] Bentham is here far from the crude logic of "unmasking," or discerning low motives—pleasure, power, envy, etc.—beneath high ethical reasons; the enigma he is confronting is a strange *eppur si muove*—even when an (ideological) fiction is clearly recognized as a fiction, it still works: "it is possible to use fictions in order to attain the real without believing in them."[24] This is the paradox of which Marx was already aware when he pointed out that "commodity fetishism" persists even after its illusory nature has become transparent. Niels Bohr provided its perfect formulation in response to a friend who asked if he really believed that the horseshoe above his door would bring him good luck: "Of course not, but I've been told it works even if one doesn't believe in it!"

What distinguishes humans from animals is their ability to pretend as opposed to simply getting caught up in an illusion: I pretend that something is *x* while knowing full well it is not *x*. Pretending (*faire-semblant*) is to be distinguished from direct attempts to create an illusion. When we watch a horror movie, we are pleasurably terrified—pleasurably, precisely because while giving ourselves up to the spectacle we know very well that that is just what it is. But imagine our shock and withdrawal if, all of a sudden, we became aware that what we were watching was in fact a snuff movie depicting real acts of horror. This is also why scarecrows can be frightening: not because we are duped into believing they are alive, but because we have to confront the fact that they work, while knowing very well they are just artifacts. A scarecrow confronts us with the efficiency of a simulacrum: "while scarecrows scare crows because they flap and shake in the wind, scarecrows scare humans because the collapse of their success at imitating a human reveals, in a sometimes abrupt and startling manner, indications that they are a simulacrum of a human."[25] What makes scarecrows terrifying is the minimal difference which makes them *in*-human:

22 Jelica Sumic, "On the Path of the Semblant," *Umbr(a)* 1 (2007), pp. 12–13.

23 This point was made already by Aristotle: we are able to enjoy the *mimesis*—say, in theatrical staging or in a painting—of something which is in itself ugly and which we would find extremely repelling were we to encounter it in reality.

24 Sumic, "On the Path of the Semblant," p. 13.

25 Russell Grigg, "Semblant, Phallus and Object in Lacan's Teaching," *Umbr(a)* 1 (2007), p. 134.

there is "nobody at home" behind the mask—as with a human who has turned into a zombie.

There is, however, a fundamental ambiguity at work here, which is why Lacan moved on from *fictions* to *semblances*. The distinction is between symbolic fiction proper and semblance in the sense of a simulacrum. Although, in both cases, the illusion works in spite of our awareness that it is only an illusion, there is a fine line separating them. It is crucial to distinguish here between pretending as a form of politeness, part of the "alienation" constitutive of the symbolic order as such, and the cynical instrumental use of norms which relies on another subject believing in them. It is one thing to greet an acquaintance with a polite "Nice to see you!" when we both know that I do not really mean it; it is another thing to play the other for a sucker, expecting him to fall for our lies. (The catch is not only that the first case cannot be dismissed as hypocrisy—in being polite, I "lie sincerely"—but also that the second case is not that of a simple lie—in duping the other, I become my own sucker …)

David K. Lewis, one of the most perspicuous American philosophers, approached the interesting problem of "truth in fiction" along just these lines: when we read a work of fiction, there is a pact between writer and reader that both will respect the illusion that the reported events are true. But what about a situation where the writer violates this fictional truth, this truth in fiction, either by violating the "truth" of his fictive universe out of sloppiness or by having the characters relate a fiction which wrongly passes for truth *within* the narrative universe of the fiction? In an epic novel, say, a minor character killed off in the first chapter pops up alive and well in a much later chapter—there is no mystery to it, the writer simply forgot that the person is dead …[26] In the more complex second case, recall the outcry provoked by the "false flashback" at the beginning of Hitchcock's *Stage Fright*: a man jumps into a car driven by the heroine and, as he starts telling her why he is running away, the events he describes are shown in flashback. At the film's end, we learn that he was lying: he is in fact the murderer. What caused the outcry was that Hitchcock had here violated one of the fundamental rules of narrative cinema: what is shown directly as a flashback must have really happened in the universe of the film; it's "cheating" if we later learn that it was a lie.[27]

26 It is said of Edgar Wallace—the English detective-fiction writer popular between the two world wars but today forgotten, who was known as a extremely fast and prolific writer—that one of his secretary's duties was to check the fate of his characters to prevent these kind of accidents, like the same person being killed twice.

27 The actress who played the victim of these lies was Jane Wyman, Ronald Reagan's first wife; later, during his presidency, Reagan specialized in such violations of even his own "fictional truth." He once told a crowd the "true" story of an heroic World War II pilot who, after all communications with his doomed plane were lost, did not eject, but

So what is the properly ontological problem here? Lewis asks a very simple but pertinent question: "why does this iteration of fiction not collapse into itself? How do we distinguish pretending [that fiction is true] from pretending to pretend?"[28] It is here that Lacan enters, with his distinction between imaginary lure and symbolic fiction proper: it is only within the symbolic space that we can pretend to pretend, or, lie in the guise of truth. Lewis's question is thus ultimately a question about the "truthful lie" of the symbolic order itself: how is it that the symbolic does not "fall into the real"? How is it that it cannot be reduced to simple signs, to an inner-worldly relation between signs and what they designate, as is the case with smoke signifying fire? The solution is a Platonic one: human language proper only functions when fiction counts for more than reality, when there is more truth in a mask than in the stupid reality beneath the mask, when there is more truth in a symbolic title (father, judge …) than in the reality of the empirical bearer of this title. This is why Lacan is right when he points out that a Platonic supra-sensible Idea is an imitation of imitation, appearance as appearance—something that *appears* on the surface of substantial reality.

The key formula of semblance was proposed by J-A. Miller: semblance is a mask (veil) of nothing.[29] Here, of course, the link with the fetish offers itself: a fetish is also an object that conceals the void. Semblance is like a veil, a veil which veils nothing—its function is to create the illusion that there is something hidden beneath the veil. This brings us back to the anecdote, repeatedly evoked by Lacan and mentioned above, about Zeuxis and Parrhasius, two painters from Ancient Greece, who compete to determine who can paint the more convincing illusion.[30] Zeuxis produced such a realistic picture of grapes that birds tried to eat them. But Parrhasius won by painting a curtain on the wall of his room so realistic that Zeuxis asked him to draw it back so that he could see the painting behind it. In Zeuxis's painting, the illusion was so convincing that the image was mistaken for the real thing; in Parrhasius's painting, the illusion resided in the very notion that what the viewer saw in front of him was just a veil covering up the hidden truth. This is also how, for Lacan, feminine masquerade works: the woman wears a mask in order to make us react like Zeuxis in front of Parrhasius's painting—*OK, now take off the mask and show us what you really*

---

tried to save his co-pilot, with the result that both were killed. When asked how he knew this, since both pilots had died, Reagan mumbled something like, "It must have been like this, he was a true American …" No wonder Jane and Ronald split up—Nancy was obviously more at home with such redoubled lies.

28 See David K. Lewis, "Truth in Fiction," in *Philosophical Papers*, Vol. 1, Oxford: Oxford University Press 1983, p. 23.

29 Jacques-Alain Miller, "Of Semblants in the Relation Between Sexes," *Psychoanalytical Notebooks* 3 (1999), p. 10.

30 See Lacan, *The Four Fundamental Concepts of Psycho-Analysis*, p. 103.

are! Developing these reflections of Lacan, Bernard Baas was right to point out that

> the formula "all discourse is semblance" can also be understood according to the logic articulated in the mathemes of sexuation: the affirmative universal proposition "all x verifies the function f(x)" implies—contrary to strict mathematical logic—the exception that makes the rule and that, in a certain way, founds it: "there exists at least one x that does not verify the function f(x)" . . . the universal law that states that "all discourse is semblance" demands, for that discourse, that there exists *at least one* discourse that would not be "semblance," because such a discourse is precisely that which forbids all discourse from escaping this law.[31]

Strangely, Baas does not supplement this masculine version with the feminine one: "there is no discourse which is not a discourse of semblance" implies that "not-all discourse is a discourse of semblance." This indicates how we are to reach a "discourse which is not semblance": not through the exception (one discourse which is not . . .), but through treating the multiplicity of discourses as "non-All," through discerning their inconsistency, their points of impossibility. This is what Lacan, in his late teaching, called "to vacillate the semblances": not to reach beyond, to an exception, but to reach their inconsistent non-All.

Therein resides the deadlock reached by Nietzsche who, in one and the same text (*Beyond Good and Evil*), seems to advocate two opposed epistemological positions: on the one hand, the notion of truth as the unbearable Real Thing—as dangerous, lethal even, like directly gazing into Plato's sun—so that the problem becomes how much truth a man can endure without diluting or falsifying it; on the other hand, the "postmodern" notion that appearance is more valuable than stupid reality, and that, ultimately, there is no final Reality, only the interplay of multiple appearances, so that the very opposition between reality and appearance should be abandoned.[32] Does not humanity's greatness lie in its ability to prioritize brilliant aesthetic appearance over gray reality? This, in Badiou's terms, is the passion of the Real versus the passion of semblance. How are we to read these two opposed positions together? Is Nietzsche here simply inconsistent, oscillating between two mutually exclusive views? Or is there a "third way"? That is to say, what if the two opposed options (passion of the Real / passion of the semblance) render palpable Nietzsche's struggle, his failure to articulate the "right" position whose formulation eluded him? There is not just the interplay of appearances, there is a Real—this Real, however, is not the inaccessible

31 Bernard Baas, "Semblance: Putting Philosophizing to the Test," *Umbr(a)* 1 (2007), p. 86.

32 I rely here on Alenka Zupančič, "Truth According to Nietzsche," an intervention at the symposium *Antinomies of Postmodern Reason*, Essen, March 15, 2002.

Thing, but the *gap* which prevents our access to it, the "rock" of the antagonism which distorts our view of the perceived object through a partial perspective. The "truth" is thus not the "real" state of things, accessed by a "direct" view of the object without any perspectival distortion, but the very Real of the antagonism which causes the perspectival distortion itself. Again, the site of truth is not the way "things really are in themselves," beyond perspectival distortion, but the very gap or passage which separates one perspective from another, the gap (in this case, social antagonism) which makes the two perspectives radically *incommensurable*. The "Real as impossible" is the cause of the impossibility of our ever attaining the "neutral" non-perspectival view of the object. There *is* a truth, and not everything is relative—but this truth is the truth of the perspectival distortion *as such*, not a truth distorted by the partial view from a one-sided perspective.

This brings us back once again to Plato: in the history of philosophy, the first exemplary case of "vacillating the semblances" occurs in the second part of Plato's *Parmenides*, with the deployment of eight hypotheses on the relation between Being and One. Each hypothesis, of course, describes the contours of a semblance—however, taken all together, they are not "mere semblances," but "semblances vacillated." And is not the Hegelian dialectical process the climax of this strategy of "vacillating the semblances"? Each figure of consciousness, each notion, is described and denounced in its semblance, without any reliance on an external standard of truth.

Dialectical gymnastics? No, thanks!

Parmenides is a dialogue from Plato's middle period—in a much more literal sense than is usually meant. Its very form is that of a composite: the first part is a typical "Socratic dialogue," this time turned against Socrates himself; the second part is exemplary of Plato's late dialogues in which one of the interlocutors develops his line of reasoning, with his partner limited to exclamatory punctuations like "So it is!" or "By Zeus, you are right!" and so on. However, this "middle period" character of the text in no way reduces it to a transitional work—it is, in a way, more radical than Plato's later dialogues because it brings about the collapse of the big Other, revealing its cracks and inconsistencies.

Parmenides first demonstrates to Socrates the weaknesses of his theory of Ideas, pointing out that, before risking such a grand theory, Socrates should first engage in some conceptual exercise, introducing movement into Ideas themselves. What then follows is a kind of philosophical counterpoint to Satie's "gymnopédies"—a vast network of "dialectical gymnastics," logical exertions actualizing the matrix of all possible relations between One and Being. The exact status of this exercise is not clear; what is clear, however, is that there is no positive result, as if the exercise were its own point. The only result is that there is no consistent totality, no "big Other." The whole interpretive problem arises when this result is read as merely negative: such a reading generates the need to fill the gap, to propose a new positive theory—which is what the late Plato then attempts to do, passing from one supplement to another, from *chora* in *Timaeus* to ... But what if such a reading is conditioned by a kind of perspectival illusion, involving a failure to see how the result is not merely negative, but is in itself already positive, already what we were looking for? To see this, one has only to effect a parallax shift and grasp the problem as (containing) its own solution.

One often hears talk of Plato's "esoteric teaching" which runs counter to his official idealism—the two main candidates are, for New Agers, a Gnostic dualism positing the feminine material principle as a counterpoint to idealism, and, for Leo Strauss, a ruthless and cynical realism, downgrading the theory of Ideas to the status of a "noble lie." What if it is *Parmenides* that delivers Plato's true teaching—not as something hidden, but in plain view? The trick is to take seriously (literally), as true ontology, what is usually seen as a playful dialectical exercise in following all possible hypotheses *ad absurdum*. The truth is not hidden behind the logical exercises, it is not the negative-theological message that the ineffable One is beyond the grasp of logic; it is simply that Plato really means what he says.

A parallel with Hegel could be of some use here. One way to determine exactly when "Hegel became Hegel" is to look at the relationship between logic and metaphysics: the early "pre-Hegelian" Hegel distinguishes between Logic (the study of pure notions as *organon*, the means to ontological analysis proper) and Metaphysics (the study of the basic ontological structure of reality), and he "becomes Hegel" the moment he drops this distinction and realizes that Logic *already is* Metaphysics: what appears as an introductory analysis of the tools required to grasp the Thing is already the Thing.[33] In an homologous way, we should not read the second part of *Parmenides* as a mere logical exercise preparing the way for the ontology proper—it *is* already this ontology. Does not Plato himself not point in this direction in the following Hegelian-sounding passage?

> By Heaven, can we be ready to believe that the absolutely real has no share in movement, life, soul or wisdom? That it does not live or think, but in solemn holiness,

33 Note the reversal of the usual reflexive move: it is not that what we thought to be the Thing reveals itself to be merely a step towards the Thing; it is that what appeared to be a mere preparatory move reveals itself to be already the Thing itself. And, needless to add, this reflexive move compels us to change the very definition of what "the Thing itself" is—it is no longer a substantial In-itself.

> unpossessed of mind, stands entirely at rest? That would be a dreadful thing to admit. (248e)

Such a radical "Hegelian" conclusion is, however, too much for the majority of interpreters. Traditional readings of the second part of *Parmenides* move between two interpretive extremes: they see in it either an exercise in pure logical gymnastics, or the negative-theological indication of the Unsayable One. For the Neoplatonists, who were the first to propose the latter reading, the purpose of *Parmenides*

> goes far beyond the making of subtle linguistic distinctions. The exercise in dialectic provides symbolic and numinous adumbrations of the nature of the super-essential One and how one might approach it. The negative conclusions of the first Hypothesis, for example, are not illustrations of the nonsensical nature of the pure One. Rather, they demonstrate the failure of reason and language to grasp the ineffable non-relative One that rises above all forms of relative knowledge. The dialectical exercise, which ranges over the whole field of discourse and considers all the logical permutations of any proposition, is a meditation for freeing the mind from clinging to any one philosophical position or assumption, thereby opening it up to mystical illumination. It is the Platonic *via negativa*.[34]

Or, as Findlay put it: "Those unable or unwilling to draw conclusions from more or less palpable hints, or constitutionally unable to understand metaphysical or mystical utterances, or to enter into mystical feelings ... should certainly *never* engage in the interpretation of Plato."[35] Badiou calls this Neoplatonic move from the inconsistent multiplicity of (logical) reasoning to the trans-discursive One (whatever its name, from Substance to Life) "the Great Temptation" of materialist thought. Both Hegel and Lacan, two great admirers of *Parmenides*, rejected this "misunderstood ecstasy" (Hegel), this "Neoplatonic confusion" (Lacan). But is the only alternative to reading *Parmenides* as a piece of mystical negative theology—its lesson being that the Absolute is ineffable, that it eludes the grasp of our categories, that we san say anything and/or nothing about it—to reduce it to a jokey logical exercise (non-substantial reasoning with no connection with reality), perhaps not even intended seriously (surely Plato must have been aware of the logical fallacies in some of the arguments)? Perhaps Hegel was right to see in this dialogue the summit of the Greek dialectic. What if we reject

34 Thomas J. McFarlane, "Plato's *Parmenides*," Center for Integral Science, December 1, 1988, revised March 3, 2004, available at integralscience.org.

35 J. N. Findlay, *Plato: The Written and Unwritten Doctrines*, New York: Humanities Press 1974, p. 26.

both options and treat the "contradictions" not as signs of the limitation of our reason, but as belonging to the "thing itself"? What if the matrix of all possible relations between the One and Being is also effectively the matrix of the "impossible" relations between the signifier and the Real?

Crucial here is the shift from the first to the second part of the dialogue. In the first part, Socrates tries to resolve the paradox that opposites can be attributed to the same entity (oneness and multiplicity, rest and movement, etc.) by way of distinguishing between the eternal order of Ideas and empirical reality. The same empirical thing can be one and multiple—it can simultaneously participate in the Idea of oneness and the Idea of multiplicity: a man is at once one, this individual, and multiple, a combination of parts or organs—but the *Ideas* of oneness or of multiplicity cannot. In the second part, Parmenides (in a supreme example of Platonic irony, given what we know of the "real" historical Parmenides) introduces the dynamics of relating, mutual participation, and "contradiction" into the real of Ideas themselves. In order to be One, one has to be multiple (to participate in multiplicity), and so on—"everything would fall apart, and great havoc would follow, if it turned out that there could be a contradiction in the order of forms themselves"[36]—"if someone could show that kinds and forms themselves have in themselves these opposite properties, that would call for astonishment. But if someone should demonstrate that I am one thing and many, what's astonishing about that?" (129c).

The succession of eight hypotheses in the second part should thus be conceived like the succession of categories in Hegel's logic, where each categorial determination is developed so that its inherent "contradiction" (inconsistency) is brought out. So what if we conceive the passage from the first to the second part of *Parmenides* as homologous to the Hegelian passage from phenomenology to logic? The first part works like any other of Plato's early dialogues: someone who pretends to know is questioned by the Socratic figure who compels him to admit the inconsistency of his position and thus the vanity of his knowledge; the exceptional feature here is that this procedure has become self-reflexive: the figure who pretends to know is now Socrates himself, whose teaching on Ideas is submitted to criticism in dialogue with Parmenides. In the second part, we pass from phenomenological dialogue to the logical self-deployment of notional determinations.

In her detailed introduction to *Parmenides*, Mary Louise Gill tries to avoid both predominant readings (*Parmenides* as a treatise on negative theology or as a logical exercise) by taking the second part literally, as an attempt to resolve the deadlock of the first part (where Parmenides has shown up the inconsistencies of Socrates' theory of forms, while nonetheless unequivocally asserting that the

36 Dolar, "In Parmenidem Parvi Commentarii," p. 67.

forms are needed if we are to understand being).[37] This heroic effort leads her to differentiate between the strength and pertinence of the various hypotheses: for her, the third hypothesis (asserting that the One and Many [the others] are not incompatible, that others can partake in the One as wholes, as parts, and get from this partaking their limit) points towards the solution: "Deduction 3 produced some highly constructive results by assuming that the one is altogether one and that the others somehow partake of it."[38] Parmenides destroys this promise in the fourth hypothesis only by accepting the unwarranted premise that the One and the others are totally incompatible.

Sympathetic and rigorous as Gill's attempt is, it seems to miss the point of the entire matrix of the eight hypotheses in their structural unity: what is the meaning of the matrix itself, irrespective of the varying quality of particular lines of argumentation? This brings us back to a reading of the entire set of hypotheses as a formal matrix of eight possible worlds: each hypothesis formulates a world's "immanent transcendental" (in Badiou's precise meaning of the term). *Parmenides* is thus Plato's "logics of worlds." The eight worlds implied by the eight hypotheses are not some kind of forerunner of a postmodern "plurality of universes": they arise against the background of a certain impossibility or deadlock which generates them—the impossibility of "reconciling" Being and the One, the Real and the Signifier, of making them overlap symmetrically. There are many worlds because Being cannot be One, because a gap persists between the two. What we should bear in mind here is that the couple of the One and Being prefigures the couple of Plato himself and Aristotle: in contrast to Aristotelian ontology, with its orientation towards being as the most basic notion in theory,

> Platonism identifies unity as the central concept from which all reasoning begins. One could say that Platonism is "henology" (*to hen* = the One) as opposed to "ontology." "The One" (an artificial philosophical word, which was not there before the school of Parmenides) is used here as a subject, not as a predicate or a numeral. For Aristotle, the concept of oneness is only an aspect of the particular. Every particular is "one," insofar as it is indivisible and individual. "Oneness," in this view, basically depends on the meaning of "Being." In Platonism, the reverse is true: the concept of the One is self-sufficient, so to speak, preceding the domain of particulars. Accordingly, the One accounts for the existence of particulars in a manifold that is somehow unified, structured, and determinate. It is a variant of the One. All these basic predicates of the particular can be interpreted in terms of the One that precedes all being.[39]

---

37 Mary Louise Gill, introduction to Plato's *Parmenides*, trans. Mary Louise Gill and Paul Ryan, Indianapolis: Hackett 1996.

38 Ibid., p. 107.

39 Dieter Henrich, *Between Kant and Hegel*, Cambridge, MA: Harvard University Press 2008, pp. 85–6.

There is yet another way to understand the link between *Parmenides*'s two parts: to focus on what the dialogue itself claims is the goal of the second part, namely to lay the ground for the proper understanding of the doctrine of Ideas whose critique has been laid out in the first part. Viewed in this way, the "pessimistic" conclusion that nothing at all exists, etc., should be qualified as a rejection of pre-Platonic cosmic monism: nothing fully exists, reality is a confused mess about which nothing consistent can be said; and if we remain within the coordinates of cosmic monism and do not posit a realm of Ideas external to Cosmos—if we limit ourselves to the One-All of the eternally changing reality—this One-All ultimately reveals itself to be nothing at all.

From the One to *den*

Parmenides's dialectical exercise is divided into eight parts: apropos of each of the two basic hypotheses—*if the One is* and *if the One is not*—he examines *the consequences for the One*, and *the consequences for the Others*; plus he adds a subtle but crucial distinction between the One which has being and the bare One, so that altogether we get eight hypotheses:

Hypothesis	*If …*	*Consequences for …*	*Result*
1	There is One	the One	negative
2	One *is*	the One	positive
3	One *is*	the Others	positive
4	There is One	the Others	negative
5	One *is not*	the One	positive
6	There is no One	the One	negative
7	One *is not*	the Others	positive
8	There is no One	the Others	negative

In the case of hypotheses 2, 3, 5, and 7, which predicate being (or non-being) of the One, the result is positive: predication is possible; that is, positive statements can be made of the One (or of the not One). In the case of hypotheses 1, 4, 6, and 8, which put the One out of the sphere of being (or non-being), the result is negative: predication is not possible; that is, nothing can be asserted of the One (or of the not One):

(1) "There is One," but a totally ineffable-unpredictable *One* without Being, a One which is neither true nor false—Dolar is right to point out that this One is not the non-symbolic Real, but the lack of a signifier, the "barred" signifier ($), which is as such still inherent to the order of the signifier.[40]

40 Dolar, "In Parmenidem Parvi Commentarii," p. 67.

(2) *One* with Being, "One *is*": we can predicate it, we are dealing with One which is; but crucial here is the implied *difference* between One and Being: "If one is, it participates in being, and is therefore something different from being, for otherwise it would make no sense to assert that one is."[41] But the moment we concede this difference, we are compelled to repeat it indefinitely, i.e., within each of its poles: every One again is and is One, every being is and is one, etc.: "'The one that is' falls apart into one and being, but in such a way that each part includes the other as its part. This inner division, once it has started, cannot be stopped: the moment we have two parts, we have infinitely many of them." Or, to put it in Hegelese, each term has two species, itself and the other term; each term is the encompassing unity of itself and its other. We enter thereby the problematic space of self-referential paradoxes: "One is now at one and the same time the whole and the part, and so into infinity, it is both limited and unlimited, it both moves and stands still, it is both identical and different, like and unlike itself and others, both equal and unequal to itself and to others etc." If the result of the first hypothesis is that we cannot predicate anything of the One, the result of the second hypothesis is that "anything goes," we can predicate all possible, even mutually exclusive, predicates. Dolar draws here exactly the opposite conclusion to Armand Zaloszyc: Lacan's *Y a d'l'Un* is a paraphrase not of the first, but of the second of *Parmenides*'s hypotheses:

> Lacan's famous dictum *Y a d'l'Un* can be read as a paraphrase of this second hypothesis. Translating it simply by "There is One" one loses the paradox of the French formulation, where the partitive article (*de*) treats the one as an indefinite quantity (as in *Il y a de l'eau*, "There is water," i.e. an indefinite quantity of it), implying, first, that there can be an immeasurable quantity of one, i.e. of what is itself the basis of any measuring, and second, if the quantity is indefinite, then it is divisible (like water)—but into what, if one is the minimal unity?[42]

But does this weird immeasurable quantity not mean that the One of the second hypothesis should *not* be linked to Lacan's *Y a d'l'Un*, that the "One which is," the unary signifier, S_1, should rather be *opposed* to the immeasurable "there is (something of the) One," which is characterized by a divisibility and thus a multiplicity not composed of Ones? The paradox is here a very elegant Hegelian one: although Plato is *the* philosopher of the One, what he is unable to think (as opposed to just "represent") is precisely the One as a concept. To do this, one needs not only a self-relating reflexive predication (the One is a "one One," an x which partakes of the Idea of One with regard

41 Ibid., p. 81.
42 Ibid., p. 82.

to Oneness itself)—which Plato possesses—but also the positive concept of zero (which Plato does not possess): to get a pure concept of the One, not just the notion of one thing, the x which "partakes of the idea of One with regard to Oneness itself" has to be zero, a void, devoid of all content. Or, to put it in a more descriptive way: being-a-One adds nothing to the content of an object; its only content is the form of self-identity itself.

In Dolar's reading, the first two hypotheses are two circles which partially intersect, so that the first hypothesis stands for the One without Being, that is, the One from which the part of it which intersects with Being is subtracted, and the second hypothesis stands for the narrow intersection of the two circles of One and Being.

(3) One with Being does not preclude Others with Being: there can be Others with predicates.

(4) One without Being precludes Others and thus also their predication.

(5) It concerns a One, something that is an entity, but which does not exist, i.e., does not have Being. Even if One is *not*, we can still predicate it, i.e., negative predication is possible, we know what we are saying when we negate a predicate.

(6) The One is here not only deprived of Being, but deprived of its very character of One: it is no longer a non-existent entity, but a nonentity—and, as such, cannot be predicated.

(7) What does the fact that the One is a non-existing entity mean for Others? As in the case of the hypothesis 5, Others can be predicated.

(8) If, however, One is not only a non-existent entity, but a nonentity, then there are also no Others, existing or non-existing—there is nothing at all.

To account for the difference between hypothesis 5—one can talk (make propositions, say true things) about non-being; truth has a structure of (symbolic) fiction—and hypothesis 7—everything is a fluid appearance—we must introduce a tripartite distinction between *symbolic* fiction, *imaginary* illusion, and the appearance of the *Real*: the One of hypothesis 5, the One that does not exist, but which we can talk about, is the symbolic fiction; the dispersed not-One of hypothesis 7 is that of imaginary illusion; and, we may add, the One that is not One of hypothesis 8 is the Real as impossible.

Radically opposed to Dolar's reading of *Parmenides* is that of Armand

Zaloszyc, according to whom "*Y a d'l'Un*" is the formula for the pure *jouissance*-One, that is, a *jouissance* not yet mediated by the Other, the symbolic order, not yet "departmentalized," accountable. The missing link which legitimizes us in establishing a connection between this thesis of Lacan and the first hypothesis of Plato's *Parmenides* (which asserts the One totally external to Being, with no relation to or participation in Being) is provided by the Neoplatonist "mysticism" of Plotinus—recall that, for Lacan, the mystical ex-stasis is the paradigmatic example of the *jouissance*-One. *Parmenides* was the Neoplatonists' favorite of Plato's texts, and they read it as a powerful assertion of the ineffability of the One with which the mystical experience reunites us:

> The demonstration of the first hypothesis of the Parmenides leads to the conclusion that it is impossible that the One exists. So it is, the One of this first hypothesis, being one by definition, could neither have parts nor be a whole. Therefore, it will have neither beginning, nor end, nor limits. For the same reason, it will not participate in time. It will therefore have no being since to be implies the participation in a time. And, if it is not at all, then can it have something that belongs to it or comes from it? Most certainly not. Therefore it has no name; there is no definition, no perception, and no knowledge of it. Is it possible that this be so of the One? No. From this demonstration of impossibility it can surely be legitimately introduced that "since the One in no way participates with being," it does not exist, that there is nothing beyond being, that being is therefore all. The Neoplatonists chose to read the Parmenides demonstration of impossibility differently. They agreed that there is an incompatibility between the One and being, but rather than deducing that the One does not exist, they concluded that no doubt the One did not exist in terms of being, but that beyond being, there is the One, that the One ex-sists from being.
>
> In this way, "there is the One" constitutes a formula that opposes ontology and leads towards the notion of the not-all of a radical Other, in terms of the otherness with which there is no relation, where emerges the logic of the Parmenides demonstration.
>
> Being on one side, and on the other, the there is—they are incompatible. Being on one side, the real on the other. We immediately see that this opposition is the one at work in negative theologies, in the pursuit of a non-knowledge that equals itself to learned ignorance, in the accounts given by the great Christian mystics of their experience, using oxymorons drawn from The Mystic Theology of Pseudo-Dionysius the Aeropagite.[43]

There are two arguments for this reading. When Lacan talks about *jouissance feminine*, he always qualifies it—"if a thing like that were to exist (but it does

43 Armand Zaloszyc, "Y a d'l'Un," intervention at the Congress of the World Association of Psychoanalysis, Rome, July 13–16, 2006.

not)"—thereby confirming its incommensurability with the order of being (existence). Plus, his formula is *Y a d'l'Un*, and the impersonal *il y a* is, like the German *es gibt* which plays such a key role in late Heidegger, clearly opposed to being (in English, this distinction gets blurred, since one cannot avoid the verb "to be" in translation). There is, however, one conclusive counter-argument which pretty much ruins the case: Zaloszyc refers to the Neoplatonic mystics as the missing link between Plato and Lacan, yet, as we have already seen, Lacan explicitly rejects the Neoplatonist reading of *Parmenides*. It thus seems that Dolar's opposed reading—wherein the One versus Being is, in Lacanese, the symbolic versus the Real—is much more convincing. But let us see where Zaloszyc's reading leads him:

> The One that there is, is the one of the jouissance One, that is, the jouissance designated in the terms of the first hypothesis of the Parmenides … it is opposed to a jouissance developed *partes extra partes* that is consequentially accountable and numerable according to the measurements of the signifier. If we think about it, the being itself is only determined by meaningfulness, whereas we refer the jouissance One to the real. The real as impossible, as we have already seen.
>
> So there is a jouissance that is not without a relation to the Other of the signifier (that is alienated to the signifier), and there is an autistic jouissance, separated from the signifier and separated from the Other, for which the paradigm is the non-relation. That is the jouissance One. From there, there are two ways to go: either maintain that there is no other being than being, with the will to foreclose the jouissance One, or support the idea that there is the One that exists apart from being, in which case the demonstration of impossibility takes into account the trace that this One leaves in the Other, in the form of "there is no sexual relation" …
>
> The passage from the jouissance One to the Name-of-the-Father is the passage from the not-all to an all, but this passage leaves an un-sublated remainder/excess, the trace that the jouissance One will leave there. One of the forms of this excess is jouissance feminine, the other is the Freudian Ur-Vater, the one who enjoys all the women.[44]

Insofar as, for Lacan, this One is (also) an "indivisible remainder" which makes the sexual relationship inexistent, one can understand how *Y a d'l'Un* is strictly correlative to *il n'y a pas de rapport sexuel*: it is the very object-obstacle to it; it is not primarily the mystical all-encompassing One of the infamous "oceanic feeling" derided by Freud, but a "little piece of the Real," the excremental remainder which disturbs the harmony of the Two. The equation of the two excesses (*jouissance feminine* and *Ur-Vater*) also makes sense: it points towards Lacan's statement that "woman is one of the names of the father."

44 Ibid.

What makes Zaloszyc's solution problematic is that it is ultimately incompatible with the very logic of the non-All to which it refers: it reduces it to the "masculine" logic of exception; symptomatically, Zaloszyc himself uses the term "exception" to designate the feminine position: "The feminine side of sexuation will present itself, not without a tie to the phallic signifier, but also not without having preserved a relation with the jouissance One"; this is what "makes a woman an exception," namely an exception to the phallic-symbolic order.

How are we to relate the One of *Y a d'l'Un* ("there is [some] One, something of a One," developed by Lacan in *Seminar XX [Encore]*) to the series of unary signifiers, prior to their unification through a phallic Master-Signifier—the infinitely self-divisible series of S_1 (S_1 (S_1 (S_1...))), which also replicates the frame of the materialist ontology of multiplicities and Void? There is a good reason Lacan uses the common French expression *Y a d'l'Un*, which is as far as possible from the elevated mystical assertion of the One beyond all being(s), *epekeina tes ousias* (like "there is water there"—an unspecified quantum). However, the One of *Y a d'l'Un* is not yet the One of counting: the diffuse "there is something of the One" precisely prevents the fixation of limits which would render possible the counting of Ones. What if one reads Lacan's *Y a d'l'Un* as the formula of the minimal libidinal fixation (on some One) constitutive of drive, as the moment of the emergence of drive from the pre-evental One-less multiplicity? As such, this One is a "*sinthome*," a kind of "atom of enjoyment," the minimal synthesis of language and enjoyment, a unit of signs permeated with enjoyment (like a tic we compulsively repeat). Are such Ones not *quanta of enjoyment*, its smallest, most elementary packages?

Obscurantist idealists like to vary the motif of "almost nothing": a minimum of being which nonetheless bears witness to divinity ("God is also present in the tiniest speck of dust ..."). The materialist answer to this is the *less than nothing*. The first to propose this answer was Democritus, the father of Ancient Greek materialism (and also, incidentally, one of the first to formulate the principle of equality—"Equality is everywhere noble," as he put it). To express this "less than nothing," Democritus took recourse to a wonderful neologism *den* (first coined by the sixth-century-BC poet Alcaeus), so the basic axiom of his ontology is: "Nothing is no less than Othing," or, as the German translation goes, "*Das Nichts existiert ebenso sehr wie das Ichts.*"[45] It is crucial to note how, contrary to the late Wittgensteinian thrust towards ordinary language, towards language as part of a life world, materialism begins by violating the rules of ordinary language, by

45 This translation probably relies on Meister Eckhart, who had already coined "*Ichts*" as a positive version of "*Nichts*," i.e., the void in its positive/generating dimension—the *nihil* out of which every creation proceeds. What Eckhart saw was the link between the subject and negativity.

thinking against language. (Since *med'hen* does not literally mean "nothing," but rather "not-one," a more adequate transposition of *den* into English would have been something like "otone" or even "tone."[46])

The Ancient Greeks had two words for nothing, *meden* and *ouden*, which stand for two types of negation: *ouden* is a factual negation, something that is not but could have been; *meden* is, on the contrary, something that in principle cannot be. From *meden* we get to *den* not simply by negating the negation in *meden*, but by displacing negation, or, rather, by supplementing negation with a subtraction. That is to say, we arrive at den when we take away from *meden* not the whole negating prefix, but only its first two letters: *meden* is *med'hen*, the negation of *hen* (one): not-one. Democritus arrives at *den* by leaving out only *me* and thus creating a totally artificial word *den*. *Den* is thus not nothing without "no," not a thing, but an *othing*, a something but *still within the domain of nothing*, like an ontological living dead, a spectral nothing-appearing-as-something. Or, as Lacan put it: "Nothing, perhaps? No—perhaps nothing, but not nothing";[47] to which Cassin adds: "I would love to make him say: *Pas rien, mais moins que rien (Not nothing, but less than nothing)*"[48]—*den* is a "blind passenger" of every ontology.[49] As such, it is "the radical real," and Democritus is a true materialist: "No more materialist in this matter than anyone with his senses, than me or than Marx, for example. But I cannot swear that this also holds for Freud"—Lacan suspects Freud's link to kabbala obscurantism.[50]

In characterizing *den* as the result of "subtraction after negation" (*something—nothing—othing*), Cassin, of course, cannot resist the temptation to have a stab at Hegel: "It cannot be dialecticized precisely insofar as it is not an assumed and sublated negation of negation, but a subtraction after negation."[51] The rise of *den* is thus strictly homologous to that of *objet a* which, according to Lacan, emerges when the two lacks (of the subject and of the Other) coincide, that is, when alienation is followed by separation: *den* is the "indivisible remainder" of the signifying process of double negation—something like Sygne de Coûfontaine's tic, this minimal *eppur si muove* which survives her utter *Versagung* (renunciation). The later reception of Democritus, of course, immediately "renormalized" *den* by way of ontologizing it: *den* becomes a positive One, atoms are now entities in the empty space, no longer spectral "othings"(less-than-nothings).

---

46 Not to mention the weird fact that, in English, *den* means "cave, hideout, nest, safe place."

47 Lacan, *The Four Fundamental Concepts of Psycho-Analysis*, p. 62.

48 Alain Badiou and Barbara Cassin, *Il n'y a pas de rapport sexuel*, Paris: Fayard 2010, p. 82.

49 Jacques Lacan, "L'Étourdit," *Scilicet* 4, Paris: Seuil 1973, p. 51.

50 Ibid.

51 Badiou and Cassin, *Il n'y a pas de rapport sexuel*, p. 83.

The neologism *den* evokes density and thus points towards the primordial, pre-ontological, contraction: *den* is, arguably, the first name for Lacan's *Y a d'l'Un*—there are ones, minimal points of contraction, of *ens* which is not yet the ontologically constituted One. Perhaps, an anachronistic reference to Kant can nonetheless be of some help here: *meden* follows the logic of negative judgment, it negates being as a predicate, while *den* asserts non-being as a (positive) predicate—*den* is nothingness (the void) which somehow "is" in itself, not only as a negation of (another) being. In other words, *den* is the space of indistinction between being and non-being, "a thing of nothing," as the "undead" are the living dead. (The well-known "*Panta rei, ouden menei*" of Heraclitus can thus be read as: "everything flows, nothing remains"—"nothing" as the very space of indistinction of things and no-thing.)

Predictably, the Eleatic Melissus, in his critique of Democritus, dismissed *den* with the scathing remark that "far from being a necessary existent, [it] is not even a word." In a way, he is right: we need a non-word to designate something that, precisely, does not yet exist (as a thing)—*den* lies outside the scope of the unity of *logos* and being. Democritean atomism is thus the first materialist answer to Eleatic idealism: Eleatics argue from the logical impossibility of the void to the impossibility of motion; Democritean atomists seem to reason in reverse, deducing from the fact that motion exists the necessity that the void (empty space) exists. The ultimate divide between idealism and materialism does not concern the materiality of existence ("only material things really exist"), but the "existence" of nothingness/the void: the fundamental axiom of materialism is that the void/nothingness is (the only ultimate) real, i.e., there is an indistinction of being and the void. If, for Parmenides, only being is, for Democritus, nothing is as much as being. In order to get from nothing to something, we do not have to add something to the void; on the contrary, we have to subtract, take away, something from nothing. Nothing and othing are thus not simply the same: "Nothing" is the generative void out of which othings, primordially contracted pre-ontological entities, emerge—at this level, nothing is more than othing, negative is more than positive. Once we enter the ontologically fully constituted reality, however, the relationship is reversed: something is more than nothing, in other words, nothing is purely negative, a privation of something.

This, perhaps, is how one can imagine the zero-level of creation: a red dividing line cuts through the thick darkness of the void, and on this line, a fuzzy something appears, the object-cause of desire—perhaps, for some, a woman's naked body (as on the cover of this book). Does this image not supply the minimal coordinates of the subject-object axis, the truly primordial axis of evil: the red line which cuts through the darkness is the subject, and the body its object?

"Nothing exists"

Hypotheses 1 and 2—*if the One is* and *if the One is not*—are followed by a brief argument (155e–157b) which is sometimes taken as a hypothesis of its own (so that we get nine instead of eight hypotheses), but more often as a mere appendix to the first two. This reasoning effectively provides a kind of mediation between hypotheses 1 and 2: if the result of hypothesis 1 was that the One, taken solely in virtue of itself, apart from everything else, is nothing at all (or totally undescribable), and if the result of hypothesis 2 was that the One, taken in virtue of others, is everything indiscriminately (large and small, similar and dissimilar, in movement and at rest ...), the appendix tries to resolve this antinomy by introducing the temporal dimension. A One which exists in time can without any contradiction change in time from one state to another (it can move, say, and then be at rest). But the interest of this otherwise commonsensical solution is that it again arrives at a paradoxical result when Parmenides focuses on the simple question: when does the One in question change? "If it is in motion, it has not yet changed. If it is at rest, it has already changed. When it changes must it not be neither in motion nor at rest? But there can be no time when a thing is neither in motion nor at rest." Parmenides proposes that the change between the two states occurs in an instant, and that the instant is not in time. At that instant, the object is neither in motion nor at rest, but is poised for both alternatives:

> The instant seems to signify something such that changing occurs from it to each of two states. For a thing doesn't change from rest while rest continues, or from motion while motion continues. Rather, this queer creature, the instant, lurks between motion and rest—being in no time at all—and to it and from it the moving thing changes to resting and the resting thing changes to moving. (156d–e)

Parmenides goes on to complicate the issue when he applies the same notion of the instant to the change from being to non-being or vice versa: at that instant, a thing neither is nor is not. (The problem with this solution is that it violates the Law of Excluded Middle which says that, at any instant, a thing should be either F or not F.) In this middle space, many weird things can take place—how can we not think of Gramsci's remark: "the crisis lies precisely in the fact that the old is dying and the new cannot be born. In the interregnum, a variety of morbid symptoms appear"?

The Real we are dealing with here is the Real of the pure virtual surface, the "incorporeal" Real, which is to be opposed to the Real in its most terrifying imaginary dimension, the primordial abyss which swallows up everything, dissolving all identities—a figure well known in literature in multiple guises, from Edgar Allan Poe's maelstrom and Kurtz's "horror" at the end of Conrad's *Heart of*

Darkness, to Pip from Melville's *Moby Dick* who, cast to the bottom of the ocean, experiences the demon God:

> Carried down alive to wondrous depths, where strange shapes of the unwarped primal world glided to and fro before his passive eyes … Pip saw the multitudinous, God-omnipresent, coral insects, that out of the firmament of waters heaved the colossal orbs. He saw God's foot upon the treadle of the loom, and spoke to it; and therefore his shipmates called him mad.[52]

This Real (whose best-known Freudian case is the dreamer's look into Irma's throat from *Traumdeutung*), this over-abundant obscene-morbid vitality of the primordial Flesh, is *not* the Real of pure appearance which is the truth of the Platonic Idea. It is again Deleuze who can help us draw a clearer line of distinction between these two Reals. On the very first page of his *Logic of Sense*, Deleuze describes pure becoming with a reference to *Alice in Wonderland*: when Alice "becomes larger,"

> she becomes larger than she was. By the same token, however, she becomes smaller than she is now. Certainly, she is not bigger and smaller at the same time. She is larger now; she was smaller before. But it is at the same moment that one becomes larger than one was and smaller than one becomes. This is the simultaneity of a becoming whose characteristic is to elude the present. Insofar as it eludes the present, becoming does not tolerate the separation or the distinction of before and after, or of past and future. It pertains to the essence of becoming to move and to pull in both directions at once: Alice does not grow without shrinking, and vice versa.[53]

Temporarily, the Sense-Event, its Becoming, is a pure Instant, the borderline between the past and the future, the point at which opposites coincide, at which a thing simultaneously grows bigger and smaller, etc.—the Instant is precisely the accumulation of the opposite predicates Plato is struggling with. One should thus not be surprised that Deleuze links this notion of becoming to Plato's *Philebos* and *Parmenides*, where Plato describes a process in which

> hotter never stops where it is but is always going a point further, and the same applies to "colder," whereas definite quality is something that has stopped going on and is fixed. (*Philebos* 24d)
>
> the younger becoming older than the older, the older becoming younger than the younger—but they can never finally become so; if they did they would no longer be becoming, but would be so. (*Parmenides* 154e–155a)

52 Herman Melville, *Moby Dick; or, The White Whale*, Boston: St. Botolph Society 1892, p. 391.

53 Deleuze, *The Logic of Sense*, p. 1.

As Deleuze shows in *The Logic of Sense*, the Sense-Event as pure insubstantial Becoming takes place on the borderline between the two "positive" domains (of things and of words):

> *Sense is both the expressible or the expressed of the proposition, and the attribute of the state of affairs.* It turns one side towards things and one side towards propositions ... It is exactly the boundary between things and propositions. It is this *aliquid* at once extra-Being and inherence, that is, this minimum of being which befits inherences.[54]

Deleuze introduces here the opposition between two modes of time, Chronos (the time of bodily substances) and Aion (the time of immaterial becoming): the cyclic time of material transformations, of the generation and corruption of things—which is, at its most basic level, the "terrifying, measureless present" of the primordial Chaos—and the pure linearity of the flux of becoming. In Chronos, "only the present exists in time. Past, present and future are not three dimensions of time; only the present fills time, whereas past and future are two dimensions relative to the present in time."[55] This Now of Chronos should be opposed to the Instant of Aion:

> In accordance with Aion, only the past and future inhere or subsist in time. Instead of a present which absorbs the past and future, a future and past divide the present at every instant and subdivide it ad infinitum into past and future, in both directions at once. Or, rather, it is the instant without thickness and without extension, which subdivides each present into past and future, rather than vast and thick presents which comprehend both future and past in relation to one another.[56]

This difference between the two becomings, the becoming-mad of the depths of the primordial formless Chaos and the surface of the infinite divisibility of the Instant, is "almost the difference between the second and third hypotheses of *Parmenides*—that of the 'now' and that of the 'instant'"[57]:

> Whereas Chronos was inseparable from circularity and its accidents—such as blockages or precipitations, explosions, disconnections, and indurations—Aion stretches out in a straight line, limitless in either direction. Always already passed and eternally yet to come, Aion is the eternal truth of time: *pure empty form of time*, which has freed itself of its present corporeal content and has thereby unwound its own circle, stretching itself out into a straight line.[58]

54 Ibid., p. 22.
55 Ibid., p. 162.
56 Ibid., p. 164.
57 Ibid., p. 165.
58 Ibid.

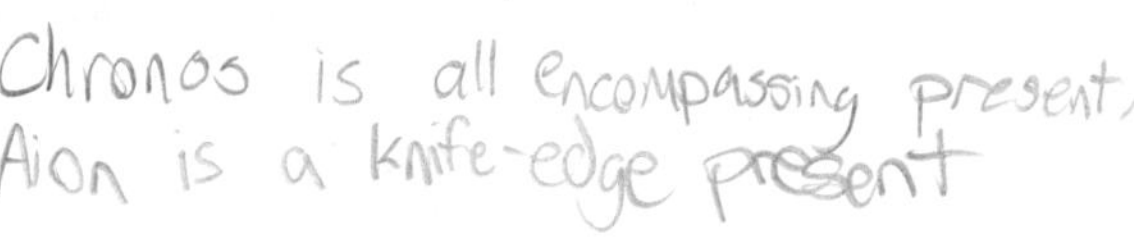

Hypothesis 3 proper, which then follows ("if one is, what are the consequences for the others"), avoids this paradox by way of outlining a common-sense, realistic ontology: although the others are not the One, they can have some relation to the One, they can partake of the form of the One: when they are combined into a Whole, this Whole is One; as parts of this Whole, each of them is also One, etc. The form of One thus delimits the parts in relation to each other and to the whole; it "accounts for the organization of parts in a unified whole,"[59] that is, it acts as the "*principle of structure* for the entities it combines."[60] If we take the form of the One away from the others, we get a chaotic unlimited multitude.

Can Plato's "illogical" change of order between hypotheses 3 and 4 be explained as an after-effect of the mysterious appendix (or hypothesis 3) which follows hypothesis 2 and is a kind of symptomal excess of the entire matrix, its "part of no-part," a something (an hypothesis) which counts for nothing? If we correct the order of hypotheses and exchange the places of 3 and 4, the underlying pattern emerges: entities that result from the hypothesis are describable/sayable if the One is *or* if it is not, that is, if we are within the order of positive being (asserted or negated), whereas the result is negative if we are within the order of "there is (or is no) One." The reason for this repartition is that, to put it in Deleuzian terms, for Plato, predication (insofar as it is possible) within the order of being is at the level of bodies and their properties/qualities, not at the level of becoming: its basic form is substance-copula-predicate, not substance-verb or even directly impersonal verb—it is "Alice is green," not "Alice greens" or even "it greens (on Alice)."

In order to grasp properly the key distinction between the next two hypotheses, 5 and 6, one should focus on a detail which may appear minor but on which everything hinges: the status of predication. Hypotheses 5 and 6 explore the consequences for the One if "One is not"; 5 reads "is not" as the assertion of a non-predicate, while 6 reads "is not" as a direct outright negation. In other words, in 5, "One is not" means that the One partakes of many characteristics (is unlike the others, like itself, and so on), among them non-being. The consequences of this triplicity are far-reaching: when we say "x is large," this does not mean that the object x is large because it directly participates in the Idea of largeness; it rather means that x *partakes of being in relation to largeness*. This triplicity holds not only for the predicative use of the verb "being": if we say that Socrates and Plato are similar in that they are both Greek, they are not similar because they both partake of the Idea of Greek—*they are similar because they both partake of the Idea of similarity in relation to being-Greek*.

So it is not only a question of the distinction between the transitive-predicative and the intransitive-existential use of "is" ("Socrates is ugly" versus

59 Gill, introduction to *Parmenides*, p. 90.

60 Ibid., p. 91.

"Socrates is")—in the logic that rules hypothesis 5, the very being is reflected-into-itself: when we say that "Socrates is," it means "Socrates is 'is', he partakes in being." We are thus dealing with *two different modes of being*, the immediate, direct existence-in-reality, and the fluid surface "being" which is indifferent to "real" being or non-being. So, what if we follow Deleuze and read these two types of being anachronistically, through the later Stoic distinction between material bodies that exist in spatio-temporal reality, and the famous "immaterials," pure surface-events which comprise what is sayable, what we can speak about? The moment we speak about something, its immediate existence is suspended, its being becomes a reflexive predicate, which is why we can speak about things which are in the mode of being or in the mode of non-being—or, to quote Gill's conclusion: "Many more things exist in Plato's ontology than exist in ours. For him anything describable is."[61] A unicorn can have one horn, four legs, and so on, and not exist. (We can also discern in this Deleuzian reading an echo of Parmenides's founding formula of philosophy which asserts the sameness of thinking/speaking—*logos*—and being.)

The next step in our interpretation of *Parmenides* should be to link this opposition between material bodies and the "immaterial" to the enigmatic difference between the first two hypotheses: "if it is One" and "if One is." Perhaps we should read "if it is One" as Lacan does, as the impersonal "*s'il y a d'l'Un*," as a "there is …," not the full assertion of being. The difference between the first two hypotheses is thus the difference between "there is One" and "the One is."

So, if we can properly talk only about entities suspended in limbo between being and non-being, of being in the mode of non-being, why can we not say anything about this One of the first hypothesis? In other words, if we can only describe and talk about that which partakes of One, when is the result of "there is one" the impossibility of saying anything at all? The negative results of some of the hypotheses in *Parmenides* should be read in a Hegelian way, as a determinate negation: each time we get a very specific negative result not to be confused with the others. The negative result of hypothesis 1 is thus to be opposed to the result of the last hypothesis, which is also total nothingness: the void of hypothesis 1 is not the ultimate abyss of reality (the Buddhist *sunyata*), but a pure One which, lacking any further qualifications, immediately erases itself. To put it in Lacanese, it is the lack of signifier-One which is still inherent to the order of the signifier-One, $, the barred signifier … in short, the void of subjectivity. $ is not the unsayable beyond the sayable, but the unsayable that is inherent to the sayable.

The last two hypotheses (7 and 8) explore the consequences of "One is not" for the others, and what makes them so interesting is not the logical (in)accuracy

61 Ibid., p. 99.

of the underlying reasoning, but the fact that, taken together, they come uncannily close to describing what we in the West perceive as the Buddhist ontology of pure fleeting substance-less appearances (hypothesis 7) beneath which there is nothing but the void of Nothingness (hypothesis 8). Gill is right to point out how "the effort required to make one's way through the previous deductions is rewarded by vivid imagery here":

> The others appear one and many, but aren't so really. They appear large, small, and equal, and they appear like and unlike themselves and each other, but they aren't really … if the others are other, they must be other than something. They can't be other than the one, if it is not, so they must be other than each other … they are other than each other, and they are unlimited in multitude … You take some small mass that seems to be one, but it suddenly disintegrates into many little bits. The small mass you started with now seems immense in relation to them. These are mere appearances, because without oneness to determine the individuality of things and the relations between them, the properties and relations we observe alter with our perspective … Imagine looking at a distant galaxy with the naked eye and then looking at it with a powerful telescope. At first you see only one tiny glowing object, but then a multitude of stars. What you see depends on your perspective.[62]

The result of the last hypothesis is the reality beneath this twinkling play of appearances—nothing. So why do we get first the play of appearances and then just outright Nothingness? It all hinges again on the difference between "there is no One" and "the One is not": hypothesis 7 considers the consequences for the others if the One is not, while hypothesis 8 considers the consequences for the others if there is no One. If the One is not (as full ontological reality), the space remains open for Ones which just are, that is, for the fluid play of appearances in which others can partake of the One and thus acquire a temporary fragile consistency. If, however, there is no One, not even a temporary delusive appearance of Oneness is possible, leaving just the void of Nothingness.

We can take the conclusion of *Parmenides* (the result of hypothesis 8: "nothing exists") in two opposed ways: either literally, as the conclusion of the entire matrix of hypotheses, i.e., as the ultimate ontological statement, or as a *reductio ad absurdum* which in a negative way demonstrates the necessity of some kind of stable forms: "The lesson is that there must be forms, or stable objects of some sort, if there is to be any world at all."[63] Is this alternative not the alternative between materialism and idealism at its purest? Here are the very last lines of *Parmenides*:

---

62 Ibid., pp. 102–3.

63 Ibid., p. 106.

> Then may we not sum up the argument in a word and say truly: If one is not, then nothing is?
>
> Certainly.
>
> Let thus much be said; and further let us affirm what seems to be the truth, that, whether one is or is not, one and the others in relation to themselves and one another, all of them, in every way, are and are not, and appear to be and appear not to be.
>
> Most true.

Is this not the most succinct, minimal definition of dialectical materialism? If there is no One, just multiplicities of multiplicities, then the ultimate reality is the Void itself; all determinate things "are and are not."[64] Should we then add to the eight hypotheses a ninth one, which, although not explicitly posited as a hypothesis, is the truth of the entire series: "Nothing is"? (Or is it rather that "nothing is" is the truth of the eighth hypothesis alone?)

It all depends on what, precisely, we mean by zero, nothing, or the void. First, there are two zeroes, the zero of measure (like a zero degree, the point of reference chosen to establish a quantitative difference, which is arbitrary—for measuring temperature, Celsius and Fahrenheit posit a different zero) and zero as the neutral element, like 0 in addition and subtraction: whichever number we add 0 to or subtract 0 from, this number remains the same. This, perhaps, offers one approach to the "analyst's neutrality": the analyst is just there as an inert *objet a*, s/he does not actively intervene. However, we should add to this neutrality of 0 the opposite case of multiplication wherein 0 is, on the contrary, the absorbing element: whichever number we multiply with 0, the result is 0. What this means is that it is nonetheless the analyst's mere *presence* which has the magic effect of transforming the patient's flow of speech into a prosopopoeia. Imagine the patient telling his analyst a passionate story about some of his recent adventures or fantasies: the very presence of the analyst, her "ironic" stance, desubjectivizes the patient; it transubstantiates his authentic subjective expression into a puppet-like delivery of a *bric-a-brac* of falsified memories and fragments lifted from totally different situations, originally addressed to different persons (like the patient's father), or even originally spoken by others. In this sense, the

64 Haas's notion of "manys" (multiple multiplicities) is effectively close to Badiou: "manys" means that multiplicity cannot be reduced to a multiplicity of Ones, so that their correlative is Nothing, the Void. (See Andrew Haas, *Hegel and the Problem of Multiplicity*, Evanston: Northwestern University Press 2000.) The key dilemma here is whether this multiple multiplicity is sustained only by the Void as the ultimate ontological reference, or whether we need a correlative notion of One. If we do, then what *kind* of One? The barred One, the One of pure Difference? Lacan's *Y a d'l'Un*?

analyst's neutral presence functions as the absorbing element: no matter how well thought out and planned the patient's speech is, once it is performed in the analytic setting (frame), its status is that of prosopopoeia and is "absorbed" into a free association.[65]

This distinction between the neutral/absorbing zero and the zero of measure is not to be confused with another distinction which also relates to the psychoanalytic practice: the distinction between *nothing* and the *void*. Nothing is localized, like when we say "there is nothing here," while the void is a dimension without limits.[66] In psychoanalytic clinics, this couple is clearly operative in the distinction between psychosis and hysteria: in psychosis, we encounter so-called "depersonalization" or the feeling of the loss of reality, which refers to a void; while in hysteria, this void is localized as a nothing, a specific dissatisfaction. What this means is that nothing is always a nothing within some specific framework: there is nothing within a frame where we expected something.[67] The first task in the analysis of a psychotic is thus arguably the most difficult, but also the most crucial: that of "hystericizing" the psychotic subject, that is, transforming the void of his "depersonalization" into a hysterical dissatisfaction. The opposite of this transformation is the case of psychotic *forclusion*, where the excluded element throws the subject back into the void. But why? Because the excluded element—the Name-of-the-Father—is not just one among the signifiers, but a signifier-frame, a signifier which sustains the texture of an entire symbolic framework.

So, to conclude, if we return from the second to the first part of *Parmenides*, i.e., to the status of Ideas, then the result should be that Ideas do not exist, do not have ontological reality of their own: they persist as purely virtual points of reference. That is to say, the only appropriate conclusion is that eternal Ideas are Ones and Others which do not participate in (spatio-temporal) Being (which is the only actual being there is): their status is purely virtual. This virtual status was made clear by Deleuze, one of the great anti-Platonists. Deleuze's notion of the Virtual is to be opposed to the all-pervasive topic of virtual reality: what matters to Deleuze is not virtual reality, but *the reality of the virtual* (which, in Lacanian terms, is the Real). Virtual Reality in itself is a rather miserable idea:

65 It is crucial not to confuse this neutral/absorbing zero with the zero of measure, as do those inauthentic analysts who endeavor to impose some normative standard of psychic "sanity" onto the patient in order to measure his or her deviation from it.

66 I rely here on Jacques-Alain Miller, "Logique du non-savoir en psychanalyse," *La cause freudienne* 75 (July 2010), pp. 169–84.

67 It is only this nothing, and not the void, which can then be counted as 1. One should apply this lesson to the key problem of Neoplatonist mystics: how to pass from the primordial abyss of the limitless Void to the One? By way of framing it and thus turning it into a nothing which can be counted as One.

that of imitating reality, of reproducing experience in an artificial medium. The reality of the Virtual, on the other hand, stands for the reality of the Virtual as such, for its real effects and consequences.

Gorgias, not Plato, was the arch-Stalinist!

From this concluding point, we can return to Gorgias and raise again the question of the relationship between Plato and the sophists. Let us approach the problem in the terms of the Platonic *dieresis*: the gradual subdivision of a genus into species which allows us to define the particular entity we are trying to grasp (to arrive at humans, we divide beings into living and non-living; the living into plants and animals; animals into mammals and all others; mammals into those who have speech and those who do not ...). When such division involves an "antagonistic" either/or (Good against Evil, freedom against oppression, morality against hedonism, etc.), there are, roughly speaking, two philosophical approaches to it: either one opts for one pole against the other, or one adopts the "deeper" attitude of emphasizing the complicity of the opposites, and of advocating a proper balanced measure or unity. Although Hegel's dialectic seems like a version of the second approach (the "synthesis" of opposites), he actually opts for an unheard-of *third* version: the way to resolve the deadlock is neither to engage in fighting for the "good" side against the "bad," nor to try to bring them together in a balanced "synthesis," but to opt for the *bad* side of the initial either/or. Lacan made the same point in his seminar *...ou pire*: in the choice between "*le père ou pire*" (the father or worse), the ethical choice opts for what is worse. Of course, this "choice of what is worse" fails, but in that failure it undermines the entire field of the alternative and thus enables us to overcome its terms. (Say, in politics, in the choice between organic unity and destructive terror, the only way to arrive at the truth is to begin with the "wrong" choice of destructive terror.)

Therein resides the insurmountable difference between Hegel and the New Age notion of balancing opposites. Take the classic case of the French revolutionary Terror: according to the common perception, Hegel condemns the French Revolution as the immediate assertion of an abstract-universal Freedom which, as such, has to end in its opposite: a universal terror directed at all particular content. To this abstract freedom—so the story goes—Hegel opposes the "concrete Freedom" of the modern rational state in which one's individual freedom is grounded in assuming one's place within the articulated totality of the social order ... The problem with this common perception is that it does not take into account the immanent temporal dimension of the dialectical process. A historical agent is never directly confronted with the choice: either revolutionary terror or organic rational state. On the eve of the revolution, the only choice is between the old "organic" order and revolution, inclusive of its terror. What tips the balance of choice towards revolution in this situation is the insight into how the organic harmony of the *ancien régime* is itself a fake, an illusion concealing the reality of brutal violence, division, and chaos.

Adolphe de Custine's experience of visiting Russia in the 1830s illustrates an interesting, properly Hegelian point: the very object of his inquiry alienated itself from him when he approached it. Custine went to Russia searching for an immediate organic order, that is, he wanted to find a society which, unlike modern Western Europe after the French Revolution, remained hierarchically ordered and grounded in tradition. However, what he found there was the exact opposite: not an organic social unity, but a fragile mixture of brutal order and chaos. Not only was there an immense chaos behind the appearance of total power and order; the state power itself functioned chaotically, exposed as it was to the whims of the Tsar. (This feature—chaos in the guise of order and totalitarian control—persists even today and was strikingly present in the Soviet era.)[68] "Organic unity" thus reveals itself to be the mode in which its opposite, inherent instability, appears. The "secret" of despotic societies is that they did not find their "*inneres Gestalt*," their inner form; this holds also for fascism which was always torn between modernism and a return to tradition. Against any kind of "organic" temptation, it is absolutely crucial for emancipatory politics to remain faithful to the universalist/secular project of modernity.

Our first choice thus has to be revolution, because it is only after we pass through the zero-level of revolution that the space for the modern rational state (always referred to by Hegel as the "post-revolutionary" state) opens up: only the "wrong" choice of abstract terror creates the space for the choice of rational state. We can see now how the infamous Hegelian triad is grounded in the temporal structure of a repeated choice: in this case, the "triad" of *ancien régime*, its abstract negation in the Revolutionary Terror, and its sublation in the post-revolutionary rational state, is set in motion by two consecutive choices—first, the choice of revolution against the *ancien régime*; then, the choice of the modern rational state with its concrete freedom. How are we to square these dialectical reversals with the Platonic dieresis? One has to go back from Plato to Gorgias, the first to propose a dieretic matrix of divisions; his *On Nature, or the Non-existent* (the text survived only in summary form in Sextus Empiricus and Aristotle's *On Melissus, Xenophanes, and Gorgias*) can be summed up in three propositions: (a) nothing exists; (b) if anything existed, it could not be known; (c) if anything did exist, and could be known, it could not be communicated to others. If ever there was a clear case of the Freudian logic of the borrowed

68 See Irena Gross, *The Scar of Revolution*, Berkeley: University of California Press 1991.

kettle (providing mutually exclusive reasons), this is it: (1) nothing exists; (2) what exists cannot be known; (3) what we know cannot be communicated to others … But more interesting is the repeated "diagonal" mode of division of genre into species: Things either exist or do not. If they exist, they can either be known or can not. If they can be known, they can either be communicated to others or can not. Surprisingly, we find the same progressive differentiation at the opposite end of the history of Western philosophy, in the twentieth-century sophistics called "dialectical materialism." Stalin's "Dialectical and Historical Materialism" enumerates four features of Marxist dialectics:

The principal features of the Marxist dialectical method are as follows:

> Contrary to metaphysics, dialectics does not regard nature as an accidental agglomeration of things, of phenomena, unconnected with, isolated from, and independent of, each other, but as a connected and integral whole, in which things, phenomena are organically connected with, dependent on, and determined by, each other.
>
> Contrary to metaphysics, dialectics holds that nature is not a state of rest and immobility, stagnation and immutability, but a state of continuous movement and change, of continuous renewal and development, where something is always arising and developing, and something always disintegrating and dying away.
>
> Contrary to metaphysics, dialectics does not regard the process of development as a simple process of growth, where quantitative changes do not lead to qualitative changes, but as a development which passes from insignificant and imperceptible quantitative changes to fundamental qualitative changes; a development in which the qualitative changes occur not gradually, but rapidly and abruptly, taking the form of a leap from one state to another; they occur not accidentally but as the natural result of an accumulation of imperceptible and gradual quantitative changes.
>
> Contrary to metaphysics, dialectics holds that internal contradictions are inherent in all things and phenomena of nature, for they all have their negative and positive sides, a past and a future, something dying away and something developing; and that the struggle between these opposites, the struggle between the old and the new, between that which is dying away and that which is being born, between that which is disappearing and that which is developing, constitutes the internal content of the process of development, the internal content of the transformation of quantitative changes into qualitative changes.[69]

First, nature is not a conglomerate of dispersed phenomena, but a connected whole. Then, this Whole is not immobile, but in a state of constant movement and change. Next, this change is not only a gradual quantitative drifting, but

69 Josef Stalin, "Dialectical and Historical Materialism," in *History of the Communist Party of the Soviet Union (Bolsheviks): Short Course*, ed. Commission of the Central Committee of the C.P.S.U.(B.), New York: International Publishers 1939, pp. 106–7.

involves qualitative jumps and ruptures. Finally, this qualitative development is not a matter of harmonious deployment, but is propelled by the struggle of the opposites … The trick here is that we are effectively *not* dealing merely with the Platonic dieresis, the gradual subdivision of a genus into species and then species into subspecies: the underlying premise is that this "diagonal" process of division is really vertical, i.e., that we are dealing with different aspects of the *same* division. To put it in Stalinist jargon: an immobile Whole is not really a Whole, but just a conglomerate of elements; development which does not involve qualitative jumps is not really a development, but just an immobile stepping at the same place; a qualitative change which does not involve a struggle of the opposites is not really a change, but just a quantitative monotonous movement. Or, to put it in more ominous terms: those who advocate qualitative change without a struggle of the opposites *really* oppose change and advocate the continuation of the same; those who advocate change without qualitative jumps *really* oppose change and advocate immobility … The political aspect of this logic is clearly discernible: "those who advocate the transformation of capitalism into socialism without class struggle *really* reject socialism and want capitalism to continue," and so on.

There are two famous quips by Stalin which are both grounded in this logic. When he answered the question "Which deviation is worse, the rightist or the leftist one?" with "They are both worse!" the underlying premise was that the leftist deviation was *really* ("objectively," as Stalinists liked to put it) not leftist at all, but a concealed rightist one! When Stalin wrote, in a report on a party congress, that the delegates unanimously approved the Central Committee resolution by a large majority, the underlying premise was, again, that there was really no minority within the party: those who had voted against thereby excluded themselves from the party. In all these cases, *the genus repeatedly overlaps (fully coincides) with one of its species.* This is also what allows Stalin to read history retroactively, so that things "become clear" retroactively: it was not that Trotsky first fought for the revolution alongside Lenin and Stalin and then, at a certain stage, opted for a different strategy than the one advocated by Stalin; this last opposition (Trotsky/Stalin) "makes it clear" how, "objectively," Trotsky was against revolution from the beginning.

We find the same procedure in the classificatory impasse the Stalinist ideologists and political activists faced in their struggle for collectivization in the years 1928–33. In their attempt to account for their effort to crush the peasants' resistance in "scientific" Marxist terms, they divided peasants into three categories (classes): *bednyaki*, the "miserable ones," the poor peasants (no land or minimal land, working for others), natural allies of the workers; *serednyaki*, the "middle ones," the autonomous middle peasants (owning land, but not employing others), rich but oscillating between the exploited and exploiters; and "kulaks" (*kulaki*) who, apart from employing other workers to work on their land, were also lending them money or seeds, etc.—they were the exploiters proper, the "class enemy" which, as such, has to be "liquidated." However, in practice, this classification became more and more blurred and inoperative: in the generalized poverty, clear criteria no longer applied, and peasants in the other two categories often joined kulaks in their resistance to forced collectivization. An additional category was thus introduced, that of a "subkulak," a peasant who, although too poor to be considered a kulak proper, nonetheless shared the kulak "counter-revolutionary" attitude. "Subkulak" was thus

> a term without any real social content even by Stalinist standards, but merely rather unconvincingly masquerading as such. As was officially stated, "by 'kulak,' we mean the carrier of certain political tendencies which are most frequently discernible in the subkulak, male and female." By this means, any peasant whatever was liable to dekulakisation; and the "subkulak" notion was widely employed, enlarging the category of victims greatly beyond the official estimate of kulaks proper even at its most strained.[70]

The "subkulak" was thus the paradoxical intersection of species: a subspecies of the species "kulaks" whose members came from the other two species. As such, "subkulak" was the embodiment of the ideological lie (falsity) of the entire "objective" classification of farmers into three categories: its function was to account for the fact that *all* strata of farmers, not only the wealthy ones, resisted collectivization. No wonder that the official ideologists and economists finally gave up trying to provide an "objective" definition of kulak: "The grounds given in one Soviet comment are that 'the old attitudes of a kulak have almost disappeared, and the new ones do not lend themselves to recognition.'"[71] The art of identifying a kulak was thus no longer a matter of objective social analysis; it became the matter of a complex "hermeneutics of suspicion," of identifying an individual's "true political attitudes" hidden beneath their deceptive public proclamations, so that *Pravda* had to concede that "even the best activists often cannot spot the kulak."[72]

What all this points towards is the dialectical mediation of the "subjective" and "objective" dimension: "subkulak" no longer designates an "objective" social category but rather the point at which objective social analysis breaks down and the subjective political attitude directly inscribes itself into the "objective" order—in Lacanese, *"subkulak" is the point of subjectivization of the*

70 Robert Conquest, *The Harvest of Sorrow*, New York: Oxford University Press 1986, p. 119.

71 Ibid., p. 120.

72 Ibid.

"objective" chain: poor peasant—middle peasant—kulak. It is not an "objective" sub-category (or sub-division) of the class of "kulaks," but simply the name for the subjective political attitude of the "kulak." This accounts for the paradox that, although it appears as a subdivision of the class of "kulaks," "subkulaks" is a species that overflows its own genus (that of kulaks), since "subkulaks" are also to be found among middle and even poor farmers. In short, "subkulak" names political division as such, the Enemy whose presence traverses the *entire* social body of peasants, which is why he can be found everywhere, in all three peasant classes.

This brings us back to the procedure of Stalinist dieresis: "subkulak" names the excessive element that traverses all classes, the outgrowth which has to be eliminated. There is, in every "objective" classification of social groups, an element which functions like "subkulak"—the point of subjectivization masked as a subspecies of "objective" elements of the social body. It is this point of subjectivization which, in the strictest sense of the term, *sutures* the "objective" social structure—and one should bear in mind the contrast between this notion of suture and the predominant use of the term (the element which "sutures" the ideological space, obliterating the traces of its dependence on its decentered "Other Scene," enabling it to present itself as self-sufficient): the point of subjectivization "sutures" not the ideological Inside, but *the Outside itself*: the "suture" is the point of subjectivization which guarantees the consistency of the "objective" field itself. What this also means is that the procedure of dieresis is not endless: it reaches its end when a division is no longer a division into two species, but a division into a species and an excremental leftover, a formless stand-in for nothing, a "part of no-part." At this final point, the singular excrement reunites with its opposite, the universal; that is, the excremental leftover functions as a direct stand-in for the Universal.

In his polemic against Badiou's reading of Paul, Agamben defines the singularity of the Christian position with regard to the opposition between Jews and Greeks (pagans) not as a direct affirmation of an all-encompassing universality ("there are neither Jews nor Greeks"), but as an additional divide that cuts diagonally across the entire social body and *as such* suspends the lines of separation between social groups: a ("Christian") subdivision of each group is directly linked with a ("Christian") subdivision of all other groups. (The difference between Badiou and Agamben is that, for Badiou, this new "Christian" collective is the site of singular universality, the self-relating universality of naming, of subjective recognition in a name, while Agamben rejects the title of universality.) The common-sense classificatory approach would say, what's the big deal? Being Christian or non-Christian is simply another classification that cuts across and overlaps with other classifications, like the fact that there are men and women, which also cuts across all ethnic, religious, and class divides. There is, however, a crucial difference here: for Paul, "Christian" does not designate yet another predicate (property or quality) of the individual, but a "performative" self-recognition grounded only in its own naming; in other words, it is a purely subjective feature—and, Badiou adds, only as such can it be truly universal. The opposition between the objective-neutral universal approach and the subjective-partisan approach is false: only a radical subjective engagement can ground true universality. The constellation here is therefore exactly the same as that of the "subkulaks" in the Stalinist discourse: "subkulaks" are also the "remainder" of kulaks which cuts across the entire field, a subjective-political category masked as a social-objective quality.

So, when Agamben defines "Christians" not directly as "non-Jews," but as "non-non-Jews,"[73] this double negation does not bring us back to the starting positive determination; it should rather be read as an example of what Kant called "infinite judgment," which, instead of negating a predicate, asserts a non-predicate: instead of saying that Christians *aren't Jews*, one should say that they *are non-Jews*, in the same sense that horror fiction talks about the "undead." The undead are alive *while dead*, they are the living dead; in the same way, Christians are non-Jews *while remaining Jews* (at the level of their pre-evental, positive social determination)—they are Jews who, as Paul put it, "died for [in the eyes of] the [Jewish] Law."

To go even further back, Gorgias's argumentation should be read in the same way. It may appear that Gorgias proceeds in three consecutive divisions: first, things either exist or do not; then, if they exist, they can either be known or can not; finally, if they can be known, we can either communicate this knowledge to others or can not. However, the truth of this gradual subdivision is again the repetition of one and the same line of division: if we cannot communicate something to others, it means that we "really" do not know it ourselves; if we cannot know something, it means that it "really" does not exist in itself. There is a truth in this logic; as Parmenides, Gorgias's teacher and reference point here, already put it: thinking (knowing) is the same as being, and thinking (knowing) itself is rooted in language (communication)—"The limits of my language are the limit of my world."

The lesson of Hegel and Lacan is that one should turn this dieresis around: we can only speak about things that *do not* exist (Bentham himself was on the right track here with his theory of fictions)—or, more modestly and precisely, speech (presup)poses a lack/hole in the positive order of being. So not only can we think about non-existing things (which is why religion is consubstantial with "human nature," its eternal temptation), we can also talk without thinking—not only in the vulgar sense of just babbling incoherently, but in the Freudian sense

73 Giorgio Agamben, *Le temps qui reste*, Paris: Payot & Rivages 2000, p. 168.

of "saying more than we intended," of making a symptomatic slip of the tongue. It is not that we know something but cannot communicate it to others—rather that we can communicate to others things we don't know (or, more precisely, to paraphrase Donald Rumsfeld, things we do not know we know, since, for Lacan, the unconscious as *une bévue* is *un savoir qui ne se sait pas*).

This is why the Hegelian-Lacanian position is neither that of Plato nor that of his sophist opponents: against Plato, it asserts that we not only *can* talk about things that we do not understand or think, but that ultimately we talk *only* about them, about fictions; while against the sophists it asserts that this in no way devalues truth, since, as Lacan put it, truth has the structure of a fiction.

Does so-called "postmodern relativism" thus only reach a deadlock that Plato was already struggling with in his repeated attempts to distinguish true philosophical knowledge from sophistic trickery? Is the very drawing of such a line not the highest act of sophistic trickery (in the same way it is claimed that the very attempt to draw a strict line between ideology and "true" non-ideological knowledge is the most ideological act of all)? Does this then mean that Lacan himself effectively *was* a sophist, in this sense, when he asserted that "there is no Other of the Other," no ultimate guarantee of Truth exempted from the circular (self-referential) play of language? If every such line of separation is "undecidable," does this mean that Badiou's desperate struggle against post-modernist-deconstructionist "sophists," and his heroic Platonic insistence on Truth as independent of historical language games, amounts to an empty gesture with no foundation? Badiou can nonetheless be defended here: the opposition between Truth and doxa occurs *within* the "undecidable" self-referential field of language, so when Badiou emphasizes the undecidability of a Truth-Event, his conception is radically different from the standard deconstructionist notion of undecidability.[74] For Badiou, undecidability means that there are no neutral "objective" criteria for an Event: an Event appears as such only to those who recognize themselves in its call; or, as Badiou puts it, an Event is self-relating, including itself—its own nomination—among its components. While this does mean that one has to *decide* about an Event, such an ultimately groundless decision is not "undecidable" in the standard sense. It is, rather, uncannily similar to the Hegelian dialectical process in which—as Hegel had already made clear in the Introduction to his *Phenomenology*—a "figure of consciousness" is not measured by any external standard of truth but in an absolutely immanent way, through the gap between itself and its own exemplification/staging. An Event is thus "non-All" in the precise Lacanian sense of the term: it is never fully verified precisely because it is infinite, that is, because there is no external limit to it. The

74 See Alain Badiou, *L'être et l'évenement*, Paris: Minuit 1989.

conclusion to be drawn is that, for the very same reason, the Hegelian "totality" is also "non-All."

The reference to Hegel is crucial here, since, especially in the Anglo-Saxon tradition, he is often perceived as the ultimate "sophist," abandoning any objective rational criteria of truth and succumbing to the mad self-referential play of the Absolute Idea. The element of truth in this reproach is that, for Hegel, the truth of a proposition is inherently notional, determined by the immanent notional content, not a matter of comparison between notion and reality—in Lacanian terms, there is a non-All (*pas-tout*) of truth. It may sound strange to invoke Hegel with regard to the non-All—is he not the philosopher of All par excellence? The Hegelian truth, however, is precisely without an external limitation/exception that would serve as its measure or standard, which is why its criterion is absolutely immanent: a statement is compared with itself, with its own process of enunciation.

Badiou and Barbara Cassin are engaged in an ongoing dialogue which can best be characterized as a new version of the ancient dialogue between Plato and the sophists: the Platonist Badiou against Cassin's insistence on the irreducibility of the sophists' rupture. The fact that Badiou is a man and Cassin a woman takes on a special significance here: the opposition between the Platonist's trust in the firm foundation of truth and the sophists' groundless play of speech is connoted by sexual difference. So, from the strict Hegelian standpoint, perhaps Cassin is right to insist on the irreducible character of the sophist's position: the self-referential play of the symbolic process has no external support which would allow us to draw a line, within the language game, between truth and falsity. Sophists are the irreducible "vanishing mediators" between *mythos* and *logos*, between the traditional mythic universe and philosophical rationality, and, as such, they are a permanent threat to philosophy. Why is this the case?

The sophists broke down the mythic unity of words and things, playfully insisting on the gap that separates words from things; and philosophy proper can only be understood as a reaction to this, as an attempt to close the gap the sophists opened up, to provide a foundation of truth for words, to return to mythos but under the new conditions of rationality. This is where one should locate Plato: he first tried to provide this foundation with his teaching on Ideas, and when, in *Parmenides*, he was forced to admit the fragility of that foundation, he engaged in a long struggle to re-establish a clear line of separation between sophistics and truth.[75] The irony of the history of philosophy is that the line of

75 The opposition between the sophists and Plato is also linked to the opposition between democracy and corporate organic order: the sophists are clearly democratic, teaching the art of seducing and convincing the crowd, while Plato outlines a hierarchic corporate order in which every individual has his or her proper place, allowing for no

philosophers who struggle against the sophistic temptation ends with Hegel, the "last philosopher," who, in a way, is also the ultimate sophist, embracing the self-referential play of the symbolic with no external support of its truth. For Hegel, there is truth, but it is immanent to the symbolic process—the truth is measured not by an external standard, but by the "pragmatic contradiction," the inner (in)consistency of the discursive process, the gap between the enunciated content and its position of enunciation.

---

position of singular universality.

CHAPTER 2

"Where There Is Nothing, Read That I Love You"

When an atheist philosopher writes about religion, she should take great care to resist the temptation formulated long ago by Rousseau: "By accusing me of being religious you excuse yourself for being a philosopher; it is as if I were to renounce wine when it would make you drunk."[1] This temptation is at its most seductive when a philosopher encounters cases which reveal the obscene disavowed underside of a religious edifice, as is the case with *The Gathering* (2003), a modest but interesting horror film set in the English countryside. The remains of an old Christian church are discovered buried beneath the earth, revealing stone statues and reliefs of the suffering Christ and a heterogeneous group of individuals observing him dying. It takes the local clergy and archaeologists some time to get the point: the sculpture is not about Christ (who is, strangely, shown from behind) but about those who came to see him die. A priest from the local church links the sculpture to the words allegedly written by St. Aristobulus (a first-century bishop) about "those who came to watch": "From the east and the west they came, from the city and the plain. Not in holy reverence to our Lord, but in lust." At the same time, the film shows us people wandering around the city whose faces strangely resemble those on the statues, and, furthermore, a researcher finds the same faces on many depictions of the crucifixion from the Middle Ages and the Renaissance. The conclusion is clear: those who came to the crucifixion not to mourn or worship, but for entertainment or out of mere curiosity, were cursed to walk the Earth immortal and bear witness to the suffering of men—as in the case of the Wandering Jew, immortality is here not a blessing but a curse. (Recall that Hamlet's father also returns as a ghost because he was murdered in the full flower of his sins.) The movie then takes a predictable turn: the immortal witnesses are gathering in the city because they have a premonition that something terrible is about to happen there.

1 "Vous vous excusez d'être philosophe en m'accusant d'être dévote; c'est comme si j'avois renoncé au vin lorsqu'il vous eut enivré." Jean-Jacques Rousseau, *Julie; ou, La Nouvelle Héloïse*, Amsterdam: Marc Michel Rey 1769, p. 284.

A Christian tragedy?

There is a deeper question that has to be raised here: is there not *always* a moment of lust (Freud called it *Schaulust*) in witnessing a traumatic event like a crucifixion? And does not the claim that we come to watch out of compassion and respect make it even (hypocritically) worse? Such a perverse logic was brought to its peak by Nicolas Malebranche, for whom, in the same way that the saintly person uses the suffering of others to bring about his own narcissistic satisfaction in helping those in distress, God also ultimately *loves only himself*, and merely uses man to promulgate his own glory. Malebranche here draws a consequence worthy of Lacan's reversal of Dostoyevsky ("*If God doesn't exist, then nothing is permitted*"): it is not true that, had Christ not come to Earth to deliver humanity, everyone would have been lost—quite the contrary, *nobody* would have been lost; in other words, *every* human being had to fall so that Christ could come and deliver *some* of them. Malebranche's conclusion is here properly perverse: since the death of Christ is a key step in realizing the goal of creation, at no time was God (the Father) happier then when he was observing his Son suffering and dying on the Cross.

Is this perversion inscribed into the very core of Christianity, or can the Christian edifice be read in a different way? And if so, is this path opened up by the specifically Christian notion of love? The wager of properly Christian love is to demonstrate to the Other (God) that it exists by way of loving it unconditionally, beyond the Good; in this way, the anxiety and incertitude over the Other's desire is "sublated" in the *act* of love. François Balmès draws attention here to the parallel with Descartes's *cogito* and its doubt: In the same way that the incertitude of radical doubt turns into the certitude of *cogito ergo sum*, the incertitude over God's desire/will, taken to the extreme, turns into the certitude of love, regardless of my exposure to damnation. This extreme form of ecstatic love is to be radically opposed to (Ancient) tragedy: in pure love, I freely consent to my own damnation or disappearance, I ecstatically assume it, while in tragedy, I (also) accept my Fate, but I accept it as an external force without consenting to it—the tragic hero rejects it absolutely, protesting against it to the end (Oedipus at Colonus—the case of Antigone is here more ambiguous). In other words, in contrast to the notion of *amor fati*, there is no love in the tragic hero's acceptance of his damnation by Fate. Therein resides the tragic hero's uncompromising fidelity to his desire: not in the acceptance of Fate, but in holding on to his desire *against* Fate, in a situation where everything is lost.

Is there, then, no properly Christian tragedy? Here, Antigone is to be opposed to Sygne de Coûfontaine from Paul Claudel's *L'Otage*: if Oedipus and Antigone are the exemplary cases of Ancient tragedy, Sygne stands for the

Christian tragedy.[2] Sygne lives in the modern world where God is dead: there is no objective Fate, our fate is our own choice, we are fully responsible for it. Sygne first follows the path of ecstatic love to the end, sacrificing her good, her ethical substance for God, for his pure Otherness; and she does it not on account of some external pressure, but out of the innermost freedom of her being—hence she cannot blame Fate when she finds herself totally humiliated, deprived of all ethical substance. This, however, is why her tragedy is much more radical than that of either Oedipus or Antigone: when, mortally wounded after taking the bullet meant for her despicable and hated husband, she refuses to confer any deeper sacrificial meaning on her suicidal intervention, there is no tragic beauty in this refusal—her "*No*" is signaled merely by a repellent grimace, a compulsive facial tic. There is no tragic beauty because her total sacrifice has deprived her of all inner beauty and ethical grandeur, so that all that remains is a disgusting excremental stain, a living shell deprived of life. There is no love here either; all her love was consumed in her previous renunciations. In a way, Sygne is here crucified, her "*No*" akin to Christ's "Father, why have you forsaken me?"—which is also a gesture of defiance, a kind of "Up yours!" directed at the God-Father. Balmès is right to point out that this properly Christian "*No*" in all its forms is the "unthinkable" traumatic core of pure love, a scandal which undermines it from within. Here is his breathtakingly precise formulation:

> The unthinkable in pure love is, in a sense, Christianity itself, the scandal of the Cross, the Passion and the death of Christ, the "Why did you abandon me?" from the psalm taken over by Christ and on which the mystics of pure love conferred a radicality intolerable for the Church.[3]

This moment of tragedy, this return of the tragic at the very heart of Christianity as the religion of love, is also the point which the self-erasing mysticism of ecstatic love cannot properly grasp: when mystics talk about the "Night of the World," they directly identify this Night (the withdrawal from external reality into the void of pure innerness) with the divine Beatitude, with the self-erasing immersion into Divinity; for Christianity, in contrast, the unbearable

2 As a matter of fact, Christian tragedy is no longer a tragedy proper; its horror reaches beyond the tragic. When Terry Eagleton wrote, "For many a tragic theorist, Agamemnon is tragic but Auschwitz is not," he meant it as a sarcastic stab at those postmodern elitists who celebrate the ethical grandeur of a solitary hero's suicidal passion, ignoring the much less heroic plight of the suffering of millions of ordinary people. One should nonetheless read his statement as simply being true: Auschwitz is not tragic; it is a blasphemy to call it tragic, since its victims were deprived of the minimum of personal dignity which enables the subject to pose as a tragic hero.

3 François Balmès, *Dieu, le sexe et la vérité*, Ramonville Saint-Agne: Érès 2007, p. 196.

and unsurpassable tension remains, there is an ex-timate "*No*" at the very heart of the loving "*Yes*" to it all. This "*No*" has nothing to do with the imaginary logic of *hainamoration*, the reversal of narcissistic love into hatred.

Claudel himself found Sygne's refusal of reconciliation with Turelure at the end of *L'Otage* mysterious: it imposed itself on him while he was writing the drama, since it was not part of the original plan (first, he intended the marriage of Sygne and Turelure to mark the reconciliation of the *ancien régime* and the new regime in the Restoration; later, he planned to have Badillon convince the dying Sygne to give the demanded sign of pardon and reconciliation to Turelure). Significantly, most critics perceived Sygne's refusal as a mark not of her radicality but of her failure to follow through with the sacrifice demanded of her, that is, to give her full consent to marriage with the despicable Turelure. The idea is that, by refusing to give any sign of consent and dying in ice-cold silence, Sygne disavows the religious principles which had hitherto dictated her behavior. As Abel Hermant wrote:

> Turelure tries to extract from Sygne a word, a sign of pardon, which would be for him the sign that he has definitely conquered her and reached the end of his ambitions. But Sygne refuses this pardon, on which nonetheless her eternal salvation seems to depend. She thus renders all her sacrifices worthless in the last minute.[4]

Claudel feebly protested such readings: "I believe she is saved," but conceded that the meaning of her final act was not clear even to him: "At the play's end, the characters escape all psychological investigation: at the human level, Sygne of course refused to fulfill her sacrifice; we do not know any more about it, and the author himself can only 'suppose' a meaning for her final gesture."[5]

In "The Ancient Tragical Motif as Reflected in the Modern," a chapter of Volume I of *Either/Or*, Kierkegaard proposed his fantasy of what a modern Antigone would have been.[6] The conflict is now entirely internalized: there is no longer a need for Creon. While Antigone admires and loves her father Oedipus, the public hero and savior of Thebes, she knows the truth about him (his murder of the father, his incestuous marriage). Her deadlock is that she is prevented from sharing this accursed knowledge (like Abraham, who likewise could not communicate to others the divine injunction to sacrifice his son): she cannot complain, or share her pain and sorrow with others. In contrast to Sophocles's Antigone, who acts (to bury her brother and thus actively assume her fate), she is unable to act, condemned forever to impassive suffering. The

4 Quoted from Jean-Pierre Kempf and Jacques Petit, *L'Otage*, Paris: Archives des Lettres Modernes 1966, p. 65.

5 Ibid., p. 53.

6 Søren Kierkegaard, *Either/Or*, Vol. 1, New York: Anchor Books 1959, pp. 137–62.

unbearable burden of her secret, of her destructive *agalma*, finally drives her to death, in which alone she finds the peace that would otherwise have come with symbolizing or sharing her pain and sorrow. Kierkegaard's point is that this situation is no longer properly tragic (again, in a similar way, Abraham is also not a tragic figure).

We can imagine the same shift also in the case of Abraham. The God who commands him to sacrifice his son is the superego-God, the perverse "version of the father," the God who, for his own pleasure, submits his servant to the ultimate test. What makes Abraham's situation non-tragic is that God's demand cannot be made public, shared with the community of believers, included in the big Other, unlike the sublime tragic moment which occurs precisely when the hero addresses the public with his terrible plight, when he puts his predicament into words. To put it succinctly, the demand addressed to Abraham has a status similar to that of a ruler's "dirty secret" when solicited to commit a crime which the State needs, but which cannot be admitted publicly. When, in the fall of 1586, Queen Elizabeth I was under pressure from her ministers to agree to the execution of Mary Stuart, she replied to their petition with the famous "answer without an answer": "If I should say I would not do what you request, I might say perhaps more than I think. And if I should say I would do it, I might plunge myself into peril, whom you labor to preserve."[7] The message was clear: she was not ready to say that she did not want Mary executed, since this would be "more than I think"; but while she clearly wanted her dead, she did not want to affirm this act of judicial murder publicly. The implicit message is thus also clear: "If you are my true and faithful servants, do this crime for me, kill her without making me responsible for her death, allow me to protest my ignorance and even punish some of you to maintain this false appearance ..." Can we not imagine God himself giving a similar answer were Abraham to ask him publicly, in front of his fellow elders, if he really wanted him to kill his only son? "If I should say I do not want you to kill Isaac I might say perhaps more than I think. And if I should say you should do it, I might plunge myself into peril (that of appearing to be an evil barbaric God, asking you to violate my own sacred Laws), from which you, my faithful follower, labor to save me."

Furthermore, insofar as Kierkegaard's Antigone is a paradigmatically modernist figure, we can extend his mental experiment and imagine a postmodern Antigone, with a Stalinist twist: in contrast to the modernist one, she would find herself in a position in which, to quote Kierkegaard himself, the ethical itself would be the temptation. One version would undoubtedly be for Antigone to publicly renounce, denounce, and accuse her father (or, in a different version, her brother Polynices) of his terrible sins *out of her unconditional love for him.*

Kierkegaard's Abraham is an example of Christian tragedy.

Christian tragic hero cannot express self in universal

Observation: Zizek does not mention the aftermath of these Christian tragedies – Kierkegaard runs down hill with Isaac in joy, Sygne presumably in heaven saved, and, most obviously, Christ resurrected!

The knight of faith is in a Stalinist phenomenon

7 Robert Hutchinson, *Elizabeth's Spymaster*, London: Orion Books 2006, p. 168.

The Kierkegaardian catch is that such a *public* act would render Antigone even more *isolated*, absolutely alone: no one—with the exception of Oedipus himself, were he still alive—would understand that her act of betrayal is the supreme act of love ... Is this predicament of the "postmodern" Antigone not also that of Judas, who was secretly enjoined by Christ to publicly betray him and pay the full price for it?

Antigone would thus be entirely deprived of her sublime beauty—all that would signal the fact that she was not a pure and simple traitor to her father, but that she acted out of love for him, would be some barely perceptible repulsive tic, like Sygne de Coûfontaine's hysteric twitch of the lips, a tic which no longer belongs to the face, but whose insistence disintegrates the unity of a face. Can we not imagine a similar tic on Judas's face—a desperate twitch of his lips signaling the terrible burden of his role?

Far from just throwing herself into the jaws of death, possessed by a strange wish to die or to disappear, Sophocles's Antigone insists up to her death on performing a precise symbolic gesture: the proper burial of her brother. Like *Hamlet*, *Antigone* is a drama of a failed symbolic ritual—Lacan insisted on this continuity (he had analyzed *Hamlet* in the seminar that preceded *The Ethics of Psychoanalysis*, which deals with *Antigone*). Antigone does not stand for some extra-symbolic real, but for the pure signifier—her "purity" is that of a signifier. This is why, although her act is suicidal, the stakes are symbolic: her passion is the death drive at its purest—but here, precisely, we should distinguish between the Freudian death drive and the Oriental nirvana. What makes Antigone a pure agent of the death drive is her unconditional demand for the symbolic ritual to be performed, an insistence which allows for no displacement or other form of compromise—this is why Lacan's formula of drive is $-D: the subject unconditionally insisting on a symbolic demand.

The problem with Antigone is not the suicidal purity of her death drive but, quite the opposite, that the monstrosity of her act is covered up by its aestheticization: the moment she is excluded from the community of humans, she turns into a sublime apparition evoking our sympathy by complaining about her plight. This is one of the key dimensions of Lacan's move from Antigone to Sygne de Coûfontaine: there is no sublime beauty in Sygne at the play's end—all that marks her as different from common mortals is the tic that momentarily disfigures her face. This feature which spoils the harmony of her beautiful face, the detail that sticks out and renders it ugly, is the material trace of her resistance to being co-opted into the universe of symbolic debt and guilt.

This, then, should be the first step in a consistent reading of Christianity: the dying Christ is on the side of Sygne, not of Antigone; Christ on the Cross is not a sublime apparition but an embarrassing monstrosity. Another aspect of this monstrosity was clearly perceived by Rembrandt, whose "Lazarus," one of the most traumatic classic paintings, depicts Christ in the act of raising Lazarus from the dead. What is striking is not only the portrayal of Lazarus, a monstrous living-dead figure returning to life, but, even more so, the terrified expression on Christ's face, as if he were a magician shocked that his spell has actually worked, disgusted by what he has brought back to life, aware that he is playing with forces better left alone. This is a true Kierkegaardian Christ, shocked not by his mortality but by the heavy burden of his supernatural powers which border on blasphemy, the blasphemy at work in every good biography: "Biography is in fact one of the occult arts. It uses scientific means—documentation, analysis, inquiry—to achieve a hermetic end: the transformation of base material into gold. Its final intention is the most ambitious and blasphemous of all—to bring back a human being to life."[8]

The death of God, as is well known, can be experienced in a plurality of modes: as a tragic loss generating a deep melancholy; as a joyful opening into a new freedom; as a simple fact to be coldly analyzed ... But in its most radical dimension, the death of God is strictly correlative to—is the other side of—the *immortalization of the body* signaled by "Christ is not dead": there is something in the human body which is more than a human body, an obscene undead partial object which is more in the body than this body itself.[9] To explain this paradox, let me cite "Joe Hill," the famous Wobblies song from 1925 (words by Alfred Hayes, music by Earl Robinson) about the judicial murder of Hill, a Swedish-born trade union organizer and singer. In the following decades, it became a true folk song, popularized around the world by Paul Robeson; here are the (slightly shortened) lyrics which present in a simple but effective way the Christological aspect of the emancipatory collective, a struggling collective bound by love:

I dreamed I saw Joe Hill last night
Alive as you or me.
Says I, "But Joe, you're ten years dead."
"I never died," says he.

"The copper bosses killed you, Joe,
They shot you, Joe," says I.
"Takes more than guns to kill a man."
Says Joe, "I didn't die."

---

8 Richard Holmes, "The Biographical Arts," review of *Truth to Life*, by A. O. J. Cockshut, *The Times* (London), May 30, 1974, p. 11.

9 When (in Romans 7:4) Paul says that Christians die to the law through the *body* of Christ, one should take note of the paradox: "law has been overcome through that which is closely tied up with sin among humans." The site of struggle and overcoming is the body, not the law.

And standing there as big as life,
And smiling with his eyes,
Joe says, "What they forgot to kill
Went on to organize."

"Joe Hill ain't dead," he says to me,
"Joe Hill ain't never died.
Where working men are out on strike,
Joe Hill is at their side."

Crucial here is the subjective reversal: the mistake of the anonymous narrator who does not believe that Joe Hill is still alive is that he forgets to include himself, his own subjective position, in the series: Joe Hill is not alive "out there," as a separate ghost; he is alive here, in the very minds of the workers remembering him and continuing his fight—he is alive in the very gaze which (mistakenly) looks for him out there. The same mistake of "reifying" the searched-for object is made by Christ's disciples, a mistake which Christ corrects with the famous words: "Where two or three are gathered in my name, I will be there."

The big Other

Is this, then, the Christian Holy Spirit—the Lacanian "big Other," the virtual, ideal agency kept alive by the work of individuals participating in it? Back in 1956, Lacan offered a short and clear definition of the Holy Ghost along these lines: "The Holy Ghost is the entry of the signifier into the world. This is certainly what Freud brought us under the title of death drive."[10] What Lacan means, at this stage of his thought, is that the Holy Ghost stands for the symbolic order as that which cancels (or, rather, suspends) the entire domain of "life"—lived experience, the libidinal flux, the wealth of emotions, or, to put it in Kant's terms, the "pathological." When we locate ourselves within the Holy Ghost, we are transubstantiated—we enter another life beyond the biological one. The status of this big Other is ironic, an agency of objective irony—in what sense? In the introduction to my book *The Fright of Real Tears*, I relate an experience of mine to illustrate the sad state of Cultural Studies today:

> Some months before writing this, at an art round table, I was asked to comment on a painting I had seen there for the first time. I did not have *any* idea about it, so I engaged in total bluff, which went on something like this: the frame of the painting in front of us is not its true frame; there is another, invisible, frame, implied by the

10 Jacques Lacan, *Le séminaire, Livre IV: La relation d'objet*, Paris: Seuil 1994, p. 48.

> structure of the painting, the frame that enframes our perception of the painting, and these two frames do not overlap—there is an invisible gap separating the two. The pivotal content of the painting is not rendered in its visible part, but is located in this dis-location of the two frames, in the gap that separates them. Are we, today, in our post-modern madness, still able to discern the traces of this gap? Perhaps more than the reading of a painting hinges on it; perhaps, the decisive dimension of humanity will be lost when we will lose the capacity to discern this gap ... To my surprise, this brief intervention was a huge success, and many following participants referred to the dimension in-between-the-two-frames, elevating it into a term. This very success made me sad, really sad. What I encountered here was not only the efficiency of a bluff, but a much more radical apathy at the very heart of today's Cultural Studies.[11]

However, 125 pages later, in the book's last chapter, I reintroduce the same notion of "between-the-two-frames," this time without irony, as a straightforward theoretical concept:

> One of the minimal definitions of a modernist painting concerns the function of its frame. The frame of the painting in front of us is not its true frame; there is another, invisible, frame, the frame implied by the structure of the painting, the frame that enframes our perception of the painting, and these two frames by definition never overlap—there is an invisible gap separating them. The pivotal content of the painting is not rendered in its visible part, but is located in this dis-location of the two frames, in the gap that separates them.[12]

What distressed me was how even some of my friends and followers missed the point—most of those who noticed this repetition read it either as a self-parodic indication of how I do not take my own theories seriously, or as a sign of my growing senility (assuming I had simply forgotten by the end of the book that I had mocked the very same notion in the introduction). Was it really so difficult to perceive how my procedure here perfectly illustrated the point I was (and am) repeatedly trying to make apropos of today's predominant attitude of cynicism and of not-taking-oneself-seriously? Even when a subject mocks a certain belief, this in no way undermines the belief's symbolic efficacy—the belief often continues to determine the subject's activity. When we make fun of an attitude, the truth is often in this attitude, not in the distance we take towards it: I make fun of it to conceal from myself the fact that it actually determines my activity. Someone who mocks his own love for a woman, say, often thereby expresses his uneasiness at being so deeply attached to her.

11 Slavoj Žižek, *The Fright of Real Tears*, London: BFI 1999, pp. 5–6.
12 Ibid., p. 130.

Peter Sellars's version of *Così fan tutte* takes place in the present (a US naval base, with Despina as a local bar owner, and the two gentlemen—naval officers —returning not as "Albanians," but as violet-and-yellow-haired punks). The main premise is that the only true passionate love is that between the philosopher Alfonzo and Despina, who experiment with two young couples in order to act out the impasse of their own desperate love. This reading hits the very heart of the Mozartean *irony* which is to be opposed to cynicism. If, to simplify it to the utmost, a cynic fakes a belief that he privately mocks (preaching sacrifice for the fatherland, say, while privately amassing profits …), an ironist takes things more seriously than he appears to—he secretly believes in what he publicly mocks. Alfonzo and Despina, the cold philosophical experimenter and the corrupt, dissolute servant girl, are the true passionate lovers using the two pathetic couples and their ridiculous erotic *imbroglio* as instruments to confront their traumatic attachment. And it is only today, in our postmodern age, allegedly full of irony and lacking all belief, that the Mozartean irony reaches its full actuality, confronting us with the embarrassing fact that—not in our interior lives, but in our acts themselves, in our social practice—we believe much more than we are aware of. Apropos of Molière's *Tartuffe*, Henri Bergson emphasized how Tartuffe is funny not on account of his hypocrisy, but because he gets caught in his own mask of hypocrisy:

> He enters so thoroughly into the role of a hypocrite that he plays it almost sincerely. In this way, and this way only, can he become comic. Were it not for this material sincerity, were it not for the language and attitudes that his long-standing experience as a hypocrite has transformed into natural gestures, Tartuffe would be simply odious.[13]

Bergson's precise expression "material sincerity" fits perfectly with the Althusserian notion of the Ideological State Apparatus, the external ritual which materializes ideology: the subject who maintains his distance towards the ritual is unaware of the fact that the ritual already dominates him from within. Even if it is misrecognized or simply "not taken seriously," this big Other is nonetheless *effective*—an efficacy clearly discernible in the case of the big Other as the "subject supposed to *not* know," as the agency of innocent appearance whose ignorance should be maintained.[14] This

13 Henri Bergson, *Laughter: An Essay on the Meaning of the Comic*, trans. Cloudesley Brereton and Fred Rothwell, New York: MacMillan 1913, p. 144–5.

14 The "subject supposed to believe" can also be defined as the "subject supposed *not* to know": in a delicate situation, the polite thing to do is to pretend to believe what my partner in conversation is claiming, in other words to pretend not to know that what he claims is not true, to act as if it were true. For example, when a foreigner desperately

point is nicely expressed in the distinction between mere politeness and tact proper:

> Following the rules of politeness is never quite enough, it requires tact. In a wonderful scene in one of Truffaut's early movies, Delphine Seyrig, a *femme du monde*, tries to teach the young Jean-Pierre Léaud the difference between politeness and tact. "Imagine you inadvertently enter a bathroom where a woman is standing naked under a shower. Politeness requires that you quickly close the door and say 'Pardon, Madame!' Whereas tact would be to quickly close the door and say 'Pardon, Monsieur!'" In both cases there is the respect for the other, for the other's intimacy upon which one has unwittingly intruded, and this requires a polite excuse. The rules are satisfied in the first case. But in the second case, one makes more: one pretends not to have seen, one pretends that the intrusion was so marginal that one couldn't even make out the sex of the exposed person, and even though the hapless lady may well know that you are pretending, she will still very much appreciate your effort.[15]

Such discretion can appear in unexpected forms and places. In China, the local party bosses are popular targets of obscene jokes mocking their vulgar tastes and sexual obsessions. (Far from originating with ordinary people, these jokes mostly express the attitude of the higher *nomenklatura* towards the lower cadres.) In one joke, a small provincial party boss has just returned from the big city with a pair of shiny new black shoes. When his young secretary brings him tea, he wants to impress her with the quality of his shoes; so when she leans over his table he moves his foot just under her skirt and tells her he can see (reflected in his shoe) that her underpants are blue. The next day the flirting goes on, and he tells her that today her underpants are green. On the third day, the secretary decides not to wear any underwear at all; looking at his shoes for the reflection, the party boss desperately exclaims: "I've just bought these shoes, and already the surface is cracked!" In the final displacement, precisely when the boss is able to see the reflected "thing itself," he withdraws from recognizing it and reads it as a feature of the mirror reflecting it. One might even detect here, beneath the surface of the boss's vulgar boastfulness, a gesture of hidden politeness: in a gentle misrecognition, he prefers to appear an idiot than to comment rudely on what he can see. The procedure is here different from that of fetishistic displacement: the subject's perception does not stop at the last thing he sees before the direct view of the vaginal opening (as in the fetishistic fixation), for his shoe

---

trying to understand me emphatically nods, signaling that he is following what I am saying, even if it is clear from his replies that he is not, it would be very impolite to brutally point this out.

15 Mladen Dolar, "The Art of the Unsaid" (unpublished paper).

is not his fetish, the last thing he sees before seeing the vaginal crack; when, unexpectedly and inadvertently, he does get the view of the crack, he as it were assumes it as his own, as his own deficiency.

In politics, a supreme case of discretion or the art of the unsaid took place during the secret meeting between Alvaro Cunhal, the leader of the Portuguese Communist Party, and Melo Antunes, the pro-democracy member of the army body which de facto ran the country after the coup against the old Salazar regime in 1974. The situation was extremely tense: on the one side there was the Communist Party and the radical army officers, ready to start the real socialist revolution, taking over factories and land (arms were already being distributed to the people, etc.); on the other side conservatives and democratic liberals were ready to stop the revolution by any means necessary, including military intervention. In their meeting, Antunes and Cunhal, both highly respected intellectuals, made a deal without stating it: there was no agreement whatsoever—explicitly, they *only* disagreed—but they left the meeting with the understanding that the communists would not start a revolution, thereby allowing the "normal" democratic state to fully form, and that the anti-socialist military would not ban the Communist Party, but accept it as a key player in the Portuguese democratic process. One can claim that this discreet meeting literally saved Portugal, preventing a bloody civil war at the very last minute. The logic of their discretion later extended to how the two participants treated their meeting. When asked about it (by a journalist friend of mine), Cunhal said that he would confirm it only if Antunes did not deny it—if Antunes denied it, then the thing never took place. When my friend then visited Antunes, he did not confirm the meeting, but listened silently as my friend told him what Cunhal had said—thus, by way of not denying it, he met Cunhal's condition and implicitly confirmed it. This is how gentlemen of the Left act in politics.

There are, of course, limits to this logic of polite ignorance. Some decades ago, a woman was slowly beaten to death in the courtyard of a big apartment block in Brooklyn; of the more than seventy witnesses who clearly saw what was going on from their windows, not one called the police. Why not? As the later investigation established, the most prevalent excuse by far was that each witness thought someone else would surely have already reported it. This fact should not be dismissed moralistically as a mere excuse for moral cowardice and egotistic indifference: what we encounter here is also a function of the big Other—this time not as Lacan's "subject supposed to know," but as what one might call "the subject supposed to call the police."

The mechanism at work here is the same as that underlying Golda Meir's famous reply when asked whether she believed in God: "I believe in the Jewish people, and they believe in God." This formula of transitive belief is today universalized: one does not believe oneself, but, relying on another "subject supposed to believe," one can act as if one believes. Furthermore, one should read Meir's statement in a very precise way: it does not imply the position of the elitist leader who feeds his naïve-believing subjects with Platonic "beautiful lies." The State of Israel is here exemplary: the fetishist disavowal is inscribed into its very foundations. Although it has, according to surveys, the most atheistic population in the world (more than 60 percent of the Jews in Israel do not believe in God), its basic legitimization (claiming the land given to them by God) is theological —the implicit formula is thus: "We know very well there is no God, but we nonetheless believe he gave us the holy land."

The "subject supposed to believe" thus does not have to exist; it suffices that its existence is presupposed as a purely virtual entity, "the Jewish people." And this was also the fatal mistake of the witnesses of the drawn-out Brooklyn murder: they misread the symbolic (fictional) function of the "subject supposed to call the police" as an empirical function, wrongly concluding that there must be at least someone who would actually make the call, that is, they overlooked the fact that the function is operative even if there is no actual subject who enacts it. One could even imagine an empirical test for this claim: if the circumstances could be recreated so that each of the witnesses were to think that he or she was alone in observing the gruesome scene, one could predict that, despite their opportunistic avoidance of "getting involved in something that isn't my business," the majority of them would have called the police.

So, again, what is the big Other? A lady from Germany once told me that her sex life was minimal: she had to seduce her husband once every couple of weeks, "just so that I can tell my psychoanalyst that I still have sex life"—the analyst is here the big Other, the agency for which one has to maintain the appearance (of an active sex life). Here is a more ominous version of the same logic: in 2009, an unfortunate Greek man wrote several letters to a Greek civil servant over several months, complaining that he had yet to receive his pension; the civil servant finally replied with a letter informing him that the reason for the delay was that he was dead.[16] The shocking nature of the message lies not only in its obvious contradiction with the fact that the addressee was actually alive, and the performative paradox that this fact implies (the message saying that I am dead is addressed to me, that is, it presupposes that I am alive). The very fact that this paradox can occur implies a more complex situation: the message addresses the dimension in me which makes me dead even while I am still alive, the "mortifying" dimension of the signifier, of being inscribed into (reduced to) the network of symbolic representation. In other words, what the message is saying is something like the following: even if you are biologically alive, you no longer exist for the big Other; as far as the state network is concerned, you are dead.

16 I owe this reference to Nikitas Fessas, Athens.

Apropos of the multiple meanings of the "big Other" in Lacan, Balmès was right to emphasize that the solution is not to attempt to distinguish clearly between the various meanings (the Other as the place of speech, the desiring Other, etc.).[17] What is much more important is to analyze what Hegel would have called the "self-movement of the notion," the way one meaning, on account of its inherent tensions and implications, passes into another (often its opposite). For example, what differentiates hysteria from psychosis is their different relation to the "enjoyment of the Other" (not the subject's enjoyment of the Other, but the Other who enjoys [in] the subject): a hysteric finds it unbearable to be the object of the Other's enjoyment, she finds herself "used" or "exploited," while a psychotic willfully immerses himself in it and wallows in it. (A pervert is a special case: he posits himself not as the object of the Other's enjoyment, but as the *instrument* of the Other's enjoyment—he *serves* the Other's enjoyment.) The root of these shifts in the meaning of big Other is that, in the subject's relation to it, we are effectively dealing with a closed loop best rendered by Escher's famous image of two hands drawing each other. The big Other is a virtual order which exists only through subjects "believing" in it; if, however, a subject were to suspend its belief in the big Other, the subject itself, its "reality," would disappear. The paradox is that symbolic fiction is constitutive of reality: if we take away the fiction, we lose reality itself. This loop is what Hegel called "positing the presuppositions." This big Other should not be reduced to an anonymous symbolic field—there are many interesting cases where an individual stands for the big Other. One should think not primarily of leader-figures who directly embody their communities (king, president, master), but rather of the more mysterious *protectors of appearances*—such as otherwise corrupted parents who desperately try to keep their child ignorant of their depraved lives, or, if it is a leader, then one for whom Potemkin villages are built.[18]

When, in David Lean's *Brief Encounter*, the lovers meet for the last time at the desolate train station, their solitude is immediately disturbed by Celia Johnson's noisy and inquisitive friend who, unaware of the underlying tension between the couple, goes prattling on about ridiculously insignificant everyday incidents. Unable to communicate directly, the couple can only stare desperately. This common prattler is the big Other at its purest: while it appears as an

---

17 Balmès, *Dieu, le sexe et la vérité*.

18 Today, it seems that appearances no longer have to be protected. We all know the innocent child from Andersen's "The Emperor's New Clothes" who publicly proclaims the fact that the emperor is naked—today, in our cynical era, such a strategy no longer works, it has lost its disturbing power, since everyone now proclaims that the emperor is naked (that Western democracies are torturing terrorist suspects, that wars are fought for profit, etc., etc.), and yet nothing happens, nobody seems to mind, the system just goes on functioning as if the emperor were fully dressed.

accidental and unfortunate intrusion, its role is structurally necessary.[19] When, towards the end of the film, we see this scene a second time, accompanied by Celia Johnson's voiceover, she tells us that she was not listening to what her friend was saying, indeed she had not understood a word; however, precisely as such, her prattling provided the necessary support, as a kind of safety-cushion, for the lovers' last meeting, preventing its self-destructive explosion or, worse, its decline into banality. That is to say, on the one hand, the very presence of the naïve prattler who "understands nothing" of the situation enables the lovers to maintain a minimum of control over their predicament, since they feel compelled to "maintain proper appearances" in front of this gaze. On the other hand, in the few words privately exchanged before the big Other's interruption, they had come to the brink of confronting the unpleasant question: if they're really so passionately in love that they can't live without each other, why don't they simply divorce their spouses and get together? The prattler then arrives at exactly the right moment, enabling the lovers to maintain the tragic grandeur of their predicament. Without the intrusion, they would have had to confront the banality and vulgar compromise of their situation. The shift to be made in a proper dialectical analysis thus goes from the condition of impossibility to the condition of possibility: what appears as the "condition of impossibility," or the obstacle, is in fact the condition that enables what it appears to threaten to exist.

Two further "as if's" in *Brief Encounter*, the first in Roald-Dahl-style: what if Celia Johnson were suddenly to discover that Trevor Howard was really a bachelor who had concocted the story of his marriage and two children to add a melodramatic-tragic flavor to the affair, and to avoid the prospect of long-term commitment? Then, one in Bridges-of-Madison-County-style: what if, at the end, Celia Johnson were to discover that her husband had known all about the affair from the beginning and had just been pretending ignorance in order to maintain appearances and/or not to hurt or put additional pressure on his wife?

To a person in a state of emotional trauma, possessed by a desire to disappear or fall into the void, a superficial external intrusion (like the friend prattling on) is often the only thing standing between him and the abyss of self-destruction: what appears as a ridiculous intrusion becomes a life-saving intervention. So when, alone with her companion in a carriage compartment, Celia

19 A similar case of a character standing in for the big Other occurs in the Bond film *Casino Royale*, in the guise of the confused, intrusively friendly and comically punctual Swiss bank representative who organizes the money transfers for the poker players. Towards the end of the film—when, in the lush garden of a Montenegrin villa, the recuperating Bond and Vesper Lynd decide to stay together, and start to embrace—the Swiss banker appears, embarrassed but intrusive, with a stupid smile, asking Bond to type in the password needed to access the money he has won—the proverbial *Liebes-Stoerer* …

Johnson complains about the incessant yapping and even expresses a desire to kill the intruder ("I wish you would stop talking. … I wish you were dead now. No, that was silly and unkind. But I wish you would stop talking"), we can well imagine what would have happened had the acquaintance really stopped talking: either Celia would have immediately collapsed, or she would have been compelled to utter a humiliating plea: "Please, just carry on talking, no matter what you are saying …" Is this unfortunate intruder not a kind of envoy of (a stand-in for) the absent husband, his representative (in the sense of Lacan's paradoxical statement that woman is one of the Names-of-the-Father)? She intervenes at exactly the right moment to prevent the drift into self-annihilation (as in the famous scene in *Vertigo* where the phone rings just in time to stop Scottie and Madeleine's dangerous drift into erotic contact).

The husband and the prattler are effectively two aspects of one and the same entity, the big Other, the addressee of Celia Johnson's confession. The husband is both the ideal recipient of the confession—dependable, open, understanding—and the one who above all cannot be confessed to—he must be protected from the truth; he is the subject supposed to *not* know: "Dear Fred. There's so much that I want to say to you. You're the only one in the world with the wisdom and gentleness to understand it. … As it is, you are the only one in the world that I can never tell. Never, never. … I don't want you to be hurt." The prattler, for her part, is the wrong person at the right time and place: Celia Johnson wants to confess to her, but cannot: "I wish I could trust you. I wish you were a wise, kind friend instead of a gossiping acquaintance I've known casually for years and never particularly cared for."[20]

In dealing with the big Other, it is crucial to be attentive to the interplay between the anonymous field and the subject impersonating it. One popular myth from the late Communist era in Eastern Europe was that there existed a department of the secret police whose function was to invent and put into circulation political jokes about the regime and its representatives, for they were aware of the positive stabilizing function of such jokes (offering ordinary people an easy and tolerable way to let off steam, easing their frustrations, etc.). Attractive as it is, this myth overlooks a rarely mentioned but nonetheless crucial feature of jokes: they never seem to have an author, as if the question "who is the author of this joke?" were an impossible one. Jokes are originally "told," they are always already "heard" ("Have you heard the one about …?"). Therein resides their mystery: they are idiosyncratic; they stand for the unique creativity of language but are nonetheless "collective," anonymous, authorless, arriving all of a sudden

20 *Brief Encounter* is a cult film among gay men, on account of the way it recalls the atmosphere of gay couples secretly meeting in the darkness of train stations at night; however, what if its libidinal structure is more that of a lesbian affair (in which, as we know from Lacan, the Third who guarantees it is the paternal figure)?

out of nowhere. The idea that there has to be an author of a joke is properly paranoid: it means that there has to be an "Other of the Other," of the anonymous symbolic order, as if the unfathomable generative power of language has to be personalized, located in an agent who controls it and secretly pulls the strings. This is why, from the theological perspective, God is the ultimate jokester. This is the thesis of Isaac Asimov's charming short story "Jokester," about a group of historians of language who, in support of the hypothesis that God created man out of apes by telling them a joke, try to reconstruct this joke, the "mother of all jokes" which first gave birth to spirit. (Incidentally, for those in the Judeo-Christian tradition, this is superfluous, since we all know what the joke was: "Do not eat from the tree of knowledge!"—the first prohibition which is clearly a joke, a perplexing temptation whose point is unclear.)

Is God then the big Other? The answer is not as simple as it may appear. One can say that he is the big Other at the level of the enunciated, but not at the level of the enunciation (the level which really matters). Saint Augustine was already fully aware of this problem, when he asked the naïve but crucial question: if God sees into the innermost depths of our hearts, knowing what we really think and want better than we do ourselves, why then is a confession to God necessary? Are we not telling him what he already knows? Is God then not like the tax authorities in some countries who already know all about our income, yet still ask us to report it, just so they can compare the two lists and establish who is lying? The answer, of course, lies in the position of enunciation. In a group of people, even if everyone knows my dirty secret (and even if everyone knows that everyone else knows it), it is still crucial for me to say it openly; the moment I do, everything changes. But what is this "everything"? The moment I say it, the big Other, the instance of appearance, knows it; my secret is thereby inscribed into the big Other. Here we encounter the two opposite aspects of the big Other: the big Other as the "subject supposed to know," as the Master who sees everything and secretly pulls the strings; and the big Other as the agent of pure appearance, the agent supposed to *not* know, the agent for whose benefit appearances are to be maintained. Prior to my confession, God in the first aspect of the big Other already knows everything, but God in the second aspect does not. This difference can also be expressed in terms of subjective assumption: insofar as I merely know it, I do not really assume it subjectively, in other words, I can continue to act as if I do not know it; only when I confess to it in public can I no longer pretend not to know.[21] The theological problem is the following: does

21 In his *De Doctrina Christiana*, Augustine artfully evoked the independence of the properly symbolic-performative dimension of speech with regard to the inner psychological attitude of the speaker, in order to justify the authority of the Church and its representatives even when they are (as persons) sinful and corrupted—the moral quality of the speaker is irrelevant, what matters is that the doctrine he preaches is orthodox: "It is

not this distinction between the two Gods introduce finitude into God himself? Should not God as the absolute Subject be precisely the one for whom the enunciated and its enunciation totally overlap, so that whatever we intimately know has already been confessed to him? The problem is that such a God is the God of a psychotic, the God to whom I am totally transparent also at the level of enunciation.

The death of God

Is the Holy Spirit, then, a version of this big Other, of what Hegel calls "objective spirit" or spiritual substance? It is crucial *not* to equate them: the properly Christian-Hegelian notion of the Holy Spirit is misunderstood when reduced to the humanist claim that "God" is nothing but our (human) awareness of God, so that the Holy Spirit is simply the spiritual substance of humanity. Here are two representative passages:

> Finite consciousness knows God only to the extent to which God knows himself, spirit is *nothing other than* those who worship him.

> Man knows God only insofar as God knows himself as man. The Spirit of man, whereby he knows God, is simply the spirit of God himself.[22]

In short, from the properly Hegelian perspective, announced already in Eckhart, one should reverse the proposition that "to believe that God exists is to believe that I stand in some relation to his existence *such that his existence is itself the reason for my belief*."[23] My belief in God is, on the contrary, the reason for God's very existence, or, God qua Holy Ghost, the spiritual substance of the Christian collective, its presupposition, is alive only insofar as it is itself posited by the continuous activity of individuals. However, it is crucial *not* to confuse this gesture with the standard "materialist" notion that God is just a fiction projected by the believers, the conclusion drawn by Solomon: "there is no 'alien' God who reaches

---

possible for a person who is eloquent but evil actually to compose a sermon proclaiming the truth for another, who is not eloquent but who is good to deliver." Do we not find here an embryo of the corrupt and cynical ghostwriter composing great speeches for the naïve political leader?

22 As quoted by Robert C. Solomon in *In the Spirit of Hegel*, Oxford: Oxford University Press 1983, p. 626; based on G. W. F. Hegel, *Lectures on the Philosophy of Religion*, ed. and trans. E. B. Speirs and J. Burdon Sanderson, London: Kegan Paul, Trench, Trübner 1895. Emphasis added.

23 Sam Harris, *The End of Faith*, New York: W. W. Norton & Company 2005, p. 63.

down to us; God is Spirit and Spirit is us, nothing more."[24] What one should render problematic here is the fateful "nothing more": of course there is no Spirit as a substantial entity above and beyond individuals, but this does not make Hegel a nominalist—there is "something more" than the reality of individuals, and this "more" is the virtual Real which always supplements reality, "more than nothing, but less than something." In other words, if there is "nothing more" than us (human individuals) in Spirit, how are we to account for the central tenet of Christianity, the event of Christ's incarnation? Why do humans not directly recognize themselves—their Spirit—in the figure of an alien substantial God? Why do they not directly "kill God" as a transcendent Subject, allowing him to survive only as the virtual symbolic order kept alive by the incessant activity of each and everyone of us? Solomon confronts this problem:

> It is the "middle term" of the Trinity that exercises Hegel the most: God or "Spirit" is easily reinterpreted as immanent, and the "Holy Ghost" already has precisely the status Hegel wants it to have, as Spirit effused throughout the community. But it is the role of Jesus that distinguishes Christianity from other religions, and the notion of "incarnation" which "contradicts all understanding."[25]

But this solution avoids the problem nicely stated centuries ago by Lessing ("How is it possible that Christianity can base the whole of its faith on an historical accident?") by claiming that "Hegel's answer, in fact, is found in Goethe, who described this as an allegory, 'a particular considered only as an illustration, as an example of the universal.'"[26] Read in this way, of course, Hegel is not

> a religious man, much less the "greatest abstract thinker of Christianity." He is, perhaps, one of the first great humanists of German philosophy. That was Hegel's secret, and the source of Kierkegaard's righteous complaint: "Modern philosophy is neither more nor less than paganism. But it wants to make itself and us believe that it is Christianity."[27]

Alasdair Macintyre was thus quite correct when he claimed that "if Kierkegaard hadn't existed, it would be necessary to invent him"—or even "God invented Kierkegaard to throw light on Hegel."[28]

Hegel does indeed say that Christ is an example—but, he adds, an "example of example" and thus "the absolute example," which means, precisely, that it

---

24 Solomon, *In the Spirit of Hegel*, p. 629.
25 Ibid., p. 628.
26 Ibid.
27 Ibid., p. 634.
28 Quoted from ibid., p. 634.

is no longer a mere example, but an example which is more the "thing itself" exemplified in/by it than the thing itself—in other words, it is only through this "example" that the exemplified "thing itself" becomes what it is. This is why Christ's incarnation "contradicts all understanding": what understanding cannot grasp is how, in Christianity, its universal/eternal Truth is based "on an historical accident," namely how its necessity is itself grounded in a contingency. In this precise sense, Hegel is *not* a "humanist": for a humanist, it is easy to see how all individuals are passing contingent embodiments/examples of the eternal human Spirit.[29] What a humanist cannot grasp is that this universal Spirit, in order to become "for itself," to fully actualize itself, has to be directly incarnated in a singular contingent individual who is not its mere "example" but the full actuality of the Universal. So when this singular individual dies, it is not just the substantial In-itself of a transcendent God which dies; what dies is also God qua spiritual substance, the universal Spirit which is kept alive by the incessant activity of all passing contingent individuals—such a representation is still too "substantial."

At a more basic level, what we are dealing with here is the shift from abstract to concrete universality. At the level of abstract universality, we can oppose the universal symbolic system as a non-psychological "objective social fact" to individual subjects and their interaction. We reach concrete universality when we ask how the anonymous symbolic system exists *for* the subject, that is, how the subject *experiences it* as "objective," universal. In order for a universality to become "concrete," For-itself, it has to be experienced as such, as a non-psychological universal order, by the subject.[30] This precise distinction enables us to account for the passage of what Hegel called "objective spirit" (OS) to "absolute spirit" (AS). We do not pass from OS to AS by way of a simple subjective appropriation of "reified" OS subjectivity (in the well-known Feuerbach-young-Marx pseudo-Hegelian mode: "the collective human subjectivity recognizes in OS its own product, the reified expression of its own creative power")—this would be a simple reduction of OS to subjective spirit (SS). But neither do we accomplish this passage by positing beyond OS another, even more In-itself absolute entity that encompasses both SS and OS. The passage from OS to AS resides in nothing but the dialectical mediation between OS and

29 Even Badiou remains a "humanist" when he remarks how "the Idea is nothing other than that by which individuals discover within themselves the action of thought as immanence to the True. This discovery immediately indicates both that the individual is not the author of this thought but merely that through which it passes, and that this thought would, nevertheless, not have existed without all the incorporations which make up its materiality." (Alain Badiou, *Second Manifesto for Philosophy*, Cambridge: Polity 2011, p. 109.) Is this not the old Hegelian idea of spiritual substance as something which cannot be reduced to individuals' experience and activity, but which nonetheless only exists when it is kept alive by the individuals' incessant activity?

30 The Freudo-Lacanian answer to this question is symbolic castration.

SS, in the above-indicated inclusion of the gap that separates OS from SS within SS, so that OS has to appear (be experienced) as such, as an objective "reified" entity, by SS itself (and in the inverted recognition that, without the *subjective* reference to an In-itself of the OS, subjectivity itself disintegrates, collapses into psychotic autism).[31]

What, then, is that which does not die, the material support of the Holy Spirit? When Robeson sang "Joe Hill" at the legendary Peace Arch concert in 1952, he changed the key line from "What they forgot to kill" into: "What they can never kill went on to organize." The immortal dimension in man, that in man which it "takes more than guns to kill," the Spirit, is what went on to organize itself. This should not be dismissed as an obscurantist-spiritualist metaphor—there is a subjective truth in it: when emancipatory subjects organize themselves, it is the "spirit" itself which organizes itself through them. One should add to the series of what the impersonal "it" (*das Es, ça*) does (in the unconscious, "it talks," "it enjoys"): *it organizes itself* (*ça s'organise*—therein resides the core of the "eternal Idea" of a revolutionary party). One should also shamelessly evoke the standard scene from science-fiction horror movies in which the alien who has taken on human appearance (or invaded and colonized a human being) is exposed, its human form destroyed, so that all that remains is a formless slime, like a pool of melted metal … the hero leaves the scene, satisfied that the threat has been dealt with—and then the formless slime that the hero forgot to kill (or could not kill) starts to move, slowly organizing itself, and the old menacing figure is reconstituted. Perhaps it is along these lines that we should read the Christian practice of Eucharist,

> in which the participants in this love feast or sacrificial meal establish solidarity with one another through the medium of a mutilated body. In this way, they share at the level of sign or sacrament in Christ's own bloody passage from weakness to power, death to transfigured life.[32]

Is not what we believers consume in the Eucharist, Christ's flesh (bread) and blood (wine), precisely the same formless remainder, "what they [the Roman soldiers who crucified him] can never kill," which then goes on to organize itself as a community of believers? From this standpoint we should reread Oedipus

---

31 In the same way, in Christianity, we overcome the opposition between God as an objective spiritual In-itself and human (believers') subjectivity by way of transposing this gap into God himself: Christianity is "absolute religion" only and precisely insofar as, in it, the distance that separates God from man separates God from himself (and man from man, from the "inhuman" in him).

32 Terry Eagleton, *Trouble with Strangers: A Study of Ethics*, Oxford: Wiley-Blackwell 2009, p. 272.

himself as a precursor of Christ: against those—including Lacan himself—who perceive Oedipus at Colonus and Antigone as figures driven by the uncompromisingly suicidal death drive, "unyielding right to the end, demanding everything, giving up nothing, absolutely unreconciled,"[33] Terry Eagleton is right to point out that Oedipus at Colonus

> becomes the cornerstone of a new political order. Oedipus's polluted body signifies among other things the monstrous terror at the gates in which, if it is to have a chance of rebirth, the polis must recognize its own hideous deformity. This profoundly political dimension of the tragedy is given short shrift in Lacan's own meditations ...[34]
>
> In becoming nothing but the scum and refuse of the polis—the "shit of the earth," as St Paul racily describes the followers of Jesus, or the "total loss of humanity" which Marx portrays as the proletariat—Oedipus is divested of his identity and authority and so can offer his lacerated body as the cornerstone of a new social order. "Am I made a man in this hour when I cease to be?" (or perhaps "Am I to be counted as something only when I am nothing / am no longer human?"), the beggar king wonders aloud.[35]

Does this not recall a later beggar king, Christ himself, who, by his death as a nobody, an outcast abandoned even by his disciples, grounds a new community of believers? They both re-emerge by way of passing through the zero-level of being reduced to an excremental remainder. The notion of the Christian collective of believers (and its later versions, from emancipatory political movements to psychoanalytic societies) is an answer to a precise materialist question: how to assert materialism not as a teaching, but as a form of collective life? Therein resides the failure of Stalinism: no matter how "materialist" its teaching was, its form of organization—the Party, which is an instrument of the historical big Other—remained idealist. Only a collective of the Holy Spirit founded on the "death of God," on accepting the inexistence of the big Other, is materialist in its very form of social organization.

This "transubstantiation," by means of which our acts are experienced as drawing strength from their own result, should not be dismissed as an ideological illusion ("in reality there are simply individuals who are organizing themselves"). Here is the shortest Jacob and Wilhelm Grimm fairy tale, "The Willful Child":

---

33 Jacques Lacan, *The Ethics of Psychoanalysis, 1959–1960*, trans. David Porter, New York: W. W. Norton & Company 1992, p. 176.

34 Eagleton, *Trouble with Strangers*, pp. 185–6.

35 Ibid., p. 271.

> Once upon a time there was a child who was willful and did not do what his mother wanted. For this reason God was displeased with him and caused him to become ill, and no doctor could help him, and in a short time he lay on his deathbed. He was lowered into a grave and covered with earth, but his little arm suddenly came forth and reached up, and it didn't help when they put it back in and put fresh earth over it, for the little arm always came out again. So the mother herself had to go to the grave and beat the little arm with a switch, and as soon as she had done that, it withdrew, and the child finally came to rest beneath the earth.

Is not this obstinacy that persists even beyond death freedom—the death drive—at its most elementary? Instead of condemning it, should we not rather celebrate it as the last resort of our resistance? The death of Christ is also the death/end of human mortality, the "death of death," the negation of negation: the death of God is the rise of the undead drive (the undead partial object). Here, however, Hegel is not radical enough: since he is not able to think *objet a*, he also ignores bodily immortality ("undeadness")—both Spinoza and Hegel share this blindness for the proper dimension of the *objet a*. How can a Christian believer come to terms with this obscene excess of immortality? Is the answer, once again, love? Can one love this excess?

In what precise sense is Christianity the religion of love? Badiou provides a standard reading: while, like Plato, Christianity mobilizes the power of love to bind together subjects and sustain their fidelity to an event which marks a rupture with their utilitarian daily lives, it subordinates love proper as the rise of the Two—as the construction of a world from the Two—to a One, the One of transcendent divinity. The open risk of a love affair, the exploration of the consequences of love with no guarantee of a final success, is thus re-inscribed into the One, the God above the Two as the ultimate goal and guarantee of love. Against this intervention of a transcendent One which resolves the impossibility inscribed into the Two, Badiou insists on the immanence of love: the real of a love-encounter is transformed into a symbolic bond, contingency is transformed into necessity, by the love declaration ("I love you"), and the commitment announced in this declaration has then to be tested in the continuous work of love. The "eternity" of love is the eternity of this commitment, not the eternity of a transcendent-eternal guarantee.

But is such a reading of Christianity the only one possible? When Christ answers his disciples, "Where two or three are gathered in my name, I will be there," does this also not dispense with any transcendence? Is love, divine love, here not also reduced to the immanence of the link which unites the Two? In other words, is the passage from God to the Holy Ghost not precisely the passage from transcendence to an immanent link? The problem resides in the precise nature of this link: after the reduction of transcendence, is the big Other still here? Furthermore, can we simply get rid of the big Other, or is a detour through the illusion of the big Other inevitable? In *Seminar XXIII*, Lacan points out that "psychoanalysis, with its success, demonstrates that one can also get rid of the Name-of-the-Father. One can get rid of it (ignore it: *s'en passer*) on condition that one makes use of it (*s'en server*)."[36]

What lurks in the background here is Lacan's dictum *la vérité surgit de la méprise*—more precisely, *de la méprise du sss (sujet supposé savoir)*: one cannot get directly at the inexistence of the big Other, one has first to be duped by the Other, because *le Nom-du-Père* means that *les non-dupes errent*: those who refuse to succumb to the illusion of *sss* also miss the truth concealed by this illusion. This brings us back to "God is unconscious": "God" (as subject supposed to know, as big Other, as the ultimate addressee beyond all empirical addressees) is a permanent, constitutive structure of language; without Him, we are in psychosis—without the place of God-Father, the subject ends up in a Schreberian delirium.[37] God as *sss* is unsurpassable, in its basic dimension of big Other, of the place of Truth. The big Other is thus the zero-level of the divine, it is "properly the place where, if you allow me this play with words, god—godspeak—speaking (*le dieu—le dieur—le dire*) produces itself. It is saying which makes God out of a nothing. And as long as something will be said, the hypothesis of God will be here."[38]

The moment we speak, we (unconsciously, at least) believe in God—it is here that we encounter Lacan's "theological materialism" at its purest: it is speech (ours, ultimately) which creates God; however, God is here the moment we speak—or, to quote the Talmud: "You have made me into a single entity in the world, for it is written 'Hear O Israel, the Lord is our god, the Lord is one,' and I shall make you into a single entity in the world."[39] Therein resides the limit of Judaism: of course it can perform the humanist reversal, we—the collective of believers—create God-One by praying to him; but *Christ*, its monstrous excess, cannot be thought here. The Talmudic formula exemplifies the standard circle of subjects and their virtual substance kept alive by the subjects' incessant activity, substance as "the work of one and all." In his seminar on *The Ethics of Psychoanalysis*, Lacan opposes to the thesis of the death of God the claim that God is dead from the very beginning, it is just that he just did not know it; in Christianity he finally learns it—on the Cross. The death of Christ is thus not an actual death, but rather a becoming aware of what is already here. One should nonetheless take note of how this process unfolds in two stages, the Jewish and the Christian. While, in pagan religions, the gods are alive, Jewish believers

36 Jacques Lacan, *Le sinthome*, Paris: Seuil 2005, p. 136.

37 See Jacques Lacan, "La méprise du sujet supposé savoir," *Scilicet* 1 (1968), p. 39.

38 Jacques Lacan, *Le séminaire, Livre XX: Encore*, Paris: Seuil 1975, pp. 44–5.

39 Babylonian Talmud, Chagigah 3a.

already took God's death into account—indications of this awareness abound in the Jewish sacred texts. Recall, from the Talmud, the story about the two rabbis who basically tell God to shut up: they fight over a theological question until, unable to resolve it, one of them proposes: "Let Heaven itself testify that the Law is according to my judgment." A voice from heaven agrees with the rabbi who first appealed; however, the other rabbi then stands up and claims that even a voice from heaven was not to be regarded, "For Thou, O God, didst long ago write down in the law which Thou gavest on Sinai, 'Thou shalt follow the multitude.'" God himself had to agree: after saying, "My children have vanquished me! My children have vanquished me!" he runs away ... There is a similar story in the Babylonian Talmud (Baba Metzia 59b), but here, in a wonderful Nietzschean twist, God accepts his defeat with joyous laughter:

> R. Eliezer brought forward every imaginable argument, but the Sages did not accept any of them. Finally he said to them: "If the Halakhah [religious law] is in accordance with me, let this carob tree prove it!" Sure enough the carob tree immediately uprooted itself and moved one hundred cubits, and some say 400 cubits, from its place. "No proof can be brought from a carob tree," they retorted. And again he said to them "If the Halakhah agrees with me, let the channel of water prove it!" Sure enough, the channel of water flowed backward. "No proof can be brought from a channel of water," they rejoined. After yet another trial with a wall, R. Eliezer then said to the Sages: "If the Halakhah agrees with me, let it be proved from heaven." Sure enough, a divine voice cried out, "Why do you dispute with R. Eliezer, with whom the Halakhah always agrees?" R. Joshua stood up and protested: "'The Torah is not in heaven!' (Deut. 30:12). We pay no attention to a divine voice because long ago at Mount Sinai You wrote in your Torah at Mount Sinai, 'After the majority must one incline' (Ex. 23:2)." R. Nathan met [the prophet] Elijah and asked him, "What did the Holy One do at that moment?" Elijah: "He laughed [with joy], saying, 'My children have defeated me, my children have defeated me.'"

The outstanding feature of this story is not only the divine laughter which replaces the sorrowful complaint, but the way the Sages (who stand for the big Other, of course) win the argument against God: even God Himself, the absolute Subject, is decentered with regard to the big Other (the order of symbolic registration), so that, once his injunctions are written down, he can no longer touch them. We can thus imagine why God reacts to his defeat with joyous laughter: the Sages have learnt his lesson that God is dead, and that the Truth resides in the dead letter of the Law which is beyond his control. In short, after the act of creation is accomplished, God loses even the right to intervene in how people interpret his law.

Modern liberal-democratic readers like to refer to this story as a parable about democracy: the majority wins, God as the ultimate Master has to concede defeat. This is, however, to miss the key message: the Sages do not simply stand for the majority, they stand for the big Other, for the unconditional authority of the dead letter of the Law to which even God himself has to bow. To give this story a Christian (and, simultaneously, radical-democratic) twist, we have to suspend the reference to the big Other, accept the big Other's inexistence, and conceive the Sages as a collective which *ne s'autorise que de lui-même.* To put it in Hegelese, in the two Talmudic stories, God is dead "For us or in himself," which is why, even if believers no longer really believe in him, they continue to practice the ritual of belief—it is only in Christianity that God dies "for himself." God thus has to die twice, in itself and for itself: in Judaism, he dies in itself by way of being reduced to the performative effect of (humans) talking about him; but such a God continues to function, so has to die for itself, which happens in Christianity.

This, perhaps, is the most concise definition of the Hegelian Absolute Knowing: fully assuming the big Other's inexistence, that is to say, the inexistence of the big Other as the subject-supposed-to-know. There is a key difference between this knowing and what, in a certain Socratic or mystical tradition, is called *docta ignorantia*: the latter refers to the *subject's* knowing its ignorance, while the ignorance registered by the subject of Absolute Knowing is that of *the big Other itself.* The formula of true atheism is thus: divine knowing and existence are incompatible, God exists only insofar as he doesn't know (take note of, register) his own inexistence. The moment God knows, he collapses into the abyss of inexistence, like the familiar cartoon cat which falls only when it notices there is no ground beneath its feet.

So why did Christ have to die? The paradox is that, in order for the virtual Substance (the big Other) to die, the price had to be paid in the real of flesh and blood. In other words, God is a fiction, but for the fiction (which structures reality) to die, a piece of the real had to be destroyed. Since the big Other as a virtual order, a symbolic fiction, is effective in its very inexistence—it does not exist, but it nevertheless works—it is thus not enough to destroy the fiction from the outside, to reduce it to reality, to demonstrate how it emerged from reality (*pace* "vulgar" atheists like Richard Dawkins). The fiction has to be destroyed from within, that is, its inherent falsity has to be brought out. To put it in descriptive terms, it is not enough to prove that God does not exist—the formula of true atheism is that *God himself must be made to proclaim his own inexistence*, must stop believing in himself. Therein lies the paradox: if we destroy the fiction from outside, reducing it to reality, *it continues to function in reality*, to exert its symbolic efficacy—as in the famous joke about the aforementioned atheist Zionists who do not believe that God exists, but nonetheless believe he gave them the land of Israel. "But now thus said the Lord that created you, Jacob, and he that formed you, Israel: Fear not, for I have redeemed you, I have called you by your name; you are mine" (Isaiah 43:1). This, exactly, is what is reversed (undone) in the "subjective destitution" at work in consistent Christianity: I have to confront the terror of the big Other's non-existence, which means that I myself am deprived of my symbolic identity—as a barred subject ($), I am no one's and nameless. And the same applies to God himself, which is why, in his unpublished seminar from 1974–5, Lacan explains that Christianity is the "true" religion: in it, God ex-sists with regard to all: "He is ex-sistence *par excellence*, that is to say, in short, he is repression in person, he is even the person supposed in repression. And it is with regard to this that Christianity is true."[40] Lacan refers here to "I am what I am," the answer the burning bush on Mount Sinai gives when Moses asks it what it is; he reads it as the designation of a point at which a signifier is lacking, at which there is a hole in the symbolic order—and this should be taken in a strong reflexive sense, not only as an indication that God is a deep reality beyond the reach of our language, but that God is *nothing but* this lack in the symbolic order (big Other). As such, the divine "I am what I am" effectively prefigures the Cartesian *cogito*, the barred subject ($), this pure evanescent point of enunciation betrayed by any enunciated. This nothing—whose stand-in (or place-holder) is *objet a*—is the focus of love, or, as Simone Weil put it: "Where there is nothing, read that I love you."

It is with regard to this crucial feature that we might also locate the ultimate limitation of Malabou's notion of plasticity, which she still conceives of as the unity of opposites, of activity and passivity, of gathering and splitting. Malabou seems to be caught in the notional frame of polarity—of (the bad infinity of) two poles each reverting into the other indefinitely, along the lines of the Freudian Eros and Thanatos or the pagan notion of the universe as originating in the constant struggle of masculine and feminine, light and darkness, etc. So when she writes, in an almost programmatic passage, the following, what is missing is the assertion of the *singular punctual moment of the full identity of the opposites*:

> An integrating and informing power, an originary synthetic power, plasticity also requires a contrary power of dissociation and rupture. These two powers characterize perfectly the gait of the Hegelian text: gathering and splitting, both at work in the System's own formation. They are two inseparable powers allowing an idea of temporalizing synthesis and an idea of factual eruption to be articulated together. My whole work is invested here, as it tries to show that the Hegelian notion of temporality is located nowhere else but in the economy opened up by this articulation.[41]

40 Jacques Lacan, *Le séminaire, Livre XXII: R.S.I., 1974–1975* (unpublished).
41 Catherine Malabou, *The Future of Hegel*, London: Routledge 2005, p. 186.

When a chaotic period of gestation culminates in the explosive eruption of a new Form which reorganizes the entire field, this very imposition of the new Necessity/Order is in itself thoroughly contingent, an act of abyssal/ungrounded subjective decision. This brings us to the strict philosophical notion of subjectivity, since what characterizes the subject—in contrast to substance—is precisely such a complete coincidence of opposites: in the case of substance, synthesis and splitting remain externally opposed. While "substance" already stands for the encompassing unity of opposites, for the medium within which particular forces reproduce themselves through their struggle, in a "substantial" relationship the two aspects, synthesis and splitting, are not yet brought to self-relating, so that splitting *as such* would be that which brings about a synthesis, so that imposing a new Necessity would be the highest gesture of contingency.

Two features which cannot but appear opposed characterize the modern subject as it was conceptualized by German Idealism: (1) the subject is the power of "spontaneous" (i.e., autonomous, starting-in-itself, irreducible to a prior cause) *synthetic* activity, the force of unification, of bringing together the manifold of sensuous data we are bombarded with into a unified representation of objects; (2) the subject is the power of negativity, of introducing a gap/cut into the given-immediate substantial unity; it is the power of *differentiating*, of "abstracting," tearing apart and treating as self-sufficient what in reality is part of an organic unity. In order to truly understand German Idealism, it is crucial to think these two features not only together (as two aspects of one and the same activity—i.e., the subject first tears apart natural unity then brings the *membra disjecta* together into a new [his own "subjective"] unity), but as *stricto sensu identical*: the synthetic activity itself introduces a gap/difference into substantial reality; likewise the differentiation itself consists in imposing a unity.

But how, exactly, are we to understand this? The subject's spontaneity emerges as a disturbing *cut* into substantial reality, since the unity the transcendental synthesis imposes onto the natural manifold is precisely "synthetic" (in the standard rather than Kantian sense, i.e., artificial, "unnatural"). To evoke a common political experience: all great unifiers begin with a divisive gesture—de Gaulle, for example, unified the French by way of introducing an irreconcilable difference between those who wanted peace with Germany and those who did not.

The same goes for Christianity: we are not *first* separated from God and *then* miraculously united with him; the point of Christianity is that the very separation unites us—it is in this separation that we are "like God," like Christ on the Cross, such that our separation from God is transposed into God himself. So when Meister Eckhart speaks of how, in order to open oneself up to the grace of God, allowing Christ to be born in one's soul, one has to "empty" oneself of everything "creaturely," how is this *kenosis* related to the properly divine *kenosis*

(or, for that matter, even to the *kenosis* of alienation, of the subject being deprived of its substantial content)?

And likewise for ethics: a radical act of Good *has* to appear first as "evil," as disturbing the substantial stability of traditional mores. Kafka formulated succinctly the basic Judeo-Christian tenet concerning Good and Evil: "Evil knows of the Good, but Good does not know of Evil. Knowledge of oneself is something only Evil has."[42] This is the proper Judeo-Christian answer to the Gnostic-Socratic motto "Know yourself!" The underlying idea that Evil comes from eating the fruit of the tree of knowledge is radically opposed to the Oriental and Platonic tradition for which Evil is grounded in the lack of the evildoer's knowledge (you cannot knowingly do evil things), so that the motto "Know yourself!" is simultaneously both ethical and epistemological. (This is why, in some Gnostic readings of the Old Testament, the snake that seduces Adam and Eve into eating from the tree of knowledge is an agent of the Good, working against the evil God-Creator.) Does this mean that, in order to be good, we should limit ourselves to ignorance? The dialectical position is more radical: there is a third way, that of the primacy of Evil over the Good. It is necessary to begin by choosing Evil; or, more precisely, every true Beginning as a radical break with the past is by definition Evil, from which the Good can emerge only afterwards, in the space opened up by that Evil.[43] The infamous series of black books (of communism, capitalism, psychoanalysis ...) should be recapitulated in a black book on humanity itself—Brecht was right, humans are by nature evil and corrupt; one cannot change them, but only limit their opportunities to actualize their evil potential.

This is why, in Christianity, opposed features are attributed to Christ: he brings peace, love, etc., *and* he brings a sword, turning son against father, brother against brother. Again, this is *one and the same* gesture, not a logic of "first divide in order to unite." And, again, it is crucial not to confuse this "identity of opposites" with the standard pagan motif of a divinity having two faces, a loving one and a destructive one—we are talking about one and the same face. But this does not mean that "the difference is only in us, not in God, who dwells in his blessed Beyond" (as in the old simile that sees reality as like a painting: if we look at it from too close up, we see only blurred stains; but viewed from a proper distance we can see the global harmony)—or, rather, it *is* like that, but not as external

42 Franz Kafka, *The Blue Octavo Notebooks*, ed. Max Brod, Cambridge, MA: Exact Change 1991, p. 24.

43 This is why a true Christian should not rely too much on "Father, forgive them, for they know not what they do": ignorance is *not* an excuse, but a form of hypocrisy. The only excusable violation of the divine command not to kill is when it is done with full awareness: in the terrible solitude of the decision, one assumes the act, knowing there is no other way.

to God-in-himself: this shift is inherent to God. The dialectic of appearance holds here also: appearing is not external to God; God also is only as deep as he appears; his depth has to appear as depth, and it is this appearing that introduces a gap/cut. God has to appear "as such" in the domain of appearance itself, tearing it apart—it is *nothing but* this appearing.

This is why those who see a deep affinity between Heidegger and Buddhism miss the point: when Heidegger speaks about the "appropriating event (*Ereignis*)," he introduces a dimension which, precisely, is missing in Buddhism—that of the fundamental historicity of Being. Although what is erroneously called "Buddhist ontology" desubstantializes reality into a pure flow of singular events, what it cannot think is the "eventuality" of the Void of Being itself. To put it another way, the goal of Buddhism is to enable a person to achieve Enlightenment by "traversing" the illusion of the Self and rejoining the Void—what is unthinkable within this space is Heidegger's notion of the human being as *Da-Sein*, as the "being-there" of Being itself, as the site of the event-arrival of Being, so that it is Being itself that "needs" *Dasein*; with the disappearance of *Dasein*, there is also no Being, no place where Being can, precisely, take place. Can one imagine a Buddhist claiming that the Void (*sunyata*) itself needs humans as the site of its arrival? One perhaps can, but in a conditional form which totally differs from Heidegger's: namely in the sense that, of all sentient beings, only humans are able to achieve Enlightenment and thus break the circle of suffering.

Perhaps the clearest indication of the gap that separates Christianity from Buddhism is the difference in their respective triads. That is to say, in their respective histories, each divided itself into three main strands. In the case of Christianity, we get the triad of Orthodoxy-Catholicism-Protestantism, which neatly fits the logic of Universal-Particular-Individual. In Buddhism, by contrast, we get a case of what in Hegel occurs as a "downward synthesis" in which the third term, whose function is to mediate between the first two, does so in a disappointing-regressive way (in Hegel's *Phenomenology*, for example, the whole dialectic of observing Reason culminates in the ridiculous figure of phrenology). The main split within Buddhism is between Hinayana ("the small wheel") and Mahayana ("the great wheel"). The first is elitist and demanding, trying to maintain a fidelity to Buddha's teaching, focusing on the individual's effort to overcome the illusion of the Self and attain Enlightenment. The second, which arose from a split with the first, subtly shifts the accent onto compassion for others: its central figure is the bodhisattva, the individual who, after achieving Enlightenment, decides out of compassion to return to the world of material illusions in order to help others to achieve Enlightenment, in other words, to work to end the suffering of all sentient beings. The split here is irreducible: working for one's own Enlightenment only reasserts the centrality of the Self in the very act of striving for its overcoming, while the "great wheel" route out of this predicament just displaces the deadlock: egotism is overcome, but at the price of universal Enlightenment itself turning into an object of the instrumental activity of the Self.

It is easy to identify the inconsistency of the Mahayana move, which cannot but have fateful consequences: when the Mahayana reinterpretation focuses on the figure of the bodhisattva—the one who, after achieving Enlightenment and entering nirvana, returns to the life of illusory passions out of compassion for all those still caught in the Wheel of Craving—a simple question arises: if, as radical Buddhists emphatically point out, entering nirvana does not mean that we leave this world and enter another, higher reality—in other words, if reality remains as it is and all that changes is the individual's attitude towards it—why, then, in order to help other suffering beings, must we *return* to our ordinary reality? Why can we not continue to dwell in the state of Enlightenment in which, as we are taught, we remain living in this world? There is thus no need for Mahayana, for the "larger wheel": the small (Hinayana) wheel is itself large enough to allow the Enlightened one to help others achieve Enlightenment. In other words, is not the very concept of the bodhisattva based on a theologico-metaphysical misunderstanding of the nature of nirvana? Does it not, in an underhand way, turn nirvana into a higher meta-physical reality? No wonder that Mahayana Buddhists were the first to give a religious twist to Buddhism, abandoning the Buddha's original agnostic materialism, his explicit indifference towards the religious topic.

It would, however, be an utterly non-Hegelian reading of Buddhism if we were to locate "the Fall" in its historical development in the humanitarian "betrayal" of its original message enacted by the Mahayana turn: if there is an Hegelian axiom, it is that the flaw has to be located at the very beginning of the entire movement. What, then, is already wrong with the Hinayana itself? Its flaw is precisely that to which the Mahayana reacts, as its symmetrical reversal: in striving for my own Enlightenment, I regress into egotism in my very attempt to erase the constraints of my Self.

So, how to bring these two orientations, Hinayana and Mahayana, together? What they both exclude is a shattering proto-conservative insight: what if truth does not alleviate our suffering? What if truth *hurts*? What if the only peace attainable comes from immersing oneself in illusion? Is this conclusion not the hidden underlying premise of the third major school, the Vajrayana, which predominates in Tibet and Mongolia? Vajrayana is clearly regressive, involving the reinscription of traditional ritualistic and magical practices into Buddhism: the opposition between Self and others is here overcome, but through its "reification" in ritualized practices which are indifferent to this distinction. It is an interesting fact of historical dialectic that Buddhism, which originally dispensed with all

institutional ritual and dogma to focus solely on the individual's Enlightenment and overcoming of suffering, ended up clinging to the most mechanical and firmly entrenched institutional hierarchical framework.

The point here is not to make fun of the "superstitious" features of Tibetan Buddhism, but to become aware of how this total externalization *does the job*, "delivers the goods": is not the use of the prayer-wheel—and of ritual more generally—also a means to achieve "mindlessness," to empty one's mind and repose in peace? So, in a way, Tibetan Buddhism *is* wholly faithful to the Buddha's pragmatic orientation (ignore theological niceties, focus on helping people): sometimes, following blind ritual and immersing oneself in theologico-dogmatic hair-splitting *is* pragmatically the most effective way to achieve the goal of inner peace. The same holds for sexuality, where, sometimes, the best cure for impotence is not just to "relax and let go" (the moment one formulates this as an injunction, it has the opposite of the intended effect), but to approach sex as a bureaucratic procedure, establishing in detail what one is planning to do. This logic is also that of intelligent utilitarians who are well aware that moral acts cannot be directly grounded in utilitarian considerations ("I will do this because, in the long run, it is the best strategy for bringing me the most happiness and pleasure ..."); but the conclusion they draw is that the Kantian "absolutist" morality ("do your duty for the sake of duty") can and should be defended precisely on utilitarian grounds—it is also the one that works best in real life.

What then is the Buddhist answer to the Hegelian question: if we suffering humans need to be awakened into Enlightenment, how did we fall asleep in the first place? How did the Wheel of Desire emerge out of the eternal Void? There are three main answers which strangely echo the triad of Hinayana, Mahayana, and Vajrayana. The first, standard answer invokes the Buddha's practico-ethical attitude: instead of dwelling on metaphysical enigmas, begin with the fact of suffering and the task of helping people out of it. The next answer draws our attention to the obvious cognitive paradox implied in the question itself: our very state of ignorance makes it impossible for us to answer it—it can only be answered (or even posed in a proper way) once one reaches full Enlightenment. (Why then do we not receive an answer from those who claim to have reached Enlightenment?) Finally, there are some Tibetan Buddhist hints at dark demonic forces which disturb the balance of nirvana from within.

It is here that the gap separating Hegel from the Buddhist experience is unbridgeable: for Hegel as a Christian philosopher, the problem is not "how to overcome the split," since the split stands for subjectivity, for the gap of negativity, and *this negativity is not a problem but a solution*, it *is* already in itself *divine*. The divine is not the abyssal, all-encompassing Substance/Unity behind the multitude of appearances; the divine is the negative power tearing apart the organic unity. Christ's "death" is not overcome, but *elevated* into Spirit's negativity.[44] Imagine experiencing oneself abandoned by God, left to one's own devices, with no big Other secretly watching over one and guaranteeing a happy outcome—is this not another name for the abyss of freedom? This abandonment in a state of freedom causes anxiety—as Lacan reinterpreted Freud—not because the divine is far from us, but because it is all too close, since it is in our freedom that we are "divine"—as Lacan put it, anxiety does not signal the loss of the object-cause of desire, but its over-proximity. If freedom is God's supreme gift to us (taking the word "gift" in all its fundamental ambiguity: "present" and "poison"—a poisonous and dangerous present, then), then being abandoned by God is the most God can give us. Crucial for Christianity, in contrast to all other religions, is this immanent reversal of abandonment into proximity—or, to put it in terms of "bad news/good news" medical jokes: the bad news is that we are abandoned by God; the good news is that we are abandoned by God and left with our freedom.

What to make, then, of the standard reproach that Hegel transposes Christianity—a religion of love and passion, of total subjective engagement—into a narrative representation of "abstract" speculative truth? Although Christianity is the "true" religion, in it the truth still appears in the medium of representation (and not in its own conceptual medium), so that speculative philosophy is the truth (the true-adequate form) of the Christian truth (content); the passion and pain of subjective engagement are thus dismissed as a secondary narrative husk to be discarded if we want to reach the truth in its own conceptual element. What this critique misses is that the casting off of the pathetic-narrative existential experience—the transubstantiation of the subject from a "concrete" self immersed in its life world into the subject of pure thought—*is itself a process of "abstraction" which has to be accomplished in the individual's "concrete" experience, and which as such involves the supreme pain of renunciation.*

For Badiou, love is a "scene of the Two" as such, grounded only in itself, its own "work of love," lacking any Third which would provide a proper support or Ground: when I am in love with someone, my love is neither One nor Three (I do not form with my beloved a harmonious One in fusion, nor is our relationship grounded in a Third, a medium which would provide predetermined coordinates for our love and thus guarantee its harmony).[45] This is what makes

44 This is why there is also an homology between this necessity of Christ as the immediate embodiment of the spiritual substance and the necessity of illusion on which, among others, Bourdieu insists in his critique of Lévi-Strauss's explanation of potlatch: it is not enough just to claim that Christ is a reified-immediate materialization of the Holy Spirit, the true question is why the Holy Spirit has to appear first in the immediate form of a singular human being.

45 I rely here on Alain Badiou, "What is Love, or, The Arena of the Two," lecture at the European Graduate School, Saas-Fee, Switzerland, August 9, 2008.

love so fragile: it is, as Badiou puts it, a process of pure presentation, a radically contingent encounter incessantly in search of some form of re-presentation in the big Other that would guarantee its consistency. Therein resides the function of marriage: through its ritual, the raw real of a love passion is registered in, and thus recognized by, the big Other of the public order, and, ultimately (in a church marriage), by God, the ultimate big Other itself. This is why, as Badiou perspicuously notes, love is in its very notion *atheist*, godless: all the talk about God's love for us or our love for God should not deceive us. How, then, are we to explain the central role of love (of God's love for humanity) in Christianity? Precisely by the fact that Christianity is, at its deepest core, already atheistic, a paradoxically atheistic religion. When Christ says to his followers deceived after his death on the Cross that, whenever there is love between them, he will be there, alive among them, this should not be read as a guarantee that Christ-Love is a Third term in the relationship of love, its guarantee and foundation, but, on the contrary, as another way of proclaiming the death of God: there is no big Other which guarantees our fate; all we have is the self-grounded abyss of our love.

What this means is also that Hegel really is the ultimate Christian philosopher: no wonder he often uses the term "love" to designate the play of the dialectical mediation of opposites. What makes him a Christian philosopher and a philosopher of love is the fact that, contrary to the common misunderstanding, in the arena of dialectical struggle there is no Third which unites and reconciles the two struggling opposites.

The Atheist Wager

In Lacan's formulae of sexuation, "non-All" designates the feminine position, a field which is not totalized because it lacks the exception, the Master-Signifier. Applied to Christianity, this means that the Holy Spirit is *feminine*, a community *not* based on a leader. The shift to the feminine occurs already in Christ: Christ is not a male figure; as many subtle readers have noted, his strangely passive stance is that of feminization, not of male intervention. Christ's impassivity thus points towards the feminization of God: his sacrifice follows the same logic as that of the heroine of Henry James's *Portrait of a Lady*, or of Sygne de Coûfontaine in Claudel's *L'Otage*. Christ is not a Master figure, but the *objet a*, occupying the position of the analyst: an embarrassing excess, answering questions with jokes and riddles that only confound his listeners further, already acting as his own blasphemy.[46] Recall the strange parable of the talents from the Gospel of Matthew:

46 Paul relates to Christ a little bit like Plato does to Socrates: like Socrates, Christ does not expose a doctrine, he is a provocateur who performatively stages an attitude towards

> For it will be as when a man going on a journey called his servants and entrusted to them his property; to one he gave five talents, to another two, to another one, to each according to his ability. Then he went away. He who had received the five talents went at once and traded with them; and he made five talents more. So also, he who had the two talents made two talents more. But he who had received the one talent went and dug in the ground and hid his master's money. Now after a long time the master of those servants came and settled accounts with them. And he who had received the five talents came forward, bringing five talents more, saying, "Master, you delivered to me five talents; here I have made five talents more." His master said to him, "Well done, good and faithful servant; you have been faithful over a little, I will set you over much; enter into the joy of your master." And he also who had the two talents came forward, saying, "Master, you delivered to me two talents; here I have made two talents more." His master said to him, "Well done, good and faithful servant; you have been faithful over a little, I will set you over much; enter into the joy of your master."
>
> He also who had received the one talent came forward, saying, "Master, I knew you to be a hard man, reaping where you did not sow, and gathering where you did not winnow; so I was afraid, and I went and hid your talent in the ground. Here you have what is yours." But his master answered him, "You wicked and slothful servant! You knew that I reap where I have not sowed, and gather where I have not winnowed? Then you ought to have invested my money with the bankers, and at my coming I should have received what was my own with interest. So take the talent from him, and give it to him who has the ten talents. For to every one who has will more be given, and he will have an abundance; but from him who has not, even what he has will be taken away. And cast the worthless servant into the outer darkness; there men will weep and gnash their teeth." (Matthew 25:14–30)

It is not hard to imagine how much an American business-oriented Baptist pastor would love this parable: does it not confirm the parallel between religion and business, promoting in both the dynamic capitalist spirit of venture, circulation, risk, and expansion? Preachers who expound the word of God must act like businessmen expanding their business! However, is it not also possible to read the parable in the opposite way, especially if we bear in mind the alternative

---

life by means of pragmatic paradoxes; like Plato, Paul then articulates these provocations into a consistent doctrine. Is this attitude of Socrates, the first philosopher, towards his polis (community) not that of subtraction in the Badiouian sense: a gesture of rejecting what Kant later called the "private use of reason," of bracketing the possible uses of knowledge for the social good and welfare, of pursuing an autonomous work of self-examination wherever it will take us? In this simple sense, the ongoing "Bologna reform" of European higher education is an anti-Socratic gesture par excellence, a threat to the very foundation of the European legacy.

version in Luke 19:11–27: here the master is a nobleman who has to leave for "a distant country to receive for himself a kingdom," although he is not wanted there; the three men are not servants but (ten) slaves; the nobleman's attendants protest at his decision to give the third man's minas to the one who already has ten ("'Sir, he has ten minas already!'"); and the parable concludes with a cruel order: "'But as for these enemies of mine who did not want me to be their king, bring them here and slaughter them in front of me!'"—hardly a gesture worthy of a good man. Is it not much more appropriate to do as William Herzog proposed, and celebrate the third servant as a whistle-blower denouncing the exploitation of the poor?[47] In other words, what if we read the third man's decision to hide the talent, withdrawing it from commercial circulation, as a gesture of *subtraction* from the field of (economic) power, as a refusal to participate in it? The master's furious reaction is thus fully justified: what this servant did is much worse than stealing his money or hiding the profit—had he done that, the servant would still have participated in the business spirit of "reaping where I have not sowed." But the servant went much further: he rejected the entire "spirit" of profit and exploitation and thus attacked the very foundations of the master's existence—and was this not why Christianity had such problems coming to terms with collecting interest, which means precisely to "reap where I have not sowed"? The parable is definitely an exercise in weird humor, so John Caputo is right to refer to Kierkegaard's Johannes Climacus who says that humor serves as the incognito of the religious—the problem resides in the precise determination of this humor, a humor inextricably mixed with horror.[48]

One can conceive of the entire history of Christianity as a reaction not against preceding religion(s), but against *its own excessive/subversive core*, that of the true dimension of the Holy Ghost (the egalitarian emancipatory collective which cancels any organic-hierarchical social link): all the great theologians embraced the task of making Christianity compatible with a hierarchical social body. Saint Augustine took the first major step in this direction by way of "inventing psychological interiority," thereby withdrawing from a literal and socially dangerous interpretation of Christ's radical sayings (to follow him one must hate one's mother and father; the rich will never enter paradise; etc.). The whole art of Thomas Aquinas culminates in a form of sophistry designed to reconcile the literal meaning of the Bible with the demands of a hierarchical society. Recall, for example, his demonstration that although Christ preaches the renunciation of earthly wealth (i.e., the sinful character of private property), this holds only for people who are themselves holy (priests, etc.); if ordinary

47 William R. Herzog II, *Parables as Subversive Speech: Jesus as Pedagogue of the Oppressed*, Louisville: Westminster/John Knox Press 1995.

48 John D. Caputo and Gianni Vattimo, *After the Death of God*, ed. Jeffrey W. Robbins, New York: Columbia University Press 2007, p. 138.

people were to want to abolish private property, they would sin against God. This, however, in no way leads to a "spurious infinity" of the gap between really existing Christianity and the true Christianity, so that every really existing form of the Church necessarily misses its notion. The solution here is the properly Hegelian one: the true Idea of the Christian collective *was* realized, but outside of the Church as an institution—which, however, does not mean that it survived in intimate, authentic religious experiences which had no need for the institutional frame; rather, it survived in *other* institutions, from revolutionary political parties to psychoanalytic societies ... It is thus only in post-religious "atheist" radical-emancipatory collectives that we find the proper actualization of the Idea of the Christian collective—the necessary consequence of the "atheistic" nature of Christianity itself.

The standard reproach addressed to this project of "Christian materialism" is that it amounts to a "barred" belief: not being courageous enough to make the "leap of faith," I retain the Christian form of religious engagement without its content. My reply is that this "emptying the form of its content" already takes place in Christianity itself, at its very core—the name of this emptying is *kenosis*: God dies and resurrects itself as the Holy Ghost, as the *form* of collective belief. It is a fetishistic mistake to search for the material support of this form (the resurrected Christ)—the Holy Ghost is the very collective of believers, what they are searching for outside of the collective is already there in the guise of the love that binds them. Adrian Johnston recently formulated a pertinent critical point apropos of my project of "Christian atheism":

> You and Badiou clearly, openly, and unambiguously are thoroughgoing atheists, thinkers insisting on the non-existence of any big Other, One-All, and so on. Moreover, both of you labor to reveal, in a non-reductive manner, the material basis/genesis of "spiritual" phenomena. And, of course, you yourself vehemently insist on reading Christianity as the "religion of atheism." But, from others' texts I've read and conversations I've had these past few years, some people register you and Badiou as religious in the same fashion that audiences register Penn and Teller as magical: "I know full well that Badiou and Žižek are atheists, but nonetheless ..."; "I know that Christianity is, as the religion of atheism, an immanent self-negation of religion, but nonetheless ... (I continue to relate to it as religion, in a religious mode replete with all its established rituals, practices, etc.)." I guess one of the things I'm saying is that the tactic of employing Christianity as a tempting Trojan horse carrying within it the explosive potentials of an atheistic-materialist radical politics carries dangerous risks arising from this *je sais bien, mais quand même* reaction evident in those who latch onto you and Badiou as licensing, as displaying strains of phenomenology and its offshoots, a version of "post-secular" Continental philosophy.[49]

49 Adrian Johnston, personal communication.

Is it true, then, that what I offer is a form of belief deprived of its structure, which effectively amounts to a disavowed belief? My counter-argument here is double. First, I conceive my position not as being somewhere in between atheism and religious belief, but as the *only* true radical atheism, that is, an atheism which draws all the consequences from the inexistence of the big Other. Therein resides the lesson of Christianity: as we have seen, it is not only that we do not believe in God, but that God himself does not believe in himself, so that he also cannot survive as the non-substantial symbolic order, the virtual big Other who continues to believe in our stead, on our behalf. Second, only a belief which survives such a disappearance of the big Other is belief at its most radical, a wager more crazy than Pascal's: Pascal's wager remains epistemological, concerning only our attitude towards God, that is, we have to assume that God exists, the wager does not concern God himself; for radical atheism, by contrast, the wager is ontological—the atheist subject engages itself in a (political, artistic, etc.) project, "believes" in it, without any guarantee. My thesis is thus double: not only is *Christianity* (at its core, if disavowed by its institutional practice) *the only truly consistent atheism*, it is also that *atheists are the only true believers*.

Let us for a moment return to Pascal. The first thing of note is his rejection of all attempts to demonstrate the existence of God: Pascal concedes that "we do not know if He is," and so seeks instead to provide prudential reasons for believing in him: we should wager that God exists because it is the best bet:

> "God is, or He is not." But to which side shall we incline? Reason can decide nothing here. There is an infinite chaos which separates us. A game is being played at the extremity of this infinite distance where heads or tails will turn up … Which will you choose then? Let us see. Since you must choose, let us see which interests you least. You have two things to lose, the true and the good; and two things to stake, your reason and your will, your knowledge and your happiness; and your nature has two things to shun, error and misery. Your reason is no more shocked in choosing one rather than the other, since you must of necessity choose … But your happiness? Let us weigh the gain and the loss in wagering that God exists.[50]

Pascal appears to be aware of the immediate objection to this argument, for he imagines an opponent replying: "That is very fine. Yes, I must wager; but I may perhaps wager too much." In short, when one wagers on God, one does put something at stake, which presumably one loses if God does not exist: truth, the respect for one's worldly life … (Indeed, it is strange how utilitarian-pragmatist Pascal's reasoning is.) A series of other objections follow:

---

50 Pascal, cited in Alan Hájek, "Pascal's Wager," online entry from *The Stanford Encyclopedia of Philosophy* (Summer 2011 Edition), ed. Edward N. Zalta. I rely here extensively on this entry.

(1) Pascal assumes that the same matrix of decision and reward applies to everybody—but what if the rewards are different for different people? Perhaps, for example, there is a predestined infinite reward for the Chosen, whatever they do, and finite utility for the rest?

(2) The matrix should have more rows: perhaps there is more than one way to wager for God, and the rewards that God bestows vary accordingly. For instance, God might not reward infinitely those who strive to believe in him only for the utilitarian-pragmatic reasons that Pascal gives. One could also imagine distinguishing belief based on faith from belief based on evidential reasons, and posit different rewards in each case.

(3) Then there is the obvious many-Gods objection: Pascal had in mind the Catholic God, but other theistic hypotheses are also live options, i.e., the "(Catholic) God does not exist" column really subdivides into various other theistic hypotheses (but the Protestant God exists, Allah exists, there is no God ...). The obverse of this objection is the claim that Pascal's argument proves too much: its logical conclusion is that rationality requires believing in various incompatible theistic hypotheses.

(4) Finally, one can argue that morality requires you to wager against God: wagering for God because of the promise of future profit violates the Kantian definition of the moral act as an act accomplished for no "pathological" reasons. Voltaire, arguing along these lines, suggested that Pascal's calculations, and his appeal to self-interest, were unworthy of the gravity of the subject.

Underlying all this is the basic paradox of belief as a matter of decision: as if to believe something or not were a matter of decision and not of insight. So, if we read Pascal's wager together with his no less well-known topic of customs, one can argue that the core of his argument does not directly concern belief but rather acting: one cannot decide to believe, one can only decide to act *as if* one believes, in the hope that belief will arise by itself; perhaps this trust that if you act as if you believe, belief will arise, is itself the wager:

> You would like to attain faith, and do not know the way; you would like to cure yourself of unbelief, and ask the remedy for it. Learn of those who have been bound like you, and who now stake all their possessions. These are people who know the way which you would follow, and who are cured of an ill of which you would be cured. Follow the way by which they began; by acting as if they believed, taking the holy water, having masses said, etc.[51]

51 Pascal, cited in ibid.

Perhaps the only way out of these impasses is what, in his unpublished "secret" writings, Denis Diderot elaborated under the title of the "materialist's credo." In "Entretien d'un Philosophe avec la maréchale de ***," he concluded: "*Après tout, le plus court est de se conduire comme si le vieillard existait … même quand on n'y croit pas.*" (After all, the most straightforward way is to behave as if the old guy exists … even if one doesn't believe it.) This may appear to amount to the same as Pascal's wager with regard to rituals: even if you do not believe in them, act as if you believe. However, Diderot's point is exactly the opposite one: the only way to be truly moral is to act morally without regard to God's existence. In other words, Diderot directly inverts Pascal's wager (the advice to place your bet on the existence of God): "*En un mot que la plupart ont tout à perdre et rien à gagner à nier un Dieu rénumérateur et vengeur.*" (In a word, it is that the majority of those who deny a remunerating and revenging God have all to lose and nothing to gain.)[52] In his denial of the remunerative and vengeful God, the atheist either loses everything (if he is wrong, he will be damned forever) or gains nothing (if he is right, there is no God, so nothing happens). It is this attitude which expresses true confidence in one's belief and makes one do good deeds without regard to divine reward or "as if the old guy exists"—this old guy is, of course, God-the-Father, which recalls Lacan's formula *le père ou pire*—father or worse. It is at this level that one should oppose Pascal and Diderot: while Pascal bets on God-the-Father, Diderot enjoins us to *parier sur le pire*, to put one's wager on the worse. In true ethics, one acts from the position of the inexistence of the big Other, assuming the abyss of the act deprived of any guarantee or support.

Authentic belief is to be opposed to the reliance on (or reference to) a(nother) subject supposed to believe: in an authentic act of belief, I myself fully assume my belief and thus have no need for any figure of the Other to guarantee that belief; to paraphrase Lacan, an authentic belief *ne s'authorise que de lui-même*. In this precise sense, authentic belief not only does not presuppose any big Other (is not a belief in a big Other), but, on the contrary, presupposes the destitution of the big Other, the full acceptance of its inexistence.

This is also why a true atheist is at the opposite end from those who want to save religion's spiritual truth from its "external" dogmatic-institutional context. A profoundly religious friend once commented on the subtitle of a book of mine, "the perverse core of Christianity": "I fully agree with you there! I believe in God, but I find repulsive and deeply disturbing all the twists celebrating sacrifice and humiliation, redemption through suffering, God organizing his own son's killing by men. Can't we have Christianity without this perverse core?" I could not bring myself to answer him: "But that is precisely the point of my

52 Denis Diderot, "Observations sur Hemsterhuis," *Oeuvres*, Vol. I, Paris: Robert Laffont 1994, p. 759.

book: what I want is all those perverse twists of redemption through suffering, the death of God, etc., but without God!"

Thus, as we have said, God has to die twice, first as real, then as symbolic; first in Judaism, then in Christianity. In Judaism, the God of the real survives as Word, as the virtual-dead Other whose specter is kept alive by the ritual performance of his subjects; in Christianity, this virtual Other itself dies. In Judaism, the God perceived directly as real dies; in Christianity, the God who is unconscious dies. The passage from paganism to Judaism is one of sublimation (the dead god survives as the symbolic Other); the death of Christ is not sublimation, in other words it is not the death of the real God who is resurrected in the Holy Ghost as the symbolic Other, like Julius Caesar who returns as sublimated in the symbolic title "Caesar."

In strict parallel with this double move from paganism to Judaism and from Judaism to Christianity is the move from traditional authoritarian power to democracy and from democracy to revolutionary power: it is only in revolutionary power that the big Other really dies. In democracy, the place of power is empty, but the electoral procedure functions as a kind of *ersatz*-Other providing the legitimacy for power. That is to say, democracy—in the way this term is used today—concerns above all formal legality: its minimal requirement is the unconditional adherence to a certain set of formal rules which guarantee that antagonisms are fully absorbed into the agonistic game. "Democracy" means that, whatever electoral manipulation takes place, every political agent will unconditionally respect the results. In this sense, the US presidential elections of 2000 were effectively "democratic": in spite of the obvious electoral duplicity and the patent meaninglessness of the fact that a couple of hundred voters in Florida decided who would be the president, the Democratic candidate accepted defeat. In the weeks of uncertainty after the elections, Bill Clinton made an appropriately acerbic comment: "The American people have spoken; we just don't know what they said." This comment should be taken more seriously than Clinton himself intended: even now, we do not know what they said—maybe because there was no substantial "message" behind the result at all. Jacques-Alain Miller has elaborated on the idea that democracy implies the "barred" big Other;[53] however, the Florida example demonstrates that there nevertheless is a "big Other" which continues to exist in democracy: the procedural "big Other" of electoral rules which must be obeyed whatever the result—and *this* "big Other," this unconditional reliance on rules, is what a more radical politics threatens to suspend.

This Kantian limitation of democracy is strictly homologous to the limitation of Kojin Karatani's Kantian "transcendental" solution to the antinomy

53 Jacques-Alain Miller, *Le neveu de Lacan*, Lagrasse: Verdier 2003, p. 270.

of money (we need an X which will be money and will not be money). When Karatani reapplies this solution to power (we need some centralized power, but not fetishized into a substance which is "in itself" Power)—and when he explicitly evokes the structural homology with Duchamp (the object becomes a work of art not because of its inherent properties, but simply by occupying a certain place in the structure)—does this not all exactly fit Lefort's theorization of democracy as a political order in which the place of power is originally empty and is only temporarily occupied by the elected representatives? Along these lines, even Karatani's apparently eccentric suggestion of combining elections with selection by lot is more traditional than it may appear (he himself mentions Ancient Greece)—paradoxically, it fulfills the same function as does Hegel's theory of monarchy.

Karatani here takes a heroic risk in proposing a crazy-sounding definition of the difference between the dictatorship of the bourgeoisie and the dictatorship of the proletariat: "If universal suffrage by secret ballot, namely, parliamentary democracy, is the dictatorship of the bourgeoisie, the introduction of lottery should be deemed the dictatorship of the proletariat." In this way, "*the center exists and does not exist at the same time*"[54]: it exists as an empty place, a transcendental X, and it does not exist as a substantial positive entity. But is this really enough to undermine the "fetishism of power"? When an ordinary individual is allowed temporarily to occupy the place of power, the charisma of power is bestowed on him, following the usual logic of fetishistic disavowal: "I know very well that this is an ordinary person like me, *but nonetheless* … (while in power, he becomes the instrument of a transcendent force, power speaks and acts through him)!" Does this not fit the general matrix of Kant's solutions, where metaphysical propositions (God, immortality, etc.) are asserted, "under erasure," as postulates? Consequently, would not the true task be precisely to get rid of the very mystique of the *place* of power? This is why, in his writings of 1917, Lenin reserves his most acerbic irony for those who engage in an endless search for some kind of "guarantee" for the revolution. This guarantee takes two main forms, in terms of either the reified notion of social Necessity (the revolution must not be risked too early; one has to wait for the right moment, when the situation is "mature" with regard to the laws of historical development) or the idea of normative ("democratic") legitimacy ("the majority of the population is not on our side, so the revolution would not really be democratic")—as if, before the revolutionary agent risks the seizure of state power, it should seek permission from some figure of the big Other (organize a referendum to ascertain whether the majority supports the revolution). Not surprisingly, a very Christian point.

54 Kojin Karatani, *Transcritique: On Marx and Hegel*, trans. Sabu Kosho, Cambridge, MA: MIT Press 2003, p. 183.

"DO NOT COMPROMISE YOUR DESIRE"

It is only against this background of the fall of the big Other that one can properly grasp Lacan's famous formulation of the basic ethical axiom implied by psychoanalysis:

> It is because we know better than those who went before how to recognize the nature of desire, which is at the heart of our experience, that a reconsideration of ethics is possible, that a form of ethical judgment is possible, of a kind that gives this question the force of a Last Judgment: Have you acted in conformity with the desire that is in you?[55]

This is Lacan's maxim of the ethics of psychoanalysis: "the only thing of which one can be guilty is of having given ground relative to one's desire."[56] This maxim, simple and clear as it appears, becomes elusive the moment one tries to specify its meaning. For Lacan, properly ethical acts are rare: they occur like "miracles" which interrupt the ordinary run of things; they do not "express" the entire "personality" of the subject, but function as a break in the continuity of "personal identity." Take the case of Maximilian Kolbe, which confronts us with a weird but crucial ethical dilemma. Kolbe was a Polish Franciscan monk who, during the 1920s and 1930s, was involved in writing and organizing mass propaganda for the Catholic Church, with a clear anti-Semitic and anti-Masonic edge. With the outbreak of World War II, he helped people threatened by the Nazis, among them many Jews, and for this he was arrested and sent to Auschwitz. When, in the summer of 1941, after the escape of a prisoner, the Germans selected ten others to be starved to death as a punishment, one of them broke down in tears, claiming he had a family which needed him; Kolbe voluntarily offered himself in the man's stead and died three weeks later of starvation. For this, he was later beatified by Pope John Paul II. How to fit these two aspects of Kolbe's life together? Most commentators take one of the many easy ways out. Some simply try to deny or minimize Kolbe's anti-Semitism (even dismissing the rumors about it as a KGB plot). Some insist on the scholastic distinction between anti-Semitism proper and anti-Judaism—a "mere" prejudice against Jews, not a murderous hatred of them—claiming that Kolbe's error was of the second, minor sort. Others interpret his helping the Jews and final sacrifice as acts of repentance: having witnessed the suffering of the Jews under the Nazi occupation, Kolbe changed his view and tried to assuage his guilt. Still others take the risky step of minimizing not his anti-Semitism, but his final self-sacrificial gesture, pointing out that the man he saved was not a Jew but a Catholic Pole. All these versions

55 Lacan, *The Ethics of Psychoanalysis*, p. 314.
56 Ibid., p. 319.

are desperate attempts to avoid the embarrassing fact that the two attitudes (and activities) can easily coexist: a person who is anti-Semitic can also be capable of a dignified act of ethical self-sacrifice—and, even more embarrassingly, the (explicit) motivation for Kolbe's noble self-sacrifice may well have been the very conservative-Catholic ideology which had sustained his anti-Semitism.

An ethical act is one that does not comprise or express the entire person, but is a moment of grace, a "miracle" which can occur also in a non-virtuous individual. This is why such acts are difficult to imagine, and why, when they do occur, one often tends to invent a narrative which normalizes them. Recall the "Assassins," the Ismaili sect, part of the Shia orientation of Islam, that fascinated the Western gaze from the twelfth century on: according to myth they were ruthless murderers who obeyed their master's orders unconditionally, without regard for their own lives; after they had killed their target (always in public and with a dagger), they did not run away, but waited to be apprehended and punished. They were able to perform these ruthless acts because they were under the influence of hashish. In the mysterious mountain fortress of Alamut in northern Iran, they were manipulated by their leader, who first drugged them and then, while they were comatose, moved them to a secluded garden decked out with all the features of the Muslim paradise, including beautiful girls ready for sex. On being returned to ordinary life, they were convinced they had experienced a heavenly episode—so when their leader told them that, if they succeeded in assassinating the designated target, they would return to paradise, they willingly complied. A closer historical study, however, quickly dispels the myth: the name *hashishi* is local to Syria only, where it functions as a general term of popular abuse; it was applied to "Assassins" as "an expression of contempt for the wild beliefs and extravagant behaviour of the sectaries—a derisive comment on their conduct."[57] The standard explanation (they were called "assassins" because they used hashish to ready themselves for their ruthless acts) has thus to be inverted: "*it was the name that gave rise to the story*, rather than the reverse ... For Western observers in particular, such stories may also have served to provide a rational explanation for behavior that was otherwise totally inexplicable."[58] The story about the recreated paradise was thus a fantasy concocted to rationalize the traumatically "incomprehensible" fact that the Ismaili followers were ready to function as perfect killing machines, willing to sacrifice their own lives in the accomplishment of the task—a fantasy, in short, that enabled Westerners to re-translate a pure "ethical" act into an act determined "pathologically" (in the Kantian sense of the term). How, then, does such an ethics stand with regard to the panoply of today's ethical options? It seems to fit three of its main versions:

57 Bernard Lewis, *The Assassins*, New York: Basic Books 2003, p. 12.

58 Ibid.

liberal hedonism, immoralism, and "Western Buddhism."[59] Let us run through these positions one by one.

The first thing to state categorically is that Lacanian ethics is not an ethics of hedonism: whatever "do not compromise your desire" means, it does *not* mean the unrestrained rule of what Freud called "the pleasure principle," the functioning of the psychic apparatus that aims at achieving pleasure. For Lacan, hedonism is in fact *the* model of postponing desire on behalf of "realistic compromises": it is not only that, in order to attain the greatest amount of pleasure, I have to calculate and economize, sacrificing short-term pleasures for more intense long-term ones; what is even more important is that *jouissance hurts*. So, first, there is no break between the pleasure principle and its counterpart, the "reality principle": the latter (compelling us to take into account the limitations that thwart our direct access to pleasure) is an inherent prolongation of the former. Second, even (Western) Buddhism is not immune to the lures of the pleasure principle; the Dalai Lama himself wrote: "The purpose of life is to be happy"—*not true for psychoanalysis*, one should add.[60] It was Nietzsche who observed that "human beings do not desire happiness, only the Englishmen desire happiness"—today's globalized hedonism is thus merely the obverse of the fact that, in the conditions of global capitalism, we are ideologically "all Englishmen" (or, rather, Anglo-Saxon Americans ...). So what is wrong with the rule of the pleasure principle? In Kant's description, ethical duty functions like a foreign intruder that disturbs the subject's homeostatic balance, its unbearable pressure forcing the subject to act "beyond the pleasure principle," ignoring the pursuit of pleasures. For Lacan, exactly the same description holds for desire, which is why enjoyment is not something that comes naturally to the subject, as a realization of his or her inner potential, but is the content of a traumatic superegoic injunction.

If hedonism is to be rejected, is Lacanian ethics then a version of the heroic immoralist ethics, enjoining us to remain faithful to ourselves and persist on our chosen way beyond good and evil? Think of don Giovanni in the last act of Mozart's opera, when the Stone Guest confronts him with a choice: he is near death, but if he repents of his sins, he can still be redeemed; if, however, he does not renounce his sinful life, he will burn in hell forever. Don Giovanni heroically refuses to repent, although well aware that he has nothing to gain, except eternal suffering, for his persistence. Why does he do it? Obviously not for any profit or

59 The larger problem here is that psychoanalysis seems able to accommodate itself to all today's predominant ethical stances—the three mentioned above plus a further two: the Levinasian-Derridean ethics of responsibility to Otherness; and the conservative advocacy of the need to reassert the symbolic law (in the guise of paternal authority) as the only way to resolve the deadlock of hedonistic permissiveness.

60 Dalai Lama (Tenzin Gyatso), foreword to Mark Epstein, *Thoughts Without a Thinker*, New York: Basic Books 1996, p. xiii.

promise of pleasure to come. The only explanation is his utmost fidelity to the dissolute life he has chosen. This is a clear case of immoral ethics: don Giovanni's life was undoubtedly immoral; however, as his fidelity to himself proves, he was immoral not for pleasure or profit, but out of principle, acting the way he did in accordance with a fundamental choice.

Or, to take a feminine example also from opera: George Bizet's *Carmen*. Carmen is, of course, immoral (ruthlessly promiscuous, ruining men's lives, destroying families), but nonetheless thoroughly ethical (faithful to her chosen path to the end, even when this means certain death). Along these lines, Lee Edelman has developed the notion of homosexuality as involving an ethics of "now," of unconditional fidelity to *jouissance*, of following the death drive by totally ignoring any reference to the future or engagement with the practical complex of worldly affairs. Homosexuality thus stands for the thorough assumption of the negativity of the death drive, of withdrawing from reality into the real of the "night of the world." Along these lines, Edelman opposes the radical ethics of homosexuality to the predominant obsession with posterity (i.e., children): children are the "pathological" moment which binds us to pragmatic considerations and thus compels us to betray the radical ethics of *jouissance*.[61] (Incidentally, does this line of thought—the idea that homosexuality at its most fundamental involves the rejection of children—not justify those who argue that gay couples should not be allowed to adopt children?) The figure of an innocent and helpless child is the ultimate ethical trap, the emblem-fetish of betraying the ethics of *jouissance*.

Friedrich Nietzsche (a great admirer of *Carmen*) was the great philosopher of immoral ethics, and we should always remember that the title of Nietzsche's masterpiece is "genealogy of morals," *not* "of ethics": the two are not the same. Morality is concerned with the symmetry of my relations to other humans; its zero-level rule is "do not do to me what you do not want me to do to you."[62] Ethics, in contrast, deals with my consistency in relation to myself, my fidelity to my own desire. On the back flyleaf of the 1939 edition of Lenin's *Materialism and Empirio-Criticism*, Stalin made the following note in red pencil:

> 1) Weakness
> 2) Idleness
> 3) Stupidity
> These are the only things that can be called vices. Everything else, in the absence of the aforementioned, is undoubtedly *virtue*.

61 See Lee Edelman, *No Future: Queer Theory and the Death Drive*, Durham: Duke University Press 2005.

62 Which is why the best psychoanalytic reply to this moral maxim is to imagine what it would mean for a *masochist* to promise us that he will follow it in relating to us.

> NB! If a man is 1) strong (spiritually), 2) active, 3) clever (or capable), then he is good, regardless of any other "vices"!
> 1) plus 3) make 2).[63]

This is as concise as ever a formulation of *immoral ethics*; in contrast, a weakling who obeys moral rules and worries about his guilt stands for *unethical morality*, the target of Nietzsche's critique of resentment. It is a supreme irony (and one of the greatest cases of poetic justice) that, among American writers, the one who provided the most precise formulation of the same immoral ethics was none other than the rabidly anti-Communist Russian emigrant Ayn Rand, in her first (still moderate) US success, the play *Night of January 16th*. Although written in a traditional realist mode, this courtroom (melo)drama engages its spectators in a very contemporary, almost Brechtian, manner: at the beginning, the twelve jury members are randomly selected from among the theater audience; they are seated on the stage and, at the play's end, they briefly withdraw before returning to deliver the verdict of guilty or not guilty—Rand provided different final lines depending on which it was. The decision they have to make is not only about the murder of Bjorn Faulkner, a ruthless Swedish tycoon: did Karen Andre, his devoted mistress and secretary, do it or not? It is also about two opposed ethics—to quote the play itself:

> if you value a strength that is its own motor, an audacity that is its own law, a spirit that is its own vindication—if you are able to admire a man who, no matter what mistakes he may have made in form, had never betrayed his essence: his self-esteem—if, deep in your hearts, you've felt a longing for greatness and for a sense of life beyond the lives around you, if you have known a hunger which gray timidity can't satisfy ...[64]

---

63 First published in Russian in *Pravda*, December 21, 1994. Beneath this note, Stalin appended in blue pencil: "Alas, what do we see, what do we see?" The translation quoted from Donald Rayfield, *Stalin and His Hangmen*, London: Penguin Books 2004, p. 22.

64 Ayn Rand, *Night of January 16th*, New York: Signet Books 1968, p. 118. Rand herself was aware of the limitations of this early attempt of hers; as she wrote in the 1968 "Introduction" to the play first performed in 1934, at this stage in her career, she was not yet ready to portray directly (her vision of) the ideal man (her first version is Howard Roar in *The Fountainhead*, New York: Signet Books 1992): "What I *was* ready to write about was a woman's feeling for her ideal man, and this is what I did in the person of Karen Andre" (p. 6). However, the fact that the portrayal of the woman's longing for such an ideal man precedes the direct portrayal of this ideal clearly indicates how Rand's figure of the ideal man is ultimately a *feminine fantasy*—no wonder that we find already in this early play noir-sounding feminine-masochist dialogues which are one of the trademarks of her later style, like the following exchange: "KAREN: He seemed to take a delight in giving me orders. He acted as if he were cracking a whip over an animal he

In short, if you advocate immoral ethics, you will find Karen not guilty; if, however, you believe in social respectability, in a life of service, duty, and unselfishness, etc., then you will find Karen guilty.

There is, however, a limit to this Stalinist immoral ethics: not that it is too immoral, but that it is secretly too moral, still relying on a figure of the big Other. In what is arguably the most intelligent legitimization of Stalinist terror, Maurice Merleau-Ponty's *Humanism and Terror* from 1946, the terror is justified as a kind of wager on the future, almost in the mode of Pascal: if the final result of today's horror turns out to be a bright communist future, then this outcome will retroactively redeem the terrible things a revolutionary has to do today. Along similar lines, even some Stalinists themselves—when forced to admit (mostly in private) that many of the victims of the purges were innocent, that they were accused and killed because "the Party needed their blood to fortify its unity"—imagined a future moment of final victory when all the victims would be given their due, and their innocence and sacrifice for the Cause would be recognized. This is what Lacan, in his seminar on Ethics, refers to as the "perspective of the Last Judgment," a perspective even more clearly discernible in two key terms of the Stalinist discourse, "objective guilt" and "objective meaning": while you can be an honest individual who acts with the most sincere intentions, you are nonetheless "objectively guilty" if your acts serve reactionary forces—and it is, of course, the Party that decides what your acts "objectively mean."

Here, again, we get not only the perspective of the Last Judgment (from which the "objective meaning" of your acts is formulated), but also the agent in the present who already has the unique ability to judge today's events and acts from this perspective.[65] The name of Raskolnikov (the hero of Dostoyevsky's *Crime and Punishment*) evokes a split (*raskol*); Raskolnikov is "the split one"—but split between what and what? The standard answer is that he is "torn between the 'Napoleonic idea,' the notion that all is permitted to a strong person, and the 'Russian idea' of selfless devotion to humanity"[66]—however, this version misses the properly "totalitarian" *coincidence* of the two ideas: it is my very selfless devotion to humanity, my awareness that I am an instrument of Humanity, which justifies my claim that all is permitted to me. The paradox is thus that

wanted to break. And I was afraid. STEVENS: Because you didn't like that? KAREN: Because I liked it …" (p. 82).

65 The same goes for such a radical hedonist atheist like the Marquis de Sade: perspicuous readers of his work (such as Pierre Klossowski) guessed long ago that the compulsion to enjoy which drives the Sadean libertine implies a hidden reference to a hidden divinity, to what Lacan called the "Supreme-Being-of-Evil," an obscure God demanding to be fed with the suffering of the innocents.

66 Ulrich Schmidt, quoted in Fyodor Dostoyevsky, *The Brothers Karamazov*, Norton Critical Edition, trans. and ed. Susan McReynolds Oddo, second edition, New York: W. W. Norton & Company 2011, p. 779.

what Raskolnikov lacks is *the split itself*, the distance between the two ideas, the "Napoleonic" and the "Russian."

We can see now why Lacan's motto "*il n'y a pas de grand Autre*" (there is no big Other) takes us to the very core of the ethical problematic: what it excludes is precisely this "perspective of the Last Judgment," the idea that somewhere—even if as a thoroughly virtual reference point, even if we concede that we can never occupy its place and pass the actual judgment—there must be a standard which would allow us to take the measure of our acts and pronounce on their "true meaning," their true ethical status. Even Derrida's notion of "deconstruction as justice" seems to rely on a utopian hope which sustains the specter of "infinite justice," forever postponed, always to come, but nonetheless here as the ultimate horizon of our activity.

The harshness of Lacanian ethics lies in its demand that we thoroughly relinquish this reference to the big Other—and its further wager is that not only does this renunciation not plunge us into ethical insecurity or relativism (or even sap the very fundamentals of ethical activity), but that renouncing the guarantee of some big Other is the very condition of a truly autonomous ethics. Recall that the exemplary dream Freud used to illustrate his procedure of dream analysis was a dream about responsibility (Freud's own responsibility for the failure of his treatment of Irma)—this fact alone indicates that responsibility is a crucial Freudian notion. But how are we to conceive of this responsibility? How are we to avoid the common misperception that the basic ethical message of psychoanalysis is, precisely, that we should relieve ourselves of responsibility and instead place the blame on the Other ("since the Unconscious is the discourse of the Other, I am not responsible for its formations, it is the big Other who speaks through me, I am merely its instrument")? Lacan himself pointed the way out of this deadlock by referring to Kant's philosophy as the crucial antecedent of psychoanalytic ethics.

Lacan against Buddhism

According to the standard critique, the limitation of the Kantian universalistic ethic of the "categorical imperative" (the unconditional injunction to do one's duty) resides in its formal indeterminacy: the moral Law does not tell me *what* my duty is, it merely tells me *that* I should accomplish my duty, and so leaves room for an empty voluntarism (whatever I decide will be my duty *is* my duty). However, far from being a limitation, this very feature brings us to the core of Kantian ethical autonomy: it is not possible to derive the concrete obligations pertaining to one's specific situation from the moral Law itself—which means that the subject himself must assume the responsibility of translating the abstract injunction into a series of concrete obligations. The full acceptance of this paradox compels us to reject any reference to duty as an excuse: "I know this is heavy and can be painful, but what can I do, this is my duty ..." Kant's ethics is often taken as justifying such an attitude—no wonder Adolf Eichmann himself referred to Kant when trying to justify his role in planning and executing the Holocaust: he was just doing his duty and obeying the Führer's orders. However, the aim of Kant's emphasis on the subject's full moral autonomy and responsibility was precisely to prevent any such maneuver of putting the blame on some figure of the big Other.

During an unfortunate debate I had with Bernard-Henri Lévy (in the premises of *Le Nouvel Observateur* in Paris), he related (what maybe was, or not) a personal experience to illustrate his opposition to killing. During the Bosnian war in the early 1990s, he had visited the besieged Sarajevo, where he was taken to a frontline trench by an officer of the Bosnian government. From here, looking through the scope of a gun, he was able to see a Serb soldier on a nearby hill occasionally shooting at civilians in the city. Looking at the soldier with his finger on the trigger, Lévy was tempted to shoot, but he resisted—the injunction "Do not kill!" is for him unconditional. To me, such a reaction was moralistic hypocrisy at its purest: Lévy fully supported the Bosnian side in the conflict (as did I, so there was no disagreement there), but his refusal to take the shot meant that, while he would have expected a Bosnian soldier in the same position to pull the trigger, he wanted to keep his hands clean and leave the necessary dirty work to others. In the face of such a dilemma, the only truly universalistic stance is to be ready to dirty one's own hands.

The core of Lacan's atheism is best discerned in the conceptual couple of "alienation" and "separation" which he develops in his *Four Fundamental Concepts of Psycho-Analysis.*[67] In a first approach, the big Other stands for the subject's alienation in the symbolic order: the big Other pulls the strings; the subject does not speak, he is "spoken" by the symbolic structure. In short, this "big Other" is the name for the social substance, for all that on account of which the subject never fully controls the effects of his acts, so that their final outcome is always other than what he aimed at or anticipated. Separation takes place when the subject takes note of how the big Other is in itself inconsistent, lacking ("barred," as Lacan liked to put it): the big Other does not possess what the subject lacks. In separation, the subject experiences how his own lack with regard to the big Other is already the lack that affects the big Other itself. To recall Hegel's immortal dictum concerning the Sphinx: "The enigmas of the Ancient Egyptians were enigmas also for the Egyptians themselves." Along the same lines, the elusive, impenetrable *Dieu obscur* has to be

67 See Chapter 11 in Jacques Lacan, *The Four Fundamental Concepts of Psycho-Analysis*, New York: W. W. Norton & Company 1978.

impenetrable also to himself; he has to have a dark side, something that is in him more than himself.[68]

During the Chinese Cultural Revolution, the Red Guards referred to suicide as "alienating oneself from the Party and people."[69] One is tempted to ask here, with regard to the Lacanian couple of alienation and separation: what, then, would *separation* from the Party and people have been? The question is not as meaningless as it may appear, insofar as, for Lacan, separation stands for redoubled alienation: the subject enacts separation when his lack coincides with the lack in the Other, that is, when he recognizes that the Other also does not have what he is missing. In short, in this context, separation involves the insight that the distance separating the subject from the Party and people is already immanent to the Party and people themselves—in other words, *the Party itself is already alienated from the people.*

So what does it mean to abandon the topic of the Last Judgment? As is often the case, Kafka provides the key here: "It is only our conception of time that makes us call the Last Judgment by this name. It is, in fact, a kind of martial law."[70] In other words, the absence of the Last Judgment does not mean that there is merely historical evolution with no moments of what Benjamin called "suspended dialectics," when the continuous flow is momentarily immobilized: the Last Judgment does not come at the end of times, it is the martial law—the state of exception—here and now.

The only other school of thought that fully accepts the inexistence of the big Other is Buddhism. Is the solution then to be found in Buddhist ethics? There are reasons to consider this option. Does not Buddhism lead us to "traverse the fantasy," overcoming the illusions on which our desires are based and confronting the void beneath each object of desire? Furthermore, psychoanalysis shares with Buddhism the insistence that there is no Self as a substantive agent of psychic life: no wonder Mark Epstein, in his book on Buddhism and psychoanalysis, refers positively to Lacan's early essay on the "mirror stage," with its notion of the Ego as an object, the result of the subject's identification with the idealized fixed image of itself:[71] the Self is the fetishized illusion of a substantial core of subjectivity where, in reality, there is nothing. This is why, for Buddhism, the point is not to discover one's "true Self," but to accept that there is no such thing, that the "Self" as such is an illusion, an imposture. In more psychoanalytic

---

68 The same goes for women in psychoanalysis: the masquerade of femininity means that there is no inaccessible feminine x beneath the multiple layers of masks, since these masks ultimately conceal the fact that there is nothing to conceal.

69 Quoted from Niall Ferguson, *The War of the World*, London: Penguin Books 2007, p. 620.

70 Kafka, *The Blue Octavo Notebooks*, p. 90.

71 Epstein, *Thoughts Without a Thinker*, p. 152.

terms: not only should one analyze resistances, but, ultimately, "there is really *nothing but* resistance to be analyzed; there is no true self waiting in the wings to be released."[72] The self is a disruptive, false, and, as such, unnecessary metaphor for the process of awareness and knowing: when we awaken to knowing, we realize that all that goes on in us is a flow of "thoughts without a thinker." The impossibility of figuring out who or what we really are is inherent, since there is nothing that we "really are," just a void at the core of our being. Consequently, in the process of Buddhist Enlightenment, we do not quit this terrestrial world for another truer reality—we just accept its non-substantial, fleeting, illusory character; we embrace the process of "going to pieces without falling apart." In the Gnostic mode, for Buddhism, ethics is ultimately a question of knowledge and ignorance: our craving (desire), our attachment to terrestrial goods, is conditioned by our ignorance, so that deliverance comes with proper knowing. (What Christian love means, on the contrary, is that there is a decision not grounded in knowledge—Christianity thus breaks with the entire tradition of the primacy of Knowledge which runs from Buddhism through Gnosticism to Spinoza.)

Crucial to Buddhism is the reflexive change from the object to the thinker himself: first, we isolate the thing that bothers us, the cause of our suffering; then we change not the object but ourselves, the way we relate to (what appears to us as) the cause of our suffering: "What was extinguished was only the *false view* of self. What had always been illusory was understood as such. Nothing was changed but the perspective of the observer."[73] This shift involves great pain; it is not merely a liberation, a step into the incestuous bliss of the infamous "oceanic feeling"; it is also the violent experience of losing the ground under one's feet, of being deprived of the most familiar stage of one's being. This is why the path towards Buddhist Enlightenment begins by focusing on the most elementary feelings of "injured innocence," of suffering an injustice without cause (the preferred topic of narcissistic, masochistic thoughts: "How could she do this to me? I don't deserve to be treated that way").[74] The next step is to make the shift to the Ego itself, the subject of these painful emotions, rendering clear and palpable its own fleeting and irrelevant status—the aggression directed against the object causing the suffering should be turned against the Self itself. We do not repair the damage; rather, we gain the insight into the illusory nature of that which appears to need repair.[75]

72 Ibid., p. 121.

73 Ibid., p. 83.

74 Ibid., p. 211.

75 Although, even here, there is a fundamental ambiguity in the Buddhist edifice: is the goal of the Buddhist meditation nirvana as the shift in the subject's stance towards reality, or is this goal the fundamental transformation of reality itself, so that all suffering disappears and all living beings are relieved of their suffering? That is to say, is not the

What, then, is the nature of the gap that separates psychoanalysis from Buddhism? In order to answer this question, we need to confront the basic enigma of Buddhism, its blind spot: how did the fall into *samsara*, the Wheel of Life, occur? This enigma is the exact *opposite* of the main Buddhist concern: how can we break out of the Wheel of Life and attain nirvana?[76] The nature and origin of the impetus by means of which desire (deception) emerged out of the Void is the big unknown in the heart of the Buddhist edifice: it points towards an act that "breaks the symmetry" within nirvana itself and thus makes something appear out of nothing (as in quantum physics with its notion of symmetry-breaking). The Freudian answer is the *drive*: what Freud calls the "drive" is not, as it may appear, the Buddhist Wheel of Life, the craving that enslaves us to the world of illusions. The drive, on the contrary, goes on even when the subject has "traversed the fantasy" and broken out of its illusory craving for the (lost) object of desire. And therein lies the difference between Buddhism and psychoanalysis, reduced to its formal minimum: for Buddhism, after Enlightenment (or "traversing the fantasy"), the Wheel no longer turns, the subject de-subjectivizes itself and finds peace; for psychoanalysis, on the other hand, *the wheel continues to turn*, and this continued turning-of-the-wheel is the drive (as Lacan put it in the last pages of *Seminar XI*: after the subject traverses the fantasy, desire is transformed into drive). What psychoanalysis adds to Buddhism is thus in fact a new version of Galileo's *eppur si muove*: imagine a Lacanian being tortured by a New Age Western Buddhist into admitting that inner peace can be achieved; after the forced concession, as he leaves the room, he quietly mumbles: "But nonetheless, it continues to move!"[77]

This is what Lacan is aiming at when he emphasizes the difference between the Freudian death drive and the so-called "nirvana principle" according to

---

effort to enter nirvana caught between two radically opposed extremes, the minimalist and the maximalist? On the one side, reality remains as it is, nothing changes, it is just fully perceived as what it is, a mere insubstantial flow of phenomena that does not really affect the void at the core of our being; on the other side, the goal is to transform reality itself so that there will be no suffering in it, so that all living beings will enter nirvana.

76 This shift is homologous to Hegel's reversal of the classic metaphysical question: how can we see through false appearances to their underlying essential reality? For Hegel, *the* question is, on the contrary: how has appearance emerged out of reality?

77 Of course, the Buddhist nirvana is not to be confused with the Western mystical ascension into a higher reality beyond this world: the Wheel continues to turn, things in their reality remain exactly as they are, they are just perceived in a new way, i.e., the individual existentially accepts the non-substantial character of reality. We are thus not dealing with the "purification" of desires, but with a different way of relating to desire. The fact is nonetheless that, in nirvana, the "enlightened" individual extracts himself from the Wheel of Craving: even if the Wheel goes on turning, he is no longer caught in that turning.

which every life system tends towards the lowest level of tension, ultimately towards death. To put it in terms of the Higgs field in quantum physics, "nothingness" (the void, being deprived of all substance) and the lowest level of energy paradoxically no longer coincide; at the lowest level of tension, or in the void, the dissolution of all order, it is "cheaper" (it costs the system less energy) to persist in "something" than to dwell in "nothing." It is this distance that sustains the death drive (namely, the drive as such, since "every drive is virtually a death drive").[78] Far from being the same as the nirvana principle (the striving towards the dissolution of all tension, the longing for a return to original nothingness), the death drive is the tension which persists and insists beyond and against the nirvana principle. In other words, far from being opposed to the pleasure principle, the nirvana principle is its highest and most radical expression. In this precise sense, the death drive stands for its exact opposite, for the dimension of the "undead," of a spectral life which insists beyond (biological) death. So does the paradox of the Higgs field not also prefigure the mystery of symbolic castration in psychoanalysis? What Lacan calls "symbolic castration" is a deprivation, a gesture of taking away (the loss of the ultimate and absolute—"incestuous"—object of desire) which is *in itself giving*, productive, generative, opening up and sustaining the space of desire and of meaning. The frustrating nature of our human existence, the very fact that our lives are forever out of joint, marked by a traumatic imbalance, is what propels us towards permanent creativity.

This is why psychoanalysis is firmly entrenched in the Western Judeo-Christian tradition, not only against Oriental spirituality but also against Islam, which, like Oriental spirituality, endorses the thesis on the ultimate vanity and illusory nature of every object of desire. On the 614th night of *One Thousand and One Nights*, Judar, following the orders of a Moroccan magician, had to open seven doors that would lead him to a treasure. When he came to the seventh door,

> there issued forth to him his mother, saying, "I salute thee, O my son!" He asked, "What art thou?" and she answered, "O my son, I am thy mother who bare thee nine months and suckled thee and reared thee." Quoth he, "Put off thy clothes." Quoth she, "Thou art my son, how wouldst thou strip me naked?" But he said "Strip, or I will strike off thy head with this sword;" and he stretched out his hand to the brand and drew it upon her saying, "Except thou strip, I will slay thee." Then the strife became long between them and as often as he redoubled on her his threats, she put off somewhat of her clothes and he said to her, "Doff the rest," with many menaces;

78 Jacques Lacan, "Position of the Unconscious," trans. Bruce Fink, in Richard Feldstein, Bruce Fink, and Maire Jaanus, eds, *Reading Seminar XI: Lacan's Four Fundamental Concepts of Psychoanalysis*, New York: SUNY Press 1995, p. 275.

> while she removed each article slowly and kept saying, "O my son, thou hast disappointed my fosterage of thee," till she had nothing left but her petticoat trousers. Then said she, "O my son, is thy heart stone? Wilt thou dishonour me by discovering my shame? Indeed, this is unlawful, O my son!" And he answered, "Thou sayest sooth; put not off thy trousers." At once, as he uttered these words, she cried out, "He hath made default; beat him!" Whereupon there fell upon him blows like rain drops and the servants of the treasure flocked to him and dealt him a funding which he forgot not in all his days.[79]

On 615th night, we learn that Judar was given another chance and tried again; when he came to the seventh door,

> the semblance of his mother appeared before him, saying, "Welcome, O my son!" But he said to her, "How am I thy son, O accursed? Strip!" And she began to wheedle him and put off garment after garment, till only her trousers remained; and he said to her, "Strip, O accursed!" So she put off her trousers and became a body without a soul. Then he entered the hall of the treasures, where he saw gold lying in heaps...[80]

Fethi Benslama has pointed out how this passage indicates that Islam knows what our Western universe denies: the fact that incest is not forbidden, but inherently impossible (when one finally gets the naked mother, she fades away as a bad specter). Benslama refers here to Jean-Joseph Goux,[81] who demonstrated how the Oedipus myth is a Western myth and as such an exception with regard to other myths; its basic feature is precisely that "behind the prohibition, the impossible withdraws itself":[82] the very prohibition is read as an indication that incest is possible.

Here, however, we should remain faithful to the Western "Oedipal" tradition: of course every object of desire is an illusory lure; of course the full *jouissance* of incest is not only prohibited, but in itself impossible; nevertheless, Lacan's *les non-dupes errent* must still be asserted. Even if the object of desire is illusory, there is a real in this illusion: the object of desire in its positive content is vain, but not the place it occupies, the place of the Real; which is why there is more truth in the unconditional fidelity to one's desire than in the resigned insight into the vanity of one's striving.

As we have seen, at the core of this paradox is a formal structure homologous to that of the Higgs field in quantum physics: what, in the Higgs field,

---

79 Richard Francis Burton (trans.), *The Arabian Nights: Tales from A Thousand and One Nights*, New York: Random House 2001, p. 441.

80 Ibid., p. 443.

81 See Jean-Joseph Goux, *Oedipe philosophe*, Paris: Aubier 1990.

82 Fethi Benslama, *La psychanalyse à l'épreuve de l'Islam*, Paris: Aubier 2002, p. 259.

is called the double vacuum[83] appears here in the guise of the irreducible gap between ethics (understood as the care of the self, as striving towards authentic being) and morality (understood as the care for others, responding to their call). Insofar as the authenticity of the Self is taken to the extreme in Buddhist meditation, whose goal is precisely to enable the subject to overcome (or, rather, suspend) its Self and enter the vacuum of nirvana, one should remember the Zen Buddhist claim that "Zen and the sword are one and the same," a principle grounded in the opposition between the reflexive attitude of our ordinary daily lives (in which we cling to life and fear death, strive for egotistic pleasures and profits, hesitate instead of acting directly) and the enlightened stance in which the difference between life and death no longer matters, in which we regain the original self-less unity and become directly our acts. In a unique short-circuit, militaristic Zen masters interpret the basic Zen message (that liberation entails losing one's Self, uniting immediately with the primordial Void) as being identical with total military fidelity, with immediately following orders and performing one's duty without concern for the Self and its interests. The standard anti-militaristic cliché about soldiers being drilled into a state of mindless subordination is here asserted as being identical to Zen Enlightenment. Within this attitude, the warrior no longer acts as a person; he is thoroughly desubjectivized; or, as D. T. Suzuki himself put it: "it is really not he but the sword itself that does the killing. He had no desire to do harm to anybody, but the enemy appears and makes himself a victim. It is as though the sword performs automatically its function of justice, which is the function of mercy."[84]

Does this description not provide the ultimate example of the phenomenological attitude which, instead of intervening into reality, just lets things appear as they are? The sword itself does the killing; the enemy just appears and makes himself a victim—the warrior is in it for nothing, reduced to being the passive observer of his own acts. No wonder that, "struck by his leader's cold demeanor and his utter ruthlessness towards their enemies, one of his comrades once compared Pol Pot with a Buddhist monk who had attained the 'third level' of consciousness: 'You are completely neutral. Nothing moves you. This is the highest level.'"[85] One should not dismiss this as an obscene false parallel: Pol Pot did indeed come from a Buddhist cultural background, and there is a long tradition of militarist discipline in Buddhism. We find the same authoritarian streak in Tibetan Buddhism—for example, in a traditional Tibetan custom which has undergone a strange transformation over the last half-century:

---

83 For a closer elaboration of this notion, see Chapter 10 of the present book.
84 Quoted in Brian Victoria, *Zen at War*, New York: Weatherhill 1998, p. 110.
85 Quoted from Ferguson, *The War of the World*, p. 623.

> During the Cultural Revolution, if an old landowner met emancipated serfs on the road he would stand to the side, at a distance, putting a sleeve over his shoulder, bowing down and sticking out his tongue—a courtesy paid by those of lower status to their superiors—and would only dare to resume his journey after the former serfs had passed by. Now things have changed back: the former serfs stand at the side of the road, bow and stick out their tongues, making way for their old lords. This has been a subtle process, completely voluntary, neither imposed by anyone nor explained.[86]

In short, the ex-serfs somehow detected that with Deng Xiaoping's "reforms," they were once again at the bottom of the social scale; however, much more interesting than the redistribution of social hierarchy signaled by this change is the fact that the same traditional ritual survived such tremendous social transformations. In order to dispel any illusions about Tibetan society, is it not enough to note the distasteful nature of this custom. Over and above the usual stepping aside and bowing—to add insult to injury, as it were—the subordinated individual had to fix his face in an expression of humiliating stupidity (open mouthed with tongue stretched out, eyes turned upwards, etc.) in order to signal with this grotesque grimace his worthless stupidity. The crucial point here is to recognize the violence of this practice, a violence that no consideration of cultural differences and no respect for otherness should wash over.

The point here is not to criticize Buddhism, but merely to emphasize the irreducible gap between subjective authenticity and moral goodness (in the sense of social responsibility): the difficult thing to accept is that one can be totally authentic in overcoming one's false Self and yet still commit horrible crimes—and vice versa, of course: one can be a caring subject, morally committed to the full, while existing in an inauthentic world of illusion with regard to oneself. This is why all the desperate attempts by Buddhists to demonstrate how respect and care for others are necessary steps towards (and conditions of) Enlightenment misfire: Suzuki himself was much more honest in this regard when he pointed out that Zen is a meditation technique which implies no particular ethico-political stance—in his political life, a Zen Buddhist may be a liberal, a fascist, or a communist. Again, the two vacuums never coincide: in order to be fully engaged ethico-politically, it is necessary to exit the "inner peace" of one's subjective authenticity.

86 Wang Lixiong and Tsering Shakya, *The Struggle for Tibet*, London: Verso Books 2009, p. 77.

CHAPTER 3

Fichte's Choice

Perhaps the most productive way to deal with an "official" history of philosophy is to consider how a philosopher who was "overcome" by his successor (according to this "official" line) *reacted (or would have reacted) to his successor*. How would Plato react to Aristotle, or Wagner to Nietzsche, or Husserl to Heidegger, or Hegel to Marx?[1] The most intriguing case of this "rebellion of the vanquished" was German Idealism, wherein each of the "predecessors" in the "official" line of progress (Kant-Fichte-Schelling-Hegel-late Schelling) reacted to the critique or interpretation of his work by his successor. Fichte wanted merely to complete Kant's philosophy with his *Wissenschaftslehre*, and Kant's disparaging remarks about Fichte are well known: he rejected as meaningless and tautological the very term *Wissenschaftslehre* ("doctrine about knowledge"). Fichte's "subjective idealism" was then followed by Schelling's philosophy of identity, which supplements the transcendental-subjective genesis of reality with a philosophy of nature. Fichte bitterly rejected this "supplement" as a misreading of his *Wissenschaftslehre*, as one can read in their correspondence. (On the other hand, Schelling himself was not slow to retort that Fichte had radically changed his position in reaction to Schelling's critique.) Hegel's "overcoming" of Schelling is a case in itself: Schelling's reaction to Hegel's idealist dialectic was so strong that it has increasingly come to be seen as the next (even final) step in the inner development of German Idealism—indeed, there is a book (by Walther Schulze) with the title *The Accomplishment of German Idealism in Schelling's Late Philosophy*. Schelling's first and decisive break out of the constraints of his early philosophy of identity occurs with his *Treatise on the Essence of Human Freedom* from 1807 (the year of Hegel's *Phenomenology of Spirit*!), to which Hegel reacted in his (posthumously published) lectures on the history of philosophy with a brief and ridiculously inadequate dismissal which totally misses the point of Schelling's masterpiece. What is today considered a highpoint in the entire history of philosophy appeared to Hegel as an insignificant minor essay. No wonder, then, that the topic among contemporary Hegel scholars is "What would Hegel's rejoinder have been to Schelling's critique of dialectics as a mere 'negative philosophy'?"

---

1 As to the last example, there have been attempts to reconstruct Hegel's answer to Marx's "materialist reversal" of dialectics—I myself have elsewhere proposed a demonstration of why one should speak of Marx's *idealist* reversal of Hegel.

Among others, Dieter Henrich and Frederick Beiser have tried to reconstruct a Hegelian answer.

When, in 1841, it was announced that the old Schelling would go to Berlin and start teaching there, answering the call by the Prussian king himself to fight the "dragonseed of Hegelian pantheism" with its "facile omniscience," Karl Rosenkranz, a leading pupil of Hegel, wrote that he was "delighted" by this prospect:

> I looked forward to the fight that this occasion must cause. I rejoiced in quiet over what by all appearances would be the toughest test of the Hegelian system and its adherents. I revelled in the feeling of progress, which for philosophy must spring from this. I greeted this challenge as a phenomenon never before encountered in philosophy, where a philosopher should have the power to step beyond the circle of his creation and grasp its consequences, which in the history of philosophy until now is without precedent.[2]

It is effectively as if, on such occasions, an impossible encounter takes place: a philosopher is somehow able to step onto his own shoulders and see himself, his thought, "objectively," as part of a larger movement of ideas, interacting with what comes after. What is the philosophical status of these "retroactive" rejoinders? It is all too easy to claim (in the postmodern vein of the "end of the grand narratives") that they bear witness to the failure of every general scheme of progress: they do not so much undermine the underlying line of succession (from Kant to late Schelling) as, rather, highlight its most interesting and lively moment, the moment when, as it were, a thought rebels against its reduction to a term in the chain of "development" and asserts its absolute right (or claim).

Sometimes, such reactions are mere outbursts of a helpless disorientation; sometimes, they are themselves the true moments of progress. That is to say, when the Old is attacked by the New, this first appearance of the New is, as a rule, flat and naïve—the true dimension of the New arises only when the Old reacts to (the first appearance of) the New. Pascal reacted from a Christian standpoint to scientific secular modernity, and his "reaction" (his struggling with the problem of how to remain a Christian in the new conditions) tells us much more about modernity than its direct partisans.[3] True "progress" emerges from the reaction

---

2 Karl Rosenkranz, *Über Schelling und Hegel: Ein Sendschreiben an Pierre Leroux*, Königsberg: Gebrüder Bonträger 1843, p. 7, as quoted and translated by Bruce Matthews in his introduction to F. W. J. Schelling, *The Grounding of Positive Philosophy*, Albany: SUNY Press 2007, p. 8.

3 Likewise, in cinema history, it was the silent directors who resisted sound, from Chaplin to Eisenstein, who brought to light the truly shattering dimension of sound cinema.

of the Old to progress. True revolutionaries are always reflected conservatives. As Roman Bainton, Luther's commentator, put it: "The most intrepid revolutionary is the one who has a fear greater than anything his opponents can inflict upon him"[4]—a version of Racine's "I fear God, and I have no other fears," from his *Athalie*.

One of the great cases of a philosopher answering his successor is that of Husserl vis-à-vis Heidegger. Husserl is often reproached for trying to cling onto the "abstract" Cartesian subject, that is, for failing to fully grasp *In-der-Welt-Sein*, the subject's active engagement in its life world—only Heidegger, it is said, was able to make this move, in *Sein und Zeit*. What if, however, it is Heidegger who is not "concrete" enough in his critique of Husserl? What if he overlooks the existential base of Husserl's phenomenological reduction? Husserl's phenomenological reduction is an exemplary case of the gap between the pure logical process of reasoning and the corresponding spiritual attitude. If one limits oneself to the process of reasoning, Husserl's deduction cannot but appear an extravagant exercise in "abstract reasoning" at its worst: all we can be sure that really exists is the process of thinking that is I; so if we want an absolutely scientific starting point, we will have to bracket the naïve-realist notion of things existing out there in the world and take into account only their pure appearance, the way they appear to us and are correlative to our (transcendental) acts. What such an understanding misses is that the state described by Husserl in terms of the "phenomenological reduction" is much more than this, approaching an existential experience and attitude close to some currents within early Buddhism: the attitude of *Realitätsverlust*, of experiencing reality as a dream, a totally desubstantialized flow of fragile and ephemeral appearances, in relation to which I am not an engaged agent, but a stunned passive observer observing my own dream. Even when I act, it is not the core of me that acts—I observe my "self," another ethereal appearance, interacting with other appearances.

Husserl should thus also be read against the background of the unity of philosophy and the existential position in actual life, which was for the first time explicitly posited by Fichte, who "proposed to develop a philosophical theory from the perspective of the living mind that directly reflected the actual life of the mind."[5] This attitude is best expressed in Fichte's saying that the kind of philosophy one has depends on what kind of man one is: philosophy is not a neutral world-view, but a reflective appropriation of one's pre-theoretical existential attitudes. And is not Hegel's *Phenomenology of Spirit* a systematic deployment of this stance? Is not every "figure of consciousness" described by Hegel a unity of

4 Quoted from James Gaines, *Evening in the Palace of Reason*, London: Harper Collins 2005, p. 19.

5 Dieter Henrich, *Between Kant and Hegel*, Cambridge, MA: Harvard University Press 2008, p. 16.

a philosophical notion and a practical life-world position?[6] This brings us back to Balmès and the reasons why Lacan retained the term "subject": Husserl's phenomenological reduction implicitly refers to the existential experience of a kind of "psychotic" disengagement for which there is no place in the Heideggerian edifice. This is why Husserl's manuscripts on passive synthesis and time-consciousness are so precious.

Far from being mere footnotes in the history of philosophy or pathetic dead ends, these detours of the Old which, instead of graciously conceding defeat and leaving the scene, persist and counter-attack the New, are in fact the very catalysts of its "development." To grasp a philosophy at its most radical, one should imagine, for example, how Kant would have answered Hegel, how Hegel would have answered the late Schelling or Marx, how Husserl would have answered Heidegger.

From Fichte's *Ich* to Hegel's Subject

Arguably the most interesting case of such a retroactive rejoinder is presented by Fichte's late philosophy in which he (implicitly or explicitly) answers his critics, primarily Schelling. Let us then focus on Fichte's shift from the self-positing I to the asubjective divine Being as the ultimate ground of all reality. Here is Günter Zöller's succinct description of this basic shift in Fichte's doctrine from the Jena period (1794–99) to the Berlin period (1799–1814): in the Jena period,

> the I, in its capacity as absolute I, had functioned as the principle of all knowledge. After 1800, the I provides the form (*Ichform*: "I-form"), of knowledge as such. The ground is now no longer identified with the I *qua* absolute I but with something absolute prior to and originally independent of the I (*Seyn*, "Being," or *Gott*, "God"). By contrast, the I *qua* I-form is the basic mode for the appearance of the absolute, which does not appear itself and as such.[7]

One should be very precise in reading this shift: it is not simply that Fichte "abandons" the I as the absolute ground, reducing it to a subordinate moment of the trans-subjective Absolute, to a mode or form of appearance of this Absolute. If anything, it is only now (after Jena) that Fichte correctly grasped the basic

6 As we have already seen, one should read even Plato's *Parmenides* in the same way: the only way to properly understand the logical gymnastics of its second part is by reading the eight (or nine) hypotheses as descriptions of concrete experiences of reality.

7 Günter Zöller, "Thinking and Willing in the Later Fichte," in Daniel Breazeale and Tom Rockmore, eds, *After Jena: New Essays on Fichte's Later Philosophy*, Evanston: Northwestern University Press 2008, p. 55.

feature of the I: the I is "as such" a split of the Absolute, the "minimal difference" of its self-appearing. In other words, the notion of I as the absolute Ground of all being secretly but unavoidably "substantivizes" the subject.

Fichte is, however, unable to formulate this insight clearly—his limitation is discernible in the wrong answer he gives to the crucial question: to whom does the Absolute appear in the I-form? Fichte's answer is: to (subjective) appearance, to the subject to whom the Absolute appears. What he is not able to assert is that, in appearing to the subject, the Absolute also appears *to itself*, i.e., that the subjective reflection of the Absolute is the Absolute's self-reflection.

The key text is here the *Wissenschaftslehre* from 1812, in contrast to the Jena versions of *Wissenschaftslehre* from 1794–99. In these early versions, Fichte's strategy is the standard subjective-idealist one of critically denouncing the "reified" notion of objective reality, of things existing out there in the world of which the subject is also part: one should dispel this necessary illusion of independent objective reality by way of deploying its subjective genesis. Here, the only Absolute is the spontaneous self-positing of the absolute I: the absolute I designates the coincidence of being and acting (*Tat-Handlung*), it is what it does. Against this version of the Fichtean I, Hegel made the well-known remark that it has the same relation to things as an empty purse has to money. One should not dismiss this parallel as simply a case of mocking aggression, implying that Fichte's self-positing of the absolute I which engenders all its content out of itself has the same (nil) value as an empty purse expected to generate money out of itself; that is, in the same way that someone has to put money into the purse from outside, the content of the pure I should "affect" the I from outside and thus cannot be generated out of the absolute I's "self-affection." On the contrary, this parallel should be given its full weight, also taking into account Kant's use of money as an example in his criticism of the ontological proof of the existence of God—you cannot deduce existence from the concept alone, it is not the same thing to have a concept of 100 thalers and to have 100 thalers in your pocket. Hegel's reply is that, precisely, God is not the same type of object as 100 thalers: at the level of the Absolute, the containing Form *can* generate its own content.

In 1812, however, Fichte takes one further step backwards: "it is no longer the absoluteness of the things that is unveiled as an unavoidable illusion, but the absoluteness of the I itself."[8] The self-positing of the I is itself an illusory appearance, an "image" of the only true Absolute, the trans-subjective immovable absolute Being ("God"). Back in 1790s, after Fichte had explained to Madame de Stael the I's self-positing, she snapped back: "So you mean that the absolute I is like Baron Münchhausen, who saved himself from drowning in a swamp by grabbing his hair and pulling himself out with his own hands?" It is as if

8 Johannes Brachtendorf, "The Notion of Being in Fichte's Late Philosophy," in ibid., p. 157.

the late Fichte accepted this critique, conceding that the self-reflecting I is a chimera floating in mid-air, which has to be grounded in some firm positive Absolute. The critical analysis has thus to take a further step back: first from objective reality to the transcendental I, then from the transcendental I to the absolute Being: the I's self-positing is an image of the divine Absolute, not the Absolute itself:

> the Absolute appears, as life teaches us. The appearance of the Absolute means that it appears *as* the Absolute. Since determinacy comes with negation, the Absolute must bring forth its own opposite, a non-Absolute, to be able to appear *as* the Absolute. This non-Absolute is the Absolute's appearance. The appearance is also that to which the Absolute appears. Thus, the Absolute can appear to the appearance only if at the same time its opposite, namely the appearance, appears to the appearance as well. There is no appearing of the Absolute without an appearing of the appearance to itself, that is, without reflectivity of the appearance. Since the Absolute appears necessarily, the self-reflection of the appearance is necessary too.
>
> Fichte relates the unitary aspect of the appearance to the appearing of the Absolute, whereas the multiplicity aspect is linked to the appearance's self-reflection. Since self-reflection is a process, there is transmutation and genesis within the appearance when it appears to itself. Employing the notion of being as unity and immutability, Fichte concludes that the appearance *is* insofar as it is a manifestation or a self-revelation of the Absolute; and that the appearance *is* not insofar as it is self-reflective.[9]

This shift can also be formulated as one from positing to appearing: while in 1794, *the I posits itself as positing itself*, in 1812,

> *the appearance appears to itself as appearing to itself.* To appear, however, is an activity. Thus, the appearance appears to itself as being active through itself, or as a principle "from itself, out of itself, through itself." Fichte concludes that, since the appearance is constituted by the act of appearing to itself, it conceives of its own existence (its "formal being") as grounded in itself. As soon as the appearance reflects on itself, it understands itself to exist through itself, that is, to be *a se*. But this cannot be true, as the *Wissenschaftslehre* demonstrates. Only One *is* in the sense of *aseitas*, namely the Absolute, so that appearance cannot truly *be* in this sense.[10]

A double mediation has to be accomplished here. Firstly, if, in the appearing of the Absolute, the Absolute appears as the Absolute, this means that the Absolute

9 Ibid.
10 Ibid., p. 158 (emphasis to first sentence added).

has to appear as absolute *in contrast to other "mere" appearances*—so there must be a cut in the domain of appearances, a cut between "mere" appearances and the appearance through which the Absolute itself transpires. In other words, the gap between appearance and true Being must inscribe itself into the very domain of appearing.

But what this reflectivity of appearing means is that the Absolute also exposes itself to the danger of merely "appearing" to be the Absolute—the appearing *of* the Absolute turns into the (misleading, illusory) appearing *to be* the Absolute. Is not the entire history of religion (from a materialist standpoint, of course) the history of such false appearances of the Absolute? At this level, "the Absolute" *is* its own appearing, that is, an organization of appearances which evokes the mirage that there is, hidden behind it, an Absolute which appears (shines through it). Here, in effect, the illusion is no longer one of mistaking appearing for being, but of mistaking being for appearing: the only "being" of the Absolute is its appearing, and the illusion is that this appearing is a mere "image" behind which there is a transcendent true Being. So when Fichte writes the following he overlooks that error which is the exact opposite of mistaking images for being (that of taking as the true being what is effectively only its image), namely the error of *mistaking being for images* (in other words of taking as merely an image of the true being what is effectively the true being itself): "Every error without exception consists in mistaking images for being. The *Wissenschaftslehre* has for the first time pronounced how far this error extends through showing that being is only in God."[11] At this level, one should thus accept the Derridean theological conclusion: "God" is not an absolute Being persisting in itself, it is the pure virtuality of a Promise, the pure appearing of itself. In other words, *the "Absolute" beyond appearances coincides with an "absolute appearance," an appearance beneath which there is no substantial Being.*

Second mediation: if the Absolute is to appear, appearing itself must appear to itself as appearing, and Fichte conceives this self-appearing of appearance as subjective self-reflection. Fichte is right to endorse a two-step critical approach (first the move from the object to its subjective constitution, then the meta-critical step of deploying the abyssal mirage of the subject's self-positing); what he gets wrong is the nature of the Absolute that grounds subjectivity itself. The late Fichte's Absolute is an immovable transcendent In-itself, external to the movement of reflection. What Fichte cannot think is the "life," movement, mediation, in the Absolute itself: how, precisely, the Absolute's appearing is not a mere appearance, but a self-actualization, a self-revelation, of the Absolute. This immanent dynamics does *not* make the Absolute itself a subject, but it inscribes subjectivization into its very core.

---

11 Quoted in ibid., p. 158.

What Fichte was furthermore unable to grasp is the speculative identity of these two extreme poles (pure absolute Being and the appearance appearing to itself): the I's self-positing self-reflectivity is, quite literally, the "image" of the Absolute as self-grounded Being. Therein resides the objective irony of Fichte's development: Fichte, *the* philosopher of subjective self-positing, ends up reducing subjectivity to a mere appearance of an immovable absolute In-itself. The proper Hegelian reproach to Fichte is thus not that he is too "subjective," but, on the contrary, that he is unable to really think Substance also as Subject: the shift of his thought towards the asubjective Absolute is not a reaction to his earlier excessive subjectivism, but a reaction to his inability to formulate the core of subjectivity.

Hegel's true novelty can be seen with regard to the topic of "absolute" idealism, in terms of the standard history of post-Kantian thought formed by the triad of Fichte's "subjective" idealism, Schelling's "objective" idealism, and Hegel's "absolute" idealism. The designation of Schelling's *Identitätsphilosophie* as "objective" idealism is, however, deceiving: the whole point of his *Identitätsphilosophie* is that subjective idealism (transcendental philosophy) and objective idealism (philosophy of nature) are two approaches to the Third, the Absolute beyond or beneath the duality of spirit and nature, subject and object, underlying and manifesting itself in both. (The late Fichte does something similar when he passes from the transcendental I to the divine Being as the absolute Ground of all reality.) In this sense, it is meaningless to call Hegel's philosophy "absolute idealism": his point is precisely that *there is no need for a Third element*, the medium or Ground beyond subject and object-substance. We start with objectivity, and the subject is nothing but the self-mediation of objectivity. When, in Hegel's dialectics, we have a couple of opposites, their unity is not a Third, an underlying medium, but *one of the two*: a genus is its own species, or, a genus ultimately has only one species, which is why specific difference coincides with the difference between genus and species.

We can thus identify three positions: metaphysical, transcendental, and "speculative." In the first, reality is simply perceived as existing out there, and the task of philosophy is to analyze its basic structure. In the second, the philosopher investigates the subjective conditions of the possibility of objective reality, its transcendental genesis. In the third, subjectivity is re-inscribed into reality, but not simply reduced to a part of objective reality. While the subjective constitution of reality—the split that separates the subject from the In-itself—is fully admitted, this very split is transposed back into reality as its kenotic self-emptying (to use the Christian theological term). Appearance is not reduced to reality; rather the very process of appearance is conceived from the standpoint of reality, so that the question is not "How, if at all, can we pass from appearance to reality?" but "How can something like appearance arise in the midst of reality? What are the conditions for reality appearing to itself?"

For Henrich, Fichte's problem is that of recognition: how do I know that what I see when I look at myself is "me"? Lacan's solution is: I do *not* know, recognition *is* misrecognition; in other words, "I" is originally a *void*, a *failure* to locate myself in the order of Being. There is a constitutive gap between the I and the substance of I, or what I am as object—this impossibility is missed by Fichte and Henrich.

One of the standard gags in American TV comedy is the late-recognition scene—a man sees a car being towed away, laughs cruelly at the owner's misfortune, before recoiling in surprise a couple of seconds later: "But, wait, that's *my* car!" The most elementary form of this gag is, of course, that of delayed *self*-recognition: I pass a glass door and think I see behind it an ugly, disfigured guy; I laugh, and then, all of a sudden, realize that the glass was a mirror, and that the figure I saw was myself. The Lacanian thesis is that this delay is structural: there is no direct self-acquaintance; the self is empty.

The Fichtean wager

What are the philosophical roots of Fichte's error regarding the status of appearing? Let us return to the early Fichte (of the Jena period), who is usually perceived as a radical subjective idealist. On this reading, there are two possible descriptions of our reality: "dogmatic" (Spinozan deterministic materialism: we are part of reality, submitted to its laws, an object among others, our freedom is an illusion) and "idealist" (the subject is autonomous and free; as the absolute I it spontaneously posits reality). Reasoning alone cannot decide between the two, the decision is a practical one; or, to quote again Fichte's famous dictum: what philosophy one chooses depends on what kind of man one is—and, in this choice, Fichte passionately opts for idealism. However, a closer look quickly makes clear that this is *not* Fichte's position. Idealism is for Fichte not a new positive teaching which should replace materialism, but, to quote Peter Preuss's perspicuous formulation:

> merely an intellectual exercise open to anyone who accepts the autonomy of theoretical reason. Its function is to destroy the current deterministic dogma. But if it were now itself to become a theoretical understanding of reality it would be every bit as bad. While human life is no longer seen as a mere natural event it would now be seen as a mere dream. We would be no more human in the one understanding than the other. In the one understanding I am the material to which life happens as an event, in the other I am the uninvolved spectator of the dream which is my

> life. Fichte finds each of these to be equal cause for lament. No, the task is not to replace one theoretical philosophy with another one, but to get out of philosophy altogether. Philosophical reason is not autonomous, but has its foundation in practical reason, i.e., the will … Fichte is widely misunderstood as opting for idealism over realism … neither realism (of whatever kind) nor idealism (of whatever kind) yields knowledge, theoretical understanding of reality. Both yield unacceptable nonsense if taken to their final conclusions. And precisely this yields the valuable conclusion that the intellect is not autonomous. The intellect, to function properly as part of a whole human being, must relate to the activity of that being. Human beings do contemplate and try to understand reality, but not from a standpoint outside the world. Human beings are in the world and it is as agents in the world that we require an understanding of the world. The intellect is not autonomous but has its foundation in our agency, in practical reason or the will.[12]

How does the will provide this foundation?

> … in an act of faith it transforms the apparent picture show of experience into an objective world of things and of other people … faith indicates a free (i.e., theoretically unjustifiable) act of mind by which the conditions within which we can act and use our intellects come to be for us.[13]

Fichte's position is thus not that a passive observer of reality chooses determinism, while an engaged agent chooses idealism: taken as an explanatory theory, idealism does not lead to practical engagement, but to the passive position of being the observer of one's own dream (reality is already constituted by me, I only have to observe it like that, that is, not as a substantial independent reality, but as a dream). Both materialism and idealism lead to consequences which make practical activity meaningless or impossible. In order for me to be practically active, engaged in the world, I have to accept myself as a being "in the world," caught in a situation, interacting with real objects which resist me and which I try to transform. Furthermore, in order to act as a free moral subject, I have to accept the independent existence of other subjects like me, as well as the existence of a higher spiritual order in which I participate and which is independent of natural determinism. To accept all this is not a matter of knowledge—it can only be a matter of faith. Fichte's point is thus that the existence of external reality (of which I myself am a part) is not a matter of theoretical proofs, but a practical necessity, a necessary presupposition of myself as an agent intervening in reality, interacting with it.

---

12 Peter Preuss, translator's introduction to Johann Gottlieb Fichte, *The Vocation of Man*, Indianapolis: Hackett 1987, pp. viii, x–xi.

13 Ibid., p. xi.

The irony is that Fichte here comes uncannily close to Nikolai Bukharin, a die-hard dialectical materialist who, in his *Philosophical Arabesques* (one of the most tragic works in the entire history of philosophy—a manuscript written in 1937, when he was in the Lubyanka prison, awaiting execution), tries to bring together for the last time his entire life-experience into a consistent philosophical edifice. The first and crucial choice he confronts is that between the materialist assertion of the reality of the external world and what he calls the "intrigues of solipsism." Once this key battle is won, once the life-asserting reliance on the real world liberates us from the damp prison-house of our fantasies, we can breathe freely, simply going on to draw all the consequences from this first key result. The mysterious feature of the book's first chapter, in which Bukharin confronts this dilemma, is its tension between form and content: although, at the level of content, Bukharin adamantly denies that his book is dealing with a choice between two beliefs or primordial existential decisions, the whole chapter is structured like a dialogue between a healthy but naïve materialist and Mephistopheles, standing for the "devil of solipsism," a "cunning spirit" which "drapes itself in an enchantingly patterned cloak of iron logic, and … laughs, poking out its tongue."[14] "Curling his lips ironically," Mephistopheles tempts the materialist with the idea that, since all we have direct access to are our subjective sensations, the only way we can pass from them to the belief in some external reality independent of them is by a leap of faith, "a *salto vitale* (as opposed to *salto mortale*)."[15] In short, Mephistopheles's "devil of logic" tries to seduce us into accepting that the belief in independent external reality is a matter of faith, that the existence of "holy matter" is the fundamental dogma of the "theology" of dialectical materialism. After a series of arguments (which, one has to admit, although not all devoid of philosophical interest, are irredeemably marked by a pre-Kantian naïveté), Bukharin concludes the chapter with the ironic call (which, nonetheless, cannot conceal the underlying despair): "Hold your tongue, Mephistopheles! Hold your dissolute tongue!"[16] But in spite of this exorcism, the devil continues to reappear throughout the book—see the first sentence of Chapter 12: "After a long interval, the demon of irony again makes his appearance."[17] As in Fichte, external reality is a matter of faith, of breaking the deadlock of theoretical sophistry with a practical *salto vitale*.

Where Fichte is more consistent than Bukharin is in his awareness that there is an element of *credo qua absurdum* in this leap: the discord between our knowledge and our ethico-practical engagement is irreducible, one cannot bring them together in a complete "world-view." Fichte here radicalizes Kant,

14 Nikolai Bukharin, *Philosophical Arabesques*, London: Pluto 2005, p. 40.
15 Ibid., p. 41.
16 Ibid., p. 46.
17 Ibid., p. 131.

who had already conjectured that the transcendental I, in its "spontaneity," occupies a third space between phenomena and noumena. The subject's freedom/spontaneity is not the property of a phenomenal entity, hence it cannot be dismissed as a false appearance concealing the noumenal fact that we are totally caught in an inaccessible necessity; however, it is also not simply noumenal. In a mysterious subchapter of his *Critique of Practical Reason* entitled "Of the Wise Adaptation of Man's Cognitive Faculties to His Practical Vocation," Kant endeavors to answer the question of what would happen to us if we were to gain access to the noumenal domain, to the *Ding an sich*:

> instead of the conflict which now the moral disposition has to wage with inclinations and in which, after some defeats, moral strength of mind may be gradually won, God and eternity in their awful majesty would stand unceasingly before our eyes ... Thus most actions conforming to the law would be done from fear, few would be done from hope, none from duty. The moral worth of actions, on which alone the worth of the person and even of the world depends in the eyes of supreme wisdom, would not exist at all. The conduct of man, so long as his nature remained as it is now, would be changed into mere mechanism, where, as in a puppet show, everything would gesticulate well but no life would be found in the figures.[18]

In short, the direct access to the noumenal domain would deprive us of the very "spontaneity" which forms the kernel of transcendental freedom: it would turn us into lifeless automata, or, to put it in today's terms, "thinking machines." The implication of this passage is much more radical and paradoxical than it may appear. If we ignore its inconsistency (how could fear and lifeless gesticulation coexist?), the conclusion it imposes is that, at the level of phenomena as well as at the noumenal level, humans are a "mere mechanism" with no autonomy and freedom: as phenomena, we are not free, we are a part of nature, a "mere mechanism," totally subjugated by causal links, a part of the nexus of causes and effects; and as noumena, we are again not free, but reduced to a "mere mechanism."[19] Our freedom persists only in a space *between* the phenomenal and the noumenal. It is therefore not that Kant simply limited causality to the phenomenal domain in order to be able to assert that, at the noumenal level, we are free autonomous agents: we are only free insofar as our horizon is that of the phenomenal, insofar as the noumenal domain remains inaccessible to us.[20] Kant

18 Immanuel Kant, *Critique of Practical Reason*, New York: Macmillan 1956, pp. 152–3.

19 Is not what Kant describes as a person who directly knows the noumenal domain strictly homologous to the utilitarian subject whose acts are fully determined by the calculus of pleasures and pains?

20 Kant's own formulations here are misleading, since he often identifies the transcendental subject with the noumenal I whose phenomenal appearance is the

formulated this impasse in his famous statement that he had to limit knowledge in order to create space for faith. Along the same lines,

> Fichte's philosophy ends in total cognitive skepticism, i.e., in the abandonment of philosophy proper, and looks instead to a kind of quasi-religious faith for wisdom. But he thinks that this is not a problem, since all that matters is practical: to produce a world fit for human beings, and to produce myself as the person I would be for all eternity.[21]

The limitation of this position resides in Kant's and Fichte's inability to conceive positively of the ontological status of this neither-phenomenal-nor-noumenal autonomous-spontaneous subject (this is already Heidegger's reproach in *Sein und Zeit*: traditional metaphysics cannot think the ontological status of *Dasein*). Hegel's solution here involves the transposition of the epistemological limitation into ontological fact: the void of our knowledge corresponds to a void in being itself, to the ontological incompleteness of reality.

This transposition enables us to cast new light on the Hegelian definition of freedom as "conceived necessity": the consistent notion of subjective idealism compels us to invert this thesis and conceive of necessity as (ultimately nothing but) conceived freedom. The central tenet of Kant's transcendental idealism is that it is the subject's "spontaneous" (i.e., radically *free*) act of transcendental apperception that changes the confused flow of sensations into "reality," which obeys necessary laws. The point is even clearer in moral philosophy: when Kant claims that moral Law is the *ratio cognoscendi* of our transcendental freedom, does he not literally say that necessity is conceived freedom? In other words, the only way for us to get to know (conceive of) our freedom is via the fact of the unbearable pressure of the moral Law, of its *necessity*, which enjoins us to act against the compulsion of our pathological impulses. At the most general level, one should posit that "necessity" (the symbolic necessity that regulates our lives) relies on the abyssal free act of the subject, on its contingent decision, on what Lacan calls the *point de capiton*, the "quilting point," which magically turns confusion into a new Order. Is this freedom that is not yet caught up in the web of necessity not the abyss of the "night of the world"?

For this reason, Fichte's radicalization of Kant is consistent, not just a subjectivist eccentricity. Fichte was the first philosopher to focus on the uncanny contingency at the very heart of subjectivity: the Fichtean subject is not the overblown Ego = Ego as the absolute Origin of all reality, but a finite subject thrown

---

empirical "person," thus recoiling from his radical insight that the transcendental subject is a pure formal-structural function beyond the opposition of the noumenal and the phenomenal.

21 Preuss, introduction to *The Vocation of Man*, p. xii.

into, caught up in, a contingent social situation forever eluding mastery.[22] The *Anstoss*, the primordial impulse that sets in motion the gradual self-limitation and self-determination of the initially void subject, is not merely a mechanical external impulse: it also points towards another subject who, in the abyss of its freedom, functions as the challenge (*Aufforderung*) compelling me to limit/specify my freedom, that is, to accomplish the passage from the abstract egotistic freedom to concrete freedom within the rational ethical universe; perhaps this intersubjective *Aufforderung* is not merely the secondary specification of the *Anstoss*, but its exemplary original case. It is important to bear in mind the two primary meanings of *Anstoss* in German: check, obstacle, hindrance, something that resists the boundless expansion of our striving; and an impetus or stimulus, something that incites our activity. *Anstoss* is not simply the obstacle the absolute I posits for itself in order to stimulate its activity, so that by overcoming the obstacle it can assert its creative power (like the games the proverbial ascetic saint plays with himself, inventing increasingly perverse temptations in order to confirm his strength by successfully resisting them). If the Kantian *Ding an sich* corresponds to the Freudian-Lacanian Thing, *Anstoss* is closer to the *objet petit a*, to the primordial foreign body that "sticks in the throat" of the subject, to the object-cause of desire that splits it up: Fichte himself defines *Anstoss* as the non-assimilable foreign body that causes the subject's division into the empty absolute subject and the finite determinate subject, limited by the non-I.

Anstoss thus designates the moment of the "run-in," the hazardous knock, the encounter with the Real in the midst of the ideality of the absolute I: there is no subject without Anstoss, without the collision with an element of irreducible facticity and contingency—"the I is supposed to encounter within itself something foreign." The point is thus to acknowledge "the presence, within the I itself, of a realm of irreducible otherness, of absolute contingency and incomprehensibility ... Ultimately, not just Angelus Silesius's rose, but every *Anstoss* whatsoever *ist ohne Warum*."[23] In clear contrast to the Kantian noumenal *Ding* that affects our senses, *Anstoss* does not come from outside, it is *stricto sensu* ex-timate: a non-assimilable foreign body in the very core of the subject. As Fichte himself emphasizes, the paradox of *Anstoss* resides in the fact that it is simultaneously "purely subjective" and not produced by the activity of the I. If *Anstoss* were not "purely subjective," if it were already the non-I, part of objectivity, we would fall back into "dogmaticism"; that is, *Anstoss* would effectively amount to no more than a shadowy remainder of the Kantian *Ding an sich* and would thus only confirm Fichte's inconsequentiality (the most common reproach against him).

22 See Daniel Breazeale, "Check or Checkmate? On the Finitude of the Fichtean Self," in Karl Ameriks and Dieter Sturma, eds, *The Modern Subject: Conceptions of the Self in Classical German Philosophy*, Albany: SUNY Press 1995.

23 Ibid., p. 100.

If *Anstoss* were simply subjective, it would be a case of the subject's vacuous playing with itself, and we would never reach the level of objective reality; that is, Fichte would effectively be a solipsist (another commonplace reproach against his philosophy). The crucial point is that *Anstoss* sets in motion the constitution of "reality": at the beginning is the pure I with the non-assimilable foreign body at its heart; the subject constitutes reality by way of assuming a distance towards the Real of the formless *Anstoss* and conferring on it the structure of objectivity. What imposes itself here is the parallel between the Fichtean *Anstoss* and the Freudian-Lacanian scheme of the relationship between the primordial *Ich* (*Ur-Ich*) and the object, the foreign body in its midst, which disturbs its narcissistic balance, setting in motion the long process of the gradual expulsion and structuration of this inner snag, through which (what we experience as) "external, objective reality" is constituted.

If Kant's *Ding an sich* is not Fichte's *Anstoss*, what is the difference? Or, to put it in another way: where *do* we find in Kant something prefiguring Fichte's *Anstoss*? One should not confuse Kant's *Ding an sich* with the "transcendental object," which (contrary to some confused and misleading formulations found in Kant himself) is not noumenal but the "nothingness," the void on the horizon of objectivity, of that which stands against the (finite) subject, the minimal form of resistance that is not yet any positive determinate object that the subject encounters in the world—Kant uses the German expression *Dawider*, what is "out there opposing itself to us, standing against us." This *Dawider* is *not* the abyss of the Thing, it does not point to the dimension of the unimaginable, but is, on the contrary, the very horizon of openness towards objectivity within which particular objects appear to a finite subject.

Anstoss and *Tat-Handlung*

To recapitulate, *Anstoss* is formally homologous to the Lacanian *objet a*: like a magnetic field, it is the focus of the I's positing activity, the point around which this activity circulates, yet it is in itself entirely insubstantial, since *it is created-posited, generated, by the very process which reacts to it and deals with it*. It is like in the old joke about the conscript who pleaded insanity in order to avoid military service: his "symptom" was to compulsively examine every paper within reach and exclaim, "That's not it!" When examined by the military psychiatrists, he does the same, so the psychiatrists finally gave him a paper confirming his release from military service. The conscript reaches for it, examines it, and exclaims: "That's it!" Here, also, the search itself generates its object. And therein resides the ultimate paradox of the Fichtean *Anstoss*: it is not immediately external to the circular movement of reflection, but an object which is posited by this very (self-referential) movement. Its transcendence (impenetrability, irreducibility to an ordinary represented object) coincides with its absolute immanence.

Is *Anstoss* then immanent or transcendent? Does it "provoke/disturb" the I from the outside, or is it posited by the I itself? In other words: do we have, first (ideally), the pure Life of the self-positing I, which then posits the obstacle? If it is transcendent, we have the finite subject limited by *Anstoss* (be it in the form of the Kantian Thing-in-itself, or in the form, today much more acceptable, of intersubjectivity, of another subject as the only true Thing, as the ethical *Anstoss*); if it is immanent, we get the boring, perverse logic of the I which posits an obstacle in order to overcome it. So the only solution is: absolute simultaneity/overlapping of self-positing and obstacle; that is, the obstacle is the excremental "reject" of the process of self-positing, not so much posited as ejected, excreted/secreted, as the obverse of the activity of self-positing. In this sense, *Anstoss* is the transcendental *a priori* of positing, that which incites the I to endless positing, the only non-posited element. Or, in Lacanese, following Lacan's logic of "non-All": the (finite) I and the non-I (object) limit each other, while, at the absolute level, there is nothing which is not I, the I is unlimited, and for that reason non-All—the *Anstoss* is that which makes it non-All.

Sylvain Portier formulated this crucial point clearly: "If we are trying to account for the 'limit,' we should be careful never to represent it in an *objective*, or, rather, *objectivized* way."[24] The standard assertion that Kant was aware of the necessity of presupposing an external X that affects us when we experience sensations, while Fichte closed the circle of transcendental solipsism, misses the point, the finesse of Fichte's argumentation: Fichte dispenses with the *Ding an sich* not because he posits the transcendental subject as an infinite Absolute, but precisely on account of the transcendental subject's *finitude*—or, as the early Wittgenstein put it: "Our life has no end in just the way in which our visual field has no limits." Like the field of vision, life is finite, and, for that very reason, we cannot ever see its limit—in this precise sense, "eternal life belongs to those who live in the present" (*Tractatus* 6.4311): precisely because we are *within* our finitude, we cannot step out of it and perceive its limitation. This is what Fichte aims at when he emphasizes that one should not conceive of the transcendental I as a closed space surrounded by another external space of noumenal entities.

This point can be made very clearly in terms of Lacan's distinction between the subject of the enunciated and the subject of the enunciation: when I directly posit/define myself as a finite being, existing in the world among other beings, at the level of enunciation (the position from which I speak) I already objectivize the limit between myself and the rest of the world; that is, I adopt the infinite position from which I can observe reality and locate myself in it. Consequently,

24 Sylvain Portier, *Fichte et le dépassement de la "chose en soi" (1792–1799)*, Paris: L'Harmattan 2005, p. 30.

the only way for me to truly assert my finitude is to accept that my world is infinite, since I cannot locate its limit *within* it.[25] As Wittgenstein points out, this is also the problem with death: death is the limit of life which cannot be located *within* life—and only a true atheist can fully accept this fact, as was made clear by Ingmar Bergman in his great manifesto for atheism, which he develops precisely apropos of his "religious" film *The Seventh Seal*:

> My fear of death was to a great degree linked to my religious concepts. Later on, I underwent minor surgery. By mistake, I was given too much anaesthesia. I felt as if I had disappeared out of reality. Where did the hours go? They flashed by in a microsecond.
>
> Suddenly I realized, *that is how it is*. That one could be transformed from *being* to *non-being*—it was hard to grasp. But for a person with a constant anxiety about death, now liberating. Yet at the same time it seems a bit sad. You say to yourself that it would have been fun to encounter new experiences once your soul had had a little rest and grown accustomed to being separated from your body. But I don't think that is what happens to you. First you *are*, then you are *not*. This I find deeply satisfying. That which had formerly been so enigmatic and frightening, namely, what might exist beyond this world, does not exist. Everything is of this world. Everything exists and happens inside us, and we flow into and out of one another. It's perfectly fine like that.[26]

There is thus a truth in Epicurus's well-known argument against the fear of death (there is nothing to fear: while you are still alive, you are not dead, and when you are dead, you feel nothing): the source of the fear of death is the power of imagination; death as an event is the ultimate anamorphosis—in fearing it, we experience a non-event, a non-entity (our passage to non-being), as an event.

Ernesto Laclau has developed the idea that, in an antagonistic relationship, external difference coincides with internal difference: the difference that separates me from other entities around me, and thus guarantees my identity, simultaneously cuts into my identity, leaving it flawed, unstable, truncated.[27] This tension should be extended to the full dialectical identity of opposites: the condition of possibility of identity is, at the same time, its condition of impossibility; the assertion of self-identity is based on its opposite, on an irreducible remainder that truncates every identity.

This is why Fichte is right to claim that the arch-model for all identity is I = I, the subject's identity with itself; the formal-logical notion of (self-)identity

25 This is also what makes Fichte's notion of *Anstoss* so difficult: *Anstoss* is not an object *within* the represented reality, but the stand-in, within reality, for what is outside reality.
26 Ingmar Bergman, *My Life in Film*, London: Faber and Faber 1995, pp. 240–1.
27 See Ernesto Laclau, *Emancipation(s)*, London: Verso Books 1995.

comes second, it has to be grounded in a *transcendental* logical notion of the self-identity of the I. When Fichte emphasizes that the absolute I is not a fact (*Tatsache*) but a deed (*Tat-Handlung*)—that its identity is purely and thoroughly processual—he means precisely that the subject is the result of its own failure to become a subject: I try to fully actualize myself as a subject, I fail (to become a subject), and this failure *is* the subject (that I am). *Only* in the case of the subject do we get this full coincidence of failure and success, of identity as grounded in its own lack; in all other cases, there is the appearance of a substantial identity that precedes or underlies processuality. And the point of Fichte's critique of realist "dogmatism" is to assert the transcendental-ontological priority of this pure processuality of the I over every substantial entity: every appearance of substantial identity has to be accounted for in terms of transcendental genesis, as the "reified" result of the pure I's processuality. The passage from I = I to the delimitation between the I and the non-I is thus the passage from immanent antagonism to external limitation that guarantees the identity of the opposed poles: the pure self-positing I does not simply divide itself into the posited non-I and the finite I opposed to it; it posits the non-I and the finite I as mutually limiting opposites in order to resolve the immanent tension of its processuality.

The claim that the limitation of the subject is simultaneously external and internal, that the subject's external limit is always its internal limitation, is, of course, developed by Fichte into the main thesis of his "absolute transcendental idealism": every external limit is the result of an internal self-limitation. This is what Kant does not see: for him, the Thing-in-itself is directly the external limit of the phenomenal field constituted by the subject, in other words the limit that separates the noumenal from the phenomenal is not the transcendental subject's self-limitation, but simply its external limit.

However, does all this endorse the standard reading, according to which Fichte marks the passage to transcendental absolute idealism wherein every external limit of subjectivity is co-opted, re-inscribed as a moment of the subject's infinite self-mediation/limitation? We should read the thesis that every limit of the subject is (grounded in) the subject's self-limitation in conjunction with the thesis on the overlapping of external and internal limitation; if we do so, then the accent of the subject's "self-limitation" shifts from the subjective to the objective genitive: the "limitation of the self" not in the sense that the subject is the full agent and master of its own limitation, encompassing its limits within the activity of its self-mediation, but in the sense that the external limitation of the self truncates from within the very identity of the subject. It is (again) Portier who clearly spells out this point:

> What the I, insofar as it is precisely the "absolute I," is not, that is to say, the "non-I" itself, is thus (for the I) absolutely nothing, a pure nothingness or, as Fichte himself

> put it, a kind of "non-being" … we should thus take care not to represent to ourselves the non-I as an *other level* than that of the I: outside the "transcendental field" of the positing I, there is truly nothing but the absence of all space, in other words, the *non-level*, the *void* that is proper to the non-I.[28]

What this means is that, since there is nothing outside the (self-)positing of the absolute I, the non-I can only emerge—can only be posited—as correlative to the I's non-positedness: *the non-I is nothing but the non-positedness of the I*. Or, translated into terms closer to our common experience: since, in Fichte's absolute egological perspective, all positing activity is the activity of the I, when the I encounters the non-I as active, as objective reality exerting active pressure on the I, actively resisting it, this can only be the result of the I's own passivity: *the non-I is active only insofar as I render myself passive and thus let it act back upon me*.[29] Therein lies, for Fichte, the fatal flaw of Kant's Thing-in-itself: insofar as the Kantian Thing is conceived as existing independently of the I and, as such, exerting pressure on it, we are dealing here with *an activity in the non-I to which no passivity in the I itself corresponds*—and this is totally unthinkable for Fichte, a remainder of metaphysical dogmatism.

This brings us to the topic of the subject's finitude: in Fichte, the *a priori* synthesis of the finite and the infinite is the *finitude* of the positing I:

> the I, that is to say, the "act of reflection-into-itself," always has to "posit something absolute outside itself," all the while recognizing that this entity can only exist "for it," that is to say, relatively to the finitude and the precise mode of intuition of the I.[30]

Fichte thus resumes the basic insight of the philosophy of reflection, which is usually formulated in a critical mode: the moment the subject experiences itself as redoubled in reflection, caught in oppositions, and so on, it has to relate this split/mediated condition of its own to some presupposed Absolute inaccessible to it, set up as the standard which the subject tries to rejoin. The same insight can also be made in more common-sense terms: when we humans are caught in a turmoil of activity, it is our propensity to imagine an external absolute point of reference that would provide an orientation for, and bring some stability to, that activity. What Fichte does here, in the best tradition of transcendental

28 Portier, *Fichte et le dépassement de la "chose en soi,"* pp. 134, 136.

29 With regard to Fichte's intense ethico-practical stance, this means that whenever I succumb to the pressure of circumstances, *I let myself* be determined by this pressure—I am determined by external causes only insofar as I let myself be determined by them; in other words, my determination by external causes is never direct, it is always mediated by my acquiescing to them.

30 Portier, *Fichte et le dépassement de la "chose en soi,"* p. 54.

phenomenology, is to read this constellation in a purely immanent way: we should never forget that this Absolute, precisely insofar as it is experienced by the subject as the presupposition of its activity, is actually *posited* by it, that is "can only exist 'for it.'" Two crucial consequences follow from such an immanent reading: first, the infinite Absolute is the presupposition of a finite subject; its specter can only arise within the horizon of a finite subject experiencing its finitude as such. Second, this experience of the gap that separates the subject from the infinite Absolute is inherently practical, compelling the subject to incessant activity. Seidel perspicuously concludes that, with this practical vision, Fichte also opens up the space for a new radical despair: not only the despair that I cannot realize the Ideal; not only the despair that reality is too hard for me; but despair at the suspicion that the Ideal is *in itself* invalidated, not worth the effort.[31]

Division and limitation

One can see now the absolutely central role of the notion of *limitation* in Fichte's entire theoretical edifice: in contrast to dogmatic realism which posits the substantial non-I as the only true and independent agency, and in contrast to "idealist realism" *à la* Descartes or Leibniz—for which the only true reality is that of monadic spiritual substance, and all activity of the non-I is a mere illusion—for Fichte, the relationship of the I and the non-I is one of mutual limitation. Although this mutual limitation is always posited *within* the absolute I, the key point is to conceive of this I *not* in a realist way, as a spiritual substance which "contains in itself everything," but as an abstract, purely transcendental-ideal *medium* in which the I and the non-I delimit themselves mutually. It is not the absolute I which is "(the highest) reality"; on the contrary, the I itself *only acquires reality through/in its real engagement with the opposing force of the non-I which frustrates and limits it*—there is no reality of the I outside its opposition to the non-I, outside this shock, this encounter of an opposing/frustrating power (which, in its generality, encompasses everything, from the natural inertia of one's own body to the pressure of social constraints and institutions upon the I, not to mention the traumatic presence of *another* I). Depriving the I of the non-I equals depriving it of its reality. The non-I is thus primordially not the abstract object (*Objekt*) of the subject's distanced contemplation, but the object as *Gegenstand*, what stands there against me, as an obstacle to my effort. As such, the subject's passivity in the face of an object that frustrates its practical effort of

31 George J. Seidel, *Fichte's* Wissenschaftslehre *of 1794: A Commentary on Part 1*, West Lafayette: Purdue University Press 1993, pp. 116–17.

positing, its *thetic* effort, is properly *pathetic*, or, rather, *pathic*.[32] Or, to put it in yet another way, the subject can only be frustrated (and experience the object as an obstacle) insofar as it is itself oriented towards the outside, "pushing" outside in its practical effort.

So, within the (absolutely positing) I, the (finite) I and the non-I are posited as divisible, limiting each other—or, as Fichte put it in his famous formula: "*I oppose in the I a divisible non-I to the divisible I.*" Jacobi was thus in a way right when, in a unique formula from his famous letter to Fichte, he designated the latter's *Wissenschaftslehre* as a "materialism without matter": the "pure consciousness" of the absolute I within which the I and the non-I mutually delimit each other effectively functions as the idealist version of matter in abstract materialism, that is, as abstract (mathematical) space endlessly divided between the I and the non-I.

Nowhere is the proximity of (and, simultaneously, the gap between) Fichte and Hegel more clearly discernible than in the difference between their respective notions of limitation. What they both share is the insight into how, paradoxically, far from excluding each other, limitation and true infinity are two aspects of the same constellation. In Hegel, the overlapping of true infinity and self-limitation is developed in the notion of self-relating: in true infinity, the relation-to-other coincides with self-relating—this is what, for Hegel, defines the most elementary structure of life. A number of contemporary researchers in the life sciences, from Lynn Margulis to Francisco Varela, assert that the true problem of biology is not how an organism and its environment interact or connect, but, rather, how a distinct self-identical organism emerges out of its environs. How does a cell form the membrane which separates its inside from its outside? The true problem is thus not how an organism adapts to its environment, but how there comes to be something, a distinct entity, which must adapt itself in the first place. At this crucial point, the language of contemporary biology starts to resemble, quite uncannily, the language of Hegel. When Varela, for example, explains his notion of autopoiesis, he repeats almost verbatim the Hegelian notion of life as a teleological, self-organizing entity. His central notion of the loop or bootstrap points towards the Hegelian *Setzung der Voraussetzungen* (positing the presuppositions):

> Autopoiesis attempts to define the uniqueness of the emergence that produces life in its fundamental cellular form. It's specific to the cellular level. There's a circular or network process that engenders a paradox: a self-organizing network of biochemical reactions produces molecules, which do something specific and unique: they create a boundary, a membrane, which constrains the network that has produced

32 Portier, *Fichte et le dépassement de la "chose en soi,"* p. 154.

> the constituents of the membrane. This is a logical bootstrap, a loop: a network produces entities that create a boundary, which constrains the network that produces the boundary. This bootstrap is precisely what's unique about cells. A self-distinguishing entity exists when the bootstrap is completed. This entity has produced its own boundary. It doesn't require an external agent to notice it, or to say, "I'm here." It is, by itself, a self-distinction. It bootstraps itself out of a soup of chemistry and physics.[33]

The conclusion to be drawn is thus that the only way to account for the emergence of the distinction between the "inside" and "outside" constitutive of a living organism is to posit a kind of self-reflexive reversal by means of which—to put it in Hegelese—the One of an organism as a Whole retroactively "posits" as its result, as that which it dominates and regulates, the set of its own causes (i.e., the very multiple processes out of which it emerged). In this way, and only in this way, an organism is no longer limited by external conditions, but is fundamentally self-limited—again, as Hegel would have articulated it, life emerges when the external limitation (of an entity by its environs) turns into self-limitation. This brings us back to the problem of infinity: for Hegel, true infinity does not stand for limitless expansion, but for active self-limitation (self-determination) in contrast to being-determined-by-the-other. In this precise sense, life (even at its most elementary, as a living cell) is the basic form of true infinity, since it already involves the minimal loop through which a process is no longer simply determined by the Outside of its environs but is itself able to (over)determine the mode of this determination and thus "posits its presuppositions." Infinity acquires its first actual existence the moment a cell's membrane starts to function as a self-boundary. So, when Hegel includes minerals in the category of "life," as the lowest form of organisms, does he not anticipate Lynn Margulis, who also insists on forms of life preceding vegetable and animal life?

In Fichte, however, the link between infinity and limitation is completely different: the Fichtean infinity is an "acting infinity," the infinity of the subject's practical engagement.[34] Although, obviously, an animal can also be frustrated by objects/obstacles, it does not experience its predicament as *stricto sensu* limited; it is not aware of its limitation, since it is simply constrained by/in it. But man does experience his predicament itself as frustratingly limited, and this experience is sustained by his infinite striving to break out of it. In this way, man's "acting infinity" is directly grounded in his experience of his own finitude. Or, to put it in a slightly different way, while an animal is simply/immediately limited, namely while its limit is external to it and thus invisible from within its

33 Francisco Varela, "The Emergent Self," in John Brockman, ed., *The Third Culture: Beyond the Scientific Revolution*, New York: Simon & Schuster 1996, p. 212.

34 Portier, *Fichte et le dépassement de la "chose en soi,"* p. 158.

constrained horizon (if an animal were to speak, it would not be able to say, "I am limited to my small, poor world, unaware of what I am missing"), a man's limitation is "self-limitation" in the precise sense that it cuts into his very identity from within, frustrating it, "finitizing" it—and this prevents man not only from "becoming the world," but from becoming *himself*. This is the (often overlooked) counterpart of Fichte's basic thesis on how "*I oppose in the I a divisible non-I to the divisible I.*" The fact that the limit between the I and the object/obstacle falls within the I entails not only the triumphant conclusion that the I is the encompassing unity of itself and its objective other; it also entails the much more unpleasant and properly traumatic conclusion that the object/obstacle cuts into the I's identity itself, rendering it finite/frustrated.

This crucial insight enables us to approach what some interpreters see as *the* problem for Fichte: how to pass from the I to the non-I as an In-itself that has a consistency outside the I's reflexive self-movement? Does the I's circular self-positing hang in mid-air, unable ever to really ground itself? (Recall Madame de Stael's comparison of Fichte's self-positing I to Baron Münchhausen.) Pierre Livet proposed an ingenious solution:[35] since there *must* be a kind of external point of reference for the I (without it, the I would simply collapse into itself), and since this point nonetheless cannot be directly external to the I (since any such externality would amount to a concession to the Kantian Thing-in-itself that impedes the I's absolute self-positing), there is only one consistent way out of this deadlock: to ground the circular movement of reflexivity in itself—not by way of the impossible Münchhausen trick in which the founded X retroactively provides its own foundation, but by way of referring to *another* I. In this way, we get a point of reference which is external to a singular I, and which the latter experiences as an opaque impenetrable kernel, yet which is nonetheless *not* foreign to the reflexive movement of (self-)positing, since it is merely *another* circle of such (self-)positing. (In this manner, Fichte can ground the *a priori* necessity of intersubjectivity.)

One can only admire the elegant simplicity of this solution which calls to mind the Lacanian-Freudian notion of the neighbor as the impenetrable traumatic Thing. However, ingenious as the solution is, it nonetheless fails, in neglecting the fact that the I's relating to the object, in the strict formal sense of transcendental genesis, precedes the I's relating to another I: the primordial Other, the Neighbor qua Thing, is *not* another subject. The *Anstoss* which awakens (what will have been) the subject out of its pre-subjective status is an Other, but not the Other of (reciprocal) intersubjectivity.

35 See Pierre Livet, "Intersubjectivité, réflexivité et récursivité chez Fichte," in *Archives de philosophie* 50:4 (October–December 1987).

The finite Absolute

We can see now the fatal flaw in dismissing Fichte's thought as the extreme point of German Idealism, as representing idealism "at its worst." According to this commonplace, Hegel represents the moment of madness, the dream of a System of Absolute Knowledge; but, as this view goes, his work nonetheless contains a lot of useful historical material as well as many valuable insights on history, politics, culture, and aesthetics. Fichte, on the contrary, as an earlier, crazier version of Hegel, represents *nothing more* than madness (see Bertrand Russell in his *History of Western Philosophy*). Even Lacan refers in passing to the radical position of solipsism as a form of madness advocated by no wise man. Even those who praise Fichte see in his thought an extreme formulation of modern subjectivity. And, upon skimming Fichte's work, it cannot but appear to be so: we start with *Ich = Ich*, the I's self-positing; then we pass to not-I; then … In other words, pure abstract ratiocinations, supported by ridiculous arguments and references to mathematics, oscillating between weird jumps and poor common sense.

However, the paradox is that, as in Kant, Schelling, and all of German Idealism, what appears as abstract speculation becomes a source of substantial insight the moment we relate it to our most concrete experience. For example, when Fichte claims that it is because the absolute/ideal self is posited by the finite self that the op-positing of the non-self occurs, this makes sense as a speculative description of the finite subject's concrete practical engagement: when I (as finite subject) "posit" an ideal/unattainable practical goal, the finite reality outside me appears as "not-self," as an obstacle to my goal to be overcome, transformed. This is Fichte's version (after Kant) of the "primacy of practical reason": the way I perceive reality depends on my practical projects. An obstacle is not an obstacle to me as an entity, but to me as engaged in realizing a project: "if my ideal as a health professional is to save lives, then I will begin to see in my patients the things I need to be concerned about: I will begin to see 'things' such as high blood pressure, high cholesterol levels, etc."[36] Or, an even more perspicuous example: "If … I am a rich capitalist being driven through a slum district in my air-conditioned limousine, I do not see the poverty and misery of the local inhabitants. What I see is people on welfare who are too lazy to work, etc."[37] Sartre was thus really in a Fichtean mood when, in a famous passage from *Being and Nothingness*, he claimed that

> whatever may be the situation in which he finds himself, the for-itself must wholly assume this situation with its peculiar coefficient of adversity, even though it be

36 Seidel, *Fichte's* Wissenschaftslehre *of 1794*, p. 102.

37 Ibid., pp. 87–8.

> insupportable. Is it not I who decides the coefficient of adversity in things and even their unpredictability by deciding myself?[38]

The weird-sounding syntagm "coefficient of adversity" belongs to Gaston Bachelard, who subjected to critique Husserl's notion of noematic objectivity as constituted by the transcendental subject's noetic activity, arguing that this notion ignores the object's "coefficient of adversity," the inertia of objects resisting subjective appropriation. While conceding the point about the inertia of the In-itself, the idiocy of the real, Sartre points out, in a Fichtean manner, that one experiences this inertia of the Real as adversity, as an obstacle, only with regard to one's determinate projects:

> my freedom to choose my goals or projects entails that I have also chosen the obstacles I encounter along the way. It is by deciding to climb this mountain that I have turned the weakness of my body and the steepness of the cliffs into obstacles, which they were not so long as I was content simply to gaze at the mountain from the comfort of my chair.[39]

It is only this primacy of the practical which provides the key to the proper understanding of how Fichte reduces the perceived thing to the activity of its perceiving, that is, how he endeavors to generate the (perceived) thing out of its perception. From this phenomenological standpoint, the In-itself of the object is the result of the long arduous work through which the subject learns to distinguish, within the field of its representations, between mere illusory appearance and the way the appearing thing is itself. The In-itself is thus also a category of appearing: it does not designate the immediacy of the thing independent of its appearing to us, but the most mediated mode of appearing. But how?

The I transfers a certain quantum of reality outside of itself; it externalizes part of its activity in a non-I which is thereby "posited as non-posited," that is, appears as "independent" of the I. Fichte's paradox here is that "it is the I's *finitude* … and not its *reflexivity* proper, which renders necessary the different modalities of the objectivization of the non-I to which this I relates itself."[40] To put it in somewhat simplified terms, the I is caught in its self-enclosed circle of objectivizations not because it is the infinite Ground of all being, but precisely because it is finite. The key point here is the paradoxical link between infinity (in the sense of the absence of external limitation) and finitude: every limitation has to be self-limitation not because the I is an infinite divine ground of all being, but precisely because of its radical finitude: as such, as finite, it cannot

38 Jean-Paul Sartre, *Being and Nothingness*, London: Methuen 1957, p. 327.

39 Robert Bernasconi, *How to Read Sartre*, London: Granta Books 2006, p. 48.

40 Portier, *Fichte et le dépassement de la "chose en soi*," p. 222.

"climb upon its own shoulders" (or "jump over its own shadow") and perceive its own external limitation. Portier is fully justified in speaking of the "'circle' of the finite absolute Knowing": finitude and infinity are here no longer opposed; it is our very encounter with the obstacle (and thus our brutal awareness of our finitude) that, simultaneously, makes us aware of the infinity in ourselves, of the infinite Duty that haunts us in the very core of our being.[41]

The standard interpretation claiming that Fichte cannot deduce the necessity of the "shock," of the encounter with the obstacle which triggers the subject's activity, thus simply misses his point: this "shock" *has* to arise "out of nowhere" because of the subject's radical finitude—it stands for the intervention of the radical Outside which by definition cannot be deduced (if it were deducible, we would be back with the metaphysical subject/substance which generates its entire content out of itself):

> Fichte's stroke of genius resides undoubtedly in the fact that he makes out of the inevitable *lack* that pertains to his categorical deduction, not the weakness, but the supreme force of his system: the fact that Necessity can only be deduced from the practical point of view is itself (theoretically and practically) *necessary*.[42]

It is here, in this coincidence of contingency and necessity, of freedom and limitation, that we effectively encounter the "acme of Fichte's edifice."[43] In this "shock," in the impact of the non-I on the I—described by Fichte as simultaneously "impossible" and "necessary"—finitude (being constrained by an Other) and freedom are no longer opposed, since it is only through the shocking encounter with the obstacle that I become free.

This is why, for Fichte, it is the infinite I, not the non-I, which has to "finitize" itself, to appear as the (self-)limited I, to split itself into the absolute I and the finite I opposed to non-I. What this means is that, as Portier puts it in a wonderfully concise way, "every non-I is the non-I of an I, but no I is the I of a non-I."[44] This, however, does not mean that the non-I is simply internal to the I, the outcome of its self-relating. One should be very precise here: over and above the standard "dogmatic" temptation to conceive of the I as part of the non-I, as part of objective reality, there is the much more tricky and no less "dogmatic" temptation of transcendental realism itself, of hypostasizing the absolute I into a kind of noumenal meta-Subject/Substance which engenders the finite subject as its phenomenal/empirical appearance. In this case, there would be no truly "real" objects: the objects would be ultimately mere phantom-objects,

41 Ibid., p. 244.
42 Ibid., p. 230.
43 Ibid., p. 238.
44 Ibid., p. 253.

specters engendered by the absolute I in its circular play with itself. This point is absolutely crucial if we are to avoid the notion of Fichte as the ridiculous figure of the "absolute idealist": the absolute I is not merely playing with itself, positing obstacles and then overcoming them, all the while secretly aware that it is the only player/agent in the house. The absolute I is *not* the absolute real/ideal Ground of everything; its status is radically *ideal*, it is the ideal presupposition of the practically engaged finite I as the only "reality" (since, as we have seen, the I becomes "real" only through its self-limitation in encountering the obstacle of the non-I). This is why Fichte is a moralist-idealist, an idealist of infinite Duty: freedom is not something that substantially coexists with the I, but something that has to be acquired through arduous struggle, through the effort of culture and self-education. The infinite I is nothing but the process of its own infinite becoming.

This brings us to Fichte's solution of the problem of solipsism: although at the level of theoretical observation we are passive receivers and at the level of practice we are active (we intervene in the world, impose our projects onto it), we cannot overcome solipsism from a theoretical standpoint, but only from a practical one: "[if] no effort, [then] no object."[45] As a theoretical I, I can easily imagine myself as a solitary monad caught in an ethereal, non-substantial web of my own phantasmagorias; but the moment I engage in practice, I have to struggle with the object's resistance—or, as Fichte himself put it: "The coercion on account of which belief in reality imposes itself is a moral coercion, the only one possible for a free being."[46] Or, as Lacan put it much later: ethics is the dimension of the Real, the dimension in which imaginary and symbolic balances are disturbed. This is why Fichte can and has to reject the Kantian solution of the dynamic antinomies: if we resolve them in the Kantian way, by simply assigning each of the two opposed theses to a different level (phenomenally we are subject to necessity, while noumenally we are free), we obfuscate the fact that *the world into which we intervene with our free acts is the very world of phenomenal reality in which we struggle for our freedom*. This is also why Fichte can avoid the above-mentioned impasse reached by Kant in his *Critique of Practical Reason*, where he endeavors to answer the question of what would happen to us were we to gain access to the noumenal domain, to the *Ding an sich* (we would be mere puppets deprived of our freedom). Fichte allows us to clarify this confusion which arises when we insist on the opposition between the noumenal and the phenomenal: the I is not a noumenal substance, but the pure spontaneity of self-positing; this is why its self-limitation does not need a transcendent God who manipulates our terrestrial situation (limiting our knowledge) in order to foster our moral growth—one can deduce the subject's limitation in a totally immanent way.

45 Ibid., p. 232.
46 Cited in ibid., p. 224.

Interpreters like to emphasize the radical break or "paradigm shift" that takes place between Kant and Fichte; however, Fichte's focus on the subject's finitude compels us to acknowledge a no less radical break between Fichte and Schelling. Schelling's idea (shared also by the young Hegel) is that Fichte's one-sided subjective idealism should be supplemented by objective idealism, since only such a two-sided approach can give us a complete image of the absolute Subject-Object. What gets lost in this shift from Fichte to Schelling is the unique standpoint of the subject's finitude (the finitude that determines Fichte's basic attitude towards reality as an engaged-practical one: the Fichtean synthesis can only be given as practical effort, as endless striving). In Fichte, the synthesis of the finite and the infinite is given in the infinite effort of the finite subject, and the absolute I itself is a hypo-thesis of the "thetic" practical-finite subject; whereas, in Schelling, the original *datum* is the Absolute qua indifference of the subject-object, and the subject as opposed to the object emerges as the *Abfall*, a falling-off, from the Absolute, which is why rejoining the Absolute is for Schelling no longer a matter of the I's practical effort, but of an aesthetic submergence into the Absolute's indifference, which amounts to the subject's self-overcoming. In other words, from Fichte's standpoint, Schelling regresses to a pre-Kantian "idealist realism": his Absolute is again the noumenal absolute Entity, and all finite/delimited entities are its results/fall-offs. For Fichte, on the contrary, the status of the Absolute (the self-positing I) remains thoroughly transcendental-ideal; it is the transcendental condition of the finite I's practical engagement, its hypo-thesis, never a positively given *ens realissimus*.

It is precisely because the status of the Absolute is, for Fichte, transcendental-ideal that he remains faithful to the basic Kantian insight that time and space are *a priori forms* of sensibility; this prohibits any naïve-Platonic notion of finite/material/sensuous reality as the secondary "confused" version of the true intelligible/noumenal universe. For Kant (and Fichte), material reality is *not* a blurred version of the true noumenal world, but a fully constituted reality of its own. In other words, the fact that time and space are *a priori forms* of sensibility means that what Kant called "transcendental schematism" is irreducible: the orders/levels of sensibility and intelligibility are irreducibly heterogeneous, and one cannot deduce anything about material reality from the categories of pure reason themselves.

Fichte's position with regard to the status of nature nonetheless remains the radicalized Kantian one: if reality is primordially experienced as the obstacle to the I's practical activity, this means that nature (the inertia of material objects) exists only as the stuff of our moral activity, that its justification can only be practical-teleological, not speculative. This is why Fichte rejected all attempts at a speculative philosophy of nature—and why Schelling, the great practitioner of the philosophy of nature, ridiculed Fichte: if nature can only be justified teleologically, this means that air and light exist only so that moral individuals can see each other and thus interact. Well aware of the difficulties such a view poses to our sense of what is credible, Fichte replied with sarcastic laughter:

> They answer me: "Air and light a priori, just think of it! Ha ha ha! Ha ha ha! Ha ha ha! Come on, laugh along with us! Ha ha ha! Ha ha ha! Ha ha ha! Air and light a priori: *tarte à la crème*, ha ha ha! Air and light a priori! *Tarte à la crème*, ha ha ha! Air and light a priori! *Tarte à la crème*, ha ha ha!" et cetera ad infinitum.[47]

The weird nature of this outburst in part resides in its contrast to the more typical common-sense laughter at the philosopher's strange speculations, the kind of laughter whose exemplary case is the joke told in poor taste about the philosopher-solipsist: "Let him hit his head against a wall and he will soon discover if he is alone in the world, ha ha ha!" Here, the philosopher-Fichte laughs at the common-sense argument that air and light are obviously not here just to enable our moral activity, but just *are* out there, whether we act or not. Fichte's laughter is all the more strange for resembling the traditional realist philosopher's direct appeal to the obviousness of reality as the best argument against abstract speculations. When Zeno the Cynic was confronted with Eleatic proofs of the non-existence of movement, he simply raised and moved his middle finger, or so the story goes … (In another version, he simply stood up and started to walk about.) However, according to Hegel, when one of the students present applauded the master for this proof that movement exists, Zeno beat him up—appeals to immediate reality do not count in philosophy, only conceptual thinking can do the job of demonstration. What, then, could Fichte's laughter mean, since he laughs not *from* the standpoint of common-sense realism (which tells us that movement exists and that air and light are out there independently of our activity), but *at* this standpoint? The key to the answer is (as is often the case with philosophers who hide their crucial formulation in a footnote or a secondary remark) squeezed between parentheses. Here is Fichte's decisive explanation of the non-I:

> ([According to the usual opinion,] the concept of the non-self is merely a general concept which emerges through abstraction from everything represented [*allem Vorgestellten*]. But the shallowness of this explanation can easily be demonstrated. If I am to represent anything at all, I must oppose it to that which represents [the representing self]. Now within the object of representation [*Vorstellung*] there can and must be an X of some sort, whereby this object discloses itself as something to be represented, and not as that which represents. But *that* everything wherein this X

47 J. G. Fichte, *Fichte: Early Philosophical Writings*, ed. and trans. Daniel Breazeale, Ithaca: Cornell University Press 1988, p. 347.

may be is not that which represents but something to be represented, is something that no object can teach me; for merely to be able to posit something as an *object*, I have to know this already; hence it must lie initially in myself, that which represents, prior to any possible experience.—And this is an observation so striking that anyone who fails to grasp it and is not thereby uplifted into transcendental idealism, must unquestionably be suffering from mental blindness.)[48]

The logic of this argumentation may appear surprising to anyone not well-versed in German idealism: it is precisely because there is something more in the non-Self, in the object, than the subject's representations (*Vorstellungen*); precisely because it cannot be reduced to a general, shared, feature abstracted from representations; and precisely because it "discloses itself as something to be represented, and not as that which represents," that this surplus over my representations must lie *in me*, in the representing subject.[49]

Seidel is thus fully justified in emphasizing that Fichte's *Nicht-Ich* should be read according to what Kant called "infinite judgment." Kant introduced the key distinction between negative and indefinite judgment: the positive judgment "the soul is mortal" can be negated in two ways, when a predicate is denied to the subject ("the soul is not mortal"), and when a non-predicate is affirmed ("the soul is non-mortal")—the difference is exactly the same as the one, known to every reader of Stephen King, between "he is not dead" and "he is undead." The indefinite judgment opens up a third domain which undermines the underlying distinction: the "undead" is neither alive nor dead, but precisely the monstrous "living dead." And the same goes for "inhuman": "he is not human" is not the same as "he is inhuman"—"he is not human" means simply that he is external to humanity, animal or divine, while "he is inhuman" means something thoroughly different, namely that he is neither human nor not-human, but marked by a terrifying excess which, although negating what we understand as "humanity," is inherent to being human. And, perhaps, one should risk the hypothesis that this is what changes with the Kantian revolution: in the pre-Kantian universe, humans were simply humans, beings of reason, fighting the excess of animal lust and divine madness; only with Kant and German Idealism does the excess to be fought become absolutely immanent, located at the very core of subjectivity itself (which is why, with German Idealism, the metaphor for that core is the night, the "night of the world," in contrast to the Enlightenment notion of the Light of Reason dispelling the surrounding darkness). So when, in the

48 Quoted from Seidel, *Fichte's* Wissenschaftslehre *of 1794*, pp. 50–1.

49 Kant had already made the same point in his account of transcendental synthesis: how do we get from the confused multitude of passive subjective impressions to the consistent perception of objective reality? By way of supplementing this subjective multitude with, again, the subject's act of transcendental synthesis ...

pre-Kantian universe, a hero goes mad, it means he is deprived of his humanity, as the animal passions or divine madness take over; with Kant, by contrast, madness signals an explosion of the very core of a human being. In precisely the same way, the Fichtean non-Self is not a negation of the predicate, but an affirmation of a non-predicate: it is not "this isn't a Self," but "this *is* a non-Self," which is why it should be translated into English more often as "non-Self" rather than "not-Self."[50] (More precisely: the moment we arrive at Fichte's third proposition—the mutual delimitation/determination of Self and non-Self—the non-Self effectively turns into a *not*-Self, something.)

Fichte starts with the thetic judgment: *Ich* = *Ich*, pure immanence of Life, pure Becoming, pure self-positing, *Tat-Handlung*, the full coincidence of posited with positing. I am only through the process of positing myself, and I am nothing but this process—*this* is intellectual intuition, this mystical flow inaccessible to consciousness: every consciousness needs something opposed to itself. Now—and here is the key—the rise of *Non-Ich* out of this pure flow is not (yet) delimited from *Ich*: it is a pure formal conversion, like Hegel's passage from Being to Nothingness. *Both Ich and non-Ich are unlimited, absolute.* How, then, do we pass from *non-Ich* to Object as not-*Ich*? Through *Anstoss*, this ex-timate obstacle. *Anstoss* is neither *Nicht-Ich* (which comprises me) nor Object (which is externally opposed to me). *Anstoss* is neither "absolutely nothing" nor something (a delimited object); it is (to refer to the Lacanian logic of suture, as deployed by Miller in his classical text) nothing *counted as* something (in the same way as the number one is zero counted as one). The distinction between form and content on which Fichte insists so much is crucial here: as to its content, *Anstoss* is nothing; as to its form, it is (already) something—it is thus "nothing in the form of something." This minimal distinction between form and content is already at work in the passage from the first to the second thesis: A = A is the pure form, the formal gesture of self-identity, the self-identity of a form with itself; non-Self is its symmetrical opposite, a formless content. This minimal reflexivity is also what makes the passage from A = A (*Ich* = *Ich*) to the positing of non-Self necessary: without this minimal gap between form and content, the absolute Self and the absolute non-Self would simply and directly overlap.

In the Preface to the second edition of the *Critique of Pure Reason*, Kant contends that

> all possible speculative knowledge of reason is limited to mere objects of *experience*. But our further contention must also be duly borne in mind, namely, that though we cannot *know* these objects as things in themselves, we must yet be in the position at least to *think* them as things in themselves; otherwise we should

50 See Seidel, *Fichte's* Wissenschaftslehre *of 1794*, p. 89.

> be landed in the absurd conclusion that there can be *appearance without anything that appears*.[51]

Is this not exactly the Hegelian-Lacanian thesis, however? Is not the supersensible which is "appearance qua appearance" precisely an appearance in which nothing appears? As Hegel put it in his *Phenomenology*: beyond the veil of appearances, there is only what the subject puts there. This is the secret of the Sublime that Kant was not ready to confront. So we turn back to Fichte: is not the *Anstoss* precisely such an appearance without anything that appears, a nothing which appears as something? This is what brings the Fichtean *Anstoss* uncannily close to the Lacanian *objet petit a*, the object-cause of desire, which is also a positivization of a lack, a stand-in for a void.

Some decades ago, Lacan invited ridicule when he stated that the meaning of the phallus is "the square of -1"—but Kant had already compared the Thing-in-itself as *ens rationis* to a "square root of a negative number."[52] It is insofar as we apply this comparison also to Fichte's *Anstoss* that the Kantian distinction between what we can only think and what we can know assumes all its weight: we can only think the *Anstoss*, we cannot know it as a determinate object-of-representation.

The Posited Presupposition

To recapitulate, Fichte's attempt to get rid of the Thing-in-itself follows a very precise logic and intervenes at a very precise point in his critique of Kant. Let us recall that, for Kant, the Thing is introduced as the X that affects the subject when it experiences an object through its senses: the Thing is primarily the source of sensuous affections. If we are to get rid of the Thing, it is thus absolutely crucial to show how the subject can affect and act upon itself, not only at the intelligible level but also at the level of (sensuous) affections; the absolute subject must be capable of temporal *auto-affection*.

For Fichte, this I's "sentimental auto-affection" by means of which the subject experiences its own existence, its own inert given character, and thus relates to itself (or, rather, is for itself) as passive, as affected, is the ultimate foundation of all reality. This does not mean that all reality, all experience of the other as inert/resisting, can be reduced to the subject's self-experience; it means that it is only the subject's passive self-relation which opens the subject up to the experience of otherness.

---

51 Immanuel Kant, *Critique of Pure Reason*, trans. Norman Kemp Smith, London: MacMillan 1929, p. 27 (emphasis in last sentence added).

52 Kant, quoted in Leo Freuler, *Kant et la métaphysique spéculative*, Paris: Vrin 1992, p. 223.

Therein culminates Fichte's entire effort, in the deployment of the notion of the subject's *"sensuous auto-affection" as the ultimate synthesis of the subject and the object*. If this is feasible, then there is no longer the need to posit, behind the transcendental I's spontaneity, the unknowable "noumenal X" that the subject "really is": if there is genuine self-affection, then the I is also able to fully *know* itself, that is, we no longer have to refer to a noumenal "I or he or it, the Thing that thinks," as Kant does in *The Critique of Pure Reason*. And, thereby, we can also see how Fichte's urgency to get rid of the Thing-in-itself is linked to his focus on the ethico-practical engagement of the subject as grounded in its *freedom*: if the subject's phenomenal (self-)experience is just the appearance of an unknown noumenal substance, then our freedom is just an illusory appearance and we are really like puppets whose acts are controlled by an unknown mechanism. Kant was fully aware of this radical consequence—and, perhaps, all of Fichte can be read as an attempt to avoid this Kantian deadlock.

But, one may ask, does this assertion of the subject's capacity to get to know itself fully not contradict Fichte's focus on the subject as practically engaged, struggling with objects/obstacles that frustrate its endeavors, and thereby as finite? So can only an infinite being fully know itself? The answer is that the Fichtean subject is precisely the paradoxical conjunction of these two features, finitude and freedom, since *the subject's infinity (the infinite striving of its ethical engagement) is itself an aspect of its finite condition*.

The key here is again provided by Fichte's notion of the mutual delimitation of subject and object, Self and not-Self: every activity is posited in/as the object only insofar as the Self is posited as passive; and this positing of the Self as passive is still an *act* of the Self, its self-limitation. I am only a passive X affected by objects insofar as I (actively) posit myself as a passive recipient. Seidel ironically calls this the "law of the conservation of activity": "when reality (activity) is canceled in the self, that quantum of reality (activity) gets posited in the non-self. If activity is posited in the non-self, then its opposite (passivity) is posited in the self: I (passively) see the (actively) blooming apple." However, this can only happen "because I (actively) posit passivity in my-self so that activity may be posited in the non-self … The non-self cannot act upon my consciousness unless I (actively, that is, freely) allow it to do so."[53]

Kant had already prefigured this in his so-called "incorporation thesis": causes only affect me insofar as I allow them to affect me. This is why "you can because you must": every external impossibility (to which the excuse "I know I must, but I cannot, it is impossible …" refers) relies on a disavowed self-limitation. Applied to the sexual opposition of the "active" male and "passive" female stance, this Fichtean notion of the activity of the non-I as strictly

---

53 Seidel, *Fichte's* Wissenschaftslehre *of 1794*, p. 104.

correlative to the I's passivity brings us directly to Otto Weininger's notion of woman as the embodiment of man's fall: woman exists (as a thing out there, acting upon man, disturbing his ethical stance, throwing him off the rails) only insofar as man adopts the stance of passivity; she is literally the *result* of man's withdrawal into passivity, so there is no need for man to actively fight woman—his adoption of an active stance automatically pulls the ground out from under woman's existence, since her entire being is nothing but man's non-being.

Here "Fichte asks himself whether the quantity (that is, the activity) of the self can ever equal zero (= 0), whether the self can ever be totally at rest, ever totally passive." Fichte's answer, of course, is no: "For the non-self has reality only to the extent that the self is affected by it; otherwise, as such, it has no reality at all ... I do not see anything I do not *will* to see."[54] However, the way we read the exact status of the non-Self is crucial here: if we read it in accordance with the Kantian infinite judgment, that is, as a non-Self that *comprises* Self itself (in the same way that the "undead" comprises the dead), then, prior to positing objectivity, the constituting/constitutive gesture of *Ich* should be an immobilization, a withdrawal, a self-emptying of the non-Self, a self-reduction to a zero which *is* the Self; this reduction to zero opens up the space, literally, for *Ich*'s activity of positing/mediating.

Fichte gets caught in a circle here. His first proposition is: A = A, *Ich* = *Ich*, i.e., absolute self-positing, pure substanceless becoming, *Tat-Handlung* (deed-activity), "intellectual intuition." Then comes the second proposition: A = non-A, *Ich* = *non-Ich*, the self posits a non-self which is absolutely opposed to it—here enters the absolute contradiction. Then comes the mutual limitation which resolves this self-contradiction in its double form, practical (the Self posits the not-self as limited by the self) and theoretical (the self posits itself as limited by the not-self)—the Self and the not-self are at the same level, divisible.[55] The ambiguity here lies in the fact that "the absolute self of the first principle is not *something* ... it is simply *what* it is."[56] Only with delimitation,

> [b]oth are something: the not-self is what the self is not, and *vice versa*. As opposed to the absolute self (though, as will be shown in due course, it can only be opposed to it insofar as it is represented [by it], not insofar as it is in itself), the non-self is *absolutely nothing* (*schlechthin Nichts*); as opposed to the limitable self, it is a *negative quantity*.[57]

---

54 Ibid.

55 Note the finesse of Fichte's reflexive formulation: in theoretical form, the self posits itself as limited, it does not directly posit the object as limiting the self; in practical form, it posits the object as limited/determined by the self, it does not directly posit itself as limiting/forming the object.

56 Henrich, *Between Kant and Hegel*, p. 64.

57 Ibid., pp. 64–5.

However, from the practical standpoint, the finite Self posits the infinite Self in the guise of the Ideal of Unity of Self and not-Self, and, with it, the non-self as an obstacle to be overcome. We thus find ourselves in a circle: the absolute Self posits non-self and then finitizes itself by its delimitation; however, the circle closes itself, the absolute presupposition itself (the pure self-positing) returns as presupposed, that is, as the presupposition *of* the posited, and, in this sense, as depending on the posited. Far from being an inconsistency, this is the crucial, properly speculative, moment in Fichte: the presupposition itself is (retroactively) posited by the process it generates.

THE FICHTEAN BONE IN THE THROAT

So perhaps, before dismissing his philosophy as the climactic point of subjectivist madness, we should give Fichte a chance. To properly understand his passage to full idealism it is necessary to bear in mind how he radicalizes the primacy of practical reason, which had already been asserted by Kant. Kant's first critics had already noticed the ambiguous relationship, in his practical philosophy, between the categorical imperative itself as the direct "fact of reason" and the postulates of pure practical reason (the immortality of the soul, the existence of God …), in other words the so-called "moral image of the world" which alone makes our moral activity meaningful: we have to trust that the reality in which we intervene is already in itself structured in such a way that will enable us to achieve our practical goals and progress to a better world. Kant's premise is that these postulates—the entire "moral image of the world"—do not have the same direct and unconditional status as does our moral awareness (of the categorical imperative), but are the result of a secondary reasoning on the cognitive implications of our moral awareness. Once we concede this point, the parallel imposes itself between the postulates of practical reason which guarantee the meaningfulness of our moral activity and the regulative ideas of pure (theoretical) reason which guarantee the consistency of our knowledge. The divine teleology that we can obscurely discern in nature is not a cognitive category, it just helps us systematize our knowledge of nature; that is, we proceed *as if* there was a God who rules the world, but without knowing this for sure. And the same holds also for practical reason: when we act morally, we proceed *as if* there is a "moral world order." It was, as Henrich notes, Schulze who developed this critique in detail, likening

> the structure of Kant's moral theology to the cosmological proof of the existence of God, in which one moves from the unavoidability of thinking the idea of God to the belief in the existence of what we are thinking … In Kant's moral theology, we have, first, the fact of the moral law that we presuppose. We then infer from this fact of

> reason, which is merely the awareness of the categorical imperative, the existence of a moral world order … the inference pursues the same illegitimate course of reasoning as the cosmological proof. Both infer from something given something else that is inaccessible to our experience.[58]

This gap thus leaves open the possibility that our moral freedom is just an illusion, that we are noumenally blind automata. Fichte's answer to this reproach is very precise and refined: the reproach itself silently presupposes the primacy of theoretical over practical reason. It is only for theoretical reason that objective reality is more than "mere" subjective certainty; from the standpoint of theoretical reason, the self-positing I (which exists only in the subjective mode, "for itself") does not exist at all, there is no such thing in "objective reality." Furthermore, insofar as the space of practical activity involves the opposition/conflict between subject and object, the I and the non-I—that is, the endless effort of the I to impose its mould on objective reality—"the entire existence of practical reason is founded on the *conflict* between the self-determining element within us and the theoretical-knowing element. And practical reason would itself be canceled if this conflict were eliminated."[59] Therein resides the difference between the ontological proof of God's existence and the postulates of practical reason: "the cosmo-theological one is based entirely upon theoretical reason, whereas the moral proof is based upon the conflict between theoretical reason and the I in itself."[60]

This Fichtean primacy of practical over theoretical reason is much more radical than the Kantian one: while Kant asserts the primacy of practical reason, he still keeps the two spheres apart—his point is ultimately that one has to limit the scope of (theoretical) knowledge to make space for (practical) beliefs. With Fichte, on the contrary, practical philosophy "becomes for the first time a part of epistemology": he finds "elements to be basic in cognition itself that traditionally had been separated from cognition and connected instead with pleasure and action."[61]

It is only by taking into account this primacy of practical philosophy that we can answer the key question: how does Fichte pass from the I's self-positing to the I's self-limitation by way of positing the non-I? In simpler terms, how does he pass from the absolute subject's self-positing to the mutual delimitation of subject and object? The problem resides in the fact that Fichte does not subscribe to the founding axiom of the post-Hegelian transcendental philosophy of finitude, which asserts the correlation between subject and object as the ultimate

58 Ibid., p. 161.
59 Ibid., p. 76.
60 Ibid., p. 161.
61 Ibid., p. 208.

horizon of our experience: for him, the two relata of the subject-object relationship are not of equal weight, one of them—the I—is absolutely privileged, since the I is all reality. For this reason, Fichte can only designate the object as "not-I," that is, its status has to be purely negative, with no positive force to it. The relationship is here that of a logical negation: the object is a non-subject *and nothing above that*. However, Fichte's thought in its entirety is a gigantic effort to conceive of all reality as originating from the I's (mind's) self-relating and the I's endless "practical" struggle with its opposite (the object, not-I) as the unsurpassable fact of our lives—and the category which fits this relation is not that of negation, but that of what Kant called "real opposition" (in his "Attempt to Introduce the Concept of Negative Magnitude into Philosophy" from his pre-critical phase, 1763–4). When two opposed forces collide, each can diminish the intensity ("quantity of a quality") of the opposite, but this diminishing is by definition the effect of the opposed positive force. To give a thoroughly simplified example: two groups of boys pull a rope in opposite directions; if the rope moves left, this means that the "negative magnitude" of the right group's force is the result of the overwhelming power of the left group's force (the rope not only did not move in the direction in which they pulled it, but moved away from them). According to Henrich (who is worth quoting *in extenso* on this point), Fichte ultimately cheats here: his whole construction of the not-I is based upon confusing (or jumping between) logical negation and real opposition—in other words, he treats what he introduces as the result of a logical negation (and as such a purely negative entity, a non-entity) as a positive counter-force:

> Kant takes it for granted that such a reduction of reality in one particular is due to a *real* force in another particular … the ontological status of being a negative particular depends, in some respect, on some other particular's being positive. By way of contrast, Fichte assumes that *all* reality has to be found in the self. He therefore cannot avoid saying that the non-self is nothing but an X that reduces the self's reality. This is the origin of Fichte's infamous and unsettling theory of the *Anstoss*—the impulse that takes place in the activity of the self and brings about its reflecting on itself …
>
> Fichte's assumption that there is absolute reality in the self depends entirely on his smuggling in a real ontological negation, by way of the negative element in the term "not-self." Fichte simply calls the object the not-self, and then he introduces the idea of its being negative. Now he means that the being negative of the not-self is an *ontological* negativity, and *only* negative in this sense. This is obviously a philosophical sleight-of-hand, a shell game, in which Fichte shifts the meaning of his terms.[62]

62 Ibid., p. 194.

Note Henrich's excessively aggressive dismissal of *Anstoss*, betraying traces of uneasiness (to be contrasted to Daniel Breazeale's much more subtle analysis) and bearing witness to his inability to perceive the inner necessity of *Anstoss*. True, Fichte himself was not able fully to account for the precise status of *Anstoss* (is it the last remainder of the Thing-in-itself, absolutely external to the I and thus limiting it, or just a self-posited obstacle?); however, the urge that pushed him to introduce this notion was absolutely consistent with the deepest logic of his thought. What Fichte failed to see was that, in the subject-object relationship, the *subject* is a negative entity, a pure self-relating negativity—which is why, in order not to "implode into itself," it needs a minimum of objectal support. That is to say, although Fichte repeatedly emphasizes how the subject is not a thing but a self-relating process, a *Tat-Handlung*, he conceives of the subject in an all-too-positive way when he claims that the absolute I (subject) is all reality—the subject is, on the contrary, a *hole* in reality. As such, the I (subject) is in no position to "transfer" its reality onto the not-I (object); on the contrary, it is itself in need of a "little bit of reality" (of an object) to regain its minimum consistency. What this means is that the subject by definition cannot be "complete": it is in itself "thwarted," the paradoxical result of its own failure-to-be. To describe it in the simplified terms of the loop of symbolic representation: the subject endeavors to adequately represent itself, this representation fails, and the subject *is* the result of this failure. Recall what one might be tempted to call the "Hugh Grant paradox" (referring to the famous scene from *Four Weddings and a Funeral*): the hero tries to express his love to his beloved, only to get caught in stumbling and confused repetitions; yet it is in this very failure to deliver his message in a perfect way that he bears witness to its authenticity. Is not Fichte himself unexpectedly on the track of this same insight when he

> shifts from the term *vorstellen* (representation) to the word *darstellen* (presentation). But what now does representation present? As soon as I have arrived at presentation from representation, the question "*What* is represented?" has an entirely different meaning. In representation, of course, it would be the object that is represented. But what is presented in the representation in the sense of *darstellen*? The answer is obvious: the self![63]

And here we come to the crucial point: the otherness, the "stranger in my very heart," which Fichte endeavored to discern under the name of *Anstoss*, is this "bone in the throat" which prevents the direct expression of the subject (and

63 Ibid., p. 200. Note how the Derridean metaphysics-of-presence relationship between presentation and re-presentation is inverted here: the "presentation" is more mediated, evasive, than the re-presentation of the object; i.e., the subject is "presented" through the lacunae, distortions, repetitions, twists, etc., of the object's re-presentation.

which—since the "subject" *is* the failure of its own direct expression—is strictly correlative to the subject). Which means that the minimal emptying of subject, the reduction of its reality (of its "thingness"), is constitutive of subjectivity: the subject is caught in its loop because it is not-All, finite, lacking, because a loss-of-reality is co-substantial with it, and *Anstoss* is the positivization of this gap. *Anstoss* is the In-itself in the mode of For-the-subject/self.

A century and a half later, Lacan called this same "bone in the throat" the *objet petit a*. Insofar as the "subject" is the name for self-relating absolute negativity, *Anstoss* as the minimal form of not-I is not a (logical) negation of the subject's (full and only) reality, but, on the contrary, the result of the negation of the negation which "is" the subject. One does not begin with a positivity which is then negated; one begins with negation, and the object's positivity is the result of the (self-related) negation of this negation. Or, to put it in Lacanese, the object *a* has no positive substantial being of its own, is nothing but the positivation of a lack: not a lacking object, but an object which positivizes a lack (negativity), whose positivity is nothing but a positivized negativity. It is here that *imagination* enters: this positivization of a lack is the zero-level imagination. At its most radical ontological level, imagination fills in the void/lack that "is" the subject, that is, what the subject originally "imagines" is its own objectal counterpoint, itself as a determinate being.

It is crucial to grasp correctly here the link between imagination (*Einbildung*) and representation (*Vorstellung*). Although closely connected, they are not simply the same (in the simplified "transcendental" sense that, since all reality is subjective, its status has to be that of the subject's imagination); there is a very precise distinction between the two. First, representation: how does Fichte come to re-presentation as the mediating moment between subject and object, between the I and the not-I? Again, his idea is not the simple commonsensical notion of representation as the subjective stand-in (representative) of a (represented) object. Here Henrich is again worth quoting in detail:

> if the Self is absolute reality itself, its reality *cannot* be reduced. Since the relation between the subject and the object is the relation between the real and the negative, no real relation between the real and the negative is possible. Therefore, only a logical relation that excludes any real relation between the two of them will do. A real relation between the two of them presupposes some third mediating element. This element must have the character of the subject to a certain degree, and just as this element has the character of the self only to a certain degree, so also it is affected by the object. … In this third element, the Self itself is not limited: the limitation of the Self would be impossible, if the Self really is *all* reality. Nonetheless, there is something that is limitation … So conceived, limitation is an entity that makes the relation between subject and object possible. In this respect the

> limited relation between subject and object is the elementary ontological status of representation."[64]

So why can the subject not simply be limited by the object? Not because the subject is absolute in the naïve sense of being the all-encompassing reality, but precisely because it is finite, caught in its self-relating loop and therefore unable to step out of itself and draw a line of delimitation between subjective and objective: every limit the subject draws is already "subjective." In other words, for the subject to be able to draw a clear "objective" limit between itself and the not-I, its objectivity, it would have to break out of its own loop and adopt a neutral position from which it would have been possible for the subject to compare itself with objectivity. The subject cannot simply be limited by the object because it is caught in its own loop, that is, because every relation it entertains with objectivity is already a mode of self-relating; the subject's direct relation to the object cannot be a relation of real opposition between two positive forces delimiting each other, but only a purely logical relation between the subject and an empty-negative X, not even the Kantian Thing-in-itself.

We can now see why representation needs to be supplemented by imagination proper: since the field of representations remains within the loop of the subject's self-relating, it is by definition always inconsistent, full of lacunae, which the subject must somehow fill in to create a minimally consistent Whole of a world—and the function of imagination is precisely to fill in these gaps. Now we can also see clearly the difference between representation and imagination: representation is the subjective mode of objectivity (objects are "represented" for the subject), while imagination is the objective mode of subjectivity (the subject's void is present[ifi]ed as an [imagined] object). In other words, while representation represents something (its object), imagination represents nothing (which "is" the subject). Fichte did not see all of this clearly, which explains why he often seems to be using "imagination" simply as a name for the subjective positing of objectivity, that is, for "subjective objectivity." But Kant already had a presentiment of the underlying true *raison d'être* of imagination: it arises because the subject is finite *and* boundless, with no externality—this is why the synthesis through imagination is needed to constitute reality: "No psychologist has yet thought that the imagination is a necessary ingredient of [the] perception [of reality] itself."[65]

Even Heidegger fell short here in his elaboration of the difference between the Ancient Greek and the modern understanding of fantasy: in Greek thought, *phantasia* referred to the coming-into-appearance of entities, to their

---

64 Ibid., p. 195.

65 Immanuel Kant, *Critique of Pure Reason*, ed. and trans. Paul Guyer and Allen W. Wood, Cambridge: Cambridge University Press 1998, p. 239.

un-concealment against the background of withdrawal/concealment. As such, *phantasia* concerns Being itself—in contrast to modern subjectivism, wherein fantasy designates man's "merely subjective" fantasizing, disconnected from "objective" reality:

> In unconcealment *fantasia* comes to pass: the coming-into-appearance, as a particular something, of that which presences—for man, who himself presences toward what appears. Man as representing subject, however "fantasizes," i.e., he moves in *imaginatio*, in that his representing imagines, pictures forth, whatever is, as the objective, into the world as picture.[66]

Lacan's precise use of fantasy restores something of the original Greek meaning: "fantasy" has for him a kind of transcendental status; it is constitutive of reality itself, a frame which guarantees the ontological consistency of reality. Heidegger nonetheless falls short here: what he fails to see is how imagination as opposed to the "objective"—that is, precisely in its "merely subjective" aspect—is needed to constitute the phenomenal "objective reality." Things become even more complex when Fichte tries to show how, out of the play of subjective imagination which is entirely contained within the loop of the mind's self-relating, the necessary belief in an external world independent of our perception/imagination arises. The I's self-limitation and its constant overcoming first constitute a play of imagination within which "consciousness in a state of dreaming can be understood as related to itself so that it experiences itself as wavering, or as moving into and out of states freely. It is thus not really determined by anything that could adequately be described as an object."[67] So, again, how do we pass from here to the (belief in the) external world? Fichte's answer is beautifully paradoxical: it is not that, in its representations, the I stumbles upon something which so resists the free play of its imagination that it can only be accounted for as an external counter-force; on the contrary, the problem the I resolves with the (hypo-)thesis of external reality is that of its own full self-awareness as a mind—what happens in the mind must be posited for it as "mental." Here again, a longer passage from Henrich is unavoidable:

> First, sensations are nothing but states of the mind. In order to know them as mental, that is, to have them *for* the mind as such, we must distinguish sensations from something that is not mental at all … In order to become aware of itself, the mind has to introduce freely a mental construct of something that corresponds to

---

66 Martin Heidegger, *The Question Concerning Technology and Other Essays*, New York: Harper & Row 1977, p. 147. I owe this reference to Heidegger to André Nusselder, *Frameworks: Fantasy in Lacanian Psychoanalysis* (unpublished manuscript).

67 Henrich, *Between Kant and Hegel*, p. 213.

> the sensations, which is the image of the external world … once we are able to think of sensations as somehow having something corresponding to them, we have *perceptions*. So construed, sensations are not now states of the mind; they are correlated to something that is not mental: they are *of* something. At this point, the closed, self-relating system of the mind is opened for the first time … To the question "What is the world?" we may now offer the following answer: it is the indeterminate dimension of correlates to the states of our minds.[68]

It is easy to see the paradox here: the mind has to posit something as not-mental in order to become aware of itself as mind, and this non-mental X is again "a *mental* construct of something that corresponds to the sensations"; so "the closed, self-relating system of the mind is opened for the first time"—but it is obviously a false opening, because it is opened towards something which is again a mental construct. Is the absurd-subjectivist sleight-of-hand not clearly discernible here, i.e., is Fichte not clearly claiming that "what is outside the mind is nothing but a construct of the self-reference of the mind itself"?[69] The mistake again is to conceive of this constellation only in a theoretical mode of subjectivity: if one adopts the stance of a passive-neutral observer, then the objective correlations to our sensations remain purely mental, lacking any real counter-force able to resist the subject—within this mode, of course, all I have direct access to are my sensations, and all other entities are my "mental constructs." In short, if Fichte were to have remained at this level, he would have really been a Berkeleyan subjectivist (as Lenin wrongly assumed in his *Materialism and Empirio-Criticism*). So the key question is: how does the relationship between subject and object become one of real opposition, that is, how does the external world become a real opposing force to the I? According to Fichte, this happens only when our mind adopts a practical stance towards the world. In the theoretical-observational stance, it is easy to conceive of reality as a mere dream that unfolds in front of our eyes—but reality "hurts" and resists us once we start intervening in it and trying to change it. Here enters, of course, Fichte's infamous "spurious infinity": the practical Self can never totally overcome the resistance of the not-I, so "the self's original practical constitution is a striving (*Streben*)"—ultimately the endless ethical striving to create a reality that would fully conform to the moral ideal.[70]

Here, however, another surprise awaits us. Fichte does not remain at the level of abstract/indeterminate striving, but tries to show how this striving (corresponding to pure subjective inwardness) becomes determinate in the guise of a particular object—and the name he chooses for this object-which-is-determinate-striving is none other than *drive*: "What begins as indeterminate

68 Ibid., pp. 214–15.

69 Ibid., p. 221.

70 Ibid., p. 213.

striving becomes determinate, once it is an object of thought. We may well wonder what this object is which simultaneously has the nature of striving. Fichte's answer: 'This object is a drive (*Trieb*).'"[71] The parallel with Freud is here truly breathtaking: in exactly the same way that, in Fichte's conception of drive, striving is posited as such (i.e., in its limitation-determination), the drive for Freud is always irreducibly linked to a partial object. Fichte accomplishes here a crucial step beyond subjectivism which Lacan himself was not able to make until his *Seminar XI* (1963–4). Prior to this date, Lacan really did not know what to do with the Freudian drive or "libido"—basically, he reduced it to the scientific objectification/"reification" of the authentic intersubjective reality of desire. Only with *Seminar XI* was Lacan able to *think* the Freudian drive as an uncanny "undead" partial object.

The first modern theology

Only against this background of Fichte's complex position can we properly approach the genealogical topic of Jacobi's necessary role in the passage from Kant to Fichte. Fichte's reaction to Jacobi's criticism of Kant is paradigmatic of how a true philosopher proceeds, fearlessly running against the grain of the predominant common sense. Jacobi claimed that Kant was inconsistent in his clinging to the notion of a Thing-in-itself: the only truly consistent transcendental philosophy would have been "transcendental egoism"—the denial of the real givenness of other minds, and of any knowledge of an external world: we are never in contact with anything other than our own minds, even our most immediate sensations are nothing but qualifications of our mental states. "Kant should have had the courage to teach this theory, but he shrank from it."[72] For Jacobi, of course, this result is patently absurd, self-refuting, a clear example of the kind of blind alley down which philosophical speculation can lead; he mentions it merely in order to step out of the domain of philosophy and advocate a return to the original "irrational" beliefs of humanity: "philosophy could never be a satisfactory explication of reality," since "any philosophy whatsoever, once made consistent, inevitably denies fundamental beliefs that no human life can abandon."[73] Fichte, however, did *not* shrink from the full implications of Kant's transcendentalism: he met Jacobi's challenge and openly endorsed what Jacobi had deemed an absurd (im)possibility. Note how the triad Kant-Jacobi-Fichte reverses the expected "normal" succession of philosophical positions: it is not that a half-way position is first radicalized to its consistent-but-absurd

71 Ibid., p. 218.
72 Ibid., p. 111.
73 Ibid., p. 109.

conclusion and then rejected; on the contrary, what is first treated as a *reductio ad absurdum*, proposed ironically as a plainly nonsensical and self-defeating radicalization, is then taken seriously and fully endorsed. The truly tragic position here is Jacobi's: he outlined the contours of an extreme position he abhorred (transcendental egoism), with the critical intent of combating tendencies that might lead towards it, but his efforts had the unintended consequence of providing a program for his opponents to follow—to "understand the world in terms of the self-referential nature of the mind."[74]

The key question is thus: how did what appeared to Jacobi (and also to Kant) as a nonsensical "transcendental egoism" suddenly become a viable philosophical option? What changed in the underlying presuppositions? This brings us to what Henrich repeatedly analyzes as "Fichte's fundamental insight," the core of which is the critical rejection of the self-reflective model of self-consciousness: self-consciousness cannot be accounted for as a second-level consciousness, a mind turning its eye upon itself, taking itself as its object; that is, it is not that there is first a consciousness of objects and then the mind bends back and makes itself its object—this would involve an infinite regress, plus it would leave unanswered the simple question: when I see myself as an object, how do I recognize it as "myself"? It is, rather, that I must in a certain way already be pre-reflexively acquainted with myself (what Henrich calls *Selbst-Vertrautheit*) in order to be able to recognize "myself" in the object of reflection. But Fichte does not stop here, with this vague notion of a pre-reflexive self-awareness or self-acquaintance; he develops all the consequences of the failure of the self-reflexive model of self-consciousness, the first of which is his own version of Lacan's axiom *il n'y a pas de méta-langage*: self-consciousness is caught in an inescapable circle or, rather, a self-referential loop—a human mind is not only aware of itself, *it exists only through this (self-)awareness, for itself*:

> the faculty of representation (i.e., the mind) does not exist at all except *for* the faculty of representation. There is no mind *plus* something for which it is that would entail a separation between the mind and its being-for-X. There is no access to the mind from the outside; and there is no mind that is not already for itself. The very essence of the mind is its self-referential character.[75]

There is thus no "objective" approach to self-consciousness (I): if we look at it from the outside, it disappears, dissolving into an objective psycho-physical process:

74 Ibid., p. 209.
75 Ibid., p. 171.

> The faculty of representation exists *for* the faculty of representation and *through* the faculty of representation: this is the circle within which every finite understanding, that is, every understanding that we can conceive, is necessarily confined. Anyone who wants to escape from this circle does not understand himself and does not know what he wants.[76]

Note here the absolutely crucial invocation of finitude: the circle holds for "every *finite* understanding." What this means is that the self-relating loop of the I is not a sign of its absolute/infinite power (as in primitive solipsistic subjectivism, where the I is the only absolute/infinite reality which creates everything else), but, on the contrary, the sign of its finitude. So when we read in Fichte what can only appear to common sense as ridiculously overblown statements about the absolute I positing itself and then, within the absolute I, op-positing the finite I and the finite non-I, we should always bear in mind that the I's self-positing is not a miracle performed by a quasi-divine infinite entity which acts as *causa sui* (like Baron Münchhausen pulling himself out of the swamp by his own hair)—on the contrary, the closed loop of self-relating is the sign of the I's ultimate finitude, of its being caught within its own horizon, of being itself only for itself.

The key term "positing" is to be opposed here to "reflecting": in self-consciousness, the I does not reflect upon itself as its own object, it directly posits itself—which means that we cannot even distinguish between the positing subject and the subject as the result of this positing. As Fichte puts it, the I absolutely posits itself *as positing*, it "is" nothing but the process of its (self-) positing. Fichte's formulation is very precise and has to be taken literally: it is not just that the mind (I) relates to itself—the mind (I) is *nothing but* this process of self-relating. Therein lies the circle or loop Fichte talks about: the relating itself not only creates what it relates to, it also *is* what it relates to.

But even this—the notion of the I's absolute self-positing—is only the first step. Around 1800, Fichte engaged in a closer and very refined analysis of the I's self-positing, and arrived at a further surprising result, a kind of "splitting the atom" of the absolute I's self-positing: he discovered that the most elementary structure of self-consciousness—the I's self-positing—is more complex than it initially appears, and displays a precise structure. Fichte's starting point is that the Self is not a product of some pre-subjective activity that generates it—the Self comes immediately with the activity. Already in 1795, Fichte employed the metaphor of the eye (*das Auge*): the Self is an activity into which an eye is inserted, an activity which sees itself and is only through seeing itself. His next step is to admit that "we cannot *account* for the duality of the activity and the eye in terms of one of them alone": "Neither the eye nor the activity can provide this account. In this moment, the idea of a ground of the structure becomes

76 Ibid., pp. 66–7.

indispensable."[77] In other words, the concept of the Self loses its explanatory power: it can no longer be the ultimate *explanans*, but is itself in need of explanation. It is here that Fichte confronts his greatest theoretical challenge: how can one conceive this Ground of the Self without betraying the basic insight into the I's self-positing, into how the I exists only for the I, and without thereby regressing into a pre-Kantian metaphysics in which the Ground is God as a noumenal Thing which *de facto* cancels the I's freedom, deprecating it as a mere "subjective" illusion?

The only solution is for self-consciousness (i.e., the I) to be "incorporated into the ground rather than only being … an effect of it":[78] in self-consciousness, the Ground itself "enters into a relationship of self-reference," that is, the I's self-consciousness is simultaneously and immediately the self-consciousness of the Ground itself.[79] The interdependence of the Ground and self-consciousness is here radically ontological and not merely epistemological: it is not only that the Ground becomes aware of itself through the I's self-consciousness; insofar as the Ground constitutes self-consciousness, we should say that the Ground "is what it is only *in* what it constitutes."[80]

In his very subtle reading in which he tries to reconstruct Fichte's implicit reasoning, Henrich points out that Fichte here imperceptibly introduces a notion of self-relating that is radically different from the self-relating of the absolute I who is nothing but its own self-positing: because of this new notion of relation, we have to interpret "the knowledge *of* the product about itself and its origin as an ontological relation between the ground and itself, by way of its essential product, the mind":[81] "self-consciousness relates itself to the absolute ground and presupposition of its activity; but self-consciousness also relates itself to *itself*, because the ultimate ground and activity is nothing but the manifestation of itself *in self-consciousness*."[82]

God not only has to manifest itself, but is *nothing but* its own self-manifestation (in an exact homology to the I which not only posits itself, but is nothing but its self-positing); only in this way is God not a Thing-in-itself which as such limits human freedom. A being which exists only through its self-manifestation is a living being, and so it is because of this thoroughly processual character of God that Fichte calls the Ground of the Self life: "God is nothing but spiritual life."[83]

---

77 Ibid., p. 267.
78 Ibid.
79 Ibid., p. 269.
80 Ibid., p. 267.
81 Ibid., p. 270.
82 Ibid., p. 272.
83 Ibid., p. 271

But in spite of this full immanence of the free self-consciousness to the Ground, "this process of the world is absolutely justified by virtue of itself. *We* are only essential elements in it, 'essential' only as vehicles *for* it. The manifestation takes place in and by ourselves, but what is manifested is not our own individual nature."[84] What this means is that, with his fateful step towards the Ground of the I, Fichte nonetheless violates the basic axiom of his project of the science of knowledge, the thesis that the I exists only for the I as absolutely self-positing, i.e., that there cannot be any external ground for it.

Fichte's passage to theology is thus again not simply a consequence of the insight into how the self-positing I is an illusion of groundless self-relating which would have imploded into nothingness without an external supporting Ground. Henrich provides a detailed analysis of the line of reasoning which brought Fichte to pass from the absolute I to God as the ultimate ground of being. Fichte's problem here is this: how can one conceive of a trans-subjective God, a God who grounds subjectivity, but who is nonetheless *not* a Thing-in-itself? The problem is strictly homologous to that of the Marxist notion of class (self-)consciousness (or, more generally, ideological consciousness): how to conceive of the self-consciousness's dependence on the Ground (the "economic base," the material process of social life) without falling into "economic reductionism" and conceiving self-consciousness as a mere "ideological effect" of the economic material process which is the only "real"?[85]

Henrich is right to try to explicate Fichte's implicit reasoning, but perhaps he is not clear enough in showing how Fichte's oscillations and ambiguities demonstrate two things simultaneously: (1) that there is a deep necessity involved in accomplishing the step to the Ground of the Self's freedom, and to the irreducible multiplicity of Selves which coexist within this Ground; and (2) that, within Fichte's horizon, it is impossible to accomplish this step, in other words, that all of Fichte's reasoning is false and ultimately irrelevant here. In short, Fichte is confronting the Real of his thought—something simultaneously both necessary and impossible. And—to make a leap of thought, if not of faith—there is a concept which fits perfectly Fichte's requirements for the Ground of freedom: Lacan's concept of the "big Other." (We leave aside here the complex relationship between the big Other and Hegel's "objective Spirit.") This is why Fichte can conceive God as the spiritual Life in which individual self-consciousnesses participate; it is not a limitation of the I's freedom, but its very ground. This is how he tries to realize the project of the "Spinozism of freedom," and this is why his theology is

---

84 Ibid., p. 272.

85 No wonder, then, that Fichte's description of the relationship between Ground and self-consciousness often sounds like the young Lukács's attempt to conceive of class-consciousness not as a passive "reflection" of its economic ground-base but as its immanent constituent.

> the first *modern* theology and perhaps the only one—Hegel's, of course, being the alternative. It qualifies as the first modern theology because it contains a potential for overcoming the antagonism between freedom and religion. Fichte conceives of the concept of God in such a way that, by definition, God cannot impose any restriction upon freedom. God is manifestation, and manifestation takes place in free self-reference. For this reason, it is absolutely unintelligible to think of God as a person who imposes demands on human beings. Fichte's conception of God precludes this antagonism.[86]

As Henrich demonstrates, Fichte cannot resolve the problem of the multiplicity of I's—not only how to account for it, i.e., describe its genesis, but how even to conceive of it. That is to say, the moment Fichte introduces the idea of a pre-subjective Ground of the I, he has to confront the question of how a multitude of I's can coexist and interact within this shared Ground. The problem here is that, once we accept the premise of a pre- and trans-subjective order which serves as the subjects' shared Ground,

> the order in which these distinct selves exist would prove not to be mental at all. In other words, any individual self is a closed system, and while there are many individual selves, the manifestation takes place in all selves individually. In order for us to account for the existence of such an order of different selves, we would have to violate Fichte's methodological principle, because now we would invoke a non-mental structure that is, nevertheless, essential for understanding what the mind is.[87]

This leads Fichte to postulate—in a wholly justified immanent way—an a- or pre-subjective knowledge: insofar as the divine Ground is not a blind mechanical substance, but a spiritual order, an order of knowledge, and, simultaneously, anonymous/pre-subjective, we must presuppose that "something that is already knowledge precedes the individual selves."[88] In other words, against any kind of phenomenological deduction of this knowledge out of inter-subjective interaction, we must presuppose that,

> rather than all knowledge somehow belonging to the knower (the self-asserting self), now the knowing subjects have to *belong to this non-individual epistemic process* ... the primary, anonymous knowledge, which Fichte always tried to render plausible by appeal to the paradigm of mathematical evidence (a somewhat Platonic move), is a form of knowledge that we cannot in any way claim to be individualized.[89]

---

86 Henrich, *Between Kant and Hegel*, p. 273.
87 Ibid., p. 281.
88 Ibid.
89 Ibid., pp. 281–3.

And it is only here that Fichte reaches the true limit of his daring endeavor: although this structure of anonymous knowledge is pre-subjective, it *has* to include "a dimension with respect to which we can distinguish a multitude of individual knowers ... This means that any of these selves knows, in advance, that there *are* other selves, despite having no direct access to their minds."[90] The problem Fichte struggles with (and cannot resolve) here corresponds perfectly to the problem in Claude Lévi-Strauss's "structural anthropology" solved by Lacan: what kind of subject fits the symbolic structure? How can we think the immanence of the excluded subject to the anonymous symbolic structure (big Other)? Or, to put it the other way round: what kind of structure do we have to think so that it effectively involves the subject, not only as its epiphenomenal "effect," but as its immanent constituent? Lacan's answer, of course, is that the condition of freedom (of a free subject) is the "barred" big Other, a structure which is inconsistent, with gaps.

As Henrich demonstrates in a detailed reconstruction of Fichte's reasoning, the close analysis of the structure of subjective self-relating reveals a split in the midst of subjectivity: a split between the subject's immediate (but pre-conceptual) self-acquaintance (self-awareness) and a moment of knowledge which is not yet subjectivized but remains "anonymous"—is this not precisely the split between $\$$ and S_2, the signifying chain of knowledge? How can the two be mediated? Through S_1, which represents the subject in the chain of knowledge at the site of its inconsistency.

The Lacanian notion of *le grand Autre* (the big Other, vaguely corresponding to what Hegel called "objective spirit" or the "spiritual substance" of individual lives), triumphantly resolves this problem. The big Other is a totally subjectivized substance: not a Thing-in-itself, but a Substance which exists only insofar as it is continuously sustained by the work of "all and everyone." Reproducing Fichte's formula of the subject's self-positing, the big Other is the Ground-presupposition which *is* only as permanently "posited" by subjects.

Fichte cannot resolve the status of Ground because he does not have at his disposal a term which would designate an entity that is not-mental, that is asubjective, and yet at the same time is not a material "thing," but purely ideal. This, however, is exactly what the Lacanian "big Other" is: it is definitely not-mental (Lacan repeatedly emphasizes that the status of the big Other is not psychological), it does not belong to the order of the subject's experience; but it is also not the pre-symbolic material Real, a thing or process in reality independent of subjectivity—the status of the big Other is purely *virtual*, as an ideal structure of reference; that is, it exists only as the subject's presupposition. (The big Other is thus close to what Karl Popper, in his late writings, designated as

90 Ibid., p. 283.

the Third World, neither objective reality nor subjective inner experience.) The Lacanian "big Other" also resolves the problem of the plurality of subjects: its role is precisely that of the Third, the very medium of the encounter between subjects.

This is also how one should approach Hegel's outrageously "speculative" formulations about Spirit as its own result, as a product of itself: while "Spirit has its beginnings in nature in general,"

> the extreme to which spirit tends is its freedom, its infinity, its being in and for itself. These are the two aspects; but if we ask what Spirit is, the immediate answer is that it is this motion, this process of proceeding from, of freeing itself from, nature; this is the being, the substance of spirit itself.[91]

Spirit is thus radically de-substantialized: Spirit is not a positive counter-force to nature, a different substance which gradually breaks and shines through the inert natural stuff; it is *nothing but* this process of freeing-itself-from. Hegel explicitly disowns the notion of Spirit as some kind of positive Agent which underlies the process:

> Spirit is usually spoken of as subject, as doing something, and apart from what it does, as this motion, this process, as still something particular, its activity being more or less contingent … it is of the very nature of spirit to be this absolute liveliness, this process, to proceed forth from naturality, immediacy, to sublate, to quit its naturality, and to come to itself, and *to free itself*, it being itself only as it comes to itself as such a product of itself; *its actuality being merely that it has made itself into what it is.*[92]

If "it is *only* as a result of itself that it is spirit,"[93] then this means that the standard talk about the Hegelian Spirit which alienates itself to itself and then recognizes itself in its otherness and thus reappropriates its content is deeply misleading: the Self to which spirit returns is produced in the very movement of this return; or, that to which the process of return returns to is produced by the very process of returning. Recall here the concise and unsurpassed formulations from Hegel's *Logic* on how essence

> presupposes itself and the sublating of this presupposition is essence itself; conversely, this sublating of its presupposition is the presupposition itself. Reflection

91 G. W. F. Hegel, *Hegels Philosophie des subjektiven Geistes/Hegel's Philosophy of Subjective Spirit*, trans. and ed. M. J. Petry, Dordrecht: D. Reidel 1978, pp. 6–7.
92 Ibid.
93 Ibid.

> therefore *finds before it* an immediate which it transcends and from which it is the return. But this return is only the presupposing of what reflection finds before it. What it thus found only *comes to be* through being *left behind* ... For the presupposition of the return-into-self—that from which essence *comes*, and is only as this return—is only in the return itself.[94]

When Hegel says that a Notion is the result of itself, that it provides its own actualization, this claim which at first cannot but appear extravagant (the notion is not simply a thought activated by the thinking subject, but that it possesses a magic property of self-movement ...), loses its mystery the moment we grasp that the Spirit as the spiritual substance is a substance, an In-itself, which sustains itself *only* through the incessant activity of the subjects engaged in it. Say, a nation exists *only* insofar as its members take themselves to be members of this nation and act accordingly; it has absolutely no content, no substantial consistence, outside this activity. The same goes for, say, the notion of communism—this notion "generates its own actualization" by way of motivating people to struggle for it.

Henrich raises here what is for him a key question: can Hegel (and Schelling, we have to add) account for the central problem with which Fichte struggled through his entire life, that of self-relating subjectivity? Fichte and Hegel share the project of grasping the basic ontological structure of reality *simultaneously* as complete self-reference and as the struggle of oppositions. So while both their systems are based on a self-referential structure, the specific matrix of self-reference is different in each case: Fichte focuses on the mental self-reference that constitutes the I and on the I's self-identification (How do I know who I am?), whereas Hegel's matrix is that of the self-relating negation. With this shift of focus, Hegel never even encountered the problem Fichte struggled with his whole life; so the crucial question (ignored by Hegel) is: can one demonstrate, from the Hegelian premises, that once we move within the matrix of self-relating negation, the Fichtean problem of mental self-relating can either be resolved or else dismissed as an illusory pseudo-problem? Henrich's reply is a negative one, which is why he insists that we bear in mind "not only the correspondence between the failures of Fichte and the merits of Hegel, but also that between the merits of Fichte and the failures of Hegel."[95] In other words, there is no unilateral progress in German Idealism: each of its four great names (Kant,

94 G. W. F. Hegel, *Hegel's Science of Logic*, Atlantic Highlands: Humanities Press International 1989, p. 402. Various nationalist movements with their striving to "return to the origins" are exemplary here: it is the very return to the "lost origins" which literally constitutes what was lost, and, in this sense, the Nation/notion—as a spiritual substance—is the "product of itself."

95 Henrich, *Between Kant and Hegel*, p. 330.

Fichte, Schelling, Hegel) struggled with a fundamental problem and ultimately failed to resolve it, but this does not mean that each linear successor resolved his predecessor's problem in a move of *Aufhebung*—rather, the successor radically changed the field, so that the problem itself disappeared. Fichte "missed the point" of Kant's thought; Schelling and Hegel "missed the point" of Fichte's (and of each other's).

Measured by his own inherent standards, the passage in Fichte from the self-positing subject to its ground (God as infinite Life) is not a compromise, a withdrawal from his earlier assertion of radical subjectivity, but a necessary consequence of thinking through the implications of the very notion of subjectivity. The subject is not only or principally the active agent who "posits" (creates, dominates, exploits) objectivity (Heidegger), but a site of "abstraction," tearing apart the links of organic totality, illusion, finitude—of what we refer to as "merely subjective." Subject only emerges as a gap in substance, as an effect of its incompleteness/inconsistency. This is what Hegel *celebrates* as the absolute power of Understanding: "The action of separating the elements is the exercise of the force of Understanding, the most astonishing and greatest of all powers, or rather the absolute power." This celebration is in no way qualified; that is, Hegel's point is not that this power is nonetheless later "sublated" into a subordinate moment of the unifying totality of Reason. The problem with Understanding is rather that it does not unleash this power to the end, that it takes it as external to the thing itself—like, in the above-quoted passage from the *Phenomenology*, the standard notion that it is merely *our* Understanding ("mind") that separates in its imagination what in "reality" belongs together, so that the Understanding's "absolute power" is merely the power of our imagination which in no way concerns the reality of the thing analyzed. We pass from Understanding to Reason not when this analyzing, or tearing apart, is overcome in a synthesis which brings us back to the wealth of reality, but when this "tearing apart" is displaced from being "merely a power of our mind" onto things themselves, as their inherent power of negativity.—And the key dialectical insight is that the "synthesis," the bringing-together of what was torn apart by Understanding, is the absolute, most radical, act of tearing apart—a violent imposition of unity.

Henrich correctly locates Hegel's great breakthrough, the moment "Hegel became Hegel," at the precise point where he dropped the "methodological distinction between the critical and the systematic discourses (*reflectionis* and *rationis*),"[96] between the critical analysis of the notions of Understanding and the positive deployment of the categories in the guise of a constructive system of Reason: the positive system of Reason is nothing but the "way towards itself" through the dialectical analysis of the categories of Understanding. He also

96 Ibid., p. 313.

correctly claims that this tension nonetheless persists in the guise of the difference between the *Phenomenology of Spirit* and the *Science of Logic*: how does the *Phenomenology* relate to the system? Is it an external introduction to it or part of it? The problem is not only an abstract one; it gets complicated by the fact that many of the analyses of the *Phenomenology* are (sometimes almost verbatim) included in the system (for example, the dialectic of the struggle of consciousness[es] for recognition reappears at the beginning—second chapter of part one—of the *Philosophy of Spirit*).

What makes Henrich's reflections so interesting is that he relies on them in his critique of Marx (and of Marx's critique of Hegel); his basic claim is that Marx's project of the critique of ideology "depends on the conceptual apparatus of the *Phenomenology of Spirit*," which is why, in his critique of Hegel's *Philosophy of Right*, Marx cannot properly get Hegel's notion of the State (which already presupposes the notional structure of the *Science of Logic*).[97] The problem Hegel struggles with in his *Philosophy of Right* is that a fully realized autonomy and freedom do not consist only in

> accepting and following the will's own law, but also involve requiring that there be a reality that corresponds structurally to the will's own structure … Hegel's answer is that it is the rational state whose good constitution respects the freedom of its citizens. This is the *structure* in reality that corresponds to the internal structure of the will.[98]

For this precise reason, a state is not only an instrument of civil society destined to guarantee the satisfaction of its subjects' particular needs: the subjects do not accept the laws of their rational state "*because* it provides for the fulfillment of all the needs of the natural individual. Instead, the will accepts the state because *only* with reference to it can the self-reference of the will's own structure be completed."[99] Henrich's critique of Marx should thus in no way be dismissed as a proof that he "remains caught up in bourgeois ideology."

The Marxist analysis of the state as a structure of class domination (and, in this sense, as an instrument of civil society) misses the crucial problem Hegel was struggling with, "leaving the *objective* issue between Hegel's institutionalism of freedom and socialism (with its spontaneity) entirely unsettled."[100] The price paid for this neglect was that the problem returned with a vengeance in the guise of the Stalinist "totalitarian" state.

---

97 Ibid., p. 328.
98 Ibid., p. 326.
99 Ibid., p. 327.
100 Ibid., p. 329.

Part 2

THE THING ITSELF: HEGEL

CHAPTER 4

Is It Still Possible to Be a Hegelian Today?

The main feature of historical thought proper is not "mobilism" (the motif of the fluidification or historical relativization of all forms of life), but the full endorsement of a certain *impossibility*: after a true historical break, one simply cannot return to the past, or go on as if nothing happened—even if one does, the same practice will have acquired a radically changed meaning. Adorno provided a nice example with Schoenberg's atonal revolution: after it took place, it was (and is), of course, possible to go on composing in the traditional tonal way, but the new tonal music has lost its innocence, since it is already "mediated" by the atonal break and thus functions as its negation. This is why there is an irreducible element of *kitsch* in twentieth-century tonal composers such as Rachmaninov—something of a nostalgic clinging to the past, something fake, like the adult who tries to keep alive the naïve child within. And the same goes for all other domains: with the emergence of Plato's philosophical analysis of notions, mythical thought loses its immediacy, any revival of it becomes fake; after Christianity, revivals of paganism become nostalgic simulacra.

Writing, thinking, or composing as if a Rupture has not occurred is more ambiguous than it may appear and cannot be reduced to a non-historical denial. Badiou once famously wrote that what unites him with Deleuze is that they are both classical philosophers for whom Kant, the Kantian break, did not happen—but is this really so? Maybe this holds for Deleuze, but definitely not for Badiou.[1] Nowhere is this clearer than in their different handling of the Event. For Deleuze, an Event really is a pre-Kantian cosmological One which generates a multitude, which is why the Event is absolutely immanent to reality, while the Badiouian Event is a break in the order of being (transcendentally constituted phenomenal reality), the intrusion of a radically heterogeneous ("noumenal") order, so that we are clearly in (post-)Kantian space. This is why one can even define Badiou's systematic philosophy (developed in his last masterpiece, *Logics of Worlds*) as Kantianism reinvented for the epoch of radical contingency: instead of one

1 Even with Deleuze, one can claim that his Spinoza is a post-Kantian Spinoza, a Spinoza imperceptibly re-read through a post-Kantian frame. Deleuze does something like Fellini in *Satyricon*, where he stages the Roman pagan universe the way it appears retrospectively, from the Christian standpoint—with the underlying idea that one can really grasp what paganism was only in this retrospective way.

transcendentally constituted reality, we get a multiplicity of worlds, each delineated by its transcendental matrix, a multiplicity which cannot be mediated/unified into a single larger transcendental frame; instead of the moral Law, we get fidelity to the Truth-Event, which is always specific with regard to a particular situation of a World.

Is not Hegel's speculative idealism *the* exemplary case of such a properly historical impossibility? Can one still be a Hegelian after the post-Hegelian break with traditional metaphysics which occurred more or less simultaneously in the works of Schopenhauer, Kierkegaard, and Marx? After all this, is there not something inherently false in advocating a Hegelian "absolute Idealism"? Will not any re-affirmation of Hegel fall victim to the same anti-historical illusion, by-passing the impossibility of being a Hegelian after the post-Hegelian break, writing as if that break had not happened? Here, however, one should complicate things a little bit: under certain conditions, one can and should write as if a break had not happened. What are these conditions? To put it simply and directly: when the break in question is not a true but a false break, in fact one which obliterates the true break, the true point of impossibility. Our wager is that this, precisely, is what happened with the "official" post-Hegelian anti-philosophical break (Schopenhauer-Kierkegaard-Marx): although it presents itself as a break with idealism as embodied in its Hegelian climax, it ignores a crucial dimension of Hegel's thought; that is, it ultimately amounts to a desperate attempt to *go on thinking as if Hegel had not happened*. The hole left by this absence of Hegel is then, of course, filled in with the ridiculous caricature of Hegel the "absolute idealist" who "possessed Absolute Knowledge." The re-assertion of Hegel's speculative thought is thus not what it may appear to be—a denial of the post-Hegelian break—but rather a bringing-forth of that very dimension whose denial sustains the post-Hegelian break itself.

Hegel versus Nietzsche

Let us develop this point apropos of Gérard Lebrun's posthumously published *L'envers de la dialectique*, one of the most convincing and forceful attempts to demonstrate the impossibility of being Hegelian today—and, for Lebrun, "today" stands under the sign of Nietzsche.[2]

Lebrun accepts that one cannot "refute" Hegel: the machinery of his dialectics is so all-encompassing that nothing is easier for Hegel than to demonstrate

2 See Gérard Lebrun, *L'envers de la dialectique: Hegel à la lumière de Nietzsche*, Paris: Seuil 2004. The irony is that, three decades earlier, Lebrun published one of the greatest books on Hegel, defending him against his critics: *La patience du concept* (Paris: Gallimard 1973).

triumphantly how all such refutations are inconsistent, to turn them against themselves ("one cannot refute an eye disease," as Lebrun quotes Nietzsche approvingly). Most ridiculous among such critical refutations is, of course, the standard Marxist-evolutionist idea that there is a contradiction between Hegel's dialectical method—which demonstrates how every fixed determination is swept away by the movement of negativity, how every determinate shape finds its truth in its annihilation—and Hegel's system: if the destiny of everything is to pass away in the eternal movement of self-sublation, does the same not hold for the system itself? Is not Hegel's own system a temporary, historically relative formation which will be overcome by the progress of knowledge? Anyone who finds such a refutation convincing is not to be taken seriously as a reader of Hegel.

How, then, can one move beyond Hegel? Lebrun's solution goes by way of Nietzschean historical philology: one should bring to light the "eminently infra-rational" lexical choices which are grounded in how living beings cope with threats to their vital interests. Before Hegel sets in motion his dialectical machinery, which "swallows up" all content and elevates it to its truth by destroying it in its immediate being, a complex network of semantic decisions has already been taken imperceptibly. In uncovering these, one begins to "unveil the obverse of the dialectics. Dialectics is also partial. It also obfuscates its presuppositions. It is not the meta-discourse it pretends to be with regard to the philosophies of 'Understanding.'"[3] Lebrun's Nietzsche is decidedly anti-Heideggerian: for Lebrun, Heidegger re-philosophizes Nietzsche by way of interpreting the Will to Power as a new ontological First Principle. More than Nietzschean, Lebrun's approach may appear Foucauldian: what he aims at is an "archaeology of the Hegelian knowledge," its genealogy in concrete life-practices.

But is Lebrun's "philological" strategy radical enough in philosophical terms? Does it not amount to a new version of historicist hermeneutics or, rather, of a Foucauldian succession of epochal *epistemi*? Does this not, if not legitimize, at least render understandable Heidegger's re-philosophization of Nietzsche? That is to say, one should raise the question of the ontological status of the "power" which sustains particular "philological" configurations—for Nietzsche himself, it is the Will to Power; for Heidegger, it is the abyssal game of "there is" which "sends" different epochal configurations of the disclosure of the world. In any case, one cannot avoid ontology: historicist hermeneutics cannot stand on its own. Heidegger's history of Being is an attempt to elevate historical (not historicist) hermeneutics directly into transcendental ontology: there is for Heidegger nothing behind or beneath what Lebrun calls infra-rational semantic choices; they are the ultimate fact/horizon of our being. Heidegger, however,

3 Lebrun, *L'envers de la dialectique*, p. 23.

leaves open what one might call the *ontic* question: there are obscure hints all through his work of a "reality" which persists out there prior to its ontological disclosure. That is to say, Heidegger in no way equates the epochal disclosure of Being with any kind of "creation"—he repeatedly concedes as an un-problematic fact that, even prior to their epochal disclosure or outside it, things somehow "are" (persist) out there, although they do not yet "exist" in the full sense of being disclosed "as such," as part of a historical world. But what is the status of this ontic persistence outside of ontological disclosure?[4]

From the Nietzschean standpoint, there is more in the "infra-rational" semantic decisions than the fact that every approach to reality has to rely on a pre-existing set of hermeneutic "prejudices" or, as Heidegger would have put it, on a certain epochal disclosure of being: these decisions effectuate the vital pre-reflexive strategy of the Will to Power. For such an approach, Hegel remains a profoundly Christian thinker, a nihilist whose basic strategy is to repackage a profound defeat, the withdrawal from life in all its painful vitality, as a triumph of the absolute Subject. That is to say, from the standpoint of the Will to Power, the effective content of the Hegelian process is one long story of defeats and withdrawals, of sacrifices of vital self-assertion: again and again, one has to renounce vital engagement as still too "immediate" and "particular." Exemplary is here Hegel's passage from the Revolutionary Terror to the Kantian morality: the utilitarian subject of civil society, the subject who wants to reduce the State to being the guardian of his private safety and well-being, has to be crushed by the Terror of the revolutionary State which can annihilate him at any moment for no reason whatsoever (the subject is not punished for something he has done, for some particular content or act, but for the very fact of being an independent individual opposed to the universal)—this Terror is his "truth." So how do we pass from Revolutionary Terror to Kant's autonomous and free moral subject? By way of what, in more contemporary language, one could call a full identification with the aggressor: the subject should recognize in the external Terror, in this negativity which constantly threatens to annihilate him, the very core of his (universal) subjectivity; in other words, he should fully identify with it. Freedom is thus not freedom *from* a Master, but the replacement of one Master with another: the external Master is replaced with an internal one. The price for this identification is, of course, the sacrifice of all "pathological" particular content—duty should be accomplished "for the sake of duty."

4 And, incidentally, Lacan's *prima facie* weird decision to stick to the term "subject" in spite of Heidegger's well-known critique of subjectivity is grounded precisely in this obscure excess of the ontic over its ontological disclosure: "subject" is for Lacan not the self-present autonomous agent reducing the whole of reality to its object, but a *pathetic* subject, that which suffers, which pays the price for being the site of the ontological disclosure in ontic flesh—the price whose Freudian name is, of course, "castration."

Lebrun demonstrates how this same logic holds also for language:

> State and language are two complementary figures of the Subject's accomplishment: here as well as there, the sense that I am and the sense that I enunciate are submitted to the same imperceptible sacrifice of what appeared to be our "self" in the illusion of immediacy.[5]

Hegel was right to point out again and again that, when one talks, one always dwells in the universal—which means that, with its entry into language, the subject loses its roots in the concrete life world. To put it in more pathetic terms, the moment I start to talk, I am no longer the sensually concrete I, since I am caught up in an impersonal mechanism which always makes me say something different from what I wanted to say—as the early Lacan liked to say, I am not speaking, I am being spoken by language. This is one way to understand what Lacan called "symbolic castration": the price the subject pays for its "transubstantiation" from being the agent of a direct animal vitality to being a speaking subject whose identity is kept apart from the direct vitality of passions.

A Nietzschean reading easily discerns in this reversal of Terror into autonomous morality a desperate strategy of turning defeat into triumph: instead of heroically fighting for one's vital interests, one pre-emptively declares total surrender and gives up all content. Lebrun is here well aware how unjustified the standard critique of Hegel is according to which the dialectical reversal of utter negativity into a new higher positivity, of catastrophe into triumph, functions as a kind of *deus ex machina*, precluding the possibility that the catastrophe might be the final outcome of the process—the well-known common-sense argument: "But what if there is no reversal of negativity into a new positive order?" This argument misses the point, which is that this is, precisely, what happens in the Hegelian reversal: there is no real reversal of defeat into triumph but only a purely formal shift, a change of perspective, which tries to present defeat itself as a triumph. Nietzsche's point is that this triumph is a fake, a cheap magician's trick, a consolation prize for losing all that makes life worth living: the real loss of vitality is supplemented by a lifeless specter. In Lebrun's Nietzschean reading, Hegel thus appears as a kind of atheist Christian philosopher: like Christianity, he locates the "truth" of all terrestrial finite reality in its (self-)annihilation—reality reaches its truth only through/in its self-destruction; unlike Christianity, Hegel is well aware that there is no Other World in which we will be repaid for our terrestrial losses: transcendence is absolutely immanent, *what is "beyond" finite reality is nothing but the immanent process of its self-overcoming.* Hegel's name for this absolute immanence of transcendence is "absolute negativity," as

5 Lebrun, *L'envers de la dialectique*, p. 83.

he makes clear in an exemplary way in the dialectics of Master and Servant: the Servant's secure particular/finite identity is unsettled when, in experiencing the fear of death during his confrontation with the Master, he gets a whiff of the infinite power of negativity; through this experience, the Servant is forced to accept the worthlessness of his particular Self:

> For this consciousness was not in peril and fear for this element or that, nor for this or that moment of time, it was afraid for its entire being; it felt the fear of death, the sovereign master. It has been in that experience melted to its inmost soul, has trembled throughout its every fibre, and all that was fixed and steadfast has quaked within it. This complete perturbation of its entire substance, this absolute dissolution of all its stability into fluent continuity, is, however, the simple, ultimate nature of self-consciousness, absolute negativity, pure self-relating existence, which consequently is involved in this type of consciousness.[6]

What, then, does the Servant get in exchange for renouncing all the wealth of his particular Self? *Nothing*—in overcoming his particular terrestrial Self, the Servant does not reach a higher level of a spiritual Self; all he has to do is to shift his position and recognize in (what appears to him as) the overwhelming power of destruction which threatens to obliterate his particular identity the absolute negativity which forms the very core of his own Self. In short, the subject has to fully identify with the force that threatens to wipe him out: what he feared in fearing death was the negative power of his own Self. There is thus no reversal of negativity into positive greatness—the only "greatness" here is this negativity itself. Or, with regard to suffering: Hegel's point is not that the suffering brought about by the alienating labor of renunciation is an intermediary moment that must be patiently endured while we wait for our reward at the end of the tunnel—there is no prize or profit to be gained at the end for our patient submission; suffering and renunciation are their own reward, all that has to be done is to change our subjective position, to renounce our desperate clinging to our finite Selves with their "pathological" desires, to purify our Selves towards their universality. This is also how Hegel explains the overcoming of tyranny in the history of states: "One says that tyranny is overturned by the people because it is undignified, shameful, etc. In reality, it disappears simply because it is superfluous."[7] It becomes superfluous when people no longer need the external force of the tyrant to make them renounce their particular interests, but when they become "universal citizens" by directly identifying the core of their being with this universality—in short, people no longer need the external

6 G. W. F. Hegel, *Phenomenology of Mind*, second revised edition, trans. J. B. Baillie, Mineola: Dover 2003, p. 110.

7 G. W. F. Hegel, *Jenaer Realphilosophie*, Hamburg: Felix Meiner Verlag 1969, pp. 247–8.

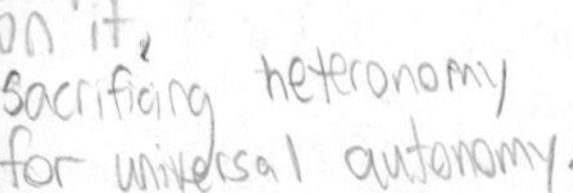

master when they are educated into doing the job of discipline and subordination themselves.

The obverse of Hegel's "nihilism" (all finite/determinate forms of life reach their "truth" in their self-overcoming) is its apparent opposite: in continuity with the Platonic metaphysical tradition, he is not ready to give negativity full rein, that is, his dialectics is ultimately an effort to "normalize" the excess of negativity. For late Plato already, the problem was how to relativize or contextualize non-being as a subordinate moment of being (non-being is always a particular/determinate lack of being measured by the fullness it fails to actualize; there is no non-being as such, there is always only, e.g., "green" which participates in non-being by not being "red" or any other color, etc.). In the same vein, Hegelian "negativity" serves to "proscribe absolute difference" or "non-being":[8] negativity is limited to the obliteration of all finite/immediate determinations. The process of negativity is thus not just a negative process of the self-destruction of the finite: it reaches its *telos* when finite/immediate determinations are mediated/maintained/elevated, posited in their "truth" as ideal notional determinations. What remains after negativity has done its work is the eternal *parousia* of the ideal notional structure. What is missing here, from the Nietzschean standpoint, is the affirmative *no*: the *no* of the joyous and heroic confrontation with the adversary, the *no* of struggle which aims at self-assertion, not self-sublation.

Struggle and Reconciliation

This brings us back to the incompatibility between Hegel's thought and any kind of evolutionary or historicist "mobilism": Hegel's dialectics "in no way involves the recognition of the irresistible force of becoming, the epopee of a flux which takes everything with it":

> The Hegelian dialectics was often—but superficially—assimilated to a *mobilism*. And it is undoubtedly true that the critique of the fixity of determinations can give rise to the conviction of an infinite dialectical process: the limited being has to disappear again and always, and its destruction extends to the very limit of our sight … However, at this level, we are still dealing with a simple going-on (*Geschehen*) to which one cannot confer the inner unity of a history (*Geschichte*).[9]

To recognize this, to thoroughly reject the "mobilist" topic of the eternal flux of Becoming which dissolves all fixed forms, is the first step towards dialectical reason in its radical incompatibility with the allegedly "deep" insight that

8 Lebrun, *L'envers de la dialectique*, p. 218.

9 Ibid., p. 11.

everything comes out of the primordial Chaos and is again swallowed by it, a form of Wisdom which persists from ancient cosmologies up to and including Stalinist "dialectical materialism." The most popular form of "mobilism" is the traditional view of Hegel as the philosopher of "eternal struggle," popularized by Marxists from Engels to Stalin and Mao: the well-known "dialectical" notion of life as an eternal conflict between reaction and progress, old and new, past and future. This belligerent view, which advocates our engagement on the "progressive" side, is totally foreign to Hegel, for whom "taking sides" as such is illusory (since it is by definition unilateral).

Let us take social struggle at its most violent: war. What interests Hegel is not struggle as such, but the way the "truth" of the engaged positions emerges through it, namely how the warring parties are "reconciled" through their mutual destruction. The true (spiritual) meaning of war is not honor, victory, defense, etc., but the emergence of absolute negativity (death) as the absolute Master which reminds us of the false stability of our organized, finite lives. War serves to elevate individuals to their "truth" by making them renounce their particular self-interests and identify with the State's universality. The true enemy is not the enemy we are fighting but our own finitude—recall Hegel's acerbic remark on how easy it is to proclaim the vanity of our finite terrestrial existence, but how much more difficult it is to accept when enforced by a wild enemy soldier who breaks into our home and starts to slice up members of our family with a saber.

In philosophical terms, Hegel's point here concerns the primacy of "self-contradiction" over the external obstacle (or enemy). We are not finite and self-inconsistent because our activity is always thwarted by external obstacles; we are thwarted by external obstacles because we are finite and inconsistent. In other words, what the subject engaged in a struggle perceives as the enemy, the external obstacle he has to overcome, is the materialization of the subject's immanent inconsistency: the struggling subject needs the figure of the enemy to sustain the illusion of his own consistency, his very identity hinges on his opposing the enemy, so much so that his (eventual) victory amounts to his own defeat or disintegration. As Hegel likes to put it, in fighting the external enemy, one (unknowingly) fights one's own essence. So, far from celebrating engaged struggle, Hegel's point is rather that every embattled position, every taking of sides, has to rely on a necessary illusion (the illusion that, once the enemy is annihilated, I will achieve the full realization of my being). This brings us to what would have been a properly Hegelian notion of ideology: the misapprehension of the condition of possibility (of what is an inherent constituent of your position) as the condition of impossibility (as an obstacle which prevents your full realization)—the ideological subject is unable to grasp how his entire identity hinges on what he perceives as the disturbing obstacle. This notion of ideology is not just an abstract mental exercise: it fits perfectly with fascist anti-Semitism as the most elementary form of ideology—one is even tempted to say: as ideology as such, *kat' exochen*. The anti-Semitic figure of the Jew, the foreign intruder who disturbs and corrupts the harmony of the social order, is ultimately a fetishistic objectivization, a stand-in, for the "inconsistency" of the social order itself, for the immanent antagonism ("class struggle") which generates the dynamic of its instability.

Hegel's interest in the "conflict of the opposites" is thus that of the neutral dialectical observer who discerns the "Cunning of Reason" at work in struggle: a subject engages in struggle, is defeated (as a rule, in his very victory), *and this defeat brings him to his truth*. We can clearly measure here the distance that separates Hegel from Nietzsche: the innocence of exuberant heroism that Nietzsche wants to resuscitate, the passion of risk, of fully engaging in a struggle, of victory or defeat—these are all absent; the "truth" of the struggle emerges only in and through defeat.

This is why the standard Marxist denunciation of the falsity of the Hegelian reconciliation (already made by Schelling) misses the point. According to this critique, the Hegelian reconciliation is false because it occurs only in the Idea, while real antagonisms persist—in the "concrete" experience of the "real life" of individuals who cling to their particular identity, state power remains an external compulsion. Therein resides the crux of the young Marx's critique of Hegel's political thought: Hegel presents the modern constitutional monarchy as a rational State in which antagonisms are reconciled, as an organic Whole in which every constituent finds, or can find, its proper place, but he thereby obfuscates the class antagonism which continues in modern societies, generating the working class as the "non-reason of the existing Reason," as the part of modern society which has no proper part in it, as its "part of no-part" (Rancière).

What Lebrun rejects in this critique is not its diagnosis (that the proposed reconciliation is dishonest, an "enforced reconciliation" [*erpresste Versöhnung*]—the title of one of Adorno's essays—which obfuscates the antagonisms' persistence in social reality), rather: "what is so admirable in this portrait of the dialectician rendered dishonest by his blindness is the supposition that he could have been honest."[10] In other words, instead of rejecting the Hegelian reconciliation as false, Lebrun rejects as illusory the very notion of dialectical reconciliation, renouncing the demand for a "true" reconciliation itself. Hegel was fully aware that reconciliation does not alleviate real suffering and antagonisms—his formula from the foreword to his *Philosophy of Right* is that one should "recognize the Rose in the Cross of the present"; or, to put it in Marx's terms: in reconciliation one does not change external reality to fit some Idea, one recognizes this Idea as the inner "truth" of the miserable reality itself. The

10 Ibid., p. 115.

Marxist reproach that, instead of transforming reality, Hegel merely proposes a new interpretation of it, thus in a way misses the point—it is knocking on an open door, since, for Hegel, in order to pass from alienation to reconciliation, we do not have to change reality, but rather the way we perceive and relate to it.

The same insight underlies Hegel's analysis of the passage from labor to thought in the subchapter on Master and Servant in the *Phenomenology of Spirit*. Lebrun is fully justified in emphasizing, against Kojève, that Hegel is far from celebrating (collective) labor as the site of the productive self-assertion of human subjectivity, as the process of forceful transformation and appropriation of natural objects, their subordination to human goals. All finite thought remains caught in the "spurious infinity" of the never-ending process of the (trans)formation of objective reality which always resists the full subjective grasp, so that the subject's work is never done: "As an aggressive activity deployed by a finite being, labor signals above all man's impotence to integrally take possession of nature."[11] This finite thought is the horizon of Kant and Fichte: the endless practico-ethical struggle to overcome external obstacles as well as the subject's own inner nature. Their philosophies are the philosophies of struggle, while in Hegel's philosophy, the fundamental stance of the subject towards objective reality is not that of practical engagement, of confrontation with the inertia of objectivity, but that of letting-it-be: purified of its pathological particularity, the universal subject is certain of itself, it knows that its thought already is the form of reality, so it can renounce enforcing its projects upon reality, it can let reality be the way it is.

This is why my labor gets all the more close to its truth the less I work to satisfy my need, that is, to produce objects I will consume. This is why industry which produces for the market is spiritually "higher" than production for one's own needs: in market-production, I manufacture objects with no relation to my needs. The highest form of social production is therefore that of a *merchant*: "the merchant is the only one who relates to the Good as a perfect universal subject, since the object in no way interests him on behalf of its aesthetic presence or its use value, but only insofar as it contains a desire of an other."[12] And this is also why, in order to arrive at the "truth" of labor, one should gradually abstract from the (external) goal it strives to realize.

The parallel with war is appropriate here: in the same way that the "truth" of the military struggle is not the destruction of the enemy, but the sacrifice of the "pathological" content of the warrior's particular Self, its purification into the universal Self, the "truth" of labor as the struggle with nature is also not victory over nature, compelling it to serve human goals, but the self-purification of the laborer itself. Labor is simultaneously the (trans)formation of external objects

11 Ibid., p. 207.

12 Ibid., p. 206.

and the disciplinary self-formation/education (*Bildung*) of the subject itself. Hegel here celebrates precisely the alienated and alienating character of labor: far from being a direct expression of my creativity, labor forces me to submit to artificial discipline, to renounce my innermost immediate tendencies, to alienate myself from my natural Self:

> Desire has reserved to itself the pure negating of the object and thereby unalloyed feeling of self. This satisfaction, however, just for that reason is itself only a state of evanescence, for it lacks objectivity or subsistence. Labour, on the other hand, is desire restrained and checked, evanescence delayed and postponed; in other words, labour shapes and fashions the thing.[13]

As such, labor prefigures thought, it achieves its *telos* in thinking which no longer works on an external stuff, but is already its own stuff, or, which no longer imposes its subjective/finite form onto external reality but is already in itself the infinite form of reality. For finite thought, the concept of an object is a mere concept, the subjective goal one actualizes when, by way of labor, one imposes it onto reality. For speculative thought, on the contrary, thought is not merely subjective, it is in itself already objective—it renders the objective conceptual form of the object. This is why inner Spirit, certain of itself, "no longer needs to form/shape nature and to render it spiritual in order to fixate the divine and to make its unity with nature externally visible: insofar as the free thought thinks externality, it can leave it the way it is (*kann er es lassen wie es ist*)."[14]

This sudden retroactive reversal from not-yet to already-is (we never directly realize a goal—we pass from striving to realize a goal to a sudden recognition that it is already realized) is what distinguishes Hegel from all kinds of historicist tropes, including the standard Marxist critical reproach that the Hegelian ideal reconciliation is insufficient, since it leaves reality (real pain and suffering) the way it is, and that what is needed is actual reconciliation through radical social transformation. For Hegel, the illusion is not that of the enforced "false reconciliation" which ignores the persisting divisions; the true illusion resides in not seeing that, in what appears to us as the chaos of becoming, the infinite goal *is already realized*: "Within the finite order, we cannot experience or see that the goal is truly achieved. The accomplishment of the infinite goal resides only in overcoming the illusion [*Täuschung*—deception] that this goal is not yet achieved."[15]

13 Hegel, *Phenomenology of Mind*, p. 111.

14 G. W. F. Hegel, *Vorlesungen über die Philosophie der Geschichte* (Werke, Vol. 12), Frankfurt: Suhrkamp 1970, p. 323.

15 G. W. F. Hegel, *Encyklopädie der philosophischen Wissenschaften im Grundrisse, Vol. 1: Die Logik*, Berlin: Dunder and Humblot 1843, p. 384 (§212).

In short, the ultimate deception lies in the failure to see that one already has what one is looking for—like Christ's disciples awaiting his "real" reincarnation, blind to the fact that their collective already was the Holy Spirit, the return of the living Christ. Lebrun is thus justified in noting that the final reversal of the dialectical process, as we have seen, far from involving the magical intervention of a *deus ex machina*, is a purely formal turnaround, a shift in perspective: the only thing that changes in the final reconciliation is the subject's standpoint—the subject endorses the loss, re-inscribes it as its triumph. Reconciliation is thus simultaneously both less and more than the standard idea of overcoming an antagonism: less, because nothing "really changes"; more, because the subject of the process is deprived of its very (particular) substance.

Here is an unexpected example: at the end of Howard Hawks's classic Western *Red River*, a "psychologically unfounded" twist occurs which is usually dismissed as a simple weakness of the script. The entire film moves towards the climactic confrontation between Dunson and Matt, a duel of almost mythic proportions, predestined by fate, as an inexorable conflict between two incompatible subjective stances; in the final scene, Dunson approaches Matt with the determination of a tragic hero blinded by his hatred and marching towards his ruin. The brutal fist fight which then ensues is unexpectedly ended when Tess, who is in love with Matt, fires a gun into the air and shouts at the two men: "anybody with half a mind would know you two love each other." A quick reconciliation follows, with Dunson and Matt chatting like old buddies: this "transition of Dunson from anger incarnate, all Achilles all the time, to sweetness and light, happily yielding to Matt … is breathtaking in its rapidity."[16] Robert Pippin is fully justified in detecting beneath this technical weakness of the script a deeper message:

> the struggle for power and supremacy that we have been watching … *has* been a kind of shadow play … a fantasy largely staged by Dunson to justify himself. There never was any great struggle, never any real threat of a fight to the death … The mythic struggle we have been watching is itself the result of a kind of self-mythologization … a fantasy narrative frame that is also demythologizing itself in front of us.[17]

This is how Hegelian reconciliation works—not as a positive gesture of resolving or overcoming the conflict, but as a retroactive insight into how *there never really was a serious conflict*, how the two opponents were always on the same side (a little bit like the reconciliation between Figaro and Marcellina in *The Marriage of Figaro*, where they are brought together by the realization that they

16 Robert Pippin, *Hollywood Westerns and American Myth*, New Haven: Yale University Press 2010, p. 52.

17 Ibid., pp. 54–5.

are mother and son). This retroactivity accounts also for the specific temporality of reconciliation. Recall the paradox of the process of apologizing: if I hurt someone by making an unkind remark, the proper thing for me to do is to offer a sincere apology, and the proper thing for her to do is to say something like, "Thanks, I appreciate it, but I wasn't offended, I knew you didn't mean it, so you really owe me no apology!" The point, of course, is that despite this final result, one still has to go through the entire process of offering the apology: "you owe me no apology" can only be said after I *have* offered an apology, so that although, formally, "nothing happens," and the offer of apology is proclaimed unnecessary, something is gained at the end of the process (perhaps, even, a friendship is saved).[18]

Perhaps this paradox provides a clue to understanding the twists and turns of the Hegelian dialectical process. Let us take Hegel's critique of the Jacobin Revolutionary Terror, understood as an exercise in the abstract negativity of absolute freedom which, unable to stabilize itself in a concrete social order, has to end in a fury of self-destruction. One should bear in mind here that, insofar as we are dealing with a historical choice (between the "French" path of remaining within Catholicism, and thus being obliged to engage in Revolutionary Terror, and the "German" path of Reformation), this choice involves exactly the same elementary dialectical paradox as that, also from the *Phenomenology of Spirit*, between the two readings of "the Spirit is a bone" which Hegel illustrates by the phallic metaphor (phallus as the organ of insemination or phallus as the organ of urination): Hegel's point is *not* that, in contrast to the vulgar empiricist mind which sees only urination, the proper speculative attitude has to choose insemination. The paradox is that to choose insemination directly is the infallible way to miss it: it is not possible to choose directly the "true meaning," in other words, one *has* to begin by making the "wrong" choice (of urination)—the true speculative meaning emerges only through the repeated reading, as the after-effect (or by-product) of the first, "wrong," reading.[19]

And the same goes for social life in which the direct choice of the "concrete universality" of a particular ethical life world can only end in a regression to

18 A scene in Ernst Lubitsch's wonderful *To Be or Not to Be*, a short dialogue between the two famous Polish theater actors, Maria Tura and her self-centered husband Josef, playfully subverts this logic. Josef tells his wife: "I gave orders that, in the posters announcing the new play we are starring in, your name will be at the top, ahead on mine—you deserve it, darling!" She kindly replies: "Thanks, but you really didn't have to do it, it was not necessary!" His answer is, of course: "I knew you would say that, so I already canceled the order and put my name back on top ..."

19 This logic of urination/insemination holds also for Hegel himself, for the two images of Hegel: the "corporate organicist Hegel" is the urination aspect, wrong but necessary: one has to begin the reading of Hegel with the "wrong Hegel," only in this way can one arrive at the right one.

premodern organic society that denies the infinite right of subjectivity as the fundamental feature of modernity. Since the subject-citizen of a modern state can no longer accept his immersion in some particular social role that confers on him a determinate place within the organic social Whole, the only route to the rational totality of the modern State leads through Revolutionary Terror: one should ruthlessly tear up the constraints of premodern organic "concrete universality" and fully assert the infinite right of subjectivity in its abstract negativity.

In other words, the point of Hegel's analysis of the Revolutionary Terror is not the rather obvious insight into how the revolutionary project involved the unilateral assertion of abstract Universal Reason and was as such doomed to perish in self-destructive fury, being unable to transpose its revolutionary energy into a stable social order; Hegel's point is rather to highlight the enigma of why, in spite of the fact that Revolutionary Terror was a historical deadlock, we have to pass through it in order to arrive at the modern rational State.

Here also, then, one has to do something (offer an apology, enact a reign of Terror) in order to see how it is superfluous. This paradox is sustained by the distinction between the "constative" and the "performative" dimensions of speech, between the "subject of the enunciated" and the "subject of the enunciation": at the level of the enunciated content, the whole operation is meaningless (why do it—offer an apology, go through the Terror—when it is superfluous?); however, what this common-sense insight forgets is that only the "wrong" superfluous gesture creates the subjective conditions which make it possible for the subject to really see *why* the gesture is superfluous. It only becomes possible to say that my apology is unnecessary after I have offered it, to see how the Terror is superfluous and destructive after one has gone through it. The dialectical process is thus more refined than it may appear: the standard notion is that one can only arrive at the final truth along the path of error, so that the errors along the way are not simply discarded, but "sublated" in the final truth, preserved in it as its moments. The evolutionary notion of dialectical process tells us that the result is not just a dead body, that it does not stand alone, in abstraction from the process that engendered it: in this process, different moments first appeared in their unilateral immediate form, while the final synthesis gathers them as sublated, maintaining their rational core. What this standard notion misses is how the previous moments are preserved *precisely as superfluous*. In other words, while the preceding stages are indeed superfluous, we need time to arrive at the point from which we can see that they are so.

A STORY TO TELL

How are we to counter this diagnosis of the "disease called Hegel," which centers on the dialectical reversal as an empty formal gesture of presenting defeat as victory? The first observation that imposes itself is that reading "infra-rational" semantic choices as strategies for coping with obstacles to the assertion of life is in itself already an "infra-rational" semantic choice. But more important is to note how such a reading subtly perpetuates a narrow view of Hegel which obliterates many key dimensions of his thought. Is it not possible to read Hegel's systematic "sublation" of each and every shape of consciousness or social life-form as, precisely, a description of all possible life-forms, with their vital "semantic choices," and their inherent antagonisms ("contradictions")?[20] If there is a "semantic choice" that underlies Hegel's thought, it is not the desperate wager that, retroactively, one will be able to tell a consistent, all-encompassing and meaningful story in which every detail will be allotted its proper place, but, on the contrary, the weird certainty (comparable to the psychoanalyst's certainty that the repressed will always return, that a symptom will always spoil every figure of harmony) that, with every figure of consciousness or form of life, things will always somehow "go wrong," that each position will generate an excess which will augur its self-destruction.

Does this mean that Hegel does not advocate any determinate "semantic choice," since, for him, the only "truth" is the endless process of the "generation and corruption" of determinate "semantic choices"? Yes, but on condition that we do not conceive this process in the usual "mobilist" sense.

How, then, does the truly historical thought break with such universalized "mobilism"? In what precise sense is it historical and not simply the rejection of "mobilism" on behalf of some eternal Principle exempted from the flow of generation and corruption? The key resides in the concept of retroactivity which concerns the very core of the relationship between Hegel and Marx: it is the main reason why, today, one should return from Marx to Hegel and enact a "materialist reversal" of Marx himself.

To approach this complex issue, let me begin with Gilles Deleuze's notion of a *pure past*: not the past into which things present pass, but an absolute past "where all events, including those that have sunk without trace, are stored and remembered as their passing away,"[21] a virtual past which already contains things

---

20 In this precise sense, the eight hypotheses of the second part of Plato's *Parmenides* form a systematic Hegelian exercise: they deploy the matrix of all possible "semantic choices" in the relationship between the One and Being, with the final "nihilistic" outcome that there is no ultimate Ground guaranteeing the consistent unity of reality, i.e., that the ultimate reality is the Void itself.

21 James Williams, *Gilles Deleuze's* Difference and Repetition*: A Critical Introduction and Guide*, Edinburgh: Edinburgh University Press 2003, p. 94.

which are still present (a present can become past because in a way it is already, it can perceive itself as part of the past; "what we are doing now is [will have been] history"). "It is with respect to the pure element of the past, understood as the past in general, as an a priori past, that a given former present is reproducible and the present present is able to reflect itself."[22] Does this mean that the pure past involves a thoroughly deterministic notion of the universe in which everything that is still to happen (to come), all actual spatio-temporal deployment, is already part of an immemorial/atemporal virtual network? No, and for a very precise reason: because "the pure past must be all the past but must also be amenable to change through the occurrence of any new present."[23] It was none other than T. S. Eliot, that great conservative, who first clearly formulated this link between our dependence on tradition and our power to change the past:

> [tradition] cannot be inherited, and if you want it you must obtain it by great labour. It involves, in the first place, the historical sense, which we may call nearly indispensable to anyone who would continue to be a poet beyond his twenty-fifth year; and the historical sense involves a perception, not only of the pastness of the past, but of its presence; the historical sense compels a man to write not merely with his own generation in his bones, but with a feeling that the whole of the literature of Europe from Homer and within it the whole of the literature of his own country has a simultaneous existence and composes a simultaneous order. This historical sense, which is a sense of the timeless as well as of the temporal and of the timeless and of the temporal together, is what makes a writer traditional. And it is at the same time what makes a writer most acutely conscious of his place in time, of his contemporaneity.
>
> No poet, no artist of any art, has his complete meaning alone. His significance, his appreciation is the appreciation of his relation to the dead poets and artists. You cannot value him alone; you must set him, for contrast and comparison, among the dead. I mean this as a principle of aesthetic, not merely historical, criticism. The necessity that he shall conform, that he shall cohere, is not one-sided; what happens when a new work of art is created is something that happens simultaneously to all the works of art which preceded it. The existing monuments form an ideal order among themselves, which is modified by the introduction of the new (the really new) work of art among them. The existing order is complete before the new work arrives; for order to persist after the supervention of novelty, the *whole* existing order must be, if ever so slightly, altered; and so the relations, proportions, values of each work of art toward the whole are readjusted; and this is conformity between the old and the new. Whoever has approved this idea of order, of the form of European, of English literature, will not find it preposterous that the past should be altered by the

22 Gilles Deleuze, *Difference and Repetition*, trans. Paul Patton, London: Continuum 2001, p. 81.

23 Williams, *Gilles Deleuze's* Difference and Repetition, p. 96.

> present as much as the present is directed by the past. And the poet who is aware of this will be aware of great difficulties and responsibilities …
>
> What happens is a continual surrender of himself as he is at the moment to something which is more valuable. The progress of an artist is a continual self-sacrifice, a continual extinction of personality. There remains to define this process of depersonalization and its relation to the sense of tradition. It is in this depersonalization that art may be said to approach the condition of science.[24]

When Eliot says that in judging a living poet "*you must set him among the dead*," he formulates a precise example of Deleuze's pure past. And when he writes that "the existing order is complete before the new work arrives; for order to persist after the supervention of novelty, the *whole* existing order must be, if ever so slightly, altered; and so the relations, proportions, values of each work of art toward the whole are readjusted," he no less clearly formulates the paradoxical link between the completeness of the past and our capacity to change it retroactively: precisely because the pure past is complete, each new work re-sets its entire balance. This is how one should read Kafka's critique of the notion of the Day of Judgment as something which will arrive at the end of time: "Only our concept of time makes it possible for us to speak of the Day of Judgment by that name; in reality it is a summary court in perpetual session." Every historical moment contains its own Judgment in the sense of its "pure past" which allocated a place to each of its elements, and this Judgment is being constantly rewritten. Recall Borges's precise formulation of the relationship between Kafka and his multitude of precursors, from ancient Chinese authors to Robert Browning:

> Kafka's idiosyncrasy, in greater or lesser degree, is present in each of these writings, but if Kafka had not written we would not perceive it; that is to say, it would not exist … each writer *creates* his precursors. His work modifies our conception of the past, as it will modify the future.[25]

In the same way, a radical revolution does (what previously appeared as) the impossible and thereby creates its own precursors—this, perhaps, is the most succinct definition of what an authentic *act* is. Such an act proper should be located in the trilogy (which strangely reflects the "European trinity" of English, French, and German): *acting out*, *passage à l'acte, Tat-Handlung* (Fichte's neologism for the founding gesture of the subject's self-positing in which the activity and its result fully overlap). *Acting out* is a hysterical outburst within the same

---

24 T. S. Eliot, "Tradition and the Individual Talent," in *The Sacred Wood: Essays on Poetry and Criticism*, London: Methuen 1920, pp. 43–5, 47.

25 Jorge Luis Borges, "Kafka and His Precursors," in *Other Inquisitions: 1937–1952*, trans. Ruth L. C. Simms, New York: Simon & Schuster 1964, p. 108.

big Other; *passage à l'acte* destructively suspends the big Other; *Tat-Handlung* retroactively rearranges it. As Jacques-Alain Miller put it, "the status of the act is retroactive":[26] a gesture "will have been" an act; it becomes an act if, in its consequences, it succeeds in disturbing and rearranging the "big Other." The properly dialectical solution of the dilemma "Is it really there, in the source, or did we just read it into the source?" is thus: it is there, but we can only perceive and state this retroactively, from the perspective of the present.[27]

One of the standard procedures of de-fetishizing/de-reifying critique is to denounce (what appears as) a direct property of the perceived object as the subject's (the observer's) "reflexive determination": the subject ignores how her gaze is already included in the perceived content. An example from recent theory: post-structuralist deconstructionism does not exist (in itself, in France), since it was invented in the US, for and by the American academic gaze with all its constitutive limitations.[28] In short, an entity like "post-structuralist deconstructionism" (a term not used in France) comes into existence only for a gaze that is unaware of the details of the philosophical scene in France: this gaze brings together authors (Derrida, Deleuze, Foucault, Lyotard, and so on) who are simply not perceived as part of the same episteme in France, just as the concept of film noir posits a unity which did not exist "in itself." And in the same way, the French gaze, ignorant of the ideological tradition of American individualist, anti-combo populism, and looking through existentialist lenses, mistook the heroic-cynical, pessimist-fatalist stance of the noir hero for a socially critical attitude. Likewise, the American perception inscribed the French authors into the field of radical cultural criticism, thereby conferring on them a feminist, etc., critical social stance for the most part absent in France itself. So just as film noir

26 Jacques-Alain Miller, "L'acte entre intention et conséquence," *La cause freudienne* 42 (May 1999), pp. 7–16.

27 The traditional definition of a good lover (the one who, by gently playing with my body, makes me aware of new capacities for intense enjoyment) also perfectly exemplifies the gap between the In-itself and For-itself: the point is neither that the lover merely brings to the light a capacity to enjoy which is already fully constituted deep within me but that I am simply unaware of, nor that the lover moulds, actively shapes, my capacity to enjoy. The point is rather that the lover actualizes that which was already in me in the status of an In-itself.

28 The prefix "post-" in "post-structuralism" is thus a reflexive determination in the strict Hegelian sense of the term: although it seems to designate a property of its object—the change, the cut, in the French intellectual orientation—it effectively involves a reference to the gaze of the subject perceiving it: "post-" here refers to what went on in French theory after the American (or German) gaze had been turned its way, while "structuralism" *tout court* designates French theory "in itself," before it was noticed by the foreign gaze. In short, "post-structuralism" is structuralism from the moment it was noted by the foreign gaze.

is not a category of American cinema, but primarily a category of the French cinema criticism and (later) of the historiography of cinema, so too "post-structuralist deconstructionism" is not a category of French philosophy, but primarily a category of the American (mis)reception of the French theorists designated as such.

This, however, is only the first step, at the level of (external) reflection. In the next and crucial step, these subjective determinations are developed precisely as not merely "subjective" but as simultaneously affecting the "thing itself." The notion of "post-structuralist deconstructionism," although resulting from a limited foreign perspective, draws out of its object potentials invisible to those directly engaged within it. Therein resides the ultimate dialectical paradox of truth and falsity: sometimes, the aberrant view which misreads a situation from its limited perspective can, on account of this very limitation, perceive the "repressed" potential of the observed constellation. And, furthermore, the external misperception can sometimes have a productive influence on the misperceived "original" itself, forcing it to become aware of its own "repressed" truth (arguably, the French notion of noir, although the result of a misperception, exerted a strong influence on later American movie-making). Is not the American reception of Derrida a supreme example of this productivity of the external misperception? Although it clearly *was* a misperception, did it not have a retroactive but productive influence on Derrida himself, forcing him to confront ethico-political issues more directly? Was the American reception of Derrida in this sense not a kind of *pharmakon*, a supplement to the "original" Derrida himself—a poisonous stain-fake, distorting the original but at the same time keeping it alive? In short, would Derrida still be so "alive" today had it not been for the American misperception of his work?

Here, Peter Hallward falls short in his otherwise excellent *Out of This World*, where he stresses only the aspect of the pure past as the virtual field in which the fate of all actual events is sealed in advance, since "everything is already written" in it.[29] At this point, where we view reality *sub specie aeternitatis*, absolute freedom coincides with absolute necessity and its pure automatism: to be free means to let oneself freely flow in/with the substantial necessity. This topic reverberates even in today's cognitivist debates on the problem of free will. Compatibilists such as Daniel Dennett have an elegant solution to the incompatibilists' complaints about determinism:[30] when incompatibilists complain that our freedom cannot be combined with the fact that all our acts are part of the great chain of natural determinism, they secretly make an unwarranted ontological assumption: first, they assume that we (the Self, the free agent) somehow stand *outside* reality, then they go on to complain about how they feel oppressed by the notion

29 Peter Hallward, *Out of This World*, London: Verso Books 2006.

30 See Daniel Dennett, *Freedom Evolves*, Harmondsworth: Penguin Books 2003.

that reality in its determinism controls them totally. This is what is wrong with the notion of us being "imprisoned" by the chains of natural determinism: we thereby obfuscate the fact that we are *part of* reality, that the (possible, local) conflict between our "free" striving and the external reality that resists it is a conflict inherent in reality itself. That is to say, there is nothing "oppressive" or "constraining" about the fact that our innermost strivings are (pre)determined: when we feel thwarted in our freedom by the pressure of external reality, there must be something in us, some desire or striving, which is thus thwarted, but where do such strivings come from if not this same reality? Our "free will" does not in some mysterious way "disturb the natural course of things," it is part and parcel of this course. For us to be "truly" and "radically" free would entail that there be no positive content involved in our free act—if we want nothing "external" and particular or given to determine our behavior, then "this would involve being free of every part of ourselves."[31] When a determinist claims that our free choice is "determined," this does not mean that our free will is somehow constrained, that we are forced to act *against* our will—what is "determined" is the very thing that we want to do "freely," that is, without being thwarted by external obstacles.

To return to Hallward: while he is right to emphasize that, for Deleuze, freedom "isn't a matter of human liberty but of liberation *from* the human,"[32] of fully submerging oneself in the creative flux of absolute Life, the political conclusion he draws from this seems too facile:

> The immediate political implication of such a position ... is clear enough: since a free mode or monad is simply one that has eliminated its resistance to the sovereign will that works through it, so then it follows that the more absolute the sovereign's power, the more "free" are those subject to it.[33]

But does Hallward not overlook here the retroactive movement on which Deleuze also insists, namely how this eternal pure past which fully determines us is itself subjected to retroactive change? We are thus simultaneously less free and more free than we think: we are thoroughly passive, determined by and dependent on the past, but we have the freedom to define the scope of this determination, to (over)determine the past which will determine us. Deleuze is here unexpectedly close to Kant, for whom I am determined by causes, but I (can) retroactively determine which causes will determine me: we, subjects, are passively affected by pathological objects and motivations; but, in a reflexive way,

31 Nicholas Fearn, *Philosophy: The Latest Answers to the Oldest Questions*, London: Atlantic Books 2005, p. 24.

32 Hallward, *Out of This World*, p. 139.

33 Ibid.

we have the minimal power to accept (or reject) being affected in this way, that is, we retroactively determine the causes allowed to determine us, or, at least, the *mode* of this linear determination. "Freedom" is thus inherently retroactive: at its most elementary, it is not simply a free act which, out of nowhere, starts a new causal link, but a retroactive act of determining which link or sequence of necessities will determine us. Here, one should add a Hegelian twist to Spinoza: freedom is not simply "recognized/known necessity," but recognized/assumed necessity, the necessity constituted/actualized through this recognition. So when Deleuze refers to Proust's description of Vinteuil's music that haunts Swann—"as if the performers not so much played the little phrase as executed the rites necessary for it to appear"—he is evoking the necessary illusion: generating the sense-event is experienced as ritualistic evocation of a pre-existing event, as if the event was already there, waiting for our call in its virtual presence.

The key philosophical implication of Hegelian retroactivity is that it undermines the reign of the Principle of Sufficient Reason: this principle only holds in the condition of linear causality where the sum of past causes determines a future event—retroactivity means that the set of (past, given) reasons is never complete and "sufficient," since the past reasons are retroactively activated by what is, within the linear order, their effect.

Changing the destiny

What directly resonates in this topic is, of course, the Protestant motif of predestination: far from being a reactionary theological motif, predestination is a key element of the materialist theory of sense, on condition that we read it along the lines of the Deleuzian opposition between the virtual and the actual. That is to say, predestination does not mean that our fate is sealed in an actual text existing from eternity in the divine mind; the texture which predestines us belongs to the purely virtual eternal past which, as such, can be retroactively rewritten by our acts. In predestination, fate is substantialized into a decision that precedes the process, so that the burden of individuals' activities is not to performatively constitute their fate, but to discover (or guess) their pre-existing fate. What is thereby obfuscated is the dialectical reversal of contingency into necessity, that is, the way the outcome of a contingent process takes on the appearance of necessity: things retroactively "will have been" necessary.

This, perhaps, would have been the ultimate meaning of the singularity of Christ's incarnation: it is an *act* which radically changes our destiny. Prior to Christ, we were determined by Fate, caught up in the cycle of sin and its payment; but Christ's erasure of our past sins means precisely that his sacrifice changes our virtual past and thus sets us free. When Deleuze writes that "my wound existed before me; I was born to embody it," does not this variation on the theme of the Cheshire cat and its smile from *Alice in Wonderland* (the cat was born to embody its smile) provide a perfect formula for Christ's sacrifice: Christ was born to embody his wound, to be crucified? The problem is with the literal teleological reading of this proposition: as if the actual deeds of a person merely actualize their atemporal-eternal fate inscribed in their virtual idea:

> Caesar's only real task is to become worthy of the events he has been created to embody. *Amor fati.* What Caesar actually does adds nothing to what he virtually is. When Caesar actually crosses the Rubicon this involves no deliberation or choice since it is simply part of the entire, immediate expression of Caesarness, it simply unrolls or "unfolds something that was encompassed for all times in the notion of Caesar."[34]

But what about the retroactivity of a gesture which (re)constitutes this past itself? This, perhaps, is the most succinct definition of what an authentic *act* is: in our ordinary activity, we effectively just follow the (virtual-fantasmatic) coordinates of our identity, while an act proper involves the paradox of an actual move which (retroactively) changes the very virtual "transcendental" coordinates of its agent's being—or, in Freudian terms, which not only changes the actuality of our world but also "moves its underground." We have thus a kind of reflexive "folding back of the condition on to the given it was the condition for":[35] while the pure past is the transcendental condition for our acts, our acts not only create new actual reality, they also retroactively change this very condition.

This brings us to the Deleuzian notion of the *sign*: actual expressions are signs of a virtual Idea which is not an ideal but, rather, a *problem*. Common sense tells us that there are true and false solutions to every problem; for Deleuze, on the contrary, there are no definitive solutions to problems, solutions are just repeated attempts to deal with the problem, with its impossible-real. *Problems themselves, not solutions, are true or false.* Each solution not only reacts to "its" problem, but retroactively redefines it, formulating it from within its own specific horizon. Which is why the problem is universal and the solutions or answers are particular. Deleuze is here unexpectedly close to Hegel: for Hegel, the Idea of the State, say, is a problem, and each specific form of the state (Ancient republic, feudal monarchy, modern democracy ...) simply proposes a solution, redefining the problem itself. The passage to the next "higher" stage of the dialectical process occurs precisely when, instead of continuing to search for a solution, we problematize the problem itself, abandoning its terms—when, for example, instead of continuing to search for a "true" State, we drop the very reference

---

34 Ibid., p. 54.

35 Williams, *Gilles Deleuze's* Difference and Repetition, p. 109.

to the State and look for a communal existence beyond the State. A problem is thus not only "subjective," not just epistemological, a problem for the subject who tries to solve it; it is *stricto sensu* ontological, inscribed into the thing itself: the structure of reality is "problematic." That is to say, actual reality can only be grasped as a series of answers to a virtual problem—in Deleuze's reading of biology, for instance, the development of the eye as an organ must be grasped as a solution to the problem of how to deal with light. And this brings us back to the sign—actual reality appears as a "sign" when it is perceived as an answer to virtual problem: "Neither the problem nor the question is a subjective determination marking a moment of insufficiency in knowledge. Problematic structure is part of objects themselves, allowing them to be grasped as signs."[36]

This explains the strange way in which Deleuze opposes signs and representations: for common sense, a mental representation directly reproduces the way a thing is, while a sign just points towards it, designating it with a (more or less) arbitrary signifier. (In a representation of a table, I "see directly" a table, while its sign just points towards the table.) For Deleuze, on the contrary, representations are mediate, while signs are direct, and the task of a creative thought is that of "making movement itself a work, without interpositions; of substituting direct signs for mediate representations."[37] Representations are figures of objects as objective entities deprived of their virtual support or background, and we pass from representation to sign when we are able to discern in an object that which points towards its virtual ground, towards the problem with regard to which it is an answer. To put it succinctly, every answer is a sign of its problem. This brings us to Deleuze's notion of the "blind seer": blind to actual reality, sensible only to the virtual dimension of things. Deleuze resorts to a wonderful metaphor of a spider deprived of eyes and ears but infinitely sensitive to whatever resonates through its virtual web. As Hallward paraphrases it:

> Actual or constituted forms slip through the web and make no impression, for the web is designed to vibrate only on contact with virtual or intensive forms. The more fleeting or molecular the movement, the more intense its resonance through the web. The web responds to the movements of a pure multiplicity before it has taken on any definite shape.[38]

This brings us to the central problem of Deleuze's ontology: how are the virtual and the actual related? "Actual things express Ideas but are not caused by them."[39] The notion of causality is limited to the interaction of actual things

---

36 Deleuze, *Difference and Repetition*, pp. 63–4.

37 Ibid., p. 8.

38 Hallward, *Out of This World*, p. 118.

39 Williams, *Gilles Deleuze's* Difference and Repetition, p. 200.

and processes; on the other hand, this interaction also causes virtual entities (sense, Ideas): Deleuze is not an idealist, Sense is for him always an ineffective, sterile shadow accompanying actual things. What this means is that, for Deleuze, (transcendental) *genesis and causality are totally opposed*: they move at different levels:

> Actual things have an identity, but virtual ones do not, they are pure variations. An actual thing must change—become something different—in order to express something. Whereas, the expressed virtual thing does not change—only its relation to other virtual things, other intensities and Ideas changes.[40]

How does this relation change? *Only through the changes in actual things which express Ideas, since the entire generative power lies in actual things*: Ideas belong to the domain of Sense which is "only a vapor which plays at the limit of things and words"; as such, Sense is "the Ineffectual, a sterile incorporeal deprived of its generative power."[41] Think of a group of dedicated individuals fighting for the Idea of communism: in order to grasp their activity, we have to take into account the virtual Idea. But this Idea is in itself sterile, it has no proper causality: all causality lies in the individuals who "express" it.

The lesson to be drawn from the basic paradox of Protestantism (how is it possible that a religion which taught predestination sustained capitalism, the greatest explosion of human activity and freedom in history) is that freedom is neither grasped necessity (the vulgata from Spinoza to Hegel and traditional Marxists) nor overlooked (ignored) necessity (the thesis of the cognitive and brain sciences: freedom is the "user's illusion" of our consciousness, which is unaware of the bio-neuronal processes that determine it), but *a Necessity which is presupposed and/as unknown/unknowable*. We know that everything is predetermined, but we do not know *what* our predetermined destiny is, and it is this uncertainty which drives our incessant activity. Freud's infamous statement "anatomy is destiny" should also be read along these lines, as a Hegelian speculative judgment in which the predicate "passes over" into the subject. That is to say, its true meaning is not the obvious one, the standard target of feminist critique ("the anatomical difference between the sexes directly determines the different socio-symbolic roles of men and women"), but rather the opposite: the "truth" of anatomy is "destiny," in other words a symbolic formation. In the case of sexual identity, an anatomic difference is "sublated," turned into the medium of appearance/expression—more precisely, into the material support—of a certain symbolic formation.

---

40 Ibid.

41 Deleuze, *Difference and Repetition*, p. 156.

This is how one should differentiate historicity proper from organic evolution. In the latter, a universal Principle is slowly and gradually differentiating itself; as such, it remains the calm, underlying, all-encompassing ground that unifies the bustling activity of struggling individuals, the endless process of generation and corruption that is the "cycle of life." In history proper, on the contrary, the universal Principle is caught in an "infinite" struggle with itself; that is, the struggle is each time a struggle for the fate of the universality itself. In organic life, particular moments are in struggle with one another, and through this struggle the Universal reproduces itself; in Spirit, the Universal is in struggle with itself.

This is why the eminently "historical" moments are those marked by great collisions in which a whole form of life is threatened, when the established social and cultural norms no longer guarantee a minimum of stability and cohesion; in such open situations, a new form of life has to be invented, and it is at this point that Hegel locates the role of great heroes. They operate in a pre-legal, stateless zone: their violence is not bound by the usual moral rules, they enforce a new order with the subterranean vitality which shatters all established forms. According to the usual *doxa* on Hegel, heroes follow their instinctual passions, their true motifs and goals are not clear to themselves, they are the unconscious instruments of a deeper historical necessity giving birth to a new spiritual life form. However, as Lebrun points out, here one should not impute to Hegel the standard teleological notion of a hidden hand of Reason pulling the strings of the historical process, following a plan established in advance and using the passions of individuals as instruments for its implementation. First, since the meaning of their acts is a priori inaccessible to the individuals who accomplish them, heroes included, there is no "science of politics" able to predict the course of events: "nobody ever has the right to declare himself a depositary of the Spirit's self-knowledge,"[42] and this impossibility "spares Hegel the fanaticism of 'objective responsibility'"[43]—in other words, there is no place in Hegel for the Marxist-Stalinist figure of the communist revolutionary who understands the historical necessity and posits himself as the instrument of its implementation. However, it is crucial to add a further twist here: if we merely assert this impossibility, we are still "conceiving the Absolute as Substance, not as Subject"—we are still surmising that there is some pre-existing Spirit imposing its substantial Necessity on history, while accepting that knowledge of this Necessity is denied us. To be consistently Hegelian, however, we must take a crucial step further and insist that historical Necessity does not pre-exist the contingent process of its actualization, that is, that the historical process is also in itself "open," undecided —this confused mixture "generates sense *insofar as it unravels itself*":

42 Lebrun, *L'envers de la dialectique*, p. 40.

43 Ibid., p. 41.

> It is people, and they only, who make history, while Spirit explicates itself through this making ... The point is not, as in a naïve theodicy, to find a justification for every event. In actual time, no heavenly harmony resonates in the sound and fury. It is only once this tumult recollects itself in the past, once what took place is conceived, that we can say, to put it briefly, that the "course of History" is a little bit better outlined. History runs forward only for those who look at it backwards; it is linear progression only in retrospect ... Hegelian "providential necessity" has so little authority that it seems as if it learns from the run of things in the world which were its goals.[44]

This is how one should read Hegel's thesis that, in the course of the dialectical development, things "become what they are": it is not that a temporal deployment merely actualizes some pre-existing atemporal conceptual structure—this atemporal conceptual structure is itself the result of contingent temporal decisions. Let us take an exemplary case of a contingent decision whose outcome defined the agent's entire life—Caesar's crossing of the Rubicon:

> It is not enough to say that crossing the Rubicon is part of the complete notion of Caesar. One should rather say that Caesar is defined by the fact that he crossed the Rubicon. His life didn't follow a scenario written in the book of some goddess: there is no book which would already have contained the relations of Caesar's life, for the simple reason that his life itself is this book, and that, at every moment, an event is in itself its own narrative.[45]

But why should we not then say that there is simply no atemporal conceptual structure, that all there is is a gradual temporal deployment? Here we encounter the properly dialectical paradox which defines true historicity as opposed to evolutionist historicism, and which was much later, in French structuralism, formulated as the "primacy of synchrony over diachrony." Usually, this primacy was taken to mean the ultimate denial of historicity in structuralism: a historical development can be reduced to the (imperfect) temporal deployment of a pre-existing atemporal matrix of all possible variations/combinations. This simplistic notion of the "primacy of synchrony over diachrony" overlooks the properly dialectical point, made long ago by, among others, T. S. Eliot (see the long quote above) with regard to how each truly new artistic phenomenon not only designates a break with the entire past, but retroactively changes this past itself. At every historical conjuncture, the present is not only present, it also encompasses a perspective on the past immanent to it—after the disintegration of the Soviet Union, say, the October Revolution is no longer the same historical

44 Ibid., pp. 41–4.
45 Ibid., p. 87.

event: it is (from the triumphant liberal-capitalist view) no longer the beginning of a new progressive epoch in the history of humanity, but the beginning of a catastrophic swerving off-course of history which reached its end in 1991.

This is the ultimate lesson of Hegel's anti-"mobilism": dialectics has nothing whatsoever to do with the historicist justification of a particular politics or practice at a certain stage of historical development, a justification which may then be lost at a later "higher" stage. Reacting to the revelation of Stalin's crimes at the twentieth congress of the Soviet Communist Party, Brecht noted how the same political agent who had earlier played an important role in the revolutionary process (Stalin) had now become an obstacle to it, and praised this as a proper "dialectical" insight—but one should thoroughly reject this logic. In the dialectical analysis of history, on the contrary, each new "stage" "rewrites the past" and retroactively de-legitimizes the previous one.

The owl of Minerva

Back to Caesar: once he crossed the Rubicon, his previous life appeared in a new way, as a preparation for his later world-historical role; that is, it was transformed into part of a totally different life story. This is what Hegel calls "totality" or what structuralism calls "synchronic structure": a historical moment which is not limited to the present but includes its own past and future, in other words, the way the past and the future appeared to and from this moment. The main implication of conceiving the symbolic order as such a totality is that, far from reducing it to a kind of transcendental a priori (a formal network, given in advance, which limits the scope of human practice), one should follow Lacan and focus on how the gestures of symbolization are entwined with and embedded in the process of collective practice. What Lacan elaborates as the "twofold moment" of the symbolic function reaches far beyond the standard theory of the performative dimension of speech, as developed in the tradition from J. L. Austin to John Searle:

> The symbolic function presents itself as a twofold movement in the subject: man makes his own action into an object, but only to return its foundational place to it in due time. In this equivocation, operating at every instant, lies the whole progress of a function in which action and knowledge alternate.[46]

The historical example evoked by Lacan to clarify this "twofold movement" is indicative in its hidden references: "in phase one, a man who works at the level of

46 Jacques Lacan, *Écrits: A Selection*, trans. Bruce Fink, New York: W. W. Norton & Company 2002, pp. 72–3.

production in our society considers himself to belong to the ranks of the proletariat; in phase two, in the name of belonging to it, he joins in a general strike."[47] Lacan's (implicit) reference here is to Lukács's *History and Class Consciousness*, a classic Marxist work from 1923 whose widely acclaimed French translation was published in the mid-1950s. For Lukács, consciousness is opposed to mere knowledge of an object: knowledge is external to the known object, while consciousness is in itself "practical," an act which changes its very object. (Once a worker "considers himself to belong to the ranks of the proletariat," this changes his very reality: he acts differently.) One does something, one counts oneself as (declares oneself) the one who did it, and, on the base of this declaration, one does something new—the proper moment of subjective transformation occurs at the moment of declaration, not at the moment of the act. This reflexive moment of declaration means that every utterance not only transmits some content, but also, simultaneously, *determines how the subject relates to this content*. Even the most down-to-earth objects and activities always contain such a declarative dimension, which constitutes the ideology of everyday life.

However, Lukács remains all too idealist when he proposes simply replacing the Hegelian Spirit with the proletariat as the Subject-Object of History: Lukács is here not really Hegelian, but a pre-Hegelian idealist.[48] One is even tempted to talk here of Marx's "idealist reversal of Hegel": in contrast to Hegel, who was well aware that the owl of Minerva takes wing only at dusk, after the fact—that Thought follows Being (which is why, for Hegel, there can be no scientific insight into the future of society)—Marx reasserts the primacy of Thought: the owl of Minerva (German contemplative philosophy) should be replaced by the singing of the Gaelic rooster (French revolutionary thought) announcing the proletarian revolution—in the proletarian revolutionary act, Thought will precede Being. Marx thus sees in Hegel's motif of the owl of Minerva an indication of the secret positivism of Hegel's idealist speculation: Hegel leaves reality the way it is.

The Hegelian reply is that the delay of consciousness does not imply a naïve objectivism which claims that consciousness is caught in a transcendent objective process. A Hegelian accepts Lukács's notion of consciousness as opposed to mere knowledge of an object; what is inaccessible to consciousness is the impact of the subject's act itself, its own inscription into objectivity. Of course thought is immanent to reality and changes it, but not as fully self-transparent self-consciousness, not as an Act aware of its own impact. Marx himself nonetheless comes close to this paradox of non-teleological retroactivity when, in his *Grundrisse* manuscripts, apropos the notion of labor, he pointed out how

---

47 Ibid., p. 73.

48 See Georg Lukács, *History and Class Consciousness*, Cambridge, MA: MIT Press 1972.

> even the most abstract categories, despite their validity—precisely because of their abstractness—for all epochs, are nevertheless, in the specific character of this abstraction, themselves likewise a product of historic relations, and possess their full validity only for and within these relations.
>
> Bourgeois society is the most developed and the most complex historic organization of production. The categories which express its relations, the comprehension of its structure, thereby also allows insights into the structure and the relations of production of all the vanished social formations out of whose ruins and elements it built itself up, whose partly still unconquered remnants are carried along within it, whose mere nuances have developed explicit significance within it, etc. Human anatomy contains a key to the anatomy of the ape. The intimations of higher development among the subordinate animal species, however, can be understood only after the higher development is already known.[49]

In short, to paraphrase Pierre Bayard, what Marx is saying here is that the anatomy of the ape, although it was formed earlier in time than the anatomy of man, nonetheless in a certain way *plagiarizes by anticipation the anatomy of man*. The question, however, remains: does Hegel's thought harbor such an openness towards the future, or does the closure of his System a priori preclude it? In spite of misleading appearances, we should answer yes, Hegel's thought is open towards the future, but precisely on account of its closure. That is to say, Hegel's opening towards the future is a *negative*: it is articulated in his negative/limiting statements like the famous "one cannot jump ahead of one's time" from his *Philosophy of Right*. The impossibility of directly borrowing from the future is grounded in the very fact of retroactivity which makes the future a priori unpredictable: we cannot climb onto our own shoulders and see ourselves "objectively," in terms of the way we fit into the texture of history, because this texture is again and again retroactively rearranged. In theology, Karl Barth extended this unpredictability to the Last Judgment itself, emphasizing how the final revelation of God will be totally incommensurable with our expectations:

> God is not hidden to us; He is revealed. But what and how we shall be in Christ, and what and how the World will be in Christ at the end of God's road, at the breaking in of redemption and completion, that is not revealed to us; that is hidden. Let us be honest: we do not know what we are saying when we speak of Jesus Christ's coming again in judgment, and of the resurrection of the dead, of eternal life and eternal death. That with all these there will be bound up a piercing revelation—a seeing, compared to which all our present vision will have been blindness—is too often testified in Scripture for us to feel we ought to prepare ourselves for it. For

49 Karl Marx, *Grundrisse: Foundations of the Critique of Political Economy*, trans. Martin Nicolaus, London: Penguin Books 1993, p. 105.

> we do not know what will be revealed when the last covering is removed from our eyes, from all eyes: how we shall behold one another and what we shall be to one another—men of today and men of past centuries and millennia, ancestors and descendants, husbands and wives, wise and foolish, oppressors and oppressed, traitors and betrayed, murderers and murdered, West and East, Germans and others, Christians, Jews, and heathen, orthodox and heretics, Catholics and Protestants, Lutherans and Reformed; upon what divisions and unions, what confrontations and cross-connections the seals of all books will be opened; how much will seem small and unimportant to us then, how much will only then appear great and important; for what surprises of all kinds we must prepare ourselves.
>
> We also do not know what Nature, as the cosmos in which we have lived and still live here and now, will be for us then; what the constellations, the sea, the broad valleys and heights, which we see and know now, will say and mean then.[50]

With this insight, it becomes clear how false, how "all too human," is the fear that the guilty will not be properly punished—here, especially, we must abandon our expectations: "Strange Christianity, whose most pressing anxiety seems to be that God's grace might prove to be all too free on this side, that hell, instead of being populated with so many people, might some day prove to be empty!"[51] And the same uncertainty holds for the Church itself—it possesses no superior knowledge, it is like a postman who delivers the mail with no idea what it says: "The Church can only deliver it the way a postman delivers his mail; the Church is not asked what it thinks it is thereby starting, or what it makes of the message. The less it makes of it and the less it leaves on it its own fingerprints, the more it simply hands it on as it has received it—and so much the better."[52] There is only one unconditional certainty in all this—the certainty of Jesus Christ as our savior, which is a "rigid designator" remaining the same in all possible worlds:

> We know just one thing: that Jesus Christ is the same also in eternity, and that His grace is whole and complete, enduring through time into eternity, into the new world of God which will exist and be recognized in a totally different way, that it is unconditional and hence is certainly tied to no purgatories, tutoring sessions, or reformatories in the hereafter.[53]

No wonder Hegel formulated this same limitation apropos politics: especially as communists, we should abstain from any positive imagination of the future communist society. We are, of course, borrowing from the future, but how we

50 Karl Barth, *God Here and Now*, London: Routledge 2003, pp. 45–6.
51 Ibid., p. 42.
52 Ibid., p. 49.
53 Ibid., p. 46.

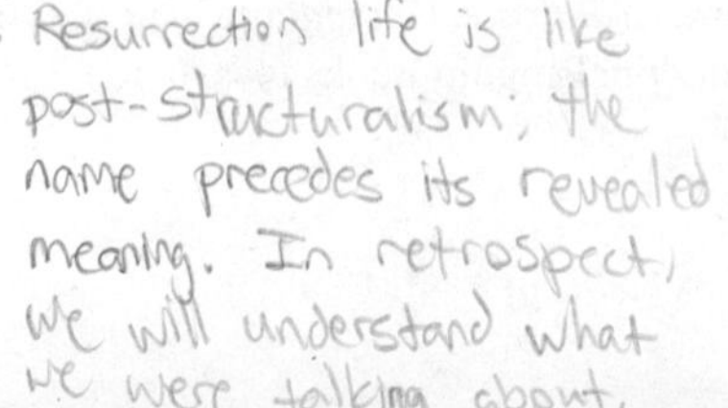
Suggestion: Resurrection life is like post-structuralism; the name precedes its revealed meaning. In retrospect, we will understand what we were talking about.

are doing so will only become readable once the future is here, so we should not put too much hope in the desperate search for the "germs of communism" in today's society.

Is the ultimate consequence of our awareness of the "retroversive effect" thus a negative one? Should we limit, reject even, ambitious social actions, since they always, for structural reasons, lead to unintended (and as such potentially catastrophic) results? A further distinction has to be drawn here: between the "openness" of the ongoing symbolic activity which is caught up in the "retroversive effect," with the meaning of each of its elements decided retroactively, and the act in a much stronger sense of the term. In the first case, the unintended consequences of our acts are simply due to the big Other, the complex symbolic network which overdetermines (and thus displaces) their meaning. In the second case, the unintended consequences emerge from the very failure of the big Other, that is, from the way our act not only relies on the big Other, but radically challenges and transforms it. The awareness that the power of a proper act is to retroactively create its own conditions of possibility should not make us afraid to embrace what, prior to the act, appears as impossible: only in this way does our act touch the Real. Replying to Judith Butler's reproach that it is not clear to what moral or political end his effort at exploring and problematizing liberal notions of freedom and justice is directed, Talal Asad offers a wonderful Hegelian answer:

> there can be no abstract answer to this question because it is precisely the implications of things said and done in different circumstances that one tries to understand … one should be prepared for the fact that what one aims at in one's thinking may be less significant than where one ends up … in the process of thinking one should be open to ending up in unanticipated places—whether these produce satisfaction or desire, discomfort or horror.[54]

We are free only against the background of this non-transparency: if it were possible for us to fully predict the consequences of our acts, our freedom would effectively be only "known necessity" in the pseudo-Hegelian way, for it would consist in freely choosing and wanting what we know to be necessary. In this sense, freedom and necessity would fully coincide: I act freely when I knowingly follow my inner necessity, the instigations that I find in myself as my true substantial nature. But if this is the case, we are stepping back from Hegel to Aristotle, for we are no longer dealing with the Hegelian subject who produces ("posits") its own content, but with an agent bent on actualizing its immanent potentials, its positive "essential forces," as the young Marx put it in his deeply

54 Talad Asad, Wendy Brown, Judith Butler, Saba Mahmood, *Is Critique Secular?*, Berkeley: University of California Press 2009, pp. 138–9.

Aristotelian critique of Hegel. What gets lost here is the dialectics of the constitutive retroactivity of sense, of the continuous retroactive (re)totalization of our experience.

Such openness for radical contingency is difficult to maintain—even a rationalist like Habermas was not able to do so. His late interest in religion breaks with the traditional liberal concern for the humanist, spiritual, etc., content hidden in the religious form; what interests him is this form itself: in particular, among those who really fundamentally believe and are ready to put their lives at stake for their beliefs, displaying the raw energy and unconditional commitment missing from the anemic sceptical-liberal stance—as if the influx of such unconditional engagement could revitalize the post-political dessication of democracy. Habermas is reacting here to the same problem as Chantal Mouffe does with her "agonistic pluralism"—namely, how to reintroduce passion into politics. Is he not, however, thereby engaged in a kind of ideological vampirism, sucking the energy from naïve believers without being ready to abandon his own basic secular-liberal stance, so that full religious belief retains a kind of fascinating and mysterious Otherness? As Hegel already showed apropos the dialectic of Enlightenment and faith in his *Phenomenology of Spirit*, such an opposition of formal Enlightenment and fundamental-substantial beliefs is false, an untenable ideologico-existential position. What should be done is to fully assume the identity of the two opposed moments, which is precisely what apocalyptic "Christian materialism" can do: it brings together the rejection of divine Otherness and the unconditional commitment.

It is, however, at this very point—after fully conceding Hegel's radical break with traditional metaphysical theodicy, and fully admitting Hegel's openness towards the yet-to-come—that Lebrun makes his critical move. Lebrun's fundamental Nietzschean strategy is, first, to admit the radical nature of Hegel's undermining of traditional metaphysics, but then, in a crucial second step, to demonstrate how this radical sacrifice of metaphysical content saves the minimal form of metaphysics. The accusations concerning Hegel's theodicy, of course, fall short: there is no substantial God who writes the script of History in advance and watches over its realization; the situation is open, truth emerges only through the very process of its deployment, and so on and so forth—but what Hegel nonetheless maintains is the much deeper presupposition that, as dusk falls over the events of the day, *the owl of Minerva will take wing*, that there always is a story to be told at the end, a story which ("retroactively" and "contingently" as much as one wants) reconstitutes the Sense of the preceding process. Likewise, with regard to domination, Hegel is of course against every form of despotic domination, so the critique of his thought as a divinization of the Prussian monarchy is ridiculous; however, his assertion of subjective freedom comes with a catch: it is the freedom of the subject who undergoes a violent "transubstantiation" from the individual stuck on his particularity to the universal subject who recognizes in the State the substance of his own being. The mirror-obverse of this mortification of individuality as the price to be paid for the rise of the "truly" free universal subject is that the State's power retains its full authority—all that changes is that this authority (as in the entire tradition from Plato onwards) loses its tyrannical-contingent character and becomes a rationally justified power.

The question is thus whether or not Hegel is effectively pursuing a desperate strategy of sacrificing everything, all metaphysical content, in order to save the essential, the form itself (the form of a retrospective rational reconstruction, the form of authority which imposes on the subject the sacrifice of all particular content, etc.). Or is it rather that Lebrun himself, in making this type of reproach, enacts the fetishistic strategy of *je sais bien, mais quand meme* ...—"I know very well that Hegel goes to the end in destroying metaphysical presuppositions, but nonetheless ..."? The answer to this kind of reproach takes the form of a pure tautology which marks the passage from contingency to necessity: there is a story to be told *if* there is a story to be told. That is to say, *if*, due to contingency, a story emerges at the end, *then* this story will appear as necessary. Yes, the story is necessary, but its necessity is itself contingent.

Nevertheless, is there not a grain of truth in Lebrun's critical point? Does Hegel not effectively presuppose that, contingent and open as history may be, a consistent story can always be told after the event? Or, to put it in Lacan's terms, is not the entire edifice of Hegelian historiography based on the premise that, no matter how confused the events themselves, a *subject supposed to know* will emerge at the end, magically converting nonsense into sense, chaos into a new order? Recall simply his philosophy of history with its narrative of world history as the story of the progress of freedom ... And is it not true that, if there is a lesson to be learned from the twentieth century, it is that all the extreme phenomena that occurred in it can never be unified in a single encompassing philosophical narrative? One simply cannot write a "phenomenology of the Spirit of the twentieth century," uniting technological progress, the rise of democracy, the failed communist experiment, the horrors of fascism, the gradual end of colonialism ... But why not? Is this *really* the case? What if one can and should write precisely such a Hegelian history of the twentieth century, this "age of extremes" (Eric Hobsbawm), as a global narrative delimited by two epochal constellations, with its starting point in the (relatively) long peaceful period of capitalist expansion from 1848 till 1914, whose subterranean antagonisms then exploded with the First World War, and its conclusion in the ongoing global-capitalist "New World Order" which emerged after 1990, as a return to a new all-encompassing system signaling a kind of Hegelian "end of history," but whose antagonisms already announce new explosions? Are the great reversals and unexpected explosions of the topsy-turvy twentieth century, its numerous "coincidences of the opposites"—the reversal of liberal capitalism into fascism, the even more weird reversal of the October Revolution into the Stalinist nightmare—not the very privileged stuff which seems to call for a Hegelian reading? What would Hegel have made of today's struggle of liberalism against fundamentalist faith? One thing is sure: he would not have simply taken the side of liberalism, but would have insisted on the "mediation" of the opposites.[55]

Potentiality versus Virtuality

Convincing as it may appear, Lebrun's critical diagnosis of the Hegelian wager that there is always a story to tell nonetheless once again falls short: Lebrun misses an additional twist which complicates the image of Hegel. Yes, Hegel sublates time in eternity—but this sublation itself has to appear as (hinges on) a contingent temporal event. Yes, Hegel sublates contingency in a universal rational order—but this order itself hinges on a contingent excess (the State as a rational totality, say, can only actualize itself through the "irrational" figure of the king at its head). Yes, struggle is sublated in the peace of the reconciliation (mutual annihilation) of the opposites, but this reconciliation itself has to appear as its opposite, as an act of extreme violence. So Lebrun is right in emphasizing that Hegel's topic of the dialectical struggle of the opposites is as far as possible from an engaged attitude of "taking sides": for Hegel, the "truth" of the struggle is always, with an inexorable necessity, the mutual destruction of the opposites—the "truth" of a phenomenon always resides in its self-annihilation, in the destruction of its immediate being. But Lebrun here nonetheless misses the paradox proper: not only did Hegel have no problem taking sides (with an often very violent partiality) in the political debates of his time, his entire mode of thinking is deeply "polemical"—always intervening, attacking, taking sides, and, as such, a long way from the detached position of Wisdom observing the ongoing struggle from a neutral distance, aware of its nullity *sub specie aeternitatis*. For Hegel, the true ("concrete") universality is accessible only from an engaged "partial" standpoint.

55 And let us not forget that, for Hegel himself, his philosophical reconstruction of history in no way pretends to "cover everything," but consciously leaves blanks: the medieval period, for example, is for Hegel one big regression—no wonder that, in his lectures on the history of philosophy, he dismisses the whole of medieval thought in a couple of pages, flatly denying any historical greatness to figures like Thomas Aquinas. Not to mention the destruction of great civilizations like the Mongols' wiping out so much of the Muslim world (the destruction of Baghdad, etc.) in the thirteenth century—there is no "meaning" in this destruction, the negativity unleashed here did not create the space for a new shape of historical life.

The Hegelian relationship between necessity and freedom is usually read in terms of their ultimate coincidence: true freedom has nothing to do with capricious choice; it means the priority of self-relating to relating-to-other; in other words, an entity is free when it can deploy its immanent potential without being impeded by any external obstacle. From here, it is easy to develop the standard argument against Hegel: his system is a fully "saturated" set of categories, with no place for contingency and indeterminacy, for in Hegel's logic, each category follows with an inexorable immanent-logical necessity from the preceding one, with the entire series of categories forming a self-enclosed Whole. We can see now what this argument misses: the Hegelian dialectical process is not this "saturated", self-contained, necessary Whole, but the *open and contingent process through which such a Whole forms itself.* In other words, the reproach confuses being with becoming: it perceives as a fixed order of Being (the network of categories) what is for Hegel the process of Becoming which, *retroactively*, engenders its necessity.

The same point can also be made in terms of the distinction between potentiality and virtuality. Quentin Meillassoux has outlined the contours of a post-metaphysical materialist ontology whose basic premise is the Cantorian multiplicity of infinities which cannot be totalized into an all-encompassing One. He relies here on Badiou, who also pointed out how Cantor's great materialist breakthrough concerns the status of infinite numbers (and it was precisely because this breakthrough was materialist that it caused so much psychic trauma for Cantor, a devout Catholic): prior to Cantor, the Infinite was linked to the One, the conceptual form of God in religion and metaphysics; after Cantor, the Infinite enters the domain of the Multiple—it implies the actual existence of infinite multiplicities, as well as an infinite number of different infinities.[56] Does, then, the choice between materialism and idealism concern the most basic scheme of the relationship between multiplicity and the One in the order of the signifier? Is the primordial fact that of the multiplicity of signifiers, which is then totalized through the subtraction of the One; or is the primordial fact that of the "barred One"—more precisely, that of the tension between the One and its empty place, of the "primordial repression" of the binary signifier, so that multiplicity emerges to fill in this emptiness, the lack of the binary signifier? Although it may appear that the first version is materialist and the second idealist, one should resist this easy temptation: from a truly materialist position, multiplicity is only possible against the background of the Void—it is only this which makes the multiplicity non-All. The (Deleuzian) "genesis" of the One out of primordial multiplicity, this prototype of "materialist" explanation of how the totalizing One arises, should therefore

56 Alain Badiou, *Second manifeste pour la philosophie*, Paris: Fayard 2009, pp. 127–8.

be rejected: no wonder that Deleuze is simultaneously the philosopher of the (vitalist) One.

With regard to its most elementary formal configuration, the couple of idealism and materialism can also be rendered as the opposition between primordial lack and the self-inverted curvature of being: while, for "idealism," lack (a hole or gap in the order of being) is the unsurpassable fact (which can then either be accepted as such, or filled in with some imagined positive content), for "materialism," lack is ultimately the result of a curvature of being, a "perspectival illusion," a form of appearance of the torsion of being. Instead of reducing one to the other (instead of conceiving the curvature of being as an attempt to obfuscate the primordial lack, or the lack itself as a mis-apprehension of the curvature), one should insist on the irreducible parallax gap between the two. In psychoanalytical terms, this is the gap between desire and drive, and here also, one should resist the temptation to give priority to one term and reduce the other to its structural effect. That is to say, one can conceive the rotary motion of the drive as a way to avoid the deadlock of desire: the primordial lack/impossibility, the fact that the object of desire is always missed, is converted into a profit when the aim of libido is no longer to reach its object, but to repeatedly turn around it—satisfaction is generated by the very repeated failure of direct satisfaction. And one can also conceive desire as a mode of avoiding the circularity of the drive: the self-enclosed rotary movement is recast as a repeated failure to reach a transcendent object which always eludes its grasp. In philosophical terms, this couple echoes (not the couple of Spinoza and Hegel, but) the couple of Spinoza and Kant: the Spinozan drive (not grounded in a lack) versus Kantian desire (to reach the noumenal Thing).

But does Hegel really begin with contingent multiplicity? Does he not rather offer a "third way," through the point of non-decision between desire and drive? Does he not actually begin with Being, and then deduce the multiplicity of existents (beings-there), which emerges as the result of the first triad (or, rather, quadruple) being-nothing-becoming-existent? Here, one should bear in mind the key fact that, when he writes about the passage from Being to Nothingness, Hegel resorts to the past tense: Being does not pass into Nothingness, it has *always already passed* into Nothingness, and so on. The first triad of the Logic is not a dialectical triad, but a retroactive evocation of a kind of shadowy virtual past, of something which never passes since it has always already passed: the actual beginning, the first entity which is "really here," is the contingent multiplicity of beings-there (existents). To put it another way, there is no tension between Being and Nothingness which would generate the incessant passage of one into the other: in themselves, prior to dialectics proper, Being and Nothingness are directly and immediately the same, they are indiscernible; their tension (the tension between form and content) appears only retroactively, if one looks at them from the standpoint of dialectics proper.

Such an ontology of the non-All asserts a radical contingency: not only are there no laws which hold of necessity, every law is in itself contingent—it can be overturned at any moment. This amounts to a suspension of the Principle of Sufficient Reason: a suspension not only epistemological, but also ontological. That is to say, it is not only that we can never get to know the entire network of causal determinations, but this chain is in itself "inconclusive," opening up the space for the immanent contingency of becoming—such a chaos of becoming, subjected to no pre-existing order, is what defines radical materialism. Along these lines, Meillassoux proposes a precise distinction between *contingency* and *chance*, linking it to the distinction between *virtuality* and *potentiality*:

> *Potentialities* are the non-actualized cases of an indexed set of possibilities under the condition of a given law (whether aleatory or not). *Chance* is every actualization of a potentiality for which there is no univocal instance of determination on the basis of the initial given conditions. Therefore I will call *contingency* the property of an indexed set of cases (not of a case belonging to an indexed set) of not itself being a case of sets of cases; and *virtuality* the property of every set of cases of emerging within a becoming which is not dominated by any pre-constituted totality of possibles.[57]

A clear case of potentiality is the throw of a die through which what was already a possible case becomes a real case: it was determined by the pre-existing order of possibilities that there is a one in six chance of number six turning up, so when number six does actually turn up, a pre-existing possible is realized. Virtuality, on the contrary, designates a situation in which one cannot totalize the set of possibles, so that something new emerges, a case is realized for which there was no place in the pre-existing set of possibles: "time creates the possible at the very moment it makes it come to pass, it brings forth the possible as it does the real, it inserts itself in the very throw of the die, to bring forth a seventh case, in principle unforeseeable, which breaks the fixity of potentialities."[58] One should note here Meillassoux's precise formulation: the New arises when an X emerges which does not merely actualize a pre-existing possibility, but *whose actualization creates (retroactively opens up) its own possibility*:

> If we maintain that becoming is not only capable of bringing forth cases on the basis of a pre-given universe of cases, we must then understand that it follows that such

57 Quentin Meillassoux, "Potentiality and Virtuality," *Collapse: Philosophic Research and Development* 2 (2007), pp. 71–2.

58 Ibid., p. 74.

cases irrupt, properly speaking, *from nothing*, since no structure contains them as eternal potentialities before their emergence: *we thus make irruption* ex nihilo *the very concept of a temporality delivered to its pure immanence.*[59]

In this way, we obtain a precise definition of time in its irreducibility: time is not only the "space" of the future realization of possibilities, but the "space" of the emergence of something radically new, outside the scope of the possibilities inscribed into any atemporal matrix. This emergence of a phenomenon *ex nihilo*, not fully covered by the sufficient chain of reasons, is thus no longer—as in traditional metaphysics—a sign of the direct intervention of some supernatural power (God) into nature, but, on the contrary, a sign of the *inexistence* of God, that is, a proof that nature is not-All, not "covered" by any transcendent Order or Power which regulates it. A "miracle" (whose formal definition is the emergence of something not covered by the existing causal network) is thus converted into a *materialist* concept: "*Every 'miracle' thus becomes the manifestation of the inexistence of God*, insofar as every radical rupture of the present in relation to the past becomes the manifestation of the absence of any order capable of overseeing the chaotic power of becoming."[60]

On the basis of these insights, Meillassoux brilliantly undermines the standard argument against the radical contingency of nature and its laws (in both senses: of the hold of laws and of the laws themselves), namely: if it is so radically contingent, how is it that nature is so permanent, that it (mostly) conforms to laws? Is this not highly improbable, the same improbability as that of the die always falling with six face up? This argument relies on a possible totalization of possibilities/probabilities, *with regard to which* the uniformity is improbable: if there is no standard, nothing is more improbable than anything else. This is also why the "astonishment" on which the Strong Anthropic Principle in cosmology counts is false: we start from human life, which could have evolved only within a set of very precise preconditions, and then, moving backwards, we cannot but be astonished at how our universe was furnished with precisely the right set of characteristics for the emergence of life—only a slightly different chemical composition, density, etc., would have made life impossible. This "astonishment" again relies on the probabilistic reasoning which presupposes a pre-existing totality of possibilities.

This is how one should read Marx's aforementioned thesis about the anatomy of man as a key to the anatomy of ape: it is a profoundly materialist thesis in that it does not involve any teleology (which would propose that man is "in germ" already present in ape; that the ape immanently tends towards man). It is precisely because the passage from ape to man is radically contingent and

59 Ibid., p. 72.

60 Ibid., p. 75.

unpredictable, because there is no inherent "progress" involved, that one can only retroactively determine or discern the conditions (not "sufficient reasons") for man in the ape. And, again, it is crucial to bear in mind here that the non-All is ontological, not only epistemological: when we stumble upon "indeterminacy" in nature, when the rise of the New cannot be fully accounted for by the set of its pre-existing conditions, this does not mean that we have encountered a limitation of our knowledge, our inability to understand the "higher" reason at work here, but, on the contrary, that we have demonstrated the ability of our mind to grasp the non-All of reality:

> The notion of virtuality permits us ... to *reverse the signs*, making of every radical irruption the manifestation, not of a transcendent principle of becoming (a miracle, the sign of a Creator), but of a time that nothing subtends (an emergence, the sign of non-All). We can then grasp what is signified by the impossibility of tracing a genealogy of novelties directly to a time before their emergence: not the incapacity of reason to discern hidden potentialities, but, quite on the contrary, the capacity of reason to accede to the ineffectivity of an All of potentialities which would pre-exist their emergence. In every radical novelty, time makes manifest that it does not actualize a germ of the past, but that it brings forth a virtuality which did not pre-exist in any way, in any totality inaccessible to time, its own advent.[61]

For we Hegelians, the crucial question here is this: where does Hegel stand with regard to this distinction between potentiality and virtuality? On a first approach, there is massive evidence that Hegel is *the* philosopher of potentiality: is not the whole point of the dialectical process as the development from In-itself to For-itself that, in the process of becoming, things merely "become what they already are" (or were from all eternity)? Is not the dialectical process the temporal deployment of an eternal set of potentialities, which is why the Hegelian System is a self-enclosed set of necessary passages? This mirage of overwhelming evidence dissipates, however, the moment we fully take into account the radical *retroactivity* of the dialectical process: the process of becoming is not in itself necessary, but is the *becoming* (the gradual contingent emergence) *of necessity itself*. This is also (among other things) what "to conceive substance as subject" means: the subject as the Void, the Nothingness of self-relating negativity, is the very *nihil* out of which every new figure emerges; in other words, every dialectical passage or reversal is a passage in which the new figure emerges *ex nihilo* and retroactively posits or creates its necessity.

61 Ibid., p. 80.

The Hegelian circle of circles

The stakes in this debate—is Hegel a thinker of potentiality or a thinker of virtuality?—are extremely high: they concern the (in)existence of the "big Other" itself. That is to say, the atemporal matrix which contains the scope of all possibilities is one name of the "big Other," and another is the totalizing story we can tell after the fact, or the certainty that such a story will always emerge. Nietzsche reproaches modern atheism precisely for the fact that, in it, the "big Other" survives—true, no longer as the substantial God, but as the totalizing symbolic frame of reference. This is why Lebrun contends that Hegel is not an atheist conveniently presenting himself as a Christian, but effectively the ultimate Christian philosopher. Hegel always insisted on the deep truth of the Protestant saying "God is dead": in his own thought, the substantial-transcendent God dies, but is resurrected as the symbolic totality which guarantees the meaningful consistency of the universe—in a strict homology with the passage from God qua substance to the Holy Spirit as the community of believers in Christianity. When Nietzsche talks about the death of God, he does not have in mind the pagan living God, but precisely *this* God qua Holy Spirit, the community of believers. Although this community no longer relies on a transcendent Guarantee of a substantial big Other, the big Other (and thereby the theological dimension) is still here as the symbolic frame of reference (in Stalinism, say, in the guise of the big Other of History which guarantees the meaningfulness of our acts).

But is *this* shift from the living gods of the real to the dead God of the Law really what happens in Christianity? Is it not that this shift already takes place in Judaism, so that the death of Christ cannot stand for this shift, but for something much more radical—precisely for the death of the symbolic-"dead" big Other itself? The key question is thus: is the Holy Spirit still a figure of the big Other, or is it possible to conceive it outside of this frame? If the dead God were to morph directly into the Holy Ghost, then we would still have the symbolic big Other. But the monstrosity of Christ, this contingent singularity interceding between God and man, is proof that the Holy Ghost is not the big Other surviving as the spirit of the community after the death of the substantial God, but a collective link of love without any support in the big Other. Therein resides the properly Hegelian paradox of the death of God: if God dies directly, as God, he survives as the virtualized big Other; only if he dies in the guise of Christ, his earthly embodiment, does he also disintegrate as the big Other.

As Christ died on the Cross, the earth shook and darkness descended, signs that the heavenly order itself—the big Other—was disturbed: not only did something horrible happen in the world, but the very coordinates of the world itself were shaken. It was as if the *sinthome*, the knot tying the world together, had been unraveled, and the audacity of the Christians was to take this as a good

omen, or, as Mao would put it much later: "there is great disorder under heaven, the situation is excellent." Therein resides what Hegel calls the "monstrosity" of Christ: *the insertion of Christ between God and man is strictly equivalent to the fact that "there is no big Other"—Christ is inserted as the singular contingency on which the universal necessity of the "big Other" itself hinges.* In claiming that Hegel is the ultimate Christian philosopher, Lebrun is thus—to paraphrase T. S. Eliot—right for the wrong reason.

Only if we bear in mind this dimension can we really see why the Darwinian (or other evolutionary) critics of Hegel miss the point when they ridicule his claim that there is no history in nature, that there is history only in human societies: Hegel does not imply that nature is always the same, that forms of vegetal and animal life are forever fixed, so that there is no evolution in nature—what he claims is that there is no history proper in nature: "The living conserves itself, it is the beginning and the end; the product in itself is also the principle, it is always as such active."[62] Life eternally repeats its cycle and returns to itself: substance is again and again reasserted, children become parents, and so on. The circle here is perfect, at peace with itself. It is often perturbed—from without: in nature we do of course have gradual transformations of one species into another, and we do get clashes and catastrophes which obliterate entire species; but what we do not perceive in nature is the Universal appearing (posited) as such, in contrast to its own particular content—a Universal in conflict with itself. In other words, what is missing in nature is what Hegel called the "monstrosity" of Christ: the direct embodiment of the *arkhe* of the entire universe (God) in a singular individual who walks around as one among the mortals. It is in this precise sense that, in order to distinguish natural from spiritual movement, Hegel uses the strange term "insertion": in an organic process, "nothing can insert itself between the Notion and its realization, between the nature of the genus determined in itself and the existence which is conformed to this nature; in the domain of the Spirit, things are wholly different."[63] Christ is such a figure which "inserts itself" between God and its creation. Natural development is dominated and regulated by a principle, *arkhe*, which remains the same throughout the movement of its actualization, be it the development of an organism from its conception to its maturity or the continuity of a species through the generation and decay of its individual members—there is no tension here between the universal principle and its exemplification, the universal principle is the calm universal force which totalizes and encompasses the wealth of its particular content; however, "life doesn't have history because it is totalizing only *externally*"[64]—it is a

62 G. W. F. Hegel, *Vorlesungen über die Philosophie der Religion* (Werke, Vol. 16), Frankfurt: Suhrkamp 1970, pp. 525–6.

63 Hegel, *Vorlesungen über die Philosophie der Geschichte*, p. 90.

64 Lebrun, *L'envers de la dialectique*, p. 250.

universal genus which encompasses the multitude of individuals who struggle, but this unity is not posited *in* an individual. In spiritual history, on the contrary, this totalization occurs for itself, it is posited as such in the singular figures which embody universality against its own particular content.

Or, to put it another way, in organic life, substance (the universal Life) is the encompassing unity of the interplay of its subordinate moments, that which remains the same through the eternal process of generation and corruption, that which returns to itself through this movement; with subjectivity, however, *predicate passes into subject*: substance does not return to *itself*, it is re-totalized by what was originally its predicate, its subordinated moment. The key moment in a dialectical process thus involves the "transubstantiation" of its focal point: what was at first just a predicate, a subordinate moment of the process (say, money in the development of capitalism), becomes its central moment, retroactively degrading its presuppositions, the elements out of which it emerged, into its subordinate moments, elements of its self-propelling circulation.

Robert Pippin exemplifies in what sense the Hegelian Spirit is "its own result" with reference to the finale of Proust's *À la Recherche*: how does Marcel finally "become what he is"? By way of breaking with the Platonic illusion that his Self can be "secured by anything, any value or reality that transcends the wholly temporal human world":

> It was … by failing to become "what a writer is," to realize his inner "writerly essence"—as if that role must be some transcendentally important or even a definite, substantial role—that Marcel realizes that such a becoming is important by *not* being secured by the transcendent, *by* being wholly temporal and finite, always and everywhere in suspense, and yet nonetheless capable of some illumination … If Marcel has become who he is, and this somehow continuous with and a product of the experience of his own past, it is unlikely that we will be able to understand that by appeal to a substantial or underlying self, now discovered, or even by appeal to successor substantial selves, each one linked to the future and past by some sort of self-regard.[65]

It is thus only by way of fully accepting this abyssal circularity, in which the search itself creates what it is looking for, that the Spirit "finds itself." This is why the verb "failing," as used by Pippin, is to be given full weight: the failure to achieve the (immediate) goal is absolutely crucial to, constitutive of, this process—or, as Lacan put it: *la vérité surgit de la méprise*. If, then, "it is *only* as a result of itself that it is spirit,"[66] this means that the standard talk about the Hegelian Spirit

---

65 Robert Pippin, *The Persistence of Subjectivity*, Cambridge: Cambridge University Press 2005, pp. 332–4.

66 Hegel, *Hegels Philosophie des subjektiven Geistes*, pp. 6–7.

which alienates itself to itself, then recognizes itself in its otherness and thus re-appropriates its content, is deeply misleading: the Self to which Spirit returns is produced in the very movement of this return, or, that to which the process of return is returning is produced by the very process of returning. In a subjective process, there is no "absolute subject," no permanent central agent playing with itself the game of alienation and disalienation, losing or dispersing itself and then re-appropriating its alienated content: after a substantial totality is dispersed, it is another agent—previously its subordinated moment—which re-totalizes it. It is this shifting of the center of the process from one moment to another which distinguishes a dialectical process from the circular movement of alienation and its overcoming; it is because of this shift that the "return to itself" coincides with accomplished alienation (when a subject re-totalizes the process, its substantial unity is fully lost). In this precise sense, substance returns to itself as subject, and this trans-substantiation is what substantial life cannot accomplish.

The logic of the Hegelian triad is thus not the externalization of Essence followed by the recuperation of the alienated Otherness by Essence, but a wholly different one. The starting point is the pure multiplicity of Being, a flat appearing with no depth. Through self-mediation of its inconsistency, this appearing constructs or engenders the Essence, the depth, which appears in and through it (the passage from Being to Essence). Finally, in the passage from Essence to Concept, the two dimensions are "reconciled" so that Essence is reduced to the self-mediation, cut, within appearing itself: Essence appears as Essence within appearing, this is its entire consistency, its truth. Consequently, when Hegel talks about how the Idea "externalizes" (*entäussert*) itself in contingent appearances, and then re-appropriates its externality, he applies one of his many misnomers: what he is actually describing is the very opposite process, that of "internalization," the process whereby the contingent surface of being is posited as such, as contingent-external, as "mere appearance," by way of generating, in a self-reflective movement, (the *appearance* of) its own essential "depth." In other words, the process in which Essence externalizes itself is simultaneously the process which generates this very essence: "externalization" is strictly the same as the formation of the Essence which externalizes itself. The Essence retroactively constitutes itself through its process of externalization, through its loss—this is how one should understand the much-quoted statement of Hegel that the Essence is only as deep as it is wide.

This is why the pseudo-Hegelian topic of the subject which first externalizes itself and then re-appropriates its alienated substantial Otherness is to be rejected. First, there is no pre-existing subject which alienates itself by way of positing its otherness: the subject *stricto sensu* emerges through this process of alienation in the Other. This is why the second move—Lacan calls it separation—in which the subject's alienation in the Other is posited as correlative to the separation of the Other itself from its ex-timate core, this overlapping of two lacks, has nothing to do with the subject integrating or internalizing its otherness. (However, a problem remains here: Lacan's duality of alienation and separation obviously also displays the formal structure of a kind of "negation of negation," but how is this redoubled negation related to the Hegelian negation of negation?)

Perhaps what is missing in Lebrun is the proper image of a circle that would render the unique circularity of the dialectical process. For pages, he fights with different images to differentiate the Hegelian "circle of circles" from the circularity of traditional (premodern) Wisdom, from the ancient topic of the "cycle of life," its generation and corruption. How, then, are we to read Hegel's description, which seems to evoke a full circle in which a thing merely becomes what it is? "Necessity only shows itself at the end, but in such a way precisely that this end reveals how it was equally the First. Or, the end reveals this priority of itself by the fact that, in the change actualized by it, nothing emerges which was not already there."[67] The problem with this full circle is that it is too perfect, that its self-enclosure is double—its very circularity is re-marked in yet another circular mark.

In other words, the very repetition of the circle undermines its closure and surreptitiously introduces a gap into which radical contingency is inscribed: if the circular closure, in order to be fully actual, has to be re-asserted as closure, this means that, in itself, it is not yet truly a closure—it is only (the contingent excess of) its repetition which makes it a closure. (Recall again the paradox of the monarch in Hegel's theory of the rational State: one needs this contingent excess to actualize the State as a rational totality. This excess is, in Lacanese, that of the signifier without the signified: it adds no new content, it just performatively registers something that is already here.) As such, this circle undermines itself: it only works if we supplement it with an additional internal circle, so that we get the figure of the "inside-inverted eight" (regularly referred to by Lacan, and also invoked once by Hegel). This is the true figure of the Hegelian dialectical process, a figure missing in Lebrun's book.

This brings us finally to Hegel's absolutely unique position in the history of philosophy. The ultimate anti-Hegelian argument invokes the very fact of the post-Hegelian break: what even the most fanatical partisan of Hegel cannot deny is that something changed after Hegel, that a new era of thought began which can no longer be accounted for in Hegelian terms of absolute conceptual mediation; this rupture occurs in different guises, from Schelling's assertion of the abyss of pre-logical Will (vulgarized later by Schopenhauer) and Kierkegaard's insistence on the uniqueness of faith and subjectivity, through Marx's assertion

67 G. W. F. Hegel, *Phänomenologie des Geistes*, second edition, Berlin: Dunder and Humblot 1843, p. 190 (§257).

of the actual socio-economic life-process, and the full autonomization of the mathematicized natural sciences, up to Freud's motif of the "death drive" as a repetition that insists beyond all dialectical mediation. Something happened here, for there is a clear break between before and after, and while one can argue that Hegel already announces this break, that he is the last idealist metaphysician and the first post-metaphysical historicist, one cannot really be a Hegelian after this break, for Hegelianism has lost its innocence forever. To act like a full Hegelian today is equivalent to writing tonal music after the Schoenbergian revolution. Hegel is the ultimate "bad guy" in this grand narrative, his work the final achievement of metaphysics. In his thought, system and history thoroughly overlap: the consequence of the equation of the Rational and the Actual is that the conceptual system is nothing but the notional structure of history, and history is nothing but the external deployment of this system.

The predominant Hegelian strategy that is emerging as a reaction to this scarecrow image of Hegel the Absolute Idealist offers a "deflated" image of Hegel freed of ontological-metaphysical commitments, reduced to a general theory of discourse, of possibilities of argumentation. This approach is best exemplified by so-called Pittsburgh Hegelians (Brandom, McDowell), and is ultimately advocated also by Robert Pippin, for whom the point of Hegel's thesis on Spirit as the "truth" of Nature "is simply that at a certain level of complexity and organization, natural organisms come to be occupied with themselves and eventually to understand themselves in ways no longer appropriately explicable within the boundaries of nature or in any way the result of empirical observation."[68] Consequently, the "sublation" of Nature in Spirit ultimately means that "natural beings which by virtue of their natural capacities can achieve it are spiritual: having achieved it and maintaining it *is* being spiritual; those which cannot are not."[69] So, far from describing an ontological or cosmic process through which an entity called Notion externalizes itself in nature and then returns to itself from it, all Hegel tried to do was to provide "some manageable account of the nature of the categorical (if not ontological) necessity for spirit-concepts in making sense of what these [human] organisms are doing, saying, and building."[70] This kind of avoidance of full ontological commitment, of course, brings us close to Kantian transcendentalism—which Pippin willingly concedes, conceiving Hegel's system as a systematic exposition of all possible forms of intelligibility:

> The idea is that the structure "Logic—Philosophy of nature—Philosophy of spirit" is an attempt at comprehending the possibility of all determinate intelligibility (the

68 Robert Pippin, *Hegel's Practical Philosophy*, Cambridge: Cambridge University Press 2008, p. 46.
69 Ibid., p. 53.
70 Ibid., pp. 52–3.

> possibility of representational or conceptual content, of objective purport, whatever one's most general statement of such possibility amounts to) … So for the Concept to be in or to underlie something is to claim that the thing has a principle of intelligibility, it can be rendered intelligible, given an account of, illuminated as what it truly is, where intelligibility is itself a logical notion and one inseparable from self-knowledge, knowledge of what explanatory satisfaction amounts to. I have already mentioned the similarity with Kant's *Critique*—"Metaphysics of Nature"—"Metaphysics of Morals" structure, although for many reasons Hegel would certainly insist that he is not presenting Kantian-like subjective conditions of intelligibility. But the issue is still, I am suggesting, intelligibility, a rendering of accounts, and Hegel clearly believed he could provide something like the comprehensive possibility of *any* account-giving.[71]

The Hegelian passage from Nature to Spirit is thus not a movement in the "thing itself," but occurs in the domain of the self-reflective movement of thinking about nature:

> Nature *itself*, that is, does not "develop into spirit." Thinking through accounts of nature can be said to lead one to spirit's own standards ("for itself") of account-giving, and therewith to the nature of normative authority in general, the central issue in our achievement of collective like-mindedness, in spirit's own self-realization.[72]

If, then, in ontological terms, spirit naturally evolves as a capacity of natural beings, why not simply endorse materialist evolutionism? That is to say, if—to quote Pippin—"at a certain level of complexity and organization, natural organisms come to be occupied with themselves and eventually to understand themselves," does this not mean that, precisely, in a certain sense nature itself *does* "develop into spirit"? What one should render problematic is precisely Pippin's fragile balance between ontological materialism and epistemological transcendental idealism: he rejects the direct idealist ontologization of the transcendental account of intelligibility, but he also rejects the epistemological consequences of the ontological evolutionary materialism. (In other words, he does not accept that the self-reflection of knowledge should construct a kind of bridge to materialist ontology, accounting for how the normative attitude of "accounting for" itself could have emerged out of nature.)

The same ambiguity can be discerned already in Habermas: no wonder he praises Brandom, since Habermas also avoids directly approaching the "big" ontological question ("are humans *really* a subspecies of animals, is Darwinism true?"), the question of God or Nature, of idealism or materialism. It would be

71 Ibid., pp. 49–50.

72 Ibid., p. 49.

easy to prove that Habermas's neo-Kantian avoidance of ontological commitment is in itself necessarily ambiguous: while Habermasians treat naturalism as an obscene secret not to be publicly admitted ("of course man developed from nature, of course Darwin was right ..."), this obscure secret is a lie, it covers up the idealist *form* of their thought (the a priori normative transcendentals of communication which cannot be deduced from natural being). While Habermasians secretly think they are really materialists, the truth resides in the idealist form of their thinking.

To avoid a fatal misunderstanding: the point is not that one should take sides and opt for one consistent stance, either evolutionary materialism or speculative idealism. The point is rather that one should fully and explicitly accept the gap which manifests itself in the incompatibility of the two stances: the transcendental standpoint is in a sense irreducible, for one cannot look "objectively" at oneself and locate oneself in reality; and the task is to *think this impossibility itself as an ontological fact*, not only as an epistemological limitation. In other words, the task is to think this impossibility not as a limit, but as a positive fact—and this, perhaps, is what at his most radical Hegel does.

Such a "deflated" image of Hegel is not enough; the post-Hegelian break must be approached in more direct terms. True, there is a break, but in it Hegel is the "vanishing mediator" between its "before" and its "after," between traditional metaphysics and post-metaphysical nineteenth- and twentieth-century thought. That is to say, something happens in Hegel, a breakthrough into a unique dimension of thought, which is obliterated, rendered invisible in its true dimension, by post-metaphysical thought.[73] This obliteration leaves an empty space which has to be filled in so that the continuity of the development of philosophy can be re-established. But, we may ask, filled in with what? The index of this obliteration is the absurd image of Hegel as the "absolute idealist" who "pretended to know everything," to possess Absolute Knowledge, to read the mind of God, to deduce the whole of reality out of the self-movement of (his) Mind—an image which is an exemplary case of what Freud called *Deck-Erinnerung* (screen-memory), a fantasy-formation destined to cover up a traumatic truth. In this sense, the post-Hegelian turn to "concrete reality, irreducible to notional mediation," should rather be read as a desperate posthumous revenge of metaphysics, as an attempt to reinstall metaphysics, although in the inverted form of the primacy of concrete reality.[74]

73 So why did Hegel's thought occur when it did, not earlier or later? It appeared in the unique historical moment of the passage between the ancient (premodern) and the new (modern) world—in this in-between. Hegel, for a brief moment, saw something that was not visible either before or after. Today, we find ourselves in another such passage, which is why there is a need to repeat Hegel.

74 Another way to deal with this embarrassing excess, this outgrowth of philosophy

Perhaps, however, we encounter here also the limit of Hegel, although not in the Nietzschean sense deployed by Lebrun. If life is a substantial universality, is not then what inserts itself in the gap between its Notion and the Notion's actualization, and what thereby breaks the substantial circularity of life, *death*? To put it bluntly: if Substance is Life, is the Subject not Death? Insofar as, for Hegel, the basic feature of pre-subjective Life is the "spurious infinity" of the eternal reproduction of the life substance through the incessant movement of the generation and corruption of its elements—that is, the "spurious infinity" of a repetition without progress—the ultimate irony we encounter here is that Freud, who called this excess of death over life the "death drive," conceived it precisely as repetition, as a compulsion to repeat. Can Hegel think this weird repetition which is not progress, but also not the natural repetition through which substantial life reproduces itself? A repetition which, by its excessive insistence, breaks precisely with the cycle of natural repetition?

which fits neither the coordinates of preceding metaphysics nor those of post-Hegelian "antiphilosophy" (Badiou), is to cast Hegel as a freak who should simply be forgotten or ignored. To give just one example, from Mehdi Belhaj Kacem: "Hegel is nothing but a parenthesis—a grandiose one, but still a parenthesis—between Kant and Badiou" (quoted from *Marianne* 671, February 27, 2010, p. 24).

Marx as a Reader of Hegel, Hegel as a Reader of Marx

The big political shift in Hegel's development occurred when he abandoned his early fascination with the Romantic vision of the non-alienated society of Ancient Greece as a beautiful organic community of love (as opposed to the modern society of the Understanding, with its mechanical interaction between autonomous egotistical individuals). With this shift, Hegel began to appreciate the very thing that had previously repelled him: the "prosaic," non-heroic character of modern societies with their complex division of professional and administrative labor, in which "no one simply could be heroically responsible for much of anything (and so could not be beautiful in action)."[1] Hegel's full endorsement of the prose of modern life, his ruthless dismissal of all longing for the heroic old times, is the (often neglected) historical root of his thesis about the "end of art": art is no longer an adequate medium for expressing such a "prosaic" disenchanted reality, reality deprived of all mystery and transcendence.[2]

The young Hegel, especially in his *System der Sittlichkeit*, was still fascinated by the Greek polis as the organic unity of individual and society: here, social substance does not yet stand opposed to individuals as a cold, abstract, objective legality imposed from outside, but appears as the living unity of "customs," of a collective ethical life in which individuals are "at home," recognizing it as their own substance. From this perspective, cold universal legality is a regression from the organic unity of customs—the regression from Greece to the Roman empire. Although Hegel soon accepted that the subjective freedom of modernity has to be accepted, that the organic unity of the polis was forever lost, he nonetheless insisted on the need for some kind of return to a renewed unity, to a new polis that would offer individuals a deeper sense of social solidarity and organic unity beyond the "mechanistic" interaction and individualist competition of civil society.

1 Robert Pippin, *The Persistence of Subjectivity*, Cambridge: Cambridge University Press 2005, p. 296.

2 Hannah Arendt's refusal to carry out this shift is what links her to Heidegger: she rejected the "prosaic" character of modern "bourgeois" life.

Hegel's crucial step towards maturity occurs when he really "abandons the paradigm of the polis" by reconceptualizing the role of civil society.[3] First, civil society is for Hegel the "state of Understanding," the state reduced to the police-apparatus regulating the chaotic interaction of individuals each of whom pursues his egotistic interests. This individualistic-atomistic notion of freedom and the notion of a legal order imposed on individuals as an external limitation of that freedom are strictly correlative. The need thus arises to pass from this "state of Understanding" to the true "state of Reason," in which individuals' subjective dispositions are harmonized with the social Whole, in which individuals recognize the social substance as their own. The key move occurs when Hegel fully develops the mediating role of civil society: the "system of multilateral dependence" whose ultimate modern form is the market economy—in which particular and universal are separated and opposed, in which every individual pursues only his private goals, in which organic social unity decomposes into external mechanical interaction—is in itself already the reconciliation of the particular and the universal in the guise of the famous "invisible hand" of the market, on account of which, by pursuing his private interests at the expense of others, every individual contributes to the welfare of all. It is thus not simply that one has to "overcome" the mechanical or external interaction of civil society in a higher organic unity: civil society and its disintegration plays a crucial mediating role, so that the true reconciliation (which does not abolish modern subjective freedom) has to recognize how this disintegration is in itself already its opposite, a force of integration. Reconciliation is thus radically *immanent*: it implies a shift of perspective with regard to what first appeared as disintegration. In other words, insofar as civil society is the sphere of alienation, of the separation between subjectivity persisting in its abstract individuality and an objective social order opposing it as an external necessity limiting its freedom, the resources for reconciliation should be found in this very sphere (in what appears, "at first sight, as the least spiritual, as the most alienating: the system of needs"[4]), not in the passage to another "higher" sphere. The structure here is that of the Rabinovitch joke: Rabinovitch wants to emigrate from the Soviet Union for two reasons: "First, I fear that, if the socialist order disintegrates, all the blame for the communist crimes will be put on us, the Jews." To the state bureaucrat's objection: "But nothing will ever change in the Soviet Union! Socialism is here to stay forever!" Rabinovitch calmly answers: "This is my second reason." The true (second) reason can be enunciated only insofar as it is produced as a reaction to the bureaucrat's rejection of the first reason. The civil society version

3 Jean-François Kervégan, " 'La vie éthique perdue dans ses extrêmes…' Scission et réconciliation dans la théorie hégélienne de la 'Sittlichkeit,'" in Olivier Tinland, ed., *Lectures de Hegel*, Paris: Le Livre de Poche 2005, p. 283.

4 Ibid., p. 291.

is: "There are two reasons modern society is reconciled with itself. The first is the interaction within civil society …" "But civil-society interaction is a matter of constant strife, the very mechanism of disintegration, of ruthless competition!" "Well, this is the second reason, since this very strife and competition makes individuals thoroughly interdependent and thus creates the ultimate social link …"

The whole perspective thus changes: it is no longer that the organic *Sittlichkeit* of the polis disintegrates under the corrosive influence of modern abstract individuality in its multiple modes (the market economy, Protestantism, etc.), and that this unity should somehow be restored at a higher level: the point of Hegel's analyses of antiquity, best exemplified by his repeated readings of *Antigone*, is that the Greek polis itself was already marked, cut through, by fatal immanent antagonisms (public-private, masculine-feminine, human-divine, free men-slaves, etc.) which belie its organic unity. Abstract universal individualism (Christianity), far from causing the disintegration of the Greek organic unity, was, on the contrary, the necessary first step towards *true* reconciliation. Likewise the market, far from being simply a corrosive force, provides the mediating process which forms the basis of a *true* reconciliation between the universal and the singular. Market competition really brings people together, while organic order divides them. The best indication of this shift in the mature Hegel concerns the opposition of customs and law: for the early Hegel, the transformation of customs into institutionalized law is a regressive move from organic unity to alienation (the norm is no longer experienced as part of my substantial ethical nature, but as an external force that constrains my freedom), while for the mature Hegel, this transformation is a crucial step forward, opening up and sustaining the space of modern subjective freedom.

The problem here, of course, is whether the market dynamic really provides what it promises. Does it not in fact generate a permanent destabilization of the social body, especially by increasing class distinctions and giving rise to a "mob" deprived of the basic conditions of life? Hegel's solution here was very pragmatic—he opted for secondary palliative measures like colonial expansion and, especially, the mediating role of estates (*Stände*). And his dilemma is still ours today, two hundred years later. The clearest indication of Hegel's historical limit lies in his double use of the same term *Sitten* (customs, social ethical order): it stands for the immediate organic unity that has to be left behind (the Ancient Greek ideal), and for the higher organic unity which should be realized in a modern state.

It is easy to play the historicist card here and claim that Hegel was unable to grasp the capitalist dynamic proper because of the limitation of his historical experience. Jameson is right to draw attention to the fact that, "despite his familiarity with Adam Smith and emergent economic doctrine, Hegel's conception of work and labor—I have specifically characterized it as a handicraft ideology—betrays no anticipation of the originalities of industrial production or the factory system"[5]—in short, Hegel's analyses of work and production cannot be "transferred to the new industrial situation."[6] There is a series of interconnected reasons for this limitation, all grounded in the constraints of Hegel's historical experience. First, his notion of the industrial revolution involved only Adam-Smith-type manufacturing where the work process was still that of a group of individuals using tools, not yet that of the factory in which the machinery sets the rhythm and individual workers are de facto reduced to organs serving the machinery, to its appendices. Second, he could not yet imagine the way abstraction rules would develop in capitalism: when Marx describes capital's mad self-enhancing circulation, which reaches its apogee in today's meta-reflexive speculations on futures, it is far too simplistic to claim that the specter of this self-engendering monster pursuing its interests with no regard for human or environmental concerns is an ideological abstraction, and that, behind this abstraction, there are real people and natural objects on whose productive capacities and resources capital's circulation is based and on which it feeds like a gigantic parasite. The problem is that this "abstraction" is not only characteristic of our (the financial speculator's) misperception of social reality, but that it is "real" in the precise sense of determining the structure of material social processes themselves: the fate of whole swathes of the population and sometimes of whole countries can be decided by the "solipsistic" speculative dance of Capital, which pursues its goal of profitability with blessed indifference to how its movements will affect social reality. Therein lies the fundamental systemic violence of capitalism, much more uncanny than the direct pre-capitalist socio-ideological violence: it is no longer attributable to concrete individuals and their "evil" intentions, but is purely "objective," systemic, anonymous.

Here we encounter the Lacanian difference between reality and the Real: "reality" is the social reality of the actual people involved in interaction and in the productive processes, while the Real is the inexorable "abstract" spectral logic of Capital that determines what goes on in social reality. This gap is tangible in the way the economic situation of a country can be considered to be good and stable by the international financial experts, even when the majority of its people are worse off than before—reality does not matter, what matters is the situation of Capital. And, again, is this not more true than ever today? Do not phenomena usually classed as features of "virtual capitalism" (future trading and similar financial speculations) point towards the reign of "real abstraction" at its purest, much more radical than in Marx's time? In short, the highest form of ideology does not involve getting caught in ideological

5 Fredric Jameson, *The Hegel Variations*, London: Verso Books 2010, p. 68.
6 Ibid.

spectrality, forgetting about real people and their relations, but precisely in overlooking this Real of spectrality and in pretending to address directly "real people with their real problems." Visitors to the London Stock Exchange are given a free leaflet explaining how the stock market is not about mysterious fluctuations, but about real people and their products—*this* is ideology at its purest.

Here, in the analysis of the universe of Capital, we should not only push Hegel towards Marx, Marx himself should be radicalized: it is only today, in relation to global capitalism in its "post-industrial" form, that, to put it in Hegelian terms, really existing capitalism is reaching the level of its notion. Perhaps, we should once again follow Marx's old anti-evolutionist motto (incidentally, taken verbatim from Hegel) that the anatomy of man provides the key to the anatomy of a monkey—i.e., that, in order to describe the inherent notional structure of a social formation, we must start with its most developed form. Marx located the elementary capitalist antagonism in the opposition between use-value and exchange-value: in capitalism, the potential of this opposition is fully realized, the domain of exchange-value acquires autonomy, is transformed into the specter of self-propelling speculative capital which uses the productive capacities and needs of actual people only as its temporary disposable embodiment. Marx derived his notion of economic crisis from this very gap: a crisis occurs when reality catches up with the illusory self-generating mirage of money begetting more money—this speculative madness cannot go on indefinitely, it has to explode in ever more serious crises. The ultimate root of the crisis is for Marx the gap between use- and exchange-value: the logic of exchange-value follows its own path, its own mad dance, irrespective of the real needs of real people. It may appear that this analysis is highly relevant today, when the tension between the virtual universe and the real is reaching almost unbearable proportions: on the one hand, we have crazy solipsistic speculations about futures, mergers, etc., following their own inherent logic; on the other hand, reality is catching up in the guise of ecological catastrophes, poverty, the collapse of social life in the Third World, and the spread of new diseases.

This is why cyber-capitalists appear as the paradigmatic capitalists today—why Bill Gates can dream of cyberspace as providing the frame for what he calls "frictionless capitalism." What we have here is an ideological short-circuit between two versions of the gap between reality and virtuality: the gap between real production and the virtual or spectral domain of Capital, and the gap between experiential reality and the virtual reality of cyberspace. The real horror of the motto "frictionless capitalism" is that, even though actual "frictions" continue to insist, they become invisible, forced into a netherworld outside our "postmodern" and post-industrial universe; this is why the "frictionless" universe of digitalized communication, technological gadgets, etc., is constantly haunted by the notion of a global catastrophe lurking just around the corner, threatening to explode at any moment.

It seems as if the gap between my fascinating cyberspace persona and the miserable flesh which is "me" off-screen translates into the immediate experience of the gap between the Real of the speculative circulation of capital and the drab reality of the impoverished masses. However, is this recourse to a "reality" which will sooner or later catch up with the virtual game really the only way to pursue a critique of capitalism? What if the problem of capitalism is not this solipsistic dance, but precisely the opposite: that it continues to disavow its gap with "reality," that it presents itself as serving the real needs of real people? The paradox of this virtualization of capitalism is ultimately the same as that of the electron in particle physics. The mass of each elementary particle is composed of its mass at rest plus the surplus provided by the acceleration of its movement; however, an electron's mass at rest is zero, its mass consists only of the surplus generated by the acceleration, as if we are dealing with a nothing which acquires some deceptive substance only by magically spinning itself into an excess of itself. Does not today's virtual capitalist function in a homologous way—his "net value" is zero, he just operates with the surplus, borrowing from the future?

This compels us to thoroughly reformulate the standard Marxist topic of "reification" and "commodity fetishism," insofar as the latter still relies on a notion of the fetish as a solid object whose stable presence obfuscates its social mediation. Paradoxically, fetishism reaches its acme precisely when the fetish itself is "dematerialized," turned into a fluid "immaterial" virtual entity; money fetishism will culminate with the passage to its electronic form, when the last traces of its materiality will disappear—electronic money is the third form, after "real" money, which directly embodies its value (in gold or silver), and paper money which, although a "mere sign" with no intrinsic value, still clings to a material existence. And it is only at this stage, when money becomes a purely virtual point of reference, that it finally assumes the form of an indestructible spectral presence: I owe you $1000, and no matter how many material notes I burn, I still owe you $1000, the debt is inscribed somewhere in virtual digital space.

Does the same not hold also for warfare? Far from pointing towards twenty-first-century warfare, the attack on the World Trade Center in September 2001 was rather the last spectacular act of twentieth-century warfare. What awaits us is something much more uncanny: the specter of an "immaterial" war in which the attacks are invisible—viruses, poisons, which can be everywhere and nowhere. At the level of visible material reality, nothing happens, there are no big explosions, and yet the known universe starts to collapse, life disintegrates. We are entering a new era of paranoid warfare in which the greatest task will be to identify the enemy and his weapons. It is only with this thoroughgoing "dematerialization"—when Marx's famous thesis from *The Communist Manifesto*, that in capitalism "all that is solid melts into air," acquires a much more literal meaning than the one he had in mind, when our material social reality is not only dominated by the spectral or speculative movement of Capital but is itself progressively "spectralized" (the "Protean Self" replacing the old self-identical Subject, the elusive fluidity of its experiences superseding the stability of owned objects), in short, when the usual relationship between solid material objects and fluid ideas is inverted (objects are progressively dissolved in fluid experiences, while the only stable things are virtual symbolic obligations)—it is only at this point that what Derrida called the spectral aspect of capitalism is fully actualized.

This is why the key feature of contemporary capitalism is not only the hegemony, but also the (relative) autonomy of financial capital: it may seem like the banks are just engaging in speculation, shuffling numbers here and there, and nobody is exploited, since exploitation happens in "real" production. But why did we have to give billions of dollars to the banks in 2008 and 2009? Because, without a functioning banking system, the entire (capitalist) economy collapses. Banks should thus also count as privatized commons: insofar as private banks control the flow of investments and thus represent, for individual companies, the universal dimension of social capital, their profit is really a rent we pay for their role as universal mediator. This is why state or other forms of social control over banks and collective capital in general (like pension funds) are crucial in taking a first step towards the social control of commons. Apropos the reproach that such control is economically inefficient, we should recall not only those cases in which such control was very effective (this was, for example, how Malaysia avoided crisis in the late 1990s), but also the obvious fact that the 2008 financial crisis was triggered precisely by the failure of the banking system.

Let us take a closer look at Marx's classical description of the passage from money to capital, with its explicit allusions to the Hegelian and Christian background. First, there is the simple act of market exchange in which I sell in order to buy—I sell the product I own or have made in order to buy another one which is of some use to me: "The simple circulation of commodities—selling in order to buy—is a means of carrying out a purpose unconnected with circulation, namely, the appropriation of use-values, the satisfaction of wants."[7] What happens with the emergence of capital is not just the simple reversal of C-M-C (Commodity-Money-Commodity) into M-C-M, i.e., of investing money in some commodity in order to sell it again and thus get back to (more) money; the key effect of this reversal is the *eternalization* of circulation: "The circulation of money as capital is, on the contrary, an end in itself, for the expansion of value

7 Karl Marx, *Capital: A Critique of Political Economy*, trans. Samuel Moore and Edward Aveling, New York: Random House 1906, p. 169.

takes place only within this constantly renewed movement. The circulation of capital has therefore no limits."[8] Crucial here is the difference between the traditional miser, hoarding his treasure in secret, and the capitalist who augments his treasure by throwing it into circulation:

> The restless never-ending process of profit-making alone is what he aims at. This boundless greed after riches, this passionate chase after exchange-value, is common to the capitalist and the miser; but while the miser is merely a capitalist gone mad, the capitalist is a rational miser. The never-ending augmentation of exchange-value, which the miser strives after, by seeking to save his money from circulation, is attained by the more acute capitalist, by constantly throwing it afresh into circulation.[9]

This madness of the miser is nonetheless not something which simply disappears with the rise of "normal" capitalism, nor is it a pathological deviation. It is rather *inherent* to it: the miser has his moment of triumph in the economic *crisis*. In a crisis, it is not—as one would expect—money which loses its value, so that we have to resort to the "real" value of commodities; commodities themselves (the embodiment of "real [use] value") become useless, because there is no one to buy them. In a crisis,

> money suddenly and immediately changes from its merely nominal shape, money of account, into hard cash. Profane commodities can no longer replace it. The use-value of commodities becomes value-less, and their value vanishes in the face of their own form of value. The bourgeois, drunk with prosperity and arrogantly certain of himself, has just declared that money is a purely imaginary creation. "Commodities alone are money," he said. But now the opposite cry resounds over the markets of the world: only money is a commodity ... In a crisis, the antithesis between commodities and their value-form, money, is raised to the level of an absolute contradiction.[10]

It is crucial how, in describing this elevation of money to the status of the only true commodity ("The capitalist knows that all commodities, however scurvy they may look, or however badly they may smell, are in faith and in truth money, inwardly circumcised Jews"[11]), Marx resorts to the precise Pauline definition of Christians as "inwardly circumcised Jews": Christians do not need actual circumcision (the abandonment of ordinary commodities with use values, dealing

8 Ibid., pp. 169–70.

9 Ibid., pp. 170–1.

10 Karl Marx, *Capital: A Critique of Political Economy*, Vol. 1, trans. Ben Fowkes, Harmondsworth: Penguin Books 1976, pp. 236.

11 Marx, *Capital: A Critique of Political Economy*, trans. Moore and Aveling, p. 172.

only with money), since they know that each of these ordinary commodities is already "inwardly circumcised," that its true substance is money. In a certain sense, this self-engendering speculative movement of Capital can also be said to indicate a limit of the Hegelian dialectical process, and one that eludes Hegel's grasp. It is in this sense that Lebrun mentions the "fascinating image" of Capital presented by Marx (especially in his *Grundrisse*): "a monstrous mixture of the good infinity and the bad infinity, the good infinity which creates its presuppositions and the conditions of its growth, the bad infinity which never ceases to surmount its crises, and which finds its limit in its own nature."[12] Actually, it is in *Capital* itself that we find this Hegelian description of the circulation of capital:

> in the circulation M-C-M, both the money and the commodity represent only different modes of existence of value itself, the money its general mode, and the commodity its particular, or, so to say, disguised mode. It is constantly changing from one form to the other without thereby becoming lost, and thus assumes an automatically active character. If now we take in turn each of the two different forms which self-expanding value successively assumes in the course of its life, we then arrive at these two propositions: Capital is money: Capital is commodities. In truth, however, value is here the active factor in a process, in which, while constantly assuming the form in turn of money and commodities, it at the same time changes in magnitude, differentiates itself by throwing off surplus-value from itself; the original value, in other words, expands spontaneously. For the movement, in the course of which it adds surplus-value, is its own movement, its expansion, therefore, is automatic expansion. Because it is value, it has acquired the occult quality of being able to add value to itself. It brings forth living offspring, or, at the least, lays golden eggs.
>
> Value, therefore, being the active factor in such a process, and assuming at one time the form of money, at another that of commodities, but through all these changes preserving itself and expanding, it requires some independent form, by means of which its identity may at any time be established. And this form it possesses only in the shape of money. It is under the form of money that value begins and ends, and begins again, every act of its own spontaneous generation.[13]

Note how Hegelian references abound here: with capitalism, value is not a mere abstract "mute" universality, a substantial link between the multiplicity of commodities; from the passive medium of exchange, it turns into the "active factor" of the entire process. Instead of just passively assuming the two different forms of its actual existence (money—commodity), it appears as the subject "endowed

12 Gérard Lebrun, *L'envers de la dialectique: Hegel à la lumière de Nietzsche*, Paris: Seuil 2004, p. 311.

13 Marx, *Capital: A Critique of Political Economy*, trans. Moore and Aveling, pp. 171–2.

with a motion of its own, passing through a life-process of its own": it differentiates itself from itself, positing its otherness, and then again overcomes this difference—the entire movement is *its own* movement. In this precise sense, "instead of simply representing the relations of commodities, it enters ... into private relations with itself": the "truth" of its relating to its otherness is its self-relating, in its self-movement, capital retroactively "sublates" its own material conditions, changing them into subordinate moments of its own "spontaneous expansion"—in pure Hegelese, it posits its own presuppositions.

Crucial in the quoted passage is the expression "an automatically active character," an inadequate translation of the German words used by Marx to characterize capital as "*automatischem Subjekt*," an "automatic subject," an oxymoron uniting living subjectivity and dead automatism. This is what capital is: a subject, but an automatic one, not a living one—and, again, can Hegel think this "monstrous mixture," a process of subjective self-mediation and retroactive positing of presuppositions which, as it were, gets caught up in a substantial "spurious infinity," a subject which itself becomes an alienated substance?

This is perhaps also the reason why Marx's reference to Hegel's dialectics in his "critique of political economy" is ambiguous, oscillating between taking it as a mystified expression of the logic of capital and taking it as a model for the revolutionary process of emancipation. First, there is the dialectic as the "logic of capital": the development of the commodity-form and the passage from money to capital are clearly formulated in Hegelian terms (capital is money-substance turning into the self-mediating process of its own reproduction, etc.). Then, there is the Hegelian notion of the proletariat as "substance-less subjectivity," the grandiose Hegelian scheme of the historical process moving from pre-class society to capitalism in a gradual separation of the subject from its objective conditions, so that the overcoming of capitalism means that the (collective) subject re-appropriates its alienated substance. Perhaps this oscillation between the two is conditioned by a third term: the precise status of the social antagonism ("class struggle"). The problem here is whether Hegel can think the class struggle, or whether Kant gets closer to it with his antinomies, which just have to be ontologized, conceived as a paradoxical feature of reality itself. But does not such an ontologization contradict Marx's notion of class struggle as historically limited, as an antagonism to be overcome with the disappearance of capitalism? In response, one can argue that neither Marx nor Freud are really able to think antagonism: ultimately, they both reduce it to a feature of (social or psychic) reality, unable to articulate it as constitutive of reality itself, as the impossibility around which reality is constructed—the only thought able to do this comes later, originating in the differential logic of "structuralism."

Marx's reading of Hegel's dialectic as an idealist formulation of the logic of capitalist domination fails to go all the way: what the Hegelian dialectical process deploys is the (mystified) expression of the *mystification* immanent to the circulation of capital, or, in Lacanian terms, of its "objectively-social" fantasy—to put it in somewhat naïve terms, for Marx, capital is not "really" a subject-substance which reproduces itself by way of positing its own presuppositions and so on; what this Hegelian fantasy of capital's self-generating reproduction obliterates is workers' exploitation, that is, how the circle of capital's self-reproduction draws its energy from the external (or, rather, "ex-timate") source of value, how it has to parasitize workers. So why not pass directly to a description of workers' exploitation, why bother with fantasies which sustain the functioning of capital? It is crucial for Marx to include in his description of capital this intermediary level of "objective fantasy," which is neither the way capitalism is actually experienced by its subjects (they are good empirical nominalists unaware of the "theological niceties") nor the "real state of things" (workers exploited by capital). But the problem is how to think together the Hegelian circulation of capital and its decentered cause, the labor force, that is, how to think the causality of a productive subject external to the circulation of capital without resorting to the Aristotelian positivity of workers' productive potential? For Marx, the starting point is precisely such a positivity: the productive force of human labor; and he accepts this starting point as unsurpassable, rejecting the logic of the dialectical process which, as Hegel put it, progresses "from nothing through nothing to nothing."

In short, capital is money which is no longer a mere substance of wealth, its universal embodiment, but value which, through its circulation, generates more value, value which mediates or posits itself, retroactively positing its own presuppositions. First, money appears as a mere means for the exchange of commodities: instead of endless bartering, we first exchange our product for the universal equivalent of all commodities, which can then be exchanged for any commodity we may need. Then, once the circulation of capital is set in motion, the relationship is inverted, the means turns into an end-in-itself, the very passage through the "material" domain of use-values (the production of commodities which satisfy individuals' particular needs) is posited as a moment of what is substantially the self-movement of capital itself. From this moment on, the true aim is no longer the satisfaction of individuals' needs, but simply more money, the endless repeating of the circulation as such. This arcane circular movement of self-positing is then equated with the central Christian tenet of the identity of God-the-Father and his Son, of the immaculate conception in which the single Father directly (without a female spouse) begets his only Son and thus forms what is arguably the ultimate single-parent family.

Is capital then the true Subject or Substance? Yes and no: for Marx, this self-engendering circular movement is—to put it in Freudian terms—precisely the "unconscious fantasy" of capitalism which parasitizes the proletariat as "pure substanceless subjectivity"; for this reason, capital's speculative self-generating dance has a limit, and brings about the conditions for its own collapse. This insight allows us to solve the key interpretive problem of the passage quoted above: how are we to read its first three words, "*in truth, however*"? First, of course, they imply that this truth has to be asserted against some false appearance or experience: the everyday assumption that the ultimate goal of capital's circulation is still the satisfaction of human needs, that capital is just a means to bring about this satisfaction in a more efficient way. However, this "truth" is *not* the reality of capitalism: in reality, capital does not engender itself, but extracts the worker's surplus-value. There is thus a necessary third level to be added to the simple opposition of subjective experience (of capital as a means of satisfying people's needs) and objective social reality (of exploitation): namely, the "objective deception," the disavowed "unconscious" fantasy (of the mysterious self-generating circular movement of capital), which is the *truth* (although not the *reality*) of the capitalist process. Again, to quote Lacan, truth has the structure of fiction: the only way to formulate the truth of capital is through a reference to this fiction of its "immaculate" self-generating movement. And this insight also allows us to locate the weakness of the above-mentioned "deconstructionist" appropriation of Marx's analysis of capitalism: although it emphasizes the endless process of deferral which characterizes this movement, as well as its fundamental inconclusiveness, its self-blockage, the "deconstructionist" retelling still describes the *fantasy* of capital—it describes what individuals believe, although they do not know it.

What all this means is that the urgent task is to *repeat* Marx's "critique of political economy," but without succumbing to the temptation of the multiple ideologies of "post-industrial" society. The key change concerns the status of private property: the ultimate element of power and control is no longer the last link in the chain of investment—the firm or individual who "really owns" the means of production. The ideal capitalist today functions in a wholly different way: investing borrowed money, "really owning" nothing, maybe even indebted, but nonetheless still controlling things. A corporation is owned by another corporation, which again borrows money from banks, which may ultimately manipulate money owned by ordinary people like ourselves. With Bill Gates, the notion of "private property of the means of production" becomes meaningless, at least in its standard sense.

It is easy to miss the irony here: the fact that Marx needed Hegel to formulate the logic of capital (the crucial breakthrough in Marx's work occurred in the mid-1850s, when, after the failure of the 1848 revolutions, he started to read Hegel's *Logic* again) means that what Hegel was not able to see was not some post-Hegelian reality but rather the properly *Hegelian* aspect of the capitalist economy. Here, paradoxically, Hegel was not *idealist* enough, for what he did not see was the properly *speculative* content of the capitalist economy, the way financial capital functions as a purely virtual notion processing "real people." And does not exactly the same hold for modern art? Robert Pippin endorses Hegel's thesis on the "end of art"—with a qualification: it does not refer to art as such, but only to representational art, to the art which relies on some pre-subjective substantial notion of "reality" that art should reflect, re-present in the medium of sensuous materials:

> *Representational art cannot adequately express the full subjectivity of experience, the wholly self-legislating, self-authorizing status of the norms that constitute such subjectivity, or, thus, cannot adequately express who we (now) are.* Only philosophy can "heal" such a self-inflicted wound and allow the self-determining character of experience its adequate expression. ("Only philosophy," that is, on Hegel's official account. I am trying to suggest here that there is no reason a form of art, like abstraction, could not make such a point in a nondiscursive way.)[14]

This is how Pippin reads—in a consciously anachronistic way, with the benefit of the hindsight of those who live two centuries after Hegel—Hegel's prophecy, in his *Lectures on Aesthetics*, that post-Romantic art will enact the "self-transcendence of art but within its own sphere and in the form of art itself":[15] art transcends itself as representational art, it overcomes its limitation to the representational sphere. What Hegel could not grasp (insofar as his thought was, as every thought is, "his time conceived in thought") was the notional possibility of an art that would overcome *in itself, as art*, the medium of representation, and thus function as an art adequate to the total reflexivization (subjective mediation) of life conceptualized in his absolute Idealism.[16]

The interest of Pippin's gesture resides in the fact that he rejects the standard story which goes something like this: with Hegel, Western metaphysics reached its apogee in the figure of Absolute Knowing, the actual infinity of the total conceptual mediation of all reality—nothing can any longer resist the power of notional conceiving; God himself is, as Hegel put it with an implicit but all the more unsurpassable acerbic irony, "an interesting representation" (meaning: a mere representation, *Vorstellung*, whose truth is its notional content). However, post-Hegelian philosophy, in all its versions, is a reaction against this totality of

14 Pippin, *The Persistence of Subjectivity*, p. 300.

15 G. W. F. Hegel, *Aesthetics: Lectures on Fine Arts*, Vol. 1, trans. T. M. Knox, Oxford: Clarendon Press 1975, p. 80.

16 It would be interesting for Hegelian Higher Criticism to engage in a debate about the possible candidates for this post-Hegelian artistic version of the total subjectivization of substance: is it only the modernist break proper—Schoenberg's atonality in music, Kandinsky's abstraction in painting, etc.—or can figures like Richard Wagner also be read in this way?

absolute notional self-mediation, against this all-powerful Spirit which swallows everything up. Finitude (either human finitude as such, man's separatedness from God; or the finitude of man's sensual life and material production) is fully reasserted, meaning, among other things, that art regains its rights against philosophy. The first step in this direction was already taken by Schelling in his *System of Transcendental Idealism*, where he places art above philosophy as the highest synthesis of Spirit and Nature, of Subject and Object, of thought and senses: philosophy is limited to the thinking subject opposed to nature, to sensuous reality; the harmonious balance of the two sides is achieved only in a work of art.

When, however, Pippin envisages a new possibility for art after Hegel, he does not ground it in any limitation of Reason, of reflexive mediation: for him, the modernist break (abstract art) has nothing to do with the reassertion of the unsurpassable horizon of finitude. Pippin remains faithful to Hegel: there is no transcendent Truth from which we, as finite humans, remain forever cut off, either in the form of an Infinite Reality which art cannot properly represent, or in the form of a Divinity too sublime to be grasped by our finite mind. In other words, the point of Pippin's rehabilitation of art is not that the Absolute cannot be directly conceptually grasped, that it can only be hinted at, evoked as an unfathomable X, in artistic metaphors; his rehabilitation of art has nothing to do with the assertion of an irrational spirituality, too subtle to let itself be caught in the crude analytical categories of human Reason, of a spirituality which can only be experienced in the form of artistic intuition. Modernist art is thoroughly reflexive, in contrast to traditional art which still relies on a non-reflected acceptance of some substantial medium or reality; it is reflexive in the radical sense of questioning its own medium. This is what "abstraction" means: a reflexive questioning of the very medium of artistic representation, so that this medium loses its natural transparency. Reality is not just "out there," reflected or imitated by art, it is something constructed, something contingent, historically conditioned—and therein resides the legacy of German Idealism, which

> destroyed the classical picture of the sensible-intelligible relation. Sensibility could not now be understood as an unclear representation of the world that reason could work to clarify or could represent better, nor could it be understood as a vivid, "lively" impression, guiding the abstracting and generalizing intellect ... The content of sensibility was, after Kant, to be understood as the material object of the understanding's synthesizing, active work ... Sensory data became representative as a result of this work by the understanding, and considered apart from such enforming, conceptualizing activity, it counted as mere stuff, preintelligible materiality.[17]

---

17 Pippin, *The Persistence of Subjectivity*, p. 297.

The consequence of all this for the visual arts is that "painterly and indeed sensible representations cannot be understood on some mimetic model of seeing through the image (or sensation) to the object itself":[18]

> "Abstraction" in this Hegelian sense does not mean abstraction of "everything that was not intrinsic to art as such," but abstraction from dependence on sensual immediacy, and so a kind of enactment of the modernist take on normativity since Kant: self-legislation ... Paintings by Pollock and Rothko are not presentations of paint drips and color fields and flat canvas. They thematize and so render self-conscious components of sensible meaning that we traditionally would not see and understand as such, would treat as given. Said another way, they present the materiality of such components in their conceptual significance; such materiality is mentioned, cited, or quoted, as well as used, as well as occupying space on a stretched canvas. And this can make sense because the "result" character of even sensible apprehension ... has come to be part of the intellectual habits of mind of modern self-understanding, even if unattended to as such.[19]

This is why one can only agree with Pippin's endorsement of Michael Fried's rejection of modernism and postmodernism as consecutive "stages" of historical development; "postmodernism" is rather the name for a regression, for a refusal to follow the consequences of the modernist break:

> There was no failure of modernism, no exhaustion by the end of abstract expressionism. Rather, there was (and still is) a failure to appreciate and integrate the self-understanding reflected in such art (the same kind of failure to appreciate modernism, or the same kind of straw-men attacks, in what we call postmodernism). The aftermath—minimalism, "literalism," op and pop art, postmodernism—can be understood better as evasions and repressions than as alternatives.[20]

Or, to put it in Badiou's terms, *there is no postmodernist Event*: postmodernism is not an Event proper, but, at its most basic, a *reactive* formation, a way of betraying the modernist break, of re-integrating its achievement into the dominant field. The apparent "radicality" of some postmodern trends should not deceive us here: this—often spectacular—"radicality" is there to fascinate us with its deceptive lure, and thus to blind us to the fundamental *absence of thought proper*. Suffice it to recall recent trends in the visual arts: gone are the days of simple statues or framed paintings—what we see now are the frames themselves without paintings, dead cows and their excrement, videos of the

18 Ibid., p. 304.
19 Ibid., pp. 304–5.
20 Ibid., p. 301.

inside of the human body (gastroscopy and colonoscopy), the inclusion of odors in the exhibition, and so on and so forth. Here, again, as in the domain of sexuality, perversion is no longer subversive: the shocking excesses are part of the system itself, what the system feeds on in order to reproduce itself. Perhaps this gives us one possible definition of postmodern art as opposed to modernist art: in postmodernism, the transgressive excess loses its shock value and is fully integrated into the established art market.

This weird postmodern space where excesses lose their subversive edge brings us to a further critical point which concerns the properly modern capitalist class struggle in its difference from traditional caste and feudal hierarchies: since Hegel's notion of domination was limited to the traditional struggle between master and servant, what he could not envisage was the kind of relationship of domination which persists in a post-revolutionary situation (referring here to the "bourgeois" revolution doing away with traditional privileges), where all individuals recognize each other as autonomous free subjects. This "prodigious social leveling" of a modern democracy

> certainly does not exclude the emergence of wealth and of profound distinctions between rich and poor, even in the socialist countries. Nor is it in any way to be understood as the end of classes in their economic sense: there are still workers and managers in these societies, there is still profit and exploitation, reserve armies of the unemployed, and so on and so forth. But the new cultural equality ... is infused with a powerful hatred of hierarchy and special privileges and with a passionate resentment of caste distinctions and inherited cultural superiority. It is permitted to be wealthy, so long as the rich man is as vulgar as everyone else.[21]

A situation which, one might add, opens up the unexpected possibility of a genuinely proletarian re-appropriation of "high culture."

All these cases of Hegel's historical limitation seem to themselves call for an Hegelian analysis: laborers reduced to an appendix of machinery; reality dominated by the virtual/ideal self-movement of capital's circulation; a hierarchy persisting in the very form of "plebeianization"—paradoxical reversals which seem to give body to all the twists and turns of the most sophisticated dialectic. What kind of "reconciliation" can we then imagine in these new conditions? Apropos Hegel's "reconciliation" in a modern post-revolutionary state, Jameson outlines a higher, "enlarged" version of Hegelian reconciliation, a version appropriate for our global capitalist epoch: the project of a "human age" characterized by "production-for-us" (the end of classes) and ecology.[22] Jameson's view is that, far from standing for the ultimate "end of history," the reconciliation proposed

21 Jameson, *The Hegel Variations*, p. 101.

22 Ibid., pp. 113–15.

at the end of the chapter on Spirit in the *Phenomenology* is a temporary, fragile synthesis—Hegel himself was aware that this reconciliation was under threat, as is clear from his panicky reaction to the revolution of 1830 and the first signs of universal democracy (recall his furious rejection of the British electoral Reform Bill, the first step towards universal elections). Is it then not consistent that, in view of the new contradictions of the nineteenth-century capitalist system which exploded the fragile Hegelian synthesis, a renewed Hegelian approach which remains faithful to the idea of concrete universality, of universal rights for all, "calls in its very structure for the subsequent enlargements of later history"[23] and for a new project of reconciliation? Such a move is nonetheless illegitimate: it does not take into account in a sufficiently radical way that the same paradox as that of the retroactive positing of presuppositions holds also for the future.

This is why Hegel was right to insist that the owl of Minerva takes flight only at dusk; and also why the twentieth-century communist project was utopian precisely insofar as it was not radical enough—that is, insofar as the fundamental capitalist thrust of unleashed productivity survived in it, deprived of its concrete contradictory conditions of existence. The inadequacy of Heidegger, Adorno and Horkheimer, and so on, lies in their abandonment of the concrete social analysis of capitalism: in their very critique or overcoming of Marx, they in a certain way repeat Marx's mistake—like him, they take unleashed productivity as something ultimately independent of the concrete capitalist social formation. Capitalism and communism are not two different historical realizations, two species, of "instrumental reason"—instrumental reason as such is capitalist, grounded in capitalist relations, and "really existing socialism" failed because it was ultimately a subspecies of capitalism, an ideological attempt to "have one's cake and eat it," to break out of capitalism while retaining its key ingredient. Marx's notion of the communist society is itself the inherent capitalist fantasy; that is, a fantasmatic scenario for resolving the capitalist antagonisms he so aptly described. In other words, our wager is that, even if we take away the teleological notion of communism (the society of fully unleashed productivity) as the implicit standard by which Marx measures the alienation of existing society, the bulk of his "critique of political economy," his insights into the self-propelling vicious cycle of capitalist (re)production, survives.

The task of contemporary theory is thus double: on the one hand, to repeat the Marxist "critique of political economy" without the utopian-ideological notion of communism as its inherent standard; on the other hand, to imagine really breaking out of the capitalist horizon without falling into the trap of returning to the eminently premodern notion of a balanced, (self-)restrained society (the "pre-Cartesian" temptation to which most contemporary ecology

23 Ibid., p. 115.

succumbs). A return to Hegel is crucial in order to perform this task, a return which dispenses with all the classic anti-Hegelian topics, especially that of Hegel's voracious narcissism, of the Hegelian Idea swallowing up or internalizing the whole of reality. Instead of trying to undermine or overcome this "narcissism" from the outside, emphasizing the "preponderance of the objective" (or the fact that "the Whole is the non-true," and every other similar motif in Adorno's rejection of "identitarian" idealism), one should rather problematize this figure of Hegel by asking a simple question: *which* Hegel is our point of reference here? Do not both Lukács and Adorno refer to the "idealist-subjectivist" (mis)reading of Hegel, to the standard image of Hegel as the "absolute idealist" who posited Spirit as the true agent of history, its Subject-Substance? Within this framework, Capital can effectively appear as a new embodiment of the Hegelian Spirit, an abstract monster which moves and mediates itself, parasitizing the activity of actual, really existing individuals. This is why Lukács also remains all too idealist when he proposes simply replacing the Hegelian Spirit with the proletariat as the Subject-Object of History: Lukács is here not really Hegelian, but a pre-Hegelian idealist.

If, however, one problematizes this figure, another Hegel appears, a more "materialist" Hegel for whom the reconciliation between subject and substance does not mean that the subject "swallows" its substance, internalizing it into its own subordinate moment. Reconciliation rather amounts to a much more modest overlapping or redoubling of the two separations: the subject has to recognize in its alienation from substance the separation of substance from itself. This overlapping is what is missed in the Feuerbachian-Marxian logic of dis-alienation in which the subject overcomes its alienation by recognizing itself as the active agent which has itself posited what appears to it as its substantial presupposition. In the Hegelian "reconciliation" between subject and substance, there is no absolute Subject which, in total self-transparency, appropriates or internalizes all objective substantial content. But "reconciliation" also does not mean (as it does in the line of German Idealism from Hölderlin to Schelling) that the subject should renounce the hubris of perceiving itself as the axis of the world and accept its constitutive "de-centering," its dependency on some primordial, abyssal Absolute beyond or beneath the subject/object divide, and, as such, also beyond the subject's conceptual grasp. The subject is not its own origin: Hegel firmly rejects Fichte's notion of the absolute I which posits itself and is nothing but the pure activity of this self-positing. But the subject is also not just a secondary accidental appendix or outgrowth of some pre-subjective substantial reality: there is no substantial Being to which the subject can return, no encompassing organic Order of Being in which the subject has to find its proper place. "Reconciliation" between subject and substance means the acceptance of this radical lack of any firm foundational point: the subject is not its own origin, it comes second, it is dependent upon its substantial presuppositions; but these presuppositions also do not have a substantial consistency of their own but are always retroactively posited.

What this also means is that communism should no longer be conceived as the subjective (re)appropriation of the alienated substantial content—all versions of reconciliation as "subject swallows the substance" should be rejected. So, again, "reconciliation" is the full acceptance of the abyss of the de-substantialized process as the only actuality there is: the subject has no substantial actuality, it comes second, it emerges only through the process of separation, the overcoming of its presuppositions, and these presuppositions are also just a retroactive effect of the same process of their overcoming. The result is thus that there is, at both extremes of the process, a failure or negativity inscribed in the very heart of the entity we are dealing with. If the status of the subject is thoroughly "processual," this means that it emerges only through the failure to fully actualize itself. This brings us again to one possible formal definition of the subject: a subject tries to articulate ("express") itself in a signifying chain, this articulation fails, and in and through this failure, the subject emerges: the subject is the failure of its signifying representation—which is why Lacan writes the subject of the signifier as $, as "barred." In a love letter, the very failure of the writer to formulate his declaration in a clear and effective way, his vacillations, the letter's fragmentary style, and so on, can in themselves be proof (perhaps the necessary and only reliable proof) that the love he professes is authentic—here, the very failure to deliver the message properly is the sign of its authenticity. If the message is delivered too smoothly, it will arouse the suspicion that it is part of a well-planned approach, or that the writer loves himself, the beauty of his writing, more than his love-object, that the latter is effectively reduced to a pretext for engaging in the narcissistically satisfying activity of writing.

And the same goes for substance: substance is not only always already lost, it only comes to be through its loss, as a secondary return-to-itself—which means that substance is always already subjectivized. In the "reconciliation" between subject and substance, both poles thus lose their firm identity. Take the case of ecology: radical emancipatory politics should aim neither at complete mastery over nature nor at humanity's humble acceptance of the predominance of Mother Earth. Rather, nature should be exposed in all its catastrophic contingency and indeterminacy, and the unpredictable consequences of human agency fully assumed—viewed from this perspective of the "other Hegel," the revolutionary act no longer involves the Lukácsian substance-subject as its agent, as the agent who knows what it is doing while acting.

Hegel is, of course, fully aware of the fact that our thinking wants to "jump ahead of its time" and project a future; his point is that such thinking is always and by definition "ideological," mistaken: its intervention into Being generates something unexpected, totally different from what was projected. Therein resides the lesson of the French Revolution: the pure thought of universal equality and freedom, imposing itself onto social Being, generated the Terror. Marx's counter-argument here is that his revolutionary theory is not a utopian projection into the future: it merely extrapolates tendencies and possibilities from the antagonisms of the present. Hegel is wrong in his basic presupposition that one can rationally grasp the Present as a Totality: it cannot be done because our historical Present is in itself split, traversed by antagonisms, incomplete—the only way to concretely grasp it as a rational totality is from the standpoint of the revolutionary agent which will resolve those antagonisms. Present antagonisms are not "readable" on their own terms; they are like the Benjaminian traces which are readable only from the future. What Hegel rejects is precisely such a totalization-from-the-future: the only totality accessible to us is the flawed totality of the present, and the task of Thought is to "recognize the Heart in the Cross of the present," to grasp how *the Totality of the Present is complete in its very incompleteness*, how this Totality is sustained by those very features which appear as its obstacles or fatal flaws.

The task here is to leave behind the standard "subjectivist" reading of Hegelian "reconciliation" whose clearest instance is Lukács's *History and Class Consciousness* but which also underlies Marx's reference to Hegel.[24] According to this reading, in reconciliation, the subject recognizes itself in the alienated substance (substantial content); that is, it recognizes in it the reified product of its own work, and thereby re-appropriates it, transforms it into a transparent medium of its self-expression. The key feature here is that the subject, the agent of re-appropriation, is in the singular (even if it is conceived as a collective subject); what thereby disappears is the dimension of what Lacan calls the "big Other," the minimally "objectivized" symbolic order, the minimal self-transcendence which alone sustains the dimension of intersubjectivity—intersubjectivity can never be dissolved into the direct interaction of individuals.

This is why one should reject not only the (in)famously stupid "dialectical-materialist" substitution of "idea" with "matter" as the absolute (so that dialectics becomes a set of dialectical "laws" of matter's movement), but also Lukács's more refined "materialist reversal of Hegel," his substitution of Hegel's "idealist" subject-object (the absolute Idea) with the proletariat as the "actual" historical subject-object. Lukács's "reversal" also implies a formalist and non-Hegelian separation of the dialectical method from the material to which it is applied: Hegel was right to describe the process of the subject's alienation and re-appropriation of the "fetishized" or reified substantial content, he just did not see that what he described as the Idea's self-movement is actually an historical

---

24 See Georg Lukács, *History and Class Consciousness*, London: Merlin Press 1975.

development which culminates in the emergence of the substanceless subjectivity of the proletariat and its re-appropriation of the alienated substance through a revolutionary act. The reason we should reject this "materialist reversal" is that it remains all too idealist: locating Hegel's idealism in the "subject" of the process (the "absolute Idea"), it fails to see the subjectivist "idealism" inherent in the very matrix of the dialectical process (the self-alienated subject which re-appropriates its "reified" substantial content, positing itself as the absolute subject-object).

There are two ways to break out of this "idealism": either one rejects Hegel's dialectics as such, dismissing the notion of the subjective "mediation" of all substantial content as irreducibly "idealist," proposing to replace it with a radically different matrix (Althusser: structural (over)determination; Deleuze: difference and repetition; Derrida: *différance*; Adorno: negative dialectics with its "preponderance of the objective"); *or* one rejects such a reading of Hegel (focused on the idea of "reconciliation" as the subjective appropriation of the alienated substantial content) as "idealist," as a misreading which remains blind to the true subversive core of Hegel's dialectic. This is our position: the Hegel of the absolute Subject swallowing up all objective content is a retroactive fantasy of his critics, starting with late Schelling's turn to "positive philosophy." This "positivity" is found also in the young Marx, in the guise of the Aristotelian reassertion of positive forces or potentials of Being pre-existing logical or notional mediation. One should thus question the very image of Hegel-the-absolute-idealist presupposed by his critics—they attack the wrong Hegel, a straw man. What are they unable to think? The pure processuality of the subject which emerges as "its own result." This is why talk about the subject's "self-alienation" is deceptive, as if the subject somehow precedes its alienation—what this misses is the way the subject emerges through the "self-alienation" of the substance, *not* of itself. We should therefore reject the young Marx's celebration of the subject's productive powers or potentials, of its essential nature—Marx is here secretly Aristotelian, presupposing a "substantial" subject which pre-exists the deployment of these potentials in history; that is, his critical move

> represents a kind of regression to an Aristotelian or naturalist essentialism, one which borrows a teleological logic of such "natures" that abandons rather than completes the Hegelian project. The key and very controversial point to be defended is: Hegel's self-making model is not derived from the Aristotelian notions of natural growth and maturation into some flourishing state.[25]

---

25 Robert Pippin, *Hegel's Practical Philosophy*, Cambridge: Cambridge University Press 2008, p. 17.

One standard criticism addressed by some late partisans of "dialectical materialism" against the "subjectivist" Marxism of the young Lukács is that there is at least one key advantage of "dialectical materialism": since it locates human history in the general frame of an all-encompassing "dialectics of nature," it is much more appropriate for grasping the ecological problematic. But is this really so? Is it not, on the contrary, that the dialectical-materialist vision with its "objective laws of nature" justifies a ruthless technological domination over and exploitation of nature? While the philosophically much more refined Adornian view of nature as the encompassing Other of humanity, out of which humanity emerged and to which it forever remains indebted (from *Dialectic of Enlightenment*), clearly sees this, it does not offer much more than the well-known clichés of the "critique of instrumental reason": it fails to provide a clear way to think "nature" philosophically, in its priority to humanity.

We can see now why Adorno's project of "negative dialectics," which sees itself as the overcoming of Hegel's "positive" dialectics, misses the point. "Negative dialectics" wants to break out of the confines of the "principle of identity" which enslaves or subordinates every otherness through conceptual mediation. In Hegel's idealism, negativity, alterity, and difference are asserted, but only as subordinate secondary moments serving their opposite—the absolute Subject re-appropriates all otherness, "sublating" it into a moment of its own self-mediation. Adorno counters this with his "primacy of the objective": instead of appropriating or internalizing all otherness, dialectics should remain open towards it, granting ultimate primacy to the objective over the subjective, to difference over identity. What if, however, the image of Hegel's dialectic this critique presupposes is wrong? What if, in its innermost core, Hegel's dialectic is not a machine for appropriating or mediating all otherness, for sublating all contingency into a subordinated ideal moment of the notional necessity? What if Hegelian "reconciliation" already is the acceptance of an irreducible contingency at the very heart of notional necessity? What if it involves, as its culminating moment, the setting-free of objectivity in its otherness? In this case, it is Adorno's "negative dialectics" which, paradoxically, remains within the confines of "identitarian" thought: the endless critical "work of the negative" which is never done, since it presupposes Identity as its starting point and foundation. In other words, Adorno does not see how what he is looking for (a break-out from the confines of Identity) is already at work at the very heart of the Hegelian dialectic, so that it is Adorno's very critique which obliterates the subversive core of Hegel's thought, retroactively cementing the figure of his dialectic as the pan-logicist monster of the all-consuming Absolute Notion.

Does this mean that the ultimate subjective position we can adopt is that of a split which characterizes the fetishistic disavowal? Is it the case that all we can do is take the stance of: "although I know very well that there is no big Other, that the big Other is only the sedimentation, the reified form, of intersubjective interactions, I am compelled to act as if the big Other is an external force which controls us all"? It is here that Lacan's fundamental insight into how the big Other is "barred," lacking, in-existent even, acquires its weight: the big Other is not the substantial Ground, it is inconsistent or lacking, its very functioning depends on subjects whose participation in the symbolic process sustains it. In place of both the submersion of the subject in its substantial Other and the subject's appropriation of this Other we thus have a mutual implication through lack, through the overlapping of the two lacks, the lack constitutive of the subject and the lack of/in the Other itself. It is perhaps time to read Hegel's famous formula "One should grasp the Absolute not only as substance, but also as subject" more cautiously and literally: the point is not that the Absolute is not substance, but subject. The point is hidden in the "not only … but also," that is, in the interplay between the two, which also opens up the space of freedom—we are free because there is a lack in the Other, because the substance out of which we grew and on which we rely is inconsistent, barred, failed, marked by an impossibility.

But what kind of freedom is thereby opened up? Here we should raise a clear and brutal question in all its naïveté: if we reject Marx's critique and embrace Hegel's notion of the owl of Minerva which takes flight only at dusk—that is, if we accept Hegel's claim that the position of an historical agent able to identify its own role in the historical process and to act accordingly is inherently impossible, since such self-referentiality makes it impossible for the agent to factor in the impact of its own intervention, of how this act itself will affect the constellation—what are the consequences of this position for the act, for emancipatory political interventions? Does it mean that we are condemned to acting blindly, to taking risky steps into the unknown whose final outcome totally eludes us, to interventions whose meaning we can establish only retroactively, so that, at the moment of the act, all we can do is hope that history will show mercy (grace) and reward our intervention with at least a modicum of success? But what if, instead of conceiving this impossibility of factoring in the consequences of our acts as a limitation of our freedom, we conceive it as the zero-level (negative) condition of our freedom?

The notion of freedom as known necessity found its highest expression in Spinoza's thought, and no wonder that Spinoza also provided the most succinct definition of the personalized notion of God: the only true God is nature itself—that is, substance as *causa sui*, as the eternal texture of causes-effects. The personalized notion of God as a wise old man who, sitting somewhere up there in the heavens, rules the world according to his caprice, is nothing but the mystified positive expression of our ignorance—when our knowledge of actual natural causal networks is limited, we as it were fill in the blanks by projecting a supreme Cause onto an unknown highest entity. From the Hegelian view,

Spinoza just needs to be taken more literally than he was ready to take himself: what if this lack or incompleteness of the causal network is not only epistemological but also ontological? What if it is not only our knowledge of reality but reality itself which is incomplete? In this case, is not the personalized notion of God also an indication (a mystified indication, but nonetheless an indication) of the ontological incompleteness of reality itself? Or, to put it in terms of the classical Hegelian distinction between what I want or mean to say and what I actually say, when I say "God," I want to name the transcendent absolute Person who governs reality, but what I really say is that reality is ontologically incomplete, that it is marked by a fundamental impossibility or inconsistency.

In this sense Dostoyevsky was right: it is only the personalized God—insofar as he is the name for a desiring/lacking Other, for a gap in the Other—who gives freedom: I am not free by being the creator and master of all reality, when nothing resists my power to appropriate all heterogeneous content; I am free if the substance of my being is not a full causal network, but an ontologically incomplete field. This incompleteness is (or, rather, can also be) signaled by an opaque desiring God, a God who is himself marked by imperfections and finitude, so that when we encounter him, we confront the enigma of "What does he want?" an enigma which holds also for God himself (who does not know what he wants).

But, again, what does this mean for our ability to act, to intervene in history? There are in French two words for the "future" which cannot be adequately rendered in English: *futur* and *avenir*. *Futur* stands for the future as the continuation of the present, as the full actualization of tendencies which are already present, while *avenir* points more towards a radical break, a discontinuity with the present—*avenir* is what is to come (*à venir*), not just what will be. For example, in the contemporary apocalyptic situation, the ultimate horizon of the "future" is what Jean-Pierre Dupuy calls the dystopian "fixed point," the zero-point of ecological breakdown, global economic and social chaos, etc.—even if it is indefinitely postponed, this zero-point is the virtual "attractor" towards which our reality, left to itself, tends. The way to combat the future catastrophe is through acts which interrupt this drifting towards the dystopian "fixed point," acts which take upon themselves the risk of giving birth to some radical Otherness "to come." We can see here how ambiguous the slogan "no future" is: at a deeper level, it designates not the impossibility of change, but precisely what we should be striving for—to break the hold the catastrophic "future" has over us, and thereby to open up the space for something New "to come."

CHAPTER 5

Parataxis: Figures of the Dialectical Process

The widespread use of the notion of "intellectual intuition" in post-Kantian German Idealism is *not* the sign of a regression to pre-critical metaphysics (as orthodox Kantians claim). For post-Kantian Idealists, "intellectual intuition" is not a passive intuitive reception or vision of noumenal reality: on the contrary, it always designates an *active*, productive, spontaneous faculty, and, as such, it remains firmly rooted in the Kantian topic of the active synthesis of transcendental imagination (which is why those who rehabilitate this notion enthusiastically refer to sections 76 and 77 of Kant's *Critique of Judgment*).[1] So why did Kant reject this notion? What threshold did he refuse to cross?

In 1804, towards the end of his life, Kant wrote that the two hinges on which his entire thought turns are the ideality of space and time and the reality of the concept of freedom.[2] Kant's opposition to the common-sense attitude is clear here: for common-sense naturalism, space and time are real (real objects and processes "are" in space and time, space and time are not merely the transcendental horizon of our experience of reality), while freedom is ideal (a form of the self-perception of our conscious Self with, perhaps, no foundation in basic reality where only matter really exists). For Kant, on the contrary, space and time are ideal (not properties of things in themselves, but forms of perception imposed on phenomena by the transcendental Self), while freedom is real in the most radical (even Lacanian) sense: freedom is an inexplicable, "irrational," unaccountable "fact of reason," a *Real* which disturbs our notion of (phenomenal) spatio-temporal *reality* as governed by natural laws. For this reason, our experience of freedom is properly *traumatic*, even for Kant himself, who mistakes the Real as the impossible which *happens* (that which "I cannot not do") for the Real as the impossible-to-happen (that which "I cannot ever fully accomplish"). That is to say, in Kantian ethics, the true tension is not between the subject's idea that he is acting only for the sake of duty and the hidden fact that there was actually some pathological motivation at work (vulgar psychoanalysis); the true tension

1 See Robert Pippin, *The Persistence of Subjectivity*, Cambridge: Cambridge University Press 2005, p. 43.

2 See Dieter Henrich, *Between Kant and Hegel: Lectures on German Idealism*, Cambridge, MA: Harvard University Press 2008, p. 53.

is exactly the opposite one: the abyssally free act is unbearable, traumatic, in that when we accomplish an act out of freedom, and in order to sustain it, we experience it as conditioned by some pathological motivation. One is tempted to refer here to the key Kantian concept of schematization: a free act *cannot be schematized*, integrated into our experience, so, in order to schematize it, we have to "pathologize" it. And Kant himself, as a rule, misreads the true tension (the difficulty in endorsing and assuming a free act) as the standard tension affecting the agent who can never be sure if his act really was free, rather than motivated by hidden pathological impulses. This is why, as Kierkegaard put it, the true trauma lies not in our mortality, but in our immortality: it is easy to accept that we are just a speck of dust in the infinite universe; what is much more difficult to accept is that we effectively *are* immortal free beings who, as such, cannot escape the terrible responsibility of our freedom.

The root of this trouble lies with the deadlock at the heart of the Kantian edifice, as noted by Henrich: Kant starts with our cognitive capacity—the Self with its three features (unity, synthetic activity, emptiness) is affected by noumenal things and, through its active synthesis, organizes impressions into phenomenal reality; however, once he arrives at the ontological result of his critique of knowledge (the distinction between phenomenal reality and the noumenal world of Things-in-themselves), "there can be no return to the self. There is no plausible interpretation of the self as a member of one of the two worlds."[3] This is where practical reason comes in: the only way to return from ontology to the Self is via freedom: freedom unites the two worlds, and provides for the unity or coherence of the Self—this is why Kant repeated again and again the motto: "subordinate everything to freedom."[4] Here, however, a gap between Kant and his followers occurs: for Kant, freedom is an "irrational" fact of reason, it is simply and inexplicably given, something like an umbilical cord inexplicably rooting our experience in the unknown noumenal reality, not the First Principle out of which one can develop a systematic notion of reality, while the Idealists from Fichte onwards cross this limit and endeavor to provide a systematic account of freedom itself. The status of this limit changes with the Idealists: what was for Kant an a priori limitation, so that the very notion of "going over" is *stricto sensu* meaningless, becomes for the Idealists just an indication that Kant was not yet ready to pursue his project to the end, to draw all the consequences from his breakthrough. For the Idealists, Kant got stuck half-way, while for Kant, his Idealist followers totally misunderstood his critique and fell back into pre-critical metaphysics or, worse, mystical *Schwarmerei*.

There are thus two main versions of this passage:[5] (1) Kant asserts the gap

3 Ibid., p. 52.

4 Ibid., p. 59.

5 Which is still one of the great dividing lines among philosophers: those—mostly of

of finitude, transcendental schematism, the negative access to the Noumenal (via the Sublime) as the only one possible, and so forth, while Hegel's absolute idealism closes the Kantian gap and returns to pre-critical metaphysics. (2) It is Kant who goes only half-way in his destruction of metaphysics, still maintaining the reference to the Thing-in-itself as an external inaccessible entity, and Hegel is merely a radicalized Kant, who moves from our negative access to the Absolute to the Absolute itself as negativity. Or, to put it in terms of the Hegelian shift from epistemological obstacle to positive ontological condition (our incomplete knowledge of the thing becomes a positive feature of the thing which is in itself incomplete, inconsistent): it is not that Hegel "ontologizes" Kant; on the contrary, it is Kant who, insofar as he conceives the gap as merely epistemological, continues to presuppose a fully constituted noumenal realm existing out there, and it is Hegel who "deontologizes" Kant, introducing a gap into the very texture of reality. In other words, Hegel's move is not to "overcome" the Kantian division, but, rather, to assert it "as such," to *remove the need for its "overcoming,"* for the additional "reconciliation" of the opposites, that is, to gain the insight—through a purely formal parallax shift—into how positing the distinction "as such" already *is* the looked-for "reconciliation." Kant's limitation lies not in his remaining within the confines of finite oppositions, in his inability to reach the Infinite, but, on the contrary, in his very search for a transcendent domain beyond the realm of finite oppositions: Kant is not unable to reach the Infinite—what he is unable to see is how he *already has what he is looking for*. Gérard Lebrun has clarified this crucial point in his analysis of Hegel's critique of Kant's antinomies.[6]

The commonplace among defenders of Kant is that Hegel's critique, although apparently more audacious (Hegel sees contradictions everywhere), only domesticates or blunts the Kantian antinomies. Kant is, so the story goes (as retold from Heidegger to postmodernists), the first philosopher who really confronted the subject's finitude not only as an empirical fact, but as the very ontological horizon of our being. This led him to conceive antinomies as genuine unresolvable deadlocks, inescapable scandals of reason, in which human reason becomes involved by its very nature—the scandal of what he even calls "euthanasia of Reason." The impasse is here irreducible, there is no mediation between the opposites, no higher synthesis. We thus get the very contemporary image of a

---

the analytic orientation—who think that Kant is the last "continental" philosopher who "makes sense," and that the post-Kantian turn of German Idealism is one of the greatest catastrophes, regressions into meaningless speculation, in the history of philosophy, and those for whom the post-Kantian speculative-historical approach is the highest achievement of philosophy.

6 Gérard Lebrun, "L'antinomie et son contenu," in Olivier Tinland, ed., *Lectures de Hegel*, Paris: Le Livre de Poche 2005.

human subject caught in a constitutive deadlock, marked by an a priori ontological split or gap. As for Hegel, although he may appear to radicalize antinomies by conceiving them as "contradictions" and universalizing them, seeing them everywhere, in every concept we use, and, going even further, ontologizing them (while Kant locates antinomies in our cognitive approach to reality, Hegel locates them in reality itself), Hegel's radicalization is a ruse: once reformulated as "contradictions," antinomies are caught in the machinery of the dialectical progress, reduced to an in-between stage, a moment on the road towards the final reconciliation. Hegel thus effectively blunts the scandalous edge of the Kantian antinomies which threatened to bring Reason to the edge of madness, renormalizing them as part of a global ontological process.

Lebrun demonstrates that this commonly shared conception is thoroughly wrong: it is Kant himself who actually defuses the antinomies. One should always bear in mind Kant's result: *there are no antinomies as such*, they emerge simply out of the subject's epistemological confusion between phenomena and noumena. After the critique of Reason has done its work, we end up with a clear and unambiguous, non-antagonistic, ontological picture, with phenomena on one side and noumena on the other. The whole threat of the "euthanasia of Reason," the spectacle of Reason as forever caught in a fatal deadlock, is ultimately revealed as a mere theatrical trick, a staged performance designed to confer credibility on Kant's transcendental solution. This is the feature that Kant shares with pre-critical metaphysics: both positions remain in the domain of Understanding and its fixed determinations, and Kant's critique of metaphysics spells out the final result of metaphysics: as long as we move in the domain of Understanding, Things-in-themselves are out of reach, our knowledge is ultimately in vain.

In what, then, does the difference between Kant and Hegel with regard to antinomies effectively reside? Hegel changes the entire terrain: his basic reproach concerns not what Kant says, but Kant's unsaid, Kant's "unknown knowns" (to use Donald Rumsfeld's newspeak)—Kant cheats, his analysis of antinomies is not too poor, but rather *too rich*, for he smuggles into it a whole series of additional presuppositions and implications. Instead of really analyzing *the immanent nature of the categories involved in antinomies* (finitude versus infinity, continuity versus discontinuity, etc.), he shifts the entire analysis onto the way we, as thinking subjects, *use* or *apply* these categories. Which is why Hegel's basic reproach to Kant concerns not the immanent nature of the categories, but, in an almost Wittgensteinian way, their illegitimate *use*, their application to a domain which is not properly theirs. *Antinomies are not inscribed into categories themselves, they only arise when we go beyond the proper domain of their use (the temporal-phenomenal reality of our experience) and apply them to noumenal reality*, to objects which cannot ever become objects of our experience. In short, antinomies emerge the moment we confuse phenomena and noumena, objects of experience with Things-in-themselves.

Kant can only perceive finitude as the finitude of the transcendental subject who is constrained by schematism, by the temporal limitations of transcendental synthesis: for him, the only finitude is the finitude of the subject; he does not consider the possibility that *the very categories he is dealing with may be "finite,"* i.e., that they may remain categories of abstract Understanding, not yet the truly infinite categories of speculative Reason. And Hegel's point is that this move from categories of Understanding to Reason proper is not an illegitimate step beyond the limits of our reason; it is rather Kant himself who oversteps the proper limits of the analysis of categories, of pure notional determinations, illegitimately projecting onto this space the topic of temporal subjectivity, and so forth. At its most elementary, Hegel's move is a reduction, not an enrichment, of Kant: a *subtractive* move, a gesture of taking away the metaphysical ballast and of analyzing notional determinations in their immanent nature.

In praise of Understanding

So what, precisely, is Understanding? Jameson characterizes Understanding (*Verstand*) as a kind of spontaneous ideology of our daily lives, of our immediate experience of reality. As such, it is not merely a historical phenomenon to be dissolved through dialectical critique and the practical transformation of the relations which engender it, but a permanent, trans-historical fixture of our everyday reality. True, Reason (*Vernunft*) "has the task of transforming the necessary errors of *Verstand* into new and dialectical kinds of truths,"[7] but this "transformation" leaves intact the everyday efficacy of Understanding, its formative role in our ordinary experience—all Reason can achieve is a kind of Kantian critical delimitation of the proper sphere of Understanding; in other words, it can only make us aware of how, in our daily lives, we are victims of necessary ("transcendental") illusions. Underlying this reading of the opposition of Reason and Understanding is a profoundly non-Marxian notion of ideology (or, rather, a profoundly non-Marxian splitting of this notion) probably taken from Althusser (and, maybe, Lacan): in a Kantian mode, Jameson seems to imply that there are two modes of ideology, a historical one (forms linked to specific historical conditions which disappear when these conditions are abolished, like traditional patriarchy) and an a priori transcendental one (a kind of spontaneous tendency to identitarian thinking, to reification, etc., which is co-substantial with language as such, and which, for this reason, can be assimilated to the

7 Fredric Jameson, *The Hegel Variations*, London: Verso Books 2010, p. 119.

illusion of the big Other as the "subject supposed to know"). Closely linked to this notion of ideology is Jameson's (rarely noticed, but all the more persistent) motif of the unsayable, of things better left unsaid—for example, in his review of my *Parallax View* in the *London Review of Books*, his argument against the notion of parallax is that, as the name for the most elementary split/diffraction, it endeavors to name something which is better left unnamed. In a similar way, Jameson subscribes to the Kantian tendency of (some of) today's brain scientists to insist on the a priori structural unknowability of consciousness:

> what Hegel's contemporaries called the not-I is that which consciousness is conscious of as its other, and not any absence of consciousness itself, something inconceivable except as a kind of science-fictional picture-thinking, a kind of thought of otherness. But it is hard to understand how we could know something without knowing what its absence entails: and it may well be, as Colin McGinn argues, that consciousness is one of those philosophical problems which human beings are structurally unfit to solve; and that in that sense Kant's was the right position to take: that, although its existence is as certain as the Cartesian cogito, consciousness must also remain perpetually unknowable as a thing-in-itself.[8]

The least one can say about these lines is that they are profoundly non-Hegelian, even taking into account Jameson's unexpected dialectical point: since an element can be properly grasped only through its difference to its opposite, and since the I's opposite—the not-I—is inaccessible to the I as it is in itself, the consequence of the unknowability of the not-I as it is In-itself, independently of the I, is *the unknowability of consciousness (the I) itself* as it is In-itself. The standard solipsist-empiricist claim that "the subject can only know itself, its sensations" is thus proven wrong: if the not-I is unknowable, the I itself suffers the same lot. The question to be raised here is whether this circle is inescapable. Are we caught in it right to the end, so that every speculation about the Outside is always already a retroactive fantasy from the standpoint of the Inside? Or, as Hegel would have put it, is every presupposition already posited? Jameson develops this impossibility of breaking out in his perspicuous reading of the concept of *positing* as the key to what Hegel means by "idealism." His first move is to dialectically mediate the very opposition of positing and presupposing: the core of "positing" is not the direct production of objects, since such a production remains abstractly opposed to what is simply given (I as a finite subject find in front of me material objects and then proceed to "positing" by working on them); the core of "positing" concerns these presuppositions themselves; that is, what are primordially posited are presuppositions themselves. Recall Heidegger's notion of the essence of modern technology as *Gestell*: in order for

8 Ibid., p. 32.

the subject to technologically manipulate and exploit reality, this reality has to be "posited"/presupposed (or, as Heidegger puts it, disclosed) in advance as an object of possible technological exploitation, as a reserve of raw materials and energies, and so on. It is in this sense that one should conceive what is posited "in terms of presuppositions: for positing somehow always takes place 'in advance' of other kinds of thinking and other kinds of acts and events,"[9] or, even more pointedly, "in terms of theatrical settings or pro-filmic arrangements, in which, ahead of time, a certain number of things are placed on stage, certain depths are calculated, and an optical center also carefully provided, the laws of perspective invoked in order to strengthen the illusion to be achieved":[10]

> Kant's theory—phenomenon and noumenon—looks somewhat different if it is grasped as a specific way of positing the world … it is no longer a question of belief: of taking the existence of objective reality, of the noumenon, of a world independent of human perceptions, on faith. But it is also not a question of following in Fichte's footsteps and affirming that objective reality—the noumenon, which has now become the not-I—is summoned into being by the primal act of the I, which "posits" it (now using the term in a metaphysical sense).
>
> Rather, that beyond as which the noumenon is characterized now becomes something like a category of thinking … It is the mind that posits *noumena* in the sense in which its experience of each phenomenon includes a beyond along with it … The *noumenon* is not something separate from the phenomenon, but part and parcel of its essence; and it is within the mind that realities outside or beyond the mind are "posited."[11]

We should introduce here a precise distinction between the presupposed or shadowy part of what appear as ontic objects and the ontological horizon of their appearing. On the one hand, as was brilliantly developed by Husserl in his phenomenological analysis of perception, every perception of even an ordinary object involves a series of assumptions about its unseen back-side, as well as about its background; on the other hand, an object always appears within a certain horizon of hermeneutic "prejudices" which provide an a priori frame within which we locate the object and which thus make it intelligible—to observe reality "without prejudices" means to understand nothing. This same dialectic of "positing the presuppositions" plays a crucial role in our understanding of history: "just as we always posit the anteriority of a nameless object along with the name or idea we have just articulated, so also in the matter of historical temporality we always posit the pre-existence of a formless object which is the raw

9 Ibid., p. 27.
10 Ibid., p. 28.
11 Ibid., p. 29.

material of our emergent social or historical articulation."[12] This "formlessness" should also be understood as a violent erasure of (previous) forms: whenever a certain act is "posited" as a founding one, as a historical cut or the beginning of a new era, the previous social reality is as a rule reduced to a chaotic "ahistorical" conundrum—say, when the Western colonialists "discovered" black Africa, this discovery was read as the first contact of "pre-historical" primitives with civilized history proper, and their previous history basically blurred into a "formless matter." It is in this sense that the notion of "positing the presuppositions" is "not only a solution to the problems posed by critical resistance to mythic narratives of origin … it is also one in which the emergence of a specific historical form retroactively calls into existence the existence of the hitherto formless matter from which it has been fashioned."[13]

This last claim should be qualified, or, rather, corrected: what is retroactively called into existence is not the "hitherto formless matter" but, precisely, matter which was well articulated before the rise of the new, and whose contours were only blurred, or became invisible, from the horizon of the new historical form—with the rise of the new form, the previous form is (mis)perceived as "hitherto formless matter," that is, *the "formlessness" itself is a retroactive effect*, a violent erasure of the previous form.[14] If one misses the *retroactivity* of such positing of presuppositions, one finds oneself in the ideological universe of evolutionary teleology: an ideological narrative thus emerges in which previous epochs are conceived as progressive stages or steps towards the present "civilized" epoch. This is why the retroactive positing of presuppositions is the materialist "substitute for that 'teleology' for which [Hegel] is ordinarily indicted."[15]

What this means is that, although presuppositions are (retroactively) posited, the conclusion to be drawn is not that we are forever caught in this circle of retroactivity, so that every attempt to reconstruct the rise of the New out of the Old is nothing but an ideological narrative. Hegel's dialectic itself is not yet another grand teleological narrative, but precisely an effort to avoid the narrative illusion of a continuous process of organic growth of the New out of the Old; the historical forms which follow one another are not successive

12 Ibid., pp. 85–6.

13 Ibid., p. 87.

14 So what about the obvious counter-argument, invoking the abundance of ethnological studies of these pre-historical societies, with detailed descriptions of their rituals, systems of kinship, myths, etc.? Classic ethnology and anthropology were precisely studies of "pre-historic" societies, studies which systematically overlooked the specificity of these societies, interpreting them as a contrast to the civilized societies. Recall how, in their description of the primitive myths of origin, the early anthropologists read, say, the statement that a tribe originates from the owl, as a literal belief ("they really believe their predecessors were owls"), totally missing the way such statements effectively functioned.

15 Jameson, *The Hegel Variations*, p. 87.

figures within the same teleological frame, but successive re-totalizations, each of them creating ("positing") its own past (as well as projecting its own future). In other words, Hegel's dialectic is the science of the gap between the Old and the New, of accounting for this gap; more precisely, its true topic is not directly the gap between the Old and the New, but its self-reflective redoubling—when it describes the cut between the Old and the New, it simultaneously describes the gap, within the Old itself, between the Old "in-itself" (as it was before the New) and the Old retroactively posited by the New. It is because of this redoubled gap that every new form arises as a *creation ex nihilo*: the Nothingness out of which the New arises is the very gap between the Old-in-itself and the Old-for-the-New, the gap which makes impossible any account of the rise of the New in terms of a continuous narrative.[16]

We should add a further qualification here: what escapes our grasp is not the way things were before the arrival of the New, but *the very birth of the New*, the New as it was "in itself," from the perspective of the Old, before it managed to "posit its presuppositions." This is why fantasy, the fantasmatic narrative, always involves an *impossible gaze*, the gaze by means of which the subject is already present at the scene of its own absence—the illusion is here the same as that of "alternate reality" whose otherness is also "posited" by the actual totality, which is why it remains within the coordinates of the actual totality. The way to avoid this utopian reduction of the subject to the impossible gaze witnessing an alternate reality from which it is absent is not to abandon the topos of alternate reality as such, but to reformulate it so as to avoid the mystification of the theosophic mytho-poetic narrative which pretends to render the genesis of the cosmos (of the fully constituted reality, ruled by *logos*) out of the proto-cosmic pre-ontological chaos. Such attempts only obfuscate the point that the repressed spectral "virtual history" is not the "truth" of the official public history, but the fantasy which fills in the void of the *act* that brought about history. At the level of family life, this distinction is palpable in so-called False Memory Syndrome: the "memories" unearthed (being seduced or molested by a family member), the repressed stories that haunt the imagination of the living, are precisely such "primordial lies" destined to forestall the encounter with the ultimate rock of impossibility, the fact that "there is no sexual relationship." And the same goes, at the level of social life, for the notion of the primordial Crime that grounds the legal Order: the secret narrative that tells its story is purely fantasmatic.

In philosophy proper, this fantasmatic mystification resides at the very core of Schelling's *Weltalter* project. What Schelling endeavored to accomplish in *Weltalter* is precisely such a mytho-poetic fantasmatic narrative that would

16 Marx himself was aware of this gap when, in the last chapter of Volume 1 of *Capital*, he confronted the chaotic brutality of the actual rise of capitalism with the narrative of "so-called primordial accumulation."

account for the emergence of *logos* itself out of the pre-logical proto-cosmic Real; however, at the very end of each of the three successive drafts of *Weltalter*—that is to say, at the very point at which the passage from *mythos* to *logos*, from the Real to the Symbolic, should have been deployed—Schelling was compelled to posit an uncanny *act* of *Ent-Scheidung* (decision or separation), an act in a way more primordial than the Real of the "eternal Past" itself. The repeated failure of his *Weltalter* drafts signals precisely Schelling's honesty as a thinker—the fact that he was radical enough to acknowledge the impossibility of grounding the act or decision in a proto-cosmic myth. The line of separation between materialism and obscurantist idealism in Schelling thus concerns precisely the relationship between the act and the proto-cosmos: idealist obscurantism deduces or generates the act from the proto-cosmos, while materialism asserts the primacy of the act and denounces the fantasmatic character of the proto-cosmic narrative.

So, apropos Schelling's claim that man's consciousness arises from the primordial act which separates the present-actual consciousness from the spectral, shadowy realm of the unconscious, one has to ask a seemingly naïve but crucial question: what, precisely, is the unconscious here? Schelling's answer is unambiguous: the "unconscious" is not primarily the rotary motion of drives ejected into the eternal past; the "unconscious" is rather the very act of *Ent-Scheidung* by means of which drives were ejected into the past. Or, to put it in slightly different terms: what is truly "unconscious" in man is not the immediate opposite of consciousness, the obscure and confused vortex of "irrational" drives, but the very founding gesture of consciousness, the act of decision in which I "choose myself," by which I combine this multitude of drives into the unity of my Self. The "unconscious" is not the passive stuff of inert drives to be used by the creative "synthetic" activity of the conscious Ego; the "unconscious" in its most radical dimension is rather the highest Deed of my self-positing, or (to resort to later "existentialist" terms) the choice of my fundamental "project" which, in order to remain operative, must be "repressed," kept out of the light of day. To quote from the admirable final pages of the second draft of *Weltalter*:

> That primordial deed which makes a man genuinely himself precedes all individual actions; but immediately after it is put into exuberant freedom, this deed sinks into the night of unconsciousness. This is not a deed that could happen once and then stop; it is a permanent deed, a neverending deed, and consequently it can never again be brought before consciousness. For man to know of this deed, consciousness itself would have to return into nothing, into boundless freedom, and would cease to be consciousness. This deed occurs once and then immediately sinks back into the unfathomable depths; and nature acquires permanence precisely thereby. Likewise that will, posited once at the beginning and then led to the outside, must

> immediately sink into unconsciousness. Only in this way is a beginning possible, a beginning that does not stop being a beginning, a truly eternal beginning. For here as well, it is true that the beginning cannot know itself. That deed, once done, is done for all eternity. The decision that in some manner is truly to begin must not be brought back to consciousness; it must not be called back, because this would amount to being taken back. If, in making a decision, somebody retains the right to reexamine his choice, he will never make a beginning at all.[17]

What we encounter here is, of course, the logic of the "vanishing mediator": of the founding gesture of differentiation which must sink into invisibility once the difference between the vortex of "irrational" drives and the universe of *logos* is in place. Schelling's fundamental move is thus not simply to ground the ontologically structured universe of *logos* in the horrible vortex of the Real; if we read him carefully, there is a premonition in his work that this terrifying vortex of the pre-ontological Real is itself (accessible to us only in the guise of) a fantasmatic narrative, a lure destined to detract us from the true traumatic cut, that of the abyssal act of *Ent-Scheidung*.

It is against this background that one can raise two further critical points about Jameson's notion of Understanding as an eternal or unsurpassable form of ideology. The first thing to note is that this unsurpassable character is in itself redoubled: first, there is Understanding as the a priori tendency of human thinking towards identitarian reification; then, there is the unsurpassability of the circle of "positing the presuppositions" which prevents us from stepping outside ourselves and grasping the not-I in all its forms, spatial and temporal (from external reality as it is independently of us, to our own historical past). The first critical point to be made here is that the features Jameson attributes to Understanding ("common-sense empirical thinking of externality, formed in the experience of solid objects and obedient to the law of non-contradiction") clearly *are* historically limited: they designate modern-secular empiricist common sense, which is very different from, say, a "primitive" holistic notion of reality permeated by spiritual forces.

However, a much more important critical point concerns the way Jameson formulates the opposition between Understanding and Reason: Understanding is understood as the elementary form of analyzing, of fixing differences and identities, reducing the wealth of reality to an abstract set of features; this spontaneous tendency towards identitarian reification has to be then corrected by dialectical Reason, which faithfully reproduces the dynamic complexity of reality by outlining the fluid network of relations within which every identity is located. This network both generates every identity and, simultaneously, causes

17 Slavoj Žižek and F. W. J. von Schelling, *The Abyss of Freedom / Ages of the World*, trans. Judith Norman, Ann Arbor: University of Michigan Press 1997, pp. 181–2.

its ultimate downfall. This, however, is emphatically *not* the way Hegel conceives the difference between Understanding and Reason—let us read carefully a well-known passage from the "Foreword" to the *Phenomenology*:

> To break up an idea into its ultimate elements means returning upon its moments, which at least do not have the form of the given idea when found, but are the immediate property of the self. Doubtless this analysis only arrives at thoughts which are themselves familiar elements, fixed inert determinations. But what is thus separated, and in a sense is unreal, is itself an essential moment; for just because the concrete fact is self-divided, and turns into unreality, it is something self-moving, self-active. The action of separating the elements is the exercise of the force of Understanding, the most astonishing and greatest of all powers, or rather the absolute power. The circle, which is self-enclosed and at rest, and, *qua* substance, holds its own moments, is an immediate relation, the immediate, continuous relation of elements with their unity, and hence arouses no sense of wonderment. But that an accident as such, when cut loose from its containing circumference,—that what is bound and held by something else and actual only by being connected with it,—should obtain an existence all its own, gain freedom and independence on its own account—this is the portentous power of the negative; it is the energy of thought, of pure Self.[18]

Understanding, precisely in its aspect of analyzing, tearing the unity of a thing or process apart, is here celebrated as "the most astonishing and greatest of all powers, or rather the absolute power"—as such, it is, surprisingly (for those who stick to the commonly held view of dialectics), characterized in exactly the same terms as Spirit which is, with regard to the opposition between Understanding and Reason, clearly on the side of Reason: "Spirit is, in its simple truth, consciousness, and forces its moments apart." Everything turns on how we are to understand this identity-and-difference between Understanding and Reason: it is not that Reason adds something to the separating power of Understanding, re-establishing (at some "higher level") the organic unity of what Understanding has sundered, supplementing analysis with synthesis; Reason is, in a way, not more but *less* than Understanding, it is—to put it in the well-known terms of Hegel's opposition between what one wants to say and what one actually says—what Understanding, in its activity, *really does*, in contrast to what it wants or means to do. Reason is therefore not another faculty supplementing Understanding's "one-sidedness": the very idea that there is something (the core of the substantial content of the analyzed thing) which eludes Understanding, a trans-rational Beyond out of its reach, is the fundamental illusion of Understanding. In other

18 G. W. F. Hegel, *Phenomenology of Mind*, trans. J. B. Baillie, Mineola: Dover 2003, p. 18; translation modified.

words, all we have to do to get from Understanding to Reason is to *subtract* from Understanding its constitutive illusion.

Understanding is not too abstract or violent, it is, on the contrary, as Hegel remarked of Kant, *too soft towards things*, too afraid to locate its violent movement of tearing things apart in the things themselves.[19] In a way, it is epistemology versus ontology: the illusion of Understanding is that its own analytical power—the power to make "an accident as such ... obtain an existence all its own, gain freedom and independence on its own account"—is only an "abstraction," something external to "true reality" which persists out there intact in its inaccessible fullness. In other words, it is the standard critical view of Understanding and its power of abstraction (that it is just an impotent intellectual exercise which misses the wealth of reality) which contains the core illusion of Understanding. To put it in yet another way, the mistake of Understanding is to perceive its own negative activity (of separating, tearing things apart) only in its negative aspect, ignoring its "positive" (productive) aspect—Reason is Understanding itself in its productive aspect.[20]

Let us indulge in an excursus at this point. What is abstract thinking? Recall Samuel Maoz's *Lebanon*, a recent film about the 1982 Lebanon war which draws on Maoz's own memories as a young soldier, rendering the war's fear and claustrophobia by shooting most of the action from inside a tank. The movie follows four inexperienced soldiers dispatched to "mop up" enemies in a Lebanese town that has already been bombarded by the Israeli Air Force. Interviewed at the 2009 Venice festival, Yoav Donat, the actor who played Moaz as a young soldier, said: "This is a movie that makes you feel like you've been to war." Maoz himself said his film was not a condemnation of Israel's policies, but a personal account of what he went through: "The mistake I made is to call the film 'Lebanon' because the Lebanon war is no different in its essence from any other war and for me any attempt to be political would have flattened the film."[21] This is

19 There is a wonderfully vulgar Jewish joke about a Polish-Jewish wife, tired after a hard day's work. When her husband comes home, also tired but aroused, he says to her: "I cannot make love to you now, but I need some kind of release—can you suck me off and swallow my sperm? This would help me a lot." The wife replies: "I am too tired to do that now, darling—why don't you just masturbate and finish in a glass, and I will drink it in the morning?" Does not this wife—contrary to the cliché about the holistic-intuitive reasoning of women as opposed to masculine rational analysis—provide an example of the ruthless feminine use of Understanding, of its power to separate what naturally belongs together?

20 In a strict homology to this Hegelian logic, it is meaningless to demand that psychoanalysis should be supplemented by psycho-synthesis, re-establishing the organic unity of the person shattered by psychoanalysis: psychoanalysis already *is* this synthesis.

21 Silvia Aloisi, "Israeli Film Relives Lebanon War from Inside Tank," Reuters, September 8, 2009.

ideology at its purest: the focus on the perpetrator's traumatic experience enables us to ignore the entire ethico-political background of the conflict: what was the Israeli army doing deep in Lebanon? and so on. Such a "humanization" thus serves to obfuscate the key question: the need for a ruthless political analysis of the stakes involved in the deployment of armed forces.

Here one immediately encounters the ideological moron's riposte: but why shouldn't the depiction of the horror and perplexity of combat be a legitimate topic for art? Is not such personal experience also part of war? Why should artistic depictions of war be limited to the great political divisions which determine such conflicts? Is not war a multi-faceted totality? In an abstract way, all this is of course true; however, what gets lost is that the true global meaning of a war and one's personal experience of it cannot coexist within the same space: an individual's experience of war, no matter how "authentic," inevitably narrows its scope and as such is in itself *a violent abstraction from the totality*. Like it or not, refusing to fight is not the same for a Nazi murdering Jews in the ghetto as for a partisan resisting the Nazis; likewise, in the Lebanon war of 1982, the "trauma" of the Israeli soldier in the tank is not the same as the trauma of the Palestinian civilian he is shelling—focusing on the former only serves to obfuscate what was at stake in the Israeli invasion.

Fredric Jameson has argued that Saint Augustine's most celebrated achievement—his invention of the psychological depth of the believer, with all the complexity constituted by inner doubt and despair—is strictly correlative to (or is the other side of) his legitimization of Christianity as a state religion, as fully compatible with the obliteration of the last remnants of radical politics from the Christian edifice.[22] The same holds for, among others, the anti-communist renegades of the Cold War era: as a rule, their turn against communism went hand in hand with a turn towards a certain Freudianism, with their discovery of the psychological complexity of individual lives.

But does this mean that the only truthful account is a de-subjectivized one, with no place for subjective experience? It is here that the key Lacanian distinction between the subject ($, the "barred" non-psychological agent) and the "person" has to be mobilized: what lies behind the screen of the wealth of a person's "inner life" is not "objective reality" but the subject itself—the *political* subject, in our case.

The act of abstraction, of tearing apart, can also be understood as an act of self-imposed blindness, of refusing to "see it all." In his *Blindness and Insight*, Paul de Man developed a refined reading of Derrida's "deconstruction" of Rousseau

22 See Fredric Jameson, "On the Sexual Production of Western Subjectivity; or, Saint Augustine as a Social Democrat," in Renata Salecl and Slavoj Žižek, eds, *Gaze and Voice as Love Objects*, Durham: Duke University Press 1996.

in *On Grammatology*.[23] De Man's thesis is that, in presenting Rousseau as a "logocentrist" caught in the metaphysics of presence, Derrida overlooks how the motifs and theoretical moves involved in deconstructing that metaphysics are already operative in Rousseau's text—often, the "deconstructive" point Derrida is making about Rousseau has already been articulated by Rousseau himself. Furthermore, this oversight is not an accident, but a structural necessity: Derrida can only see what he sees (deploy his deconstructive reading) through such blindness. And it would be easy to demonstrate the same paradoxical overlapping of blindness and insight in other great Derridean readings—say, for his detailed reading of Hegel in *Glas*. Here also, the price for the complex theoretical move of demonstrating how Hegel fails to see that a condition of impossibility is a condition of possibility—how he produces something whose status he has to disavow in order to maintain the consistency of his edifice, and so forth—is a violent simplification of the underlying frame of Hegel's thought. The latter is reduced by Derrida to the absolute-idealist "metaphysics of presence," where the Idea's self-mediation is able to reduce all Otherness, and all Hegel's formulations which run against this image are read as so many signs of his symptomatic inconsistency, of Hegel not being able to control his own theoretical production, of being forced to say more, or something different, than what he wanted to say.

But how, exactly, are we to read this co-dependence of insight and blindness? Is it possible to avoid the standard reading that imposes itself with an apparently self-evident force: the reading according to which the co-dependence of insight and blindness is an indication of our unsurpassable finitude, of the radical impossibility of our reaching the standpoint of infinity, of an insight no longer marred by any kind of blindness? It is our wager that Hegel offers another way here: what he calls "negativity" can also be couched in terms of insight and blindness, as the "positive" power of "blindness," of ignoring parts of reality. How does a notion emerge out of the confused network of impressions we have of an object? Through the power of "abstraction," of blinding oneself to most of the features of the object, reducing it to its constitutive key aspects. The greatest power of our mind is not to see more, but to see *less* in a correct way, to reduce reality to its notional determinations—only such "blindness" generates the insight into what things really are.

The same principle of "less is more" holds for reading the body of a book: in his wonderful *How to Talk About Books You Haven't Read*, Pierre Bayard demonstrates (taking an ironic line of reasoning which is ultimately meant quite seriously) that, in order to really formulate the fundamental insight or achievement of a book, it is generally better *not* to read it all—too much data only blurs

23 See Paul de Man, *Blindness and Insight: Essays in the Rhetoric of Contemporary Criticism*, second rev. ed., Minneapolis: University of Minnesota Press 1983.

our clear vision.[24] For example, many essays on Joyce's *Ulysses*—and often the best ones—were written by scholars who had not read the whole book; the same goes for books on Kant or Hegel, where a truly detailed knowledge often only gives rise to a boring specialist exegesis, rather than living insights. The best interpretations of Hegel are always partial: they extrapolate the totality from a particular figure of thought or of dialectical movement. As a rule, it is not a reading of a thick book by Hegel himself, but some striking, detailed observation—often wrong or at least one-sided—made by an interpreter that allows us to grasp Hegel's thought in its living movement.

The tension between insight and blindness accounts for the fact that Hegel uses the term *Begriff* (notion) with two opposed meanings: "notion" as the very core, the essence, of the thing, and "notion" as "mere notion" in contrast to "the thing itself." And one should bear in mind that the same goes for his use of the term "subject": the subject as elevated above the objective, as the principle of life and mediation of objects, and the subject as designating something "merely subjective," a subjectively distorted impression in contrast to the way things really are. It is all too simple to treat these two aspects in terms of the "lower"—pertaining to the abstract approach of Understanding (the reduction of the subject to the "merely subjective")—and the "higher"—involving the truly speculative notion of the Subject as the mediating principle of Life or reality. The point is, rather, that the "lower" aspect is the key constituent of the "higher": one overcomes the "merely subjective" precisely by fully endorsing it. Recall again the passage from the Preface to the *Phenomenology* celebrating the disjunctive power of "abstract" Understanding: Hegel does not overcome the abstract character of Understanding by substantially changing it (replacing abstraction with synthesis etc.), but by perceiving in a new light this same power of abstraction: what at first appears as the weakness of Understanding (its inability to grasp reality in all its complexity, its tearing apart of reality's living texture) is in fact its greatest power.

PHENOMENA, NOUMENA, AND THE LIMIT

Although Kant makes it clear that antinomies result from the misapplication of categories, and that they disappear the moment we clarify this confusion and respect the gap that separates noumena from phenomena, he nonetheless has to insist that this misapplication is not a contingent mistake, but a kind of necessary illusion inscribed into the very functioning of our Reason. One thus needs to be very precise in describing the true contours of the passage from Kant to Hegel: with his philosophical revolution, Kant made a breakthrough the radicality of which he was himself unaware; so, in a second move, he withdraws from

24 See Pierre Bayard, *How to Talk About Books You Haven't Read*, London: Granta 2009.

this radicality and desperately tries to navigate into the safe waters of a more traditional ontology. Consequently, in order to pass "from Kant to Hegel," we have to move not "forward" but backward: back from the deceptive envelope to identify the true radicality of Kant's breakthrough—in this sense, Hegel was literally "more Kantian than Kant himself." One of the points where we see this clearly is in the distinction between phenomena and noumena: Kant's explicit justification of why we need to introduce noumena remains well within the confines of traditional ontology with its distinction between appearance and true reality—appearances cannot stand on their own, there must be something behind them which sustains them:

> The cause of our not being satisfied with the substrate of sensibility, and of our therefore adding to the phenomena noumena which only the pure understanding can think, is simply as follows. The sensibility (and its field, that of the appearances) is itself limited by the understanding in such fashion that it does not have to do with things in themselves but only with the mode in which, owing to our subjective constitution, they appear. The Transcendental Aesthetic, in all its teaching, has led to this conclusion; and the same conclusion also, of course, follows from the concept of an appearance in general; namely, that something which is not in itself appearance must correspond to it. For appearance can be nothing by itself, outside our mode of representation. Unless, therefore, we are to move constantly in a circle, the word appearance must be recognized as already indicating a relation to something, the immediate representation of which is, indeed, sensible, but which, even apart from the constitution of our sensibility (upon which the form of our intuition is grounded), must be something in itself, that is, an object independent of sensibility.[25]

There is, however, an implicit clash between this account, in which phenomena and noumena are distinguished as two types (spheres) of (positively existing) objects, and Kant's key thesis that, since noumena are radically transcendent, never given as objects of our experience, the concept of a noumenon is "a merely *limiting concept*, the function of which is to curb the pretensions of sensibility; and it is therefore only of negative employment":[26]

> The division of objects into phenomena and noumena, and the world into a world of the senses and a world of the understanding, is therefore quite inadmissible in the positive sense although the distinction of concepts as sensible and intellectual is certainly legitimate. For no object can be determined for the latter concepts, and consequently they cannot be asserted to be objectively valid ... What our understanding

25 Immanuel Kant, *Critique of Pure Reason*, trans. Norman Kemp Smith, London: Macmillan 1929, pp. 269–70.
26 Ibid., p. 272.

> acquires through this concept of a noumenon, is a negative extension; that is to say, understanding is not limited through sensibility; on the contrary, it itself limits sensibility by applying the term noumena to things in themselves (things not regarded as appearances). But in so doing it at the same time sets limits to itself, recognizing that it cannot know these noumena through any of the categories, and that it must therefore think them only under the title of an unknown something.[27]

True, we can read these lines as simply restating the standard division of all objects into phenomena and noumena: the "negative employment" of "noumenon" merely reasserts the radical transcendence of the In-itself, its inaccessibility to our experience: there is an endless field of positive things out there, which can never become objects of our experience, so we can refer to them only in a negative way, well aware that they are "in themselves" fully positive, the proper cause and foundation of phenomena. But is there not another, much more radical notion lurking behind the concept of a noumenon—that of the *pure negativity, that is, the self-limitation, of phenomena as such*, as opposed to their limitation by another positive transcendent domain? In this case, negativity is not a mirror-like effect of transcendent positivity (so that we can only grasp the transcendent In-itself in a negative way); on the contrary, every positive figure of the In-itself is a "positivization" of negativity, a fantasmatic formation we construct in order to fill in the gap of negativity. As Hegel put it with unsurpassable clarity in his *Phenomenology*: behind the curtain of phenomena, there is only what we put there. Negativity thus precedes transcendent positivity, the self-limitation of phenomena precedes what is beyond the limit—this is the deep speculative sense of Kant's thesis that the "division of objects into phenomena and noumena, and the world into a world of the senses and a world of the understanding, is … inadmissible in the positive sense": the limit between phenomena and noumena is not the limit between two positive spheres of objects, since *there are only phenomena and their (self-)limitation, their negativity*. The moment we get this, the moment we take Kant's thesis on the negative employment of "noumena" more literally than he did himself, we pass from Kant to Hegel, to Hegelian negativity.

This is how one should read the key statement that understanding "limits sensibility by applying the term noumena to things in themselves (things not regarded as appearances). But in so doing it at the same time sets limits to itself, recognizing that it cannot know these noumena through any of the categories." Our understanding first posits noumena as the external limit of "sensibility" (that is, of the phenomenal world, objects of possible experience): it posits another domain of objects, inaccessible to us. But in doing so, it "limits itself": it admits that, since noumena are transcendent, never to be an object of possible experience, it cannot legitimately treat them as positive objects. That is to say,

27 Ibid., p. 272–3.

in order to distinguish noumena and phenomena as two positive domains, our understanding would have to adopt the position of a meta-language, exempt from the limitation of phenomena, dwelling somewhere above the division. Since, however, the subject dwells within phenomena, how can it perceive their limitation (as Wittgenstein also noted, we cannot see the limits of our world from within our world)? The only solution is that *the limitation of phenomena is not external but internal*, in other words that the field of phenomena is *in itself* never "all," complete, a consistent Whole; this self-limitation of phenomena assumes in Kant the form of the antinomies of pure reason. There is no need for any positive transcendent domain of noumenal entities which limit phenomena from outside—phenomena with their inconsistencies, their self-limitations, are "all there is." The key conclusion to be drawn from this self-limitation of phenomena is that it is strictly correlative to subjectivity: there is a (transcendental) subject only as correlative to the inconsistency, self-limitation, or, more radically, "ontological incompleteness," of phenomenal reality. The moment we conceive the inconsistency and self-limitation of phenomenal reality as secondary, as the effect of the subject's inability to experience the transcendent In-itself the way it "really is," the subject (as autonomous-spontaneous) becomes a mere epi-phenomenon, its freedom becomes a "mere appearance" conditioned by the fact that noumena are inaccessible to it (to put it in a somewhat simplified way: I experience myself as free insofar as the causality which effectively determines me is inaccessible to me). In other words, the subject's freedom can be ontologically grounded only in the ontological incompleteness of reality itself.

And, to avoid the obvious reproach, this purely negative use of noumena in no way implies a naïve "subjective idealism," a universe in which there is nothing but (self-)limited subjective phenomena: of course there are things-processes out there not yet known or discovered by us, there is what naïve realism designates as "objective reality," but it is wrong to designate it as noumenal—this designation is *all too "subjective."* Noumena designate the In-itself *as it appears to us, embedded in phenomenal reality*; if we designate our unknowns as "noumena," we thereby introduce a gap which is not warranted by their mere unknowability: there is no mysterious gap separating us from the unknown, the unknown is simply unknown, indifferent to being-known. In other words, we should never forget that what we know (as phenomena) is not separated from things-in-themselves by a dividing line, but is *constitutive* of them: phenomena do not form a special ontological domain, they are simply part of reality.

This brings us to Hegel's basic criticism of Kant, of his insistence on the limitation that our finitude imposes on our knowledge. It is that, beneath Kant's modesty, there is a hidden arrogance: when Kant claims that we humans, constrained by our finite Understanding, cannot ever come to know the totality of the universe, he continues to represent this infinite task as one that another,

infinite, Understanding would be able to accomplish, as if the problem is simply one of extending or extrapolating our capacity to infinity, rather than changing it qualitatively. The model for such false reasoning is the well-known naturalist-determinist idea that, were an infinite mind able to know extensively all the atoms in the universe, their position, force, and movement, it would be able to predict their future behavior with the utmost precision—as if the very notion of a finite mind extended to infinity were not in itself nonsensical. When we represent to ourselves a mind able to grasp infinity, the image we refer to is that of a mind somehow able to count an infinite number of elements in the same way we are able to count a finite number of them. In a wonderfully vicious image, Hegel likens Kant's notion of an infinite mind to the way a poor church organist tries to explain God's greatness to a simple peasant: "In the same way you know every individual in our village by name, God intimately knows every single fly among the infinite number of flies that buzz around the globe ..."[28]

This brings us to the gap between what is explainable-in-principle and what is actually explained-in-fact—this gap is fully operative in the cognitive sciences: thought is a product of the brain and can in principle be accounted for in terms of neuronal processes; it is only a matter of fact that we are not yet there. According to this view, this gap is purely cognitive: it is simply the gap between the empirical limitation of our knowledge of reality and reality itself. For Hegel, on the contrary, this gap is notional, categorical:

> The proposition which states that our actual, real knowledge, the way it exists at this moment, articulated in causal explanations, is finite and even no knowledge in the absolute meaning of the word, but a mere certainty, is ultimately not really a proposition about the limits of our knowledge, but a proposition about the form of our knowledge. It is a notional, tautological, proposition.[29]

The mistake resides in the fact that the limit pertaining to the form itself (to the categories used) is misperceived as a contingent empirical limitation. In the case of cognitivism: it is not that we already have the categorial apparatus necessary to explain consciousness (neuronal processes, etc.), and our failure to have yet done so pertains only to the empirical limitation of our knowing the relevant facts about our brain; the true limitation lies in the very form of our knowledge, in the very categorial apparatus we are using. In other words, the gap between the form of knowledge and its empirical limitation is inscribed in this form itself. It is because Kant locates the limitation in the finitude of our

28 G. W. F. Hegel, *Vorlesungen über die Philosophie der Religion I* (Werke, Vol. 16), Frankfurt: Suhrkamp 1986, pp. 493–4.

29 Pirmin Stekeler-Weithofer, *Philosophie des Selbstbewusstseins*, Frankfurt: Suhrkamp 2005, p. 23.

temporal-empirical experience that he is inconsistent in his dealing with the antinomies of pure reason.

Here, then, possibility is narrowed down: what appears as possible-in-principle, rendered impossible only on account of our empirical limitations, is revealed to be impossible also in principle, in its very notional-formal determinations. However, the obverse of this narrowing-down of the field of the possible is its extension: the Hegelian totality is not merely the totality of the actual content; it includes the immanent possibilities of the existing constellation. To "grasp a totality" one should include its possibilities; to grasp the truth of what there is, one should include its failure, what might have happened but was missed. But why should this be the case? Because the Hegelian totality is an "engaged" totality, a totality disclosed to a partial partisan view, not a "neutral" overview transcending engaged positions—as Georg Lukács recognized, such a totality is accessible only from a practical standpoint that considers the possibility of changing it. Hegel has thus a lot to teach us about the topic of possibility versus actuality. What is involved in a dialectical analysis of, say, a past event, such as a revolutionary break? Does it really amount to identifying the underlying necessity that governed the course of events in all their apparent confusion? What if the opposite is true, and dialectical analysis *reinserts possibility into the necessity of the past*? There is something of an unpredictable miraculous emergence in every passage from "negation" to "negation of negation," in every rise of a new Order out of the chaos of disintegration—which is why for Hegel dialectical analysis is always the analysis of *past* events.[30] No deduction will bring us from chaos to order; and to locate this moment of the magical turn, this unpredictable reversal of chaos into Order, is the true aim of dialectical analysis. For example, the aim of the analysis of the French Revolution is not to unearth the "historical necessity" of the passage from 1789 to the Jacobin Terror and then to Thermidor and Empire, but rather *to reconstruct this succession in terms of a series of (to use this anachronistic term) existential decisions made by agents who, caught up in a whirlwind of action, had to invent a way out of the deadlock* (in the same way that Lacan reconceptualizes the succession of oral, anal, and phallic stages as a series of dialectical reversals).

As a rule, Hegel's famous suggestion that one should conceive the Absolute not only as substance but also as subject conjures up the discredited notion

30 One of the paradoxes of this properly dialectical tension between possibility and actuality is that, in a situation involving an ultimate choice (to live or to die, to kill oneself or to go on living and struggling), the choice of suicide can help the subject to postpone actually killing themselves: "Now that I've decided to kill myself, I know that the escape from my desperate situation is open to me, and till that moment, I can take life more easily since I am rid of the unbearable pressure to choose ..."—in this way, I gain time to eventually reconsider my decision and go on living.

of some kind of "absolute Subject," a mega-Subject creating the universe and keeping watch over our destiny. For Hegel, however, the subject, at its very core, also stands for finitude, the cut, the gap of negativity, which is why God only becomes subject through Incarnation: he is not already in himself, prior to Incarnation, a mega-Subject ruling the universe. Kant and Hegel are usually contrasted along the lines of finite versus infinite: the Hegelian subject as the totalizing and infinite One which mediates all multiplicity; the Kantian subject marked by finitude and the gap that forever separates it from the Thing. But, at a more fundamental level, is not exactly the opposite the case? The basic function of the Kantian transcendental subject is to continuously enact the transcendental synthesis of apperception, to bring into One the multitude of sensible impressions; while the Hegelian subject is, in its most basic dimension, the agent of splitting, division, negativity, redoubling, the "fall" of Substance into finitude.

Consequently, it is crucial not to confuse Hegel's "objective spirit" with the Diltheyan notion of a life-form, a concrete historical world, as "objectivized spirit," the product of a people, its collective genius: the moment we do this, we miss the point of "objective spirit," which is precisely that it is spirit in its objective form, experienced by individuals as an external imposition, a constraint even—there is no collective or spiritual super-Subject that would be the author of "objective spirit," whose "objectivization" this spirit would have been. In short, for Hegel there is no collective Subject, no Subject-Spirit beyond and above individual humans. Therein resides the paradox of "objective spirit": it is independent of individuals, encountered by them as given, pre-existent, as the presupposition of their activity; yet it is nonetheless spirit, that is, something that exists only insofar as individuals relate their activity to it, only as *their* (pre)supposition.[31]

The differend

Such a reading cannot but appear to be at odds with the standard reading of Hegel as an "absolute idealist." There is a nice exercise in the genre of Žižek-bashing which perfectly illustrates this gap that separates me from the common-sense notion of Hegel; the author takes as his starting point a passage from my Preface to the new edition of *For They Know Not What They Do* which allegedly demonstrates "how badly Žižek mishandles Hegel." I originally wrote:

> Hegel has nothing to do with such a pseudo-Hegelian vision (espoused by some conservative Hegelians like Bradley and McTaggart) of society as an organic

31 See Myriam Bienenstock, "Qu'est-ce que 'l'esprit objectif' selon Hegel?," in Tinland, *Lectures de Hegel*.

> harmonious Whole, within which each member asserts his or her "equality" with others through performing his or her particular duty, occupying his or her particular place, and thus contributing to the harmony of the Whole. For Hegel, on the contrary, the "transcendent world of formlessness" (in short: the Absolute) is at war *with itself*; this means that (self-)destructive formlessness (absolute, self-relating negativity) must appear as such in the realm of finite reality. The point of Hegel's notion of the revolutionary Terror [in the *Phenomenology*] is precisely that it is a necessary moment in the deployment of freedom.[32]

From this, my critic generates his scathing commentary:

> We correct: Bradley (and the British Idealists generally) were not bad readers of Hegel when it came to political philosophy ... Hegel was very much concerned, from his student days up through his mature System, with the possibility of life in a society as a harmonious existence, of being reconciled to the world and to one's life in it. Early-on, this takes the form of a Romantic idolization of Greek life as a sort of *naturliche Harmonie*; by the point of his Jena writings, Hegel had already become critical of this tendency in the thought of his contemporaries.
>
> If a modern man was to be reconciled to his world, then it could only be through a *moralische Harmonie*, a harmony which was not merely given but which was comprehended in thought; a man had to not merely be an harmonious part of his society, but had to recognize this harmony, had to comprehend his own existence (including what is most "inward" and private for him, such as his feelings & religious sentiments) as being integrated with the whole of life. The bulk of Hegel's criticisms of his contemporary society make the complaint that it does not make sufficient allowance for this reconciliation to become possible; the life of private individuals is too abstract from the affairs of the state (or the church, or various other social organizations), or else the state (or the church, or various other social organizations) does not make sufficient allowance for the free self-determination of individual actors to do as they judge best. Hegel does not think that *moralische Harmonie* is impossible; on the contrary, the possibility of this harmony is the highest achievement of modern civilization (and its philosophical handmaiden, Hegel's System, is directed towards helping this *Harmonie* come about more fully). This is the "end of History": with modernity Spirit knows its world as its own product, comprehends what is given to it as always already implicitly Spirit, as capable of being rationally comprehended, and the social world of "Objective Spirit" is a place where Spirit can feel "at home with itself in its other," where the individual peculiarities of a particular

32 Slavoj Žižek, *For They Know Not What They Do*, second ed., London: Verso Books 2002, p. xliv. Passage reproduced in Daniel Lindquist, "Christianity and the Terror; or, More Žižek-Bashing," at sohdan.blogspot.com, October 17, 2007. However, Lindquist misquotes the reference to "self-relating negativity" as "self-*negating* negativity."

> subject are recognized as determinations of the "universal" of society, and not something over and against it.
>
> Zizek is one hundred eighty degrees wrong about Hegel's "the Absolute": it is not a *nihil*, a "transcendent world of formlessness," or any other ding-an-sich-like transcendence. Hegel's Absolute is not the Schellingian "night in which all cows are black"; the Absolute is the most contentful thing there is. The Absolute is a concrete universal; it has its being, its truth, only in the particular determinations ("moments") which make up Hegel's system—those which make up the triad of Logic, Nature, and Spirit. The Absolute is not "at war with itself"; the Absolute particularizes itself in the asunderness of nature and returns to unity with itself in the reconciliation of asunderness with unity. To put it in religious terms, the Father begets the Son, and they are united in the Spirit of charity which proceeds from both; God creates a "fallen" world of disorder, enters into it in His only Son, and the world is reconciled to God through the life of the Spirit; the sinful individual, separated from God, becomes an adopted child of God in the community of the Spirit. The Absolute does not wage war in the divine comedy.
>
> The "absolute, self-negating negativity" [sic] of the Terror is a moment of history, just as the Fall of Adam is a moment in the Christian story of salvation-history. For Hegel, the Terror is an exemplar of the "abstract universal": in "absolute freedom" one refuses to recognize any "given" content as adequate to the universal, to Reason,—thus the purely formal "Supreme Being" of the French Revolution, and its trumpeting of "Liberty, Equality, and Fraternity" while the actual state was rank tyranny of the lowest sort. The "point" of Hegel's reference to the Terror is not "that it is a necessary moment in the deployment of freedom" (for this would apply to everything Hegel includes in his System), but that the Terror shows what happens when the drive for the Universal in human life takes a utopian form, trying to build everything up anew out of pure thought rather than recognizing and cultivating what is already rational in human life.[33]

Here we have the *differend* at its purest, and, insofar as we remain within the confines of the standard-textbook interpretation, the notion of Hegel which underlies this critique will appear not only convincing but even obvious—as if what I am offering is an eccentric reading against which it suffices to recall the basic facts known to any student of Hegel. This is why, for me, replying to this critique is almost embarrassing: everything it claims about Hegel is, of course, well known to me, since it consists in precisely the predominant image of Hegel that I endeavor to undermine—so one cannot simply invoke it against me … The question nonetheless remains: what justifies me rejecting this image? Let us begin with the last sentence from the quoted passage: after admitting that Revolutionary Terror was necessary (in a purely formal sense, as a subordinate

33 Lindquist, "Christianity and the Terror."

moment in the development), my critic reduces it to the outcome of a wrong choice: the Terror "shows what happens when the drive for the Universal in human life takes a utopian form, trying to build everything up anew out of pure thought"—it explodes when, instead of "recognizing and cultivating what is already rational in human life," that is, instead of searching for and endorsing the underlying rationality of the existing order and imposing changes in continuity with this tradition, people want to enact a violent rupture with the past, turn the world on its head and start again from year-zero. The problem here is that it is precisely this quality of the French Revolution that Hegel unambiguously celebrated to the end of his life—here are his sublime words from the *Lectures on the Philosophy of World History*:

> It has been said that the French revolution resulted from philosophy, and it is not without reason that philosophy has been called *Weltweisheit* [world wisdom]; for it is not only truth in and for itself, as the pure essence of things, but also truth in its living form as exhibited in the affairs of the world. We should not, therefore, contradict the assertion that the revolution received its first impulse from philosophy ... Never since the sun had stood in the firmament and the planets revolved around him had it been perceived that man's existence centers in his head, i.e. in thought, inspired by which he builds up the world of reality ... not until now had man advanced to the recognition of the principle that thought ought to govern spiritual reality. This was accordingly a glorious mental dawn. All thinking being shared in the jubilation of this epoch. Emotions of a lofty character stirred men's minds at that time; a spiritual enthusiasm thrilled through the world, as if the reconciliation between the divine and the secular was now first accomplished.[34]

This, of course, did not prevent Hegel from coldly analyzing the inner necessity of this explosion of abstract freedom turning into its opposite, the self-destructive Revolutionary Terror; however, one should never forget that Hegel's critique is immanent, accepting the basic principle of the French Revolution (and its key supplement, the Haitian Revolution). One should be very clear here: Hegel in no way subscribes to the standard liberal critique of the French Revolution which locates the wrong turn in 1792–3, whose ideal is 1789 without 1793, the liberal phase without the Jacobin radicalization—for him 1793–4 is a necessary immanent consequence of 1789; by 1792, there was no possibility of taking a more "moderate" path without undoing the Revolution itself. Only the "abstract" Terror of the French Revolution creates the conditions for post-revolutionary "concrete freedom."

---

34 G. W. F. Hegel, *Lectures on the Philosophy of History* (translation of *Vorlesungen über die Philosophie der Weltgeschichte*), trans. J. Sibree, London: Henry G. Bohn 1861, pp. 465–6.

If one wants to put it in terms of choice, then Hegel here follows a paradoxical axiom which concerns logical temporality: the first choice has to be the wrong choice. Only the wrong choice creates the conditions for the right choice. Therein resides the temporality of a dialectical process: there is a choice, but in two stages. The first choice is between the "good old" organic order and the violent rupture with that order—and here, one should take the risk of opting for "the worse." This first choice clears the way for the new beginning and creates the condition for its own overcoming, for only after the radical negativity, the "terror," of abstract universality has done its work can one choose between this abstract universality and concrete universality. There is no way to obliterate the temporal gap and present the choice as threefold, as the choice between the old organic substantial order, its abstract negation, and a new concrete universality.

It is this paradoxical priority of the wrong choice that provides the key to the Hegelian "reconciliation": it is not the organicist harmony of a Whole within which every moment sticks to its particular place, as opposed to a field torn apart, in which every moment strives to assert its one-sided autonomy. Every particular moment *does* fully assert itself in its one-sided autonomy, but this assertion leads to its ruin, to its self-destruction—and *this* is the Hegelian "reconciliation": not a direct reconciliation in mutual recognition, but a reconciliation in and through the struggle itself. The "harmony" Hegel depicts is the strange harmony of "extremes" themselves, the mad violent dance of every extreme turning into its opposite. Within this mad dance, the Absolute is not the all-encompassing container, the space or field within which particular moments are at war with each other—it is itself caught up in the struggle. Here, again, my critic misreads my claim that "the 'transcendent world of formlessness' (in short: the Absolute) is at war with itself; this means that (self-)destructive formlessness (absolute, self-relating negativity) must appear as such in the realm of finite reality": he reads these lines as if I am asserting that the Hegelian Absolute is the abstract negativity of a Universal suspending all its particular content, the proverbial night in which all cows are black, and then triumphantly makes the elementary point that, on the contrary, the Hegelian Absolute is a concrete universal. But the choice proposed here by my critic—the choice between abstract universality and concrete organic system in which the universal engenders and contains the wealth of its particular determinations—is a false one: what is missing here is the third, properly Hegelian, choice, precisely the one I invoked in the quoted passage, namely the choice of *abstract universality as such, in its opposition to its particular content, appearing within its own particular content* (as one of its own species), encountering among its species as its own "oppositional determination." It is in *this* sense that "the 'transcendent world of formlessness' (in short: the Absolute) is at war with itself" and that "(self-)destructive formlessness (absolute, self-relating negativity) must appear as such in the realm of finite reality": this abstract universality becomes "concrete" not only by deploying itself in the series of its particular determinations, but by *including itself in this series*. It is because of this self-inclusion (self-referentiality) that the Absolute is "at war with itself," as in the case of Revolutionary Terror, where abstract negativity is no longer a transcendent In-itself, but appears "in its oppositional determination," as a particular force opposed to and destroying all (other) particular content. In more traditional Hegelian terms, this is what it means to say that, in a dialectical process, every external opposition, every struggle between the subject and its external opposite, gives way to an "internal contradiction," to a struggle of the subject with itself: in its struggle against Faith, Enlightenment is at war with itself, it opposes itself to its own substance. Denying that the Absolute is "at war with itself" means denying the very core of the Hegelian dialectical process, reducing it to a kind of Oriental Absolute, a neutral or impassive medium in which particulars struggle against each other.

This is also why my critic is wrong when he claims that the Absolute

> is not "at war with itself"; the Absolute particularizes itself in the asunderness of nature and returns to unity with itself in the reconciliation of asunderness with unity. To put it in religious terms, the Father begets the Son, and they are united in the Spirit of charity which proceeds from both; God creates a "fallen" world of disorder, enters into it in His only Son, and the world is reconciled to God through the life of the Spirit; the sinful individual, separated from God, becomes an adopted child of God in the community of the Spirit.[35]

Although this may appear a faithful summary of Hegel's deployment of the Absolute, it misses the key feature—the fact that, as Hegel repeats again and again, the Absolute is the "result of itself," the outcome of its own activity. What this means is that, in the strict sense of the term, there is no Absolute which externalizes or particularizes itself and then unites itself with its alienated Otherness: the Absolute emerges out of this process of alienation; that is, as the result of its own activity, the Absolute "is" nothing but its "return to itself." The notion of an Absolute which externalizes itself and then reconciles itself with its Otherness presupposes the Absolute as given in advance, prior to the process of its becoming; it posits as the starting point of the process what is effectively its result. The insufficiency of this standard notion of the Hegelian process becomes palpable when my critic puts it in religious terms: on a close reading, one cannot fail to note how he evokes two different "triads," first the triad of the Father begetting the Son and then uniting with him in the Spirit, then the triad of God creating a fallen world and then reconciling himself with it by entering into it in the guise

35 Lindquist, "Christianity and the Terror."

of Christ, his Son. It is true that, in this way, "the sinful individual, separated from God, becomes an adopted child of God in the community of the Spirit"; however, the price paid for this is that God himself has to be separated from himself, that he has to die in the guise of his Son's crucifixion. Is the death of Christ not the ultimate proof that, in the tension between God and the fallen world, God is at war with himself, which is why he has to "enter" the fallen world in the guise of his oppositional determination, as a miserable individual called Jesus?

Negation of the negation

But is not the claim that the Absolute is the "result of itself," the outcome of its own activity, yet another sophism recalling Baron Münchhausen? Dieter Henrich made this point in philosophical terms when he explained how Hegel never succeeded in clearly presenting the basic "matrix" of his dialectical procedure, "a second-order discourse that could interpret what he was doing. I believe that without that key I am offering to you [my readers], the system remains ultimately inaccessible."[36] As is well known, Henrich tries to find this key in his classic essay on Hegel's logic of reflection: his claim is that Hegel came closest to articulating the basic matrix of his procedure when, at the beginning of his logic of Essence, he deals briefly with the different modes of reflection. The question, as always, is whether this key delivers what it promises: does it really open the door to the innermost secret of Hegel's dialectics? Here is how Henrich begins his explanation:

> Starting only with negation means having *nothing but negation*. Now in order to have nothing but negation, we need negation more than once. For, in Hegel's view, negation is *relational* in the sense that there must be something it negates. But inasmuch as there is nothing that negation could possibly negate—owing to the assumption that we have *only* negation—negation can only negate *itself*. Accordingly, *autonomous* negation can only be a negation *of negation*. This means that autonomous negation is originally self-referential: in order to have only negation, we have to have negation twice …
>
> We do *not* have, first, some particular proposition, and subsequent to this the negation of it, and, then, a further negation of the negation that might give us back the proposition.[37]

36 Henrich, *Between Kant and Hegel*, p. 317.

37 Ibid., pp. 317–18.

For common-sense reasoning, all this is, of course, meaningless sophistry: one cannot begin with negation, negation presupposes a positive entity that is negated. This is why it is crucial to explain what is meant by the self-referential negation through convincing examples—and here, it seems, Henrich does not live up to his own standards: a gap persists between the above-quoted abstract determination of the self-relating negation and the example of Hegel's procedure provided by Henrich some pages earlier:

> [Hegel] pursues the following strategy: he invokes Kant's idea of autonomy (complete self-determination) as his criterion, and then notes that there are various ways in which the individual agent can acquire and observe this principle ... Now the critical analysis of the philosopher can show that the discrepancy remains between the demands of autonomy and the state of consciousness or behavior that the agent has already achieved. Moreover, the proof of this discrepancy is simultaneously the justification of the demand for a higher form of moral life. This higher form eliminates the defects of the previous ones and so *completes* it ... the new form requires that the preceding one remain present, anticipating completion, even though it is no longer the ultimate form.[38]

To illustrate this very procedure (in a way which, of course, runs counter to Henrich's political orientation), let us note how the Marxist critique of "bourgeois" freedom and equality provides a perfect case of such a *pleroma* (fulfillment of the law): if we remain at the level of merely legal equality and freedom, this has consequences which lead to the immanent self-negation of freedom and equality (the un-freedom and inequality of the exploited workers who "freely" sell their labor-power on the market); the abstract legal principle of freedom and equality has thus to be supplemented by a social organization of production which will no longer allow for the self-undermining of the principle in its very enactment. The principle of freedom and equality is thereby "sublated": negated, but in such a way that it is maintained at a higher level.[39] This example enables us to clarify the paradoxical starting point of Henrich's "key": Hegel does not actually start with negation, he starts with an apparent positivity which, upon closer inspection, immediately reveals itself to be its own negation: so, in our example, positive "bourgeois" freedom and equality reveal themselves (in their actualization) as their opposites, as their own negation. This is not yet negation proper, negation as a movement of mediation—the movement proper begins when the original form (which "is" its own negation) is negated or replaced

38 Ibid., pp. 305–6.

39 Therein resides the difference between Marxist anti-capitalism and the conservative anti-capitalists who want to sacrifice the very principle of freedom and equality in order to establish a more harmonious organic society.

by a higher form; and the "negation of negation" occurs when we realize that this higher form which negated the first effectively maintains (and even asserts more strongly) the starting point, in other words truly actualizes it, confers on it some positive content: the immediate assertion of freedom and equality really *is* its opposite, its self-destruction; it is only when it is negated or elevated to a higher level (in the socially just organization of the economy, and so on) that freedom and equality become *actual.* This is why, at the end of his *Science of Logic*, Hegel says that if one wants to count the moments of a dialectical process, they can be counted either as three or as four—what is negated is already in itself negated. But there is a further point to be added here: it is not only that, as in our example, if one sticks to abstract subjective autonomy without its more concrete fulfillment, this autonomy negates itself. Much more importantly, this "sticking" is necessary, unavoidable, one cannot by-pass it and move on directly to a more concrete higher form: it is only through the "excessive" sticking to the lower form that the self-negation takes place which then creates the need (or opens up the space) for the higher form. (Recall Hegel's example of the French Revolution: the "abstract" freedom and equality *had* first to negate themselves in [or reveal themselves as] absolute Terror—only in this way was the space created for a post-revolutionary "concrete" State.)

We can clearly see here what is wrong with one of the basic common-sense criticisms of Hegel: "Hegel always presupposes that the movement goes on—a thesis is opposed by its anti-thesis, the 'contradiction' gets aggravated, we pass to the new position, etc., etc. But what if a moment refuses to get caught in the movement, what if it simply insists in (or resigns itself to) its inert particularity: 'OK, I am inconsistent with myself, but so what? I prefer to stay where I am …'" The mistake of this criticism is that it misses the point: far from being a threatening abnormality, an exception to the "normal" dialectical movement, this—the refusal of a moment to become caught in a movement, its sticking to its particular identity—is precisely what happens as a rule. A moment turns into its opposite precisely by way of sticking to what it is, by refusing to recognize its truth in its opposite.

But is there not a more radical (in theoretical *and* political terms) example which fits much better Henrich's abstract description of starting with negation and then reaching a new positivity through self-relating negation—that of *crime*? The central figure of G. K. Chesterton's religious thriller *The Man Who Was Thursday* is a mysterious chief of a super-secret Scotland Yard department who is convinced that "a purely intellectual conspiracy would soon threaten the very existence of civilization":

> He is certain that the scientific and artistic worlds are silently bound in a crusade against the Family and the State. He has, therefore, formed a special corps of

> policemen, policemen who are also philosophers. It is their business to watch the beginnings of this conspiracy, not merely in a criminal but in a controversial sense … The work of the philosophical policeman … is at once bolder and more subtle than that of the ordinary detective. The ordinary detective goes to pot-houses to arrest thieves; we go to artistic tea-parties to detect pessimists. The ordinary detective discovers from a ledger or a diary that a crime has been committed. We discover from a book of sonnets that a crime will be committed. We have to trace the origin of those dreadful thoughts that drive men on at last to intellectual fanaticism and intellectual crime.[40]

Would not thinkers as different as Popper, Adorno, and Levinas also subscribe to a slightly modified version of this idea, where the actual political crime is called "totalitarianism" and the philosophical crime is condensed in the notion of "totality"? A straight road leads from the philosophical notion of totality to political totalitarianism, and the task of the "philosophical policeman" is to discover from one of Plato's dialogues or a treatise by Rousseau that a political crime will be committed. The ordinary political policeman goes to secret meetings to arrest revolutionaries; the philosophical policeman goes to philosophical symposia to detect proponents of totality. The ordinary anti-terrorist policeman tries to detect those preparing to blow up buildings and bridges; the philosophical policeman tries to detect those about to deconstruct the religious and moral foundations of our societies. The same insight was already formulated by Heinrich Heine in his *History of Religion and Philosophy in Germany* from 1834, although as a positive, admirable fact: "Mark you this, you proud men of action, you are nothing but the unconscious henchmen of intellectuals, who, often in the humblest seclusion, have meticulously plotted your every deed."[41] As cultural conservatives would put it today, deconstructionist philosophers are much more dangerous than actual terrorists: while the latter want to undermine our politico-ethical system in order to impose their own religious-ethical regime, deconstructionists want to undermine order as such:

> We say that the most dangerous criminal now is the entirely lawless modern philosopher. Compared to him, burglars and bigamists are essentially moral men; my heart goes out to them. They accept the essential ideal of man; they merely seek it wrongly. Thieves respect property. They merely wish the property to become their property that they may more perfectly respect it. But philosophers dislike property as property; they wish to destroy the very idea of personal possession. Bigamists respect marriage, or they would not go through the highly ceremonial and even

40 G. K. Chesterton, *The Man Who Was Thursday*, Harmondsworth: Penguin Books 1986, pp. 44–5.

41 Quoted from Dan Hind, *The Threat to Reason*, London: Verso Books 2007, p. 1.

> ritualistic formality of bigamy. But philosophers despise marriage as marriage. Murderers respect human life; they merely wish to attain a greater fullness of human life in themselves by the sacrifice of what seems to them to be lesser lives. But philosophers hate life itself, their own as much as other people's ... The common criminal is a bad man, but at least he is, as it were, a conditional good man. He says that if only a certain obstacle be removed—say a wealthy uncle—he is then prepared to accept the universe and to praise God. He is a reformer, but not an anarchist. He wishes to cleanse the edifice, but not to destroy it. But the evil philosopher is not trying to alter things, but to annihilate them.[42]

This provocative analysis demonstrates the limitation of Chesterton, and the inadequacy of his Hegelianism: what he does not grasp is that *universal(ized) crime is no longer a crime—it sublates (negates/overcomes) itself as crime and turns from transgression into a new order.* He is right to claim that, compared to the "entirely lawless" philosopher, burglars, bigamists, murderers even, are essentially moral: a thief is a "conditionally good man," he does not deny property *as such*, he just wants more of it for himself and is then quite ready to respect it. However, the conclusion to be drawn from this is that *crime is as such "essentially moral,"* that it desires simply a particular illegal reordering of the global moral order which itself should remain unchanged. And, in a truly Hegelian spirit, one should take this proposition (of the "essential morality" of the crime) as far as its immanent reversal: not only is crime "essentially moral" (in Hegelese: an inherent moment of the deployment of the inner antagonisms and "contradictions" of the very notion of moral order, not something that disturbs moral order from outside, as an accidental intrusion); but *morality itself is essentially criminal*—again, not only in the sense that the universal moral order necessarily "negates itself" in particular crimes, but, more radically, in the sense that *the way morality (and, in the case of theft, property) asserts itself is already in itself a crime*—"property *is* theft," as they used to say in the nineteenth century. That is to say, we should pass from theft as a particular criminal violation of the universal form of property to this form itself as a criminal violation: what Chesterton fails to perceive is that the "universalized crime" he projects onto "lawless modern philosophy" and its political equivalent, the "anarchist" movement that aims at destroying the totality of civilized life, *already exists in the guise of the existing rule of the law*, so that the antagonism between the law and crime reveals itself to be inherent to crime, as the antagonism between universal and particular crime.[43] This point was clearly made by none other than

42 Chesterton, *The Man Who Was Thursday*, pp. 45–6.

43 We might recall here an unexpected Hegelian moment from popular culture: the (somewhat awkward) Hegelianism of the first three installments of the *Star Wars* saga: as in Chesterton's *The Man Who Was Thursday*, where the criminal mastermind is revealed

Richard Wagner who, in his draft for the play *Jesus of Nazareth*, written some time between late 1848 and early 1849, attributes to Jesus a series of alternate supplementations of the Commandments:

> The commandment saith: Thou shalt not commit adultery! But I say unto you: Ye shall not marry without love. A marriage without love is broken as soon as entered into, and whoso hath wooed without love, already hath broken the wedding. If ye follow my commandment, how can ye ever break it, since it bids you do what your own heart and soul desire?—But where ye marry without love, ye bind yourselves at variance with God's law, and in your wedding ye sin against God; and this sin avengeth itself by your striving next against the law of man, in that ye break the marriage-vow.[44]

The shift from Jesus' actual words is crucial here: Jesus "internalizes" the prohibition, rendering it much more severe (the Law says do not commit adultery, but I say if you even covet another's wife in your mind, it is the same as if you had already committed adultery, etc.); Wagner also internalizes it, but in a different way—the inner dimension is not that of intention, but of the love that should accompany the Law (marriage). True adultery is not copulating outside marriage, but copulating in marriage without love: simple adultery just violates the Law from outside, while marriage without love destroys it from within, turning the letter of the Law against its spirit. So, to paraphrase Brecht once again: what is simple adultery compared to the adultery that is a loveless marriage? It is not by chance that Wagner's underlying formula "marriage is adultery" recalls Proudhon's "property is theft"—in the stormy events of 1848, Wagner was not only a Feuerbachian celebrating sexual love, but also a Proudhonian revolutionary demanding the abolition of private property; so no wonder that, on the same page, Wagner attributes to Jesus a Proudhonian supplement to "Thou shalt not steal!":

> This also is a good law: Thou shalt not steal, nor covet another man's goods. Who goeth against it, sinneth: but I preserve you from that sin, inasmuch as I teach you: Love thy neighbour as thyself; which also meaneth: Lay not up for thyself treasures,

to be none other than God himself, we gradually discover that senator Palpatine, the leader of the Republic in its war against the separatist federation, is none other than Darth Sidius, the mysterious supreme Sith lord behind the actions of the separatists—in fighting the separatists, the Republic is fighting itself, which is why the moment of its triumph and the defeat of the separatists is the moment of the Republic's conversion into the evil Empire.

44 Richard Wagner, *Jesus of Nazareth and Other Writings*, Lincoln: University of Nebraska Press 1995, p. 303.

whereby thou stealest from thy neighbour and makest him to starve: for when thou hast thy goods safeguarded by the law of man, thou provokest thy neighbour to sin against the law.[45]

This is how the Christian "supplement" to the Book should be conceived: as a properly Hegelian "negation of negation," which resides in the decisive shift from the *distortion of a notion* to a *distortion constitutive of this notion*, that is, to this notion as a distortion-in-itself. Recall again Proudhon's dialectical motto "property is theft": the "negation of negation" is here the shift from theft as a distortion ("negation," violation) of property to the dimension of theft inscribed into the very notion of property (nobody has the right to fully own the means of production; they are by nature inherently collective, so every claim "this is mine" is illegitimate). As we have just seen, the same goes for crime and law, for the passage from crime as the distortion ("negation") of the law to crime as sustaining the law itself, the idea of the law itself as universalized crime. We should note that, in this notion of the "negation of negation," the encompassing unity of the two opposed terms is the "lowest," "transgressive" one: it is not crime which is a moment of law's self-mediation (or theft which is a moment of property's self-mediation); the opposition of crime and law is inherent to crime, law is a subspecies of crime, crime's self-relating negation (in the same way that property is theft's self-relating negation). And, ultimately, does not the same go for nature itself? Here, the "negation of negation" is the shift from the idea that we are violating some natural balanced order to the idea that imposing on the Real such a notion of balanced order is in itself the greatest violation—which is why the premise, the first axiom even, of every radical ecology is "there is no Nature." Chesterton wrote: "Take away the supernatural and what you are left with is the unnatural." We should endorse this statement, but in a sense opposite to that intended by Chesterton: we should accept that nature is "unnatural," a freak show of contingent disturbances with no inner rhyme or reason. The same dialectical reversal characterizes the notion of violence: it is not only that an outburst of violence is often a *passage à l'acte* as a sign of impotence; one could claim that this reversal is inherent to the notion of violence as such, and not only a feature or sign of a deficient violence. Violence *as such*—the need to attack the opponent—is a sign of impotence, of the agent's exclusion from what it attacks. I treat with violence only that which escapes my control, that which I cannot regulate or steer from within.

The lines quoted above from Wagner cannot but evoke the famous passages from *The Communist Manifesto* which respond to the bourgeois reproach that communism wants to abolish freedom, property, and family: it is capitalist freedom itself which, as the freedom to buy and sell on the market, is the very

45 Ibid., pp. 303–4.

form of un-freedom for those who have nothing but their labor-power to sell; it is capitalist property itself which is the "abolition" of property for those who do not own the means of production; it is bourgeois marriage itself which is universalized prostitution. In all these cases, the external opposition is internalized, so that one opposed term becomes the form of appearance of the other (bourgeois freedom is the form of appearance of the unfreedom of the majority, etc.). However, at least in the case of freedom, for Marx this means that communism will not abolish freedom but, by abolishing capitalist servitude, bring about actual freedom, the freedom which will no longer be the form of appearance of its opposite. It is thus not freedom itself which is the form of appearance of its opposite, but only a false freedom, freedom distorted by relations of domination.

Underlying the dialectic of the "negation of negation," then, a Habermasian "normative" approach immediately imposes itself: how can we talk about crime without a preceding notion of legal order that is violated by the criminal transgression? In other words, is not the notion of law as universalized or self-negated crime self-destructive? This, precisely, is what a properly dialectical approach rejects: what precedes transgression is just a neutral state of things, neither good nor bad (neither property nor theft, neither law nor crime); the balance of this state of things is then violated, and the positive norm (law, property) arises as a secondary move, as an attempt to counteract and contain the transgression. With regard to the dialectic of freedom, this means that it is "alienated, bourgeois" freedom itself which creates the conditions and opens up the space for "actual" freedom.[46]

The shift from negation to the negation of negation is thus a shift from the objective to the subjective dimension: in direct negation, the subject observes a change in the object (its disintegration, its passage into its opposite), while in the negation of negation, the subject includes itself in the process, taking into account how the process it is observing affects its own position. Let us take the "highest" example, that of the crucifixion: the subject first observes the most

46 In political terms, "negation of negation" designates the moment in a process when the agent radically shifts the blame for the deadlock, with the result that it gets even worse. A decade or so ago, when Israel was repeatedly hit by terror attacks, liberal peace-loving Jews repeated the mantra that while of course they recognized the injustice of the occupation of the West Bank, in order to have proper negotiations, the other side had to stop the attacks—their continuation would only make the Israeli establishment more obstinate and a compromise less likely. For some years now no terror attacks have been carried out in Israel; the only terror is the continuous low-level pressure on the West Bank Palestinians (crop burnings, poisoning of water supplies, even the burning of mosques), and the result is the exact opposite of Israel withdrawing from the West Bank: the expansion of Israeli settlements and a simple ignorance of the Palestinians' plight. Shall we draw the sad conclusion that, while violence does not work, renouncing it works even less?

radical "negation" imaginable, the death of God; then, it becomes aware of how the death of God opens up the space for its own (subjective) freedom.

Such a reading of the negation of negation runs counter to the commonly held notion according to which the first negation is the splitting or particularization of the inner essence, its externalization, and the second negation the overcoming of that split. No wonder that this notion caused many interpreters of Hegel to mock the negation of negation as a magical mechanism which guarantees that the final outcome of a process will always be happy. Back in 1953, the young Louis Althusser published a text in *La revue de l'enseignement philosophique* in which he congratulated Stalin for rejecting the "negation of negation" as a universal law of dialectics,[47] a rejection shared by Mao. It is easy to understand this rejection as the expression of the spirit of struggle, of "one divides into two": there is no reunification, no final synthesis, the struggle goes on forever. However, the Hegelian dialectical "synthesis" has to be clearly delimited from the "synthesis-of-the-opposites" model with which it is as a rule identified. In psychoanalysis, this model has two versions. The first is *subjectivist*: the psychoanalytical treatment is conceived as the reflexive appropriation of the alienated unconscious substance, and, on a first approach, it may appear that Freud's famous *wo es war soll ich werden* fits perfectly the process of "the unconscious substance becoming subject." The second version is *substantialist*, and it should come as no surprise to true Freudians that the first person to propose it was Jung, the arch-renegade, in his pseudo-Hegelian "compensation theory." (In the opposition between Freud and Jung, Freud was here the truer Hegelian.) The basic idea of "compensation theory" is the elevation of the Unconscious into the hidden substantial Truth of the human subject—with our one-sided rationalist subjectivism, we in the West have lost sight of this substantial Truth in the depth of our being:

> Whenever life proceeds one-sidedly in any given direction, the self-regulation of the organism produces in the unconscious an accumulation of all those factors which play too small a part in the individual's conscious existence. For this reason I have put forward the compensation theory of the unconscious as a complement to the repression theory.[48]

It is easy to see how this relates to neurotic symptoms and therapy: when the ego becomes too narrow and rigid, excluding the ("irrational") tendencies that do not fit its (self-)image, these tendencies return in the guise of neurotic

---

47 See Dominique Pagani, *Féminité et communauté chez Hegel*, Paris: Editions Delga 2010, p. 43.

48 C. G. Jung, *Civilization in Transition* (The Collected Works of C. G. Jung, Vol. 10), London: Routledge 1979, p. 14 (§20).

symptoms. For example, when a man curtails his feminine "shadow" (anima), cutting it out of his identity, it returns to haunt him in the guise of monstrous and obscene feminine figures in which he is not able to recognize himself, and which he experiences as brutal foreign intrusions. The goal of therapy is therefore not to eliminate these symptoms, but to integrate them into a wider Self that transcends the narrow confines of ego. The symptoms stand for forces that are not in themselves evil and destructive: what makes them such is the false perspective of the ego, or, as Hegel would have put it, evil resides in the very gaze that sees evil everywhere around it. So when the ego is haunted by neurotic symptoms, the task of the therapist is to get the patient to see how his ego is part of the problem, not its solution: the patient should shift his perspective and recognize in his symptoms the violent expression of the disavowed part of himself. The true illness is that of the ego itself, and the neurotic symptoms are desperate attempts at a cure, attempts to re-establish the balance disturbed by the ego's narrow frame which has excluded crucial parts of the Self's content:

> A neurosis is truly removed only when it has removed the false attitude of the ego. We do not cure it—it cures us. A man is ill, but the illness is nature's attempt to heal him, and what the neurotic flings away as absolutely worthless contains the true gold we should never have found elsewhere.[49]

No wonder that some partisans of Jung see in this "compensation theory" a Hegelian inspiration:

> It was Hegel who argued that the only way a battle could cease between a thesis and an antithesis was through the construction of a *synthesis* that would include elements from both sides and transcend the opposition. Although Jung denied that Hegel was an influence of his thought, it is hard to imagine Jungian thought without the Hegelian model that sees conflict overcome through the creation of a transcendent "third" which is neither thesis nor antithesis but a new entity in which both are included.[50]

Here, however, Jung was for once right: there really is no trace of Hegel in Jung's "compensation theory." This may appear too hasty, since many of Jung's formulations effectively recall Hegel's notion of the reconciliation of the subject with its alienated substance—how the subject has to recognize in the foreign power it fights the misrecognized part of its own substance. This dialectic of recognition effectively belongs to the young Hegel; it found its definitive expression in the Jena-period fragments on love and reconciliation, and, later, in Hegel's reading

49 Ibid., p. 170.

50 David Tracey, *How to Read Jung*, London: Granta Books 2006, p. 81.

of *Antigone* as the tragic confrontation of two opposed positions, Antigone's and Creon's, both blinded by their one-sidedness and thus each unable to recognize the moment of their own truth in the other. Here is Jung's most "Hegelian" formulation: "The individual is faced with the necessity of recognizing and accepting what is different and strange as a part of his own life, as a kind of 'also-I.'"[51]

Is it then possible to say, in line with "recognizing and accepting what is different and strange as a part of his own life," that the goal of the analytic process is, in a vaguely Hegelian way, to enable the patient to "set straight" the libidinal compromises that characterize his subjective position, and to arrive at the truth about his desire? No, for a very precise and simple reason: because there is no substantial truth to be appropriated, in which the subject or patient might recognize his authentic place. We should thus reject the matrix underlying the first philosophically relevant attempt to establish the link between Hegel and psychoanalysis, namely, that undertaken within the tradition of the Frankfurt School, first elaborated by Jürgen Habermas in *Interest and Human Knowledge*, and later acquiring its definitive formulation in Helmut Dahmer's *Libido and Society*. The basic matrix involved here is provided by the homology between the Hegelian process of alienation and its overcoming through subjective mediation, or reflexive re-appropriation, of the alienated substantial content, and the Freudian process of repression and its overcoming through the analytic process wherein the patient is brought to recognize his own content in what appeared to him as the weird formations of the unconscious. Like Hegelian reflection, psychoanalysis does not generate neutral-objective knowledge, but a "practical" knowledge which, when subjectively assumed, radically changes its bearer.

From a contemporary perspective, it is easy to see the limitations of such a notion of reconciliation—it suffices to attempt to apply it to the struggle between the Nazis and the Jews. Again, on a first approach, the Jungian notion of the "shadow" as the misrecognized alter ego seems fitting here: is there not indeed a strange echoing and redoubling between the Nazi elevation of Aryan Germans and the Jews' perception of themselves as the chosen nation? Was it not already Schoenberg who dismissed Nazi racism as a miserable imitation of the Jewish identity as the chosen people? And yet would it not be obscene to say that each of these two parties should recognize in its opponent its own truth and substance, its own second Self? For the Jews, this could only mean that they should recognize how, in the guise of the Nazi hatred of them, they suffer the reaction to the fact that they excluded themselves from organic communal life and thereby abandoned themselves to a rootless, alienated existence. It is immediately clear what is wrong here: what's missing is the radical asymmetry of the opposed poles. While the (anti-Semitic figure of the) "Jew" really is

51 C. G. Jung, *The Structure and Dynamics of the Psyche* (The Collected Works of C. G. Jung, Vol. 8), London: Routledge 1970, p. 393 (§764).

a kind of "symptom" of Nazism, Nazism is definitely not in any symmetrical way a symptom of Judaism, the return of its repressed, its inner truth, for it is an obscenity to say that, in their struggle against Nazism, the Jews "fling away as absolutely worthless the true gold they should never have found elsewhere."

The opposition of poles thus conceals the fact that one of the poles already is the unity of the two—so, for Hegel, there is no need for a third element to bring the two together.[52] This is why Hegel's dialectics is radically groundless, abyssal, a process of the self-relating of the Two which lacks any Third—for example, there is no external Third, no Ground, no shared medium in which the opposition between law and crime is "synthesized": the dialectical "truth" of their opposition is that crime is its own species, the encompassing unity of itself and its opposite. With regard to the opposition of liberal individualism and fundamentalism, today's communitarians advocate a kind of Jungian "compensation theory": we in the West put too much emphasis on individualism, neglecting the bonds of community, which then return to haunt us in the guise of the fundamentalist threat; the way to fight fundamentalism is thus to change our own view, to recognize in it the distorted image of the neglected aspect of our own identity. The solution lies in restoring the proper balance between individual and community, creating a social body in which collective and individual freedom organically supplement each other. What is wrong here is this very figure of a balanced harmony of the two opposed principles. We should start, on the contrary, with the immanent "contradiction" (antagonism) of capitalist individualism—fundamentalism is ultimately a secondary, "reactive" phenomenon, an attempt to counteract and "gentrify" this antagonism.

For Hegel, the goal is thus not to (re)establish the symmetry and balance of the two opposing principles, but to recognize in one pole the symptom of the failure of the other (and *not vice versa*): fundamentalism is a symptom of liberalism, Antigone is a symptom of Creon, etc. The solution is to revolutionize or change the universal term itself (liberalism, etc.), so that it will no longer require its symptom as the guarantee of its unity. Consequently, the way to overcome the tension between secular individualism and religious fundamentalism is not to find a proper balance between the two, but to abolish or overcome the source of the problem, the antagonism at the very heart of the capitalist individualist project.

52 Another example from contemporary political conflicts suggests itself here: in the struggle between market liberalism and state interventionism, each side should recognize its need for the other. Only an effective state guarantees the conditions for the development of the market, and only a thriving market economy provides the resources for an efficient state. However, this very example also indicates the limitation of such logic: what if the antagonism reaches such a pitch that the reconciliation is not feasible? What if the only viable solution is to change the entire system?

It is this move towards self-relating negativity that is absent in Zen Buddhism, which also relies on a kind of "negation of negation": first, we deny the substantial character of reality and assert that the only Absolute is the Void itself; then, we overcome the Void itself insofar as it is still opposed to positive reality and assert the ultimate sameness of the plurality of phenomena and the Void. This is why the basic feature of the Buddhist ontology is the notion of the radical interdependence of phenomena: phenomena are totally non-substantial, there is nothing behind them, no Ground, only the Void; that is, if we isolate a thing from its relations to other things and try to grasp it as it is "in itself," we get only Void. In nirvana, we existentially assume this Void—not by denying phenomena, but by fully assuming their non-substantial character. The ethical implication of this notion of Void is that "good has no priority over evil. The priority of good over evil is an ethical imperative but not an actual human condition."[53] "Good and evil are completely interdependent. There is no good without evil and vice versa. There is no nothingness without somethingness and vice versa."[54] When we realize this (not only notionally, but also existentially), we reach "the point where there is neither good nor evil, neither life nor death, neither nothingness or somethingness ... This is freedom."[55] At this point, "I am neither good nor bad. I am nothing whatsoever."[56] From this position, even Hegel's dialectics appears not radical enough: for Hegel, Being still has priority over Nothing, negativity is contained to the self-mediating movement of the absolute Spirit which thus maintains a minimum of substantial identity, and the Hegelian "Cunning of Reason" indicates that a substantial force underlies the interplay of phenomena, teleologically directing it.

From the Hegelian standpoint, what is missing here is the properly dialectical paradox of a Nothingness which is *prior* to Somethingness and, even more, of a weird Something which is *less* than nothing. In other words, the Buddhist inter-relation and de-substantialization of reality remains at the level of the thorough interdependence of the opposite poles: no good without evil, no something without nothing, and vice versa—and we can overcome this duality only by way of withdrawing into the abyss of the absolute and unconditional Void. But what about a properly Hegelian dialectical process in which negativity is not reduced to a self-mediation of the positive Absolute, but in which, on the contrary, positive reality appears as the result of self-relating negativity (or, with regard to ethics, in which the good is a self-negated or self-mediated evil)?

53 Masao Abe, *Zen and Western Thought*, Honolulu: University of Hawaii Press 1985, p. 191.
54 Ibid., p. 201.
55 Ibid.
56 Ibid., p. 191.

Form and content

Can the matrix of the "subjective re-appropriation of the alienated objective content" still be applied to Lacan's "return to Freud"? Is not the whole thrust of Lacan's reading of Freud directed against such a subjective re-appropriation of alienated Otherness? For Lacan, is not the alienation of the subject in the Other constitutive of subjectivity? The obvious answer is no—however, it is our aim to give this "no" a different twist from the usual one: not to cut the link which connects Lacan to Hegel (a path which was increasingly followed by Lacan himself), but to make, in reading Hegel through Lacan, a new "return to Hegel," that is, to discern the contours of a different Hegel, a Hegel who no longer fits the subjectivist matrix of the subject appropriating (internalizing through notional mediation, sublating, idealizing) all substantial content.

One of the best indicators of the dimension which resists the pseudo-Hegelian understanding of psychoanalytic treatment as the process of the patient's appropriation of repressed content is the paradox of perversion in the Freudian theoretical edifice: perversion demonstrates the insufficiency of the simple logic of transgression. The standard wisdom tells us that perverts actually do what hysterics only dream about doing, for "everything is allowed" in perversion, a pervert openly actualizes all repressed content—and yet, nonetheless, as Freud emphasizes, *nowhere is repression as strong as in perversion*, a fact amply confirmed by our late-capitalist reality in which total sexual permissiveness causes anxiety and impotence or frigidity instead of liberation. This compels us to draw a distinction between the repressed content and the form of repression, where the form remains operative even after the content is no longer repressed—in short, the subject can fully appropriate the repressed content, but repression remains. Commenting on a short dream had by one of his patients (a woman who at first refused to tell Freud the dream "because it was so indistinct and muddled"), which revealed itself to refer to the fact that the patient was pregnant but in doubt as to the baby's father (i.e., the parenthood was "indistinct and muddled"), Freud draws a key dialectical conclusion:

> the lack of clarity shown by the dream was a part of the material which instigated the dream: part of this material, that is, was represented in the *form* of the dream. *The form of a dream or the form in which it is dreamt is used with quite surprising frequency for representing its concealed subject-matter.*[57]

The gap between form and content is here properly dialectical, in contrast to the transcendental gap whose point is that every content appears within an

57 Sigmund Freud, *The Interpretation of Dreams*, trans. James Strachey, New York: Avon Books 1965, p. 367.

a priori formal frame, and hence we should always be aware of the invisible transcendental frame which "constitutes" the content we perceive—or, in structural terms, we should distinguish between the elements and the formal places these elements occupy. We only attain the level of proper dialectical analysis of a form when we conceive a certain formal procedure not as expressing a certain aspect of the (narrative) content, but as marking or signaling that part of the content which is excluded from the explicit narrative line, so that—and herein

resides the proper theoretical point—if we want to reconstruct "all" of the narrative content, we must reach beyond the explicit narrative content as such and include those formal features which act as a stand-in for the "repressed" aspect of the content.[58] To take the well-known elementary example from the analysis of melodramas: the emotional excess that cannot express itself directly in the narrative line finds its outlet in the ridiculously sentimental musical accompaniment or in other formal features.

Exemplary is here the way Claude Berri's *Jean de Florette* and *Manon des Sources* displace Marcel Pagnol's original film (and his own later novelization of it) on which they are based. That is to say, Pagnol's original retains traces of the "authentic" French provincial community life, with its old, quasi-pagan religious patterns, while Berri's films fail in their effort to recapture the spirit of this closed, premodern community. However, unexpectedly, the inherent obverse of Pagnol's universe is the theatricality of the action and the element of ironic distance and comicality, while Berri's films, though shot more "realistically," place the emphasis on destiny (the musical leitmotif of the films is based on Verdi's *La forza del destino*), and on the melodramatic excess whose hystericality often borders on the ridiculous (like the scene in which, after the rain by-passes his field, the desperate Jean cries and shouts at Heaven). So, paradoxically, the closed, ritualized, premodern community implies theatrical comicality and irony, while the modern, "realistic" rendering involves Fate and melodramatic excess. In this respect, Berri's two films are to be opposed to Lars von Trier's *Breaking the Waves*: in both cases, we are dealing with the tension between form and content; however, in *Breaking the Waves*, the excess is located in the content (the subdued pseudo-documentary form makes this excess palpable), while in Berri, the excess in the form obfuscates and thus renders palpable the flaw in the content, the impossibility today of realizing the pure classical tragedy of Destiny.

Therein lies the key consequence of the move from Kant to Hegel: the very gap between content and form is to be reflected back into the content itself, as

an indication that the content is not all, that something was repressed/excluded from it. This exclusion which establishes the form itself is the "primordial

58 The thesis that form is part of content, the return of its repressed, should be supplemented by its reversal: content is ultimately also nothing but an effect and indication of the incompleteness of the form, of its "abstract" character.

repression" (*Ur-Verdrängung*), and no matter how much we bring out all the repressed content, this primordial repression persists. How do we explain this?  The immediate answer involves the identity of the repression with the return of the repressed, which means that the repressed content does not pre-exist repression, but is retroactively constituted by the very process of repression. Through different forms of negation or obfuscation (condensation, displacement, denegation, disavowal ...), the repressed is allowed to penetrate public conscious speech, to find an echo in it (the most direct example comes from Freud: when one of his patients said, "I don't know who this woman in my dream is, but I am sure she is not my mother!" the mother, the repressed, entered into speech). What we get here is another kind of "negation of negation"; that is, the content is negated or repressed, but this repression is in the same gesture itself negated in the guise of the return of the repressed (which is why we are definitely not dealing here with the properly Hegelian negation of negation). The logic seems similar to that of the relationship between sin and Law in Paul, where there is no sin without Law, where the Law itself creates the transgression it tries to subdue, so that, if we remove the Law, we also lose what the Law tried to "repress"—or, in more Freudian terms, if we remove the "repression," we also lose the repressed content. Is the proof not provided by today's typical patient, whose reaction to the same dream would be: "I don't know who this woman in my dream is, but I am sure she has something to do with my mother!"? The patient says this, but there is no liberation, no truth-effect, no shift in his subjective position—why? Again, what remains "repressed" even when the barriers preventing access to the repressed content come down? The first answer is, of course: the form itself. That is to say, both the positive and the negative form ("this is my mother"; "this is not my mother") move within the same field, the field of the symbolic form, and what we should focus on is a more radical "repression" constitutive of this form itself, what Lacan (at some point) called symbolic castration or the prohibition of incest—a negative gesture which sustains the very symbolic form, so that even when we say, "This is my mother!" the mother is already lost. That is to say, this negative gesture sustains the minimal gap between the symbolic and the Real, between (symbolic) reality and the impossible Real.

However, insofar as we are dealing here with the properly dialectical mediation between form and content, we should not reduce primordial repression simply to the form of a gap: something insists, the weird positivity of an excessive "content" not only impervious to negation, but produced by the very process of redoubled (self-relating) negation. Consequently, this something is not simply a remainder of the pre-symbolic Real that resists symbolic negation, but a spectral X called by Lacan the *objet a* or surplus-enjoyment. Here Lacan's key distinction between pleasure (*Lust, plaisir*) and enjoyment (*Geniessen, jouissance*) comes into play: what is "beyond the pleasure principle" is enjoyment itself, the drive

as such. The basic paradox of *jouissance* is that it is both impossible *and* unavoidable: it is never fully achieved, always missed, but, simultaneously, we never can get rid of it—every renunciation of enjoyment generates an enjoyment in renunciation, every obstacle to desire generates a desire for an obstacle, and so on. This reversal provides the minimal definition of surplus-enjoyment: it involves a paradoxical "pleasure in pain." That is to say, when Lacan uses the term *plus-de-jouir*, one has to ask another naïve but crucial question: in what

does this surplus consist? Is it merely a qualitative increase of ordinary pleasure? The ambiguity of the French expression is decisive here: it can mean "surplus of enjoyment" as well as "no enjoyment"—the surplus of enjoyment over mere pleasure is generated by the presence of the very opposite of pleasure, namely pain; it is the part of *jouissance* which resists being contained by homeostasis, by the pleasure-principle; it is the excess of pleasure produced by "repression" itself, which is why we lose it if we abolish repression. This is what Herbert Marcuse, in his *Eros and Civilization*, misses when he proposes a distinction between "basic repression" ("the 'modifications' of the instincts necessary for the perpetuation of the human race in civilization") and "surplus-repression" ("the restrictions necessitated by social domination"):

> while any form of the reality principle demands a considerable degree and scope of repressive control over the instincts, the specific historical institutions of the reality principle and the specific interests of domination introduce *additional* controls over and above those indispensable for civilized human association. These additional controls arising from the specific institutions of domination are what we denote as *surplus-repression*.[59]

Marcuse offers as examples of surplus-repression "the modifications and deflections of instinctual energy necessitated by the perpetuation of the monogamic-patriarchal family, or by a hierarchical division of labor, or by public control over the individual's private existence."[60] Although he concedes that basic and surplus-repression are de facto inextricably intertwined, one should go a step further and render problematic their very conceptual distinction: it is the paradox of libidinal economy that surplus or excess is necessary for even for the most "basic" functioning. An ideological edifice "bribes" subjects into accepting "repression" or renunciation by way of offering surplus-enjoyment (Lacan's *plus-de-jouir*)—that is, enjoyment generated by the "excessive" renunciation of enjoyment itself; surplus-enjoyment is by definition enjoyment-in-pain. (Its paradigmatic case is the Fascist call "Renounce corrupt pleasures! Sacrifice yourself for your country!" a call which promises an obscene enjoyment brought

59 Herbert Marcuse, *Eros and Civilization*, Boston: Beacon Press 1974, p. 37.
60 Ibid., pp. 37–8.

about by this very renunciation.) Thus one cannot have only "basic" repression without surplus-repression, since it is the very enjoyment generated by surplus-repression which renders "basic" repression palpable to subjects. The paradox we are dealing with here is thus a kind of "less is more": "more" repression is less traumatic, more easily accepted, than less. When repression is diminished, it becomes much more difficult to endure and provokes rebellion. (This may be one of the reasons why revolutions break out not when oppression is at its height, but when it diminishes to a more "reasonable" or "rational" level—the diminishing deprives repression of the aura which makes it acceptable.)

To return to Hegel: can one really claim that this excess produced by the very process of self-relating negation is beyond his scope? In a neglected passage from the subchapter of the *Phenomenology* describing the structure of the utilitarian Enlightenment universe, Hegel (for the first time) formulates the basic paradox of the "pleasure principle": the fact that the greatest threat to pleasure is not a scarcity that prevents full access to it, but the excess of pleasure itself. In the utilitarian universe, "everything exists to pleasure and delight [man], and, as he first comes from the hand of God, he walks the earth as in a garden planted for him." But what disturbs this paradise is that, having also "plucked the fruit of the tree of knowledge of good and evil," man's

> inherently good nature is also so constituted that the superfluity of delight does it harm, or rather his singleness contains as a factor in its constitution a principle that goes beyond it; his singleness can overreach itself and destroy itself. To prevent this, he finds reason a useful means for duly restraining this self-transcendence, or rather for preserving himself when he does go beyond the determinate: for such is the force of consciousness ... The principle of measure or proportion has, therefore, the determinate function of preventing pleasure in its variety and duration from being quite broken off: i.e. the function of "measure" is immoderation.[61]

This lesson is repeatedly imparted to us by advertising: to enjoy our product fully and permanently, we must enjoy it in proper measure (drink reasonably, consume only one bar of chocolate at a time ...)—only such restraint guarantees true "immoderation," a prolonged life of pleasure; as Lacan pointed out, the Freudian pleasure principle is not a principle of unbridled ecstatic enjoyment, but a principle of restraint.

The proof that Hegel's formulation of the "beyond of the pleasure principle" is embedded in his notion of subjectivity lies in his definition of the subject as "the activity of the formal rationality of satisfying impulses."[62] This

61 Hegel, *Phenomenology of Mind*, p. 330.
62 G. W. F. Hegel, *Hegels Philosophie des subjektiven Geistes/Hegel's Philosophy of Subjective Spirit*, trans. and ed. M. J. Petry, Dordrecht: D. Reidel 1978, p. 253 (§475).

idea is developed in his Introduction to the *Lectures on the Philosophy of World History*:

> [Man] places the ideal, the realm of thought, *between* the demands of the impulse and their satisfaction. In the animal, the two coincide; it cannot sever their connection by its own efforts—only pain or fear can do so. In man, the impulse is present before it is satisfied and independently of its satisfaction; in controlling or giving rein to his impulses, man acts in accordance with *ends* and determines himself in the light of a general principle. It is up to him to decide what end to follow; he can even make his end a universal one. In so doing, he is *determined* by whatever conceptions he has formed of his own nature and volitions. It is this which constitutes man's independence: for he knows what it is that determines him.[63]

This means that rationality, at first merely interposing itself as an agency for the better satisfaction of impulses, ends up subordinating all natural goals to itself ("positing its presuppositions") and becoming its own goal: rationality first emerges as

> a hedonic calculus aiming at the general satisfaction of my impulses (in happiness); but finally, if I am to be fully satisfied in my action—in my regard that it is my own—the rationality principle that I apply must not be conditional on a contingent end like happiness (which may depend on some view of desire preference that I can't be sure is my own, since others may have influenced my selection of it). Rather, the principle of my action must involve my willing that I be present in my action as a free agent.[64]

No wonder, then, that the identity of opposites is clearly discernible in the case of pleasure and duty. Not only is it possible to elevate pleasure into a duty (*à la* the narcissistic hedonist), it is also possible to elevate duty into a pleasure (*à la* the sentimental moralist). But what about the majority of cases in which the two are simply opposed? The catch is: am I able to do my duty, not when it curtails my pleasures, but when it gives me pleasure to do it? Only if I *am* able to do so will the two domains be truly separated. If I cannot tolerate the pleasure that may result as a by-product, then my carrying out of my duty will already be contaminated by pleasure, by the economy of "moral masochism." In other words, it is crucial to distinguish between tolerating pleasure as an accidental by-product of doing my duty, and doing a duty *because* it provides me pleasure.

---

63 G. W. F. Hegel, *Lectures on the Philosophy of World History—Introduction: Reason in History*, trans. H. B. Nisbet, Cambridge: Cambridge University Press 1975, pp. 49–50.
64 Allen Speight, *Hegel, Literature and the Problem of Agency*, Cambridge: Cambridge University Press 2001, p. 129.

NEGATION WITHOUT A FILLING

The "coincidence of the opposites" thus has nothing whatsoever to do with the "eternal harmony/struggle" of opposed forces, the constituent of every pagan cosmology. In a given society, certain features, attitudes, and norms of life are not perceived as ideologically marked but appear as "neutral," as part of a non-ideological common-sense way of life. "Ideology" is then reserved for those explicitly posited ("marked" in the semiotic sense) positions which stand out from or against this background (like extreme religious zeal, dedication to some political orientation, etc.). The Hegelian point here would be that it is precisely this neutralization of certain features within a spontaneously accepted background which is ideology at its purest (and at its most effective). Here, then, is a true case of the "coincidence of the opposites": the actualization of a notion (ideology in this case) at its purest coincides with (or more precisely appears as) its opposite (as non-ideology). And, mutatis mutandis, the same goes for violence: social-symbolic violence at its purest appears as its opposite, as the spontaneity of the milieu in which we dwell, as neutral as the air that we breathe.

What this last example clearly shows is that, in the Hegelian "negation of negation," the *level* shifts: first negation directly changes the content within the same horizon, while in the negation of negation, "nothing really changes," the horizon is simply turned around, so that "the same" content appears as its opposite. Another unexpected example: in the mid-1990s, the servicing of goods organized by the state in North Korea's centralized and fully regulated economy gradually ceased to function: the food distribution system delivered increasingly smaller rations, factories simply stopped paying salaries, the medical system was without medicines, electricity and water were available for only a couple of hours per week, cinemas stopped showing films, etc. The reaction of ordinary North Koreans to this disintegration may be surprising to some: the needs which were no longer being met by the state were, up to a point, accommodated by primitive forms of a modest market capitalism, grudgingly tolerated by the state: individuals selling home-grown vegetables, fish or mushrooms, dogs and rats (or trading them for family valuables like jewelry or clothes); electronic devices and DVDs smuggled in from China. What emerged was a brutal survivalist market economy, as if the country had regressed to a kind of Hobbesian state of nature: find your market niche (from selling homemade corn noodles to hairdressing) or die. It was thus not some elementary form of solidarity but raw egoism which won the day: in a cruel irony, at this zero-point, the official ideology of total solidarity and the dedication of individuals to the community was supplemented by its pure and simple opposite. The Hegelian point to be made here is, of course, that this negation of the official ideology was not external, but internal to it: the explosion of egoism was "in itself" already there in the actual subjective economy of those who participated in the official communal rituals—they participated as a matter of survival, as part of a pure egoist strategy of avoiding state terror. A recent docu-fiction book (based on interviews with refugees) describes the moment when Jun-sang, a privileged student at a Pyongyang university, after encountering a starving homeless child, suddenly realized that he no longer believed in the North Korean official ideology:

> He now knew for sure that he didn't believe. It was an enormous moment of self-revelation, like deciding one was an atheist. It made him feel alone. He was different from everybody else, burdened by a secret he had discovered about himself.
>
> At first he thought his life would be dramatically different with his newfound clarity. In fact, it was much the same as ever before. He went through the motions of being a loyal subject. On Saturday mornings he showed up punctually at the ideological lectures at the university.[65]

However, he then noticed that the faces of his fellow students

> were still and expressionless, as blank as mannequins in a department store window.
>
> He realized suddenly he wore the same vacant expression on his face. In fact, they all probably felt exactly the same way he did about the contents of the lecture.
>
> "They know! They all know!" he nearly screamed, he was so certain … Jun-sang realized he was not the only nonbeliever out there. He was even convinced that he could recognize a form of silent communication that was so subtle it didn't even rise to the level of a wink or a nod.[66]

One should read these lines literally: far from experiencing a loss of individuality through immersion in a primordial collective identity, the individuals who participated in the obligatory ideological rituals were absolutely alone, reduced to a punctual individuality, unable to communicate their true inner subjective stance, totally divorced from the ideological big Other. What we encounter here is one of the purest examples of the shift from alienation to separation as developed by Lacan in his seminar on the four fundamental concepts of psychoanalysis: radical alienation in the public ideological order, where people seem to lose their individuality and act like puppets, is no less a form of radical separation, the total withdrawal of subjects into their mute singularity excluded from any symbolic collective—it was this singularity produced by the state-ideological machine which exploded in North Korea when the state servicing of goods ceased to function. (Perspicuous analysts of Stalinism had already

65 Barbara Demick, *Nothing to Envy: Ordinary Lives in North Korea*, New York: Spiegel & Grau 2009, pp. 195–6.
66 Ibid., p. 196.

noted that the Stalinist collective rendered individuals less solidary and more survivalist-egotist than normal bourgeois society, where elements of solidarity survive as a reaction against market competition.)[67]

The underlying logic here is that of the retroactive positing of presuppositions. This logic also allows us to see what is wrong in the Hobbesian vision of the Monarch as the One who brutally but necessarily imposes peaceful coexistence upon the multitude of individuals who, left to themelves, would descend into a state where *homo homini lupus*. This supposedly "natural" state of the war of all against all is a retroactive product of the imposed state power; that is, in order for that power to function, the One has to sever the direct lateral links between individuals: "the relation to the One makes of every subject a traitor to his fellows. It is false to assert that the One is put in the place of the third because *homo homini lupus*, as Hobbes would say. It is the fact of putting the One in the place of the transcendent lawgiver or considering him as its representative that makes a wolf out of a man."[68] A similar point was made by Sofia Näsström: it is the state itself that "frees" people from their responsibility to each other, narrowing the space of direct communal solidarity and reducing people to abstract individuals—in short, the state itself creates the problem it then strives to resolve.[69]

What this more complicated model including retroactivity indicates is that the Hegelian triad is never really a triad, that its number is not 3. There were three steps in the formation of Russian national identity: first, the substantial starting point (premodern Orthodox Russia); then, the violent modernization enforced by Peter the Great, which continued throughout eighteenth century and created a new French-speaking elite; finally, after 1812, the rediscovery of "Russianness," the return to forgotten authentic origins.[70] It is crucial to bear in

67 More generally, one of the great ironies of the fall of the communist regimes is that, while it was perceived as the end of ideology (capitalism winning over a crude ideology which had tried to impose its narrow views on society), the parties that succeeded the communists in the post-communist countries proved to be the most ruthless "non-ideological" agents of capitalism (in Poland, Hungary), while even those communists who are still in power (in China, Vietnam) endorse a brutal capitalism.

68 Moustapha Safouan, *Why Are the Arabs Not Free? The Politics of Writing*, Oxford: Wiley-Blackwell 2007.

69 See Sofia Näsström, *The An-Archical State: Logics of Legitimacy in the Social Contract Condition*, dissertation, Stockholm Series in Politics 99, Stockholm: Stockholm University 2004. Did not the same logic apply to Iraq in 2007? The only convincing argument that resurfaced towards the end of 2006 for why the US Army should not leave Iraq was that its abrupt withdrawal would plunge the country into the total chaos of a large-scale civil war with the disintegration of all state institutions. The supreme irony of this argument was that the US intervention itself created the conditions in which the Iraqi state was not able to function properly.

70 Perhaps, however, the true beginning, the first term which started the entire moment,

mind that this rediscovery of authentic roots was only possible *through* and *for* the educated eyes of the French-speaking elite: "authentic" Russia existed only for the "French gaze." This is why it was a French composer (working at the imperial court) who wrote the first opera in Russian and thus started the tradition, and why Pushkin himself had to use French words to make clear to his readers (and to himself) the true meaning of his authentic Russian terms. Later, of course, the dialectical movement goes on: "Russianness" immediately splits into liberal populism and conservative Slavophilism, and the process culminates in the properly dialectical coincidence of modernity and primitivism: the fascination of the early twentieth-century modernists with ancient barbaric cultural forms. The complexity of this example accounts for why it seems that Hegel secretly oscillates between two matrices of the negation of negation. The first matrix is: (1) substantial peace; (2) the subject's act, its one-sided intervention which disturbs the peace, disrupts the balance; (3) the revenge of Destiny which re-establishes the balance by way of annihilating the subject's excess. The second is: (1) the subject's act; (2) the failure of the act; (3) the shift of perspective which inverts this failure into success.[71] It is easy to see that the last two moments of the first triad overlap with the first two moments of the second triad—it all depends on where we start to count: if we start with substantial unity and balance, the subjective act is the negation; if we start with the subjective act as the moment of positing, negation is its failure.

What this complication implies is that, already at the abstract-formal level, we should distinguish four rather than only three stages of a dialectical process. Decades ago, *MAD* magazine published a series of variations on the topic of how a subject can relate to a norm at four levels: in fashion, say, the poor don't care how they dress; the lower middle classes try to follow the fashion but always lag behind; the upper middle classes dress in accordance with the latest fashion; those at the top, the trend-setters, also don't care how they dress since the way they dress *is* the fashion. Or, with regard to the law, the outcasts do not care what the law says, they just do whatever they want; the utilitarian egotists follow the law, but only approximately, when it suits their interests; the moralists strictly follow the law; while those at the top, like the absolute monarch, again do whatever they want since what they do or say *is* the law. In both cases, the logic is the same: we progress from ignorance to partial commitment and then to full commitment, but to these three steps another is added: the highest level which

---

the "thesis," was Peter's modernization, so that what preceded it was just its formless substantial presupposition.

71 Jean Baudrillard was therefore in a way right when—tongue in cheek, of course—he proposed a new Hegelian triad: thesis–antithesis–prothesis. The third moment which "resolves" the contradiction is by definition "prothetic" (virtual, artificial, symbolic, not substantially natural).

paradoxically coincides with the lowest—at this highest level, people do exactly the same as at the previous level, but with a subjective attitude which is the same as the attitude of those at the lowest level. Does this not fit with Augustine's saying that, if you have Christian love, you can do whatever you want since what you do will automatically be in accordance with the law? And do these four steps not also provide a model for the "negation of negation"? We start with a totally non-alienated attitude (I do what I want), then we progress through partial alienation (I restrain myself, my egotism) followed by total alienation (I surrender myself completely to the norm or law), until finally, in the figure of the Master, this total alienation is self-negated, coinciding with its opposite.

This more complex model, which distinguishes between two alienations or negations, partial and total, also enables us to answer one of the critical points often made against Hegel: namely that he cheats when he presents the inner deployment of a constellation in such a way that the lowest point of self-relating negation magically reverts into a new higher positivity—at best, what we should get, instead of the total destruction or self-erasure of the entire movement, is a return to the immediate substantial starting point, so that we would find ourselves in a cyclical universe. But the first surprise is that Hegel himself outlines this option in his *Phenomenology*, in the chapter on absolute freedom and the Terror:

> Out of this tumult spirit would be hurled back upon its starting point, the ethical world and the real world of spiritual culture, which would thus have been merely refreshed and rejuvenated by the fear of the lord, that has again entered men's hearts. Spirit would have anew to traverse and continually repeat this cycle of necessity, if only complete interpenetration of self-consciousness and the substance were the final result: an interpenetration in which self-consciousness, which has experienced the force of its universal nature operating negatively upon it, would try to know and find itself not as this particular self-consciousness but only as universal, and hence, too, would be able to endure the objective reality of universal spirit, a reality, excluding self-consciousness *qua* particular.[72]

In Revolutionary Terror, the singular consciousness experiences the destructive consequences of keeping itself separate from the universal substance: in such a separation, substance appears as a negative power which arbitrarily annihilates every singular consciousness. Here we can employ one of Hegel's famous word plays: the ambiguity of the German expression *zugrundegehen*, which means to disintegrate, fall apart, but literally also *zu Grunde gehen*, to reach one's ground—the positive outcome of the Terror is that, in the subject's very annihilation, the

72 Hegel, *Phenomenology of Mind*, pp. 348–9.

subject reaches its ground, finds its place in the ethical substance, accepts its unity with this substance. On the other hand, since ethical substance is actual only as the force which mobilizes singular subjects, the annihilation of the singular subject by the substance is simultaneously the substance's self-annihilation, which means that this negative movement of self-destruction seems compelled to repeat itself indefinitely. It is at this point, however, that the inevitable "but" enters, articulated in a precise line of argumentation:

> But this is not the form the final result assumed. For in absolute freedom there was no reciprocal interaction either between an external world and consciousness, which is absorbed in manifold existence or sets itself determinate purposes and ideas, or between consciousness and an external objective world, be it a world of reality or of thought. What that freedom contained was the world absolutely in the form of consciousness, as a universal will, and, along with that, self-consciousness gathered out of all the dispersion and manifoldness of existence or all the manifold ends and judgments of mind, and concentrated into the bare and simple self ... In the sphere of culture itself it does not get the length of viewing its negation or alienation in this form of pure abstraction; its negation is negation with a filling and a content—either honour and wealth, which it gains in the place of the self that it has alienated from itself; or the language of *esprit* and insight, which the distraught consciousness acquires; or, again, the negation is the heaven of belief or the principle of utility belonging to the stage of enlightenment. All these determinate elements disappear with the disaster and ruin that overtake the self in the state of absolute freedom; its negation is meaningless death, sheer horror of the negative which has nothing positive in it, nothing that gives a filling.
>
> At the same time, however, this negation in its actual manifestation is not something alien and external. It is neither that universal background of necessity in which the moral world is swamped, nor the particular accident of private possession, the whims and humours of the owner, on which the distraught consciousness finds itself dependent; it is universal will, which in this its last abstraction has nothing positive, and hence can give nothing in return for the sacrifice. But just on that account this will is in unmediated oneness with self-consciousness, it is the pure positive because it is the pure negative; and that meaningless death, the unfilled, vacuous negativity of self, in its inner constitutive principle, turns round into absolute positivity.[73]

In an uncanny act of what Pierre Bayard calls "plagiarizing the future," Hegel seems to quote Lacan here: how can "negation with a filling" not evoke all the Lacanian formulae for filling in the lack, for an object which serves as the placeholder of the lack (*le tenant-lieu du manque*), etc.? The infamous reversal of the negative into the positive occurs here at a very precise point: at the moment

73 Ibid., p. 349.

when the exchange breaks down. Throughout the whole period of what Hegel calls *Bildung* (culture or education through alienation), the subject is deprived of (a part of) its substantial content, yet it gets something in exchange for this deprivation, "either honour and wealth, which it gains in the place of the self that it has alienated from itself; or the language of *esprit* and insight, which the distraught consciousness acquires; or, again, the negation is the heaven of belief or the principle of utility belonging to the stage of enlightenment." In Revolutionary Terror, this exchange breaks down, the subject is exposed to the destructive abstract negativity (embodied in the State) which deprives it even of its biological substance (of life itself), without giving anything in return—death is here utterly meaningless, "the most cold-blooded and meaningless death of all, with no more significance than cleaving a head of cabbage or swallowing a draught of water," without even surviving as a noble memory in the minds of friends and family. How, then, does this pure negativity or loss "magically" turn into new positivity? What do we get when we get nothing in exchange? There is only one consistent answer: *this nothingness itself.* When there is no filling of the negation, when we are forced to confront the power of negativity in its naked purity and are swallowed by it, the only way to go on is to realize that this negativity is the very core of our being, that the subject "is" the void of negativity. The core of my being is not some positive feature, but merely the capacity to mediate or negate all fixed determinations; it is not what I am, but the negative way I am able to relate to what(ever) I am.[74] But does Hegel not thereby endorse what one is tempted to call the mother of all ideological mystifications of the French Revolution, first formulated by Kant, for whom, more important than the often bloody reality of what occurred on the streets of Paris, was the enthusiasm that the Revolution gave rise to among sympathetic observers throughout Europe?

74 This power is not a merely negative one, but the positive power of negativity itself, the power to generate new forms, to create entities *ex nihilo*. Apropos labor as thwarted desire and the forming of objects, Jameson makes a perspicuous observation on the difference between Master and Servant: the Servant's negativity, his renouncing of immediate satisfaction and the forming of objects, "trumps idealism and constitutes a philosophically more satisfactory force of the dissolution of the physical (and of everything else) than the Master's ignorant Samurai-like fearlessness" (Jameson, *The Hegel Variations*, p. 56). In short, while the Master fearlessly risks his life and assumes the negativity of death, the life he leads is a life enslaved to sensual satisfaction (to consuming the objects produced by the Servant), while the Servant effectively annihilates immediate material existence through its de-formation—the Servant is thus more "idealist" than the Master, since he is able to force Ideas onto reality.

But, again, Lebrun voices a gnawing suspicion that this triumph of negativity conceals a bitter taste: is such a reversal of the negative into the positive not yet another case of "if you can't beat them, join them," of the desperate strategy of turning total defeat into victory by way of "identifying with the enemy"?

> The revolution which we have seen taking place in our own times in a nation of gifted people may succeed, or it may fail. It may be so filled with misery and atrocities that no right-thinking man would ever decide to make the same experiment again at such a price, even if he could hope to carry it out successfully at the second attempt. But I maintain that this revolution has aroused in the hearts and desires of all spectators who are not themselves caught up in it a *sympathy* which borders almost on enthusiasm, although the very utterance of this sympathy was fraught with danger. It cannot therefore have been caused by anything other than a moral disposition within the human race.[75]

The mystification resides in the reversal of the external negativity of the Revolutionary Terror into the sublime internal power of the moral Law within each of us—but can this *sublation* (*Aufhebung*) actually be accomplished? Is the violence of the Terror not too strong for such a domestication? Kant himself is fully aware of this excess: in the *Metaphysics of Morals* (1797), he characterizes the central defining event of the French Revolution (regicide) as a "suicide of the state," as a pragmatic paradox opening up an "abyss" into which reason falls, as an indelible crime (*crimen immortale, inexpiable*) which precludes forgiveness in this world or in the next:

> Of all the atrocities involved in overthrowing a state by rebellion … it is the formal *execution* of the monarch that strikes horror in a soul filled with the idea of human rights, a horror that one feels repeatedly as soon and as often as one thinks of such scenes as the fate of Charles I or Louis XVI.[76]

All the oscillations involved in the encounter with the Real are here: a regicide is something so terrible one cannot fully represent it to oneself in all its dimensions; it cannot really happen (people cannot be so evil), it should only be constructed as a necessary virtual point; the actual regicide was not a case of diabolical evil, of an evil accomplished for no pathological reason (and thus indistinguishable from the Good), since it was in fact done for a pathological reason (the fear that, if the king were allowed to live, he might return to power and exact revenge). It is interesting to note how the standard Kantian suspicion about an act being truly good or ethical is here weirdly mobilized in the opposite direction: we cannot be sure that an act really was "diabolically evil," that some pathological motivation did not make it a normal case of evil. In both cases, empirical causality appears to be suspended, the excess of another noumenal dimension seems to intrude

75 Immanuel Kant, "The Contest of Faculties," in *Political Writings*, second ed., trans. H. B. Nisbet, Cambridge: Cambridge University Press 1991, p. 182.

76 Immanuel Kant, *The Metaphysics of Morals*, in *Practical Philosophy*, trans. and ed. Mary J. Gregor, Cambridge: Cambridge University Press 1996, pp. 464–5.

violently into our reality. Kant is thus unable to assume this ultimate political infinite judgment.

Hegel is the only one who fully asserts the identity of the two extremes, of the Sublime and of the Terror: "Hegel's unflinching identification of the Terror as the inauguration of political modernity does not prevent him from affirming the Revolution in its entirety as inevitable, comprehensible, justifiable, horrible, thrilling, mind-numbingly boring, and infinitely productive."[77] Hegel's sublime words on the French Revolution from his *Lectures on the Philosophy of World History* are, if anything, even more enthusiastic than Kant's, and he rejects the easy way out of the traumatic "infinite judgment" in both its versions: First, the liberal dream of "1789 without 1793" (the idea that we could have had the Revolution without the Terror, with the latter seen as an accidental distortion). Second, the conditional endorsement of 1793 as the price that had to be paid in order for the nation to enjoy the institutions of modern civil society as the "rational kernel" which remains after the repellent shell of the revolutionary upheaval has been discarded.[78] (Marx reverses this relationship: he praises the enthusiasm of the Revolution, treating the later prosaic, commercial order as its banal truth.)

Furthermore, Hegel also clearly registers the limit of what may appear to be his own solution: the above-mentioned *Aufhebung* of the abstract freedom or negativity of the Revolution in the concrete post-revolutionary rational state. As Rebecca Comay summarizes this argument (not without irony): "Hegel loves the French Revolution so much he needs to purge it of the revolutionaries."[79] However, as Comay makes clear, a close reading of the last part of the chapter on Spirit in the *Phenomenology* reveals how, far from celebrating the *Aufhebung* of Terror in the inner freedom of the subject obeying only his autonomous voice of conscience, Hegel is fully aware that

> such freedom on its own terms does nothing to redeem the blocked promise of the Revolution. Hegel makes it bitterly clear that the sublime purity of the moral will can be no antidote to the terrifying purity of revolutionary virtue. He demonstrates that all the features of absolute freedom are carried over into Kantian morality: the obsessionality, the paranoia, the suspicion, the surveillance, the evaporation of objectivity within the sadistic vehemence of a subjectivity bent on reproducing itself within a world it must disregard.[80]

77 Rebecca Comay, *Mourning Sickness: Hegel and the French Revolution*, Palo Alto: Stanford University Press 2011, p. 76.

78 Ibid., pp. 76–7.

79 Ibid., p. 90.

80 Ibid., p. 93.

The excess of the Revolution thus resists its *Aufhebung* in both its dimensions: not only is inner moral freedom not strong enough to pacify the Revolutionary Terror (to account for it, to justify it), it is also—and this is the obverse of the same failure—not strong enough to actualize the Revolution's emancipatory promise. Inner moral freedom, even when overblown in the Romantic absolute subject, always and by definition conceals a resigned acceptance of the existing social order of domination:

> Hegel has relentlessly dismantled every attempt to displace or dissolve the traumatic rupture of the French Revolution within a spiritual, philosophical, or aesthetic upheaval. Political revolution can no longer be absorbed into the Copernican revolution of Kant or Fichte, or into the various cultural revolutions projected from Schiller on ... Hegel is as unforgiving here as Marx: every retreat from politics to the freedom of moral self-consciousness rehearses the Stoic impasse, provokes the sceptical rejoinder, and culminates in a self-serving misery in which can be discerned a secret collusion with the existent.[81]

Comay notes how this brutal critique of Kant's practical thought reveals Hegel at his most Freudo-Nietzschean, deploying the "hermeneutics of suspicion" at its most radical: "The catalogue of Freudian concepts (and at times even vocabulary) marshalled by Hegel throughout this section is impressive: repression, perversion, isolation, splitting, disavowal, fetishism, projection, introjection, incorporation, masochism, mourning, melancholia, repetition, death drive."[82] With Hegel's analysis of the steps which follow his critique of the Kantian ethical edifice (Fichtean concrete duty, the Schillerian aestheticization of ethics, the hypocrisy of the Beautiful Soul), we are just caught further in this downward spiral, right down to the solipsistic madness of "vaporized subjectivity" and its self-ironic mirroring. Even when describing how this self-destructive pathological Narcissism reaches its peak, admitting the void in its heart, Hegel is well aware that the fetish is not only an object filling in the void: "The void carved by the missing object turns into a filling for itself: even absence provides its own bitter consolation."[83] Referring to Origen, Hegel "goes so far as to suggest gleefully, on Enlightenment's behalf, that even castration can be a defence against castration: the florid example of Origen shows how an all too literal injury can serve to preempt the ultimate traumatic wounding"[84]—a thesis fully confirmed by psychoanalysis, which demonstrates how a castration in reality (cutting off one's penis or testicles) can function as a way of avoiding the wound of symbolic

81 Ibid., p. 149.
82 Ibid., p. 96.
83 Ibid., p. 114.
84 Ibid., p. 124.

castration (this was the strategy of the "skopci" sect in Russia and Eastern Europe during the late nineteenth century).

We touch here on a problematic nerve, highlighted by the Young Hegelian reproach that Hegel surrenders to the existing social misery. Does Hegel not detect a hidden conformism in the critical stance itself? This is why, in a profoundly Hegelian way, Catherine Malabou calls for the abandonment of the *critical* stance towards reality as the ultimate horizon of our thinking, under whatever name it may appear, from the Young Hegelian "critical critique" to twentieth-century Critical Theory.[85] What such a critical stance fails to accomplish is the fulfillment of its own gesture: the radicalization of the subjective negative-critical attitude towards reality into a full critical self-negation. Even if it leaves one open to the accusation of having "regressed" to the Old Hegelian position, one should adopt the authentically Hegelian *absolute* position which, as Malabou points out, involves a kind of speculative "surrender" of the Self to the Absolute, albeit in a Hegelian-dialectical way: not the immersion of the subject in the higher unity of an all-encompassing Absolute, but the inscription of the "critical" gap separating the subject from the (social) substance into this substance itself, as its own antagonism, or self-distance. The "critical" stance is thus not directly canceled in some higher-level *Yes* to a positive Absolute; it is rather inscribed into the Absolute itself as its own gap. This is why Hegelian Absolute Knowledge, far from signaling a kind of subjective appropriation or internalization of all substantial content, should be read against the background of what Lacan called "subjective destitution." In the very last pages of the chapter on Spirit, this "surrender to the Absolute" takes the form of an unexpected and abrupt gesture of *reconciliation*: "The reconciling *Yes*, in which the two I's let go their antithetical existence, is the existence of the 'I' which has expanded into a duality, and therein remains identical with itself."[86] While this formulation may sound emptily abstract, the worst kind of exercise in formal-dialectical thinking, it pays to read it closely, bearing in mind its precise context. Just before the quoted passage, Hegel characterizes reconciliation as "externalization," a kind of counter-move to the standard dialectical internalization of the external opposition: here, it is the inner contradiction of the subject which is externalized in the relationship among subjects, indicating the subject's acceptance of itself as part of the outer social world over which it does not exert control. What is accepted in the *Yes* of reconciliation is thus a basic alienation in an almost Marxist sense: the meaning of my acts does not depend on me, on my intentions, it is decided afterwards, retroactively. In other words, what is accepted,

85 See Judith Butler and Catherine Malabou, *Sois mon corps. Une lecture contemporaine de la domination et de la servitude chez Hegel*, Paris: Bayard 2010.

86 G. W. F. Hegel, *Phenomenology of Spirit*, trans. A. V. Miller, Oxford: Oxford University Press 1977, p. 409.

what the subject has to assume, is its radical and constitutive decentering in the symbolic order.

"The two" in the passage just quoted refers to the opposition between the acting and the judging consciousness: to act is to err, the act is by definition partial, it involves guilt, but the judging consciousness does not admit that its judging is also an act, it refuses to include itself in what it judges. It ignores the fact that the true evil lies in the neutral gaze which sees evil everywhere around itself, so that it is no less tainted than the acting consciousness. In geopolitical terms, this gap between the judging consciousness and the acting consciousness, between knowing and doing, is the gap between Germany and France: reconciliation is the reconciliation of the two nations, where the Word of reconciliation should be pronounced by Germany—German thought should reconcile itself with the acting French hero (Napoleon). We are dealing here with a purely performative formal gesture of abandoning purity and accepting the "stain" of one's complicity with the world. The one who pronounces the word of reconciliation is the judging consciousness, renouncing its critical attitude. But far from amounting to conformism, only such a *Yes* (expressing a readiness to accept the evil, to dirty one's hands) opens up the space for real change. As such, this reconciliation is simultaneously both precipitous and belated: it occurs all of a sudden, as a kind of flight forward, before the situation seems ready for it, and, at the same time, like Kafka's Messiah, it comes one day too late, when it no longer matters.

But how does such an elementary gesture of accepting (oneself as part of) the contingency of the world open up the space for real change? Towards the end of the "Preface" to his *Philosophy of Right*, Hegel defines the task of philosophy: like the owl of Minerva which takes flight at dusk, philosophy can only paint "gray on gray," in other words it only translates into a lifeless conceptual scheme a form of life which has already reached its peak and entered its decline (is becoming "gray" itself). Comay perspicuously reads this "gray on gray" as a figure of "minimal difference"[87] (or, as Nietzsche would have put it, of the "shortest shadow," although Nietzsche speaks of midday, of course): the difference between the decrepit reality and its notion when the difference is *at its minimal*, purely formal, in contrast to when a wide gap exists between an ideal and the misery of its actual existence.

How can such a tautology open up the space for the New? The only solution to this paradox is that the New we are dealing with is not primarily the future New, but *the New of the past itself*, of the thwarted, blocked, or betrayed possibilities ("alternate realities") which have disappeared in the actualization of the past: the actualization (*Verwirklichung*)—that is, the acceptance of actuality—brought about by Reconciliation involves the "*deactivation* of the

87 Comay, *Mourning Sickness*, p. 142.

existent and the reactivation and reenactment (in every sense) of the thwarted futures of the past. Actuality thus expresses precisely the presence of the virtual: it opens history to the 'no longer' of a blocked possibility and the persistence of an unachieved 'not yet.'"[88] The Hegelian tautology "gray on gray" should be linked to the Deleuzian notion of pure repetition as the rise of the New: what emerges in the repetition of the same actual "gray" is its virtual dimension, the lost "alternate histories" of what might have happened but did not. "The French Revolution is the French Revolution" does not add any new positive knowledge, any new positive determinations, but it reminds us of the spectral dimension of the hopes that the Revolution evoked and which were thwarted by its outcome. Such a reading also enables us to see how we can think together Reconciliation as internalizing memory (*Er-Innerung*) *and* the retroactive healing of the wounds of the Spirit which undoes (*ungeschehenmachen*) catastrophes of the past in an act of radical *forgetting*:

> Forgetting is not opposed to the work of remembrance but proves here to be its most radical achievement: oblivion brings memory itself to a point beyond its own beginning. To forget, to undo the past, to make it all "un-happen," is precisely to remember a moment *before* it all happened, to undo the inexorability of fate by restaging the beginning, even if only in imagination and in proxy: to act *as if* we could take it over again, as if we could cast aside the legacy of dead generations, as if we could refuse the mourning work of cultural succession, as if we could cast off our patrimony, rewrite our origins, as if every moment, even those long vanished, could become a radically new beginning—unprecedented, unrehearsed, unremembered.[89]

Reconciliation as pure repetition does not bring us back to some mythical beginning, but to the moment just before the beginning, before the flow of events organized itself into a Fate, obliterating other alternative possibilities. For example, in the case of Antigone, the point is not to somehow restore the organic unity of mores (*Sittlichkeit*), since there never was such a unity—a split is constitutive of the very order of *Sittlichkeit*. *Antigone* is a story about this division constitutive of power, and one should avoid the boring moralistic topic of who is right or who is worse, Antigone or Creon, the representative of respect for the sacred or the representative of secular power. As Stalin would have put it, they are both worse (than what? Than the power of the people!), part of the same hierarchic power machine. The only way to break the deadlock of their conflict is to step outside of their common ground and imagine a third option from which to reject the entire conflict as false—something like the Chorus taking over, arresting both Antigone and Creon for posing a threat to the people,

88 Ibid., p. 145.
89 Ibid., pp. 147–8.

putting at risk their very survival, and establishing itself as a collective body of revolutionary justice, a kind of Jacobin committee for public safety keeping the guillotine busy.

The problem here is: how does this negation of negation which changes the entire field relate to the Freudo-Lacanian negation of negation which ends with the spectral not-not-nothingness? Does not the shift from the first negation ("negation with a filling"), where I sacrifice the core of my being in exchange for something (heaven of belief, honor, utility, wealth ...), to the negation of negation ("negation without a filling") point towards what Lacan, in his reading of Claudel, deployed as the structure of *Versagung*, where we pass from the sacrifice made for something to the sacrifice made for nothing?

Let us clarify this crucial point by way of a detour through literature: not Claudel's *L'Otage* (Lacan's own reference in his explication of *Versagung*), but J. M. Coetzee's *Disgrace*, a profoundly Hegelian novel set in post-apartheid South Africa. David Lurie is a divorced, middle-aged scholar of Romantic poetry whose unrealized ambition is to write a chamber opera about Byron's life in Italy. He has become a victim of "the great rationalization" of his Cape Town university, which has been turned into a technical college, where he now teaches courses in "communication skills" that he finds nonsensical. He is such a nonentity that not only do his students look straight through him, even the prostitute he patronizes weekly, and for whom he has begun buying gifts, stops receiving him. When he is hauled before an academic tribunal after a misbegotten affair with Melanie, a beautiful black student, he refuses to defend himself against charges of sexual harassment, although his conduct towards Melanie has fallen only a little short of rape. He finally blurts out an apology, but the members of the tribunal are not satisfied, and demand to know whether it reflects his sincere feelings and comes from the heart. He rashly tells his judges that his liaison with the pretty and almost totally passive Melanie transformed him, if only briefly: "I was no longer a fifty-year-old divorcé at a loose end. I became a servant of Eros."

To escape this suffocating situation, David moves in with his daughter Lucy, a stolid lesbian who, like him, seems to have been abandoned by the world, and lives in an isolated farm on the South African plain, surviving by selling flowers and vegetables at a local market. Their relations with Petrus, the African farmer who is their nearest neighbor, become increasingly troubled. Once Lucy's servant, he now owns his own plot of land, and is conspicuously absent when David and Lucy become the victims of a vicious criminal assault: three black youngsters beat David and burn his face, while Lucy is gang raped. We are given hints that the attacks are part of Petrus's plan to take over Lucy's farm. In the wake of these brutal attacks, David's angry demands for justice receive no response from the overstretched police, and his attempts to confront one of the assailants (whom Petrus is protecting) are met with silence and evasive lies.

Finally, Petrus informs David that he plans to marry Lucy and take control of her farm to provide her with protection. To David's shock and surprise, Lucy tells him that she will accept Petrus's offer and give birth to the child she bears as the result of the rape. Lucy seems to understand what David cannot: that to live where she lives she must tolerate brutalization and humiliation and simply keep going. "Perhaps that is what I must learn to accept," she tells her father. "To start at ground level. With nothing ... No cards, no weapons, no property, no rights, no dignity ... Like a dog."

Again needing to escape a terrible deadlock, David volunteers to work for Bev, a friend of Lucy's who runs the local veterinary clinic. He soon comes to realize that Bev's primary role, in this impoverished land, is not to heal animals but to kill them with as much love and mercy as she can summon. He becomes Bev's lover, although she is conspicuously ugly. He returns briefly to Cape Town, where he visits Melanie's family and apologizes to her father. At the novel's end, David is also reconciled to his life with Lucy; he thus reclaims a kind of dignity based on the very fact that he has given up everything: his daughter, his notion of justice, his dream of writing an opera on Byron, and even his favorite dog, which he helps Bev to put down. He no longer needs a dog, since he has himself accepted to live "like a dog" (echoing the final words of Kafka's *The Trial*).

Perhaps this is what true Hegelian reconciliation looks like—and maybe this example enables us to clear up some confusions about what that reconciliation actually involves.[90] David is portrayed as a disenchanted cynic who exploits his power over students, and the rape of his daughter seems a kind of repetition which establishes a certain justice: what he did to Melanie happens again to his daughter. However, it is all too simple to say that David should recognize his own responsibility for the predicament he finds himself in—such a reading of David as a "tragic" character who gets his comeuppance in his final humiliation still relies on a kind of moral balance or justice being established at the end, and thus avoids the deeply disturbing fact that the novel in fact has no clear moral compass. This ambiguity is condensed in the character of Petrus who, while ruthlessly ambitious and manipulative beneath his polite exterior, nonetheless

90 A particularly cruel variation of the bad news/good news medical joke, encompassing the entire triad of good-bad-good news, usefully illustrates the Hegelian triad inclusive of the final "reconciliation": After his wife has undergone a long and risky operation, the husband approaches the doctor to inquire about the outcome. The doctor begins: "Your wife survived, she will probably live longer than you. But there are some complications: she will no longer be able to control her anal muscles, so excrement will dribble continuously out of her anus; there will also be a flow of bad-smelling yellow jelly from her vagina, so any sex is out. Plus her mouth will malfunction and food will fall out ..." Noting the expression of rising panic on the husband's face, the doctor taps him kindly on the shoulder and smiles: "Don't worry, I was only joking! Everything is OK—she died during the operation."

stands for a kind of social stability and order. The political message implied by his ascendance to power within the small local community is not a racist one ("this is what happens if you allow the blacks to take over: no real change, just a reorganization of domination which makes things even worse than before"), but one that highlights the re-emergence of a gangster-like patriarchal-tribal order which, one can argue, is the result of white rule which kept the blacks in a state of apartheid, preventing their inclusion in modern society.

The wager of the novel is that the very radicality of the white hero's utter resignation and acceptance of this new oppressive order confers on him a kind of ethical dignity. If David can be seen as a contemporary Sygne de Coûfontaine, *Versagung* is enacted here in a reversed way: it is not that the subject renounces everything for a higher Cause and then notices he has thereby lost the Cause itself; it is rather that the subject *simply loses everything*, his egoist interests as well as his higher ideals, and his wager is then that this total loss itself will be converted into some kind of ethical dignity.

But something is missing at the end of *Disgrace*, something that would correspond to the repulsive tic on the face of the dying Sygne, as a mute gesture of protest, of the refusal to reconcile, or to Julie's "Happiness is boring" at the end of *La Nouvelle Héloïse*. One can imagine the boy in *Der Jasager* or in *Massnahme*, when he accepts his death, doing the same—emitting a barely perceptible repetitive gesture of resistance, an *eppur si muove* that persists, a pure figure of the undead drive. Here the *objet a* is generated through the process of the negation of negation as its excess or product. But is not the process of *Versagung* as the loss of a loss precisely the process of the loss of the *objet a*, the object-cause of desire? In *Vertigo*, Scottie first loses the object of his desire (Madeleine), and then, when he learns that Madeleine was a fake from the very beginning, loses his desire itself. Is there a way out of this abyss to a new *objet a*? Can we say that what is lost in *Versagung* is the fantasmatic status of the *objet a* (the fantasy-frame which sustained the subject's desire), so that the *Versagung*, which equals the act of traversing the fantasy, opens up the space for the emergence of the pure drive beyond fantasy?

INTERLUDE 2

Cogito in the History of Madness

Levinas's early critique of Hegel and Heidegger in his *Totality and Infinity* is a model of the anti-philosophical procedure: for Levinas, the infinity of relating to the divine Other is the excess which breaks out of the circle of philosophical totality. It is crucial to note here that Derrida is *not* an antiphilosopher—on the contrary, Derrida at his best (say, in his detailed "deconstructive" readings of Levinas, Foucault, Bataille, etc.) convincingly demonstrates how, in their effort to break out of the closed circle of philosophy, to assert a point of reference outside the horizon of philosophy (infinity versus totality in Levinas, madness versus *cogito* in the early Foucault, sovereignty versus Hegelian domination in Bataille), they remain within the field they try to leave behind.[1] No wonder, then, that Foucault reacted so violently to Derrida's critical analysis of his *History of Madness*, accusing Derrida of remaining within the confines of philosophy: yes, Derrida does, but therein lies his strength with regard to those who pretend all too easily to have reached a domain beyond philosophy. What Derrida does is not only "deconstruct" philosophy, demonstrating its dependence on an external Other; even more so, he "deconstructs" the attempt to locate a sphere outside philosophy, demonstrating how all anti-philosophical efforts to determine this Other remain indebted to a frame of philosophical categories.

Cogito, madness, and *religion* are interlinked in Descartes (see his thought experiment with the *malin génie*) as well as in Kant (his notion of the transcendental subject emerged from the critique of Swedenborg, whose religious dreams stand for madness). Simultaneously, the *cogito* emerges through a differentiation from (or a reference to) madness, *and* the *cogito* itself (the idea of the *cogito* as the point of absolute certainty, "subjective idealism") is perceived (not only) by common sense as the very epitome of the madness of philosophy, of its crazy paranoid system-building (cf. the "philosopher as madman" motif in the late Wittgenstein). Simultaneously, religion (direct faith) is evoked as a form of madness (Swedenborg for Kant, or religion generally for Enlightenment

1 For example, Levinas's—and, later, Marion's—talk about God "beyond Being" simply reduces being to the domain of positive reality, including its transcendental-ontological horizon, failing to raise the phenomenological question of how the divine dimension "beyond being" nonetheless appears within a certain horizon of the disclosure of being.

rationalists, up to Dawkins today), *and* religion (God) enters as the solution to (solipsistic) madness (Descartes).

This triangle of *cogito*, religion, and madness is the focus of the polemic between Foucault and Derrida, in which they both share the key underlying premise: that the *cogito* is inherently related to madness. The difference is that, for Foucault, the *cogito* is grounded in the exclusion of madness, while, for Derrida, the *cogito* itself can only emerge through a "mad" hyperbole (universalized doubt), and remains marked by this excess: before it stabilizes itself as *res cogitans*, the self-transparent thinking substance, the *cogito* explodes as a crazy punctual excess.[2]

Foucault's starting point is a fundamental change in the status of madness which took place in the passage from the Renaissance to the classical Age of Reason (the beginning of the seventeenth century). During the Renaissance (Cervantes, Shakespeare, Erasmus, etc.), madness was a specific phenomenon of the human spirit which belonged to the series of prophets, possessed visionaries, saints, clowns, those obsessed by demons, and so on. It was a meaningful phenomenon with a truth of its own: even if madmen were vilified, they were treated with awe, as if messengers of a sacred horror. With Descartes, however, madness is excluded; in all its varieties, it comes to occupy a position that was formerly the preserve of leprosy. It is no longer a phenomenon to be interpreted, its meaning searched for, but a simple illness to be treated under the well-regulated laws of a medicine or a science that is already sure of itself, sure that it cannot be mad. This change concerns not only theory, but social practice itself: from the Classical Age on, madmen were interned, imprisoned in psychiatric hospitals, deprived of the full dignity of a human being, studied and controlled like a natural phenomenon.

In his *Histoire de la folie*, Foucault dedicated three or four pages to the passage in the *Meditations* in which Descartes arrives at *cogito ergo sum*. Searching for the absolutely certain foundation of knowledge, Descartes analyses the main forms of delusion: delusions of the senses and sense perception, the illusions of madness, dreams. He ends with the most radical delusion imaginable, the hypothesis that everything that we experience is not true, but a universal dream, an illusion staged by an evil genius (*malin génie*). From here, he arrives at the certainty of the *cogito* (I think): even if I can doubt everything, even if all I see is an illusion, I cannot doubt that I think all this, so the *cogito* is the absolutely certain starting point for philosophy. Foucault's objection here is that Descartes does not really confront madness, but rather avoids thinking it: he *excludes* madness from the domain of reason. In the Classical Age, Reason is thus based on the exclusion of madness: the very existence of the category "madness" is

2 A solid, balanced account of this polemic is given in Roy Boyne, *Foucault and Derrida: The Other Side of Reason*, London: Unwin Hyman 1990.

historically determined, along with its opposite "reason"; that is, it is determined through power relations. Madness in the modern sense is not directly a phenomenon we can observe, but a discursive construct which emerges at a certain historical moment, together with its double, Reason in the modern sense.

In his reading of *Histoire de la folie*, Derrida focused on these four pages on Descartes which, for him, provided the key to the entire book. Through a detailed analysis, he tries to demonstrate that, far from excluding madness, Descartes pushes it to an extreme: universal doubt, where I suspect that the entire world is an illusion, is the greatest madness imaginable. Out of this universal doubt the *cogito* emerges: even if everything is an illusion, I can still be sure that I think. Madness is thus not excluded by the *cogito*: it is not that the *cogito* is not mad, but the *cogito is true even if I am totally mad*. Extreme doubt, the hypothesis of universal madness, is not external to philosophy, but strictly internal to it, a hyperbolic moment, the moment of madness, which grounds philosophy. Of course, Descartes later "domesticates" this radical excess with his image of man as a thinking substance, dominated by reason; he constructs a philosophy which is clearly historically conditioned. But the excess, the hyperbole of universal madness, is not itself historical; it is the excessive moment which grounds philosophy in all its historical forms. Madness is thus not excluded by philosophy: it is internal to it. Of course, every philosophy tries to control this excess, to repress it—but in repressing it, it represses its own innermost foundation: "Philosophy is perhaps the reassurance given against the anguish of being mad at the point of greatest proximity to madness."[3]

In his reply, Foucault first tries to prove, through a detailed reading of Descartes, that the madness he evokes does not have the same status as sensory illusions and dreams. When I suffer sensory illusions of perception or when I dream, I *remain normal and rational*, I only deceive myself with regard to what I see. In madness, on the contrary, I myself am no longer normal, I lose my reason. So madness has to be excluded if I am to be a rational subject. Derrida's refusal to exclude madness from philosophy bears witness to the fact that he remains a philosopher who is unable to think the Outside of philosophy, who is unable to think how philosophy itself is determined by something that escapes it. Apropos the hypothesis of universal doubt and the Evil Genius, we are not dealing with true madness, but with the rational subject who feigns to be mad, who makes a rational experiment, never losing his control over it.

Finally, on the very last page of his reply, Foucault tries to identify the true difference between himself and Derrida. He attacks (without naming it) the practice of deconstruction and textual analysis, for which "there is nothing outside the text," so that we are caught in an endless process of interpretation.

3 Jacques Derrida, "Cogito and the History of Madness," in *Writing and Difference*, trans. Alan Bass, Chicago: University of Chicago Press 1978, p. 59.

Foucault, on the contrary, does not practice textual analysis, but analyses discourses, "*dispositifs*," formations in which texts and statements are interlinked with extra-textual mechanisms of power and control. What we need is not deeper textual analyses, but analyses of the way discursive practices are combined with practices of power and domination. But does this rejection of Derrida hold? Let us go through the debate once again, this time taking Derrida as the starting point. As Derrida made clear in his essay on Foucault's *Histoire de la folie*, madness is inscribed in the history of *cogito* at two levels. First, throughout the entire philosophy of subjectivity from Descartes through Kant, Schelling, and Hegel, up to Nietzsche and Husserl, the *cogito* is related to its shadowy double, the *pharmakon*, which is madness. Second, madness is inscribed into the very (pre)history of the *cogito* itself, as part of its transcendental genesis:

> the Cogito escapes madness only because at its own moment, under its own authority, it is valid even if I am mad, even if my thoughts are completely mad … Descartes never interns madness, neither at the stage of natural doubt nor at the stage of metaphysical doubt … Whether I am mad or not, *Cogito, sum* … even if the totality of the world does not exist, even if nonmeaning has invaded the totality of the world, up to and including the very contents of my thought, I still think, I am while I think.[4]

Derrida leaves us in no doubt that, "as soon as Descartes has reached this extremity, he seeks to reassure himself, to certify the Cogito through God, to identify the act of the Cogito with a reasonable reason."[5] This withdrawal sets in "from the moment when he pulls himself out of madness by determining natural light through a series of principles and axioms."[6] The term "light" is here crucial in measuring Descartes's distance from German Idealism, in which, precisely, the core of the subject is no longer light, but the abyss of darkness, the "Night of the World." This, then, is Derrida's fundamental interpretive gesture: one of

> separating, within the Cogito, *on the one hand*, hyperbole (which I maintain cannot be enclosed in a factual and determined historical structure, for it is the project of exceeding every finite and determined totality), and, *on the other hand*, that in Descartes's philosophy (or in the philosophy supporting the Augustinian Cogito or the Husserlian Cogito as well) which belongs to a factual historical structure.[7]

Here, when Derrida asserts that "the historicity proper to philosophy is located and constituted in the transition, the dialogue between hyperbole and the finite

---

4 Ibid., pp. 55–6.
5 Ibid., p. 58.
6 Ibid., p. 59.
7 Ibid., p. 60.

structure, … in the difference between history and historicity," he perhaps falls too short.[8] This tension may appear very "Lacanian": is it not a version of the tension between the Real—the hyperbolic excess—and its (ultimately always failed) symbolization? The matrix we thus arrive at is that of an eternal oscillation between the two extremes, the radical expenditure, hyperbole, excess, and its later domestication (as in Kristeva, the oscillation between Semiotic and Symbolic). Both extremes are illusionary: pure excess as well as pure finite order would disintegrate, cancel themselves out. Such an approach misses the true point of "madness," which is not the pure excess of the "night of the world," but the madness of the passage to the symbolic itself, of imposing a symbolic order onto the chaos of the Real.[9] If madness is constitutive, then *every* system of meaning is minimally paranoid, "mad." Recall again Brecht's slogan "What is the robbing of a bank compared to the founding of a new bank?"—therein resides the lesson of David Lynch's *Straight Story*: what is the ridiculously pathetic perversity of figures like Bobby Peru in *Wild at Heart* or Frank in *Blue Velvet* compared to deciding to cross the US central plane on a lawnmower to visit a dying relative? Measured against this act, Frank's and Bobby's outbreaks of rage are but the impotent theatrics of old and sedate conservatives. In the same way, we should say: what is the mere madness caused by the loss of reason compared to the madness of reason itself?

This step is the properly "Hegelian" one—which is why Hegel, the philosopher who made the most radical attempt to think the abyss of madness at the core of subjectivity, is also the philosopher who brought to its "mad" climax the philosophical System as the totality of meaning. This is why, for very good reasons, from the common-sense perspective "Hegel" stands for the moment at which philosophy goes "mad," explodes in a "crazy" pretense to "Absolute Knowledge."

It is thus not enough simply to oppose "madness" and symbolization: there is, in the history of philosophy itself (of philosophical "systems"), a privileged point at which the hyperbole, philosophy's ex-timate core, directly inscribes itself into it, and this is the moment of the *cogito*, of transcendental philosophy. "Madness" is here "tamed" in a different way, through a "transcendental" horizon which does not cancel it in an all-encompassing world-view, but maintains it.

"In the serene world of mental illness, modern man no longer communicates with the madman: … the man of reason delegates the physician to madness, thereby authorizing a relation only through the abstract universality of

8 Ibid.

9 Recall Freud, who, in his analysis of the paranoid Judge Schreber, points out how the paranoid "system" is not madness, but a desperate attempt to *escape* madness—the disintegration of the symbolic universe—through an ersatz universe of meaning.

disease."[10] However, what about psychoanalysis? Is not psychoanalysis precisely the point at which the "man of reason" re-establishes his dialogue with madness, rediscovering the dimension of truth in it—not the same truth as before, in the premodern universe, but a different, properly scientific, one? Foucault himself dealt with this in his later *History of Sexuality*, where psychoanalysis is conceived as the culmination of "sex-as-the-ultimate-truth" logic of confession.

In spite of the *finesse* of Foucault's reply, he ultimately falls into the trap of an historicism which cannot account for its own position of enunciation; this impossibility is redoubled in Foucault's characterization of his "object," madness, which oscillates between two extremes. On the one hand, his strategic aim is to make madness itself talk, as it is in itself, outside of the (scientific, etc.) discourse on it: "it is definitely not a question of a history of ideas, but of the rudimentary movements of an experience. A history not of psychiatry, but of madness itself, in its vivacity, before knowledge has even begun to close in on it."[11] On the other hand, the (later) model deployed in his *Discipline and Punish* and *History of Sexuality* compels him to posit the absolute immanence of the (excessive, transgressive, resisting ...) object to its manipulation by the *dispositif* of power-knowledge: in the same way that "the carceral network does not cast the inassimilable into a confused hell; there is no outside";[12] in the same way that the "liberated" man is himself generated by the *dispositif* that controls and regulates him; in the same way that "sex" as the inassimilable excess is itself generated by the discourses and practices that try to control and regulate it; madness is also generated by the very discourse that excludes, objectivizes, and studies it, there is no "pure" madness outside it. As Boyne puts it, Foucault here "effectively acknowledg[es] the correctness of Derrida's formulation,"[13] that is, of *il n'y a pas de hors-texte*,[14] providing his own version of it. When Foucault writes that "Perhaps one day [transgression] will seem as decisive for our culture, as much a part of its soil, as the experience of contradiction was at an earlier time for dialectical thought,"[15] does he not thereby miss the point, which is that this day has already arrived, that permanent transgression already *is* a key feature of late

10 Michel Foucault, *Madness and Civilization*, trans. Richard Howard, London: Tavistock 1967, p. x.

11 Michel Foucault, *Folie et déraison: Histoire de la folie à l'âge classique*, Paris: Plon 1961, p. vii; as translated in Boyne, *Foucault and Derrida*, pp. 55–6.

12 Michel Foucault, *Discipline and Punish*, trans. Alan Sheridan, Harmondsworth: Penguin Books 1977, p. 301.

13 Boyne, *Foucault and Derrida*, p. 118.

14 "Reading ... cannot legitimately transgress the text toward something other than it ... *There is nothing outside the text*." (Jacques Derrida, *Of Grammatology*, Baltimore: Johns Hopkins University Press 1976, p. 158.)

15 Michel Foucault, *Language, Counter-Memory, Practice*, trans. Donald F. Bouchard and Sherry Simon, Oxford: Blackwell 1977, p. 33.

capitalism? And this is why his concluding objection to Derrida's *il n'y a pas de hors-texte* seems to miss the mark, when he characterizes it in terms of a

> reduction of discursive practices to textual traces; elision of the events which are produced in these practices, so that all that remains of them are marks for a reading; inventions of voices behind the texts, so that we do not have to analyze the modes of the implication of the subject in the discourses; the assignation of the originary as [what is] said and not-said in the text, so that we do not have to locate discursive practices in the field of transformations in which they effectuate themselves.[16]

No wonder that some Marxists took Foucault's side here, conceiving his polemic with Derrida as the latest chapter in the eternal struggle between materialism and idealism: Foucault's materialist analysis of discursive practices versus Derrida's endless self-reflexive textual games. A further point in favor of Foucault seems to be that he remains a radical historicist, reproaching Derrida for his inability to think the exteriority of philosophy. This is how he sums up the stakes of their debate:

> could there be something prior or external to the philosophical discourse? Can the condition of this discourse be an exclusion, a refusal, an avoided risk, and, why not, a fear? A suspicion rejected passionately by Derrida. *Pudenda origo*, said Nietzsche with regard to religious people and their religion.[17]

However, Derrida is much closer to thinking this externality than Foucault, for whom exteriority involves a simple historicist reduction which cannot account for itself (when Foucault was asked from what position he was speaking, he employed the cheap rhetorical trick of claiming that this was a "police" question, "who are you to say that"—but he combined this reply with the opposite claim that genealogical history is an "ontology of the present"). It is easy to submit philosophy to such a historicist reduction (philosophers can easily dismiss such external reduction as relying on a confusion between genesis and value); it is much more difficult to think its *inherent* excess, its ex-timate core. These, then, are the true stakes of the debate: ex-timacy or direct externality?

This dark core of madness at the heart of the *cogito* can also be determined in a more genetic way. Daniel Dennett draws a convincing and insightful parallel between an animal's physical environment and the human environment, including not only human artifacts (clothes, houses, tools) but also the "virtual" environment of the discursive web: "Stripped of [the 'web of discourses'], an

16 Michel Foucault, "Mon corps, ce papier, ce feu," in *Histoire de la folie à l'âge classique*, Paris: Gallimard 1972, p. 602.

17 Ibid., p. 584.

individual human being is as incomplete as a bird without feathers, a turtle without its shell."[18] A naked man is the same nonsense as a shaved ape: without language (and tools and ...), man is a crippled animal—it is this lack which is supplemented by symbolic institutions and tools, so that the point made obvious today in popular culture figures like Robocop (man as simultaneously super-animal and crippled) holds from the very beginning. How do we pass from the "natural" to the "symbolic" environment? This passage is not direct, one cannot account for it within a continuous evolutionary narrative: something has to intervene between the two, a kind of "vanishing mediator," which is neither Nature nor Culture—this in-between is not the spark of *logos* magically conferred on *homo sapiens*, enabling him to form his supplementary virtual symbolic environment, but precisely something which, although it is also no longer nature, is not yet *logos*, and has to be "repressed" by *logos*—the Freudian name for this in-between is, of course, the death drive.

Perhaps, even more than Descartes, the philosopher who stands for one extreme of "madness" is Nicolas Malebranche, with his "occasionalism." Malebranche, a disciple of Descartes, drops the latter's ridiculous reference to the pineal gland as the point of contact between material and spiritual substance, body and soul; but how, then, are we to explain their coordination, if there is no contact between the two, no point at which a soul can act causally on a body or vice versa? Since the two causal networks (that of ideas in my mind and that of bodily interconnections) are totally independent, the only solution is that a third, true Substance (God) continuously coordinates and mediates between the two, thereby maintaining the semblance of continuity: when I think about raising my hand and my hand then rises, my thought causes the raising of my hand not directly but only "occasionally"—upon noticing my thought directed at raising my hand, God sets in motion the other, material, causal chain which leads to my hand actually being raised.

If we replace "God" with the big Other, the symbolic order, we can see the proximity of occasionalism to Lacan's position: as Lacan put it in his polemic against Aristotle in "Television," the relationship between soul and body is never direct, since the big Other always interposes itself between the two.[19] Occasionalism is thus essentially a name for the "arbitrariness of the signifier," for the gap that separates the network of ideas from the network of bodily (real) causality, for the fact that it is the big Other which accounts for the coordination of the two networks, so that, when my body bites into an apple, my soul experiences a pleasurable sensation. This same gap was targeted by the ancient Aztec priests who organized human sacrifices to ensure that the sun would rise again: the human sacrifice was an appeal to God to sustain the coordination between

18 Daniel C. Dennett, *Consciousness Explained*, New York: Little, Brown 1991, p. 416.
19 See Jacques Lacan, "Television," *October* 40 (Spring 1987).

the two series, bodily necessity and the concatenation of symbolic events. "Irrational" as the Aztec priest's sacrifice may appear, its underlying premise is far more insightful than our commonplace intuition according to which the coordination between body and soul is direct, i.e., that it is "natural" for me to have a pleasurable sensation when I bite into an apple since this sensation is caused directly by the apple: what gets lost is the intermediary role of the big Other in guaranteeing the coordination between reality and our mental experience of it. And is it not the same with our immersion in Virtual Reality? When I raise my hand in order to push an object in virtual space, this object effectively moves—my illusion, of course, is that it was the movement of my hand which directly caused the relocation of the object, for in my immersion, I overlook the intricate mechanisms of computerized coordination, homologous to the role of God guaranteeing the coordination between the two series in occasionalism.[20]

It is a well-known fact that the "close the door" button in most elevators is a totally non-functioning placebo, placed there just to give us the impression that we can somehow speed things up—when we push the close button, the door closes in exactly the same amount of time as it would had we only pressed the floor button. This extreme and clear case of fake participation is an appropriate metaphor for the participation of individuals in our "postmodern" political process. And it represents occasionalism at its purest: from Malebranche's perspective, we are effectively pressing such buttons all the time, and it is God's incessant activity that coordinates between our action and the event that follows, while we think the event results from our action.

For this reason, it is crucial to keep open the radical ambiguity involved in how cyberspace will affect our lives: it does not depend on technology as such but on the mode of its social inscription. Immersion in cyberspace can intensify our bodily experience (a new sensuality, a new body with more organs, new sexes ...), but it also opens up the possibility for someone manipulating the cyberspace machinery to literally *steal* our own (virtual) body, depriving us of control over it, so that one no longer relates to one's body as to "one's own." What we encounter here is the constitutive ambiguity of the notion of mediatization.[21] Originally this referred to the gesture by means of which a subject was stripped of its direct, immediate right to make decisions; the great master of political mediatization was Napoleon, who left to the monarchs he conquered the appearance of power, while they were effectively no longer in a position to exercise it. At a more general level, one could say that just such a "mediatization" of the monarch defines constitutional monarchy: in it, the monarch is

20 The main work of Nicolas Malebranche is *De la recherches de la vérité*, Paris: Vrin 1975 (originally published 1674–5).

21 As to this ambiguity, see Paul Virilio, *The Art of the Motor*, Minneapolis: University of Minnesota Press 1995.

reduced to the point of a purely formal symbolic gesture of "dotting the i's," of signing and thereby conferring performative force on the edicts whose content has been determined by the elected governing body. And, *mutatis mutandis*, does not the same hold also for the progressive digitalization of our everyday lives, in the course of which the subject is also more and more "mediatized," imperceptibly stripped of his power, all the while under the false impression that it is being increased? When our body is mediatized (caught in the network of electronic media), it is simultaneously exposed to the threat of a radical "proletarianization": the subject is potentially reduced to the pure $, since even my own personal experience can be stolen, manipulated, regulated by the mechanical Other.

One can see, again, how the prospect of radical virtualization bestows on the computer a position strictly homologous to that of God in Malebranchean occasionalism: since the computer coordinates the relationship between my mind and (what I experience as) the movement of my limbs (in virtual reality), one can easily imagine a computer which runs amok and starts to act like an Evil God, disturbing that coordination—when the mental signal to raise my hand is suspended or even counteracted in (the virtual) reality, the most fundamental experience of the body as "mine" is undermined. It thus seems that cyberspace effectively realizes the paranoid fantasy elaborated by Schreber, the German judge whose memoirs were analyzed by Freud: the "wired universe" is psychotic insofar as it seems to materialize Schreber's hallucination of the divine rays through which God directly controls the human mind. In other words, does not the externalization of the big Other in the computer account for the inherent paranoiac dimension of the wired universe? Or, to put it another way: the commonplace is that the ability to upload consciousness into a computer finally frees people from their bodies—*but it also frees the machines from "their" people* ... Which brings us to the Wachowski brothers' *Matrix* trilogy: much more than Berkeley's God who sustains the world in his mind, the *ultimate* Matrix is Malebranche's occasionalist God.

What, then, is the Matrix? Simply the Lacanian "big Other," the virtual symbolic order, the network that structures reality for us. This dimension of the "big Other" is that of the constitutive *alienation* of the subject in the symbolic order: the big Other pulls the strings, the subject does not speak, he "is spoken" by the symbolic structure. In short, this "big Other" is the name for the social Substance, for the agency thanks to which the subject never fully dominates the effects of his acts, thanks to which the final outcome of his activity is always something other than what he aimed at or anticipated. However, it is crucial to note that, in the key chapters of his *Four Fundamental Concepts of Psycho-Analysis*, Lacan struggles to delineate the operation that follows alienation and is in a sense its counterpoint, that of *separation*: alienation *in* the big Other is followed by the separation *from* the big Other. Separation takes place when the subject takes note of how the big Other is in itself inconsistent, purely virtual, "barred," deprived of the Thing—and fantasy is an attempt to fill out this lack *of the Other, not of the subject*, that is, to (re)constitute the consistency of the big Other.

Following the same paranoid twist, the thesis of *The Matrix* is that this big Other is externalized in the really existing Mega-Computer. There is—there *has* to be—a Matrix because "things are not right, opportunities have been missed, something goes wrong all the time," in other words, the film's idea is that it is so because the Matrix obfuscates the "true" reality behind it all. The problem with the film is that it is *not* "crazy" enough, because it supposes another "real" reality behind our everyday reality sustained by the Matrix. One is tempted to claim, in Kantian fashion, that the mistake of conspiracy theory is homologous to the "paralogism of pure reason," to the confusion between the two levels: suspicion (of received scientific, social, etc., opinion) as the formal methodological stance, and the positivization of this suspicion in another global all-explanatory para-theory.

The excess of madness at the heart of the *cogito* is thus closely linked to the topic of freedom. The "antagonism" of the Kantian notion of freedom (as the most concise expression of the antagonism of freedom in bourgeois life itself) does not lie where Adorno locates it (the self-imposed law means that freedom coincides with self-enslavement and self-domination, that Kantian "spontaneity" is in actuality its opposite, utter self-control, the thwarting of all spontaneous impetuses), but is, as Robert Pippin put it, "*much more on the surface*."[22] For Kant as for Rousseau, the greatest moral good is to lead a fully autonomous life as a free rational agent, and the worst evil is subjection to the will of another; however, Kant has to concede that man does not emerge as a free mature rational agent spontaneously, through his natural development, but only through an arduous process of maturation sustained by harsh discipline and education which cannot but be experienced by the subject as an external coercion:

> Social institutions both to nourish and to develop such independence are necessary and are consistent with, do not thwart, its realization, but with freedom understood as an individual's causal agency this will always look like an external necessity that we have good reasons to try to avoid. This creates the problem of a form of dependence that can be considered constitutive of independence and that cannot be understood as a mere compromise with the particular will of another or as a separate, marginal topic of Kant's dotage. *This* is, in effect, the antinomy contained within the bourgeois notions of individuality, individual responsibility …[23]

22 Robert Pippin, *The Persistence of Subjectivity*, Cambridge: Cambridge University Press 2005, p. 118.

23 Ibid., pp. 118–19.

Here one can indeed imagine Kant as an unexpected precursor of Foucault's thesis, in his *Discipline and Punish*, on the formation of the free individual through a complex set of disciplinary micro-practices—and, as Pippin does not hesitate to point out, this antinomy explodes even more intensely in Kant's socio-historical reflections, focused on the notion of "unsocial sociability": what is Kant's notion of the historical relation between democracy and monarchy if not this same thesis (of the link between freedom and submission to a higher authority) applied to the historical process itself? In the long term (or in its notion), democracy is the only appropriate form of government; however, because of the immaturity of the people, the conditions for a functioning democracy can only be established through a non-democratic monarchy which, in the exertion of its benevolent power, brings the people to political maturity. And, as to be expected, Kant does not fail to mention the Mandevillean rationality of the market in which each individual's pursuit of his or her egotistic interests is what works best (much better than direct altruism) for the common good. At its most extreme, this leads Kant to the notion that human history itself is governed by an inscrutable divine plan, within which we mortals are destined to play a role unbeknownst to us—here, the paradox grows even stronger: our freedom is  linked to its opposite not only "from below" but also "from above"; that is, not only can it arise only through our submission and dependence, but our freedom as such is a moment in a larger divine plan—our freedom is not truly an aim-in-itself, but serves a higher purpose.

We can clarify—if not to resolve—this dilemma by introducing some further distinctions into the notion of "noumenal" freedom itself. Upon a closer look, it becomes evident that, for Kant, discipline and education do not directly work  on our animal nature, forging it into human individuality: as Kant points out, animals cannot be properly educated, since their behavior is already predestined by their instincts. What this means is that, paradoxically, in order to be educated into freedom (qua moral autonomy and self-responsibility), *I already have to be free* in a sense much more radical, "noumenal," monstrous even. The Freudian name for this monstrous freedom is, again, the death drive. It is interesting to note how philosophical narratives of the "birth of man" are always compelled to presuppose a moment in human (pre)history when (what will become) man  is no longer a mere animal but also not yet a "being of language," bound by symbolic Law; a moment of thoroughly "perverted," "denaturalized," "derailed" nature which is not yet culture. In his anthropological writings, Kant emphasized that the human animal needs disciplinary pressure in order to tame that uncanny "unruliness" which seems to be inherent to human nature—a wild,  unconstrained propensity to insist stubbornly on one's own will, whatever the cost. It is on account of this that the human animal needs a Master to discipline him: discipline targets this "unruliness," not the animal nature in man. In Hegel's

Lectures on Philosophy of History, a similar role is played by the reference to "negroes": significantly, Hegel deals with "negroes" before history proper (which starts with ancient China), in the section entitled "The Natural Context or the Geographical Basis of World History": "negroes" here stand for the human spirit in its "state of nature," they are described as a kind of perverted, monstrous children, simultaneously naïve and corrupted, living in a pre-lapsarian state of innocence, and, precisely as such, the cruelest of barbarians; part of nature and yet thoroughly denaturalized; ruthlessly manipulating nature through primitive sorcery, yet simultaneously terrified by raging natural forces; mindlessly brave cowards.[24]

This in-between is the "repressed" of the narrative form (in this case, of Hegel's "grand narrative" of the world-historical succession of spiritual forms): not nature as such, but the very break with nature which is (later) supplemented by the virtual universe of narratives. According to Schelling, prior to its assertion as the medium of the rational Word, the subject is the "infinite lack of being" (*unendliche Mangel an Sein*), the violent gesture of contraction that negates every being outside itself. This insight also forms the core of Hegel's notion of madness: when Hegel determines madness to be a withdrawal from the actual world, the closing of the soul onto itself, its "contraction," he all too quickly conceives of this withdrawal as a "regression" to the level of the "animal soul" still embedded in its natural environment and determined by the rhythm of nature (night and day, etc.). But does not this withdrawal, on the contrary, amount to a severing of links with the *Umwelt*, the end of the subject's immersion in its immediate natural environment, and is it not, as such, the founding gesture of "humanization"? Was not this withdrawal-into-the-self accomplished by Descartes with his universal doubt and reduction to the *cogito*, which, as Derrida pointed out, also involves a passage through the moment of radical madness?

This brings us to the necessity of the Fall: given the Kantian link between dependence and autonomy the Fall is unavoidable, a necessary step in the moral progress of man. That is to say, in precise Kantian terms: the "Fall" is the very renunciation of my radical ethical autonomy; it occurs when I take refuge in a heteronomous Law, in a Law experienced as imposed on me from the outside. The finitude in which I search for support to avoid the dizziness of freedom is the finitude of the external-heteronomous Law itself. Therein resides the *difficulty of being a Kantian.* Every parent knows that the child's provocations, wild and "transgressive" as they may appear, ultimately conceal and express a demand for the figure of authority to set firm limits, to draw a line which means "This far and no further!" thus enabling the child to clearly map what is possible and what is not possible. (And does the same not go also for hysteric's provocations?)

24 See G. W. F. Hegel, *Lectures on the Philosophy of World History—Introduction: Reason in History*, trans. H. B. Nisbet, Cambridge: Cambridge University Press 1975, pp. 176–90.

This, precisely, is what the analyst refuses to do, and this is what makes him so traumatic for the analysand—paradoxically, it is the setting of a firm limit which is liberating, and it is the very absence of a firm limit which is experienced as suffocating.

This is why the Kantian autonomy of the subject is so difficult—its implication is precisely that there is no one else, no external agent of "natural authority," who can do the job for me, that I myself have to set the limit to my natural "unruliness." Although Kant famously wrote that man is an animal which needs a master, this should not deceive us: what Kant was aiming at was not the philosophical commonplace according to which, in contrast to animals whose behavioral patterns are grounded in their inherited instincts, man lacks such firm coordinates which, therefore, have to be imposed on him from outside, through a cultural authority; rather, Kant's true aim is to point out how *the very need for an external master is a deceptive lure*: man needs a master in order to conceal from himself the deadlock of his own difficult freedom and self-responsibility. In this precise sense, a truly enlightened "mature" human being is a subject who *no longer needs a master*, who can fully assume the heavy burden of defining his own limitations. This basic Kantian (and also Hegelian) lesson was put very clearly by Chesterton: "Every act of will is an act of self-limitation. To desire action is to desire limitation. In that sense every act is an act of self-sacrifice."[25]

The lesson here is thus in a precise sense an Hegelian one: the external opposition between freedom (transcendental spontaneity, moral autonomy, and self-responsibility) and slavery (submission, either to my own nature, its "pathological" instincts, or to an external power) *has to be transposed into freedom itself*, as the "highest" antagonism between monstrous freedom qua "unruliness" and the true moral freedom. However, a possible counter-argument here would be that this noumenal excess of freedom (Kantian "unruliness," the Hegelian "night of the world") is a retroactive result of the disciplinary mechanisms themselves (along the lines of the Paulinian motif of "Law creates transgression," or the Foucauldian topic of how the very disciplinary measures that try to regulate sexuality generate "sex" as the elusive excess)—the obstacle creates that which it endeavors to control.

Are we then dealing with the closed circle of a process positing its own presuppositions? Our wager is that the Hegelian dialectical circle of positing presuppositions, far from being closed, generates its own opening and thus the space for freedom. In order to see this, one has to begin with what appears to be the very opposite of freedom: blind mechanical habit. In the shift from Aristotle to Kant, to modernity with its subject as pure autonomy, the status of habit changes from organic inner rule to something mechanical, the opposite of

25 G. K. Chesterton, *Orthodoxy*, San Francisco: Ignatius Press 1995, p. 45.

human freedom: freedom can never become habit(ual); if it becomes a habit, it is no longer true freedom (which is why Thomas Jefferson wrote that if people are to remain free, they have to rebel against the government every couple of decades). This eventuality reaches its apogee in Christ, who is "the figure of a pure event, the exact opposite of the habitual."[26]

Hegel here provides the immanent corrective to Kantian modernity. As Catherine Malabou notes, Hegel's *Philosophy of Spirit* begins with a study of the same topic with which *Philosophy of Nature* ends: the soul and its functions. This redoubling offers a clue as to how Hegel conceptualizes the transition from nature to spirit: "not as a sublation, but as a *reduplication*, a process through which spirit constitutes itself in and as a *second nature*."[27] The name for this second nature is *habit*. So it is not that the human animal breaks with nature through the creative explosion of spirit, which then gets "habituated," alienated, turned into a mindless routine; the reduplication of nature in "second nature" is primordial, it is only this reduplication that opens up the space for spiritual creativity.

Perhaps this Hegelian notion of habit allows us to account for the figure of the zombie, slowly dragging itself around in a catatonic mode but persisting forever: are zombies not figures of pure habit, of habit at its most elementary, prior to the rise of intelligence (language, consciousness, and thinking)?[28] This is why a zombie par excellence is always someone we knew before, when he was still normally alive—the shock for a character in a zombie movie comes when they recognize the formerly friendly neighbor in the creeping figure relentlessly stalking them.[29] What Hegel says about habits thus has to be applied to zombies: at the most elementary level of human identity, *we are all zombies*; our "higher" and "free" human activities are dependent on the reliable functioning of our zombie-habits—in this sense, being-a-zombie is a zero-level of humanity, humanity's inhuman or mechanical core. The shock of meeting a zombie is thus not the shock of encountering a foreign entity, but the shock of being confronted by the disavowed foundation of our own humanity.[30]

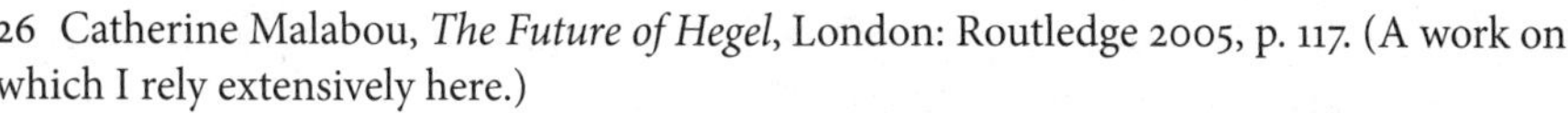

26 Catherine Malabou, *The Future of Hegel*, London: Routledge 2005, p. 117. (A work on which I rely extensively here.)

27 Ibid., p. 26.

28 I owe this observation to Caroline Schuster, Chicago.

29 Zombies, these properly un-canny (*un-heimlich*) figures, are therefore to be opposed to aliens who invade the body of a terrestrial: while aliens look and act like humans, but are really foreign to the human race, zombies are humans who no longer look and act like humans; while, in the case of an alien, we suddenly become aware that someone close to us—wife, son, father—has been colonized by an alien, in the case of a zombie, the shock is that this strange creep is someone close to us.

30 There is, of course, a big difference between sluggish, automated, zombie-like movements and the subtle plasticity of habits proper, of their refined know-how;

Hegel's conception of habit is unexpectedly close to the logic of what Derrida called *pharmakon*, the ambiguous supplement which is simultaneously a force of death and a force of life. Habit is, on the one hand, the dulling of life, its mechanization (Hegel characterizes it as a "mechanism of self-feeling"[31]): when something turns into a habit, it means that its vitality is lost, we just mechanically repeat it without being aware of it. Habit thus appears to be the very opposite of freedom: freedom means making creative choices, inventing something new, in short, precisely *breaking with (old) habits*. Think about language, whose "habitual" aspect is best exemplified by standard ritualized greetings: "Hello, how are you? Nice to see you!"—we do not really mean it, there is no living intention in it, it is just a "habit."

On the other hand, Hegel emphasizes again and again that there is no freedom without habit: habit provides the background and foundation for every exercise of freedom. Take language again: in order for us to exercise freedom in using language, we have to get fully accustomed to it, habituated (in)to it, we have to learn to practice it, to apply its rules "blindly," mechanically, as a habit: only when a subject externalizes what he learns in mechanized habits is he "open to be otherwise occupied and engaged."[32] Not only language, but a much more complex set of spiritual and bodily activities have to be turned into a habit in order for a human subject to be able to exert his "higher" functions of creative thinking and working—all the operations we perform all the time mindlessly, such as walking, eating, holding things, and so on and so forth, have to be learned and turned into mindless habits. Through habits, a human being transforms his body into a mobile and fluid means, the soul's instrument, which serves us without our having to focus consciously on it. In short, through habits, the subject appropriates his body. As Alain points out in his commentary on Hegel:

> When freedom comes it is in the sphere of habit … Here the body is no longer a foreign being, reacting belligerently against me; rather it is pervaded by soul and has become soul's instrument and means; yet at the same time, in habit the corporeal self is understood as it truly is; body is rendered something mobile and fluid, able to express directly the inner movements of thought without needing to involve thereby the role of consciousness or reflection.[33]

---

however, habits proper arise only when the level of habit is supplemented by the level of consciousness proper and speech. What the "blind" zombie-like behavior provides is, as it were, the "material base" for the refined plasticity of habits proper: the stuff from which these habits proper are made.

31 G. W. F. Hegel, *Philosophy of Mind*, trans. William Wallace, "Additions" trans. A. V. Miller, Oxford: Clarendon Press 1971, §410 Remark.

32 Ibid., §410.

33 Alain, *Idées: Introduction à la philosophie*, Paris: Flammarion 1983, p. 200; as translated in Malabou, *The Future of Hegel*, p. 36.

More radically even, for Hegel, living itself (leading a life) is for us something we must learn as a habit, starting with birth itself. Recall how, seconds after birth, the baby has to be shaken and thereby reminded to breathe—otherwise, forgetting to breathe, it will die. Indeed, as Hegel reminds us, a human being can also die of habit: "Human beings even die as result of habit—that is, if they have become totally habituated to life, and spiritually and physically blunted."[34] Nothing thus comes "naturally" to human being, including walking and seeing:

> The form of habit applies to spirit in all its degrees and varieties. Of all these modifications, the most external is the determination of the individual in relation to space; this, which for man means *an upright posture*, is something which by his will he has made into a habit. Adopted *directly, without thinking*, his upright stance continues through the persistent involvement of his will. Man stands upright only because and insofar as he wants to stand, and only as long as he wills to do so without consciousness of it. Similarly, to take another case, the act of *seeing*, and others like it, are concrete habits which combine in a single act the multiple determinations of sensation, of consciousness, intuition, understanding, and so forth.[35]

Habit is thus "depersonalized" willing, a mechanized emotion: once I become habituated to standing, I will it without consciously willing it, since my will is embodied in the habit. In a habit, presence and absence, appropriation and withdrawal, engagement and disengagement, interest and disinterest, subjectivization and objectivization, consciousness and unconsciousness, are strangely interlinked. Habit is the unconsciousness necessary for the very functioning of consciousness:

> in *habit* our consciousness is at the same time *present* in the subject-matter, *interested* in it, yet conversely *absent* from it, *indifferent* to it; ... our Self just as much *appropriates* the subject-matter as, on the contrary, it draws away from it; ... the soul, on the one hand, completely pervades its bodily activities and, on the other hand, *deserts* them, thus giving them the shape of something *mechanical*, of a merely natural *effect*.[36]

And the same goes for my emotions: their display is not purely natural or spontaneous; we learn to cry or laugh at appropriate moments (recall how, for the Japanese, laughter functions in a different way than for us in the West: a smile can also be a sign of embarrassment and shame). The external mechanization

34 G. W. F. Hegel, *Elements of the Philosophy of Right*, trans. H. B. Nisbet, Cambridge: Cambridge University Press 1991, p. 195 (§151).

35 Hegel, *Philosophy of Mind*, §410 Addition.

36 Ibid.

of emotions—from the ancient Tibetan prayer wheel which prays for me to "canned laughter" where the TV set laughs for me, turning my emotional display quite literally into a mechanical display—is thus based in the fact that emotional displays, including the most "sincere," are already in themselves "mechanized."

However, the highest level (and, already, the self-sublation) of habit is *language* as the medium of thought—in it, the couple of possession and withdrawal is taken to the limit. The point is not only that, in order to speak a language "fluently," we have to master its rules mechanically, without thinking about it; much more radically, the co-dependence of insight and blindness determines the very act of understanding: when I hear a word, I not only immediately abstract from its sound and "see through it" to its meaning (recall the weird experience of becoming aware of the non-transparent vocal materiality of a word—it appears as intrusive and obscene ...), but I have to do so if I am to experience meaning at all.

If, for Hegel, man is fundamentally a being of habit, if habits actualize themselves when adopted as automatic reactions which occur without the subject's conscious participation, and, finally, if we locate the core of subjectivity in its ability to perform intentional acts, to realize conscious goals, then, paradoxically, the human subject is at its most fundamental a "disappearing subject."[37] The habit's "unreflective spontaneity"[38] accounts for the well-known paradox of *subjectively choosing an objective necessity*, of *willing what unavoidably will occur*: through its elevation into a habit, a reaction which was first something imposed on me from outside is internalized, transformed into something that I perform automatically and spontaneously, "from inside":

> If an external change is repeated, it turns into a tendency internal to the subject. The change itself is transformed into a disposition, and receptivity, formerly passive, becomes activity. Thus habit is revealed as a process through which man ends by *willing* or choosing what came to him from outside. Henceforth the will of the individual does not need to oppose the pressure of the external world; the will learns gradually to want what is.[39]

What makes habit so central is the temporality it involves: having a habit involves a relationship to the future, prescribing how I will react to some future event. Habit is a feature of the organism's economizing of its forces, of building up a reserve for the future. That is to say, in its habits, subjectivity "embraces in itself

37 Malabou, *The Future of Hegel*, p. 75.

38 Ibid., p. 70.

39 Ibid., pp. 70–1.

its future ways of being, the ways it will become actual."[40] This means that habit also complicates the relationship between possibility and actuality: it is *stricto sensu* the *actuality of a possibility*. This means is that habit belongs to the level of virtuality (defined by Deleuze precisely as the actuality of the possible): habit is actual, a capacity to react in a certain way that I fully possess here and now, and simultaneously a possibility pointing towards my reacting a certain way in the future.

Interesting conceptual consequences follow from this notion of habit. Ontologically, with regard to the opposition between particular accidents and universal essence, habit can be described as the "becoming-essential of the accident":[41] once an externally caused accident has been repeated enough times, it is elevated into the universality of the subject's inner disposition, into a feature that belongs to and defines its inner essence. This is why we can never determine the precise beginning of a habit, the point at which external occurrences change into habit—once a habit has been formed, its origins are obliterated and it appears as if it was always already there. The conclusion is thus clear, almost Sartrean: man has no permanent substance or universal essence; he is to his very core a creature of habit, a being whose identity is formed through the elevation of contingent external accidents or encounters into an internal(ized) universal habit. Does this mean that only humans have habits? Here, Hegel is much more radical—he takes a decisive further step and leaves behind the old opposition of nature as fully determined in its closed circular movement versus man as a being of openness and existential freedom: "for Hegel, nature is always *second nature*."[42] Every natural organism has to regulate its exchange with its environment, the assimilation of the environment into itself, through habitual procedures which "reflect" into the organism, as its inner dispositions, its external interactions.

Because of the virtual status of habits, adopting a (new) habit is not simply a matter of changing an actual property of the subject; rather, it involves a kind of reflexivity, a change in the subject's disposition which determines his reaction to changes, a change in the kind of changes to which the subject is submitted: "Habit does not simply introduce mutability into something that would otherwise continue without changing; it suggests change within a disposition, within its potentiality, within the internal character of that in which the change occurs, which does not change."[43] This is what Hegel means by self-differentiation as the "sublation" of externally imposed changes into self-changes, of external into

40 Ibid., p. 76.

41 Ibid., p. 75.

42 Ibid., p. 57.

43 Félix Ravaisson, *De l'habitude*, Paris: Fayard 1984, p. 10; as translated in Malabou, *The Future of Hegel*, p. 58.

internal difference—only organic bodies differentiate themselves: an organic body maintains its unity by internalizing an externally imposed change into a habit to deal with future such changes.

If this is the case, however, if the whole of (organic, at least) nature is already second nature, in what does the difference between animal and human habits consist? Hegel's most provocative and unexpected contribution concerns this very question of the genesis of *human* habits: in his *Anthropology* (which opens the *Philosophy of Spirit*) we find a unique "genealogy of habits" reminiscent of Nietzsche. This part of the *Philosophy of Spirit* is one of the hidden, not yet fully exploited, treasures of the Hegelian system, where we find the clearest traces of what one can only call the dialectical-materialist aspect of Hegel: the passage from nature to (human) spirit is developed here not as a direct external intervention of Spirit, as the intervention of another dimension disturbing the balance of the natural circuit, but as the result of a long and tortuous "working through" by means of which intelligence (embodied in language) emerges from natural tensions and antagonisms. This passage is not direct, for Spirit (in the guise of speech-mediated human intelligence) does not directly confront and dominate biological processes—Spirit's "material base" forever remains pre-symbolic (pre-linguistic) habit.

So how does habit itself arise? In his genealogy, Hegel conceives habit as the third, concluding, moment of the dialectical process of the Soul, whose structure follows the triad of notion–judgment–syllogism. At the beginning, there is Soul in its immediate unity, in its simple notion, the "feeling soul": "In the sensations which arise from the individual's encounter with external objects, the soul begins to awaken itself."[44] The Self is here a mere "sentient Self," not yet a subject opposed to objects, but just experiencing a sensation in which the two sides, subject and object, are immediately united: when I experience a sensation of touch, it is simultaneously the trace of the external object I am touching and my inner reaction to it; sensation is a Janus-faced entity in which subjective and objective immediately coincide. Even in later stages of the individual's development, this "sentient Self" survives in the guise of what Hegel calls a "magical relationship," referring to phenomena that, in Hegel's times, were designated with terms like "magnetic somnambulism" (hypnosis), all the phenomena in which my Soul is directly—in a pre-reflexive, non-thinking way—linked to external processes and affected by them. Instead of bodies influencing each other at a distance (Newtonian gravity), we have spirits influencing each other at a distance. Here, the Soul remains at the lowest level of its functioning, directly immersed in its environment. (What Freud called "oceanic feeling," the source of religious experience, is thus for Hegel a feature of the lowest level of the Soul.) What the

44 Malabou, *The Future of Hegel*, p. 32.

Soul lacks here is a clear self-feeling, a feeling of itself as distinguished from external reality, which is what happens in the next moment, that of judgment (*Urteil*—Hegel here mobilizes the word-play of *Urteil* with *Ur-Teil*, "primordial divide/division"):

> The sensitive totality is, in its capacity as an individual, essentially the tendency to distinguish itself in itself, and to wake up to the *judgment in itself*, in virtue of which it has *particular* feelings and stands as a *subject* in respect of these aspects of itself. The subject as such gives these feelings a place as *its own* in itself.[45]

All problems arise from this paradoxical short-circuit of the feeling of Self becoming a specific feeling among others, and, simultaneously, the encompassing container of all feelings, the site where all dispersed feelings can be brought together. Malabou provides a wonderfully precise formulation of this paradox of the feeling of Self:

> Even if there is a possibility of bringing together feeling's manifold material, that possibility itself becomes part of the objective content. The form needs to be the content of all that it forms: subjectivity does not reside in its own being, it "haunts" itself. The soul is possessed by the possession of itself.[46]

This is the crucial feature: possibility itself has to actualize itself, to become a fact; or, the form needs to become part of its own content (or, to add a further variation on the same motif, the frame itself has to become part of the framed content). The subject is the frame/form/horizon of his world *and* part of the framed content (of the reality it observes), and the problem is that it cannot see or locate itself within its own frame: since all there is is already within the frame, the frame as such is invisible. The possibility of locating oneself within one's reality has to remain a possibility—however, and herein lies the crucial point, this possibility itself has to actualize itself *qua possibility*, to be active, to exert influence, *qua possibility*.

There is a link to Kant here, to the old enigma of what exactly Kant had in mind with his notion of "transcendental apperception," of self-consciousness accompanying every act of my consciousness (when I am conscious of something, I am thereby always also conscious of the fact that I am conscious of it). Is it not an obvious fact that this is empirically not true, that I am not always reflexively aware of my awareness itself? Interpreters of Kant try to resolve this problem by claiming that every conscious act of mine can potentially be rendered self-conscious: if I want to, I always can turn my attention to what I am

45 Hegel, *Philosophy of Mind*, §407.
46 Malabou, *The Future of Hegel*, p. 35.

doing. But this is not strong enough: transcendental apperception cannot be an act that never need actually happen, that just could have happened at any point. The solution to this dilemma lies precisely in the notion of virtuality in the strict Deleuzian sense, as the actuality of the possible, as a paradoxical entity the very possibility of which already produces or has actual effects. Is not this Virtual ultimately the symbolic as such? Take symbolic authority: in order to function as an effective authority, it has to remain not-fully-actualized, an eternal threat.

This, then, is the status of the Self: its self-awareness is, as it were, the actuality of its own possibility. Consequently, what "haunts" the subject is his inaccessible noumenal Self, the "Thing that thinks," an object in which the subject would fully "encounter himself."[47] Of course, for Kant, the same goes for every object of my experience which is always phenomenal, that is inaccessible in its noumenal dimension; however, with the Self, the impasse is accentuated: all other objects of experience are given to me phenomenally, but, in the case of the subject, I cannot even get a phenomenal experience of me—since I am dealing with "myself," in this unique case, phenomenal self-experience would equal noumenal access; that is, if I were to be able to experience "myself" as a phenomenal object, I would thereby *eo ipso* experience myself in my noumenal identity, as a Thing.

The underlying problem here is the impossibility of the subject's objectivizing himself: the subject is singular *and* the universal frame of "his world," for every content he perceives is "his own"; so how can the subject include himself (count himself) in the series of his objects? The subject observes reality from an external position and is simultaneously part of this reality, without ever being able to attain an "objective" view of reality with himself included it. The Thing that haunts the subject is *himself* in his objectal counterpoint, qua object. Hegel writes: "The subject finds itself in contradiction between the totality systematized in its consciousness, and the particular determination which, in itself, is not fluid and is not reduced to its proper place and rank. This is mental derangement [*Verrücktheit*]."[48] This has to be read in a very precise way. Hegel's point is not simply that madness signals a short-circuit between totality and one of its particular moments, a "fixation" of totality in this moment on account of which the totality is deprived of its dialectical fluidity—although some of his formulations may appear to point in this direction.[49] The "particular determina-

---

47 Hume drew a lot of mileage—too much—out of this observation regarding how, upon introspection, all I perceive in myself are my particular ideas, sensations, emotions, never my "Self" itself.

48 As quoted in Malabou, *The Future of Hegel*, p. 35; translation modified from Hegel, *Philosophy of Mind*, §408.

49 Is not paranoid fixation such a short-circuit, in which the totality of my experience becomes non-dialectically "fixated" on a particular moment, the idea of my persecutor?

tion which, in itself, is not fluid" and resists being "reduced to its proper place and rank" is *the subject himself*, or, more precisely, the feature (signifier) that re-presents him (holds his place) within the structured ("systematized") totality; and since the subject cannot ever objectivize himself, the "contradiction" here is absolute.[50] With this gap, the possibility of madness emerges—and, as Hegel puts it in proto-Foucauldian terms, madness is not an accidental lapse, a distortion, or an "illness" of human spirit, but is inscribed into an individual spirit's basic ontological constitution, for to be human means to be potentially mad:

> This interpretation of insanity as a necessarily occurring form or stage in the development of the soul is naturally not to be understood as if we were asserting that *every* mind, *every* soul, must go through this stage of extreme derangement. Such an assertion would be as absurd as to assume that because in the Philosophy of Right crime is considered as a necessary manifestation of the human will, therefore to commit crime is an inevitable necessity for *every* individual. Crime and insanity are *extremes* which the human mind *in general* has to overcome in the course of its development.[51]

Although not a factual necessity, madness is a formal possibility constitutive of human mind: it is something whose threat has to be overcome if we are to emerge as "normal" subjects, which means that "normality" can only arise as the overcoming of this threat. This is why, as Hegel puts it a couple of pages later, "insanity must be discussed before the healthy, intellectual consciousness, although it has that consciousness for its *presupposition*."[52] Hegel here evokes the relationship between the abstract and the concrete: although, in the empirical state of things, abstract determinations are always already embedded in a concrete Whole as their presupposition, the notional reproduction or deduction of this Whole has to progress from the abstract to the concrete: crimes presuppose the rule of law, they can only occur as their violation, but must be nonetheless grasped as an abstract act that is "sublated" through the law; abstract legal relations and morality are *de facto* always embedded in some concrete totality of

50 Upon a closer look, it becomes clear that the Hegelian notion of madness oscillates between the two extremes which one is tempted to call, with reference to Benjamin's notion of violence, constitutive and constituted madness. First, there is constitutive madness: the radical "contradiction" of the human condition itself, between the subject as "nothing," as the evanescent punctuality, and the subject as "all," as the horizon of its world. Then, there is "constituted" madness: the direct fixation upon, identification with, a particular feature as an attempt to resolve (or, rather, cut short) the contradiction. In a way homologous with the ambiguity of the Lacanian notion of the *objet petit a*, madness names at the same time the contradiction or void and the attempt to resolve it.

51 Hegel, *Philosophy of Mind*, §408 Addition.

52 Ibid.

Customs, but, nonetheless, the Philosophy of Right has to progress from the abstract moments of legality and morality to the concrete Whole of Customs (family, civil society, state). The interesting point here is not only the parallel between madness and crime, but the fact that madness is located in a space opened up by the discord between actual historical development and its conceptual rendering, that is, in a space which undermines the vulgar-evolutionist notion of dialectical development as a conceptual reproduction of factual historical development which purifies the latter of its insignificant empirical contingencies. Insofar as madness *de facto* presupposes normality while conceptually preceding it, one can say that the "madman" is precisely a subject who wants to "live"—to reproduce in actuality itself—the conceptual order, to act as if madness also *effectively* precedes normality.

We can now see in what precise sense habits form the third, concluding, moment of the triad, its "syllogism": *in a habit, the subject finds a way to "possess itself,"* to stabilize its own inner content in "having" as its property a habit, not a positive actual feature, but a virtual entity, a universal disposition to (re)act in a certain way. Habit and madness are thus to be thought together: habit is a way of stabilizing the imbalance of madness. Another way to approach the topic is via the relationship between soul and body as the Inner and the Outer, as a circular relationship in which body expresses the soul and the soul receives impressions from the body—the soul is always already embodied and the body always already impregnated with its soul:

> What the sentient self finds within it is, on the one hand, the naturally immediate, as "ideally" in it and made its own. On the other hand and conversely, what originally belongs to the central individuality ... is determined as natural corporeity, and is so felt.[53]

So, on the one hand, through feelings and perceptions, I internalize objects that affect me from outside: in a feeling, they are present in me not in their raw reality, but "ideally," as part of my mind. On the other hand, through grimaces, etc., my body immediately "gives body" to my inner soul which thoroughly impregnates it. However, if this were the entire truth, then man would have been simply a "prisoner of this state of nature,"[54] moving in the closed loop of absolute transparency provided by the mutual mirroring of body and soul.[55] What happens with the moment of "judgment" is that the loop of this closed circle is broken—not by the intrusion of an external element, but by a self-referentiality

53 Ibid., §401; translation modified via Malabou, *The Future of Hegel*, pp. 32–3.

54 Malabou, *The Future of Hegel*, p. 67.

55 Physiognomy and phrenology remain at this level, as do contemporary New Age ideologies enjoining us to express or realize our true Selves.

which twists this circle into itself. In other words, the problem is that, "since the individual is at the same time only what he has done, his body is also the expression of himself which he has himself produced."[56] This means that the process of corporeal self-expression has no pre-existing referent as its mooring point: the entire movement is thoroughly self-referential, it is only through the process of "expression" (externalization in bodily signs) that the expressed Inner Self (the content of these signs) is retroactively created—or, as Malabou puts it concisely: "Psychosomatic unity results from an auto-interpretation independent of any referent."[57] The transparent mirroring of the soul and the body in the natural expressivity thus turns into total opacity:

> If a work signifies itself, this implies that there is no "outside" of the work, that the work acts as its own referent: it presents what it interprets at the same moment it interprets it, forming one and the same manifestation … The spiritual bestows form, but only because it is itself formed in return.[58]

What this "lack of any ontological guarantee outside the play of signification"[59] means is that the meaning of our gestures and speech acts is always haunted by the spirit of irony: when I say A, it is always possible that I do it in order to conceal the fact that I am non-A—Hegel refers to Lichtenberg's well-known aphorism: "You certainly act like an honest man, but I see from your face that you are forcing yourself to do so and are a rogue at heart."[60] The ambiguity is here total and undecidable, because the deception is the one that Lacan designates as specifically human, namely the possibility of lying in the guise of truth. Which is why it goes even further than the quote from Lichtenberg—the reproach should rather be: "You act like an honest man in order to convince us that you mean it ironically, and thus to conceal from us the fact that you really *are* an honest man!" This is what Hegel means in his precise claim that, "for the individuality, it is as much its countenance as its mask which it can lay aside":[61] in the gap between appearance (mask) and my true inner stance, the truth can be either in my inner stance or in my mask. This means that the emotions I perform through the mask (the false persona) I adopt can in a strange way be more authentic and truthful than what I really feel in myself. When I construct a false image of myself which stands in for me in a virtual community in which I participate

56 G. W. F. Hegel, *Phenomenology of Spirit*, trans. A. V. Miller, Oxford: Oxford University Press, 1977, p. 185–6.

57 Malabou, *The Future of Hegel*, p. 71.

58 Ibid., p. 72.

59 Ibid., p. 68.

60 Hegel, *Phenomenology of Spirit*, p. 193.

61 Ibid., p. 191.

(in virtual sexual interaction, for example, a shy man often assumes the screen persona of an attractive, promiscuous woman), the emotions I feel and feign as part of my screen persona are not simply false: although (what I think of as) my true self does not feel them, they are nonetheless in a sense "true." For example, what if, deep inside, I am a sadistic pervert who dreams of beating up other men and raping women; in my real-life interaction with other people, I am not allowed to enact this true self, so I adopt a more humble and polite persona—in this case, is not my true self much closer to what I adopt as a fictional screen persona, while the self of my real-life interactions is a mask concealing the violence of my true self?

Habit provides the way out of this predicament. How? Not as the subject's "true expression," but by locating the truth in "mindless" expression—recall Hegel's constant motif that truth is in what you *say*, not in what you *mean* to say. Consider again the enigmatic status of what we call "politeness": when, upon meeting an acquaintance, I say, "Glad to see you! How are you today?" it is clear to both of us that, in a way, I "do not mean it seriously."[62] However, it would nonetheless be wrong to label my act as simply "hypocritical," since, in another way, I *do* mean it: the polite exchange does establish a kind of pact between the two of us; in the same sense as I do "sincerely" laugh through the canned laughter (the proof being that I effectively do "feel relieved" afterwards). This brings us to one possible definition of a madman, as a subject unable to participate in this logic of "sincere lies," so that when a friend greets him with "Nice to see you! How are you?" he explodes: "Are you really glad to see me or are you just pretending? And who gave you the right to probe into my state?"

The same overlapping of appearance with truth is often at work in ideological self-perception. Recall Marx's brilliant analysis of how, in the French revolution of 1848, the conservative-republican Party of Order functioned as a coalition of the two branches of royalism (Orleanists and Legitimists) in the "anonymous kingdom of the Republic."[63] The parliamentary deputies of the Party of Order saw their republicanism as a mockery: in parliamentary debates, they frequently made royalist slips of the tongue and ridiculed the Republic to let it be known that their true aim was to restore the monarchy. What they were not aware of was that they themselves were duped as to the true social impact of their rule. What they were effectively doing was establishing the conditions of the bourgeois republican order they despised so much (by, for instance, guar-

62 If my interlocutor suspects that I am really interested, he may even be unpleasantly surprised, as though I were aiming at something too intimate and of no concern to me—or, to paraphrase the old Freudian joke, "Why are you saying you're glad to see me, when you're *really* glad to see me!?"

63 See Karl Marx, "Class Struggles in France," in Karl Marx and Friedrich Engels, *Collected Works*, Vol. 10, London: Lawrence & Wishart 1978, p. 104.

anteeing the safety of private property). So it is not that they were just royalists wearing a republican mask: although they experienced themselves as such, it was their very "inner" royalist conviction that was the deceptive front masking their true social role. In short, far from being the hidden truth of their public republicanism, their sincere royalism was the fantasmatic support of their actual republicanism—it was what added the passion to their activity. Is it not the case, then, that the deputies of the Party of Order were also *feigning to feign* to be republicans, to be what they really were?

Hegel's radical conclusion is that the sign with which we are dealing here, in corporeal expressions, "in truth signifies nothing" (*in Wahrheit nicht bezeichnet*).[64] Habit is thus a strange sign which "signifies the fact that it signifies nothing."[65] What Hölderlin proposed as the formula for our destitute predicament—for an era in which, because the gods have abandoned us, we are "signs without meaning"—acquires here an unexpected positive interpretation. And we should take Hegel's formula literally: the "nothing" in it has a positive weight; that is, the sign which "in truth signifies nothing" is what Lacan calls the *signifier*, that which represents the subject for another signifier. The "nothing" is the void of the subject itself, so that the absence of an ultimate reference means that absence itself is the ultimate reference, and this absence is the subject itself. This is why Malabou writes: "Spirit is not that which is expressed by its expressions; it is that which originally terrifies spirit."[66] The dimension of haunting, the link between spirit qua the light of Reason and spirit qua obscene ghost, is crucial here: spirit or Reason is, by a structural necessity, forever haunted by the obscene apparitions of its own spirit.

> The human being is this night, this empty nothing, that contains everything in its simplicity—an unending wealth of many representations, images, of which none belongs to him—or which are not present. This night, the interior of nature, that exists here—pure self—in phantasmagorical representations, is night all around it, in which here shoots a bloody head—there another white ghastly apparition, suddenly here before it, and just so disappears. One catches sight of this night when one looks human beings in the eye—into a night that becomes awful.[67]

---

64 Hegel, *Phenomenology of Spirit*, p. 191; translation modified via Malabou, *The Future of Hegel*, p. 67.

65 Malabou, *The Future of Hegel*, p. 67.

66 Ibid., p. 68.

67 G. W. F. Hegel, "Jenaer Realphilosophie," in *Frühe politische Systeme*, Frankfurt: Ullstein 1974, p. 204; translation quoted from Donald Phillip Verene, *Hegel's Recollection*, Albany: SUNY Press 1985, pp. 7–8. Hegel also mentions the "night-like abyss within which a world of infinitely numerous images and presentations is preserved without being in consciousness" (G. W. F. Hegel, *Hegels Philosophie des subjektiven Geistes/Hegel's Philosophy of Subjective Spirit*, Vol. 3, trans. and ed. M. J. Petry, Dordrecht: D. Reidel 1978,

Again, one should not be blinded by the poetic power of this description, but read it precisely. The first thing to note is how the objects which freely float around in this "night of the world" are *membra disjecta*, partial objects, objects detached from their organic Whole—is there not a strange echo between this passage and Hegel's description of the negative power of Understanding which is able to abstract an entity (a process, a property) from its substantial context and treat it as if it has an existence of its own? "That an accident as such, detached from what circumscribes it, what is bound and is actual only in its context with others, should attain an existence of its own and a separate freedom—this is the tremendous power of the negative."[68] It is thus as if, in the ghastly scenery of the "night of the world," we encounter something like *the power of Understanding in its natural state*, spirit in the guise of a *proto-spirit*—this, perhaps, is the most precise definition of horror: when a higher state of development violently inscribes itself in the lower state, in its ground/presupposition, where it cannot but appear as a monstrous mess, a disintegration of order, a terrifying unnatural combination of natural elements.

In the context of contemporary science, we encounter this horror at its purest when genetic manipulations go awry and generate objects never seen in nature, freaks like goats with a gigantic ear instead of a head or a head with one eye, meaningless accidents which nonetheless touch our deeply repressed fantasies and thus trigger wild interpretations. The pure Self as the "inner of nature"[69] stands for this paradoxical short-circuit of the supernatural (spiritual) in its natural state. Why does it occur? The only consistent answer is a *materialist* one: *because spirit is part of nature*, and can occur or arise only through a monstrous self-ffliction (distortion, *derangement*) of nature. Therein lies the paradoxical materialist edge of cheap spiritualism: it is precisely because spirit is part of nature, because spirit does not intervene into nature—which is already constituted, ready-made somewhere else—but has to emerge out of nature through its derangement, that there is no spirit (Reason) without spirits (obscene ghosts), that spirit is forever haunted by spirits.

It is from this standpoint that we should (re)read Sartre's deservedly famous description in *Being and Nothingness* of the café waiter who, with an exaggerated theatricality, performs the clichéd gestures of a waiter and thus "plays at being a waiter in a café":

---

p. 153 [§453]). Hegel's historical source here is Jacob Bohme.

68 Hegel, *Phenomenology of Spirit*, p. 19.

69 A strange expression, since, for Hegel, nature, precisely, *has no interior*: its ontological status is that of externality, not only externality with regard to some presupposed Interior, but externality with regard to itself.

> His movement is quick and forward, a little too precise, a little too rapid. He comes toward the patrons with a step a little too quick. He bends forward a little too eagerly; his voice, his eyes express an interest a little too solicitous for the order of the customer. Finally there he returns, trying to imitate in his walk the inflexible stiffness of some kind of automaton ...[70]

Does not Sartre's underlying ontological thesis—that "the waiter in the café can not be immediately a café waiter in the sense that this inkwell *is* an inkwell"—point forward towards Lacan's classic thesis that a madman is not only a beggar who thinks he is a king, but also a king who thinks he is a king? We should be very precise in this reading: as Robert Bernasconi notes in his commentary, there is much more to Sartre's thesis than a simple point about *mauvaise foi* and self-objectivization (in order to cover up—or escape from—the void of his freedom, a subject clings to a firm symbolic identity); what Sartre does is show how, through the very exaggeration of his gestures, through his very over-identification with the role, the waiter in question signals his distance from it and thus asserts his subjectivity. True, this French waiter

> plays at being a waiter by acting like an automaton, just as the role of a waiter in the United States, by a strange inversion, is to play at acting like one's friend. However, Sartre's point is that, whatever game the waiter is called upon to play, the ultimate rule that the waiter follows is that he must break the rules, and to do so by following them in an exaggerated manner. That is to say, the waiter does not simply follow the unwritten rules, which would be obedience to a certain kind of tyranny, but, instead, goes overboard in following those rules. The waiter succeeds in rejecting the attempt to reduce him to nothing more than being a waiter, not by refusing the role, but by highlighting the fact that he is playing it to the point that he escapes it. The waiter does this by overdoing things, by doing too much. The French waiter, instead of disappearing into the role, exaggerates the movements that make him something of an automaton in a way that draws attention to him, just as, we can add, the quintessential North American waiter is not so much friendly as overfriendly. Sartre uses the same word, *trop*, that we saw him using in *Nausea* to express this human superfluity.[71]

And it is crucial to supplement this description with its symmetrical opposite: one is *truly* identified with one's role precisely when one does not "over-identify" with it, but accompanies one's role-playing, following the rules, with small violations or idiosyncrasies designed to signal that, beneath the role, there is a real person who cannot be directly identified with it or reduced to it. In other

70 Jean-Paul Sartre, *Being and Nothingness*, London: Methuen 1957, p. 59.

71 Robert Bernasconi, *How to Read Sartre*, London: Granta 2006, p. 38.

words, it is totally wrong to read the waiter's behavior as a case of *mauvaise foi*: his exaggerated act opens up, in a negative way, the space for his authentic self, since its message is "I am not what I am playing at being." True *mauvaise foi* consists precisely in embellishing my playing a role with idiosyncratic details—it is this "personal touch" which provides the space for false freedom, allowing me to accommodate myself to my self-objectivization in the role I am playing. (So what about those rare and weird moments in an American cafeteria when we suddenly suspect that the waiter's friendliness is genuine?)[72]

This brings us back to our original question: in what does the difference between animal and human habits consist? Only humans, spiritual beings, are haunted by spirits—why? Not simply because, in contrast to animals, they have access to universality, but because this universality is for them *simultaneously necessary and impossible*; that is, it is a problem. In other words, while for human subjects the place of universality is prescribed, it has to remain empty, it can never be filled in with its "proper" content. The specificity of man thus concerns the relationship between universal essence and its accidents: for animals, accidents remain mere accidents; only the human being posits universality as such, relates to it, and can therefore reflectively elevate accidents into universal essence. *This is why* man is a "generic being" (Marx): to paraphrase Heidegger's definition of *Dasein*, man is a being for which its genus is for itself a problem: "Man can 'present the genus' to the degree that habit is the unforeseen element of the genus."[73]

This formulation opens up an unexpected link to the notion of *hegemony* as developed by Ernesto Laclau: there is forever a gap between the universality of man's genus and the particular habits which fill in its void; habits are always "unexpected," contingent, accidents elevated to universal necessity. The predominance of one or another habit is the result of a struggle for hegemony, a struggle over which accident will occupy the empty place of the universality. That is to say, with regard to the relationship between universality and particularity, the "contradiction" in the human condition—a human subject perceives reality from a singular subjective viewpoint and, simultaneously, perceives

72 Sartre also draws attention to a crucial distinction between this kind of "playing a role" and a theatrical "playing a role" where the subject merely imitates the gestures of a waiter for the amusement of spectators or as part of a stage performance: in clear opposition to the theatrical imitation, the waiter who "plays being a waiter" *really is a waiter*. As Sartre put it, the waiter "realizes" the condition of being a waiter, while an actor who plays a waiter on stage is "irrealized" in his role. In linguistic terms, what accounts for this difference is the performative status of my acts: in the case of an actor, the performative "efficacy" is suspended. A psychotic is precisely one who does not see (or, rather, "feel") this difference: for him, both the real waiter and the actor are just "playing a role."

73 Malabou, *The Future of Hegel*, p. 74.

himself as included in this same reality as a part, as an object in it—means that the subject has to presuppose universality (there is a universal order, some kind of "Great Chain of Being," of which he is a part), while, simultaneously, it is forever impossible for him to entirely fill in this universality with its particular content, to harmonize the Universal and the Particular (since his approach to reality is forever marked—colored, twisted, distorted—by his singular perspective). Universality is always simultaneously *necessary* and *impossible.*

Laclau's concept of hegemony offers an exemplary matrix of the relationship between universality, historical contingency, and the limit of an impossible Real—and one should always keep in mind that we are dealing here with a distinct concept whose specificity is often missed (or reduced to some vague quasi-Gramscian generality) by those who refer to it. The key feature of the concept of hegemony resides in the contingent connection between intra-social differences (elements *within* the social space) and the limit that separates society itself from non-society (chaos, utter decadence, the dissolution of all social links)—the limit between the social and its exteriority, the non-social, can only articulate itself in the guise of a difference (by mapping itself onto a difference) between elements within social space. In other words, radical antagonism can only be represented in a distorted way, through particular differences internal to the system. External differences are thus always already also internal, and, furthermore, the link between the internal and external difference is ultimately contingent, the result of political struggle for hegemony.

The standard anti-Hegelian counter-argument here is, of course, that this irreducible gap between the universal (frame) and its particular content is what characterizes Kantian finite subjectivity. Is not Hegelian "concrete universality" the most radical expression of the fantasy of full reconciliation between the universal and the particular? Is not its basic feature the self-generation of the entire particular content out of the self-movement of universality itself? Against this common reproach, we should insist on the closeness of Laclau's notion of hegemony to the Hegelian notion of "concrete universality." In the latter, the specific difference overlaps with the difference constitutive of the genus itself, just as, in Laclau's notion of hegemony, the antagonistic gap between society and its external limit, non-society, is mapped onto an intra-social structural difference. Laclau himself rejects the Hegelian "reconciliation" between universal and particular on behalf of the gap that forever separates the empty or impossible universal from the contingent particular content that hegemonizes it. If, however, we take a closer look at Hegel, we see that—insofar as every particular species does not "fit" its universal genus—when we finally arrive at a particular species that fully fits its notion, that universal notion itself is transformed into another notion. No existing historical State fully fits the notion of the State—the necessity of a dialectical passage from the State ("objective spirit," history) into Religion ("absolute spirit") involves the fact that the only existing State that effectively fits its notion is a religious community—which, precisely, is no longer a State. Here we encounter the properly dialectical paradox of "concrete universality" qua historicity: in the relationship between a genus and its subspecies, one of these subspecies will always be the element that negates the very universal feature of the genus. Different nations have different versions of soccer; Americans do not (or did not) have soccer, because "baseball *is* their soccer." Hence also Hegel's famous claim that modern people do not pray in the morning, because reading the newspaper *is* their morning prayer. In the same way, in disintegrating "socialist" states, writers' and other cultural clubs did act as political parties. In the same way, "woman" becomes one of the subspecies of man, Heideggerian *Daseinsanalyse* one of the subspecies of phenomenology, "sublating" the preceding universality.

The impossible point of "self-objectivization" would be precisely the point at which universality and its particular content are fully harmonized—in short, where there would be no struggle for hegemony. And this brings us back to madness: its most succinct definition is that of a *direct* harmony between universality and its accidents, of a cancellation of the gap that separates the two—for the madman, the object which is his impossible stand-in within objectal reality loses its virtual character and becomes a fully integral part of that reality. In contrast to madness, habit avoids this trap of direct identification thanks to its virtual character: the subject's identification with a habit is not a direct identification with some positive feature, but an identification with a disposition, with a virtuality. Habit is the outcome of a struggle for hegemony: it is *an accident elevated to an "essence," to universal necessity*, made to fill in its empty place.

CHAPTER 6

"Not Only as Substance, But Also as Subject"

Concrete universality

> Hegel's great originality is that he shows exactly how an interpretation that aims at nothing more than universality, that disallows any role for the singularity of the exegete, an interpretation, indeed, that refuses to be plastic, in the sense of both "universal and individual," would be in reality particular and arbitrary.[1]

The stakes are very precise in this passage from Catherine Malabou's groundbreaking book on Hegel. Every interpretation is partial, "embedded" in an interpreter's ultimately contingent subjective position; however, far from blocking access to the universal truth of the interpreted text, full acceptance of this contingency and of the need to work through it is the only way the interpreter can access the universality of the content of the text. The interpreter's contingent subjective position provides the impetus, the urge or urgency, which sustains an authentic interpretation. If we want to attain the universality of the interpreted text directly, as it is "in itself," bypassing, erasing, or abstracting from the engaged position of the interpreter, then we either have to admit defeat and accept historicist relativism, or elevate into a fixed universal In-itself what is effectively a particular and arbitrary reading of the text. In other words, the universality we arrive at in this way is *abstract* universality, a universality which excludes rather than encompasses the contingency of the particular. The true "concrete universality" of a great historical text like *Antigone* (or the Bible or a play by Shakespeare) lies in the very totality of its historically determined readings. The crucial feature to bear in mind here is how *concrete universality is not true concrete universality without including in itself the subjective position of its reader-interpreter as the particular and contingent point from which the universality is perceived.* That is to say, in the Hegelian deployment of a process of cognition, the subject of cognition is not only the universal medium of reflection in which particular thoughts occur, a kind of receptacle containing thoughts about determinate objects as its particular content. The opposite also holds: the object of cognition is a universal In-itself, and the subject stands precisely for what the word "subjective" means in its standard use, as when we talk about

1 Catherine Malabou, *The Future of Hegel*, London: Routledge 2005, p. 181.

"subjective perceptions which distort the way a thing really is." Hence the true particularity of a universal Notion is not simply one of its species which can, as such, be grasped by a neutral subject observing this universality (as when, in reflecting upon the notion of the State, I see that the state in which I live is a particular species, and that there are also other kinds of states); rather, the true particularity is, primarily, *the particular subjective position from which the universal Notion is acceptable to me* (in the case of State: the fact that I am a member of some particular state, rooted in its particular ideological structure, "colors" my universal notion of the State). And, as Marx knew very well, this dialectic holds also for the rise of universality itself: it is only in a specific, particular, historical constellation that the universal dimension of a Notion can appear "as such." Marx's example is that of labor: only in capitalism, in which I exchange my labor power for money as the universal commodity, do I relate to my specific profession as one contingent particular form of employment; only here does the abstract notion of work become a social fact, in contrast to medieval societies in which the laborer does not choose his field of work as a profession, since he is directly "born" into it. (The same goes for Freud and his discovery of the universal function of the Oedipus complex.) In other words, the very gap between a universal notion and its particular historical form appears only in a certain historical epoch. What this means is that we truly pass from abstract to concrete universality only when the knowing subject loses its external position and itself becomes caught up in the movement of its content—only in this way does the universality of the object of cognition lose its abstract character and enter into the movement of its particular content.

Concrete universality should thus be strictly distinguished from historicism. In relation to the notion of human rights, a Marxist symptomal reading can convincingly identify the particular content that gives it a specifically bourgeois ideological spin: universal human rights are effectively the rights of white male property owners to exchange freely on the market, exploit workers and women, as well as exert political domination. The identification of the particular content that hegemonizes the universal form is, however, only half the story. The other half, no less crucial, consists in asking a much more difficult question concerning the emergence of the form of universality itself. How and under what specific historical conditions does abstract Universality itself become a "fact of (social) life"? Under what conditions do individuals experience themselves as subjects of universal human rights? This is the point of Marx's analysis of commodity fetishism: in a society in which commodity exchange predominates, individuals in their daily lives relate to themselves, as well as to the objects they encounter, as contingent embodiments of abstract and universal notions. What I am, in terms of my concrete social or cultural background, is experienced as contingent, since what ultimately defines me is the abstract universal capacity to think and/or to work. Any object that can satisfy my desire is experienced as contingent, since my desire is conceived as an abstract formal capacity, indifferent towards the multitude of particular objects that may satisfy it, but never fully do. The modern notion of a profession, as just noted, implies that I experience myself as an individual who is not directly "born into" his social role. What I will become depends on the interplay between contingent social circumstances and my free choice. The contemporary individual has a profession—he is an electrician or a professor or a waiter—but it would be meaningless to claim that a medieval serf was a peasant by profession. The crucial point here is that, again, in the specific social conditions of commodity exchange within a global market economy, "abstraction" becomes a direct feature of actual social life. It has an impact on the way individuals behave and relate to their fate and to their social surroundings. Marx shares Hegel's insight into how Universality becomes "for itself" only insofar as individuals no longer fully identify the kernel of their being with their particular social situation: they experience themselves as forever "out of joint" with regard to this situation. In other words, in a given social structure, Universality becomes "for itself" only in those individuals who lack a proper place in it. The mode of appearance of an abstract Universality, its entering into actual existence, thus produces violence, disrupting the former organic equilibrium.

It is thus not only that every universality is haunted by a particular content that taints it; it is also that every particular position is haunted by its implicit universality, which undermines it. Capitalism is not just universal In-itself, it is universal For-itself, as the tremendous corrosive power which undermines all particular life worlds, cultures, and traditions, cutting across them, sucking them into its vortex. It is meaningless to ask, "Is this universality genuine or merely a mask for particular interests?" This universality is directly actual as universality, as the negative force of mediating and destroying all particular content. And the same logic holds for emancipatory struggle: the particular culture desperately trying to defend its identity has to repress the universal dimension which is active at its very heart, that is, the gap between the particular (its identity) and the universal which destabilizes it from within. This is why the "leave our culture alone" argument fails. Within every particular culture, individuals *do* suffer and *do* protest—women protest when forced to undergo clitoridectomy, for example—and *these protests against the parochial constraints of one's culture are formulated from the standpoint of universality.* Actual universality is not the "deep" feeling that different cultures ultimately share the same basic values, etc.; *actual universality "appears" (actualizes itself) as the experience of negativity, of the inadequacy-to-itself, of a particular identity.* "Concrete universality" does not concern the relationship of a particular to the wider Whole, the way it relates to others and to its context, but rather *the way it relates to itself,* the way its very particular identity is split from within. The standard problem of universality (how can I be sure that what I perceive as universality is not colored by my particular identity) thereby disappears: "concrete universality" means precisely that my particular identity is corroded from within, that the tension between particularity and universality is inherent to my particular identity—or, to put it in more formal terms, that specific difference overlaps with generic difference.

In short, a universality arises "for itself" only through or at the site of a *thwarted particularity*. Universality inscribes itself into a particular identity as its inability to fully become itself: I am a universal subject insofar as I cannot realize myself in my particular identity—this is why the modern universal subject is by definition "out of joint," lacking its proper place in the social edifice. This thesis has to be taken literally: it is not only that universality inscribes itself into my particular identity as its rupture, its out-of-jointness; universality "in itself" is in its actuality *nothing but* this cut which blocks from within all and every particular identity. Within a given social order, a universal claim can be made only by a group that is prevented from realizing its particular identity—women thwarted in their effort to realize their feminine identity, an ethnic group prevented from asserting its identity, and so on. This is also why, for Freud, "everything has a sexual connotation," why sexuality can infect everything: not because it is "the strongest" component in people's lives, exerting a hegemony over all other components, but because it is the one most radically thwarted in its actualization, marked by that "symbolic castration" on account of which, as Lacan put it, there is no sexual relationship. Every universality that arises, that is posited "as such," bears witness to a scar in some particularity, and remains forever linked to this scar.

Recall Krzysztof Kieslowski's passage from documentary to fiction cinema: we do not simply have two species of cinema, documentary and fiction; the fiction cinema emerged out of the inherent limitations of the documentary cinema. Kieslowski's starting point was the same as for all filmmakers in the "socialist" countries: the conspicuous mismatch between the drab social reality and the bright, optimistic images which pervaded the heavily censored official media. Kieslowski's initial reaction to the fact that Polish social reality was, as he put it, "unrepresented" was, of course, to pursue a more adequate representation of real life in all its drabness and ambiguity—in short, to adopt an authentic documentary approach. But Kieslowski soon came to reject this, for reasons best captured by the end of the documentary *First Love* (1974). Here the camera follows a young unmarried couple through the girl's pregnancy, their wedding, and the delivery of the baby, ending by showing the father holding the newborn baby and crying. Kieslowski reacted to the obscenity of such unwarranted intrusion into the intimate lives of others with the "fright of real tears": there is a domain of fantasmatic intimacy marked by a "No trespassing!" sign and which should be approached only via fiction. This is also the why the French Véronique in *The Double Life of Véronique* rejects the puppeteer: he wants to probe too far, which is why, after he tells her the story of her double life, she is deeply hurt and escapes back to her father towards the end of the film.[2] "Concrete universality" is a name for this process through which fiction explodes documentary *from within*, for the way the emergence of fiction cinema resolves the inherent deadlock of the documentary cinema.[3] Another example from cinema history is provided by one of its great mysteries: the sudden eclipse of the Western in the mid-1950s. Part of the answer lies in the fact that, at the same moment, space opera emerged as a genre—so one can venture the hypothesis that space opera took the place of the Western in the late 1950s. The dialectical point here is that the Western and space opera are not two subspecies of the genre "adventure." Rather, we should shift the perspective and start *only* with the Western—in the course of its development, the Western then encounters a deadlock and, in order to survive, has to "reinvent" itself as space opera—space opera is thus structurally a subspecies of the Western, in the same way that, for Kieslowski, fiction is a subspecies of documentary.

And does the same not hold for the passage from the State to the religious community in Hegel? They are not simply two species of the genre of "large socio-ideological communities"; it is rather that the State, in its particular forms, cannot ever resolve the deadlock inscribed in its notion (i.e., cannot adequately represent and totalize the community—in the same way that, for Kieslowski, documentary cannot adequately render the core of social reality) and so needs to pass over into another notion, that of the Church. The Church is, in this sense, "more State than the State itself," it actualizes the notion of the State by shifting to another notion. In all these cases, universality is located in the enchainment or overlapping of particularities: A and B are not parts (species) of their encompassing universality; A cannot fully become A, actualize its notion, without passing into B, which is formally its subspecies, but a subspecies which undermines the very species under which it is formally subsumed. Every species contains a subspecies which, precisely insofar as it effectively realizes the notion of this species, explodes its frame: the space opera is "a Western at the level of its notion" and, for that very reason, no longer a Western. Instead of a universality subdivided into two species, we thus get a particular species which generates another

2 For a more detailed account of this passage, see Chapter 1 of Slavoj Žižek, *The Fright of Real Tears: Krzysztof Kieslowski Between Theory and Post-Theory*, London: British Film Institute 2001.

3 Or, in philosophy, the point is not to conceive eternity as being opposed to temporality, but to conceive it as something that emerges from within our temporal experience. (This paradox can also be turned around, as was done by Schelling: one can conceive of time itself as a subspecies of eternity, as the resolution of a deadlock of eternity.)

species as its own subspecies, and true ("concrete") universality is nothing but this movement in the course of which a species engenders a subspecies which negates its own species. The same dialectical mediation between the universal and the particular can also be formulated in terms of a universal notion and its examples. The difference between the idealist and the materialist use of examples is that, in the Platonic-idealist approach, examples are always imperfect, they never perfectly render what they are supposed to exemplify, while for a materialist there is always more in the example than in what it exemplifies, in other words, the example always threatens to undermine what it is supposed to exemplify since it gives body to what the exemplified notion itself represses or is unable to cope with. (Therein resides Hegel's materialist procedure in the *Phenomenology*: each "figure of consciousness" is first exemplified and then undermined through its own example.) This is why the idealist approach always demands a multitude of examples—since no single example really fits, one has to enumerate a great many of them in order to indicate the transcendent wealth of the Idea they exemplify, the Idea being the fixed point of reference for the floating examples. A materialist, on the contrary, tends to return obsessively to one and the same example: it is the particular example which remains the same in all symbolic universes, while the universal notion it is supposed to exemplify continually changes its shape, so that we get a multitude of universal notions circulating around a single example. Is this not what Lacan does, returning to the same exemplary cases (the guessing-game with five hats, the dream of Irma's injection, etc.), each time providing a new interpretation? The materialist example is thus a *universal Singular*: a singular entity which persists as the universal through the multitude of its interpretations.

This dialectic reaches its apogee when the universal as such, in contrast to its particular content, enters into being, acquires real existence—this is the rise of subjectivity described in Hegel's theory of the Notion as the first moment of his "subjective logic." Two introductory remarks should be made here. First, one should note the paradox of the fundamental difference between the logic of Essence and the logic of the Notion: precisely because the logic of Essence is the logic of Understanding—and, as such, sticks to fixed oppositions, being unable to grasp their self-mediation—it results in a mad dance of self-destruction in which all fixed determinations are dissolved. The logic of the Notion, by contrast, is the logic of fluid self-mediations which, precisely for this reason, is able to generate a stable structure. Second, the term "subjective logic" is fully justified in the precise sense that, for Hegel, the "Notion" is not the usual abstract universality designating a common feature of an empirical multiplicity—*the original "Notion" is the "I," the subject itself.* Hegel provides the most concise presentation of the "subjectivity" of the Notion at the beginning of his "Subjective Logic," where he first defines individuality as "the reflection of the Notion out of its determinateness *into itself*. It is the self-*mediation* of the Notion insofar as its *otherness* has made itself into an *other* again, whereby the Notion has reinstated itself as self-identical, but in the determination of absolute negativity."[4]

It is easy to see how universality and particularity are co-present in every Notion: every Notion is by definition universal, designating a single abstract feature that unites a series of particulars, and precisely as such, it is always already particular—not in addition to its universality, but by virtue of it. "Human" is a universal Notion, designating the universal dimension of all human beings, and as such it is particular, or determinate—it designates a certain feature, ignoring endless others (not only are there beings who are not human, but every human being has an endless number of other properties which can also be designated by other determinate Notions. Universality and particularity are thus two aspects of one and the same Notion: its very "abstract" universality makes it particular. A Notion is thus an immediate unity of indeterminacy and determination: it is both elevated above, or subtracted from, the texture of spatio-temporal reality, and simultaneously a fixed abstract determination. Why and how is the Notion subjective? First in the simple sense that it is posited as such only in the mind of a subject, a thinking being who possesses the power of abstraction: only a thinking being can subtract or abstract from the empirical multitude a single uniting feature and designate it as such. Then, in a much more radical sense: the passage to individuality is *the passage from subjective Notion to Subject (Self, I) itself as a pure Notion*. What can this mean? Is not the subject in its singularity what Kierkegaard emphasizes as the singularity irreducible to all universal mediation?

In a determinate Notion, universality and particularity immediately coexist; that is, the notion's universality immediately "passes" into its particular determination. The problem here is not how to reconcile or "synthesize" the opposites (the universal and the particular aspects of a Notion), but, on the contrary, how to pull them apart, how to separate universality from its "otherness," from its particular determinations. The absolute contradiction between universality and particularity can only be resolved, their immediate overlapping can only be mediated, when the Notion's universality is asserted or posited (or appears) as such, in opposition to its otherness, to every particular determination. In such a move, the Notion returns "out of its determinateness *into itself*," it reinstates itself "as self-identical, but in the determination of absolute negativity"—absolutely negating all and every positive content, all and every particular determination. The pure I (the Cartesian *cogito*, or Kantian transcendental apperception) is just such an absolute negation of all determinate content: it is the void of radical abstraction from *all* determinations, the form of "I think" emptied of

4 G. W. F. Hegel, *Hegel's Science of Logic*, trans. A. V. Miller, Atlantic Highlands: Humanities Press International 1989, p. 618.

all determinate thoughts. What happens here is what Hegel himself refers to as a "miracle": this pure universality emptied of all content is simultaneously the pure singularity of the "I"; it refers to myself as the unique evanescent point which excludes all others, which cannot be replaced by any others—my self is, by definition, only me and nothing else. The I is, in this sense, the coincidence of pure universality with pure singularity, of radical abstraction with absolute singularity.[5] And this is also what Hegel aims at when he says that in "I" the Notion as such comes to exist: the universal Notion exists in the form of the I in which absolute singularity (it is me, only me) overlaps with radical abstraction (as pure I, I am totally indistinguishable from all other I's).[6] In Paragraphs 1343 and 1344 of the *Science of Logic*, he then adds the "bad news" that accompanies the "good news" of the Notion's return-to-itself from its otherness: "Individuality is not only the return of the Notion into itself; but immediately its loss"; that is, in the guise of an individual I, the Notion not only returns to itself (to its radical universality), freeing itself from the otherness of all particular determinations; it simultaneously emerges as an actually existing "this," a contingent empirical individual immediately aware of itself, a "being-for-self":

> Through individuality, where the Notion is internal to itself, it becomes external *to itself* and enters into actuality ... The individual, therefore, as self-related negativity, is immediate identity of the negative with itself; it is *a being-for-self*. Or it is the abstraction that determines the Notion, according to its ideal moment of *being*, as an *immediate*. In this way, the individual is a qualitative *one* or *this*.[7]

We find here already the allegedly "illegitimate" move from notional determinations to actual existence whose best-known version occurs at the end of the

5 Along these lines, Hegel proposes a precise definition of consciousness: it emerges when the distinction between the universal consciousness and the individual self has been superseded: the self knows itself in its awareness of its universal duty.

6 The two sides of universality, positive and negative, are easily discernible in the case of the category of *Grund* (ground). In German as well as in English, the word has an underlying meaning that is opposed to its main meaning (reason-cause and foundation): Hegel refers to the German expression *zu Grunde gehen*, which means "to fall apart, to disintegrate"; in English, one of the meanings of "ground" as a verb is "to bring down, knock down, flatten" (with a similar legal sub-meaning of "to punish, or impose a sanction"). One should take note of the fact that the "positive" meanings (cause, foundation) mostly belong to "ground" as a substantive and the "negative" meanings to "ground" as a verb. What this tension points towards is the opposition of being and becoming, stasis and movement, substance and subject, In-itself and For-itself: as activity, as movement, ground is the activity of self-erasure: ground asserts itself against its grounded effects by destroying them.

7 Hegel, *Hegel's Science of Logic*, p. 621.

Logic, when the Idea releases itself into Nature as its externality. Let us avoid the standard idealist misunderstanding: of course, this speculative move does not "create" the flesh-and-blood individual, but it "creates" the "I," the self-relating empty point of reference that the individual experiences as "itself," as the void at the core of its being.

This is the first, theoretical, triad of the Notion; once this is accomplished and the singular universality of the Subject is in place, we face the opposite process: not U-P-I, but U-I-P—not the contradiction between Universal and Particular resolved by the I, but the contradiction between the Universal and the I resolved by the Particular. That is to say, how can the pure I break out of the abyss of radical self-relating negativity in which universality and singularity immediately coincide, excluding all determinate content? Here we enter the practical domain of will and decision: the subject qua pure Notion has to freely determine itself, to posit some determinate particular content which will count as "its own." And what we should not forget is that this determinate content (as the expression of the subject's freedom) is irreducibly arbitrary: it is ultimately grounded only in the subject's "It is so because I will it so," the moment of pure subjective decision or choice which stabilizes a world. In his *Logics of Worlds*, by way of designating this moment, Badiou proposes the concept of "point" understood as a simple decision in a situation reduced to a choice of *Yes* or *No*. He implicitly refers to Lacan's *point de capiton*, of course—and does not this imply that there is no "world" outside language, no world whose horizon of meaning is not determined by a symbolic order? The passage to truth is therefore the passage from language ("the limits of my language are the limits of my world") to the *letter*, to "mathemes" which run diagonally across a multitude of worlds. Postmodern relativism is precisely the thought of the irreducible *multitude of worlds*, each of them sustained by a specific language game, so that each world "is" the narrative its members tell themselves about themselves, with no shared terrain, no common language; and the problem of truth is how to establish something that—to use the terms popular in modal logic—remains the same in all possible worlds.

Hegel, Spinoza ... and Hitchcock

It is at this precise point that the contrast between Hegel and Spinoza appears at its purest: Spinoza's Absolute is a Substance which "expresses" itself in its attributes and modes without the subjectivizing *point de capiton*. True, Spinoza's famous proposition *omnis determinatio est negatio* may sound Hegelian, but the two opposed ways in which it can be read (depending on what *negatio* refers to) are both decidedly anti-Hegelian: (1) if it refers to the Absolute itself, it makes a negative-theological point: every positive determination of the Absolute, every predicate we attribute to it, is inadequate, fails to grasp its essence and thus already negates it; (2) if it refers to particular empirical things, it makes a point about their transient nature: every entity delimited from others by a particular determination will sooner or later join the chaotic abyss out of which it arose, for every particular determination is a negation not only in the sense that it will involve the negation of other particular determinations (if a rose is red, it is not blue, green, yellow ...), but in a more radical sense that refers to its long-term instability. Is Hegel's point then that these two readings are in fact simply identical, something like: "the Absolute is not a positive entity persisting in its impermeable identity beyond the transient world of finite things; the only true Absolute is nothing but this very process of the rising and passing away of all particular things"? Such a vision remains, however, all too close to a pseudo-Oriental Heraclitean wisdom concerning the eternal flow of the generation and corruption of all things under the sun—in more philosophical terms, such a vision relies on the univocity of being.

In defense of Spinoza, one could definitely claim that Substance is not simply the eternal generative process which continues without any interruption or cut, but that it is, on the contrary, the universalization of a cut or fall (*clinamen*): Substance is nothing but the constant process of "falling" (into determinate/particular entities); everything there is, is a fall (if we are permitted to read the famous proposition from Wittgenstein's *Tractatus*—"*Der Welt ist was der Fall ist*"—more literally than he meant it, discerning in *der Fall* also the meaning "fall"). There is no Substance which falls, curves, interrupts the flow, etc.; substance simply *is* the infinitely productive capacity of such falls/cuts/interruptions, they are its only reality.[8] In such a reading of Spinoza, Substance and *clinamen* (the curvature of the Substance which generates determinate entities) directly coincide; in this ultimate speculative identity, Substance is nothing but the process of its own "fall," the negativity that pushes towards productive determination; or, in Lacanian terms, the Thing is directly the *objet a*.

However, the problem with such a universalization of the *clinamen* (what the late Althusser called "aleatory materialism") is that it "renormalizes" the *clinamen* and thus turns into its opposite: if all that there is are interruptions or falls,

---

8 Spinoza's thought should be clearly distinguished from the Plotinian tradition of emanation: in emanation, effects fall outside of the One, the Supreme Being, they are ontologically inferior to it, the process of creation is the process of gradual degradation/corruption, while Spinoza asserts the absolute univocity of being, which means that all reality is not only caused by Substance, but remains *within* Substance, it never falls out of it. The standard Plotinian program of reversing degradation—in short, the teleological program of returning effects to their Origin—is meaningless for Spinoza: why return to something we never left in the first place?

then the key aspect of surprise, of the intrusion of an unexpected contingency, is lost, and we find ourselves in a boring, flat universe whose contingency is totally predictable and necessary. When Quentin Meillassoux insists on contingency as being the only necessity, he finds himself in the same predicament: his mistake is to conceive the assertion of contingency according to the masculine side of Lacan's formulae of sexuation, namely according to the logic of universality and its constitutive exception: everything is contingent, *with the exception of contingency itself, which is absolutely necessary*—necessity thus becomes the external guarantee of the universal contingency. What we should oppose to this universalization of contingency is not the universalization of necessity (everything that is is necessary, except for this necessity itself, which is contingent), but the "feminine" non-All of contingency: there is nothing which is not contingent, which is why not-all is contingent. Simultaneously, there is the non-All of necessity: there is nothing which is not necessary, which is why not-all is necessary. "Not-all is necessary" means that, from time to time, a contingent encounter occurs which undermines the predominant necessity (the space of possibilities sustained by this necessity), so that in it, the "impossible" happens.[9] The key point is that, if there is to be a moment of surprise in the cut or fall, it can only occur against the background of a continuous flow, as *its* interruption.

In contrast to Spinoza, for whom there is no Master-Signifier enacting a cut, marking a conclusion, "dotting the i," but just a continuous chain of causes, the Hegelian dialectical process involves cuts, sudden interruptions of the continuous flow, reversals which retroactively restructure the entire field. In order to properly understand this relationship between a continuous process and its cuts or ends, we should ignore the stupid notion of a "contradiction" in Hegel's thought between method (endless process) and system (end); it is also not sufficient to conceive cuts as moments within an encompassing process, internal differences which arise and disappear. A parallel with the flow of speech might be of some help here: the flow of speech cannot go on indefinitely, there has to be *le moment de conclure*, like the point that concludes a sentence. It is only the dot at the end that retroactively fixes or determines the meaning of the sentence. However, it is crucial to add that this dot is not a simple fixation which removes all risk, abolishing all ambiguity and openness. It is, on the contrary, the dotting itself, its cut, which releases—sets free—meaning and interpretation: the dot always occurs contingently, as a surprise, it generates a surplus—why *here*? What does this mean?

This element of surprise emerges at its purest in tautology—Hegel himself analyzes tautology through expectation and surprise, the excess is here the unexpected lack itself: "A rose is ... a rose"—we expected something, a determination,

9 See Alenka Zupančič, "Realno in njegovo nemožno" ("The Real and its Impossible"), *Problemi* 1–2 (2010).

a predicate, but what we get is just the repetition of the subject, which makes the phrase latent with virtual meaning. Far from clarifying things, tautology gives birth to the specter of some imponderable depth which escapes words; far from being an index of perfection, it hints at an obscene contingent underside. When do we say, "The law is the law"? Precisely when the law is encountered as unjust, arbitrary, etc., and we then add, "But, nonetheless, the law is the law." The final cut is then simultaneously the opening, what triggers or sets in motion a new process of endless interpretation. And, of course, the same goes for the absolute ending, the conclusion of Hegel's system.

The consequence of asserting the radical univocity of being is that all distinctions between "essential" and "secondary," between "actual" and "virtual," and so forth, have to be dropped. With regard to the classic Marxist distinction between base and superstructure, this means that the sphere of economic production is in no way more "real" than ideology or science, that it has no ontological priority over them, so we should abandon even the notion of the "determination in the last instance" of all social life by the economy. With regard to the topic of virtual reality, this means that it is not enough to say that reality is always supplemented by virtuality; one should drop the distinction itself and claim that all reality is virtual. In the economy, one should also drop the distinction between the "real economy" (the production of material goods) and the "virtual economy" (financial speculation with no foundation in real production): the whole economy, no matter how real, is already virtual. Such a direct universalization is nonetheless too hasty. If what we experience as reality is to retain its consistency, it has to be supplemented by a virtual "fiction"—this paradox, known already to Bentham, was poignantly formulated by Chesterton: "Literature and fiction are two entirely different things. Literature is a luxury, fiction is a necessity."[10] However, it was also Bentham who saw clearly that we nevertheless can (and should) clearly distinguish between reality and fiction—therein resides the paradox he tried to capture with his notion of fictions: although we can clearly distinguish between reality and fiction, we cannot simply drop fiction and retain only reality; if we drop fiction, reality itself disintegrates, loses its ontological consistency.

A few years ago, a caricature appeared in a German daily newspaper depicting five men answering the question: "What would you like to do during your summer holiday?" Each of them gave a different answer (read a good book, visit a faraway country, rest on a sunny beach, have fun eating and drinking with friends ...), but, in a cloud above the head of each of them, depicting what they were really dreaming about, was an image of a naked woman. The point is obvious. Beneath the semblance of civilized interests, there is only one thing: sex. The caricature is formally wrong: we all know that we are "really always

10 G. K. Chesterton, "A Defence of Penny Dreadfuls," in *The Defendant*, New York: Dodd Mead 1902, p. 10.

thinking about *that*,” but the question is in what precise way, what works as the object-cause of our desire, what fantasy-frame sustains our desire? One way to make this point clear would be to invert the caricature and have each man giving the same answer—“I want to have a lot of sex!”—and putting the non-sexual ideas (resting on a sunny beach, etc.) into the clouds to represent their intimate thoughts, thus providing a clue to what precise mode of *jouissance* is being targeted: one man dreams of having sex in a faraway, exotic place like a Hindu temple, surrounded by erotic statues; another dreams about making love on a secluded, sandy beach (maybe with an exhibitionist twist such as being secretly observed by a group of children playing nearby), and so on.

At its best, cinema plays with this role of fiction (or fantasy) as a supplement to reality, guaranteeing its consistency. This is not just a case of relying on special effects to present a fantasized world as reality: cinema is at its best when, through the subtleties of *mise-en-scène*, it makes the spectator experience reality itself as something fantasmatic. In the final scene of Alfonso Cuaron's *Children of Men*, Theo and Kee, a young black illegal-immigrant woman with the first newborn baby, a hope for all humanity, board a small boat. Theo rows Kee and her baby out to the buoy that marks the rendezvous point with the *Tomorrow*, a lab-ship carrying the independent scientist who is working on solving the infertility problem. Kee sees blood dripping in the boat, and Theo admits that he was shot during their escape. As the *Tomorrow* emerges from the thick fog, Theo loses consciousness and slumps to the side of the boat. The beauty of this ending is that, although shot realistically, as an actual event, it can clearly also be read as the fantasy of the dying Theo to whom the boat magically appears out of the mystic fog—in reality, they are just alone in a drifting boat, going nowhere.

A more complex procedure is that of the so-called “Hitchcockian ellipse,” whose exemplary case is the murder of Townsend in the UN building in *North by Northwest*.[11] Roger Thornhill arrives at the UN, secretly followed by the killer Valerian. In the reception hall, Thornhill asks a clerk to call Townsend, who duly arrives. When the two men are standing face to face, we see Valerian observing them from the corridor and putting on his gloves—an indication that he is about to kill someone. We do not yet know who he plans to murder, though we probably assume that it is Thornhill, since Valerian's group already tried to kill him the previous evening. The three characters are positioned in a line, with Thornhill and Townsend facing each other, and Valerian behind Townsend, so that the latter also functions as an obstacle, preventing a direct confrontation between Thornhill and Valerian, the true opponents. Thornhill suddenly draws from his pocket the photo he found in “Kaplan's” hotel room, showing

11 I rely here on the outstanding analysis in Jean-Jacques Marimbert, Éric Dufour, Laurent Jullier, and Julien Servois, *Analyse d'une oeuvre:* La mort aux trousses: *A. Hitchcock, 1959*, Paris: Vrin 2008, pp. 49–52.

Townsend, van Damme (the master criminal of the film), and a few others. Pointing at van Damme, Thornhill asks Townsend, "Do you know this man?" But there is no time for Townsend to reply: in a short blurred shot, we see a knife flying towards him, then Townsend's face distorted into a grimace of pain and surprise as he falls forward into Thornhill's arms. A brief shot of Valerian running away from the scene follows, before the film cuts back to Thornhill and Townsend, who slides down, revealing a big knife stuck in his back. Confused, Thornhill automatically grabs the knife and pulls it out. At that very moment a photographer takes a shot of Thornhill holding the knife above Townsend's body, obviously creating the impression that he is the murderer. Realizing this, Thornhill drops the knife and runs away in the confusion—clearly acting like a guilty suspect.

What is notable about this scene is that we do not really see the murder being carried out—not only do we never see Townsend and Valerian in the same shot, but the very continuity of the action is broken: we see what happens beforehand (Valerian's preparations) and afterwards (Townsend dropping into Thornhill's arms), but we do not see Valerian throwing the knife, nor even his face when he decides to act; we only see its effect, Townsend's shocked face. The causal chain seems interrupted in this "Hitchcockian abstraction": the clear link between Valerian and Townsend's death is, of course, implied, but at the same time the immediate impression is that Townsend drops dead because he has seen something terrifying and/or forbidden, something he should not have seen, in the photo shown to him by Thornhill (which, in a way, is true!), so that Thornhill's sudden gesture of reaching into his pocket and pulling out the photo becomes equivalent to the threatening gesture of pulling out a gun. This effect is reinforced by the general spatial disposition of the scene, which clearly mobilizes Hitchcock's classical division between the space of ordinary reality (the busy reception hall of the UN building with groups of people talking in the background) and the space of an obscene subterranean proto-reality in which danger lurks (the cellar in *Psycho*; in *Vertigo*, the dark room behind the mirror in the florist's reception room, from which Scottie observes Madeleine through the crack, etc.). In other words, it is as if the only reality of the scene is that of the big reception hall in which Thornhill and Townsend meet, while Valerian operates from another spectral space, visible to no one, interrupting the normal causal chain of ordinary reality, and thus dispossessing Thornhill of the act attributed to him (or, rather, attributing to him an act which was not his).

Why is this fictional supplement needed? What hole does it fill? In order to guarantee the symbolic consistency of our "sphere" of life (to use Sloterdijk's expression), something—some excremental waste—has to disappear. The paradox of radical ecology, which blames humanity for disturbing the natural homeostasis, is that, in it, a self-relating reversal of this logic of exclusion takes place: the "excrement," the destructive element which has to disappear so that the balance can be re-established, is ultimately *humanity itself*. As a result of its hubris, its will to dominate and exploit nature, humanity has become the stain in the picture of the natural idyll (as in those narratives in which ecological catastrophe is seen as the revenge of the Mother Earth or Gaia for the wounds inflicted on her by humanity). Is this not the ultimate proof of the ideological nature of ecology? What this means is that there is nothing more distant from a truly radical ecology than the image of a pure idyllic nature cleansed of all human dirt. Perhaps, then, in order to break out of this logic, we should change the very coordinates of the relationship between humanity and prehuman nature: humanity *is* anti-nature, it *does* intervene in the natural cycle, disturbing or controlling it "artificially," postponing the inevitable degeneration, buying itself time. Nevertheless, as such, it is still part of nature, since "there is no nature." If Nature conceived as the balanced cycle of Life is a human fantasy, then humanity is (closest to) nature precisely when it brutally establishes its division from nature, imposes on it its own temporary, limited order, creating its own "sphere" within the natural multiplicity.[12] Do we not find a similar logic in the radical-revolutionary imaginary? In a song originally part of *The Measure Taken*, but later left out, Brecht proposes to identify the revolutionary agent with the cannibal who ate the last of the cannibals in order to annihilate cannibalism —the Chorus sings of the wish to be the last bit of dirt in the room, which, in the final gesture of erasing itself, will make the entire space clean.

Cinema at its worst tries to fill this void not by way of fiction, but by directly depicting the excluded dirt. For example, the worst moment of vulgarity in *Schindler's List* occurs when Spielberg could not resist the temptation of directly staging the moment of Schindler's ethical transformation from a cold manipulator of the misfortunes of others to a subject overwhelmed by a sense of responsibility towards the Jews. The transformation occurs when Schindler, out on a morning ride with his mistress on a hill above Cracow, observes German units entering the Jewish ghetto. The moment of ethical awareness is accompanied by the shots of the little Jewish girl in the red coat (in a black-and-white film). This depiction is properly obscene and blasphemous: it encroaches in a vulgar way upon the abyssal mystery of the sudden rise of goodness, trying to establish a causal link where a gap should be left open. A similar vulgarity occurs

12 The ideological aspect of ecology should also be denounced in relation to architecture. Architecture should be in harmony with its natural environment? But architecture is by definition anti-nature, an act of delimitation against nature: one draws a line separating inside from outside, clearly stating to nature, "Stay outside! The inside is a domain from which you are excluded!"—the Inside is a de-naturalized space to be filled with artifacts. The effort to harmonize architecture with the rhythms of nature is a secondary phenomenon, an attempt to obliterate the traces of the original founding crime.

in *Pollock*, a film which likewise failed to resist a temptation, in this case that of depicting the very moment of the invention of action painting. Predictably enough, the drunken Pollock accidentally spills a jug of paint onto a canvas, and, surprised by the complex and strangely attractive stain that results, gets an idea for a new technique. The value of this vulgar account of the mysterious moment of creation is the same as that of Jonathan Swift's ironic account of the birth of language: at first, in order to inform others about absent objects, people carried on their backs small replicas of all objects, until someone came up with the ingenious idea of replacing the models with words designating the objects.

The relationship between reality and fiction also holds for substance and subject: true, substance is always already a subject, it emerges only retroactively, through its subjective mediation; nonetheless, we should distinguish them—the subject always, constitutively, comes second, it refers to an already given Substance, introducing into it abstract distinctions and fictions, tearing apart its organic unity. This is why, while we can interpret the Spinozan substance as the "subject at work," there is in Spinoza no subject at a distance from Substance.

If the limit has priority over what is beyond it, then all there is is (phenomenal) reality and its limitation. There is nothing beyond the limit, or, more precisely, what is beyond the limit coincides with the limit itself; this coinciding of the limit with its beyond means that the Beyond has always already passed over into the process of becoming which generates determinate (phenomenal) entities. In other words, the Beyond is like Hegel's pure Being: always already reflected/mediated, passed-over into becoming. The limit is thus not merely negative, it is the productive negativity which generates determinate reality; alternatively: negation is always already the negation of negation, the productive movement of its own disappearing.

What is beyond the limit, beyond the screen which denies us (protects us from) any direct access to the In-itself? There is only one convincing answer: what is "really" beyond the limit, on the other side of the screen, is not nothing, but rather *the same reality we find in front of the screen*. Think of a theater stage and all the machinery behind it used to generate the staged illusion: what really accounts for the latter is not this machinery as such but the frame which delimits the "magic" space of the stage from the "ordinary" reality off-stage; if we want to explore the mystery of the illusion by going backstage, we will discover there exactly the same ordinary reality as exists in front of stage. (The proof is that, even if the backstage machinery is totally visible, as in some theaters, the staged reality is still generated.) What counts is that one part of ordinary reality is separated from the rest by a frame which designates it as a magical space of illusion. We have one and the same reality, separated from itself (or, rather, redoubled) by a screen. This inversion-into-itself by way of which reality encounters itself on a fantasmatic stage is what compels us to abandon the univocity of being:

the field of (what we experience as) reality is always traversed by a cut which inscribes appearance into appearance itself. In other words, if there is a field of reality, then it is not enough to claim that reality is inherently fantasmatic, that it is always constituted by a transcendental frame; this frame has to inscribe itself into the field of reality, in the guise of a difference between "ordinary" reality and the ethereal reality: within our experience of reality (structured by fantasy), a part of reality has to appear to us as "fantasmatic," as not "real reality."

Recall the scene, from *Vertigo*, of Scottie's and Judy's first date (at Ernie's again, as with Madeleine), where the couple fails to engage in a meaningful conversation. All of a sudden, Scottie's gaze fixes on some point behind Judy, and we see that he is looking at a woman vaguely similar to Madeleine, dressed in the same gray gown. When Judy notices what has attracted Scottie's gaze, she is, of course, deeply hurt. The crucial moment here is when we see, from Scottie's point of view, the two women in the same shot: Judy on the right, close to him, the woman in gray to the left, in the background. Again, we have vulgar reality side-by-side with an ethereal apparition of the ideal. The split from the shot of Midge and the portrait of Carlotta is here externalized onto two different persons: Judy close up and the momentary spectral apparition of Madeleine behind—with the additional irony, missed by Scottie, that the vulgar Judy *is* in fact the Madeleine he is desperately seeking among the fleeting appearances of strangers. This brief moment in which Scottie is deluded into thinking that what he sees is Madeleine is the moment at which *the Absolute appears*: it appears "as such" in the very domain of appearances, in those sublime moments when a supra-sensible dimension "shines through" in our ordinary reality. When Plato introduces three ontological levels (Ideas, their material copies, and copies of these copies) and dismisses art as the "copy of a copy," what gets lost is that the Idea can only emerge in the distance that separates our ordinary material reality (the second level) from its copy. When we copy a material object, *what* we actually copy, what our copy refers to, is never this particular object itself but its Idea. It is similar to a mask which engenders a third reality, a ghost in the mask which is not the face hidden beneath it. In this precise sense, the Idea is the appearance *as* appearance (as Hegel and Lacan put it): the Idea is something that *appears* when reality (the first-level copy or imitation of the Idea) is itself copied. It is that which is in the copy more than the original itself. No wonder that Plato reacted in such a panicky way against the threat of art: as Lacan pointed out in his *Seminar XI*, art (as the copy of a copy) does not compete with material objects as "direct," first-level copies of the Idea; rather, it competes with the supra-sensible Idea itself. We should take this redoubling of reality in the strongest sense, as a fundamental feature of the ontology of our world: every field of reality contains an enframed, separated, part which is not experienced as fully real, but as fiction.

Does this cut in the univocity of being, this necessity of supplementing "ordinary reality" with fiction, demonstrate that lack is primordial with regard to curvature? One can easily generate curvature from lack and vice versa. On the one hand, we can conceive curvature (the rotary movement of the drive) as a way of avoiding the deadlock of primordial lack. What comes first is the lack: the incestuous Object of desire is always missing, it eludes the subject's grasp, all that desire can catch are the metonymies of the Thing, never the Thing itself. However, this repeated failure to reach the Thing can be inverted into success if the source of enjoyment is defined not as reaching the Thing, but as the satisfaction brought about by the repeated effort to arrive at it. This brings us to the Freudian drive, whose true aim is not its goal (object), but the repeated attempt to reach it (for example, what brings satisfaction in the oral drive is not its object [milk], but the repeated act of sucking). We can thus conceive curvature, its circular movement, as ontologically secondary, as a way of turning the failure of desire into success.

On the other hand, in a Deleuzian mode, one can conceive the experience of lack itself as a kind of perspectival illusion, as a misrecognition of the rotary movement of the drive. In this case, what comes first, the primordial fact, is the rotary movement of the drive, and desire emerges from a teleological misreading of the drive, as if its circular movement does not bring satisfaction in itself but has to be read as a reaction to some primordial lack.[13] What, then, comes first, lack or curvature? Hegel or Spinoza? This choice is a trap to be avoided: one should insist that the alternative "lack or curvature" is a kind of primordial diffraction, a parallax with no priority.

It is precisely apropos the topic of the *clinamen* that the gap separating Hegel from Spinoza can be formulated. Spinozan Substance can be conceived as the productive force which generates the multiplicity of *clinamina*, and which is as such a virtual entity totally immanent to its products, present and actual only in its products, in *clinamina*. For Hegel, however, the actually existing plurality of clinamina presupposes a more radical "clinamen"—a reversal or negativity—in the Substance itself (which is why Substance has to be conceived also as subject). To put it in Gnostic terms, the Fall, the gap between God and reality, presupposes a prior reversal in God himself. The example of alternative modernities will help make this clear: for a Spinozan, the plurality of modernities expresses the productive power of the capitalist social Substance, while for a Hegelian, there is a plurality of modernities because the capitalist social Substance is in itself "perverted," antagonistic. So why is there something rather than nothing?

13 Deleuze provided many wonderful descriptions of this reversal, in particular in his essay on Kafka, where he reads the inaccessible transcendence (of the Court or Castle) the hero tries (and fails) to reach as an inverted misperception of the surplus of immanent productivity over its object.

Because nothing itself is divided into two (the "false" and the "true" vacuum, to put it in the terms of quantum physics)—it is this tension or gap in the void which pushes it towards generating somethings.[14]

How, then, are we to think together the two moments of negativity united in the German word *Verneinung*, the Freudo-Spinozan *ver* (*clinamen* and other forms of displacement) and the more radical Hegelian *nein* (cut, negation, void)? What if the two dimensions are brought together in Lacan's formula $-*a*, which conjoins the void or negativity of the subject and the stain that blurs reality? *Ver* stands for the anamorphic distortion of reality, for the stain which inscribes the subject into reality, and *nein* is the gap, hole, in reality. They are two sides of the same coin, or, rather, the opposite sides of a Möbius band: the correlation of the empty place and the excessive object. There is no gap without a protraction or distortion of reality (no subject without its objectal counterpart), and vice versa, every anamorphic distortion of reality bears witness to a subject.

Is it then possible to describe some kind of underlying structure which allows us to generate the alternative of lack and curvature? It is here, perhaps, that the distinction between the two vacuums, the "false" one and the "real" one, can be of some use insofar as it renders a minimal structure of imbalance, of a gap that divides a thing from itself, which can be operationalized in the direction either of the "false" vacuum (full peace as the unattainable goal) or of the "true" vacuum (the balance of the circular movement). Perhaps this gap separating the two vacuums is then the ultimate word (or one of them, at least) that we can pronounce on the universe: a kind of primordial ontological dislocation or *différance* on account of which, no matter how peaceful things may appear *sub specie aeternitatis*, the universe is out of joint and *eppur si muove*.[15] So it is not enough to say, in a radical reading of Spinoza, that Substance is nothing but the process of its *clinamen*—here, Substance remains One, a Cause immanent to its effects. Here we should take a step further and reverse the relationship: there is no Substance, only the Real as the absolute gap, non-identity, and particular phenomena (modes) are Ones, so many attempts to stabilize this gap. (What this also means is that the Real at its most radical is not a contingent encounter: the encounter is how the Real—the Real of the absolute gap—returns within the constituted reality as its symptomal point of impossibility.)

This notion of two vacuums, however, brings us back to Hegel, to the gap between Substance and Subject hinted at in the famous formula about the

14 For a detailed elaboration of the notion of two vacuums, see the last chapter of the present book.

15 Although one should add that, in his theologico-political turn relating the process of *différance* to the impossible point of Messianic Justice, Derrida has privileged the side of desire/lack, conceiving the process of *différance* as always failed and lacking with regard to the goal of Messianic Justice which, like democracy, always remains "to come."

Absolute being "not *only* a Substance, but *also* a Subject." The Hegelian totality is not the ideal of an organic Whole, but a critical notion—to locate a phenomenon in its totality does not mean to see the hidden harmony of the Whole, but to include in a system all its "symptoms," antagonisms, and inconsistencies as integral parts. On this reading, the "false vacuum" designates the existing organic Whole, with its deceitful stability and harmony, while the true vacuum integrates into this Whole all the destabilizing excesses which are necessary for its reproduction (and which ultimately bring about its ruin). The Hegelian dialectical process thus functions as a repetitive undermining of a "false vacuum" by a "true" one, as a repetitive shift from Substance to Subject. At its most radical, this gap appears as the minimal ethical contrast between Buddhism and Hegelian dialectics, between the attainment of peace (the primordial Void, Symmetry, Balance, Harmony, or whatever it is called) and the persistent *eppur si muove*. Buddhism thus provides a radical answer to *the* question "Why is there something and not nothing?": there *is* only Nothing, nothing "really exists," all "somethings," all determinate entities, emerge only from a subjective perspectival illusion. Dialectical materialism here goes a step further: *even Nothing does not exist*—if by "Nothing" we mean the primordial abyss in which all differences are obliterated. What, ultimately, "there is" is only the absolute Difference, the self-repelling Gap.

In order to grasp the radical link between the subject and nothingness (the Void), one should be very precise in reading Hegel's famous statement on substance and the subject: it is not enough to emphasize that the subject is not a positively existing self-identical entity, that it stands for the incompleteness of substance, for its inner antagonism and movement, for the Nothingness which thwarts the substance from within, destroying its unity, and thus dynamizes it—the notion best rendered by Hegel's remark, apropos the "unrest" of substantial unity, that the Self is this very unrest ("*eben diese Unruhe ist das Selbst*"). This notion of the subject still presupposes the substantial One as a starting point, even if this One is always already distorted, split, and so on. And it is this very presupposition that should be abandoned: at the beginning (even if it is a mythical one), there is no substantial One, but Nothingness itself; every One comes second, emerges through the self-relating of this Nothingness. In other words, Nothing as negation is not primarily the negation of something, of a positive entity, but the negation of itself.

Hegel formulated this crucial insight at the beginning of the second book of his *Logic* (on "Essence"), when he deals with the logic of reflection.[16] Hegel begins

16 As we saw in Chapter 5, many interpreters of Hegel—exemplarily Dieter Henrich in his classic essay "Hegels Logik der Reflexion" (in *Hegel im Kontext*, Frankfurt: Suhrkamp 2010)—have argued that this part of *Logic*, which articulates the triad of positing-external-determining reflection, provides the basic matrix for the dialectical process as such.

with the opposition, constitutive of the notion of essence, between essence and its appearing in the illusory being (*Schein*): "The immediacy of the determinateness in illusory being over against essence is consequently nothing other than essence's own immediacy"[17]—beneath the flux of the illusory being (of appearing: *Schein*), there is no substantial self-identical Essence: the immediacy of illusory appearing overlaps with the immediacy of the non-illusory substance, of its "true" being; or, in Lacanian terms, "essence is this structure in which the most interior is conjoined to the most exterior in its turning."[18] What this means is that all there is is the flux of illusory being, of its passing determinations, and the nothingness beneath it:

> These two moments, namely the nothingness, but as persisting [*Bestehen*], and the being, but as a moment, or the negativity in itself and the reflected immediacy, that constitute the moments of illusory being, are thus *moments of the essence itself*; what we have here is not an illusory show of being *in* essence, or an illusory show of essence *in* being; the illusory being in essence is not the illusory being of an other, but is *illusory being in itself, the illusory being of essence itself*. Illusory being is essence itself in the determinateness of being.[19]

Hegel had already made this claim in his *Phenomenology*, where he stated that the supra-sensible essence is appearance as appearance; it is that which is in the copy more than the original itself.

The Hegelian Subject

This brings us back to the statement on substance and subject from the "Introduction" to the *Phenomenology*: Hegel does not simply say that "Substance is Subject"—what he says is that one should not conceive the Absolute "*only* as Substance, but *also* as Subject." The Subject is thus not merely a subordinated moment of Substance, of the substantial totality; but neither is Substance directly the Subject, so that we should not assert their immediate identity. ("Substance—the Origin of everything, its founding principle—is the productive power of self-relating negativity which is the core of subjectivity"; that is, Substance in its actuality is nothing but *the subject at work*.) The Subject is always already related to some heterogeneous substantial content, it always comes second, as

17 Hegel, *Hegel's Science of Logic*, p. 397.

18 Jacques-Alain Miller, "A Reading of the Seminar *From an Other to the other*," *lacanian ink* 29 (Spring 2007), p. 17.

19 Hegel, *Hegel's Science of Logic*, pp. 397–8. A. V. Miller's otherwise excellent translation has been corrected in a few places in the quotations that follow.

the negation or mediation of this content, as its splitting or distortion, and this secondary character should be maintained to the end, the subject should never be directly elevated into the grounding Principle of all reality.

This "restraining" of the subject—the idea that Hegel's Substance = Subject works as an "infinite judgment" of two incompatible terms and not as a full subjectivization of Substance, not as the direct assertion of the Subject as the productive ground of all reality, as the agent which "swallows up" or appropriates all there is—should *not* be read as a half-baked compromise, in the sense of "too much subjectivity is self-destructive, so we must maintain the proper measure." Such a compromised position is not only philosophically naïve, but outright wrong: *the move towards "restraining" the subject equals the full assertion of subjectivity*, since, at its most elementary, the "subject" is not a substantial agent generating all reality, but precisely the moment of cut, failure, finitude, illusion, "abstraction." "Not only as Substance, but also as Subject" does *not* mean simply that Substance is "really" a force of subjective self-mediation, etc., but that Substance is in itself ontologically flawed, incomplete. This is what Hegel clearly saw, against the "subjectivist" tradition which peaks in Fichte's notion of the self-positing of the absolute I: the subject does not come first, it is not a new name for the One which grounds all, but the name for the inner impossibility or self-blockage of the One.

What this means is that illusion is necessary, that it is inherent to truth: *la vérité surgit de la méprise* ("truth arises out of misrecognition"), as Lacan at his most Hegelian put it, and this is what the Spinozan cannot accept. What the Spinozan can and does think is the necessity of error; what he cannot accept is error or misrecognition as immanent to truth and prior to it—epistemologically and ontologically, the process has to begin with error, and truth can only emerge second, as a *repeated error*, as it were. Why? Because, as we have seen apropos Understanding and Reason, truth (Reason) is not a correction of error (of the unilateral abstractions of Understanding); truth is *error as such*, what we effectively do when we commit (perceive ourselves as committing) an error, so that error lies in the very gaze which perceives the act as an error. In other words, Hegel's "Substance as Subject" should thus be read in a way homologous to Lacan's re-reading of Freud's famous formula *wo es war soll ich werden*, which also should not be interpreted as a demand for the simple subjectivization of the unconscious substance ("I should appropriate my unconscious"), but as the recognition of my place within it, of how the subject exists only through the inconsistency of the unconscious.

To recapitulate, the Hegelian motif of Substance as Subject means that the Absolute qua Real is not simply different or differentiated from finite entities—the Absolute is *nothing but* this difference. At its most elementary, the Real is non-identity itself: the impossibility for X to be(come) "fully itself." The Real is not the external intruder or obstacle preventing the realization of X's identity with itself, but the absolutely immanent impossibility of this identity. It is not that X cannot fully realize itself as X because an external obstacle hinders it—the impossibility comes first, and the external obstacle ultimately just materializes this impossibility. As such, the Real is opaque, inaccessible, out of reach, *and* undeniable, impossible to by-pass or remove—in it, lack and surplus coincide. This overlapping *seems* foreign to dialectics: its coincidence of opposites appears to be not of the same nature as the reversals and mediations of the dialectical process. The Real is rather the opaque-indeterminate, abyssal, pre-logical Background that is always already there, presupposed by every properly dialectical process. No wonder that the philosopher who first comes to mind here is Schelling, who, in his critique of Hegel's "negative" philosophy, thematized the pre-logical Ground of Being as a positivity which is opaque and simultaneously unavoidable. But is this really so?

The Hegelian wager is that the dialectical process retroactively posits this presupposed Background as a sign of its own incompleteness. That is to say, in Hegel, the beginning has the status of the Lacanian Real, which is always already lost, left behind, mediated, and so on, and yet simultaneously something we can never get rid of, something which forever insists, continues to haunt us. For example, *jouissance* as real is lost for those who dwell in the symbolic order, is never given directly and so forth; however, the very loss of enjoyment generates an enjoyment of its own, a surplus-enjoyment (*plus-de-jouir*), so that *jouissance* is simultaneously something always already lost and something we cannot ever rid ourselves of. What Freud called the compulsion to repeat is grounded in this radically ambiguous status of the Real: what repeats itself is the Real itself, which, lost from the very beginning, persists in returning again and again.

Does not the Hegelian beginning have the same status, especially when he deals with the beginning of philosophy? It seems to repeat itself again and again: Oriental spirituality, Parmenides, Spinoza—all stand for the inaugural gesture of philosophy which has to be left behind if we are to progress on the long road from Substance to Subject. However, this beginning is not an obstacle pulling us back, but the very motif or instigator of "development": the true development, the passage to a new level, occurs only through settling accounts with the inaugural gesture again and again. The beginning is thus what Fichte called *Anstoss*: obstacle and incitement at the same time. The inaugural gesture always repeats itself in a new guise: the Oriental beginning (China and India, the first version of *Being and Nothingness*) stands for the pre-philosophical abyss of chaotic mythology; Parmenides stands for the philosophical beginning proper, the break with mythology and the conceptual assertion of the One; while Spinoza designates the modern beginning (Substance as the container of thriving multiplicities).

Why is Parmenides, who asserts that only Being, the One, exists, not Oriental? Why is he the first Western philosopher? The difference is not at the level of content, but at the level of form: Parmenides says the same as the Orientals, but he *says* it in conceptual form. By stating that "Being is and non-Being is not," by affirming the unity of being and thinking, he introduces difference, a minimal formal mediation, into the One, in contrast to Oriental One which is totally abyssal, which neither is nor is not.[20] The difference between Oriental thought and Parmenides's is thus the difference between the In-itself and the For-itself: Parmenides is the first "dogmatic" in Chesterton's sense. Chesterton wrote *Orthodoxy* as a reply to the critics of his previous book, *Heretics* (1908); in the very last paragraph of "Concluding Remarks on the Importance of Orthodoxy," the last chapter of *Heretics*, he says:

> Truths turn into dogmas the instant that they are disputed. Thus every man who utters a doubt defines a religion. And the scepticism of our time does not really destroy the beliefs, rather it creates them; gives them their limits and their plain and defiant shape. We who are Liberals once held Liberalism lightly as a truism. Now it has been disputed, and we hold it fiercely as a faith. We who believe in patriotism once thought patriotism to be reasonable, and thought little more about it. Now we know it to be unreasonable, and know it to be right. We who are Christians never knew the great philosophic common sense which inheres in that mystery until the anti-Christian writers pointed it out to us. The great march of mental destruction will go on. Everything will be denied. Everything will become a creed. It is a reasonable position to deny the stones in the street; it will be a religious dogma to assert them.[21]

This is a profoundly Hegelian insight: one should not confuse dogma with the immediate pre-reflexive acceptance of an attitude. Medieval Christians were not "dogmatic" (just as it is senseless to say that the ancient Greeks "dogmatically" believed in Zeus and other Olympian divinities: they were simply part of their life world), they became "dogmatic" only when modern Reason started to doubt religious truths. A "dogmatic" stance is always already mediated by its opposite, and this is also why contemporary fundamentalism really is "dogmatic": it clings to its articles of faith against the threat of modern secular rationalism. In short, "dogma" is already the result of the decomposition of a substantial organic Whole. Hegel describes this decomposition as a twofold movement. First, there

---

20 What we encounter here is again the retroactive blurring of articulations, i.e., the transformation of the past into a formless matter: for Hegel, what we have before Parmenides is a chaotic multiplicity without any proper inner conceptual articulation, like the arbitrary mixture of objects (gods, animals, symbols, etc.) in Indian mythology.

21 G. K. Chesterton, *Heretics*, New York: John Lane 1905, p. 304.

is the "autonomization" of what were originally only accidental predicates of the Substance—recall the famous passage from the *Phenomenology*:

> The circle that remains self-enclosed and, like substance, holds its moments together, is an immediate relationship, one therefore which has nothing astonishing about it. But that the accidental as such, detached from what circumscribes it, what is bound and is actual only in its context with others, should attain an existence of its own and a separate freedom—this is the tremendous power of the negative.[22]

Second, there is the opposite autonomization of substantial unity itself: Substance no longer functions as the container, the mediating unity, of its particular content, but instead posits or asserts itself as the negative unity of that content, as the power of destruction of all its particular determinations—this negativity lies at the base of spiritual freedom, since spirit is, "formally speaking, *freedom*, the concept's absolute negativity or self-identity. Considered as this formal aspect, it may withdraw itself by abstracting from everything exterior and from its own externality, its very existence."[23] This self-relating negativity of substance, its self-contraction to an empty point, is *singularity* as opposed to particularity. The speculative point here is to think these two moves together: accidents of a substance can attain an existence of their own, cut off from their substantial Whole, only insofar as Substance itself reduces or contracts itself to the point of singularity. The gap, the loosening of the links, between Substance and its accidents (particular determinations) presupposes the radical "contradiction," at the very heart of Substance itself, between its fullness and its void, between its all-inclusiveness and its all-excluding self-relationship, between S and $ (the subject as "barred" Substance, Substance dispossessed of its content). The concrete expression of this link is the speculative identity between the subject (the void of self-relating negativity) and an accidental aspect of Substance autonomized into an "organ without a body": this "partial object" is the correlate of the "pure" subject. The subject is to be opposed here to what we usually refer to as the "person": "person" stands for the substantial wealth of a Self, while the subject is this substance contracted to the singular point of negative self-relating. One should bear in mind here that the two couples, subject-object and person-thing, form a Greimasian semiotic square. That is to say, if we take the "subject" as the starting point, it has two opposites: its contrary (counterpart) is, of course, the "object," but its "contradiction" is the "person" (the "pathological"

22 G. W. F. Hegel, *Phenomenology of Spirit*, trans. A. V. Miller, Oxford: Oxford University Press, 1977, pp. 18–19.

23 As quoted in Malabou, *The Future of Hegel*, p. 160, which is modified from the translation in G. W. F. Hegel, *Philosophy of Mind*, trans. William Wallace, Oxford: Clarendon Press 1971, §382.

wealth of inner life as opposed to the void of pure subjectivity). In a symmetrical way, the opposite counterpart to a "person" is a "thing," and its "contradiction" is the subject. "Thing" is something embedded in a concrete life world, in which the entire wealth of the meaning of the life world echoes, while "object" is an "abstraction," something extracted from its embeddedness in the life world.

The subject is not the correlate of a thing (or, more precisely, a body): a person dwells in a body, while the subject is the correlate of a (partial) object, of an organ without a body. Against the standard notion of person-thing as a life-world totality from which the subject-object couple is extrapolated, one should thus insist on the subject-object couple (in Lacanese: \$-*a*, the barred subject coupled with the *objet petit a*) as primordial—the couple person-thing is its secondary "domestication." What gets lost in the passage from subject-object to person-thing is the twisted relationship of the Möbius band: "persons" and "things" are part of the same reality, while the object is the impossible equivalent of the subject itself. We arrive at the object when we pursue the side of the subject (of its signifying representation) on the Möbius track to the end and find ourselves on the other side of the same place from where we started. One should thus reject the topic of the personality as a soul-body unity or organic Whole which is dismembered in the process of reification and alienation: the subject emerges out of the person as the product of the violent reduction of the person's body to a partial object.[24]

So when Hegel writes that the concept is a "free subjective concept that is for itself and therefore possesses *personality*—the practical, objective concept determined in and for itself which, as person, is impenetrable atomic subjectivity," he may appear to be creating a meaningless short-circuit between the abstract-logical domain of concepts, of notional determinations, and the psychological domain of personality, of actual persons.[25] However, upon a closer look, one can clearly see his point: personality in its "impenetrable atomic subjectivity," the abyss or void of the "I" beyond all my positive properties, is a *conceptual* singularity: it is the "actually existing" abstraction of the concept; i.e., in it, the negative power of the concept acquires actual existence, becomes "for itself." And Lacan's \$, the "barred subject," is precisely such a conceptual singularity,

---

24 One should also bear in mind here how the Freudian notion of the "partial object" is not that of an element or constituent of the body, but of an organ which *resists* its inclusion within the Whole of a body. This object, which is the correlate of the subject, is the subject's stand-in within the order of objectivity: it is the proverbial "piece of flesh," that part of the subject that the subject had to renounce in order to emerge as subject. Is this not what Marx was aiming at when he wrote about the rise of the class consciousness of the proletariat? Proletarian subjectivity only emerges when the worker is reduced to an equivalent of money, selling the commodity "labor-power" on the market.

25 Hegel, *Hegel's Science of Logic*, p. 824. Translation slightly modified.

a singularity devoid of any psychological content. It is in this precise sense that Hegel writes: "The singular individual is, on its own terms, the transition of the category from its concept into external reality; it is pure schema itself."[26] Every word carries its full weight in this precise and condensed proposition. The subject in its uniqueness, far from standing for the singularity of existence irreducible to any universal notion (an idea varied endlessly by Kierkegaard in his critique of Hegel), stands for precisely the opposite: the way the universality of a notion passes over into "external reality," acquires actual existence as part of this temporal reality. The properly dialectical twist here is, of course, that universality acquires actual existence in the guise of its very opposite, of the retraction of the multiplicity of reality into pure singularity. Since external reality is defined by its spatio-temporal coordinates, the subject in his or her actuality has to exist in time, as the self-sublation of space in time; and since he or she is the notion that acquires temporal existence, this temporality can only be that of a "schema" in Kant's sense of the term, namely the *a priori* temporal form that mediates between the atemporal conceptual universality and the spatio-temporal "external reality." Consequently, since external reality is correlative to the subject that constitutes it transcendentally, this subject is the "pure schema" of this reality—*not* simply its transcendental horizon, the frame of *a priori* categories of Reason, but its *schema*, the *a priori* form of temporal finitude itself, *the temporal horizon of the atemporal a priori itself.* Therein resides the paradox (which Heidegger was the first to identify—in his *Kant and the Problem of Metaphysics*): the pure I as the agent of transcendental synthesis is not "above" atemporal categories of reason, but the "schema" of temporal finitude which delineates the field of their application.

But is not this subject which, through transcendental synthesis, "sutures" reality into a consistent Whole, a new version of Identity embracing its opposite? Is not radical negativity here turned into the ground of a new identity? There is a parallel between Foucault's critique of Derrida's reading of Descartes's *cogito*, and the standard "postmodern" critique of the Hegelian notion of contradiction, of the series difference-opposition-contradiction. For Foucault, Descartes (and, following him, Derrida) progresses from madness to universal doubt as a more "radical" version of madness, so that he can then self-cancel it in the rational *cogito*. Foucault's counter-argument is that madness is not less but *more* radical than the notion of universal doubt, that the passage from madness to dream silently *excludes* the unbearable excess of madness. In a homologous way, Hegel appears to "radicalize" difference in opposition, and then opposition in contradiction; however, this "progress" effectively cancels what is really troubling in the notion of difference for a monist philosopher: the notion of radical

26 As quoted in Malabou, *The Future of Hegel*, p. 18, modified from Miller's translation in Hegel, *Phenomenology of Spirit*, p. 143 (§236).

heterogeneity, of a totally contingent external otherness which cannot be related dialectically to the inwardness of the One. With the passage from (the simple external) difference (of *indifferent* units) to opposition (which already inherently relates the opposed units) and then to contradiction (in which the gap is posited *within* the One, as its inherent split, or self-inconsistency), the road is prepared for the self-sublating of the difference and for the return to the One able to internalize and thus "dialectically mediate" all differences.

Laclau also follows this line of critique when, in dealing with the Real, he seems to oscillate between the formal notion of Real as antagonism and the more "empirical" notion of the Real as that which cannot be reduced to a formal opposition: "the opposition A-B will never fully become A-not A. The 'B-ness' of the B will be ultimately non-dialectizable. The 'people' will always be something more than the pure opposite of power. There is a Real of the 'people' which resists symbolic integration."[27] The crucial question, of course, is: what, exactly, is the character of this excess of the "people" that is "more than the pure opposite of power," *what* in the "people" resists symbolic integration? Is it simply the wealth of its (empirical or other) determinations? If this is the case, then we are *not* dealing with a Real that resists symbolic integration, because the Real here is precisely the antagonism A-not A, so that "that which is in B more than not A" is not the Real in B but B's symbolic determinations. Since Laclau, of course, fully admits that every One-ness is split by an inherent gap, the dilemma is this: is the inherent impossibility of the One achieving full self-identity the result of the fact that it is always affected by heterogeneous Others, or is the One's being-affected by Others an indication of how it is split or thwarted in itself? The only way to "save the Real" is to assert the primacy of the inner split: the primordial fact is the One's inner impediment; the heterogeneous Others merely materialize, or occupy the place of, that impediment—which is why, even if they are annihilated, the impossibility (of the One reaching its full self-identity) remains. In other words, if the intrusion of heterogeneous Others were the primary fact, the annihilation of these external obstacles would allow the One to realize its full self-identity.[28]

---

27 Ernesto Laclau, *On Populist Reason*, London: Verso Books 2005, p. 152.

28 The Lacanian "logic of the signifier" even compels us to go a step further and assert that the self-identity of an entity itself implies this entity's inner split or impediment: "self-identity" involves the reflexive gesture of identifying an entity with the void of its structural place, the void filled in by the signifier identifying this entity—"A = A" can occur only within the symbolic order, where the identity of A is guaranteed-constituted by the "unary feature" that marks (stands for) the void in its core. "You are John" means: the core of your identity is the abyssal *je ne sais quoi* designated by your name. So it is not only that every identity is always thwarted, fragile, fictitious (as the postmodern "deconstructionist" mantra goes): *identity itself* is stricto sensu the mark of its opposite, of its own lack, of the fact that the entity asserted as self-identical *lacks* full identity.

Absolute Knowing

It is only this speculative notion of identity which enables us to fully grasp the thrust of Hegel's critique of Kant, namely his rejection of the need for an *a priori* formal-transcendental frame as a measure or standard which would allow us to judge from the outside the validity of all content (cognitive, ethical, or aesthetic): "we do not need to import criteria, or to make use of our own bright ideas and thoughts during the course of the inquiry; it is precisely when we leave these aside that we succeed in contemplating the matter at hand as it is *in and for itself*."[29] This is what Hegel means by "absolute" Idealism: not the magical ability of Spirit to generate all content, but Spirit's thorough passivity: adopting the stance of "Absolute Knowing," the subject does not ask if the content (some particular object of inquiry) meets some a priori standard (of truth, goodness, beauty); it lets the content measure itself, by its own immanent standards, and thus self-authorizes itself. The stance of "Absolute Knowing" thus fully coincides with thorough (absolute) historicism: there is no transcendental "big Other," there are no criteria that we can apply to historical phenomena to judge them; all such criteria must be immanent to the phenomena themselves. It is against this background that one should understand the "near-Kafkaesque" (Pippin) claim in Hegel's *Aesthetics* that a portrait of a person can be "more like the individual than the actual individual himself":[30] what this implies is that the person itself is never fully "itself," that it does not coincide with its concept.

Such a notion of Absolute Knowing is grounded already in Hegel's definition of Self-Consciousness, in the passage from Consciousness to Self-Consciousness (in the *Phenomenology*). Consciousness first experiences a failure to grasp the In-itself: the In-itself repeatedly eludes the subject, all content supposed to pertain to the In-itself reveals itself as having been put there by the subject itself, so that the subject becomes increasingly caught up in the web of its own phantasmagorias. The subject passes from the attitude of Consciousness to that of Self-Consciousness when it reflexively assumes this failure as a positive result, inverting the problem into its own solution: the subject's world *is* the result of its own "positing."[31] This is also how Hegel resolves the apparent contradiction between the reflexivity of modern art and the rise of "still life" or landscape painting, that is, depictions of nature at its most "spiritless": his solution is that the proper object of attention

29 Hegel, *Phenomenology of Spirit*, p. 54.

30 G. W. F. Hegel, *Aesthetics: Lectures on Fine Arts*, Vol. 2, Oxford: Clarendon Press 1975, pp. 866–7.

31 Does Adorno not make a similar point when he claims that the Kantian transcendental constitution is a misnomer, or, more precisely, a positive spin given to a limitation, namely to the fact that the subject is not able to reach beyond its subjective horizon?

is the landscape painting itself, not the natural landscape as such[32]—such paintings are really paintings about painting itself, a visual counterpart to poems or novels about writing literature, for what we admire in a painting of a dead fish on a kitchen table is the artifice of the painter whose mastery is displayed.[33]

Parenthetically, a dead fish is a good example for another, quite different, reason: what renders it uncanny are its eyes, which continue to stare at us, and lead us to a further consequence Hegel draws, which is more daring, almost surrealistic. Even when a painting depicts natural objects, it is always about spirit, the material appearing of spirit. There is, however, a privileged organ of the human body in which spirit reverberates most directly: the eye as the "window into the human soul," as the object which, when we look into it, confronts us with the abyss of the person's inner life. The conclusion from these two premises is that, insofar as art creates natural objects which are "ensouled" (*beseelt*), insofar as, in a painting, all objects become suffused with human meaning, it is as if the artistic treatment transforms every visible surface into an eye, so that, when we look at a painting, we look at a "thousand-eyed Argus."[34] The artwork thus becomes a monstrosity, a multiplicity of eyes staring at us from all sides—hence one can say that artistic beauty is, as Lacan put it in his *Seminar XI*, precisely an attempt to cultivate, to tame, this traumatic dimension of the Other's gaze, to "put the gaze to rest."

And is not what Hegel calls "Absolute Knowing" (*Wissen*, not *Erkenntniss* or knowledge) the end-point of these reversals, when the subject stumbles upon the final limitation, the limitation as such, which can no longer be inverted into a productive self-assertion? Absolute Knowing thus "does not mean 'knowing everything.' It rather means—recognizing one's limitations."[35] "Absolute Knowing" is the final recognition of a limitation which is "absolute" in the sense that it is not determinate or particular, not a "relative" limit or obstacle to our knowledge that we can clearly see and locate as such. It is invisible "as such" because it is the limitation of the entire field as such—that closure of the field which, from within the field itself (and we are always by definition within it, because in a way this field "is" ourselves) cannot but appear as its opposite, as the very openness of the field. The dialectical buck stops here: the subject can no longer play the game

32 G. W. F. Hegel, *Aesthetics: Lectures on Fine Arts*, Vol. 1, Oxford: Clarendon Press 1975, p. 29.

33 This is why, in his *History and Class Consciousness*, Lukács is profoundly Hegelian when he uses "(self-)consciousness" not as a term for passive reception/representation or awareness, but as referring to the unity of intellect and will: "(self-)consciousness" is inherently practical, it changes its subject-object—once the working class arrives at its adequate class consciousness, it changes into an actual revolutionary subject in its social reality.

34 Hegel, *Aesthetics*, Vol. 1, p. 153.

35 Robert C. Solomon, *In the Spirit of Hegel*, Oxford: Oxford University Press 1983, p. 639.

of the "experience of consciousness," comparing the For-us with the In-itself and thereby subverting both of them, since there is no longer any shape of the In-itself available as a measure of the truth of the For-us.

Surprisingly, Hegel here rejoins Fichte's critique of Kant's Thing-in-itself. The problem of the In-itself should thus be radically transformed: if, by the In-itself, we understand the transcendent X to which our representations refer, then this X can only be a void of Nothingness; this, however, in no way implies that there is no real, that there are only our subjective representations. All determinate being is relational, things only are what they are in relation to otherness, or, as Deleuze put it, perspectival distortion is inscribed into the very identity of the thing. The Real is not out there, as the inaccessible transcendent X never reached by our representations; the Real is here, as the obstacle or impossibility which makes our representations flawed, inconsistent. The Real is not the In-itself but the very obstacle which distorts our access to the In-itself, and this paradox provides the key for what Hegel calls "Absolute Knowing."

Absolute Knowing thus takes the impossibility of a meta-language to the extreme. In our ordinary experience, we rely on the distinction between For-us and In-itself: we attempt to draw the line between how things appear to us and how they are in themselves, outside of their relation to us: we distinguish secondary properties of things (which exist only for us, like their color or taste) from their primary properties (shape, and so on) which characterize things as they are in themselves; at the end of this road is the pure mathematical formalism of quantum physics as the only (totally non-intuitive) In-itself accessible to us. This final result, however, simultaneously renders visible the paradox which underlies all distinctions between the In-itself and the For-us: what we posit as the "In-itself" of things is a product of the centuries-long labor of scientific research—in short, a lot of subjective activity (of experimentation, creating new concepts, etc.) is needed to arrive at what is "objective." The two aspects, the In-itself and the For-itself, thus reveal themselves to be dialectically mediated—as Hegel put it, they both (along with their distinction) "fall into consciousness." What Hegel calls "Absolute Knowing" is the point at which the subject fully assumes this mediation, when he abandons the untenable project of taking up a position from which he might compare his subjective experience and the way things are independently of his experience—in other words, Absolute Knowing is a name for the acceptance of the absolute limitation of the circle of our subjectivity, of the impossibility of stepping outside of it. Here, however, we should add a crucial qualification: this acceptance in no way amounts to any kind of (individual or collective) subjectivistic solipsism. We must displace the In-itself from the fetishized "outside" (with regard to subjective mediation) to the very gap between the subjective and the objective (between For-us and In-itself, between appearances and Things-in-themselves). Our knowing is irreducibly "subjective" not because we are forever separated from reality-in-itself, but precisely because we are part of this reality, because we cannot step outside it and observe it "objectively." Far from separating us from reality, the very limitation on our knowing—its inevitably distorted, inconsistent character—bears witness to our inclusion in reality.

It is a commonplace to oppose Hegel's "ridiculous" Absolute Knowing to a modest skeptical approach which recognizes the excess of reality over every conceptualization. What if, however, it is Hegel who is much more modest? What if his Absolute Knowing is the assertion of a radical closure: there is no meta-language, we cannot climb on our own shoulders and see our own limitations, we cannot relativize or historicize ourselves? What really is arrogant, as Chesterton made clear, is precisely such self-relativization, the attitude of "knowing one's limitations," of not agreeing with oneself—as in the proverbial "wise" insight according to which we can only approach reality asymptotically. What Hegel's Absolute Knowing deprives us of is precisely this minimal self-distance, the ability to put ourselves at a "safe distance" from our own location.

This brings us to the difficult question raised by Catherine Malabou in *The Future of Hegel*—that of the historicity of Hegel's own system. There are passages in Hegel (not too many, but numerous enough to be considered systematic) which explicitly belie the notion of the "end of history," demonstrating that he in no way thought that, at his historical moment, history had come to an end. At the very end of his entire "system," in the conclusion to the *Lectures on the History of Philosophy*, he tersely states that this is, *for the time being*, the state of knowledge: "*Dies ist nun der Standpunkt der jetzigen Zeit, und die Reihe der geistigen Gestaltungen ist* für jetzt *damit geschlossen*."[36] ("This is now the standpoint of our time, and the series of spiritual formations is thereby, for now, closed.") Note the triple historical relativization (*now, our time, for now*), an over-insistence which makes the statement almost symptomatic—one thing is sure here: Hegel definitely applied also to himself the well-known lines from the "Preface" to his *Philosophy of Right*:

> As for the individual, every one is a son of his time; so philosophy also is its time apprehended in thoughts. It is just as foolish to fancy that any philosophy can transcend its present world, as that an individual could leap out of his time or jump over Rhodes. If a theory transgresses its time, and builds up a world as it ought to be, it has an existence merely in the unstable element of opinion, which gives room to every wandering fancy.[37]

---

36 G. W. F. Hegel, *Vorlesungen über die Geschichte der Philosophie*, Vol. 3, Leipzig: Philipp Reclam 1971, p. 628.

37 G. W. F. Hegel, *Hegel's Philosophy of Right*, trans. S. W. Dyde, London: George Bell 1896, pp. xxviii–xxix.

Proof abounds that this was not just a formal concession. In the Introduction to *Lectures on the Philosophy of World History*, he concludes that "America is therefore the country of the future, and its world-historical importance has yet to be revealed in the ages that lie ahead,"[38] and he makes a similar statement about Russia: both are "immature" states, states which have not yet reached the full actualization of their historical form. Even in his much-maligned philosophy of nature, he concedes his own historically conditioned limitation: "We must be content with what we can, in fact, comprehend at present. There is plenty that cannot be comprehended yet."[39] In all these cases, Hegel, "for a moment, [takes] an external point of view with respect to the (universally comprehensive) story he is telling and announces that at some later stage a more articulate (universally comprehensive) story will be available"—how, from what position, can he do this?[40] Whence comes this excess or remainder of historicist common sense which relativizes the highest speculative insights? It is clear that there is no space for it *within* the Hegelian philosophical narrative.

Is *this* then the task of a proper "materialist reversal of Hegel": to introduce this self-relativization *into* the "system" itself? To recognize traces which, for us today, *remain* unreadable traces; to recognize the irreducible parallax gap between multiple narratives (of those in power, of those oppressed ...) which cannot be brought together, etc.? What if, however, this conclusion, convincing as it may appear *prima facie*, proceeds all too fast? What if there is no external opposition between the "eternal" System of Knowing and its historicist (self-) relativization? What if this (self-)relativization does not come from outside, but is inscribed in the very heart of the System? The true "non-All" is thus not to be sought in a renunciation of systematicity that pertains to the project of "negative dialectics," in the assertion of finitude, dispersion, contingency, hybridity, multitude, and so forth, but *in the absence of any external limitation that would allow us to construct and/or validate elements with regard to an external measure.* Read in this way, the infamous "closure of the Hegelian system" is strictly correlative to (the obverse of) its thorough (self-)relativization: the "closure" of the System does *not* mean that there is nothing outside the System (the naïve notion of Hegel as the individual who claimed to have achieved "Absolute Knowledge of everything"); it means that *we are forever unable to "reflexivize" this Outside, to inscribe it within the Inside*, even in the purely negative (and deceptively modest,

38 G. W. F. Hegel, *Lectures on the Philosophy of World History—Introduction: Reason in History*, trans. H. B. Nisbet, Cambridge: Cambridge University Press 1975, p. 170.

39 G. W. F. Hegel, *Hegel's Philosophy of Nature*, trans. A. V. Miller, Oxford: Clarendon Press 1970, p. 62.

40 Ermanno Bencivenga, *Hegel's Dialectical Logic*, Oxford: Oxford University Press 2000, p. 75.

self-deprecating) mode of acknowledging that reality is an absolute Otherness which forever eludes our conceptual grasp.

Throughout his *Persistence of Subjectivity*, Pippin distinguishes between the actual, historically limited Hegel, and what he (once) refers to as the "eternal Hegel," by which he means not a trans-historical eternal truth of Hegel, but, rather, the way each post-Hegelian epoch has to reinvent the position of "Absolute Knowing" to ask the question: how would Hegel have conceptualized our predicament, how can one be Hegelian today? For example, Pippin is fully aware that Hegel's answer to the social crisis of his time (his notion of constitutional monarchy organized into "estates") is not "workable" today, does not do the job of bringing about the "reconciliation" of *our* antagonisms; however, what we can elaborate is a Hegelian "reconciliation" (dialectical mediation) of *today's* tensions. Or, in the case of abstract art (arguably Pippin's most brilliant example): of course Hegel did not predict it, there is no theory of abstract art in Hegel's aesthetics; however, one can easily and convincingly extrapolate from Hegel's reflections on the decline of the key role of art in the modern "reflexive" world the notion (and possibility) of abstract art, as a "reflexivization" of art itself, as art questioning and thematizing its own possibility and procedures.

The problem here is whether this distinction between the "actual" Hegel (some of whose solutions are obviously dated) and the "eternal" Hegel introduces a Kantian formalism, in terms of the distinction between Absolute Knowing as a formal procedure of totalized self-reflection, and its contingent, empirically conditioned, historical instantiations. Is not this idea of a form independent of its accidental content profoundly anti-Hegelian? In other words, does not this solution amount to a "historicization" of Hegel whose obverse is the "spurious infinity" of reflexive knowledge: in each epoch, humanity tries to formulate its autonomy, to grasp its predicament; it ultimately fails, but the process goes on, with the formulations getting better and better over time?

How then are we to escape from this deadlock? How to overcome the debilitating alternative of either asserting Hegel's philosophy as the moment of Absolute Knowing in the naïve sense of the term (with Hegel, history reached its end, he basically "knew everything there is to know"), or the no less naïve evolutionist historicization of Hegel in which, while dropping the obviously historically conditioned content of Hegel's thought, the notion of the "eternal Hegel" is retained as a kind of regulative Idea to be approached again and again? The properly dialectical way out is to conceive the gap that separates the "eternal" Hegel from the "empirical" Hegel not as a dialectical tension, not as the gap between the inaccessible Ideal and its imperfect realization, but as an empty, purely formal distance, as an index of their *identity*. That is to say, Hegel's ultimate point is not that, in spite of our limitation, our embeddedness in a contingent historical context, we—or Hegel himself, at least—can somehow overcome this limitation and gain access to Absolute Knowledge (to which historicist relativism then responds that we can never reach this position, that we can only aim at it as at an impossible Ideal). What he calls Absolute Knowing is, on the contrary, the very sign of our total capture—we are *condemned* to Absolute Knowing, we cannot *escape* it, since "Absolute Knowing" means that there is no external point of reference from which we could perceive the relativity of our own "merely subjective" standpoint.

What if, then, we conceive Hegel's Absolute Knowing as an act of "dotting the i" which is simultaneously the closing moment of traditional metaphysics and, by the same token, the opening moment in the extensive field of post-Hegelian thought. It is as if Hegel himself, by way of closing his system, opens up the field for the multiple rejections of his thought. The best way to encapsulate the Hegelian moment of final closure is thus to repeat the formula used by the young Georg Lukács in his *Theory of the Novel*: "The path is finished, the journey begins." The circle is closed, we have reached the end, the immanent possibilities are exhausted, and, at this same point, everything is open. This is why to be a Hegelian today does not mean to assume the superfluous burden of some metaphysical past, but to regain the ability to begin from the beginning.

One can read the formula of Absolute Knowing as an infinite judgment whose truth resides in the ridiculous dissonance between its two poles: the knowledge of the Absolute, the mind of God, the ultimate truth about the universe, was formulated by that contingent individual, Professor Hegel from Germany. Maybe we should really read this infinite judgment just like the infamous "the Spirit is a bone": "Absolute Knowing" is not the total knowledge of the universe the individual Hegel claimed to achieve, but a paradoxical name for the very absurdity of this claim, or, to paraphrase the Rabinovitch joke once again: "I possess Absolute Knowing." "But that is absurd, no finite being can possess it!" "Well, Absolute Knowing is nothing but the demonstration of that limit."

It is thus emphatically a case of shedding the "false" skin of Hegel-the-Absolute-Idealist in order to extract the "rational core" of Hegel's dialectics: Hegel *does* write and sound as if he is naïvely claiming "Absolute Knowing" (and the idealist Cunning of Reason, etc.), but this detour through a false appearance is necessary, for Hegel's point can only be made through the patent absurdity of his starting point. The same goes for our (re)assertion of dialectical materialism: that, philosophically speaking, Stalinist "dialectical materialism" is imbecility embodied is not so much beside the point as, rather, *the point itself*, since the point is precisely to conceive the identity of our Hegelian-Lacanian position and the philosophy of dialectical materialism as a Hegelian infinite judgment, a speculative identity of the highest and the lowest, like the formula of phrenology "the Spirit is a bone." In what, then, does the difference between the "highest" and the "lowest" reading of dialectical materialism consist? The steely Fourth

Teacher[41] committed a serious philosophical error when he ontologized the difference between dialectical and historical materialism, conceiving it as the difference between *metaphysica universalis* and *metaphysica specialis*, universal ontology and its application to the special domain of society. All one has to do here in order to pass from the "lowest" to the "highest" is to *displace this difference between the universal and the particular into the particular itself*: "dialectical materialism" provides another view on humanity itself, different from historical materialism. Yes, again, the relationship between historical and dialectical materialism is that of a parallax: they are substantially the same, the shift from the one to the other is purely one of perspective. It introduces topics like the death drive, the "inhuman" core of the human, which reach beyond the horizon of the collective *praxis* of humanity; the gap between historical and dialectical materialism is thus asserted as inherent to humanity itself, as the gap between humanity and *its own* inhuman excess.

The Idea's constipation?

Such a notion of Absolute Knowing enables us to avoid the trap into which even Jameson falls when he identifies *narcissism* as that which "may sometimes be felt to be repulsive in the Hegelian system as such,"[42] or, in short, as the central weakness of Hegel's thought expressed in his claim that reason should find itself in the actual world:

> We thereby search the whole world, and outer space, and end up only touching ourselves, only seeing our own face persist through multitudinous differences and forms of otherness. Never truly to encounter the not-I, to come face to face with radical otherness (or, even worse, to find ourselves in an historical dynamic in which it is precisely difference and otherness which is relentlessly being stamped out): such is the dilemma of the Hegelian dialectic, which contemporary philosophies of difference and otherness seem only able to confront with mystical evocations and imperatives.[43]

Let us take Hegel's dialectics at its most "idealist," that is, at the level which appears to confirm the accusation of narcissism: the notion of the sublation (*Aufhebung*) of all immediate material reality. The fundamental operation of *Aufhebung* is reduction: the sublated thing survives, but in an "abridged" edition,

41 Who, today, has to remain unnamed, like Benjamin's dwarf hidden within the puppet of historical materialism.

42 Fredric Jameson, *The Hegel Variations*, London: Verso Books 2010, p. 130.

43 Ibid., p. 131.

as it were, torn out of its life-world context, reduced to its essential feature, all the movement and wealth of its life reduced to a fixed mark. It is not that, after the abstraction of Reason does its mortifying job with its fixed categories or notional determinations, speculative "concrete universality" somehow returns us to the lushness of Life: once we pass from empirical reality to its notional *Aufhebung*, the immediacy of Life is lost forever. There is nothing more foreign to Hegel than lamenting the loss of the richness of reality when we grasp it conceptually—recall his unambiguous celebration of the absolute power of Understanding from his Foreword to the *Phenomenology*: "The action of separating the elements is the exercise of the force of Understanding, the most astonishing and greatest of all powers, or rather the absolute power." This celebration is in no way qualified, for Hegel's point is not that this power is nonetheless later "sublated" into a subordinate moment of the unifying totality of Reason. The problem with Understanding is rather that it does not unleash this power to the end, that it takes itself as being external to the Thing itself. The standard notion is that it is merely *our* Understanding ("the mind") that separates in its imagination what in "reality" belongs together, so that the Understanding's "absolute power" is merely the power of our imagination which in no way concerns the reality of the thing analyzed. We pass from Understanding to Reason not when this analyzing, tearing apart, is overcome in a synthesis which brings us back to the wealth of reality, but when this power of "tearing apart" is transferred from being "merely in our mind" into Things themselves, as their inherent power of negativity.

This point can also be made apropos the properly dialectical notion of abstraction: what makes Hegel's "concrete universality" infinite is that *it includes "abstractions" in concrete reality itself, as their immanent constituents.* To put it another way: what, for Hegel, is the elementary move of philosophy with regard to abstraction? It is to abandon the common-sense empiricist notion of abstraction as a step away from the wealth of concrete empirical reality with its irreducible multiplicity of features: life is green, concepts are gray, they dissect, mortify, concrete reality. (This common-sense notion even has its pseudo-dialectical version, according to which such "abstraction" is a feature of mere Understanding, while "dialectics" recuperates the rich tapestry of reality.) Philosophical thought proper begins when we become aware of how *such a process of "abstraction" is inherent to reality itself*: the tension between empirical reality and its "abstract" notional determinations is immanent to reality, it is a feature of "Things themselves." Therein lies the anti-nominalist accent of philosophical thinking—for example, the basic insight of Marx's "critique of political economy" is that the abstraction of the value of a commodity is its "objective" constituent. It is life without theory which is gray, a flat stupid reality—it is only theory which makes it "green," truly alive, bringing out the complex underlying network of mediations and tensions which makes it move.

This is how we should distinguish "true infinity" from "spurious (or bad) infinity": bad infinity is the asymptotic process of discovering ever new layers of reality—reality is posited here as the In-itself which can never be fully grasped, only gradually approached, for all we can do is discern particular "abstract" features of the transcendent and inaccessible plenitude of the "real Thing." The movement of "true infinity" is exactly the opposite: one includes the process of "abstraction" in the "Thing itself." This brings us, unexpectedly, to the question: what is involved in the dialectical self-deployment of a notion? Imagine, as a starting point, being caught in a complex and confused empirical situation which we try to understand, to bring some order to. Since we never start from the zero-point of pure pre-notional experience, we begin with the double movement of applying to the situation the abstract universal notions at our disposal, and of analyzing the situation, comparing its elements to one another and with our previous experiences, generalizing and formulating empirical universals. Sooner or later, we become aware of inconsistencies in the notional schemes we are using to understand the situation: something which should have been a subordinate species seems to encompass and dominate the entire field; different classifications and categorizations clash, without us being able to decide which is the more "true," and so on and so forth. We spontaneously dismiss such inconsistencies as signs of the deficiency of our understanding: reality is much too rich and complex for our abstract categories, we will never be able to deploy a notional network capable of capturing its diversity. Then, however, if we have a refined theoretical sense, we sooner or later notice something strange and unexpected: it is not possible to clearly distinguish the inconsistencies of our notion of an object from the inconsistencies which are immanent to the object itself. The "Thing itself" is inconsistent, full of tensions, oscillating between its different determinations, and the deployment of these tensions, this struggle, is what makes it "alive." Take a particular political state: when it malfunctions, it is as if its particular (specific) features are in tension with the universal Idea of the State; or take the Cartesian *cogito*: the difference between me as a particular person embedded in a particular life world and me as an abstract Subject is part of my particular identity itself, since to act as an abstract Subject is a feature that characterizes individuals in modern Western society. Here, again, what appears as a conflict between two "abstractions" in our mind reveals itself as a tension in the Thing itself.

A similar case of Hegelian "contradiction" may be found the notion of "liberalism," as it functions in contemporary discourse: its many meanings turn around two opposed poles: economic liberalism (free market individualism, opposition to strong state regulation, etc.) and political libertarian liberalism (where the accent is on equality, social solidarity, permissiveness, etc.)—in the US, Republicans are more liberal in the first sense and Democrats in the second.

The point, of course, is that while one cannot decide through closer analysis which is the "true" liberalism, one also cannot resolve the deadlock by trying to propose a kind of "higher" dialectical synthesis, or "avoid the confusion" by drawing a clear distinction between the two senses of the term. The tension between the two meanings is inherent in the very content that "liberalism" tries to designate, it is constitutive of the notion itself; hence this ambiguity, far from signaling the limitation of our knowledge, signals the innermost "truth" of the notion of liberalism. What happens here is not that "abstractions" lose their abstract character and are drowned in full concrete reality—they *remain* "abstractions" and relate to each other *as* "abstractions."

Back in the 1960s, one "progressive" theorist of education created a stir when he published the results of a simple experiment: he asked a group of five-year-old children to draw an image of themselves playing at home; two years later, he asked the group to do the same thing again, after they had undergone a year and a half of primary school. The difference was striking: the self-portraits of the five-year-olds were exuberant, lively, full of color, surrealistically playful, but two years later, the portraits were much more rigid and subdued, plus a large number of children spontaneously chose to use only an ordinary gray pencil, although other colors were available. Quite predictably, this experiment was invoked as proof of the "oppressiveness" of the school apparatus, of how the school drill and discipline was crushing children's spontaneous creativity, and so on. From a Hegelian standpoint, one should, on the contrary, celebrate this shift from colorful liveliness to gray order as an indication of spiritual progress: nothing is lost in the reduction of lively colorfulness to gray discipline, everything stands to be gained—the power of the spirit is precisely to progress from the "green" immediacy of life to its "gray" conceptual structure, and to reproduce in this reduced medium the essential determinations to which our immediate experience blinds us.

The same mortification occurs in historical memory and monuments of the past where what survives are objects deprived of their living souls—here is Hegel's comment apropos Ancient Greece: "The statues are now only stones from which the living soul has flown, just as the hymns are words from which belief has gone."[44] As with the passage from substantial God to Holy Spirit, the properly dialectical re-animation is to be sought in this very medium of "gray" notional determinations: "The understanding, through the form of abstract universality, does give [the varieties of the sensuous], so to speak, a *rigidity* of being ... but, at the same time through this simplification it *spiritually animates* them and so sharpens them."[45] This "simplification" is precisely what Lacan, referring

44 Hegel, *Phenomenology of Spirit*, p. 455.

45 As quoted in Malabou, *The Future of Hegel*, p. 97, modified from the translation in Hegel, *Hegel's Science of Logic*, p. 611 (§1338).

to Freud, deployed as the reduction of a thing to *le trait unaire* (*der einzige Zug*, the unary feature): we are dealing with a kind of epitomization by means of which a multitude of properties is reduced to a single dominant characteristic, so that we get "a concrete shape in which one determination predominates, the others being present only in blurred outline":[46] "the content is already the actuality reduced to a possibility (*zur Moeglichkeit getilgte Wirklichkeit*), its immediacy overcome, and the embodied shape reduced to abbreviated, simple determinations of thought."[47]

The dialectical approach is usually seen as trying to locate the phenomenon-to-be-analyzed in the totality to which it belongs, embedded in its rich historical context, and thus to break the spell of fetishizing abstraction. This, however, is the most dangerous trap to be avoided: for Hegel, the true problem is the opposite one, the fact that, when we observe a thing, we see *too much* in it, we fall under the spell of the wealth of empirical detail which prevents us from clearly perceiving the notional determination which forms the core of the thing. The problem is thus not how to grasp the wealth of determinations, but precisely how to *abstract* from them, how to restrict our gaze and learn to grasp only the notional determination.

Hegel's formulation is here very precise: the reduction to the signifying "unary feature" reduces or contracts actuality to possibility, in the precise Platonic sense in which the notion (Idea) of a thing always has a deontological dimension to it, designating *what the thing should become in order to fully be what it is*. "Potentiality" is thus not simply a name for the essence of a thing as the potentiality actualized in the multitude of empirical things of a certain genre (the Idea of a chair is a potentiality actualized in empirical chairs). The multiple actual properties of a thing are not simply reduced to the inner core of the thing's "true reality"; what is more important is that a name accentuates (profiles) the thing's inner potential. When I call someone "my teacher," I thereby outline what I expect from him; when I refer to a thing as "chair," I profile the way I intend to use it. When I observe the world around me through the lenses of a language, I perceive its actuality through the lenses of the potentialities hidden or latently present in it. Potentiality thus appears "as such," becomes actual *as potentiality*, only through language: it is the appellation of a thing that brings to light ("posits") its potentials.

Once we grasp *Aufhebung* in this way, we can immediately see what is wrong with one of the main pseudo-Freudian reasons for dismissing Hegel: the notion of Hegel's System as the highest and most over-blown expression of the oral economy. Is the Hegelian Idea not effectively a voracious eater "swallowing" every object it stumbles upon? No wonder Hegel perceived himself as Christian:

46 Hegel, *Phenomenology of Spirit*, p. 16 (§28); translation modified.
47 Ibid, p. 17.

for him, the transubstantiation of the bread into Christ's flesh signals that the Christian subject can integrate and digest God himself without remainder. Is not the Hegelian process of conceiving or grasping a sublimated version of digestion? Hegel writes:

> If the individual human being does something, achieves something, attains a goal, this fact must be grounded in the way the thing itself, in its concept, acts and behaves. If I eat an apple, I destroy its organic self-identity and assimilate it to myself. That I can do this entails that the apple in itself, already, in advance, before I take hold of it, has in its nature the determination of being subject to destruction, having in itself a homogeneity with my digestive organs such that I can make it homogeneous with myself.[48]

Is not what he describes here a lower version of the cognitive process itself, in which, as Hegel likes to point out, we can only grasp the object if this object itself already "wants to be with or by us"? One should pursue this metaphor to the end: the standard critical reading constructs the Hegelian absolute Substance-Subject as thoroughly *constipated*—retaining within itself the ingested content. Or, as Adorno put it in one of his cutting remarks (which, as is all too often the case with him, miss the mark), Hegel's system "is the belly turned mind," pretending that it has swallowed the totality of indigestible Otherness.[49] But what about the inevitable counter-movement, Hegelian defecation? Is not the subject of what Hegel calls "Absolute Knowing" also a thoroughly *emptied* subject, a subject reduced to the role of pure observer (or, rather, registrar) of the self-movement of the content itself?

> The richest is therefore the most concrete and most *subjective*, and that which withdraws itself into the simplest depth is the mightiest and most all-embracing. The highest, most concentrated point is the pure personality which, solely through the absolute dialectic which is its nature, no less *embraces and holds everything within itself*.[50]

In this strict sense, the subject itself is the abrogated or cleansed substance, a substance reduced to the void of the empty form of self-relating negativity, emptied of all the wealth of "personality"—in Lacanese, the move from substance to

48 As quoted in Malabou, *The Future of Hegel*, p. 97, modified from the translation in G. W. F. Hegel, *Lectures on the Philosophy of Religion, Vol. 3: The Consummate Religion*, trans. R. F. Brown, P. C. Hodgson and J. M. Stewart, Berkeley: University of California Press 1987, p. 127.

49 Theodor W. Adorno, *Negative Dialectics*, London: Continuum 2007, p. 23.

50 Hegel, *Hegel's Science of Logic*, p. 841.

subject is the move from S to \$, the subject is the barred substance. (Adorno and Horkheimer, in *The Dialectic of Enlightenment*, make the critical point that the Self bent on mere survival has to scarify all content that would make survival worthwhile; this very move is what Hegel asserts.) Schelling referred to this same move as *contraction* (again, with the excremental connotation): the subject is the contracted substance.

Does the final subjective position of the Hegelian System thus compel us to turn around the digestive metaphor? The supreme (and for many the most problematic) case of this counter-movement occurs at the very end of the *Logic*, when, after the notional deployment is completed, closing the circle of the absolute Idea, the Idea, in its resolution or decision, "freely releases itself" into Nature—lets it go, discards it, pushes it away from itself, and thus liberates it.[51] Which is why, for Hegel, the philosophy of nature is not a violent re-appropriation of its externality; it rather involves the passive attitude of an observer: "philosophy has, as it were, simply to watch how nature itself sublates its externality."[52]

The same move is accomplished by God himself who, in the guise of Christ, as a finite mortal, also "freely releases itself" into temporal existence. And the same goes for early modern art, where Hegel accounts for the rise of "dead nature" paintings (not only of landscapes, flowers, etc., but of food and dead animals) in the following way: precisely because, in the development of art, subjectivity no longer needs the visual as the principal medium of its expression—the accent having shifted to poetry as a more direct means of expressing the subject's inner life—the natural is "released" from the burden of expressing subjectivity and can thus now be approached, and visually depicted, on its own terms. Furthermore, as some perspicuous readers of Hegel have already pointed out, the very sublation of art itself in the philosophical sciences (in conceptual thought)—the fact that it is no longer obliged to serve as the principal medium of the expression of spirit—brings art a certain freedom, allowing it to stand on its own. Is this not the very definition of the birth of modern art proper, as a practice no longer subordinated to the task of representing spiritual reality?

The way abrogation relates to sublation is not in terms of a simple succession or external opposition: not "first you eat, then you shit." Defecation is the immanent *conclusion* of the entire process: without it, we would be dealing with the "spurious infinity" of an endless process of sublation. The process of sublation itself can only reach its end in this counter-movement:

> contrary to what one would initially imagine, these two processes of sublation and abrogation are completely interdependent. Considering the last moment of absolute spirit (*Philosophy*), one readily notes the synonymy between the verbs *aufheben* and

51 Ibid., p. 843.

52 Hegel, *Philosophy of Mind*, p. 28.

> *befreien* ("to liberate"), as well as *ablegen* ("to discard," "to remove," "to take away"). Speculative abrogation, in no way alien to the process of *Aufhebung*, is indeed its fulfillment. Abrogation is a *sublation of sublation*, the result of the *Aufhebung*'s work on itself and, as such, its transformation. The movement of suppression and preservation produces this transformation at a certain moment in history, the moment of Absolute Knowledge. Speculative abrogation is the *absolute sublation*, if by "absolute" we mean a relief or sublation that frees from a certain type of attachment.[53]

True cognition is thus not only the notional "appropriation" of its object: the process of appropriation goes on only as long as cognition remains incomplete. The sign of its completion is that it liberates its object, lets it be, drops it. This is why and how the movement of sublation has to culminate in the self-relating gesture of sublating itself.

So what about the obvious counter-argument: is not the part which is abrogated or released merely the arbitrary, temporary aspect of the object, that which the notional mediation or reduction can afford to let go as being in itself worthless? This is precisely the mistake to be avoided, for two reasons. First (if one may be permitted to extend the excremental metaphor), the released part is, precisely as discarded, the *manure* of spiritual development, the ground out of which further development will grow. The release of Nature into its own thus lays the foundation for Spirit proper, which can develop itself only out of Nature, as its inherent self-sublation. Second (and more fundamentally), what is released into its own being in speculative cognition is ultimately the object of cognition itself which, when truly grasped (*begriffen*), no longer has to rely on the subject's active intervention, but develops according to its own conceptual automatism, with the subject reduced to a passive observer who, without making any contribution (*Zutun*), allows the thing to deploy its potential and merely registers the process. This is why Hegelian cognition is simultaneously both active and passive, but in a sense which radically displaces the Kantian notion of cognition as the unity of activity and passivity. In Kant, the subject actively synthesizes (confers unity on) the content (the sensuous multiplicity) by which it is passively affected. For Hegel, on the contrary, at the level of Absolute Knowing, the cognizing subject is thoroughly passivized: it no longer intervenes in the object, but merely registers the immanent movement of the object's self-differentiation/determination (or, to use a more contemporary term, the object's autopoietic self-organization). The subject is thus, at its most radical, not the agens of the process: the agens is the System (of knowledge) itself which "automatically" deploys itself, without the need for any external impetus. This utter passivity, however, simultaneously involves the greatest activity: it takes the most strenuous effort for the subject to "erase itself" in its particular content, as an agent intervening in the object, and

53 Malabou, *Future of Hegel*, p. 156.

to expose itself as a neutral medium, as the site of the System's self-deployment. Hegel thereby overcomes the standard dualism between System and Freedom, between the Spinozist notion of a substantial *deus sive natura* of which I am a part, caught in its determinism, and the Fichtean notion of the subject as an agent opposed to inert stuff, trying to dominate and appropriate it. *The supreme moment of the subject's freedom is when it sets free its object*, leaving it alone to freely deploy itself: "The Idea's absolute freedom consists in [its resolution] to freely let go out of itself the moment of its particularity."[54] "Absolute freedom" is here literally absolute in the etymological meaning of *absolvere*: releasing, letting go. Schelling was the first to criticize this move as illegitimate: after completing the circle of the logical self-development of the Notion, and being aware that it had all taken place in the abstract medium of thought, Hegel had somehow to make the passage to real life—however, there were no categories in his logic capable of accomplishing this passage, which is why he had to resort to terms like "decision" (the Idea "decides" to release Nature from itself), which are not categories of logic, but of the will and practical life. What this critique clearly misses is the way the act of releasing the other is thoroughly *immanent* to the dialectical process, as its conclusive moment, the sign of the completion of the dialectical circle. Is this not the Hegelian version of *Gelassenheit*?

This, then, is how one should read Hegel's "third syllogism of Philosophy," Spirit-Logic-Nature: the starting point of the speculative movement is spiritual substance, into which subjects are immersed; then, through a strenuous conceptual effort, the wealth of this substance is reduced to its underlying logical or notional structure; once this task is accomplished, the fully developed logical Idea can release Nature out of itself. Here is the key passage:

> The Idea, ... in positing itself as absolute unity of the pure Notion and its reality and thus contracting itself into the immediacy of being, is the totality in this form—nature.
>
> But this determination has not issued from a process of becoming, nor is it a transition, as when above, the subjective Notion in its totality becomes objectivity, and the subjective end becomes life. On the contrary, the pure Idea in which the determinateness or reality of the Notion is itself raised into Notion, is an absolute liberation for which there is no longer any immediate determination that is not equally posited and itself Notion; in this freedom, therefore, no transition takes place; the simple being to which the Idea determines itself remains perfectly transparent to it and is the Notion that, in its determination, abides with itself. The passage is therefore to be understood here rather in this manner, that the Idea freely releases itself in its absolute self-assurance and inner poise. By reason of this freedom, the form

54 G. W. F. Hegel, *Encyklopädie der philosophischen Wissenschaften im Gründrisse, Vol. 1: Die Logik*, Berlin: Dunder and Humblot 1843, pp. 413–14 (§244).

> of its determinateness is also utterly free—the externality of space and time existing absolutely on its own account without the moment of subjectivity.[55]

Hegel here repeatedly insists how this "absolute liberation" is thoroughly different from the standard dialectical "transition." But how? The suspicion lurks that Hegel's "absolute liberation" relies on the absolute mediation of all otherness: I set the Other free after I have completely internalized it ... But is this really so?

One should reread here Lacan's critique of Hegel: what if, far from denying what Lacan calls the "subjective disjunction," Hegel on the contrary asserts an unheard-of division that *runs through the (particular) subject as well as through the (universal) substantial order of "collectivity," uniting the two*? That is to say, what if the "reconciliation" between the Particular and the Universal occurs precisely through the division that cuts across the two? The basic "postmodern" reproach to Hegel—that his dialectic admits antagonisms only to resolve them magically in a higher synthesis—strangely contrasts with the good old Marxist reproach (already formulated by Schelling) according to which Hegel resolves antagonisms only in "thought," through conceptual mediation, while in reality they remain unresolved. One is tempted to accept this second reproach at face value and use it against the first one: what if this is the proper answer to the accusation that Hegelian dialectics magically resolves antagonisms? What if, for Hegel, the point is precisely *not* to "resolve" antagonisms "in reality," but just to enact a parallax shift by means of which antagonisms are recognized "as such" and thereby perceived in their "positive" role?

The passage from Kant to Hegel is thus much more convoluted than it may appear—let us approach it again through their opposition with regard to the ontological proof of God's existence. Kant's rejection of this proof takes as its starting point the thesis that being is not a predicate: even if one knows all the predicates of an entity, its being (existence) does not follow, for one cannot conclude from a notion to being. (The argument is clearly posed against Leibniz, according to whom two objects are indiscernible if all of their predicates are the same.) The implications for the ontological proof are clear: in the same way that I can have a perfect notion of 100 thalers and still not have them in my pocket, I can have a perfect notion of God and God can still not exist. Hegel's first remark on this line of reasoning is that "being" is the poorest, most imperfect, notional determination (everything "is" in some way, even my wildest imaginings); it is only through further notional determinations that we get to existence, to reality, to actuality, which are all much more than mere being. His second remark is that the gap between notion and existence is precisely the mark of finitude, it holds for finite objects like 100 thalers, but not for God: God is not something I can have (or not have) in my pocket.

55 Hegel, *Hegel's Science of Logic*, p. 843.

On a first approach, it may seem that the opposition is here ultimately that between materialism and idealism: Kant insists on a minimum of materialism (the independence of reality with regard to notional determinations), while Hegel totally dissolves reality in its notional determinations. However, Hegel's true point lies elsewhere: it involves a much more radical "materialist" claim that a complete notional determination of an entity, to which one would only have to add "being" in order to arrive at its existence, is in itself an abstract notion, an empty abstract possibility. The lack of (a certain mode of) being is always also an inherent lack of some notional determination—for a thing to exist as part of material reality, a whole set of notional conditions or determinations have to be met (and other determinations to be lacking). With regard to 100 thalers (or any other empirical object), this means that their notional determination is abstract, which is why they possess an opaque empirical being and not full actuality. So when Kant draws a parallel between God and 100 thalers, one should ask a simple and naïve question: does Kant *really* possess a (fully developed) *concept* of God?

This brings us to the true finesse of Hegel's argumentation, which runs in both directions: against Kant but also against Anselm's classic version of the ontological proof. Hegel's argument against the latter is not that it is too conceptual, but that it is not conceptual enough: Anselm does not develop the concept of God, he just refers to it as the sum of all perfections which, as such, is precisely beyond the comprehension of our finite human mind. In other words, Anselm merely presupposes "God" as an impenetrable reality beyond our comprehension (outside the notional domain), for his God is precisely not a concept (something posited by our conceptual work), but a purely presupposed pre- or non-conceptual reality. Along the same lines, albeit in the opposite sense, we should note the irony that Kant talks about thalers, that is, *money*, whose existence *as money* is not "objective," but depends on "notional" determinations. True, as Kant says, having a concept of 100 thalers is not the same as having them in your pocket; but let us imagine a process of rapid inflation which totally devalues the pocketed 100 thalers; yes, the same objects are there in reality, but they are no longer money, just meaningless, worthless coins. In other words, money is precisely an object whose status depends on how we "think" about it: if people no longer treat this piece of metal as money, if they no longer "believe" in it as money, it no longer *is* money.[56] So when Kant argues that those who want

56 This point, incidentally, was already made by the young Marx, who noted in his doctoral thesis: "Real talers have the same existence that the imagined gods have. Has a real taler any existence except in the imagination, if only in the general or rather common imagination of man? Bring paper money into a country where this use of paper is unknown, and everyone will laugh at your subjective imagination" (Karl Marx, "The Difference Between the Democritean and Epicurean Philosophy of Nature: Fragment

to prove the existence of God from his notion are like those who think they can become richer by adding zeros to their banknotes, he misses the fact that, in capitalism, one actually *can* get rich in this way: in a successful act of fraud, say, one falsifies one's financial assets in order to get credit, then invests the money and gets rich.

With regard to material reality, the ontological proof of God's existence should thus be turned around: the existence of material reality bears witness to the fact that the Notion is not fully actualized. Things "materially exist" not when they meet certain notional requirements, but when they *fail* to meet them—material reality is as such a sign of imperfection. In this sense, as we saw in Chapter 1, for Hegel the truth of a proposition is inherently notional, determined by the immanent notional content, not a matter of comparison between notion and reality—in Lacanian terms, there is a non-All (*pas-tout*) of truth. So, to pursue the rather tasteless metaphor, Hegel was not a sublimated coprophagist, as the usual notion of the dialectical process would lead us to believe. The matrix of the dialectical process is not that of defecation-externalization followed up by a swallowing up (re-appropriation) of the externalized content; on the contrary, it is one of appropriation followed by the excremental movement of dropping, releasing, letting go. What this means is that one should not equate externalization with alienation: the externalization which concludes a cycle of dialectical process is not alienation, it is the highest point of dis-alienation: one really reconciles oneself with some objective content not when one still has to strive to master and control it, but when one can afford the supreme sovereign gesture of letting this content go, of setting it free. Which is why, incidentally, as some perceptive interpreters have pointed out, far from subduing nature totally to man, Hegel unexpectedly opens up a space for ecological awareness. For him, the drive to exploit nature technologically is still a mark of man's finitude; in such an attitude, nature is perceived as an external object, an opposing force to be dominated; adopting the standpoint of Absolute Knowing, however, the philosopher does not experience nature as a threatening other to be controlled and dominated, but as something that should be left to follow its inherent path.

Here Louis Althusser was wrong when he opposed the Hegelian Subject-Substance, as a "teleological" process-with-a-subject, to the materialist-dialectical "process without a subject." The Hegelian dialectical process is in fact the most radical version of a "process without a subject," in the sense of an agent controlling and directing it—be it God or humanity, or a class as a collective subject. In his late writings, Althusser came to recognize this, but what remained obscure to him was how the fact that the Hegelian dialectical process is "without a subject" means exactly the same as Hegel's fundamental thesis that "the Absolute must

from the Appendix," in Karl Marx and Friedrich Engels, *Marx and Engels: Collected Works*, Vol. 1, London: Lawrence & Wishart 1975, p. 104).

be grasped not only as Substance, but also as Subject": the emergence of a pure subject qua void is strictly correlative to the notion of "System" as the self-deployment of the object itself with no need for any subjective agent to drive it forward or direct it.

This is why it is a mistake to treat Hegelian self-consciousness as a kind of meta-Subject, a Mind, much larger than an individual human mind, aware of itself: once we do this, Hegel can only appear as a ridiculous spiritualist obscurantist, claiming that there is some kind of mega-Spirit controlling our history. Against this cliché, one should emphasize how fully aware Hegel is that "it is in the finite consciousness that the process of knowing spirit's essence takes place and that the divine self-consciousness thus arises. Out of the foaming ferment of finitude, spirit rises up fragrantly."[57] However, although our awareness—the (self-)consciousness of finite humans—is the only actual site of spirit, this does not entail any kind of nominalist reduction. There is another dimension at work in "self-consciousness," the one designated by Lacan as the "big Other" and by Karl Popper as the Third World. That is to say, for Hegel, "self-consciousness" in its abstract definition stands for a purely non-psychological self-reflexive fold of registering (re-marking) one's own position, of reflexively "taking into account" what one is doing.

Therein resides the link between Hegel and psychoanalysis: in this precise non-psychological sense, "self-consciousness" for psychoanalysis is an object—a tic, say, a symptom which betrays the falsity of my position of which I am unaware. For example, I do something wrong, and I consciously tell myself that I had the right to do it; but, unbeknown to me, a compulsive act which to me appears mysterious and meaningless "registers" my guilt, bears witness to the fact that, somewhere, my guilt is remarked. Along the same lines, Ingmar Bergman once noted that, towards the end of their careers, both Fellini and Tarkovsky (whom he admired) unfortunately started to make "Fellini films" and "Tarkovsky films," and that the same weakness affected his *Autumn Sonata*—it is a "Bergman film made by Bergman." In *The Autumn Sonata*, Bergman lost his creative spontaneity: he started to "imitate himself," to reflexively follow his own formula—in short, *The Autumn Sonata* is a "self-conscious" film, even if Bergman himself was psychologically totally unaware of this. This is the function of the Lacanian "big Other" at its purest: this impersonal, non-psychological, agency (or rather site) of registering, of "taking note of" what takes place.

This is how one should grasp Hegel's notion of the State as the "self-consciousness" of a people: "The state is the *self-conscious* ethical substance."[58] A State is not merely a blind mechanism applied to regulate social life, it always also contains a series of practices, rituals, and institutions that serve to "declare"

57 Hegel, *Lectures on the Philosophy of Religion, Vol.* 3, p. 233.

58 Hegel, *Philosophy of Mind*, p. 263.

its own status, in the guise of which the State appears to its subjects as what it is—parades and public celebrations, solemn oaths, legal and educational rituals which assert (and thereby enact) the subject's belongingness to the State:

> the self-consciousness of the state has nothing mental about it, if by "mental" we understand the sorts of occurrences and qualities that are relevant to *our own* minds. What self-consciousness amounts to, in the state's case, is the existence of reflective practices, such as, but not limited to, educational ones. Parades displaying the state's military strength would be practices of this kind, and so would statements of principle by the legislature, or sentences by the Supreme Court—and they would be that *even if* all individual (human) participants in a parade, all members of the legislature or of the Supreme Court were personally motivated to play whatever role they play in this affair by greed, inertia, or fear, *and* even if all such participants or members were thoroughly uninterested and bored through the whole event, and totally lacking in any understanding of its significance.[59]

So it is quite clear to Hegel that this appearing has nothing to do with conscious awareness: it does not matter what individuals' minds are preoccupied with while they are participating in a ceremony, the truth resides in the ceremony itself. Hegel made the same point apropos the marriage ceremony, which registers the most intimate link of love: "the solemn declaration of consent to the ethical bond of marriage and its recognition and confirmation by the family and community constitute the formal *conclusion* and *actuality* of marriage," which is why it belongs to "impertinence and its ally, understanding," to see "the ceremony whereby the essence of this bond is expressed and *confirmed* … as an external formality," irrelevant with regard to the inwardness of passionate feeling.[60]

This, of course, is not the whole story: Hegel also emphasized the need for a subjective element of individual self-awareness through which a State alone fully actualizes itself—there has to be an actual individual "I will!" which immediately embodies the will of the State, and therein consists Hegel's deduction of monarchy. However, here, we are in for a surprise: the Monarch is not the privileged point at which the State becomes fully aware of itself, of its own nature and spiritual content; the Monarch is rather an idiot who merely supplies the purely formal aspect of "This is my will! So be it!" to a content imposed on it from outside: "In a fully organized state … all that is required in a monarch is someone to say 'yes' and to dot the 'i'; for the supreme office should be such

59 Bencivenga, *Hegel's Dialectical Logic*, pp. 63–4.

60 G. W. F. Hegel, *Elements of the Philosophy of Right*, trans. H. B. Nisbet, Cambridge: Cambridge University Press 1991, pp. 204–5.

that the particular character of its occupant is of no significance."[61] The State's "self-consciousness" is thus irreducibly split between its "objective" aspect (the self-registration in State rituals and declarations) and its "subjective" aspect (the person of the Monarch conferring on it the form of individual will)—the two never overlap. The contrast between the Hegelian Monarch and the "totalitarian" Leader who is effectively supposed to know could not be stronger.

The animal that I am

What the critics of Hegel's voracity need is thus, perhaps, a dose of a good laxative. Hegel is much less a voracious subjectivist even with regard to the idealist topic par excellence, that of the debasement of the animality of man. Let us approach this topic through Derrida's *The Animal That Therefore I Am*.[62] Although the title was intended as an ironic stab at Descartes, one should perhaps take it with a more literal naïveté—the Cartesian *cogito* is not a separate substance different from the body (as Descartes himself misunderstood the *cogito* in his illegitimate passage from *cogito* to *res cogitans*); at the level of substantial content, I am nothing but the animal that I am. What makes me human is the very form, the formal declaration, of me *as* an animal.

Derrida's starting point is that every clear and general differentiation between humans and "the animal" in the history of philosophy (from Aristotle to Heidegger, Lacan, and Levinas) should be deconstructed: what really authorizes us to say that only humans speak, while animals merely emit signs; that only humans respond, while animals merely react; that only humans experience things "as such," while animals are just captivated by their life world; that only humans can feign to feign, while animals just directly feign; that only humans are mortal, experience death, while animals just die; or that animals enjoy a harmonious sexual relationship of instinctual mating, while for humans, *il n'y a pas de rapport sexuel*; and so on and so forth? Derrida displays here the best of what we cannot but call the "common sense of deconstruction," asking naïve questions which undermine philosophical propositions taken for granted for centuries. What, for example, allows Lacan to claim with such self-confidence, without providing any data or arguments, that animals cannot feign to feign? What allows Heidegger to claim as a self-evident fact that animals do not relate to their death? As Derrida emphasizes again and again, the point of this questioning is not to cancel the gap that separates man from (other) animals and

61 Ibid., p. 323. See Interlude 3, below, for a detailed discussion of Hegel's defense of monarchy.

62 Jacques Derrida, *The Animal That Therefore I Am*, New York: Fordham University Press 2008.

attribute also to (other) animals properly "spiritual" properties—the path taken by some eco-mystics who claim that not only animals, but even trees and plants communicate in a language of their own to which we humans are deaf. The point is rather that all these differences should be re-thought and conceived in a different way, multiplied, "thickened"—and the first step on this path is to denounce the all-encompassing category of "the animal."

Such a negative characterizations of animals (as speechless, worldless, etc.) generate the appearance of a positive determination which is false: animals as being captured within their environment, and so on. Do we not encounter the same phenomenon in traditional Eurocentric anthropology? Viewed through the lenses of modern Western "rational" thought taken as the standard of maturity, its Others cannot but appear as "primitives" trapped in magic thinking, "really believing" that their tribe originates from their totemic animal, that a pregnant woman has been inseminated by a spirit and not by a man, etc. Rational thought thus engenders the figure of "irrational" mythical thought —what we get here is (again) a process of violent simplification (reduction, obliteration) which occurs with the rise of the New: in order to assert something radically New, the entire past, with all its inconsistencies, has to be reduced to some basic defining feature ("metaphysics," "mythical thought," "ideology"…). Derrida himself succumbs to the same simplification in his deconstructive mode: the past as a whole is totalized as "phallogocentrism" or "metaphysics of presence," which—it can be argued—is secretly modeled upon Husserl. (Derrida here differs from Deleuze and Lacan, who treat philosophers one by one, without totalizing them.) Does not the same thing happen when the Western Judeo-Greek legacy is opposed to the "Oriental" stance, thereby obliterating the incredible wealth of positions covered by the term "Oriental thought"? Can we really put into the same category, say, the Upanishads, with their "corporate" metaphysics of castes, and Confucianism with its agnostic-pragmatic stance?

But is not such a violent leveling a necessary feature of every critical move, of every rise of the New? Perhaps then, instead of dismissing *en bloc* such "binary logic," one should assert it, not only as a necessary step of simplification, but as inherently true in that very simplification. To put it in Hegelese, it is not only that, say, the totalization effected under the heading "the animal" involves the violent obliteration of a complex multiplicity; it is also that the violent reduction of such a multiplicity to a minimal difference is the moment of truth. That is to say, the multiplicity of animal forms is to be conceived as a series of attempts to resolve some basic antagonism or tension which defines animality as such, a tension which can only be formulated from a minimal distance, once humans are involved. Recall the well-known elaboration of the general equivalent from the first edition of *Capital*, Volume 1, where Marx writes:

> It is as if, alongside and external to lions, tigers, rabbits, and all other actual animals, which form when grouped together the various kinds, species, subspecies, families, etc. of the animal kingdom, there existed in addition *the animal*, the individual incarnation of the entire animal kingdom.[63]

Doe not this image of money as "the animal" romping alongside all the heterogeneous instances of particular sorts of animality that exist around it capture what Derrida describes as the gap that separates the Animal from the multiplicity of actual animal life? In Hegelese again, what man encounters in *the* Animal is itself in the oppositional determination: viewed as an animal, man is *the* spectral animal existing alongside really existing animal kinds. Does this not also allow us to give a perverse twist to the early Marx's determination of man as *Gattungswesen*, a species-being: it is as if, alongside particular subspecies, the species as such comes to exist. Perhaps this is how animals view humans, and this is the reason for their perplexity.

The key point here is that it is not enough to say that, while such a determination of animals as speechless, etc., is wrong, the determination of humans as rational, speaking, etc., is right, so that we just have to provide a more adequate definition of animality—the entire field is false. This falsity can be thought in terms of the Kierkegaardian couple of becoming and being: the standard opposition animal/human is formulated from the perspective of the human as being, as already constituted; it cannot think the human in its becoming. It thinks animals from within the given human standpoint, it cannot think the human from the animal standpoint. In other words, what this human/animal difference obfuscates is not only the way animals really are independently of humans, but the very difference which effectively marks the rupture of the human within the animal universe. It is here that psychoanalysis enters: the "death drive" as Freud's name for the uncanny dimension of the human-in-becoming. This In-between is the "repressed" of the narrative form (in Hegel's case, of the "grand narrative" of the world-historical succession of spiritual forms): not nature as such, but the very break with nature which is (later) supplemented by the virtual universe of narratives. The answer to Derrida's claim that every feature attributed exclusively to "man" is a fiction could thus be that such fictions nonetheless have a reality of their own, effectively organizing human practices—that humans are precisely animals who become committed to their fictions, adhering to them scrupulously (a version of Nietzsche's claim that man is the animal capable of making promises).

---

63 As reproduced in Karl Marx, *Value: Studies*, trans. Albert Dragstedt, London: New Park 1976. Marx dropped this sentence from the second edition of *Capital*, where he rearranged the first chapter.

Derrida begins his exploration of this obscure "twilight zone" with a report on a kind of primordial scene: after waking, he goes naked to the bathroom where his cat follows him; then the awkward moment occurs—he is standing in front of the cat which is looking at his naked body. Unable to endure this situation, he puts a towel around his waist, chases the cat outside, and takes a shower. The cat's gaze stands for the gaze of the Other—an inhuman gaze, but for this reason all the more the Other's gaze in all its abyssal impenetrability. Seeing oneself being seen by an animal is an abyssal encounter with the Other's gaze, since—precisely because we should not simply project onto the animal our inner experience—something is returning the gaze which is radically Other. The entire history of philosophy is based upon a disavowal of such an encounter, right up to Badiou, who is all too quick in characterizing a human being not yet converted into a subject (to the Event) as a "human animal." Sometimes, at least, the enigma is admitted—by, among others, Heidegger, who insists that we are not yet able to determine the essence of a being which is "living." And, sporadically, we can even find direct reversals of this disavowal: not only is the gaze of the animal recognized, it is also directly elevated into the key preoccupation of philosophy, as in Adorno's surprising proclamation: "Philosophy exists in order to redeem what you see in the gaze of an animal."[64]

I remember seeing a photo of a cat after it had been subjected to some lab experiment in a centrifuge, its bones half broken, its skin half hairless, its eyes looking helplessly into the camera—this is the gaze of the Other disavowed not only by philosophers, but by humans "as such." Even Levinas, who wrote so much about the face of the helpless other as the original site of the ethical responsibility, explicitly denied that an animal's face could function like this. One of the few exceptions here is Bentham, who made a simple proposal: instead of asking, "Can animals reason and think? Can they talk?" we should rather ask, "Can they suffer?" Human industry alone is continuously causing an immense suffering to animals which is systematically disavowed—not only laboratory experiments, but special regimes to produce eggs and milk (turning lights on and off to shorten the day, the use of hormones, etc.), pigs which are half blind and barely able to walk, fattened up rapidly to be slaughtered, and so on and so forth. Many of those who visit a chicken factory find themselves no longer able to eat chicken meat, and although all of us know what goes on in such places, this knowledge has to be neutralized so that we can act as if we do not know. One way to facilitate this ignorance is with the Cartesian notion of the *animal-machine*. Cartesians warn us against having compassion for animals: when we hear an animal emitting sounds of pain, we should always bear in mind that these sounds do not express any real inner feeling—since animals do not

64 Theodor Adorno and Max Horkheimer, *Towards a New Manifesto*, London: Verso Books 2011, p. 71. Translation slightly modified.

have souls, they are just sounds generated by a complex mechanism of muscles, bones, fluids, etc., that one can clearly see through dissection. The problem is that the notion of the *animal-machine* developed into La Mettrie's *L'Homme-Machine*: for a fully committed neuro-biologist, exactly the same claim can be made about the sounds and gestures emitted by humans in pain; there is no separate interior domain of the soul where pain is "really felt," such sounds and gestures are simply produced by the complex neuro-biological mechanisms of the human organism.

In revealing the larger ontological context of this animal suffering, Derrida resuscitates the old motif of German Romanticism and Schelling, taken over by Heidegger and Benjamin, of the "great sorrow of nature": "It is in the hope of requiting that [sorrow], of redemption from that suffering, that humans live and speak in nature."[65] Derrida rejects this Schellingian-Benjaminian-Heideggerian motif of the sadness of nature, the idea that nature's numbness and muteness signals an infinite pain, as being teleologically logocentric: language becomes a *telos* of nature, nature strives towards the Word to be relieved of its sadness, to reach its redemption. But this mystical topos nonetheless raises the right question by, again, reversing the standard perspective: not "What is nature for language? Can we grasp nature adequately in or through language?" but "What is language for nature? How does its emergence affect nature?" Far from belonging to logocentrism, such a reversal is the strongest suspension of logocentrism and teleology, in the same way that Marx's thesis on the anatomy of man as the key to the anatomy of ape subverts any teleological evolutionism. Derrida is aware of this complexity: he describes how the animal sadness

> doesn't just derive from the inability to speak and from muteness, from a stupefied or aphasic privation of words. If this putative sadness also gives rise to a lament, if nature laments, expressing a mute but audible lament through sensuous sighing and even the rustling of plants, it is perhaps because the terms have to be inverted. Benjamin suggests as much. There must be a reversal, an *Umkehrung* in the essence of nature … nature (and animality within it) isn't sad because it is mute. On the contrary, it is nature's sadness or mourning that renders it mute and aphasic, that leaves it without words.[66]

Following Benjamin, Derrida thus interprets this reversal as revealing that what makes nature sad is not "a muteness and the experience of powerlessness, an inability ever to name; it is, in the first place, the fact of *receiving one's name.*"[67] Our insertion into language, our being given a name, functions as a *memento*

65 Derrida, *The Animal That Therefore I Am*, p. 19.

66 Ibid.

67 Ibid., pp. 19–20.

mori—in language, we die in advance, we relate to ourselves as already dead. Language is in this sense a form of melancholy, not of mourning: in it, we treat an object which is still alive as already dead or lost, so that when Benjamin speaks about "*a foreshadowing of mourning*," one should take this as the very formula of the melancholy.

There is, however, a barely concealed ambiguity in Derrida's claims: if sadness is prior to muteness (lack of language), if it causes muteness, is then the primordial function of language to release or abolish this sadness? But if this is the case, how can this sadness originally be the sadness of receiving one's name? Am I left without words at the unheard-of violence of someone naming me, imposing a symbolic identity on to me, without asking for my consent? And how can the sadness caused by this reduction to the passivity of being-named be experienced by nature itself? Does not such an experience presuppose that one already dwells in the dimension of naming, of language? Should one not limit such a claim to so-called domestic animals? Lacan noted somewhere that, while animals do not speak, domestic animals nonetheless already dwell in the dimension of language (they react to their names, run to their master when they hear it called, obey orders, etc.), which is why, although they do not have access to "normal" subjectivity, they can nonetheless be affected by (human) pathology: a dog can be hystericized, and so on. So, to return to the sad and perplexed gaze of the laboratory cat, what it expresses is perhaps the cat's horror at having encountered The Animal, namely ourselves, humans: what the cat sees is us in all our monstrosity, and what we see in its tortured gaze is our own monstrosity. In this sense, the big Other (the symbolic order) is already here for the poor cat: like the prisoner in Kafka's penal colony, the cat suffered the material consequences of being caught in the symbolic gridlock. It effectively suffered the consequences of being named, included in the symbolic network.

To resolve this problem, should we distinguish between *two* sadnesses: the sadness of natural life prior to and independent of language, and the sadness of being named, subjugated to language? There is, first, the "infinite melancholy of all living things," a tension or pain which is resolved when a Word is spoken; then, however, the pronunciation of a Word itself generates a sadness of its own (referred to by Derrida). Does not this insight into the intimate link between language and pain bring us close to Richard Rorty's definition of humans as beings who suffer and are able to narrate their suffering—or, as Derrida put it, to man as the autobiographical animal? What Rorty does not take into account is the additional pain (the surplus-pain) generated by language itself.

Maybe Hegel can show us a way out here, when he interprets gravity as an indication that matter (nature) has its center outside itself and is condemned to strive endlessly towards it; spirit, on the contrary, has its center in itself, with the rise of spirit, reality returns to itself from its self-externalization. Spirit, however, is only actual in human thought, whose medium is language, and language involves an even more radical externalization—nature thus returns to itself through a repeated externalization (or, as Schelling would have put it, in language, a subject contracts itself outside itself).

There is an underlying necessity at work here: every speaker—every name-giver—*has* to be named, has to be included in its own chain of nominations, or, to refer to the joke often quoted by Lacan: "I have three brothers, Paul, Ernest, and myself." No wonder that, in many religions, God's name is secret, one is prohibited from pronouncing it. The speaking subject persists in this in-between: prior to nomination, there is no subject, but once it is named, it already disappears in its signifier—the subject never is, it always *will have been*.

But what if that which characterizes humans is this very openness to the abyss of the radical Other, this perplexity of "What does the Other really want from me?" In other words, what if we turn the perspective around here? What if the perplexity a human sees in the animal's gaze is the perplexity aroused by the monstrosity of the human being itself? What if it is my own abyss I see reflected in the abyss of the Other's gaze—"*dans ses yeux, je vois ma perte écrite*," as Racine put it in *Phèdre*? Or, in Hegelese, instead of asking what Substance is for the Subject, how the Subject can grasp Substance, one should ask the obverse question: what is (the rise of the) Subject for (pre-subjective) Substance? G. K. Chesterton proposed such a Hegelian reversal precisely apropos man and animals: instead of asking what animals are for humans, for our experience, we should ask what man is for animals—in his less well-known *Everlasting Man*, Chesterton conducts a wonderful mental experiment along these lines, imagining the monster that man might have seemed at first to the merely natural animals around him:

> The simplest truth about man is that he is a very strange being; almost in the sense of being a stranger on the earth. In all sobriety, he has much more of the external appearance of one bringing alien habits from another land than of a mere growth of this one. He has an unfair advantage and an unfair disadvantage. He cannot sleep in his own skin; he cannot trust his own instincts. He is at once a creator moving miraculous hands and fingers and a kind of cripple. He is wrapped in artificial bandages called clothes; he is propped on artificial crutches called furniture. His mind has the same doubtful liberties and the same wild limitations. Alone among the animals, he is shaken with the beautiful madness called laughter; as if he had caught sight of some secret in the very shape of the universe hidden from the universe itself. Alone among the animals he feels the need of averting his thought from the root realities of his own bodily being; of hiding them as in the presence of some higher possibility which creates the mystery of shame. Whether we praise these things as

> natural to man or abuse them as artificial in nature, they remain in the same sense unique.[68]

This is what Chesterton called "thinking backwards": we have to put ourselves back in time, before the fateful decisions were made or before the accidents occurred that generated the state which now seems normal to us, and the best way to do it, to render palpable this open moment of decision, is to imagine how, at that point, history might have taken a different turn. With regard to Christianity, instead of losing time probing into how it related to Judaism—how it misunderstands the Old Testament by reading it as announcing the arrival of Christ—and then trying to reconstruct what the Jews were like prior to Christianity, unaffected by the retroactive Christian perspective, one should rather turn the perspective around and "extraneate" Christianity itself, treat it as Christianity-in-becoming and focus on what a strange beast, what a scandalous monstrosity, Christ must have appeared to be in the eyes of the Jewish ideological establishment.

A hyperbolic example is provided by those rare societies which, until now, had succeeded in avoiding contact with "civilization." In May 2008, the media reported on the discovery of an "uncontacted tribe" in the thick rainforest along the Brazilian-Peruvian frontier: they had never had any contact with the "outside world"; their way of life had probably remained unchanged for over 10,000 years. Photos of their village were released, taken from a plane. When anthropologists first flew over the area, they saw women and children in the open and no one appeared to be painted. Only when the plane returned a few hours later did they see tribesmen covered head-to-toe in red: with their skin painted bright red, heads partially shaved, arrows drawn back in the longbows and aimed square at the aircraft buzzing overhead, their gesture was unmistakable: Stay away! And the gesture was correct: contact is usually a disaster for such remote tribes. Even if the loggers do not shoot them or force them off the land, diseases against which these isolated humans have no resistance typically wipe out half an uncontacted tribe's numbers in only a few years. Our civilization is for them literally a melting pot—they melt and disappear into it, like the ancient frescoes in *Fellini's Roma* which were protected as long as they were isolated in their underground vacuum—the moment the (very careful and respectful) researchers entered their domain, they started to disintegrate. We often ask ourselves how we would react to meeting aliens much more developed than ourselves—in the case of uncontacted tribes, we ourselves are the aliens. Therein resides the horror of these pictures: we see the terrified natives observing an inhuman Other, and we ourselves are this Other.

---

68 G. K. Chesterton, *The Everlasting Man*, Mineola: Dover 2007, pp. 30–1.

How, then, do we humans affect nature? When fires raged in the Peloponnese in the summer of 2007, one photo of the ravaged area showed a field of large cacti half-burned in such a strange way that they appeared almost melted, their shape protracted in a multitude of ways, somehow like Dali's famous painting of the "melted" clock, twisted in the middle like a thick pancake. What makes such images so fascinating is the way they represent not only a destruction internal to reality, but a destruction of the very texture of reality, of reality's basic coordinates. The first effect is that of a denaturalized nature: nature half-destroyed loses its "organic" character, appearing as a *bricolage*, an artificial composite of heterogeneous elements chaotically thrown together. The second effect is that of a temporal disturbance: it seems as if we are no longer dealing with nature in its regular rhythm of generation and corruption, growth and decay, but with a twisted space in which, in an obscene way, as in the case of cancerous protuberances, new forms of life grow out of decay itself. A third effect is that of a multiple anamorphic distortion: when plants appear as partially "melted," unnaturally prolonged in different directions, it is as if the object itself, in its distorted material reality, has incorporated multiple perspectives, fractured views of how we would perceive it if we were to look at it from different standpoints. It thus appears that one can no longer clearly distinguish between the object's immediate reality and the subjective perspectives on it—the distortions involved in looking awry at the object are inscribed into its very objective reality.

In Hegelian terms, such a landscape embodies the coincidence of the extremes of In-itself and For-us: in catching sight of such a weird scene, our first impression is that we are getting a glimpse of nature In-itself in its monstrous pre-human form. However, it is precisely as such that nature inscribes, in the guise of its distortion, the monstrosity of man, his awkward place within nature. Man *is* such an anamorphic distortion of nature, a perturbance of the "natural" rhythm of generation and corruption. When we hear a statement like Hölderlin's famous "poetically dwells man on this earth," we should not imagine man's dwelling as a hut near a stream in a forest, but precisely as such a distorted "denaturalized" landscape.

INTERLUDE 3

King, Rabble, War … and Sex

The most famous passage in Jack London's *Martin Eden* is the final paragraph, describing the hero's suicide by drowning:

> He seemed floating languidly in a sea of dreamy vision. Colors and radiances surrounded him and bathed him and pervaded him. What was that? It seemed a lighthouse; but it was inside his brain—a flashing, bright white light. It flashed swifter and swifter. There was a long rumble of sound, and it seemed to him that he was falling down a vast and interminable stairway. And somewhere at the bottom he fell into darkness. That much he knew. He had fallen into darkness. And at the instant he knew, he ceased to know.

How had Martin arrived at this point? What pushed him to suicide was his very success—the novel presents the crisis of investiture in its simple but most radical form: after long years of struggle and hard work, Martin finally succeeds and becomes a famous writer; however, while he is floating in wealth and fame, one thing puzzles him,

> a little thing that would have puzzled the world had it known. But the world would have puzzled over his bepuzzlement rather than over the little thing that to him loomed gigantic. Judge Blount invited him to dinner. That was the little thing, or the beginning of the little thing, that was soon to become the big thing. He had insulted Judge Blount, treated him abominably, and Judge Blount, meeting him on the street, invited him to dinner. Martin bethought himself of the numerous occasions on which he had met Judge Blount at the Morses' and when Judge Blount had not invited him to dinner. Why had he not invited him to dinner then? he asked himself. He had not changed. He was the same Martin Eden. What made the difference? The fact that the stuff he had written had appeared inside the covers of books? But it was work performed. It was not something he had done since. It was achievement accomplished at the very time Judge Blount was sharing this general view and sneering at his Spencer and his intellect. Therefore it was not for any real value, but for a purely fictitious value that Judge Blount invited him to dinner.

This little puzzling thing grows larger and larger, turning into the central obsession of his life:

> His thoughts went ever around and around in a circle. The centre of that circle was "work performed"; it ate at his brain like a deathless maggot. He awoke to it in the morning. It tormented his dreams at night. Every affair of life around him that penetrated through his senses immediately related itself to "work performed." He drove along the path of relentless logic to the conclusion that he was nobody, nothing. Mart Eden, the hoodlum, and Mart Eden, the sailor, had been real, had been he; but Martin Eden! the famous writer, did not exist. Martin Eden, the famous writer, was a vapor that had arisen in the mob-mind and by the mob-mind had been thrust into the corporeal being of Mart Eden, the hoodlum and sailor.

Even his beloved Lizzy, who had not wanted to marry him, now desperately throws herself at him, proclaiming that she loves him totally; when she claims that she is ready to die for him, Martin tauntingly replies:

> Why didn't you dare it before? When I hadn't a job? When I was starving? When I was just as I am now, as a man, as an artist, the same Martin Eden? That's the question I've been propounding to myself for many a day—not concerning you merely, but concerning everybody. You see I have not changed, though my sudden apparent appreciation in value compels me constantly to reassure myself on that point. I've got the same flesh on my bones, the same ten fingers and toes. I am the same. I have not developed any new strength nor virtue. My brain is the same old brain. I haven't made even one new generalization on literature or philosophy. I am personally of the same value that I was when nobody wanted me. And what is puzzling me is why they want me now. Surely they don't want me for myself, for myself is the same old self they did not want. Then they must want me for something else, for something that is outside of me, for something that is not I! Shall I tell you what that something is? It is for the recognition I have received. That recognition is not I. It resides in the minds of others.

What Martin cannot accept is the radical gap that forever separates his "real" qualities from his symbolic status (in the eyes of the others): all of a sudden, he is no longer a nobody avoided by the respectable public but a famous author invited to dinner by the pillars of society, with even the beloved woman now throwing herself at his feet. But he is fully aware that nothing has changed in him in reality, he is now the same person as he was, and even all his works were already written when he was ignored and despised. What Martin cannot accept is this radical de-centering of the very core of his personality which "resides in the minds of others": he is nothing in himself, just a concentrated projection of others' dreams. This perception that his *agalma*, what now makes him desired by others, is something outside of him not only ruins his narcissism, it also kills his desire: "Something has gone out of me. I have always been unafraid of life, but I never dreamed of being sated with life. Life has so filled me that I am empty of any desire for anything." It is this "conclusion that he was nobody, nothing" which drove him to suicide.

Frank D. Gilroy's *From Noon Till Three*, a quite unique comedy Western from 1976, deals with the same topic of the consequences of symbolic alienation. Here is a summary of the plot, courtesy of Wikipedia: In the American West of the late nineteenth century, Graham Dorsey (Charles Bronson), a member of a gang, is involved in a failed bank robbery; on the run, he finds himself at the ranch of the widow Amanda Starbuck (Jill Ireland) and stays there for three hours ("from noon till three"). He tries to force himself on Amanda, who resists his advances rather inventively; the frustrated Graham decides on a ruse: he pretends he is impotent, hoping to play on Amanda's sympathy. The deception works, and they make love three times; afterwards, they have a long talk and even dance to Amanda's music box, with Graham wearing Mr. Starbuck's old tuxedo. A neighbor boy stops by to tell Amanda about an attempted bank robbery in town. On Amanda's instigation, Graham leaves to help his fellows, but he is spotted and chased. Graham eludes them when he comes upon Dr. Finger, a traveling dentist, steals his horse and wagon, and exchanges clothes with him at gunpoint. Dr. Finger is taken for Graham and shot dead; the posse, recognizing Mr. Starbuck's horse and tux, bring the dead body back to the Starbuck ranch. Amanda, seeing what she thinks is Graham's body (she cannot see the face) faints. But it turns out Dr. Finger was a quack, and the first person Graham encounters after his escape is one of Dr. Finger's dissatisfied customers, which leads to Graham being sent to prison on a year-long sentence for Dr. Finger's crimes. During this time, Amanda is at first ostracized by the townspeople, but an impassioned speech proclaiming her love for Graham leads to a surprising turnaround: the townspeople not only forgive her, they see Graham and Amanda's story as remarkable. The story then becomes a legend, spawning a popular book (entitled *From Noon Till Three*), dime novels, a stage play, and even a popular song. The legend of Graham and Amanda becomes bigger than the reality, and when her book becomes a worldwide bestseller it makes Amanda a very wealthy woman. Graham, who reads the book while in prison, is amused by the distortions. After serving his time, a disguised Graham takes one of Amanda's guided tours of her ranch and stays behind, intending to reveal himself. Amanda does not recognize him and becomes frightened: for every detail of their love encounter he tells her, she cries back: "It's in the book!" It is only when Graham shows her "something that's not in the book" (his penis) that Amanda believes him; but instead of joy, she is worried: if word got out that Graham was alive, the legend of Graham and Amanda would be done for. Even Graham's suggestion that he live with her incognito is no good; after all, if Amanda were to live with another man, the legend would still be destroyed. The encounter ends up with Amanda pointing a gun at Graham ... but at the last moment she decides to shoot herself. Graham is now heartbroken: not only has he lost Amanda, he also loses his identity: people laugh when he tells them he is Graham, since he looks nothing like his description in the book. The fact that he encounters his public figure everywhere (he hears "their song" at a local saloon and walks in on a stage production of *From Noon Till Three*) literally drives him crazy. In the end he is confined to an insane asylum, where he meets the only people who believe him and accept him as Graham: his fellow inmates. Finally, he is content. Indeed, as Lacan once remarked, every one of us always tries to transform himself into a character in the novel which is his own life.[1]

Note the symmetry with *Martin Eden*: both Graham and Amanda relate to their "legend" (their public symbolic identity), but they react differently when reality catches up with it: Amanda chooses the legend over reality, for in a weird variation of the famous line from a John Ford Western ("when reality doesn't fit the legend, print the legend"), she shoots herself to save her own legend. Graham, on the contrary, chooses reality (they should live together even if this will ruin the legend), but is unaware that the legend has a power of its own which also determines their (social) reality. The price he pays is that his symbolic identity is literally taken from him: the material proof of his identity—(the shape of) his penis—does not hold in public, since the penis should not be confused with the phallus. The only place where he is recognized as who he is is the lunatic asylum; to paraphrase Lacan: a madman is not only someone other than Graham Dorsey thinking he is Graham Dorsey, a madman is also Graham Dorsey thinking he is Graham Dorsey—a further confirmation that the denial of symbolic castration leads to psychosis.

Insofar as symbolic castration is also a name for the gap between my immediate stupid being and my symbolic title (recall the proverbial disappointment of the adolescent: is that miserable coward really my *father*?), and since a symbolic authority can only function insofar as, in a kind of illegitimate short-circuit, this gap is obfuscated and my symbolic authority appears as an immediate property or quality of me as a person, each authority has to protect itself from situations in which this gap becomes palpable. For example, political leaders know very well how to avoid situations in which their impotence might be revealed; a father knows how to hide his humiliations (when his boss shouts at him, and so

1 But does the same not also hold for philosophy? Is not the ultimate goal of a philosophical system to account for the thinker himself, to construct a narrative in which the thinker is the main character (Hegel, exemplarily)? Kierkegaard's critique is that Hegel fails precisely here.

forth) from the gaze of his son. What is protected by such "face saving" strategies is *appearance*: although I know very well my father is ultimately impotent, I refuse to believe it, which is why the effect of witnessing the open display of his impotence can be so shattering. Such humiliating moments fully deserve to be called "castrating experiences," not because father is shown to be castrated or impotent, but because the gap between his miserable reality and his symbolic authority is rendered palpable and can no longer by ignored by way of fetishistic disavowal.

Is this not the problem of *The King's Speech*, the film which triumphed at the 2011 Oscars? The problem of the soon-to-be-king, the cause of his stuttering, is precisely his inability to assume his symbolic function, to identify with his title. The king thus displays a minimum of common sense, experiencing the stupidity of seriously accepting that one is a king by divine will—and the task of the Australian voice-coach is to render him stupid enough to accept his being a king as his natural property. As usual, Chesterton got it right: "if a man says that he is the rightful King of England, it is no complete answer to say that the existing authorities call him mad; for if he were King of England that might be the wisest thing for the existing authorities to do." In the key scene of the film, the coach sits on the king's chair; the furious king demands that he stand up, and the coach refuses, asking by what right the king can command him. The king shouts back: "Divine right, if you must! I'm your king!!!" at which point the coach has won the argument—now the king believes he is a king. The solution of the film is thus, of course, a reactionary one: the king is "normalized," the force of his hysterical questioning is obliterated.

Another winner at the 2011 Oscars, *Black Swan*, the feminine counterpart to *The King's Speech*, is even more reactionary: its premise is that, while a man can be dedicated to his mission (as the king is in *The King's Speech*) and still lead a normal private life, a woman who totally dedicates herself to her mission (here, to be a ballerina) enters on the path to self-destruction—her success is paid for by her death. It is easy to recognize in this plot the old *topos* of a woman torn between her artistic vocation and a happy, calm private life, who makes the wrong choice and dies—in Michael Powell's *Red Shoes* it is also a ballerina, while in Offenbach's *Hoffman's Tales* and Kieslowski's *Double Life of Véronique* it is a singer. *Hoffman's Tales* presents the heroine's dedication to her artistic vocation as the result of manipulation by a dark devilish character, while *The Double Life of Véronique* stages both versions of the choice: the Polish Weronika, who has chosen to sing, dies during a performance, while the French Véronique withdraws into privacy and survives. The two recent films, *The King's Speech* and *Black Swan*, thus work in a complementary way as a reassertion of the traditional couple under the masculine authority: for the man, a naïve assumption of symbolic authority; for the woman, withdrawal into privacy—a clear conservative strategy designed to counteract the rise of the postmodern post-Oedipal mode of subjectivity.

For Hegel, the king is defined as a subject who accepts this radical decentering, that is, to quote Marx again, accepts the fact that he is a king because others treat him as a king, not the other way round—otherwise, if he thinks that he is a king "in himself," he is a madman. According to legend, during the decisive battle between the Prussian and the Austrian armies in the 1866 war, the Prussian king, formally the supreme commander of the Prussian army, observing the fight from a nearby hill, looked worried at (what appeared to him) the confusion on the battleground, where some of the Prussian troops even seemed to be retreating. General von Moltke, the great Prussian strategist who had planned the battle deployment, turned to the king in the middle of this confusion and said: "May I be the first to congratulate your majesty on a brilliant victory?" This exemplifies the gap between S_1 and S_2 at its purest: the king was the Master, the formal commander totally ignorant of the meaning of what was happening, while von Moltke embodied strategic knowledge—although, at the level of actual decisions, the victory was Moltke's, he was correct in congratulating the king on behalf of whom he was acting. The stupidity of the Master is palpable in this gap between the confusion of the master-figure and the objective-symbolic fact that he had already won a brilliant victory. We all know the old joke referring to the enigma about who really wrote Shakespeare's plays: "Not William Shakespeare, but someone else with the same name." This is what Lacan means by the "decentered subject," this is how a subject relates to the name which fixes its symbolic identity: John Smith is (always, by definition, in its very notion) not John Smith, but someone else with the same name. As Shakespeare's Juliet already knew, I am never "that name"—the John Smith who really thinks he is John Smith is a psychotic. This key point was missed by the young Marx in his critique of Hegel's *Philosophy of Right*; after quoting the beginning of §281:

> Both moments in their undivided unity—(a) the will's ultimate ungrounded self, and (b) therefore its similarly ungrounded objective existence (existence being the category which is at home in nature)—constitute the Idea of something against which caprice is powerless, the "majesty" of the monarch. In this unity lies the actual unity of the state, and it is only through this, its inward and outward immediacy, that the unity of the state is saved from the risk of being drawn down into the sphere of particularity and its caprices, ends and opinions, and saved too from the war of factions round the throne and from the enfeeblement and overthrow of the power of the state.[2]

2 G. W. F. Hegel, *Hegel's Philosophy of Right*, trans. T. M. Knox, Oxford: Oxford University Press 1978, p. 185.

Marx adds his (all too common-sensical) ironic commentary:

> The two moments are [a] the contingency of the will, caprice, and [b] the contingency of nature, birth; thus, His Majesty: Contingency. Contingency is thus the actual unity of the state.
>
> The way in which, according to Hegel, an inward and outward immediacy [of the state] is to be saved from collision, [due to caprice, factions,] etc., is incredible, since collision is precisely what it makes possible ...
>
> The prince's hereditary character results from his concept. He is to be the person who is specified from the entire race of men, who is distinguished from all other persons. But then what is the ultimate fixed difference of one person from all others? The body. And the highest function of the body is sexual activity. Hence the highest constitutional act of the king is his sexual activity, because through this he makes a king and carries on his body.[3]

Marx concludes with the sarcastic note that the Hegelian monarch is nothing more than an appendix to his penis—to which we should say: yes, but that is precisely Hegel's point, namely that such an utter alienation, such a reversal by which a person becomes an appendix of its biological organ of procreation, is the price to be paid for acting like the state's sovereignty embodied.[4] One can clearly see, from §281 quoted above, how the institution of hereditary monarchy is for Hegel the solution to the problem of caprice and of factions, the problem, in short, of the contingency of power. This contingency is overcome not by a deeper necessity (say, in the sense of Plato's philosopher-kings, rulers whose knowledge legitimizes their power), but by an even more radical contingency: we posit at the top a subject effectively reduced to an appendix of his penis, a subject who did not make himself what he is (through the labor of mediation), but is immediately born into it. Of course, Hegel is fully aware that there is no deeper necessity operating behind the scenes to guarantee that the monarch will be a wise, just, and courageous person—on the contrary, in the figure of the monarch, contingency (the contingency of his properties and qualifications) is taken to an extreme; all that matters is his birth.[5] In socio-political life, stability can only be gained when all subjects accept the result of this contingent process, since the contingency of birth is exempted from social struggles.

---

3 Karl Marx, *Critique of Hegel's "Philosophy of Right,"* trans. Annette Jolin and Joseph O'Malley, Cambridge: Cambridge University Press 1970, pp. 35, 40.

4 Note also the irony of the situation: insofar as the gap between my immediate bodily being and my symbolic identity is the gap of castration, being reduced to one's penis is the very formula of castration.

5 Also in inherent philosophical terms, we can see here how radical Hegel is in his assertion of contingency: the only way to overcome contingency is through its redoubling.

An obvious counter-argument arises here: does Hegel not remain caught in an illusion of purity—namely of the purity of the expert-knowledge of the state bureaucracy which only works rationally for the common good? True, he concedes an irreducible impurity (the contingent play of partial interests and factional struggles) of political life, but is not his illusory wager that, if one isolates this moment of impurity (subjective caprice) in the figure of the monarch, this exception will make the rest (the body of the state bureaucracy) rational, exempted from the play of conflicting partial interests? With this notion of state bureaucracy as the "universal class," is not the state thus depoliticized, exempted from the properly political *differend*? However, while Hegel is well aware that political life consists of a contingent "war of factions around the throne," his idea is not that the monarch takes upon himself this contingency and thus magically turns the state bureaucracy into a neutral machine, but that, on account of his being-determined by the contingency of biological descent, *the king himself* is in a formal sense elevated above political struggles.

In Lacanese, the passage from inherent notional self-development which mediates all content to the act or decision which freely releases this content is, of course, the passage from S_2 (knowledge, the chain of signifiers) to S_1 (the performative Master-Signifier). In a strictly homologous sense, the Hegelian Absolute Knowing is a knowledge which is "absolved" from its positive content—how? Jean-Claude Milner has developed a notion of Absolute Knowing (*savoir absolu*) which, without even mentioning Hegel, is simultaneously close and distant from him. Milner's starting point is the grammatical opposition between relative and absolute in the use of verbs: when I say, "I know Latin," my knowing is related to a determinate object, it is supplemented by this object, in contrast to simply saying, "I know," where knowledge is "absolved" (freed) from such attachments. Such "absolute" knowing is "the agent of its own deployment whose object is merely its occasion and whose subject is its instrument; it follows its internal law that I call surplus-knowing."[6] Milner's model of this Absolute Knowing is not Hegel, but the post-Hegelian *Wissenschaft*, university science in continuous progress: its surplus is something which is not yet here as said/known, but always to be produced. The difference that separates surplus-knowing from established knowledge is thus a pure difference immanent to knowing, with no reference to its external object: the difference between the known and the not-yet-known, the difference which makes the field of knowledge forever incomplete. Milner's objection to this notion of Absolute Knowing is that it involves only a "more" and not a "less," only a surplus and not a lack of knowing—the reason why Lacan rejects it as the pure figure of the University Discourse. So far so good—but where does Hegel, his Absolute Knowing, fit into all this? Hegel's Absolute

6 Jean Claude Milner, *Clartes de tout*, Paris: Verdier 2011, p. 54.

Knowing *does* involve a "less": it refers to a constitutive lack, the lack in the Other itself, not in our knowledge. Hegel's Absolute Knowing is not an open field of endless progress, and it is the overlapping of the two lacks (the subject's lack of knowing and the lack in the Other itself) that accounts for its "closure."

To explain the mode of functioning of the objectless knowing, Milner evokes the TV series *Dexter*, in which a father who knows his son is genetically determined to become a serial killer tells him to become a cop and thus satisfy his innate urge to kill by killing only the killers themselves.[7] In a homologous way, Milner's aim is to operate like a bird flying high up in the air, with no attachment to any particular object on the land; from time to time, the bird dives and picks out its victim—like Milner who, in his work, picks on one particular knowledge after another and tears it apart by displaying its inconsistency. But is this not precisely the mode of functioning of Hegel's own Absolute Knowing which moves from one to another shape of knowing, touching it in its Real, i.e., bringing out its immanent/constitutive antagonism?

Schelling was thus wrong in his critique of Hegel: the intervention of the act of decision is purely immanent, it is the moment of the "quilting point," of the reversal of constative into performative. Does not the same go for the king in the case of the State, according to Hegel's defense of the monarchy? The bureaucratic chain of knowledge is followed by the king's decision which, as the "completely concrete objectivity of the will," "reabsorbs all particularity into its single self, cuts short the weighing of pros and cons between which it lets itself oscillate perpetually now this way and now that, and by saying 'I will' makes its decision and so inaugurates all activity and actuality" (§281). Hegel emphasizes this apartness of the monarch already when he states that the "ultimate self-determination" can "fall within the sphere of human freedom only insofar as it has the position of a pinnacle, explicitly distinct from, and raised above, all that is particular and conditional, for only so is it actual in a way adequate to its concept" (§281). This is why "the conception of the monarch" is

> of all conceptions the hardest for ratiocination, i.e. for the method of reflection employed by the Understanding. This method refuses to move beyond isolated categories and hence here again knows only *raisonnement*, finite points of view, and deductive argumentation. Consequently it exhibits the dignity of the monarch as something deduced, not only in its form, but in its essence. The truth is, however, that to be something not deduced but purely self-originating is precisely the conception of monarchy.

In the next paragraph, Hegel further elaborates this speculative necessity of the monarch:

---

7 Ibid., p. 60.

> This ultimate self in which the will of the state is concentrated is, when thus taken in abstraction, a single self and therefore is immediate individuality. Hence its "natural" character is implied in its very conception. The monarch, therefore, is essentially characterized as this individual, in abstraction from all his other characteristics, and this individual is raised to the dignity of monarchy in an immediate, natural, fashion, i.e. through his birth in the course of nature.
>
> *Remark*: This transition of the concept of pure self-determination into the immediacy of being and so into the realm of nature is of a purely speculative character, and the apprehension of it therefore belongs to logic. Moreover, this transition is on the whole the same as that familiar to us in the nature of willing, and there the process is to translate something from subjectivity (i.e. some purpose held before the mind) into existence. But the proper form of the Idea and of the transition here under consideration is the immediate conversion of the pure self-determination of the will (i.e. of the simple concept itself) into a single and natural existent without the mediation of a particular content (like a purpose in the case of action).
>
> In the so-called "ontological" proof of the existence of God, we have the same conversion of the absolute concept into existence …
>
> *Addition*: It is often alleged against monarchy that it makes the welfare of the state dependent on chance, for, it is urged, the monarch may be ill-educated, he may perhaps be unworthy of the highest position in the state, and it is senseless that such a state of affairs should exist because it is supposed to be rational. But all this rests on a presupposition which is nugatory, namely that everything depends on the monarch's particular character. In a completely organized state, it is only a question of the culminating point of formal decision (and a natural bulwark against passion. It is wrong therefore to demand objective qualities in a monarch); he has only to say "yes" and dot the "i", because the throne should be such that the significant thing in its holder is not his particular make-up … In a well-organized monarchy, the objective aspect belongs to law alone, and the monarch's part is merely to set to the law the subjective "I will".

The speculative moment that Understanding cannot grasp is "the transition of the concept of pure self-determination into the immediacy of being and so into the realm of nature." In other words, while Understanding can well grasp the universal mediation of a living totality, what it cannot grasp is that this totality, in order to actualize itself, has to acquire actual existence in the guise of an immediate "natural" singularity.[8] One can also say that Understanding misses

---

8 The Marxists who mocked Hegel here paid the price for this negligence: in the regimes which legitimized themselves as Marxist, a Leader emerged who, again, not only directly embodied the rational totality, but embodied it fully, as a figure of full Knowledge and not merely the idiotic dotter of the i's. In other words, the Stalinist Leader is *not* a monarch, which makes him all the worse.

the *christological* moment: the necessity of a singular individual embodying the universal Spirit. The term "nature" should be given its full weight here: in the same way that, at the end of the Logic, the Idea's completed self-mediation releases from itself Nature, collapses into the external immediacy of Nature, the State's rational self-mediation has to acquire actual existence in a will which is determined as directly natural, unmediated, *stricto sensu* "irrational." Recall here Chesterton's appraisal of the guillotine (which was used precisely to behead a king):

> The guillotine has many sins, but to do it justice there is nothing evolutionary about it. The favourite evolutionary argument finds its best answer in the axe. The Evolutionist says, "Where do you draw the line?" the Revolutionist answers, "I draw it *here*: exactly between your head and body." There must at any given moment be an abstract right or wrong if any blow is to be struck; there must be something eternal if there is to be anything sudden.[9]

It is from here that one can understand why Badiou, *the* theorist of the Act, has to refer to Eternity: the Act is only conceivable as the intervention of Eternity into time. Historicist evolutionism leads to endless procrastination, the situation is always too complex, there are always further aspects to be accounted for, the pondering of pros and cons is never over. Against this stance, the passage to the act involves a gesture of radical and violent simplification, a cut like that of the proverbial Gordian knot: the magical moment when the infinite pondering crystallizes itself into a simple "yes" or "no."

This brings us to the topic of sublation versus sublimation. In *Seminar VII*, Lacan opposes sublation as dialectical mediation to sublimation: sublation includes all particulars into a dialectical totality, while sublimation takes a non-sublated remainder of the Real and elevates it directly into the embodiment of the impossible Thing that eludes all mediation. But is this move of sublimation really foreign to Hegel? With regard to the king, is not Hegel's point that, while all individuals have to "become what they are" through their work and thus to mediate or sublate their natural immediacy, the king is the only one who directly (by his nature) is that which his symbolic title designates him to be (one is a king by birth). The circle of mediation can thus only be concluded when it is supplemented by a "raw" non-mediated "irrational" element which "sutures" the rational totality.

When Hegel articulates the three parallel moves—from Logic to Nature, from the rational totality of the State to Monarch, and the ontological proof of God—does he not suggest that (a personal) God arises out of the same necessity

9 G. K. Chesterton, *Orthodoxy*, San Francisco: Ignatius Press 1995, p. 116.

as the Monarch? That God is the Monarch of the universe? This example makes it clear how the notional development can never reach its completion (in the naïve sense of the completed chain of reasons by means of which "everything is deduced")—the arbitrary intervention of the Master-Signifier designates the point at which contingency intervenes in the very heart of necessity: the very establishment of a necessity is a contingent act.[10] In a totally different field, Dennett detects the need for "conversation-stoppers" in the endless pursuit of argumentation which, because of the finitude and limitation of our situation, never comes to an end: there are always some other aspects to take into account, etc.[11] Is this need not the need for what Lacan called the Master-Signifier (Dennett himself refers to the "magic word," or to a fake dogma): for something that will cut the Gordian knot of endless pros and cons with an act of (ultimately arbitrary and imperfect) decision?

Apropos school exams, Lacan pointed out a strange fact: there must be a minimal gap, a delay, between the grading of the exam papers and the act of announcing the results. In other words, even if I know that I provided perfect answers to the questions, there will remain a minimal element of insecurity until the results are announced—this gap is the gap between constative and performative, between *measuring* the results and *taking note* of them (registering them) in the full sense of the symbolic act. The whole mystique of bureaucracy at its most sublime hinges on this gap: you know the facts, but you can never quite be sure how these facts will be registered by the bureaucracy. And, as Jean-Pierre Dupuy points out, the same holds for elections: in the electoral process also, the moment of contingency, of hazard, of a "draw," is crucial.[12] Fully "rational" elections would not be elections at all, but a transparent objectivized process. Traditional (premodern) societies resolved this problem by invoking a transcendent source which "verified" the result, conferring authority on it (God, the king ...). Therein lies the problem of modernity: modern societies perceive themselves as autonomous, self-regulated; that is, they can no longer rely on an external (transcendent) source of authority. But nevertheless, the moment of hazard has to remain operative in the electoral process, which is why commentators like to dwell on the "irrationality" of votes (one never knows where the votes will swing in the final days of an election campaign ...). In other words, democracy would not work if it were reduced to permanent opinion-polling—fully mechanized and quantified, deprived of its "performative" character; as

---

10 Descartes and other "voluntarists" were on the track of this paradox when they pointed out how universal necessary laws hold because of the arbitrary divine decision: 2 + 2 = 4 and not 5 because God willed it so.

11 Daniel Dennett, *Darwin's Dangerous Idea: Evolution and the Meanings of Life*, New York: Touchstone 1996, p. 506.

12 Jean-Pierre Dupuy, *La marque du sacré*, Paris: Carnets Nord 2008.

Lefort pointed out, voting has to remain a (sacrificial) ritual, a ritualistic self-destruction and rebirth of society.[13] The reason is that this hazard itself should not be transparent, it should be minimally externalized/reified: "the people's will" is our equivalent of what the Ancients perceived as the imponderable will of God or the hand of Fate. What people cannot accept as their direct arbitrary choice, the result of a pure hazard, they can accept if it refers to a minimum of the "Real"—Hegel knew this long ago, and this is the entire point of his defense of monarchy. And, last but not least, the same goes for love: there should be an element of the "answer of the Real" in it ("we were forever meant for each other"), I cannot really accept that my falling in love hinges on a pure contingency.[14]

Even such a superb reader of Hegel as Gérard Lebrun falls short here in inscribing Hegel into the Platonic tradition of "philosopher-kings": every exercise of power has to be justified by good reasons, the bearer of power has to be properly qualified for it by his knowledge and abilities, and power should be exercised for the good of the entire community—this notion of power sustains Hegel's concept of the state bureaucracy as the "universal class" educated to protect state interests against the particular interests of members and groups in civil society. Nietzsche counters this received notion by questioning its underlying premise: what kind of power (or authority) is it which needs to justify itself with reference to the interests of those over whom it rules, which accepts the need to provide reasons for its exercise? Does not such a notion of power undermine itself? How can I be your master if I accept the need to justify my authority in your eyes? Does this not imply that my authority depends on your approval, so that, acting as your master, I effectively serve you (recall Frederick the Great's famous notion of the king as the highest servant of his people)? Is it not rather that authority proper needs no reasons, since it is simply accepted on its own? As Kierkegaard put it, for a child to say that he obeys his father because the latter is wise, honest, and good, is a blasphemy, a total disavowal of true paternal authority. In Lacanian terms, this passage from "natural" authority to authority justified with reasons is, of course, the passage from the Master's discourse to the University discourse. This universe of the justified exercise of power is also eminently anti-political and, in this sense, "technocratic": my exercise of power should be grounded in reasons accessible to and approved by all rational human beings, for the underlying premise is that, as an agent of power, I am totally replaceable, I act in exactly the same way everyone else would have acted in my place—politics as the domain of competitive struggle, as the articulation of irreducible social antagonisms, should be replaced by rational administration which directly enacts the universal interest.

13 See Claude Lefort, *Essais sur le politique*, Paris: Seuil 1986.

14 See Slavoj Žižek, *Looking Awry*, Cambridge, MA: MIT Press 1991.

But is Lebrun right in imputing to Hegel such a notion of justified authority? Was Hegel not fully aware that true authority always contains an element of tautological self-assertion? "It is so because I say it is so!" The exercise of authority is an "irrational" act of contingent decision which breaks the endless chain of enumerating reasons *pro et contra*. Is this not the very rationale of Hegel's defense of monarchy? The state as a rational totality needs at its head a figure of "irrational" authority, an authority not justified by its qualifications: while all other public servants have to prove their capacity to exert power, the king is justified by the very fact that he is a king. To put it in more contemporary terms, the performative aspect of the state's actions is reserved for the king: the state bureaucracy prepares the content of state action, but it is the signature of the king which enacts it, enforcing it upon society. Hegel was well aware that it is only this distance between the "knowledge" embodied in the state bureaucracy and the authority of the Master embodied in the king which protects the social body against the "totalitarian" temptation: what we call a "totalitarian regime" is not a regime in which the Master imposes his unconstrained authority and ignores the suggestions of rational knowledge, but a regime in which Knowledge (the rationally justified authority) immediately assumes "performative" power—Stalin was not (did not present himself as) a Master, he was the highest servant of the people, legitimized by his knowledge and abilities.

This insight of Hegel's points towards his unique position between the Master's discourse (of traditional authority) and the University discourse (of modern power justified by reasons or by the democratic consent of its subjects): Hegel recognized that the charisma of the Master's authority is a fake, that the Master is an impostor—it is only the fact that he occupies the position of a Master (that his subjects treat him as a Master) which makes him a Master. However, he was also well aware that, if one tries to get rid of this excess and impose a self-transparent authority fully justified by expert knowledge, the result is even worse: instead of being limited to the symbolic head of state, "irrationality" spreads over the entire body of social power. Kafka's bureaucracy is just such a regime of expert knowledge deprived of the figure of the Master—Brecht was right when, as Benjamin reports in his diaries, he claimed that Kafka is "the *only genuine Bolshevik* writer."[15]

Is Hegel's position then a cynical one? Does he tells us to act as if a monarch is qualified to rule by his properties, to celebrate his glory, etc., although we know very well that he is a nobody in himself? A gap nonetheless separates Hegel's position from cynicism: the Hegelian (utopian?) wager is that one can admire a monarch not for his supposed real qualities, but on account of his very mediocrity, as a representative of human frailty. Here, however, things get

15 Quoted in Stathis Gourgouris, *Does Literature Think?*, Palo Alto: Stanford University Press 2003, p. 179.

complicated: is not the excess at the top of the social edifice (king, leader) to be supplemented by the excess at its bottom, those who have no proper place within the social body, what Rancière calls its "part of no-part," and what Hegel called the *Pöbel* (rabble)? Hegel fails to take note of how the rabble, in its very status as the destructive excess of the social totality, its "part of no-part," is the "reflexive determination" of the totality as such, the immediate embodiment of its universality, the particular element in the guise of which the social totality encounters itself among its elements, and, as such, the key constituent of its identity.[16] This is why Frank Ruda is fully justified in reading Hegel's short passages on the rabble in his *Philosophy of Right* as a symptomatic point of his entire philosophy of right, if not of his entire system.[17] If Hegel had seen the universal dimension of the rabble, he would have invented the symptom (as Marx—who saw in the proletariat the embodiment of the deadlocks of the existing society, the universal class—did).[18] In other words, what makes the notion of the rabble symptomatic is that it describes a necessarily produced "irrational" excess of the modern rational state, a group of people for whom there is no place within the organized totality, although they formally belong to it—as such, they perfectly exemplify the category of singular universality (a singular which directly gives body to a universality, by-passing the mediation through the particular):

> §244 When the standard of living of a large mass of people falls below a certain subsistence level—a level regulated automatically as the one necessary for a member of the society—and when there is a consequent loss of the sense of right and wrong, of honesty and the self-respect which makes a man insist on maintaining himself by his own work and effort, the result is the creation of a rabble of paupers. At the same time this brings with it, at the other end of the social scale, conditions which greatly facilitate the concentration of disproportionate wealth in a few hands.

---

16 Note the dialectical finesse of this last feature: what "sutures" the identity of a social totality as such is the very "free-floating" element which dissolves the fixed identity of any intra-social element. One can even establish a link between Hegel's residual anti-Semitism and his inability to think pure repetition: when he gives way to his displeasure with the Jews who stubbornly stick to their identity, instead of "moving forward" and, like other nations, allowing their identity to be sublated (*aufgehoben*) in historical progress, is not his displeasure caused by the perception that the Jews remain caught in the repetition of the same? Parenthetically, I am here in full solidarity with Benjamin Noys who, in his *The Persistence of the Negative* (Edinburgh: Edinburgh University Press 2010), emphasizes and deploys the link between the vicissitudes of the "purely philosophical" notion of negativity and the shifts and impasses of radical politics: when one talks on negativity, politics is never far behind.

17 I rely here on Frank Ruda's *Hegel's Rabble: An Investigation into Hegel's Philosophy of Right*, London: Continuum 2011.

18 I owe this formulation to Mladen Dolar.

We can easily see here the link between the eminently political topic of the status of the rabble and Hegel's basic ontological topic of the relationship between universality and particularity, that is, the problem of how to understand Hegelian "concrete universality." If we understand "concrete universality" in the usual sense of the organic subdivision of the universal into its particular moments, so that universality is not an abstract feature in which individuals directly participate, and the participation of the individual in the universal is always mediated through the particular network of determinations, then the corresponding notion of society is a corporate one: society as an organic Whole in which each individual has to find its particular place, in which I participate in the State by fulfilling my particular duty or obligation. There are no citizens as such, one has to be a member of a particular estate (a farmer, a state official, mother in a family, teacher, artisan ...) in order to contribute to the harmony of the Whole. This is the Bradleyian proto-fascist Hegel who opposes atomistic liberalism (in which society is a mechanical unity of abstract individuals) on behalf of the State as a living organism in which each part has its function. Within this space, the rabble has to appear as an irrational excess, as a threat to social order and stability, as outcasts excluded and excluding themselves from the "rational" social totality.

But is this truly what Hegel is aiming at with his "concrete universality"? Is not the core of dialectical negativity the short-circuit between the genus and (one of) its species, so that the genus appears as one of its own species opposed to others, entering into a negative relationship with them? In this sense, concrete universality is precisely a universality which includes itself among its species, in the guise of a singular moment lacking particular content—in short, it is precisely those who are without their proper place within the social Whole (like the rabble) who stand for the universal dimension of the society which generates them. This is why the rabble cannot be abolished without radically transforming the entire social edifice—and Hegel is fully aware of this; he is consistent enough to confess that a solution of this "disturbing problem" is impossible not for external contingent reasons, but for strictly immanent conceptual reasons. While he enumerates a series of measures to resolve the problem (police control and repression, charity, export of the rabble to colonies ...), he himself admits that these are only secondary palliatives which cannot really resolve the problem—not because the problem is too hard (because there is not enough wealth in society to take care of the poor), but because there is too much wealth—the more society is wealthy, the more poverty it produces:

> §245 When the masses begin to decline into poverty, (a) the burden of maintaining them at their ordinary standard of living might be directly laid on the wealthier classes, or they might receive the means of livelihood directly from other public

> sources of wealth (e.g. from the endowments of rich hospitals, monasteries, and other foundations). In either case, however, the needy would receive subsistence directly, not by means of their work, and this would violate the principle of civil society and the feeling of individual independence and self-respect in its individual members. (b) As an alternative, they might be given subsistence indirectly through being given work, i.e. the opportunity to work. In this event the volume of production would be increased, but the evil consists precisely in an excess of production and in the lack of a proportionate number of consumers who are themselves also producers, and thus it is simply intensified by both of the methods (a) and (b) by which it is sought to alleviate it. It hence becomes apparent that despite an excess of wealth civil society is not rich enough, i.e. its own resources are insufficient to check excessive poverty and the creation of a penurious rabble.

Note the finesse of Hegel's analysis: he points out that poverty is not only a material condition, but also the subjective position of being deprived of social recognition, which is why it is not enough to provide for the poor through public or private charity—in this way, they are still deprived of the satisfaction of autonomously taking care of their own lives. Furthermore, when Hegel emphasizes how society—the existing social order—is the ultimate space in which the subject finds his or her substantial content and recognition, namely how subjective freedom can actualize itself only in the rationality of the universal ethical order, the implied (although not explicitly stated) obverse is that those who do *not* find this recognition have also the right to rebel: if a class of people is systematically deprived of their rights, of their very dignity as persons, they are *eo ipso* also released from their duties towards the social order, because this order is no longer their ethical substance. The dismissive tone of Hegel's statements about the "rabble" should not blind us to the basic fact that he considered their rebellion fully justified in rational terms: the "rabble" is a class of people to whom systematically, not just in a contingent way, recognition by the ethical substance is denied, so they do not owe anything to society, and are dispensed of any duties towards it.

Negativity—the non-recognized element of the existing order—is thus necessarily produced, inherent to it, but with no place within the order. Here, however, Hegel makes an error (measured by his own standards): he does not venture the obvious thesis that, as such, the rabble should immediately stand for the universality of society. As excluded, lacking recognition of its particular position, the rabble is the universal as such. On this point at least, Marx was right in his critique of Hegel, since he was here more Hegelian than Hegel himself—as is well known, this is the starting point of the Marxian analysis: the "proletariat" designates such an "irrational" element of the "rational" social totality, its unaccountable "part of no-part," the element systematically generated by it and, simultaneously, denied the basic rights that define this totality; as such, the proletariat stands for the dimension of universality, for its emancipation is only possible in/through the universal emancipation. In a way, *every* act is proletarian: "There is only one social symptom: every individual is effectively proletarian, that is to say, he does not dispose of a discourse by means of which he could establish a social link."[19] It is only from such a "proletarian" position of being deprived of a discourse (of occupying the place of the "part of no-part" within the existing social body) that an act can emerge.

How, then, do the two excesses (at the top and at the bottom) relate to each other? Does not the link between the two provide the formula for a populist authoritarian regime? In his *Eighteenth Brumaire*, an analysis of the first such regime (the reign of Napoleon III), Marx pointed out that while Napoleon III played one class off against the other, stealing from one in order to satisfy another, the only true class base of his rule was the lumpenproletarian rabble. In a homologous way, the paradox of fascism is that it advocates a hierarchical order in which "everybody has his/her proper place," while its only true social base is a rabble (SA thugs and so forth)—in it, the only direct class link of the Leader is the one which connects him to the rabble, only among the rabble was Hitler truly "at home."

Hegel is of course aware that objective poverty is not enough to generate a rabble: this objective poverty must be subjectivized, changed into a "disposition of the mind," experienced as a radical injustice on account of which the subject feels no duty or obligation towards society. Hegel leaves no doubt that this injustice is real: society has a duty to guarantee the conditions for a dignified, free, autonomous life to all its members—this is their right, and if it is denied, they also have no duties towards society:

> *Addition*: The lowest subsistence level, that of a rabble of paupers, is fixed automatically, but the minimum varies considerably in different countries. In England, even the very poorest believe that they have rights; this is different from what satisfies the poor in other countries. Poverty in itself does not make men into a rabble; a rabble is created only when there is joined to poverty a disposition of mind, an inner indignation against the rich, against society, against the government, &c. A further consequence of this attitude is that through their dependence on chance men become frivolous and idle, like the Neapolitan lazzaroni for example. In this way there is born in the rabble the evil of lacking self-respect enough to secure subsistence by its own labour and yet at the same time of claiming to receive subsistence as its right. Against nature man can claim no right, but once society is established, poverty immediately takes the form of a wrong done to one class by another. The

19 Jacques Lacan, "La troisième," *Lettres d'Ecole freudienne* 16 (1975), p. 187.

> important question of how poverty is to be abolished is one of the most disturbing problems which agitate modern society. (§244)

It is easy to discern the ambiguity and oscillation in Hegel's line of argumentation here. He first appears to blame the poor themselves for subjectivizing their position as that of a rabble, for abandoning the principle of autonomy which obliges subjects to secure their subsistence by their own labor, and for claiming that they should receive from society the means for survival as a right. He then subtly changes the tone, emphasizing that, in contrast to his relations with nature, man can claim rights against society, which is why poverty is not just a social fact but a wrong done to one class by another. Furthermore, there is a subtle *non sequitur* in the argument: Hegel passes directly from the indignation of the rabble against the rich/society/government to their lack of self-respect—the rabble is irrational because it demands a decent life without working for it, thus denying the basic modern axiom that freedom and autonomy are based on the work of self-mediation. Consequently, the right to subsist without labor

> can only appear as irrational because [Hegel] links the notion of right to the notion of the free will that can only be free if it becomes an object for itself through objective activity. To claim a right to subsist without activity and to claim this right at the same time only for oneself, according to Hegel, therefore means to claim a right that has neither the universality nor the objectivity of a right. The right that the rabble claims is for Hegel therefore a *right without right* and ... he consequently defines the rabble as the particularity that unbinds itself also from the essential interrelation of right and duty.[20]

But indignation is not the same as lack of self-respect: it does not automatically generate the demand to be provided for without working. Indignation can also be a direct expression of self-respect: since the rabble is produced necessarily, as part of the social process of the (re)production of wealth, it is society itself which denies it the right to participate in the social universe of freedoms and rights—it is denied the right to have rights, for the "right without right" is effectively a meta-right or reflexive right, a universal right to have rights, to be in a position to act as a free autonomous subject. The demand to be provided for without working is thus a (possibly superficial) form of appearance of the more basic and in no way "irrational" demand to be given a chance to act as an autonomous free subject, to be included in the universe of freedoms and obligations. In other words, since the rabble are excluded from the universal sphere of free autonomous life, their demand is itself universal—their "claimed *right without right* contains a latent universal dimension and is itself not at all a mere particular

20 Ruda, *Hegel's Rabble*, p. 132.

right. As a particularly articulated right it is a right that latently affects anyone and offers the insight into a demand for equality beyond the existing objective statist circumstances."[21]

There is a further key distinction to be introduced here, a distinction only latent in Hegel (in the guise of the opposition between the two excesses of poverty and wealth) but elaborated by Ruda: members of the rabble (those excluded from the sphere of rights and freedoms):

> can be structurally differentiated into two types: there are the poor and there are the gamblers. Anyone can non-arbitrarily become poor, but only the one that arbitrarily decides not to satisfy his egoist needs and desires by working can become a gambler. He relies fully on the contingent movement of bourgeois economy and hopes to secure his own subsistence in an equally contingent manner—for example by contingently gaining money on the stock-market.[22]

The excessively wealthy are thus also a species of the rabble in the sense that they violate the rules of (or exclude themselves from) the sphere of duties and freedoms: they not only demand that society provide for their subsistence without work, they are *de facto* so provided. Consequently, while Hegel criticizes the position of the rabble as that of an irrational particularity egoistically opposing its mere particular interests against the existing and rationally organized universality, this differentiation between the two distinct rabbles demonstrates that only the rich rabble falls under Hegel's verdict: "While the rich rabble is, as Hegel judges correctly, a mere particular rabble, the poor rabble contains, against Hegel's judgment, a latent universal dimension that is not even inferior to the universality of the Hegelian conception of ethics."[23]

One can thus demonstrate that, in the case of the rabble, Hegel was inconsistent with regard to his own matrix of the dialectical process, *de facto* regressing from the properly dialectical notion of totality to a corporate model of the social Whole. Is this a simple empirical and accidental failure on Hegel's part, such that we can correct this (and other) similar points and thereby establish the "true" Hegelian system? The point is, of course, that here also one should apply the fundamental dialectical guideline: such local failures to properly deploy the mechanism of the dialectical process are its immanent symptomal points, they indicate a more fundamental structural flaw in the basic mechanism itself. In short, if Hegel had articulated the universal character of the rabble, his entire model of the rational State would have had to have been abandoned. Does this mean that all we have to do here is make the passage from Hegel to Marx? Is

21 Ibid.

22 Ibid.

23 Ibid., p. 133.

the inconsistency resolved when we replace the rabble with the proletariat as the "universal class"? Here is how Rebecca Comay sums up the socio-political limitation of Hegel:

> Hegel is not Marx. The rabble is not the proletariat, communism is not on the horizon, and revolution is not a solution ... Hegel is not prepared to see in the contradiction of civil society the death knell of class society, to identify capitalism itself as its own gravedigger, or to see in the disenfranchised masses anything more than a surge of blind, formless reaction, "elemental, irrational, barbarous, and terrifying" ... a swarm whose integration remains unrealized and unrealizable, an "ought" ... But the aporia, untypical for Hegel, points to something unfinished or already crumbling within the edifice whose construction Hegel declares to be completed, a failure of both actuality and rationality that undermines the solidity of the state he elsewhere celebrates, in Hobbesian language, as an earthly divinity.[24]

Is Hegel thus simply constrained by his historical context, did he come too early to see the emancipatory potential of the "part of no-part," so that all he could have done was to honestly register the unresolved and unresolvable aporias of his rational state? Perhaps; but does not the historical experience of the twentieth century also render problematic Marx's vision of the revolution? Are we not today, in the post-Fukuyama world, exactly in the late Hegel's situation? We see "something unfinished or already crumbling within the edifice" of the liberal-democratic welfare state which, in the utopian Fukuyama moment of the 1990s, may have appeared as the "end of history," the finally found best possible politico-economic form. Perhaps, then, we encounter here yet another case of non-synchronicity: in a way, Hegel was closer to the mark than Marx, the twentieth-century attempts to enact the *Aufhebung* of the rage of the disenfranchised masses into the will of the proletarian agent to resolve the social antagonisms ultimately failed, the "anachronistic" Hegel is more our contemporary than Marx.

We can also see how wrong Althusser was when, in his crude opposition between overdetermined structure and the Hegelian totality, he reduced the latter to a simple synchronicity that he called "expressive totality": for Althusser's Hegel, every historical epoch is dominated by one spiritual principle which expresses itself in all social spheres. However, as the example of the temporal discord between France and Germany demonstrated, non-contemporaneity is for Hegel a principle: Germany was politically in delay with regard to France (where the Revolution took place), which is why it could only prolong it in the domain of thought; however, the Revolution itself emerged in France only

24 Rebecca Comay, *Mourning Sickness: Hegel and the French Revolution*, Palo Alto: Stanford University Press 2011, p. 141.

because France itself was in delay with regard to Germany, that is, because France had missed the Reformation which asserts inner freedom and thus reconciles secular and spiritual domains. So, far from being an exception or an accidental complication, anachronism is the "signature" of consciousness: "experience is continually outbidding itself, perpetually making demands that it (i.e., the world) is unequipped to realize and unprepared to recognize, and comprehension inevitably comes too late to make a difference, if only because the stakes have already changed."[25] This anachronistic untimeliness holds especially for revolutions: "The 'French' Revolution that provides the measure of 'German' untimeliness is itself untimely ... There is no right time or 'ripe time' for revolution (or there would be no need of one). The Revolution always arrives too soon (conditions are never ready) and too late (it lags forever behind its own initiative)."[26] We can see now the stupidity of those "critical Marxists" who repeat the mantra that Stalinism emerged because the first proletarian revolution occurred in the wrong place (in semi-developed "Asiatic"-despotic Russia instead of Western Europe)—revolutions *always*, by definition, occur at the wrong time and place, they are always "out of place." And was not the French Revolution conditioned by the fact that, because of its absolutism, France was lagging behind England in terms of capitalist modernization? But is this non-contemporaneity irreducible? Is not Absolute Knowing, the concluding moment of the Hegelian system, the moment when, finally, history catches up with itself, when notion and reality overlap in full contemporaneity? Comay rejects this easy reading:

> Absolute knowing is the exposition of this delay. Its mandate is to make explicit the structural dissonance of experience. If philosophy makes any claim to universality, this is not because it synchronizes the calendars or provides intellectual compensation for its own tardiness. Its contribution is rather to formalize the necessity of the delay, together with the inventive strategies with which such a delay itself is invariably disguised, ignored, glamorized, or rationalized.[27]

This delay—ultimately not only the delay between the elements of the same historical totality, but the delay of the totality with regard to itself, the structural necessity for a totality to contain anachronistic elements which alone make it possible for it to establish itself as a totality—is the temporal aspect of a gap which propels the dialectical process, and far from filling in this gap, "Absolute Knowing" makes it visible as such, in its structural necessity:

---

25 Ibid., p. 6.
26 Ibid., p. 7.
27 Ibid., p. 6.

> Absolute knowing is neither compensation, as in the redemption of a debt, nor fulfilment: the void is constitutive (which does not mean that it is not historically overdetermined). Rather than trying to plug the gap through the accumulation of conceptual surplus value, Hegel sets out to demystify the phantasms we find to fill it.[28]

Therein lies the difference between Hegel and historicist evolutionism: the latter conceives historical progress as the succession of forms, each of which grows, reaches its peak, and then becomes outdated and disintegrates, while for Hegel, disintegration is the very sign of "maturity," for there is no moment of pure synchronicity when form and content overlap without delay.

Perhaps we should conceive the European trinity itself as a Borromean knot of anachronisms: the model-like excellence of each nation (British political economy, French politics, German philosophy) is grounded in an anachronistic delay in other domains (the excellence of German thought is the paradoxical result of its politico-economic backwardness; the French Revolution was grounded in the delay of capitalism due to French state absolutism, and so on. In this sense, the trinity worked like a Borromean knot: each two nations are linked only through the intermediary of the third (in politics, France links England and Germany, etc.).

We should risk taking a step further here and demystify the very notion of a world-historical nation, a nation destined to embody the level world history has reached at a certain point. It is often claimed that, in China, if you really hate someone, the curse you address to him is: "May you live in interesting times!" As Hegel was fully aware, in our history, "interesting times" are effectively times of unrest, war, and power struggles, with millions of innocent bystanders suffering the consequences: "The history of the world is not the theatre of happiness. Periods of happiness are blank pages; for they are periods of harmony, periods of the missing opposition."[29] Should we then conceive the succession of great "historical" nations which, passing the torch from one to the other, embody progress for a period (Iran, Greece, Rome, Germany ...) not as a blessing in which one nation is temporarily elevated to world-historical rank, but, rather, as the transmitting of a kind of contagious spiritual disease, a disease which a nation can only get rid of by passing it on to another nation, a disease which brings only suffering and destruction to the people contaminated by it? The Jews were a normal nation living in a happy "blank page" of history until, for reasons unknown, God selected them as his chosen people, which brought them only pain and dispersion—Hegel's solution is that this burden can be passed on,

28 Ibid., 125.

29 G. W. F. Hegel, *Lectures on the Philosophy of History*, trans. J. Sibree, London: Henry G. Bohn 1861, p. 73; translation modified.

and one can return to the happy "blank page." Or, to put it in Althusserian terms, while people live like individuals, from time to time some of them have the misfortune of being interpellated into subjects of the big Other.

So, back to rabble, one can argue that the position of the "universal rabble" perfectly captures the plight of today's new proletarians. In the classical Marxist *dispositif* of class exploitation, capitalist and worker meet as formally free individuals on the market, equal subjects of the same legal order, citizens of the same state, with the same civil and political rights. Today, this legal frame of equality, this shared participation in the same civil and political spaces, is gradually dissolving with the rise of new forms of social and political exclusion: illegal immigrants, slum-dwellers, refugees, etc. It is as if, in parallel to the regression from profit to rent, the existing system, in order to continue to function, has to resuscitate premodern forms of direct exclusion—it can no longer afford exploitation and domination in the form of legal and civil authority. In other words, while the classic working class is exploited through their very participation in the sphere of rights and freedoms—i.e., while their *de facto* enslavement is realized through the very form of their autonomy and freedom, through working in order to provide for their subsistence—today's rabble is denied even the right to be exploited through work, its status oscillating between that of a victim provided for by charitable humanitarian help and that of a terrorist to be contained or crushed; and, exactly as described by Hegel, they sometimes formulate their demand as the demand for subsistence without work (like the Somali pirates).

We should bring together here, as aspects of the same limitation, the two topics on which Hegel fails (by his own standards): the rabble and sex. Far from providing the natural foundation of human lives, sexuality is the very terrain upon which humans detach themselves from nature: the idea of sexual perversion or of a deadly sexual passion is totally foreign to the animal universe. Here, Hegel himself falls short of his own standards: he only describes how, through culture, the natural substance of sexuality is cultivated, sublated, mediated—we humans no longer just make love for procreation, we enter into a complex process of seduction and marriage in which sexuality becomes an expression of the spiritual bond between a man and a woman, and so on. However, what Hegel misses is how, in humans, sexuality is not only transformed or civilized, but, much more radically, *changed in its very substance*: it is no longer the instinctual drive to reproduce, but a drive that finds itself thwarted in relation to its natural goal (reproduction) and thereby explodes into an infinite, properly meta-physical, passion. The becoming-cultural of sexuality is thus not the becoming-cultural of nature, but the attempt to domesticate a properly un-natural excess of the meta-physical sexual passion. This excess of negativity discernible in sex and apropos the rabble is the very dimension of "unruliness" identified by Kant as the violent freedom on account of which man, in contrast to animals, needs a master. So it is not just that sexuality is the animal substance which is then "sublated" into civilized modes and rituals, gentrified, disciplined, etc.—the excess of sexuality itself, sexuality as the unconditional Passion which threatens to explode all "civilized" constraints, is the result of Culture. In terms of Wagner's *Tristan*: civilization is not only the universe of the Day, of the rituals and honors that bind us, but the Night itself, the infinite passion in which the two lovers want to dissolve their ordinary daily existence—animals know no such passion. In this way, civilization/Culture retroactively posits/transforms its own natural presupposition, retroactively "denaturalizes" nature itself—this is what Freud called the Id, libido. This is how, here also, in fighting its natural obstacle, its opposed natural substance, Spirit fights itself, its own essence.

Elisabeth Lloyd suggests that the female orgasm has no positive evolutionary function: it is not a biological adaptation with evolutionary advantages, but an "appendix," like male nipples.[30] In the embryonic stage of growth, male and female both have the same anatomical structure for the first two months, before the differences set in—the female acquires the ability to orgasm only because the male will later need it, just like the male acquires nipples only because the female will later need them. All the standard explanations (like the "uterine upsuck" thesis—the orgasm causes contractions that "suck up" sperm and thus aid conception) are false: while sexual pleasure and even the clitoris *are* adaptive, the orgasm is not. The fact that this thesis provoked a furor among feminists is in itself proof of the decline of our intellectual standards: as if the very superfluity of the feminine orgasm does not make it all the more "spiritual"—let us not forget that, according to some evolutionists, language itself is a by-product with no clear evolutionary function. One should be attentive not to miss the properly dialectical reversal of substance at work here: the moment when the immediate substantial ("natural") starting point is not only acted upon, transformed, mediated/cultivated, but changed in its very substance. We not only work upon and thus transform nature—in a gesture of retroactive reversal, nature itself radically changes its "nature."[31] This is why Catholics who insist that only sex for procreation is human, while coupling out of lust is bestial, totally miss the point, and end up celebrating the animality of men.

Why is Christianity opposed to sexuality, accepting it as a necessary evil only if it serves its natural purpose of procreation? Not because in sexuality our lower nature explodes, but precisely because sexuality competes with pure spirituality as the primordial meta-physical activity. The Freudian hypothesis

---

30 See Elisabeth Lloyd, *The Case of the Female Orgasm*, Cambridge, MA: Harvard University Press 2006.

31 In a homologous way, once we enter the domain of legal civil society, the previous tribal order of honor and revenge is deprived of its nobility and all of a sudden appears as common criminality.

is that the passage from animal instincts (of mating) to sexuality proper (to drives) is the primordial step from the physical realm of biological (animal) life to meta-physics, to eternity and immortality, to a level which is heterogeneous with regard to the biological cycle of generation and corruption.[32] Plato was already aware of this when he wrote about Eros, the erotic attachment to a beautiful body, as the first step on the way towards the supreme Good; perceptive Christians (like Simone Weil) discerned in sexual longing a striving for the Absolute. Human sexuality is characterized by the impossibility of reaching its goal, and this constitutive impossibility eternalizes it, as is the case in the myths about great lovers whose love persists beyond life and death. Christianity conceives this properly meta-physical excess of sexuality as a disturbance to be erased, so it is paradoxically Christianity itself (especially Catholicism) which wants to get rid of its competitor by reducing sexuality to its animal function of procreation: Christianity wants to "normalize" sexuality, spiritualizing it from without (imposing on it the external envelope of spirituality—sex must take place in a loving relationship and with respect for one's partner and so on), and thereby obliterating its immanent spiritual dimension, the dimension of unconditional passion. Even Hegel succumbs to this mistake when he sees the properly human-spiritual dimension of sexuality only in its cultivated or mediated form, ignoring how this mediation retroactively transubstantiates or eternalizes the very object of its mediation. In all these cases, the aim is to get rid of the uncanny double of spirituality, of a spirituality in its obscene libidinal form, of the excess which absolutizes the instinct itself into the eternal drive.

The limitation of Hegel's notion of sexuality is clearly discernible in his theory of marriage (from his *Philosophy of Right*), which nonetheless deserves a close reading: beneath the surface of the standard bourgeois notion of marriage lurk many unsettling implications. While a subject enters marriage voluntarily, surrendering his or her autonomy by way of immersion into the immediate or substantial unity of the family (which functions with regard to its outside as one person), the function of the family is the exact opposite of such a substantial unity: it is to educate those born into it to abandon their (parental) family and pursue their path independently of it. The first lesson of marriage is thus that that the ultimate goal of every substantial ethical unity is to dissolve itself by giving rise to individuals who will assert their full autonomy against the substantial unity which gave birth to them.

This surrender of autonomous individuality is the reason Hegel opposes those (including Kant) who insist on the contractual nature of marriage: "though marriage begins in contract, it is precisely a contract to transcend the standpoint

32 This is why the Catholic argument that sex without procreation, whose aim is not procreative, is animal is so erroneous: the exact opposite is true, sex spiritualizes itself only when it abstracts from its natural end and becomes an end-in-itself.

of contract, the standpoint from which persons are regarded in their individuality as self-subsistent units. The identification of personalities, whereby the family becomes one person and its members become its accidents (though substance is in essence the relation of its accidents to itself), is the ethical mind" (§163). It is clear in what sense, for Hegel, marriage is "a contract to transcend the standpoint of contract": a contract is a deal between two or more autonomous individuals each of whom retains their abstract freedom (as is the case in the exchange of commodities), while marriage is a weird contract by which the two concerned parties oblige themselves precisely to abandon or surrender their abstract freedom and autonomy and to subordinate it to a higher organic ethical unity.[33]

Hegel's theory of marriage is formulated against two opponents: his rejection of the contract theory is linked to his critique of the Romantic notion of marriage which conceives its core as the passionate love attachment of the couple, so that the form of marriage is at best merely the external registration of this attachment and at worst an obstacle to true love. We can see how these two notions supplement each other: if the true core of marriage is the passionate inner love, then, of course, marriage itself is nothing but an external contract. For Hegel, on the contrary, the external ceremony is precisely not merely external—in it resides the very ethical core of marriage:

> It is in the actual conclusion of a marriage, i.e. in the wedding, that the essence of the tie is expressed and established beyond dispute as something ethical, raised above the contingency of feeling and private inclination. If this ceremony is taken as an external formality, a mere so-called "civil requirement", it is thereby stripped of all significance except perhaps that of serving the purpose of edification and attesting the civil relation of the parties … As such it appears as something not merely indifferent to the true nature of marriage, but actually alien to it. The heart is constrained by the law to attach a value to the formal ceremony and the latter is looked upon merely as a condition which must precede the complete mutual surrender of the parties to one another. As such it appears to bring disunion into their loving disposition and, like an alien intruder, to thwart the inwardness of their union. Such a doctrine pretentiously claims to afford the highest conception of the freedom,

33 In a weird argumentative turn, Hegel deduces the prohibition of incest from the very fact that "marriage results from the free surrender by both sexes of their personality—a personality in every possible way unique in each of the parties": "Consequently, it ought not to be entered by two people identical in stock who are already acquainted and perfectly known to one another; for individuals in the same circle of relationship have no special personality of their own in contrast with that of others in the same circle. On the contrary, the parties should be drawn from separate families and their personalities should be different in origin" (§168).

> inwardness, and perfection of love; but in fact it is a travesty of the ethical aspect of love, the higher aspect which restrains purely sensual impulse and puts it in the background … In particular, the view just criticised casts aside marriage's specifically ethical character, which consists in this, that the consciousness of the parties is crystallised out of its physical and subjective mode and lifted to the thought of what is substantive; instead of continually reserving to itself the contingency and caprice of bodily desire, it removes the marriage bond from the province of this caprice, surrenders to the substantive. (§164)

Along these lines, Hegel rejects the Romantic view of Schlegel and his friends that "the wedding ceremony is superfluous and a formality which might be discarded. Their reason is that love is, so they say, the substance of marriage and that the celebration therefore detracts from its value. Surrender to sensual impulse is here represented as necessary to prove the freedom and inwardness of love—an argument not unknown to seducers" (§164). What the Romantic view thus misses is that marriage is "ethico-legal [*rechtlich sittliche*] love, and this eliminates from marriage the transient, fickle, and purely subjective aspects of love." The paradox here is that, in marriage, "the natural sexual union—a union purely inward or implicit and for that very reason existent as purely external—is changed into a union on the level of mind, into self-conscious love": the spiritualization of the natural link is thus not simply its internalization; it rather occurs in the guise of its opposite, of the externalization in a symbolic ceremony:

> the solemn declaration by the parties of their consent to enter the ethical bond of marriage, and its corresponding recognition and confirmation by their family and community, constitutes the formal completion and actuality of marriage. The knot is tied and made ethical only after this ceremony, whereby through the use of signs, i.e. of language (the most mental embodiment of mind), the substantial thing in the marriage is brought completely into being. (§164)

Here Hegel foregrounds the "performative" function of the marriage ceremony: even if it appears to the love partners as mere bureaucratic formalism, it enacts the inscription of their sexual link into the big Other, an inscription which radically changes the subjective position of the concerned parties. This explains the well-known fact that married people are often more attached to their spouses than may appear to be the case (including to themselves): a man may have secret affairs, may even dream about leaving his wife, but anxiety prevents him from doing so when the chance presents itself—in short, we are ready to cheat on our spouses on condition that the big Other does not know it (register it). The last quoted sentence is very precise here: "The knot is tied and made ethical only after this ceremony, whereby through the use of signs, i.e. of language (the most mental embodiment of mind), the substantial thing in the marriage is brought completely into being." The passage from a natural link to spiritual self-consciousness has nothing to do with "inner awareness" and everything to do with the external "bureaucratic" registration, a ritual whose true scope may be unknown to its participants, who may think they are just performing an external formality.

The key feature of marriage is not sexual attachment, but "the free consent of the persons ... to make themselves one person, to renounce their natural and individual personality to this unity of one with the other. From this point of view, their union is a self-restriction, but in fact it is their liberation, because in it they attain their substantive self-consciousness" (§162). In short, true freedom is the liberation from pathological attachments to particular objects determined by caprice and contingency. But Hegel here goes to the end, right up to the dialectical reversal of necessity into contingency: to overcome contingency does not mean to arrange a marriage on the basis of a careful examination of the future partner's mental and physical qualities (as in Plato); it is rather that, in marriage, the partner *is* contingent, and this contingency should be assumed as necessary. So when Hegel deals with the two extremes of prearranged marriages and marriages based on attraction and love, on ethical grounds he prefers the first one. At one extreme,

> the marriage is arranged by the contrivance of benevolent parents; the appointed end of the parties is a union of mutual love, their inclination to marry arises from the fact that each grows acquainted with the other from the first as a destined partner. At the other extreme, it is the inclination of the parties which comes first, appearing in them as *these* two infinitely particularized individuals. The more ethical way to matrimony may be taken to be the former extreme or any way at all whereby the decision to marry comes first and the inclination to do so follows, so that in the actual wedding both decision and inclination coalesce. (§162)

The beginning of the last sentence is worth rereading: "The more ethical way to matrimony may be taken to be the former extreme or any way at all whereby the decision to marry comes first and the inclination to do so follows ..."—in other words, the prearranged marriage is more ethical not because the benevolent elder relatives can see further and are in a better position than the young couple, blinded by their passions, to judge if they have the qualities needed to make for a happy shared life; what makes it more ethical is that, in this case, the contingency of the partner is directly and openly assumed—I am simply informed that I am expected to freely choose as a life-long partner an unknown person imposed on me by others. This freedom to choose what is necessary is more spiritual because physical love and emotional ties come as secondary:

they follow the abyssal decision to marry. Two consequences follow from this paradox: not only is the surrender of abstract freedom in marriage a double surrender (I not only surrender my abstract freedom by agreeing to immerse myself in the family unity; this surrender itself is only formally free, since the partner to whom I surrender my abstract freedom is de facto chosen by others); furthermore, the surrender of my abstract freedom is not the only surrender implied by the act of marriage—let us read carefully the following passage:

> The distinction between marriage and concubinage is that the latter is chiefly a matter of satisfying natural desire, while this satisfaction is made secondary in the former ... The ethical aspect of marriage consists in the parties' consciousness of this unity as their substantive aim, and so in their love, trust, and common sharing of their entire existence as individuals. When the parties are in this frame of mind and their union is actual, their physical passion sinks to the level of a physical moment, destined to vanish in its very satisfaction. On the other hand, the spiritual bond of union secures its rights as the substance of marriage and thus rises, inherently indissoluble, to a plane above the contingency of passion and the transience of particular caprice. (§163)

So what do we surrender in marriage?[34] Insofar as, in marriage, pathological attraction and lust are sublated into a symbolic link and thus subordinated to spirit, the consequence is a kind of *de-sublimation* of the partner: the implicit presupposition (or, rather, injunction) of the standard ideology of marriage is that, precisely, there should be no love in it. The true Pascalian formula of marriage is therefore not "You don't love your partner? Then marry him or her, embrace the rituals of a shared life, and love will emerge by itself!" but, on the contrary: "Are you too much in love with somebody? Then get married, ritualize your relationship in order to cure yourself of the excessive passionate attachment, to replace it with boring daily customs—and if you cannot resist passion's temptation, there are always extra-marital affairs ..." Marriage is thus a means of re-normalization which cures us of the violence of falling in love—in Basque, the term for falling in love is *maitemindu* which, literally translated, means "to be injured by love." In other words, what is sacrificed in marriage is the object—the lesson of marriage is that of Mozart's *Così fan tutte*: the replaceable object.

What makes *Così* the most perplexing, traumatic even, among Mozart's operas is the very ridiculousness of its content: it is almost impossible to "suspend our disbelief" and accept the premise that the two women do not recognize their own lovers in the Albanian officers. No wonder, then, that throughout the nineteenth century the opera was performed in an amended version in order to

---

34 I rely here on Jure Simoniti, "Verjetno bi pod drugim imenom dišala drugače," *Problemi* 1–2 (2010).

render the story credible. There were three main types of amendment, which fit perfectly the main modes of the Freudian negation of a certain traumatic content: (1) the staging implied that the two women knew all along the true identity of the "Albanian officers"—they just pretended not to know in order to teach their lovers a lesson; (2) the couples reunited at the end are not the same couples as at the beginning; they change places diagonally, so that, through the confusion of identities, the true, natural love links are established; (3) most radically, only the music was used, with a wholly new libretto telling a totally different story.

Edward Said drew attention to Mozart's letters to his wife Constanze from September 30, 1790, that is, at the time he was composing *Così*; after expressing his pleasure at the prospect of meeting her again soon, he goes on: "If the people were to be able to see into my heart, I would have to be almost ashamed of myself ..." At this point, as Said perceptively notes, one would have expected the confession of some dirty private secret (sexual fantasies about what he will do to his wife when they will finally meet, etc.); however, the letter goes on: "everything is cold to me—cold like ice."[35] It is here that Mozart enters the uncanny domain of "Kant avec Sade," the domain in which sexuality loses its passionate, intense character and turns into its opposite, a "mechanical" exercise in pleasure executed with a cold distance, like the Kantian ethical subject doing his duty without any pathological commitment. Is not this the underlying vision of *Così*: a universe in which subjects are determined not by their passionate engagements, but by a blind mechanism that regulates their passions? What compels us to bring *Così* close to the domain of "Kant avec Sade" is its very insistence on the universal dimension already indicated by its title: "they are *all* acting like this," all determined by the same blind mechanism. In short, Alfonso, the philosopher who organizes and manipulates the game of changed identities in *Così*, is a version of the figure of the Sadean pedagogue educating his young disciples in the art of debauchery. It is thus oversimplified and inadequate to conceive this coldness as that of "instrumental reason."

The traumatic core of *Così* lies in its radical "mechanical materialism," in the Pascalian sense alluded to above: Pascal advised non-believers to "Act as if you believe, kneel down, follow the ritual, and belief will come by itself!" *Così* applies the same logic to love: far from being external expressions of an inner feeling, love rituals and gestures are what generate love itself—so act as if you are in love, follow the procedures, and love will emerge by itself. Moralists who condemn *Così* for its alleged frivolity thus totally miss the point: *Così* is an "ethical" opera in the strict Kierkegaardian sense of the "ethical stage." The ethical stage is defined by the sacrifice of the immediate consumption of life,

35 See Edward W. Said, "Così fan tutte," *Lettre International* 39 (Winter 1997), pp. 69–70.

of our yielding to the fleeting moment, in the name of some higher universal norm. If Mozart's *Don Giovanni* embodies the aesthetic (as was developed by Kierkegaard himself in his detailed analysis of the opera in *Either/Or*), the lesson of *Così* is ethical—why? The point of *Così* is that the love that unites the two couples at the beginning of the opera is no less "artificial," mechanically brought about, than the second falling in love of the sisters with the exchanged partners dressed up as Albanian officers, which happens as the result of Alfonso's manipulations—in both cases, we are dealing with a mechanism that the subjects follow in a blind, puppet-like way. Therein consists the Hegelian "negation of the negation": first, we perceive the "artificial" love, the product of manipulation, as opposed to the initial "authentic" love; then, all of a sudden, we become aware that there is actually no difference between the two—the original love is no less "artificial" than the second. The conclusion being that, since the one love counts just as much as the other, the couples can return to their initial marital arrangement.

In Lacanian terms, marriage subtracts from the object (partner) "what is in him/her more than him/herself," the *objet a*, the object-cause of desire, it reduces the partner to an ordinary object. The lesson of marriage which follows Romantic love is: you are passionately in love with that person? So marry her and you will see what he or she is in everyday life, with his or her vulgar tics, petty meanness, dirty underwear, snoring, and so forth. One should be clear here: it is marriage whose function it is to vulgarize sex, to take all true passion out of it and turn it into a boring duty. And we should even correct Hegel on this point: sex is in itself not natural, *it is the function of marriage to reduce it to a subordinated pathological/natural moment.* Hegel should also be corrected insofar as he confuses idealization and sublimation: what if marriage is the key test of true love in which sublimation survives idealization? In blind passion, the partner is not sublimated, he or she is rather simply idealized; married life definitely de-idealizes the partner, but does not necessarily de-sublimate him or her.

The old saying "love is blind, but lovers are not" should be read in a precise way, as pointing towards the structure of disavowal: "I know very well (that my beloved is full of flaws), but nonetheless (I fully love him/her)." The point is thus not that we are more cynical realists than it may appear, but that, when in love, this realism becomes inoperative: in our acts, we follow our blind love. In an old Christian melodrama, a temporarily blinded ex-soldier falls in love with the nurse who takes care of him, fascinated by her goodness, forming in his mind an idealized image of her; when his blindness is cured, he sees that, in her bodily reality, she is ugly. Aware that his love would not survive extended contact with this reality, and that the inner beauty of her good soul has a higher value than her external appearance, he intentionally blinds himself by looking into the sun for too long, so that his love for the woman will survive. If there ever was a false celebration of love, this is it. In true love, there is no need for an idealization of its object, no need to ignore the object's discordant features: the ex-soldier would be able to see the beauty shining through the nurse's "ugliness" itself.

It is easy to see the parallel between the rabble and sex here: Hegel does not recognize in the rabble (rather than the state bureaucracy) the "universal class"; likewise, he does not recognize in sexual passion the excess which is neither culture nor nature. Although the logic is different in each case (apropos the rabble, Hegel overlooks the universal dimension of the excessive/discordant element; apropos sex, he overlooks the excess as such, the undermining of the opposition nature/culture), the two failures are linked, since excess is the site of universality, the way universality as such inscribes itself into the order of its particular content.

The underlying problem is the following: the standard "Hegelian" scheme of death (negativity) as the subordinate or mediating moment of Life can only be sustained if we remain within the category of Life whose dialectic is that of the self-mediating Substance returning to itself from its otherness. The moment we effectively pass from Substance to Subject, from Life(-principle) to Death (-principle), there is no encompassing "synthesis," death in its "abstract negativity" forever remains as a threat, an excess which cannot be economized. In social life, this means that Kant's universal peace is a vain hope, that *war* forever remains a threat to organized state Life, and, in individual subjective life, that *madness* always lurks as a possibility.

Does this mean that we are back at the standard *topos* of the excess of negativity which cannot be "sublated" in any reconciling "synthesis," or even at the naïve Engelsian view of the alleged contradiction between the openness of Hegel's "method" and the enforced closure of his "system"? There are indications which point in this direction: as has been noted by many commentators, Hegel's "conservative" political writings of his last years (such as his critique of the English Reform Bill) betray a fear of any further development which will assert the "abstract" freedom of civil society at the expense of the State's organic unity and thereby open the way to more revolutionary violence.[36] Why did Hegel step back here, why did he not dare to follow his basic dialectical rule, courageously embracing "abstract" negativity as the sole path to a higher stage of freedom?

Hegel may appear to celebrate the *prosaic* character of life in a well-organized modern state, where heroic disturbances are overcome in the tranquility of private rights and the security of the satisfaction of needs: private property is guaranteed, sexuality is restricted to marriage, the future is safe. In this organic order, universality and particular interests appear reconciled: the "infinite right" of subjective singularity is given its due, individuals no longer

36 Hegel died a year after the French Revolution of 1830.

experience the objective state order as a foreign power intruding on their rights, they recognize in it the substance and frame of their very freedom. Lebrun here poses the fateful question: "Can the sentiment of the Universal be dissociated from this appeasement?"[37] Against Lebrun, our answer should be: yes, and this is why war is necessary—in war, universality reasserts its right over and against the concrete-organic appeasement in prosaic social life. Is not the necessity of war thus the ultimate proof that, for Hegel, every social reconciliation is doomed to fail, that no organic social order can effectively contain the force of abstract-universal negativity? This is why social life is condemned to the "spurious infinity" of an eternal oscillation between stable civic life and wartime perturbation—the notion of "tarrying with the negative" acquires here a more radical meaning: not just to "pass through" the negative but to persist in it.

This necessity of war should be linked to its opposite: the necessity of a rebellion which shakes the power edifice from its complacency, making it aware of both its dependence on popular support and of its a priori tendency to "alienate" itself from its roots. Or, as Jefferson famously wrote, "a little rebellion now and then is a good thing": "It is a medicine necessary for the sound health of government. God forbid that we should ever be twenty years without such a rebellion. The tree of liberty must be refreshed from time to time with the blood of patriots and tyrants. It is its natural manure."[38] In both cases, war and rebellion, a "terroristic" potential is unleashed: in the first, it is the state that unleashes absolute negativity to shatter individual subjects out of their particular complacency; in the second, it is the people themselves who remind the state power of the terroristic dimension of democracy by shattering all particular state structures. The beauty of the Jacobins is that, in their terror, they brought these two opposed dimensions together: the Terror was simultaneously the terror of the state against individuals and the terror of the people against particular state institutions or functionaries who excessively identified with their institutional positions (the objection to Danton was simply that he wanted to rise above others). Needless to say, in a properly Hegelian way, the two opposed dimensions are to be identified; that is, the negativity of state power against individuals sooner or later inexorably turns against (the individuals who exercise) the state power itself.

Apropos war, Hegel is thus again not fully consistent with regard to his own theoretical premises: to be consistent, he would have had to accomplish the Jeffersonian move, the obvious dialectical passage from external war (between states) to "internal" war (revolution, rebellion against state power) as a sporadic explosion of negativity which rejuvenates the edifice of power. This is why, in

37 Gérard Lebrun, *L'envers de la dialectique: Hegel à la lumière de Nietzsche*, Paris: Seuil 2004, p. 214.

38 Quoted from Howard Zinn, *A People's History of the United States*, New York: HarperCollins 2001, p. 95.

reading the infamous Paragraphs 322–324 of Hegel's *Philosophy of Right*, where Hegel justifies the ethical necessity of war, one should be very careful to note the link between his argumentation here and his basic propositions on the self-relating negativity that constitutes the very core of a free autonomous individual. Here Hegel simply applies this basic self-relating negativity constitutive of free subjectivity to relations between states:

> §322 Individuality is awareness of one's existence as a unit in sharp distinction from others. It manifests itself here in the state as a relation to other states, each of which is autonomous vis-à-vis the others. This autonomy embodies mind's actual awareness of itself as a unit and hence it is the most fundamental freedom which a people possesses as well as its highest dignity.
>
> §323 This negative relation of the state to itself is embodied in the world as the relation of one state to another and as if the negative were something external. In the world of existence, therefore, this negative relation has the shape of a happening and an entanglement with chance events coming from without. But in fact this negative relation is that moment in the state which is most supremely its own, the state's actual infinity as the ideality of everything finite within it. It is the moment wherein the substance of the state—i.e. its absolute power against everything individual and particular, against life, property, and their rights, even against societies and associations—makes the nullity of these finite things an accomplished fact and brings it home to consciousness ...
>
> An entirely distorted account of the demand for this sacrifice results from regarding the state as a mere civil society and from regarding its final end as only the security of individual life and property. This security cannot possibly be obtained by the sacrifice of what is to be secured—on the contrary ...
>
> War is not to be regarded as an absolute evil and as a purely external accident, which itself therefore has some accidental cause, be it injustices, the passions of nations or the holders of power, &c., or in short, something or other which ought not to be. It is to what is by nature accidental that accidents happen, and the fate whereby they happen is thus a necessity. Here as elsewhere, the point of view from which things seem pure accidents vanishes if we look at them in the light of the concept and philosophy, because philosophy knows accident for a show and sees in it its essence, necessity. It is necessary that the finite—property and life—should be definitely established as accidental, because accidentality is the concept of the finite. From one point of view this necessity appears in the form of the power of nature, and everything is mortal and transient. But in the ethical substance, the state, nature is robbed of this power, and the necessity is exalted to be the work of freedom, to be something ethical. The transience of the finite becomes a willed passing away, and the negativity lying at the roots of the finite becomes the substantive individuality proper to the ethical substance ...

> In peace civil life continually expands; all its departments wall themselves in, and in the long run men stagnate. Their idiosyncrasies become continually more fixed and ossified. But for health the unity of the body is required, and if its parts harden themselves into exclusiveness, that is death. Perpetual peace is often advocated as an ideal towards which humanity should strive. With that end in view, Kant proposed a league of monarchs to adjust differences between states, and the Holy Alliance was meant to be a league of much the same kind. But the state is an individual, and individuality essentially implies negation. Hence even if a number of states make themselves into a family, this group as an individual must engender an opposite and create an enemy. As a result of war, nations are strengthened, but peoples involved in civil strife also acquire peace at home through making wars abroad. To be sure, war produces insecurity of property, but this insecurity of things is nothing but their transience—which is inevitable. We hear plenty of sermons from the pulpit about the insecurity, vanity, and instability of temporal things, but everyone thinks, however much he is moved by what he hears, that he at least will be able to retain his own. But if this insecurity now comes on the scene in the form of hussars with shining sabres and they actualize in real earnest what the preachers have said, then the moving and edifying discourses which foretold all these events turn into curses against the invader.

The function of what Hegel conceptualizes as the necessity of war is precisely the repeated untying of organic social links. When, in his *Group Psychology*, Freud outlined the "negativity" of untying social ties (*Thanatos* as opposed to *Eros*, the force of the social link), he (with his liberal limitations) all too easily dismissed the manifestations of this untying as the fanaticism of the "spontaneous" crowd (as opposed to artificial crowds: the Church and Army). Against Freud, we should retain the ambiguity of this movement of untying: it is a zero level that opens up the space for political intervention. In other words, this untying is the pre-political condition of politics, and, with regard to it, every political intervention proper already goes "one step too far," committing itself to a new project (or Master-Signifier).[39] Today, this apparently abstract topic is relevant once again: the "untying" energy is largely monopolized by the New Right (the Tea Party movement in the US, where the Republican Party is increasingly split between Order and its Untying). However, here also, every fascism is a sign of failed revolution, and the only way to combat this rightist untying will be for the Left to engage in its own untying—and there are already signs of it (the large demonstrations all around Europe in 2010, from Greece to France and the UK, where the student demonstrations against university fees unexpectedly turned violent). In asserting the threat of "abstract negativity" to the existing order as a

39 Badiou also jumps all too directly from mere "animal life" to the political Event, ignoring the negativity of the death drive which intervenes between the two.

permanent feature which can never be *aufgehoben*, Hegel is here more materialist than Marx: in his theory of war (and of madness), he is aware of the repetitive return of the "abstract negativity" which violently unbinds social links. Marx re-binds violence into the process out of which a New Order arises (violence as the "midwife" of a new society), while in Hegel, the unbinding remains non-sublated.

One cannot emphasize enough how these "militaristic" ruminations are directly grounded in Hegel's fundamental ontological insights and matrices. When Hegel writes that the state's negative relation to itself (its self-assertion as an autonomous agent whose freedom is demonstrated through its readiness to distance itself from all its particular content) "is embodied in the world as the relation of one state to another and as if the negative were something external," he evokes a precise dialectical figure of the unity of contingency and necessity: the coincidence of external (contingent) opposition and immanent (necessary) self-negativity—one's own innermost essence, the negative relation-to-oneself, has to appear as a contingent external obstacle or intrusion. This is why, for Hegel, the "truth" of the external contingent opposition is the necessity of negative self-relating. And this direct coincidence of the opposites, this direct overlapping (or short-circuit) between extreme internality (the innermost autonomy of the Self) and the extreme externality of an accidental encounter, cannot be "overcome," the two poles cannot be "mediated" into a stable complex unity. This is why Hegel surprisingly evokes the "solemn cycles of history," making it clear that there is no final *Aufhebung* here: the entire complex edifice of the particular forms of social life has to be put at risk again and again—a reminder that the social edifice is a fragile virtual entity which can disintegrate at any moment, not because of contingent external threats, but because of its innermost essence. This regenerating passage through radical negativity can never be "sublated" in a stable social edifice—a proof, if one is needed, of Hegel's ultimate *materialism*. That is to say, the persistent threat that radical self-relating negativity will threaten and ultimately dissolve any organic social structure points towards the *finite* status of all such structures: their status is virtual-ideal, lacking any ultimate ontological guarantee, always exposed to the danger of disintegration when, triggered by an accidental external intrusion, their grounding negativity explodes. The identity of opposites here does not mean that, in an idealist way, the inner spirit "generates" external obstacles which appear as accidental: external accidents which cause wars are genuinely accidental, the point is that, as such, they "echo" the innermost negativity that is the core of subjectivity.

CHAPTER 7

The Limits of Hegel

A LIST

Let us jump *in medias res* and confront the question head-on: can Hegel think the notion which, according to Lacan, condenses all the paradoxes of the Freudian field, the notion of the *non-All*? If we take "Hegel" as the ridiculous textbook-figure of an absolute idealist who, under the headline "the Whole is the True," claims to integrate the entire wealth of the universe into the totality of rational self-mediation, then the answer is, of course, a resounding no. If, however, we take into account the true nature of the Hegelian totality—that it designates a Whole *plus* all its "symptoms," the excesses which do not fit into its frame, antagonisms which ruin its consistency, and so on—then the answer becomes more blurred. Here is an improvised list of what Hegel "cannot think," a series of concepts mostly elaborated by psychoanalysis and Marxism: repetition; the unconscious; overdetermination; *objet a*; matheme/letter (science and mathematics); *lalangue*; antagonism (parallax); class struggle; sexual difference.[1] Upon a closer look, however, it becomes clear that one should be very precise about what Hegel "cannot do": it is never a question of simple impossibility or inability. There is, in all these cases, a tiny, imperceptible line of separation which compels us to supplement the assertion of impossibility with a qualifying "yes, but ...":

Hegel does think repetition, but not a pure non-productive one, not a "mechanical" repetition which just strives for more of the same: his notion of repetition always involves sublation; in other words, through repetition, something is idealized, transformed from an immediate contingent reality to a notional universality (Caesar dies as a person and becomes a universal title); or, at least, through repetition, the necessity of an event is confirmed (Napoleon had to lose twice to get the message that his time was over, that his first defeat was not just an accident). The fact that Hegel misses the excess of purely mechanical repetition in no way implies that he is excessively focused on the New (the progress which takes place through idealizing *Aufhebung*)—on the contrary, bearing in mind that the radically New emerges only through pure repetition, we should say that Hegel's inability to think pure repetition is the obverse of his inability to think the radically New, that is, a New, which is not potentially already in the

1 This list was suggested to me by Mladen Dolar.

Old and has just to be brought out into the open through the work of dialectical deployment.

Hegel does also think the unconscious, but it is the formal unconscious, the transcendental universal form of what I am doing as opposed to the immediate particular content which is the focus of my attention—to take the most elementary example from the beginning of the *Phenomenology*: when I say "Now!" I mean this particular moment, but what I say is every now, and the truth is in what I say. The Freudian unconscious is, on the contrary, the unconscious of particular contingent associations and links—to take a classic Freudian example, when his patient dreams about a funeral she attended the previous day, the "unconscious" of this dream was the totally contingent fact that, at the funeral, the dreamer had met an old flame for whom she still cared.

Linked to this is the impossibility, for Hegel, of thinking overdetermination: Hegel can think it, but only in the formal sense of a universal genus which includes itself as its own species and thus encounters, among its species, itself in its "oppositional determination." What he cannot think is the complex network of particular links organized along the lines of condensation, displacement, and so on. In more general terms, the Hegelian process always deals with radical clear cut (re)solutions; what is totally foreign to it is the Freudian logic of pragmatic and opportunistic compromises—something is rejected, but not quite, since it returns in a ciphered mode; it is rationally accepted, but isolated or neutralized in its full symbolic weight and so on and so forth. We thus get a mad dance of distortions which follow no clear univocal logic, but form a patchwork of improvised connections. Recall the legendary case of the forgetting of the name Signorelli from Freud's *The Psychopathology of Everyday Life*: Freud could not recall the name of the painter of the Orvieto frescos and produced as substitutes the names of two other painters, Botticelli and Boltraffio; his analysis of the blockage brings to light the signifying associations which linked Signorelli to Botticelli and Boltraffio (the Italian village of Trafoi was where he received the message informing him of the suicide of one of his patients, who had been struggling with sexual problems; *Herr*, the German word for Mister—*Signor*—is linked to a trip to Herzegovina, where an old Muslim had told Freud that if one can no longer have sex, then there is no reason to go on living). The complex rhizomatic texture of such associations and displacements has no clear triadic structure with a clear final resolution; the result of the tension between "thesis" (the name Signorelli) and "anti-thesis" (its forgetting) is the compromise-formation of falsely remembering two other names in which (and this is their crucial feature) the dimension on account of which Freud was unable to remember Signorelli (the link between sex and death) returns in an even more conspicuous way. There is no place for such logic in Hegel, who would have dismissed Freud's example as a game of trifling contingencies. The Freudian negation of negation is not a radical resolution of a deadlock, but, in its basic guise, the "return of the repressed" and, as such, by definition a compromise-formation: something is asserted and simultaneously denied, displaced, reduced, encrypted in an often ridiculously ad hoc way.

Hegel does think a kind of *objet a*, but it is merely the contingent singularity to which the rational totality clings—like the state clings to the monarch—or the indifferent pretext for a struggle. For example, one way for the subject to demonstrate its autonomy is for it to be ready to put everything, even its life, at stake for some minor object: although this object is in itself unimportant, its very indifference signals that what the struggle is about is the subject's dignity and autonomy, not its interests. This, however, is not yet the material remainder to which the subject's very consistency clings: Hegel does propose the formula "the Spirit is a bone," but as the absolute contradiction, not as a little bit of the real constitutive of subjectivity.

Although one finds in Hegel's texts surprising evocations of *jouissance* (*Geniessen*, not just pleasure, *Lust*)—for example, *Geniessen* of the believer is for him the true goal of religious rituals—there is no place in his thought for *jouissance* as the Real, as a substance (the only substance recognized by psychoanalysis). Insofar as *jouissance* is Real and truth is symbolic, one should add that, in Hegel's notional space, there is also no place for the gap that separates truth from the Real—or, as Lacan put it succinctly: "The true or the real? At this level, everything is set up as if these two terms are synonymous. But the unpleasant thing is that they are not … When we are dealing with the real, the true is in divergence."[2]

Here (as elsewhere), and as is always the case in a properly dialectical misrecognition, what Hegel does not see is not simply some post-Hegelian dimension totally beyond his grasp, but *the very "Hegelian" dimension of the analyzed phenomenon*. For example, what Marx demonstrates in *Capital* is how the self-reproduction of capital obeys the logic of the Hegelian dialectical process of a substance-subject which retroactively posits its own presuppositions. Marx designates capital as "an automatically active character"—an inadequate translation of the German words used by Marx to characterize capital as "*automatischem Subjekt*," "automatic subject," an oxymoron uniting living subjectivity and dead automatism. This is what capital is: a subject, but an automatic one, not a living one. Can Hegel think this "monstrous mixture," a process of subjective self-mediation and retroactive positing of presuppositions which as it were gets caught in a substantial "spurious infinity," a subject which itself becomes an alienated substance? Perhaps this same limitation also accounts for Hegel's inadequate understanding of mathematics, his reduction of mathematics to the

2 Jacques Lacan, *Le séminaire, Livre XXIX: L'insu que sait de l'une bevue s'aile a mourre*, December 14, 1976 (unpublished).

very model of the abstract "spurious infinity." What Hegel was unable to see is how, like the speculative movement of capital in Marx, modern mathematics also displays the same "monstrous mixture of the good infinity and the bad infinity": the "bad infinity" of repetition combined with the "true infinity" of self-relating paradoxes.

No modern science can be reduced to mathematical formalism since it always includes also a minimum of empirical testing and measuring which introduce the aspect of contingency—no one knows in advance what the measurements will show. This element is missing in mathematics, where the contingency is limited to the selection or positing of the axioms with which the theoretician begins, and all that follows are the rational consequences of those axioms. Even such an "abstract" science like quantum physics, in which dense positive materiality is dissolved into the pure virtuality of quantum waves, has to expose itself to measurement. Modern science from Galileo to quantum physics is thus characterized by two connected features: mathematization (the statements to be proven are mathematized formulae) and a reliance on measurement which introduces an irreducible element of contingency. Both aspects imply the meaningless real of the silent, infinite universe: the real of mathematized formulae deprived of sense, the real of radical contingency.[3] Is there a place for modern science in Hegel? Is his thought not the last great attempt to "sublate" empirical-formal science into speculative Reason? Is not the explosive growth of

3 Along the same lines, the time has come to declare Bach the greatest *modernizer* of European music, the key agent in inscribing music into the Newtonian scientific-formalized universe. Prior to Bach's time, music was perceived within the Renaissance horizon of *harmonia mundi*: its harmonies were conceived as part of the global harmony of the universe, expressed in the harmony of celestial spheres, of (Pythagorean) mathematics, of society as a social organism, of the human body—all these levels harmoniously reflected in each other. Around Bach's time, a totally different paradigm started to emerge: that of a "well-tempered" scale, in which musical sounds are to be arranged following an order not grounded in any higher cosmic harmony, but which has an (ultimately arbitrary) rational structure. (True, Bach was obsessed with the Pythagorean mysticism of numbers and their secret meanings, but the status of this obsession is exactly the same as that of Newton's obscurantist Gnostic fantasies which comprise more than two thirds of his written work: a reaction to the true breakthrough, an inability to assume all its consequences.) This was Bach's true *fidelity* (in the Badiouian sense): to draw all the consequences from this de-cosmologization of music. All the talk about Bach's deep spirituality, about how his oeuvre is dedicated to God, should not deceive us here: in his musical practice, he was a radical materialist (in the modern formalized-mathematized sense), exploring the immanent possibilities of the new musical formalism. It is the "Italian" re-assertion of emotional melody (pursued also by his composer-son who, in taking this line, committed a kind of parricide and was for a short while even more popular than his father) which marked the expressive-idealist reaction to Bach's materialist breakthrough.

the natural sciences from the eighteenth century onwards simply beyond of the scope of Hegel's thought?

The topic of nature confronts us with yet another problem raised by Hegel's critics: does not Hegel's deduction of nature clearly posit a limit to this retroactivity? Is not the passage from logic to nature a case of externalization, of the concept positing its otherness? Does not Hegel begin with logic, with ideal categories, and then try to "deduce" material reality from this shadowy realm? Is this not a model case of idealist mystification? The problem with this counterargument is that it knocks at an open door: Hegel himself explicitly says that his "system of logic is the realm of shadows, the world of simple essentialities freed from all sensuous concreteness."[4]

Hegel is thus no Platonic idealist for whom Ideas constitute a higher ontological realm with regard to material reality: they form a pre-ontological realm of shadows. For Hegel, spirit has nature as its presupposition and is simultaneously the truth of nature and, as such, the "absolute first"; nature thus "vanishes" in its truth, is "sublated" in the spirit's self-identity:

> This identity is absolute negativity, because the notion has its *complete* external objectivity in nature, but this, its externalization, has been sublated, and it has become identical with itself. At the same time therefore, it is *only* as this return out of nature that the concept constitutes this identity.[5]

Note the precise triadic structure of this passage, in the most orthodox "Hegelian" mode: *thesis*—the notion has its *complete* external objectivity in nature; *antithesis* ("but")—this externality is sublated and, through this sublation, the notion achieves its self-identity; *synthesis* ("at the same time therefore")—it is *only* as this return out of nature that the concept constitutes this identity. This is how one should understand identity as absolute negativity: the spirit's self-identity emerges through its negative relationship (sublation) of its natural presuppositions, and this negativity is "absolute" not in the sense that it negates nature "absolutely," that nature "absolutely" (totally) disappears in it, but in the sense that the negativity of sublation is self-related, in other words that the outcome of this work of negativity is the spirit's positive self-identity. The key words in the quoted passage are: *complete* and *only*. The notion "has its *complete* external objectivity in nature": there is no "other" objective reality, all that "really exists" as reality is nature, spirit is not another thing that adds itself to natural

4 G. W. F. Hegel, *Hegel's Science of Logic*, trans. A. V. Miller, Atlantic Highlands: Humanities Press International 1989, p. 58.

5 G. W. F. Hegel, *Hegels Philosophie des subjektiven Geistes/Hegel's Philosophy of Subjective Spirit*, Vol. 1, trans. and ed. M. J. Petry, Dordrecht: D. Reidel 1978, pp. 24–5. Emphases mine.

things. This is why "it is *only* as this return out of nature that the concept constitutes [its] identity": there is no spirit pre-existing nature which somehow "externalizes" itself in nature and then re-appropriates this "alienated" natural reality—the thoroughly "processual" nature of spirit (spirit is its own becoming, the result of its own activity) means that spirit is only (i.e., *nothing but*) its "returning to itself" from nature. In other words, "returning to" is fully performative, the movement of the return creates what it is returning to.

The passage from nature to freedom can be rendered in terms of a very precise reversal of the dialectical relationship between necessity and contingency: "nature" stands for the *contingency of necessity* (in nature, events occur necessarily, following inexorable laws; however, the very fact of these laws—why such a ratio between velocity and mass and not a different one—is utterly contingent, things are just like that, there is no "why"), while "freedom" stands for the *necessity of contingency* (freedom is not just blind contingency, an act is not free just because it is contingent, just because "I could have decided otherwise"; in true freedom, my abyssal/contingent decision grounds a new necessity of its own, actualized in the chain of reasons—I acted in such and such a way for that reason ...). To put it another way: in nature, necessity appears (realizes itself) in the form of contingency (necessity is the underlying law which regulates what appears a chaotic contingent interaction), while in freedom, contingency appears (realizes itself) in the form of necessity (my contingent decision is a decision to ground a new necessity, a necessity of a deontological—ethical—order).

Necessity and contingency thus not only dialectically supplement each other, but, in a much more stringent way, free each other into their own essence through the mediation of freedom. Mere blind necessity is best encapsulated in the formula "It is so because it is so"—no further questions asked. $E = mc^2$ because it is so—as if we are dealing with a contingent decision, since all we could add to this brute fact is that "it could (also) be otherwise." Blind natural necessity is thus "radically passive in relation to itself"[6]: it is, as it were, oppressed by its own imposition, without any space to relate to itself—and, on behalf of this imposition, it coincides with its opposite, with contingency. So how can necessity redeem itself from this contamination by blind contingency and posit itself as true necessity? Hegel's answer is: through the mediation of freedom: "Necessity does not become *freedom* by vanishing, but only because its still *inner* identity is *manifested*."[7] It is in this sense that freedom is "conceived necessity": necessity posited as such, conceived in ... In what? *In its necessity*, precisely: in its inner logic that makes it necessary and not just something that merely "is so because it is so." Freedom is thus the very "inter-," the gap that separates necessity from itself. Conversely, contingency, in its immediacy, as blind natural

6 Catherine Malabou, *The Future of Hegel*, London: Routledge 2005, p. 162.

7 Hegel, *Hegel's Science of Logic*, p. 571.

contingency, also coincides with its opposite, with necessity: that something is contingent ultimately means that it is just so according to blind natural laws. The only way for contingency to get rid of this stain of necessity and posit itself (manifest itself) as true contingency is through the mediation of freedom: it is only here that contingency is a matter of a subject's contingent decision.

Contingency is thus not externally opposed to necessity, it is the result of necessity's self-relating: when necessity loses its immediate-natural character and reflects itself as such, it acquires freedom which, in its immediate appearance, is contingency, the abyss of "It is so because I want it so, because I decided it so!" This reflection-into-itself equals the inscription of the enunciation into the enunciated content: as we saw earlier, when the Hegelian monarch announces "So be it! I want it so!" this is not only the moment of the contingent supplement which concludes the chain of necessity, but simultaneously the moment of enunciation with regard to a series of statements: through his act, statements prepared by the state bureaucracy acquire performative power, become actualized. Common sense tells us that every statement has to be enunciated in order to actualize itself, and that the moment (and location) of its enunciation is contingent; what philosophical reflection adds is the insight into how this contingent moment is not simply external but immanent: the contingent expression of a necessary truth signals the contingency of this necessary truth itself.

We should then oppose the Marxist line, from the young Lukács to Kojève, which rejected the dialectics of nature as a mistake: the philosophy of nature is a crucial and immanent part of the Hegelian system. It is also by far the most discredited part of Hegel's philosophy, the permanent butt of jokes, from quoting Hegel's alleged claim that "if theory doesn't fit the facts, so much worse for the facts" to the anecdote that he deduced the necessity of eight planets around the sun, not knowing that astronomers had already discovered the ninth (Neptune). (The irony here is that, a decade or so ago, astronomers re-categorized Neptune as a satellite, no longer as a planet—so, in fact, Hegel was right ...) The standard reproach to Hegel is that he tries to abolish the absolute heterogeneity of the Other, its thoroughly contingent character. But there *is* in Hegel a name for such irreducible contingent Otherness: *nature*. It is irreducible in the sense that, even if it is gradually more and more "conceptualized," mediated, it remains there as the irreducibly contingent background for human history. No big fuss for Hegel here: the contingency of nature means, among other things, that there is no guarantee that a meaningless asteroid will not hit the earth and kill us all. Nature is contingent, there is no secret substantial Mind overseeing things to make sure that nothing terrible will happen.

When Hegel defines nature, he says not only that it is the Otherness *of* the Idea, but that it is the Idea itself in its Otherness—however, what this "idealist" turn means is that Otherness should be displaced into nature itself: nature is not only the Other of the Idea, but Other with regard to itself. (So, insofar as the Idea returns to itself in spirit, one should raise the question: is spirit then also in some mode "Other with regard to itself"? Yes—precisely as what we usually call "second nature," spirit petrified in spiritual substance.) This is why nature at its zero level is space: not only the Otherness of the Idea (the Idea in its Otherness), but Otherness with regard to itself—a coexistence of points (extensively side-by-side), with no content to it, no difference, the same throughout in its pure extensive in-difference. Far from being the "mystery" of something containing objects, space is literally the most stupid thing there is. And it does not get "sublated" in the sense that it is no longer there: natural objects which "sublate" space remain spatial objects! Where spatiality is negated is in chemism, magnetism, and then organism, where objects are no longer dead composites of elements-parts, where we get an "eternal" ideal unity which cannot be located at a certain point in space: there is no "center" of an organism at some point in space. Here, perhaps, Hegel points towards relativity (it has been noted that his critique of Newtonian space foreshadows the Einsteinian critique): if the zero level of nature is space, then natural objects should develop out of space, not be conceived as mysterious chunks of matter that from who-knows-where "enter" space. The only thing that can happen to pure space is asymmetry, its becoming de-homogenized, "curved"—so the idea that "matter" is the effect of curved space is implied by Hegel's theory of space.

Even such a perceptive dialectician as Jameson falls into a trap here in his dismissive judgment that Hegel's concept of life, "pre-Darwinian as it is, is probably far too metaphysical and epistemological (highest form of the unity of subject and object) to be of much interest for us today."[8] What about recent biological theories which focus on self-referentiality (drawing a line between inside and outside) as a constitutive feature of the life process, and which often read as verbatim passages from Hegel's *Naturphilosophie*? However, even when, in reading Hegel's philosophy of nature, one stumbles upon many unexpected pearls (his critique of Newton uncannily pointing towards Einstein; his theory of life uncannily prefiguring theories of autopoiesis; etc.), the basic fact remains that its fundamental tenor is totally inadequate in relation to the two key features of modern Galilean science: mathematical formalization and openness to the contingency of (experimental) measurement. As Popper made abundantly clear, the very core of the modern scientific method lies in its effort to formulate a precise experimental setup capable of falsifying a prior hypothesis—and there is simply no place for such a stance in Hegel.

This inability of Hegel to think mathematical formalization is the obverse of his inability to think the overdetermined space of what Lacan called *lalangue*.

8 Fredric Jameson, *The Hegel Variations*, London: Verso Books 2010, p. 2.

What happens in late Lacan is the passage from (or the splitting of) the unity of conceptual thinking (in)to the duality of *matheme* and *lalangue*: on the one hand, mathematical or logical formulae and schemes (formulae of sexuation, the four discourses, etc.); on the other, the explosion of word-play and other forms of poetic discourse—a move unthinkable for Hegel, who insists on the priority of conceptual thinking.[9]

Necessity as self-sublated contingency

What if Kierkegaard's critique of Hegel, which endlessly varies this motif of irreducible contingency, relies on a fatal misunderstanding of Hegel's fundamental insight? The first thing that strikes the eye is that Kierkegaard's critique is based on the (thoroughly Hegelian!) opposition between "objective" and "subjective" thought: "While objective thought translates everything into results … subjective thought puts everything into process and omits the result … because an existing individual is constantly in process of coming to be."[10] For Kierkegaard, obviously, Hegel represents the ultimate achievement of "objective thought": he "does not understand history from the point of view of becoming, but with the illusion attached to pastness understands it from the point of view of a finality that excludes all becoming."[11] Here, one should be very careful not to miss Kierkegaard's point: for him, only subjective experience is effectively "in becoming," and any notion of objective reality as an open-ended process with no fixed finality still remains within the confines of being. But why, we may ask? Because any objective reality, as "processual" as it might be, is by definition ontologically fully constituted, present as a positively existing domain of objects and their interactions; only subjectivity designates a domain which is *in itself* "open," marked by an *inherent* ontological failure:

> Whenever a particular existence has been relegated to the past, it is complete, has acquired finality, and is in so far subject to a systematic apprehension … but for whom is it so subject? Anyone who is himself an existing individual cannot gain this

9 A nicely vulgar example of *lalangue* in Slovene: every (honest) Slovene knows what the Mona Lisa's smile is all about. Slovenes do not have their own dirty words, so they have to borrow them, mostly from Serbo and Croat, but also from Italian. So they know that "Mona" is a popular Italian name for vagina, and "lisa" (pronounced "leeza") is the root of the Slovene verb "to lick."

10 Søren Kierkegaard, *Concluding Unscientific Postscript*, trans. David F. Swenson and Walter Lowrie, Princeton: Princeton University Press 1968, p. 68.

11 Ibid., p. 272.

> finality outside existence which corresponds to the eternity into which the past has entered.[12]

What if, however, Hegel actually does the exact opposite? What if the wager of his dialectic is not to adopt the "point of view of finality" towards the present, viewing it as if it were already past, but, precisely, to *reintroduce the openness of the future into the past*, to *grasp that-which-was in its process of becoming*, to see the contingent process which generated existing necessity? Is this not why we have to conceive the Absolute "not only as Substance, but also as Subject"? This is why German Idealism already exploded the coordinates of the standard Aristotelian ontology structured around the vector running from possibility to actuality. In contrast to the idea that every possibility strives to fully actualize itself, one should conceive of "progress" as the movement of restoring the dimension of potentiality to mere actuality, of unearthing, in the very heart of actuality, a secret striving towards potentiality. Recall Walter Benjamin's notion of revolution as redemption through repetition of the past: apropos the French Revolution, the task of a true Marxist historiography is not to describe the events the way they really were (and to explain how these events generated the ideological illusions that accompanied them); the task is rather to unearth the hidden potentiality (the utopian emancipatory potential) which was betrayed in the actuality of revolution and in its final outcome (the rise of utilitarian market capitalism). Marx's point is not primarily to make fun of the Jacobin's wild revolutionary hopes, to point out how their enthused emancipatory rhetoric was just a means used by the historical "Cunning of Reason" to establish the vulgar commercial capitalist reality; it is rather to explain how these betrayed radical-emancipatory potentials continue to "insist" as historical "specters" that haunt the revolutionary memory, demanding their enactment, so that the later proletarian revolution should also redeem (lay to rest) these past ghosts. These alternative versions of the past which persist in a spectral form constitute the ontological "openness" of the historical process, as was—again—clear to Chesterton:

> The things that might have been are not even present to the imagination. If somebody says that the world would now be better if Napoleon had never fallen, but had established his Imperial dynasty, people have to adjust their minds with a jerk. The very notion is new to them. Yet it would have prevented the Prussian reaction; saved equality and enlightenment without a mortal quarrel with religion; unified Europeans and perhaps avoided the Parliamentary corruption and the Fascist and Bolshevist revenges. But in this age of free-thinkers, men's minds are not really free to think such a thought.

12 Ibid., p. 108.

> What I complain of is that those who accept the verdict of fate in this way accept it without knowing why. By a quaint paradox, those who thus assume that history always took the right turning are generally the very people who do not believe there was any special providence to guide it. The very rationalists who jeer at the trial by combat, in the old feudal ordeal, do in fact accept a trial by combat as deciding all human history.[13]

This, however, does not mean that, in a historical repetition in the radical Benjaminian sense, we simply return to the open moment of decision and, this time, make the right choice. The lesson of repetition is rather that our first choice was necessarily the wrong one, and for a very precise reason: the "right choice" is only possible the second time, for only the first choice, in its wrongness, literally creates the conditions for the right choice. The notion that we might have already made the right choice the first time, but just blew the chance by accident, is a retroactive illusion. A reference to Georg Büchner may be of some help here, with his great motif of Destiny as that which predetermines our lives—there is no free will, "the individual is no more than a foam on the wave" (as he put it in a letter to his fiancée in 1833): "The word *must* is one of the curses with which mankind is baptized. The saying 'It must be that offenses come; but woe to him by whom the offense cometh' is terrifying. What is it in us that lies, murders, steals? I no longer care to pursue this thought."[14] What terrified Büchner was the fact that, although our acts are predetermined, we experience ourselves as thoroughly responsible for them—the paradox resolved by Kant and Schelling with the hypothesis of an atemporal transcendental act by means of which each of us has always already chosen our eternal character: what we experience as fate is our "nature," the outcome of an unconscious choice. And it is only at this point that the true dialectic of freedom and necessity, of choice and determination, begins.

The common-sense "dialectics" of freedom and necessity conceives of their articulation in the sense of the famous lines from the beginning of Marx's *Eighteenth Brumaire of Louis Bonaparte*: "Men make their own history, but they do not make it as they please; they do not make it under self-selected circumstances, but under circumstances existing already, given and transmitted from the past."[15] We are partially, but not totally, determined: we have a space of freedom, but within the coordinates imposed by our objective situation. What

---

13 G. K. Chesterton, "The Slavery of the Mind," in *The Collected Works of G. K. Chesterton*, Vol. 3, San Francisco: Ignatius 1990, p. 290.

14 Quoted in Georg Büchner, *Complete Plays and Prose*, New York: Hill and Wang 1963, p. xiii.

15 Karl Marx, *The Karl Marx Library*, Vol. 1, trans. Saul K. Padover, New York: McGraw Hill 1972, p. 245.

this view fails to take into account is the way our freedom (free activity) retroactively creates ("posits") its objective conditions: these conditions are not simply given, they emerge as the presuppositions of our activity. (And vice versa: the space of our freedom itself is sustained by the situation in which we find ourselves.) The excess is thus double: we are not only less free than we think (the contours of our freedom are predetermined), we are simultaneously more free than we think (we freely "posit" the very necessity that determines us). This is why, to arrive at our "absolute" freedom (the free positing of our presuppositions), we have to pass through absolute determinism.

But does not Hegel's rejection of the "Cleopatra's nose" thesis in his great *Logic* (what we would call today the "butterfly-effect" thesis, the idea that small accidents can change the course of world history—as the beauty of Cleopatra's nose changed the course of ancient Roman history) point towards a view which reduces the role of contingency in history? For Hegel, the error of such reasoning involves the "inadmissible application" of a mechanical notion of cause to large-scale processes in organic or spiritual life: the "common jest" that, in history, great effects can result from ridiculously small causes is "an instance of the conversion which spirit imposes on the external; but for this very reason, this external is not a *cause in the process*, in other words, this conversion itself sublates the relationship of causality."[16] One should read these lines very closely, not as a simplistic dismissal of external mechanical causality. What does Hegel mean here by "conversion"? Recall the case of language: the leader says a simple word ("yes" or "no"), and the result can be a great war with hundreds of thousands of dead—from the external mechanistic standpoint, the vibration of a few sounds (a human voice pronouncing a brief word) "caused" a concatenation of events, leading to thousands of deaths—and in a way this is true, but only if we take into account the "conversion" which makes material elements the bearers and transmitters of meaning in a way which has nothing to do with their little bit of immediate material reality. In this sense, the relation of causality is "sublated" here: it is negated, but maintained and elevated at a higher level, for the causality is no longer immediate mechanical causality (like the proverbial billiard ball hitting another ball), but a causality mediated by meaning. But in all this, we should bear in mind that the whole process has also to take place at the level of immediate materiality: there is meaning, but this meaning can exert its "higher" causal power only as materialized in sounds or letters, it has no "pure" existence of its own.[17]

---

16 Hegel, *Hegel's Science of Logic*, pp. 562–3.

17 And it is easy to see why Hegel mentions not only spiritual life, but also organic life: organic life already points towards such a "conversion" which sublates mechanical causality. Due to the organic unity of a living body, a weak part (the brain) can direct the movements of much larger and stronger parts, i.e., to account for how an organism

What, then, is the central insight of the Hegelian dialectics of necessity and contingency? Not only does Hegel (quite consistently with his premises) deduce the *necessity of contingency*—namely how the Idea necessarily externalizes itself (acquires reality) in phenomena which are genuinely contingent—he also (and this aspect is often neglected by many commentators) develops the opposite and theoretically much more interesting thesis, that of the *contingency of necessity*. That is to say, when Hegel describes the progress from "external" contingent appearance to "inner" necessary essence, the appearance's "self-internalization" through self-reflection, he is not thereby describing the discovery of some preexisting inner Essence, something that was already there (this, exactly, would have been a "reification" of the Essence), but a "performative" process of constructing (forming) that which is "discovered." As Hegel himself puts it in his *Logic*, in the process of reflection, the very "return" to the lost or hidden Ground produces what it returns to. It is then not only inner necessity that is the unity of itself and contingency as its opposite, necessarily positing contingency as its moment; it is also contingency which is the encompassing unity of itself and its opposite, necessity; that is to say, *the very process through which necessity arises out of necessity is a contingent process.*

One can put it also in the terms of the dialectics of ontology and epistemology: if the encompassing unity of necessity and contingency is necessity, then the necessity (gradually discovered by our cognition as the underlying Notion of the phenomenal contingent multiplicity) had to be there all the time waiting to be discovered by our cognition—in short, in this case, Hegel's central idea (first clearly formulated in his Introduction to the *Phenomenology*) that our way towards truth is part of the truth itself, is canceled, and we regress to the standard metaphysical notion of Truth as a substantial In-itself, independent of subject's approach to it. Only if the encompassing unity is contingency can we claim that the subject's discovery of necessary truth is simultaneously the (contingent) constitution of this truth itself, that, to paraphrase Hegel, the very return to (rediscovery of) eternal Truth generates this Truth. So, far from being an "essentialist" who develops the entire content out of the necessary self-deployment of the Notion, Hegel is—to use today's terms—the ultimate thinker of autopoiesis, of the process of the emergence of necessary features out of chaotic contingency, the thinker of contingency's gradual self-organization, of the gradual rise of order out of chaos.

How, then, can necessity arise out of contingency? The only way to avoid the obscurantism of "emergent properties" is to bring into play negativity: at its most radical, necessity is not a positive principle of regularity that overcomes contingency, but the negative obverse of contingency: what is

---

works, one has to refer to a minimum of ideality, of links which cannot be reduced to the mechanical interaction of physical parts.

"necessary" above all is that every contingent particular entity find its truth in its self-cancellation, disintegration, death. Let us imagine an entity which persists in its singularity, endeavoring to impose itself as a lasting necessity —the actual necessity is the negativity which destroys this entity. This is Hegelian universal necessity in its actuality: the negative power which brings to its truth every particularity by way of destroying it. Necessity is thus nothing but the "truth" of contingency, contingency brought to its truth by way of its (self-)negation.

The standard view of Hegel's system is that of a closed circle of categories which succeed one another with a logical necessity, and the critical energy is focused on the "weak points" of that deduction, on passages where Hegel seems to "cheat," proposing a new category which does not really follow from what precedes it. This perspective must be radically reversed: each passage in Hegel is a moment of creative invention, the New does not arise automatically but comes as a miraculous surprise. This is what it means to reproduce a process through its dialectical analysis: to re-introduce possibility and ontological openness into what retroactively appears as a closed succession determined by its immanent necessity. So when Hegel says that, in a dialectical process, the thing becomes what it always already was, this clearly offers itself to be read as an assertion of full ontological closure: there is nothing radically new, what emerges in the dialectical movement is just the full actualization of what was *in potentia* (or in itself) already there. However, the same statement can also be read in a much more radical (and literal) way: in a dialectical process, the thing *becomes* "what it always already was"; that is, the "eternal essence" (or, rather, concept) of a thing is not given in advance, it emerges, forms itself in an open contingent process—the eternally past essence is a *retroactive* result of the dialectical process. This retroactivity is what Kant was not able to think, and Hegel himself had to work long and hard to conceptualize it. Here is how the early Hegel, still struggling to differentiate himself from the legacy of the other German Idealists, qualifies Kant's great philosophical breakthrough: in the Kantian transcendental synthesis, "the determinateness of form is nothing but the identity of opposites. As a result, the *a priori* intellect becomes, at least in principle, *a posteriori* as well; for *a posteriority* is nothing but the positing of the opposite."[18] In principle, the meaning of this dense passage seems clear: the "determinateness of form" is another name for concrete universality, for the fact that the universal form of a concept generates out of itself its particular content, that it is not merely a form imposed on an independent empirical content. And since the notional universality and the particularity of its content—in short, the a priori of the universal form and the a posteriori of its content—are the opposites (precisely the opposites

18 G. W. F. Hegel, *Faith and Knowledge*, trans. Walter Cerf and H. S. Harris, Albany: State University of New York Press 1977, p. 78.

that Kant keeps apart, ultimately external to each other, since the immanent transcendental form is imposed onto a content that affects the subject from the outside), the determinateness of form equals the unity of opposites, the fact that the content is generated by its form. The question is how, concretely, we are to read this identity of opposites. The standard critical reading is satisfied with seeing in it the very model of how the Idea mediates or posits all its particular content, that is, as the extreme "idealist" affirmation of the primacy of the a priori over the a posteriori. What such a reading clearly misses is the opposite movement, the irreducible "umbilical cord" on account of which every a priori universality remains attached to ("overdetermined" by) the a posteriori of a particular content. To put it somewhat bluntly: yes, the universal notional form imposes necessity upon the multitude of its contingent contents, but *it does so in a way which itself remains marked by an irreducible stain of contingency*—or, as Derrida would have put it, the frame itself is always also a part of the enframed content. The logic here is that of the Hegelian "oppositional determination" (*gegensätzliche Bestimmung*), in which the universal genus encounters itself among its particular and contingent species.[19]

Hegel introduces this notion of "oppositional determination" in his logic of essence, when he discusses the relationship between identity and difference; his point there is not only that identity is always the identity of identity and difference, but that difference itself is also always the difference between itself and identity; in the same way, it is not only necessity that encompasses both itself and contingency, but also—and more fundamentally—it is contingency itself which encompasses both itself and necessity. Or, with regard to the tension between essence and appearance, the fact that essence has to appear not only means that essence generates or mediates its appearances, but that the difference between essence and appearance is internal to appearance: essence has to appear within the domain of appearances, as a hint that "appearances are not all" but are "merely appearances." Insofar as this opposition appears in language as the opposition between the universal content of meaning and its expression in a contingent particular form (of the signifier), it is no wonder that language provides the ultimate example of this dialectical unity of opposites—and no wonder that Hegel rejects the idea of constructing a new, more precise, artificial language which would eliminate the imperfections of our natural languages: "There is no such thing as a superior language or benchmark idiom. Every language is an instance of the speculative. Philosophy's role is to show

19 In Marx's hands, this is rendered as follows: among the species of production, there is always one which gives a specific character to the universality of production within a given mode of production. In feudal societies, artisanal production itself is structured like another domain of agriculture, while in capitalism, agriculture itself is "industrialized"; that is, it becomes one of the domains of industrial production.

how, in each language, the essential is said and exhibited through the idiom's accidents."[20]

The starting point of a philosophical thought has to be the contingency of one's own language as the "substance" of one's thinking: there is no direct path to universal truth through abstracting from the contingencies of one's "natural" tongue and constructing a new artificial or technical language whose terms would carry precise meanings. This, however, does not mean that a thinker should naïvely rely on the resources of his own language: the starting point for his reflection should rather be the *idiosyncrasies* of this language, which are in a way redoubled contingencies, contingencies within a contingent (historically relative) order itself. Paradoxically, the path from the contingency (of one's natural language) to the necessity (of speculative thought) leads through the redoubled contingency: one cannot escape thinking in one's language, this language is one's unsurpassable substance; however, thinking means thinking *against* the language in which one thinks—language inevitably ossifies our thoughts, it is the medium of the fixed distinctions of Understanding *par excellence*. But, while one has to think against the language in which one thinks, one has to do so *within* language, there is no other option. This is why Hegel precludes the possibility (developed later especially in Anglo-Saxon analytical philosophy) of purifying our natural language of its "irrational" contingencies and constructing a new artificial language that would faithfully reflect conceptual determinations. Where, then, in language itself, can we find some support for thinking against it? Hegel's answer is: where language is not a formal system, where language is at its most inconsistent, contingent, idiosyncratic. The paradox is that one can only combat the "irrationality" of language on behalf of the immanent notional necessity if this necessity itself relies on what is most "irrational" in language, on its redoubled irrationality or contingency. The situation is similar to that of the Freudian logic of the dream, in which the Real announces itself in the guise of a dream within a dream. What Hegel has in mind here is often uncannily close to Lacan's notion of *lalangue*: word-play, double meanings, and so on—his great example in German are words with opposite or multiple meanings (like *zu Grunde gehen*, "disintegrate / fall apart" *and*, literally, "to go to, to reach, one's ground," etc., not to mention the notorious *Aufhebung* with its three meanings: to cancel/annihilate, to preserve, to elevate to a higher level). *Aufhebung* is often put forward as exemplary of everything that is "idealist-metaphysical" about Hegel: does it not signal the very operation by means of which all external contingency is overcome and integrated into the necessary self-deployment of the universal notion? Against this operation, it is fashionable to insist that there is always a remainder of contingency, of particularity, which cannot be *aufgehoben*,

20 Malabou, *The Future of Hegel*, p. 171.

which resists its conceptual (dis)integration. The irony here is that the very term Hegel uses to designate this operation is marked by the irreducible contingency of an idiosyncrasy of the German language.

There is no conceptual clarity without taking *lalangue* as a starting point—or, to put it in more conceptual terms, not only does necessity express itself in the appearance of contingency, but this necessity itself does not pre-exist the contingent multitude of appearances as their ground—it itself emerges out of contingency, as a contingency (say, the multiple meanings of *Aufhebung*) elevated into the necessity of a universal concept.[21] Does not Freud intend something strictly homologous with his notions of symptoms, jokes, and slips of tongue? An inner necessity can only articulate itself through the contingency of a symptom, *and* vice versa: this necessity (say, the constant urge of a repressed desire) comes to be only through this articulation. Here also, necessity does not simply pre-exist contingency: when Lacan says that repression and the return of the repressed (in symptomal formations) are the front and the back of one and the same process, the implication is precisely that the necessity (of the repressed content) hinges on the contingency (of its articulation in symptoms). Critics of Hegel emphasize only the first aspect, necessity as the inner principle dominating its contingent expressions, neglecting the second one, namely how this necessity itself hinges on contingency, *is* nothing but contingency elevated into the form of necessity.

This brings us to the Hegelian *Aufhebung* (sublation) as a movement through which every contingent particularity is *aufgehoben* (sublated) in its universal notion. The standard argument against *Aufhebung* is that there is always a remainder which resists it, which persists in its immediate idiocy. What if, however, this is the very point of the truly Hegelian *Aufhebung*, of the "negation of negation"? The direct attempt at *Aufhebung* is the initial "position"; it is "negated" in its failure, in the element that resists it; the "negation of negation" is then the insight into how this resisting element, this obstacle, is in itself a positive condition of possibility—the *Aufhebung* has to be sustained by its constitutive exception.

So what if the lesson of the Hegelian *Aufhebung* is that the loss itself (the failure) is to be celebrated? Hegel was fully aware of how the weight given to an event by its symbolic inscription "sublates" its immediate reality—in his *Philosophy of History*, he offers a wonderful characterization of Thucydides's

21 And Hegel was far from conceding any priority to the German language—an interesting biographical detail: when, in the 1810s, he was considering the invitation of a Dutch friend to accept a university post in Amsterdam, he not only started to learn Dutch, but immediately bombarded his friend with requests to inform him on Dutch-language idiosyncrasies like forms of word-play, so that he would be able to develop his thoughts in Dutch.

history of the Peloponnesian war: "In the Peloponnesian War, the struggle was essentially between Athens and Sparta. Thucydides has left us the history of the greater part of it, and his immortal work is the absolute gain which humanity has derived from that contest."[22] One should read this judgment in all its naïveté: in a way, from the standpoint of world history, the Peloponnesian War took place so that Thucydides could write a book on it. The term "absolute" should be given here all its weight: from the relative standpoint of our finite human interests, the numerous real tragedies of the Peloponnesian war are, of course, infinitely more important than a book; but from the standpoint of the Absolute, it is the book that matters. One should not be afraid to say the same thing about some truly great works of art: the Elizabethan era occurred in order to produce Shakespeare; Shakespeare's work is "the absolute gain which humanity has derived" from the vicissitudes of his era. And yes, why not?—Hitchcock's masterpieces of the 1950s are the "absolute gain" which humanity derived from the Eisenhower period in the US. Sometimes, even, an author's importance may be condensed not in his work, but in a book written on him—although Samuel Johnson was the author of *A Dictionary of the English Language* and the *spiritus movens* of the thriving "public sphere" of eighteenth-century London, he is today remembered almost exclusively for *The Life of Samuel Johnson*, the ample biography written by his friend James Boswell (1791).

Here a surprising link with Heidegger suggests itself. In his reading of "essence" (*Wesen*) as a verb ("essencing"), Heidegger provides a de-essentialized notion of essence: while, traditionally, "essence" refers to a stable core that guarantees the identity of a thing, for Heidegger, "essence" is something that depends on the historical context, on the epochal disclosure of being that occurs in and through language as the "house of being." The expression "*Wesen der Sprache*" does not means "the essence of language," but the "essencing" done by language,

> language bringing things into their essence, language "moving us" so that things matter to us in a particular kind of way, so that paths are made within which we can move among entities, and so that entities can bear on each other as the entities they are ... We share an originary language when the world is articulated in the same style for us, when we "listen to language," when we "let it say its saying to us."[23]

For example, for a medieval Christian, the "essence" of gold resides in its incorruptibility and divine sheen, which make it a "divine" metal, while for us, it is, among other things, a resource to be traded in commodity markets or a material

22 G. W. F. Hegel, *Lectures on the Philosophy of History*, trans. J. Sibree, London: Henry G. Bohn 1861, p. 277.

23 Mark Wrathall, *How to Read Heidegger*, New York: W. W. Norton & Company 2006, pp. 94–5.

appropriate for aesthetic purposes. (Or, to take another example, the voice of a castrato was for Catholics the very voice of an angel prior to the Fall, while for us today it is a monstrosity.) There is thus a fundamental violence in this "essencing" ability of language: our world is given a partial twist, it loses its balanced innocence, one partial color gives its tone to the Whole. The operation designated by Laclau as that of hegemony is inherent to language.

Varieties of self-relating negation

However, the question persists: does this Hegelian assertion of radical contingency open up the space for the coincidence of repression with the return of the repressed which exemplifies the properly Freudian "negation of negation" (the repression—negation—of some content only works if it is itself negated, if the repressed returns)? Lacan repeats the classic argument against the dialectical triad, the return of the starting point back to itself through its self-mediation: "When one makes two, there is never a return. It never comes back to make one again, *even if it is a new one*."[24] It may seem that Hegel's basic premise is that the two come back to One, even if we concede the key point that this One is a new One: not the One which was lost in alienation-externalization, but a new One "performatively" created in the very process of returning-to-itself. When a substantial unity dissolves into the multiplicity of its predicates, it is one of its former predicates which establishes itself as a new subject, retroactively positing its presuppositions. However, even this properly dialectical image of permanent transubstantiation remains misleading: to put it bluntly, for Hegel, there is no One at the beginning, every One is a return-to-itself from the two. The One to which one returns is constituted through return, so it is not that One splits into two—One is a Two of which one part is nothing. Here is how, in an extremely condensed passage, Hegel formulated the gap that separates the dialectical process proper from Plotinian "emanation": "The simple unity, its becoming, is that sublation of all predicates—the absolute negativity; the coming-out [emanation: *Herausgehen*] is this negativity in itself—*one should not begin with oneness and then pass to duality*."[25] The last part says it all, directly rejecting the standard notion of the dialectical process as the deployment or division of the initial or immediate One into Two—*one should not begin with oneness and then pass to duality*. Why not? Because the One is only constituted through the passage to duality, through its division. The unexpected consequence of this fact is that, contrary to the common notion that the number of Hegelian dialectics

24 Jacques Lacan, *Le séminaire, Livre XX: Encore*, Paris: Seuil 1975, p. 79.

25 G. W. F. Hegel, *Vorlesungen über die Geschichte der Philosophie* (Werke, Vol. 18), Frankfurt: Suhrkamp 1979, p. 450.

is 3, in other words that Hegel's goal is to overcome all dualisms in a higher "synthesis," to reconcile the opposites in an encompassing third medium, the proper number of dialectics is 2: not 2 as the duality of polar opposites, but 2 as the inherent self-distancing of the One itself: the One only becomes One by way of redoubling itself, by acquiring a minimal distance towards itself. This is why, when Badiou defines love as the construction of a world from the perspective of the Two, one should recognize in this definition an echo of the Hegelian dialectic: love brings the two together so that their gap is maintained, there is no pseudo-Wagnerian or mystical fusion here, the gap between the two is parallactic and as such unsurpassable. This point has already been made by Jameson when, apropos *Antigone*, he insisted that the opposition between human law and divine law has to be read

> not as a struggle between the state and the family or clan that tears society apart; but first and foremost as the division which brings society itself into being in the first place by articulating its first great differentiations, that of warrior versus priest, or of city versus clan, or even outside versus inside … Each of these larval powers brings the other into being and reinforces the distinctiveness of its opposite number … the contradiction which ultimately tears the polis apart and destroys it … is the same opposition that brings it into being as a viable structure in the first place.[26]

Here we can see again the gap that separates Hegel from historicist evolutionism: from the historicist standpoint, every historical figure has its moment of maturity which is then followed by the period of decay. For example, capitalism was progressive until the middle of the nineteenth century, when it had to be supported in its struggle against premodern forms of life; but with the aggravation of class struggle, capitalism became an obstacle to the further progress of humanity and will have to be overcome. For a real dialectician, there is no moment of maturity when a system functions in a non-antagonistic way: paradoxical as this may sound, capitalism was at the same time "progressive" and antagonistic, in decay, and the threat of its decay is the very driving force of its "progress" (capitalism has to revolutionize itself constantly to cope with its constitutive "obstacle"). The family and the state are thus not simply the two poles of the social Whole; it is rather that society has to split itself from itself in order to become One—it is this tearing apart of the social Whole, this division itself, which "brings society itself into being in the first place by articulating its first great differentiations, that of warrior versus priest." It is in this precise sense that one should read Badiou's claim: "The real is not what brings together, but what separates." Even more pointedly, one should add that the real is the separation (antagonistic split) which, as such, brings together a socio-symbolic field.

26 Jameson, *The Hegel Variations*, pp. 82–3.

The Hegelian reading of *Antigone* as a play dealing with "the emergence of an articulated society as such" thus demonstrates the radically anti-corporatist nature Hegel's social thought:[27] the underlying premise of this thought is that every social articulation is by definition always "inorganic," antagonistic. And the lesson of this insight is that, whenever we read a description of how an original unity becomes corrupted and splits, we should remember that we are dealing with a retroactive ideological fantasy which obfuscates the fact that such an original unity never existed, that it is a retroactive projection generated by the process of splitting. There never was a harmonious state which was split into warriors and priests. Or, at a different level, when we use a conventional gesture like shaking hands, we should not presume that originally such a gesture or expression had a literal meaning (I offer you my hand to demonstrate that I am not holding a knife, and so on)—the gap between literal meaning and clichéd use is there from the beginning; that is, from the moment shaking hands became a gesture, it meant more than demonstrating that one was not armed, it became a performative act of signaling an openness to social contact, and so on and so forth. We encounter here the topic of what quantum physics calls the two vacuums:[28] in order for the hierarchical power to establish itself, it has to redouble or divide itself into "true" (warrior) and "false" (priestly) power—it is this division which, far from weakening power, constitutes it. The ruling class has to divide itself in order to rule—the rule is here "divided we stand, united we fall." A certain "negation of negation" is also constitutive of the phallic signifier. That is to say, what makes the phallic signifier such a complex notion is not only that, in it, the symbolic, imaginary, and real dimensions are intertwined, but also that, in a double self-reflexive step which uncannily imitates the process of the "negation of negation," it condenses three levels: it is (1) *position*: the signifier of the lost part, of what the subject loses and lacks with its entry into (or submission to) the signifying order; (2) *negation*: the signifier of (this) lack; and (3) *negation of negation*: itself the lacking/missing signifier.[29] The phallus is the part which is lost ("sacrificed") with the entry into the symbolic order and, simultaneously, the signifier of this loss.[30]

When Badiou emphasizes that double negation is not the same as affirmation, he thereby merely confirms the old Lacanian motto "*les non-dupes errent*."[31] Let us take the affirmation "I believe." Its negation is: "I do not really believe, I am just pretending to believe." Its properly Hegelian negation of negation, however, is not the return to direct belief, but the self-relating pretense: "I pretend to

27 Ibid., p. 80.

28 For a more detailed account of the notion of two vacuums, see Chapter 14.

29 François Balmès, *Dieu, le sexe et la vérité*, Ramonville Saint-Agne: Érès 2007, p. 150.

30 Ibid., p. 166.

31 In Alain Badiou, *Logics of Worlds*, London: Continuum 2009.

pretend to believe," which means: "I really believe without being aware of it." Is not irony, then, the ultimate form of the critique of ideology today—irony in the precise *Mozartian* sense of taking statements more seriously than the subjects who utter them themselves? Or, as Descartes put it at the beginning of Chapter 3 of his *Discourse on Method*: "very many are not aware of what it is that they really believe; for, as the act of mind by which a thing is believed is different from that by which we know that we believe it, the one act is often found without the other." Again, how does this Lacanian "negation of negation" relate to the Hegelian one? Let us take negation in the guise of man's abandonment by God: there is no happy ending here; in the "negation of negation" we are no less alone and abandoned as before, all that happens is that we experience this abandonment in its positive dimension, as the space of our freedom. Another version of this reversal was discerned by Chesterton who, in his wonderful text *The Book of Job*, shows why God has to rebuke his own defenders, the "mechanical and supercilious comforters of Job":

> The mechanical optimist endeavors to justify the universe avowedly upon the ground that it is a rational and consecutive pattern. He points out that the fine thing about the world is that it can all be explained. That is the one point, if I may put it so, on which God, in return, is explicit to the point of violence. God says, in effect, that if there is one fine thing about the world, as far as men are concerned, it is that it cannot be explained. He insists on the inexplicableness of everything. "Hath the rain a father? … Out of whose womb came the ice?" (38:28). He goes farther, and insists on the positive and palpable unreason of things; "Hast thou sent the rain upon the desert where no man is, and upon the wilderness wherein there is no man?" (38:26) … To startle man, God becomes for an instant a blasphemer; one might almost say that God becomes for an instant an atheist. He unrolls before Job a long panorama of created things, the horse, the eagle, the raven, the wild ass, the peacock, the ostrich, the crocodile. He so describes each of them that it sounds like a monster walking in the sun. The whole is a sort of psalm or rhapsody of the sense of wonder. The maker of all things is astonished at the things he has Himself made.[32]

God is here overwhelmed by the miracle of his own creation—and we should not miss the negative aspect also at work here. In referring to the chaotic wealth of creatures, God is not boastfully asserting the infinite gap which separates Job from him (as in: "Who are you to complain about your little misery? You have no idea what the universe is …"); he is—implicitly, at least—also admitting that Job has nothing to complain about because his case is in no way unique: the whole world is a terrifying unreasonable mess. This "negation of negation" thus

32 G. K. Chesterton, *The Book of Job*, London: Cecil Palmer & Hayward, 1916, p. xxii–xxiii.

deprives Job even of the last solace brought by the hope that, in God's eyes at least, his suffering has some deeper meaning: what he thought to be his own perplexity reveals itself to be the perplexity of God himself. This brings us again to Lacan's key motif of the lack in the Other, best rendered by Hegel's famous remark that the secrets of the Egyptians were secrets also for the Egyptians themselves: the secret of God is also a secret for God himself.

So far so good, we may say: by way of transposing what appears as an epistemological limit into the Thing itself, Hegel shows how the problem is its own solution—but in what precise sense? To avoid a fatal misunderstanding: this crucial dialectical move from epistemological obstacle to ontological impossibility in no way implies that all we can do is reconcile ourselves to this impossibility, i.e., accept reality itself as imperfect. The premise of psychoanalysis is that one can intervene with the symbolic into the Real, because the Real is not external reality-in-itself, but a crack in the symbolic, so one can intervene with an act which re-configures the field and thus transforms its immanent point of impossibility. "Traversing the fantasy" does not mean accepting the misery of our lives—on the contrary, it means that only after we "traverse" the fantasies obfuscating this misery can we effectively change it.

Furthermore, there is a subtle difference between the two versions of the reversal of the epistemological limit into ontological impossibility, "Rabinovitch's" and "Adorno's."[33] In the first one, we get a clear solution, no antagonism persists here (if, of course, one ignores the social censorship which prevents Rabinovitch from directly stating his true reason). The truth wins, and the interesting point is how it can do so only through error (confirming Hegel's point that the path to truth is part of the truth). In other words, the elegant economy of the joke is that the very necessity of the detour through the first (false) reason confirms the second (true) reason: Rabinovitch wants to emigrate because of the social oppression exemplified by the bureaucrat's response to his first reason (communism will last forever). Although it may appear to follow the same logic, Adorno's example does not resolve the antagonism, for all that happens in its resolution is that the epistemological antinomy is displaced into the Thing itself, as its immanent antagonism—the antagonism is thereby fully confirmed. The key question here is: where in the triad of the dialectical process should one locate the precise moment of the explosion of the antagonism which underlies the entire process? Do we encounter the antagonism at its purest at the moment of the most aggravated negativity—that is, of the negativity brought to self-relation—or in the final result of the process, namely the reversal of negativity into the new positivity? Does the result assert or cancel the antagonism? Or does it, in some way, do both?

33 These two names refer to the two examples mentioned in Interlude 1 (the Soviet joke on Rabinovitch's and Adorno's antagonistic notion of society).

Insofar as the Hegelian "reconciliation" is at its core the reversal of the condition of impossibility into a condition of possibility, or the recognition that what appeared as an obstacle is a positive condition of the existence of the very thing thwarted by this obstacle, the ambiguity remains: does reconciliation reconcile in the sense of *overcoming* the antagonism, or in the sense of the reconciliation *with* the antagonism (or, in some sense, both at the same time, if we can say that the reconciliation with antagonism changes its antagonistic nature)? When, in the *Phenomenology*, Hegel introduces the notion of reconciliation as the way to resolve the deadlock of the Beautiful Soul, his term designates the acceptance of the chaos and injustice of the world as immanent to the Beautiful Soul which deplores it, the Beautiful Soul's acceptance of the fact that it participates in the reality it criticizes and judges, not any kind of magical transformation of this reality.

Does not the development of Brecht's plays from the 1920s to the early 1930s also enact an homologous kind of renunciation? The plays of the '20s, exemplarily *The Beggar's Opera*, perform a brutal sacrifice of all ideological ideals to cynical earthly interests—power, money, sex—that lie at the core of the egotistic subject; then, in the "learning plays" of the early '30s, exemplarily in *The Measure Taken*, this subject itself is obliterated in a gesture of radical sacrifice on behalf of the collective. It is crucial to note how the second sacrifice is not an external reversal of the first one (of the sacrifice of all ideological ideals), but its immanent accomplishment: first we sacrifice or renounce everything for our ego, then we realize that we have thereby lost or sacrificed the ego itself. Why? Because the subjective position of a thoroughly cynical ego is impossible: the "ego" only functions insofar as it is sustained by its fantasmatic support of illusions and dreams.[34] What makes Brecht's learning plays so uncanny and disturbing is that there is no deeper subjective condition or message beneath this mechanism (denouncing it as an oppressive ideological operation, celebrating it as an elementary ethical gesture ...)—all Brecht does is stage this mechanism of sacrifice in its formal neutrality.[35]

Or, to shift the accent slightly, can we read Hegel's "negation of negation" qua self-relating negativity also in the sense of this position of utter despair when the subject not only assumes a radical loss, but is then deprived of this loss itself—not in the sense of regaining what was lost, but in the much more radical sense of finding itself in a radical void after losing the very coordinates which made the loss meaningful? In Hitchcock's *Vertigo*, Scottie first experiences the loss of Madeleine, his fatal love; when he recreates Madeleine in Judy and then discovers that the Madeleine he knew was Judy all along pretending to be Madeleine,

34 I rely here on Mladen Dolar, "Brecht's Gesture," in *11th International Istanbul Biennial Reader: What Keeps Mankind Alive?*, Istanbul: İstanbul Kültür ve Sanat Vakfı 2009.

35 I owe this point to Fredric Jameson.

what he discovers is not simply that Judy is a fake (he knew that she was not the true Madeleine, since he had recreated a copy of Madeleine out of her), but that, *because she is not a fake—she is Madeleine; Madeleine herself was already a fake*—the *objet a* disintegrates, the very loss is lost, we get a negation of negation. It is important to remember here that the last shot of *Vertigo*—after Judy falls from the tower, Scottie stands on the edge, looking down—gave rise to radically opposed readings: for some interpreters, this shot signals that Scottie survives as a totally broken man, for others, it is a kind of happy ending (Scottie is now cured of his disease, he can look down into the abyss)—an ambivalence which perfectly reproduces the ambiguity of the outcome of the Hegelian negation of negation (utter despair or reconciliation). So, again: where does the Hegelian negation of negation stand with regard to this ambiguity?

A closer look at different modalities of the negation of negation in Hegel is needed here. First, we have the "Rabinovitch-matrix" (the reversal of the problem into its own solution: "thesis"—I want to emigrate because, after the fall of socialism, they will blame us, the Jews, for the communist crimes; "antithesis"—but socialism will never fall, it will last forever; "synthesis"—that is the true reason I want to emigrate), which ends with a positive resolution. Then we have the "Adorno-matrix" in which the reversal of the problem into its own solution (here: the transposition of an epistemological limitation into an ontological impossibility) brings no resolution, but, on the contrary, renders visible the underlying antagonism in its pure state. Finally, we have the "Irma-matrix," the logic which underlies Freud's dream of Irma's injection. The dream begins with a conversation between Freud and his patient Irma about the failure of her treatment due to an infected needle; in the course of the conversation, Freud gets closer to her, approaches her face and looks deep into her mouth, confronting the horrible sight of the red flesh of her throat. At this point of unbearable horror, the tone of the dream changes, the horror all of a sudden passes into comedy: three doctors, Freud's friends, appear, who, in a ridiculous pseudo-professional jargon, enumerate multiple (and mutually exclusive) reasons why Irma's poisoning by the infected needle was nobody's fault (there was no injection; the needle was clean ...). So there is first a traumatic encounter (the sight of Irma's throat), followed by the sudden shift into comedy, which enables the dreamer to avoid an encounter with the true trauma. It may appear that the triad of the "Irma-matrix" is that of "IRS": first, the imaginary duality; then, its aggravation into the abyss of the Real; finally, the symbolic resolution. However, a more precise reading discloses that in fact we get two Reals in the dream, in that each of its two parts concludes with a figuration of the Real. In the conclusion of the first part (the conversation between Irma and Freud), this is obvious: the look into Irma's throat renders the Real in the guise of primordial flesh, the palpitation of the life substance as the Thing itself, in its disgusting dimension as a cancerous outgrowth. However, in the second part, the comic symbolic exchange or interplay between the three doctors also ends up with the Real, this time in its opposite aspect—the Real of writing, of the meaningless formula of trimethylamine. The difference hinges on the different starting point: if we start with the imaginary (the mirror-confrontation of Freud and Irma), we get the Real in its imaginary dimension, as a horrifying primordial image that cancels the imagery itself; if we start with the symbolic (the exchange of arguments between the three doctors), we get the signifier itself transformed into the Real of a meaningless letter or formula. These two figures are the two opposite aspects of the Real: the abyss of the primordial Life-Thing and the meaningless letter or formula (as in the Real of the modern science).

How does this duality of the imaginary Real and the symbolic Real relate to the Real we encountered at the end of the "Adorno-matrix"? The Real we get in the "Adorno-matrix" is neither of the first two, but the "real Real," a purely formal Real, the Real of an antagonism ("contradiction"). And what we should add here is this Real is in itself redoubled: as we have already seen, the Real is characterized by a kind of "coincidence of opposites," of the purely material contingent remainder (the *objet a*, a little piece of reality) and the pure Real of formal antagonism. This brings us to the key question: does Hegel generate the *objet a* at the end of the process of negation of negation? That is to say: the Lacanian Real at its most radical is not a pre-symbolic substance; it rather emerges through the redoubling of the symbolic, through the passage from alienation to separation (defined as the overlapping of the two lacks). So does not the triumphant tone of the Hegelian negation of negation hinge on the fact that, while Hegel can—maybe conditionally—think antagonism, he is not able to think the ultimate speculative identity of the purely formal antagonism and the contingent remainder or excess of a little piece of reality? This limitation, this inability to think the "indivisible remainder" of the dialectical form not as an excess of the Real which simply eludes dialectical mediation, but as the product of this mediation, as its concluding moment, is clearly discernible in Hegel's theory of marriage (from his *Philosophy of Right*).[36]

The formal aspect

So, again, can Hegel think the excess of the death drive (of love as the lethal passion) which persists as a kind of "indivisible remainder" after the dialectical resolution of the process in a rational totality? And if he cannot, are we really dealing with a fundamental systemic failure? Would it not be appropriate to

36 See G. W. F. Hegel, *Hegel's Philosophy of Right*, trans. T. M. Knox, London: Oxford University Press 1978, pp. 111–16.

claim that, if Hegel were faithful to his own inner logic, he should have applied here the same reasoning as he does in his deduction of the necessity of monarchy as the peak of the rational state? When Hegel claims that the conception of the monarch is "of all conceptions the hardest for ratiocination, i.e. for the method of reflection employed by the Understanding," the speculative moment that Understanding cannot grasp is "the transition of the concept of pure self-determination into the immediacy of being and so into the realm of nature." In other words, while Understanding can well grasp the universal mediation of a living totality, what it cannot grasp is that this totality, in order to actualize itself, has to acquire actual existence in the guise of an immediate "natural" singularity. Should we then posit that, in a strictly homologous way, the rational totality of reconciled family life has to generate a "passionate attachment" to the contingent singularity of the beloved?

The difference that separates Lacan from Hegel is thus a minimal difference, a tiny, barely perceptible feature which changes everything. It is not Hegel versus another figure, but Hegel and his spectral double—in the passage from Hegel to Lacan, we do not pass from One-Hegel to another One-Lacan. They are not two, but the One-Hegel plus his *objet a*. This brings us back to the relationship between repetition and minimal difference: minimal difference is something which emerges in pure repetition. In Henning Mankel's police procedural series, Inspector Kurt Wallander has a father whose means of survival is painting—he paints all the time, making hundreds of copies of the same painting, a forest landscape over which the sun never sets (therein resides the "message" of the painting: it is possible to hold the sun captive, to prevent it from setting, to freeze a magical moment, extracting its pure appearance from nature's eternal circular movement of generation and degeneration). There is, however, a "minimal difference" in these otherwise identical paintings: in some, there is a small grouse in the landscape, while others are without the grouse, as if eternity itself, frozen time, has to be sustained by a minimal variation, a kind of stand-in for what really distinguishes each painting, its unique, purely virtual intensity.

Deleuze's most radical anti-Hegelian argument concerns this pure difference: Hegel is unable to think pure difference which is outside the horizon of identity or contradiction; Hegel conceives a radicalized difference as contradiction which is then, through its dialectical resolution, again subsumed under identity. (Here, Deleuze is also opposed to Derrida who, from Deleuze's perspective, remains caught within the vicious cycle of contradiction/identity, merely postponing resolution indefinitely.) And, insofar as Hegel is the philosopher of actuality or actualization, insofar as, for him, the "truth" of a potentiality is revealed in its actualization, Hegel's inability to think pure difference is linked to his inability to think the virtual in its proper dimension, as a possibility which already qua possibility possesses its own reality: pure difference is not actual, it does not concern different actual properties of a thing or differences among things, its status is purely virtual, it is a difference which takes place at its purest precisely when nothing changes in actuality, when, in actuality, the *same* thing repeats itself. It may appear that it is only Deleuze who formulates the truly post-Hegelian program of thinking difference: the Derridean "opening" which emphasizes the endless difference, the dissemination that can never be sublated or re-appropriated, etc., remains within the Hegelian framework, merely "opening" it up ... But, here, the Hegelian counter-argument would be: is not "pure" virtual difference the very name for actual self-identity? Is it not *constitutive* of actual identity? More precisely, in the terms of Deleuze's transcendental empiricism, pure difference is the virtual support or condition of actual identity: an entity is perceived as "(self-)identical" when (and only when) its virtual support is reduced to a *pure* difference. In Lacanese, pure difference concerns the supplement of the virtual object (Lacan's *objet a*); its most plastic experience is that of a sudden change in (our perception of) an object which, with regard to its positive qualities, remains the same: "although nothing changes, the thing all of a sudden seemed totally different"—as Deleuze would have put it, it is the thing's *intensity* which changes. (For Lacan, the theoretical problem or task is here to distinguish between the Master-Signifier and the *objet a*, both of which refer to the abyssal X in the object beyond its positive properties.) As such, pure difference is closer to antagonism than to the difference between two positive social groups, one of which is to be annihilated. The universalism that sustains an antagonistic struggle is not exclusive of anyone, which is why the highest triumph lies not in the destruction of the enemy, but in the explosion of "universal brotherhood" in which agents of the opposing camp change sides (recall the proverbial scenes of police or military units joining demonstrators). It is in such an explosion of all-encompassing brotherhood, from which no one is in principle excluded, that the difference between "us" and "the enemy" as positive agents is reduced to a *pure* formal difference.

This brings us to the topic of difference, repetition, and change (in the sense of the rise of something genuinely new). Jean-Luc Godard proposed the motto "*Ne change rien pour que tout soit différent*" ("Change nothing so that everything will be different"), a reversal of "Some things must change so that everything remains the same." In some political constellations, such as the late capitalist dynamic in which only constant self-revolutionizing can maintain the system, those who refuse to change anything are effectively the agents of true change: the change of the very principle of change. We all know the Oriental principle of the cosmic Whole which reproduces itself through the incessant movement and struggle of its parts—all the parts move and thereby maintain the deeper peace of the cosmic Whole. The most elementary formula of Western negativity is the disturbance of the Whole which occurs precisely when something gets stuck, fixed, refuses to move, thereby disturbing the cosmic balance of change, throwing it out of joint.

Deleuze's thesis according to which New and repetition are not opposed, for the New arises only from repetition, must be read against the background of the difference between the virtual and the actual: changes which concern only the actual aspect of things are only changes within the existing frame, not the emergence of something really New—the New only emerges when the virtual support of the actual changes, and this change occurs precisely in the guise of a repetition in which a thing remains the same in its actuality. In other words, things really change not when A transforms itself into B, but when, while A remains exactly the same with regard to its actual properties, it "totally changes" imperceptibly. This change is the minimal difference, and the task of theory is to subtract this minimal difference from the given field of multiplicities. In this sense, subtraction is also another name for the Hegelian sublation (*Aufhebung*) or negation of negation: in it, radical change (negation) overlaps with the pure repetition of the same. This means that the inertia of the Old and the rise of the New also coincide in the dialectical notion of repetition. The New emerges when, instead of a process just "naturally" evolving in its flow of generation and corruption, this flow becomes stuck, an element (a gesture) is fixed, persists, repeats itself and thus perturbs the "natural" flux of (de)composition. This persistence of the Old, its "stuckness," is the only possible site of the rise of the New: in short, *the minimal definition of the New is as an Old which gets stuck and thereby refuses to pass away.*

Here is the crux of the post-Hegelian rupture: its most elementary feature, from Kierkegaard to Marx, is the gap that emerges between sublation and repetition; that is, repetition acquires autonomy with regard to sublation, and the two are now opposed—either a thing is sublated into a higher mode of its existence, or it just drags on in its inertia. This "liberation" of repetition from the hold of sublation, this idea of a non-cumulative repetition which just runs on empty, not generating anything new, is usually taken as the minimal index of post-Hegelian materialism, in its break with the Hegelian circle of total conceptual mediation. Under Lacan's influence, Jean Hyppolite read in this way the philosophical foundation of the Freudian notion of death drive as the compulsion to repeat. As Lacan points out in his *Seminar II*, another name for this excess of repetition over organic progress is mechanism: what the post-Hegelian thought brings out is the notion of a non-cumulative mechanical repetition.

Is this diagnosis correct, however? Was not Hegel fully aware that the way spirit arises out of the organic natural process is through a mechanical repetition which disturbs the free organic deployment? This is the point of his discussions of habit, etc., in the "Anthropology" section of his *Philosophy of Spirit*: in the triad of mechanical process, organic process, and the properly spiritual process, the spiritual dimension needs a "regressive" support in mechanical habits ("blind" learning of the rules of language, etc.). There is no spirit without a machine, the appearance of spirit is a machine which colonizes the organism, the victory of spirit over mere life appears as a "regression" of life to a mechanism. (This fact finds its extreme expression in Descartes's "dualism": the assertion of pure thinking is correlative to the reduction of nature to a blind mechanism.)

How are we to clarify this elusive difference between Hegel and Freud? Mladen Dolar proposed to read "Hegel is Freud" as the ultimate philosophical infinite judgment, since Hegel and Freud cannot but appear absolute opposites: Absolute Knowing (the unity of the subject and the Absolute) versus the unconscious (the subject not master in his own house); excessive knowledge versus lack of knowledge. The first complication in this simple opposition is that, for Freud and Lacan, the unconscious is not a blind instinctual field but also a kind of knowledge, an unconscious knowledge, a knowledge which does not know itself ("unknown knowns," in terms of Rumsfeldian epistemology)—so what if Absolute Knowing is to be located into the very tension between the knowledge aware of itself and the unknown knowledge? What if the "absoluteness" of knowing refers not to our access to the divine Absolute-in-itself, or to a total self-reflection through which we would gain full access to our "unknown knowing" and thus achieve subjective self-transparency, but to a much more modest (and all the more difficult to think) overlapping between the lack of our "conscious" knowledge and the lack inscribed into the very heart of our unknown knowledge? It is at this level that one should locate the parallel between Hegel and Freud: if Hegel discovers unreason (contradiction, the mad dance of opposites which unsettles any rational order) in the heart of reason, Freud discovers reason in the heart of unreason (in slips of tongue, dreams, madness). What they share is the logic of retroactivity: in Hegel, the One is a retroactive effect of its loss, the very return to the lost One constitutes it; and in Freud, repression and the return of the repressed coincide, the repressed is the retroactive effect of its return.

There are also good reasons for linking the Freudian unconscious to self-consciousness as self-reflexivity: "self-consciousness is an object," for in an object-symptom, I reflexively register a truth about myself inaccessible to my consciousness. This, however, is not quite the same as the Hegelian unconscious: it is a particular (singular) unconscious, a kind of contingent transcendental, a contingent knot-*sinthome* holding together the subject's universe. In clear contrast to this Freudian unconscious, the Hegelian unconscious is formal: it is the form of enunciation invisible in the enunciated content; it is systemic, not a contingent *bricolage* of lateral links (what Lacan calls *lalangue*); that is, it resides in the universal symbolic form on which the subject unknowingly relies, not in the contingent "pathological" desire which transpires in slips of tongue. Hegel's unconscious is the unconscious of self-consciousness itself, its own necessary non-transparency, the necessary overlooking of its own *form* ("*das Formelle*") in the content it confronts. The unconscious is the universal form of particular content: when Hegel says that the truth is in what I say, not in what I mean (to say), he means that truth is in the universality of the meaning of words as opposed to the particular intention. The contrast between the Freudian unconscious (singular contingent links, word-play) and the Hegelian unconscious (the universal scheme overlooked by our conscious focusing on the particular, or what Hegel himself calls *das Formelle*) is thus obvious—Lacan speaks of the "Hegelian unconscious," opposing it to the Freudian. The most succinct definition of the Hegelian unconscious is provided towards the end of the "Introduction" to the *Phenomenology*, where Hegel determines *das Formelle* as In-itself or For-us (the philosophical observer) in contrast to the for-consciousness (how things appear to the engaged subject itself), as the process in contrast to its abstract result, and as the determinate negation in contrast to abstract negation which leaves the negated content behind:

> the result which at any time comes about in the case of an untrue mode of knowledge cannot possibly collapse into an empty nothing, but must necessarily be taken as the negation of that of which it is a result ... this origination of the new object—which offers itself to consciousness without consciousness knowing how it comes by it—that to us, who watch the process, is to be seen going on, so to say, behind its back. Thereby there enters into its process a moment of being *in itself*, or of being for us, which is not expressly presented to that consciousness which is in the grip of experience itself. The *content*, however, of what we see arising, exists for it, and we lay hold of and comprehend merely its formal character [*das Formelle*], i.e. its bare origination; *for it*, what has thus arisen has merely the character of object, while, *for us*, it appears at the same time as a process and coming into being.[37]

In short, when the subject passes from one "object" (which can also be an entire mode of life) to another, it appears to it that the new "object" (content) is simply immediately found; what the subject does not see is the process of mediation, going on behind its back, which generated the new content out of the inconsistencies of the old one. The Freudian unconscious also has a formal aspect and is not merely a matter of content: recall the cases when Freud interprets a dream so that what is repressed or excluded from its content returns as a feature of the form of the dream (in a dream about pregnancy, the fact that the dreamer is not sure who the father is articulates itself in the guise of an uncertainty about what the dream was about); furthermore, Freud emphasizes that the true secret of the dream is not its content (the "dream-thoughts"), but the form itself:

37 G. W. F. Hegel, *Phenomenology of Mind*, second rev. ed., trans. J. B. Baillie, Mineola: Dover 2003, p. 53.

> The latent dream-thoughts are the material which the dream-work transforms into the manifest dream ... The only essential thing about dreams is the dream-work that has influenced the thought-material. We have no right to ignore it in our theory, even though we may disregard it in certain practical situations. Analytic observation shows further that the dream-work never restricts itself to translating these thoughts into the archaic or regressive mode of expression that is familiar to you. In addition, it regularly takes possession of something else, which is not part of the latent thoughts of the previous day, but which is the true motif force for the construction of the dream. This indispensable addition [*unentbehrliche Zutat*] is the equally unconscious wish for the fulfillment of which the content of the dream is given its new form. A dream may thus be any sort of thing in so far as you are only taking into account the thoughts it represents—a warning, an intention, a preparation, and so on; but it is always also the fulfillment of an unconscious wish and, if you are considering it as a product of the dream-work, it is only that. A dream is therefore never simply an intention, or a warning, but always an intention, etc., translated into the archaic mode of thought by the help of an unconscious wish and transformed to fulfill that wish. The one characteristic, the wish-fulfillment, is the invariable one; the other may vary. It may for its part once more be a wish, in which case the dream will, with the help of an unconscious wish, represent as fulfilled a latent wish of the previous day.[38]

Every detail is worth analyzing in this brilliant passage, from its implicit opening motto "what is good enough for practice—namely the search for the meaning of dreams—is not good enough for theory," to its concluding redoubling of the wish. Its key insight is, of course, the "triangulation" of latent dream-thought, manifest dream-content, and the unconscious wish, which limits the scope of—or, rather, directly undermines—the hermeneutic model of the interpretation of dreams (the path from the manifest dream-content to its hidden meaning, the latent dream-thought), which travels in the opposite direction to the path of the formation of a dream (the transposition of the latent dream-thought into the manifest dream-content by the dream-work). The paradox is that this dream-work is not merely a process of masking the dream's "true message": the dream's true core, its unconscious wish, inscribes itself only through and in this very process of masking, so that the moment we re-translate the dream-content back into the dream-thought expressed in it, we lose the "true motive force" of the dream—in short, it is the process of masking itself which inscribes into the dream its true secret. One should therefore reverse the standard notion of penetrating deeper and deeper into the core of the dream: it is not that we first move from the manifest dream-content to the first-level secret, the latent dream-thought,

38 Sigmund Freud, *Introductory Lectures on Psychoanalysis*, Harmondsworth: Penguin Books 1973, pp. 261–2.

and then, taking a step further, go even deeper, to the dream's unconscious core, the unconscious wish. The "deeper" wish is located in the very gap between the latent dream-thought and the manifest dream-content.

Nonetheless, the Freudian form of the unconscious is not the same as the Hegelian one. But, more importantly, instead of automatically taking this gap that separates Freud from Hegel as an indication of Hegel's limitation ("Hegel could not see that ..."), one should reverse the underlying question: not only "Can Hegel think the Freudian unconscious?" but also "Can Freud think the Hegelian unconscious?" It is not that there is something "too radical for Hegel" missing from his thought, something with regard to which Freud is more consistent and "goes further," but the very opposite: like Hegel, Freud is a thinker of conflict, struggle, of "self-contradiction" and inherent antagonisms; but, in clear contrast to Hegel, in Freud, a conflict is not resolved by a self-contradiction being taken to an extreme and, with its self-cancellation, a new dimension emerging. On the contrary, the conflict is not resolved at all, the "contradiction" is not brought to its climax, but is rather stalled, brought to a temporary halt in the guise of a compromise-formation. This compromise is not the "unity of opposites" in the Hegelian sense of the "negation of negation," but a ridiculously *failed* negation, a negation which is hindered, derailed, distorted, twisted, sidetracked, a kind of *clinamen* of the negation (to use the neat formulation proposed by Mladen Dolar). In other words, what eludes Hegel (or what he would have dismissed as trifling or accidental) is overdetermination: in the Hegelian dialectical process, negativity is always radical or radicalized, and consistent—Hegel never considers the option of a negation that fails, so that something is just half-negated and continues to lead a subterranean existence (or, rather, insistence).[39] He never considers a constellation in which a new spiritual principle continues to coexist with the old one in an inconsistent totality, or in which a moment condenses (*verdichten*) a multiplicity of associative causal chains, so that its explicit "obvious" meaning is there to conceal the true repressed one. What would Hegel have made of Freud's dream on Irma's injection, the interpretation of which unearths a kind of *superposition* of multiple interpretive lines (getting rid of the guilt for the failure of Irma's treatment; the wish to be like the primordial father who possesses all the women; and so on)? What would Hegel have said about a dream in which the remains of the day (*Tagesreste*) are connected to the core of the dream only through verbal or similar marginal associations? What would he have said about a dream of a woman patient ("*Her husband asked her: 'Don't you think we ought to have the piano tuned?' And she replied: 'It's not worth it ...'*"), where the clue is provided by the presumed mental occurrence of the same fragment of speech in a previous

39 Maybe this is why it was a Jew who invented psychoanalysis: are not the Jews as a nation the exemplary case of the persistence of the Old which refuses its sublation?

analytic session during which she had suddenly caught hold of her jacket, one of the buttons having come undone, as though she were saying: "Please don't look [at my breasts]; *it's not worth it*." There is no notional unity here between the two levels (the dream scene and the accident during the previous session), what connects them is just a signifying bridge. Hegel does refer to *lalangue*, to word-play, but "within the limits of reason alone": *Aufhebung* contains a happy coincidence of three meanings which form the same notion, while in the dream logic, multiple meanings remain disparate.

This is also why Hegel cannot think overdetermination. For example, in the social sphere, this is how the economy plays its role of determining the social structure "in the last instance": the economy is never directly present as an actual causal agent, its presence is purely virtual, it is the social "pseudo-cause," but, precisely as such, absolute, non-relational, the absent cause, something that is never "at its own place": "that is why 'the economic' is never given properly speaking, but rather designates a differential virtuality to be interpreted, always covered over by its forms of actualization."[40] It is the absent X which circulates between the multiple levels of the social field (economic, political, ideological, legal ...), distributing them in their specific articulation. One should thus insist on the radical difference between the economic as this virtual X, the absolute point of reference of the social field, and the economic in its actuality, as one of the elements ("subsystems") of the actual social totality: when they encounter each other—or, in Hegelese, when the economic as virtual encounters itself in the guise of its actual counterpart as its "oppositional determination"—this identity coincides with absolute (self-)contradiction. However, although the Hegelian concept of oppositional determination captures the key feature of overdetermination, what gets lost is the multiplicity of "factors" (the causal links of signification) which are only parasitically exploited or manipulated, never created, by the "last instance."

At this precise point, politics enters: the space of politics is opened up by the distance of the "economy" from itself, by the gap that separates the economy as the absent Cause from the economy in its "oppositional determination," as one of the elements of the social totality. The economy is thus here doubly inscribed in the precise sense which defines the Lacanian Real: it is simultaneously the hard core (what the struggle ultimately is about) "expressed" in other struggles through displacements and other forms of distortion, and the very structuring principle of these distortions. Politics which occurs in this in-between space is non-All: its formula is not "everything is political," but "there is nothing which is not political," which means that "not-all is political." The field of the political cannot be totalized, "there is no class relationship," there is no meta-language in

40 Gilles Deleuze, *Difference and Repetition*, trans. Paul Patton, London: Continuum 2001, p. 186.

which we can "objectively" describe the whole political field, every such description is already partial (for example, Left and Right are not simply two options within a field, but two different visions of the entire field, and there is no neutral way to describe how the field "really is," the difference that constitutes it is the impossible/real of an antagonism). In this sense, Lenin was right to claim that, although the economy determines in the last instance, everything is decided in the political struggle.

There are, in Hegel, traces of the logic of *Verstellung* (not direct negation, but inconsequential complication, displacement, etc.) of a fundamental principle—such a logic is inscribed into the very heart of the Hegelian notion of totality, which is a Whole *plus* its constitutive distortions, symptoms, excesses. There are, in Hegel, traces of the "compromising" logic—its main case, significantly, is the necessary production of the rabble in the modern bourgeois society. Hegel outlines a fundamental deadlock (the more a society is rich, the less it can take care of the rabble), and then outlines three main strategies to deal with the problem (public works, private charities, export of the surplus rabble to colonies), making it clear that, in the long term, these procedures only aggravate the problem, so that all one can do is more or less successfully contain it—there is no clear logical solution here, just a compromise limiting the problem. In such cases, the only reconciliation is the (resigned) reconciliation with the fact that the problem is insoluble (within the framework of the "rational state" outlined by Hegel)—as market advocates would put it, the excess of the rabble is the price we have to pay for living in a free rational state. But is not the famous dialectic of servitude and domination also a case of compromise? The (future) servant decides not to go to the end and really risk his life; his exposure to negativity is thus thwarted, and the power of the negative is re-channeled into the formation of material objects.

Is it thus inadequate to say that Freud complicates the Hegelian negation by adding an additional twist, another turn of the screw, "negating the negation itself" not in the Hegelian sense of radicalizing negation and thus bringing it to its self-relation, but in the sense of thwarting it, introducing an obstacle to the full deployment of the power of the negative—as if the power of the negative gets caught up in a quagmire of compromises, of half-successes, and is thus diverted from its straight path? The difference between Hegel and Freud with regard to negativity can in no way be reduced to the fact that, while Hegel radicalizes negativity to its self-destructive extreme, Freud focuses on the compromise-forms which block negativity half-way: in an asymmetrical way, one should also turn things around. One of the standard reproaches to Hegel is that his radicalization of negativity is a fraud: as Georges Bataille put it, the Hegelian "work of the negative" remains within the constraints of the "restricted economy," with an in-built mechanism guaranteeing that the radicalized negativity will convert into the subordinated moment of a new mediated positive order.[41] Freud's death drive, on the contrary, asserts the *nihil unbound* up to its radical climax, the disappearance of all life (and, perhaps, the predicted implosion of the entire universe); Freudian "compromises" are thus defense mechanisms postponing the absolute catastrophe which does not even appear on Hegel's horizon. But, again, this alternative simplification is also wrong and misleading: as we have already amply demonstrated, the Hegelian "negation of negation" is far from being the simple sublation of negativity in a new positive order, while the Freudian death drive is not a push towards total disappearance or self-annihilation, but an "undead" persistence attached to a contingent particularity.

The main point is that the quagmire of obstacles which prevents the full deployment of negativity in Freud cannot be reduced to the wealth of empirical reality resisting abstract notional determinations: what it implies is not the external excess of reality over the conceptual power of the negative, but a more radical level of "negativity" itself, the level indicated by the notion of the death drive. The Freudian series of *Vers* (*Verdrängung*—repression, *Verwerfung*—foreclosure, *Verleugnung*—disavowal, *Verneinung*—denial) which supplements the Hegelian-dialectical No is thus not just a complication of that No, it points towards a more radical No, the core of negativity which escaped Hegel and which leaves its traces in different post-Hegelian versions of pure repetition. According to Freud, the multiplicity of phalli in a dream always points towards castration: multiplicity comes to fill in the gap, the lack, of the missing one. Can we then say that—insofar as the unconscious does not know negation ("no"), as Freud claims—the missing or excluded negation returns with a vengeance in the multiple forms of the process of repression: repression itself, disavowal, denial, etc.?[42] The answer is yes—on condition that we add that the very fact of the proliferation of quasi-negations bears witness to the fact that some kind of radical negation is already at work in the unconscious, even if it is excluded. The field of the unconscious—as the big Other—is structured around a loss or obstacle, around an impossibility, and the key problem is discerning the exact nature of this founding impossibility.

---

41 As we have just seen, the formal matrix of the dialectical process precludes in advance the possibility that the struggle to the death between the future master and the future servant will end with the death of one of them. It is Hegel who here defuses the destructive consequences and stages a compromise in the guise of a symbolic pact—just before the end of the struggle, one of the combatants concedes defeat, making it clear he is not ready to fight to the death.

42 Note how the Name-of-the-Father, the signifier which is also the signifier of negation (prohibition)—*le-Nom-du-Père* as *le-Non-du-Père*—is for Lacan the central signifier *in the unconscious.*

AUFHEBUNG AND REPETITION

The true move "beyond Hegel" is not to be sought in the post-Hegelian return to the positivity of "real life," but in the strange affirmation of death that occurs in the guise of *pure repetition*—an affirmation which brings into line two strange bedfellows, Kierkegaard and Freud. In Hegel, repetition plays a crucial role, but within the economy of *Aufhebung*: through a mere repetition, an immediacy is elevated into universality, a contingency is transformed into necessity—after Caesar's death, "Caesar" is repeated no longer as the designation of a particular individual, but as the name of a universal title. There is no place, within Hegel's system, for thinking "pure" repetition, a repetition not yet caught in the movement of *Aufhebung*. In a famous passage from his letter to Schiller of August 16/17, 1797, Goethe reports on an experience which made him perceive a piece of ruined reality as a symbol:

> My grandfather's house, its courtyard and its gardens had been transformed from the parochial-patrician home of an old Frankfurt elder into the most useful trading and market place by wisely enterprising people. Curious coincidence during the bombardment conspired to see the structure perish, but even today, reduced, for the most part, to a pile of rubble, it is still worth twice as much as the current owners paid my family for it 11 years ago. Conceivably, the whole thing may, in the future, be bought and restored by yet another entrepreneur, and you can easily see that it would, in more than one sense, stand as a symbol of thousands of other instances, in this industrious city and in particular in my own eyes.[43]

The contrast between allegory and symbol is crucial here. Allegory is melancholic: as Freud pointed out, a melancholic treats an object which is still here as already lost, for melancholy is pre-emptive mourning. So, in an allegoric approach, one looks at a busy market-place and sees in it already the ruins it will become—the ruins are the "truth" of the proud building we see. This is melancholy at its purest. (No wonder that it was fashionable among the rich in the Romantic era to build new houses partly as ruins, with bits of wall missing and so on.) Goethe, however, does the exact opposite: he sees (the potential for) future prosperity in the present pile of rubble.[44] Crucial here is the rise of the

---

43 Johann Wolfgang Goethe, "Brief an Friedrich Schiller, 16./17. August 1797," in *Sämtliche Werke, Briefe, Tagebücher und Gespräche*, Vol. 31: *Johann Wolfgang Goethe mit Schiller (1794–1799)*, Frankfurt: Deutscher Klassiker 1998, p. 390. I owe my thanks to Frauke Berndt (Frankfurt am Main), who proposed a perspicuous reading of this passage.

44 In a somewhat pathetic way, one could say the same about the ruins of 9/11: a melancholic would see in them the "truth" of the arrogant dreams of US grandeur; i.e., she would see already in the Twin Towers themselves the ruins that lay ahead, while a

symbol from ruin and repetition: Goethe's grandfather's house was not a symbol for its first generation of owners—for them, it was just a *zu-handenes* object, part of their environment with which they were engaged. It was only its destruction, its reduction to a pile of rubble, that made it appear as a symbol. (There is a temporal ambiguity in Goethe's last sentence: will the house become a symbol when it is renovated, or is it already a symbol now, for the one able to see in it its future renewal?) Meaning—allegoric or symbolic—arises only through destruction, through an out-of-joint experience, or a cut which interrupts the object's direct functioning in our environment.[45] We should oppose Goethe to Kierkegaard here: while, in Goethe, repetition generates meaning, for the post-idealist Kierkegaard, there is *only* repetition (of the impossibility of reaching meaning), no (rise of new) meaning. This is one of the definitions of the nineteenth-century post-idealist break: repetition is asserted as such, as a force of its own, in its mechanical quality, in no way *aufgehoben* in new Meaning—from physics and mechanics up to Kierkegaard and Freud's *Wiederholungszwang*.

But there is a paradox which complicates this critique of Hegel: is not absolute negativity, this central notion of Hegelian thought, precisely a philosophical figure of what Freud called the "death drive"? Insofar as—following Lacan—the core of Kant's thought can be defined as the "critique of pure desire," is not the passage from Kant to Hegel then precisely the passage from desire to drive? The very concluding lines of Hegel's *Encyclopedia* (on the Idea which enjoys repeatedly transversing its circle) point in this direction, suggesting that the answer to the standard critical question—"Why does the dialectical process always go on? Why does dialectical mediation always continue its work?"—is precisely the *eppur si muove* of the pure drive. This structure of negativity also accounts for the quasi-"automatic" character of the dialectical process, for the common reproach concerning its "mechanical" character: belying all the assurances that dialectics is open to the true life of reality, the Hegelian dialectic is like a processing machine which indifferently swallows up and processes all possible contents, from nature to history, from politics to art, delivering them packaged in the same triadic form.

Heidegger was thus right with his thesis that Hegel does not render thematic his basic operation of negativity, but he is, as it were, right for the wrong reason: the core of Hegelian dialectics, inaccessible to Hegel himself, is the repetitive (death) drive which becomes visible after the post-Hegelian break. But why

---

Goethean optimist would see in the ruins of 9/11 a symbol of the enterprising spirit of that other "industrious city" that will soon replace the ruins with new buildings.

45 In a strictly homologous way, for Hegel, self-consciousness arises out of the limitation of consciousness: I cannot reach the object I aim at, it eludes my grasp, in all that I can reach I discover my own product—so I turn my gaze towards my own activity and the way it "posits" what appears to me as presupposed.

should there not be at the base of dialectics a tension between dialectics and its non-dialectizable core? In this sense, the death drive or the compulsion to repeat is the heart of negativity, Hegel's non-thematized presupposition—inaccessible not only to him, but, perhaps, to philosophy as such: its outlines were first deployed by a theologian (Kierkegaard) and a (meta-)psychologist (Freud), and a century later a philosopher (Deleuze) incorporated Kierkegaard's and Freud's lesson. With regard to the precise status of negativity, the situation is thus in a way reversed: it is Hegel who offers a series of *Vers*, of displaced variations of negativity, and it is only in psychoanalysis, through Freud and Lacan, that we can formulate the elementary form of negativity.

The post-Hegelian break has two aspects which are not to be confused: the assertion of the positivity of actual being as opposed to notional mediation (affirmationism), and the assertion of pure repetition which cannot be contained in the idealist movement of sublation. Although the first aspect was much more to the fore, it is the second which bears witness to a true philosophical revolution. There is no complementarity between these two aspects, they are mutually exclusive: *repetition relies on the blockage of direct positive affirmation*, we repeat because it is impossible to directly affirm. Related to the opposition between these two aspects is the opposition between finitude and infinity: the great motif of the post-Hegelian assertion of positive being is the accent on material, actual, finitude, while the compulsion to repeat introduces an obscene infinity or "immortality"—not spiritual immortality, but an immortality of "spirits," of the living dead.

If, however, the death drive or the compulsion to repeat lies at the heart of negativity, how are we to read Freud's famous claim that the unconscious (as exemplified by the universe of dreams) knows no negation? It is all too easy to refute this claim empirically by noting that, not so many pages after making this claim, Freud himself outlines a number of ways in which dreams can effect a negation of a certain state of things. Freud's example of *Verneinung* (when a patient says, "I don't know who the woman is who appears in my dream, but one thing is sure—she is not my mother!" one should interpret this assertion as an unambiguous confirmation that the woman in the dream is the patient's mother) remains pertinent here: negation belongs to the level of consciousness/preconsciousness, it is one way for the conscious subject to admit their unconscious incestuous fixation. The Hegelian negation as the universalizing abolition of particular content (say, the negation of the empirical wealth of an object in its name), this violence inherent to idealization, is what is missing in the Freudian unconscious. However, there is also a weird negativity which pervades the entire sphere of the unconscious, from brutal aggression and self-sabotaging to hysteria, with its basic experience, apropos every object, of *ce n'est pas ça*—so that it is as if (in accordance with Freud's aforementioned insight that the multiplicity of phalli is a sign of castration) the suspension of negation is paid for by its multiplication. What is the foundation and status of this all-pervasive "negativity" which eludes the logical form of negation? Perhaps one way to read this negation itself is as a positive fact, in the same way that, in a differential system, absence itself can be a positive feature (for example, to refer to one of the best-known lines from the Sherlock Holmes stories, the fact that the dog didn't bark in the night is in itself the curious incident). The difference between the system of consciousness/preconsciousness and the unconscious is thus not simply that, in the former, there is negation, while the unconscious is too primitive to know the function of negation; it is rather that the system of consciousness/preconsciousness perceives only the negative aspect of the negation, for it sees negation only in its negative dimension (something is missing, etc.), ignoring the positive space opened up by this negation.

When confronted by a fact that clearly goes against some deep conviction of ours, we can react to it in one of two basic ways: either simply and brutally rejecting it, or endorsing it in a "subl(im)ated" form, as something not to be taken literally, but rather as an expression of a deeper or higher truth. For example, we can either reject outright the idea of Hell (as a real place where sinners suffer endless pain as punishment for their deeds), or we can claim that Hell is a metaphor for the "inner turmoil" we suffer when we do something wrong. Recall the well-known Italian expression *se non e vero, e ben'trovato*—"(even) if it is not true, it is well-founded (it hits the mark)." It is in this sense that anecdotes about famous people, even when invented, often capture the core of their personality more accurately than would an enumeration of their real qualities—here also, "truth has the structure of a fiction," as Lacan put it. There is a wonderfully obscene Serbo-Croat version of this expression which perfectly renders the proto-psychotic rejection of symbolic fiction: *se non e vero, jebem ti mater!* "Jebem ti mater" (pronounced "yebem ti mater," meaning "I'll fuck your mother") is one of the most popular vulgar insults; the joke, of course, relies on the almost perfect rhyme, with the same number of syllables, between *e ben'trovato* and *jebem ti mater*. The meaning thus changes into an explosion of obscene rage, an attack on the other's most intimate primordial object: "It better be true—if it's not true, I'll fuck your mother!" The two versions thus clearly enact the two reactions to what literally turns out to be a lie: furious rejection, or the "subl(im)ation" into a "higher" truth. In psychoanalytical terms, their difference is that between foreclosure (*Verwerfung*) and symbolic transubstantiation.

Freud deploys a whole series, a system even, of negations in the unconscious: throwing-out of the Ego (*Ausstossung*), rejection (*Verwerfung*), repression (*Verdrängung*, itself divided into primordial repression—*Ur-Verdrängung*—and "normal" repression), disavowal (*Verleugnung*), denial (*Verneinung*), up to the complex ways in which acceptance itself can function as a mode of denial, as in so-called "isolation" (*Isolierung*), where a traumatic fact is rationally accepted, but isolated from its libidinal-symbolic context.[46] What further complicates the scheme are objects and signifiers which somehow overlap with their own lack: for Lacan, the phallus is itself the signifier of castration (this introduces all the paradoxes of the signifier of the lack of signifier, of how the lack of a signifier is itself "remarked" in a signifier of this lack), not to mention *l'objet petit a*, the object-cause of desire which is nothing but the embodiment of lack, its place-holder. The relationship between object and lack is here turned around: far from lack being reducible to the lack of an object, the object itself is a spectral positivization of a lack. And one has to extrapolate this mechanism into the very (pre-)ontological foundation of all being: the primordial gesture of creation is not that of an excessive giving, of assertion, but a negative gesture of withdrawal, of subtracting, which alone opens up the space for the creation of positive entities. This is how "there is something rather than nothing": in order to arrive at something, one has to *subtract from nothing its nothing(ness) itself*, that is, one has to posit the primordial pre-ontological Abyss "as such," *as nothing*, so that, in contrast to (or against the background of) nothing, something can appear.

What precedes Nothing is less than nothing, the pre-ontological multiplicity whose names range from Democritus's *den* to Lacan's *objet a*. The space of this pre-ontological multiplicity is not between Nothing and Something (more than nothing but less than something); *den* is, on the contrary, *more than Something but less than Nothing*. The relationship between these three basic ontological terms—Nothing, Something, *den*—thus takes the form of a paradoxical circle, like Escher's famous drawing of the interconnected waterfalls forming a circular *perpetuum mobile*: Something is more than Nothing, *den* is more than Something (the *objet a* is in excess with regard to the consistency of Something, the surplus-element which sticks out), and Nothing is more than *den* (which is "less than nothing").

The underlying problem here is to determine which of the Freudian negations is the primordial one—which one opens up the space for all the others. From the Lacanian perspective, the most obvious candidate may appear to be the notorious "symbolic castration," the loss which opens up and sustains the space of symbolization—recall, in relation to the Name-of-the-Father as the bearer of symbolic castration, how Lacan, as we have seen, plays on the French homophony between *le Nom-du-Père* and *le Non-du-Père*. But it seems more productive to follow a more radical path of thinking beyond the father (*père*) to what is even worse (*pire*). Again, the most obvious candidate for this "worse"

46 An exemplary case of *Isolierung* is the way China's relation to the major famine that occurred during the Great Leap Forward relies on a specific symbolic economy: while formally admitting the horror (Mao's "mistakes"), it continues to be treated as taboo (the admission is purely formal and accompanied by a prohibition on going into any detail).

is the (death) drive, a kind of Freudian correlate of what Schelling called the primordial "contraction," an obstinate repetitive fixation on a contingent object which subtracts the subject from its direct immersion in reality.

From repetition to drive

What does the drive mean from a *philosophical* standpoint? In a vague general sense, there is a homology between the shift from Kant to Hegel and the shift from desire to drive: the Kantian universe is that of desire (structured around the lack, the inaccessible Thing-in-itself), of endlessly approaching the goal, which is why, in order to guarantee the meaningfulness of our ethical activity, Kant has to postulate the immortality of the soul (since we cannot reach the goal in our terrestrial life, we must be allowed to go on *ad infinitum*). For Hegel, on the contrary, the Thing-in-itself is not inaccessible, the impossible does happen here and now—not, of course, in the naïve pre-critical sense of gaining access to the transcendent order of things, but in the properly dialectical sense of shifting the perspective and conceiving the gap (that separates us from the Thing) as the Real. With regard to satisfaction, this does not mean that, in contrast to desire which is constitutively non-satisfied, the drive achieves satisfaction by way of reaching the object which eludes desire. True, in contrast to desire, the drive is by definition satisfied, but this is because, in it, satisfaction is achieved in the repeated failure to reach the object, in repeatedly circling around the object. Following Jacques-Alain Miller, a distinction has to be introduced here between a lack and a hole: a lack is spatial, designating a void *within* a space, while a hole is more radical, it designates the point at which this spatial order itself breaks down (as in the "black hole" in physics).[47]

Therein lies the difference between desire and drive: desire is grounded in its constitutive lack, while the drive circulates around a hole, a gap in the order of being. In other words, the circular movement of the drive obeys the weird logic of the curved space in which the shortest distance between two points is not a straight line, but a curve: the drive "knows" that the quickest way to realize its aim is to circulate around its goal-object. At the immediate level of addressing individuals, capitalism of course interpellates them as consumers, as subjects of desire, soliciting in them ever new perverse and excessive desires (for which it offers products to satisfy them); furthermore, it obviously also manipulates the "desire to desire," celebrating the very desire to desire ever new objects and modes of pleasure. However, even if it already manipulates desire in a way which takes into account the fact that the most elementary desire is the desire to

47 See Jacques-Alain Miller, "Le nom-du-père, s'en passer, s'en servir," excerpted at www.lacan.com

reproduce itself as desire (and not to find satisfaction), at this level, we do not yet reach the drive. The drive inheres in capitalism at a more fundamental, *systemic*, level: the drive is that which propels forward the entire capitalist machinery, it is the impersonal compulsion to engage in the endless circular movement of expanded self-reproduction. We enter the mode of the drive the moment the circulation of money as capital becomes an end in itself, since the expansion of value takes place only within this constantly renewed movement. (One should bear in mind here Lacan's well-known distinction between the aim and the goal of drive: while the goal is the object around which the drive circulates, its true aim is the endless continuation of this circulation as such.) The capitalist drive thus belongs to no particular individual—it is rather that those individuals who act as the direct "agents" of capital (capitalists themselves, top managers) have to display it.

Miller recently proposed a Benjaminian distinction between "constituted anxiety" and "constituent anxiety," which is crucial with regard to the shift from desire to drive: while the first designates the standard notion of the terrifying and fascinating abyss of anxiety which haunts us, its infernal circle which threatens to draw us in, the second stands for the "pure" confrontation with the *objet petit a* as constituted in its very loss.[48] Miller is right to emphasize here two features: the difference which separates constituted from constituent anxiety concerns the status of the object with regard to fantasy. In a case of constituted anxiety, the object dwells within the confines of a fantasy, while we get only the constituent anxiety when the subject "traverses the fantasy" and confronts the void, the gap, filled up by the fantasmatic object. Clear and convincing as it is, Miller's formula misses the true paradox or, rather, ambiguity of the *objet a*, the ambiguity which concerns the question: does the *objet a* function as the object of desire or of the drive? That is to say, when Miller defines the *objet a* as the object which overlaps with its loss, which emerges at the very moment of its loss (so that all its fantasmatic incarnations, from breast to voice to gaze, are metonymic figurations of the void, of nothing), he remains within the horizon of *desire*—the true object-cause of desire is the void filled in by its fantasmatic incarnations. While, as Lacan emphasizes, the *objet a* is also the object of the drive, the relationship is here thoroughly different: although in both cases the link between object and loss is crucial, in the case of the *objet a* as the object-cause of *desire*, we have an object which is originally lost, which coincides with its own loss, which emerges as lost, while, in the case of the *objet a* as the object of the drive, the "object" *is directly the loss itself*—in the shift from desire to drive, we pass from the *lost object* to *loss itself as an object*. That is to say, the weird movement called "drive" is not driven by the "impossible" quest for the lost object; it is *a drive to directly*

48 See ibid.

enact the "loss"—the gap, cut, distance—itself. There is thus a *double* distinction to be drawn here: not only between the *objet a* in its fantasmatic and post-fantasmatic status, but also, within this post-fantasmatic domain itself, between the lost object-cause of desire and the object-loss of the drive.

This is what Lacan means by the "satisfaction of the drives": a drive does not bring satisfaction because its object is a stand-in for the Thing, but because a drive, as it were, turns failure into triumph—in it, the very failure to reach its goal, the repetition of this failure, the endless circulation around the object, generates a satisfaction of its own. To put it even more pointedly, the object of the drive is not related to the Thing as a filler of its void: the drive is literally a counter-movement to desire, it does not strive towards impossible fullness and then, being forced to renounce it, get stuck onto a partial object as its remainder —the drive is quite literally the very "drive" to *break* the All of continuity in which we are embedded, to introduce a radical imbalance into it, and the difference between drive and desire is precisely that, in desire, this cut, this fixation onto a partial object, is as it were "transcendentalized," transposed into a stand-in for the void of the Thing.

So, when Hegel concludes his *Encyclopedia* with the claim that "the eternal idea which exists in and for itself, eternally sets itself to work, engenders and enjoys itself as absolute spirit" ("*die ewige an und für sich seiende Idee sich ewig als absoluter Geist betätigt, erzeugt und genießt*"[49]), does he not describe here a repetitive circular movement of alienating or losing oneself in order to regain oneself again, a movement which strangely recalls Lacan's definition of castration as a movement in which the object is lost in order to be regained on the ladder of desire? Is not the repetitive movement of losing and regaining oneself, of alienation and disalienation, a movement which, as Hegel explicitly claims, brings enjoyment, uncannily close to the circular movement of the drive?

Gregor Moder's ebullient *Hegel in Spinoza* focuses on this most elementary opposition: *lack or curvature*?[50] In Freudian terms, this opposition appears as that between *desire or drive*: desire is structured around its constitutive lack, each determinate object of desire is, as Lacan put it, a "metonymy of a lack," while the drive, instead of pursuing an impossible object which forever eludes the subject, finds satisfaction in its curved path, in circulating around its object. In more philosophical terms, applied to the notion of Substance, this difference between lack and curvature can be formulated as the following alternative: (1) Substance is lacking, thwarted, organized around absence, and the subject is located in this lack, it *is* this lack; (2) Substance is not lacking anything, there is no lack around which it is organized; Substance is just curved, inverted-into-itself, like a Möbius

49 G. W. F. Hegel, *Encyklopädie der philosophischen Wissenschaften, Vol. 3: Die Philosophie des Geistes*, Berlin: Dunder and Humblot 1845, pp. 413–14 (§577).

50 See Gregor Moder, *Hegel in Spinoza*, Ljubljana: Analecta 2009.

band. The ultimate lesson of psychoanalysis is that human life is never "just life": humans are not simply alive, they are possessed by the strange drive to enjoy life in excess, passionately attached to a surplus which sticks out and derails the ordinary run of things.

The basic paradox here is that the specifically human dimension—drive as opposed to instinct—emerges precisely when what was originally a mere by-product is elevated into an autonomous aim: man is not more "reflexive"; on the contrary, man perceives as a direct goal what, for an animal, has no intrinsic value. In short, the zero-degree of "humanization" is not a further "mediation" of animal activity, its reinscription as a subordinated moment of a higher totality (for example, we eat and procreate in order to develop our higher spiritual potentials), but a radical narrowing of focus, the elevation of a minor activity into an end-in-itself. We become "humans" when we get caught up in a closed, self-propelling loop of repeating the same gesture and finding satisfaction in it. We can all recall the archetypal cartoon scene: a cat jumps into the air and turns on its own axis; but instead of plunging back down in accordance with the normal laws of gravity, it remains suspended, turning around in the levitated position as if caught in a loop of time, repeating the same circular movement over and over again.[51] In such moments, the "normal" run of things, of being caught in the imbecilic inertia of material reality, is for a brief moment suspended; we enter the magical domain of suspended animation, of a kind of self-sustaining ethereal rotation. This rotary movement, in which the linear progress of time is suspended in a repetitive loop, is the *drive* at its most elementary. This, again, is "humanization" at its zero-level: this self-propelling loop which suspends or disrupts the linear temporal enchainment. This shift from desire to drive is crucial if one is to grasp the true nature of the "minimal difference": at its most fundamental, the minimal difference is not the unfathomable X which elevates an ordinary object into an object of desire, but, rather, the inner torsion which curves libidinal space and thus transforms instinct into drive.

Consequently, the concept of drive makes the alternative "either get burned by the Thing or maintain a safe distance" false: for a drive, the "Thing itself" is a circulation around the void (or, rather, hole). The drive as such is the death drive—not in the sense of longing for universal negation or the dissolution of all particularity, but, on the contrary, in the sense of the "spontaneous" life-flow of generation and corruption becoming "stuck" on some accidental particularity and circulating endlessly around it. If Life is a song played on an old LP (which it definitely is not), the drive arises when, due to a scratch on the LP surface, the

51 One also finds the same shot in some musical comedies which make use of the elements of slapstick: when a dancer turns around in the air, they remain up there a little bit too long, as if, for a brief moment, they had succeeded in suspending the law of gravity. And, indeed, is not such an effect the ultimate goal of the art of dancing?

needle gets stuck and the same fragment is repeated over and over. The deepest speculative insight is that universality can only emerge when a particular flow gets stuck on a singular moment. This Freudian notion of drive brings us to the radical ambiguity of Hegel's dialectic: does it follow the logic of the drive or not? Hegel's logic is a logic of purification, of "unsticking": even when a subject puts the whole of its libidinal investment into a contingent fragment of being ("I am ready to risk everything for that!"), this contingent fragment—the Lacanian *objet petit a*—is, in its indifferent accidentality, an operator of purification, of "unsticking" from all (other) particular content. In Lacanese, this object is a metonymy of lack. The subject's desire is here the transcendental void, and the object is a contingent ontic filler of this void. For the drive, in contrast, the *objet a* is not only the metonymy of lack, but a kind of transcendental stain, irreducible and irreplaceable in its very contingent singularity, not just a contingent ontic filler of a lack. While the drive involves getting stuck on a contingent stain-object, dialectical negativity involves a constant process of "un-sticking" from all particular content: *jouissance* "leans on" something, hanging on to its particularity—and this is what is missing in Hegel, but operative in Freud.

The relationship between Hegel's negativity and Freud's death drive (or compulsion to repeat) is thus a very specific one, well beyond their (hidden) outright identity: what Freud was aiming at with his notion of death drive—more precisely, the key dimension of this notion to which Freud himself was blind, unaware of the full significance of his discovery—is the "non-dialectical" core of Hegelian negativity, the pure drive to repeat without any movement of sublation or idealization. The paradox here is that pure repetition (in contrast to repetition as idealizing sublation) is sustained precisely by its *impurity*, by the persistence of a contingent "pathological" element to which the movement of repetition gets and remains stuck. The key question is thus: can Hegel think the "indivisible remainder" generated by every move of idealization or sublation? Before concluding too quickly that he cannot, we should bear in mind that, at its most radical, the Lacanian *objet a* (the name of this "indivisible remainder") is not a substantial element disturbing the formal mechanism of symbolization, but a purely formal curvature of symbolization itself.

The *objet a* and pure repetition are thus closely linked: the *a* is the excess which sets repetition in motion and simultaneously prevents its success (which would reside in fully recapturing what one tries to repeat). And, insofar as Hegel cannot think pure repetition (a repetition not yet caught in the movement of sublation or idealization), the *objet a* is simultaneously the object missing in Hegel *and the way in which this object is missing*: in the same way that, according to Derrida, the difference between the Hegelian *Aufhebung* and his own notion of *différance* is barely perceptible, almost indistinguishable, the difference between Hegel and what Hegel misses (cannot think) is barely perceptible: not a positive difference (where we could clearly identify what is missing), but just a "pure" difference, a barely perceptible shift in the virtual or spectral accent of what Hegel actually says. To produce this difference then, one need only repeat Hegel.

Paradoxically, repetition provides the (absent) Hegelian answer to Heidegger's critical point about how Hegel fails to deploy the phenomenological content of his central notion of negativity: at its zero-level, negativity is not a destructive annihilation of whatever there is; it rather appears as a sudden *immobilization* of the normal flow of things—at some point, things get stuck, a singularity persists beyond its proper term. In his reading of a fragment of Anaximander on order and disorder, Heidegger considers the possibility that an entity

> may even insist [*bestehen*] upon its while solely to remain more present, in the sense of perduring [*Beständigen*]. That which lingers persists [*beharrt*] in its presencing. In this way it extricates itself from its transitory while. It strikes the wilful pose of persistence, no longer concerning itself with whatever else is present. It stiffens—as if this were the only way to linger—and aims solely for continuance and subsistence.[52]

This is how, according to Deleuze, the New arises through repetition: things flow, they follow their usual course of incessant change, and then, all of a sudden, something gets stuck, interrupts the flow, imposing itself as New by way of its very persistence. It is thus as if the excessive attachment, the excessive *Yes* to a partial object, is a *reflexive determination of negativity*, a moment of oppositional determination in which negativity encounters itself among its species (*Verdrängung, Verwerfung* ...).

Is not the excess in Hegel, that which cannot be counted, to be located at the point where Hegel himself brings in the un-accountable? When, at the end of his *Great Logic*, he provides a kind of formal description of the dialectical process, he says that its moments can be counted as 3 or as 4—it is negativity which can be counted two times, as direct negation and as self-relating negation. This excess of negativity that is the death drive, the blind compulsion to repeat, that Hegel misses apropos sexuality as well as the rabble, perhaps accounts for his inability to think exploitation in the strict Marxist sense: Lacan had already drawn attention to the link between surplus-value and surplus-enjoyment (surplus-value being the surplus that emerges in the very equivalent exchange between worker and capitalist). The de-centered element which is "exploited" in the dialectical process is thus the third/fourth moment of self-relating negativity, this blind repetitive productive force.

---

52 Martin Heidegger, "The Anaximander Fragment," in *Early Greek Thinking*, trans. David Farrell Krell and Frank A. Capuzzi, New York: Harper & Row 1984, p. 42. Translation slightly modified.

The underlying problem here is how we are to read Hegel's occasional and tentative but nevertheless unambiguous self-relativizations and/or self-historicizations—facts waiting to be discovered by the natural sciences; the impossibility of grasping the spiritual essence of countries like North America and Russia which will deploy their potential only in the next century; the consequences of his argumentation for the necessity of war; and the characterization of his own thought as the standpoint reached by spirit "for the time being." Robert Pippin's solution, distinguishing between the "eternal Hegel" and the historical Hegel of the system, is *the* trap to be avoided insofar as it reintroduces a normative logic, a gap between the "ideal" Hegelian position and its historical realizations. The properly Hegelian move is to reject any trans-historical ideal which would enable us to measure and evaluate all empirical-historical realizations of the Hegelian system, and to consider the changes in this ideal itself. (Much more adequate is Andrew Cutrofello's notion of Gilles Deleuze, *the* great contemporary anti-Hegelian, as embodying a repetition of Hegel today.) Our starting point should be that "Absolute Knowing" involves a recognition of both radical historical closure (there is no meta-language, no way of looking at oneself from the outside) and, simultaneously, of a radical openness of the future (the focus of Catherine Malabou in her *Future of Hegel*). Furthermore, the task is to think (beyond Hegel) this radical openness with (or even as) repetition: for Hegel, repetition is sublation or idealization (say, from the Caesar-name to the Caesar-title); that is, he cannot think the pure repetition of Kierkegaard and Freud. Is not the excess of negativity over the reconciled social order also the excess of repetition over sublation? The task Hegel has left us with, the big gap in his thinking, is how to think this excess (discernible at many levels: in the necessity of war, the threat of madness ...) without falling back into a relativist historicism? This reference to the persistent excess of negativity—from the ever-present possibility of madness as constitutive of subjectivity, to the necessity of war as the social form of the explosion of abstract universality—is also crucial for understanding what Hegel means by "reconciliation" which, in contrast to a "critical" attitude, characterizes the dimension of the Absolute. Reconciliation does not mean that the subject finally succeeds in appropriating the otherness which threatens its self-identity, mediating or internalizing (i.e., "sublating") it. Quite the contrary, Hegelian reconciliation contains a resigned note: one has to reconcile oneself with the excess of negativity as a positive ground or condition of our freedom, to recognize our own substance in what appears to be an obstacle.

In Kierkegaardian-Freudian pure repetition, as we have seen, the dialectical movement of sublimation encounters itself, its own core, outside itself, in the guise of a "blind" compulsion to repeat. It is here that we should apply the great Hegelian motto concerning the internalizing of the external obstacle: in fighting its external opposite, blind non-sublatable repetition, the dialectical movement fights against its own abyssal ground, its own core; in other words, the ultimate gesture of reconciliation is to recognize in this threatening excess of negativity the core of the subject itself. This excess has different names in Hegel: the "night of the world," the necessity of war, of madness, etc. Perhaps the same holds for the basic opposition between Hegelian and Freudian negativity: precisely insofar as there is an unbridgeable gap between them (Hegelian negativity idealizes and sublates all particular content in the abyss of its universality, while the negativity of the Freudian drive is expressed in its "sticking" to a contingent particular content), Freudian negativity provides (quite literally) the "material basis" for idealizing negativity. To put it in somewhat simplified terms, every idealizing/universalizing negativity has to be attached to a singular, contingent, "pathological" content which serves as its "*sinthome*" in the Lacanian sense (if the *sinthome* is unraveled or disintegrated, universality disappears). The exemplary model for this link is Hegel's deduction of the necessity of hereditary monarchy: the rational state as a universal totality mediating all particular content has to be embodied in the contingent "irrational" figure of the monarch (and we can also apply the same matrix to Hegel's treatment of the "rabble"). This excess of the drive qua pure repetition is the "decentered" source of value that Hegel could not conceptualize, the libidinal correlate of the labor-power which produces surplus-value.

Does this mean that, once we have entered the Freudo-Kierkegaardian world of pure repetition, we can forget about Hegel? Claude Lévi-Strauss wrote that the prohibition of incest is not a question without an answer, but rather the opposite: an answer without a question, the solution of an unknown problem. The same goes for pure repetition: it is an answer to the *Hegelian* problem, its hidden core, which is why it can only be properly located within the Hegelian problematic—once we enter the post-Hegelian world, the concept of repetition is "renormalized" and loses its subversive edge. The relationship is similar to that between the finale of Mozart's *Don Giovanni* and post-Mozartian Romanticism: the scene of don Giovanni's death generates a terrifying excess which disturbs the coordinates of Mozart's universe; however, although this excess points forward towards Romanticism, it loses its subversive edge and is "renormalized" once we reach Romanticism proper.

But does this not, paradoxically and unexpectedly, bring us back to the topic of *Aufhebung*, this time applied to the very relationship between Hegel and his post-Hegelian "repetition"? Deleuze once characterized his own thought as an essay in thinking as if Hegel had not existed, repeatedly making the point that Hegel was a philosopher who should be simply ignored, not worked-through. What Deleuze missed was how his own thought of pure repetition only works as a weird sublation of Hegel. In this exemplary last revenge of Hegel, the great

Hegelian motif of the path towards truth being part of the truth—of how, in order to arrive at the right choice, one has to begin with the wrong choice—reasserts itself. The point is not so much that we should *not* ignore Hegel, but that we can only afford to ignore him after a long and arduous working-through-Hegel.

The time has thus come to *repeat Hegel.*

Part III

THE THING ITSELF: LACAN

CHAPTER 8

Lacan as a Reader of Hegel

> [The] question of the termination of an analysis is that of the moment at which the subject's satisfaction is achievable in the satisfaction of all—that is, of all those it involves in a human undertaking. Of all the undertakings that have been proposed in this century, the psychoanalyst's is perhaps the loftiest, because it mediates in our time between the care-ridden man and the subject of absolute knowledge.[1]

This passage from *Rapport de Rome* contains *in nuce* Lacan's program of the early 1950s—a program that every professional philosopher would undoubtedly dismiss as nonsense: namely, to bring together Heidegger (who defines "care" as the fundamental feature of finite *Dasein*) and Hegel (the philosopher of infinite Absolute Knowledge in which the Universal and the Particular are fully mediated).[2] The Lacanian analyst as a figure of Absolute Knowing? Is not this thesis restricted to a specific historical moment (the early 1950s), when Hegel's influence on Lacan (mediated by Alexandre Kojève and Jean Hyppolite) was at its peak? Did not Lacan soon move from Hegel to Kant, insisting on the inaccessible ("impossible") character of the Real that forever resists symbolization, on the subject's unsurpassable separation from the cause of its desire? Is not the best description of Lacan's central project that of a *critique of pure desire*, where the term "critique" is to be understood in its precise Kantian sense: maintaining the gap that forever separates every empirical ("pathological") object of desire from its "impossible" object-cause whose place has to remain empty? And is not what Lacan calls "symbolic castration" this very gap which renders every empirical object unsatisfactory? Indeed, in the following paragraphs of the *Rapport de Rome* itself, Lacan already outlines the "limits within which it

---

1 Jacques Lacan, *Écrits: The First Complete Edition in English*, trans. Bruce Fink, New York: W. W. Norton & Company 2006, p. 264.

2 If, measured by today's standards, this goal of uniting Hegel and Heidegger cannot but appear blatantly inconsistent, one should remember the crucial role of Alexandre Kojève in Lacan's development—Lacan referred to Kojève as his *maître* (the only other *maître* being the psychiatrist Clérambault). Kojève's central aim was precisely to bring together Hegel and Heidegger, i.e., to read Hegel's motifs of negativity and, exemplarily, the struggle-to-death between the (future) Master and Slave, through Heidegger's topic of being-towards-death.

is impossible for our teaching to ignore the structuring moments of Hegel's phenomenology":

> But if there is still something prophetic in Hegel's insistence on the fundamental identity of the particular and the universal, an insistence that reveals the extent of his genius, it is certainly psychoanalysis that provides it with its paradigm by revealing the structure in which this identity is realized as disjunctive of the subject, and without appealing to the future.
>
> Let me simply say that this, in my view, constitutes an objection to any reference to totality in the individual, since the subject introduces division therein, as well as in the collectivity that is the equivalent of the individual. Psychoanalysis is what clearly relegates both the one and the other to the status of mirages.[3]

We are thereby back in familiar waters: Hegelian self-consciousness, the subject of absolute notional self-mediation which supersedes or devours every alterity, versus the Lacanian divided subject of the unconscious, by definition separated from its Cause. It is not enough, however, to reduce Hegel to his grand formulae (the Absolute not only as Substance but also as Subject; the actuality of the rational; Absolute Knowing; the self-canceling force of negativity; etc.) and then to quickly reject him as the most extreme expression of the modern delirium of the total subjective-notional mediation or appropriation of all reality. One should display, apropos Hegel himself, what the author of one of the best books on Hegel, Gérard Lebrun, called the "patience of the notion" (*La patience du concept*, the book's title): to read Hegel's theoretical practice *en détail*, in miniature, following all his dialectical cuts and turns. The wager of such an operation is double: it can ground the (only serious) critique of Hegel, the immanent critique that measures him by his own standards, analyzing how he realizes his own program; but it can also serve as a means to redeem Hegel, to unearth the actual meaning of his great programmatic maxims as opposed to the standard understanding of them.

The Cunning of Reason

Where then do we stand with regard to Absolute Knowing? When, in his writings around the *Rapport de Rome*, Lacan himself defines the conclusion of a

3 Lacan, *Écrits: The First Complete Edition in English*, p. 242. Significantly, these paragraphs were rewritten for *Écrits*—it would be interesting to analyze in detail how, in his rewriting of the *rapport* for publication in 1966, Lacan desperately tried to erase (or, at least, dilute) the traces of his Hegelianism.

treatment as the position of Hegelian Absolute Knowing, how are we to read this together with Lacan's insistence on human finitude, on the irreducible *future antérieur* that pertains to the process of symbolization (every conclusion involves a gesture of precipitation; it never occurs "now," but in a now viewed backwards)? Take the following passage: "What is realized in my history is neither the past definite as what was, since it is no more, nor even the perfect of what has been in what I am, but the future anterior as what I will have been, given what I am in the process of becoming."[4] But the same goes for Hegel—when he adopts the position of the "end of history," presenting us with a coherent narrative about the entirety of history, he does not simply look at the past from the present position; although he prohibits philosophy from speculation about the future and restricts it to comprehending what *is* the case, past and present, the position from which he enacts the final "reconciliation" has a futural dimension of its own, that of a "future perfect" from which the present itself is seen from a minimal distance, in its accomplished form:

> It is a present that raises itself, it is essentially reconciled, brought to consummation through the negation of its immediacy, consummated in universality, but in a consummation that is not yet achieved, and which must therefore be grasped as *future*—a now of the present that has consummation before its eyes; but because the community is posited now in the order of time, the consummation is distinguished from this "now" and is posited as future.[5]

This "future perfect" is that of accomplished symbolization, which is why, in his *Rapport de Rome*, Lacan systematically identifies the conclusion of the analytic treatment with Hegelian "Absolute Knowing": the aim of the treatment is to achieve the same "future perfect" of accomplished symbolization. Each day's edition of *Le Monde*, the most prestigious (and proverbially haughty) French daily newspaper, appears in the early afternoon of the previous day (for example, the issue for July 4 is on sale around 3 p.m. on July 3), as if the editors wanted to signal a simultaneous move of precipitation and delay: they write from eternity, observing events from a point later than that of other daily newspapers caught up in immediate "live" reporting; however, simultaneously, they are able to see the present itself from its immediate future (i.e., in its true potential, not only the way it appears in its chaotic immediacy)—so, you can learn already in the afternoon of July 3 how things look from the perspective of July 4. No wonder *Le Monde* is accused of arrogance: this coincidence of delay and precipitation

---

4 Ibid., p. 247.

5 G. W. F. Hegel, *Lectures on the Philosophy of Religion, Vol. 3: The Consummate Religion*, trans. R. F. Brown, P. C. Hodgson, and J. M. Stewart, Berkeley: University of California Press 1987, p. 188.

effectively betrays its pretense to standing for a kind of "Absolute Knowing," in contrast to its rivals which merely report fleeting opinions.

So when, in his *Rapport de Rome*, Lacan refers to Absolute Knowing, we should look closely at how he conceives this identification of the analyst with the Hegelian master, and not succumb to the temptation of quickly retranslating Absolute Knowing into the accomplished symbolization. For Lacan, the analyst stands for the Hegelian master, the embodiment of Absolute Knowing, insofar as he renounces all forcing (*forçage*) of reality and, fully aware that the actual is already in itself rational, adopts the stance of a passive observer who does not intervene directly in the content, but merely manipulates the scene so that the content destroys itself, when confronted with its own inconsistencies. This is how one should read Lacan's indication that Hegel's work is "precisely what we need to confer a meaning on so-called analytic neutrality other than that the analyst is simply in a stupor"[6]—it is this neutrality which keeps the analyst "on the path of non-action."[7] The Hegelian wager is that the best way to destroy an enemy is to leave the field free for him to deploy his potential, so that his success will be his failure, since the lack of any external obstacle will confront him with the absolutely inherent obstacle of the inconsistency of his own position:

> Cunning is something other than trickery. *The most open activity is the greatest cunning* (the other must be taken in its truth). In other words, with his openness, a man exposes the other in himself, he makes him appear as he is in and for himself, and thereby does away with himself. Cunning is the great art of inducing others to be as they are in and for themselves, and to bring this out to the light of consciousness. Although others are in the right, they do not know how to defend it *by means of speech*. Muteness is bad, mean cunning. Consequently, a true master [*Meister*] is at bottom only he who can provoke *the other to transform himself through his act*.[8]

The wager of the Hegelian Cunning of Reason thus involves not so much a trust in the power of Reason (we can take it easy and withdraw—Reason will ensure that the good side wins out), as a trust in the power of "unreason" in every determinate agent which, left to itself, will destroy itself: "If reason is as cunning as Hegel said it was, it will do its job without your help."[9] The Cunning of Reason thus in no way involves a faith in a secret guiding hand guaranteeing

6 Lacan, *Écrits: The First Complete Edition in English*, p. 242.

7 Ibid., p. 258.

8 G. W. F. Hegel, *Jenaer Realphilosophie*, Hamburg: Felix Meiner 1969, p. 199. Incidentally, the text goes on: "Through cunning, the willing becomes *feminine* ..."—the "feminine passivity" is thus for Hegel not inferior to man's, but superior to it: it is a passivity that lets the (male) other undermine itself.

9 Lacan, *Écrits: The First Complete Edition in English*, p. 341.

that all the apparent contingency of unreason will somehow contribute to the harmony of the Totality of Reason; if anything, it involves a trust in un-Reason, the certainty that, no matter how well-planned things are, somehow they will go wrong. This is what Lacan meant by his statement that "a letter always reaches its destination": there is no repression without the return of the repressed, every totality-of-meaning is always disturbed by its symptom.

So what about the obvious counter-argument that this reference to Hegel is operative only in the early Lacan, for whom the goal of the psychoanalytic cure is the complete symbolization ("symbolic realization") of symptoms, and no longer for the Lacan who becomes aware of the "barred" big Other? For the Lacan of the 1950s, focused on the symbolic, the success of the analytic treatment relies on the liberating power of "symbolic realization," of listening to and assuming the "I, truth" which "speaks" in and through the unconscious symptoms. In a Hegelian mode, Lacan asserts the link, identity even, between language and death: in language, immediate reality is mortified or idealized in its notional sublation, and insofar as the symbolic order is sustained by death drive "beyond the pleasure-principle," one has to "subjectivize one's own death," to recognize in it the only master to be obeyed, and thereby to get rid of all other master figures.[10] The late Lacan, now focused on the Real, introduces the irreducible tension between the symbolic and the real of death: "It is possible that all language is made [to enable us] not to think death which, effectively, is the least thinkable thing."[11] Far from being the operator of death, language is here conceived as a defense against—a screen protecting us from—the confrontation with death.[12] Since this tension is irreducible, the goal of analysis is no longer Lacan's version of Hegelian Absolute Knowing, namely the ideal of a total symbolization in which the subject gets rid of its imaginary ego; it is now its very opposite (as deployed in the seminar on *The Ethics of Psychoanalysis*)—the subject's heroic "forcing" of the symbolic prohibition, his or her confrontation with the "Black Sun" of the Real Thing.

Lacan's idea of the end or goal of the analytic treatment passes through three main phases which vaguely fit the triad of symbolic, Real, and imaginary: first, the symbolization of the symptoms; then, the violent encounter with the Real; finally, the modest amelioration of our daily psychic economy. Lacan's limitation is clearly discernible in how, in his last decades, he tends to oscillate between

10 Jacques Lacan, *Écrits*, Paris: Seuil 1966, pp. 348–9.

11 Jacques Lacan, "Improvisation: désir de mort, rêve et réveil," from notes taken by Catherine Millot in 1974, published in *L'âne* 3 (1981).

12 Of course, it would be easy to unite the two opposed theses: language itself makes us "mortal," it makes us beings that relate to death as their innermost (im)possibility, so that it itself opens up the gap against which it protects us—in a strict homology with the *objet a* which is, for Lacan, at the same time the void and what fills in the void.

two poles which are both "worse," as Stalin would have put it. Sometimes (exemplarily in his reading of *Antigone*), he conceives of the ethical act as a kind of "forcing," a violent act of transgression which cuts into imaginary and symbolic semblances and makes the subject confront the terrifying Real in its blinding destructive power—such traumatic encounters, such penetrations into the forbidden or damned domain, in *Antigone*, are called *ate*, and can only be sustained for a brief moment. These authentic moments are rare; one can only survive them if one soon returns to the safe domain of semblances—truth is too painful to be sustained for more than a passing moment. At other times (especially in his ruminations about the symptom towards the end of his life), Lacan adopts the opposite (but effectively complementary) attitude of wisdom: the analyst never knows what will happen when he pushes analysis too far and dissolves the analysand's symptoms too radically—one can get more than one expected, a local interpretive intervention into a particular symptomal formation can destabilize the subject's entire symbolic economy and bring about a catastrophic disintegration of his world. The analyst should thus remain modest and respect appearances without taking them too seriously; they are ultimately all we have, all that stands between us and the catastrophe. It is easy to see how these two stances complement each other: they rely on a (rather Heideggerian) image of human life as a continuous dwelling in "inauthentic" semblances, interrupted from time to time by violent encounters with the Real. (What this entire field encompassing the two stances excludes is the Christian "work of love," the patient work of continuous fidelity to the encounter with the Real.) This modest approach of merely "making life a little bit easier," of diminishing suffering and pain, forgetting about capitalized Truth, makes the late Lacan almost a Rortyan, and clearly reverses his earlier fidelity to the biblical prescription:

> But if God so clothes the grass of the field, which is alive today and tomorrow is thrown into the furnace, will He not much more clothe you? You of little faith! Do not worry then, saying, "What will we eat?" or "What will we drink?" or "What will we wear for clothing?" For the Gentiles eagerly seek all these things; for your heavenly Father knows that you need all these things. But seek first His kingdom and His righteousness, and all these things will be added to you. So do not worry about tomorrow; for tomorrow will care for itself. Each day has enough trouble of its own. (Matthew 6:30–4)

Lacan often refers to these lines in order to denigrate healing as the primary goal of psychoanalytic treatment: health comes *par surcroît*—in addition or in excess, and by itself, as an unintended bonus. Insofar as health concerns the organism and its homeostasis, not Truth, its status is pathological in the Kantian sense, so that Lacan's motto can also be expressed in terms of focusing on ethical duty and ignoring utilitarian concerns: do your duty, and happiness and the Good will take care of themselves. There are many variations of this attitude, best rendered by the saying "Take care of the pennies, and the pounds will take care of themselves," which should be inverted into: Take care of the sounds (signifiers), and the sense (signified) will take care of itself. Lacan aims at the heroic stance of "Take care of the truth, and the healing will take care of itself": confront the Truth, risk everything, ignore the consequences, and health will come *par surcroît* ... In short: confront the Real, and reality will take care of itself. Do not compromise your desire, and your needs and demands will be provided for.

There is, however, a fundamental ambiguity which pertains to this attitude: does it mean that one should ignore health and focus on the essential, on the patient's articulation and assumption of the Truth of his or her desire, *or* does it mean, in a more refined way, that psychic health is "essentially a by-product"? In the latter case, health remains the true goal of the treatment, the point is simply that it is counter-productive, self-destructive even, to make it a direct goal—one should work on other things and count on health emerging as a by-product. But if this is the case, should we not also invert the motto accordingly: take care of the pathological reality, and the Real will take care of itself? Be modest, try to help the patient by easing his suffering, and the Truth will emerge by itself?

Furthermore, this biblical formula can also be considered a denial of the unconscious: "seek first His kingdom and His righteousness, and all these things will be added to you"—by whom? By God, who will do the work behind the scenes, in the same way He "clothes the grass of the field."[13] Lacan's thesis that "God is unconscious" is endowed here with a new meaning: do your duty, and God will be the mole, the agent of that subterranean unconscious "weaving of the spirit" which will create the conditions for my act to succeed. In other words, does Lacan himself not rely here on some kind of Cunning of Reason which will help the patient achieve health without directly looking for it?

The Lacanian prosopopoeia

The mode of appearance of this Cunning of Reason is irony, which for Hegel lies at the very core of dialectics: "All dialectics lets hold that which should hold, treats it as if it fully holds [*lässt das gelten, was gelten soll, als ob es gelte*], and, in this way, it lets it destroy itself—the general irony of the world."[14] With his method of questioning, Socrates merely pushes his opponent-partner to make his abstract idea more concrete ("what do you mean by justice, by happiness

13 François Balmès, *Dieu, le sexe et la vérité*, Ramonville Saint-Agne: Érès 2007, p. 213.
14 G. W. F. Hegel, *Vorlesungen über die Geschichte der Philosophie*, Vol. 1, Leipzig: Philipp Reclam 1971, p. 581.

...?"), and, in this way, lets him reveal the inconsistency of his position and lets this position destroy itself. The method does not impose external standards onto an idea, it measures the idea by its own standards and lets it destroy itself through its own self-explication. When Hegel writes that womankind is "the everlasting irony of the community,"[15] does he thereby not assert the feminine character of irony or dialectics?[16] What this means is that the very presence of Socrates, his questioning attitude, transforms the speech of his partner into prosopopoeia:

> When the participants in a conversation are confronted with Socrates, their words all of a sudden start to sound like quotes and clichés, like borrowed voices; the participants are confronted with the abyss of what authorizes them in their speech, and the moment they try to rely on the usual supports of authorization, authorization fails. It is as if an inaudible echo of irony adds itself to their speech, an echo which hollows out their words and their voice, and their voice appears as borrowed and expropriated.[17]

Recall the proverbial scene of a man making a speech in front of his wife, boasting of his great exploits, evoking high ideals, etc., and his wife silently observing him with a barely concealed mocking smile—her silent presence has the effect of ruining the pathos of his speech, of unmasking him in all his misery. It is in this sense that, for Lacan, the Socratic irony announces the subjective position of the analyst: does not the same hold also for the analytic session? Recall Umberto Eco's analysis of *Casablanca*, where he draws attention to a strange habit of the Resistance hero Victor Laszlo: in every scene, he orders a different drink, a Pernod, a cognac, a whisky. But why? Is this to be read as an indication that, beneath the image of a heroic anti-fascist fighter, there dwells a refined, decadent hedonist? No: it is simply that the scriptwriters did not treat Victor Laszlo as a psychologically consistent personality, but as a composite of multiple clichés. And it is the same in subjective reality: the mysterious "depth of personality" has to be demystified as the illusory effect of prosopopoeia, of the fact that the subject's discourse is a bricolage of fragments from different sources.

The status of prosopopoeia in Lacan changes radically with the shift in the status of the analyst from being the stand-in for the "big Other" (the symbolic order) to being the "small other" (the obstacle which stands for the inconsistency, failure, of the big Other). The analyst who occupies the place of the big Other is himself the medium of prosopopoeia: when he speaks, it is the big Other who speaks (or, rather, keeps silence) through him; in the intersubjective

---

15 G. W. F. Hegel, *Phenomenology of Spirit*, trans. A. V. Miller, Oxford: Oxford University Press, 1977, p. 288.

16 I owe this insight to Mladen Dolar, *Prozopopeja*, Ljubljana: Analecta 2006, p. 186.

17 Ibid., pp. 214–15.

economy of the analytic process, he is not just another subject, he occupies the empty place of death. The patient talks, and the analyst's silence stands for the absent meaning of the patient's talk, the meaning supposed to be contained in the big Other. The process ends when the patient can himself assume the meaning of his speech. The analyst as the "small other," on the contrary, magically transforms the words of the analysand into prosopopoeia, de-subjectivizing his words, depriving them of the quality of being an expression of the consistent subject and his intention-to-mean. The goal is no longer for the analysand to assume the meaning of his speech, but for him to assume its non-meaning, its nonsensical inconsistency, which implies, with regard to his own status, his de-subjectivization, or what Lacan calls "subjective destitution."

Prosopopoeia is defined as "a figure of speech in which an absent or imaginary person is represented as speaking or acting." The attribution of speech to an entity commonly perceived to be unable to speak (nature, the commodity, truth itself ...) is for Lacan the condition of speech as such, not only its secondary complication. Does not Lacan's distinction between the "subject of the enunciation" and the "subject of the enunciated" point in this direction? When I speak, it is never directly "myself" who speaks—I *have* to have recourse to a fiction which is my symbolic identity. In this sense, *all* speech is "indirect": "I love you" has the structure of: "my identity as lover is telling you that it loves you."[18] The implication of prosopopoeia is thus a weird split of which Robert Musil was aware: the "man without properties" (*der Mann ohne Eigenschaften*) has to be supplemented with properties without man (*Eigenschaften ohne Mann*), without a subject to whom they are attributed.

There are two correlative traps to be avoided here, the rightist and the leftist deviations. The first, of course, is the pseudo-Hegelian notion that this gap stands for a "self-alienation" which I should strive to abolish ideally and then fully assume my speech as directly my own. Against this version, one should

---

18 We encounter prosopopoeia in the guise of *lacrimae rerum* quite literally at the very end of part one of Kieslowski's *Decalogue*, when the father whose small son has just drowned while skating on a frozen lake goes to an empty church to vent his despair. In an impotent outburst of destructive rage, he knocks over the altar, causing the burning candles to fall; the wax from the overturned candles drips down a painting of the Virgin Mary, creating an image of tears. This "answer of the Real," the sign of the divine compassion for the hero's misery, only takes place when he reaches the depth of utmost despair, rejecting divinity itself—following the steps of Christ, one is united with God only in the experience of utter abandonment by him. Significantly, the melting wax is the last link in the chain of metonymic displacements of the motif of melting down: first, the frozen milk melts; then, the ice that covers the lake melts, causing the tragedy; finally, the wax melts—is *this* the final answer of the Real, the proof that we are not alone, that "someone is out there," or just another stupid coincidence? Whatever our reading, the effect of prosopopoeia is here, the Thing itself cries on our behalf.

insist that there is no I which can, even ideally, assume its speech "directly," bypassing the detour of prosopopoeia. Wearing a mask can thus be a strange thing: sometimes, more often than we tend to believe, there is more truth in the mask than in what we assume to be our "real self." Think of the proverbial shy and impotent man who, while playing an interactive video game, adopts the screen identity of a sadistic murderer and irresistible seducer—it is all too simple to say that this identity is just an imaginary supplement, a temporary escape from his real-life impotence. The point is rather that, since he knows that the video game is "just a game," he can "reveal his true self," do things he would never do in real-life interactions—in the guise of a fiction, the truth about himself is articulated. Therein lies the truth of a charming story like Alexandre Dumas's *The Man in the Iron Mask*: what if we invert the topic according to which, in our social interactions, we wear masks to cover our true face? What if, on the contrary, in order for us to interact in public with our true face, we have to have a mask hidden somewhere, a mask which renders our unbearable excess, what is in us more than ourselves, a mask which we can put on only exceptionally, in those carnivalesque moments when the standard rules of interaction are suspended? In short, what if the true function of the mask is not to be worn, but to be kept hidden?[19]

The opposite trap is to elevate "that through which I speak" into an authentic site of Truth, so that "something in me deeper than myself, the Truth itself, speaks through me." This is the Jungian version, involving a distinction between my Ego and the Self, a much broader ground of my subjectivity, with the task being to progress from my Ego to my true Self. Against this version, one should assert that that which speaks through me is fundamentally a lie.[20] The temptation here, of course, is to say that it is not the other through whom I speak, but that the Other itself speaks through me: the ultimate prosopopoeia is the one in which I myself am the other, the means used by X to speak. Does, then, the key dialectical reversal apropos prosopopoeia go from the subject talking through others to the subject itself as the site through which the Other speaks? The shift from me speaking through some figure of the Other to the I itself as prosopopoeia? From "I cannot tell the truth about myself directly; this most

19 The standard argument against cyberspace is that we can always step out of it and re-enter the game at will, in contrast to real life in which we are stuck, with no space to withdraw to. The lesson of Buddhism (and the reason it comes close to the notion of reality itself as a virtual fantasy space) is precisely that we *can* withdraw from reality itself, since the very notion of firm reality is an illusion—we can withdraw not into another reality, but into the primordial Void itself.

20 And then there is the third, postmodern, temptation, the most dangerous of all: the claim that there is no site of truth, that there are only layers of prosopopoeiae like the layers of an onion, that every truth which speaks through a mask in prosopopoeia is already another prosopopoeia.

intimate truth is so painful that I can only articulate it through another, by adopting the mask, talking through the mask, of another entity," to "truth itself is talking through me"? This reversal involves the dialectical shift from predicate to subject—from "what I am saying is true" to "truth is talking through me." And, furthermore, is not this shift also clearly sexualized? Woman is man's prosopopoeia: she is man's symptom, she has no substance of her own, she is a mask through which man speaks (more precisely, as Otto Weininger demonstrated, a mask through which the fallen nature of man speaks). Woman cannot relate to truth as an inherent value, she cannot tell the truth; however, truth can speak in or through her. The reversal from "I speak the truth" to "I, the truth, speak" occurs with woman's identification with the truth: men tell the truth, while in woman, truth itself speaks.

The "primordial prosopopoeia" is effectively that of the symbolic order itself, of the subject (constituting itself through) assuming a symbolic mandate—or, as Lichtenberg put it in one of his aphorisms: "There is a transcendent ventriloquism that makes people believe that something that was said on earth came from heaven." In one of the Marx brothers' films, Groucho, caught telling a lie, answers angrily: "Whom do you believe, your eyes or my words?" This apparently absurd logic renders perfectly the functioning of the symbolic order in which the symbolic mask matters more than the direct reality of the individual who wears it. It involves the by now familiar structure of what Freud called "fetishistic disavowal": "I know very well that things are the way I see them, that the person in front of me is a corrupt weakling, but I nonetheless treat him respectfully, since he wears the insignia of a judge, so that when he speaks, *it is the law itself which speaks through him*." So, in a way, I really do believe his words, not my eyes. This is where the cynic who believes only hard facts falls short: when a judge speaks, there is in a way more truth in his words (the words of the institution of law) than in the direct reality of the person of judge; if one limits oneself to what one sees, one simply misses the point. This paradox is what Lacan aims at with his *les non-dupes errent* (those in the know err): those who refuse to let themselves get caught in the symbolic fiction and believe only what they see with their own eyes are those who err most. What the cynic misses here is the efficiency of the symbolic fiction, the way it structures our (experience of) reality. A corrupt priest preaching on goodness may be a hypocrite, but if people endow his words with the authority of the Church, they may inspire them to perform good deeds.

Here one should take note of a certain paradox: it is precisely when "I speak"—when I perceive myself as the agent of my speech—that, effectively, "the big Other speaks through me," that I am "spoken," since my speech acts are totally regulated by the symbolic order in which I dwell. And, conversely, the only way for me to bring my subjective position of enunciation into words is to let myself be surprised by what I say, to experience my own words as a case of "it speaks in/through me." This is what happens in the case of a symptom: in it, my true subjective position finds a way to articulate itself against my will and intention. The opposition is thus not directly between "I speak" and "the Other speaks through me," since these are the two sides of the same coin. When "it speaks" through me, it is not the big Other which speaks: the truth that articulates itself is the truth about the failures, gaps, and inconsistencies of the big Other.[21]

The Talmud says: "The one who quotes properly brings redemption to the world." Is this not literally the formula of Stalinist argumentation? Freud also emphasizes that the unconscious in dreams can only quote—dreams are like a parrot, they are the ultimate prosopopoeia, just repeating speech fragments qua remnants of the day, while also, of course, submitting them to cruel cuts and rearrangements in order to squeeze its message into them. (The underlying premise of quotation: the big Other is always there, everything is already written, so all that we can say should, if true, be supported by a quotation.) This—and not the ridiculous notion of some mysterious Spirit secretly pulling the strings to guarantee a happy outcome—is what the Hegelian "Cunning of Reason" amounts to: I hide nothing from you, I renounce all "hermeneutics of suspicion," I do not impute any dark motives to you, I just leave the field free for you to deploy your potential and thus destroy yourself. There is more than superficial word-play in the resonance between *List der Vernunft* (Cunning of Reason) and *Lust der Vernunft* (Pleasure of Reason): the Cunning of Reason only works, the subject only allows itself to get caught in the trap of reason, if it is bribed by some surplus-pleasure, and it is this surplus that is brought out by the analytic stance.

It is easy to discern here the unexpected proximity of the Hegelian master to the analyst, to which Lacan alludes: the Hegelian Cunning of Reason means that the Idea realizes itself in and through the very failure of its realization. It is worth recalling the sublime reversal found in Charles Dickens's *Great Expectations*: when, as a young man, Pip is described as a "fellow of great expectations," everybody perceives this as a prediction of his future worldly success. At the novel's end, however, when Pip abandons London and returns to his modest childhood community, we realize that he lived up to the prediction that marked his life only by finding the strength to leave behind the vain thrill of London's high society, and thereby authenticate the notion of his being a "man of great expectations." Furthermore, as befits a Hegelian novel, the ending of *Great Expectations* is deeply ambiguous in a way which evokes the radical ambiguity of the Hegelian

21 Again, one should note a shift in Lacan: while for the Lacan of the 1950s the unconscious is the "discourse of the Other," the moment he introduces the key notion of the "barred Other" and draws out its consequences, the unconscious turns into the discourse that registers the gaps and failures of the Other.

reconciliation—here is the novel's last paragraph, describing Pip and Estella meeting again at the ruins of Satis House:

> "We are friends," said I, rising and bending over her, as she rose from the bench. "And will continue friends apart," said Estella. I took her hand in mine, and we went out of the ruined place; and, as the morning mists had risen long ago when I first left the forge, so the evening mists were rising now, and in all the broad expanse of tranquil light they showed to me, I saw no shadow of another parting from her.

How are we to read the last words, "I saw no shadow of another parting from her"? Do they mean that Estella and Pip will never part, that they will stay together forever, *or that it is only at this moment that Pip did not (or could not) see the shadow of a future parting*? Even more interestingly, we now know that this ending was a revised second version: in the original ending, Estella has remarried and Pip remains single; following the advice of certain friends (Edward Bulwer-Lytton, Wilkie Collins), Dickens wrote a more upbeat ending, suggesting that Estella and Pip would marry. Many critics not only found this new ending a concession to popular taste; some even proposed their own new ending—here is G. B. Shaw's version, describing what happens after Estella and Pip run into one another and then part again: "Since that parting, I have been able to think of her without the old unhappiness; but I have never tried to see her again, and I know I never shall." There is an ambiguity here again: "I know I never shall"—shall what? See Estella again *or try to see her again* (which leaves open the prospect of an unpremeditated encounter)? Another attempt was made by Douglas Brooks-Davies, who resolved the ambiguity of Dickens's second ending by opting for the pessimistic version: when Estella and Pip are leaving the garden together, "the evening sunlight of the moment when I left Satis holding Estella's hand was so bright that it banished all shadows—even the metaphorical shadow of the parting that we were soon (and permanently) to endure." However, this dispelling of the ambiguity does not work because, in a way, it is superfluous, it *says too much*—in an exact parallel with Hegel's "Absolute Knowing," where we also see "no shadow of another parting from it": it, of course, includes its own historicity; however, to say this explicitly is already to say too much and involves a regression to historicism. The denouement of *Great Expectations* thus relies on a kind of Hegelian reflexivity: what changes in the course of the hero's ordeal is not only his character, but also the very ethical standard by which we measure his character.

In his review of Badiou's *Ethics*, Terry Eagleton wrote:

> There is a paradox in the idea of transformation. If a transformation is deep-seated enough, it might also transform the very criteria by which we could identify it, thus

> making it unintelligible to us. But if it is intelligible, it might be because the transformation was not radical enough. If we can talk about the change then it is not full-blooded enough; but if it is full-blooded enough, it threatens to fall outside our comprehension. Change must presuppose continuity—a subject to whom the alteration occurs—if we are not to be left merely with two incommensurable states; but how can such continuity be compatible with revolutionary upheaval?[22]

The properly Hegelian solution to this dilemma is that a truly radical change is self-relating: it changes the very coordinates by means of which we measure change. In other words, a true change *sets its own standards*: it can only be measured by criteria that result from it. This is what the "negation of negation" is: a shift of perspective which turns failure into true success. And does the same not go for the Freudian *Fehlleistung* (*acte manqué*)—an act which succeeds in its very failure? Robert Pippin is right to emphasize that "the realization that only in such 'failure' is there success (success at being *Geist*) is an achievement like no other" in the history of philosophy.[23] This is where the standard reproach to Hegel (that he fails to fully confront negativity, failure, collapse, etc., since there is always a mechanism of redemption built into the dialectical process which guarantees that the utter failure will magically be converted into its opposite) falls short: the story of the Hegelian dialectical reversal is not the story of failure as a blessing in disguise, as a (painful but necessary) step or detour towards the final triumph that retroactively redeems it, but, on the contrary, the story of the necessary failure of every success (of every direct project or act), the story of how the only "success" the subject can gain is the reflexive shift of perspective which recognizes success in failure itself.

Lacan, Marx, Heidegger

Such a shift also lies at the very heart of the Hegelian relationship between lies and truth. Winston Churchill was right when he characterized truth not as something we search for, but as something upon which, occasionally, we accidentally stumble: "Men stumble over the truth from time to time, but most pick themselves up and hurry off as if nothing happened." A psychologically intuitive person may be able to recognize immediately—from a slight change of tone or of gesture—when somebody has started to lie; but perhaps what one needs much more is someone able to recognize when, in the generalized babble of daily communication, a person stumbles upon truth (or, rather, when the truth starts to

22 Terry Eagleton, *Figures of Dissent*, London: Verso Books 2003, p. 246.

23 Robert Pippin, *The Persistence of Subjectivity*, Cambridge: Cambridge University Press 2005, p. 78.

talk in or through the babble)—not, of course, factual truth, but subjective truth, which can also (even as a rule does) express itself in the guise of a (factual) lie. The reason is that, at their most radical, lies are not a simple denial of truth; they serve a much more refined protective function: to render the truth palpable, tolerable. During World War II, Churchill quipped: "In wartime, truth is so precious that she should always be attended by a bodyguard of lies." And since, in a way, life itself, especially love, is permanent warfare, lying is what keeps the world together. Joseph de Maistre wrote: "if we want to teach an error, we should … always begin with a truth."[24] De Maistre had in mind how even the most cruel sacrificial rituals of pagan religion implicitly harbor a correct insight into the efficacy of sacrifice brought out in its true form by Christianity. However, from a Hegelian standpoint, we should invert this statement: "if we want to teach a truth, we should always begin with an error."

The basic strategy of Brecht's celebrated adaptive cunning, exemplified by his behavior during his interview by the House Un-American Activities Committee (HUAC), is to "lie with (partial) truth": while all Brecht's answers to the Committee were factually true, he tailored the facts to create a false overall impression (in short: that he was not a dedicated communist propagandist, but just an anti-fascist democrat). The principle underlying Brecht's strategy is best expressed in his cynical reply to the reproach that he acted like a coward: "My profession is not a hero, but a writer." The problem here, of course, is that being a hero—that is, having courage—is precisely *not* a profession, but a characteristic that can be displayed in any situation where what is at stake is what Badiou calls fidelity to a Truth-Event. Brecht's stance should be contrasted to that of Dashiell Hammett, who found himself in a similar predicament at the same time: called to testify before the HUAC, he was asked if he really was a trustee for a fund that the Communist Party of the USA had organized to protect its persecuted members and sympathizers. The truth was that he knew nothing about the fund, but he was too proud to answer truthfully, since this would have implied that he recognized the authority of the HUAC and accepted the need to defend himself; so he refused to answer (and was duly sent to prison where, after only two weeks, the guards began to address him as "Sir"—proof of the extraordinary power and dignity of his personality). Both Brecht and Hammett lied, but where Brecht lied with (partial) truth, Hammett lied to save his dignity and truthfulness.[25]

24 Joseph de Maistre, *Éclaircissement sur les sacrifices*, Paris: L'Herne 2009, p. 29: "Il faut donc toujours partir d'une vérité pour enseigner une erreur."

25 Another case of lying in the guise of truth: a corrupt philosophy professor from my youth in Slovenia openly admitted his conformism, saying with a disarming smile: "I am scum, I know it, so what?" The lie of such an admission resides in the gap between the enunciated content and its subjective position of enunciation: by way of admitting his corruption openly, did he not adopt an honest position which somehow redeemed him

No wonder that Georg Lukács, Brecht's great Marxist opponent, displayed more ethical courage than Brecht when, after the crushing of the Hungarian rebellion at the end of 1956, he was arrested by the Soviets, who offered him freedom on one condition: they had tapes of his phone conversations with the other members of the Imre Nagy government and they knew that he had expressed his disagreement with some of the government's anti-socialist measures—all the Soviets wanted from him was to restate these disagreements publicly. Lukács declined, knowing perfectly well that to state the factual truth under such conditions would have been to lie.

In his first *Seminar*, Lacan defines error as a habitual embodiment of truth: "as long as the truth will not be revealed in its entirety, that is to say, in all probability till the end of time, it will be in its nature to propagate itself in the guise of error: error is thus a constitutive structure of the revelation of being as such."[26] The reference here, of course, is to the Freudian universe in which truth articulates itself as a rupture of the normal or regular flow of our speech or activity: the truth leaks out in the guise of slips of the tongue, failures to act, etc. Lacan wants to draw a strict distinction between this Freudian procedure and the Hegelian dialectic in which truth also arises out of errors, through the self-sublation of the latter: Hegelian truth is the absolute disclosure which can only be formulated at the end of history, when the historical process is fully actualized, while Freudian truth is partial, fragmentary, always just a rupture in the flow of ignorance, never the revealed totality. The problem here is that since psychoanalysis thus lacks the final point of total revelation which would enable it to firmly distinguish truth from error, how can it be sure that the other discourse which the psychoanalytic interpretation discerns beneath the discourse of *méprise* is not just another discourse of misrecognition? Aware of the problem, for a couple of years Lacan effectively insisted on a homology between psychoanalysis and Hegelian Absolute Knowing: the only difference being that the psychoanalyst is more modest, aware that we cannot ever reach the point of accomplished symbolization/revelation. (Later, Lacan resorted to the classic Freudian answer: the proof of the truth of a psychoanalytic interpretation is its own symbolic efficacy, the way it transforms the subject.) However, such a reading of Lacan as a "weak Hegelian," still faithful to the Hegelian goal and merely postponing indefinitely the final reconciliation, is *stricto sensu* wrong—that is, wrong with regard to Hegel. In other words, the very notion of Absolute Knowing as accomplished

from corruption? Not at all: the appropriate response is to paraphrase the old Jewish joke quoted by Freud: "If you are really scum, why are you telling us that you are scum?" Or, a more aggressive version: "You say that you are scum, but this will not fool us—you really are scum!"—in short: "Don't lie to us by telling the truth—you *are* scum!"

26 Jacques Lacan, *Le séminaire, Livre I: Les écrits techniques de Freud*, Paris: Seuil 1975, p. 289.

symbolization, the full revelation of Being, etc., totally misses the point of the Hegelian "reconciliation" by turning it into an Ideal to be reached, rather than something that *is always already here and should merely be assumed.* Hegelian temporality is crucial here: we enact "reconciliation" not by way of a miraculous healing of wounds, and so forth, but by recognizing "the rose in the cross of the present," by realizing that reconciliation is already accomplished in what we (mis)perceived as alienation.

Consequently, Hegel does deal with symptoms—in the sense that every universality in its actualization generates an excess which undermines it. The Hegelian totality is by definition "self-contradictory," antagonistic, inconsistent: the "Whole" which is the "True" (Hegel: "*das Ganze is das Wahre*") is the Whole *plus* its symptoms, the unintended consequences which betray its untruth. For Marx, the "totality" of capitalism includes crises as its integral moments; for Freud, the "totality" of a human subject includes pathological symptoms as indicators of what is "repressed" in the official image of the subject. The underlying premise is that *the Whole is never truly whole*: every notion of the Whole leaves something out, and the dialectical effort is precisely the effort to include this excess, to account for it. Symptoms are never just secondary failures or distortions of the basically sound System—they are indicators that there is something "rotten" (antagonistic, inconsistent) in the very heart of the System. This is why the anti-Hegelian rhetoric which insists on how Hegel's totality misses the details which stick out and destroy its equilibrium misses the point: the space of the Hegelian totality *is* the very space of the interaction between the ("abstract") Whole and the details that elude its grasp, although they are generated by it. So what if Hegel's thought is not a metaphysics, but a form of pataphysics in Alfred Jarry's sense, a thinking of pathological incidents which inevitably disturb the inner logic of a process?

The paradigmatic case of Understanding, of its "abstract" reasoning, is thus not primarily the isolated analysis of objects and processes, or a blindness to the complex dynamic Whole within which an object is located (even Stalin was well aware of this topic, with his endless variations on the motif of how "everything is connected with everything else"), but rather a blindness to the structural role of symptoms, of excesses and obstacles, a blindness to the productive role of these obstacles. For example, at the level of Understanding, crises appear as obstacles to capitalism's smooth functioning, obstacles that can and should be avoided by the adoption of intelligent economic policies. Likewise, for Understanding, the "totalitarian" character of the communist regimes of the twentieth century appears as a regrettable consequence of "neglecting" the central role of democratic decision-making, not as a necessary feature of the twentieth-century communist project as such. "Understanding" is thus inherently utopian (in the ideological sense of the term): it dreams of, say, a society based on money, but in which money would not be an instrument of fetishistic alienation and exploitation, but would simply mediate the exchange between free individuals; or of a society based on parliamentary democracy which would fully and effectively represent the people's will and so on.

So Hegel "cannot think the symptom" insofar as we understand the Cunning of Reason in its traditional teleological sense, as a hidden rational order controlling historical contingency, manipulatively exploiting particular moments in order to realize its hidden universal goal. However, the moment we take into account the retroactivity of universal necessity—the fact that each "use" of particular moments for some universal goal, as well as this goal itself, emerge retroactively in order, precisely, to "rationalize" the symptomal excess—we can no longer accept the Hegelian Cunning of Reason in its standard sense. In his early, Maoist-phase *Theory of Contradiction*, Badiou wrote: "To the nothing-new-under-the-sun, the thinking of revolt opposes the ever new insurgent red sun, under the emblem of which the unlimited affirmative hope of rebellious producers engenders ruptures." This upbeat statement is supplemented by a much more ominous-sounding one: "There is the radically New only because there are corpses that no trumpet of Judgment will ever reawaken."[27] The shocking brutality of this last statement should not blind us to its truth: if we really want to assert a radical break, we must abandon the Benjaminian notion of retroactive redemption, of a revolutionary act which redeems all past suffering and defeats—as the Christians say, the dead should be left to bury the dead. No Cunning of Reason can retroactively justify present suffering, as in the Stalinist idea, elaborated by Merleau-Ponty in *Humanism and Terror*, that the good life of the communist future will justify the cruelty of the contemporary revolutionary process.

Robert Pippin is the only thinker today who heroically defines his goal as the promotion of "bourgeois philosophy," that is, the philosophy of legitimizing and analyzing the "bourgeois" way of life centered on the notion of autonomous and responsible individuals leading a safe life within the confines of civil society. The problem, of course, comes back to the skeleton in the closet of every bourgeois society: Pippin as a Hegelian (*the* US Hegelian) should know that, for Hegel, modern bourgeois society could only have arisen through the mediation of Revolutionary Terror (exemplified by Jacobins); furthermore, Hegel is also aware that, in order to prevent its own death by habituation (immersion in the life of particular interests), every bourgeois society needs to be shattered from time to time by war.

A problem such as "can excesses like Auschwitz be justified, economized, as necessary detours on the road towards a free society, can they be *aufgehoben*

27 Alain Badiou, *Théorie de la contradiction*, Paris: Maspero 1975, p. 86.

as moments of historical progress?" is, therefore, from a strict Hegelian perspective, badly posed: it presupposes a position of external substantial teleology that is precluded by Hegel. There is no substantial historical Spirit weighing up in advance the costs and benefits of a prospective historical catastrophe (e.g., is the massacre of European Jewry a price worth paying for the unprecedented peace and prosperity of postwar Europe?): it is only actual humans, caught up in a historical process, who generate a catastrophe which can then give birth to new ethico-political awareness, without any claim that this unintended result in any way "justifies" or legitimizes the enormous suffering that led to it. Measured in this way, no historical progress is "worth the price": all one can say is that the ultimate outcome of historical catastrophes is sometimes a higher ethical awareness which one should accept with humility and in memory of the blood spilled on the path to realizing it. Such "blessings in disguise" are never guaranteed in advance, which is why, insofar as a symptom is the point of "irrationality" of the existing totality, a point which cannot be subsumed under any figure of totalizing Reason, we should invert Marx's famous formula of recovering the "rational core" of Hegel's dialectic and boldly propose to recover its *irrational* core.

But, again, are we not contradicting here Lacan's explicit critique of the Hegelian "Cunning of Reason"? Does not Lacan advocate Marx's "materialist reversal of Hegel": what Hegel cannot think is the radical sense of a symptom which undermines from within any Cunning of Reason? For Marx, the totality of Reason (which asserts its reign through its "cunning") is undermined in its symptom (the proletariat as the "unreason within the domain of Reason," as the non-sense that no cunning can legitimate and/or rationalize). This dimension of the symptom as "the return of truth as such into the gap of a certain knowledge"

> is highly differentiated in Marx's critique, even if it is not made explicit there. And one can say that a part of the reversal of Hegel that he carries out is constituted by the return (which is a materialist return, precisely insofar as it gives it figure and body) of the question of truth. The latter actually forces itself upon us … not by taking up the thread of the ruse of reason, a subtle form with which Hegel sends it packing, but by upsetting these ruses (read Marx's political writings) which are merely dressed up with reason.[28]

Marx "invents the symptom" when he conceptualizes the position of the proletariat as the material "figure and body" which gives body to the "un-reason" of the totality of Reason (the modern Rational State) conceptualized and legitimized by Hegelian Knowledge. Marx thus sees through the Hegelian trick of legitimizing exploitation and other horrors as necessary moments of the

28 Lacan, *Écrits*, p. 194.

progress of Reason (Reason using evil human passions as means to actualize itself), denouncing it as the legitimization of a miserable social reality which is merely "dressed up with reason." As such, the "message" of the symptom is: "Men, listen, I am telling you the secret. I, truth, speak."[29] In a symptom, "it speaks," the subject is surprised by it, taken aback, caught with his pants down; a symptom is thus something that cannot be attributed to any subject or agent. The temptation to be resisted here—the very temptation of the Cunning of Reason—is to surmise another meta-Subject or Agent who organizes these apparent failures and mistakes, turning them into steps towards the final Truth. The Cunning of Reason is the desperate wager of trusting in history, the belief that the big Other guarantees its final happy outcome—or, as Lacan put it in his acerbic way:

> The discourse of error—its articulation in action—could bear witness to the truth against the apparent facts themselves. It was then that one of them tried to get the cunning of reason accepted into the rank of objects deemed worthy of study. Unfortunately, he was a professor … Remain content, then, with your vague sense of history and leave it to clever people to found the world market in lies, the trade in all-out war, and the new law of self-criticism on the guarantee of my future firm. If reason is as cunning as Hegel said it was, it will do its job without your help.[30]

A symptom is, on the contrary, that which undermines the big Other, that in which the big Other reveals its gaps, inconsistency, failure, impotence. When Lacan writes, "I, truth, speak," this does not mean that the substantial "big Other" in me speaks, but, on the contrary, that the big Other's failure breaks through. Error is the partial un-truth which can be sublated into a subordinate moment of the truth of Totality, while a symptom is a partial break-through of the repressed truth of the Totality, a truth which belies totality. Lacan here opposes error and mistake (*méprise*): while, in the Hegelian dialectical process, truth arises through error, in the psychoanalytic process, it arises from a mistake (or, rather, mis-apprehension)—truth says: "Whether you flee from me in deceit or think you can catch me in error, I will catch up with you in the mistake from which you cannot hide."[31] When I am in error, I hold as true something that is not true; in a symptom, on the contrary, truth appears in what I hold as least true, most contingent, unworthy of universality. Again, truth says:

> I wander about in what you regard as least true by its very nature: in dreams, in the way the most far-fetched witticisms and the most grotesque nonsense of jokes defy

29 Ibid., p. 340.
30 Ibid., p. 341.
31 Ibid.

> meaning, and in chance—not in its law, but rather in its contingency. And I never more surely proceed to change the face of the world than when I give it the profile of Cleopatra's nose.[32]

The implications of such a radical notion of the symptom are much more far-reaching than it may appear: the symptom is not a secondary expression of some substantial content already dwelling deep in the subject—on the contrary, the symptom is "open," coming from the future, pointing towards a content that will only come to be through the symptom.[33] Recall Lacan's statement that "woman is a symptom of man"—does this mean that, *vulgari eloquentia*, a woman comes to ex-sist only when a man selects her as a potential object of libidinal investment? So what is she prior to this investment? What if we conceive the idea of a symptom that pre-exists what it is a symptom of, so that we can consider women as symptoms wandering around in search of something to attach themselves to as symptoms—or even just being satisfied with their role as empty symptoms?[34] One can effectively claim that a woman who withdraws from sexual contact with men is a symptom at its purest, a zero-level symptom—a nun, for example, who, in rejecting becoming the symptom of a particular man (her sexual partner), posits herself as the symptom of Christ, *the* man (*ecce homo*).

This notion of the paradoxical pre-existence of a symptom can also be given a Benjaminian twist. In the middle of Tchaikovsky's "Francesca da Rimini" (eleven minutes into it), there is a passage which sounds *almost* like Bernard Herrmann, a kind of flight into the future; then the standard Romanticism recovers itself. It is really as if Tchaikovsky produced here a symptom in the early Lacanian (or Benjaminian) sense of a message from the future, something that its own time lacked the proper means to hear or understand. (This is how modernism works: what were originally fragments of an organic Whole are

32 Ibid., p. 342.

33 Insofar as a symptom is inherently related to its interpretation, i.e., insofar as it functions, somewhat like Joyce's *Finnegans Wake*, as an attempt to take into account and answer in advance its possible interpretations, it has the intricate structure of a temporal loop: a symptom is a purely reflexive entity, a pre-emptive reaction to its own future effects.

34 What then is a man for a woman? A catastrophe, as Lacan conjectures? What if, bearing in mind the couple symptom/fantasy, man is a fantasy of a woman? Does Lacan not point in this direction when he claims that don Juan is a feminine fantasy? Both woman and man, not only woman, are thus co-dependent on each other, like Escher's two hands drawing each other. The trap to be avoided here is to conceive this relationship as being somehow complementary—as if, once a man finds his symptom in a woman and the same woman her fantasy embodied in a man, there finally is a kind of sexual relationship. We must bear in mind that fantasy and symptom are structurally incompatible.

autonomized—the same goes for Joan Miró's paintings.) No wonder that *this* is the music used for the ballet sequence at the end of *Torn Curtain*—a kind of revenge of Herrmann whose score Hitchcock discarded—a scene in which the "repressed returns." (Did he choose this piece?)[35]

There is a nice anecdote about a Latin American poet who modified the political tenor of his poetry according to whoever was his most recent mistress: when she was a proto-fascist rightist, he celebrated military discipline and patriotic sacrifice; when he got involved with a pro-communist woman, he started to celebrate guerrilla warfare; later, he moved on to a hippy mistress and wrote about drugs and transcendental meditation. *This* is what "woman as a symptom of man" means, not merely that a man uses a woman to articulate his message—on the contrary, woman is the determining factor: man orients himself towards his symptom, he clings to it to give consistency to his life. And the Hegelian Cunning of Reason works in a similar way: it is not that Reason is a secret force behind the scenes using human agents for its purposes: there are *nothing but* agents following their particular purposes, and what they do "auto-poetically" organizes itself into a larger pattern.

But did not Heidegger propose a much more radical critique of the Hegelian Cunning of Reason, in a way which differs radically from Marx's critique (and which enables us to recognize in Marx himself the presence of the Hegelian notion of history as the story of dialectical redemption[36])? For the Cunning of Reason to be operative, there is no need to resuscitate any transcendent rational agency; particular contingent finite facts must be accounted for not in terms of any such higher power, but in terms of their own intelligibility, which is the true "infinite" immanent to the finite itself. The contrast with Heidegger's own full assertion of finitude could not be clearer. Heidegger deploys all the consequences of such a radical assertion of finitude, up to and including a series of self-referential paradoxes. His claim is that the ultimate failure, the breakdown of the entire structure of meaning, the withdrawal from engagement and care—in other words the possibility that the totality of *Dasein*'s involvements "collapses

---

35 However, Hitchcock's discarding of Herrmann's score cannot simply be dismissed as a concession to Hollywood commercial pressure. In the DVD edition of *Torn Curtain*, one can also watch some scenes accompanied with the Herrmann score, among them the Gromek murder. In the released version, this scene has no musical accompaniment, all we hear are the occasional grunts and groans which render the oppressive *real presence* of the painfully prolonged activity of trying to kill Gromek much more efficiently than would Herrmann's standard score of brassy Wagnerian ostinati!

36 Which accounts for the clear presence of the motif of the "Cunning of Reason" in Marx's theoretical framework; for example, remarking on the consequences of English colonial rule in India, Marx claimed that, in spite of all its destructive effects upon Indian society, colonization would push India into modernity.

into itself; the world has the character of completely lacking significance"[37]—is the innermost possibility of *Dasein*, that *Dasein* can succeed in its engagement only against the background of a possible failure: "the interrelational structure of the world of Care can fail in such a catastrophic way that *Dasein* will appear not as the world-embedded, open-to-meaning, engaged agent in a shared world that it is, but, all at once as it were, the null basis of a nullity."[38] Here Heidegger is not just making the decisionist-existentialist point about how "being a subject means being able to fail to be one," how the choice is ours and utterly contingent, with no guarantee of success.[39] His point is rather that the historical totality-of-meaning into which we are thrown is always already, "constitutively," thwarted *from within* by the possibility of its utmost impossibility. Death, the collapse of the structure of meaning and care, is not an external limit which, as such, would enable *Dasein* to "totalize" its meaningful engagement; it is not the final quilting point that "dots the i" of one's life span, enabling us to totalize a life story into a consistent, meaningful narrative. Death is precisely that which *cannot* be included in any meaningful totality, its meaningless facticity is a permanent threat to meaning, its prospect a reminder that there is no final way out.[40] The consequence of this is that the choice is not a direct choice between success and failure, between authentic and inauthentic modes of existence: since the very notion that one can successfully totalize one's life within an all-encompassing structure-of-meaning is the ultimate inauthentic betrayal, the only true "success" *Dasein* can have is to heroically confront and accept its ultimate failure.

The "magical force" of reversal

The contrast with Hegel is thus striking. If Hegel's underlying axiom is that "the result of an untrue mode of knowledge must not be allowed to run away into an empty nothing"[41] (note the prohibitive mode: "must not be allowed to ..."!)—i.e., that, through the work of "tarrying with the negative," every outbreak of negativity can be accounted for (rendered intelligible) in a narrative of meaning and thus *aufgehoben* in an encompassing infinite totality—for Heidegger, it

37 Martin Heidegger, *Being and Time*, trans. John MacQuarrie and Edward Robinson, New York: HarperCollins 2008, p. 231.

38 Pippin, *The Persistence of Subjectivity*, p. 64.

39 Ibid., p. 67.

40 Here we touch on the topic of Heidegger and psychiatric clinics: what about that withdrawal from engagement which is *not* death but the psychotic breakdown of a living human being? What about the possibility of "living in death," of vegetating with no care, like the *Muselmannen* in the Nazi camps?

41 Hegel, *Phenomenology of Spirit*, p. 56.

is a formal (a priori) characteristic of *Dasein*'s finitude that every meaningful engagement will finally "run away into an empty nothing": all our meaningful engagements are just so many contingent attempts to postpone the inevitable; heroic acts against the background of the ultimate nullity of all human endeavor. Does this critique of Hegel hold up however? On a first approach, it may well appear justified—as Pippin has noted, when, in a famous passage from the Foreword to the *Phenomenology*, Hegel provides the most outstanding formulation of the reversal of the negative into a higher positivity, of the resurrection of the infinite life after death, he has recourse to a very strange term: "Spirit is this power only by looking the negative in the face, and tarrying with it. This tarrying with the negative is the magical force [*Zauberkraft*] that converts it into being."[42] Effectively, it is "as if Hegel cannot help giving away his dodge and his own uncertainty with that revealing (most un-Hegelian) word or Freudian slip, *Zauberkraft*"[43]—an admission that there is something magical, something like the intervention of a *deus ex machina*, in the dialectical reversal of the negative into the positive. This is why we need to be very precise in circumscribing this reversal. It is a commonplace about Hegel that he criticized the idea of the Crusades for confounding the possession of the spiritual Truth of Christianity with the possession of the physical site of Christ's tomb, the place of his crucifixion and resurrection. However, here again, the choice is not an immediate one: in order to experience the spiritual Truth of Christianity one *has to* first occupy the tomb and experience its emptiness—only in this disappointment, through this failure-in-triumph, does one reach the insight that, in order to "live in Christ," it is not necessary to travel to faraway lands and occupy empty tombs, since Christ is already here whenever there is Love between his followers. To recast this experience in the terms of the Rabinovitch joke:

> "We are going to Jerusalem to find Christ's tomb and to dwell in the presence of divinity."
>
> "But what you will discover in Jerusalem is that the tomb is empty, that there is nothing to find, that all you have is yourselves, the community of visiting Christians …"
>
> "Well, this community of spirit *is* the living Christ, and this is what we were really looking for!"

The same goes for the resurrection itself: "Christ will be resurrected!" "But we, his followers who wait for him, see nothing …" "True, you don't see—but what you don't see is that the spirit of this community of yours, the love that bonds

42 As quoted in Pippin, *The Persistence of Subjectivity*, p. 77, modified from the translation in Hegel, *Phenomenology of Spirit*, p. 19.

43 Pippin, *The Persistence of Subjectivity*, pp. 77–8.

you, *is* the resurrected Christ!" And likewise even more so for the topic of the Second Coming: nothing will "really happen," no God will miraculously appear; people will just realize that God *is already here*, in the spirit of their collective.

Christopher Nolan's film *The Prestige* (2006)—a story about the deadly rivalry between two magicians, the lower-class Alfred Borden and the upper-class Robert Angier, in *fin de siècle* London—can, surprisingly, help us to grasp clearly this "magical" aspect of Hegelian dialectics. The film can be read as an allegory of the struggle for Hegel's legacy between Right and Left Hegelians. The two magicians compete over who can deliver the best performance of the "Transported Man" trick; Borden, the first to perform it, disappears into a box, bounces a ball to another box across the stage, and instantly reappears within the second box to catch the ball. Blackmailed into revealing the source of his trick to Angier, Borden gives him one clue, the name of an inventor: "Tesla." (This, we later learn, is a lie: Borden simply used his twin brother to replace him.) Angier travels to Colorado Springs to meet Nikola Tesla and learn the secret of Borden's illusion. Tesla constructs a teleportation machine, but the device fails to work. Angier then learns from Borden's notebook that he has been sent on a wild-goose chase. Feeling he has wasted his money, he returns to Tesla's lab and discovers that the machine can in fact create and teleport a duplicate of any item placed in it. When Tesla is forced to leave Colorado Springs, Angier is left with the machine. In a letter, Tesla warns Angier to destroy it. Angier refuses to do so and returns to London to begin a final set of 100 performances with his new act, "The Real Transported Man," in which he disappears under huge arcs of electricity and "teleports" fifty yards from the stage to the balcony in a second. Borden attends Angier's performance and is baffled; he slips backstage and finds Angier inside a water tank, with a padlock on the latch that prevents his escape. At the film's end, the mortally wounded Angier reveals his secret to Borden: each time he disappeared during the illusion, he fell through a trap door into the tank and drowned; the machine created a duplicate who teleported to the balcony and basked in the applause. Angier says he suffered to become great—a philosophy Borden thought Angier had never learned.

The class rivalry between the upper-class Angier and the lower-class Borden is reflected in, among other things, the different ways in which they organize the illusion: Borden uses his twin brother to replace him, while Angier does it with the help of true scientific wizardry (he really is redoubled). There is a celebration of the aristocratic ethic of sacrifice (against cheap lower-class trickery) at work here: for the sake of his art, Angier undergoes the terrible pain of drowning during each performance. Therein resides Angier's revenge: Borden thinks that only he is ready to truly suffer to become great (when he loses some fingers on his hand, his twin brother also cuts off the same fingers to remain indiscernible from him, etc.); however, at the end, he is forced to admit that beneath Angier's corrupted-aristocrat attitude there is a much more terrible sacrifice—each performance is paid for with a suicide.

Early in the film, when a magician performs a trick with a small bird which disappears in a cage on the table, a small boy in the audience starts to cry, claiming that the bird has been killed. The magician approaches him and finishes the trick, gently producing a live bird out of his hand—but the boy is not satisfied, insisting that this must be another bird, the dead one's brother. After the show, we see the magician in a room behind the stage, bringing in a flattened cage and throwing a squashed bird into a trash bin—the boy was indeed correct. The film describes the three stages of a magic performance: the setup, or the "pledge," where the magician shows the audience something that appears ordinary but is probably not, making use of misdirection; the "turn," where the magician makes the ordinary act extraordinary; and the "prestige," where the effect of the illusion is produced. Is not this triple movement the Hegelian triad at its purest? The thesis (pledge), its catastrophic negation (turn), and the magical resolution of the catastrophe (prestige)? The catch, as Hegel was well aware, is that in order for the miracle of the "prestige" to occur, somewhere there must be a squashed bird—in *The Prestige*, it is Angier's drowned body.

We should thus have no qualms about admitting that there is something of the "cheap magician" about Hegel, in his trick of synthesis, of *Aufhebung*. Ultimately, there are only two ways to account for this trick, like the two versions of the vulgar bad news/good news medical joke: (1) the good news is good, but it concerns *another* subject ("The bad news is that you have a terminal cancer and will die in a month. The good news is: you see that beautiful nurse over there? I've been trying to get her into bed for months; finally, yesterday, she said yes and we made love the whole night like crazy ..."); (2) the good news *is* bad news for the subject, but from a different perspective ("The bad news is you have severe Alzheimer's. The good news is: you have Alzheimer's, so you will have forgotten the bad news by the time you get home"). The true Hegelian "synthesis" is the synthesis of these two options: the good news is the bad news itself—but in order for us to see that, we have to shift to a different agent (from the bird which dies to the one which replaces it; from the cancer-ridden patient to the happy doctor, from Christ as individual to the community of believers). In other words, the dead bird remains dead, it *really* dies; likewise in the case of Christ, who is reborn as *another* subject, as the Holy Ghost.

We are dealing here with jokes in which we arrive at the final line only through a dialogic undermining of a preceding position, an undermining which unexpectedly involves our subjective standpoint.[44] The basic idea of Hegel's

44 Agamben is right in pointing out the ambiguity of the apocalyptic-messianic "time that remains" as the time to end time: when we dwell in it, what appears to us as the slowing down of the final demise of the (rule of) Law, as the endless deferral of this final

dialectic is, on the contrary, that this dialogic process is not just subjective but is inscribed in the reality of the "Thing itself": the tension which is reflected in the dialogue is constitutive of reality—this is how Hegel's thesis that the path to truth is part of truth itself should be conceived. Even the remark allegedly made by Brecht in Sidney Hook's apartment, apropos the accused at the Moscow show trials in the 1930s, can be recast in these terms:

> In 1935 Brecht visited Hook's house in Manhattan. When Hook raised the question of the recent arrest and imprisonment of Zinoviev, Kamenev, and thousands of others, Brecht is alleged by Hook to have replied calmly in German: "The more innocent they are, the more they deserve to be shot." As Hook tells it, he then handed Brecht his hat and coat. Brecht left "with a sickly smile."[45]

Brecht's statement is thoroughly ambiguous—it can be read as a standard assertion of radical Stalinism (your very insistence on your innocence, your refusal to sacrifice yourself for the Cause, bears witness to your guilt, which resides in giving preference to your individual interests over the larger interests of the Party), or it can be read in a radically anti-Stalinist manner: if they were in a position to plot the assassination of Stalin and his entourage, and were "innocent" (that is, did not grasp the opportunity), then they really deserve to die for having failed to rid us of Stalin. The true guilt of the accused is thus that, instead of rejecting the very ideological framework of Stalinism and ruthlessly acting against Stalin, they narcissistically fell in love with their victimization and either protested their innocence or became fascinated by the ultimate sacrifice they could make for the Party by confessing to non-existent crimes. The properly dialectical way to grasp the imbrication of these two meanings would be to start with the first reading, followed by the common-sense moralistic reaction to Brecht: "But how can you say something so ruthless? Surely such a logic, demanding a blind self-sacrifice to satisfy the accusatory whims of the Leader, can only function within a terrifying and criminal totalitarian system—it is surely the duty of every ethical subject to fight such a system with all means possible, including the physical removal, murder if necessary, of the totalitarian leadership?" "Yes, so you can see how, if the accused were innocent, they deserve all the more to be shot—they effectively *were* in a position to rid us of Stalin and

---

point, is retroactively revealed as the very anarchic state of freedom we were waiting for. In a properly Hegelian twist, the protracted deferral that bars full access to the Thing is already the Thing itself—the structure of this unique *différance* is thus yet again that of the Rabinovitch joke: "The arrival of full *parousia* is endlessly postponed ..." "But this postponement *is* the *parousia* we strive for."

45 David Caute, *The Dancer Defects: The Struggle for Cultural Supremacy During the Cold War*, Oxford: Oxford University Press 2003, p. 299.

his henchmen, and missed this unique opportunity to spare humanity from his terrible crimes!"[46]

The same ambiguity can be discerned in the infamous statement attributed to various Nazi leaders: "When I hear the word 'culture,' I reach for my pistol." The Nazi's intended meaning was probably that he was ready to defend high German culture with arms, if necessary, against the Jews and other barbarians; the true meaning, however, is that he is himself a barbarian who explodes with violence when confronted with true works of culture.[47]

Hegel's version of "infinite judgment" is thus different from Kant's—there is a negation of negation (of the Rabinovitch type) at work in its most famous example, "the Spirit is a bone": (1) the Spirit is a bone; (2) this is nonsense, there is an absolute contradiction between these two terms; (3) well, the Spirit *is* this contradiction. One can see the opposition between this procedure and the paradox of identity as identified by Hegel, where the very occurrence of an identical term

---

46 Although the same reversal also works in the opposite direction. Recently in Slovenia, the public prosecutor started an action against an old communist functionary involved in the show trials and mass killings of members of the Slovene anti-communist units imprisoned immediately after the end of World War II. Not long after the prosecution was announced, I happened to meet another unrepentant old communist cadre and asked him for a reaction; to my surprise, he told me that the accused functionary fully deserved the harshest punishment, and added: "Not for what he is accused of, of course, but for his true crime, decades later, of allowing the communists to lose power!"

47 This, of course, in no way elevates Brecht above ethico-political suspicion. The case against him was succinctly expressed by W. H. Auden: "To offer your art in vocal support of the Party is one thing. To do so and *still* keep a bolt-hole and nest-egg is quite another ... From the moment of his espousal of Communism, Brecht stood on the sidelines, cheering on a party he most emphatically did not wish to join, recommending that others submit to a discipline which he himself refused" (quoted in Caute, *The Dancer Defects*, p. 300). So when Brecht, the GDR *Staatsdichter* with an Austrian passport and a Swiss bank account, wrote in his poem "In Dark Times" against poets who remain silent in times of oppression—"[later generations] won't say: the times were dark / Rather, why were these poets silent?"—one should indeed raise the question: "So why was he himself silent whenever the dark places of the USSR and the international Communist movement were concerned?" (ibid.) Furthermore, when Fredric Jameson (see his *Brecht and Method*, London: Verso Books 1998, p. 10) defends Brecht against the accusation that he relied heavily on anonymous collaborators, even copying from them the majority of some of his works, with the counter-argument that "these attacks depreciate politics altogether—as the action of collectives—in the name of the personal and of individual ownership," adding how, in this way, "the properly utopian features of Brecht's collective work, and of collective and collaborative work of all kinds, are occulted and repudiated," one cannot but take note of the oxymoron "Brecht's collective work"—a collective work which Brecht nonetheless, in a very pragmatic and totally non-utopian way, sold on the market as his own, resorting to all the finesse of "bourgeois" copyright law, and demanding high sums of money as befitting one who sells his "individual ownership."

causes surprise: A rose is … (we expect a predicate, but get) a rose. The Hegelian move is to treat this surprise/paradox as constitutive of identity: there is surprise (and a temporal logic) in both cases, but of a different kind.[48]

This in turn means that Heidegger's notion of death as the ultimate point of impossibility that cannot be dialectically "sublated" or included in a higher totality is no argument against Hegel: the Hegelian response is just to shift the perspective in order to recognize this negativity itself in its positive aspect, as a condition of possibility: what appears as the ultimate obstacle is in itself a positive condition of possibility, for the universe of meaning can only arise against the background of its annihilation. Furthermore, the properly dialectical reversal is not only the reversal of negative into positive, of the condition of impossibility into the condition of possibility, of obstacle into enabling agency, but, simultaneously, the reversal of transcendence into immanence, and the inclusion of the subject of enunciation in the enunciated content.

This reversal-into-itself—the shift in the status of what-is-at-stake from sign to Thing, from predicate to subject—is crucial for the dialectical process: what first appears as a mere sign (property, reflection, distortion) of the Thing turns out to be the Thing itself. If the Idea cannot adequately represent itself, if its representation is distorted or deficient, then this simultaneously signals a limitation or deficiency of the Idea itself. Furthermore, not only does the universal Idea always appear in a distorted or displaced way; this Idea is *nothing but* the distortion or displacement, the self-inadequacy, of the particular with regard to itself.

This brings us to the most radical dimension of the (in)famous "identity of opposites": insofar as "contradiction" is the Hegelian name for the Real, this means that the Real is *simultaneously* the Thing to which direct access is impossible *and* the obstacle which prevents this direct access; the Thing which eludes our grasp *and* the distorting screen which makes us miss the Thing. Is this not how trauma works? On the one hand, trauma is the X that the subject is unable to approach directly, that can only be perceived in a distorted way, through some kind of protective lens, that can only be alluded to in a roundabout way, never confronted head on, etc. On the other hand, however, for a subject who has experienced a traumatic shock, the trauma also functions as the very opposite of the inaccessible Thing-in-itself which eludes its grasp: it functions as something here, in me, that distorts and disturbs my perspective on reality, twisting it

48 An unexpected version of the Rabinovitch joke circulated in ex-Yugoslavia: an officer wants to educate a Gypsy soldier by teaching him poetry; so, in order to explain rhyme to him, he gives an example: "I play balalaika, I screw your mother" (the line rhymes in the original: *Igram balalaiku, yebem tvoiu maiku.*) The Gypsy answers: "Oh, I get it! Here's another one: I play balalaika, I screw your wife." The officer comments: "But this doesn't rhyme!" The Gypsy retorts: "No, it doesn't rhyme, but it is true." The catch is that, in Serb, this last line loosely rhymes (*Nije rima, ali je istina*), so that we do finally get a rhyme.

in a particular way. A woman who has been brutally raped and humiliated not only cannot directly recall the rape scene; the repressed memory of the rape also distorts her approach to reality, making her oversensitive to some of its aspects, ignoring others and so on.

And is not this shift structurally homologous to that of the Rabinovitch joke quoted above? The very problem (obstacle) retroactively appears as its own solution, since what prevents us from directly accessing the Thing is the Thing itself. The only change here lies in the shift of perspective. In exactly the same way, the final twist in Kafka's parable "Before the Law" relies on a mere shift of perspective: the man from the country, confronted with the door of the Law that prevents his access to the terrifying Thing (the Law), is told that from the very beginning the door was there only for him, in other words that he was from the beginning *included* in the Law—the Law was not just the Thing which fascinated his gaze, it always already returned his gaze. And, to go a step further, the gap that separates me from God is the gap that separates God from himself: the distance is not abolished (I do not miraculously rejoin God), it is merely displaced into God himself.

Yet another way to articulate this key moment is in the more traditional terms of the dialectical tension between the epistemological and the ontological dimensions: the gap that separates the knowing subject from the known object is inherent to the object itself, my knowing a thing is part of a process internal to the thing, which is why the standard epistemological problem should be turned around: not "How is my knowledge of the thing possible?" but "How is it that knowledge appears within the thing as a mode of the thing's relating to itself?" With regard to God, the problem is not "How can I know God?" but "How and why does God generate in humans knowledge about himself?" that is, how does my knowledge (and ignorance) of God function within God himself? Our alienation from God is God's self-alienation. When we lose God, it is not only that God abandons us, God abandons himself.

Reflection and supposition

Hegelian reflection is thus the opposite of the transcendental approach which reflexively regresses from the object to its subjective conditions of possibility. Even the philosophy of the "linguistic turn" remains at this transcendental level, addressing the transcendental dimension of language—that is, how the horizon of possible meaning sustained by language in which we dwell functions as the transcendental condition of possibility for all our experience of reality. Here, then, "the signified falls into the signifier," for the signified is an effect of the signifier, it is accounted for in the terms of the symbolic order as its transcendentally constitutive condition.[49] What dialectical reflection adds to this is another reflexive twist which grounds the very subjective-transcendental site of enunciation in the "self-movement" of the Thing itself: here, "the signifier falls into the signified," the act of enunciation falls into the enunciated, the sign of the thing falls into the Thing itself. When asked to explain the meaning of a term X to someone who, while more or less fluent in our language, does not know this specific term, we invariably respond with a potentially endless series of synonyms, paraphrases, or descriptions of situations in which the use of the term would be appropriate. In this way, through the very failure of our endeavor, we circumscribe an empty place, the place of the right word—precisely the word we are trying to explain. So at some point, after our paraphrases fail, all we can do is to conclude in exasperation: "In short, it is X!" Far from functioning as a simple admission of failure, however, this can effectively generate an insight—*if*, that is, through our failed paraphrases we have successfully circumscribed the *place* of the term to be explained. At this point, as Lacan would have put it, "the signifier falls into the signified," the term becomes part of its own definition. It is a little bit like listening to old mono recordings: the very crackling sounds that filter and disturb the pure reproduction of the human voice generate an effect of authenticity, the impression that we are listening to (what was once) a real person singing, while the very perfection of modern recordings, with their stereo and other effects, strangely de-realize what we hear. This is why the "enlightened" New Ager who implores us to fully realize or express our true Self cannot but appear as its opposite—as a mechanical, depthless subject blindly repeating his or her mantra.

To recapitulate: dialectical reversal is more complex than it may appear; at its most radical, it is not only the reversal of a predicate (the reason against

---

49 A brief note should be added here. The partisans of "discourse analysis" often rail against those who continue to emphasize the key structural role of the economic mode of production and its dynamics, raising the specter of "vulgar Marxism" (or, another popular catchword, "economic essentialism"): the insinuation is that such a view reduces language to a secondary factor, locating historical efficacy only in the "reality" of material production. There is, however, a symmetrical simplification which is no less "vulgar": that of proposing a direct parallel between language and production, i.e., of conceiving—in Paul de Man style—language itself as another mode of production, the "production of meaning." According to this approach, in parallel with the "reification" of productive labor in its result, the common-sense notion of speech as a mere expression of some pre-existing meaning also "reifies" meaning, ignoring how meaning is not only reflected in speech, but generated by it—it is the result of "signifying practice," as it was once fashionable to say. One should reject this approach as the worst example of non-dialectical *formalism*, involving a hypostasis of "production" into an abstract-universal notion encompassing economic and "symbolic" production as its two species, and neglecting their radically different status.

becomes the reason for), but the shift of the predicate itself into the position of the subject. This key feature of the Hegelian dialectic can be clarified by way of the well-known male-chauvinist notion of how, in contrast to man's firm self-identity, "the essence of woman is dispersed, elusive, displaced." The appropriate response here is to move from this claim that the essence of woman is forever dispersed to the more radical claim that *this dispersion or displacement as such is the "essence of femininity."* This is a shift which, once again, can be retold in terms of the Rabinovitch formula: "I have found the essence of femininity." "But one cannot find it, femininity is dispersed, displaced …" "Well, this dispersion *is* the essence of femininity …" One should again insist here on the irreducible character of this dialogical process: the fact that one cannot directly pass to the "essence of femininity," but must pass through the illusory assertion "I have found the essence of femininity" and its failure, is not only a necessity which affects our cognitive approach, but constitutes the Thing itself (the "essence of femininity"). And the "subject" is not just an example here, but the name for a formal structure: the subject "as such" is a subjectivized predicate; the subject is not only always already displaced, and so on, it *is* this displacement. What this means is, again, that the above-described dialogical structure is inscribed into the very being of subject: the subject aims at representing itself; this representation fails; the subject *is* this failure of its own representation.

The supreme case of this shift constitutive of the dimension of subjectivity is that of *supposition*. Lacan began with the notion of the analyst as the "subject supposed to know," which arises through transference (the analyst is the one supposed to know the meaning of the patient's symptoms). However, he soon realized that he was dealing with a more general structure of supposition, in which a figure of the Other is not only supposed to know, but can also believe, enjoy, cry, and laugh, or even *not* know for us (from Tibetan prayer mills to canned laughter). This structure of presupposition is not infinite: it is strictly limited, constrained by the four elements of the discourse. S_1—the subject supposed to believe; S_2—the subject supposed to know; *a*—the subject supposed to enjoy; and … what about $? Is it a "subject supposed to be a subject"? What would this mean? What if we read it as standing for the very structure of supposition: it is not only that the subject is supposed to have a quality, to do or undergo something (to know, to enjoy …)—*the subject itself is a supposition*, for the subject is never directly "given," as a positive substantial entity, we never directly encounter it, it is merely a flickering void "supposed" between the two signifiers. (We encounter here again the Hegelian passage from subject to predicate: from the subject supposed to … to the subject itself as a supposition.) That is to say, what, precisely, is a "subject"? Think of a proposition, a statement—how, when, does this statement become "subjectivized"? It becomes so when some reflexive feature inscribes into it the subjective attitude—in this precise sense, a signifier "represents the subject for another signifier." The subject is the absent X that has to be supposed in order to account for this reflexive twist, for this distortion. And Lacan pushes on here to the end: the subject is not only supposed by the external observer-listener of a signifying chain; it is *in itself a supposition*. The subject is inaccessible to itself as a Thing, in its noumenal identity, and, as such, it is forever haunted by itself as object: what are all *Doppelgänger* figures if not figures of myself as an object that haunts me? In other words, not only are others a supposition for me (I can only suppose their existence beneath the reflexive distortion of a signifying chain), *I myself am no less a supposition for myself*: something to be presumed (there must be an X that "I am," the "I or It or a Thing that thinks," as Kant put it) and never directly accessible. Hume's famous observation that, no matter how closely or deeply I look into myself, all I will find are specific ideas, particular mental states, perceptions, emotions, etc., never a "Self," misses the point: this non-accessibility of the subject to itself as an object is constitutive of being a "self."

One could even claim that, formally, this reversal from the subject supposed to … to the subject itself as a supposition *defines* subjectivity: substance appears in phenomena, while a subject is *nothing but* its own appearance. (And these formulae can be multiplied: the universal is *nothing but* the inadequacy, the non-identity, of the particular to/with itself; the essence is *nothing but* the inadequacy of the appearance to itself, and so on and so forth.) This does not mean that the subject is the stupid tautology of the Real ("things just are what they seem to be"), but, much more precisely, that the subject is *nothing but its own appearing, the appearing reflected-into-itself*[50]—a paradoxical torsion in which a Thing starts to function as a substitute *for itself*. As Robert Pfaller observes apropos this substitution:

> What is substituted can also appear itself, in a 1:1 scale, in the role of the substitute—there only must be some feature ensuring that it is not taken to be itself. Such a feature is provided for by the threshold which separates the place of what is substituting from what is being substituted—or symbolizes their detachment. Everything that appears in front of the threshold is then assumed to be the ersatz, as everything that lies behind it is taken to be what is being substituted.

50 This is why the Kantian transcendental I, its pure apperception, is a purely formal function which is neither noumenal nor phenomenal—it is empty, no phenomenal intuition corresponds to it, since, if it were to appear to itself, its self-appearance would be the "Thing itself," i.e., the direct self-transparency of a noumenon. The parallel between the void of the transcendental subject ($) and the void of the transcendental object, the inaccessible X that causes our perceptions, is misleading here: the transcendental object is the void *beyond* phenomenal appearances, while the transcendental subject *already appears as a void*.

> There are scores of examples of such concealments that are obtained not by miniaturization but only by means of clever localization. As Freud observed, the very acts that are forbidden by religion are practiced in the name of religion. In such cases—as, for instance, murder in the name of religion—religion also can do entirely without miniaturization. Those adamantly militant advocates of human life, for example, who oppose abortion, will not stop short of actually murdering clinic personnel. Radical right-wing opponents of male homosexuality in the USA act in a similar way. They organize so-called "gay bashings" in the course of which they beat up and finally rape gays. The ultimate homicidal or homosexual gratification of drives can therefore also be attained, if it only fulfils the condition of evoking the semblance of a counter-measure. What seems to be "opposition" then has the effect that the x to be fended off can appear itself and be taken for a non-x.[51]

What we encounter here yet again is the Hegelian "oppositional determination": in the figure of the gay-basher raping a gay man, the gay encounters himself in his oppositional determination; that is, tautology (self-identity) appears as the highest contradiction.[52] In other words, the structure is again that of the Möbius band: if we progress far enough on one side, we reach our starting point again (a gay sex act), but on the other side of the band. Lewis Carroll was therefore right: a country *can* serve as its own map insofar as the model or map is the thing itself in its oppositional determination, that is, insofar as an invisible screen ensures that the thing is not taken to be itself. In this precise sense, the "primordial" difference is not between things themselves, also not between things and their signs, but between the thing and the void of an invisible screen which distorts our perception of the thing so that we do not take the thing for itself. The movement from things to their signs is not that of a replacement of the thing by its sign, but that of the thing itself becoming the sign of—not another thing, but—*itself*, the void at its very core.[53]

This paradox brings us to the relationship between man and Christ: the tautology "man is man" is to be read as a Hegelian infinite judgment, as the encounter of "man" with its oppositional determination, with its counterpart on

51 Robert Pfaller, "The Potential of Thresholds to Obstruct and to Facilitate: On the Operation of Displacement in Obsessional Neurosis and Perversion" (unpublished paper, 2002).

52 In a homologous way, the very excess of ecological catastrophism (the end of the world is nigh, etc.) functions as a defense, a way to obfuscate the true dangers. This is why the only appropriate reply to an ecologist trying to convince us of the impending threat is to suggest that the true target of his desperate argument is *his own* non-belief—in other words, our answer should be something like "Don't worry, the catastrophe is sure to come!"

53 For a more detailed account of this structure, see my *The Puppet and the Dwarf*, Cambridge, MA: MIT Press 2003.

the other side of the Möbius band. In the same way that, already in our everyday understanding, "the law is the law" means its opposite, the coincidence of law with arbitrary violence ("What can you do, even if it is unjust and arbitrary, the law is the law, you have to obey it!"), "man is man" signals the non-coincidence of man with man, the properly *inhuman* excess which disturbs its self-identity—and what, ultimately, is Christ but the name of this excess inherent to man, man's extimate kernel, the monstrous surplus which, following the unfortunate Pontius Pilatus, one of the few ethical heroes of the Bible (the other being Judas, of course), can only be designated as "*ecce homo*"?

Beyond intersubjectivity

What is the status of this in-human excess? In his attempt to describe the genesis of our search for meaning, Wolfram Hogrebe claims that the subject's relation to objectivity has to be grounded in intersubjectivity: "without a dark You [*das dunkle Du*], we do not have a chance to begin developing objective relations with things."[54] "Objectivity" can only arise as the notion of an X that remains the same under different subjective perspectives or descriptions—it is the *result* of such abstraction from subjective standpoints. What precedes it is the "mantic" animist experience of reality as meaningful, full of unknown meaning. It is not that I begin with the encounter with objects around me, and then notice how some of these objects have an inner life like me, so transfer onto them my inner life; on the contrary, the transference comes first, objectivization comes after.

Against this background, Hogrebe interprets popular-culture figures like vampires, zombies, aliens, and replicants as uncanny figures of intelligent beings deprived of emotions and of a horizon of meaning, lacking the searching-for-meaning attitude, properly "world-less" beings. As Markus Gabriel points out, there is a shift here from Romanticism, in which uncanny monstrous doubles stand for the "inhuman" abyss of the subject itself, to our own time in which replicants, etc., stand for worldless "thinking machines."[55] But is there not an ambiguity present also in today's replicants or robots, from "terminators" onwards? Are they not, beneath the appearance of desubjectivized "thinking machines," figures of the subject in its pure in-human state? Is not the alien or terminator today's image of the "dark I" beyond human empathy?

---

54 Wolfram Hogrebe, *Die Wirklichkeit des Denkens*, Heidelberg: Universitätsverlag Winter 2007, p. 13.

55 Markus Gabriel, "The Mythological Being of Reflection," in Markus Gabriel and Slavoj Žižek, eds., *Mythology, Madness, and Laughter: Subjectivity in German Idealism*, London: Continuum 2009.

One of the strategies for taming this "dark I" is a kiss. Sándor Márai's *Embers* ends with a definition of the kiss as "an answer, a clumsy but tender answer to a question that eludes the power of language."[56] This short definition effectively circumscribes the key dimension of a kiss: crucially, it is given by the mouth, the very organ of speech (and, in a full erotic kiss, also contacts the other's mouth), depriving it of its ability to talk, shutting it off. As such, the kiss is an answer to the "question that eludes the power of language," which is nothing other than what Lacan calls "*Che vuoi?*" (What do you want?), the question which concerns the abyss of the Other's desire, the abyss opened up by speech but for which every word fails. A kiss is a clumsy and desperate measure to pacify this abyss by way of closing off its source through a direct intervention into the bodily Real: "Shut up! Let my closeness to you close the gap which threatens to ruin our relationship!" This is the truth in the cliché about prostitutes who allow their customers to penetrate them but not to kiss them on the mouth—a signal that they do not want to surrender the abyss of their subjectivity to the closeness of a stranger.

Is the traumatic encounter with the "divine"—in the guise of a meaningless (or pre-meaning) Absolute which triggers, as a reaction, the search for meaning—effectively the primordial fact? Psychoanalysis provides a key insight here. Let us approach it through *The Perplexity of Hariya Hercules*, an extraordinary short novel by Manohar Shyam Joshi, and one of the classics of twentieth-century Indian literature.[57] Set in Delhi around 1960, the novel tells the story of Harihar Datt Twari (mockingly known as Hariya Hercules after the name of his bicycle, which contrasts with Hariya's utterly non-heroic nature), an infinitely patient, unmarried, middle-aged man who spends all his time attending to his blind, infirm, and chronically constipated old father, who was once a pillar of society. Hariya's care for his father includes regularly cleansing his rectum to clean out the dried excrement. One day, while visiting a relative, Hariya hears that there is a town called Goomalling in Australia; he hallucinates that his own double lives there. The word "Goomalling," a signifier of father's desire, thus disturbs Hariya's inner peace and triggers his perplexity, not only about his father but about all things sexual. Having up to now simply ignored sexuality, he becomes intrigued by how and why the sexual act brings pleasure, and tries to learn from his older female relatives all about it. When his father dies soon afterwards, Hariya inherits one of his most precious possessions, a trunk containing jewelry, pornographic pictures of group sex acts in which his father participated, and a letter from a Tibetan lama. The letter describes the curse brought by the father upon a Twari family when, in the mythic Himalayan town of Goomalling

56 Sándor Márai, *Embers*, London: Penguin Books 2003, p. 249.

57 Manohar Shyam Joshi, *The Perplexity of Hariya Hercules*, New Delhi: Penguin Books 2009.

(the same name as the real Australian town!), he stole the trunk that belonged to the terrible deity of Goomalling. As a dutiful son, Hariya goes looking for Goomalling to return the trunk to the deity. After he mysteriously vanishes, members of his community back in Delhi compose a multitude of stories, some describing him as a self-sacrificing saint, others as a victim of manipulation and robbery. In spite (or, rather, because) of all the disgusting details, this novel is one of the most beautiful and touching stories about the rise of desire out of an encounter with what Jean Laplanche would have called an "enigmatic signifier," a signifier which condenses the mystery of the Other's desire. As we know from Freud and Lacan, the father is not simply a bearer of prohibition—the price he has to pay for occupying this place is that he himself gets prohibited, and what triggers Hariya's desire is this dark, prohibited side of the father. Furthermore, a similar self-reflexive reversal of subject into object affects Hariya himself: after he becomes perplexed by the mystery, he himself turns into an object of mystery, for his disappearance triggers a multitude of inconsistent narratives concerning his fate.

However, from a strict materialist standpoint, Laplanche's notion of the "enigmatic signifier" should be critically supplemented: it is not a primordial fact, an "original trauma" which sets the human animal on the path of subjectivization; it is, rather, a secondary phenomenon, a reaction to the primordial fact of the over-proximity of the other, of his or her intrusive presence or bodily-material too-much-ness. It is this intrusive presence which is then interpreted as an "enigma," as an obscure "message" from the other who "wants something" from me. In this sense, the "Neighbor" refers not primarily to the abyss of the Other's desire, the enigma of "*Che vuoi?*" of "What do you really want from me?" but to an intruder who is always and by definition too near. This is why for Hitler the Jew was a neighbor: no matter how far away the Jews were, they were always too close; no matter how many were killed, the remnants were always too strong.[58] As usual, Chesterton made this point with utmost clarity: "The Bible tells us to love our neighbors, and also to love our enemies; probably because they are generally the same people."

There is a problem to be clarified here: no matter how intrusively one touches a dog or a cat, the intrusion will never be interpreted by it as an "enigmatic signifier"; which means that something, some radical change, must have already happened in a living being for it to experience something as an intrusion. It seems obvious that a violation is always a violation with regard to some presupposed norm. Should one then say that, in order for something to be experienced by the body as intrusion, a kind of primordial Ego already has to be constituted, implying a line of division between the Inside and the Outside? Is it then the

58 I owe this idea to Alenka Zupančič.

homeostasis of the primordial Ego which is disturbed, derailed, by the intrusion of the (death) drive, so that the opposition between Ego and drive is the opposition between Life and Death? Which norm is violated in too-muchness? The properly Freudian materialist solution would be to turn this relationship around and to posit the paradox of an original excess, an excess "in itself" rather than in relation to a presupposed norm. The Freudian drive is just such an excess-in-itself: there is no "normal" drive. The formation of the Ego with its borderline between Inside (Ego) and Outside (non-Ego) is already a defense-formation, a reaction against the excess of the drive. In short, it is not the excess of the drive which violates the "norm" of the Ego, it is the "norm" (proper measure) itself which is a defense against the excess of the drive.

It is for this reason that intersubjectivity is not a primordial or "natural" state of human being. To find traces of a dimension "beyond intersubjectivity" in Hegel, one should look for them in the very place which is the central reference for the partisans of recognition: the famous chapter on servitude and domination from the *Phenomenology*. Malabou has noted perceptively that, in spite of the precise logical deduction of the plurality of subjects out of the notion of life, there is an irreducible *scandal*, something traumatic and unexpected, in the encounter with *another* subject, that is, in the fact that the subject (a self-consciousness) encounters outside itself, in front of it, another living being in the world which also claims to be a subject (a self-consciousness).[59] As a subject, I am by definition alone, a singularity opposed to the entire world of things, a punctuality to which all the world appears, and no amount of phenomenological description of how I am always already "together-with" others can cover up the scandal of another such singularity existing in the world. In the guise of the living being in front of me who claims to be also a self-consciousness, infinity assumes a determinate form, and this coincidence of opposites (the infinity of self-relating consciousness is this particular living being) points towards the infinite judgment "the Spirit is a bone," which concludes the section on observing reason in the *Phenomenology*.

The source of this scandal is that self-consciousness breaks with the oscillation between attachment and detachment that characterizes the process of life: life is at the same time the life of the species which reproduces itself through the life and death of its members, and the life of each member. Each member's attachment is thus split, divided between an attachment to its own particular finite being and an attachment to its species (which means a detachment from its particular being). Once we enter Spirit proper, however, this dialectic of attachment and detachment which characterizes the life of a species radically changes: in the life of Spirit, a singularity interposes itself between the species and its

59 See Judith Butler and Catherine Malabou, *Sois mon corps: Une lecture contemporaine de la domination et de la servitude chez Hegel*, Paris: Bayard 2010.

individual members. This means that an individual can no longer be reduced to being a particular member of its species, subordinated to its higher universal interest: a spiritual individual ("self-consciousness") has the "infinite right" to universality, because his singular existence is not merely that of a member of the species—in it, the universality of the species becomes "for itself," assumes a determinate form. So when I encounter in front of me another self-consciousness, there is something in me (not simply my egotism, but something in the very notion of self-consciousness) which resists the reduction of both myself and the opposed self-consciousness to simple members of the human species: what makes the encounter shocking is that in it, *two universalities meet where there is room only for one.*[60]

In the original encounter, the Other is thus not simply another subject with whom I share the intersubjective space of recognition, but a traumatic Thing. This is why this excess cannot be properly counted: subjects are never 1 + 1 + 1..., there is always an objectal excess which adds itself to the series. We find an echo of this excess in those science-fiction or horror stories where strange things start to happen (murders, as a rule) among a group of people in an isolated place (a small island or spaceship, say) and everything points to something else being present—not another human, all of whom can be counted without ever grasping the excess, but an alien monster which is less than One but more than zero. (The psychoanalytic treatment recreates this scene: the analyst is not another subject, there is no face to face, s/he is an object which adds itself to the patient.) This excessive spectral object is, of course, a stand-in for the subject, the subject itself as object, the subject's impossible-real objectal counterpart.

60 The rather boring criticism of Hegel's starting point in the dialectic of servitude and domination (the struggle to the death between the future master and the future servant) is that Hegel cheats by silently ignoring the obvious radical solution: the two of them really fight to the death, i.e., until one of them is actually killed—the "critical" point being that since this result would have brought the dialectical process to a halt, the Hegelian struggle to death is not really fought without restraint, but presupposes a certain implicit symbolic pact that the result will not be death. But here, one cannot cheat and pretend to fight to the death knowing that nobody will die: the (future) master's readiness to die must be fully actual. The only solution is to accept that many struggles do end in death and deadlock, so that, in order for the historical process to be set in motion by the proper dialectic of servitude and domination, many individuals had to die a meaningless death which amounted to a pure expenditure, lost without trace in the dark past of (pre)history, as so many nameless skulls strewn across the long road of history, to paraphrase Hegel.

Drive versus Will

The Freudian name for this excessive attachment to the objectal excess is the drive, which brings us to the key question: can Hegel think the drive? Hegel comes close to the Freudian drive in his elaboration of the notion of Force (towards the end of the chapter on Consciousness in the *Phenomenology*).[61] The dialectic of the (substantial) Thing and its properties dissolves into the "unconditioned universal" beneath the flow of phenomena; this universal gives a positive form to the void at the heart of every Thing, the void that accounts for the One-ness of the Thing and that can only be accounted for by the Thing's name. "In itself," this void is already the subject, the universal dimension of subjectivity; however, it "is still an *object* of consciousness," "the result has to be given an objective significance *for consciousness.*" Consciousness does not yet know that there is nothing behind the veil of appearances—nothing but what consciousness itself puts there. This feature captures the acephalous character of the drive: it is not "mine," the subject's, it is the very core of my being insisting "out there," as a partial object which is not me. This remaining split between consciousness and objective being has to be reflected into the object itself; it appears there in the guise of the distinction between form and content: the form of universality and its content, multiple particular "independent" elements. The two moments of this distinction, of course, are not fixed opposites, but are caught in an endless process of passing-into-each-other, in an oscillation typical of "spurious infinity":

> the "matters" posited as independent directly pass over into their unity, and their unity directly unfolds its diversity, and this once again reduces itself to unity. But this movement is what is called *Force*. One of its moments, the dispersal of the independent "matters" in their [immediate] being, is the *expression* of Force; but Force, taken as that in which they have disappeared, is *Force proper*, Force which has been driven back into itself from its expression. First, however, the Force which is driven back into itself *must* express itself; and, secondly, it is still Force remaining within itself, just as much as it is expression in this self-containedness.[62]

Does this being "driven back into itself" of the Force already point towards the Freudo-Lacanian drive? Is the drive a Force in its being-driven-back-into-itself? Does the rhythm of Force point towards the repetitive movement of the drive? Hegel's Force is driven back into itself as the very power of annihilating the appearances in which it expresses itself; it is not yet the potentiality of virtual Power which retains its authority only as virtual, as the threat of its actualization.

61 I owe this reference to Force to Benjamin Bliumis, NYU.

62 Hegel, *Phenomenology of Spirit*, p. 81.

More precisely, the drive is not Power, but also not Force. It is a Force thwarted in its goal, finding its aim in repeating the very failure to reach its goal. The drive does not express itself, it stumbles upon an external element or obstacle; it does not pass from one to another of its manifestations or expressions, it gets stuck on one of them. It is not driven back to itself through overcoming or annihilating its expressions, but through *not being able to do so*.

The drive has nothing whatsoever to do with psychology: the death drive (and the drive as such is the death drive) is not a psychic (or biological) striving for death and destruction—as Lacan emphasizes repeatedly, the death drive is an ontological concept, and it is this properly ontological dimension of the death drive which is so difficult to think. Freud defined *Trieb* (drive) as a limit-concept situated between biology and psychology, or nature and culture—a natural force known only through its psychic representatives. But we should take a step further here and read Freud more radically: the drive is natural, but the natural thrown out of joint, distorted or deformed by culture; it is culture in its natural state. This is why the drive is a kind of imaginary focus, or meeting place, between psychoanalysis and cognitive brain sciences: the paradox of the self-propelling loop on which the entire Freudian edifice is based and which the brain sciences approach in metaphoric formulations, without being able to define it precisely. Due to this in-between status, the insistence of the drive is "immortal," an "undead" striving that insists beyond life and death. In the classic German poem about two naughty children, Wilhelm Busch's "Max und Moritz" (first published in 1865), the children continually act in a disgraceful way towards respected authorities, until finally they both fall into a wheat mill and come out cut up into tiny grains. But when the grains fall on the floor, they form into the shapes of the two boys:

Rickeracke! Rickeracke!
Geht die Mühle mit Geknacke.
Hier kann man sie noch erblicken,
Fein geschroten und in Stücken.

In the original illustration, the shapes are sneering obscenely, insisting in their evil even after death ... (Adorno was right when he wrote that when one encounters a truly evil person, it is difficult to imagine that this person can ever die.) The formula of the drive is thus the same as Kant's formula of duty, "Du kannst, denn du sollst!" (You can, because you must!)—a deeply ambiguous formula that can be read in two ways which may appear to overlap, but are in fact very different: (1) no matter how hard or impossible the task appears, you simply *have* to do it!; (2) since you should do it, although you really cannot, you are forever condemned to feel guilty for not having done it. The first version is the formula of the unconditional drive which insists beyond life and death; the second is its superego perversion.

This obstinacy can also be embodied in a particular organ, like a fist or the feet, as in Hans Christian Andersen's "Red Shoes," the story of Karen, a poor little girl adopted by a rich old lady after her mother's death. Growing up vain, she buys a pair of red shoes and wears them to church, where she pays no attention to the service. When her adoptive mother becomes ill, Karen deserts her, preferring to attend a party in her red shoes. But once she begins dancing, she cannot stop—the shoes take over: she cannot control them, they are stuck to her feet and continue to dance, through fields and meadows, come rain or shine, night and day. She cannot even attend her adoptive mother's funeral. An angel appears to her, condemning her to dance until she grows cold and pale, as a warning to vain children everywhere. Karen then asks the executioner to chop off her feet. He does so and gives her a pair of wooden feet and crutches. Thinking that she has suffered enough for the red shoes, Karen decides to go to church, but the chopped-off feet still wearing the red shoes dance before her, barring the way. The following Sunday she tries again, thinking herself at least as good as the others in church, but again the dancing shoes bar the way. Karen then goes to do service in the parsonage, and when Sunday comes she dares not go to church. As she sits alone at home and prays to God, it is as though the church comes home to her and her heart becomes so filled with peace and joy that it bursts. She dies, and her soul flies on rays of sunlight to heaven, where no one asks her about the red shoes.[63]

In his film *The Red Shoes*, Michael Powell transposed Andersen's fairy tale into a modern ballet-company setting, but with a strange twist: the dancing shoes bring death to the heroine (called Vicky) not because they enact her fidelity to her vocation, but because they push her towards the suicidal act of sabotaging her return to a dancing career. Towards the film's end, Vicky is torn between the charismatic-demoniac Lermontov, the director of the ballet company, and Julian, a young composer for whom she gave up her career. Lermontov convinces her to return to the company to dance in a revival of *The Red Shoes*, Julian's ballet based on Andersen's fairy tale. On the opening night, as she is preparing to perform, Julian appears in her dressing room to take her back with him. Lermontov arrives, and he and Julian contend for Vicky's soul. Torn between her love for Julian and

63 Andersen himself located the origins of the story in an incident he witnessed as a small child—in a wonderful example of the self-destructive, uncompromising stance: His father was sent a piece of red silk by a rich customer, to make a pair of dancing slippers for her daughter. Using red leather along with the silk, the father worked very carefully on the shoes, only to have the rich lady tell him they were inadequate. She said he had done nothing but spoil her silk. "In that case," he said, "I may as well spoil my leather too," and cut up the shoes in front of her.

her need to dance, she cannot decide what to do. Julian, realizing that he has lost her, leaves for the railway station, while Lermontov consoles Vicky: "Sorrow will pass, believe me. Life is so unimportant. And from now onwards, you will dance like nobody ever before." However, while being escorted to the stage by her dresser, and wearing the red shoes, Vicky is suddenly seized by an irresistible impulse and runs out of the theater. Julian, on the platform at the train station, sees her and runs helplessly towards her. Vicky jumps from a balcony and falls in front of an approaching train. While lying on a stretcher, bloody and battered, Vicky asks Julian to remove the red shoes. Shaken by Vicky's death and broken in spirit, Lermontov appears before the audience to announce that "Miss Page is unable to dance tonight, nor indeed any other night." Nevertheless, the company performs *The Red Shoes* with a spotlight on the empty space where Vicky would have been.

This ending is deeply ambiguous with regard to the role of the shoes: did Vicky run out of the theater to join Julian *against* (the will of) the red shoes, and the shoes merely sabotaged the reunion of lovers by causing her deadly fall, or did the shoes also lead her to run away? The key to this ambiguity is provided by the difference between the drive and the Will: it is not that "drive" suggests an unfocused pressure or impulse, while "will" implies concentration and domination; for Freud, the "drive" is no less focused than the "will," it always has an object, the X onto which it is stuck and to which it repetitively returns, around which it circulates. The "drive" is in many ways almost a photographic negative of the "will": it is the push to eject its object, to lose it, to introduce a gap, not to overcome it. Thus, we could even say that the will is a counter-movement to the drive, an attempt to re-inscribe the "asubjectal" drive into the economy of the Ego as the agency of control and domination.

In the standard description of the circular process of alienation and re-appropriation, the subject loses itself in its otherness in order to re-appropriate its alienated substantial content; the drive is, at its most fundamental, this gesture of loss itself, not as externally imposed, but as "willed" by the subject. In every heroic narrative of recuperation, there is a moment of loss or betrayal which enables the later redemption: Adam and Eve had to fall in order for Christ to redeem us; Judas had to betray Christ in order for Christ to fulfill his mission, and so on. There is a perverse core that we always stumble upon in these narratives: was the Fall not a *felix culpa*? Did not God play a perverse game with humans, provoking the Fall so that he would then be able to display his mercy and love for fallen humanity? Was not Christ's betrayal by Judas a key moment that enabled humanity's redemption through Christ's crucifixion, that is, an act that *had* to happen and that was clearly, if ambiguously, willed by Christ? This negative act is the manifestation of the drive at its purest.

This, perhaps, is what Nietzsche had in mind when he insisted that the Will was unconditional, a matter of willing it all (the idea underlying the Eternal Return of the Same): we should also will, fully assume as what we wanted, the dirty work that we prefer to leave to others in order to enjoy the result while hypocritically condemning the way it was obtained. The pure Will to Will means that Christ willed Judas to betray him, that God willed Adam and Eve to fall. On the other hand, we should also avoid the perverse temptation of willing the Fall in order to cast oneself as the Savior, like the nanny from Patricia Highsmith's very first short story "The Heroine," who sets the house on fire in order to be able to save the children from death and thus earn the love and respect of their parents. There lies the thin line that separates the drive from perversion: in the drive proper, the loss is willed as such, in itself, not on account of its instrumentalization.

One could thus venture the hypothesis that, if desire is as such, in its innermost essence, hysterical—that is, marked by the hysterical "this is not that"—then the drive is as such (almost) perverse. This is where Lacan's reading of Antigone as exemplifying the ethics of desire ("do not give way on your desire") should be corrected. In his *écrit* "Subversion of the Subject and Dialectics of Desire," Lacan proposes $-D as the formula of the drive: instead of moving beyond demand to its gaps, to what is "in demand more than demand," the drive insists on the literality of the demand—which is exactly what Antigone does: her unconditional demand is for the proper symbolic burial of her brother, and she insists on it up to *pereat mundus*. Whatever she is, she is not hysterical: she wants what she wants *literally*. As such, her act is beyond the opposition between consciousness and the unconscious, and also beyond any figure of the big Other, inclusive of the eternal unwritten Laws—it is an act of abyssal freedom and, as such, *political*. Lacan proposes as the true formula of atheism "God is unconscious": "God could be unconscious. The hypothesis of the unconsciousness of God reflects the hypothesis that knowledge is not gifted with reflexivity of consciousness."[64] How, precisely, are we to grasp this ambiguous formula? Is it that God is *our* unconscious (unconscious *for us*, operating as our "unknown knowns," as the "unconscious prejudices" or magical beliefs which determine our activity), or is it that God in himself "has" an unconscious, that his activity and knowledge are not transparent to himself? Does not the tradition from Boehme to Schelling point in this second, more radical, direction? Insofar as *deus sive natura*, the encompassing universe of reality, is "unconscious," and insofar as the Freudian unconscious belongs to the pre-ontological level, this leads us to the conclusion that reality is in itself not fully ontologically constituted, non-All.[65] Furthermore, should we not read the thesis "God is the unconscious"

64 Balmès, *Dieu, le sexe et la vérité*, p. 53.

65 As Lacan points out in his *Four Fundamental Concepts of Psycho-Analysis* (New York: W. W. Norton & Company 1998). See also Schelling's transposition of the distinction

together with the thesis "the unconscious is politics"? "I am not even saying 'politics is the unconscious,' but only 'the unconscious is politics.'"[66] The difference is crucial here. In the first case, the unconscious is elevated into the "big Other" which exists: it is posited as a substance which really dominates and regulates political activity, in the sense of "the true mobilizers of our political activity are not ideology or interests, but unconscious libidinal motivations." In the second case, the big Other itself loses its substantial character, it is no longer "*the* Unconscious," it changes into a fragile inconsistent field overdetermined by political struggles.

The unconscious of self-consciousness

It is along these lines that we can discern the contours of the theologico-political in Lacan: the political nature of the unconscious means that it is not an underlying deeper force secretly governing what appear as contingencies, expressing itself through them: contingencies are irreducible, primary, they really are contingencies, and the unconscious is strictly parasitic, opportunistically exploiting unexpected contingencies to deliver its message. Freud is here radically opposed to that Jungian New Age obscurantism for which, precisely, "there are no accidents," and everything has a deeper meaning—therein resides the difference between idealism and materialism (and, unexpectedly, Hegel is here on the side of materialism: for him, speculative meaning articulates itself by way of exploiting the contingent ambiguities or double meanings of our ordinary language). This is why the Lacanian "de-centered subject" does *not* imply the kind of de-centering usually associated with psychoanalysis: "there is something in me more than myself, some foreign power which runs the show, so that I am not responsible for my acts …" If anything, Lacan insists on the subject's total responsibility: I am responsible even for acts and decisions of which I am not aware.

Apropos the fear that the brain sciences will eventually demonstrate that humans are in reality merely neuro-biological mechanisms, that there is "nobody home" beneath the surface of our phenomenal (self-)experience, one should fully accept this fear and avoid the primordial idealist lure which tempts

---

between Existence (ontologically fully-constituted reality) and the dark spectral pre-ontological Ground of Existence into God himself, so that we must distinguish God's existence from his chaotic pre-ontological "nature." The whole of late Schelling could be condensed into this reversal of *deus sive natura*: where Spinoza sees identity, synonymity, "God *or* nature," Schelling sees irreducible tension and struggle.

66 Lacan, seminar of May 10, 1967, in *Le séminaire, Livre XIV: La logique du fantasme* (unpublished).

us to substantialize our consciousness in some determinate component of reality (the temptation to which David Chalmers succumbed in an exemplary way). There effectively is nothing "beneath" or "behind," since consciousness is entirely phenomenal: the moment one brackets the phenomenal level of (self-) awareness and limits oneself to "reality," consciousness by definition disappears. It is as if one were to take a close look at a rainbow in order to locate some mysterious X in reality that corresponds to "rainbow in itself." Consciousness thus confronts us with the hard task of grasping the effectiveness, the (quasi-) causal power, of the appearance as such—and the Freudian unconscious should also be understood along these lines: not as a substance behind the appearances of consciousness, but as itself a mode of appearing. In other words, the term "unconscious" must be understood in terms of the Kantian infinite judgment rather than negative judgment: it is not that what it designates "is not conscious," it is rather that what it designates "is unconscious." This is what differentiates the Freudian unconscious from the neuronal unconscious of the material processes going on in our brain when we think: the neuronal unconscious is merely not conscious, while the Freudian unconscious is like the "undead," it is inherent to the psyche.

Here the Freudian hypothesis of the unconscious confronts us with the limits of any torture or truth serum procedure designed to extract from the subject his true position, "what he really thinks." A truth serum may get results if there is an ultimate truth the subject is trying to conceal—it may work if we are dealing with facts the subject knows and is trying to hide—but what if the subject is radically *divided*? For example, what if I pretend to believe in God, while sincerely thinking that there is no God, but this sincere conviction of mine is itself mistaken, and the truth lies in the external rituals I follow? In other words, what if I believe more than I believe I believe? Or, what if, while loving a person, I hate loving her—what would the truth serum make me say?

We can see from this last example that the division of the subject is not to be taken as a simple separation into two parts where "the right hand does not know what the left hand is doing." The division rather relies on a kind of reflexivity: when I hate to love someone, my love is reflexively mediated by hatred. Pippin indicates this reflexivity when he provides a concise definition of what Hegel means by "spiritual" being, that is, of how the subject is a "spiritual" entity: "The subject 'taking itself' to be a certain way is the 'object' to be such a way."[67] Spirit means that a human being, in its specific being-human, ultimately is what it "takes itself to be." The key problem, of course, is how, exactly, we are to understand this "taking oneself." Perhaps Pippin all too quickly reduces it to a "normative" dimension: "taking myself to be a father" means that a behavior

67 Robert Pippin, *Hegel's Practical Philosophy*, Cambridge: Cambridge University Press 2008, p. 51.

which follows certain norms (taking care of and educating my children, etc.) is expected of me. But is it not more appropriate to conceive this "taking as" as the act of assuming a certain symbolic identity (or title) conferred upon me, as the "symbolic registration" of my identity? A "father" is someone who takes himself (and is taken by others) as a father; normative demands or expectations are here secondary: even if I do not meet or follow them, I am still a father, just a "bad father," one who fails to act the way his title obliges him to act. In other words, for the normative dimension to be operative, the "big Other"—the scene of symbolic inscriptions and actions different from my immediate physical or psychic identity—already has to be in place, and for Lacan, it is this reflexive "giving account," the inscription of what a subject does in the symbolic texture, which is the proper locus of the unconscious.

There is thus a reflexivity inscribed into the very heart of psychoanalysis. What Pippin fails to take into account is how the Freudian unconscious is not raw stuff to be "mediated," reflexively appropriated, by the subject, but the very site of this reflective inscription. No wonder, then, that in his critical remarks on psychoanalysis Pippin reduces it to yet another mode of the "substantial" determination of the subject which misses the Kantian-Hegelian dimension of reflexivity that sustains the subject's autonomy and self-responsibility: as a subject, I cannot refer to the unconscious that determines me as a direct motivation—if unconscious motives effectively determine me *as an autonomous subject*, I should be the one who freely endorses the force of such motifs, who *accepts* them as motives—in short, every reference to the irresistible force of such motives has to involve a minimum of what Sartre called *mauvaise foi*. What if, however, it is Pippin himself who misses a crucial homology between the reflexivity inscribed into the very heart of Kantian-Hegelian subjectivity and the "reflexivity" of desire elaborated in detail by Lacan? What we have in mind here with regard to Kant is the so-called "incorporation thesis," the inextricable normativity of even the most elementary perceptions: even when I merely state the obvious, making the most basic statement of fact, "a table is there in front of me," I am not purely passive, I also *declare* a fact, I reflectively signal that I *uphold* this statement. This, however, is exactly what Lacan has in mind when he insists that, in every statement, the subject's position of enunciation is inscribed: when I state: "I wear stone-washed jeans," my statement always also renders how I relate to this fact (I want to appear as having a down-to-earth attitude, or following a fashion …). This inherent reflexive moment of "declaration" (the fact that every communication of a content always simultaneously "declares itself" as such) is what Heidegger designated as the "as such" that specifies the properly human dimension: an animal perceives a stone, but it does not perceive this stone "as such." This is the "reflexivity" of the signifier: every utterance not only transmits some content, but, simultaneously, renders how the subject relates to this content (in the terms of German Idealism, every consciousness is always already self-consciousness).[68]

Pippin is sympathetic to Manfred Frank's rejection of "neostructuralism" as unable to account for subjectivity or meaning, but critical of Frank's version of pre-reflexive self-acquaintance as a crucial dimension of subjectivity. Pippin sees this dimension in Kantian-Hegelian reflexivity/autonomy/self-responsibility, but what he fails to see is how this Kantian reflexivity opens up a space for the Lacanian subject of the unconscious.[69] The Freudian "unconscious" is inscribed into this very reflexivity; take, for example, someone I "love to hate," such as a villain in a Hitchcock film: consciously, I just hate his guts, yet unconsciously I (do not love him, but) love to hate him; that is, what is unconscious here is the way I reflexively relate to my conscious attitude. (Or take the opposite case of someone I "hate to love"—like the hero in a film noir who cannot help loving the evil *femme fatale* but hates himself for loving her.) This is what Lacan means when he says that man's desire is always a desire to desire: in an exact formal replica of Kantian reflexivity, I never simply and directly desire an object, I always reflexively relate to this desire—I can desire to desire it, I can hate to desire it, I can be indifferent to this desire of mine, just tolerating it neutrally. The philosophical consequence of this reflexivity of desire is crucial: it tells us how the opposition between the conscious and the unconscious is related to the opposition between consciousness and self-consciousness: the unconscious is not some kind of pre-reflexive, pre-thetic, primitive substrate later elaborated upon by conscious reflexivity; quite the contrary, what is most radically "unconscious" in a subject is his self-consciousness itself, the way he reflexively relates to his conscious attitudes. The Freudian subject is thus identical to the Cartesian *cogito*, or, more precisely, to its later elaboration in Kantian-Hegelian self-consciousness.

During a recent multi-lingual public debate in Spain, Gianni Vattimo's remarks were by mistake translated back to him in English, to which he mockingly replied: "I don't need a translator to understand myself!" The Freudian *divided* subject is someone who, precisely, *does* need a translator to understand him or herself—which is exactly the role the psychoanalyst plays for them. There is a joke which tells us more about what Lacan means with regard to the "divided

68 This self-declaratory reflexivity is also discernible in regard to fame: people can be famous for this or that, but they can also be famous simply *for being famous*. Recall the phenomenon of Paris Hilton, an absolute nobody adored by the trashy media, who report on her every step. She is not famous for doing or being something special; the dialectical reversal in her case consists in the fact that the media report on her most banal behavior—jumping over a car in a crowded parking lot, eating a hamburger, shopping at a discount store—simply because she is a celebrity. Her ordinariness, vulgarity even, is directly transubstantiated into the feature of a celebrity.

69 See "On Not Being a Neo-Structuralist" in Pippin, *The Persistence of Subjectivity*, pp. 168–85.

subject" than pages and pages of theoretical elaboration (though, in order to understand what it tells us, of course we need pages and pages of theoretical elaboration ...): Two men, having had a drink or two, go to the theater, where they become thoroughly bored with the play. One of them feels an urgent need to urinate, so he tells his friend to mind his seat while he goes to find a toilet: "I think I saw one down the corridor outside." The man wanders down the corridor, but finds no WC; wandering ever further into the recesses of the theater, he walks through a door and sees a plant pot. After copiously urinating into it and returning to his seat, his friend says to him: "What a pity! You missed the best part. Some fellow just walked on stage and pissed in that plant pot!"[70] The subject necessarily misses its own act, it is never there to see its own appearance on the stage, its own intervention is the blind spot of its gaze.

What, then, divides the subject? Lacan's answer is simple and radical: its (symbolic) identity itself—prior to being divided between different psychic spheres, the subject is divided between the void of its *cogito* (the elusively punctual pure subject of enunciation) and the symbolic features which identify it in or for the big Other (the signifier which represents it for other signifiers). In Agnieszka Holland's *Europa, Europa*, the hero (a young German Jew who passes as an Aryan and fights in the Wehrmacht in Russia) asks a fellow soldier who had been an actor prior to the war: "Is it hard to play someone else?" The actor answers: "It's much easier than playing oneself." We encounter this otherness at its purest when we experience the other as a neighbor: as the impenetrable abyss beyond any symbolic identity. When a person I have known for a long time does something totally unexpected, disturbingly evil, so that I have to ask myself, "Did I really ever know him?" does he not effectively become "another person with the same name"?

One strategy for coping with this gap that separates me from my name is to add another (secret) name designed to capture the core of my being which eludes my public name. In a German film about high-school delinquency, a gang member says to his apprentice: "My name is Jack. But you can call me Jack." A nice play with tautology: in the closed gang universe, the norm is that one is only allowed to call the boss by his nickname: "My name is Jack, but you can call me Jacko!"—the pseudo-intimacy of this invitation to use the nickname implies an injunction to accept and participate in the relations of domination and servitude that characterize the gang universe. The permission to address the boss directly by his proper name is thus the highest privilege. Imagine God telling you, "My name is God, but you can call me God!"—something definitely much more frightening than "My name is God, but you can call me the Old One in the Sky."

70 I owe this joke to Simon Critchley, who used it in a (very) critical review of a book of mine.

INTERLUDE 4

Borrowing from the Future, Changing the Past

In his wonderful *Le plagiat par anticipation*, Pierre Bayard developed in detail the idea that writers can plagiarize not only works from the past, but also works from the future.[1] The accusation of plagiarism is grounded on a resemblance between two works which is so strong that it cannot be dismissed as a mere coincidence or a sharing of the same style—so when we have two works from different periods which very closely resemble each other, what is the key argument for taking this as a paradoxical case of the earlier work plagiarizing the not-yet existing work from its future, and not, as in the standard approach, treating the latter as plagiarizing the former? Bayard proposes the criterion of dissonance: if we can clearly establish that, in relation to the features shared by the two works, the later one contains these features in a more fully developed form, while the earlier one contains only undeveloped fragments which do not fit into the totality of the work, but appear to strike a dissonant tone (or if this work itself, as a whole, strikes a dissonant tone in its own cultural context), then we can assume with reasonable certainty that the earlier work is a plagiarism of the later one. Among other amusing references (like a passage from Voltaire's *Zadig* which clearly points forward to Sherlock Holmes's method of deduction), Bayard's great example is from a lesser-known novel by Guy de Maupassant which contains an uncannily "Proustian" passage on how a contingent encounter with an everyday object can trigger a multiplicity of half-forgotten memories about the past. This novel was written three decades before Proust began to publish his great cycle, and the passage is clearly "out of sync" with the rest of the novel, so it really is as if Maupassant plagiarized Proust—as if, in a weird rupture of the linear temporal continuum, a door into the future momentarily opened up, giving Maupassant a glimpse into what lay ahead in literature.

There is an uncanny moment of plagiarizing the future in Hitchcock's work. *Vertigo* contains an enigmatic episode in which Madeleine is seen by Scottie as she opens a window and then inexplicably disappears from the house. Does this scene not point forward to *Psycho*, to the appearance of the mother's silhouette in the window—in both cases, a body appears out

1 See Pierre Bayard, *Le plagiat par anticipation*, Paris: Éditions de Minuit 2009.

of nowhere and disappears back into the void? The fact that in *Vertigo* this episode remains unexplained tempts one to read it in a kind of *futur antérieur*, as already pointing towards *Psycho*: is not the old lady who is the hotel clerk of the house in *Vertigo* a kind of strange condensation of Norman Bates and his mother, the clerk (Norman) who is at the same time the old lady (mother), thus providing in advance a clue to their identity, which is the great mystery of the film?

The question which immediately arises here is, of course, how seriously we should take these claims. Surely not too seriously, since, in this case, we would have to embrace the New Age topic of synchronicity and mystical communion between spirits from different epochs, able to converse with each other in an eternal present. Nonetheless, the idea of a "plagiarism by anticipation" should not to be dismissed as a mere provocation; still less so does it imply any kind of a hidden teleology in which the present points towards a future determined in advance. On the contrary, this idea is profoundly anti-teleological and materialist—all that needs adding to it is the key concept of retroactivity. Italo Calvino's story "A Beautiful March Day" offers an idiosyncratic description of the conspiracy against Julius Caesar. Calvino focuses on the unintended consequences of the act of killing Caesar: while the conspirators' intention was to kill a tyrant and thereby restore Rome to its republican glory, their act effectively abolishes the very conditions which sustained its intended meaning. As Molly Rothenberg explains:

> The very world in which it made sense to get rid of Caesar also vanishes with those dagger strokes—not because Caesar held that world together, but because the assassins could not foresee that their act would also transform the way the act would be judged. They could not factor in the historicity of their action; neither they nor anyone else could predict or govern how the future would interpret the assassination. Put another way, we could say that there simply was no way for them to take into account the *retroversive* effect of future interpretations.[2]

Here we encounter the key feature of the symbolic: the fundamental "openness" it introduces into a closed order of reality. Once we enter the symbolic, things never simply are, they all "will have been," they as it were borrow (part of) their being from the future. Rothenberg employs a simple example of a tender statement: "Carl smiled as he gently stroked the velvety skin of his lover …," which continues with a supplement that brutally changes the meaning of the first part: "…with the keen edge of a steak knife." The cause of this irreducible "openness" of the symbolic is not its excessive complexity (we never know into what

2 Molly Anne Rothenberg, *The Excessive Subject: A New Theory of Social Change*, Cambridge: Polity Press 2010, p. 1.

decentered context our statement will be inscribed), but the much more refined, properly dialectical impossibility of taking into account the way our own intervention will transform the field. The speaking subject cannot take into account the way it is itself "counted" in the signifying series; with regard to its own inclusion, it is irreducibly split, redoubled.

How, then, to resolve this enigma without resorting to New Age obscurantism? The key is the properly dialectical notion of repetition through which things "become what they are." Maupassant becomes a plagiarist-in-advance of Proust, he becomes what he is (a Proustian *avant la lettre*), only *once Proust arrives*. In Hegelese, the shift is from In-itself to For-itself: through his repetition in Proust, Maupassant retroactively becomes Proustian. This means that we have to introduce a radical split between Maupassant's book as it is in itself and his book as it is when read retroactively, after Proust—i.e., the fact of Proust's text generates *another* Maupassant, the Proustian one. We are thus dealing with three (and not two) texts here: Maupassant's original novel, Proust's cycle of novels, and the Proustian Maupassant. But why talk like this, why not simply say that Proust influences our reading of Maupassant? Because such a retroactive reading does not simply add another dimension to how we receive Maupassant: rather, we need to grasp Maupassant's text as not-All, as open towards the future, as full of gaps and inconsistencies waiting to be filled in.

Bayard himself retreats here with regard to his own theory when, in an all too naïve way, he tries to outline the future Kafka was plagiarizing by anticipation. What should make us suspicious of his attempt is the image of Kafka's universe to which he refers—the boring standard image of Kafka as the precursor of twentieth-century "totalitarianism" (an oppressed individual exposed to the whims of arbitrary power, etc.). Invoking the even greater oppression of women described in Kafka's texts, Bayard engages in a ridiculously Politically Correct speculation that Kafka had plagiarized a future (not yet written) novel about an oppressed Muslim woman. This is Bayard at his worst, ignoring all the profound ambiguities concerning the role of women in Kafka's texts: they are not only servants, but also corrupted with lust, helping those in power to harass the hero. As Reinhard Stach demonstrated long ago, Kafka's image of women is deeply indebted to Otto Weininger, the ultimate anti-feminist (and anti-Semite). In outlining his ridiculous proposal, Bayard ignores his own basic rule: instead of looking for dissonances in Kafka's work, he simply extrapolates the contours of the future work from the standard clichés about Kafka. The great dissonances in Kafka's work are constituted by his animal stories (about dogs, and so forth), which clearly stand apart from the clichéd image of the hero caught up in a totalitarian machine. Among them, one should especially focus on the very last literary text he was writing while close to death, the story about the singing mouse Josephine—in this dissonant image of the role of the artist in a communist society, we find a woman of the future different from all the corrupted seductive heroines from Kafka's great novels.[3]

Another version of the same retroactive mechanism is at work in cases where a substantial decision, involving the rise of a new Master-Signifier which rearranges the agent's entire symbolic economy, is taken and then undone, like sending a letter which commits me to a new relationship and then, when I discover that the letter was lost in the post, reneging on the commitment. A case of undoing can be found in *Two Lovers* (James Gray, 2008), a film loosely based on Dostoyevsky's "White Nights," which takes place in the Russian Jewish part of the Brighton beach suburb of New York. The hero, Leonard, emotionally unstable, makes several unsuccessful suicide attempts (acts and then changes his mind). At the start of the film, he jumps into the water in an attempted suicide, then changes his mind and surfaces to be helped by a passer-by. He is split between two women. His parents set him up with Sandra, the daughter of their potential business partner, who is loving and caring, but conventional; the other woman is Michelle, his outrageously daring and unconventional new neighbor. When he learns that Michelle is dating Ronald, a married partner in her law firm, he tries to break all contact with her and becomes more deeply involved with Sandra. However, when a desperate Michelle calls him from the hospital where she is being treated for a miscarriage, they become attached again; disappointed with Ronald for not helping her enough in her distress, Michelle informs Leonard that she has broken off the relationship and is going to San Francisco. Deciding to go with her, Leonard buys two tickets online, purchases an engagement ring, and packs for his trip. At a party the next day, Sandra's father, believing that Leonard is planning to marry Sandra, offers him a partnership in the soon-to-be merged family businesses. Leonard ducks out to meet Michelle, who tells him that she is not going to San Francisco after all because Ronald has left his wife and will marry her. Distraught, Leonard goes to the beach to kill himself; however, as he steps in the ocean, he drops a glove that Sandra had bought for him earlier; picking it up, he returns to the party and gives Sandra the engagement ring he bought for Michelle.

The movie deals with the standard theme of the choice between a secure, emotionally stable marriage and a wild passionate bond destined to end in catastrophe. It is a choice between happiness and what Lacan calls *jouissance*,

3 With regard to Weininger, we should risk the hypothesis that his masterpiece *Sex and Character* is in a kind of *negative* dialogue with future, not directly borrowing from it but rather reacting furiously to the prospect of emancipated feminine subjectivity. Along similar lines, F. W. J. Schelling noted somewhere that the explosion of decadent Evil in Ancient Rome just before the rise of Christianity obeyed a deep necessity: it was as if, suspecting what lay ahead, it made a last vicious attempt to assert itself. The same holds for Weininger's negative plagiarism-by-anticipation: he attacks what has not yet arrived.

excessive enjoyment beyond the pleasure principle, with the underlying implication that, against the excess of *jouissance*, hedonism (the reign of pleasure) and law (in the narrower sense of public morality) are *on the same side*. To be able to put everything at risk and jump into the unknown waters of a passionate affair requires an act which may irreparably change the most basic coordinates of a subject's life. However, the true interest and originality of the plot lies elsewhere: in the precise temporality of the hero's decision and its retroactive cancellation. After making the fateful decision (the choice of Michelle) and thus apparently reaching the point of no return, Leonard learns that his decision has been rendered meaningless (Michelle is no longer available), and so undoes it. Since Sandra knows none of this, Leonard just acts as if nothing has happened, as if there was no decision, and even opportunistically gives her the ring meant for Michelle. The appearance of a smooth and seamless relationship with Sandra is restored.

To get at the core of this situation, we can imagine three different versions of the same plot, three what-ifs:

(1) What if, even after learning that Michelle will return to Ronald, Leonard were to stick to his decision and drop Sandra, in recognition of the authenticity of his love for Michelle? Perhaps, this would have been a true act?

(2) What if, after the decision is taken, Leonard is overcome with anxiety as he becomes fully aware of the consequences of his act? In a panic, he would then desperately search for a way out and find that he can undo the decision, retroactively erasing its traces. (The difference with the film plot is that, in this version, he undoes the act not because Michelle dropped him, but of his own accord.)

(3) Finally, what if, secretly knowing about Leonard's distress and his commitment to Michelle, Sandra helped him by feigning ignorance? Let us imagine that Leonard had written Sandra a letter informing her of his decision to leave with Michelle, but Sandra pretended that she missed the letter, thus giving him the chance to undo his "mad" decision with grace and without a scandal. Such an act of ignoring, of pretending not to know, is what is usually referred to as wisdom.

The circular relationship between the future and the past that we encounter here goes "all the way down," to the very emergence of the speaking subject out of the "human animal": in Lacan's account of this emergence, it sometimes appears that the primordial fact is the encounter with the symbolic order, the parasitic intrusion of the signifier which upsets the balance of the "human animal," introducing a gap into it, engendering a pathological excess of "undead" life over mere biological life; sometimes, it appears that it is, on the contrary, the derailment of life itself, the emergence of a traumatic excess of "more than life," which is the primordial fact, and the symbolic order's function is rather to "normalize" and tame this excess. The solution to this alternative is retroactive causality: the excess of life comes first, but it can be recognized as such only retroactively, once the symbolic order is already there; without this after-effect, the excess of life is merely a natural accident. On a first approach, it may appear that the first account is the "idealist" one (the signifying order intervenes into animal life from a mysterious outside, like a hand of God imparting spirit into bodies), while the second narrative is the "materialist" one (the disturbance of material-biological life comes first, the symbolic order arises as a secondary defense mechanism). However, the properly Hegelian (that is, dialectical-materialist) solution is more complex as it involves retroactivity. True, there is first an excess, a derailing, of the natural circuit of instincts; however, this derailment is confirmed as the foundation of being-human (as its inhuman core) only by its effect, by the rise of the symbolic order which endeavors to normalize it. Without the symbolic order, the excess remains an aberration of nature, a meaningless freakish accident. The search for this "pure" excess of life not yet contaminated/obfuscated by the symbolic order is thus a mythical search for a fantasmatic entity: it is not that such a search is condemned to failure—we may well succeed in isolating this excess; but there would be nothing "human" about it, it would be just a meaningless deformation.

We encounter here yet again the innermost paradox of the symbolic order, namely its retroactivity. The symbolic order is not a cause which intervenes from the outside, violently derailing the human animal and thus setting in motion its becoming-human; it is an effect, but a paradoxical effect which retroactively posits its presupposition, its own cause.[4] This temporal paradox holds even more strongly for the relationship between a literary text and real life: in his *Tomorrow is Written*, written before *Plagiarizing the Future*, Bayard prefigures the analyses of the later book, focusing on those literary texts in which the author seems to predict his own future, especially the mode of his death.[5] Here it is not a future text which is plagiarized, but reality itself which is (not plagiarized but) described before it has happened. (Note how, in Bayard's own case, the later book seems to precede the earlier one.) Apart from the obvious case of Oscar Wilde who, in his *The Picture of Dorian Gray*, displayed an uncanny awareness of the catastrophe which awaited him years later, the most interesting

4 And, incidentally, the same solution can be proposed to resolve the ambiguity of the relation between an Event and its nomination in Badiou's thought: the Event is not the same as its nomination, it is a Real to which nomination reacts, fixing it within the symbolic space; however, there is nonetheless no Event prior to its nomination, since only a nomination turns something which merely happened into an Event.

5 Pierre Bayard, *Demain est écrit*, Paris: Éditions de Minuit 2005.

example here is Jack London's *Martin Eden*, with its description of the writer's suicide by drowning—a weird case of an autobiography which stretches into the writer's future. An author usually writes his autobiography in old age, when his life has come full circle, recapitulating his trajectory from the perspective of maturity which allows him to see it in its totality, assigning each event to its proper place. The extraordinary thing about *Martin Eden* (a novel, but clearly an autobiographical one) is that Jack London wrote it in the middle of his life, at the height of his success and creative powers—at this point, instead of ending in the present, he did not stop but courageously went on, continuing his life story into the future, right up to its tragic end.[6]

Perhaps a little prematurely, Bayard opposes his approach to that of psychoanalysis, which sees the roots of the present narrative in the real of a past trauma which can only be described (and may even be constituted) *après coup*, retroactively. Here, by contrast, the trauma lies not in the past but in the future, from where it mysteriously casts its shadow over the present writing. In his conceptual elaborations which follow the analyses of literary cases, Bayard proposes two new grammatical-temporal categories in order to account for such strange occurrences: *the past to come* (in the future) and *the future which already happened* (in the past), that is, which belongs to the past.

What, then, changes in the passage from the Real of an accident to its inscription into a narrative as a part of the subject's Fate? The Real accident is purely contingent, while its symbolic inscription into a life narrative makes it not so much necessary as an expression of the subject's will. Even if the future is that of a terrifying catastrophe, the subject wills it in the sense of willingly accepting the coming catastrophe, of freely assuming its necessity.[7] Bayard is not a spiritual obscurantist: when he talks about "the future being already written," he is not invoking some kind of divine big Other able to see across time into the past as well as the future; on the contrary, he emphasizes human finitude and contingency, which means that the gap between the symbolic (narrative) and the Real is irreducible—the future that has a retroactive causality on the present can also *not* happen, due to some totally unforeseen contingency:

> What then happens with the events—and which is the world that is sufficiently generous to gather them?—for which the writing shows that they should have been produced, but which were in the last moment stopped in their path towards realization? The life of Kafka, the very symbol of the precursor, bears witness to how an entire human existence can be organized in such a way that it points towards an event which should take place, but is finally thwarted.[8]

6 Ibid., pp. 123–4.
7 Ibid., pp. 128–9.
8 Ibid., p. 142.

The future Real which causes its present literary registration (inverting the proper temporal order, so that the future cause precedes its effect, the present narrative) may be a catastrophe that will befall the author (death, social disgrace, etc.), but may also be a happy culmination of his efforts. The subject (author) can thus relate in two ways to the future event: he can fully engage in bringing it about, in realizing his Fate, but be thwarted by (what appears as, but may not be) a pure external contingency; or, aware of his Fate as the catastrophe awaiting him at the end of the path, he works desperately to thwart (or at least postpone) its arrival—until, as in the well-known twist of the Oedipus myth or the appointment in Samara, he discovers that the very effort to avoid his Fate ensures that it will actually be realized. This basic temporal paradox of the symbolic order, its "borrowing from the future"—or how the goal towards which our activity is directed does not precede it but emerges through this very activity of trying to reach it—brings us back to Hegel, to the link between intention and act which lies at the core of his literary references.

One of the enigmas of Hegel's *Phenomenology* is how, in roughly the middle of the book, there is a sudden surge in references to literary examples, which had been absent up to that point. Allen Speight was right to identify as the key factor the topic of *agency*, of the subject as an autonomous agent who has to justify its acts with reasons and then assume their unexpected consequences—and the narrative (the story told in literature or in a theatrical piece) is ultimately always the drama of the subject's action, relating the subject's (painful or ridiculous, tragic or comic) experience of the unintended consequences set in motion by his action.[9] A story is the story of things gone wrong, of intervening to achieve A and getting B. This is why literary references arise not only in the long section on "Spirit," the quantitative and qualitative center of the entire book, but already in the preceding section on "Reason," with its second division on "The actualization of rational self-consciousness through its own activity," which follows the weird climax on "Observing Reason," the notorious subdivision on physiognomy and phrenology. As Speight perceptively notices, the passage is announced in Hegel's brief reference to Hamlet's meditations on Yorick's skull: in contrast to the section on phrenology, where the skull as a dead object, in its immediate material being, is supposed to provide the key to the human mind, Yorick's skull is for Hamlet a self-erasing sign, a reminder of all the past acts and experiences of the dead subject.

The three main figures from literature that are then referred to are Goethe's *Faust*, Schiller's *Karl Moor*, and Cervantes's *Don Quixote*. In all these cases, it is as if "Spirit" casts its shadow backwards onto the chapter on Reason: the literary references contained in the latter point forward, towards their proper form

9 I rely here on Allen Speight, *Hegel, Literature and the Problem of Agency*, Cambridge: Cambridge University Press 2001.

in Spirit. In other words, at the level of Reason, we do not yet have a proper spiritual substance, a historical totality which exists as an actual form of life, but just abstract forms of subjective life, forms which can appear within different historical epochs: it is only with Spirit that the succession of figures ("shapes of consciousness") reproduces the succession of actual historical formations from Greek Antiquity through Rome and the medieval self-alienation of Spirit, up to the struggle of the Enlightenment against Belief, the French Revolution and the post-revolutionary morality of the emerging bourgeois order—in short, the section on Spirit is Hegel's first systematic exposition of a philosophy of history.

The inner structure of the section on Spirit is, as expected, triadic. It starts with the Ancient Greek substantial order of customs (*Sittlichkeit*), and the reading of *Antigone* confronts us with the subterranean antagonism which leads to the collapse of this order, to the split of its substantial unity into abstract individuals opposed to the alienated objectivity. The next stage, Culture or self-alienated Spirit, deals with the painful process of the subject's gradual overcoming of this alienation through the hard work of *Bildung*, of the self-sacrificing "education" destined to elevate the subject to the level of universality: to become a universal subject reconciled with Substance, one has to renounce any direct identification with the particular nature of one's identity. The reading of Diderot's *Rameau's Nephew* then shows how the self-renouncing sacrifice of serving a noble Cause shifts into a different self-alienation, the sacrifice of one's ethical substance itself in the vain flattery of the Monarch. The logic is again that of the immanent self-relating reversal: one begins with a sincere readiness to sacrifice everything for the honor of serving a noble Cause, and one ends by sacrificing this Cause itself, of losing the honor itself.[10] Finally, the third part describes the post-revolutionary "Spirit certain of itself": the rise of the (Kantian) subject who directly knows itself as the bearer of the universal moral Law. This direct identification with the Universal again leads to an antagonism: the conflict between the acting subject who, as is the case with every act, imposes on objectivity its partial project, and the judging subject who condemns the acting subject (the "beautiful souls"), but whose position is no less unilateral and false. The judging subject refuses to see how he participates in the corrupted world he so vigorously condemns—as Hegel deploys it through implicit references to Rousseau

10 Does not the same shift repeat itself in the passage from Leninism to Stalinism: dedicated self-sacrificing service to the revolutionary Cause turns into an unprincipled opportunist flattering of the Leader? It would be interesting to explore how the passage from tragedy to comedy in Antiquity is repeated here in the guise of the passage from medieval epics about heroes serving an honorable Cause (El Cid, Roland, Nibelungs) to early modern comedy (from *Don Quixote* to Diderot's *Rameau*) which describes the inherent reversal of heroic service into flattery and theatricality.

(*The New Heloise*) and Jacobi (not his philosophical works, but his novels), evil is also in the eye of those who perceive evil everywhere around them.

Speight develops in detail how each of the three epochs has its own literary genre which articulates the core of its socio-ethical antagonism (Greek tragedy, Roman and then early modern comedy, the Romantic novel), as well as a notion which formulates the lesson of this antagonism. The lesson of the antagonisms which lead to the hero's tragic fate in Greek drama is the immanent *retrospectivity* of the true meaning of our acts (or, as we would put it today, "moral luck"): it is only retrospectively, through accomplishing the act, that the subject becomes aware of its true dimension (and of its own true motivations for accomplishing it.) The lesson of comedy is the inherent *theatricality* of our social lives: every act is acting, even when we (think we) just are who we are, we "act ourselves," we play a socially mediated role. And, finally, the lesson of the Romantic novel concerns Evil and its forgiveness, namely the possibility of *reconciliation*: while in Greek tragedy reconciliation was only possible in the guise of *amor fati*, as the tragic-heroic acceptance of Fate, the Romantic universe opens up the possibility of resolving the conflict not with the agent's destruction, but with the mutual reconciliation between the agent and its judge, both sides admitting their fatal limitation.

We can now also see how referring to literature is an immanent part of the Hegelian procedure: the way Hegel undermines a certain "shape of consciousness" is by first presenting it "in itself," in its abstract notion (the way it perceives itself as a consistent socio-ethical project), and then problematizing it, not by measuring it against a pre-existing higher standard nor by submitting it to an abstract-logical analysis which would unearth its "contradictions," but by *staging* it as a concrete stance of subjectivity in a historical life world: in today's terminology, Hegel is not interested only in logical contradictions, but more so in pragmatic contradictions, in the tension between what we claim we are doing and what we are actually doing. *Antigone* describes what happens when a subject effectively acts upon the premises of the ethics of immediate substantial customs, and thereby brings out the inconsistency of this ethical figure, the inconsistency which leads to its self-destruction. The reference to *Antigone* provides a model of Hegel's reading. He begins with Antigone before her act of disobedience to Creon's prohibition: her starting point is the simple substantial ethical awareness that there are higher (or, rather, deeper) laws than the public laws of the city, laws which are "irrational," coming from nowhere, but nonetheless have to be obeyed unconditionally:

> Zeus did not announce those laws to me.
> And Justice living with the gods below
> sent no such laws for men. I did not think

anything which you proclaimed strong enough
to let a mortal override the gods
and their unwritten and unchanging laws.

They're not just for today or yesterday,
but exist forever, and no one knows
where they first appeared. So I did not mean
to let a fear of any human will
lead to my punishment among the gods.

But once she engages in the forbidden act (performing the funeral rite for Polynices) and faces the consequences, the threat that she will "die while still alive," only then does she become aware of the actual rule that guided her:

What law do I appeal to, claiming this?
If my husband died, there'd be another one,
and if I were to lose a child of mine
I'd have another with some other man.
But since my father and my mother, too,
are hidden away in Hades' house,
I'll never have another living brother.
That was the law I used to honor you.

How are we to read this descent from the highly principled appeal to universal eternal unwritten laws to the "apparently contingent and prudential reasoning" which refers to quite precise particular pragmatic considerations?[11] These scandalous lines, which have bothered interpreters up to and including Judith Butler (Goethe and many others even suggested they must be a later intrusion), are crucial for the "concrete universality" Hegel is aiming at: for a sister, the brother is *the particular which directly stands for the universal*, he is a pure Other not marked by any (sexual or power) interest, and love for him is pure love.[12] It is this anchoring of her persistence in the figure of the brother that provides Antigone with the "highest intuition of ethical essence," and it is crucial that Antigone was able to formulate this insight only after she accomplished her act: only then did she become aware of what she had done, of what had really motivated her—there

11 Speight, *Hegel, Literature and the Problem of Agency*, p. 59.

12 The obvious rebuke arises here: but what about incestuous desire? After all, we are in Oedipus's family. It is here that we should invoke the good old Lévi-Straussian example of a tribe that treats all dreams as having a sexual meaning—except those which deal directly with sexual matters. In the same way, we should suspect incestuous desire in all families with close links—except for the Oedipus family.

is no prior "goal" or "norm" which is merely executed in the act. We should not read this retroactivity as Antigone simply becoming-aware of what was already there in her unconscious, of what unconsciously she always already knew (such a reading merely moves the pre-existing goal/norm into the unconscious), but in a more radically "decentered" fashion: the very norm that effectively guided her comes-to-be only through its actualization, for the act generates its own norm, the passage from intention to act is the passage from the "abstract universality" of the Law (respect for the dead, they all deserve funeral rites) to the "concrete universality" which exposes the particular content that sustains the universality of the Law.

At the level of speech, this means that our thought—our intention-to-mean, what we want to say—is dependent on the process of its "expression": I discover what I want to say only by saying it. In today's cognitive sciences, this dependence of thought on the linguistic process of its articulation was most clearly pointed out by Daniel Dennett, who quotes Lincoln's famous line "You can fool all the people some of the time, and some of the people all the time, but you cannot fool all the people all of the time," drawing attention to its logical ambiguity: does it mean that there are some people who can always be fooled, or that, on every occasion, someone or other is bound to be fooled? His point is that it is wrong to ask, "What did Lincoln really mean?"—in all probability, Lincoln himself was not aware of the ambiguity.[13] He simply wanted to make a witty point, and the phrase "imposed itself on him" because "it sounded good." Here we have an exemplary case of how, when the subject has a vague intention-to-signify and is "looking for the right expression" (as we usually put it), the influence goes both ways: it is not only that, among the multitude of contenders, the best expression wins, but some expression might impose itself which changes more or less considerably the very intention-to-signify. Is this not what Lacan referred to as the "efficacy of the signifier"? The thought itself formulates itself through the process of its articulation:

> We don't first apprehend our experience in the Cartesian Theater and then, on the basis of that acquired knowledge, have the ability to frame reports to express ... The emergence of the expression is precisely what creates or fixes the content of the higher-order thought expressed. There need be no additional episodic "thought." The higher-order state literally depends on—causally depends on—the expression of the speech act.[14]

The perfect example is a situation in which I become aware of a "deep" attitude of mine, when, in a totally unexpected way, without any premeditation, I simply

13 Daniel C. Dennett, *Consciousness Explained*, New York: Little, Brown 1991, p. 244.
14 Ibid., p. 315.

blurt something out. Dennett himself refers to the famous passage from one of Bertrand Russell's letters to Lady Ottoline in which he recalls the circumstances of his declaration of love to her: "I did not know I loved you till I heard myself telling you so—for one instant I thought 'Good God, what have I said?' and then I knew it was the truth."[15] For Dennett, this is not an exceptional feature but the basic mechanism which generates meaning: a word or a phrase forces itself upon us, and thereby imposes a semblance of narrative order on our confused experience; there is no pre-existing "deep awareness" expressed in this phrase—it is, on the contrary, this very phrase which organizes our experience into a "deep awareness."

In literature, an outstanding example is provided by the very last lines of Patricia Highsmith's *Strangers on a Train*: in contrast to Hitchcock's film version, Guy does also kill Bruno's father, and, at the end of the novel, the detectives who have been closely monitoring him for some time finally approach him to take him in for questioning. Guy, who has been preparing for this moment for a long time and has memorized his alibi in detail, reacts with a confessionary gesture of surrender which takes even him by surprise: "Guy tried to speak, and said something entirely different from what he had intended. 'Take me.'"[16] Again, Dennett's point would be that it is wrong to "substantialize" the attitude expressed in Guy's last words, as if, "deep within himself," he was all the time aware of his guilt and nourished a desire to be arrested and punished for it. There was, of course, a confessional "disposition" in Guy, but it was competing with other dispositions, ambiguous, not clearly defined, and it won out due to a concrete contingent constellation—not unlike Kieslowski's early film *Blind Chance* (1981), which deals with three different outcomes of a man running for a train: he catches it and becomes a communist official; he misses it and becomes a dissident; there is no train and he settles down to a mundane life. This notion of mere chance determining the course of a man's life was unacceptable to both communists and dissidents (it deprives the dissident attitude of its deep moral foundation). The point is that in all three cases, the contingency which gave the "spin" to his life is "repressed"; that is, the hero constructs his life story as a narrative leading to its final result (a dissident, an ordinary man, a communist apparatchik) with a "deep necessity." Is this not what Lacan referred to as the *futur antérieur* of the unconscious which "will have been"?

In Hegel's own time, this properly dialectical self-relating in which meaning emerges through the retroactive influence of its "expression" was formulated in an unsurpassable way by Heinrich von Kleist, in his essay "On the Gradual

15 Ibid., p. 246, quoting from R. W. Clark, *The Life of Bertrand Russell*, London: Weidenfeld & Nicolson 1975, p. 176.

16 Patricia Highsmith, *Strangers on a Train*, Harmondsworth: Penguin Books 1982, p. 256.

Formation of Thoughts in the Process of Speech" (from 1805, first published posthumously in 1878), which deserves to be quoted in full:

> The French say *l'appétit vient en mangeant*, and this empirical maxim remains true if one makes a parody of it and says *l'idée vient en parlant.*
>
> Often I sit over my papers and I try to find out from what angle a given conflict has to be judged. Usually, I look into the light, as the brightest spot I can find, as I try to enlighten my inner being. Or else I seek out the first approach, the first equation which expresses the obtaining relations, and from which the solution may be derived simply through plain arithmetic. And look what happens: as soon as I talk to my sister—who is sitting and working behind me—about this matter, I realize what hours of hard thinking have not been able to make clear to me. It isn't as if she was telling me in any direct sense. She does not know the law, and has never studied her Euler and her Kästner. Neither is that what she leads me to the crucial point through deft questions—although this latter case may occasionally occur. But since I have some vague thoughts that are in some way connected with what I am looking for, then once I have embarked on the formulation of the thought it is as if the need to lead what has been begun to some conclusion transforms my hazy imaginations into complete clarity in such a way that my insight is completed together with my rambling sentence. I mix in inarticulate noises, I draw out my sentence connectives, I use appositions where they are not strictly necessary and I use other rhetorical tricks that will draw out speech: in this way I gain the time to fabricate my idea in this workshop of reason.
>
> Nothing in all this is more useful than some movement on the part of my sister, a movement indicating that she intends to interrupt me. For my strained mind becomes even more excited by the need to defend this inherent right to speak against attack from the outside. The mind's abilities grow like those of a great general who is faced with a very difficult situation.
>
> It is against this background that I understand how useful Molière found his maid. For if, as he claims, he trusted her judgment more than his own, this would indicate a degree of modesty on his part which I refuse to believe was there.
>
> The other person's face is a curious source of inspiration for a person who speaks. A single glance which indicates that a half-expressed thought is already understood, bestows on us the other half of the formulation.
>
> I believe that many a great orator, before he opened his mouth, did not know what he was going to say. But the conviction that the necessary wealth of thought would be naturally inspired by the conditions surrounding his speech and his resulting excitement, causes him to be bold enough to make a beginning with his speech.
>
> This makes me think of that "thunderbolt" of Mirabeau. Mirabeau sent the Master of Ceremonies packing when the latter after the last national meeting led by the King on June 23, in which the King had ordered the members of the assembly

to disperse, returned to the meeting room where the assembly had not dispersed, and asked whether they had received the King's orders. "Yes," Mirabeau replied, "we have understood the King's orders."—I am convinced that when he made this humane start he did not think of those bayonets with which he closed his speech. "Yes, Sir," he repeated, "we have understood them."—One can see that he has no idea of where he is going. "However, on what authority do you think you are entitled" he continues, and a sudden source of amazing thoughts began to flow for him, "to address orders to us? We are the representatives of the nation!"—Ah, this was what he needed! "The nation gives orders. It does not receive orders."—And he surges up the heights of hubris. "And to make everything perfectly plain to you,"—And only at this point he finds the proper expression for the act of defiance for which his soul is prepared, "you should go and tell your King that we shall not leave our places here except when forced with bayonets." Upon which he settled, utterly satisfied, into a chair.

Thinking about the Master of Ceremonies it is impossible to visualise him except in a state of complete spiritual bankruptcy. The law is the same as that by which an electrically neutral body, when entering the atmosphere of a charged body, will acquire the opposite (negative, bankrupt) electrical charge. And just as the energy charge in the charged body is strengthened through interaction, so in the case of this annihilation of the opponent, Mirabeau's enthusiasm knew no bounds.

Perhaps it was just the twitching of the upper lip or an ambiguously uncertain movement about the sleeves that caused the change of the course of events in France.

One reads that Mirabeau stood up, as soon as the Master of Ceremonies had left, and proposed that the assembly should constitute itself as the national assembly and as inviolable. For since he had lost his charge, like a Kleistian bottle, he had become neutralized and he gave room in his mind to fear of the judiciary at Chatelet and to carefulness in political action.

This is a curious convergence between the phenomena of the natural and the moral world which, if one wished to pursue the matter, could be shown to apply even in the minor subplots of this episode. But I shall leave my simile, and I shall return to my subject.

Even La Fontaine gives a very fine example of the gradual constitution of thought in the process of speaking in his fable entitled *Les animaux malades de la peste*. In this fable the fox is forced to give a speech in defence of the lion without knowing where on earth he should find support for his defence. The well-rounded idea is born from a beginning which is dictated by necessity.

The fable is well known. The plague is ravaging the animal kingdom. The lion assembles the "important" animals and explains that it must be offered Heaven with a sacrifice in order to get it to relent. The lion maintained that there were many sinners among the animals, and the greatest of these would have to be sacrificed for the survival of the others. He therefore suggested that everyone should confess their sins to him. He, for his part, had to admit that in the heat of hunger he had killed many a sheep and even some dogs who had come too close. Moreover, he had once by chance—in a gourmet mood—feasted on a shepherd. If no one else could show greater weaknesses he was ready to die.

"Sir," said the fox, who was trying to avert disaster from himself, "You are too generous. Your honest endeavour leads you too far. What's wrong with strangling a sheep? Or a dog, worthless creature!" And then: "quant au berger" he continues, for this is the main point, "on peut dire" although he has no idea what to say about him!, "qu'il méritait tout mal": he says that on the off chance that he can think of something, and now he is in trouble. "Étant" he continues, a poor phrase to use, but it does give him time: "de ces gens là" and only at this point does he hit that thought which gets him out of trouble: "qui sur les animaux se font un chimérique empire"— And now for the demonstration that the ass, the bloodthirsty one! (who eats away at the herbs), that the ass was the proper sacrificial victim. And everyone pounces on the ass, tears him to pieces.

Such speech is truly thought in the vocal medium. The sequences of thoughts and expressions go alongside each other, and the underlying psychological realities converge. Language, under these conditions, is not manacles, it is not like some impediment on the wheel of the spirit. Language is a second wheel on the same axle!

The situation is quite different if the mind is finished already with a thought before the speaking starts. Then the spirit stays back in the process of mere articulation and this business of articulation, far from exciting the spirit, on the contrary reduces the mental intensity. If therefore a thought is expressed in a fuzzy way, then it does not at all follow that this thought was conceived in a confused way. On the contrary it is quite possible that the ideas that are expressed in the most confusing fashion are the ones that were thought out most clearly.

One often sees, in social company where congenial conversation inspires everyone with continuous fresh ideas, that people who usually feel linguistically inept feel inspired to break into flickering of unstable articulation, to take hold of language—and produce something utterly incomprehensible. And when these people have the others' attention they show through their embarrassed gestures that they have no idea what they were really trying to say. It is quite probable that these people have thought up something quite apt and clear. But the abrupt change in activity, the passage of the mind from thinking to articulation, this abrupt change dampened that very excitement which was necessary for keeping the thought in mind as well as for putting it into words. In such cases it is all the more necessary that language is available to us with facility and ease so that what we have just thought and are unable to articulate at that very same time, can at least be put into words as soon as possible afterwards.

Quite generally, someone who—with the same degree of clarity—speaks faster than his opponent, will have a distinct advantage over him. The reason is that the fast talker is leading more troops into the field.

When, in examinations, one abruptly examines open-minded and well-educated people, without introduction, on questions like "What is the state?" or "What is property?", one realizes how necessary it is that the mind be excited in a certain way for us to be able to recreate in our minds even thoughts that we have had before. If the same people whom we examine in this way are found in congenial company where the talk has been about questions of the state and of property for a while, then perhaps these people would have no trouble through comparisons, contrasts and summary of the concepts concerned to find acceptable definitions. But under examination conditions, where the preparation of the mind is missing, one finds that they falter. Only an ignorant examiner will conclude that they do not know.

For it is not we who know. It is a certain state of us that knows.

Only truly vulgar spirits, people who have learnt by heart yesterday what the state is supposed to be and who have forgotten it tomorrow, will have a ready answer. Perhaps there is no more inappropriate occasion to show oneself in a positive light than a public examination. I disregard the fact that public examinations are disgusting and hurtful to the sensitive mind. I disregard the fact that it is provoking to be faced with a hack who looks at our knowledge in order to decide whether to buy us if the number is five and to send us away if the number is six.

It is very hard to play on the instrument of the human mind, to elicit its proper sound from it. The mind gets so easily out of tune under clumsy hands. So much so, that the greatest connoisseur of men, the consummate specialist in the midwifery of thoughts—as Kant calls it—might well commit serious mistakes with the young soul entrusted to him.

What ensures good results for such young people, by the way, even the most ignorant among them, is the circumstance that the examiners' minds, in the case of public examinations, are far too preoccupied to be able to pass a free judgment. Not only do they often feel the indecency of the whole procedure: it would be indecent enough to ask someone to open his purse before our eyes, but how much more indecent it is to ask him to open up his soul for examination! There is another thing: the examiners themselves have to pass a severe test in these examinations, and they may often thank the Lord for being able to leave examinations without showing weaknesses that are greater, perhaps, than those disclosed in the youth that has just emerged from the university and whom they have examined.[17]

---

17 Heinrich von Kleist, "On the Gradual Formation of Thoughts in the Process of Speech," translation by Christoph Harbsmeier of "Über das Verfertigen der Gedanken beim Reden," in *Werke in einem Band*, Munich: Carl Hanser 1966, pp. 810–14. I owe this reference to Kleist to Mladen Dolar.

Kleist thus inverts the common wisdom according to which one should open one's mouth and say something only when one has a clear idea of what one wants to say: "If therefore a thought is expressed in a fuzzy way, then it does not at all follow that this thought was conceived in a confused way. On the contrary it is quite possible that the ideas that are expressed in the most confusing fashion are the ones that were thought out most clearly." Let us return to his comment on the famous episode from the French Revolution which occurred on June 23, 1789, when the king ordered the members of the assembly to disperse and then left; the members refused to leave, so the king sent the Master of Ceremonies back to the assembly, asking the members whether they had received the king's orders:

> "Yes," Mirabeau replied, "we have understood the King's orders."—I am convinced that when he made this humane start he did not think of those bayonets with which he closed his speech. "Yes, Sir," he repeated, "we have understood them."—One can see that he has no idea of where he is going. "However, on what authority do you think you are entitled," he continues, and a sudden source of amazing thoughts began to flow for him, "to address orders to us? We are the representatives of the nation!"—Ah, this was what he needed! "The nation gives orders. It does not receive orders."—And he surges up the heights of hubris. "And to make everything perfectly plain to you,"—And only at this point he finds the proper expression for the act of defiance for which his soul is prepared, "you should go and tell your King that we shall not leave our places here except when forced with bayonets." Upon which he settled, utterly satisfied, into a chair.[18]

What Kleist makes clear is the presence, in the Hegelian space, of another *Ver-* which supplements the Freudian list of *Ver-*s (*Verdrängung*, *Verneinung*, *Verwerfung* …): the *Ver-* of *Versprechen*, of saying more than one wanted to say. Is not the same mechanism, the same panicky reversal from *impasse* into *passe*, at work in many legendary revolutionary gestures? In a famous speech in *Assemblée nationale*, Robespierre claimed that there were traitors of the Revolution even in the very hall, and then went on: "I say that anyone who trembles at this moment is guilty; for innocence never fears public scrutiny." We can imagine his reasoning: after the first statement, he noticed signs of unrest and fear among the listeners; he quickly thought about how to exploit this fear—should he offer a carrot by adding something like, "If you are innocent, you have nothing to fear"? No, better to use this fear itself as an argument for guilt.

Perhaps the same goes for the late Lenin's programmatic note: "What if the complete hopelessness of the situation, by stimulating the efforts of the workers and peasants tenfold, offered us the opportunity to create the fundamental

---

18 Ibid.

requisites of civilization in a different way from that of the West European countries?"[19] After conceding the complete hopelessness of the situation in which the Bolshevik state found itself in 1922, with no realistic option of building socialism, Lenin thought in panic about how to block the obvious conclusion (that the Bolsheviks should simply step down), and, suddenly, the idea came to him of presenting this hopeless situation itself as offering an unexpected opportunity. There is a passage in one of Stalin's speeches from the early 1930s where he proposes radical measures against all those who even secretly oppose the collectivization of farms: "We should detect and fight without mercy even those who oppose collectivization only in their thoughts—yes, I mean this, we should fight even people's thoughts." One can safely presume that this passage was not prepared in advance: Stalin got caught up in his rhetorical enthusiasm and was spontaneously carried away into adding that even people's private thoughts should be controlled and fought; then he immediately become aware of what he had just said, but, instead of admitting that he had gotten carried away, quickly decided to stick heroically to his hyperbole. Looking further back, does not exactly the same hold for Antigone's confrontation with Creon? At the outset, Antigone grounds her insistence on the proper burial for Polynices in the simple substantial ethical awareness that there are higher (or, rather, deeper) laws than the public laws of the city; it is only through her act that she becomes aware of the specific motive that guided her (she was ready to do what she did only for her brother, not for all the oppressed and excluded).

Mirabeau and Antigone: two exemplary cases of how "truth is an effect of surprise triggered by its enunciation"[20]—or, as Althusser put it, referring to the word-play between *prise* and *surprise*, every authentic "grasping" (*prise*) of some content comes as a surprise to the one who accomplishes it. Althusser locates this insight in the same Kierkegaardian opposition between the open contingent process of becoming and the retroactive systemic illusion: "The world is an accomplished fact. Once it is accomplished, sense etc. take over in it. But the accomplishment of the fact is an effect of contingency."[21] The irony is that, for Althusser as for Kierkegaard, Hegel is *the* systemic philosopher of the *fait accompli*, while, as we have just seen, the point of Hegelian dialectical analysis is not to reduce the chaotic flow of events to a deeper necessity, but to unearth the contingency of the rise of necessity itself—this is what it means to grasp things "in their becoming." So when, in his late text "The Subterranean Current of the Materialism of Encounter," Althusser endeavors to discern, beneath the hegemonic idealist orientation of Origins/Sense, etc., the subterranean tradition

19 V. I. Lenin, "Our Revolution," in *Collected Works*, Vol. 33, Moscow: Progress Publishers 1966, p. 478.

20 Gregor Moder, *Hegel in Spinoza*, Ljubljana: Analecta 2009, p. 240.

21 Louis Althusser, *Philosophy of the Encounter*, London: Verso Books 2006, p. 162.

of "aleatory materialism"—Epicurus (and the Stoics?) versus Plato, Machiavelli versus Descartes, Spinoza versus Kant and Hegel, Marx, Heidegger—the least one can say is that he is wrong to locate Hegel in the hegemonic "idealist" line.

Everything is thus here, in Kleist's refined description, up to and including the temporal dialectic of transference and the proto-Lacanian invocation of the cut (the analyst's sudden intervention) into the flow of analysand's rambling ("free associations") as generative of the sudden emergence of new meaning: "Nothing in all this is more useful than some movement on the part of my sister, *a movement indicating that she intends to interrupt me*. For my strained mind becomes even more excited by the need to defend this inherent right to speak against attack from the outside." It is easy to miss the complexity of Kleist's point: it is not simply that the effort to put one's thought into words clarifies and forms it, but that, for this to happen, my speech should be addressed to an Other who, in the transferential illusion, is presupposed to already know the meaning I struggle to formulate—in order to formulate a thought, we must presuppose that this thought already exists in the Other's mind: "The other person's face is a curious source of inspiration for a person who speaks. A single glance *which indicates that a half-expressed thought is already understood*, bestows on us the other half of the formulation."

This, then, brings us back to Hegel: the structure of the Hegelian "dialectical process" is not the automatic deployment of consequences regulated by an inexorable conceptual necessity, but precisely the process of getting lost and then improvising an invention described by Kleist. One plans to say (do) something, things go wrong, one gets lost and, to escape the deadlock, one invents an improvised solution. And one should go to the end here: does not exactly the same hold for the crucifixion itself? Christ's plan was to give himself up to the Roman authorities via the delicate negotiations carried out by Judas; however, things took an unexpected turn for the worse and, in a truly Kleistian twist, as a desperate attempt to get something out of the fiasco, the story of redemption-through-death was duly concocted. And, in exactly the same way, it was only Creon's interruption which made Antigone aware of her true intention.

There is, however, a limitation in this figure of the brother as the stand-in for the universality of a human being deserving funeral rites: the brother as Other is deprived of all personal features, for Antigone's deed "no longer concerns the living but the dead, the individual who, after a long succession of separate disconnected experiences, concentrates himself into a single completed shape, and has raised himself out of the unrest of the accidents of life into the calm of simple universality."[22] Speight is right to add wryly that "to love someone for what he *is*,

22 G. W. F. Hegel, *Phenomenology of Spirit*, trans. A. V. Miller, Oxford: Oxford University Press 1977, p. 270.

for his being, is to love him in his inaction, is to love a corpse."[23] This limitation is the necessary result of Antigone's immediate immersion in the ethical substance: there is no call of duty here exerting pressure on us, so that, in order to act upon it, we have to fight our spontaneous pathological impulses—Antigone's pathos *is* directly substantially ethical. This is why, as Hegel puts it, experiencing the limited character of this ethical identity can only happen through suffering: in experiencing the contingency of this identity, the subject has to separate itself from its very ethical "nature."

However, in an exemplarily Hegelian way, this utter tragedy, this loss of our very ethical ground, turns into comedy. In other words, Hegel noticed something weird happening to Antigone after she pathetically assumes her fate—to put it bluntly, she starts to *act*, for her statements display a level of self-awareness and reflexivity about her "role" which undermine her immediate ethical spontaneity from within:

> I've heard about a guest of ours,
> daughter of Tantalus, from Phrygia—
> she went to an excruciating death
> in Sipylus, right on the mountain peak.
> The stone there, just like clinging ivy,
> wore her down, and now, so people say,
> the snow and rain never leave her there,
> as she laments. Below her weeping eyes
> her neck is wet with tears. God brings me
> to a final rest which most resembles hers.

Antigone is using metaphors to designate herself—do not these lines display a "self-consciously *artistic* ability involved in *playing the role* of a character"?[24] Antigone is acting here, modeling her predicament on mythical examples—in short, she is aware of the immanent theatricality of her tragic predicament, a theatricality which by definition confers on it a minimal touch of comedy—one can (and should) imagine her interrupting her pathetic complaint, worrying briefly whether her outburst of spontaneous passion is well acted. Indeed, the tragic characters

> are artists, who do not express with unconscious naturalness and naivety the *external* aspect of their resolves and enterprises, as happens in the language accompanying ordinary actions in actual life; on the contrary, they give utterance to the inner essence, they prove the rightness of their action, and the "pathos" which moves them

23 Speight, *Hegel, Literature and the Problem of Agency*, p. 62.
24 Ibid., p. 67.

> is soberly asserted and definitely expressed in its universal individuality, free from the accidents of circumstance and personal idiosyncrasies.[25]

The lesson concerns the "inherent theatricality involved in self-knowledge and action. No action or motivation of [the agent] is *directly* his own, but must be assessed in the light of others' reactions to it; he understands himself by constantly looking at his actions in the light of the mask that he wears in them."[26] In other words, the lesson concerns "the mediation of desire and feeling by the imagination or fiction inherent in the relation between actor and spectator," namely the "inherently socially mediated character of desire formation itself."[27] What Lacan calls "the big Other" is this agency of social rules and appearances which confers on everything we do a minimal aspect of theatricality: no matter how passionately we act, our desire is always a desire of the Other, mediated by the Other (the symbolic texture which provides the scripts for possible desires); we are not directly ourselves, we play the role of ourselves, we imitate a fiction of what we are.

We should link this topic with Hegel's lectures on aesthetics, where he describes how the passage from tragedy to comedy concerns overcoming the limits of representation: while in a tragedy the individual actor represents the universal character he plays, in a comedy he immediately *is* this character. The gap of representation is thus closed, which, however, does not mean that, in a comedy, the actor coincides with the person he plays in the way that he plays himself on the stage, that there he just "is what he really is." It is rather that, in a properly Hegelian way, the gap which separates the actor from his stage persona in a tragedy is transposed into the stage persona itself: a comic character is never fully identified with his role, he always retains the ability to observe himself from outside, "making fun of himself."[28] Speight notices the inversion of theatricality that occurs in modernity, when the alienating process of *Bildung* reaches its climax: "in ancient comedy, it was the recognition of real life coming onto the stage that was at issue in the comic actor's dropping of his mask, whereas here we will be concerned with how the theatrical comes into life"—the artificial social world of modernity confronts us with "roles and imitation in social life itself."[29] This reversal is in itself deeply dialectical: the *intrusion of reality onto the stage* (an actor distancing himself from his role, showing his awareness of playing a

25 Hegel, *Phenomenology of Spirit*, p. 444.

26 Speight, *Hegel, Literature and the Problem of Agency*, p. 70.

27 Ibid., p. 81.

28 Recall the immortal Lucy from *I Love Lucy* whose trademark gesture, when something unusual happened, was to slightly bend her neck and cast a surprised look direct to the camera—this was not Lucille Ball, the actress, mockingly addressing the public, but an attitude of self-estrangement that was part of "Lucy" (as a screen persona) herself.

29 Speight, *Hegel, Literature and the Problem of Agency*, p. 77.

role) is paid for by the *theatricalization of real life itself*: you start claiming that we should not get caught up in the theatrical fiction, that we should be aware of how theater is part of our real lives, and you end up claiming that real life itself is a theater.

CHAPTER 9

Suture and Pure Difference

More than forty years ago, a short debate between Jacques-Alain Miller and Alain Badiou took place in *Cahiers pour l'Analyse*, a journal that stands for everything in "French theory" that resists being incorporated into "deconstruction." The debate focused on the notion of "suture": to Miller's seminal text "Suture (Elements of the Logic of the Signifier)," Badiou replied with "The Mark and the Lack." Lurking in the background was the status of the *subject*, the relationship between the subject/lack and structure, and one can say that this was *the* key problem of the entire field of "structuralism." Its founding gesture is to assert the differential or self-relational structure in its formal purity, purifying it of all "pathological" imaginary elements. Here is Lacan's classic formulation:

> it is the specific law of [the symbolic] chain which governs those psychoanalytic effects that are decisive for the subject: such as foreclosure, repression, denial itself—specifying with appropriate emphasis that these effects follow so faithfully the displacement of the signifier that imaginary factors, despite their inertia, figure only as shadows and reflections in the process.[1]

The question is: after this purification, is there a subject to this structure? The predominant answer was a resounding no. Even post-structuralist deconstruction, with its emphasis on gaps, ruptures, differences, and deferrals, etc., conceived the subject as the culmination of the metaphysics of self-presence, and its self-identity as something to be deconstructed (by way of demonstrating how its condition of impossibility is its condition of possibility, how the subject's identity is always already deferred, how it has to rely on the very process that undermines it). Derrida's early analyses of Husserl's phenomenology are exemplary here: the subject's self-presence and self-identity, whose supreme and founding case is the experience of *s'entendre-parler* (of hearing or understanding-oneself-talking), is always already undermined by the process of "writing," which stands for the deferral of self-identity, for the "dead letter" in the very heart of the living spirit. Although "deconstruction" endlessly insists on the gap, rupture,

1 Jacques Lacan, "Seminar on the 'Purloined Letter,'" in John P. Muller and William J. Richardson, eds., *The Purloined Poe*, Baltimore: Johns Hopkins University Press 1988, pp. 28–9.

deferral, lack, failure, etc., it conceives the subject as the agent and result of the obfuscation of this lack.

So what were the positions taken up in this struggle? The ultimate reason for the breathtaking resonance of Miller's "Suture" was that, by systematizing Lacan's dispersed statements (let us not forget that Lacan uses the term only once, and even then in a verbal form), Miller for the first time proposed and elaborated the concept of a subject which belongs to the very "abstract," purely differential notion of structure. In fierce and rigorous opposition to this notion of a subjectivized structure, Badiou insisted on the anonymous or asubjective structure: structure renders the knowledge of the real; there is no lack in it, so the concept of the subject should be strictly limited to the level of imaginary misrecognition; it is the way we illusorily live or experience anonymous structural causality.

From differentiality to the phallic signifier

In order to elaborate on the idea of a subjectivized structure, we need to radicalize the notion of differentiality, bringing it to self-referentiality. Ferdinand de Saussure was the first to formulate the notion of differentiality, pointing out that the identity of a signifier resides only in a series of differences (the features which distinguish it from other signifiers)—there is no positivity in a signifier, it "is" only a series of what it is *not*. The crucial consequence of differential identity is that the very absence of a feature can itself count as a feature, as a positive fact—if every presence arises only against the background of potential absence, then we can also talk about the presence of absence as such. For example, something not happening can also be a positive event—recall the famous dialogue from "Silver Blaze" between Scotland Yard detective Gregory and Sherlock Holmes about the "curious incident of the dog in the night-time":

> "Is there any other point to which you would wish to draw my attention?"
> "To the curious incident of the dog in the night-time."
> "The dog did nothing in the night-time."
> "That was the curious incident."

This positive existence of the absence itself, the fact that the absence of a feature is itself a positive feature which defines the thing in question, is what characterizes a differential order, and, in this precise sense, differentiality is the core feature of dialectics proper. Consequently, Jameson was right to emphasize, against the standard Hegelian-Marxist rejection of structuralism as "undialectical," that the role of the structuralist explosion in the 1960s was "to signal a reawakening or a rediscovery of the dialectic."[2] This is also why, in a nice jab at cultural studies' fashionable rejection of "binary logic," Jameson calls for "a generalized celebration of the binary opposition" which, brought to self-referentiality, is the very matrix of structural relationality or differentiality.[3] Furthermore, insofar as Hegel is *the* dialectician and his *Phenomenology of Spirit* is the unsurpassed model of dialectical analysis, Jameson is fully justified in drawing his non-intuitive conclusion: "it is certain that the *Phenomenology* is a profoundly structuralist work *avant la lettre*."[4] This background should be borne in mind when considering Adorno's very last course on the "Introduction to Sociology" from 1968, where Adorno twice signals his interest in French structuralism (which at that point was exploding in popularity in France).[5] First, after opposing the methods of Weber and Durkheim and endorsing the then current cliché about the French Durkheimean tradition as "chosisme," he says: "Traces of this notion survive today in French structuralism, to which, by the way, I plan to dedicate one of the next main seminars, because I think German students of sociology should be able to obtain a first-hand knowledge of precisely these things."[6] Forty pages later, Adorno makes it clear that sociological theory deals with phenomena which cannot be reduced to the purely social:

> To refer to a recent phenomenon within social thinking, structuralism, French structuralism, which is linked above all to the names of Lévi-Strauss and Lacan, and which influences very strongly sociological thinking—I hope I will be able to hold a seminar on structuralism in the semester after the next one—for essential reasons, fully justified by the development of its theory, this structuralism takes its material above all from anthropology and, over and above that, from a very specific orientation of language research, phonology, whose main representative was Trubetzkoj in Vienna. When one wants to separate structuralism, which understands itself essentially as a theory of society, from this ethnological or anthropological material, then basically nothing at all remains from its conception.[7]

Is not this announcement that the topic for a later semester will be Claude Lévi-Strauss and Jacques Lacan a clear sign of Adorno's awareness that something important was going on in France at that moment? Without casting him as a German John the Baptist with regard to Lacan, and without speculating on his reading of the latter, we can nevertheless assume that Adorno's confrontation

2 Fredric Jameson, *The Hegel Variations*, London: Verso Books 2010, p. 48.
3 Ibid.
4 Ibid.
5 See Theodor W. Adorno, *Einleitung in die Soziologie*, Frankfurt: Suhrkamp 1993.
6 Ibid., p. 133.
7 Ibid., pp. 174–5.

would have been much more substantial than was either Alfred Schmidt's or Jürgen Habermas's facile dismissal of structuralism as a regression to an unhistorical and non-dialectical mode of thinking. The very term *chosisme* should make us suspicious: if there is a purely relational thought which dispenses with any reference to the positivity of "things" it is structuralism with its basic notion of the identity of X as reducible to a *faisceau* of its differences from other elements, which is why the absence of a feature can itself function as a positive property (the link between this differentialist approach and Hegelian dialectics was clearly perceived by Roman Jakobson).

But if absence itself can function as presence or as a positive fact—if, for example, woman's lack of a penis is in itself a "curious incident"—then presence (man's possession of a penis) can also arise only against the background of its (possible) absence. But how, precisely? Here we need to introduce self-reflexivity into the signifying order: if the identity of a signifier is nothing but the series of its constitutive differences, then every signifying series has to be supplemented—"sutured"—by a reflexive signifier which has no determinate meaning (signified), since it stands only for the presence of meaning as such (as opposed to its absence). The first to fully articulate the necessity of such a signifier was Lévi-Strauss, in his famous interpretation of "mana"; his achievement was to demystify mana, reducing its irrational connotation of a mythic or magical power to a precise symbolic function. Lévi-Strauss's starting point is that language as a bearer of meaning by definition arises at once, covering the entire horizon: "Whatever may have been the moment and the circumstances of its appearance in the ascent of animal life, language can only have arisen all at once. Things cannot have begun to signify gradually."[8] This sudden emergence, however, introduces an imbalance between the two orders of the signifier and the signified: since the signifying network is finite, it cannot adequately cover the endless field of the signified in its entirety. In this way,

> a fundamental situation perseveres which arises out of the human condition: namely, that man has from the start had at his disposition a signifier-totality which he is at a loss to know how to allocate to a signified, given as such, but no less unknown for being given. There is always a non-equivalence or "inadequation" between the two, a non-fit and overspill which divine understanding alone can soak up; this generates a signifier-surfeit relative to the signifieds to which it can be fitted. So, in man's effort to understand the world, he always disposes of a surplus of signification ... That distribution of a supplementary ration ... is absolutely necessary to insure that, in total, the available signifier and the mapped-out signified may remain in

8 Claude Lévi-Strauss, *Introduction to the Work of Marcel Mauss*, London: Routledge 1987, p. 59.

> the relationship of complementarity which is the very condition of the exercise of symbolic thinking.[9]

Every signifying field thus has to be "sutured" by a supplementary zero-signifier, "a *zero symbolic value*, that is, a sign marking the necessity of a supplementary symbolic content over and above that which the signified already contains."[10] This signifier is "a symbol in its pure state": lacking any determinate meaning, it stands for the presence of meaning *as such* in contrast to its absence; in a further dialectical twist, the mode of appearance of this supplementary signifier which stands for meaning as such is non-sense (Deleuze developed this point in his *Logic of Sense*). Notions like mana thus "represent nothing more or less than that *floating signifier* which is the disability of all finite thought."[11]

The first thing to note here is Lévi-Strauss's commitment to scientific positivism: he grounds the necessity of mana in the gap between the constraints of our language and infinite reality. Like the early Badiou and Althusser, he excludes science from the dialectics of lack that generates the need for a suturing element. For Lévi-Strauss, mana stands for the "poetic" excess which compensates for the constraints of our finite predicament, while the effort of science is precisely to suspend mana and provide direct adequate knowledge. Following Althusser, one can claim that mana is an elementary operator of ideology which reverses the lack of our knowledge into the imaginary experience of the ineffable surplus of Meaning. The next step towards "suture" proper consists of three interconnected gestures: the *universalization* of mana (the zero-signifier is not just a mark of ideology, but a feature of every signifying structure); its *subjectivization* (re-defining mana as the point of the inscription of the subject into the signifying chain); and its *temporalization*[12] (a temporality which is not empirical but logical, inscribed into the very signifying structure). With this subjectivization, the standard Althusserian difference between science and ideology is left behind—no wonder Badiou introduces the Truth-Event and the subject as the agent of fidelity to the Truth-Event in terms which strangely resemble Althusser's analysis of ideological interpellation as the transformation of (human-animal) individuals into subjects: the Truth-Event is the big Other which requires the fidelity of the subject who recognizes itself in it.

9 Ibid., pp. 62–3.

10 Ibid., p. 64.

11 Ibid., p. 63.

12 For Lévi-Strauss, the symbolic structure is an atemporal matrix of all possible permutations of a structure, while the radicalized mana introduces into the structure an irreducible temporality: the "floating" zero-signifier alternates endlessly between 1 and 0, between being and non-being, the fullness of ineffable meaning and non-sense, providing the most elementary formula of what Freud called the compulsion to repeat.

This triple gesture, a crucial step from mana to "suture," was gradually accomplished by Lacan, starting with his articulation of the concept of the "*point de capiton*" (quilting point) whose apparent reference obviously points towards suture. As in Lévi-Strauss, the "quilting point" sutures the two fields, that of the signifier and that of the signified, acting as the point at which, as Lacan put it in a precise way, "the signifier falls into the signified."[13] This is how one should read the tautology "socialism is socialism"—recall the old Polish anti-communist joke: "Socialism is the synthesis of the highest achievements of all previous historical epochs: from tribal society, it took barbarism, from Antiquity, it took slavery, from feudalism, it took relations of domination, from capitalism, it took exploitation, and from socialism, it took the name …" Does not the same hold for the anti-Semitic image of the Jew? From the rich bankers, it took financial speculation, from capitalists, it took exploitation, from lawyers, it took legal trickery, from corrupt journalists, it took media manipulation, from the poor, it took indifference towards hygiene, from sexual libertines it took promiscuity, and from the Jews it took the name. Or take the shark in Spielberg's *Jaws*: from immigrants, it took the threat to small-town daily life, from natural catastrophes, it took their blind destructive rage, from big capital, it took the ravaging effects of an unknown cause on the daily lives of ordinary people, and from the shark it took its image. In all these cases, the "signifier falls into the signified" in the precise sense that the name is included in the object it designates—the signifier has to intervene *into* the signified to enact the unity of meaning. What unites a multitude of features or properties into a single object is ultimately its *name*.[14] (In a strictly homologous way, for Badiou, an Event includes its name in its definition.)

This is why every name is ultimately tautological: a "rose" designates an

---

13 We should note here the link between Lacan's "quilting point" and the concept of a *point* deployed by Badiou in his *Logics of Worlds*, as the moment when the complexity of a situation is reduced to a simple choice of "yes" or "no," when we have to decide—war or peace, attack or withdraw, accept or reject an offer ...

14 Many theorists sympathetic to communism mention what one could call a PR-objection: in most countries, especially post-socialist ones, the very word "communism" has such a bad press, evoking traumatic memories, that, if one aims at a serious social movement, another word should be found, one more acceptable to the general public. It is hard not to be reminded here of Ernst Jones's negotiations on the fate of psychoanalysis in Germany after 1933, when Jones reached a compromise with the Nazi regime to the effect that, in order to save psychoanalytic practice (on top of excluding Jewish analysts, of course), the term "psychoanalysis" would be replaced with the term "dynamic psychology." In other words, the problem with this easy solution is that the very taboo with regard to the word "communism" is the result of the defeat of the radical emancipatory struggle, so that when one abandons the word, one sooner or later also betrays the content covered by this word.

object with a series of properties, but what holds all these properties together, what makes them the properties of the same One, is ultimately the name itself. Imagine a situation of social disintegration and confusion in which the cohesive power of ideology loses its efficacy: in such a situation, the Master is the one who invents a new signifier, the famous "quilting point," which stabilizes the situation and makes it readable. The "university discourse" that then elaborates the network of Knowledge which sustains this readability by definition presupposes and relies on the initial gesture of the Master. The Master adds no new positive content—he merely adds a signifier which all of a sudden turns disorder into order, into a "new harmony," as Rimbaud would have put it. Take anti-Semitism in the Germany of the 1920s: following their "undeserved" military defeat, the German people were disoriented, thrown into a situation of economic crisis, political inefficiency, and moral degeneration—and the Nazis offered a single agent which accounted for it all: the Jew, the Jewish plot. Therein resides the magic of a Master: although there is nothing new at the level of positive content, "nothing is quite the same" after he pronounces his Word. Recall how, to illustrate the *point de capiton*, Lacan quotes the famous lines from Racine's *Athalie*: "*Je crains Dieu, cher Abner, et je n'ai point d'autre crainte*" ("I fear God, my dear Abner, and I have no other fears")—all fears are exchanged for one fear, it is the very fear of God which makes me fearless in all worldly matters. The same reversal that gives rise to a new Master-Signifier is at work in ideology: in anti-Semitism, all fears (of economic crisis, of moral degradation ...) are exchanged for the fear of the Jew—*je crains le Juif, cher citoyen, et je n'ai point d'autre crainte.*[15]

Lacan is here a radical Hegelian (unbeknownst to himself, no doubt): there is multiplicity because the One does not coincide with itself. We can now see the precise sense of Lacan's thesis according to which what is "primordially repressed" is the binary signifier (that of *Vorstellungs-Repräsentanz*): what the symbolic order precludes is the full harmonious presence of the couple of Master-Signifiers, S_1-S_2, as *yin-yang* or any other two symmetrical "fundamental principles." The fact that "there is no sexual relationship" means precisely that the secondary signifier (that of the Woman) is "primordially repressed," and *what we get in place of this repression, what fills the gap, are the multiple "returns of the*

15 In clear opposition to the idea that anti-capitalism is today really a form of anti-Semitism, one should assert more than ever the notion of anti-Semitism as the elementary form of a compromise with capitalism, of accepting capitalism: if a "leftist" movement resorts to anti-Semitism, this *eo ipso* means that it displaces the cause of capitalist antagonisms onto a (pseudo-)concrete intrusive (racial) Other, thereby evoking the fantasy that, once we get rid of this Other, we will get capitalism *without* its antagonisms. So if, indeed, one can find elements of anti-Semitism in today's anti-imperialist struggles, what they indicate is simply the depth of the global victory of capitalism, the way capitalism pervades our ideological imagination: even those who profess to be anti-capitalist cannot really escape the most basic coordinates of the capitalist universe.

repressed," the series of "ordinary" signifiers. Watching Woody Allen's parody of Tolstoy's *War and Peace*, the first association that springs to mind is, of course: "If this is Tolstoy, where is Dostoyevsky?" In the film, Dostoyevsky (the "binary signifier" to Tolstoy) remains "repressed"—however, the price to be paid for that appears in a conversation in the middle of the film which, accidentally as it were, includes the titles of all Dostoyevsky's main novels: "Is that man still in the underground?" "You mean one of the Karamazov brothers?" "Yes, that idiot!" "Well, he did commit his crime and was punished for it!" "I know, he was a gambler who always risked too much!" and so on. Here we encounter the "return of the repressed," the series of signifiers which fills in the gap of the repressed binary signifier "Dostoyevsky." This is why the standard deconstructionist criticism according to which Lacan's theory of sexual difference falls foul of "binary logic" totally misses the point: Lacan's *la Femme n'existe pas* aims precisely at undermining the "binary" polar couple of Masculine and Feminine—the original split is not between the One and the Other, but is strictly inherent to the One, as the split between the One and its empty place of inscription (this is how we should read Kafka's famous statement that the Messiah arrives one day too late). This is also how one should conceive the link between the split inherent to the One and the explosion of the multiple: the multiple is not the primordial ontological fact; the "transcendental" genesis of the multiple resides in the lack of the binary signifier; that is, the multiple emerges as a series of attempts to fill in the gap of the missing binary signifier. The difference between S_1 and S_2 is thus not the difference of two opposed poles within the same field, but, rather, the cut within this field (the cut of the level at which the process occurs) inherent to the one term: the original couple is not that of two signifiers, but that of the signifier and its *reduplicatio*, the minimal difference between a signifier and the place of its inscription, between one and zero.

According to Thomas Schelling, real human interactions are governed not only by a pure strategic calculus (which can be formalized), but also by focal points that are "invisible under a mathematical formulation of the problem. Schelling did not believe that game theory was useless, merely that most human interactions were so shot through with ambiguity that these focal points could be the ultimate guide to what might or should happen."[16] Here is Schelling's most famous example: I arrange with a friend to meet him the next day in New York, but, due to a breakdown of all communication systems, neither of us knows where and when to meet. When Schelling asked his students what to do, the majority suggested going to the clock at the Grand Central Station at noon—it is the meeting point which imposed itself as the most "obvious" one (to a person from our culture, of course) independently of all strategic calculations. The

16 Tim Harford, *The Logic of Life*, London: Abacus 2009, p. 52.

reasoning is here more complex than it may appear: in choosing a focal point, I do not merely try to guess which will be the most obvious point for both of us—the question I try to answer is "What do I expect the other to expect that I will expect of him?" In other words, when I go to the Grand Central clock at noon, I do so because I expect that my friend expects me to expect him to go there.

In negotiations, the "focal point" can be an "irrational" commitment (in the sense of not being grounded in any rational strategic calculation) which fixes a non-negotiable feature: for the State of Israel, control over the whole of Jerusalem is "non-negotiable"; ahead of salary negotiations, a trade union leader announces that he will never settle for a pay raise of less than 5 percent, and so on. While there are, of course, always ways to compromise while sticking to the letter of one's engagement (the trade union leader, say, can accept a 5 percent rise spread over five years), such an engagement rises the stakes: one cannot abandon it altogether without "losing face." In contrast to purely strategic reasoning, such commitment is not psychological but properly *symbolic*: it is "performative," grounded in itself ("I say so because I say so!"). As such, the "focal point" is another name for what Lacan called the "quilting point" and, later, the Master-Signifier.

We can also say that, in contrast to the particular features of a thing, a name is a symptom of the thing it names: insofar as it is a signifier which falls into the signified, it stands for *objet a*, the X, the *je ne sais quoi*, which makes a thing a thing. The name names the universality of a thing in its impossible objectal counterpoint. Recall again Lacan's precise reading of Freud's concept of *Vorstellungs-Repräsentanz*: not simply (as Freud probably intended it) a mental representation or idea which is the psychic representative of the biological instinct, but (much more ingeniously) the representative (stand-in, place-holder) of a missing representation. Every name is in this sense a *Vorstellungs-Repräsentanz*: the signifying representative of that dimension in the designated object which eludes representation, that which cannot be covered by our ideas-representations of the positive properties of this object. There is "something in you more than yourself," the elusive *je ne sais quoi* which makes you what you are, which accounts for your "specific flavor"—and the name, far from referring to the collection of your properties, ultimately refers to that elusive X. An act does have a cause: it is caused by the *objet a*, by the *je ne sais quoi* which pushes me to do it. The moment one asks, "What to do?" this cause is lost.[17]

Does not the formula of love—"You are … you!"—rely on the split which is

---

17 This is why an act as a proper symbolic intervention has to be strictly distinguished from a performative one (a speech act): while a speech act remains firmly embedded in a "big Other," relying for its effect on pre-established rules, an intervention proper intervenes in the big Other itself, attacking it at the point of its inconsistency, changing its very rules.

at the core of every tautology? You—this empirical person, full of defects—are *you*, the sublime object of love, for the tautology itself renders visible the radical split or gap. This tautology surprises the lover again and again: how can you be *you*?[18] But we should take a step further here and recall that Lacan defines *Vorstellungs-Repräsentanz* as the representative of the missing binary signifier, the feminine Master-Signifier which would be the counterpart of the phallic Master-Signifier, guaranteeing the complementarity of the two sexes, each at its own place—*yin* and *yang*, etc. Lacan's thesis is that the starting point is the self-deferral of the One, its non-coincidence with itself, and that the two sexes are two ways of dealing with this deadlock.

It is in this precise sense that one can agree with Brecht when he wrote that there is no dialectics without humor: dialectical reversals are deeply connected to comical twists and unexpected shifts of perspective. In his book on jokes, Freud refers to the well-known story of a go-between who tries to convince a young man to marry a woman he represents; his strategy is to turn every objection into a positive feature: When the man says, "But the woman is ugly!" he answers: "So you will not have to worry about her deceiving you with others!" "She is poor!" "So she will be used to not spending lots of your money!" and so on until, finally, when the young man formulates a reproach impossible to reinterpret in this way, the middleman explodes: "What do you want? Perfection? Nobody is totally without faults!" Is it not also possible to discern in this joke the underlying structure of the legitimization of a "really existing" socialist regime? "There is too little meat and rich food in the stores!" "So you don't have to worry about getting fat and suffering a heart attack!" "There are not enough interesting films or good books available!" "So you are all the more able to cultivate a rich social life, visiting friends and neighbors!" "The secret police exert total control over my life!" "So you can just relax and lead a life safe from worries!" and so on, until … "But the air is so polluted from the nearby factory that all my children have life-threatening lung diseases!" "What do you want? No system is without its faults!"[19] For Lacan, the phallic signifier is such a suturing element: Lacan's concept of the phallus is exemplary of the dialectic of the priority of lack over

18 If love is, as Lacan put it, giving what one does not have, how then does a true Master who loves you give you what he does not have? He gives you, his pupil, *yourself*, the possibility of becoming what you are. But recall here the apparently opposite use of tautology in everyday practice: when one says "a man is a man," this means precisely that no man is at the level of its notion, that every actual man is full of imperfections; or, again, when we say "the law is the law," the implication is that we have to obey it even when it obviously violates our sense of justice—"the law is the law" means that the law is fundamentally grounded on an illegal violence.

19 It is similar with the series seventeen, eighteen, nineteen, tenteen—twenty: the reversal from "tenteen" to "twenty" signals the self-reflexive gesture of an inscription of the maximum at a lower level into a higher encompassing level.

the element that fills it in—and, as Lacan points out, for a very precise reason (known to all Lacanians), the phallus is the very signifier of this lack:

> the nature of the phallus itself is "nothing but the site of the lack it indicates in the subject." A lack in being provided in its index, in its signifier, is presented to us then as the ultimate nature of the phallus. Also, to define it as lack in being in Lacan's clinical practice makes it equivalent to the barred subject. This radical position of the nature of the phallus as lack in being allows for the equivalence between this lacking phallus and subjective lack itself.[20]

Insofar as the phallic Master-Signifier is the point of the subject's symbolic identification, identification is ultimately always *identification with a lack*. Sometimes, mentioning the so-called excesses of Political Correctness is justified—not to make cheap jibes about it, but to identify at its purest the logic which underlies our social space. Take the case of Deaf Nation:

> Today deaf activists, who argue that being deaf is not a disability but a distinguishing mark of separateness, are in the process of creating a Deaf Nation. They resist medical interventions, such as cochlear implants, or attempts to train deaf children to speak ("Oralism," they say with contempt) and insist that sign language is a fully fledged language in its own right. Capitalizing the D in "Deaf" symbolizes the view that deafness is a culture and not simply the loss of hearing.[21]

The entire academic identity-politics machine is thus set in motion: scholars give courses and publish books on "deaf history" dealing with the oppression of the deaf and celebrating victims of Oralism, organize Deaf conventions, denounce speech therapists and hearing-aid manufacturers as a powerful lobby which wants to grind the deaf minority down, and so on and so forth. It is easy to make fun of this case—and one can imagine going several steps further: if Deaf Nation, why not Blind Nation, fighting the tyranny of Visualism? Why not Impotent and Frigid nation, oppressed by Sexualism? Why not the Fat Nation, terrorized by the health-food and the fitness lobbies? Why not Stupid Nation, brutally oppressed by the academic lobby? The sky is the limit here ... However, it is much more interesting to see the formation of the Deaf Nation as a repetition of the very matrix of the rise of a specifically human community—as an attempt to elevate (what is from a biological standpoint) a lack into a distinguishing feature of collective identification, and then to mobilize creative energy to invent new modes of supplanting this lack. In a way, we humans *are* a

---

20 Jacques-Alain Miller, "Phallus and Perversion," *lacanian ink* 33 (Spring 2009), p. 58.

21 Margaret MacMillan, *The Uses and Abuses of History*, London: Profile 2009, p. 60.

"Deaf Nation"—Lacan's name for the "deafness" (the malfunction) constitutive of being-human is, of course, symbolic castration.

This brings us to the paradox of how sexual difference relates to the phallic signifier: the moment we conceive the phallus as signifier and not only as an image ("symbol") of potency, fertility, or whatever, we should conceive it primarily as something that, due to the very fact that a woman lacks a penis, belongs to her (or, more precisely, to the mother). It is thus not that, in a first moment, man "has it" and woman does not, and, in a second moment, woman fantasizes about "having it." As Lacan puts it on the very last page of his *Écrits*: "the lack of penis in the mother is 'where the nature of the phallus is revealed.' We must give all its importance to this indication, which distinguishes precisely the function of the phallus and its nature."[22] And it is here that we should rehabilitate Freud's deceptively "naïve" notion of the fetish as the last thing the subject sees before it sees the lack of a penis in a woman: what a fetish covers up is not simply the absence of a penis in a woman (in contrast to its presence in a man), but the fact that this very structure of presence/absence is differential in the strict "structuralist" sense.[23]

What makes the phallic signifier such a complex notion is not only that, in it, the symbolic, imaginary, and Real dimensions are intertwined, but also that, in a double self-reflexive step which uncannily imitates the process of the "negation of the negation," it condenses three levels: (1) *position*: the signifier of the lost part, of what the subject loses and lacks with its entry into (or submission to) the signifying order; (2) *negation*: the signifier of (this) lack; and (3) *negation of the negation*: the lacking/missing signifier itself.[24] The phallus is the part which is lost ("sacrificed") with the entry into the symbolic order and, simultaneously, the signifier of this loss.[25] (Therein is grounded the link between the phallic signifier and the Name-of-the-Father, the paternal Law; here also, Lacan accomplishes the same self-relating reversal, for the paternal prohibition is itself prohibited.) Why is this the case? Why should the prohibition itself be prohibited? The answer is: *because there is no meta-language.*

---

22 Cited in Miller, "Phallus and Perversion," p. 58.

23 Against the standard feminist critiques of Freud's "phallocentrism," Boothby makes clear Lacan's radical reinterpretation of the notorious notion of "penis envy": "Lacan enables us finally to understand that penis envy is most profoundly felt precisely by those who have a penis" (Richard Boothby, *Freud as Philosopher*, London: Routledge 2001, p. 292).

24 François Balmès, *Dieu, le sexe et la vérité*, Ramonville Saint-Agne: Érès 2007, p. 150.

25 The properly Freudian reply to the common-sense dig at alleged "psychoanalytic symbolism" ("Sometimes a cigar is just a cigar!") is undoubtedly: "Sometimes a phallus is just a phallus!" It should be added, however, that the subject for whom a phallus is just a phallus has a precise name: the pervert.

The idea(l) of a symbolic order which clearly and explicitly states its prohibitions presupposes a level at which prohibitions that ground the symbolic space are canceled, a level free of prohibitions at which we can, in this space of "communication free of domination," establish the very rules of domination. It is as if we are not fully caught up in relations of domination but are able to occupy the neutral position of a meta-language from which we can view domination from the outside, observing it without our position of enunciation already being affected by it. Recall a typical child's strategy when confronted with his father's stern prohibition: in a (sometimes touching) gesture of trying to ensure a level of basic solidarity above (or, rather, beneath) their conflict, he tries to address the father as an equal partner, to secure the conditions under which he will accept the paternal prohibition. At his show trial, Nikolai Bukharin found himself in exactly the same predicament when he heroically insisted that the core of his subjectivity should be exempted from his confessions. In his letter to Stalin of December 10, 1937, while making clear that he would obey the ritual of confession *in public* ("In order to avoid any misunderstandings, I will say to you from the outset that, as far as the world at large [society] is concerned … I have no intention of recanting anything I've written down [confessed]"[26]), he desperately addressed Stalin as a person, professing his innocence. Bukharin's fatal mistake was to think that he could in a sense have his cake and eat it: to the very end, while professing utter devotion to the Party and to Stalin personally, he was not ready to renounce the minimum of subjective autonomy. He was ready to plead guilty *in public* if the party needed his confession, but in the inner circle, among comrades, he wanted it to be made clear that he was not really guilty, but just willing to play the necessary role in the public ritual. This, precisely, the Party could not allow him: the ritual loses its performative power the moment it is explicitly designated as a mere ritual.

Far from being a symbol of power and fertility, the phallic signifier thus gives body to the structural fault of the system; that is, it stands for the point at which a fault can no longer be recast as a positive feature, the point of "What do you want? No system is without faults!" the point at which castration is inscribed into a system. This is why it has to be covered up: its disclosure equals the disclosure of castration. This covering-up has "two essential recourses: the wall—which is the phobic solution—or the veil—which is the fetishistic solution."[27] We can even take a step further and conceive the veil as a *painted wall*, like the Berlin Wall, which was painted on its Western side, or the wall that separates the (very diminished and fragmented) West Bank from Israel proper. The dream that underlies this politics of "painting the wall" is best illustrated

26 J. Arch Getty and Oleg V. Naumov, *The Road to Terror: Stalin and the Self-Destruction of the Bolsheviks, 1932–39*, New Haven and London: Yale University Press 1999, p. 556.
27 Miller, "Phallus and Perversion," p. 61.

by a wall that separates a Jewish settler's town from the Palestinian town on a nearby hill somewhere in the West Bank. The Israeli side of the wall is painted with the image of the countryside beyond the wall—but minus the Palestinian town. Is this not ethnic cleansing at its purest, imagining the outside beyond the wall as it should be, empty, virginal, waiting to be settled? Who is devouring whom here? Afraid of being devoured by the Arabs surrounding it, Israel is effectively gradually devouring the West Bank.[28]

And the same goes for the so-called "non-castrated" omnipotent devouring mother: apropos the real mother, Lacan noted that "not only is there an unsatisfied mother but also an all-powerful one. And the terrifying aspect of this figure of the Lacanian mother is that she is all-powerful and unsatisfied at the same time."[29] Therein resides the paradox: the more "omnipotent" a mother appears, the more unsatisfied (which means: lacking) she is: "The Lacanian mother corresponds to the formula *quaerens quem devoret*: she looks for someone to devour, and so Lacan presents her then as the crocodile, the subject with the open mouth."[30] This devouring mother does not respond (to the child's demand for a sign of love), and it is as such that she appears omnipotent: "Since the mother does not respond … she is transformed into the real mother, that is to say, into power … if the Other does not respond, he is transformed into a devouring power."[31] The lesson from all this is a surprisingly feminist one: being a mother is not the ultimate destiny or path of fulfillment for a woman, but a secondary substitute. Being-a-mother makes a woman "the one who has," it obfuscates her lack, but

> behind the mother there is always a Medea; this is always in the order of the possible. And even if the mother is exemplary, the child is only a substitute, to such a point that one must assume the question which is presented here: is maternity the only path or the privileged path of the realization of the female? … Lacan surely had the idea that maternity is not the path, it is a metaphorical part for the woman, to the point that I think that the ethics of psychoanalysis cannot really impose this ideal that is more on the side of substitution, even for Freud himself.[32]

---

28 It would be appropriate if the Zionists who want to annex the West Bank were to remember passages from the Old Testament like the following: "Do not oppress an alien; you yourselves know how it feels to be aliens, because you were aliens in Egypt" (Exodus 23:9); "When an alien lives with you in your land, do not ill-treat him. The alien living with you must be treated as one of your native-born. Love him as yourself, for you were aliens in Egypt" (Leviticus 19:33–4).

29 Miller, "Phallus and Perversion," p. 23.

30 Jacques-Alain Miller, "The Logic of the Cure," *lacanian ink* 33 (Spring 2009), p. 19.

31 Ibid., p. 28.

32 Ibid., p. 31.

The "good" mother fills in her lack with a child-fetish; the "evil" devouring mother fills it in with her phobic-terrifying figure—again, two modes of obfuscating the void that is (feminine) subjectivity.[33]

But this description opens up the space for a standard reproach to the Lacanian notions of the phallus and castration, which is that they involve an ahistorical short-circuit: Lacan directly links the limitation of human existence as such to a particular threat (that of castration) which relies on a specific patriarchal gender constellation. The next move is usually to try to get rid of the idea of castration—this "ridiculous" Freudian notion—by claiming that the threat of castration is, at best, just a local expression of the global limitation of the human condition, which is that of human finitude, experienced in a whole series of constraints (the existence of other people who limit our freedom, our mortality, and, also, the necessity of "choosing one's sex"). This move from castration to an anxiety grounded in the finitude of the human condition is, of course, the standard existential-philosophical move of "saving" Freud by getting rid of the embarrassing topic of castration and penis envy ("who can take this seriously today?"). Psychoanalysis is thus redeemed, magically transformed into a respectable academic discipline that deals with how suffering human subjects cope with the anxieties of finitude. The (in)famous advice given to Freud by Jung as their boat was approaching the US coast in 1912—that Freud should leave out or at least limit his emphasis on sexuality, in order to render psychoanalysis more acceptable to the American medical establishment—is resuscitated here.

Why, then, is it not sufficient to emphasize how "castration" is just a particular instance of the general limitation of the human condition? Or, to put it in a slightly different way, how should one cut the link between the universal symbolic structure and the particular corporeal economy? The old reproach against Lacan is that he conflates two levels, the allegedly neutral-universal-formal symbolic structure and the particular-gendered-bodily reference: true, he emphasizes that the phallus is not the penis as an organ, but a signifier, even a "pure" signifier—so why then call this "pure" signifier a "phallus"? However, as was clear to Deleuze (and not only to Lacan), the notion of castration answers a very specific question: how does the universal symbolic process detach itself from its corporeal roots? How does it *emerge* in its relative autonomy? "Castration" designates the violent bodily cut which enables us to enter the domain of the incorporeal. And the same goes for the topic of finitude: "castration" is not simply one local case of the experience of finitude—the concept of castration tries to answer a more fundamental "arche-transcendental" question, namely, *how do we, as humans, experience ourselves as marked by finitude in the first place?* This fact is not self-evident: Heidegger was right to emphasize that only humans exist in the mode

33 So is there a vagina with teeth? There is, of course, and it is called virginity—the point of losing virginity is precisely that the vaginal teeth get broken.

of "being-towards-death." Of course, animals are also somehow "aware" of their limitations, of their limited power, and so on—the hare *does* try to escape the fox. And yet, this is not the same as human finitude, which emerges against the background of the small child's narcissistic attitude of illusory omnipotence (of course, we do indeed say that, in order to become mature, we have to accept our limitations). What lurks behind this narcissistic attitude is, however, the Freudian death drive, a kind of "undead" stubbornness denounced already by Kant as a violent excess absent in animals—which is why, for Kant, only humans need education through discipline. The symbolic Law does not tame and regulate nature, but, precisely, applies itself to an unnatural excess. Or, to approach the same complex from another direction: at its most radical, the helplessness of the small child about which Freud speaks is not physical helplessness, the inability to provide for one's own needs, but a helplessness in the face of the enigma of the Other's desire, a helpless fascination with the excess of the Other's enjoyment, and the ensuing inability to account for its meaning in the terms available.

So what is symbolic castration, with the phallus as its signifier? We should begin by conceiving of the phallus as a signifier—which means what? From the traditional rituals of investiture, we know the objects which not only "symbolize" power, but put the subject who acquires them into the position of effectively *exercising* power—if a king holds the scepter and wears the crown, his words will be taken as the words of a king. Such insignia are external, not part of my nature: I don them; wear them in order to exert power. As such, they "castrate" me: they introduce a gap between what I immediately am and the function that I exercise (thus I am never fully at the level of my function). This is what the infamous "symbolic castration" means: not "castration as symbolic, as just symbolically enacted" (in the sense in which we say that one is "symbolically castrated" when deprived of something), but the castration which occurs by the very fact of being caught up in the symbolic order, assuming a symbolic mandate. Castration is the gap between what I immediately am and the symbolic mandate which confers on me this "authority." In this precise sense, far from being the opposite of power, it is synonymous with power; it is that which confers power on me. And, one has to think of the phallus not as the organ which immediately expresses the vital force of my being, my virility, and so on, but precisely as such an insignia, as a mask which I put on in the same way a king or judge puts on his insignia—the phallus is an "organ without a body" which I put on, which gets attached to my body, without ever becoming its "organic part," forever sticking out as an incoherent, excessive supplement.

But the fact remains that the notion of the "phallic signifier" enacts a short-circuit between pure difference (the form of meaning prior to meaning) and a contingent bodily element. How to justify this? The point is, precisely, that the short-circuit is thoroughly contingent: to become operative, pure difference, its pure form, has to attach itself to a contingent bodily element (the absence/presence of a penis). This short-circuit between the opposites is the same as that of the rational order of the State, which only acquires full actuality in the contingent monarch's body, which is thereby transubstantiated/*aufgehoben*, turned into a "reflexive determination" of its opposite. One should recall here the phenomenon of the phantom limb: the sensation that an amputated limb or organ, like a hand, is still attached to the body and moving appropriately with other body parts. In contrast to the phantom organ (which we feel even if it is cut off), the phallus is the organ which men effectively possess (as a penis), but they do not feel it as such, always experiencing it as missing, cut off, separated.

Can this identity between pure form and a contingent bodily element be broken? Can the contingent objectal moment be separated from the symbolic form of a pure signifier? This, for Lacan, is precisely what happens in what he calls *separation*, the separation of the object from the signifier, which renders visible the utter contingency of their link.

From the Phallic Signifier to *Objet a*

The concept of *point de capiton* underwent many transformations in Lacan's later work before finding its definite form in the notion of the Master-Signifier. This, finally, brings us to back to Miller: in "Suture," first delivered as an intervention at Jacques Lacan's seminar on February 24, 1965, he elevated a casual word that occurs once in Lacan into a concept designating the relationship between the signifying structure and the subject of the signifier. Miller's implicit starting point is Lacan's definition of the signifier as that which "represents the subject for another signifier": all signifiers are not on the same level—since no structure is complete, since there is, in a structure, always a lack, this lack is filled in, remarked, sustained even, by a "reflexive" signifier which is the signifier of the lack of the signifier. Identifying the subject with the lack, we can thus say that the reflexive signifier of the lack represents the subject for the other signifiers. If this sounds abstract, recall numerous examples from the history of science, from phlogiston (a pseudo-concept which merely betrayed the scientist's ignorance of how light really travels) to Marx's "Asiatic mode of production" (which is a kind of negative container: the only true content of this concept being "all those modes of production which do not fit Marx's standard categorization of modes of production"). Miller generates the notion of the subject without any reference to the imaginary level: this "subject of the signifier" involves no lived experience, consciousness, or any other predicates we usually associate with subjectivity.[34]

34 In the later development of Lacanian theory, of course, complications arise: there is a pathological "stain" that is the subject's equivalent—not imaginary, but real, the *objet petit*

The basic operation of suture is thus that 0 is counted as one: the absence of a determination is counted as a positive determination of its own, as in Borges's famous classification of dogs which includes, as a species, all the dogs not included among the previous species, in other words, the "part of no-part" of the canine genus. While all this is well known, what is usually left out of consideration is the formal homology (as well as substantial difference) between this reflexive logic of the Master-Signifier—the signifier of the lack of the signifier, the signifier which functions as a stand-in (filler) of a lack—and the logic of the *objet petit a* which is also repeatedly defined by Lacan as the filler of a lack: an object whose status is purely virtual, with no positive consistency of its own, only a positivization of a lack in the symbolic order. Something escapes the symbolic order, and this X is positivized as the *objet a*, the *je ne sais quoi* which makes me desire a certain thing or person. It is all too easy to counter the hermeneutic circle of Meaning with reference to the external reality of the voice (or some other material medium) itself, emphasizing how the presence of this external reality is an a priori condition of every re-presentation—every hermeneutician will fully endorse this point, adding only that we should repeat the same move in the opposite direction and concede that every such presence always already appears to us within a certain symbolic horizon of understanding, never in its virgin factuality. The true task is to see how Meaning is corroded *from within* by an ex-timate object, an object inherent to it, a stranger within.

However, this formal parallel between the Master-Signifier and the *objet petit a* should not deceive us: although, in both cases, we seem to be dealing with an entity which fills in the lack, what differentiates the *objet a* from the Master-Signifier is that, in the case of the former, the lack is redoubled, that is, the *objet a* is the result of the overlapping of the two lacks, the lack in the Other (the symbolic order) and the lack in the object—in the visual field, say, the *objet a* is what we cannot see, our blind spot in relation to the picture. Each of the two lacks can operate independently of the other: we can have the lack of the signifier, as when we have a rich experience for which "words are missing," or we can have the lack in the visible for which, precisely, there *is* a signifier, namely the Master-Signifier, the mysterious signifier which seems to recapture the invisible dimension of the object. Therein resides the illusion of the Master-Signifier: it coalesces with the *objet a*, so that it appears that the subject's Other/Master possesses what the subject lacks. This is what Lacan calls alienation: the confrontation of the subject with a figure of the Other possessing what the subject lacks. In separation, which follows alienation, the *objet a* is separated also from the Other, from the Master-Signifier; that is, the subject discovers that the Other

---

a, the "stain in the picture," the non-signifying remainder of the signifying operation. In this way, we arrive at the four elements of Lacan's concept of discourse: the chain of ordinary signifiers (S_2), the Master-Signifier (S_1), the "barred" subject ($), the object (*a*).

also does not have what he is lacking. The axiom Lacan follows is "no I without *a*": wherever an I (unary feature, signifying mark that represents the subject) emerges, it is followed by an *a*, the stand-in for what was lost in the signification of the real.[35]

Is, then, the *objet a* the signified of the S_1, of the Master-Signifier? It may appear so, since the Master-Signifier signifies precisely that imponderable X which eludes the series of positive properties signified by the chain of "ordinary" signifiers (S_2). But, upon a closer look, we see that the relationship is exactly the inverse: with regard to the division between signifier and signified, the *objet a* is on the side of the signifier, it fills in the lack in/of the signifier, while the Master-Signifier is the "quilting point" between the signifier and the signified, the point at which the signifier falls into the signified.

How, then, does One divide into Two? Gilbert Ryle once played with the idea that the only way to bring to an end the interminable division of an entity into smaller and smaller parts would be to reach the point of the "last division," the point at which One no longer divides into two positive parts, but into *a part and nothingness*. For Lacan, this nothingness positivizes itself as the *objet a*. This nothingness which supplements every positive identity is not to be confused with the differentiality constitutive of every identity: the relation between the One and the *objet a* is not that of differentiality, but that of diffraction at its most elementary: the One (the clearly delineated object) plus its *teleiosis*, its blurred virtual supplement, "more than one but less than two."[36] This two-ness, the doubling of an entity into itself and its *teleiosis*, the nothingness of its objectal shadow, precedes any relationship to the big Other (the symbolic order) as well as to a complementary other (a polar opposite: masculine and feminine, light and darkness, left and right ...). The *objet a* is not complementary to the One, but its supplement; a strange supplement which makes the One to which it is attached not so much more as less than One, corroding it from within; it is an excess which subtracts.[37]

---

35 Years ago, on the Santa Cruz campus, one of the capitals of Political Correctness, I was told that they had developed jokes which were funny without hurting, humiliating, or even making fun of anyone, like, "What happens when a triangle meets a circle?..." Predictably, I immediately exploded: "I don't care what happens when a triangle meets a circle, the whole point of a joke is that there must be someone who gets hurt, humiliated ...!" But what if I was wrong, what if it is the purely formal aspect of a joke which makes it funny much more than its content, in the same way that sexuality is not a matter of direct content, but of the way this content is formally treated? The problem, of course, is whether this form can work alone, or whether it needs "a little piece of reality" added to it, in the sense of some contingent positive content related to "dirty" topics (sex, violence, etc.).

36 For a more detailed account of *teleiosis*, see Chapter 14.

37 The relationship between anorexia and bulimia is a supreme example of the link

This nothingness which attaches itself to every entity as its shadowy double is the zero-level of negativity and is as such inaccessible to Hegel, as the non-thematized presupposition of his entire deployment of negativity. Hegel does formulate the overlapping of two lacks, the subject's lack and the lack of/in the substance itself (recall his famous statement that the secrets of the Ancient Egyptians were secrets also for the Egyptians themselves); however, he does not see this overlapping (dis-alienation) as separation, but as a cancellation of the lack—for example, if my distance from God is God's distance from himself, then there is a reconciliation between me and God. In other words, what Hegel misses is the *objet a*, the object produced by the overlapping of the two lacks. Furthermore, it is because of his inability to think the *objet a* that Hegel cannot conceive pure repetition: pure repetition is sustained by the nothingness of the *objet a* which haunts every One, for the One repeats itself in the attempt to recapture its shadow.

Although the *objet a* is the non-signifying glitch within a symbolic edifice, it can thus only be conceived against the background of the gap that separates a formal structure from the elements that fill in its places. Jacques-Alain Miller recently elaborated this gap apropos the topic of structure and change. He took Lacan's matrix of the four discourses—in which, in an anti-clockwise movement, each of the four terms (the subject—$; the Master-Signifier—$S_1$; the chain of knowledge—S_2; the object—*a*) gradually occupies all four places in the structure (agent, other, truth, production)—as the exemplary case of how

> something remains constant and, at the same time, something changes. What remains constant? The places, the relationships and the relationships between the places. What changes are the terms that occupy these places … This is what allows us to say that precisely in the structure the transformation is a permutation, that speaking of permutation is the attempt, the way of making the structure dynamic and, I would say, it is a certain structural solution for the articulation of one and of multiple. The places are fixed and, with the permutation of terms, we obtain the variants.[38]

This difference between (fixed) structural places and the (variable) terms that occupy these places is crucial in order to break the fetishistic coagulation of a

---

between lack and excess: anorexics as a rule turn into bulimics and then, in order to punish themselves, return to anorexia. Bulimics eat to excess while, for anorexics, *all* food is already an excess, a disgusting foreign body to be rejected. Which is why the two coincide: they both lack the "common measure" of the "normal" habit of eating; they both bear witness to the imbalance introduced into the animal rhythm of digestion by the emergence of subjectivity.

38 Miller, "The Logic of the Cure," p. 11.

term with its place, to make us aware of the extent to which the aura emanating from an object hinges not on the object's direct properties, but on the place it occupies. The classic example of this dependency on place is, of course, Marcel Duchamp's well-known urinal, which became an art object by being exhibited as such. Duchamp's achievement was not just to extend the scope of what counts as a work of art (even a urinal), but—as a formal condition of such universalization—to introduce the distinction between an object and the (structural) place it occupies: what makes a urinal a work of art is not its immanent properties, but the place it occupies (in an art gallery)—or, as Marx put it long ago apropos commodity fetishism, people do not treat a person as a king because he is a king, he is a king because people treat him as such.[39] In everyday life, we are victims of a kind of reification: we misperceive a purely formal or structural determination as a direct property of an object. This is why one can imagine a quite justified provocation at a Duchamp exhibition: a spectator starts to urinate into the urinal; when the shocked bystanders remind him that this is an art gallery, not a toilet, he replies: "No, you don't get it: when I entered the space of the art object, my activity also became an art performance—what I did was not vulgar desublimation, I merely filled the sublime space of art with new content ..." This logic was taken to an extreme in Hal Ashby's film *Being There* (based on Jerzy Koziński's short novel) in which Peter Sellers plays the US president's autistic, socially isolated gardener. When the president dies unexpectedly, Sellers is mistaken for the president's wise confidante. His naïve sayings about how to cultivate a garden are taken as encoded deep insights into how to run international affairs simply because he "is there"—finds himself in the wrong place, like Roger O. Thornhill who is mistaken for the inexistent George Kaplan at the beginning of Hitchcock's *North by Northwest*.[40]

This purely formal boundary between daily life in which we engage with objects and the aesthetic stance in which we suspend the functional use of objects can also be registered in non-artistic ways. Recall *chindogu*, the Japanese movement popular a decade or more ago, devoted to inventing objects which are useless in their very over-functionality (like spectacles with small wiper-blades, enabling one to see clearly while walking in rain; or a lipstick-tube filled

39 The difference between a structural place and the element filling it out is also discernible in the subtle distinction between "we are waiting for X" and "X is what we were waiting for." For example, if we are eagerly expecting a new book from an author, and the book, when it finally appears, turns out to be a disappointment, we can say: "Although we were waiting for this book, this is not the book we were waiting for."

40 Or, as Will Self wrote apropos his *The Book of Dave*: "The book is arguing that what you need for a revealed religion is any old bollocks, it just has to be there in the right place at the right time" (quoted in Helen Brown, Interview with Will Self, *Daily Telegraph*, May 28, 2006).

with butter, allowing me to butter a slice of bread without a knife)—through this procedure, a kind of technological counterpart to ideological over-identification, our engagement with technology itself is turned into a means of releasing ourselves from its grip. Although the shift from a sexual to an aesthetic attitude towards a naked body is often taken as a model for such disengagement, one should not forget the fundamental lesson of psychoanalysis, namely that sexuality itself emerges from a similar disengagement: the disengagement from the procreative functionality of mating. Sexuality proper occurs only when the process of mating is cut off from its procreative goal and posited as an end-in-itself, caught in the vicious cycle of repetitive insistence which cannot ever be fully satisfied.[41]

This difference between place and term opens up the possibility (or, rather, structural *necessity*) of an empty place lacking any element to fill it in; for this place to occur, it must itself be "marked" as empty, in other words, within it, form and content are mediated. This place is not simply empty or without content, emptiness *is* its content (or, to put it in structuralist jargon, absence—of content—is itself present in it). We thus get two emptinesses: direct pre-symbolic emptiness and emptiness marked as such within the symbolic space; or, in terms of music, we get two silences, direct silence and marked silence, a silence heard as such: the "sound of silence." In the old days of the jukebox, some diners offered a simple solution for those guests who preferred silence to the noisy music: the machine would contain a disc with nothing recorded on it lasting the length of an average song, so the customer who wanted peace just had to slip in the appropriate coins and select the silent disc—a nice structural mechanism for "marking" silence itself as present: after the empty disc was selected, not only was there no longer music playing, but, in a way, *silence itself was playing*.

But does this difference between place and content not remain too formalistic? Do we not, as card-carrying Hegelians, have to take a further step towards the full dialectical overlapping of form and content? Here is Miller's concise description of this overlapping apropos what one can only call Lévi-Strauss's Hegelianism (ironically, in view of the latter's opposition to dialectics):

> It is a matter of a logic, a logic of detail, it is a matter of assuming some details. Lévi-Strauss had already said it, long ago, that it was the superiority of structuralism over

41 Architecture (together with design) is here unique: it has to generate this effect of the suspension of everyday functioning, of disengagement, while simultaneously constructing buildings which still meet the material needs of the people using it and thus function as part of everyday functional reality. At its best, it succeeds in pervading our utilitarian use of the object with a kind of disengagement, so that, in a utopian way, our daily business is elevated to an aesthetic experience.

> formalism. He said it in an introduction to Vladimir Propp, who had proposed a formalization of fairy tales. He said: for the formalist there is a form, and the details are like an amorphous material that does not count; for a structuralist, on the contrary, there is no distinction between material and form and the structure is found in the things themselves, so everything counts; one cannot be satisfied with an abstract formula.[42]

We are dealing here with the properly dialectical paradox of *an object which "is" only its formal structure*, a paradox that offers a solution to the problem of structural change stronger than the permutation of terms within a fixed set of places: permutations come to an end when an element intervenes *whose emergence (or disappearance) changes the structure itself.* Such an element is the Lacanian *objet a*: an element to which—since its status is thoroughly non-substantial—the form(al matrix) itself is linked as to its umbilical cord. At the (admittedly rather abstract) level of social dynamics, such an element is what Badiou calls the "symptomal torsion" of the social edifice, its Rancièrian "part of no-part": this element cannot just be submitted to permutation and made to occupy different places within the same formal edifice—the change in its position necessarily brings about a radical transformation of the entire edifice itself. One can only talk about the "part of no-part" against the background of the topic of suture.

This brings us, finally, to the most speculative aspect of the notion of suture: the purely formal difference between an element and its place functions as a *pure difference* which is no longer a difference between two positive entities; and, as we have already seen, this pure difference is the condition of symbolic differentiality. The paradox is thus that what sutures a field is not a unifying feature but the pure difference itself—how?

Sibelius's silence

One aspect of the difference between modernism and postmodernism, not only in music, is that modernism involves a logic of prohibition and/or limitation—what is dodecaphony if not a self-imposed set of limitations on and prohibitions of harmonies? The paradox here, noted already by Adorno, is that the liberation from the chains of tonality assumes the form of a self-imposed set of limitations and prohibitions which demand a strict discipline. Postmodernism, on the contrary, stands for a massive return to the stance of "everything is permitted." But why? Our awareness that the authentic Thing is irrevocably lost, that no substantial relationship towards it is possible, generates an attitude of playfulness in which the old forms can be reenacted in the form of pastiche, deprived of their

42 Miller, "The Logic of the Cure," p. 29.

substantial content. In this sense, was not Stravinsky (as opposed to Schoenberg) the first postmodern composer, playing freely with all inherited styles?[43]

If the couple of Schoenberg and Stravinsky exemplifies the opposition of modernity and postmodernity, who then is emblematic of the missing third option, that of a persistent traditionalism? The answer is the third S, Sibelius, so utterly despised by Adorno; not any old Sibelius, but Sibelius once he had outgrown the influence of Tchaikovsky, the Sibelius of the fourth symphony. Here one encounters the notion of "substance"—of being immersed in the ethnic substance of one's being—at its most radical, beyond all cheap late-Romantic nationalism. And here we should counterpose Sibelius and Mahler, in particular, the two similar movements from their symphonies: Mahler's notorious Adagietto from his fifth symphony, and what is arguably Sibelius's supreme achievement, the third movement (Il tempo largo) from his fourth symphony. In spite of the striking similarity, one can feel here the gap succinctly expressed in the famous dialogue between the two composers that took place during Mahler's visit to Helsinki: Mahler emphasized how a symphony has to encompass the entire world, while Sibelius pleaded for restraint and reserve.[44]

The proof of Sibelius's artistic integrity, the proof that his case is not straightforwardly that of a phony conservative, lies in his ultimate *failure*: his silence from the mid-1920s onwards when, for thirty years, he composed practically nothing.[45] At what precise point in his development did Sibelius fall into silence?—at the point when the parallax that provided the basic tension of his work collapsed, when the distance between the two lines of his music, symphonic and narrative, dissolved. His last two substantial compositions are the seventh symphony and the tone poem "Tapiola" (which, as was often remarked,

---

43 In Lacanian terms, this difference is that between alienation and separation: modernism enacts alienation, the loss of one's roots in tradition, but only with postmodernism do we truly separate ourselves from tradition: its loss is no longer experienced as a loss, which is why we can playfully return to it.

44 This, perhaps, is what makes Sibelius similar to Maurice Ravel, the other great composer of restraint and reserve: Stephan in Claude Sautet's *Un coeur en hiver* is in a way a portrait of Ravel himself, of the proper "spirit" of his music. The difference between Ravel and Sibelius is the difference of the two types of reserve: refined and sensitive French bourgeois self-constraint versus Nordic rural reticence and distrust of metropolitan society. Recall Ravel's ironic statement apropos his "Trio," one of his greatest masterpieces, that he had in his head the whole piece already composed—he just had to invent and insert the melodic lines. This priority of structure over the melodic line is perhaps the best characterization of the "reserve" of Ravel's musical style.

45 All great composers fail—Beethoven's ninth is a failure, Wagner's *Parsifal* is a failure, the finale of Mozart's *Cosi* is a failure—failure is a sign that the composer is dealing with the *Real* of the musical matter. It is only the "light" *kitsch* composers who can pass from one smooth triumph to the next.

is to the forest what Debussy's "La mer" is to the sea), and their crucial feature is their similarity (both are of approximately same length, in one long movement internally subdivided, but deeply interconnected), as if Sibelius approached the same ideal-impossible point of encounter from two different directions. This impossible/ideal Sibelius composition is the one which would "sublate" the tension between "absolute music" (symphonies) and "programmatic music" (tone poems), between music as representing (depicting, evoking ...) a determinate "content" and music as rendering its spiritual content directly by means of its formal articulation, between the wealth of personal experience (of nature) and the void of subjectivity. ("Tapiola" internalizes the experience of forest into a purely spiritual, "abstract" inner journey, while the seventh symphony comes imperceptibly close to being a tone poem.) This synthesis, of course, is a priori impossible, the failure is structural, and Sibelius, to retain his artistic integrity, had to remain silent. But it is precisely on account of this uncanny proximity and resemblance that the *difference* between absolute and programmatic music, between symphony and tone poem, becomes more palpable than ever: the last symphony renders a state of inner calm and satisfaction, of a battle finally won, of the assertion of Life (no wonder that it often resembles the fifth symphony), while "Tapiola"—far from falling into the Romantic trap of an immersion in the healing flux of Nature—renders the restlessness and horror at the raw power of nature, man's vain attempt to resist the power of nature and his ultimate breakdown. The final outcome of the cycle of symphonies is thus assertion and reconciliation, and of the tone poems failure and loss, with no further mediation possible between these two poles.

The third movement of Sibelius's fourth symphony exemplifies his intense relationship towards musical "stuff": it is a kind of musical counterpart to the statues of Rodin (or even late Michelangelo) in which the shape of the body painfully, with strenuous effort, endeavors to emerge from the inert captivity of the stone, never quite getting rid of the oppressive weight of material inertia. The great effort of this movement is to give birth to the central melodic motif (melodic line), which occurs only a couple of times towards the end of the movement. This procedure offers the greatest possible contrast to Viennese classicism in which the motif, the main melodic line, is directly given and rendered (in Mozart's famous third movement of *Gran Partita*, the melodic line literally "emerges from up above," "from heaven," delivered of any material weight).

If we reach even further back in time, we enter a period in which there was no melody in the strict sense of the term. Take a popular baroque piece like Pachelbel's "Canon": today, the first notes are automatically perceived as the accompaniment, so that we wait for the moment when the melody proper will emerge; since we get no melody but only a more and more intricate polyphonic variation of (what we perceived as) the pre-melodic accompaniment, we somehow feel "disappointed." Where does this horizon of expectation, which sustains our feeling that the melody proper is missing, come from? The moment of the birth of a melody proper is, of course, the event of Viennese classicism; suffice it to recall again the third movement of the *Gran Partita* serenade: after the first notes, whose status is uncertain (*today*, we perceive them as accompaniment preparing the way for the melody proper, while in its own time, there probably was uncertainty as to its status, for it was probably perceived as already the main melodic line), the melody proper enters as if "from above," from the "heavenly heights." And where does then the melody proper end? The answer is also clear: in late Beethoven (especially his last piano sonatas), in Romanticism proper, whose true breakthrough resides precisely in rendering the melody proper "impossible," in marking it with a bar of impossibility (the flowering of "beautiful Romantic melodies" is nothing but the kitschy obverse of this fundamental impossibility). So we have an apparently universal phenomenon (melody) which is, "as such," nonetheless constrained, limited to a precisely defined historical period. What is perhaps the ultimate achievement of late Romantic expressionism is precisely the notion of the melodic line, of the main motif, as something which has to be "wrought out," sculpted, extracted from the inertia of vocal material by means of painful labor: far from functioning as the starting point for a series of variations which then form the main part of the piece, the main musical motif results from the painful perlaboration of the musical matter which forms the main body of the piece. Perhaps this intense relationship towards the inertia of stuff or matter is what brings together Sibelius and Tarkovsky, for whom, also, the earth, in its inert, humid nature, is not opposed to spirituality but is its very medium.

In this respect, the third movement of Sibelius's fourth symphony has to be contrasted with its concluding fourth movement. Each of them renders a specific mode of failure. As we have just seen, the third movement displays a painful effort to extract the main melody, an effort which twice comes to the very verge of succeeding, yet ultimately fails: "what purports to be the main theme … as the movement evolves tries twice to achieve the status of a fully fashioned melody, but backs off each time, first when dissuaded by the return of the opening motif, secondly when crushed by the brass."[46] This failure, this inherent blockage which prevented the ultimate assertion of the melody, must have been especially difficult to bear for Sibelius, who is otherwise known for his capacity to build tension slowly and then release it with the final emergence of the full melodic motif—suffice it to recall the triumphant finales of his second and fifth symphony.

The fourth movement fails in a much more disturbing way:

46 Burnett James, *The Music of Jean Sibelius*, Rutherford: Fairleigh Dickinson University Press 1983, p. 77.

> the first part of the finale appears to be on the point of releasing melodic and impulsive generosities, as though the principle of laying longer, more pliable sentences alongside the concentrated thematic nuclei is about to be honored. But it does not come out like that: before long an unnerving process of disintegration begins which by the end has become total and irreconcilable. The last pages die away into a kind of resigned nothingness, with a thrice repeated figure from a solo oboe as of some mythical creature uttering a cry of infinite loneliness in the frozen wastes of the spirit ...[47]

The last part of this appreciation is not only pseudo-poetically awkward, but *stricto sensu* false: what effectively happens in the last part of the finale of Sibelius's fourth is something much more uncanny than the standard expressionist rendering of the utterly isolated individual's scream heard by no one in the void of an empty wasteland. We rather witness a kind of musical cancer or virus triggering the gradual progressive decomposition of the very musical texture—as if the very foundation, the "stuff" of (musical) reality, loses its consistency; as if, to use another poetic metaphor, the world we live in is gradually losing its color, its depth, its definite shape, its most fundamental ontological consistency.

What happens in the last movement of Sibelius's fourth is thus something homologous to the scene towards the end of Josef Rusnak's *The Thirteenth Floor* (1999), when Hall, the film's hero, drives to a place he would never have considered going to otherwise; at a given point during the trip, he stops the car after seeing that everything within it has been replaced with wireframe models. He has approached the limit of our world, the domain where our dense reality dissolves into abstract digital coordinates, and he finally grasps the truth: that 1990s Los Angeles—his world—is a simulation.

So, instead of becoming engaged, like the third movement, in a struggle to wrest out the melody, the fourth movement begins as if everything is alright, as if the melodic starting point is already at our disposal, and the full organic deployment of its potential is promised; but what happens next is that the material does not resist our effort to mould it properly (as in the third movement)—it rather directly disintegrates, slips away, gradually losing its material substance, turning into a void. We can do anything we want with it, the problem is that the stuff on which we work progressively implodes, collapses, simply fading out. Is not this tension between third and fourth movement of the fourth symphony comparable to the tension between Hitchcock's *Vertigo* and his *Psycho*?[48] It is

---

47 Ibid., p. 75.

48 In short, the passage here is that from Romanticism to modernism. From the standpoint of the new materialism, we should also rehabilitate musical Romanticism: its basic feature is not the celebration of spiritual longing, but the gradual and painful

the difference between the human and the inhuman, or rather the post-human: while the third movement renders the human dimension at its most melancholic, the fourth movement shifts into a dimension beyond, in which a mad post-human playfulness coincides with subjective destitution.

The pure difference

Deleuze often varies the motif of how, in becoming post-human, we should learn to practice "a perception as it was before men (or after) … released from their human coordinates":[49] those who fully endorse the Nietzschean "return of the same" are strong enough to sustain a vision of the "iridescent chaos of a world before man."[50] Although Deleuze openly resorts here to Kantian language, talking about the direct access to "things (the way they are) in themselves," his point is precisely that one should subtract the opposition between phenomena and things-in-themselves, between the phenomenal and the noumenal, from its Kantian context, where noumena are transcendent things that forever elude our grasp. What Deleuze refers to as "things-in-themselves" are in a way *even more phenomenal* than our shared phenomenal reality: they are the impossible phenomena, the phenomena excluded from our symbolically constituted reality. The gap that separates us from noumena is thus primarily not epistemological, but practico-ethical and libidinal: there is no "true reality" behind or beneath phenomena; noumena are phenomenal things which are "too strong," too intense or intensive, for our perceptual apparatus, attuned as it is to constituted reality. Here, epistemological failure is a secondary effect of libidinal terror, its underlying logic a reversal of Kant's "You can, because you must!": "You cannot (know noumena), because you must not!" Think of someone being forced to witness terrifying acts of torture: in a way, the monstrosity of what they see would make this an experience of the noumenal impossible-real that shatters the coordinates of our common reality. (The same holds for witnessing intense sexual activity.)

In this sense, if we were to discover films shot in a concentration camp among the *Musulmannen*, showing scenes from their daily life, how they were

---

emergence of a melody out of a struggle with the musical material. In this sense, musical Romanticism is deeply materialist: in Mozart and (most of) Beethoven, a melody is unproblematically there, simply given as the starting point for its variations, while in Romanticism, the melody only gradually emerges through the struggle with and work on the material. In modernism proper, something even more radical happens: the material itself loses its substantial density and weight.

49 Gilles Deleuze, *Cinema 1: The Movement-Image*, trans. Hugh Tomlinson and Barbara Hammerjam, Minneapolis: University of Minnesota Press 1986, p. 122.

50 Ibid., p. 81.

systematically mistreated and deprived of all dignity, we would have "seen too much," seen the prohibited, we would have entered a forbidden territory of what should have remained unseen. Is this not an example of intensity growing so strong that it undermines or explodes the very transcendental coordinates of the world in which it occurs? This, perhaps, is what is missing in Badiou's notion of intensity as a feature of all entities that belong to a world: they participate in this world with more or less intensity, down to the minimum of the "part of no-part," of the element which is formally part of a world, but deprived of any intense participation in it.[51] But what about the idea of *excessive intensity*? Such an intensity explodes a world, but not from outside, as a simple external catastrophe; it explodes it from within, overburdening its inherent or constitutive intensity. (For example, a community can disintegrate when its rulers take the omnipotence of their role too literally and engage in a murderous annihilation of their subjects.)

This is also what makes it so unbearable to witness the last moments of people who know they are about to die and are in this sense already living-dead. Again, imagine that we discovered intact, among the ruins of the Twin Towers, a video camera from one of the planes containing footage of what went on among the passengers in the minutes before the plane crashed into one of the towers.[52] In all these cases, we would effectively see things as they are "in themselves," outside human coordinates, outside our human reality—we would see the world with inhuman eyes. It is against this background that we should also locate Claude Lanzmann's famous statement that, if by chance he were to stumble upon some documentary footage depicting the actual process of Jews being killed in Auschwitz, he would destroy it immediately—this is Jewish iconoclasm at its purest, as a prohibition on showing images of the raw Real. The lesson here is profoundly Hegelian: the difference between the phenomenal and the noumenal has to be reflected or transposed back into the phenomenal, as the split between the normal "gentrified" phenomenon and the "impossible" phenomenon.

Robert Altman's universe, best exemplified in his masterpiece *Short Cuts*, is effectively one of contingent encounters between a multitude of series, a universe in which different series communicate and resonate at the level of what Altman himself refers to as "subliminal reality" (meaningless mechanical shocks, encounters, and impersonal intensities which precede the level of social meaning). One should thus avoid the temptation to reduce Altman to a poet

51 An Event, of course, turns around this disposition, so that the "part of no-part" becomes the most intense element of the new world—proletarians who were nothing become everything, abstract form which was nothing in realistic painting becomes the hegemonic style, etc.

52 Maybe the US authorities do possess such footage and, for understandable reasons, are keeping it secret.

of American alienation, rendering the silent despair of everyday lives: there is another Altman, for whom the focus is on opening oneself up to joyful aleatory encounters. Just as Deleuze and Guattari read the absence of the inaccessible and elusive transcendent Center (Castle, Court, God) in Kafka as the presence of multiple passages and transformations, one is tempted to read Altmanian "despair and anxiety" as the deceptive obverse of a more affirmative immersion in a multitude of subliminal intensities. The difference is precisely that between human and inhuman: the story read as one of despair and alienation is the story reduced to its human coordinates, while the same story appears as an interplay of contingent encounters between a multitude of series when it is released from those coordinates and read as part of the "iridescent chaos of a world before man."

This "iridescent chaos" is pure Life as the flux of virtual creativity, the flux in which Spinoza's substance as *causa sui* overlaps with the Fichtean self-positing of the pure absolute I: "The concept posits itself to the same extent that it is created. What depends on a free creative activity is also that which, independently and necessarily, posits itself in itself: the most subjective will be the most objective."[53] Consequently, the most succinct definition of Deleuze's late philosophy would be that it amounts to a "Fichteanized Spinozism"—and we should just bear in mind that Fichte was (or perceived himself as) the absolute anti-Spinozist. The purely virtual self-referential act of creation moves at infinite speed, since it needs no externality in/through which to mediate its self-positing movement: "Infinite speed thus describes a movement that no longer has anything to do with actual movement, a purely virtual 'movement' that has always reached its destination, whose moving is itself its own destination."[54] This is why Deleuze insists that desire has no object (whose lack would trigger and sustain its movement): desire itself is "a purely virtual 'movement' that has always reached its destination, whose moving is its own destination." This is also the thrust of Deleuze's reading of masochism and courtly love—in both cases what is at stake is not the logic of sacrifice, but rather how to sustain desire. According to the standard reading of masochism, the masochist, like everyone else, is also looking for pleasure; his problem is that, because of his internalized superego, he has to access pleasure with pain, to pacify the oppressive agency which finds pleasure intolerable. For Deleuze, on the contrary, the masochist chooses pain in order to

> dissolve the pseudo-link of desire with pleasure as its extrinsic measure. Pleasure is in no way something that can only be reached via the detour of pain, but that which has to be delayed to the maximum since it is something which interrupts the

53 Gilles Deleuze and Félix Guattari, *What is Philosophy?*, trans. Hugh Tomlinson and Graham Burchell, New York: Columbia University Press 1994, p. 11.
54 Peter Hallward, *Out of This World*, London: Verso Books 2006, p. 142.

> continuous process of the positive desire. There is an immanent joy of desire, as if desire fills itself with itself and its contemplations, and which does not imply any lack, any impossibility.[55]

And the same goes for courtly love: its eternal postponement of fulfillment does not obey a law of lack or an ideal of transcendence: here also, it signals a desire which lacks nothing, since it finds its fulfillment in itself, in its own immanence; every pleasure is, on the contrary, already a re-territorialization of the free flux of desire.[56] Therein resides the ultimate irony of Deleuze's critique of Hegel: when, against Hegel, Deleuze claims that creation "is immediately creative; there is no transcendent or negating subject of creation that might need time in order to become conscious of itself or otherwise catch up with itself," he thereby imputes to Hegel a substantialization-reification which was never there, and, in this way, obliterates precisely that dimension in Hegel which is closest to Deleuze himself.[57] Hegel repeatedly insists that Spirit is "a product of itself": it is not a pre-existing Subject intervening into objectivity, sublating-mediating it, but the result of its own movement, that is, pure processuality. As such, it needs time not to "catch up with itself," but simply to generate itself.[58]

Deleuze's second reproach to Hegel is the obverse of this first misreading: "whereas according to Hegel any given 'thing differs with itself because it differs first with all that it is not,' namely with all the objects to which it relates, Deleuze's Bergson affirms that a 'thing differs with itself first, immediately,' on account of the 'internal explosive force' it carries within itself."[59] If ever there was a straw man, it is Deleuze's Hegel: is not Hegel's basic insight precisely that every external opposition is grounded in the thing's immanent self-opposition, that every external difference implies self-difference? A finite being differs from other (finite) things because it is already not identical with itself.

When Deleuze talks about a process which creates and sees in a single movement, he thereby consciously evokes the formula of intellectual intuition, the prerogative of God alone. Deleuze pursues a pre-critical agenda, passionately defending Spinoza's and Leibniz's metaphysical "realism" (direct insight into the very core of things-in-themselves) against Kant's "critical" limitation of our knowledge to the domain of phenomenal representations. However, the Hegelian reply to this would be as follows: what if the distance of re-presentation,

---

55 Gilles Deleuze and Félix Guattari, *Mille plateaux*, Paris: Minuit 1980, p. 192.

56 Ibid., p. 193.

57 Hallward, *Out of This World*, p. 149.

58 Furthermore, does not Deleuze's argument against the (Hegelian) negative hold only if we reduce the negative to the negation of a pre-existing positive identity? What about a negativity which is in itself positive, giving, "generative"?

59 Hallward, *Out of This World*, p. 15.

the distance that renders the Thing inaccessible to us, is inscribed into the heart of the Thing itself, so that the very gap that separates us from the Thing includes us in it? Therein lies the core of Hegelian Christology, in which our alienation from God coincides with the alienation of God from himself. Deleuze says that propositions do not describe things but are the verbal actualization of those things, namely these things themselves in their verbal mode—would not Hegel claim, in the same way, that our re-presentation of God is God himself in the mode of representation, that our erroneous perception of God is God himself in erroneous mode?[60]

The exemplary case of such a creative process is *art* which "allows for an absolute and genuinely transformative liberation-expression, precisely because what it liberates *is* nothing other than the liberating itself, the movement of pure spiritualization or dematerialization":[61] what has to be liberated is ultimately liberation itself, the movement of "deterritorializing" all actual entities. This self-relating move is crucial—and, along the same lines, what desire desires is not a determinate object but the unconditional assertion of desiring itself (or, as Nietzsche put it, the will is at its most radical the will to will itself). Another name for this process is *individuation* as "a relation conceived as a pure or absolute between, a between understood as fully independent of or external to its terms—and thus a between that can just as well be described as 'between' nothing at all."[62]

The status of this "absolute between" is that of a pure *antagonism.* Its structure was deployed by Lacan apropos sexual difference which, as a difference, precedes the two terms between which it is the difference: the point of Lacan's "formulae of sexuation" is that both masculine and feminine positions are ways of avoiding the deadlock of the difference as such. This is why Lacan's claim that sexual difference is "real-impossible" is strictly synonymous with his claim that "there is no sexual relationship." Sexual difference is for Lacan not a firm set of "static" symbolic oppositions and inclusions or exclusions (heterosexual normativity that relegates homosexuality and other "perversions" to some secondary role), but the name of a deadlock, of a trauma, of an open question, of something that *resists* every attempt at its symbolization. Every translation of sexual difference into a set of symbolic opposition(s) is doomed to fail, and it is

60 The gist of Deleuze's critique of Aristotle's notion of specific difference is that it privileges identity over difference: specific difference always presupposes the identity of a genre in which opposed species coexist. But what about the "Hegelian complication" here? What about *a specific difference which defines the genre itself,* a difference of species which coincides with the difference between genus and species, thus reducing the genus itself to one of its species?

61 Hallward, *Out of This World*, p. 122.

62 Ibid., p. 154.

this very "impossibility" that opens up the terrain of the hegemonic struggle for what "sexual difference" will mean. And the same goes for political difference (class struggle): the difference between Left and Right is not only the difference between the two terms within a shared field, it is "real" since a neutral description of it is not possible—the difference between Left and Right appears differently if perceived from the Left or from the Right: for the first, it signals the antagonism which cuts across the entire social field (the antagonism concealed by the Right), while the Right perceives itself as a force of moderation, social stability, and organic unity, with the Left reduced to the position of an intruder disturbing the organic stability of the social body—for the Right, the Left is as such "extreme." In this precise sense, sexual (or political) difference is the "dark precursor," never present, a purely virtual "pseudo-cause," the X which always (constitutively) "lacks at its own place" (all its actualizations already displace it) and, as such, distributes the two actual series (masculine and feminine in sexuality, the Right and the Left in politics). In this sense, Lacan advocates a non-relational concept of the phallus: the phallic signifier "founds sexuality in its entirety as system or structure": it is in relation to the phallic object

> that the variety of terms and the variation of differential relations are determined in each case ... The *relative* places of the terms in the structure depend first on the *absolute* place of each, at each moment, in relation to the object = x that is always circulating, always displaced in relation to itself ... Distributing the differences through the entire structure, making the differential relations vary with its displacements, the object = x constitutes the differentiating element of difference itself.[63]

Here, however, one should be careful to avoid the same trap that lurks apropos Deleuze's notion of the "pure past": this fixed element which, as the "absent cause," distributes the elements is a purely virtual element which is present only in its effects and is, as such, retroactively posited (pre-sup-posed) by its effects; it has no substantial independent existence prior to this process.[64] It is because

---

63 Gilles Deleuze, *Desert Islands and Other Texts, 1953–1974*, Los Angeles: Semiotext(e) 2004, pp. 185–6.

64 This brings us to the dimension of symbolic castration: the phallus as the signifier of the pure virtuality of meaning has to be a "signifier without a signified": it is non-sense, the absence of any determinate meaning, which stands for the virtuality of pure meaning. (Or, to put it in more Deleuzian terms: the very counter-actualization, the move backwards from actuality to the virtual field that is its transcendental condition, has to occur *within* actuality, as a displacement or disorder, out-of-joint of the elements within this order.) This is why it is not nonsensical to speak of the "signifier without a signified": this absence of meaning is in itself a positive feature, inscribed into the field of meaning as a gaping hole in its midst. (In a homologous way, the Jews are the "phallic" nation, the "phallic" element among nations: they are a nation without a land, such that

of this "minimalist"—purely formal and insubstantial—status of the Real that, for Lacan, *repetition precedes repression*—or, as Deleuze put it succinctly: "We do not repeat because we repress, we repress because we repeat."[65] It is not that, first, we repress some traumatic content, and then, since we are unable to remember it and thus to clarify our relationship to it, this content continues to haunt us, repeating itself in disguised forms. If the Real is a minimal difference, then repetition (which establishes this difference) is primordial; the primacy of repression emerges with the "reification" of the Real into a Thing that resists symbolization—only then does it appear that the excluded or repressed Real insists and repeats itself. The Real is primordially nothing but the gap that separates a thing from itself, the gap of repetition.[66]

Deleuzian "pure difference" at its purest, if we may put it in this tautological way, is the purely virtual difference of an entity which repeats itself as totally identical with regard to its actual properties: "there are significant differences in the virtual intensities expressed in our actual sensations. These differences do not correspond to actual recognizable differences. That the shade of pink has changed in an identifiable way is not all-important. It is that the change is a sign of a re-arrangement of an infinity of other actual and virtual relations."[67] Does not such a pure difference take place in the repetition of the same actual melodic line in Robert Schumann's "Humoresque"? This piece is to be read against the background of the gradual loss of the voice in Schumann's songs: it is not a simple piano piece, but a song without the vocal line, with the vocal line reduced to silence, so that all we actually hear is the piano accompaniment. This is how one should read the famous "inner voice" (*innere Stimme*) added by Schumann

this absence is inscribed into their very being, as the absolute reference to the virtual land of Israel.)

65 Gilles Deleuze, *Difference and Repetition*, trans. Paul Patton, London: Continuum 2001, p. 105. The consequence of this also involves an inversion in the relationship between repetition and re-memoration. Freud's famous motto "what we do not remember, we are compelled to repeat" should thus be reversed: *what we are unable to repeat, we are haunted with and are compelled to memorize*. The way to get rid of a past trauma is not to rememorize it, but to fully *repeat* it in the Kierkegaardian sense.

66 Especially in the context of political struggle, detecting the minimal difference in all its guises is crucial: the difference between authentic enthusiasm and reactionary fanaticism, between the pursuit of national liberation and anti-immigrant populism, between obscene solidarity and racist jokes, etc. This difference is difficult to define because there are often no clear criteria, no positive properties which allow us to decide—it is all a matter of proper contextualization. For example, Badiou's formula "*qui est içi est d'içi*" (those who are here are from here) works in France against the anti-immigrant populists, but a similar formula is also invoked by Jewish settlers in the West Bank: we are here, so we are from here no less than the Palestinians.

67 James Williams, *Gilles Deleuze's* Difference and Repetition*: A Critical Introduction and Guide*, Edinburgh: Edinburgh University Press 2003, p. 27.

(in the written score) as a third line between the two piano lines, higher and lower: as the vocal melodic line which remains a non-vocalized "inner voice" (which exists only as *Augenmusik*, music for the eyes only, in the guise of written notes). This absent melody is to be reconstructed on the basis of the fact that the first and third levels (the right and the left hand piano lines) do not relate to each other directly; that is, their relationship is not that of an immediate mirroring: in order to account for their interconnection, one is thus compelled to (re)construct a third, "virtual" intermediate level (melodic line) which, for structural reasons, cannot be played. Schumann takes this use of the absent melody to an apparently absurd level of self-reference when, later in the same fragment of "Humoresque," he repeats the same two actually played melodic lines, yet this time the score contains no third absent melodic line, no inner voice—so that what is absent here is the absent melody, absence itself. How are we to play these notes when, at the level of what is actually to be played, they repeat the previous notes exactly? The actually played notes are deprived only of what is not there, of their constitutive lack; or, to refer to the Bible, they lose even that which they never had.[68] Consequently, when we suspend the symbolic efficiency of the inexistent "third melody," we do not simply return to the explicit line; what we get is a double negation—in the terms of the Lubitch joke, we do not get straight coffee, but a no-no-milk coffee;[69] in terms of Schumann's piece, we do not get a straight melody, but a melody which lacks the lack itself, in which the lacking "third line" is itself lacking.

On a closer analysis, we could say that "Humoresque" can be played in four ways: (1) simply ignoring the third (absent) line; (2) playing it so that the absent line resonates in the other two lines; (3) playing it without the resonance of the third line, but so that this absence of resonance is felt, that is, playing the two lines with active ignorance of the third; (4) playing the piece so that the third absent line resonates in it, but in an active and reflected way, generating the impression that the third line does not just organically resonate, but somehow imposes itself—this last option is, of course, the most difficult.[70]

68 Another everyday example of pure difference: when watching a movie on DVD with the subtitles for the hearing-impaired turned on, which also describe all the sounds, one often encounters a strange moment: what to do when a scene occurs which usually generates a clearly recognizable sound, but, on the soundtrack, we (whose hearing is not impaired) do *not* hear it? (Say someone on screen shouts, but we do not hear any shout?) At such moments, the only solution for the subtitles is to *note the absence itself* (automatically assumed by the spectator), something like "no cry heard" or "no ringing of the phone heard." Is not the difference here also a purely virtual one, a difference between me not hearing anything because I am hearing-impaired, and me not hearing a sound which, if I were not hearing-impaired, I would have heard?

69 See Chapter 11 (on the non-All) of the present book.

70 We should introduce the same quadruple structure into *Antigone*: the conflict is not

In Natsume Soseki's *The Three-Cornered World*, a painter (the narrator), wandering over the mountains, finds himself drawn to O-Nami, the strange and beautiful daughter of an innkeeper rumored to have abandoned her husband after falling in love with a priest at a nearby temple. He wants to paint her, but, troubled by a certain quality in her expression which condenses the enigma of her life, fails to capture it:

> "I could paint it now really. But it's just that there's something missing, and I think it would be a pity to paint you without that something."
>
> "What do you mean, 'something missing'? Since this is the face I was born with, there is nothing I can do about it, is there?"
>
> "Even the face you were born with can be varied in many ways."[71]

Towards the end of the novel, the painter observes O-Nami giving some money to a destitute bearded soldier who, she later tells him, is her ex-husband. The soldier then departs on a train to the front. The narrator sees how—and these are the very last lines of the novel—the soldier,

> filled with the sadness of parting, was taking one last look out of the window. Just then, he and O-Nami happened to catch sight of each other, but the engine continued to chug on, and very soon his face disappeared from view.
>
> O-Nami gazed after the train abstractedly, but strangely enough the look of abstraction was suffused with that "compassion" which had hitherto been lacking.
>
> "That's it! That's it! Now that you can express that feeling, you are worth painting," I whispered, patting her on the shoulder. It was at that very moment that the picture in my mind received its final touch.[72]

Is not this story a beautiful parable of a "pure" parallax shift—a shift *which does not relate to the change in any of the object's positive properties*? Badiou's (and Deleuze's) name for this shift is "a minimal difference." In Lacanese, what occurs is the addition or subtraction of the *objet a* from the thing, of that unfathomable

---

only between Antigone (standing for the family principle) and Creon (standing for the principle of the *polis*, the state). Two other positions must be added to render this conflict understandable: that of Haimon (who stands for neither family nor state, but for erotic love) and that of the Chorus (which stands for community in its distance from state power). What is crucial here is not the tension between family and state, but the tension which determines each of these two terms from within: in the "private" domain, family versus the singularity of erotic love (a couple ultimately always betrays their respective families), and, in the "public" domain, state versus society outside the state structure.

71 Natsume Soseki, *The Three-Cornered World*, London: Peter Owen 2002, pp. 178–9.

72 Ibid., p. 184.

X which stands for the inscription of the subject itself (its gaze or desire) into the object. This minimal difference can only be detected at the moment of shortest shadow when, as Nietzsche put it in *Beyond Good and Evil*, "at midday it happened, at midday one became two."

This logic of virtual difference can also be discerned in another paradox. The cinema version of Doctorow's *Billy Bathgate* is basically a failure, but an interesting one: a failure which nonetheless evokes in the viewer the specter of a much better novel. However, when one then goes on to read the novel on which the film is based, one is disappointed—this is *not* the novel the film evoked as the standard with regard to which it failed. The repetition (of a failed novel in the failed film) thus gives rise to a third, purely virtual, element: the better novel. This is an exemplary case of what Deleuze describes in a crucial passage from *Difference and Repetition*:

> while it may seem that the two presents are successive, at a variable distance apart in the series of reals, in fact they form, rather, *two real series which coexist in relation to a virtual object of another kind*, one which constantly circulates and is displaced in them ... Repetition is constituted not from one present to another, but between the two coexistent series that these presents form in function of the virtual object (object = x).[73]

With regard to *Billy Bathgate*, the film does not "repeat" the novel on which it is based; rather, they both "repeat" the unrepeatable virtual X, the "true" novel whose specter is engendered in the passage from the actual novel to the film. This virtual point of reference, although "unreal," is in a way more real than reality: it is the *absolute* point of reference of the failed real attempts. This is how, from the perspective of materialist theology, the divine emerges from the repetition of terrestrial material elements, as their "cause" retroactively posited by them. Deleuze is right to refer to Lacan here: this "better book" is what Lacan calls the *objet petit a*, the object-cause of desire that "one cannot recapture in the present, except by capturing it in its consequences," the two really existing works, the book and the film.

> Why is structuralism serious? For the serious to be truly serious, there must be the serial, which is made up of elements, of results, of configurations, of homologies, of repetitions. What is serious for Lacan is the logic of the signifier, that is to say the opposite of a philosophy, inasmuch as every philosophy rests on the appropriateness, transparency, agreement, harmony of thought with itself. There is always some part hidden, in a philosophy, an I = I, which constitutes what Lacan called at some

73 Deleuze, *Difference and Repetition*, pp. 104–5.

> moment "the initial error in philosophy," which consists in privileging this equality and thus making one believe that the "I" is contemporary with itself, while its constitution is always after the emergence of its cause, of *petit a*.
>
> The unconscious means that thought is caused by the non-thought that one cannot recapture in the present, except by capturing it in its consequences. This is how Georges Dandin recaptures the consequence of stopped time when he stops to say: "*Tu l'as voulu, Georges Dandin!*" (You wanted it, Georges Dandin!) He makes time stop to recapture in the consequence what was caused by the non-thought.[74]

The only thing with which one cannot fully agree in this quoted passage concerns Miller's (and Lacan's) all too quick and slick condemnation of philosophy: Fichte, the very German idealist who articulated the infamous I = I, the formula of the I's self-identity from which Lacan is distancing himself, also made clear the subject's dependence on a cause which is de-centered with regard to the subject—the subject needs an absolutely contingent object-cause, what Fichte called *Anstoss*, obstacle or solicitation. The temporality of the subject's cause is not that of the linear deployment of time (and of the corresponding notion of causality in which past causes determine the present); it is the temporality of a circular time in which "time stops" when, in a convoluted self-relating, the subject posits its own presupposed cause. Miller himself concedes this when he points out that the cause of desire is "a cause moreover which is posed by retroaction."[75] It is in this precise sense that subject and object are correlative: the subject's emergence, its breaking of (cut into, suspension of) the linear causality of "reality" has a cause, but a cause which is retroactively posited by its own effect. It is this minimal retroactivity, not just some kind of structural "complexity," which allows us to pass from linear natural causality, no matter how complex it is, to structural causality proper.

"You wanted it, Georges Dandin," quoted by Miller, is a line from Molière in which the subject is reminded that the deadlock he finds himself in is the unintended consequence of his own past acts; Miller gives it an additional twist: the subject should recapture in the consequences he encounters in reality the results of their absent and non-thought cause—in the case of *Billy Bathgate*, he should recapture in the two "real" objects, the novel and the film, the consequences of their virtual cause, the spectral "better novel."

The underlying movement is thus here more complex than it may appear. It is not that we should simply conceive the starting point (the novel) as an "open work," full of possibilities which can later be deployed, actualized in other versions; or—even worse—that we should conceive the original work as a pre-text

74 Jacques-Alain Miller, "Profane Illuminations," *lacanian ink* 28 (Fall 2006), pp. 22–3.
75 Jacques-Alain Miller, "Detached Pieces," *lacanian ink* 28 (Fall 2006), p. 37.

to be later incorporated in other con-texts and given a meaning totally different from the original one. What is missing here is the retroactive, backwards movement: the film inserts back into the novel the possibility of a different, much better novel. And the irony is that this logic of repetition, elaborated by Deleuze, *the* anti-Hegelian, lies at the very core of the Hegelian dialectic: it relies on the properly dialectical relationship between temporal reality and the eternal Absolute. The eternal Absolute is the immobile point of reference around which temporal figurations circulate, their presupposition; however, precisely as such, it is posited by these temporal figurations, since it does not pre-exist them: it emerges in the gap between the first and the second one—in the case of *Billy Bathgate*, between the novel and its repetition in the film. Or, to return to Schumann's "Humoresque": the eternal Absolute is the third unplayed melodic line, the point of reference of the two lines played in reality: it is absolute, but fragile—if the two positive lines are played wrongly, it disappears. This is what one is tempted to call "materialist theology": temporal succession creates eternity.

It is along these lines that one should interpret the (often noted) weird impassivity of the figure of Christ, its "sterility": what if Christ is an Event in the Deleuzian sense—an occurrence of pure individuality without proper causal power? Which is why Christ suffers, but in a thoroughly impassive way. Christ is "individual" in the Deleuzian sense: he is a pure individual, not characterized by positive properties which would make him "more" than an ordinary human; the difference between Christ and other humans is purely virtual. Christ is, at the level of actuality, the same as other humans, only the unplayed "virtual melody" that accompanies him is added. And with the Holy Spirit, we get this "virtual melody" on its own: the Holy Spirit is a collective field of pure virtuality, with no causal power of its own. Christ's death and resurrection is the death of the actual person which confronts us directly with the ("resurrected") virtual field that sustained it. The Christian name for this virtual force is "love": when Christ says to his worried followers after his death "where two or more are gathered in my name, I will be there," he thereby asserts his virtual status.

Does this virtual dimension which sustains actuality allow us to bring together Lacan and Deleuze? The starting point for a Lacanian reading of Deleuze should be a brutal and direct substitution: whenever Deleuze and Guattari talk about "desiring machines" (*machines désirantes*), we should replace this term with *drive*. The Lacanian drive—this anonymous/acephalous immortal insistence-to-repeat of an "organ without a body" which precedes the Oedipal triangulation and its dialectic of the prohibitory Law and its transgression—fits perfectly what Deleuze tries to circumscribe as the pre-Oedipal nomadic machines of desire: in the chapter dedicated to the drive in his *Seminar XI*, Lacan himself emphasizes the "machinal" character of a drive, its anti-organic nature of an artificial composite or montage of heterogeneous parts.[76]

However, this should be only the starting point. What immediately complicates the issue is the fact that, in this substitution, something gets lost: the very irreducible difference between drive and desire, the parallax nature of this difference which makes it impossible to deduce or generate one from the other. In other words, what is totally foreign to Lacan is Deleuze's anti-representationalist notion of desire as the primordial flux which itself creates its scene of representation or repression. This is also why Deleuze talks about the liberation of desire, of liberating desire from its representationalist frame, something which is totally meaningless within Lacan's horizon: for Deleuze, desire at its purest stands for the free flow of the libido, while the Lacanian drive is constitutively marked by a basic insoluble deadlock—the drive is an impasse, which finds satisfaction ("passé") in the very repetition of the impasse.

To put it in Deleuze's own terms, his flux of desire is a BwO, a body without organs, while Lacan's drive is an OwB, an organ without body. Desire is not a partial object, while the drive *is* such an object. As Deleuze emphasizes, what he is fighting against are not organs but *organism*, the articulation of a body into a hierarchical-harmonious Whole of organs, each "in its place," with its function: "the BwO is in no way the contrary of the organs. Its enemies are not organs. The enemy is the organism."[77] He is fighting corporatism/organicism. For him, Spinoza's substance is the ultimate BwO: the non-hierarchical space in which a chaotic multitude (of organs?), all equal (the univocity of being), float. Nonetheless, there is a strategic choice made here: why BwO, why not (also) OwB? Why not the Body as the space in which autonomous organs freely float? Is it because "organs" evoke a function within a wider Whole, a subordination to a goal? But does not this very fact make their autonomization, OwB, all the more subversive?

The price Deleuze pays for his preference of the body over organs is clearly discernible in his acceptance of the Leibnizian hierarchy of monads: the difference between monads is ultimately quantitative, for every monad is substantially the same, it expresses the whole infinite world, but with a different, always specific, quantitative intensity and adequacy: at the one extreme, the lowest, there are "darkened monads" with only one clear perception, their hatred of God; at the highest extreme, there are "reasonable monads" which can open themselves

76 For both Lacan and Deleuze, the drive has an ethical status. So when I am in doubt about whether I can perform some difficult task, and a teacher tells me, "I trust you! I know you can do it!" he is referring not only to my symbolic identity beneath my miserable psychological reality, but also to "what is in me more than myself," to the impossible-real of the acephalous drive that is me.

77 Deleuze and Guattari, *Mille plateaux*, p. 196.

to reflect the entire universe. What, in a monad, resists the full expression of God is its stubborn attachment to its creatural delusion, to its particular (ultimately material) identity. Humanity occupies here the place of the highest tension: on the one hand, humans are, even more than other living beings, caught up in the thrall of absolute egotism, obstinately focused on the preservation of the identity of their Self (which is why, for Deleuze, the highest task of philosophy is to elevate man above his human condition, to the "inhuman" level of the "overman"); on the other hand, Deleuze agrees with Bergson that man stands for a unique breakthrough and the highest point in the evolution of life—with the emergence of consciousness, a living being is finally able to by-pass its material (organic) limitations and advance to a purely spiritual plane of unity with the divine All.

From a Hegelian standpoint, what Deleuze fails to fully perceive is what Schelling, among others, saw clearly: *the ultimate identity of these two features*, of the lowest and the highest. It is precisely *through* its stubborn attachment to its singular Self that a human subject is able to extract itself from the particular convolutions of actual life (with its circular movement of generation and corruption) and enter into relation with virtual eternity. This is why (insofar as "Evil" is another name for this stubborn egotistical attachment) Evil is a formal condition of the rise of the Good: it literally creates the space for the Good. And do we not encounter here the ultimate case of suture: in order to retain its consistency, the field of the Good has to be sutured by the singularity of Evil?

The rest, as they say, is history: already in the late 1960s, the concept of "suture" was imported into cinema theory by Jean-Pierre Oudart;[78] later, when it was again taken over and elaborated by the English *Screen* theorists, it became a global concept within cinema theory, the subject of wide discussion. Finally, years later, it lost its specific mooring in cinema theory and became part of the deconstructionist jargon, functioning as a vague notion rather than a strict concept, as synonymous with "closure": "suture" signaled that the gap, the opening, of a structure was obliterated, enabling the structure to (mis)perceive itself as a self-enclosed totality of representation.

Miller's suture thus made history (in social and cinema theory), while Badiou's reply was largely ignored, or, rather, drowned out by the Althusserian orthodoxy. Furthermore, soon after the *Cahiers* debate, Badiou shifted his position, introducing his own theory of the subject (elaborated in detail in his first masterpiece, *Théorie du sujet*). In a crucial difference from Lacan and Miller, Badiou's subject is not universal (co-extensive with the structure as such, since every structure involves a lack), but a rarity, something which arises only in

78 Jean-Pierre Oudart, "La suture," *Cahiers du cinéma* 211 (April 1969), pp. 36–9; and Jean-Pierre Oudart, "La suture," *Cahiers du cinéma* 212 (May 1969), pp. 50–5.

exceptional conditions when a Truth-Event disrupts the ordinary run of things. Although Badiou's notion of the subject involves a reflexivity which is vaguely homologous to the reflexivity of the subject of the signifier (the site of the emergence of a subject is the "supernumerary" element of the situation, its "part of no-part," homologous to the empty signifier), the gap that separates Badiou from Miller thus remained after Badiou introduced his concept of the subject.

So did Miller "win" in the debate? The catch here is that the very triumph of Miller's concept of suture was inextricably mixed up with a radical misunderstanding of the concept: paradoxically, what won out was a kind of perverted synthesis of the two positions, Althusser's and Lacan's. As we have seen, what triumphed was the Althusserian notion of the subject as the site of an imaginary or ideological (mis)recognition of structural necessity, and the notion of "suture" was, in its predominant popular reception and use, interpreted as the very operator of this misrecognition; that is, it designated the operation by means of which the field of ideological experience gets "sutured," its circle closed, and the de-centered structural necessity rendered invisible. In this reading, "suturing" means that all disturbing traces of the radical Outside within the field of ideological experience are obliterated, so that this field is perceived as a seamless continuity—a grand historical process, say, is (over)determined by a complex network of "anonymous" structural causes, and this complexity is obfuscated when we posit a Subject (humanity, consciousness, life, God ...) which dominates and directs the process. This misunderstanding emerges when one reads suture against the background of the conceptual couple presence/representation.

Where do we stand today, then, with regard to the debate between Miller and Badiou? In contrast to Badiou, we should insist on a "universal" subject, since anxiety is co-extensive with the human condition, and it is this anxiety which is the site of primordial subjectivization—subjective fidelity to a Truth-Event comes later. There is, however, also a crucial limitation to Miller's position (which, one can argue, is the limitation of psychoanalysis as such). For Miller (who here follows Lacan), anxiety remains the only affect which does not cheat (as Freud already put it), which means that there is in every (political) enthusiasm for a Cause an element of imaginary misrecognition—as Miller has insisted especially in the last few years, politics is a domain of imaginary or symbolic identifications and as such the domain of illusions. Such a position unavoidably ends up in some kind of cynical pessimism (which can be also masked as a tragic grandeur): all collective enthusiastic engagement ends in fiasco, the truth can only be experienced momentarily, in self-blinding acts of tragic authenticity in which we "traverse the fantasy." These moments cannot be sustained permanently, so the only thing we can do is to "play the (social) game," aware that it is ultimately a mere game of illusions. Badiou enables us to break out of this ennobled tragic cynicism: enthusiasm is no less "authentic" than anxiety, a collective political engagement does not *eo ipso* involve imaginary misrecognition.

This difference is absolutely crucial today—it is the difference between political death and life, between endorsing the reigning post-political cynicism and gathering the courage for a radical emancipatory engagement.

INTERLUDE 5

Correlationism and Its Discontents

Quentin Meillassoux, in his *After Finitude*, made a forceful return to the "naïve" question of the existence and cognizability of reality in its independence from our (human) mind.[1] Meillassoux's argumentation often sounds like a repetition of Lenin's ill-famed *Materialism and Empirio-Criticism* (such as when, in an exact echo of Lenin, he ultimately reduces Kantian transcendentalism to a repackaged version of Berkeley's solipsism). Indeed, *After Finitude* can effectively be read as *Materialism and Empirio-Criticism* rewritten for the twenty-first century. This is why Meillassoux starts with the naïve but urgent question of the status of so-called "ancestrality": how can transcendental philosophy (for which all reality is subjectively constituted) account for statements about natural processes which occurred prior to the rise of humanity, from the beginning of our universe (the Big Bang) to fossils from the early stages of life on Earth? Within the transcendental approach, the ultimate horizon of subjectivity is that of our finitude, for we cannot reach beyond (or abstract from) our engagement with the world. Here is Heidegger's ambiguous formulation of this obscure point: "I often ask myself—this has for a long time been a fundamental question for me—what nature would be without man—must it not resonate through him in order to attain its ownmost potency."[2]

Meillassoux is well aware of the finesses of the transcendental approach; that is, he is well aware that Kant's transcendental constitution is not the same as the pre-transcendental Berkeleyian notion of the observer who directly (ontically)

---

1 Quentin Meillassoux, *After Finitude: An Essay on the Necessity of Contingency*, London: Continuum 2008.

2 Letter from October 11, 1931, in *Martin Heidegger/Elisabeth Blochmann: Briefwechsel 1918–1969*, Marbach: Deutsches Literatur-Archiv 1990, p. 44; as quoted in Meillassoux, *After Finitude*, p. 137. Note that this passage is from the time immediately after Heidegger's lectures on *The Fundamental Concepts of Metaphysics* from 1929–30, where a Schellingian hypothesis is also formulated that, perhaps, animals are, in a hitherto unknown way, aware of their lack, of the "poorness" of their relating to the world—perhaps there is an infinite pain pervading the entire living nature: "if deprivation in certain forms is a kind of suffering, and poverty and deprivation of world belongs to the animal's being, then a kind of pain and suffering would have to permeate the whole animal realm and the realm of life in general." (Martin Heidegger, *The Fundamental Concepts of Metaphysics*, Bloomington: Indiana University Press 1995, p. 271.)

"creates" what it observes. He is furthermore well aware that the minimal feature of the position he is attacking is so-called "correlationism": the idea that subject and object (or, to put it in less subjectivist terms, man and reality) only exist (more precisely: are only given to us) as correlated, in their inter-relationship. There is no subject outside its engagement with reality, we are "beings-in-the-world," and, for this very reason, every reality disclosed to us is always already a reality disclosed within a certain life world—or, as the young Georg Lukács put it in Marxist terms, nature is always already a social-historical category.

This "correlationism" can be further grounded in a multitude of positions: subjectivism (the subject's self-division as the origin of the subject-object distinction—as Fichte put it, every object which opposes a subject is the result of the subject's self-limitation); the positing of the subject-object (cor)relation itself as the Absolute (basically post-Kantian German Idealism, especially Schelling's "philosophy of identity"); and, finally, the standard twentieth-century position, involving an acceptance of the correlation itself as the unsurpassable horizon, the mark of the finitude of the human condition. However, what all these positions share is their inability to provide a satisfying account of the status of "ancestrality": a cosmological description of what occurred millions of years ago, before the formation of our solar system, is not really what it claims to be, i.e., a description of what went on millions of years ago, before the rise of humanity, but a description of how this past appears within the horizon of our human existence—our position is always already included in what is described.

Against this background, Meillassoux convincingly argues that the recent rise of irrational religious orientations within philosophy (so-called "post-secular" thought) is not a regression to premodern times, but a necessary outcome of Western critical reason. In the Kantian version of the Enlightenment, the critical use of reason was always aimed also at reason itself: the critique of religion ended up as the critique of reason, as reason's self-limitation which again opened up a space for religious faith, only this time not for the "God of Philosophers," the God whose existence or features can be demonstrated or at least circumscribed by our reasoning, but for the paradoxically abyssal God qua radical Otherness, totally beyond *logos*. The first to make this move was Kant himself, when he famously claimed that he had to limit reason (human knowledge) to create the space for morality; today, the emblematic figure of this orientation is, of course, Levinas, the central point of reference for all postmodern-deconstructionist theologies of a "God beyond Being." Derrida's theological turn brought this orientation to its climax: the radical deconstruction of the entire metaphysical tradition has to accomplish a reflexive turn and render thematic its own "undeconstructible" conditions. The presupposition of this "death of the death of God" is thus that the Enlightenment, to be consistent, leads to its self-negation: the critique which first targets religious and all other metaphysical superstitions has to end up by negating its own metaphysical presuppositions, its own trust in a rational deterministic world which inexorably leads to progress: "In Kierkegaard and Nietzsche, the world of Enlightenment Reason and Hegelian Absolute Knowledge is left far behind. They each foresee in his own way the madness of the twentieth century whose genocidal violence made a mockery of Hegel's sanguine view of history as the autobiography of the Spirit of time."[3] In this way, as one might expect, even Nietzsche, the fiercest critic of Christianity, can be enlisted in support of the postmodern "theological turn":

> When Nietzsche says "God is dead," he's saying that there is no center, no single, overarching principle that explains things. There's just a multiplicity of fictions or interpretations. Well, if there's no single overarching principle, that means science is also one more interpretation, and it doesn't have an exclusive right to absolute truth. But, if that's true, then non-scientific ways of thinking about the world, including religious ways, resurface.[4]

It is indeed true that the now predominant "skepticism" about the secular narratives of the Enlightenment is the obverse of the so-called "post-secular" turn in which religion appears as a key "site of resistance" against the alienations of what is perceived as a singularly Western modernity. Religion stands here for an "auratic" belief in "God," a word here deprived of any positive onto-teleological status: God is no longer the Highest Being watching over our destiny, but a name for radical openness, for the hope of change, for the Otherness always-to-come, etc. According to Meillassoux, what lies at the origin of this "death of the death of God" is the mistake inherent in the Kantian criticism: Kant confused the rejection of philosophical dogmaticism (*à la* Leibniz) with the rejection of all philosophical (rational, conceptual) reference to the Absolute, as if the Absolute and radical contingency were incompatible. When Kant prohibits us to think the Absolute (since the noumenal is beyond the grasp of our reason), the Absolute itself does *not* thereby disappear—such a critical delimitation of human knowledge opens up a new discursive space for the access to the Absolute, "*the only proviso being that nothing in these discourses resembles a rational justification of its validity*."[5] In this way, "the victorious critique of ideologies has been transformed into a renewed argument for blind faith":[6] the ruthless critique of every dogmaticism culminated in an unexpected resurgence of *credo qua absurdum*. However, when Meillassoux sarcastically notes how the Kantian critique

3 John D. Caputo, *On Religion*, London: Routledge 2001, p. 55.

4 John D. Caputo and Gianni Vattimo, *After the Death of God*, ed. Jeffrey W. Robbins, New York: Columbia University Press 2007, p. 133.

5 Meillassoux, *After Finitude*, pp. 44–5.

6 Ibid., p. 49.

of idealist rational metaphysics opens up the space for irrational fideism, he strangely overlooks how the same is true of his own position: does not his materialist critique of correlationism also open up the path to a new divinity (as we know from his mostly unpublished texts on the inexistent virtual God)?

We will have to leave aside here many wonderful lines of thought in *After Finitude*—for example, Meillassoux's precise and perspicuous deduction of why it follows from the assertion of the radical contingency of Being that "there is something and not nothing": the jump from universal notion to actual empirical reality is always contingent; that is, the actual existence of an entity cannot be deduced from the inner necessity of its notion. What this means is that, if a being is necessary, then it can always not exist. If, however, a being is radically contingent, then something (contingent) *has* to exist.[7] This insight is connected to Meillassoux's reversal of the ontological proof of God: it is the radical contingency of Being itself which allows us to make a jump from notion to reality, to prove that some (contingent) entity necessarily *has* to exist. And, in contrast to the standard opinion on Hegel (unfortunately shared by Meillassoux), Hegel's rehabilitation of the ontological proof of God in no way also rehabilitates the "illegitimate" jump from notion to actual existence: Hegel can pass to the existence of "something and not nothing" precisely because his starting point is the pure contingency of Being.

In another ambiguous (mis)reading of Hegel, Meillassoux claims that the dialectical principle of contradiction (contradictions are really present in things) excludes any change: change means a transformation of p into non-p, of a feature into its opposite, but since, in a contradiction, a thing already *is* its opposite, it has nowhere to develop into. The universe which fully embodied the reality of contradiction would be an immovable self-identical universe in which contradictory features would immediately coincide. In the actual universe, things move, change in time, precisely because they *cannot* be directly A and non-A—they can only gradually *change* from A to non-A. There is time because the principle of identity, of non-contradiction, resists the direct assertion of contradiction. This is why Hegel is not a philosopher of evolution, of movement and development: Hegel's system is "static," every evolution is contained in the atemporal self-identity of a Notion.

Here, however, Meillassoux misses the point of Hegelian dialectical movement: contradiction is necessary *and at the same time impossible*; that is, a finite thing precisely *cannot* be simultaneously A and non-A, which is why the process through which it is compelled to assume contradiction equals its annihilation.

7 Is this not a variation on the old insight into how existence does not follow from a true universal judgment? If a "unicorn has one horn" is true, it can still be true that no unicorn exists; but if "some unicorns have one horn" is true, then at least one unicorn has to exist.

No wonder, then, that Hegel was the first to outline the contours of a *logical temporality*: even in the sphere of pure conceptual reasoning, the succession of moves does not work as an atemporal chain of consequences—some logical moves (precisely the right ones) can be made only after other (erroneous) moves have been done. Meillassoux thus reads the "atemporality" of the dialectical process in an all too "immediate" way: he fails to grasp how, for Hegel, "contradiction" is not opposed to identity, but is its very core. "Contradiction" is not only the Real-impossible on account of which no entity can be fully self-identical; "contradiction" is pure self-identity as such, the tautological coincidence of form and content, of genus and species, in the assertion of identity. There is time, there is development, precisely because opposites *cannot* directly coincide. Therein resides already the lesson of the very beginning of the Logic: how do we pass from the first identity of opposites, Being and Nothing, to Becoming (which then stabilizes itself in Something[s])? If Being and Nothing are identical, if they overlap, why move forward at all? Precisely because Being and Nothing are not directly identical: Being is a form, the first formal-notional determination, whose only content is Nothing; the couple Being/Nothing forms the highest contradiction which is impossible, and to resolve this impossibility, this deadlock, one passes into Becoming, into oscillation between the two poles.

But let us return to the crux of *After Finitude*, the mutual implication of the *contingency of necessity* and the *necessity of contingency*: not only is every necessity contingent (groundless, "without reason," and under the shadow of the permanent possibility of its collapse), but, even more strongly, the *only* thing that is absolutely necessary is the contingency (of the laws of nature, of their necessity). The beauty and strength of Meillassoux's argument is that the conclusion he draws from this unconditional assertion of contingency is not some kind of universalized agnostic relativism, but, on the contrary, the assertion of the cognitive accessibility of reality-in-itself, the way it is independently of human existence. The "finitude" to which the book's title alludes is the finitude of the Kantian transcendental subject which constitutes the phenomenal "objective reality": Meillassoux's aim is no less than to demonstrate—*after* Kant, taking into account the Kantian revolution—the possibility of the cognition of the noumenal In-itself. He rehabilitates the old distinction between the "primary" properties of objects (which belong to objects independently of their being-perceived by humans) and their "secondary" properties (color, taste), which exist only in human perception; the basic criterion of this distinction is a scientific one, namely the possibility of describing an object in mathematicized terms: "*all those aspects of the object that can be formulated in mathematical terms can be meaningfully conceived as properties of the object in itself.*"[8]

8 Meillassoux, *After Finitude*, p. 3.

According to Meillassoux, the greatest irony in the entire history of philosophy is the naming of the Kantian turn as a "Copernican revolution": his turn is, on the contrary, a Ptolemaic *counter-revolution* against the Galilean decentering of the universe from the meaningful medieval Earth-centered and teleologically ordered Whole to the "gray" infinite universe of science adequately rendered only in mathematicized formulae. Although Kant's original task (as formulated in his *Critique of Pure Reason*) was to provide ontological grounding for the (obvious) universal validity of modern (Newtonian) science, his "grounding" is nothing but the negation of the most basic ontological premise of modern science: while natural science purports to describe reality the way it "really is," independently of our observations and of the meanings we introject into it on account of the interested character of those observations, the transcendental "grounding" of the natural sciences claims that the very "objective reality" described by sciences hinges on a subjective transcendental frame, is subjectively constituted, or that the "disinterested," neutral character of science is itself sustained by certain interests or practical attitudes (say, for Heidegger, the attitude of technological manipulation and exploitation of nature).

Meillassoux is very clear about how his primary target here is not so much Kant himself as those twentieth-century philosophers, from Husserl to Heidegger, who emphasize the "naïveté" of the natural sciences, their crude "naturalism," the "abstract" character of their description of reality. As was exemplarily asserted by the late Husserl and early Heidegger, the scientific "objective" approach to reality is always already grounded in our (human) immersion into a concrete historical life world (*Lebenswelt*), for we do not encounter things primarily as objects of neutral observation, but as something "ready-at-hand," something which belongs to the whole of our practical-engaged existence.[9]

The dilemma that arises here can also be expressed in terms of the traditional distinction between genesis and value (of a scientific proposition). A partisan of scientific objectivism would in all probability accept most of the claims about how science is always already rooted in a concrete historical life world, and so on; he would simply add that, while these claims adequately describe the empirical genesis of the natural sciences, it is epistemologically illegitimate to see them as affecting also their cognitive validity. A somewhat simplified example: while it is probably true that Galilean physics could not have arisen outside of the development of the capitalist market economy and of the prospect of technological domination over nature, this fact does not invalidate the objective truth of Galileo's scientific discoveries—they hold independently of their contingent origins. For a transcendental philosopher, however, the link between

9 This transcendental critique-grounding of the natural sciences and their "objectivism" can also be given a distinctly Marxist touch when the natural sciences are grasped as rooted in a historical collective *praxis*.

scientific knowledge and its historical presuppositions concerns the very epistemological status of scientific knowledge: the natural sciences do not describe and/or explain reality "the way it is independently of us"; they describe and/or explain reality they way it appears *only* from within a certain historically specified horizon of meaning and are therefore *stricto sensu* meaningless outside of this horizon.

However, are things as clear as all that with regard to Kant's "Ptolemaic counter-revolution"? Both Kant and Freud claim to repeat the "Copernican turn" in their respective domains. With regard to Freud, the meaning of this reference seems simple enough: in the same way that Copernicus demonstrated that our Earth is not the center of the universe, but a planet revolving around the Sun, and in this sense "de-centered," turning around *another* center, Freud also demonstrated that the (conscious) Ego is not the center of the human psyche, but ultimately an epiphenomenon, a satellite turning around the true center, the Unconscious or the Id. With Kant, things are more ambiguous—in a first approach (on which Meillassoux relies), it appears that he actually did the exact *opposite* of the Copernican turn: is not the key premise of his transcendental philosophy that the conditions of possibility of our experience of objects are at the same time the conditions of possibility of these objects themselves, so that, instead of a subject who, in his cognition, has to accommodate itself to some external, "decentered" measure of truth, the objects have to follow the subject, for it is the subject itself who, from its central position, constitutes the objects of knowledge? However, if one reads Kant's reference to Copernicus closely, it becomes clear that his emphasis is not on the shift of the substantial fixed Center, but on something quite different—on the status of the subject itself:

> We here propose to do just what Copernicus did in attempting to explain the celestial movements. When he found that he could make no progress by assuming that all the heavenly bodies revolved round the spectator, he reversed the process, and tried the experiment of assuming that the spectator revolved, while the stars remained at rest.[10]

The precise German terms ("*die Zuschauer sich drehen*"—not so much turn around another center as *turn or rotate around themselves*[11]) make it clear what interests Kant: the subject loses its substantial stability or identity and is reduced to the pure substanceless void of the self-rotating abyssal vortex called "transcendental apperception." And it is against this background that one can locate

10 Immanuel Kant, *Critique of Pure Reason*, trans. J. M. D. Meiklejohn, London: Henry G. Bohn 1855, p. xxix.

11 For a good account of the false translations of this key passage, see Gérard Guest, "La tournure de l'événement," *Heidegger Studies* 10 (1994).

Lacan's "return to Freud": to put it as succinctly as possible, Lacan reads the Freudian reference to the Copernican turn *in the original Kantian sense*, as asserting not the simple displacement of the center from the Ego to the Id or the Unconscious as the "true" substantial focus of the human psyche, but as *the transformation of the subject itself from the self-identical substantial Ego, the psychological subject full of emotions, instincts, dispositions, etc., into what Lacan calls the "barred subject ($)," the vortex of the self-relating negativity of desire.* In this precise sense, the subject of the unconscious is none other than the Cartesian *cogito*.

How, then, does Meillassoux accomplish the shift, the reversal, from transcendental-correlationist closure to the opening of our knowledge towards the In-itself, to the accessibility of the In-itself? The ultimate horizon of transcendental correlationism is that of *facticity*: things are the way they are "*ohne Warum*," as Angelus Silesius put it. Our unsurpassable finitude means that, ultimately, things appear to us the way they do for no reason, there is no necessity in the specific mode of their appearing, there is always the possibility that they could (have) turn(ed) otherwise. It was Heidegger who pushed this line of reasoning to the extreme, a line which has a long history in modern thought, from its beginnings in Duns Scotus and Descartes (who both advocated the radical "voluntarism" of divine creation: there is no Reason whose necessity limits God's freedom; if God were to decide 2 + 2 = 5 and not 4 it would be so) through to figures like the late Schelling (who, against Hegel, insisted on the utter contingency of the act of creation: God could also have decided not to create the world; the ultimate reality is the abyss of the divine freedom). There is a link here between the apparent opposites of the "irrational" (decisionist/voluntarist) assertion of radical contingency and of the scientific universe of natural laws: for modern mathematicized science, every (discovered) necessity is contingent, there is no necessity of the necessity itself (which is why Pope Benedict was in a way right to accuse modern science of "irrationalism" and to see in Christianity a defense of Reason against scientific "irrationality"). Heidegger's "*Er-Eignis*," the Event/Arrival of a new historical epoch, of a new mode of the disclosure of Being—or, to put it in inadequate but nonetheless appropriate terms: of a new transcendental horizon of meaning—asserts the radical facticity or contingency of the Transcendental. There is no Necessity, no Reason, no Why in why reality is disclosed to us within this and not another transcendental horizon of meaning, no deeper logical process which regulates the succession of the epochs of Being; the history of Being is an abyssal game; that is, *Er-Eignis* is not a "deeper" Ground or Agent regulating the succession of the historical appearances of Being, it is these appearances themselves as abyssal Events, as things which, in the most radical sense imaginable, "just happen."

The mistake of transcendental correlationism does not reside in this full assertion of facticity (of radical ontological contingency), but, on the contrary, in the (philosophically inconsistent, self-contradictory) *limitation* of this facticity. Correlationism reads the ultimate facticity, the "*ohne Warum*," of our reality, as the indelible mark of our finitude, on account of which we are forever condemned to remain trapped behind the Veil of Ignorance separating us from the unknowable Absolute. It is here that Meillassoux pulls off a properly speculative-Hegelian *tour de force*, demonstrating how the way out of this deadlock is not to by-pass it by claiming that we can nonetheless penetrate the Veil of Ignorance and reach the Absolute, but to assert it and extrapolate all its consequences. The problem with transcendental agnosticism concerning the In-itself is not that it is too radically skeptical, that it "goes too far," but, on the contrary, that it remains stuck half-way.

In what, then, does Meillassoux's operation consist? The very problem—the obstacle—retroactively appears as its own solution, since what prevents us from directly accessing the Thing is the Thing itself. Is the logic of the final reversal not exactly the same as that of Adorno's analysis of the antagonistic character of the notion of society? On a first approach, the split between the two notions of society (Anglo-Saxon individualistic-nominalistic and Durkheimian organicist notions of society as a totality which pre-exists individuals) seems irreducible, we seem to be dealing with a true Kantian antinomy which cannot be resolved via a higher "dialectical synthesis" and which elevates society into an inaccessible Thing-in-itself. On a second approach, however, one merely need take note of how this radical antinomy which seems to preclude our access to the Thing *already is the Thing itself*—the fundamental feature of today's society *is* the irreconcilable antagonism between Totality and the individual.

Meillassoux does exactly the same with regard to the experience of facticity and/or absolute contingency: he transposes what appears to transcendental partisans of finitude as the limitation of our knowledge (the insight that we can be totally wrong about our knowledge, that reality in itself can be totally different from our notion of it) into the most basic positive ontological property of reality itself—the absolute "*is simply the capacity-to-be-other as such, as theorized by the agnostic*. The absolute is the *possible transition*, devoid of reason, of my state towards any other state whatsoever. But this possibility is no longer a 'possibility of ignorance,' viz., a possibility that is merely the result of my inability to know ... rather, it is the *knowledge* of the very real possibility"[12] in the heart of the In-itself:

> We must show why thought, far from experiencing its intrinsic *limits* through facticity, experiences rather its *knowledge* of the absolute through facticity. We must grasp in fact not the inaccessibility of the absolute but the unveiling of the in-itself and the

12 Meillassoux, *After Finitude*, p. 56.

> eternal property of what is, as opposed to the perennial deficiency in the thought of what is … [In this way,] facticity will be revealed to be a knowledge of the absolute *because we are going to put back into the thing itself what we mistakenly mistook to be an incapacity in thought*. In other words, instead of construing the absence of reason inherent in everything as a limit that thought encounters in its search for the ultimate reason, we must understand that this absence of reason *is*, and can *only* be the *ultimate* property of the entity.[13]

The paradox of this quasi-magical reversal of epistemological obstacle into ontological premise is that "it is through facticity, and through facticity alone, that we are able to make our way towards the absolute":[14] the radical contingency of reality, this "open possibility, this 'everything is equally possible,' is an absolute that cannot be de-absolutized without being thought as absolute once more."[15]

Here, one should also establish a link with the great conflict over how to interpret indeterminacy in quantum physics: for the "orthodox" quantum physicists, this epistemological indeterminacy is simultaneously ontological, a property of "reality" itself which is "in itself" indeterminate, while for those, from Einstein onwards, who hold to the classical "realism-of-necessity," the epistemological indeterminacy can only mean that quantum physics does not offer a complete description of reality, that there must be some hidden variables it does not take into account. To put it in a somewhat problematic and exaggerated way, the Einsteinian critics try to re-Kantianize quantum physics, excluding from its grasp reality-in-itself.

Meillassoux is well aware that quantum physics, with its uncertainty principle and emphasis on the role the observer plays in the collapse of the wave function, seems to undermine the notion of objective reality independent of any observer and thus give an unexpected boost to Kantian transcendentalism; however, as he points out, their similarity is deceptive, and obfuscates a fundamental difference: "Certainly, the presence of an observer may eventually affect the effectuation of a physical law, as is the case for some of the laws of quantum physics—but the very fact that an observer can influence the law is itself a property of the law which is not supposed to depend upon the existence of an observer."[16] In short, while in Kant's transcendentalism the "observer"-subject constitutes what he observes, in quantum physics, the observer's active role itself is re-inscribed into physical reality.

How, then, can this access to the absolute be reconciled with the obvious

---

13 Ibid., pp. 52–3.

14 Ibid., p. 63.

15 Ibid., p. 58.

16 Ibid., p. 114.

limitation of our knowledge of reality? A reference to Brecht may be of some use here: in one of his reflections about the stage, Brecht ferociously opposed the idea that the background of the stage should render the impenetrable depth of the All of Reality as the obscure Origin of Things out of which everything we see and know appear as fragments. For Brecht, the background of a stage should ideally be empty, white, signaling that, behind what we see and experience, there is no secret Origin or Ground. This in no way implies that reality is transparent to us, that we "know all"; of course there are infinite blanks, but the point is that these blanks *are just that, blanks*, things we simply do not know, not a substantial "deeper" reality.

Now we come to the properly *speculative* crux of Meillassoux's argument: how to justify this passage from (or reversal of) epistemological limitation to (or into) positive ontological feature? As we have seen, the transcendental criticism conceives facticity as the mark of our finitude, of our cognitive limitations, of our inability to access the absolute In-itself: to us, to our finite reason, reality appears contingent, *ohne Warum*, but considered in itself, it may well be true that reality is non-contingent (regulated by a deep spiritual or natural necessity), so that we are mere puppets of a transcendent mechanism, or that our Self is itself generating the reality it perceives, etc. In other words, for the transcendentalist, there is always the radical "*possibility of ignorance*":[17] we are ignorant of how reality really is, there is always the possibility that reality is radically other than how it appears to us. How, then, does Meillassoux make the step from this epistemological limitation to the unique access to the absolute? In a deeply Hegelian way, he locates in this very point the paradoxical overlapping of possibility and actuality: "How are you able to *think* this 'possibility of ignorance'...? The truth is that you are only able to think this possibility of ignorance because you have *actually* thought the *absoluteness* of this possibility, which is to say, its non-correlational character."[18] The ontological proof of God is here inverted in a materialist way: it is not that the very fact that we can think the possibility of a Supreme Being entails its actuality; it is, on the contrary, that the very fact that we can think the possibility of the absolute contingency of reality, the possibility of its being-other, of the radical gap between the way reality appears to us and the way it is in itself, entails its actuality, that is, entails that reality in itself is radically contingent. In both cases, we are dealing with the direct passage from the notion of existence to existence which is part of the notion; however, in the case of the ontological proof of God, the term that mediates between possibility (of thinking) and actuality is "perfection" (the very notion of a perfect being includes its existence), while in the case of Meillassoux's passage from notion to existence, *the mediating term is imperfection*. If we can *think* our knowledge

17 Ibid., p. 58.
18 Ibid.

of reality (the way reality appears to us) as having radically failed, as radically different from the Absolute, *then this gap (between For-us and In-itself) must be part of the Absolute itself*, so that the very feature that seemed forever to keep us away from the Absolute is the *only* feature which *directly* unites us with the Absolute. And does not exactly the same shift lie at the very core of the Christian experience? It is the radical separation of man from God which unites us with God, since, in the figure of Christ, God is thoroughly separated *from itself*—the point is thus not to "overcome" the gap which separates us from God, but to take note of how *this gap is internal to God himself* (Christianity as the ultimate version of the Rabinovitch joke)—only when I experience the infinite pain of separation from God do I share an experience with God himself (Christ on the Cross).

Two things must be noted here. First, when Meillassoux asserts contingency as the only necessity, his mistake is to conceive this assertion according to the masculine side of Lacan's formulae of sexuation, that is, according to the logic of universality and its constitutive exception: everything is contingent—with the exception of contingency itself, which is absolutely necessary. Necessity thus becomes the external guarantee of the universal contingency—but what about the non-All of contingency: there is nothing which is not contingent, which is why not-All is contingent? Simultaneously, there is the non-All of necessity: there is nothing which is not necessary, which is why not-All is necessary. Not-All is necessary, which means that, from time to time, a contingent encounter occurs which undermines the predominant necessity (the space of possibilities sustained by this necessity), so that in it, the "impossible" happens.[19] How do these two non-Alls relate? Since reality is contingent, we should begin with the non-All of contingency: it is out of contingency that, contingently, necessities arise.

Second, we should take note of Meillassoux's frequent and systematic use of Hegelian terms, even (and especially) in his critique of Hegel. For example, he repeatedly characterizes his own position as "speculative" (in the sense of the post-Kantian assertion of the accessibility to our knowledge of the absolute) in contrast to "metaphysical" pre-critical dogmatism (which claims access to transcendent absolute necessity). Paradoxically, Hegel counts for him as "metaphysical," although it was precisely Hegel who deployed the "metaphysical," the "critical" (in the sense of Kantian criticism), and the "speculative" as the three basic stances of thought towards reality, making it clear that his own "speculative" stance can only arise when one has fully accepted the lesson of the critical stance. No wonder that Meillassoux, following Hegel, designates his own position as that of "Absolute Knowledge," characterized in a thoroughly Hegelian

19 See Alenka Zupančič, "Realno in njegovo nemožno" ("The Real and its Impossible"), *Problemi* 1–2 (2010).

way as "the principle of an *auto-limitation* or *auto-normalization of the omnipotence of chaos*"[20]—in short, as the rise of necessity out of contingency:

> We can only hope to develop an absolute knowledge—a knowledge of chaos which would not simply keep repeating that everything is possible—on condition that we produce necessary propositions about it besides that of its omnipotence. But this requires that we discover norms or laws to which chaos itself is subject. Yet there is nothing over and above the power of chaos that could constrain it to submit to a norm. If chaos is subject to constraints, then this can only be a constraint which comes from the nature of chaos itself, from its own omnipotence … in order for an entity to be contingent and un-necessary in this way, *it cannot be anything whatsoever*. This is to say that in order to be contingent and un-necessary, the entity must conform to *certain determinate conditions*, which can then be construed as *so many absolute properties of what is*.[21]

Is this not exactly Hegel's program? For Hegel, necessary laws are contingent in the simple sense that "they are because they are"—there is no question of why. In a Hegelian-speculative manner the regularities of nature are precisely the highest assertion of contingency: the more nature behaves regularly, following its "necessary laws," the more contingent is this necessity. Radical contingency not only does not preclude, but even *prefers* the stability of laws: the highest contingency is when laws are eternal, unchangeable—but contingently so, for no reason at all. At the beginning of Hegel's *Logic*, we have the process of Becoming (the unity of Being and Nothingness), which is the thoroughly contingent process of generating the multiplicity of Somethings. The "spurious infinity" of Somethings and Something-Others is chaos at its purest, with no necessity whatsoever underlying or regulating it, and the entire development of Hegel's *Logic* is the deployment of the immanent process of "*auto-limitation* or *auto-normalization of the omnipotence of chaos*": "We then begin to understand what the rational discourse about unreason—an unreason which is not irrational—would consist in: it would be discourse that aims to establish the constraints to which the entity must submit in order to exercise its capacity-not-to-be and its capacity-to-be-other."[22]

This "capacity-to-be-other," as expressed in the gap that separates For-us and In-itself (in the possibility that reality-in-itself is totally different from the way it appears to us), is the self-distance of the In-itself, the *negativity* in the very heart of Being—this is what Meillassoux signals in his wonderfully dense proposition that "the thing-in-itself is nothing other than the facticity of the

20 Meillassoux, *After Finitude*, p. 66.

21 Ibid.

22 Ibid.

transcendental forms of representation," nothing other than the radically contingent character of our frame of reality.[23] To see reality the way it "really is" is not to see another "deeper" reality beneath it, but to see this same reality in its thorough contingency.

So why does Meillassoux not openly acknowledge the Hegelian nature of his breakthrough? The first reason, at least, is a simple one: he endorses the standard reading of Hegelian dialectics as the description of the necessary self-deployment of the Notion:

> Hegelian metaphysics maintains the necessity of a moment of irremediable contingency in the unfolding of the absolute; a moment which occurs in the midst of nature as the pure contingency, the reality devoid of actuality, the sheer finitude whose chaos and gratuitousness are recalcitrant to the labour of the Notion ... But this contingency is deduced from the unfolding of the absolute, which in itself, *qua* rational totality, is devoid of contingency. Thus, in Hegel, the necessity of contingency is not derived from contingency as such and contingency alone, but from a Whole that is ontologically superior to the latter.[24]

Meillassoux here crucially simplifies the properly Hegelian relationship between necessity and contingency. On a first approach, it appears that their encompassing unity is necessity, that necessity itself posits and mediates contingency as the external field in which it expresses or actualizes itself—contingency itself is necessary, the result of the self-externalization and self-mediation of notional necessity. However, it is crucial to supplement this unity with the opposite, with contingency as the encompassing unity of itself and necessity: the very elevation of a necessity into the structuring principle of the contingent field of multiplicity is a contingent act; one can almost say: the outcome of a contingent ("open") struggle for hegemony. This shift corresponds to the shift from S to $, from substance to subject. The starting point is a contingent multitude; through its self-mediation ("spontaneous self-organization"), contingency engenders or posits its immanent necessity, in the same way that Essence is the result of the self-mediation of Being. Once Essence emerges, it retroactively "posits its own presuppositions," that is, it sublates its presuppositions into subordinated moments of its self-reproduction (Being is transubstantiated into Appearance); however, this positing is retroactive.

This brings us to Meillassoux's basic strategic move (and a deeply Hegelian one, at that) from the gap that separates us (finite humans) from the In-itself to the gap that is immanent to the In-itself; this move is strictly correlative to Lacan's move from desire to drive: the drive is "transcendental," its space is that

23 Ibid., p. 76.
24 Ibid., p. 80.

of the fantasy which fills in the void of the lost primordial Object (Thing)—in short, desire is Kantian, the drive is Hegelian. The Lacanian *objet a* as the object which overlaps with its loss, which emerges at the very moment of its loss (so that all its fantasmatic incarnations, from breast to voice and gaze, are metonymic figurations of the void, of nothing), remains within the horizon of *desire*—the true object-cause of desire is the void filled in by its fantasmatic incarnations. While, as Lacan emphasizes, the *objet a* is also the object of the drive, the relationship is here thoroughly different: although, in both cases, the link between object and loss is crucial, in the case of the *objet a* as the object-cause of *desire*, we have an object which is originally lost, which coincides with its own loss, which emerges as lost, while, in the case of the *objet a* as the object of the drive, the "object" *is directly the loss itself*—in the shift from desire to drive, we pass from the *lost object* to *loss itself as an object*. In other words, the weird movement called "drive" is not driven by the "impossible" quest for the lost object; it is *a push to directly enact the "loss"—the gap, cut, distance—itself*. There is thus a *double* distinction to be drawn here: not only between the *objet a* in its fantasmatic and post-fantasmatic status, but also, within this post-fantasmatic domain itself, between the lost object-cause of desire and the object-loss of the drive.

It is thus wrong to claim that the "pure" death drive would be the impossible "total" will to (self-)destruction, an ecstatic self-annihilation in which the subject would rejoin the fullness of the maternal Thing, but that this will is not realizable, that it gets blocked, stuck to a "partial object." Such a notion retranslates the death drive into the terms of desire and its lost object: it is in desire that the positive object is a metonymic stand-in for the void of the impossible Thing; it is in desire that the aspiration to fullness is transferred to partial objects—this is what Lacan called the metonymy of desire. We have to be very precise here in order not to miss Lacan's point (and thereby confuse desire and drive): the drive is not an infinite longing for the Thing which gets fixated onto a partial object—the "drive" *is* this fixation itself in which resides the "death" dimension of every drive. The drive is not a universal thrust (towards the incestuous Thing) checked and broken up, it *is* this brake itself, a brake on instinct, its "stuckness," as Eric Santner would put it.[25] The elementary matrix of the drive is *not* that of transcending all particular objects towards the void of the Thing (which is then accessible only in its metonymic stand-in), but that of our libido getting "stuck" onto a particular object, condemned to circulate around it forever.

Consequently, as we have seen, the concept of drive makes the alternative "either get burned by the Thing or maintain a safe distance" false: in a drive, the "Thing itself" is a circulation around the void (or, rather, hole, not void). To put it even more pointedly, the object of the drive is not related to the Thing as a

25 See Eric Santner, *On the Psychotheology of Everyday Life*, Chicago: University of Chicago Press 2001.

filler of its void: the drive is literally a counter-movement to desire, it does not strive towards impossible fullness and, being forced to renounce it, get stuck onto a partial object as its remainder—the drive is quite literally the very "drive" to *break* the All of continuity in which we are embedded, to introduce a radical imbalance into it, and the difference between drive and desire is precisely that, in desire, this cut, this fixation onto a partial object, is as it were "transcendentalized," transposed into a stand-in for the void of the Thing.

From this paradox of the drive, we can discern the limitation of speculative realism, a limitation signaled in the fact that it immediately split into four orientations which form a kind of Greimasian semiotic square: Meillassoux's "speculative materialism," Harman's "object-oriented philosophy,"[26] Grant's neo-vitalism,[27] and Brassier's radical nihilism. The two axes along which these four positions are placed are divine/secular and scientific/metaphysical. Although both Meillassoux and Brassier advocate a scientific view of reality as radically contingent and apprehensible through formalized science, Brassier also endorses scientific reductionism, while Meillassoux leaves the space open for a non-existent divinity which will redress all past injustices. On the other side, both Harman and Grant advocate a non-scientific metaphysical approach, with Harman opting for a directly religious (or spiritualist, at least) panpsychism, outlining a program of investigating the "cosmic layers of psyche" and "ferreting out the specific psychic reality of earthworms, dust, armies, chalk, and stone," while Grant, in Deleuzian fashion, locates the meta-physical dimension in nature itself, conceiving the world of objects as the products of a more primordial process of becoming (will, drive, etc.). What stands out in this square are the two positions which unsettle the expected overlapping of the two axes (metaphysical divinity versus secular scientific reductionism): Meillassoux's scientistic assertion of radical contingency which nonetheless leaves open the space for a non-existing God who may emerge in order to redress past injustices, and Grant's anti-scientistic vitalist metaphysics which nonetheless remains naturalist/materialist. The gap filled in by these two additional options signals that the price speculative realism pays for leaving behind transcendental correlationism is that it remains caught up in the traditional pre-critical antinomies, i.e., that a dimension is missing in the basic opposition which defines speculative realism: realism versus correlationism. What is this dimension?

Ray Brassier was right with his programmatic slogan of *nihil unbound*—one should definitely go all the way in "unbounding" nothingness, or, in other words, pushing "secularization" to the end. One of the names of the enemy today is "post-secular thought": the idea that the process of "disenchantment"

26 Graham Harman, *The Quadruple Object*, Ropley: Zero Books 2011.

27 Iain Hamilton Grant, *Philosophies of Nature After Schelling*, London: Continuum 2006.

has reached its limit and that a new, post-metaphysical, return of the Sacred is on the way, no longer grounded in the access to an infinite Absolute, but in our very finitude, in our irreducible rootedness in the finite *Lebenswelt* with its concrete experience of bodily life permeated with meaning. In order to overturn this tendency, we should begin at the very beginning, with the reversal of the identity of being and *logos* first formulated by Parmenides in what is the inaugural gesture of philosophy: "being and thinking/speaking are the same." This sameness should be conceived as negative: contrary to Plato's notion that what one talks about has to exist in some way, one can only talk about what (potentially, at least) is not, for there is no speech without a hole in the texture of the Real; the very fact of affirming something locates this something against the background of its potential disappearance, or, to paraphrase Parmenides, thinking/speaking and non-being are the same. Furthermore, this hole in the texture of the Real can only arise if the Real itself is ultimately nothing but a void, if "all there is" is, precisely, not-All, a distorted fragment which is ultimately a "metonymy of nothing."

The problem here is how we compound this full deployment of nothingness with the big dilemma of contemporary thought, which is (to paraphrase Brassier): do we conceive the scientific explanation of reality as grounded in our concrete experience of reality, in our *Lebenswelt*, or do we endorse a version of "scientific reductionism" which tries to explain our very experience of reality in scientific terms (in terms of cognitive science, Darwinism, etc.)? The first approach is a version of what Meillassoux calls "correlationism," which can also have a pointedly "materialist" accent (as in what was once called "humanist Marxism," where science was seen as part of the practical engagement of humanity with nature), so the problem is, again, how to break out of the correlationist constraints. In short: can science think radical Nothingness? Meillassoux claims that my (and "perhaps" Badiou's) positions

> consist at bottom in making of materialism a "misfired correlationism". Ever since Derrida in particular, materialism seems to have taken the form of a "sickened correlationism": it refuses both the return to a naïve pre-critical stage of thought *and* any investigation of what prevents the "circle of the subject" from harmoniously closing in on itself. Whether it be the Freudian unconscious, Marxist ideology, Derridean dissemination, the undecidability of the event, the Lacanian Real considered as the impossible, etc., these are all supposed to detect the trace of an impossible coincidence of the subject with itself, and thus of an extra-correlational residue in which one could localize a "materialist moment" of thought. But in fact, such misfires are only further correlations among others: it is always *for* a subject that there is an undecidable event or a failure of signification. Unless we fall back on naïve realism, we cannot treat these misfires as "effects" of a cause that could definitely

> be established as external to the subject or even to consciousness. In any case, a correlationist would have no difficulty in retorting that this genre of materialism is either a disingenuous idealism or a dogmatic realism of the "old style". When a chair is wobbly, the "wobbly" exists only in relation to the chair, not independently of it. When one clogs up the Subject, one does not go outside it: instead, one merely constructs a transcendental or speculative Wobbly Subject—a subject that is assured *a priori*, and according to a properly absolute Knowing, for which things always turn out badly in its world of representations.[28]

As usual with Meillassoux, this argumentation is precise and to the point; my (day)dream is that if Lenin were alive and had time to read my *Parallax View*, something like this would have been his reaction to my "dialectical materialism"—beneath the rhetorical materialist surface, there lies good old-fashioned subjective idealism. But is this really the case? On the face of it, the argument is convincing: do I not claim that, beneath the transcendental correlation between (the conscious) subject and reality, there is the correlative between the subject (of the unconscious) and its Real/impossible objectal counterpoint, S-*a*? Strange as this correlation is, it still makes sense only if a subject is already there, that is, it does not enable us to think reality *without* a subject. But, again, is this truly the case? The point Meillassoux misses is that this impossible/Real object is the very mode of inscription of the subject into trans-subjective reality; as such, it is not transcendental, but (what Derrida would have called) arche-transcendental, an attempt to circumscribe the "subject in becoming," the trans-subjective process of the emergence of the subject.

The critical implication with regard to Meillassoux is that the true problem is not to think pre-subjective reality, but to think how something like a subject could have emerged within it; without this (properly Hegelian) gesture, any objectivism will remain correlationist in a hidden way—its image of "reality in itself" remains correlated (even if in a negative way) with subjectivity. To make this gesture, it is not enough to posit the subject (or, rather, presuppose it) as a contingent emergence—while this is true, one should locate traces of this contingency in a kind of umbilical cord which links the subject to its

28 Quentin Meillassoux, interview in Graham Harman, *Quentin Meillassoux: Philosophy in the Making*, Edinburgh: Edinburgh University Press, p. 166. Incidentally, if there is a philosopher who effectively seems to be caught in the circle of what Meillassoux calls "failed correlationism," it is Derrida, whose thought oscillates in its deconstructive analyses between two poles: on the one hand, he emphasizes that there is no direct outside (of metaphysics), that the very attempt to directly break out of the circle of logocentrism has to rely on a metaphysical conceptual frame; on the other hand, he sometimes treats writing and difference as a kind of general ontological category, talking about "traces" and "writing" in nature itself (genetic codes, etc.).

pre-subjective Real, and thus breaks the circle of transcendental correlationism. In other words, what Meillassoux calls "sickened" or "failed" correlationism, far from being a half-hearted break-out from the correlationist constraint, is the key component of any true escape: it is not enough to oppose to transcendental correlation a vision of reality-in-itself—transcendental correlation itself has to be grounded in reality-in-itself; i.e., its possibility has to be accounted for in the terms of this reality. As Niels Bohr (who is sometimes misunderstood as having wanted to "transcendentalize" physics) liked to repeat, at the level of the physics of micro-particles, there is no "objective" measurement, no access to "objective" reality—not because we (our mind) constitutes reality, but because we are part of the reality which we measure, and thus lack an "objective distance" towards it.

It is against this background of the radical asymmetry or non-correlation between subject and object (or thinking and reality) that one can clearly see where Meillassoux's critique of correlationism falls short. In his very anti-transcendentalism, Meillassoux remains caught up in the Kantian topic of the accessibility of the Thing-in-itself: is what we experience as reality fully determined by our subjective-transcendental horizon, or can we get to know something about the way reality is independently of our subjectivity? Meillassoux's claim is to have achieved the breakthrough into independent "objective" reality. But there is a third Hegelian option: the true problem that follows from Meillassoux's basic speculative gesture (transposing the contingency of our notion of reality into the Thing itself) is not so much what more we can say about reality-in-itself, but how our subjective standpoint and subjectivity itself fit into reality. The problem is not "Can we penetrate the veil of subjectively constituted phenomena to Things-in-themselves?" but "How do phenomena themselves arise within the flat stupidity of reality which just is; how does reality redouble itself and start to appear to itself?" For this, we need a theory of the subject which involves neither transcendental subjectivity nor a reduction of the subject to a part of objective reality; such a theory also enables us to formulate in a new way what Meillassoux calls the problem of correlationism (ancestrality). Here, both Lacan and Hegel are anti-Leninists, for their problem is not "how to reach objective reality which is independent of (its correlation to) subjectivity," but how subjectivity is already inscribed into reality—to quote Lacan again, not only is the picture in my eye, but I am also in the picture.

To make this key point again, in his rejection of transcendental correlationism (the claim that in order to think reality, there must already be a subject to whom this reality appears), Meillassoux remains trapped within the confines of the Kantian-transcendental opposition between reality the way it appears to us and the transcendent beyond of reality-in-itself, independently of us. In a Lenin-like manner (the Lenin of *Materialism and Empirio-Criticism*), he then asserts that we can access and think reality in itself. But something is lost in this very field of the transcendental dilemma, something which concerns the very core of the Freudian discovery (or the way this discovery was formulated by Lacan): the inherent twist/curvature that is constitutive of the subject itself. In other words, what Lacan asserts is precisely the irreducible (constitutive) discord, or non-correlation, between subject and reality: in order for the subject to emerge, the impossible object-that-is-subject must be excluded from reality, since it is this very exclusion which opens up the space for the subject. The problem is not to think the Real outside of transcendental correlation, independently of the subject; the problem is to think the Real *inside* the subject, the hard core of the Real in the very heart of the subject, its ex-timate center.

The true problem of correlationism is not whether we can reach the In-itself the way it is outside of any correlation to the subject (or the way the Old is outside its perception from the standpoint of the New); but the true problem is to think the New itself "in becoming." The fossil is not the Old the way it was/is in itself, the true fossil is the subject itself in its impossible objectal status—the fossil is myself, the way the terrified cat sees me when it looks at me. This is what truly escapes correlation, not the In-itself of the object, but the subject as object.

Usually we have the split in the object (between the object for us and the way the object is in itself), but thinking and the subject are conceived as homogeneous. Lacan, however, introduces a split also into the subject, between its thinking and its (not actual life-being but its) non-thought thought, its non-non-thought, between discourse and the Real (not reality). So the point is not only to overcome the inaccessible In-itself by claiming that "there is nothing beyond the veil of semblances except what the subject itself put there," but to relate the In-itself to the split in the subject itself.

Meillassoux ironically mentions the ridiculously ingenious Christian reply to the Darwinist challenge: one of Darwin's contemporaries proposed a neat reconciliation between the Bible and evolutionary theory: the Bible is literally true, the world was created c.4000 years BC—but how then do we explain the fossils? They were *directly created by God as fossils*, to give humanity a false sense of living in an older universe—in short, when God created the universe, he also included in it traces of an imaginary past. Meillassoux's point is that post-Kantian transcendentalism answers the challenge of objective science in a similar way: if, for the theological literalists, God directly created fossils in order to expose men to the temptation of denying the divine creation, to test their faith, the post-Kantian transcendentalists conceive the spontaneous everyday "naïve" notion of objective reality existing independently of us as a similar trap, exposing humans to the test, challenging them to see through this "evidence" and grasp how reality is constituted by the transcendental subject.[29] We

29 Meillassoux, *After Finitude*, p. 62.

should nonetheless insist that the Christian solution, meaningless though it is as a scientific theory, contains a grain of truth: what Lacan calls the *objet a*, the subject's impossible-Real objectal counterpart, is precisely such an "imagined" (fantasmatic, virtual) object which never positively existed in reality—it emerges through its loss, it is directly created as a fossil.

Simultaneously, the exclusion of this object is constitutive of the appearance of reality: since reality (not the Real) is correlative to the subject, it can only constitute itself through the withdrawal from it of the object which "is" the subject; that is, through the withdrawal of the subject's objectal correlate. Or, to put it in the old jargon of the logic of the signifier, the subject is only possible out of its own impossibility, the impossibility of becoming an object. What breaks up the self-closure of transcendental correlation is thus not the transcendent reality that eludes the subject's grasp, but the inaccessibility of the object that "is" the subject itself.[30] This is the true "fossil," the bone that is the spirit, to paraphrase Hegel, and this object is not simply the full objective reality of the subject (the successful scientific reduction of subjective experience to objective processes, such as in biogenetics), but the non-corporeal, fantasmatic *lamella*.

Why this primordial loss, why this constitutive withdrawal from reality of a part of the Real? Precisely because the subject is a part of reality, because it emerges out of it. This is why, if the subject is to emerge as the non-substantial *cogito*, its being must be elevated into a spectral impossible object which forever haunts it (and which can assume many fantasmatic forms, from the *lamella* to the double). The "official" transcendental subject-object correlation is thus redoubled by a kind of negative correlation of the subject and the impossible-Real object: before relating to objects which are part of external reality, the subject is haunted by its own objectal shadow; in the guise of this additional virtual object, the subject is ex-posed to the Real, constitutively "de-centered," much more radically even than in the symbolic order. This is how we can read one of Lacan's re-formulations of Descartes's *cogito ergo sum*: "I am at that impossible piece of the real where I cannot think." We can also see in what way two lacks overlap in this impossible object: the constitutive lack of the subject (what the subject has to lose in order to emerge as the subject of the signifier) and the lack in the Other itself (what has to be excluded from reality so that reality can appear). Again, the object is not simply there at the intersection of the two lacks: it literally and much more radically emerges through the overlapping of the two lacks. (Once Lacan got this point, he changed the status of the *objet a* from imaginary to Real.) So the Real is not some kind of primordial Being which is lost with the opposition of subject and object (as Hölderlin put it in his famous *Ur-Fragment* of German Idealism); the Real is, on the contrary, a product (of the overlapping

30 See Zupančič, "Realno in njegovo nemožno."

of the two lacks). *The Real is not lost, it is what we cannot get rid of,* what always sticks on as the remainder of the symbolic operation.

It is here that Meillassoux is also too hasty in dismissing the transcendental position: (what we experience as) reality is always transcendentally constituted. The remainder of the Real is the price we pay for the inversion of the "natural" order that pertains to the symbolic order: although language is ultimately part of reality, reality (the way it appears to us) is always already transcendentally constituted through language. Or, to put it another way: we cannot gain full neutral access to reality *because we are part of it.* The epistemological distortion of our access to reality is the result of our *inclusion* in it, not of our distance from it. The *objet a* is the splinter in the eye which distorts our clear perception of reality, and the agent of this distortion is desire (recall that the *objet a* is the object-cause of desire). This brings us to the unique "short-circuit between epistemology and ontology": the very epistemological failure (to reach reality) is an indication and effect of our being part of reality, of our inclusion within it.[31]

In the opposition between the symbolic order and reality, the Real is on the side of the symbolic—it is the part of reality which clings to the symbolic (in the guise of its inconsistency/gap/impossibility). The Real is the point at which the external opposition between the symbolic order and reality is immanent to the symbolic itself, mutilating it from within: it is the non-All of the symbolic. There is a Real not because the symbolic cannot grasp its external Real, but because the symbolic cannot fully become *itself.* There is being (reality) because the symbolic system is inconsistent, flawed, for the Real is an impasse of formalization. This thesis must be given its full "idealist" weight: it is not only that reality is too rich, so that every formalization fails to grasp it, stumbles over it; the Real *is* nothing but an impasse of formalization—there is dense reality "out there" *because* of the inconsistencies and gaps in the symbolic order. The Real is nothing but the non-All of formalization, not its external exception.

Since reality is in itself fragile and inconsistent, it needs the intervention of a Master-Signifier to stabilize itself into a consistent field; this Master-Signifier marks the point at which a signifier falls into the Real. The Master-Signifier is a signifier which not only designates features of reality, but performatively intervenes into reality. As such, the Master-Signifier is the counterpart of the *objet a*: if the *objet a* is the Real which is on the side of the symbolic, the Master-Signifier is the signifier which falls into the Real. Its role is exactly homologous to that of the transcendental synthesis of apperception in Kant: its intervention transforms the inconsistent multiplicity of fragments of the Real into the consistent field of "objective reality." In the same way that, for Kant, it is the

31 At a different level, therein resides the basic epistemological lesson of quantum physics: we cannot get to know reality the way it is independently of us because we are part of reality.

addition of the subjective synthesis which transforms the multiplicity of subjective impressions into objective reality, for Lacan, it is the intervention of the Master-Signifier which transforms the confused field of impressions into "extra-linguistic reality." This, then, should be the Lacanian answer to correlationism: while transcendental correlationism can think the intervention of the Master-Signifier as constitutive of reality, it misses this other inverted correlation between the Master-Signifier and the *objet a*; that is, it cannot think the stain of the Real which de-centers the subject from within.

So, to repeat Meillassoux's fossil question in the most direct way: is a dinosaur fossil proof that dinosaurs existed on Earth independently of any human observer, whether empirical or transcendental? If we can imagine transposing ourselves into the pre-historical past, would we encounter dinosaurs the way we reconstruct them today? Before rushing to an answer, we should remember how relative "external reality" is with regard to our point of view, which does not mean that we "created" it, but that out of the infinite complexity of the Real-in-itself a part or slice of reality was selected as correlative to our perceptual apparatus. So we cannot ever escape the circle: the reality of a fossil is "objective" insofar as it is observed from our standpoint, in the same way that a rainbow "objectively exists" from our standpoint—what "objectively exists" is the entire field of interaction between subject and object as part of the Real.

CHAPTER 10

Objects, Objects Everywhere

SUBTRACTION, PROTRACTION, OBSTRUCTION … DESTRUCTION

Back in 2008, when confronted with his low position in the opinion polls, the Republican presidential candidate Mike Huckabee (a figure who seemed to have stepped right out of an old Frank Capra film, if not a Dickens novel) said: "I know the pundits and I know what they say, the math doesn't work out. Well I didn't major in math, I majored in miracles. And I still believe in those, too." This anecdote is worth quoting not just to make fun of the standard of political debate in the US, but because, in a negative way, it points to a central component of Badiou's thinking which, precisely, brings together mathematics and miracles. When talking about miracles, we should of course bear in mind Lacan's qualification that the only "irrationality" he admits is that of irrational numbers in mathematics—in a homologous way, the only "miracles" a radical materialist allows for are mathematical ones. A "miracle" is simply the sudden emergence of the New, irreducible to its preceding conditions, of something which retroactively "posits" its conditions. Every authentic act creates its own conditions of possibility.

But what is this "irrational" element? As Badiou has pointed out, what defines a "world" is not primarily its positive features, but the way its structure relates to its own inherent (point of) impossibility. Classical mathematics dismissed the square root of -1 as an irrelevant externality, as nonsense to be ignored, while modern mathematics makes this impossible calculable, marking it with the letter I ("imaginary number"): "mathematics historically splits and remakes itself by creating constants that occupy these impossible places: the root square of -1 is baptized an imaginary number which is then used in a new space of calculations."[1]

Things are similar with Cantor's conceptualization of different modalities of the infinite: the transfinite and so forth. The distinction between "transfinite" and "infinite" as elaborated by Cantor roughly fits the Hegelian distinction between "true" and "bad" (or "spurious") infinity: with the "bad infinity," we never actually reach the infinite, another unit can be added to every number, and "infinity"

1 Oliver Feltham, "On Changing Appearances in Lacan and Badiou," *Umbr(a)* 1 (2007), p. 121.

here refers precisely to this constant possibility of adding, to the impossibility of ever reaching the ultimate element in the series. What if, however, we treat this set of elements forever "open" to addition as a closed totality and posit the infinite as an element of its own, as the external frame of the endless set of elements it contains? The transfinite is thus a number or an element with the paradoxical property of being insensitive to addition or subtraction: whether we add a unit to it or subtract one from it, it remains the same.[2] Did not Kant in a similar way construct the concept of the "transcendental object"? One is tempted to risk a pun here: Kantor. The transcendental object is external to the endless series of empirical objects: we arrive at it by way of treating this endless series as closed, and positing an empty object outside of it, the very form of an object, that frames the series. It is also easy to discern a further homology with the *objet petit a*, the Lacanian object-cause of desire: the latter is also "transfinite," namely an empty object that frames the endless set of empirical objects. In this precise sense, our two *objets petit a*, voice and gaze, are "transfinite": in both cases, we are dealing with an empty object that frames the "bad infinity" of the field of the visible and/or audible by giving body to what constitutively eludes this field (on this account, the object-gaze is a blind spot within the field of the visible, whereas the object-voice par excellence is of course silence).[3]

In his debate with the Athenians related in *Acts*, Paul makes deft use of the fact that the Athenians, in their pragmatic opportunism, built a statue to an unknown god on top of the statues of all their known gods—they just wanted to be sure that their series of statues also included a reference to a divinity ignored by them, a reference to what might be excluded or missing from their pantheistic

---

2 On a first approach, it may appear that we are here as far as possible from Hegel: does not Cantor's concept of the transfinite as that which persists outside the finite, which stands side by side with it, which is exempted from it as its external frame, provide an exemplary case of what Hegel calls the "abstract infinite" which, insofar as it is externally opposed to the finite and excludes it, is in itself again finite? And, in contrast, is not the Hegelian "true infinite" immanent to the finite, is it not the very organic totality of the finite in its movement of self-sublation? It is, however, precisely such an "organic" notion of the infinite as the living totality of the finite that remains at the level of Substance since, in it, the infinite is not yet for itself: it is crucial for Hegel that the infinite must appear, that it be "posited as such," in its difference to the finite—only thus do we pass from Substance to Subject. For Hegel, the "subject" qua the power of absolute negativity designates the point at which the infinite is posited as such, in its negative relationship to everything finite.

3 Strictly speaking, the same goes also for the transcendental dimension as such. The field of our experience is in principle "open," infinite, there is always something to be added to it; we arrive at the transcendental dimension when we decide to treat this "open" field of experience as a closed, framed totality and to render thematic the frame which, although not part of our experience, a priori delineates its contours.

pandemonium. Paul cunningly remarks that there already is in Athens a statue of the unique God of whom he speaks; the trick is that he replaces the indefinite article with a definite one: not a statue of *an* unknown god (like the monument to the unknown soldier, referring to the anonymous fallen generally), but a statue of *the* unknown god, meaning the (one true) god who is/remains unknown, obfuscated by the glittering chaos of polytheism. Did not Paul also thereby internalize the point of impossibility of the pagan universe?

The same holds for capitalism: its dynamic of perpetual self-revolutionizing relies on the endless postponement of its point of impossibility (its final crisis or collapse). What for earlier modes of production was a dangerous exception is for capitalism normality: in capitalism, crisis is internalized, taken into account, as the point of impossibility which impels it into continuous activity. Capitalism is structurally always in crisis—which is why it is expanding all the time: it can only reproduce itself by "borrowing from the future," in a *fuite en avant* into the future. The final settling of accounts when all its debts will have been paid will never arrive. Marx proposed his own name for the social point of impossibility: "class struggle."

Perhaps, one should extend this to the very definition of humanity: what ultimately distinguishes humans from animals is not some positive feature (speech, tool-making, reflexive thinking, etc.), but the rise of a new point of impossibility designated by Freud and Lacan as *das Ding*, the impossible-real ultimate reference point of desire. The often noted experimental difference between humans and apes acquires here all its significance: when an ape is presented with an object out of reach, it will abandon it after a few failed attempts to grasp it and move on to a more modest object (a less attractive sexual partner, say), while a human will persist in its effort, remaining transfixed on the impossible object.

This is why the subject as such is hysterical: precisely a subject who posits *jouissance* as an absolute; it responds to the absolute of *jouissance* in the form of unsatisfied desire. Such a subject is capable of relating to a term that remains outside the limits of the game; indeed, this relationship to a term "out-of-play" is constitutive of the subject itself. Hysteria is thus the elementary "human" way of installing a point of impossibility in the guise of absolute *jouissance*. Is not Lacan's *il n'y a pas de rapport sexuel* also such a point of impossibility constitutive of being human?

When cognitivists from Dennett onwards try to explain consciousness, they enumerate a whole series of specifically human capacities which "cannot really function without consciousness"—what if, however, instead of focusing on "what we can (only) do with consciousness," we should shift the terrain and ask: what is the specific point of impossibility of consciousness? What is it that we *cannot* do with consciousness? How is consciousness related to what we *a priori* cannot become conscious of? And what unsurpassable failure gave birth to consciousness? Is consciousness at its zero-level not consciousness of a failure—of coming up against a radical impossibility? Here, the topic of mortality re-emerges: when Heidegger claims that only man is mortal, not animals, this again means that death is the ultimate possibility of impossibility for a human being, its inherent point of impossibility, something one calculates with, relates to, in contrast to the animal for whom death is simply external.

Many a cognitivist (from Pinker to McGinn) tries to account for the paradox of (self-)consciousness by claiming that its inability to "know itself," to account for itself as an object in the world, is co-substantial with consciousness itself, its inherent constituent. (Pinker offers a more scientific, evolutionist version—consciousness did not emerge with the aim of understanding/explaining itself, but with other evolutionary functions—while McGinn offers a more purely theoretical version of why consciousness is necessarily an enigma to itself.)[4] What we get here is nothing less than an evolutionary biological explanation for the emergence of metaphysics. However, a Heideggerian counter-question, issuing from the framework of *Being and Time*, immediately pops up here: does not consciousness *necessarily* question itself, asking itself about the enigma it is a priori unable to answer? (As Heidegger himself puts it: *Dasein* is an entity that questions its own being.) How did *this* property emerge within the evolutionary logic? The point is not only that, *on top* of its adaptive functions (how to find one's way in the environment, etc.), consciousness is *also* bothered by enigmas having no evolutionary, adaptive function (humor, art, metaphysical questions). The further (and crucial) point is that this useless supplement, this compulsive fixation on problems which a priori cannot be solved, retroactively enabled an explosion of procedures (techniques, insights) which themselves had a major survival value. It is as if, in order to assert its priority over other living beings in the struggle for survival, the human animal has to forsake the struggle for survival itself and focus on other questions. Victory in the struggle for survival can only be gained as a by-product: if one focuses directly on the struggle, one loses. Only a being obsessed with impossible or insoluble problems can make a breakthrough in possible knowledge. This means that, in contrast to the animal's struggle for survival, man's struggle is already "reflective," as Heidegger would have put it, experienced as the horizon of meaning for his existence. The development of technology, the struggle for power, occur within and as a certain disclosure of Being, rather than being an immediate "fact of life."[5]

---

4 See Colin McGinn, *The Mysterious Flame: Conscious Minds in a Material World*, New York: Basic Books 2000.

5 Also, it is incredible how directly Kantian these formulations are (recall Kant's famous "I or he or it, the thing that thinks"), which is why one is tempted to apply to them the Hegelian solution or turn: this unknowableness of consciousness to itself is its own solution, since consciousness *is* this gap in/of being.

When McGinn claims that there is, in reality, nothing mysterious about how the brain generates consciousness (we are just forever cognitively closed to understanding this process in the same way an understanding of quantum mechanics lies beyond the cognitive capacities of monkeys), the irony here is double: not only do we incessantly *try* to understand consciousness, in clear contrast to monkeys (who do not care about quantum physics)—even humans themselves cannot really understand quantum physics (in the strict sense of translating it into their horizon of meaning). If we claim that what we are dealing with here is a "mismatch between the very nature of these problems and the computational apparatus that natural selection has fitted us with,"[6] the true enigma is not the enigma of the meaning of life as such, but, rather, *why do we persistently probe into the meaning of life in the first place?* If religion and philosophy are (in part, at least) "the application of mental tools to problems they were not designed to solve," how did this misapplication occur, and why is it so persistent?[7] Note the Kantian background of this position: it was already Kant who claimed that the human mind is burdened by metaphysical questions that, a priori, it cannot answer. These questions cannot be suspended; they are part of human nature itself.

Imagine scientists have discovered a gigantic asteroid which they are certain will hit Earth in thirty-five years' time, not only destroying all life but throwing the planet itself off its track around the sun. How would people react? Would the social and ethical order collapse? Would people lose all shame and quickly try to realize their sexual and other fantasies? And yet, the true question is: do we not all know that, in a much more distant (let us hope so) future, something like this *will indeed* happen and humanity will disappear without a trace? So what is the difference? The situation is akin to that in the famous anecdote about George Bernard Shaw—at a dinner party, he asked the upper-class beauty at his side if she would spend a night with him for 10 million pounds; when she laughingly said yes, he went on and asked if she would do it for 10 pounds; when the lady exploded in rage at being treated like a cheap whore, he calmly replied: "Come on, we have already established that your sexual favors can be bought—now we are only haggling over the price ..." The difference is the same as with death of course: the event should be far enough in the future that we can ignore it, pretend not to know about it, and thus act as if we know nothing about it. This is why almost everyone, though they know very well they will die at some point, would refuse to know in advance the exact moment of their death: they secretly refuse to believe they will die, and the knowledge of the exact moment of their death would made this future death fully actual. Kafka wrote: "The lamentation around the deathbed is actually the lamentation over the fact that here no

6 Steven Pinker, *How the Mind Works*, New York: W. W. Norton & Company 1997, p. 565.
7 Ibid., p. 525.

dying in the true sense has taken place."[8] But what if there is no dying "in the true sense," what if dying is always and by definition "improper," arriving at the wrong time and place?

This point of impossibility is one feature of the Lacanian *objet a*: it designates that which is *subtracted* from reality (as impossible) and thus gives it consistency—if it gets included in reality, it causes a catastrophe. In what sense is the *objet a* as the frame of reality surplus-enjoyment? In relation to cinema, think about the "production of a couple"—a motif which frames many a Hollywood narrative about a grand historical event like a war or natural catastrophe: this topic is, quite literally, the film's ideological surplus-enjoyment. Although in a direct sense we enjoy the spectacular shots of the catastrophe (the battle, the tidal wave, the sinking ship ...), the surplus-enjoyment is provided by the subnarrative about the couple which forms a "frame" for the spectacular event—the asteroid which hits Earth in *Deep Impact* materializes the daughter's rage at her father's new marriage; the October Revolution in *Reds* reunites the lovers; the ferocious dinosaurs in *Jurassic Park* materialize the father-figure's aggressive rejection of paternal authority and care; etc. It is this frame, through its surplus-enjoyment, that "libidinally bribes" us to accept the ideology of the story. An example of subjectivity ruined by such a catastrophic inclusion is provided by the hero of *Perfume* (Patrick Süskind's novel and Tom Tykwer's film).[9] Lacan supplemented Freud's list of partial objects (breasts, feces, penis) with two further objects: the voice and the gaze. Perhaps, we should add another item to this series: smell. *Perfume* seems to point in this direction. Grenouille, the novel's unfortunate hero, is odorless, others cannot smell him; but he himself possesses such an extraordinary sense of smell that he is able to detect persons far away. When his ideal woman dies in an accident, he tries to recreate not the woman in her bodily existence—*Perfume* is a true anti-*Frankenstein*, but her odor by killing twenty-five pretty young women and scratching the surface of their skin to subtract their odors, mixing them into *the* ideal perfume. This irresistible perfume is the ultimate *odor di femina*, the extracted "essence" of femininity: whenever ordinary humans smell it, they suspend all rational restraint and engage in a sexual orgy. So when, towards the novel's end, Grenouille is arrested for the murders and sentenced to death, it is enough for him to wave a napkin soaked in the perfume in front of the crowd, who then, instantly forgetting their cries for his death, start undressing to take part in an orgy. The extracted essence of femininity is what Lacan called the *objet petit a*, the object-cause of desire, that which is "in you more than yourself" and thus makes me desire you; this is why Grenouille has to kill the virgins in order to extract from them their

8 Franz Kafka, *The Blue Octavo Notebooks*, ed. Max Brod, Cambridge, MA: Exact Change 1991, p. 53.

9 See Patrick Süskind, *Perfume: The Story of a Murderer*, London: Penguin Books 2006.

"essence," or, as Lacan put it: "I love you, but there is something in you more than yourself that I love, the *objet petit a*, so I destroy you."

Grenouille's fate is tragic, however: being odorless, he is a *pure subject*, without an object-cause of desire in himself, and as such never desired by others. What he gains from this predicament is the direct access to the object-cause of desire: while ordinary individuals desire another person because of the lure of the *objet a* in him, Grenouille has direct access to this object. Ordinary individuals can only desire insofar as they become victims of an illusion: they think they desire another individual because of the person they are; that is, they are not aware that their desire is caused by the "essence" or odor which has nothing to do with the person as such. Since Grenouille can by-pass the person and directly target the object-cause of desire, he can avoid this illusion—which is why for him eroticism is a ridiculous game of lures. The price he pays for it, however, is that he can never accept the inverse illusion that someone loves him: he is always aware that it is not him but his perfume that makes people adore him. The only way out of this predicament, the only way to posit himself as an object of the others' desire, is suicidal: in the final scene of the novel, he spills perfume on himself and is literally torn apart and devoured by a bunch of thieves, beggars, and whores.

Is not this violent reduction of the thing to its *objet a* also an example of what Badiou calls *subtraction*? One subtracts from the thing its decentered core, leaving behind its dead body. The opposite of this subtraction, and also a way to generate the *objet a*, is *protraction*. An example from cinema is provided by one of Tarkovsky's formal techniques which, ironically given his Soviet origins, cannot but evoke the (in)famous dialectical "law" of the inversion of quantity into quality, supplementing it with a kind of "negation of the negation" (which was excluded by Stalin from the list of these "laws" as being too Hegelian, not properly "materialist"). As Sean Martin put it:

> Tarkovsky proposed that if a take is lengthened, boredom naturally sets in for the audience. But if the take is extended even further, something else arises: curiosity. Tarkovsky is essentially proposing giving the audience time to inhabit the world that the take is showing us, not to *watch* it, but to *look* at it, to explore it.[10]

Perhaps the ultimate example of this procedure is the famous scene in Tarkovsky's *Mirror*, in which the heroine, who works as a proofreader for a daily newspaper in the Soviet Union of the mid-1930s, runs from her home to the printing office fearing she has missed an obscene misprint of Stalin's name.[11] Martin is

---

10 Sean Martin, *Andrei Tarkovsky*, Harpenden: Pocket Essentials 2005, p. 49.

11 Tarkovsky refers here to the legend according to which, at the height of the purges, an issue of *Pravda* was almost printed in which Stalin's name was misspelled "Sralin"—the

right to emphasize an unexpected feature of this scene —its immediate physical beauty:

> it is as if Tarkovsky were content just to watch Margarita Terekhova running through the rain, down steps, across yards, into corridors. Here, Tarkovsky reveals the presence of beauty in something that is apparently mundane and, paradoxically (given the period), also potentially fatal for Maria if the mistake she thinks she's made has gone to press.[12]

This effect of beauty is generated precisely by the excessive length of the scene: instead of just watching Maria running and, immersed in the narrative, worrying whether she will arrive on time to prevent the catastrophe, we are seduced into looking at the scene, taking note of its phenomenal features, the intensity of movements, and so forth.

Cristian Mungiu's *4 Months, 3 Weeks and 2 Days* (Romania 2007), set in 1987 during the last years of Ceauşescu's rule, tells the story of Otilia and Gabita, two university friends in Bucharest. When Gabita falls pregnant, Otilia arranges for her friend a meeting with Mr. Bebe in a hotel, where he is to perform the abortion (abortion was prohibited and severely punished at that time). The frighteningly repulsive Mr. Bebe (a kind of Romanian version of the Javier Bardem figure in *No Country for Old Men*) demands sexual favors from Otilia as the price for performing the operation. Otilia agrees for the sake of her friend, the abortion is performed, but at the film's end she remains alone, having lost even the respect of her friend for whom she made the sacrifice. Throughout the film, the threat that Mr. Bebe will do something terrifying (butcher Gabita and bleed her to death, etc.) lurks in the background; however, the elegance of the film is such that this threat remains purely virtual, nothing happens, everything basically goes as planned, and yet nevertheless the final result is bitter despair. This endless postponement of the threatened act functions in a similar way to the Tarkovskian protraction: it elevates Mr. Bebe to the *objet a*, to a sublime figure of Evil.

Tarkovsky, however, all too often succumbs to the temptation of re-inscribing this excess of phenomenality into hermeneutics. Recall the difference between Stanislaw Lem's classic science-fiction novel *Solaris* and Tarkovsky's cinema version. Solaris is a planet with an oceanic fluid surface which moves incessantly and, from time to time, imitates recognizable forms, not only elaborate geometric structures, but also gigantic children or human buildings. Although all attempts to communicate with the planet fail, scientists entertain

---

"shitter," from the verb "srat," to shit. At the scene's end, relieved that the fatal mistake had not taken place, the actress whispers the word into her friend's ear.

12 Martin, *Andrei Tarkovsky*, p. 135.

the hypothesis that Solaris is a massive brain which somehow reads our minds. Soon after his arrival there, Kelvin, the hero, finds at his side in his bed his dead wife, Harey, who, years ago on Earth, killed herself after he had abandoned her. Kelvin grasps that Harey is a materialization of his own innermost traumatic fantasies. Solaris, this gigantic Brain, directly materializes the innermost fantasies which support our desire. Read in this way, the story is really about the hero's inner journey, about his attempt to come to terms with a repressed truth, or, as Tarkovsky himself put it in an interview: "Maybe, effectively, the mission of Kelvin on Solaris has only one goal: to show that love of the other is indispensable to all life. A man without love is no longer a man." In clear contrast to this, Lem's novel focuses on the inert external presence of the planet Solaris, of this "Thing that thinks" (to use Kant's expression, which fully fits here): the point of the novel is precisely that Solaris remains an impenetrable Other with which communication is impossible—true, it returns us our innermost disavowed fantasies, but it remains thoroughly impenetrable (Why does It do it? As a purely mechanical response? To play demonic games with us? To help us—or compel us—to confront our disavowed truths?). It would thus be interesting to put Tarkovsky's film in the same bracket as Hollywood commercial rewritings of novels which have served as the base for a movie: Tarkovsky does exactly the same as the lowest Hollywood producer, reinscribing the enigmatic encounter with Otherness into the framework of the production of the couple.

But there is, perhaps, a link between these two aspects of Tarkovsky. In standard pre-critical metaphysics, "finitude" was associated with materialist empiricism ("only material finite objects really exist"), while "infinity" was the domain of idealist spiritualism. In an unexpected reversal, today, the main argument for spiritualism relies on the irreducibility of human finitude as the unsurpassable horizon of our existence, while it is the contemporary forms of radical scientific materialism which keep the spirit of infinity alive. The standard spiritualist argument is as follows: we should not forget that the technological dream of total mastery over nature and our lives is indeed just a dream, that we humans remain forever grounded in our finite life world with its unfathomable background, and that it is this finitude, this very limitation of our horizon, which opens up the space for spirituality proper. All today's predominant forms of spirituality thus paradoxically emphasize that we are not free-floating spirits but are irreducibly embodied in a material life world; they all preach respect for this limitation and warn against the "idealist" hubris of radical materialism—exemplary here is the case of ecology. In contrast to this spiritualist attitude of limitation, the radical scientific attitude which reduces man to a biological mechanism promises the full technological control over human life, its artificial recreation, its biogenetic and biochemical regulation, ultimately its immortality in the guise of the reduction of our inner Self to a software program that can be copied from one piece of hardware to another. The scientific basis of the claim that such immortality is feasible lies in the hypothesis of so-called "substrate independence": "conscious minds could in principle be implemented not only on carbon-based biological neurons (such as those inside your head) but also on some other computational substrate such as silicon-based processors."[13]

The third figure of the *objet a*, after *subtraction* and *protraction*, is that of *obstruction*: the *objet a* as an agent of the Cunning of Reason, the obstacle which always perturbs the realization of our goals. Another example from cinema: the libidinal focus of the Coen brothers' *No Country for Old Men* (2007) is the figure of the pathological assassin played by Javier Bardem—a ruthless killing machine, with an ethic all his own, sticking to his word, a figure of what Kant called diabolical Evil. When, at the film's end, he forces the hero's wife to choose head or tails to decide whether she lives or dies, she replies that he should not hide behind the contingency of flipping a coin—it is his will that will decide to kill her. He replies that she has not understood: he, his will, *is* like the coin. The key to this character is the fact that it represents not a real-life person, but a fantasy-entity, an embodiment of the pure object-obstacle, that unfathomable "X" of Blind Fate which always, in a weird mixture of chance and inexorable necessity, as the necessity of chance (of bad luck), intervenes to undermine the fulfillment of the subject's plans and intentions, guaranteeing that, one way or another, things will always somehow go wrong.

The Bardem character is thus the opposite of the resigned old Sheriff (Tommy Lee Jones), who complains all the time about the crazy violence of modern times—it is to him that the film's title refers. They are the obverse of each other: the Sheriff as the Master rendered impotent, the failure of paternal authority; the Bardem figure as embodying the cause of his collapse. The proper way to read *No Country for Old Men* is therefore first to imagine the same story *without* the Bardem figure: just the triangle of the hero who runs away with the money after stumbling upon the site of the gangsters' gunfight, the gangsters hiring a freelancer (Woody Harrelson) to get the money back, and the Sheriff observing their interplay from a safe distance, playing off one against the other, and guaranteeing a happy (or at least just) outcome. The Bardem figure is the fourth element, the *objet a* which ruins the game.

Another way to put it is that the *objet a* prevents the letter arriving at its destination—but does it? Is there not a Cunning of Reason at work here, such that the very failure to reach the destination compels us to change our perspective and redefine the latter? The 2001 Darwin award for the most stupid act of the year was posthumously conferred on an unfortunate Romanian woman who

13 Nick Bostrom, "Playthings of a Higher Mind," *Times Higher Education Supplement*, May 16, 2003. Also known as "The Simulation Argument: Why the Probability that You Are Living in a Matrix is Quite High."

awoke in the middle of her funeral procession; after crawling out of her coffin and seeing what was going on, she ran from the procession in terror and, crossing a busy road, was hit by a truck and instantly killed—so they put her back in the coffin and the funeral procession carried on. Is this not the ultimate example of what we call fate—of a letter arriving at its destination?

The fate of Nikolai Bukharin's "testament," a letter he wrote to his wife Anna Larina in 1938, on the eve of his execution, is a tragic case of the same thing. Bukharin exhorts his wife to "Remember that the great cause of the USSR lives on, and *this* is the most important thing. Personal fates are transitory and wretched by comparison."[14] The letter disappeared into the secret Soviet archives and was delivered to Anna Larina only in 1992—she was able to read it only after the fall of the Soviet Union. Bukharin's letter *did* arrive at its destination—did reach its addressee—at precisely the right moment; one can even say that it was delivered as soon as was possible, that is, as soon as the historical situation made it possible for its delivery to produce a truth-effect. Bukharin saw his personal fate as insignificant in comparison to the success of the great historical cause of the USSR—the continuity of this cause guaranteed that his death was not meaningless. Read after the USSR has disappeared, the letter confronts us with the meaninglessness of Bukharin's death: there is no big Other to redeem it, he literally died in vain.

The general lesson of this is that, in order to interpret a scene or an utterance, sometimes the key thing to do is to *locate its true addressee.* In one of the best Perry Mason novels, the lawyer witnesses a police interrogation of a couple in the course of which the husband explains in unusually great detail what happened, what he saw, and what he thinks happened—why this excess of information? The answer is that the couple themselves committed the murder, and since the husband knew that they would both soon be arrested on suspicion and kept separated, he used the opportunity to tell his wife the (false) story they should both stick to—the true addressee of his interminable discourse was thus not the police, but his wife.

Subtraction, protraction, obstruction: three versions of the same excessive/lacking object, an object which is never at its own place, always missing and exceeding it. One finds all three dimensions of the *objet a* in the formal structure of capitalism itself: *subtraction* (of surplus-value as the *movens* of the entire process); *protraction* (the capitalist process is by definition interminable, for its ultimate goal is the reproduction of the process itself); and *obstruction*: the gap between the subjective experience (of individuals pursuing their interests) and objective social mechanisms (which appear as an "irrational" and uncontrollable Fate) is inscribed into the very notion of capitalism, and, on account of

14 Anna Larina, *This I Cannot Forget: The Memoirs of Nikolai Bukharin's Widow*, New York: W. W. Norton & Company 1993, p. 355.

this gap, there always lurks the threat that individuals' intentions and plans will be sabotaged, obstructed. It is in this gap that one should locate the systemic violence proper to capitalism.

To the three modes of the *objet a*, of how it distorts reality by inscribing itself into it, one should then add a fourth: *destruction*. Is what happens in the case of a post-traumatic subject not the *destruction* of the *objet a*? This is why such a subject is deprived of engaged existence and reduced to "vegetative" state of indifference. What we should nonetheless bear in mind is that this destruction results also in the loss of reality itself, which is sustained by the *objet a*—when the subject is deprived of the excess, it at once loses that with regard to which the excess is an excess. This is why the "Muslims," the "living dead" of the concentration camps, were simultaneously reduced to "bare life" *and* stood for the pure excess (the empty form) which remains when all the content of human life is taken away from the subject. To properly understand the world-historical dimension of the post-traumatic subject, one should recognize in this extreme form of subjectivity the actualization of a possibility that announces itself in the Cartesian *cogito*: is not the radical de-substantialization of the subject, its reduction to the evanescent point of "I think," the very operation that gives birth to the *cogito*? As such, the *cogito*—the modern subject or, rather, the subject of modernity—should not be too hastily dismissed as "Eurocentric": one can argue that the *cogito* stands for a kind of un-historical excess which underlies and sustains every historical life-form.

THE *OBJET A* BETWEEN FORM AND CONTENT

What these paradoxes indicate is that, in the *objet a*, form and content coincide: the *objet a* is the "indivisible remainder" which escapes the symbolic form, and, simultaneously, pure form, a purely formal distortion (protraction, etc.) of the content. More precisely, this oscillation of the *objet a* between form and content involves four consecutive dialectical reversals, in a kind of complex negation of the negation. It is symptomatic that, when Lacan and his followers describe some process that clearly has the structure of a "negation of the negation," they almost compulsively hasten to add that this is not meant in the Hegelian sense—is this not a defense mechanism par excellence, the disavowal of an uncomfortable proximity? How, then, does it stand with the "negation of the negation" in Lacan? Is his version compatible with Hegel's? Since, in Lacan, in apparent contrast to Hegel, the double movement of "negation of negation" produces an excess or remainder, that of the *objet a*, let us begin with Miller who, in his commentary on Lacan's *Seminar XVI*, elaborated the crucial change in the status of the *objet petit a*, the object-cause of desire: the passage from corporeal specimen (partial object: breasts, feces ...) to a pure logical function. In this seminar, "Lacan does not really describe *objets a* as corporeal specimens, he constructs them as a logical consistency, logic being there in the place of biology. The logical consistency is like a function that the body must satisfy through different bodily deductions."[15]

This passage is the passage from the foreign intruder, the grains of sand in the signifying machine which prevent its smooth functioning, to something which is totally immanent to the machine. When Lacan is describing the loops and twists of the symbolic space on account of which its interiority overlaps with its exteriority ("ex-timacy"), he does not merely describe the structural place of the *objet a* (surplus-enjoyment): surplus-enjoyment is *nothing but this structure itself*, this "inward loop" of the symbolic space. This can be clarified in relation to the gap that separates drive from instinct: while drive and instinct have the same "object," the same goal, what differentiates them is that the drive finds satisfaction not in reaching its goal, but in circulating around it, repeating its failure to reach it. One can say, of course, that what prevents the drive from reaching its goal is the *objet a* which is decentered with regard to it, so that, even if we reach the goal, the object eludes us and we are condemned to repeat the procedure; however, this *objet a* is purely formal, it is the curvature of the space of the drive, hence the "shortest way" to reach the object is not to aim directly at it but to encircle it, to circle around it.

This shift is deeply Hegelian, forming a kind of "negation of the negation": we begin with the consistent "big Other," the self-enclosed symbolic order; then, in a first negation, this consistency is disturbed by the remainder of the Real, a traumatic left-over which resists being integrated into the symbolic and thus disturbs its balance, rendering it "barred," introducing into it a gap, flaw, or antagonism; in short, inconsistency; the second negation, however, requires a shift of perspective in which we grasp this intrusive left-over of the Real as itself the only element that guarantees the minimal consistency of the inconsistent big Other. Take the logic of class struggle: it renders society "inconsistent," antagonistic, perturbing its balance; however, it is simultaneously that which holds the entire social body together, its underlying structuring principle, since all social phenomena are overdetermined by class struggle. At a more prosaic level, is it not often struggle itself, a basic tension, that keeps different elements together? When struggle disappears, the elements drift apart into a sterile, indifferent coexistence. In the same way, while trauma is, of course, what disturbs the balance of a subject's symbolic space, it is simultaneously the ultimate reference point of the subject's psychic life—all its symbolizing activity ultimately aims at coping with the trauma, repressing it, displacing it, and so on.

---

15 Jacques-Alain Miller, "A Reading of the Seminar *From an Other to the other*," *lacanian ink* 29 (Spring 2007), p. 13.

There is more: not only does the intruding element "hold together" the big Other which, in the absence of this intruder, would have fallen apart; this element, the *objet a*, has no positive objectal reality, its status is purely that of logical consistency: it is logically implied, presupposed, as the cause of the inconsistencies of/in the big Other; that is, it can only be discerned retroactively, through its effects. Take an attractor in mathematics: all positive lines or points in its sphere of attraction can only endlessly approach it, never actually reaching its form—the existence of this form is purely virtual, being nothing more than the shape towards which the lines and points tend. However, precisely as such, the virtual form is the Real of this field: the immovable focal point around which all elements circulate.

The Hegelian logic of these twists can thus be rendered even more precise: there are not only three, but four moments at work here. First, the consistent big Other; then, the big Other rendered inconsistent by the *objet a* as intrusive remainder; then, this object as guaranteeing the "consistency" of the big Other (multiple inconsistent symbolizations can only be "totalized" as a network of reactions to the intruding object); finally, we are back at the beginning, although at a different level—there is no object that, from outside, disturbs the consistency of the big Other; the *objet a* as the "Real" is only a name for the purely formal twist, the internal loop, of the symbolic order itself.

Insofar as it lacks its mirror image, is the *objet a* then the vampiric object (vampires, as we know, are not reflected in a mirror)? It may seem so: are not vampires versions of *lamella*, of the undead partial object? However, perhaps the exact opposite would be more appropriate as an image of the *objet a*: when we look at a thing directly, in reality, we do not see "it"—this "it" only appears when we look at the thing's mirror image, as if here there were something more than in reality, as if only the mirror image can bring out that mysterious ingredient for which we search in vain in the object's reality. To put it in Deleuzian terms: the mirror image desubstantializes a thing, depriving it of its density and depth, reducing it to a flat surface, and it is only through this reduction that the purely non-substantial *objet a* becomes perceptible.[16]

Perhaps this double status of the *objet a* also provides a clue to the relationship between the death drive and the superego. Some time ago, Eric Santner raised a critical point about my work, questioning "The link, even at times identity … of the organ without body and the superego. Should we just collapse the superego

16 One story in the classic British horror omnibus *Dead of Night* plays on this very register: a couple moves into a renovated house with a large, old mirror in the living room; when, in the evening, the husband looks into the mirror, he sees a scene totally different from the reality of the living room, an old-fashioned room with a fireplace. The explanation is that, two centuries earlier, a terrible murder was committed in this very room, which is "remembered" by the mirror.

and the death drive like this? Doesn't everything depend on keeping at least a thin line between them? Shouldn't we speak of a superegoization of drive?"[17] As Santner emphasizes, we are dealing here with a parallax split, not with the cosmic polarity of two opposed forces: the organ without a body and the superego are not like *yin* and *yang* or the principles of light and dark. Furthermore, the tension in question is asymmetric, the two poles are not balanced, the OwB aspect somehow has priority—but what kind of priority exactly? What we are not dealing with here is yet another case of the logic of self-alienation, at work from Marx and Nietzsche to Deleuze, of a generative power which misrecognizes itself in its own product, i.e., in the same way that, for Marx, capital is the result of collective labor turned against itself, its own origin, or, for Nietzsche, moral resentment is the productivity of life turned against itself, the superego excess is the excess of the OwB turned against itself. Read in this way, the task becomes one of returning the alienated result back to its origin, re-establishing the excess of OwB without its superego distortion. This, however, is the very logic one should avoid at all costs.[18]

One path to take here would be to link this duality of the superego and the drive to the duality in the status of the *objet petit a*: is not the "superego," as the name for the excess of the drive, the object in its aspect of material reality, the foreign intruder that "drives me crazy" with its impossible requests; and is not the OwB the object in its aspect of a purely formal structure? Both aspects display the same self-propelling structure of a loop: the more the subject obeys the superego, the more he is guilty, caught up in a repetitive movement homologous to that of the drive circulating around its object. The passage from the first to the second aspect is itself structurally homologous to that of the Rabinovitch joke, or of the problem which is its own solution: what, at the level of the superego, appears as a deadlock (the more I obey, the more I am guilty ...) turns into the very source of satisfaction (which is not the object of the drive, but the very activity of repeatedly encircling it).[19]

---

17 Private communication.

18 A direct reference to the formulae of sexuation (the "masculine" superego versus the "feminine" drive) also has its limits.

19 According to Freud, love arises out of the inhibited desire: the object whose (sexual) consummation is prevented is then idealized as a love object. This is why Lacan establishes a link between love and drive: the space of the drive is defined by the gap between its goal (object) and its aim, which is not to directly reach its object, but to circulate around the object, to repeat the failure to reach it—what the drive and love share is this structure of inhibition. And does not the same shift determine also the status of the Badiouian Event with regard to how it relates to the order of Being? An Event inscribes itself into the order of Being, leaving its traces in it, or rather, an Event is *nothing but* a certain distortion or twist in the order of Being. The four stages in the development of the *objet a* can effectively be applied to the Event in its relation to Being: (1) there is the order of

So, back to the two aspects of the *objet a*, its corporeal reality and its logical consistency: although antinomic, they fit together—but how, exactly? Miller's first formulation is that of a hole (empty place) and the contingent element filling it in: "The small a, when it is designated as topological structure and as logical consistency, has, if I may say so, the substance of a hole, and then some detached pieces of the body are molded in this absence."[20] This formulation, however, appears all too simplistic. Does not the paradox of an object which "is" only its formal structure disappear here? How, then, are we to accomplish that move which, in the terms of the classical Teachers, one could call the move from metaphysical/mechanical materialism to dialectical materialism? In his *Logic of Sense*, Deleuze provided a model which allows one to grasp the mediation of form and content in showing how the two series (of the signifier and the signified) always contain a paradoxical entity that is "doubly inscribed" (that is simultaneously surplus and lack): a surplus of the signifier over the signified (the empty signifier without a signified) and the lack of the signified (the point of nonsense within the field of Sense). In other words, as soon as the symbolic order emerges, a minimal difference is introduced between a structural place and the element that occupies or fills out this place: an element is always logically preceded by the place in the structure it fills out. The two series, therefore, can also be described as the "empty" formal structure (signifier) and the series of elements filling out the empty places in the structure (signified). From this perspective, the paradox consists in the fact that the two series never overlap: we always encounter an entity that is simultaneously (with regard to the structure) an empty, unoccupied place and (with regard to the elements) a rapidly moving, elusive object, an occupant without a place. We have thereby produced Lacan's formula of fantasy $-*a*, since the matheme for the subject is $, an empty place in the structure, an elided signifier, while the *objet a* is, by definition, an excessive object, an object that lacks a place in the structure. Consequently, the point is not simply that there is a surplus of an element over the places available in the structure, or the surplus of a place that has no element to fill it out. An empty place in the structure would still sustain the fantasy of an element that will emerge to fill the place; an excessive element lacking its place would still

---

Being; (2) this order is rendered incomplete or inconsistent by the miracle of an Event; (3) this Event appears as the virtual point of consistency which only renders readable the inconsistently distorted texture of Being; finally, 4) the Event appears as *nothing but* this distortion of Being. But perhaps this reference to Lacan also enables us to identify what is missing in Badiou's scheme: is it not possible to think this distortion of Being *independently of* (or as prior to) the Event, so that the "Event" ultimately names a minimal "fetishization" of the immanent distortion of the texture of Being into its virtual object-cause? And is not the Freudo-Lacanian name of this distortion the *drive*, the death drive?

20 Miller, "A Reading of the Seminar *From an Other to the other*," p. 25.

sustain the fantasy of some yet unknown place waiting to be filled. The point is, rather, that the empty place in the structure is strictly correlative to the errant element lacking its place: they are not two different entities, but the two sides of one and the same entity, that is, one and the same entity inscribed onto the two surfaces of a Möbius strip. In short, the subject qua $ does not belong to the depths: it emerges from a topological twist of the surface itself. Does not Miller himself point in this direction later in the same text?

> When Lacan speaks of a hole at the level of the big Other, he must say that the hole is not a lack, but it is what permits, on the contrary, in Lacan's logical elucubrations, the interior circle of the Other to be considered as conjoined to the most exterior circle, almost as its inversion. Lacan says in passing that it is the structure itself of the *objet a*, or rather that the *objet a* is this structure in which the most interior is conjoined to the most exterior in its turning.[21]

The "or rather" has to be given full weight here: from the structure *of* the object to a strange object which *is* nothing but this structure, its substantial identity merely a reified specter. This object "is" the subject, the subject's impossible/Real objectal correlate. This weird correlation subverts the standard transcendental correlation between subject and object: in it, the subject is correlated with the very impossible/Real object that has to be excluded from the field of reality so that the subject can relate to this field. In order to delineate this unique character of the *objet a* as the embodiment of a void, of the lack or loss of the primordial object which can only emerge as always already lost, Lacan opposes it to two other figures of nothingness, the nothingness of destruction and the Hegelian negativity which is the "nullification" constitutive of subjectivity, the nothing as the initial moment in the instauration of the subject. In contrast to these two versions, he relates the *objet a* to what Kant called "*der Gegenstand ohne Begriff*," the object without concept (not covered by any concept). The *objet a* is as such "irrational," in the strictly literal sense of being outside all *ratio*, all relation as proportion. In other words, when a particular element resists being subsumed under a universal concept, the *objet a*, "what is in you more than yourself," is precisely that *je ne sais quoi* which prevents this subsumption.

Here, however, one must remain a consistent Hegelian and resist the empiricist temptation: the fact that the assertion of the existence of a particular element goes against the universal notion supposed to cover or contain this element should not be dismissed as a case of the wealth of particular content overwhelming abstract notional frameworks. The empirical excess should rather be read as an indication of the inherent inconsistency or failure of the universal notion itself. So when Lacan says that "only with the analytic discourse can a universal find its

---

21 Ibid., p. 18.

true ground in the existence of an exception, which is why it is certain that we can in any case distinguish the universal which is thus grounded from all use of this same universal rendered common by the philosophical tradition,"[22] he (as usual) ignores the uniqueness of Hegelian "concrete universality." Let us risk a political example here. When, in order to generate hope among radical leftists, certain intellectuals point out that there indeed exists today some authentic emancipatory agent (usually far away, in Haiti or Venezuela or Nepal ...), this triumphant assertion ("You see, we are not dreaming, there is an authentic revolutionary process going on!") serves precisely as a fetish enabling us to avoid confronting the inadequacy of the standard notion of radical emancipatory agency for today's global struggle. What this means is that, in the opposition between concept and reality (real existence), the *objet a* is on the side of the concept: it is not the excess of reality, but an immanent hole or crack in the conceptual edifice.

The *objet a* is thus not the core of reality which resists being subsumed by the conceptual frame imposed by the subject; it is, on the contrary, the objectivization of the subject's desire: the status of that which makes me desire an object is irreducibly linked to my "subjective" perspective, it is not simply an objective property of the beloved—that X which fascinates me in the beloved exists only for me, not for an "objective" view. We can even go a step further and argue that the subjective mediation here is *double*: far from simply standing for the excess in the object eluding the subject's grasp, the *objet a* is, at its most elementary, what I see in the other's gaze. In other words, what eludes me in a libidinal object is not some transcendent property, but the inscription into it of my own desire: what I see in the other is his or her desire for me; that is, I read in his or her eyes my own status as an object (of desire), the way I appear to the other.

Voice and gaze

This brings us to the paradoxical status of the voice and the gaze, the paradigmatic *objets a* in Lacan's theory. As noted above, the voice and the gaze are the two objects added by Lacan to Freud's list of "partial objects" (breasts, feces, phallus). As objects, they are not on the side of the looking/hearing subject but on the side of what the subject sees or hears. Recall the archetypal scene from Hitchcock: a heroine (Lilah in *Psycho*, Melanie in *The Birds*) approaches a mysterious, apparently empty house; she looks at it, yet what makes a scene so disturbing is that we, the spectators, get the vague impression that the house is somehow returning her gaze. The crucial point, of course, is that this gaze should not be subjectivized: it is not simply that "there is somebody in the house," we are rather dealing with a kind of empty, a priori gaze which cannot be traced

22 Jacques Lacan, seminar of March 3, 1972, ... *ou pire* (unpublished).

to a determinate reality—the heroine "cannot see it all," there is a blind spot in what she is looking at, and the object returns her gaze from this blind spot. The situation is homologous with the voice: it is as if, when we are talking, whatever we say is already an answer to a primordial address by the Other—we are always already addressed, and, again, this address is blank, it cannot be attributed to a specific agent but is a kind of empty a priori, the formal "condition of possibility" of our speaking, just as the object returning the gaze is a kind of formal "condition of possibility" of our seeing anything at all. What happens in psychosis is that this empty point in the other, in what we see and/or hear, is actualized, becomes part of effective reality: the psychotic actually hears the voice of the primordial Other addressing him, knows that he is being observed all the time. Usually, psychosis is conceived as a form of lack with reference to the "normal" state of things: something is missing, the key signifier (the "paternal metaphor") is rejected, foreclosed, excluded from the symbolic universe and thence returns in the Real in the guise of psychotic apparitions. However, we should not forget the obverse of this exclusion: the inclusion. Lacan pointed out that the consistency of our "experience of reality" depends on the exclusion of the *objet petit a* from it: in order for us to have a normal "access to reality," something must be excluded, "primordially repressed." In psychosis, this exclusion is undone: the object (in this case, the gaze or voice) is included in reality, the outcome of which is the disintegration of our "sense of reality," the loss of reality.[23]

François Balmès draws attention to the radical ambiguity in how the Lacan of the 1950s defines the relationship between the Real, the symbolic, and the lack: he shifts between the thesis that the symbolic introduces the *lack-of-being* into the Real—prior to the rise of the symbolic, there is no lack, just a flat positivity of the Real—and the thesis that *being* arises only with the symbolic—prior to the symbolic, there is no being.[24] Confronted with this ambiguity, we would be

---

23 Insofar as this object is the elementary fantasmatic object (see Lacan's matheme of fantasy, $-a), another way to make the same point is to say that our sense of reality disintegrates the moment reality approaches too closely our fundamental fantasy. We should be careful not to miss the paradox here: when, exactly, does the experience of the "loss of reality" take place? Not, as one would expect, when the abyss that separates "words" and "things" grows too large, so that "reality" no longer seems to fit the frame or horizon of our symbolic pre-understanding, but, on the contrary, when "reality" fits "words" too closely, when the content of our words is realized in an excessively "literal" way. Suffice it to recall Freud's uncanny reaction when, after many years of fantasizing about the Acropolis, he visited it for the first time: he was so amazed by the fact that what he had read about since his youth really existed and looked exactly the way it was described in the books, that his first reaction was an overwhelming feeling of a "loss of reality"—"No, this cannot be real ..."

24 See François Balmès, *Ce que Lacan dit de l'être*, Paris: Presses Universitaires de France 1999.

wise to avoid the all-too-easy Heideggerian solution that we are simply dealing with two different meanings of "being": Being in the ontological sense of the openness within which things appear, and being in the ontic sense of reality, of entities existing in the world (what arises with the symbolic is the ontological horizon of Being, while its obverse is the lack-of-being, i.e., the fact that a human being as the there-of-Being (*Dasein*) lacks its place in the positive order of reality, that it cannot be reduced to an entity within the world, because it is the place of the very openness of a world). Balmès seeks the solution along a totally different path: he notes perceptively that Lacan resolves the problem, the question, by way of "*making a response out of this question*,"[25] of perceiving the question as its own answer. That is to say, being and the lack-of-being coincide, they are the two sides of the same coin—the clearance of the horizon within which things fully "are" only emerges on condition that something is excluded ("sacrificed") from it, that something in it is "missing at its own place." More precisely, what characterizes a symbolic universe is the minimal gap between its elements and places they occupy: the two dimensions do not directly coincide, as is the case in the flat positivity of the Real, which is why, in the differential order of signifiers, absence as such can count as a positive feature. This brings us back to Lacan's basic "ontological" hypothesis: in order for this gap between elements and their structural places to occur, *something—some element—has to be radically (constitutively) excluded*; Lacan's name for this object which is always (by definition, structurally) missing at its own place, which coincides with its own lack, is, of course, the *objet petit a*, as the object-cause of desire or surplus-enjoyment, a paradoxical object which gives body to the very lack-of-being. The *objet petit a* is that which should be excluded from the frame of reality, that whose exclusion constitutes and sustains the frame itself. And, as we have just seen, what happens in psychosis is precisely the *inclusion* of this object into the frame of reality: it appears within reality as the hallucinated object (the voice or gaze which haunts a paranoiac, etc.).[26]

Is it possible to conceive of this tension between the *objet a* and the frame of reality at the level of the relationship between the visual and auditive dimensions themselves, so that the voice itself would function as the *objet a* of the visual, as the blind spot from which the picture returns the gaze? Therein seems to lie the lesson of "the talkies." That is to say, the effect of adding a spoken soundtrack to the silent film was the exact opposite of the expected "naturalization," of an even more "realistic" imitation of life. What occurred from the very beginning

25 Ibid., p. 138.

26 Balmès also notes this asymmetrical circularity in the relationship between the Real, reality, and symbolization: reality is the Real as domesticated—more or less awkwardly—by the symbolic; within this symbolic space, the Real returns as its cut, gap, point of impossibility (see, for example, ibid., p. 177).

of the talking movie was an uncanny autonomization of the voice, baptized by Chion as "acousmatization":[27] the emergence of a voice that is neither attached to an object (a person) within diegetic reality nor simply the voice of an external commentator, but a spectral voice which floats freely in a mysterious intermediate domain and thereby acquires a horrifying dimension of omnipresence and omnipotence, the voice of an invisible Master—from Fritz Lang's *Testament of Dr. Mabuse* to the "mother's voice" in Hitchcock's *Psycho*. In the final scene of *Psycho*, the "mother's voice" literally cuts a hole in the visual reality: the screen-image becomes a delusive surface, a lure secretly dominated by the bodiless voice of an invisible or absent Master, a voice that cannot be attached to any object in the diegetic reality—as if the true subject of enunciation of Norman's/mother's voice is death itself, the skull that we perceive for a brief moment in the fade-out of Norman's face.

In his *Lectures on Aesthetics*, Hegel mentions an Ancient Egyptian sacred statue which, every sunset, as if by a miracle, issued a deeply reverberating sound. This mysterious sound magically resonating from within an inanimate object is a good metaphor for the birth of subjectivity. However, we must be careful here not to miss the tension, the antagonism, between the silent scream and the vibrant tone, the moment when the silent scream resounds. The true object-voice is mute, "stuck in the throat," and what actually reverberates is the void: resonance always takes place in a vacuum—the tone as such is originally the lament for the lost object. The object is there as long as the sound remains silent; the moment it resounds, the moment it "spills out," the object is evacuated, and this voidance gives birth to $, the barred subject lamenting the loss of the object. This lament, of course, is deeply ambiguous: the ultimate horror would be that of an object-voice coming too close to us, so that the reverberation of the voice is at the same time a conjuration destined to keep the voice-object at sufficient distance. We can now answer the simple question "Why do we listen to music?": in order to avoid the horror of the encounter with the voice qua object. What Rilke said of beauty goes also for music: it is a lure, a screen, the last curtain protecting us from directly confronting the horror of the (vocal) object. When the intricate musical tapestry disintegrates or collapses into a pure unarticulated scream, we approach voice qua object. In this precise sense, as Lacan points out, voice and silence relate as figure and ground: silence is not (as one would might think) the ground against which the figure of a voice emerges; quite the contrary, the reverberating sound itself provides the ground which renders visible the figure of silence. We have thus arrived at the formula of the relationship between voice and image: the voice does not simply persist at a different level with regard to what we see, it rather points towards a gap in

27 See Michel Chion, *La voix au cinéma*, Paris: Cahiers du Cinéma 1982.

the field of the visible, towards the dimension of what eludes our gaze. In other words, their relationship is mediated by an impossibility: ultimately, we hear things because we cannot see everything.[28]

The next step is to reverse the logic of the Voice as the filler of the body's constitutive gap: the obverse of the Voice that gives body to what we can never see, to what eludes our gaze, is an image that makes present the failure of the voice—an image can emerge as the place-holder for a sound which does not yet resonate but remains stuck in the throat. Munch's *Scream*, for example, is by definition silent: in front of this painting, we "hear (the scream) with our eyes." However, the parallel is here by no means perfect: to see what one cannot hear is not the same as to hear what one cannot see. Voice and gaze relate to each other as life and death: the voice vivifies, whereas the gaze mortifies. For that reason, "hearing oneself speaking" (*s'entendre-parler*), as Derrida has demonstrated, is the very kernel, the fundamental matrix, of experiencing oneself as a living being, while its counterpart at the level of the gaze, "seeing oneself looking" (*se voir voyant*), unmistakably stands for death: when the gaze qua object is no longer the elusive blind spot in the field of the visible but is included in this field, one meets one's own death. Suffice it to recall how, in the uncanny encounter with a double (Doppelgänger), what eludes our gaze is always his eyes: the double strangely seems always to look askew, never to return our gaze by looking straight into our eyes—the moment he were to do so, our life would be over.[29]

It was Schopenhauer who claimed that music brings us into contact with the *Ding an sich*: it renders directly the drive of the life substance that words can only signify. For that reason, music "seizes" the subject in the Real of his or her being, by-passing the detour of meaning: in music, we hear what we cannot see, the vibrating life force beneath the flow of *Vorstellungen*. But what happens when this flux of life substance is itself suspended, discontinued? At this point, an image emerges, an image that stands for absolute death, for death beyond the cycle of death and rebirth, corruption and generation. Far more horrifying than to see with our ears—to hear the vibrating life substance beyond visual

28 If we imagine the respective domains of what we see and of what we hear as two intersecting circles, their intersection is not simply what we hear and see; it has two sides: the voice that we see (but do not hear) and the image that we hear (but do not see).

29 However, although it is not possible to "see oneself looking," it is, for that very reason, possible to "see oneself [being-]seen" (*se voir être vu*)—therein, in seeing oneself being exposed to the other's gaze, consists the exhibitionist's enjoyment. On the other hand, the very possibility of "hearing oneself speaking" renders it impossible to "hear oneself being heard" (*s'entrendre être entendu*)—as Lacan pointed out, those who do "hear themselves being heard" are precisely those who "hear voices," psychotics with auditory hallucinations (see Jacques Lacan, *Le séminaire, Livre VIII: Le transfert*, Paris: Seuil 1991, p. 360).

representation, this blind spot in the field of the visible—is to hear with our eyes, to see the absolute silence that marks the suspension of life, as in Caravaggio's *Testa di Medusa*: is not the scream of the Medusa by definition silent, "stuck in the throat," and does not this painting provide an image of the moment at which the voice fails?[30]

Against this background of "hearing what one cannot see" and "seeing what one cannot hear," it is possible to delineate the illusory locus of the "metaphysics of presence." Let us return for a brief moment to the difference between "hearing oneself speaking" and "seeing oneself looking": only the second case involves reflection proper, namely the act of recognizing oneself in an (external) image, while in the first case we are dealing with the illusion of an immediate auto-affection which precludes even the minimal self-distance implied by the notion of recognizing oneself in one's mirror-image. In contrast to Derrida, one is tempted to assert that the founding illusion of the metaphysics of presence is not simply that of "hearing oneself speaking," but rather a kind of short-circuit between "hearing oneself speaking" and "seeing oneself looking": a "seeing oneself looking" in the mode of "hearing oneself speaking," a gaze that regains the immediacy of vocal auto-affection. In other words, we should always bear in mind that, from Plato's *theoria* onwards, metaphysics relies on the predominance of seeing—so how are we to combine this with "hearing oneself speaking"? "Metaphysics" resides precisely in the notion of a self-mirroring seeing which would abolish the distance of reflection and attain the immediacy of "hearing oneself speaking." In other words, "metaphysics" stands for the illusion that, in the antagonistic relationship between "seeing" and "hearing," it is possible to abolish the discord, the impossibility, that mediates between the two terms (we hear things because we cannot see it all, and vice versa) and to conflate them in a unique experience of "seeing in the mode of hearing."

True, the experience of *s'entendre-parler* grounds the illusion of the transparent self-presence of the speaking subject; however, is not the voice at the same time that which undermines most radically the subject's self-presence and self-transparency? I hear myself speaking, yet what I hear is never fully myself but a parasite, a foreign body at the very heart of me. This stranger in myself acquires positive existence in different guises, from the voice of conscience and the voice of the hypnotist to the persecutor in paranoia. The voice is that which,

---

30 Georges Balanchine staged a short orchestral piece by Webern (they are all short) in which, once the music is over, the dancers continue to dance for some time in complete silence, as if they had not noticed that the music providing the substance for their dance was already over. Like the living dead who dwell in the interstices of empty time: their movements, lacking vocal support, allow us to see not only the voice but silence itself.

in the signifier, resists meaning; it stands for the opaque inertia which cannot be recuperated by meaning. It is only the dimension of writing which accounts for the stability of meaning, or, to quote the immortal words of Samuel Goldwyn: "A verbal agreement isn't worth the paper it's written on." As such, the voice is neither dead nor alive: its primordial phenomenological status is rather that of the living dead, of a spectral apparition which somehow survives its own death, namely the eclipse of meaning. In other words, while it is true that the life of a voice can be opposed to the dead letter of the written word, this life is the uncanny life of an undead monster, not the "healthy," living self-presence of Meaning.

To make manifest this uncanny voice, it is sufficient to cast a cursory glance at the history of music—which reads as a kind of counter-history to the usual story of Western metaphysics as the domination of voice over writing. What we encounter here again and again is a voice that threatens the established Order and which thus has to be brought under control, subordinated to the rational articulation of the spoken and written word, fixed in writing. In order to designate the danger that lurks here, Lacan coined the neologism *jouis-sens*, enjoyment-in-meaning—the moment at which the singing voice cuts loose from its anchoring in meaning and accelerates into destructive self-enjoyment. The problem is thus always the same: how are we to prevent the voice from sliding into a destructive self-enjoyment that "effeminizes" the reliable masculine Word? The voice functions here as a "supplement" in the Derridean sense: one tries to restrain it, to regulate it, to subordinate it to the articulated Word, yet one cannot dispense with it altogether, since a proper dosage is vital for the exercise of power (suffice it to recall the role of patriotic-military songs in the construction of a totalitarian community). However, this brief description may create the wrong impression that we are dealing with a simple opposition between the "repressive" articulated Word and the "transgressive" voice: on the one hand, the articulated Word that disciplines and regulates the voice as a means of asserting social discipline and authority, on the other, the self-enjoying Voice which acts as the medium of liberation, breaking the disciplinary chains of law and order. But what about the US Marine Corps' mesmeric "marching chants"—with their debilitating rhythm and sadistically sexualized content are they not an exemplary case of consuming self-enjoyment in the service of Power? The excess of the voice is thus radically undecidable.

The grandmother's voice

The magic power of the voice as object is perhaps best rendered towards the end of Chapter 1 of Marcel Proust's "The Guermantes Way," part of his *In Search of*

Lost Time.[31] In a memorable scene, the narrator Marcel, using the phone for the first time, talks to his grandmother:

> after a few seconds of silence, suddenly I heard that voice which I supposed myself, mistakenly, to know so well; for always until then, every time that my grandmother had talked to me, I had been accustomed to follow what she was saying on the open score of her face, in which the eyes figured so largely; but her voice itself I was hearing this afternoon for the first time. And because that voice appeared to me to have altered in its proportions from the moment that it was a whole, and reached me in this way alone and without the accompaniment of her face and features, I discovered for the first time how sweet that voice was … It was sweet, but also how sad it was, first of all on account of its very sweetness, a sweetness drained almost—more than any but a few human voices can ever have been—of every element of resistance to others, of all selfishness; fragile by reason of its delicacy it seemed at every moment ready to break, to expire in a pure flow of tears; then, too, having it alone beside me, seen, without the mask of her face, I noticed for the first time the sorrows that had scarred it in the course of a lifetime.

Proust's very precise description here uncannily points forward to Lacanian theory: the voice is subtracted from its "natural" totality of the body to which it belongs, out of which it emerges as an autonomous partial object, an organ magically capable of surviving without the body whose organ it is—it is as if it stands "alone beside me, seen, without the mask of her face." This subtraction withdraws it from (our ordinary) reality into the virtual domain of the Real, where it persists as an undead specter haunting the subject: "'Granny!' I cried to her, 'Granny!' and would have kissed her, but I had beside me only that voice, a phantom, as impalpable as that which would come perhaps to revisit me when my grandmother was dead." As such, this voice signals simultaneously a distance (Granny is not here) and an obscene over-proximity, a presence more intimate, more penetrating, than that of a body in front of us:

> A real presence indeed that voice so near—in actual separation. But a premonition also of an eternal separation! Over and again, as I listened in this way, without seeing her who spoke to me from so far away, it has seemed to me that the voice was crying to me from depths out of which one does not rise again, and I have known the anxiety that was one day to wring my heart when a voice should thus return (alone, and attached no longer to a body which I was never more to see).

---

31 Marcel Proust, *The Guermantes Way*, trans. C. K. Scott Moncrieff, New York: Modern Library 1952.

The term "anxiety" is to be read in the precise Lacanian sense: for Lacan, anxiety does not signal the loss of the object, but, on the contrary, its over-proximity. Anxiety arises when the *objet a* falls directly into reality, appears in it—which is precisely what happens when Marcel hears the grandmother's voice separated from her body and discovers "for the first time how sweet that voice was": this sweetness is, of course, the extracted quintessence which led to Marcel's intense libidinal investment in the grandmother. This, incidentally, is how psychoanalysis approaches the libidinal-subjective impact of new technological inventions: "technology is a catalizer, it enlarges and enhances something which is already here"[32]—in this case, a fantasmatic virtual fact, like that of a partial object.[33] And, of course, this realization changes the entire constellation: once a fantasy is realized, once a fantasmatic object directly appears in reality, reality is no longer the same.

Here we might mention the sex-gadget industry: one can find today on the market a so-called "Stamina Training Unit," a masturbatory device which resembles a battery light (so that one will not be embarrassed carrying it around). It works by putting the erect penis into the opening at the top and moving the device up and down until satisfaction is achieved. The product is available in different colors, widths, and forms that imitate all three main orifices (mouth, vagina, anus). What one is offered here is simply the partial object (erogenous zone) alone, minus the embarrassing additional burden of a whole person. The fantasy (of reducing the sexual partner to a partial object) is thus directly realized, which changes the entire libidinal economy of sexual relations.

This brings us to the key question: what happens to the body when it is separated from its voice, when the voice is subtracted from the wholeness of the person? For a brief moment, we see "a world robbed of fantasy, of the affective frame and sense, a world out of joint."[34] Grandmother appears to Marcel outside the fantasmatic horizon of meaning, the rich texture of his previous long experience of her as a warm, charming person. All of a sudden, he sees her "red-faced, heavy and common, sick, lost in thought, following the lines of a book with eyes that seemed hardly sane, a dejected old woman whom I did not know." Seen after the fateful phone conversation, deprived of the fantasy frame, the grandmother is like a beached squid—a creature which moves elegantly in the water but turns into a disgusting piece of slimy flesh once out of it. Here is Proust's precise description of this effect:

---

32 Mladen Dolar, "Telephone and Psychoanalysis," *Filozofski Vestnik*, Vol. 29, No. 1 (2008), p. 12. I rely here heavily on this text.

33 Something like this happens in a psychoanalytic session where, precisely, the patient is reduced to a voice: "psychoanalysis makes out of the ordinary voice a telephone voice" (ibid., p. 22).

34 Ibid., p. 11.

> entering the drawing-room before my grandmother had been told of my return, I found her there, reading. I was in the room, or rather I was not yet in the room since she was not aware of my presence, and, like a woman whom one surprises at a piece of work which she will lay aside if anyone comes in, she had abandoned herself to a train of thoughts which she had never allowed to be visible by me. Of myself—thanks to that privilege which does not last but which one enjoys during the brief moment of return, the faculty of being a spectator, so to speak, of one's own absence,—there was present only the witness, the observer, with a hat and traveling coat, the stranger who does not belong to the house, the photographer who has called to take a photograph of places which one will never see again. The process that mechanically occurred in my eyes when I caught sight of my grandmother was indeed a photograph. We never see the people who are dear to us save in the animated system, the perpetual motion of our incessant love for them, which before allowing the images that their faces present to reach us catches them in its vortex, flings them back upon the idea that we have always had of them, makes them adhere to it, coincide with it … But if, in place of our eye, it should be a purely material object, a photographic plate, that has watched the action, then what we shall see, in the courtyard of the Institute, for example, will be, instead of the dignified emergence of an Academician who is going to hail a cab, his staggering gait, his precautions to avoid tumbling upon his back, the parabola of his fall, as though he were drunk, or the ground frozen over. So is it when some casual sport of chance prevents our intelligent and pious affection from coming forward in time to hide from our eyes what they ought never to behold, when it is forestalled by our eyes, and they, arising first in the field and having it to themselves, set to work mechanically, like films, and show us, in place of the loved friend who has long ago ceased to exist but whose death our affection has always hitherto kept concealed from us, the new person whom a hundred times daily that affection has clothed with a dear and cheating likeness … I, for whom my grandmother was still myself, I who had never seen her save in my own soul, always at the same place in the past, through the transparent sheets of contiguous, overlapping memories, suddenly in our drawing-room which formed part of a new world, that of time, that in which dwell the strangers of whom we say "He's begun to age a good deal," for the first time and for a moment only, since she vanished at once, I saw, sitting on the sofa, beneath the lamp, red-faced, heavy and common, sick, lost in thought, following the lines of a book with eyes that seemed hardly sane, a dejected old woman whom I did not know.

This passage should read against its implicit Kantian background: a network screens our raw perceptions of beloved persons; that is, "before allowing the images that their faces present to reach us catches them in its vortex, [it] flings them back upon the idea that we have always had of them, makes them adhere to it, coincide with it"; this network—the complex web of past experiences, affections, etc., which colors our raw perceptions—plays exactly the role of a transcendental horizon which makes our reality meaningful. When deprived of this network, of the fantasmatic coordinates of meaning, we are no longer engaged participants in the world, we find ourselves confronted with things in their *noumenal* dimension: for a moment, we see them the way they are "in themselves," independently of us—or, as Proust puts it in a wonderful formula, one becomes "a spectator, so to speak, of one's own absence." Once the fantasy-object is subtracted from reality, it is not only the observed reality which changes, but also the observing subject himself: he is reduced to a gaze observing how things look in his own absence (recall the old Tom Sawyer/Huck Finn fantasy about being present at one's own funeral). And is not this, precisely, the feature which makes the camera so uncanny? Is not a camera our eye separated from our body, drifting around and recording how things look in our absence?

So, to recapitulate: the grandmother's voice, heard on the telephone, separated from her body, surprises Marcel—it is a voice of a frail old woman, not the voice of the grandmother he remembers. And the point is that this experience colors his perception of the grandmother: when he later visits her in person, he perceives her in a new way, as a strange old woman drowsing over her book, overburdened with age, flushed and coarse, no longer the charming and caring grandmother he remembered. This is how voice as an autonomous partial object can affect our entire perception of the body to which it belongs. The lesson is precisely that the direct experience of the unity of a body, where the voice seems to fit its organic whole, involves a necessary mystification; in order to get to the truth, one has to tear this unity apart, to focus on one of its aspects in isolation, and then to allow this element to color our entire perception. In other words, what we find here is another case of Freud's anti-hermeneutic motto that one should interpret *en détail*, not *en masse*. To locate every feature of a human being in the organic Whole of the person is to miss not only its meaning, but the true meaning of the Whole itself. In this sense also, person and subject are to be opposed: the subject is de-centered with regard to person, it obtains its minimal consistency from a singular feature ("partial object"), the *objet petit a*, the object-cause of desire.

What we have to renounce is thus the common-sense notion of a primordial, fully constituted reality in which sight and sound harmoniously complement each other: the moment we enter the symbolic order, an unbridgeable gap separates forever a human body from "its" voice. The voice acquires a spectral autonomy, it never quite belongs to the body we see speaking, there is always a minimum of ventriloquism at work: it is as if the speaker's own voice hollows him out and in a sense speaks "by itself," through him.[35] In other words, their

35 The point is therefore not only that voice fills out the hole in the image: the voice simultaneously cuts out this hole. What we encounter here is again the fundamental

relationship is mediated by an impossibility: ultimately, *we hear things because we cannot see everything*. When, in narrating the myth of the cave, Socrates describes the prisoners who can see only shadows on the wall in front of them, he asks: "And if their prison had an echo from the wall opposite them, when one of the passers-by uttered a sound, do you think that they would suppose anything else than the passing shadow to be the speaker?"[36] Does he not thereby refer to the gap between the speaking body and the speaking voice which is constitutive of our experience of a speaking subject?

One can thus even go on to claim that this gap is that of castration, so that the ultimate modernist dream of "seeing voices" is the dream of entering a universe where castration is suspended—no wonder the Talmud declares that the elect "have seen the voices." This is why directors like Eisenstein, Chaplin, and even Hitchcock were so resistant to embracing sound—as if they wanted to prolong their sojourn in the silent paradise in which castration is suspended. Hitchcock himself expected his spectators "to have auditory eyes."[37] The disembodied seductive voice which threatens to swallow us thus simultaneously bears witness to the fact of castration.

This same lesson, concerning the tension between bodily appearance and the voice as ex-centric partial object, is given a sexualized twist in the story of Jacob. Jacob fell in love with Rachel and wanted to marry her; her father, however, wanted him to marry Leah, Rachel's elder sister. So that Jacob would not be tricked by the father or by Leah, Rachel taught him how to recognize her at night in bed. Before the sexual act, Rachel felt guilty towards her sister and told her what the signs were. Leah asked Rachel what would happen if Jacob recognized her voice. So the decision was taken that Rachel would lie under the bed, and while Jacob was making love to Leah, Rachel would

---

paradox of a fantasy which fills out the gap it itself opens up: the element which conceals is simultaneously that which reveals; i.e., the very process of concealing creates the concealed content, creates the impression that there is something to conceal. A scene from Mel Brooks's *High Anxiety* takes place at a psychoanalytical conference, with a couple of young children occupying seats in the first row. The speaker, scrutinized by the inquisitive children, feels embarrassed when he comes to talk about perversions, the phallus, castration, and so on, so he gets around the problem by translating his complex psychoanalytical jargon into "childspeak" ("papa threatens to cut off the little boy's pipi," etc.). The blunder here resides in the fact that the very attempt to adapt the content to accommodate the children (and thus to neutralize its traumatic impact) renders it accessible to them—had the speaker simply read his original text, the children would have had no idea as to its content.

36 Plato, *The Republic*, Vol. 2, trans. Paul Shorey, Cambridge, MA: Harvard University Press 1935, p. 123 (Book VII, 515b).

37 Peter Conrad, *The Hitchcock Murders*, London: Faber & Faber 2000, p. 159.

make the sounds, so he would not recognize that he was having sex with the wrong sister.[38]

In Shakespeare's *All's Well That Ends Well*, we can also imagine Diana hidden beneath the bed where Helen and Bertram are copulating, making the appropriate sounds so that Bertram will not realize he is not having sex with her, her voice serving as the support for the fantasmatic dimension. Shakespeare's *As You Like It* proposes a different version of this logic of double deception. Orlando is passionately in love with Rosalind who, in order to test his love, disguises herself as Ganymede and, as a male companion, interrogates Orlando about his love. She even takes on the personality of Rosalind (in a redoubled masking, she pretends to be herself, as Ganymede playing Rosalind) and persuades her friend Celia (disguised as Aliena) to marry them in a mock ceremony. Here Rosalind literally feigns to feign to be what she is: truth itself, in order to win, has to be *staged* in a redoubled deception—in a homologous way to *All's Well* in which marriage, in order to be asserted, has to be consummated in the guise of an extramarital affair.[39]

What then is the relation between the voice (and the gaze) and the triad imaginary-symbolic-Real? When Pascal, as a Jansenist, says that the authentic image of God is speech, we should take this claim literally and insist on "image" as the encompassing term whose subspecies is speech: Pascal's point is not simply the standard iconoclastic one that speech, not the visual image, is the domain of the divine; it is rather that speech remains a paradoxical image which sublates itself as image and thus avoids the trap of idolatry. Speech (the symbolic) deprived of its mediation by image (the imaginary) disintegrates in itself, as meaningful speech. (Recall the last words of *Moses und Aaron*, Schoenberg's great iconoclastic work and one candidate for the honorific title of the "last opera": "*O Wort, das mir fehlt!*" [O the word which I lack!]—a quite appropriate description of Moses's predicament following his furious rejection of images.) For a Lacanian, the solution is simple (or, rather, elementary in the Holmesian sense): we should read the claim about speech being the true image of God together with the Jansenist's basic thesis on the "*dieu caché*" (the hidden

38 Galit Hasan-Rokem, *Web of Life: Folklore and Midrash in Rabbinic Literature*, Palo Alto: Stanford University Press 2000.

39 In the fall of 2007, the Bosnian media reported on a crazy communicational short-circuit: A wife disappointed by her marriage established a passionate link with a no less disappointed married man via an internet chat-room; they both found in their virtual partner (each known only by pseudonyms) what they were missing in their real-life partner, and fell wildly in love. The wife wrote: "I believed that I had finally found someone who understood me, since he was like me caught in an unhappy marriage." The virtual couple finally decided to risk meeting in real life—and discovered that the virtual partner *was* the real-life spouse! The disappointed real-life couple had constructed in the virtual space an ideal couple.

god)—the word changes (the image of) God into the void in the image, into what is hidden in and by the image we see. The image thus becomes a screen which offers itself as visible in order to conceal what is invisible—in the sense of the dialectic of appearance deployed by Lacan: the symbolic is appearance as appearance, a screen which hides not another true content, but the fact that there is nothing to hide. In other words, the true function of a deceptive screen is not to conceal what lies behind it, but, precisely, to create and sustain the illusion that there is something it is hiding.

The Master and its specter

This notion of the lacking Other also opens up a new approach to fantasy, conceived as precisely an attempt to fill out this lack of the Other, to reconstitute the consistency of the big Other.[40] For that reason, fantasy and paranoia are inherently linked: at it most elementary, paranoia is a belief in an "Other of the Other," in another Other who, hidden behind the Other of the explicit social reality, controls (what appears to us as) the unforeseen effects of social life and thus guarantees its consistency. This paranoid stance has acquired a further boost with the ongoing digitalization of our daily lives: it is easy to imagine, once our (social) existence is entirely externalized, materialized in the big Other of the global computer network, an evil programmer erasing our digital identity and thus depriving us of our social existence, turning us into non-persons.

In the domain of ideology, the primordial fantasmatic object, the mother of all ideological objects, is the object of anti-Semitism, the so-called "conceptual Jew": beneath the chaos of the market, the degradation of morals, and so on, there lies the Jewish plot. According to Freud, the attitude of the male subject towards castration involves a paradoxical splitting: I know that castration is not an actual threat, that it will not really occur, yet I am nonetheless haunted by its prospect. And the same goes for the figure of the "conceptual Jew": he does not exist (as part of our experience of social reality), but for that reason I fear him even more—in short, the very non-existence of the Jew in reality functions as the main argument for anti-Semitism. That is to say, anti-Semitic discourse constructs the figure of the Jew as a phantom-like entity to be found nowhere in reality, and then uses this very gap between the "conceptual Jew" and actually

40 A patient from Latin America reported to his analyst a dream in which he felt an unbearable compulsion to eat caramel sweets. The analyst was wise enough to resist any quick reference to the oral drive, etc., and instead focused on the Spanish expression "to eat a caramel," which means to swallow a lie or a fantasy (to say that someone "gave me a caramel to eat" means that he put me off with solacing lies). The dream was thus revealing the patient's urge to be protected by a cobweb of fantasies to soften the impact of the Real.

existing Jews as the ultimate argument for anti-Semitism. We are thus caught in a kind of vicious circle: the more things appear to be normal, the more suspicion they arouse and the more panic-stricken we become. In this respect, the Jew is like the maternal phallus: there is no such thing in reality, but for that very reason, its phantom-like, spectral presence gives rise to an unbearable anxiety. Therein consists also the most succinct definition of the Lacanian Real: the more my (symbolic) reasoning tells me that X is not possible, the more its specter haunts me—like the proverbial courageous Englishman who not only didn't believe in ghosts but was not even afraid of them.

A homology imposes itself here between the "conceptual Jew" and the Name-of-the-Father: in the latter case, we also have a split between knowledge and belief ("I know very well that my father is actually an imperfect, confused, impotent creature, yet I nonetheless believe in his symbolic authority"). The empirical father never lives up to his Name, to his symbolic mandate—and insofar as he does live up to it, we are dealing with a psychotic constellation (Schreber's father, from the case analyzed by Freud, was a clear case of a father who did live up to his Name). Is not the "transubstantiation," the "sublation" (*Aufhebung*), of the real father into the Name-of-the-Father therefore strictly homologous to the "transubstantiation" of the empirical Jew into (the form of appearance of) the "conceptual Jew"? Is not the gap that separates actual Jews from the fantasmatic figure of the "conceptual Jew" of the same nature as the gap that separates the empirical, always deficient person of the father from the Name-of-the-Father, from his symbolic mandate? In both cases, a real person acts as the personification of an irreal, fictitious agency—the actual father as a stand-in for the agency of symbolic authority and the actual Jew as a stand-in for the fantasmatic figure of the "conceptual Jew."

Convincing as it may sound, this homology has to be rejected as deceptive: in the case of the Jew, the standard logic of symbolic castration is reversed. In what, precisely, does symbolic castration consist? A real father exerts authority only insofar as he posits himself as the embodiment of a transcendent symbolic agency, that is, insofar as he accepts that it is not himself, but the big Other who speaks through him (like the millionaire from one of Claude Chabrol's films who inverts the standard complaint about being loved only for his wealth: "If only I were able to find a woman who would love me only for my millions, not for myself!"). Therein lies the ultimate lesson of the Freudian myth of parricide, of the primordial father who, after his violent death, returns stronger than ever in the guise of his Name, as a symbolic authority: if the real father is to exert paternal symbolic authority, he must in a sense die while alive—it is his identification with the "dead letter" of the symbolic mandate that bestows authority on his person, or, to paraphrase the old anti–Native American slogan: "Only a dead father is a good father!"

For this reason, our experience of the paternal figure necessarily oscillates between lack and surplus: there is always "too much" or "not enough" of the father, never the right measure—"either he is wanting as presence or, in his presence, he is all too much here."[41] On the one hand, we have the recurrent motif of the absent father, blamed for everything up to and including the crime rate among adolescents; on the other hand, when the father is effectively "there," his presence is necessarily experienced as disturbing, vulgar, boastful, indecent, incompatible with the dignity of parental authority, as if his presence as such is already an obtrusive excess.

This dialectic of lack and excess accounts for the paradoxical inversion in our relationship to a figure of Power: when this figure (father, king ...) no longer successfully performs his function, when he no longer fully exerts his power, this lack is necessarily (mis)perceived as an excess, the ruler is reproached for having "too much authority," as if we were dealing with a "brutal excess of Power." This paradox is typical of the pre-revolutionary situation: the more a regime (say, the *ancien régime* in France in the years before 1789) is uncertain of itself, of its legitimacy—the more it hesitates and makes concessions to the opposition—the more it is attacked by the opposition as a tyranny. The opposition, of course, acts here as a hysteric, since its reproach concerning the regime's excessive exercise of power conceals its exact opposite—its true reproach is that the regime is not strong enough, that it does not live up to its mandate of power.

Another homology that has to be rejected for the same reasons is that between the Name-of-the-Father and the fantasmatic Woman. Lacan's "Woman doesn't exist" (*la Femme n'existe pas*) does not mean that no empirical, flesh-and-blood woman is ever "She," that she cannot ever live up to the inaccessible ideal of Woman (in the way that the empirical, "real" father never lives up to his symbolic function, to his Name). The gap that forever separates any empirical woman from Woman is not the same as the gap between an empty symbolic function and its empirical bearer. The problem with woman is, on the contrary, that it is not possible to formulate her empty ideal-symbolic function—this is what Lacan has in mind when he asserts that "Woman does not exist." The impossible "Woman" is not a symbolic fiction, but again a fantasmatic specter whose support is *objet a*, not S_1. The one who "does not exist" in the same sense as Woman does not exist is the primordial Father-enjoyment (the mythic pre-Oedipal father who had a monopoly over all women in his group), which is why his status is correlative to that of Woman.

The trouble with most criticisms of Lacan's "phallocentrism" is that, as a rule, they refer to the "phallus" and/or "castration" in a pre-conceptual, common-sense metaphorical way: within standard feminist film-studies, for example,

41 Jacques Lacan, *Le séminaire, Livre VIII: Le transfert*, Paris: Seuil 1991, p. 346.

every time a man behaves aggressively towards a woman or asserts his authority over her, one can be fairly sure his actions will be designated as "phallic"; every time a woman is framed, rendered helpless, cornered, and so forth, her experience will most likely be designated as "castrating." What gets lost here is precisely the paradox of the phallus as the signifier of castration: if we are to assert our (symbolic) "phallic" authority, the price to be paid is that we have to renounce the position of agent and consent to function as the medium through which the big Other acts and speaks. Insofar as the phallus qua signifier designates the agency of symbolic authority, its crucial feature therefore resides in the fact that it is not "mine," the organ of a living subject, but a place at which a foreign power intervenes and inscribes itself onto my body, a place at which the big Other acts through me—in short, the fact that the phallus is a signifier means above all that it is structurally an organ without a body, somehow "detached" from my body. This crucial feature of the phallus, its detachability, becomes clearly visible in the use of the plastic artificial phallus ("dildo") in lesbian sadomasochistic practices, where it circulates as a plaything—the phallus is far too serious a thing for its use to be left to stupid creatures like men.[42]

There is, however, a pivotal difference between this symbolic authority guaranteed by the phallus as the signifier of castration and the spectral presence of the "conceptual Jew": although in both cases we are dealing with the split between knowledge and belief, the two splits are of a fundamentally different nature. In the first case, the belief concerns the "visible" public symbolic authority (notwithstanding my awareness of the father's imperfection and debility, I still accept him as a figure of authority), whereas in the second case, what I believe in is the power of an invisible spectral apparition.[43] The fantasmatic "conceptual Jew" is

42 If we were to indulge in speculation as to why the phallus qua organ has been chosen to function as the phallic signifier, then the characteristic that "predisposes" it for this role would be the feature evoked by Saint Augustine: the phallus is an organ of power-potency, yet one whose display of potency essentially eludes the subject's control—with the alleged exception of some Hindu priests, one cannot bring about an erection at will, hence it bears witness to some foreign power at work in the very heart of the subject.

43 The other (mis)reading, closely linked to the first, concerns the opposition between the phallic economy and the polymorphous plurality of subject positions: according to the standard view, the task of the phallic economy is to mold the dispersed pre-Oedipal plurality of subject-positions into a unified subject subordinated to the rule of the Name-of-the-Father (the bearer and relay of social authority) and is as such the ideal subject of (social) Power. What should be called into question here is the underlying assumption that social Power exerts itself via the unified Oedipal subject entirely submitted to the phallic paternal Law and, inversely, that the dispersion of the unified subject into a multitude of subject-positions as it were automatically undermines the authority and exercise of Power. Against this commonplace, one has to point out again and again that Power always interpellates us, addresses us, as split subjects, that, in order to reproduce

not a paternal figure of symbolic authority, a "castrated" bearer or medium of public authority, but something decidedly different, a kind of uncanny double of the public authority that perverts its proper logic: he has to act in the shadow, invisible to the public eye, irradiating a phantom-like, spectral omnipotence. On account of this unfathomable, elusive status of the kernel of his identity, the Jew is—in contrast to the "castrated" father—perceived as *uncastratable*: the more his actual, social, public existence is cut short, the more threatening his elusive fantasmatic ex-sistence becomes.[44]

This fantasmatic logic of an invisible and for that very reason all-powerful Master was clearly at work in the way the figure of Abimael Guzmán—"Presidente Gonzalo," the leader of Sendero Luminoso in Peru—functioned prior to his arrest: the fact that his very existence was doubted (people were not sure if he actually existed or was just a myth) only added to his power. The mysterious master criminal "Keyser Söze," from Bryan Singer's *The Usual Suspects*, is another example. Again, it is not clear whether he exists at all: as one of the characters in the film puts it, "I don't believe in God, but I'm nonetheless afraid of him." People are afraid to see him or, once forced to confront him face to face, to mention this to others—his identity is kept highly secret. At the end of the film, it is disclosed that Keyser Söze is in fact the most miserable of the group of suspects, a limping, self-humiliating wimp, like Alberich in Richard Wagner's *Ring des Nibelungen*. What is crucial is this very contrast between the omnipotence of the invisible agent of power and the way this same agent is reduced to a crippled weakling once his identity is made public. The fantasmatic feature that accounts for the power exerted by such a Master figure is not his symbolic place but an act in which he has displayed his ruthless will and readiness to dispense altogether with ordinary human considerations (Keyser Söze supposedly shot his own wife and children in cold blood in order to prevent an enemy gang from blackmailing him by threatening to kill them—an act strictly homologous to Alberich's renunciation of love).

---

itself, it relies upon our splitting: the message the power discourse bombards us with is by definition inconsistent, there is always a gap between public discourse and its fantasmatic support. Far from being a kind of secondary weakness, a sign of the Power's imperfection, this splitting is constitutive of its exercise. With regard to the so-called "postmodern" form of subjectivity that befits late capitalism, we must even go a step further: the "postmodern" subject is directly, at the level of the public discourse itself, constituted as an inconsistent bundle of multiple "subject positions" (economically conservative but sexually "enlightened" yuppie, etc.).

44 For a classic statement of the different versions of "I know very well, but still ..." see Octave Mannoni, "Je sais bien, mais quand meme ...," in *Clefs pour l'imaginaire; ou, L'autre scène*, Paris: Seuil 1968. For a political reading of it, see Chapter 6 of Slavoj Žižek, *For They Know Not What They Do*, London: Verso Books 2002.

In short, the difference between the Name-of-the-Father and the "conceptual Jew" is the difference between a symbolic fiction and a fantasmatic specter: in Lacanian algebra, between S_1, the Master-Signifier (the empty signifier of symbolic authority), and the *objet petit a*.[45] When the subject is endowed with symbolic authority, he acts as an appendix of his symbolic title; that is, it is the big Other who acts through him. In the case of the spectral presence, in contrast, the power I exert relies on "something in me more than myself," best exemplified by numerous science-fiction thrillers from *Alien* to *Hidden*: an indestructible foreign body that stands for the pre-symbolic life substance, a nauseous mucous parasite that invades my insides and takes over.

So, back to Chabrol's joke about the millionaire: when someone says they love me not because of myself but because of my symbolic standing (power, wealth), my predicament is decidedly better than when I am told that I am loved because somebody feels the presence in me of "something more than myself." If a millionaire loses his millions, the partner who loved him for his wealth will simply lose interest and abandon him, with no deep trauma involved; if, however, I am loved because of "something in me more than myself," the very intensity of this love can easily convert into a no less passionate hatred, a violent attempt to annihilate the surplus-object in me that disturbs my partner.[46] One can therefore sympathize with the poor millionaire's plight: it is far more comforting to know that a woman loves me for my millions (or power or glory)—this

45 The same logic seems to be at work in the anti-communist, right-wing populism that has recently been gaining strength in the ex-socialist East European countries: its answer to the present economic and other hardships is that, although they have officially lost power, the communists continue to pull the strings, to control the levers of economic power, to dominate the media and state institutions. Communists are thus perceived as a fantasmatic entity à la the Jews: the more they lose public power and become invisible, the stronger their phantom-like omnipresence, their shadowy control. This idée fixe of the populists—according to which what is now emerging in post-socialist countries is not "true" capitalism but a false imitation in which actual power and control remain in the hands of ex-communists dressed up as new capitalists—also offers an exemplary case of the illusion whose mechanism was laid bare for the first time by Hegel: what the populists fail to recognize is that their opposition to this "false" capitalism is effectively an opposition to capitalism tout court, i.e., that they, not the ex-communists, are the true ideological inheritors of socialism—no wonder that the populists are compelled to resuscitate the old communist opposition between "formal" and "true" democracy. In short, we are dealing with yet another example of the irony that pertains to the revolutionary process, already described by Marx: all of a sudden, the amazed revolutionaries realize that they were mere vanishing mediators whose "historical role" was to prepare the terrain for the old masters to take over in a new guise.

46 A classic example of this opposition between symbolic authority and the spectral, invisible Master is provided by Wagner's *Das Rheingold*, in the guise of opposition between Wotan and Alberich.

awareness allows me to maintain a safe distance, to avoid getting caught up in the relationship too intensely, exposing to the other the very kernel of my being. When the other sees in me "something more than myself," the path is wide open for the paradoxical short-circuit between love and hate for which Lacan coined the neologism *l'hainamoration*.[47]

The two sides of fantasy

This duality of symbolic fiction and spectral apparition can also be discerned in the utter ambiguity that surrounds the notion of fantasy. The latter offers an exemplary case of the dialectical *coincidentia oppositorum*: on the one hand, fantasy on its beatific side, in its stabilizing dimension, the dream of a state without disturbances, out of reach of human depravity; on the other hand, fantasy in its destabilizing dimension whose elementary form is envy—all that "irritates" me about the Other, images that haunt me of what he or she might be doing when out of my sight, of how he or she deceives me and plots against me, of how he or she ignores me and indulges in an enjoyment so intense it lies beyond my capacity to represent it, and so on (this, for example, is what bothers Swann apropos Odette in *Un amour de Swann*). Does not the fundamental lesson of so-called totalitarianism concern the co-dependence of these two aspects of the notion of fantasy? Those who claimed to have fully realized fantasy 1 (the symbolic fiction) had to have recourse to fantasy 2 (the spectral apparition) in order to explain their failure—the foreclosed obverse of the Nazi's harmonious *Volksgemeinschaft* returned in the guise of their paranoiac obsession with the Jewish plot. Similarly, the Stalinists' compulsive discovery of ever new enemies of Socialism was the inescapable obverse of their pretense to have realized the ideal of the "new Socialist man." (Perhaps freedom from the infernal hold of fantasy 2 provides the most succinct criterion for sainthood.)

Fantasy 1 and fantasy 2, symbolic fiction and spectral apparition, are thus two sides of the same coin: insofar as a community experiences its reality as regulated or structured by fantasy 1, it has to disavow its inherent impossibility,

---

47 The millionaire's position is in fact even more complex. That is to say, when a woman says to a man, "I don't love you for your millions [or your power ...] but for what you really are!" what does this amount to? The more she "means it sincerely" the more she is the victim of a kind of perspectival illusion, failing to notice how the very fact that (people know that) I am a millionaire (or a man of power) affects people's perception of what I am "in myself," irrespective of this property of mine. As long as I remain rich, people perceive me as a strong, independent personality, whereas the moment I lose my millions, they all of a sudden see in me a dull weakling (or vice versa). In short, the paradox lies in the fact that only a woman who (knows that she) loves me for my millions is able to see me the way I truly am, since my wealth no longer distorts her perception.

the antagonism at its very heart—and fantasy 2 gives body to this disavowal. In short, the success of fantasy 1 in maintaining its hold depends on the effectiveness of fantasy 2. Lacan rewrote Descartes's "I think, therefore I am" as "I am the one who thinks 'therefore I am'"—the point being, of course, the noncoincidence of the two "am's," and the fantasmatic nature of the second. The pathetic assertion of ethnic identity should be submitted to the same reformulation: the moment "I am French (German, Jewish, American ...)" is rephrased as "I am the one who thinks 'therefore I am French,'" the gap at the core of my self-identity becomes visible—and the function of the "conceptual Jew" is precisely to render this gap invisible.

What, then, is fantasy? The desire "realized" (staged) in fantasy is not the subject's own but the other's desire—that is to say, fantasy, a fantasmatic formation, is an answer to the enigma of "*Che vuoi?*" (What do you want?), which renders the subject's primordial, constitutive position. The original question of desire is not directly "What do I want?" but "What do others want from me? What do they see in me? What am I for others?" A small child is embedded in a complex network of relations, serving as a kind of catalyst and battlefield for the desires of those around him; his father, mother, brothers, and sisters, and so on, fight out their battles around him. While being well aware of this role, the child cannot fathom what object he is for the others, or the exact nature of the games they are playing around him. Fantasy provides him with an answer to this enigma—at its most fundamental level, fantasy tells me what I am for my others. It is again anti-Semitism, anti-Semitic paranoia, which reveals in an exemplary way this radically intersubjective character of fantasy: the social fantasy of the Jewish plot is an attempt to provide an answer to the question "What does society want from me?" to unearth the meaning of the murky events in which I am forced to participate. For that reason, the standard theory of "projection," according to which the anti-Semite "projects" onto the figure of the Jew the disavowed part of himself, is inadequate—the figure of "conceptual Jew" cannot be reduced to being an externalization of the anti-Semite's "inner conflict"; on the contrary, it bears witness to (and tries to cope with) the fact that the subject is originally decentered, part of an opaque network whose meaning and logic elude its control.

On that account, the question of *la traversée du fantasme* (of how to gain a minimal distance from the fantasmatic frame which organizes one's enjoyment, of how to suspend its efficacy) is not only crucial for the psychoanalytic cure and its conclusion—in our era of renewed racist tension, of universalized anti-Semitism, it is perhaps also the foremost political question. The impotence of the traditional Enlightenment attitude is best exemplified by the anti-racist who, at the level of rational argumentation, produces a series of convincing reasons for rejecting the racist Other but is nonetheless clearly fascinated by the object of his critique. Consequently, all his defenses disintegrate the moment a real crisis occurs (when "the fatherland is in danger," for example), like in the classical Hollywood film in which the villain, though he will be "officially" condemned at the end, is nonetheless the focus of our libidinal investment (Hitchcock emphasized that a film is only as alluring as its bad guy). The foremost problem is not how to denounce and rationally defeat the enemy—a task which can easily result in its strengthening its hold upon us—but how to break its (fantasmatic) spell. The point of *la traversée du fantasme* is not to get rid of *jouissance* (in the mode of old-style leftist Puritanism): taking a minimal distance towards fantasy rather means that I, as it were, "unhook" *jouissance* from its fantasmatic frame and acknowledge it as that which is properly undecidable, as an indivisible remainder which is neither inherently "reactionary," supporting historical inertia, nor a liberating force enabling us to undermine the constraints of the existing order.

In his movie version of Kafka's *The Trial*, Orson Welles accomplishes such a breaking of the fantasmatic spell in an exemplary way by reinterpreting the place and the function of the famous parable "Before the Law." In the film, we hear the story twice: at the very beginning, it serves as a kind of prologue, read and accompanied by (fake) ancient engravings projected from lantern-slides; then, shortly before the end, it is told to Josef K., not by the priest (as in the novel), but by K.'s lawyer (played by Welles himself), who unexpectedly joins the priest and K. in the Cathedral. The action then takes a strange turn and diverges from Kafka's novel—even before the lawyer has warmed to his theme, K. cuts him short: "I've heard it. We've heard it all. The door was meant only for him." What ensues is a painful dialogue in which the lawyer advises K. to "plead insanity" by claiming that he is the victim of a diabolical plot hatched by a mysterious State agency. K., however, rejects the role of victim: "I don't pretend to be a martyr." "Not even a victim of society?" "No, I'm not a victim, I'm a member of society ..." In his final outburst, K. then asserts that the true conspiracy (of Power) consists in the very attempt to persuade subjects that they are victims of irrational, impenetrable forces, that everything is crazy, that the world is absurd and meaningless. When K. thereupon leaves the Cathedral, two plain-clothes policemen are already waiting for him; they take him to an abandoned building site and blow him up. In Welles's version, the reason K. is killed is therefore the exact opposite of the reason implied in the novel—he represents a threat to power the moment he unmasks, "sees through," the fiction upon which the existing power structure is founded.

Welles's reading of *The Trial* thus differs from both predominant approaches to Kafka, the obscurantist-religious as well as the naïve enlightened humanist perspectives. According to the former, K. is effectively guilty: what makes him guilty is the very protestation of his innocence, his arrogant reliance on naïve-rational argumentation. The conservative message of this reading that sees K. as representative of an enlightened questioning of authority is unmistakable: K. himself is the true nihilist, who acts like the proverbial elephant in the china shop—his confidence in public reason renders him totally blind to the Mystery of Power, to the true nature of bureaucracy. The Court appears to K. as a mysterious and obscene agency bombarding him with "irrational" demands and accusations exclusively on account of K.'s distorted subjectivist perspective: as the priest in the Cathedral points out to K., the Court is in fact indifferent, it wants nothing from him. In the contrary reading, Kafka is seen as a deeply ambiguous writer who revealed the fantasmatic basis of the totalitarian bureaucratic machinery yet was himself unable to resist its fatal attraction. Therein resides the uneasiness felt by many "enlightened" readers of Kafka: in the end, did he not participate in the infernal machinery he was describing, thereby strengthening its hold instead of breaking its spell?

Although it may seem that Welles aligns himself with the second reading, things are by no means so unequivocal: he, as it were, adds another turn of the screw by raising "conspiracy" to the power of two—as K. puts it in the Welles's version, the true conspiracy of Power resides in the very notion of conspiracy, in the notion of some mysterious Agency that effectively runs the show, that behind the visible, public Power, there lies another obscene, invisible, "crazy" power structure. This other, hidden Law acts the part of the "Other of the Other" in the Lacanian sense, the part of the meta-guarantee of the consistency of the big Other (the symbolic order that regulates social life). "Totalitarian" regimes were especially skilled in cultivating the myth of a secret parallel power, invisible and for that very reason all-powerful, a kind of "organization within the organization"—the KGB, freemasons, or whatever—that compensated for the blatant inefficiency of the public, legal Power and thus assured the smooth operation of the social machine. This myth is not only in no way subversive, it serves as the ultimate support of Power. The perfect American counterpart to it is (the myth of) J. Edgar Hoover, the personification of the obscene "other power" behind the president, the shadowy double of the legitimate Power. Hoover held onto power by compiling secret files that allowed him to keep the entire political and power elite in check, while he himself regularly indulged in homosexual orgies dressed up as a woman. When K.'s lawyer offers him, as a desperate last resort, the role of playing the martyr-victim of a hidden conspiracy, K. turns it down, being well aware that by accepting it he would walk into the most perfidious trap of Power.

This obscene mirage of the Other Power brings into play the same fantasmatic space as the famous advertisement for Smirnoff vodka, which also deftly manipulates the gap between reality and the "other surface" of the fantasy space: the camera, placed behind a bottle of vodka on a tray carried by a waiter, wanders around the deck of a luxurious ocean-liner; every time it passes an object, we first see it as it is in its everyday reality, and then, as the transparent glass of the bottle comes between our gaze and the object, we see it distorted in a fantasy dimension—two gentlemen in black evening attire become two penguins, the necklace around a lady's neck a living snake, stairs a set of piano keys, etc. The Court in Kafka's *The Trial* possesses the same purely phantasmagorical existence; its predecessor is Klingsor's Castle in Wagner's *Parsifal*. Since its hold upon the subject is entirely fantasmatic, it is sufficient to break its spell via a gesture of distantiation, and the Court or Castle falls to dust. Therein resides the political lesson of *Parsifal* and of Welles's *The Trial*: if we are to overcome the "effective" social power, we have first to break its fantasmatic hold upon us.[48]

"Traversing the fantasy" does not mean going outside reality, but "vacillating" it, accepting its inconsistent non-All. The notion of fantasy as a kind of illusory screen blurring our relation to partial objects may seem to fit perfectly the common-sense idea of what psychoanalysis should do: of course it should liberate us from the hold of idiosyncratic fantasies and enable us to confront reality the way it is. This, precisely, is what Lacan does *not* have in mind—what he is aiming at is almost the exact opposite. In our daily existence, we are immersed in "reality" (structured or supported by the fantasy), but this immersion is disturbed by symptoms which bear witness to the fact that another repressed level of our psyche resists the immersion. To "traverse the fantasy" therefore means, paradoxically, *to fully identify oneself with the fantasy*—with the fantasy which structures the excess that resists our immersion in daily reality. In Richard Boothby's succinct formulation:

> "Traversing the fantasy" thus does not mean that the subject somehow abandons its involvement with fanciful caprices and accommodates itself to a pragmatic "reality," but precisely the opposite: the subject is submitted to that effect of the symbolic lack that reveals the limit of everyday reality. To traverse the fantasy in the Lacanian sense is to be more profoundly claimed by the fantasy than ever, in the sense of being brought into an ever more intimate relation with that real core of the fantasy that transcends imaging.[49]

Boothby is right to emphasize the Janus-like structure of a fantasy: a fantasy is simultaneously pacifying, disarming (providing an imaginary scenario which

48 What if there is—as indeed there always is—an actual conspiracy or corruption scandal in which state power itself is involved? The fantasmatic logic of Conspiracy effectively hinders the public revelation of actual conspiracies, corruption cases, etc.—the efficacy of the fantasmatic logic of Conspiracy demands that the Enemy remain an unfathomable entity whose true identity can never be fully disclosed.

49 Richard Boothby, *Freud as Philosopher*, London: Routledge 2001, pp. 275–6.

enables us to endure the abyss of the Other's desire) *and* shattering, disturbing, inassimilable into our reality. The ideologico-political dimension of this notion of "traversing the fantasy" was made clear by the unique role the rock group *Top lista nadrealista* (*The Top List of the Surrealists*) played during the Bosnian war in the besieged Sarajevo: their ironic performances which, in the midst of the war and hunger, satirized the predicament of the Sarajevan population, acquired a cult status not only in the counterculture, but also among the citizens of Sarajevo in general (the group's weekly TV show was broadcast throughout the war and became extremely popular). Instead of bemoaning their tragic fate, they daringly mobilized all the clichés about "stupid Bosnians" common in Yugoslavia, fully identifying with them—the point thus made was that the path to true solidarity goes via a direct confrontation with obscene racist fantasies circulating in symbolic space, through a playful identification with them, not through the denial of them on behalf of "what people are really like."

This brings us to what, for Lacan, is the ultimate ethical trap: to confer on the fantasmatic gesture of deprivation some sacrificial value, something that can only be justified with a reference to a deeper meaning. This seems to be the trap into which *The Life of David Gale* fell, a film which has the dubious distinction of being the first big Hollywood production to include an explicit Lacanian reference.[50] Kevin Spacey plays a philosophy professor and opponent of the death penalty who, very early on, is seen delivering a course on Lacan's "graph of desire." Later, he sleeps with one of his students, loses his job, is shunned by the community, and then gets blamed for the murder of a close female friend, ending up on death row, where a reporter (Kate Winslet) comes to interview him. Initially certain that he his guilty, she begins to have doubts when he tells her: "Think about it—I was one of the biggest opponents of the death penalty, and now I'm on death row." Pursuing her research, Winslet discovers a tape which reveals that he didn't commit the murder—but too late, since he has already been executed. She makes the tape public, however, and the inadequacies of the death penalty are duly revealed. In the last moments of the film, Winslet receives another version of the tape in which the whole truth becomes clear: the allegedly murdered woman in fact killed herself (she was dying anyway of cancer), and Spacey was present as she did so. In other words, Spacey was engaged in an elaborate anti-death-penalty activist plot: he sacrificed himself for the greater good of exposing the horror and injustice of death penalty. What makes the film interesting is that, retroactively, we see how this act is grounded in Spacey's reading of Lacan at the film's beginning: from the (correct) insight into the fantasmatic support of desire, it draws the conclusion that all human desires are vain, and proposes helping others, right up to sacrificing one's life for them, as

50 *The Life of David Gale*, 2003, directed by Alan Parker and written by Charles Randolph, a native from Texas who taught philosophy at Webster University in Vienna.

the only proper ethical course. Here, measured by the proper Lacanian standards, the film fails: it endorses an ethic of radical self-sacrifice for the good of others; this is why the hero makes sure Winslet receives the final tape—because ultimately he needs the symbolic recognition of his act. No matter how radical the hero's self-sacrifice, the big Other is still there.

Image and Gaze

It is against this background that we should read the mediation between the imaginary and the symbolic in Lacan: the imaginary relates to the seen, while the symbolic as it were redoubles the image, shifting the focus onto what cannot be seen, onto what the image that we see obfuscates or blinds us to. Lacan spells out very precisely the implications of this redoubling: it is not only that, with the symbolic, the imaginary turns into the appearance concealing a hidden reality—the appearance the symbolic generates is that of appearance itself, namely the appearance that there is a hidden reality beneath the visible appearance. The precise name for this appearance of something that has no existence in itself, that exists only in its effects and thus only appears to appear, is virtuality—the virtual is the invisible X, the void whose contours can only be reconstructed from its effects, like a magnetic pole which only exists inasmuch as it attracts the small metal pieces that gather around it. With regard to sexual difference, the fundamental virtual entity, the most elementary invisible X which only "appears to appear," is the maternal phallus: the maternal phallus is imagined—not directly, but as a forever invisible virtual point of reference:

> When Lacan spoke of the imaginary register, he was talking about images that could be seen. The pigeon is not interested in the void; if there is a void in the place of the image, the pigeon does not develop there, the insect does not reproduce. But it is a fact that Lacan does not stop talking about the imaginary once he has introduced the symbolic. He still talks a great deal about it, but it is an imaginary that has completely changed its definition. The post-symbolic imaginary is very different from the pre-symbolic imaginary from before the introduction of this register. How is the concept of the imaginary transformed after the symbolic has been introduced? In a very precise way. The most important part of the imaginary is what cannot be seen. In particular, taking the pivot of the clinical practice that, for example, is developed in Seminar IV, *La relation d'objet*, it is the female phallus, the maternal phallus. It is a paradox to call it the imaginary phallus when precisely one cannot see it; it is almost as if it were a question of imagination. In Lacan's celebrated observations and theorizations on the mirror stage, Lacan's imaginary register was essentially linked to perception. While now, when the symbolic is introduced, there is a disjunction

> between the imaginary and perception, and in some way this imaginary of Lacan is linked to the imagination. … This implies the connection of the imaginary and the symbolic and thus a thesis that is separated from perception: the image is a screen for what cannot be seen.[51]

Insofar as the maternal phallus is by definition veiled, this brings us to the positive/constitutive ontological function of the veil: the image/screen/veil itself creates the illusion that there is something behind it—as one says in everyday language, with the veil, there is always "something left to the imagination." One should take this ontological function at its strongest and most literal: by hiding nothing, the veil creates the space for something to be imagined—the veil is the original operator of creation ex nihilo, or, as Hegel put it in his *Phenomenology*: "behind the so-called curtain which is supposed to conceal the inner world, there is nothing to be seen unless we go behind it ourselves, as much in order that we may see, as that there may be something behind there which can be seen."[52] Ten pages earlier, he puts it in even stronger terms: our perception is limited to the sensible world; beyond this world, there is only the void, and in order that, "in this complete void, which is even called the holy of holies, there may yet be something, we must fill it up with reveries, appearances, produced by consciousness itself. It would have to be content with being treated so badly for it would not deserve anything better, since even reveries are better than its own emptiness."[53] What Hegel is saying here is, of course, not that the sensible world is the only real one, and that the "true supra-sensible Beyond" is only a product of our imagination; the sensible world is a world of vanishing, self-canceling appearances—therein lies Hegel's idealism—but there is no separate "true reality" beneath it. The only "true reality" is the fact that appearances are "mere appearances," the transformation of immediate sensible reality into appearance: "The suprasensible is therefore appearance qua appearance."[54] We thus have two levels of appearance: the appearances of the direct sensible world, and the appearance, within this world of appearances, of objects which are "elevated to the dignity of a Thing," that is, which give body to—or point beyond themselves towards—what is beyond appearance: "Thanks to the veil, the lack of object is transformed into object, and the beyond makes its entrance in the world"[55]—this gap is crucial, and is missed by Buddhist "nihilism" where we have only flat appearances and the Void. And, in the same way that, as Freud

51 Jacques-Alain Miller, "The Prisons of *Jouissance*," *lacanian ink* 33 (Spring 2009), p. 39.
52 G. W. F. Hegel, *Phenomenology of Spirit*, trans. A. V. Miller, Oxford: Oxford University Press 1977, p. 103.
53 Ibid., pp. 88–9.
54 Ibid., p. 89.
55 Miller, "The Prisons of *Jouissance*," p. 45.

put it, the real inscribes itself in a dream in the guise of a dream within a dream, the real beyond appearances appears as an appearance within appearance, as what Plato called the "imitation of imitation." As Lacan perceptively notes, this is why Plato was so adamantly opposed to painting: not because painting is even further away from true reality than the sensible reality it imitates, but because, in it, true reality appears within ordinary sensible reality:

> The painting doesn't compete with appearance, it competes with what Plato designated as the Idea which is beyond appearance. It is because the painting is this appearance which says that it is what gives appearance that Plato rises against painting as against an activity which competes with his own.[56]

This is why Hitchcock's *Vertigo* is the ultimate anti-Platonic film, a systematic materialist undermining of the Platonic project: the murderous fury that seizes Scottie when he finally discovers that Judy, whom he has tried to make into Madeleine, *is* (the woman he knew as) Madeleine is the fury of the deceived Platonist when he perceives that the original he wants to remake in a perfect copy is itself already a copy. The shock here is not that the original turns out to be merely a copy—a standard deception against which Platonism continually warns us—but that (what we took to be) the copy turns out to be the original. Scottie's shock at the moment of recognition is also a Kafkaesque one. In the same way that, at the end of the parable "Before the Law," the man from the country learns that the door was there only for him, in *Vertigo* too, Scottie has to accept that the fascinating spectacle of Madeleine, which he was secretly following, was staged for his gaze only, that his gaze was included in it from the very beginning.

This brings us to Lacan's (and Hegel's) implicit theology: if God is the ultimate ground of all things, the reason why "there is something rather than nothing," then God is the veil itself: there is something and not nothing thanks to the veil which separates us from the void of Nothing. The statement "God is the veil" has to be read as a Hegelian speculative judgment which unites two opposite contents: (1) God is the ultimate reverie with which our imagination fills in the void behind the veil; (2) God is this veil itself as the ultimate creative power:

> the image conceals; the image that is showing is both an image that conceals, and that shows in order to conceal. All of Lacan's commentaries on images from that moment revolve around this idea ... So the image is something that is presented, and a fortiori when it is a matter of the image in a tableau, the image that is given

56 Jacques Lacan, *Le séminaire, Livre XI: Les quatre concepts fondamentaux de la psychanalyse*, Paris: Seuil 1973, p. 103.

> to be seen is a deception because it veils what is found behind. In this way it repeats a whole classic rhetoric that invites people to be wary, to reject images as deceitful. But at the same time—I have said that the image hides at first, I've commented on this—the veil that hides causes what cannot be seen to exist. This is the schema that Lacan presents in Seminar IV, La relation d'objet: on the left, the subject, a point; then the veil; and on the other side, another point, nothingness. Without the veil it is as if there is nothingness. But with a veil between the subject and nothingness everything is possible. One can play with the veil, imagine things, a little bit of simulacra can also help. Where there was nothing before the veil there is, perhaps, something and at least there is the beyond of the veil and in this way, through this "perhaps," the veil creates something ex nihilo.
>
> The veil is a God. Leibniz asks quietly why things exist rather than not—I say "quietly" because it's a little late, there already is something, and he should have thought about this a little before, before developing this world. I am addressing the God … who creates *ex nihilo*. But the veil is how one can respond to Leibniz: if there is something and not nothing, it is because there is a veil somewhere. With this function of the veil, the screen is introduced, this screen that converts the nothing into being. This is important to all of us inasmuch as we have come here dressed. One can hide what there is and, at the same time and in the same manner, what there is not: hiding the object and hiding, at the same time and with the same facility, the lack of the object. Clothing itself is in this movement of showing and hiding. The transvestite shows something and hides it at the same time. Which is to say he gives something other than what he shows to be seen. Thanks to the veil, the lack of object is transformed into object, and the beyond makes its entrance in the world in such a way that with the veil, as Lacan says, already in the imaginary there is the symbolic rhythm of the subject, the object and the beyond.[57]

The consequence of this insight is nothing less than an undermining of both the basic pre-Hegelian philosophical positions, the pre-critical metaphysics of a "true" substantial reality behind appearances as well as Kant's critical transcendentalism. In order to fully grasp this consequence, we should take the crucial step from the veil masking the Void to the gaze of the Other, the gaze as object: the In-itself beyond the veil, what the veil masks, is not some substantial transcendent reality but the Other's gaze, the point from which the Other returns the gaze. What I do not see in what I see is the gaze itself, the gaze as object.

Hence Lacan's axiom: in every picture, there is a blind spot, and the picture at which I look returns the gaze (stares back at me) from this point. It is against this background that one should read Lacan's thesis on the reflexive character of the Freudian drive, as the stance of "*se faire* …" (the visual drive is not the drive to see, but, in contrast to the desire to see, the drive to *make oneself* seen,

57 Miller, "The Prisons of *Jouissance*," pp. 44–5.

etc.). Does not Lacan here point towards the most elementary *theatricality* of the human condition? Our fundamental striving is not to observe, but to be part of a staged scene, to expose oneself to a gaze—not the determinate gaze of a person in reality, but the non-existing pure Gaze of the big Other. This is the gaze for which, on ancient Roman aqueducts, the details were carved on the reliefs at the top, invisible to any human eye; the gaze for which the ancient Incas made their gigantic drawings out of stones whose form could be seen only from high up in the air; the gaze for which the Stalinists organized their gigantic public spectacles. To specify this gaze as "divine" is already to "gentrify" its status, to deprive it of its "acousmatic" nature, of the fact that it is a gaze of no one, a gaze freely floating, with no bearer. The two correlative positions, that of the actor on stage and that of the spectator, are not ontologically equivalent or contemporary: we are not originally observers of the drama of reality, but part of the tableau staged for the void of a non-existing gaze, and it is only in a secondary moment that we assume the position of those who look at the stage. The unbearable "impossible" position is not that of the actor, but that of the observer, of the public.

Presence

This brings us to a possible Lacanian definition of fantasy as an imaginary scenario which stages an impossible scene, something that could only be seen from the point of impossibility.[58] A fantasy scene is what fully deserves the term "auratic *presence*." Insofar as it involves the point of impossibility, it can also be said to stage the *objet petit a*. And, indeed, does not the Lacanian couple of signifier and *objet a* correspond to the difference between representation and presence? While both are stand-ins, place-holders, of the subject, the signifier re-presents it, while object shines in its presence. In this sense, we can talk about—I quote Jacques-Alain Miller here—"the representation of the subject through the *objet a*, except that the word 'representation' does not suit. Must one posit an expression, a presentation, an identification?"[59] Precisely because the *objet a* does not represent the subject, we should not conjoin them (as in the formula of fantasy: $-*a*), limiting ourselves to

> putting only *a* and putting rays about it, rays because of the implicit presence, of presence as effacement of the subject, since, rather than of representation, of expression,

58 Here, we encounter the limit of Descartes's procedure of the exhaustion of fiction: I cannot feign that I am not. This, precisely, is what happens in fantasy, whose elementary coordinates are the subject's contraction to a gaze observing the world as it is imagined to be in the absence of the subject.

59 Miller, "The Prisons of *Jouissance*," p. 45.

> of identification, it is a question here of effacement ... The subject is present here essentially in its effacement, in its fashion of being effaced, what [Lacan] calls, with a great economy of words, using this neologism: the *effacon*.[60]

Lacan's twist here is that this presence of the *objet a* fills in the gap, the failure, of representation—his formula is that of the *objet a* above the bar, beneath which there is S(A), the signifier of the barred, inconsistent other. The present object is a filler, a stop-gap; so when we confront the tension between the symbolic and the Real, between meaning and presence—the event of presence which interrupts the smooth running of the symbolic, which transpires in its gaps and inconsistencies—we should focus on the way the Real corrodes from within the very consistency of the symbolic. And, perhaps, we should pass from the claim that "the intrusion of the Real corrodes the consistency of the symbolic" to the much stronger claim that "the Real is *nothing but* the inconsistency of the symbolic."

Heidegger liked to quote a line from Stefan George: "*Kein Ding sei wo das Wort gebricht*"—there is no thing where the word breaks down. When talking about the Thing, this line should be reversed: "*Ein Ding gibt es nur wo das Wort gebricht*"—there is a Thing only where the word breaks down. The standard notion according to which words represent absent things is here turned around: the Thing is a presence which arises where words (symbolic representations) fail, it is a thing standing for the missing word. In this sense, a sublime object is "an object elevated to the dignity of the Thing": the void of the Thing is not a void in reality, but, primarily, a void in the symbolic, and the sublime object is an object at the place of the failed word.[61] This, perhaps, is the most succinct definition of aura: aura envelops an object when it occupies a void (hole) within the symbolic order. What this implies is that the domain of the symbolic is not-All—is thwarted from within.[62]

60 Ibid., pp. 45–6.

61 Pippin noted the contrast between the Kantian and the religious sublime: while the latter aims at provoking a humbling awe (confronted with the infinite and inconceivable divine power, I am a nobody), in Kant's "heretical" view, the experience of the sublime is a two-step process which culminates in the assertion of "man's absolute supremacy over all of nature by virtue of his moral vocation and its independence from any natural condition or power." Robert Pippin, *The Persistence of Subjectivity*, Cambridge: Cambridge University Press 2005, p. 294.

62 This lack or imperfection of the (big) Other is rendered in a wonderfully simple way in a joke about two friends playing a game of trying to hit a can with a ball. After repeated hits, one of them says: "For devil's sake, I missed!" His friend, a religious fanatic, complains: "How dare you talk like that, this is blasphemy! May God strike you down with a lightning bolt as punishment!" A moment later, lightning does strike, but it hits the religious boy who, badly hurt and barely alive, turns to the heavens to ask: "But why

So, again, what is presence? Imagine a group conversation in which all the participants know that one of them has cancer and also know that everyone in the group knows it; they talk about everything, the new books they have read, movies they have seen, their professional disappointments, politics ... just to avoid the topic of cancer. In such a situation, one can say that cancer is fully *present*, a heavy presence that casts its shadow over everything the participants say and that gets all the heavier the more they try to avoid it.

What if, then, the true line of separation is not the one dividing presence and symbolic representation, but the one which runs across this division, splitting from within each of the two moments? It is to the eternal credit of "structuralism" to have "de-hermeneuticized" the very field of the symbolic, to have treated the signifying texture as independent of the universe of the experience of meaning; and it is the great achievement of the late Lacan's elaborations of the Real to have uncovered a traumatic intrusive "presence" which wreaks havoc upon every meaningful auratic experience of Presence. Recall Sartre's *Nausea*, one of the paradigmatic literary approaches to the Real: it is very difficult, counter-intuitive, to subsume the disgusting slime of the inert Real under the category of "aura." Is not aura precisely a "domestication" of the Real, a screen that protects us from its traumatic impact? The motif of a presence "this side of hermeneutics" is central for Lacan, for whom psychoanalysis is not hermeneutics, especially not a deep form. Psychoanalysis deals with the subject contemporary to the rise of the modern Real which emerges when meaning is evacuated from reality: not only the scientific real accessible in mathematical formulae, but also, from Schelling to Sartre, the proto-ontological abyss of the inertia of the "mere real" deprived of any meaning. For Lacan, there is thus no need for a psychoanalytic hermeneutics—religion does this job perfectly well.

Here Meaning and Sense should be counterposed: Meaning belongs to the big Other, it is what guarantees the consistency of our entire field of experience, while Sense is a local, contingent occurrence in the sea of non-sense. In Lacanian terms, Meaning belongs to the level of All, while Sense is non-All: ultimate Meaning is guaranteed by religion (even if things appear meaningless, like killings, famine, disasters, all this confusion has a higher Meaning from God's standpoint), while Sense is materialist, something which arises "out of nowhere" in a magical explosion of, say, an unexpected metaphor. Meaning is an affair of hermeneutics, Sense is an affair of interpretation, such as interpreting the sense of a symptom which, precisely, belies and undermines the totality of Meaning. Meaning is global, the horizon encompassing details which, in themselves, appear meaningless; Sense is a local occurrence in the field of non-sense. Meaning is threatened from the outside by non-Meaning; Sense is internal to

did you strike me, my Lord, and not the real culprit?" A deep voice resonates from above: "For devil's sake, I missed!"

non-Sense, the product of a nonsensical, contingent, or lucky encounter. Things have Meaning, but they make Sense.

Lacan's notion of interpretation is thus opposed to hermeneutics: it involves the reduction of meaning to the signifier's nonsense, not the unearthing of a secret meaning.[63]

Even "lower," if I may put it in this way, there is the level of what Lacan calls *sinthomes*, as opposed to symptoms—signifying knots of *jouis-sens*, enjoy-meant, "meaning" which directly penetrates the materiality of a letter.[64] Heinrich Kleist's short story "St Cecilia or the Power of the Voice" renders perfectly the (singing) voice in its uncanny embodiment of "ugly" *jouissance*. It takes place in a German town, torn between Protestants and Catholics, during the Thirty Years' War. The Protestants plan to trigger a slaughter in a large Catholic church during midnight mass; four people are planted to start making trouble and thus give the signal to the others to cause havoc. However, things take a strange turn when a beautiful nun, allegedly dead, miraculously awakens and leads the chorus in a sublime song. The song mesmerizes the four thugs: they are unable to start making trouble and so, since there is no signal, the night passes peacefully. Even after the event, the four Protestants remain numbed: they are locked into an asylum where for years they just sit and pray all day long. At midnight each night, they all promptly stand up and sing the sublime song they had heard on that fateful night. Here, of course, the horror arises, as the original divine singing which exerted such a miraculous, redemptive, pacifying effect becomes, in its repetition, a repulsive and obscene imitation. What we have here is an exemplary case of the Hegelian tautology as the highest contradiction: "Voice is … voice," the ethereal-sublime voice of a Church choir encounters itself in its otherness in the grotesque singing of the madmen. This effectively inverts the standard version of the obscene turn—that of the gentle girl's face all of a sudden

63 There is a certain anti-hermeneutic literalism which belongs to the very core of Jewish spirituality. David Grossman told me a nice personal anecdote: when, just prior to the 1967 Israeli-Arab war, he heard on the radio about the Arab threat to throw the Jews into the sea, his reaction was to take swimming lessons—a paradigmatic Jewish reaction if there ever was one, in the spirit of the long talk between Josef K. and the priest (the prison chaplain) that follows the parable "Before the Law."

64 The *sinthome* should be opposed to the *matheme*: although they both belong to the enigmatic space "between nature and culture," between senseless data and meaning—they are both pre-semantic, outside the domain of meaning, and yet nonetheless are signifiers and as such irreducible to the meaningless texture of positive data—"sinthome" is a name for the minimal formula which fixates/registers what Eric Santner called the "too-muchness of life." A *sinthome* is a formula which condenses the excess of *jouissance*, and this dimension is clearly missing in the *matheme*, whose exemplary cases are mathematically formalized scientific statements—*mathemes* do not imply any libidinal investment, they are neutral, desubjectivized.

distorted by rage as she starts to swear and spit out unspeakable blasphemies (the possessed girl in *The Exorcist*, etc.). This common version reveals the horror and corruption beneath the gentle surface: the semblance of innocence disintegrates, all of a sudden we perceive the intense obscenity behind it—what can be worse than this? Precisely what takes place in Kleist's story: the ultimate horror does not occur when the mask of innocence disintegrates, but rather when the sublime text is (mis)appropriated by the wrong speaker. In the standard version, we have the right object (a gentle, innocent face) in the wrong place (engaged in blasphemous profanities), while in Kleist the wrong object (the brutal thugs) in the right place (trying to imitate the sublime religious ritual) produces a much stronger profanation.

Two questions nonetheless arise here: how does this subversive practice relate to the similar (though definitely not subversive) practice of obscene "marching chants"? Where is the difference? Why is the first practice subversive and the second not? Furthermore, what would have been a parallel procedure for subverting the ruling ideology in the state-socialist regimes? There is a song which comes pretty close to it: the 8.40-minute-long *Gruess an die Partei (Chormusik Nr. 5 fuer grossen Chor, Bass-Solo und grosses Orchester)*, composed in 1976 by Paul Dessau (Brecht's last collaborator), with words by—again!—Heiner Müller (Brecht's unofficial successor as the leading dramatist of the GDR), putting together quotes from a speech by Erich Honecker, then general secretary of the *Socialist Unity-Party of Germany* (*Sozialistische Einheits-Partei Deutschlands*, SED—the tone-series "Es-E-D" appears again and again in the music!). The legend of Honecker as a misrecognized poet was one of the GDR's standard jokes: the idea was to take a passage from one of his speeches and add a new line every few words, thereby creating an abstract modern poem. In Müller-Dessau's "Greeting to the Party," a supreme example of what the Germans called *Polit-Byzantinismus*, this joke is realized in such a way that (as was often the case in the communist countries) it is not clear whether Müller intended it as a secret parody, whether he wrote (or chose) the words with his fingers crossed. What stands out is the extreme disparity, tension even, between the thoroughly modernist, non-melodic, atonal music and the utter banality of the words. Here are the first three Honecker "poems":

Great things were achieved
With the force of the people and
For the well-being of the people
In the fraternal link with the Soviet Union

Never was so much done
In the community of
Socialist states

For peace and security
For the freedom of the people
Many things remain to be done
In the Communist way
Year after year

The obscenity reaches its peak in the last "poem" where, towards its end, in a celebration of the ongoing passage from socialism to communism, the harsh declarations and injunctions, accompanied by rather brutal drum beatings, momentarily morph into a much softer and silent chant, like the climax of a religious hymn, signaling how, after the hard struggle of our epoch of socialism, the harmony of communism will win the day.

Today everybody can see:
Imperialism is in retreat
Progress is
Marching forward
With the power of the entire people
From the present of Socialism
To the future
Of Communism[65]

The frontier between the (state-byzantine) Sublime and the ridiculous is here effectively undecidable—one need only imagine Honecker, after a speech at the Party congress, *singing* these words accompanied by a chorus (composed of the delegates) and orchestra, to find oneself in the middle of the Marx Brothers' *Duck Soup*. But perhaps laughing at such spectacles is all too easy—perhaps it makes us miss their true addressee, the same imagined or inexistent gaze as the Incas' impossible gaze from above. In short, the most elementary fantasmatic notion is not that of a fascinating scene to be looked at, but the notion that "there is someone out there looking at us"; not a dream but the notion that "we are characters in someone else's dream." Far from signaling a subjective pathology, such a fantasmatic gaze is a *sine qua non* of our normality, in contrast to psychosis, where this gaze appears as part of reality. To make this crucial point clear, let us begin by clarifying the status of the gaze and the voice in psychoanalytic theory, where we must always keep in mind their different status in neurosis, psychosis, and perversion:[66]

65 Song and text available on the CD *Die Partei hat immer Recht: Eine Dokumentation in Liedern*, Amiga, BMG 74321394862.

66 I rely here on Paul-Laurent Assoun, *Leçons psychanalytiques sur le regard et la voix*, Vols. 1 and 2, Paris: Anthropos 2001.

(1) In neurosis, we are dealing with hysterical blindness or loss of the voice, that is, the voice or gaze are incapacitated; in psychosis, on the contrary, there is a surplus of the gaze or voice, for a psychotic experiences himself as gazed upon (paranoiac) or he hears (hallucinates) non-existing voices.[67] In contrast to both these stances, a pervert uses the voice or gaze as an instrument, he "does things" with them.

(2) The couple gaze and voice should also be linked to the couple *Sach-Vorstellungen* and *Wort-Vorstellungen*: the "representations-of-things" involve the gaze—we see things, while the "representations-of-words" involve the voice ("vocal images")—we hear words.

(3) Furthermore, the gaze and the voice are linked, respectively, to the Id (drive) and the superego: the gaze mobilizes the scopic drive, while the voice is the medium of the superego agency which exerts pressure on the subject. But one should also bear in mind here that the superego draws its energy from the Id, which means that the superego voice also mobilizes drives. In terms of the drives, the voice and the gaze are thus related as Eros and Thanatos, life drive and death drive: the gaze "siderates," side-tracks, transfixes, or immobilizes the subject's face, turning the subject into a Medusa-like petrified entity. The insight into the Real mortifies, it stands for death (the Medusa's head is itself a transfixed/petrified gaze, and seeing it does not blind me—on the contrary, I myself turn into a transfixed gaze), while the seductive voice stands for the pre-Oedipal maternal link beyond/beneath the Law, for the umbilical cord which vivifies (from the maternal lullaby to the hypnotist's voice).

(4) The relationship between the four partial objects (oral, anal, voice, gaze) is that of a square structured along the two axes of demand/desire and to the Other/from the Other. The oral object involves a demand addressed to the Other (the mother, to give me what I want), while the anal object involves a demand from the Other (in the anal economy, the object of my desire is reduced to the Other's demand—I shit regularly in order to satisfy the parents' demand). In a homologous way, the scopic object involves a desire addressed to the Other (to show itself, to allow to be seen), while the vocal object involves a desire from the Other (announcing what it wants from me). To put it in a slightly different way: the subject's gaze involves its attempt to see the Other, while the voice is an invocation (Lacan: "invocatory drive"), an attempt to provoke the Other (God, the king, the beloved) to respond; this is why the gaze mortifies-pacifies-immobilizes the Other, while the voice vivifies it, tries to elicit a gesture from it.

---

67 This difference can also be linked to the difference between the inability to act and the *passage à l'acte*: the hysteric position involves a blocked act, procrastination, oscillation, empty gestures (which function like "acting out," a theatrical gesture instead of a true act); the psychotic position involves the Real of a violent *passage à l'acte* which suspends the big Other itself.

(5) How, then, are the gaze and the voice inscribed into the social field? Primarily as shame and guilt: the shame of the Other seeing too much, seeing me in my nakedness; the guilt triggered by hearing what others say about me.[68] Is not the opposition of voice and gaze thus linked to the opposition of superego and Ego Ideal? The superego is a voice which haunts the subject and finds it guilty, while the Ego Ideal is the gaze in front of which the subject is ashamed. There is thus a triple chain of equivalences: gaze–shame–Ego Ideal, and voice–guilt–superego.

"The picture is in my eye, but me, I am in the picture"

This brings us to the properly ontological lesson of psychosis, of psychotic hallucinations in which "what was foreclosed from the symbolic returns in the Real," the lesson which effectively undermines the Cartesian *cogito* as the *percipiens* (perceiving subject) external to the *perceptum*. The lesson is that

> the *percipiens* is not exterior to the *perceptum* but that it is included, that there is a being in the *perceptum* itself that is not exterior to it; that it is not necessary to depart from the idea of a representation in which the exterior world would be convoked facing the subject sure of his existence, but that one must consider the inclusion of the subject of perception in the perceived. With hallucinations, for example … it is not enough to say that the subject perceives what is not found in the *perceptum* or of only asking if the subject believes this, and of thinking that this is not consistent. Why doesn't someone other than the subject experience it? … What Lacan stresses in verbal hallucinations is that they have their own linguistic structure and that it is not necessary to consider them as an error or a malady of the subject, but as exploitation of the structure itself of language. The subject does not unify perception; it is not a power of exterior synthesis of the perceived, but he is included …
>
> When the question is one of perception and more precisely of visual perception, of the relationship with the scopic, it is a matter of re-establishing the *percipiens* in the *perceptum*, of assuring and of basing the presence of the *percipiens* in the *perceptum*. One more presence, one "more" left out of classic theory. But there is also an absence. We must refer to Freud's concept of reality. The objectivity of reality implies, according to Freud … that the libido does not invade the perceptive field. This means that for Freud, the condition of objectivity of reality is a libidinal disinvestment. Its ingenuous translation is the ethics of the sensible scientist to

68 The most disturbing thing here is the Other's ignorance, as in the well-known dream in which I walk naked in the street or some other public place, but everyone ignores me and behaves as if nothing extraordinary is taking place—such a predicament is much more disturbing than expressions of shock at my nakedness.

> meticulously try not to employ his personal passion and to efface any libido, or at least the *libido sciendi*, to describe or investigate reality. But the ethical supposition of the scientist is translated into the exigency of delibidinalization of perception that Lacan renders in his code as extraction of the *objet petit a* and there, the condition of "the objectivity of reality"—in quotations, because the subject is always included, as Lacan says the *perceptum* is always impure—extorts that reality be a desert of *jouissance*.
>
> This *jouissance* is condensed in the *objet petit a* in such a way that the presence of the *percipiens* in the *perceptum* is correlative to what appears as an absence of surplus-*jouir*. When one studies vision, which one studies in psychology, in medicine, in ophthalmology, it is a relationship to reality without *jouissance*. This is why Lacan distinguishes the field of vision from what he calls the scopic field. What he calls the scopic field is reality and *jouissance*. Lacan developed a theory of the scopic field by studying how the drive presents itself in this field.[69]

This structure of the scopic field as opposed to the field of vision, this experience of "when I look at the world, I always somehow feel that things stare back at me"—as opposed to the pure Cartesian subject who perceives the world along clear geometric lines—provides the underlying minimal *dispositif* of religion. "God" is, at its most elementary, this Other's gaze returned by objects, an imagined gaze, for sure (we look for it in vain in reality), but no less real. This gaze exists only for a desiring subject, as the object-cause of its desire, not in reality (except for a psychotic). In passionate love, there are moments when the beloved feels that her lover sees in her something of which she herself is not aware—it is only through his gaze that she becomes aware of this dimension in her. What the beloved feels in those moments is "what is in herself more than herself," the *je ne sais quoi* which causes the lover's desire for her and which exists only for the lover's gaze, which is in a way the desire's objectal counterpart, the inscription of desire into its object. What the lover sees is the lost part of himself contained in (enveloped by) the Other. As such, the object-gaze cannot be reduced to an effect of the symbolic order (the big Other): "the gaze of the Other remains, even if the Other has ceased to exist."[70]

Due to its inexistence, the status of this immaterial object-cause is not ontological, but purely ethical—perhaps this feeling of an Other's gaze which "sees in me more than myself" is the zero-level deontological experience, what originally pushes me towards ethical activity whose goal is to render me adequate to the expectation written into the Other's gaze. One cannot but recall here the last two verses of Rilke's famous sonnet "Archaic Torso of Apollo": "*denn da ist keine Stelle / die dich nicht sieht. Du musst dein Leben aendern*" (for here there

69 Miller, "The Prisons of *Jouissance*," pp. 48–50.

70 Ibid., p. 55.

is no place that does not see you. You must change your life). Peter Sloterdijk, who used the second line as the title for a book,[71] noted the underlying enigmatic interdependence of the two statements: from the fact that there is no place (in the Thing which is Auguste Rodin's torso of Apollo) which does not gaze back at you, the call somehow follows that you (the viewer of the statue) must change your life—how? In his grandiose reading of Rilke's poem, in a subchapter entitled "The Order Out of the Stone," Sloterdijk illustrates how the torso regards or concerns me, addresses me, how the object returns the gaze—this gaze returned by the object is the "aura," the minimum of "religiosity," this ability to be affected by the Other/Thing's gaze, to "see it as seeing."[72] Subject and object exchange places here—but not wholly: I remain subject and the object remains object, for I do not become an object of the subjectivized big Other—this happens only in perversion. As Sloterdijk puts it, this gazing Other is fantasized, never part of reality, it is only "supposed" (*unterstellt*)—a supposed gaze.[73] Authentic religion never takes the fateful step beyond this supposed status of the Other gazing at us—the moment we accomplish this step, we find ourselves in psychosis: a psychotic knows himself to be looked at in reality. Therein also resides the ultimate difference between knowledge and belief: I can know the objects I look at (Descartes's perspective), but I can only believe that they return my gaze. More precisely, what returns the gaze is by definition the object and *not* another subject, as in psychosis. This is why, perhaps, there is nonetheless a psychotic core in every religion, insofar as every *religio* transforms the *Ding* into another Subject from which the gaze emanates. The clinical implications of this purely virtual status of the gaze (and the voice) are thus clear: what characterizes psychosis, the psychotic experience, is that this gaze is precisely no longer a virtual Real but falls into perceptible reality—a psychotic can "see" the object-gaze (or "hear" the object-voice). The key point to bear in mind is that the counterpoint to the psychotic is not a "normal" subject who sees only "what is really out there," but a subject of desire who relates to a virtual Real of the gaze or the voice:

> What Lacan designates as objects we cannot perceive. What he calls gaze or voice are objects whose substance, the substantiality, cannot be captured. What he calls voice is not the tone, it is not the breath, not even the feeling; the voice is what is already present in each signifying chain, and what he calls gaze is not something that is found in the eye or that comes out of the eye. That is, he gives to these objects, gaze and voice, a definition exterior to perception. We can all approach these two terms through perception but they are only really constituted when perception is not possible.

71 See Peter Sloterdijk, *Du mußt dein Leben ändern*, Frankfurt: Suhrkamp 2009.

72 Ibid., p. 45.

73 Ibid., p. 44.

> It is in the experience of the psychotic that the voice that no one can hear, that the gaze that no one can see, find their existence. It is in relation to the psychotic that Lacan finally introduces the theory of perception in order to detonate it, in order not to reduce the experience of the psychotic to supposedly normal experience. In the psychotic experience voice and gaze are not elided. It is the privilege of the psychotic to perceive Lacanian objects, voice and gaze. He perceives the voice present in each signifying chain. It is enough to have a signifying chain to have a voice, and it is enough to have an articulated thought in order to perceive the presence of a voice. Painfully, the psychotic experiences the gaze that comes from the world, but these are the "things themselves that gaze on him," something shows "itself." Thus the well known example of the sardine box, Lacan's famous little anecdote we remember that gives precisely a simulacrum of a psychotic experience. This object gazes at me myself and I am, myself, in the *perceptum* of this object. Lacan says that the frame is in my eye, and this is the truth of the theory of representation, but myself, I, am in the frame.[74]

It is at this point that Lacan's theory of visual art intervenes: with regard to the traumatic gaze embodied in an object, a painting is the process of "taming a shrew," it imprisons or tames this gaze:

> a tableau gives pleasure to the spectator who finds in reality something beautiful, and this appeases in him the anxiety of castration because nothing is lacking. The spectator can see the gaze in the tableau but it is an imprisoned gaze, the gaze materialized in the form of the stroke of the brush. Thus the tableau … is like a prison for the gaze. Lacan makes an exception for expressionist painting inasmuch as expressionist painting tries to activate the gaze that is in the tableau and inasmuch as the spectator feels gazed upon and captured by the spectacle.[75]

No wonder expressionism is usually associated with anxiety: anxiety arises when the gaze-object is displayed too directly.[76] Benjamin noted that the aura surrounding an object signals that it returns the gaze; he simply forgot to add that the auratic effect arises when this gaze is covered up, "gentrified"—the moment this cover is removed, the aura changes into a nightmare, the gaze becomes that of Medusa.

This brings us again to the key difference between the Cartesian subject of the geometric perspective and the Freudian subject of the curved space of desire:

74 Miller, "The Prisons of *Jouissance*," pp. 51–3.

75 Ibid., p. 54.

76 Note how for Lacan, in contrast to Heidegger and Freud, anxiety *has* its object, which is the object-cause of desire, the *objet petit a* in all its versions. Anxiety does not arise when the object is missing, but in the case of its over-proximity.

the object-gaze (or the object-voice) does not exist for a neutral gaze observing reality, but for a gaze sustained by desire; what I see in the object that I desire is the objectal counterpoint to my desire itself—in other words, I see my gaze itself as an object. Kant is here all too Cartesian, which is why the faculty of desire is for him thoroughly "pathological": there is for Kant no a priori object-cause of desire, every desire is a desire for some contingent "pathological" object. Lacan supplements Kant by way of extending the notion of transcendental critique to the faculty of desire: in the same way that, for Kant, our pure (theoretical) reason implies a priori universal forms, and in the same way that our "practical" faculty is also "pure," motivated by the a priori universality of the moral law, for Lacan, our faculty of desire is also "pure" since, beyond all "pathological" objects, it is sustained by non-empirical objects, which is why the most succinct formula for Lacan's endeavor is, in precise Kantian terms, the *critique of pure desire*. But what we should add (since this is not always clear to Lacan himself) is that this addition of a "pure faculty of desire" not only completes the Kantian edifice, but sets in motion its radical reconfiguration—in short, we have to move *from Kant to Hegel*. It is only with Hegel that the fundamental and constitutive "reflexivity" of desire is taken into account (a desire which is always already desire of/for a desire, that is a "desire of the Other" in all variations of this term: I desire what my Other desires; I want to be desired by my Other; my desire is structured by the big Other, the symbolic field in which I am embedded; my desire is sustained by the abyss of the real Other-Thing). What functions as an object in the curved space of such reflexivity of desire is an X which undermines the most elementary coordinates of modern philosophy, the opposition between objectivist realism and transcendental idealism. The object-cause of desire is neither part of substantial "objective reality" (we look for it in vain among the properties and components of the things around us) nor another subject, but the impossible/insubstantial "object" that is the desiring subject itself. The intervention of this purely virtual, inexistent but real, object which "is" the subject means that the subject cannot be located in "objective reality" as a part of it, that I cannot include myself in reality and see myself as part of reality, but neither can the subject posit itself as the agent of the transcendental constitution of reality. It is here that the move from Kant to Hegel has to be accomplished, the move from transcendental constitution to the dialectical self-inclusion of the subject into substance. Lacan's most succinct formula for this inclusion is: "The picture is in my eye, but me, I am in the picture." The picture is in my eye: as the transcendental subject I am the always already given horizon of all reality, but, at the same time, I myself am in the picture: I exist only through my counterpoint or counterpart in the very picture constituted by me; I as it were have to fall into my own picture, into the universe whose frame I constitute, in the same way that, in the Christian Incarnation, the creator God falls into his own creation.

From the transcendental standpoint, such an inclusion of the subject into its own *perceptum* can only be thought as the transcendental subject's constitution of itself as an element of (constituted) reality: I constitute "myself" as an inner-worldly entity, the "human person" that is "me," with a set of positive ontic properties, etc. But the self-inclusion of the transcendental I itself into the field of its own *perceptum* is nonsensical from the transcendental standpoint: the transcendental I is the a priori frame of reality which, for that very reason, is exempted from it. For Lacan, however, such a self-referential inclusion is precisely what happens with the *objet petit a*: the very transcendental I, $, is "inscribed into the picture" as its point of impossibility.

A statement is attributed to Hitler: "We have to kill the Jew within us." A. B. Yehoshua has provided an adequate commentary: "This devastating portrayal of the Jew as a kind of amorphous entity that can invade the identity of a non-Jew without his being able to detect or control it stems from the feeling that Jewish identity is extremely flexible, precisely because it is structured like a sort of atom whose core is surrounded by virtual electrons in a changing orbit."[77] In this sense, Jews are effectively the *objet petit a* of the Gentiles: what is "in the Gentiles more than the Gentiles themselves," not another subject that I encounter in front of me but an alien, a foreigner, within me, what Lacan called the lamella, an amorphous intruder of infinite plasticity, an undead "alien" monster which can never be pinned down to a determinate form. In this sense, Hitler's statement says more than it wants to say: against its intended sense, it confirms that the Gentiles need the anti-Semitic figure of the "Jew" in order to maintain their identity. It is thus not only that "the Jew is within us"—what Hitler fatefully forgot to add is that he, the anti-Semite, his identity, is also in the Jew.[78] Here we can again locate the difference between Kantian transcendentalism and Hegel: what they both see is, of course, that the anti-Semitic figure of the Jew is not to be reified (to put it naïvely, it does not fit "'real Jews"), but is an ideological fantasy ("projection"), it is "in my eye." What Hegel adds is that the subject who fantasizes the Jew is itself "in the picture," that its very existence hinges on the fantasy of the Jew as the "little bit of the Real" which sustains the consistency of its identity: take away the anti-Semitic fantasy, and the subject whose fantasy it is itself disintegrates. What matters is not the location of the Self in objective reality, the impossible-real of "what I am objectively," but *how I am located in my own fantasy*, how my own fantasy sustains my being as subject.

In philosophical terms, the task is to think the subject's emergence or becoming from the self-splitting of substance: the subject is not directly the

77 A. B. Yehoshua, "An Attempt to Identify the Root Cause of Antisemitism," *Azure* 32 (Spring 2008), p. 71.
78 I am here, of course, paraphrasing Lacan's statement: "The picture is in my eye, but me, I am in the picture."

Absolute, it emerges out of the self-blockage of substance, out of the impossibility of substance fully asserting itself as One. Hegel's position here is unique: the subject is the operator of the Absolute's (self-)finitization, and to "conceive the Absolute not only as Substance, but also as Subject" means to conceive the Absolute as failed, marked by an inherent impossibility. Or, to borrow terms from one interpretation of quantum physics: the Hegelian Absolute is *diffracted*, splintered by an inherent—virtual/real—impossibility/obstacle. The key turning point in the path towards Hegel is Fichte: the late Fichte was struggling with the right problem resolved later by Hegel. After radicalizing the Kantian transcendental subject into the self-positing "absolute I," Fichte then struggled till the end of his life with how to limit this absolute I, how to think the primacy of the trans-subjective absolute ("God") over the I without falling back into a pre-critical "dogmatism." (This problem is first outlined in Hölderlin's famous system-fragment.) Frederick Beiser is right to point out that the basic problem of all post-Kantian German Idealism is how to limit subjectivity: Fichte's attempt to think a trans-subjective Absolute is based on a correct insight, but he is unable to accomplish his task successfully; later, Schelling and Hegel offer two different ways out of this Fichtean deadlock.

Leave the screen empty!

The external gaze is "impossible" in the precise sense that its place is libidinally too strongly invested to be occupied by any human subject. Recall the magic moment from Hitchcock's *Vertigo* when, in Ernie's restaurant, Scottie sees Madeleine for the first time: this fascinating shot is *not* Scottie's point-of-view shot. It is only after Elster rejoins Madeleine, with the couple moving away from Scottie and approaching the restaurant exit, that we get, as a counter-shot to the shot of Scottie behind the bar, his point-of-view shot of Madeleine and Elster. This ambiguity of subjective and objective is crucial. Precisely insofar as Madeleine's profile is not Scottie's point of view, the shot of her profile is totally subjectivized, depicting, in a way, not what Scottie really sees, but what he imagines, that is, his hallucinatory inner vision (recall how, while we see Madeleine's profile, the red background of the restaurant wall seems to get even more intense, almost threatening to explode in red heat turning into a yellow blaze—as if Scottie's passion is directly inscribed into the background). No wonder, then, that although Scottie does not see Madeleine's profile he acts as if he is mysteriously captivated by it, deeply affected by it. In these two excessive shots, we encounter the "kino-eye" at its purest: as the shot which is somehow "subjectivized," without the subject being given.[79]

79 Such an impossible point of view is often mobilized in jokes. One contemporary

We thus have, twice, the same movement from the excess of "subjectivity without subject-agent" to the standard procedure of "suture" (the exchange of objective and subjective shots—we are first shown the person looking and then what he sees). The excess is thus "domesticated," captivated in being caught within the subject-object mirror relationship as exemplified by the exchange of objective shot and point-of-view counter-shot. This scene can be connected to another wonderful moment in the film, the evening scene in Judy's Empire Hotel room, to which the couple returns after dinner at Ernie's. In this scene, we see Judy's profile, which is completely dark (in contrast to Madeleine's dazzling profile at Ernie's). From this shot, we pass to a front shot of her face, the left half completely dark, and the right half a weird green (from the neon light outside the room).

Instead of reading this shot as simply designating Judy's inner conflict, it should be allowed its full ontological ambiguity: Judy is depicted here as a proto-entity, not yet ontologically constituted in full (a greenish ectoplasm plus darkness), as can be found in some versions of Gnosticism. It is as if, in order to fully exist, her dark half waits to be filled in with the ethereal image of Madeleine. In other words, here we have literally the other side of the magnificent profile shot of Madeleine at Ernie's, its negative: the previously unseen dark half of Madeleine (the green anguished face of Judy), plus the dark half to be filled in by Madeleine's dazzling profile. At this very point at which Judy is reduced to less-than-an-object, to a formless pre-ontological stain, she is *subjectivized*—this anguished half-face, totally unsure of itself, designates the birth of the subject. Recall the proverbial imaginary resolution of Zeno's paradox of infinite divisibility: if we continue the division long enough, we will finally stumble upon a point at which a part will no longer be divided into smaller parts, but into a (smaller) part *and nothing*—this nothing "is" the subject. Is this not, exactly, the division of Judy in the above-mentioned shot? We see half of her face, while the other half is a dark void. And, again, the task is to leave this void empty, not to fill it up by projecting onto it the disgusting slime called the "wealth of personality."

This void is not the result of an "abstraction" from the concrete fullness of human existence; this void is primordial, constitutive of subjectivity, it precedes any content which might fill it up. And it poses a limit to the common-sense idea that our conversation with others should follow the path of straightforward sincerity, avoiding the extremes of both hypocritical etiquette and unwarranted

---

Chinese sexual joke relates a conversation between twin brothers who are still fetuses in their mother's womb. One says to the other: "I love it when our father visits us, but why is he so rude at the end of each visit, spitting all over us?" The other replies: "True, our uncle is much nicer: he always comes with a nice hat made of rubber on his head, so that he doesn't spit on us!"

intrusive intimacy. Perhaps the time has come to acknowledge that this *imaginary* middle road has to be supplemented with both its extreme poles: the "cold" discretion of *symbolic* etiquette which allows us to maintain a distance towards our neighbors, as well as the (exceptional) risk of obscenity which allows us to establish a link with the other in the *Real* of his/her *jouissance*.

Let us conclude with a more political example of resisting the urge to project. The theologico-political topic of the King's Two Bodies (developed by Ernst Kantorowicz in his classic work of the same title) returns violently in Stalinism, in the guise of the Leader's two bodies (recall the Stalinist procedures for dealing with the Leader's body, from retouching photos to conserving the body in a mausoleum). As Eric Santner has pointed out, the sublime body's obverse is a rotting undead body, disgusting in the literal German sense of *entsetzlich*, de-posed, what remains after the king loses his title. This remainder is not the king's biological body, but the excess of an "undead" horrible specter; this is why the Stalinists put the dead Leader's body in a mausoleum: to prevent its putrefaction.[80]

When the sovereignty of the State shifts from King to People, the problem becomes that of the people's Body, of how to incarnate the People, and the most radical solution is to treat the Leader as the People incarnated. In between these two extremes, there are many other possibilities—consider the uniqueness of Jacques-Louis David's *The Death of Marat*, "the first modernist painting," according to T. J. Clark. The oddity of the painting's overall structure is seldom noted: its upper half is almost totally black. (This is not a realistic detail: the room in which Marat actually died had lively wallpaper.) What does this black void stand for? The opaque body of the People, the impossibility of representing the People? It is as if the opaque background of the painting (the People) invades it, occupying its entire upper half. What happens here is structurally homologous to a formal procedure often found in *film noir* and Orson Welles movies, when the discord between figure and background is mobilized: when a figure moves in a room, the effect is that the two are somehow ontologically separated, as in a clumsy rear-projection shot in which one can clearly see that the actor is not really in a room, but just moving in front of a screen onto which the image of a room is projected. In *The Death of Marat*, it appears as if we see Marat in his bathtub in front of a dark screen onto which the fake background

80 The scandal of Dominique Strauss-Kahn's alleged rape of a chambermaid in New York, which erupted in early 2011, confronted us with a new variation on the topic of the "king's two bodies." Here we had the banker's two bodies: the "infinite judgment on DSK" asserts the ultimate identity of the sublime body of a top banker and the ridiculous tumescent body of a compulsive seducer. Something similar can be found in films like *Percy Jackson* and *Thor*, where, respectively, an Ancient Greek and a Nordic god (Perseus, Thor) find themselves in the body of a confused US adolescent.

has not yet been projected—this is why the effect can also be described as one of anamorphosis: we see the figure, while the background remains an opaque stain; in order to see the background, we would have to blur the figure. But what is impossible is to get the figure and the background in the same focus.

Is this not also the logic of the Jacobin Terror—individuals must be annihilated in order to make the People visible; the People's Will can be made visible only through the terrorist destruction of the individual's body? Therein resides the uniqueness of *The Death of Marat*: it concedes that one cannot blur the individual in order to represent the People directly—all one can do to come as close as possible to an image of the People is to show the individual at the point of his disappearance—his tortured, mutilated dead body against the background of the blur that "is" the People.

There is nonetheless a minimal sublimation at work here: what we see in *The Death of Marat* is Marat's (sublime) body, not his (scarred) flesh. That is to say, we all know Marat suffered from a disease which covered his skin with scars and caused constant itching—his flesh was almost literally burning. The only way to avoid the pain and the constant pressure to scratch was to be submerged in water. The "real" Marat was thus like a "creature from the lagoon" incapable of surviving in fresh air and light, who can thrive only in an "unnatural" aquatic element. Significantly, David omits this feature in his portrait (just as portraits of Stalin omit the scars which besmirch his face): Marat's skin on the parts of his body that we can see (face, shoulders, and arms) is smooth and shiny, plus there is a clear desexualization of his face, with its softly rounded, almost feminine features. Referring to the Paulinian opposition between body and flesh (a Christian gets rid of flesh and enters Corpus Christi, the body of the Church), where flesh belongs to the Jews caught up in the cycle of the Law and its transgression (the Law makes flesh out of the body), one can say that *The Death of Marat* also transforms the flesh of the "real" Marat into a body, in accordance with the Christological aspects of the painting (Marat's hand hanging in a Christ-like way; his sacrifice for the People, bringing them freedom and thus redeeming them, etc.). One usually talks here about a failed Christ—but why failed? As Thomas Altizer pointed out, in Christianity also only suffering can be vividly represented, not the heavenly bliss that comes afterwards.

It is quite impressive that this uneasy and disturbing painting was adored by the revolutionary crowds in Paris—proof that Jacobinism was not yet "totalitarian," that it did not yet rely on the fantasmatic logic of a Leader who *is* the People. Under Stalin, such a painting would have been unimaginable, the upper part would have had to have been filled in—with, say, the dream of the dying Marat, depicting the happy life of a free people dancing and celebrating their freedom. The greatness of the Jacobins lay in their attempt to keep the screen empty, to resist filling it in with ideological projections. They thereby set in motion a process which, in art, culminated in the minimalism of Kazimir Malevich, with his reduction of painting to the act of registering the minimal, purely formal difference between the frame and its background: Malevich is to the October Revolution what Marat was to the French Revolution.

After the minimalist radicality of his paintings of the 1910s and the early 1920s, with their variations on the motif of a square on a surface, Malevich's last decade (1925–35) is marked by a return to figurative painting; it is, of course, not the old realism, the figures are "flat," composed of abstract color patches, but the patches are nonetheless clearly recognizable as figures (mostly of women and peasants). Can this return be written off as a mere compromise with the new cultural politics, as bowing to official pressure? Malevich himself signals his persistence, his fidelity to his "minimalist" breakthrough, in his late realistic *Self-Portrait* (1933), where the open hand with outstretched fingers sketches the outline of the absent square. The same goes for *Portrait of the Artist's Wife* and *Woman Worker* from the same year: the virgin Mary becomes a worker, the child Christ disappears, but the hands retain the imprint of the child's form.[81] We should bear in mind that the minimalism of the "square and surface" paintings was not an asymptotic zero-point, but a starting point, a clearing-of-the-decks ahead of a new beginning. The end is always a new beginning, which is why we should reject the topic of the asymptotic approach to zero: one is never quite there, where the Real Thing is, one can only reach the point of minimal difference/distance, of being almost there. The Hegelian lesson is that the zero-point is the point one must pass through in order to start again "from zero"—in art, Malevich's black square on a white surface is such a marking of the liminal zero-point of minimal difference which creates the conditions for a new beginning.

What, however, does his return to figurality indicate? From the late 1920s, Malevich not only made many paintings of peasants (and also workers and sportsmen), he himself started to dress like one. His peasants are painted in an abstract-desubjectivized mode: figures reduced to brightly colored flat forms, with faces simplified to a black circle or divided geometrically into symmetric colored parts, as in *Young Girls in the Fields* (1928–32), *Sportsmen* (1928–32), *Peasant Woman* (1930), *Peasants* (1930), *Red Figure* (1928–32), and *Running Man* (early 1930s—behind the figure of the running man there is a red cross). How to read this desubjectivization? Do we really have here a defense of the peasantry against brutal mechanization and collectivization? "Faces without faces, faces that have lost their beards, dummies without arms, stigmatised or crucified beings: Malevich's icons show humanity to be the victim of some nihilistic apocalyptic devastation. They are as if frozen in expectation of world's end."[82]

---

81 It is significant that persistence is signaled by the hand acting as an autonomous "organ without a body," delivering a message of its own.

82 Gilles Neret, *Malevich*, Köln: Taschen 2003, p. 84.

But if this is the message, then it presupposes as its standard a fully realistic portrait of peasants with rich features; in other words, such a reading would imply that Malevich abandoned his minimalist breakthrough, retroactively reinterpreting it as a depiction of the "soullessness" of modern man, not as an act of artistic liberation. If, on the contrary, we take into account Malevich's continuing fidelity to his minimalism, then the peasants' "faceless faces" can be read as the instantiation of a new dimension of subjectivity, of the post-psychological "desubjectivized subject."

Such a reading allows us to establish an unexpected link between Malevich and Hitchcock's *Vertigo*: the black patches which depict faces in Malevich's late paintings belong to the same series as the black profile of Judy's head in *Vertigo*. Furthermore, with regard to the history of painting, one can posit Malevich as the third, concluding, term in the series David–Munch–Malevich. Recall Munch's *Madonna*, where the voluptuous feminine body is drawn within a double-lined frame; in the tiny space between the two lines of the frame, among the floating sperm-like drops, we recognize a small homunculus, none other than the figure from *The Scream*. This homunculus is desperate not because of a lack or void, but because it is overwhelmed by the flux of excessive enjoyment: the Madonna versus the sperm in the frame stands for the incestuous Enjoyment-Thing versus the remainders of surplus-enjoyment.

The line that runs from David through Munch to Malevich is thus clear. In Munch, the figure of "Marat" is squeezed into the frame, reduced to a homunculus, while the dark void that covers most of David's painting is here filled in by the impossible incestuous object. In Malevich's square, we get a kind of ironic negation of the negation: the reduction is total, both the frame and the center are reduced to nothing, all that remains is the minimal difference, the purely formal line which separates the frame from the content it encircles.

INTERLUDE 6

Cognitivism and the Loop of Self-Positing

When a certain discipline is in crisis, attempts are made to change or supplement its theses *within* its basic framework—a procedure one might call "Ptolemization" (after data poured in which clashed with Ptolemy's Earth-centered astronomy, his supporters introduced additional complications to account for the new data); then, the true "Copernican" revolution takes place, which, instead of just adding additional complications and modifying minor premises, changes the basic framework itself. So when we are dealing with a self-professed "scientific revolution," the question to ask is always whether it is truly a Copernican revolution, or merely a Ptolemization of the old paradigm. Two examples of the latter: there are good reasons to claim that "string theory," which pretends to provide the foundations of the unified theory (combining relativity theory and quantum physics by accounting in a single theoretical framework for all four elementary forces), is still an attempt at Ptolemization, and that we are still waiting for a new beginning which will require an even more radical change in our basic presuppositions (something like abandoning time or space as the basic constituent of reality).[1] In social theory, there are also good reasons for claiming that all the "new paradigm" proposals about our epoch (that we are entering a post-industrial, postmodern, risk, or informational society, and so on) remain so many Ptolemizations of the "old paradigm" of the classic sociological models.

The question is: how do things stand with psychoanalysis? Although Freud presented his discovery as a Copernican revolution, the fundamental premise of the cognitive sciences is that psychoanalysis remains a "Ptolemization" of classical psychology, failing to really abandon its most basic premises.[2] Only with today's brain sciences do we have the true revolution, namely that, for the first time, we are approaching a scientific understanding of the emergence of consciousness. Catherine Malabou draws a radical consequence from the cognitivist standpoint: the task now is not to supplement the Freudian unconscious with the cerebral unconscious, but to replace the former with the latter—once we accept the cerebral unconscious, there is no longer any space for the Freudian version.

1 See Lee Smolin, *The Trouble with Physics*, New York: Houghton Mifflin Company 2006.

2 And, incidentally, post-classical economists make the same claim about Marx: his critique of Smith and Ricardo amounts to their Ptolemization.

There is, however, one problem with this easy and clear solution: reading the classic cognitivists, one cannot help noting how their description of consciousness at the phenomenal-experiential level is very traditional and pre-Freudian. Recall Damasio's narrative of the gradual emergence of Self: first there is the "proto-Self" as the agent which regulates the homeostasis of the body, the self-organizing agent which maintains the body within the limits of stability and self-reproduction. This, however, is not yet the domain of the "mental" proper: the "proto-Self" is followed by the emergence of self-awareness, the singular "I," and, finally, by the "autobiographic Self," the organization of the narrative-history of "what I am."[3] Two related points should be noted here. First, the common-sense simplicity of this description, which perfectly fits the naïve-evolutionist notion of how the Self must have developed. Second: as such, this description stands on its own, it is fully understandable without its neurological-scientific foundation (without the precise description of the neuronal foundations of the psychic life). The key question here is what happens when this description is replaced with the much more counter-intuitive Freudo-Lacanian description, with its paradoxes of the "death drive," formations of the unconscious, and so forth? One cannot avoid the simple fact that the epistemological function of the development of the neuronal foundation of the Self is to enable us to get rid of the paradoxes of the Freudian subject, so that we can return to the naïve pre-Freudian figure of the Self, this time legitimized by the neurological-scientific notional edifice.

Against this cognitivist dismissal, we should rehabilitate psychoanalysis in its philosophical core—as a theory indebted to Hegel's dialectic and only readable against this background. This may well appear as the worst possible move to make: trying to save psychoanalysis, a discredited theory (and practice), with reference to an even more discredited theory, the worst of speculative philosophy rendered irrelevant by the progress of modern science. However, as Lacan pointed out, when we are confronted with an apparently clear choice, the correct thing is sometimes to choose the worst.

We are dealing here with four basic positions: (1) our common everyday understanding of what we are as Selves; (2) the philosophical understanding of the Self (which reaches its peak in German Idealism and its notion of the transcendental I); (3) theories of the Self in contemporary cognitivism and brain sciences; (4) the psychoanalytic (Freudian, Lacanian) notion of the subject. The implicit premise of the brain sciences is that positions (2) and (4) are historical curiosities which have no inherent role to play in our knowledge of the human mind—all we really need is our everyday understanding of the Self (which, even if false, is part of our pre-theoretical experience and, as such, has to be accounted

3 See Chapters V and VI of Antonio Damasio, *The Feeling of What Happens*, London: Vintage 2000.

for) and scientific theories which explain that Self.[4] The task is to see if (2) and (4) are really basically irrelevant, or if they indicate a dimension missed not only in our everyday experience, but also by cognitivism and the brain sciences.

Let us begin with some strange echoes between cognitivism and German Idealism. Does not the title of Douglas Hofstadter's book on the paradoxes of (self-)consciousness, *I Am a Strange Loop*, best capture Fichte's early thought?[5] Hofstadter understands his work as a contribution to the "self-referentialist" theory of consciousness—the underlying idea is not a simple "reductionist" neurological materialism (a search for the material-neuronal substrate of consciousness), but a much more interesting one: independently of its material (neuronal) support, a certain abstract-formal paradoxical structure of self-referentiality at the level of thinking itself is constitutive of consciousness. As is usually the case, Hofstadter understands this self-referentiality in terms of Gödel's theorem.

In order to explain the illusion of consciousness, of the Self as a clearly delimitated self-identical entity, Hofstadter reports on a personal experience which, at first glance, may appear convincing as a metaphor but is much more weird in its presuppositions and consequences. Taking hold of a pack of envelopes in a box, all of a sudden he "felt, between my thumb and fingers, something very surprising. Oddly enough, there was a *marble* sitting (or floating?) right in the middle of that flimsy little cardboard box!"[6] He inspected the package envelope by envelope, looking for the small, firm object which must have somehow found its way there, but there was nothing. Finally, "it dawned on me that there wasn't any marble in there at all, but that there was something that *felt* for all the world exactly like a marble":

> It was an *epiphenomenon* caused by the fact that, for each envelope, at the vertex of the "V" made by the flap, there is a triple layer of paper as well as a thin layer of glue. An unintended consequence of this innocent design decision is that when you squeeze down on a hundred such envelopes all precisely aligned with each other, you can't compress that little zone as much as the other zones.[7]

Hofstadter's point, of course, is that the Self in its firm self-identity—the Cartesian Ego—is an exactly homologous "large-scale illusion created by the

---

4 Even if some theories in (3) and (4) are treated with sympathy by brain scientists—see, for example, Damasio's celebration of Spinoza—they are reduced to precursors of brain sciences: Damasio's point is simply, "Look how much Spinoza had already guessed about what we know today about the Self!"

5 Douglas Hofstadter, *I Am a Strange Loop*, New York: Basic Books 2007.

6 Ibid., p. 92.

7 Ibid., p. 93.

collusion of many small and indisputably non-illusory events."[8] Our everyday experience finds it difficult to accept that my "*me*-ness is more like a shimmering elusive rainbow than it is like a solid, mass-possessing rock":[9] "We believe in marbles that disintegrate when we search for them but that are as real as any genuine marble when we're not looking for them."[10] Recall the famous formula of phrenology from Hegel's *Phenomenology*: "the Spirit is a bone (crane)." Hofstadter here offers as a common-sense view of the Self a similar formula: "The spirit is a stone (marble)." But was not this common-sense view of the Self as a substantial thing undermined long ago by David Hume? Here is his classic formulation:

> It must be some one impression that gives rise to every real idea. But self or person is not any one impression, but that to which our several impressions and ideas are supposed to have a reference. If any impression gives rise to the idea of self, that impression must continue invariably the same, through the whole course of our lives; since self is supposed to exist after that manner. But there is no impression constant and invariable. Pain and pleasure, grief and joy, passions and sensations succeed each other, and never all exist at the same time. It cannot therefore be from any of these impressions, or from any other, that the idea of self is derived; and consequently there is no such idea ... For my part, when I enter most intimately into what I call myself, I always stumble on some particular perception or other, of heat or cold, light or shade, love or hatred, pain or pleasure. I never can catch myself at any time without a perception, and never can observe any thing but the perception ... If any one, upon serious and unprejudiced reflection, thinks he has a different notion of himself, I must confess I can reason no longer with him. All I can allow him is, that he may be in the right as well as I, and that we are essentially different in this particular. He may, perhaps, perceive something simple and continued, which he calls himself; though I am certain there is no such principle in me.[11]

The mention of Hume is important here because his position on the non-existence of a substantial Self draws attention to another key distinction which is ignored by Hofstadter, for whom the only alternative is that between (1) our higher-level, spontaneously illusory (self-)perception of the I as an isolated monad, a firm, self-identical mental agent who is exempted from the laws of material reality and, as such, "freely" causes its actions, and (2) the lower-level reality of neuronal loops etc.—all that which the I "really is" but is unable to perceive itself as such. However, what Hume does when he turns his gaze upon

8 Ibid.

9 Ibid., p. 360.

10 Ibid., p. 363.

11 David Hume, *A Treatise of Human Nature*, Book I, Part 4, Section 6, available online at anselm.edu.

the Self and discovers the illusory character of its substantial identity is neither (1) nor (2): he undermines the perception of Self as a stable "marble," but *not* through any scientific insight into the neuronal basis of consciousness—he simply provides a close description of our stream-of-consciousness itself, demonstrating that the stable identity of the Self is not a spontaneous illusion of our experience, but the result of our imposing upon our immediate experience a set of metaphysical concepts. As James Giles notes, Hofstadter thereby confounds scientific reductionism and the no-self theory which is

> more phenomenologically based than are the reductionist theories. To borrow Husserl's phrase, it goes back to the things themselves. That is, it starts with an examination of experience rather than with an attachment to the project of how to account for personal identity. This does not mean, of course, that the no-self theory need not face the issue of why someone might come to believe in his own identity. For if there is no such thing as personal identity, then it is essential that we can offer some other account of why someone might be led to think there is …

In the earliest texts of Buddhism, we come across a distinction drawn between two types of discourse: that of direct meaning and that of indirect meaning. The former type of discourse is said to be one whose meaning is plain while the latter type needs to have its meaning inferred with reference to the former. In the discourses of indirect meaning, words are used which apparently refer to persisting entities such as a self or an I which, according to the Buddha, are merely "expressions, turns of speech, designations in common use in the world which the Tathagata (i.e., the Buddha) makes use of without being led astray by them." That is, although we may use words like "self" and "I," we should not be led into thinking that they actually refer to something, for they are but grammatical devices. This non-denoting aspect of these expressions is something which must be inferred in light of the discourses of direct meaning. In this latter type of discourse, the non-existence of anything permanent or enduring, such as the self or I, is asserted, and the misleading features of language—those features which lead us astray into the belief in an I—are made explicit. Here there is no need for inference, since the meaning of such discourse is plain.

Although the Buddha cites various characteristics that something must have if it is to be considered a self, the most important is that of permanence or identity over time. But when we look to our experience, there is nothing but impermanence: our bodies, feelings, and thoughts are forever coming and going. In this sense the Buddha is in complete agreement with Hume: where there is diversity there can be no identity.[12]

12 James Giles, "The No-Self Theory: Hume, Buddhism, and Personal Identity," *Philosophy East and West*, Vol. 43 (1993), available online at http://ccbs.ntu.edu.tw.

This brings us to the passage from Hume to Kant: while Hume endeavors to demonstrate how there is no Self (when we look into ourselves, we only encounter particular ideas, impressions, etc.—no "Self" as such), Kant claims that this void *is* the Self. The proper Kantian answer to Hume's argument against the Self (when I look into myself, I see a multitude of particular affects, notions, etc., but I never find a "Self" as an object of my perception) is a kind of Rabinovitch joke: "When you look into yourself, you can discover your Self." "But I see no Self there, there is nothing in me beyond the multiplicity of representations!" "Well, the subject is precisely this Nothing!" The limitation of Buddhism is that it is not able to accomplish this second step—it remains stuck at the insight that "there is no true Self." All the German Idealists insist on this point: while Kant just leaves it empty (as the transcendental Ego—the inaccessible Thing), Fichte endlessly emphasizes that the I is not a thing, but purely processual, only a process of its appearing-to-itself; Hegel does the same. They would have been the first to laugh at what Hofstadter presents as the idealist (dualist) view:

> The problem is that, in a sense, an "I" is something created out of nothing. And since making something out of nothing is never possible, the alleged something turns out to be an illusion, in the end, but a very powerful one, like the marble among the envelopes. However, the "I" is an illusion far more entrenched and recalcitrant than the marble illusion, because in the case of "I," there is no simple revelatory act corresponding to turning the box upside down and shaking it, then peering in between the envelopes and finding nothing solid and spherical in there. We don't have access to the inner workings of our brains. And so the only perspective we have on our "I"-ness marble comes from the counterpart to squeezing all the envelopes at once, and *that* perspective says it's real![13]

This is patently wrong: we *do* have an exact counterpart to the "simple revelatory act corresponding to turning the box upside down and shaking it, then peering in between the envelopes and finding nothing solid and spherical in there," namely, the simple act of focusing our gaze upon our Self itself and discovering precisely that there is "nothing solid and spherical in there," the act performed in modern philosophy in an exemplary way by Hume (but performed long ago already by Buddhist thinkers).

The post-Humean critical-transcendental idealists, from Kant to Hegel, do *not* return to the pre-critical, rock-like, solid, substantial identity of the Ego—what they struggled with was precisely how to describe the Self which has no substantial identity (as was stated by Kant in his critique of Descartes's own reading of *cogito* as *res cogitans*, "a thing that thinks"), but nonetheless functions

---

13 Hofstadter, *I Am a Strange Loop*, p. 292.

as the irreducible point of reference—here is Kant's unsurpassable formulation in his *Critique of Pure Reason*:

> The simple, and in itself completely empty, representation 'I' ... we cannot even say that this is a concept, but only that it is a bare consciousness which accompanies all concepts. Through this I or he or it (the thing) which thinks, nothing further is represented than a transcendental subject of the thoughts = X. It is known only through the thoughts which are its predicates, and of it, apart from them, we cannot have any concept whatsoever, but can only revolve in a perpetual circle, since any judgment upon it has always already made use of its representation.[14]

Kant thus prohibits the passage from "I think" to "I am a thing that thinks": of course there has to be some noumenal basis for (self-)consciousness, of course I must be "something" objectively, but the point is precisely that this dimension is forever inaccessible to the I—and co-substantial with the very (f)act of the I. A Self that "knew itself objectively" would no longer be a Self.[15]

So when Hofstadter proposes to "see the 'I' as a hallucination perceived by a hallucination, which sounds pretty strange, or perhaps even stranger: the 'I' as a hallucination *hallucinated* by a hallucination," the problem with this statement is not its strangeness, its shocking impact for common-sense understanding, nor its apparent paradox (at the end of the line, there must be some reality in which hallucinations are grounded; that is, the loop of self-relating hallucinations cannot be complete—it would imply the same nonsensical paradox as Escher's two hands drawing each other; or, as Descartes would have put it, even if everything is just hallucinated, there must be some X which does the hallucinating), but, on the contrary, that it remains all too much within the confines of the *common-sense* distinction between basic reality and higher-level illusions.[16] What Hofstadter cannot see is how it is the higher-level "illusion" which transforms the pre-ontological blur of the Real into substantial reality. In Hegelese, in "a hallucination *hallucinated* by a hallucination," hallucinating is self-sublated through its very self-relating, and a new "reality" is established.

In a way, Fichte says the same thing when he claims that the I exists only for the I, that mental representation exists only for the mental representation,

14 Immanuel Kant, *Critique of Pure Reason*, trans. Norman Kemp Smith, London: Macmillan 1929, p. 331.

15 The passage from Kant to post-Kantian idealism is crucial here, involving as it does *not* a return to pre-critical access to the absolute reality of the I, but a radical shift in perspective, so that the problem itself appears as its own solution—what if the negativity that pertains to the I, its constitutive inability to locate itself "objectively," is not just epistemological but ontological, and as such its *positive* feature? What if the I *is* the void of negativity?

16 Hofstadter, *I Am a Strange Loop*, p. 293.

that it has no "objective" existence external to this loop. So when Hofstadter defines (self-)consciousness as a hallucination perceived by a hallucination, he is here not "too radical," pushing things towards a paradox unacceptable to our common sense, but *not radical enough*: what he does not see (and what Fichte clearly saw), is that the paradoxical redoubling of hallucination (a hallucination itself perceived by a hallucination, that is by a hallucinatory entity) cancels (sublates) itself, generating a new reality of its own.

There is, of course, a way to account for the paradox of "a hallucination itself perceived by a hallucination" without getting caught up in a meaningless, vicious cycle: *stricto sensu*, it is not a hallucination that perceives a hallucination; it is just that the asubjective neuronal process (the "really existing" foundation of the process of perception), together with the illusion that we directly perceive reality, generates the illusion that the agent of perception is a Self—both poles of the perceptual process, the perceived content and the perceiving subject, are in this sense hallucinations, and there is no paradox involved here. Thomas Metzinger has developed this position in detail;[17] according to him, human phenomenal experience is a dynamic multi-dimensional map of the world—but with a twist: "like only very few of the *external* maps used by human beings, it also has a little red arrow ... the phenomenal self *is* the little red arrow in your conscious map of reality."[18] Metzinger here refers to city, airport, or shopping-mall maps in which a little red arrow indicates the observer's location within the mapped space ("You are here!"):

> Mental self-models are the little red arrows that help a phenomenal geographer to navigate her own complex mental map of reality ... The most important difference between the little red arrow on the subway map and the little red arrow in our neurophenomenological troglodyte's brain is that the external arrow is *opaque*. It is always clear that it is only a representation—a placeholder for something else ... The conscious self-model in the caveman's brain itself, however, is in large portions transparent: ... it is a phenomenal self characterized not only by full-blown prereflexive embodiment but by the comprehensive, all-encompassing subjective experience of *being situated*.[19]

This "red arrow," of course, is what Lacan called the signifier which represents the subject for other signifiers. Metzinger illustrates our total immersion in the map with the metaphor of a *total flight simulator*:

---

17 Thomas Metzinger, *Being No One: The Self-Model Theory of Subjectivity*, Cambridge, MA: MIT Press 2004, p. 331.

18 Ibid., p. 551.

19 Ibid., p. 552.

> The brain differs from the flight simulator in not being used by a student pilot, who episodically "enters" it ... A total flight simulator is a self-modeling airplane that has always flown without a pilot and has generated a complex internal image of itself within its *own* internal flight simulator. The image is transparent. The information that it is an internally generated image is not yet available to the system as a whole ... Like the neurophenomenological caveman, "the pilot" is born into a virtual reality right from the beginning—without a chance to ever discover this fact.[20]

Again, how to avoid the vicious circle in this version of Plato's Cave argument? A cavern projects an image of itself onto the cave wall, and *it generates-simulates the observer itself*—but is it not the case that, while the cave can simulate the substantial identity or content of the observer, it cannot simulate the *function* of the observer, since, in this case, we would have a fiction observing itself? In other words, while what the observer immediately identifies with in the experience of self-awareness is a fiction, something with no positive ontological status, *his very activity of observing is a positive ontological fact.* Metzinger's (and Hofstadter's) solution is to distinguish between the reality of the observing process (there is no "observer" as an autonomous Self, just the asubjective neuronal process) and the "transparent" (self-)perception of the agent of this process as a Self. In other words, the distinction between appearance (of phenomenal "transparent" reality) and reality in transposed into the perceiving process itself.

But does this solution actually work? In his analysis of the Cartesian "I am certain that I exist," Metzinger introduces a distinction very close to Lacan's own between the "subject of the enunciation" and the "subject of the enunciated."[21] Crucial for Metzinger is the distinct status of the two "I"s in "I am certain that I exist": while the second "I" simply designates the content of the *transparent* self-model—Lacan's "subject of the enunciated," the ego as an *object*—the first "I" stands for the *opaque* component of the very thinker that thinks (i.e., generates) this thought—Lacan's "subject of the enunciation." The Cartesian confusion is that the self-transparent thinking substance which directly experiences itself is generated by the illegitimate identification of the two I's, where the first is embedded in the second: the opaque component "has already been *embedded* in the continuously active background of the transparent self-model."[22] In other words, although the first "I" (the X that thinks this very thought) undoubtedly refers to *something*, to a system that generates this thought, "[w]hat is not clear is if this system is actually a *self*."[23]

20 Ibid., p. 557.
21 Ibid., pp. 398–403.
22 Ibid., p. 401.
23 Ibid., p. 405.

But here we are in for a surprise: this distinction was already known to Kant, who, as we have seen, emphasized the thoroughly non-substantial character of the subject and defined its noumenal substratum as the "I or he or it that thinks," effectively implying that the ignorance of one's own noumenal nature is a positive condition of thinking subjectivity. There is, however, something more in Kant, a key element which missing in Metzinger: the thoroughly non-substantial "I," to be distinguished from its noumenal substratum, is also not what Kant calls a "person," the positive phenomenal content of subjectivity, including all the psychological wealth of desires, dreams, knowledge, abilities, etc., which form my personality and which is what Metzinger calls the conscious "self-model" of the brain. The "I" is neither noumenal nor phenomenal, neither the I's asubjective neuronal substratum nor my representation of myself. This is what is missing in Metzinger. Let us quote him again: "The most important difference between the little red arrow on the subway map and the little red arrow in our neurophenomenological troglodyte's brain is that the external arrow is *opaque*. It is always clear that it is only a representation—a place-holder for something else." The Kantian reply is that the "red arrow" that holds the place of the I in the I's cognitive mapping is also "only a representation—a place-holder for something else"—however, this "something else" is not the I's neuronal substratum, but the I itself as the empty point of (self-)reference, what Lacan calls the "barred subject," $. This subject precisely *cannot* be in the map—to put it in the map would amount to the subject's full self-objectivization, for in it, I would be able to see myself "objectively," as a part of the world. The paradox is here a very precise one: the "red arrow" that holds the place of the I in the I's cognitive map is "only a representation—a place-holder for something else," but a representation of what? Not of something, but of *nothing*. "I" am not just my self-model, the content of my self-representation, but that elusive X to which this content appears, the "myself" which cannot be yet another appearance, since it is that to which/whom appearance appears *as* appearance. In other words, for the distance between noumenal and phenomenal, between my neuronal substratum and my self-model, to persist, a *third* virtual term is needed—appearance cannot appear to another appearance, but it also cannot appear to reality itself. The "subject" is *the non-phenomenal support of appearance*: it is not part of reality, since, as Fichte clearly saw, a subject exists only for a subject; that is, there is no subject for an external "objective" view; but it is also not another appearance.

In order to account for the Self, we should thus problematize the standard opposition between appearance and reality (where appearance is precisely a "mere appearance") and accept the embarrassing paradox encountered by the twentieth-century "hard" sciences: in (among others) quantum physics, the "appearance" (perception) of a particle determines its reality—the very emergence of "hard reality" out of the quantum fluctuation through the collapse of the wave function is the outcome of observation, of the intervention of consciousness. This notion of the ontological superiority of appearances is difficult to accept—no wonder it is often shared by otherwise fierce opponents: Hofstadter here shares a key premise with his official opponent, David Chalmers, whom he often mocks. When, in his argument against the reductive explanation of consciousness, Chalmers writes that "even if we knew every last detail about the physics of the universe—the configuration, causation, and evolution among all the fields and particles in the spatiotemporal manifold—*that* information would not lead us to postulate the existence of conscious experience," he commits the standard Kantian mistake: such total knowledge is strictly nonsensical, epistemologically *and* ontologically.[24] It is the obverse of the vulgar determinist notion, articulated in Marxism by Nikolai Bukharin when he wrote that, if we knew all physical reality, we would also be able to predict precisely the emergence of a revolution. This line of reasoning—consciousness as an excess, surplus, over the physical totality—is misleading, since it has to evoke a meaningless hyperbole: when we imagine the Whole of reality, there is no longer any place for consciousness (and subjectivity). There are two options here: either subjectivity is an illusion, or reality is *in itself* (and not only epistemologically) not-All. The premise Hofstadter shares is that of the theoretical possibility of a total description of reality at the most basic level—the difference is that he draws from it the opposite conclusion: he thinks that at this level, it would be possible to account for consciousness.

Hofstadter conceives of the I as an agent in parallel with how we spontaneously perceive higher-level processes, ignoring their lower-level substratum. When a high wave approaches the seashore, we perceive it as a substantial entity moving across the surface of the water; but this wave has no substantial identity, its atoms are changing all the time—what is "really going on" is that an infinitely complex interaction of water and other molecules generates the effect of the same wave moving across the ocean. This is an effect of the spontaneous "thinkodynamics" of our psychic life: to avoid the infinite complexity of what really is going on, we construct higher-level entities and perceive them as "agents." The same goes for the I: when we see a person perform an act, we cannot afford to analyze the infinitely complex interaction of brain and muscle (and, at an even lower level, of the elementary particles) which constitutes this act, so we construct the "I" to which we attribute the power to cause the act in question.[25] We

24 David Chalmers, *The Conscious Mind*, New York: Oxford University Press 1997, p. 101.

25 When, in an otherwise "realistic" video game, we get too close to a single figure, we all of a sudden see that it has no face at all, but just crude abstract contours, like an imprecise drawing; our common sense tells us that this is so because we are not dealing with a real human person, but just an artificial, virtual copy. However, does the same not

thus have two levels. First, there is what Hofstadter calls the "God's eye view," the view which perceives reality in its endless complexity and can establish the full fundamental causal chain—here, we "see it all," the causal network is complete, nothing is left out. Then, we have the "highly compressed simplification in which vast amounts of information are thrown away"; this simplification "might seem to be the more *useful* one for us mortals, as it is so much more efficient (even though some things seem to happen 'for no reason'—that's the tradeoff)."[26] The feeling of "freedom" (the perception that we did something "for no reason at all," just because the urge to do it popped into our mind) is grounded precisely in our ignoring all the details we lose when we perceive things at the higher level of simplification. When we perceive some acts as "intentional," we commit the same spontaneous simplification: when I raise a glass to my mouth and drink water from it, the true answer to the question "Why did I raise the glass?" would involve the complex of neuronal processes, reacting to (what I experience as) thirst, which send signals to my hand muscles, and so on—at this level, there is no intention, just pure (although extremely complex) natural causality. In order to simplify things, I posit intention as a cause and say: "I raised the glass in order to have a drink."

So, what is wrong with this premise? Its initial presupposition, that there *is* something like a "God's eye view," that the idea of an intelligence which "sees it all," although (for an atheist) epistemologically impossible, is ontologically grounded: the infinitely complex network of "all reality" really is out there, it is the ultimate true reality, it is just inaccessible to our finite minds. But what if there simply *is no basic level*, what if divisions go on indefinitely, what if the quantum level marks the beginning of the "blurring" of "basic" full reality, so that the only ultimate reality is a Void?[27]

This brings us to Hofstadter's limitation: he is precisely unable to think the "downward causality" displayed by the collapse of the wave function in quantum physics, for his opposition between reality and appearance remains the traditional one. The gap that separates the quantum level from our ordinary perceived reality is *not* a gap between ultimate hard reality and a higher-level unavoidable-but-illusory hallucination. On the contrary, it is the quantum

hold also for real human persons? When we approach them too closely, do we also not discover that, beneath the surface, there are just organs, blood, bones, that our thought "is" just the flesh of the brain, and, when we get even closer, just mindless atoms and empty space?

26 Hofstadter, *I Am a Strange Loop*, p. 98.

27 What makes nanotechnology so thrilling is the prospect of constructing objects and processes in such a small dimension that all correlation with our ordinary life world is lost, so that it is effectively as if we are dealing with an alternate reality: there are no shared scales between nano-reality and our ordinary reality, and yet nonetheless we can influence our reality through nano-processes.

level which is effectively "hallucinated," not yet ontologically fully constituted, floating and ambiguous, and it is the shift to the "higher" level of appearances (appearing perceived reality) that makes it into a hard reality.

Furthermore, when Hofstadter defines the Self not as a substantial thing, but as a higher-level pattern which can flow between a multitude of material instantiations, he is not consistent enough and repeats the mistake of the brain-in-the-vat fantasy: the "pattern" which forms my Self is not only the pattern of self-referential loops in my brain, but the much larger pattern of interactions between my brain-and-body and its entire material, institutional, and symbolic context. What makes me "my-Self" is the way I relate to the people, things, and processes around me—and this is what by definition would be lost if only my brain-pattern were transposed from my brain here on Earth to another brain on Mars: this other Self would definitely not be me, since it would be deprived of the complex social network which makes me my-Self.

Hofstadter's alternative is: either my Self is somehow directly linked to a mysterious, unknown physical property of my brain and thus irreducibly rooted in it, or it is a higher-level formal pattern of self-relating loops which is not limited to my individuality but can be transposed into others. What Hofstadter lacks here is simply the notion of the I as the singular universality, the abstract-universal point of reference which, of course, is not to be identified with its material support (my brain) in a Searle-like way, but is also not just a pattern floating around and capable of being transposed into other individuals.[28] This purely formal-negative self-identity is the core of the Cartesian *cogito*, and this is why, whenever Hofstadter speaks (in the usual mocking way) of the Cartesian Ego, he *substantializes* it into a Thing. No wonder, then, that things get complicated when, in order to account for the threshold which separates humans from animals, Hofstadter refers to Turing's notion of a "universal (computing) machine":

> the critical threshold for this kind of computational universality comes at exactly that point where a machine is flexible enough to read and correctly interpret a set of data that describe its own structure. At this critical juncture, a machine can, in principle, explicitly watch how it does any particular task, step by step. Turing realized that a machine that has this critical level of flexibility can imitate any another [*sic*] machine, no matter how complex the latter is. In other words, there is nothing *more* flexible than a universal machine ... We human beings, too, are universal machines

28 Incidentally, the strange thing about the constellation described in Searle's (in)famous Chinese Box thought experiment is that it can also be taken as a description of how our mind works: if we take a close look at our brain, we will never locate the exact place where the brain "understands" the symbol input, but just a dispersed network for the "meaningless" transmission and manipulation of signs ...

> of a different sort: our neural hardware can copy arbitrary patterns, even if evolution never had any grand plan for this kind of "representational universality" to come about.[29]

How do we become "universal machines"? Through a self-referential loop. This is philosophically the crucial insight: it is the very "limitation" of universality, the fact that universality involves a short-circuit with a singularity, which enables the universality to be posited "for itself," to appear as such, to cut its links with a particular content.[30] The standard notion of self-referentiality remains at the level of the "spurious infinity": an image endlessly mirrors itself—say, on a TV screen, we see a table with a TV set whose screen shows a table with a TV set whose screen shows ... and so on. In order to distinguish the "true infinity" that gives rise to the Self from this infinite regress, Hofstadter evokes a nice old example, namely:

> the famous label of a Morton Salt box, which shows a girl holding a box of Morton Salt. You may think you smell infinite regress once again, but if so, you are fooling yourself! The girl's arm is covering up the critical spot where the regress would occur. If you were to ask the girl to please hand you her salt box so that you could actually *see* the infinite regress on its label, you would wind up disappointed, for the label on *that* box would show her holding a yet smaller box with her arm once again blocking the regress.
>
> And yet we still have a self-referential picture, because customers in the grocery store understand that the little box shown on the label is the same as the big box they are holding. How do they arrive at this conclusion? By using analogy. To be specific, not only do they have the large box in their own hands, but they can see the little box the girl is holding, and the two boxes have a lot in common (their cylindrical shape, their dark-blue color, their white caps at both ends); and in case that's not enough, they can also see salt spilling out of the little one. These pieces of evidence suffice to convince everyone that the little box and the large box are identical, and there you have it: self-reference without infinite regress![31]

Through such self-referential inclusion, we get "the elephant into a matchbox": the frame is inscribed as an element in the framed content, the whole becomes part of itself. The price to be paid for this victory over infinite regress

---

29 Hofstadter, *I Am a Strange Loop*, p. 242, p. 245.

30 Another way to define the terms of the famous Turing Test on how to gauge whether our partner in a conversation is human or a machine would have been to focus on the ability of the machine to generate a true (Freudian) slip: not only a meaningless glitch, but *a failure with meaning*, an uncontrolled "malfunction" which bears a message.

31 Hofstadter, *I Am a Strange Loop*, pp. 144–5.

is that the second image-within-the-image is incomplete, curtailed, not fully the same but recognized as the same only by analogy (we see only partially the box within the picture)—the supplementary self-reflexive image has to be minimally "metonymic." And—to simplify things to the utmost—the idea is that the same curtailed symbolic self-representation is constitutive of what we call "Self": the Self is constituted through its (self-)representation; that is, the two meanings of the term "self," substantial and predicative (self as the "I" and self as designating self-relation), are closely linked. There is "human speech" only insofar as the speaking subject who uses language to designate objects and processes self-reflexively inscribes itself into its speech. This self-inscription which constitutes the subject cannot be reduced to a simple inclusion of a representation (an image or sign) of me into the chain of my speech—the catch is that this representation has to function as the stand-in of "me," the speaker itself as the unique point from which I perceive the world and engage with it, the point for which words have meaning. Since this operation is basically impossible (I cannot fully objectivize myself in my speech and see/represent myself in it as speaking) and yet necessary, it can only be performed in a truncated way—to put it in Lacanese, the signifier which signifies "me" (the very subject of the enunciation) is a signifier without a signified. Lacan's name for this exceptional signifier is the Master-Signifier (S_1), as opposed to the chain of "ordinary" signifiers (S_2), and we can see now how the topic of "downward causality" can be translated into Lacanian terms: this exceptional signifier exerts "downward causality" insofar as it "falls into the signified," that is, insofar as it constitutes the very unity of the signified object (a Jew becomes a Jew when the *name* "Jew" is added to him, for the name is not just his external designation, it constitutes him ontologically). This causality runs "downward" in contrast to the standard "upward" causality of signs which "reflect" the reality they designate: causality runs here "upward," things cause words, they determine their signs, while in the case of the Master-Signifier, a word determines/causes the designated thing.

Does this then mean that the "Self" is the X caused (posited) through its nomination in the same way a "Jew" emerges through his nomination? We must introduce a key distinction here: the Self is *not* self-referential in the direct sense of referring to itself and thus being accessible to itself—the Self is the void that enables the infinite regress to be cut short, and the sign that directly represents the Self (I) is therefore an empty sign, a sign which holds the place of a void. This is the dimension missing in the Metzinger metaphor of the subject as the red arrow on the map—here is the key passage again:

> The most important difference between the little red arrow on the subway map and the little red arrow in our neurophenomenological troglodyte's brain is that the external arrow is *opaque*. It is always clear that it is only a representation—a

> placeholder for something else ... The conscious self-model in the caveman's brain itself, however, is in large portions transparent: ... it is a phenomenal self characterized not only by full-blown prereflexive embodiment but by the comprehensive, all-encompassing subjective experience of *being situated*.[32]

What Metzinger misses is that, in contrast to ordinary signs, which are "placeholders for something else," the "red arrow" which stands in for the Self is a place-holder for *nothing* (the nothing which "is" the subject itself). Here one should correct the standard notion of the I as a set of features in which I (the subject) recognize myself: I by definition experience myself as *absent*, as an emptiness towards which my stand-ins point, I never directly identify myself with my stand-ins or with my self-model. It is here that the (otherwise fashionable and much misused) reference to Gödel's theorem acquires a precise meaning: in the same way that, for Gödel, the lack of proof of the "undecidable" proposition is a direct consequence of its truth, the very failure of the subject's representation is a proof that we are dealing with the dimension of subjectivity. This brings us back to one of our formal definitions of the subject: a subject tries to articulate ("express") itself in a signifying chain, this articulation fails, and *by means and through this failure, the subject emerges*: the subject is the failure of its signifying representation—this is why Lacan writes the subject of the signifier as $, as "barred." In this precise sense, the subject is a non-provable presupposition, something whose existence cannot be demonstrated but only inferred through the failure of its direct demonstration. This weird coincidence of the inaccessible Thing with the very obstacle which prevents direct access to it signals that the status of the subject is that of a Real—that, as Lacan would have put it, the subject is an "answer of the Real" to the failed attempts to enforce its symbolization. The reason Hofstadter misses this dimension is that, when he describes "upside-down causality," he ultimately presents it as a kind of necessary illusion:

> evolution tailored human beings to be perceiving entities—entities that filter the world into macroscopic categories. We are consequently fated to describe what goes on about us, including what other people do and what we ourselves do, not in terms of the underlying particle physics (which lies many orders of magnitude removed from our everyday perceptions and our familiar categories), but in terms of such abstract and ill-defined high-level patterns as mothers and fathers, friends and lovers, grocery stores and checkout stands, soap operas and beer commercials, crackpots and geniuses, religions and stereotypes, comedies and tragedies.[33]

32 Metzinger, *Being No One*, p. 552.

33 Hofstadter, *I Am a Strange Loop*, p. 172.

Applied to ourselves, the same mechanism accounts for the emergence of the Self: "We are powerfully driven to create a term that summarizes the presumed unity, internal coherence, and temporal stability of all the hopes and beliefs and desires that are found inside our own cranium—and that term, as we all learn very early on, is 'I.'"[34] And since "we perceive not particles interacting but macroscopic patterns in which certain things push other things around with a blurry causality, and since the Grand Pusher in and of our bodies is our 'I,' and since our bodies push the rest of the world around, we are left with no choice but to conclude that the 'I' is where the causality buck stops ... This is ... a surprisingly reliable and totally indispensable distortion."[35] The I is thus "a useful shorthand standing for a myriad of infinitesimal entities and the invisible chemical transactions taking place among them."[36]

As a description of our innermost self-experience, this is wrong: the "I" does not stand for any unity-coherence-stability of the substantial content of my personality, but for an evanescent, self-referential singularity which is at a distance from all substantial content. Furthermore, when Hofstadter talks about the tendency of our mind to reduce complex reality to "abstract and ill-defined high-level patterns," he seems to confuse two levels of ontologically different nature:

> Mature human brains are constantly trying to reduce the complexity of what they perceive, and this means that they are constantly trying to get unfamiliar, complex *patterns* made of many symbols that have been freshly activated in concert to trigger just *one* familiar pre-existing symbol (or a very small set of them). In fact, that's the main business of human brains—to take a complex situation and to put one's finger on *what matters* in it, to distill from an initial welter of sensations and ideas what a situation really is about. To spot the gist.[37]

Here, we have to be precise: the reduction of complexity Hofstadter is talking about is not the same as the reduction of lower-level neuronal processes to the higher-level perceptions and symbols, but a reduction, inherent to this level of symbols, of complex patterns to the simple choice (point of decision) which condenses the entire situation to a simple feature. These two levels are, of course, linked, but in a way which escapes Hofstadter: the "upward leap from *raw stimuli* to *symbols*," namely the emergence of the symbolic order, can only occur when, within this order (what Lacan calls) a Master-Signifier "quilts" and thus stabilizes the field of meaning. In a perceptive observation, Hofstadter suggests that

---

34 Ibid., p. 179.
35 Ibid., p. 182.
36 Ibid., p. 203.
37 Ibid., p. 277.

it is this "level-shifting" which accounts for the difference between the simple feedback loop (like the TV mirror-image of the TV set infinitely reflected in itself) and the "strange loop" that constitutes a Self: in the second case,

> the level-shifting acts of perception, abstraction, and categorization are central, indispensable elements. It is the upward leap from *raw stimuli* to *symbols* that imbues the loop with "strangeness" ... What makes a strange loop appear in a brain and not in a video feedback system, then, is an ability—the ability to think—which is, in effect, a one-syllable word standing for the possession of a sufficiently large repertoire of triggerable symbols.[38]

We should add here a key feature noted by Hofstadter elsewhere: in contrast to the infinite reiteration of a simple feedback loop (a picture within a picture within a picture ...), the "strange loop" is precisely *not* infinite, the infinite series is cut short by a stop-gap, a "reflexive" symbol, the odd-one-out in the series. Furthermore, as Hofstadter is quick to note, this very ability is grounded in an inability which is its obverse: the "inability to peer below the level of our symbols. It is our inability to see, feel, or sense in any way the constant, frenetic churning and roiling of micro-stuff, all the unfelt bubbling and boiling that underlies our thinking."[39] Consequently, "the combination of these two ingredients—one an ability and the other an inability—gives rise to the strange loop of selfhood, a trap into which we humans all fall, every last one of us, willy-nilly."[40] Here, Hofstadter again displays his eternal oscillation: he as a rule dismisses downward causality as an indispensable distortion, as in the following passages:

> The "I,"—yours, mine, everyone's—is a tremendously effective illusion, and falling for it has fantastic survival value. Our "I"s are self-reinforcing illusions that are an inevitable by-product of strange loops, which are themselves an inevitable by-product of symbol-possessing brains that guide bodies through the dangerous straits and treacherous waters of life ... The "I" is a necessary, indispensable concept to all of us, even if it's an illusion, like thinking that the sun is circling the earth because it rises, moves across the sky, and sets ... Ceasing to believe altogether in the "I" is in fact impossible, because it is indispensable for survival. Like it or not, we humans are stuck for good with this myth.[41]

There is thus an unbridgeable gap between my spontaneous self-experience which tells me that "I" am the agent of my acts, and the scientific

38 Ibid., p. 187, p. 203.

39 Ibid., p. 204.

40 Ibid., p. 205.

41 Ibid., pp. 291–2, p. 294.

knowledge which tells me that there is no "I," just a complex network of neuronal processes—in this sense, the "I" is literally a fetish, for we are stuck in a situation of fetishistic disavowal: "I know very well [that what science tells me is true], but nonetheless ..."—At the same time, however, Hofstadter often reiterates that "high-level, emergent, self-referential meanings in a formal mathematical system can have a causal potency just as real as that of the system's rigid, frozen, low-level rules of inference."[42] "Indispensable illusion" or "just as real"?

We encounter the same problem with the question "How do choice and genetic determinism relate?" If I stop smoking by genetic intervention, not through my strenuous effort, does this deprive me of my freedom of choice? The spontaneous mystification here is: if my attitude (say, desire to smoke) is just a contingent fact, I perceive it as my choice and myself as responsible for it; if, on the contrary, my ceasing to smoke is the result of a biogeneticist's intervention, it is as if I am deprived of my freedom, under the control of others. But, if my ceasing to smoke is conditioned by the geneticist's meddling with my genes, then my previous smoking was also determined by the previous constellation of my genes. If, on the contrary, my previous smoking was my choice, then even after the geneticist's meddling I am still free to stop smoking, even if this now takes more effort. If genes determine me, then they determine me *always*, whether their constellation is the result of natural blind chance or the result of the intervention of another person who changed my genome. Why, then, does it appear that the geneticist's meddling deprives me of my freedom? There is only one consistent answer: if my genome depends on blind chance, then I can *pretend* that I am free, save the appearances. In my spontaneous perception, I thus secretly believe in the truth of determinism—what I want to save is not freedom but the *appearance* of freedom.

One should thus reject the "positive" ontology which presupposes some zero-level of reality where things "really happen" and dismisses the higher levels as mere abbreviations, illusory self-perception, and so forth. There is no such zero-level: if we go "all the way down," we arrive at the Void. Back in 1959, Richard Feynman announced nanotechnology in a speech entitled "There's Plenty of Room at the Bottom"—from the standpoint of the incompleteness of reality, we can even make a step further and claim that, at the very bottom, there is all the room we want, since there is nothing else there, just the void.

And it is only within such an incompleteness that the notion (and actuality) of the Self is thinkable. In other words, what is the Self? When we see a table, we accept that there is nothing behind its components, no secret X that stands for the core of its identity beyond and independently of all its properties, while, when dealing with a Self, we spontaneously assume that the Self is not simply

---

42 Ibid., p. 206.

a combination of its properties and of things that happens to and in it—there has to be some X beneath all this wealth that gives the Self its uniqueness. The problem is that, after we abstract all determinate qualities from the Self, what remains is just plain nothing, a void. So we should accept that our Self is, like a table, nothing but the network of its properties, of its contents, or, to put it in a more postmodern vein, of stories it tells itself about itself—as Nietzsche put it, there is no mysterious doer behind the multitude of deeds. There is, however, one option that this account leaves out of consideration: what if our Self is *this void itself*, what if its core is not some positive content, but the "self-relating negativity" (Hegel), the very ability to negate every determinate content?

The dilemma here is that between the "upward" or "downward" status of freedom. That is to say, on the one hand, there are the attempts to account for freedom as a higher-level property "emerging" out of the complex interaction of lower-level elements which are part of a determinist network—the problem is then to determine what the status of freedom is if the same process which, at this higher level (the level of what Dennett calls "design"), involves freedom, can also be described at the lower level of its constituent elements in deterministic terms. On the other hand, there are attempts to ground freedom in the fact that the deterministic interaction is not the lowest ontological level: in terms of quantum physics, it takes place at the level of constituted reality, beneath which there are quantum oscillations which do not obey deterministic laws—the problem here is that freedom in no way involves pure contingency, for if an event is underdetermined, if it is genuinely accidental, this in no way means that it is free, since freedom is not the lack of causal determination, but a *sui generis* form of determination.

Furthermore, Hofstadter distinguishes the I from a content-free feedback loop (the "vanilla" loop): if one points a TV camera at the middle of a blank screen to which the camera is linked, all that we shall see on the screen is a fixed white image, the endless series of self-reflected images indistinguishable from each other. When, however, the camera turns or zooms out enough to take in something external to the blank screen, this non-blank patch gets sucked into the video loop and cycled around, populating the screen with many bits of color forming a complex pattern. Similarly, "a 'bare' strange loop of selfhood does not give rise to a distinct self—it is just a generic, vanilla shell that requires contact with something else in the world in order to start acquiring a distinctive identity, a distinctive 'I.'"[43] Is this not what Lacan was aiming at with his formula $-*a*? What Hofstadter calls a "bare strange loop of selfhood" is the void of self-relating negativity, the empty form of self-reflexivity deprived of all content—to fill in this form with content ("personal identity"), to pass from a pure/empty subject

43 Hofstadter, *I Am a Strange Loop*, p. 208.

to a "person," one needs a minimum of contingent external input, what Lacan calls *le peu de réel*, (or what Fichte called *Anstoss*). From a strict Lacanian point, however, is not this scheme of the relationship between $ and *a*, between the empty form of a subject (or, rather, subject *as* an empty form of self-relating) and the "pathological" content which fills it in, too close to common sense? What it misses is the proper dialectical twist: *le peu de réel* of minimal content is not merely the stain which spoils the purity of the "bare strange loop of selfhood," but its formal condition of possibility—it is the very minimal motivation, the "cause" which sets in motion the self-reflecting of the pure I. And vice versa, the "bare strange loop of selfhood," the pure form of self-relating negativity, always accompanies every positive content that forms a "personality" as a permanent threat of radical negativity, that is, of the erasure of all content. In Hegelese, the pure-empty form of self-relating negativity and the minimal "stain" of a contingent content without form that affects the Self from outside are the two sides of the same coin, they are identical in the sense of an "infinite judgment." Therein resides the difference from the TV set endlessly reflecting itself: in the case of the I, the "bare" loop is formally, not only empirically, impossible—if one erases the stain, the Self implodes, collapses in on itself.

The problematic nature of identifying a Self with the individuals' self-model (the complex network of memories, attitudes, opinions, ideals, fears, etc., that form a particular personality) becomes clear when Hofstadter approaches the topic of the interpenetration of Selves: "The more intimately someone comes to know you, the finer-grained will be the 'portrait' of you inside their head. The highest-resolution portrait of you is of course your own self-portrait—your own mosaic of yourself, your self-symbol, built up over your entire life."[44] From this notion of the Self as self-model, Hofstadter draws the logical conclusion that, when I know another person intimately enough, part of his Self is effectively in me—once the Self is defined as the texture of psychic features, there is no longer any strong qualitative difference between my feature and the same feature as it reverberates in the minds of those close to me, it is just that, for the obvious reasons (lack of all the background "murmur" of innumerable other features), I am present in others in a much reduced way. Hofstadter goes on to draw other conclusions—first, Selves are not equal, there is an infinite variety of Selves, up to persons with "great souls" (the meaning of Mahatma, Gandhi's name) who can integrate elements of numerous other Selves. Second, one can rehabilitate the old topic of the soul's immortality: once a Self is defined in this way, the biological death of an individual does not automatically entail the death of his

---

44 Ibid., p. 255. But what about the (Freudian) hypothesis of the unconscious? Does it not imply precisely that a subject is *not* the one whose self-portrait has the highest resolution. An external observer can see unconscious patterns which determine my activity much more clearly than I do, precisely *because* he is not "me."

Self, since parts of his Self literally survive in the lasting memory of all those who remember him and continue to mentally interact with him.

This apparently neutral and benevolent notion that there are large and small souls is not without potentially dangerous political consequences: if there is no underlying equality between Selves, why should we all be politically equal? Hofstadter is aware of the problematic character of the "distinctions between the values of souls": "any hint at such a distinction risks becoming inflammatory, because in our culture there is a dogma that states, roughly, that all human lives are worth exactly the same amount."[45] Hofstadter's counter-argument is here a common-sense comparison of the difference between human souls with the difference between human and animal souls: "Most people I know would rate ... cat souls as higher than cow souls, cow souls higher than rat souls ... And so I ask myself, if soul-size distinctions *between* species are such a commonplace and non-threatening notion, why should we not also be willing to consider some kind of ... spectrum of soul-sizes *within* a single species, and in particular within our own?"[46] Is then political equality just an illusion, a pure ethico-political presupposition without any foundation in reality? The solution is to focus on the "I" as the pure subject, the evanescent point of self-relating negativity—at this level (and at this level only), we effectively are all equal. One should thus nonetheless endorse our common-sense intuition which tells us that something is missing in Hofstadter's account: not some mysterious para-natural ingredient, but simply the self-relating singularity of "me" in which a Self is only *actualized*. There is no substance to this One: it is neither some minimal feature of my psychic content nor the biological base (brain) which instantiates it—it is merely the abstract form of self-relating, but a form which is as such essential for the Self's actuality. It is this One-ness which makes us equal in the moral and political sense: no matter how rich or pure our content, we are all Ones, points of irreducible singularity.

Sara Baartman was a young woman from the Khoi Khoi tribe who, in 1810, was taken from Cape Town to London and then exhibited as a freak across Britain, where the image of "The Hottentot Venus" (focused on her broad behind) fascinated the public. After a court battle waged by abolitionists to free her from her exhibitors failed, she was in 1814 taken to France, where she became the object of "scientific" research: Cuvier himself (who, after seeing her head, said that he never saw a human being whose physiognomy was so close to that of an ape) measured and examined her body in detail, and was especially fascinated by her extended *labia minora*. Sara died a year later, but her body remained an object of "scientific" fascination for decades after her death: her sexual organs and brain were displayed in the *Musée de l'Homme* in Paris

45 Ibid., p. 343.
46 Ibid., p. 344.

until 1985. Two outstanding films on Sara Baartman were made recently, a documentary *The Life and Times of Sara Baartman* by Zola Maseko (South Africa 2001), and a fictional film *Black Venus* by Abdellatif Kechiche (France 2010) with Yahima Torres playing Sara. Torres rendered with disturbing and breathtaking force the feature emphasized by many witnesses: although Sara was hurt and felt betrayed when she was examined, she stood with silent dignity when "scientists" touched her behind and poked and measured her labia. The contrast here is absolute between her poise and the vulgarity of her "explorers": if the word "civilization" has any meaning after its history of abuses, it is Sara who was truly civilized when confronted with the barbarism of European scientists, and the difference between barbarism and civilization is here not only quantitative, but qualitative and, as such, absolute.

The very fact of Sara's dignity refutes one of the more disgusting books of European cultural conservatism, Max Scheler's *Ressentiment*, an attempt to Christianize Nietzsche.[47] When Scheler debates the issue of slavery, he introduces the distinction between a mere human being and a free person: for Aristotle, slaves are of course human, but they are not persons, since they do not possess the inner dignity and free autonomy of a true person—and, as he adds to dispel any ambiguity, this does not mean only or primarily that a slave is not treated as a free person, but that he does not *treat himself as a person*, that he does not truly respect himself, has no sense of the dignity of his person, is not mortally offended when something is done to him that would deprive a free person of their dignity. What Scheler misses here is that this lack of dignity of a slave is not a simple fact, but something imposed on him or her by education and harsh discipline exerted by the masters: if a slave displays dignity, it is either brutally suppressed or mocked, taken as a ridiculous imitation of true dignity. This was Sara's position: her (evident) dignity was simply ignored by her ordinary and "scientific" observers. And this brings us to the dimension Hofstadter misses: the unique dignity of a person has nothing to do with the "greatness" of his or her soul in Hofstadter's sense of integrating elements of numerous other Selves.

47 See Max Scheler, *Ressentiment*, New York: Schocken 1972.

CHAPTER 11

The Non-All, or, the Ontology of Sexual Difference

Sexual difference in the disenchanted universe

On a first approach, there is nothing shocking about the link between ontology and sexual difference. Is not such a link the defining feature of all premodern cosmologies which explain the origin of the universe in terms of a primordial conflict between a masculine and a feminine principle (yin and yang, light and darkness, Heaven and Earth...)? Back in the hippie era of 1960s, I remember reading a book by Alan Watts, the zen popularizer, in which he explained how, in the simple activity of love-making, the whole cosmos resonates, the two opposing cosmic principles, yin and yang, dancing with each other—a message which no doubt boosted the confidence of adolescents wanting sex as well as spiritual fulfillment.

What we call the modern "disenchantment" of the universe involves not only the assertion of the gap between the meaningless and cold "objective reality" accessible to mathematicized science and the "subjective" universe of meanings and values which we "project" onto reality; underlying this gap is the de-sexualization of reality. It is against this background that Lacan's achievement should be measured: he reasserts the ontological status of sexual difference *within the field of modern science*—how can this be done without regressing into a pre-scientific mythology? That is to say, for modern transcendental philosophy, sexual difference is deontologized, reduced to the ontic sphere of the human race—if one ontologizes it, one is accused of "anthropomorphism," of projecting onto the universe what is merely an empirical (biological and psychic) feature of human beings. This is why neither the Kantian transcendental subject nor the Heideggerian *Dasein* is sexualized: in his analytic of *Dasein*, Heidegger totally ignores sexuality. (Typically, when philosophers deal with Freudian notions like "castration," they read them as ontic metaphors for the ontological a priori of our finitude, limitation, powerlessness...)

So how exactly does Lacan succeed in re-ontologizing sexual difference without regressing to a premodern sexualized cosmology? Clearly, for Lacan, "sexuality" does not designate a particular ontic sphere of human reality: it stands for a certain displacement, an anamorphic distortion, whose status is strictly formal. Every "sphere" of human reality can get "sexualized," not because sexuality is so "strong" that it can spill over and contaminate all other spheres, but for the very opposite reason: because it does *not* have its own "proper" sphere, because it is primordially "out of joint," marked by a constitutive gap or discord.[1] The first philosopher to articulate this deadlock (though he was unaware of its link with sexual difference, of course) was Kant, when, in his *Critique of Pure Reason*, he described the "ontological scandal" of the antinomies of pure reason, the inner inconsistency of the basic ontologico-transcendental framework we use to approach reality: "mathematical" antinomies render the deadlock which characterizes the feminine position, and "dynamic" antinomies the deadlock of the masculine position.[2] Kant himself, as we have seen, was unable to confront and assume the radicality of his breakthrough: he ultimately confers on these antinomies a merely epistemological status. Antinomies are indications of the inability of our finite reason to grasp the noumenal reality: the moment we apply our categories to what can never become an object of our experience, we become caught up in insoluble contradictions and antinomies. As Hegel put it with his acerbic irony, Kant, the great destroyer of metaphysics, all of a sudden developed a tenderness towards Things-in-themselves and decided to spare them from antinomies. Here, however, Lacan is at the level of modern science—what he does with Kant is, in a way, to raise his Newtonianism to the level of quantum physics.

The passage from Einstein to Bohr repeats the logic of the passage from Kant to Hegel: for Einstein, in a thoroughly Kantian way, the "antinomy" of velocity and position demonstrates that quantum physics does not reach the noumenal reality of Things-in-themselves; for Hegel, "antinomy" is the very sign that we have touched the noumenal Real. In the first case, ontological incompleteness is transposed into an epistemological form, the incompleteness is perceived as an effect of the fact that another (secret, but fully real) agency has constructed our reality as a simulated universe. The truly difficult thing is to accept the second choice, the ontological incompleteness of reality itself. Common sense will immediately complain loudly: but how can this ontological incompleteness hold for reality itself? Is not reality *defined* by its ontological completeness?[3] If

1 Lacan has many names for this discord, some Freudian, some his own: symbolic castration, "there is no sexual relationship," the difference between the aim and the goal of a drive, etc.

2 See Joan Copjec, *Read My Desire: Lacan Against the Historicists*, Cambridge, MA: MIT Press 1994; and Slavoj Žižek, *Tarrying With the Negative*, Durham: Duke University Press 1993.

3 The opposition to this notion of ontological completeness defines Hegel's Idealism: its core lies in the assertion that finite (determinate, positive-substantial) reality is in itself empty, inconsistent, self-sublating. However, it does not follow from this that finite reality is just a shadow, a secondary reflection, etc., of some higher reality: there is *nothing but* this reality, and the "suprasensible is appearance qua appearance," i.e., the very movement

reality "really exists out there," it *has* to be complete "all the way down," otherwise we are dealing with a fiction which just "hangs in the air," like appearances which are not appearances of a substantial Something. Here, precisely, quantum physics enters in, offering a model of how to think (or at least imagine) such an "open" ontology. Alain Badiou formulated the same idea with his notion of pure multiplicity as the ultimate ontological category: reality is the multiplicity of multiplicities which cannot be generated or constituted from (or reduced to) some form of Ones as its elementary ("atomic") constituents. Multiplicities are not multiplications of One, they are irreducible multiplicities, which is why their opposite is not One but zero, the ontological void: no matter how far we progress in our analysis of multiplicities, we never reach the zero-level of its simple constituents—the only "background" for multiplicities is thus zero, the void.[4] Therein resides Badiou's ontological breakthrough: the primordial opposition is not that of One and Zero, but that of Zero and multiplicities, and the One emerges later. To put it even more radically, since only Ones "really exist," multiplicities and Zero are the same thing (not *one and* the same thing): Zero "is" multiplicities without the Ones which would guarantee their ontological consistency. This ontological openness of the One-less multiplicity also allows us to approach in a new way Kant's second antinomy of pure reason: "Every composite substance in the world consists of simple parts; and there exists nothing that is not either itself simple, or composed of simple parts."[5] Here is Kant's proof:

> For, grant that composite substances do not consist of simple parts; in this case, if all combination or composition were annihilated in thought, no composite part, and (as, by the supposition, there do not exist simple parts) no simple part would exist. Consequently, no substance; consequently, nothing would exist. Either, then, it is impossible to annihilate composition in thought; or, after such annihilation, there must remain something that subsists without composition, that is, something that is simple. But in the former case the composite could not itself consist of substances, because with substances composition is merely a contingent relation, apart from

of the self-sublation of this reality. So we really pass "from nothing through nothing to nothing": the starting point, immediate reality, deploys its nothingness, it cancels itself, negates itself, but there is nothing beyond it. This is why Hegel cannot be situated with regard to the opposition between transcendence and immanence: his position is that of the *absolute immanence of transcendence*. In other words, his position can only be grasped in a temporal shift: first, one asserts transcendence (in an apophatic way)—immanent/immediate positive reality is not all, it has to be negated/overcome, it points beyond itself; then, this overcoming is posited as thoroughly immanent: what is beyond immediate reality is not another higher reality, but the movement of its negation as such.

4 See Alain Badiou, *Being and Event*, London: Continuum 2005.

5 Immanuel Kant, *Critique of Pure Reason*, trans. J. M. D. Meiklejohn, London: Henry G. Bohn 1855, p. 271.

> which they must still exist as self-subsistent beings. Now, as this case contradicts the supposition, the second must contain the truth—that the substantial composite in the world consists of simple parts.
>
> It follows, as an immediate inference, that the things in the world are all, without exception, simple beings—that composition is merely an external condition pertaining to them—and that, although we never can separate and isolate the elementary substances from the state of composition, reason must cogitate these as the primary subjects of all composition, and consequently, as prior thereto—and as simple substances.[6]

What if, however, we accept the conclusion that ultimately "nothing exists"? (A conclusion which, incidentally, exactly matches that of Plato's *Parmenides*: "Then may we not sum up the argument in a word and say truly: If one is not, then nothing is?") Such a move, although rejected by Kant as obvious nonsense, is not as un-Kantian as it may appear: it is here that we should apply yet again the Kantian distinction between negative and infinite judgment.

The statement "material reality is all there is" can be negated in two ways, in the form of "material reality *is not all there is*" and "material reality *is non-all*." The first negation (of a predicate) leads to standard metaphysics: material reality is not everything, there is another, higher, spiritual reality. As such, this negation is, in accordance with Lacan's formulae of sexuation, inherent to the positive statement "material reality is all there is": as its constitutive exception, it grounds its universality. If, however, we assert a non-predicate and say "material reality *is non-all*," this merely asserts the non-All of reality without implying any exception—paradoxically, one should thus claim that the axiom of true materialism is not "material reality is all there is," but a double one: (1) there is nothing which is not material reality, (2) material reality is non-All.[7]

6 Ibid., pp. 271–3.

7 Perhaps the incompatibility between Derrida and Deleuze can also be accounted for in terms of Lacan's "formulae of sexuation." What makes Derrida "masculine" is the persistence, throughout his work, of totalization-with-exception: the search for a post-metaphysical way of thinking, for an escape from metaphysical closure, presupposes the violent gesture of universalization, of a leveling-equalization-unification of the whole field of intra-metaphysical struggles ("all attempts to break out of metaphysics, from Kierkegaard to Marx, from Nietzsche to Heidegger, from Levinas to Lévi-Strauss, ultimately remain within the horizon of the metaphysics of presence"). This same gesture is clearly discernible in Heidegger (for whom all reversals of metaphysics from Marx to Nietzsche, from Husserl to Sartre, remain within the horizon of the forgetting of Being, ultimately caught in the technological nihilism of the accomplishment of metaphysics) as well as in Adorno and Horkheimer (for whom all Western, and not only Western, thought is totalized-equalized as the gradual deployment of the dialectic of Enlightenment which culminates in today's "administered world"—from Plato to NATO, as one used to say).

If we want to simulate reality within an artificial (virtual, digital) medium, we do not have to go all the way: we just have to reproduce those features which will make the image realistic from the spectator's point of view. For example, if there is a house in the background, we do not have to program the house's interior, since we expect that the participant will not want to enter the house; or, the construction of a virtual person in this space can be limited to his exterior—no need to bother with inner organs, bones, etc. We just need to create a program which will promptly fill in this gap if the participant's actions necessitate it (say, if he plunges a knife deep into the virtual person's body). It is similar to scrolling down a long passage of text on a computer screen: the pages do not pre-exist our viewing them. The truly interesting idea here is that the quantum indeterminacy we encounter when inquiring into the tiniest components of our universe can be read in exactly the same way, as a feature of the limited resolution of our simulated world, as the sign of the ontological incompleteness of (what we experience as) reality itself. Imagine a god creating the world for us, its human inhabitants, to dwell in. His task

> could be made easier by furnishing it only with those parts that its inhabitants need to know about. For example, the microscopic structure of the Earth's interior could be left blank, at least until someone decides to dig down deep enough, in which case the details could be hastily filled in as required. If the most distant stars are hazy, no one is ever going to get close enough to them to notice that something is amiss.[8]

The idea is that the god who created or "programmed" our universe was too lazy (or, rather, he underestimated our intelligence): he thought that we humans would not succeed in probing into the structure of nature beyond the level of

---

In Derrida, this logic of totalizing exception finds its highest expression in the formula of justice as the "indeconstructible condition of deconstruction": everything can be deconstructed—with the exception of the indeconstructible condition of deconstruction itself. Perhaps it is this very gesture of a violent equalization of the entire field, against which one's own position as Exception is then formulated, which is the most elementary gesture of metaphysics. In clear contrast to Derrida, this gesture of violent equalization is absent from Deleuze's work—his gaze upon the tradition of philosophy is something like the gaze of God upon Creation in God's reply to Job (as described by Chesterton): there is no norm which would allow us to level the field, miracles are everywhere, every phenomenon, perceived properly (from a position which "estranges" it from its standard context) is an exception. (This is also why what both Deleuze and Badiou call the "minimal difference" is not the gesture of "totalizing the enemy" performed by critics of metaphysics from Heidegger to Adorno and Derrida, but its very opposite: a de-totalization of the enemy.)

8 See Nicholas Fearn, *Philosophy: The Latest Answers to the Oldest Questions*, London: Atlantic Books 2005, p. 77.

atoms, so he programmed the Matrix of our universe only to the level of its atomic structure—beyond that, he simply left things fuzzy.[9] This theologico-digital interpretation, however, is not the only way to read the paradox in question. It can be read as a sign that we already live in a simulated universe, but it can also be taken as a signal of the ontological incompleteness of reality itself. Does not this ontological "fuzziness" of reality also offer us a new approach to modernism in painting? Are not the "stains" which blur the transparency of a realist representation, which impose themselves *as* stains, precisely indications that the contours of constituted reality are blurred, that we are approaching the pre-ontological level of fuzzy proto-reality? Therein lies the crucial shift a viewer has to accomplish: stains are not obstacles that prevent our direct access to represented reality, they are, on the contrary, "more real than reality," something that undermines its ontological consistency from within—or, to put it in old-fashioned philosophical terms, their status is not epistemological but ontological.

Along these lines we can also address the standard problem of how to unite the causal description of an event with its reading as a free human act: where, in the network of natural necessity, is the space for freedom? Is the "teleological" causality of motivation (I acted in such a way because I aimed at such and such a goal) just an epiphenomenon, the mental translation of a process which can (also) be fully described at the purely physical level of natural determinism, or does such a "teleological" causation actually possess a power of its own, which fills in a gap in physical causality? The underlying premise here is that the causality of natural necessity reaches "all the way down"—but is this level of total determinism really the zero-level of the ontological structure of reality? The lesson of quantum physics is that, beneath solid material reality, there is a quantum level at which determinism breaks down. Hence the claim that the indeterminacy discovered by quantum physics opens up a space within which the "higher level" teleological causality can determine the "lower level" material events, without relying on any spiritualist notion of the power of our minds to magically suspend natural causality.

The only true alternative to this ontological fuzziness is the aforementioned and no less paradoxical idea that, at some point, the endless progress of dividing reality into its components reaches its end when the division is no longer a division into two (or more) parts, but a division into a part (something) and *nothing*. This would be proof that we had reached the most elementary constituent of reality: when something can only be further divided into a something and a nothing. Do not these two options relate again to Lacan's "formulae of sexuation," so that the irreducible-multiplicity option is "feminine" and the division

9 Ibid., pp. 77–8.

of the last term into a something and a nothing is "masculine"? Furthermore, is it not the case that, if we could reach the point of the last division (and thus the ultimate one, the last constituent of reality), then there would be no "creation" proper, nothing really new would emerge, there would be only a (re)combination of existing elements, while the feminine "fuzziness" of reality leaves open the space for creation proper? The underlying problem here is how to pass from the multitude-that-is-Zero to the emergence of One. Is it that One is a multiple which "stands for nothing," is it that Ones only exist at the level of re-presentation?

The Real of Sexual Difference

On a first approach, sexuality is thus a force of disfiguration, something which distorts our "objective" view of reality. As such, it points towards an irreducible, unsurpassable, ontological scandal, the true "euthanasia of reason" by which Kant was so shocked: every attempt to think reality in its totality has to end in a deadlock, an inconsistency. The paradox—and the properly Hegelian insight—is to accept that this distorting "sexual bias" of our perception, far from separating us from reality-in-itself, provides a direct link to it: "sexuality" is the way the ontological deadlock, the incompleteness of reality in itself, is inscribed into subjectivity. It is not a subjective distortion of objective reality, but a subjective distortion which is directly identical with the non-All, the inconsistency/out-of-jointness, of reality itself. This is why sexuality is, at its most radical, not human, but the point of in-humanity, the "*operator of the inhuman.*"[10] Pagan sexualized cosmology is a fantasmatic attempt to supplement and obfuscate the ontological scandal inherent in the deadlock of human sexuality.

An old Slovene joke: a young schoolboy has to write a short composition with the title "There is only one mother!" in which he is expected to illustrate, apropos a singular experience, the love which links him to his mother; here is what he writes: "One day I returned home earlier than expected, because the teacher was ill; I looked for my mother and found her naked in bed with another man who was not my father. My mother angrily shouted at me: 'What are you staring at, you idiot? Why don't you run to the refrigerator and get us two cold beers!' I ran to the kitchen, opened the refrigerator, looked into it and shouted back to the bedroom: 'There is only one, mother!'" Is this not a supreme case of an interpretation in which a single diacritical sign simply changes everything, as in the well-known parody of the first words of *Moby Dick*: "Call me, Ishmael!" We can find the same operation in Heidegger (the way he reads "Nothing is

10 Alenka Zupančič, "Sexuality and Ontology," *Filozofski Vestnik*, Vol. 29, No. 1 (2008), p. 63. I rely here heavily on this text.

without reason" [*nihil est sine ratione*], by shifting the accent to "Nothing[ness] *is* without reason"), or in the superego displacement of the prohibitive injunction of the symbolic law (from "Don't kill!" to "Don't!" ... "Kill!"). However, here one should risk a more detailed interpretation. The joke stages a Hamlet-like confrontation of the son with the enigma of the mother's excessive desire; in order to escape this deadlock, the mother as it were takes refuge in (the desire for) an external partial object, the bottle of beer, designed to divert the son's attention from the obscene Thing he has just stumbled upon—the message of her demand is: "You see, even if I am in bed with a man, my desire is for something else that only you can bring me, I am not excluding you by getting completely caught up in the circle of passion with this man!" The two bottles of beer (also) stand for the elementary signifying dyad, like Lacan's famous two restroom doors observed by two children from the train window in his "Instance of the Letter in the Unconscious." From this perspective, the child's riposte is to be read as giving the mother an elementary Lacanian lesson: "Sorry, mother, but there is *only one signifier*, for the man only, there is no binary signifier (for the woman), this signifier is *ur-verdrängt*, primordially repressed!" In short: you have been caught naked, you are not covered by the signifier. And what if this is the fundamental message of monotheism—not the reduction of the Other to the One, but, on the contrary, the acceptance of the fact that the binary signifier always already lacks? This imbalance between the One and its "primordially repressed" counterpart is the radical difference, in contrast to the great cosmological couples (*yin* and *yang*, etc.) which can only emerge within the horizon of the undifferentiated One (*tao*, etc.). Even attempts to introduce a balanced duality into trivial spheres of consumption, like the small blue and red bags of artificial sweetener found in many cafes, betray yet another desperate effort to provide a symmetrical signifying couple for sexual difference (blue "masculine" bags versus red "feminine" bags). The point is not that sexual difference is the ultimate signified of all such couples, but rather that their proliferation is an attempt to compensate for the *lack* of the founding binary signifying couple that would directly stand for sexual difference.

This is also why the Lacanian problematic of sexual difference—of the unavoidability of sexuation for human beings ("beings of language")—has to be strictly distinguished from the (de)constructionist problematic of the "social construction of gender," the contingent discursive formation of gender identities which emerge in being performatively enacted. An analogy with class antagonism may be of some help in grasping the crucial distinction: class antagonism (the unavoidability of the individual's "class inscription" in a class society, the impossibility of remaining unmarked by its central antagonism) also cannot be reduced to the notion of the "social construction of class identity," since every determinate "construction of class identity" is already a "reactive" or "defense" formation, an attempt to "cope with" (to come to terms with, to pacify…) the trauma of class antagonism. Every symbolic "class identity" already displaces the class antagonism by way of translating it into a positive set of symbolic features: the conservative organicist notion of society as a collective Body, with different classes as bodily organs (the ruling class as the benevolent and wiser "head," workers as the "hands," etc.) is only the most obvious case. For Lacan, things are the same with sexuation: it is impossible to "stay outside" of it, the subject is always already marked by it, always already "takes sides," always already "partial" with regard to it. The paradox of the problematic of the "social construction of gender" is that, while presenting itself as a break with "metaphysical" and/or essentialist constraints, it implicitly accomplishes a return to the pre-Freudian philosophical (i.e., non-sexualized) subject. The problematic of the "social construction of gender" presupposes the subject as given, presupposes the space of contingent symbolization, while, for Lacan, "sexuation" is the price to be paid for the very constitution of the subject, for its entry into the space of symbolization. Therein lies the crucial difference between psychoanalysis and philosophy concerning the status of sexual difference: for philosophy, the subject is not inherently sexualized, sexualization only occurs at the contingent, empirical level, whereas psychoanalysis raises sexuation into a kind of formal a priori condition for the very emergence of the subject. We should thus defend the claim that what philosophy cannot think is sexual difference *in its philosophical (ontological) dimension*: sexual difference stands for the primordial antagonism, for the non-All that subverts any totality, and this is what philosophy, up to Heidegger, has to ignore:

> The Greeks had two words for what we call life: *bios* and *zôê*. They used *bios* in a twofold sense. First, in the sense of biology, the science of life. Here we think of the organic growth of the body, glandular activity, sexual difference, and so on … Another sense of *bios* for the Greeks is the course of a life, the history of a life, more or less in the sense that the word "biography" still has for us today. *Bios* here means human history and existence—so there can be no *bios* of animals. *Bios*, as human *bios*, has the peculiar distinction of being able either to stand above the animal or to sink beneath it.[11]

If there is a lesson of psychoanalysis, it is that sexual difference belongs to the domain of *bios* as history, not to the domain of glandular activity, and so forth.

Even the "mystical" experience of "depersonalization" is marked by sexual difference. In this experience, I see myself as part of a picture which is not "mine," does not involve my standpoint—in short, I see myself "objectively" (even if this

11 Martin Heidegger, "*Hegel und der Staat*," unpublished seminar from 1933/34; my thanks to Gregory Fried, who provided me with this translation.

objectivity is, of course, fantasmatic). Recall Lacan's formula: "The picture is in my eye, but I am in the picture." If, in the common subjectivist perspectival view, every picture is mine, "in my eye," while I am not (and by definition cannot be) in the picture, the mystical experience inverts this relation: I am in the picture that I see, but the picture is not mine, "in my eye." This is how Lacan's formula of the male version of the mystical experience should be read: it identifies my gaze with the gaze of the big Other, for in it I see myself directly through the eyes of the big Other. This reliance on the big Other makes the male version of the mystical experience false, in contrast to the feminine version in which the subject identifies her gaze with the *small* other.

When Lacan claims that sexual difference is "real," he is therefore far from elevating a historically contingent form of sexuation into a trans-historical norm ("if you do not occupy your proper pre-ordained place in the heterosexual order, as either man or woman, you are excluded, exiled into a psychotic abyss outside the symbolic domain"): the claim that sexual difference is "real" equals the claim that it is "impossible": impossible to symbolize, to formulate as a symbolic norm. In other words, it is not that we homosexuals, fetishists, and other perverts are proof of the failure of sexual difference to impose its norm; it is not that sexual difference is the ultimate point of reference which anchors the contingent drifting of sexuality; it is, on the contrary, on account of the gap which forever persists between the real of sexual difference and the determinate forms of heterosexual symbolic norms that we have the multitude of "perverse" forms of sexuality. Therein lies the problem with the accusation that sexual difference involves a "binary logic": insofar as sexual difference is real/impossible, it is precisely *not* "binary," but, again, that on account of which every "binary" interpretation (every translation of sexual difference into symbolic dualisms: reason versus emotion, active versus passive, etc.) always fails.[12]

In short, what marks the difference between the two sexes is not a direct reference to the series of symbolic oppositions, but a different way of coping with the necessary inconsistency involved in the act of assuming one and the same universal symbolic feature (ultimately that of "castration"). It is not that man stands for *logos* as opposed to the feminine emphasis on emotions; it is rather that, for man, *logos* as the consistent and coherent universal principle of all reality relies on the constitutive exception of some mystical ineffable X ("there are things one should not talk about"), while, in the case of woman, there is no exception, "one can talk about everything," and, for that very reason, the

12 As Joan Copjec demonstrated in *Read My Desire*, herein resides the limit of the Butlerian motif of sexual difference as being always incomplete, as a performative process which never arrives at its end (i.e., in fixed identities). Here one has to take only a (Hegelian) step further into self-relating: sexual difference is not always incomplete, etc., *it is this incompleteness itself which makes a difference sexual.*

universe of *logos* becomes inconsistent, incoherent, dispersed, "non-All." Or, with regard to the assumption of a symbolic title, a man who tends to identify with his title absolutely, to put everything at stake for it (to die for his Cause), nonetheless relies on the myth that he is not only his title, the "social mask" he is wearing, that there is something beneath it, a "real person"; in the case of a woman, on the contrary, there is no firm, unconditional commitment, everything is ultimately a mask, and, for that very reason, there is nothing "behind the mask." Or again, with regard to love: a man in love is ready to give everything for it, the beloved is elevated into an absolute, unconditional Object, but, for that very reason, he is compelled to sacrifice Her for the sake of his public or professional Cause; while a woman is entirely, without restraint or reserve, immersed in love, there is no dimension of her being which is not permeated by love—but, for that very reason, "love is not all" for her, it is forever accompanied by an uncanny fundamental indifference.

If, then, the active-passive contrast cannot serve to differentiate the two sexes, is the contrast between interactivity (in the sense of the Cunning of Reason, of the subject transposing his/her activity onto another) and interpassivity more appropriate? Interactivity is "feminine," according to the cliché about women knowing how to remain in the background and, with their cunning plots, how to manipulate men into doing their dirty work (destroying their enemies, say). Agatha Christie's *Curtain: Poirot's Last Case* (published in 1975, although written decades earlier) concludes with a self-relating twist: the final murder is committed by Poirot himself. The true criminal of the novel, Norton, is responsible for a series of deaths but without getting blood on his hands: he has perfected the Iago-like technique of manipulating someone psychologically to provoke them into commiting a murder. In the middle of the novel, Hastings himself, Poirot's Watsonesque companion, plans a poisoning and is prevented at the last minute by Poirot. Since Poirot, himself close to death, cannot bring Norton to court, he shoots him in cold blood and then lies down to die, denying himself the pills that would have saved his life. No wonder the author of this story is a woman: Norton is interactive Evil at its purest. Interpassivity, on the contrary, is more a masculine strategy: since men are not expected to display their emotions in public, they let women to do it for them (weepers hired to mourn at funerals are always women), while they retain their self-constraint.

The traditional metaphysics of subjectivity opposes man and woman as "pure" subject (man is rational, delivered of sensuality and bodily passions) and "impure" subject (woman is unable to cut her links with sensuality, her mind at the mercy of obscure irrational passions, a passive receiver of sensual impressions, etc.)—to paraphrase Hegel, woman is a substance which has failed to fully become a subject, to purify itself into subject (or a subject who has failed to cut its links with its substance). For example, in the domain of ethics, only a man is able to abstract from his substantial family ties and reason according to universal principles, that is, to act in a truly ethical way; while with women, universality is always coloured by their particular interests: if a woman acquires universal political power, she uses it to promote the interests of her particular kin—a wisdom endlessly varied by anti-feminists like Otto Weininger (and traces of which are discernible even in Hegel's famous remarks, apropos *Antigone*, of femininity as the "eternal irony" of history).

Lacan introduces a key complication into this traditional scheme: for him, a subject (as $, a barred one) *is* the failure of its own actualization—a subject endeavors to actualize-express itself, it fails, and the subject *is* this failure. What Lacan calls the *objet petit a* gives body to this failure, it is the substantial remainder of the process of the subjectivization of substance, of the latter's *Aufhebung* in a subjective order; this is why, for Lacan, the subject is constitutively linked to the remainder, it is strictly correlative to it, as registered in Lacan's formula of fantasy: $-*a*. Insofar as woman is an "impure" subject, and insofar as the *objet petit a* is the index of this impurity, we can therefore conclude that, on account of her very "impurity," only woman is a pure subject, the subject as such, in contrast to masculine subjectivity whose "purity" is by definition fake, sustained by a hidden substantialization. In Cartesian terms, only a woman is a *cogito*, while a man is always already a *res cogitans*.

So, how does all this relate to our "concrete," "lived" experience of sexual difference? Let us begin with an archetypal melodramatic scene: that of a woman writing a letter explaining the situation to her lover, and then, after some vacillation, tearing it apart, throwing it away, and (usually) going to him, offering herself, in flesh, in her love, instead of the letter. The content of the letter is strictly codified: as a rule, it explains to the beloved why the woman he fell in love with is not who he thinks she is, and, consequently, why, precisely because she loves him, she must leave him in order not to deceive him. The tearing up of the letter then functions as a retreat: the woman cannot go right to the end and tell the truth, she prefers to go on with her deception. This gesture is fundamentally false: the woman's presence is offered as a screen destined to repress the traumatic truth which was to be articulated in the letter—as in transference in psychoanalysis, where the patient offers herself to the analyst as the ultimate form of defense, in order to block the emergence of truth.[13] In other words, love emerges when the analysis gets too close to the unconscious traumatic truth: at this point, the analysand offers herself to the analyst as the object of love, instead

13 In this sense, love is the "interpretation of the other's desire": by way of offering myself to the other, I interpret his desire as the desire for myself and thereby obfuscate the enigma of the other's desire. Put another way: when a woman offers her presence instead of the symbolic message, she thereby posits her body as the envelope of a secret, for her presence becomes a "mystery."

of the authentic letter to the analyst which would articulate the traumatic truth. In transferential love, I offer myself as object instead of knowledge: "here you have me (so that you will no longer probe into me)."[14]

This, however, is only one way to interpret the enigma of the letter which is written but not posted. In his *Why Do Women Write More Letters Than They Post?*, Darian Leader proposes a series of answers to this question,[15] which can be systematized by grouping them into two couples:

(1) With regard to its addressee, the true addressee of a woman's love letter is the Man, the absent symbolic fiction, its ideal reader, the "third" in the scene, not the flesh-and-blood man to whom it is addressed; alternatively, its true addressee is the gap of absence itself, for the letter functions as an object, it is its very play with absence (the absence of the addressee) which provides *jouissance*, since *jouissance* is contained in the act of writing itself, and since its true addressee is thus the writer herself.

(2) With regard to the way it relates to its author, the letter remains unposted because it did not say all (the author was unable to express some crucial trauma which would account for her true subjective position); or, it remains in itself forever unfinished, for there is always something more to say, since—like modernity for Habermas—woman is in herself an "unfinished project," and the non-posting of the letter acknowledges this fact that woman, like truth, cannot be "all told," that this is, as Lacan put it, "materially impossible."

Do we not encounter here the split between the phallic economy and the non-phallic domain? Not posting a letter as a false act of "repression" (of suppressing the truth and offering oneself as a love object in order to maintain the lie) is clearly correlated to the split between the man, its flesh-and-blood addressee, and some third Man, the bearer of phallic power, its ultimate addressee. In an homologous way, not posting a letter because it is an object which contains its own *jouissance* is correlated to the non-All of *feminine jouissance*, to the *jouissance* which can never be "said" in its entirety.

The direct sexualization of the gap itself which characterizes feminine

14 In contrast to such a letter which, apparently, does *not* arrive at its destination, there are (at least) two types of letters which *do* arrive at their destinations. One is the "Dear John" letter, in which the woman explains to the husband or boyfriend not love but the end of love, the fact that she is leaving him. The other is the suicidal letter destined to reach its addressee when the woman is already dead, as in Zweig's "Letter From an Unknown Woman."

15 See Darian Leader, *Why Do Women Write More Letters Than They Post?*, London: Faber & Faber 1996.

sexuality—namely the fact that, in it, much stronger than in man, the absence as such (the withdrawal, the non-act) is sexualized—also accounts for the gesture of feminine withdrawal at the very moment when "she could have had it all" (i.e., the longed-for partner) in a series of novels from Madame de Lafayette's *Princesse de Cleves* to Goethe's *Elective Affinities* (or, in the obverse or complementary case, the woman's non-withdrawal, her inexplicable perseverance in the unhappy marriage, even when the possibility has arisen for her to get out of it, as in James's *The Portrait of a Lady*).[16] Although ideology gets invested in this gesture of renunciation, the gesture itself is non-ideological. One reading of this gesture to be rejected is the standard psychoanalytic interpretation according to which we are dealing with the hysterical logic of the object of love (the lover) who is desired only insofar as he is prohibited, only insofar as there is an obstacle in, e.g., the guise of the husband—the moment the obstacle disappears, the woman loses interest in the love object. In addition to this hysterical economy of being able to enjoy the object only insofar as it remains prohibited, in other words in the guise of fantasies about what "might be," this withdrawal (or insistence) can also be interpreted in a multitude of other ways: as the expression of so-called "feminine masochism" (which can be further read as an expression of the eternal feminine nature, or as the internalization of patriarchal pressure) preventing a woman from fully "seizing the day"; as a proto-feminist gesture of breaking with the phallic economy which posits happiness in a relationship with a man as the woman's ultimate goal, and so on. However, all these interpretations seem to miss the point, which consists in the absolutely fundamental nature of the gesture of withdrawal or substitution as constitutive of the subject herself. If, following the great German Idealists, we equate the subject with freedom and autonomy, is not such a gesture of withdrawal—not as a sacrificial gesture addressed to some version of the big Other, but as a gesture which generates its own satisfaction, finding *jouissance* in the very gap that separates the subject from the object—the ultimate form of autonomy?[17]

---

16 Furthermore, the Princess of Cleves subverts the logic of adultery as inherent transgression by reversing the standard adulterous procedure of "doing it" (having sex with another man) and not telling the husband: on the contrary, she tells her husband, but does not "do it."

17 Although here again the obverse also holds: is not the famous *an die ferne Geliebte*, to the distant beloved, the motto of all love poetry? Is not male love poetry therefore the exemplary case of the sexualization of the gap which separates the poet from the beloved, so that, when the barrier disappears and the beloved comes too close, the consequences can be catastrophic? The thing to do would be, again, to construct two almost-symmetrically inverted couple of opposites: men prefer their beloved to remain distant in contrast to women who want their man close to them; but, simultaneously, men want to enjoy directly the partner's body, while women can enjoy the very gap which separates them from the partner's body. What is wrong with the male version? One of Schubert's

The conclusion to be drawn from this is that it is wrong to contrast man and woman in an immediate way, as if man directly desires an object, while woman's desire is a "desire to desire," the desire for the Other's desire. We are dealing here with sexual difference as real, which means that the opposite also holds, albeit in a slightly displaced way. True, a man directly desires a woman who fits the frame of his fantasy, while a woman alienates her desire much more thoroughly in a man—her desire is to be the object desired by man, to fit the frame of his fantasy, which is why she endeavors to look at herself through the other's eyes and is permanently bothered by the question "What do others see in her/me?" However, a woman is simultaneously much less dependent on her partner, since her ultimate partner is not the other human being, her object of desire (the man), but the gap itself, that distance from her partner in which the *jouissance féminine* is located. *Vulgari eloquentia*, in order to cheat on a woman, a man needs a (real or imagined) partner, while a woman can cheat on a man even when she is alone, since her ultimate partner is solitude itself as the locus of *jouissance féminine* beyond the phallus.

Sexual difference is thus real also in the sense that no symbolic opposition can directly and adequately render it. The real difference is not a difference between opposed symbolic features, but a difference between two types of opposition: a woman is essential to a man's sexual life, yet for that very reason he has a domain outside his sexual life which matters more to him; to a woman, sexuality tends to be the feature which permeates her entire life, there is nothing which—potentially, at least—is not sexualized, yet for that very reason a woman's sexuality involves much more that the presence of a man. The point, of course, is that this reversal is not purely symmetrical, but slightly displaced—and it is this displacement which points towards the Real of sexual difference. Again, the underlying structure here is that of Lacan's formulae of sexuation, the universality (a woman who is essential, all…) with an exception (career, public life) in man's case; the non-universality (a man is not-all in woman's sexual life) with no exception (there is nothing which is not sexualized) in woman's case. This paradox of the feminine position is captured by the ambiguity of Emily Dickinson's celebrated Poem 732:

key songs, "The Wanderer" (D 493, words by Georg Philipp Schmidt von Luebeck), describing the search for the beloved homeland where "my friends walk, where my dead rise again," ends with: "I wander, silent and joyless, / my sighs forever asking: Where? / A ghostly whisper answers me: / 'There where you are not, there happiness lies.'" The final "*Dort, wo du nicht bist, dort ist das Glück!*" is the most concise formulation of what is wrong with Romantic love, of why this love is false.

She rose to His Requirement—dropt
The Playthings of Her Life
To take the honorable Work
Of Woman, and of Wife—

If ought she missed in Her new Day,
Of Amplitude, or Awe—
Or first Prospective—Or the Gold
In using, wear away,

It lay unmentioned—as the Sea
Develop Pearl, and Wheed,
But only to Himself—be known
The Fathoms they abide—[18]

This poem, of course, can be read as alluding to the sacrifice of the *agalma*—the *objet petit a*, the "playthings" of feminine *jouissance*—which occurs when the woman becomes a Woman, when she assumes the subordinate role of Wife: underneath, inaccessible to the male gaze, the part of "she" which does not fit her role as "Woman" (which is why, in the last stanza, she refers to herself as "Himself") continues to lead its secret "unmentioned" existence. However, it can also be read in an opposite, and far more uncanny, way: what if the status of this "secret treasure" sacrificed when the woman becomes a Wife is purely fantasmatic? What if she evokes this secret in order to fascinate His (her husband's, the male) gaze? Is it not also possible to read "but only to Himself" in the sense that the notion of the feminine treasure sacrificed when a woman enters into a sexual liaison with a man is a semblance intended to fascinate His gaze, and thus stands for the loss of something which was never present, never possessed? (The very definition of the *objet a* is: an object which emerges in the very gesture of its loss.) In short, does not this "lost treasure" follow the line of the male fantasy about the feminine secret which lies beyond the limit of the symbolic order, beyond its reach? Or, in Hegelese: the feminine In-itself, out of reach of the male gaze, is already "for the Other," an inaccessible Mystery imagined by the male gaze itself. This is why Badiou is fully justified in rejecting the standard version of Lacan's *jouissance féminine* which links its infinity to the mystical Unsayable as the remainder of the "cultural": "That feminine enjoyment ties the infinite to the unsayable, and that mystical ecstasy provides evidence for this, is a theme I would characterize as cultural. One feels that, even in Lacan, it has not yet been submitted to a radical test by the ideal of the matheme."[19]

18 *The Complete Poems of Emily Dickinson*, Boston: Little, Brown 1960, p. 359.
19 Alain Badiou, *Theoretical Writings*, London: Continuum 2004, p. 129.

All one should add here is that there is also a more literal reading of the *jouissance féminine* which totally breaks with the topos of the Unsayable—on this opposite reading, the "non-All" of the feminine implies that there is nothing in feminine subjectivity which is not marked by the phallic-symbolic function: if anything, woman is *more* fully "in language" than man. Which is why any reference to pre-symbolic "feminine substance" is misleading. According to a recently popular theory, the (biological) male is just a (falsely emancipated) detour in female self-reproduction, which, in principle, is possible without men. Elisabeth Badinter claims that, biologically, we are all essentially feminine (the X chromosome is the pattern for all humanity, the Y chromosome an addition, not a mutation); for that reason, development into a male implies a labor of differentiation that female embryos are spared.[20] Furthermore, in relation to social life, males start off as citizens in a female homeland (the uterus) before being forced to emigrate and live their lives as homesick exiles. That is to say, since men were originally created female, they must have become differentiated from women by means of social and cultural processes—so it is man, not woman, who is the culturally formed "second sex."[21] This theory can be useful as a kind of political myth accounting for the contemporary insecurity of male identity. Badinter is at a certain level right to point out that the true social crisis today is the crisis of male identity, of "what it means to be a man": women are more or less successfully invading man's territory, assuming male functions in social life without losing their feminine identity, while the obverse process, the male (re)conquest of the "feminine" territory of intimacy, is far more traumatic. While the figure of publicly successful woman is already part of our "social imaginary," problems with a "gentle man" are far more unsettling. This theory, however, while it seems to assert in a "feminist" way the primacy of the feminine, reproduces fundamental metaphysical premises concerning the relationship between the masculine and the feminine; Badinter herself associates the male position with the values of being prepared to take the risk of exile, to leave the safe haven of Home, and of the need to create one's identity through labor and cultural mediation—is this not a pseudo-Hegelian theory which, on account of the fact that labor and mediation are on the male side, clearly privileges man? In short, the notion that woman is the Base and man the secondary mediation/deviation with no proper/natural identity, lays the ground for the anti-feminist argument par excellence,

20 See Elisabeth Badinter, *XY: On Masculine Identity*, New York: Columbia University Press 1996.

21 At a more elementary biological (and also scientifically more convincing) level, some scientists claim that complex forms of organic life result from the malignancy of simple (monocellular) life-forms which, at a certain point, "ran amok" and started to multiply in a pathological way—complex life is thus inherently, in its very notion, a pathological formation.

since, as Hegel never tires of repeating, spirit itself is, from the standpoint of nature, "secondary," a pathological deviation, "nature sick unto death," and the power of spirit resides in the very fact that a marginal/secondary phenomenon, "in itself" a mere detour within some larger natural process, can, through the labor of mediation, elevate itself into an End-in-itself which "posits" its own natural presupposition as part of its own "spiritual" totality. On that score, the apparently "depreciating" notions of femininity as a mere masquerade, lacking any substantial identity and inner shape, of woman as a "castrated," deprived, degenerated, incomplete man, are potentially of far greater use for feminism than the ethical elevation of femininity—in short, Otto Weininger is more useful than Carol Gilligan.

Formulae of sexuation: the All with an exception

Lacan elaborated the inconsistencies which structure sexual difference in his "formulae of sexuation," where the masculine side is defined by the universal function and its constitutive exception, and the feminine side by the paradox of "non-All" (*pas-tout*) (there is no exception, and for that very reason, the set is non-All, non-totalized). Recall the shifting status of the Ineffable in Wittgenstein: the passage from early to late Wittgenstein is the passage from All (the order of the universal All grounded in its constitutive exception) to non-All (the order without exception and for that reason non-universal, non-All). That is to say, in the early Wittgenstein of the *Tractatus*, the world is comprehended as a self-enclosed, limited, bounded Whole of "facts" which precisely as such presupposes an Exception: the mystical Ineffable which functions as its Limit. In late Wittgenstein, on the contrary, the problematic of the Ineffable disappears, yet for that very reason the universe is no longer comprehended as a Whole regulated by the universal conditions of language: all that remains are lateral connections between partial domains. The notion of language as a system defined by a set of universal features is replaced by the notion of language as a multitude of dispersed practices loosely interconnected by "family resemblances."[22]

A certain type of ethnic cliché renders perfectly this paradox of the non-All: the narratives of Origin in which a nation posits itself as being "more X than X itself," where X stands for another nation commonly regarded as the paradigmatic case of some property. The myth of Iceland is that it became inhabited

22 In Yu-Gi-Oh, a massively popular card game of neo-Gothic mythical content, the rules are endless: new cards are always added, each card containing its own precise rule of application. All the cards together thus can never be subsumed under a general set of rules—they form a kind of Lacanian "non-All" multiplicity, in clear contrast to the classic games with their limited number of cards and clear finite rules.

when those who found Norway, the freest land in the world, too oppressive, fled to Iceland; the myth about Slovenes being miserly claims that Scotland (the proverbial land of misers) became populated when Slovenes expelled to Scotland someone who had spent too much money. The point is not that Slovenes are the most avaricious or Icelanders the most freedom-loving—Scots remain the most miserly, but Slovenes are even more so; the people of Norway remain the most freedom-loving, but Icelanders are even more so. This is the paradox of the "non-All": if we totalize all nations, then the Scots are the most miserly, yet if we compare them one by one, as "non-All," Slovenes are more miserly. A variation on the same motif occurs in Rossini's famous statement on the difference between Beethoven and Mozart: when asked, "Who is the greatest composer?" Rossini answered, "Beethoven"; when asked the additional question "What about Mozart?" he added, "Mozart is not the greatest, he is the only composer..." This opposition between Beethoven ("the greatest" of them all, since he struggled with his compositions with titanic effort, overcoming the resistance of the musical material) and Mozart (who freely floated in the musical stuff and composed with spontaneous grace) points towards the well-known opposition between the two notions of God: God as "the greatest," above all Creation, the Ruler of the World, and so on, and God who is not the greatest but simply the only reality, who does not relate to finite reality as separate from him, since he is "all there is," the immanent principle of all reality.[23]

The famous first paragraph of Deleuze and Guattari's *Anti-Oedipus* contains another unexpected example of universality grounded in an exception: it begins with a long list of what the unconscious ("it," not the substantialized "Id," of course) does: "It is at work everywhere, functioning smoothly at times, at other times in fits and starts. It breathes, it heats, it eats. It shits and fucks."[24] Talking is conspicuously missing from this series: for Deleuze and Guattari, there is no "ça parle," the unconscious does not talk. The plethora of functions is in place to cover up this absence—as was clear already to Freud, multiplicity (of phalluses in a dream, of the wolves the Wolf-man sees through the window in his

23 Nietzsche's famous claim that Christ was the only true Christian also relies on a reversal of the usual role of the founding figure which is that of the constitutive exception: Marx was not a Marxist, since he himself was Marx and could not entertain towards himself the reflexive relationship implied by the term "Marxist." Christ, on the contrary, not only was a Christian, but—for that very reason, following an inexorable necessity—has to be the only (true) Christian. How is this possible? Only if we introduce a radical gap between Christ himself and Christianity and assert that Christianity is grounded in the radical misrecognition, even active disavowal, of Christ's act. Christianity is thus a kind of defense-formation against the scandalous nature of Christ's act.

24 Gilles Deleuze and Félix Guattari, *Anti-Oedipus: Capitalism and Schizophrenia*, trans. R. Hurley, M. Seem, and H. R. Lane, Minneapolis: University of Minnesota Press 1983, p. 1.

famous dream) is the very image of castration. Multiplicity signals that the One is lacking.[25]

The logic of universality and its constitutive exception should be deployed in three moments: (1) First, there is the exception to universality: every universality contains a particular element which, while formally belonging to the universal dimension, sticks out, does not fit its frame. (2) Then comes the insight that *every* particular example or element of a universality is an exception: there is no "normal" particularity, every particularity sticks out, is in excess and/or lacking with regard to its universality (as Hegel showed, no existing form of state fits the notion of the State). (3) Then comes the proper dialectical twist: the exception to the exception—still an exception, but the exception as singular universality, an element whose exception is its direct link to universality itself, which stands directly for the universal. (Note here the parallel with the three moments of the value-form in Marx.)

The starting point for Lacan's formulae of sexuation is Aristotle—why? Aristotle oscillates between two notions of the relationship between form and matter: either form is conceived as universal, a possibility of particular beings, and matter as the principle or agent of individualization (what makes a table this particular table is the particular matter in which the universal form of Table is actualized), or matter is conceived as neutral-universal stuff, a possibility of different beings, and form as the principle of individualization, as the agent which transforms neutral matter into a particular entity (the form of a table makes wood—which could have become many other things—a table). For Hegel, of course, the first notion is that of abstract universality (universality as a neutral form shared by many particular entities), while the second notion already contains the germ of concrete universality: the form (i.e., universal concept) is in itself the principle or agent of its own individualization, of its concrete self-articulation. *It is in order to resolve or obfuscate this deadlock that Aristotle has to have recourse to sexual difference*: being (a substantial entity) is the unity of form and hyle, of masculine and feminine, of active and passive.

This point is crucial to bear in mind: Lacan's claim is not the rather obvious one that the Aristotelian couple of form and hyle is "sexualized," that Aristotelian ontology remains in the lineage of the ancient sexualized cosmologies. It is, on the contrary, that Aristotle has to have recourse to a sexualized couple in order to resolve a strictly conceptual problem—and that this solution does not work, since the paradox of gender is that it disturbs the clear division into genus and species: we cannot say that humanity is a genus (gender) composed of two

25 However, how are we to read this thesis together with Badiou's basic ontological axiom on primordial multiplicity which is not the multiplicity of Ones? The identity of this multiplicity and the Void is clearly *not* the sign of the lack of the One, but a primordial ontological fact.

species, men and women, since a species is a unity which can reproduce itself—no wonder our everyday use of these terms turns this hierarchical distinction around: we talk about the human *species* composed of (divided into) two *genders*.[26] What this confusion indicates is that there is indeed "gender trouble," but not in Judith Butler's sense: the point is not only that the identity of each sex is not clearly established, neither socially nor symbolically nor biologically—it is not only that sexual identity is a symbolic norm imposed onto a fluid and polymorphous body which never fits the ideal—the "trouble" is rather that this ideal itself is inconsistent, masking a constitutive incompatibility. Sexual difference is not simply a particular difference subordinated to the universality of the human genus/gender, but has a stronger status inscribed into the very universality of the human species: a difference which is the constitutive feature of the universal species itself, and which, paradoxically, for this reason, precedes (logically/conceptually) the two terms it differentiates between: "perhaps, the difference which keeps apart one [sex] from the other belongs neither to the one nor to the other."[27]

So how do Lacan's formulae of sexuation relate to Aristotle? Lacan proposes a reading of the Aristotelian "logical square" different from the predominant one: he introduces a subtle change into each of the four propositions. First, in his reading (here Lacan follows Peirce), the truth of the universal affirmation does not imply existence: it is true that "all x are Fx" even if no x exists. Second, he does not read the particular affirmation (some x are Fx) in the standard "minimal" way ("at least some x—but maybe all x—are Fx"), but in the "maximal" way, that is, as excluding the universal affirmation, as in contradiction with it ("some x are Fx means that all x are *not* Fx"). Third, he changes the formulation of the universal negative statement into a double negation: instead of the standard "all x are not Fx," he writes, "there is no x which is not Fx." Fourth, he changes the formulation of the negative particular statement, displacing the negation from the function to the quantifier: not "some x are not Fx," but "not-all x are Fx."

What immediately stands out is how contradiction is displaced. In the classic Aristotelian logical square, contradiction is vertical, between the left side ("all x are Fx" and "some x are Fx") and the right side ("all x are not Fx" and "some x are not Fx"): the two universal propositions are contrary (all x are Fx or not Fx), while the two diagonals are contradictory ("some x are nonFx" is in contradiction with "all x are Fx"; and "some x are Fx" is in contradiction with "all x are nonFx"). Furthermore, the relation between each universal and particular

26 A further indication of this confusion is found in German, where the word *Geschlecht* means species (like *Menschengeschlecht*, human species) or even tribe, *and* sex (*Geschlechtdifferenz* is sexual difference).

27 Guy Le Gaufey, *Le Pastout de Lacan: consistance logique, conséquences cliniques*, Paris: EPEL 2006, p. 11.

proposition is one of implication: "all x are Fx" implies that "some x are Fx," and "all x are not Fx" implies that "some x are not Fx"; plus the relation between the two particular propositions is one of compatibility ("some x are Fx" and "some x are not Fx" can both be true). The standard example: "all swans are white" and "all swans are not-white" is contrary; "all swans are white" and "some swans are non-white" is contradictory, as well as "all swans are non-white" and "some swans are white"; "some swans are white" is compatible with "some swans are non-white."

In the square as rewritten by Lacan, contradictions are only between the upper and the lower levels (directly and diagonally): "all x are Fx" is in contradiction with "there is at least one x which is nonFx" as well as with "not-all x are Fx," and vice versa for "there is no x which is not Fx"; the relationship between the two horizontal couples, the upper and the lower, is, on the contrary, one of equivalence: "all x are Fx" is equivalent to "there is no x which is nonFx," and "there is at least one x which is nonFx" is equivalent to "not-all x are Fx." This lesson is crucial: "there is no sexual relationship" means that there is no direct relationship between the left (masculine) and the right (feminine) side, not even that of contrariness or contradiction; the two sides, set side by side, are equivalent, which means they just coexist in a non-relationship of indifference. Contradiction only occurs *within* each of the sexes, between the universal and the particular of each sexual position ("all x are Fx" is in contradiction with "there is at least one x which is not Fx," and "there is no x which is not Fx" is in contradiction with "not-all x are Fx"). Sexual difference is thus ultimately not the difference between the sexes, but the difference which cuts across the very heart of the identity of each sex, stigmatizing it with the mark of impossibility. If sexual difference is not the difference between the two sexes, but a difference which cuts from within each sex, how then do the two sexes relate to each other? Lacan's answer is "indifference": there is no relationship, *il n'y a pas de rapport sexuel*—the two sexes are out of sync. Recall that, on very last page of *Seminar XI*, Lacan defines the desire of the analyst not as a pure desire (a self-critical remark, clearly—he had himself claimed this in *Seminar VII*), but as a desire to obtain absolute difference.[28] In order for the difference to be "absolute," it

28 The structural role of Lacan's seminar on the four fundamental concepts of psychoanalysis is comparable to that of Shakespeare's late plays, Mozart's *Magic Flute*, or Wagner's *Parsifal*: after the lowest point of despair (Shakespeare's mature tragedies, Mozart's *Cosi fan tutte*, Wagner's *Twilight of the Gods*), the mood changes, we enter a fairy-tale space where problems are magically resolved, where the tragic deadlock dissolves into bliss. This shift is similar to the one in the middle of Freud's dream on Irma's injection: the darkest moment of nightmare, as Freud looks into Irma's throat, which stands for the abyss of the primordial Real, suddenly shifts into comedy, the lighthearted conversation between the three doctors who try to pass the blame for the treatment's failure onto each other. And is it not similar with the passage from Lacan's

must be a redoubled, self-reflected difference, a difference of differences, and this is what the formulae of sexuation offer: the "dynamic" antinomy of All and its exception, and the "mathematic" antinomy of non-All without exception. In other words, there is no direct way to formulate sexual difference: sexual difference names the Real of an antagonism which can only be circumscribed through two different contradictions.[29]

Let us take a closer look at the first antinomy: Lacan refers here to Peirce's logical square of universal and particular positive and negative propositions, which implies that the truth of a universal affirmative proposition does not imply the existence of a term to which it refers, in contrast to a particular affirmative proposition ("all unicorns have one horn" is true even if there are no unicorns, but not "some unicorns have one horn"—for the second proposition to be true, at least one unicorn has to exist).[30] What are the consequences for psychoanalysis of the purely logical point that the true of a universal affirmation does not imply that a particular element which exemplifies this truth exists? It is true that unicorns have only one horn, but there are nonetheless no unicorns... and if we go by way of a little wild analysis insisting on the phallic value of the single horn growing out of the forehead, this brings us to the paternal phallic authority, to what Lacan calls the Name-of-the-Father. "All fathers are Fx" is true, but this means that no existing father is "really father," that—in Hegelese—there is no father at the level of his notion: every father that exists is an exception to the universal notion of father:

> the order of the function which we introduced here as that of the name-of-the-father is something which has universal value, but, simultaneously, puts on you the charge to control if there is or not a father who fits this function. If there is no such father,

---

Seminar X (on anxiety) to *Seminar XI*? *Seminar X* marks the lowest point of nightmare, the confrontation with the Real of anxiety, while, in *Seminar XI*, the mood changes—stylistically also—from the tragic-pathetic elaboration of concepts that characterizes Lacan's "mature" seminars of the late 1950s and early 1960s, to the hermetic "playfulness" of the seminars that follow the eleventh.

29 There are even two approaches to the inner logic of the four formulae: either we start on the masculine side, where it all begins with the maximal particular (existential) judgment, and the feminine side then emerges as the consequence, or we begin with the feminine non-All, which is then totalized through exception.

30 During one of Boris Yeltsin's visits abroad in the mid-1990s, a foreign dignitary asked him: "Can you describe, very briefly, in one word, the situation in Russia?" Yeltsin replied: "Good." Surprised, the foreign dignitary went on: "And a little bit more in detail, in two words?" "Not good." Yeltsin's answer demonstrated a surprising dialectical *finesse*: both of his replies were true; i.e., in order to pass from the positive judgment to negativity ("not"), all one has to do is expand the judgment into the particular, since particularity is as such "negative," the negation of its universal dimension.

> it still remains true that the father is God, it is simply that this formula is confirmed only by the empty sector of the square.[31]

The implications of this paradox for the individual's psychic economy are crucial: the paternal function is universal, each of us is determined by it, but there is always a gap between the universal paternal function and the individual who occupies this symbolic place: no father is "really a father," every "real" father is either not-enough-father, a deficient father, failing to play the role properly, or too-much-father, an overbearing presence which stains the paternal symbolic function with pathological obscenity. The only father who fully exists is the exception to the universal function, the "primordial father" external to the symbolic Law.[32] Or, a more problematic example: one curious story about Hitler reported in the (in)famous record of his "table conversations" is that, one morning in the early 1940s, he awoke terrified and then, with tears running down his cheeks, explained to his doctor the nightmare that had haunted him: "In my dream, I saw the future overmen—they are so totally ruthless, without any consideration for our pains, that I found it unbearable!" The very idea of Hitler, our main candidate for the most evil person of all time, being horrified at a lack of compassion is, of course, weird—but, philosophically, the idea makes sense. What Hitler was implicitly referring to was the Nietzschean passage from Lion to Child: it is not yet possible for us, caught as we are in the reflective attitude of nihilism, to enter the "innocence of becoming," the full life beyond justification; all we can do is engage in a "self-overcoming of morality through truthfulness."[33] So it is all too easy to dismiss the Nazis as inhuman and bestial—what if the problem was precisely that they remained "human, all too human"? But let us go further and move to the opposite end of the spectrum, to Jesus Christ: is not Jesus also a case of the singular exception ("there is one God who is an exception to divinity, who is fully human") which implies the inexistence of the universal God?

This affirmation of existence as an exception to (its) universal notion cannot but appear anti-Hegelian, Kierkegaardian even: is not Hegel's point precisely that every existence can be subsumed under a universal essence through notional mediation? But what if we conceive it as the elementary figure of what Hegel called "concrete universality"? Concrete universality is not the organic

31 Jacques Lacan, seminar of January 17, 1962, in *Le séminaire, Livre XI: L'identification* (unpublished).

32 The Lacanian exception is nicely captured in a vulgar wisdom popular among soldiers: "No matter how hard you shake your peg, you'll always have a drop upon your leg!"

33 Friedrich Nietzsche, *Ecce Homo*, trans. R. J. Hollingdale, London: Penguin Books 1992, p. 98.

articulation of a universality into its species or parts or organs; we approach concrete universality only when the universality in question encounters, among its species or moments, itself in its oppositional determination, in an exceptional moment which denies the universal dimension and is as such its direct embodiment. Within a hierarchical society, the exceptional element are those at the bottom, like the "untouchables" in India. In contrast to Gandhi, Dr. Ambedkar "underlined the futility of merely abolishing Untouchability: this evil being the product of a social hierarchy of a particular kind, it was the entire caste system that had to be eradicated: 'There will be out castes [Untouchables] as long as there are castes.' … Gandhi responded that, on the contrary, here it was a question of the foundation of Hinduism, a civilization which, in its original form, in fact ignored hierarchy."[34] Although Gandhi and Ambedkar respected each other and often collaborated in the struggle to defend the dignity of the Untouchables, their difference here is insurmountable: it is the difference between the "organic" solution (solving the problem by returning to the purity of the original uncorrupted system) and the truly radical solution (identifying the problem as the "symptom" of the entire system, a symptom which can only be resolved by abolishing the entire system). Ambedkar saw clearly how the four-caste structure does not unite four elements which belong to the same order: while the first three castes (priests, warrior-kings, merchants-producers) form a consistent All, an organic triad, the Untouchables are, like Marx's "Asiatic mode of production," the "part of no-part," the inconsistent element which, within the system, occupies the place of what the system as such excludes—and, as such, the Untouchables stand for universality. Effectively, there are no castes without outcasts—as long as there are castes, there will be an excessive, excremental zero-value element which, while formally part of the system, has no proper place within it. Gandhi obfuscates this paradox, clinging to the (im)possibility of a harmonious structure that would fully integrate all its elements. The paradox of the Untouchables is that they are doubly marked by the excremental logic: not only do they deal with impure excrement, their own formal status within the social body is that of excrement. Hence the properly dialectical paradox: to break out of the caste system, it is not enough to reverse the Untouchable's status, elevating them into the "children of God." The first step should rather be exactly the opposite one: to *universalize* their excremental status to the whole of humanity.

But is there an inconsistency here?—First, the claim was that *every* particular entity is an exception, unfit as an example of its universality; then we posited the exception as the singular Master-Signifier which holds, within a structure, the place of its lack. The solution lies in the redoubled exception: every particular entity is in the position of an exception with regard to its universality;

34 Christophe Jaffrelot, *Dr Ambedkar and Untouchability: Analysing and Fighting Caste*, New Delhi: Permanent Black 2005, pp. 68–9.

with regard to the series of "normal" exceptions, the Master-Signifier which represents the subject is the *exception to the exception*, the only place of direct universality. In other words, in the Master-Signifier, the logic of exception is taken to its reflexive extreme: the Master-Signifier is totally excluded from the universal order (as its "part of no-part," with no proper place in it), and, as such, it immediately stands for universality as opposed to its particular content. (It is in this sense that Hegel characterizes Christ as an "example of example" and, as such, as the "absolute example.")

Such "oppositional determination" subjectivizes a structure—how? To grasp this logic of subjectivization, one has to introduce the difference between the enunciated (content) and its process of enunciation, that is, Lacan's difference between the subject of the enunciated and the subject of enunciation: *the exception with regard to the universal order is the subject itself*, its position of enunciation. To put it in somewhat simplistic terms, insofar as universality is in front of me, the object of my thought or speech, I occupy by definition a place of minimal externality with regard to it—no matter how much I locate myself as a *res cogitans*, as a determinate object within the reality I am grasping, that tiny spot in my world is not me as the point of "self-consciousness," the point from which I speak or think. Of course, all my positive properties or determinations can be "objectivized," but not "myself" as the singular self-reflexive point of enunciation. In this simple but strict sense, the subject is more universal than universality itself: it may be a tiny part of reality, a tiny speck in the "great chain of being," but it is simultaneously the singular (stand)point encompassing reality as something that appears within its horizon. We experience this exception in a pointed way apropos statements which concern our mortality: "every human is mortal" implicitly excludes *me* as mortal, excepts me from the universality of mortals, although I know very well that (as a human animal) I am also mortal. One should take a step further here: not only is the subject a crack in universality, an X which cannot be located in a substantial totality—there is universality (universality "for itself," as Hegel would have put it) only for the subject: only from the minimally exempted subjective standpoint can an All, a universality (as different from its particular instantiations), appear as such, never to someone or something fully embedded in it as its particular moment. In this sense exception literally grounds universality.

Formulae of sexuation: the non-All

What if there is no such exception? Then we are dealing with particularities which, by definition (or, in Hegelese, in their very notion), *cannot be universalized*. The most interesting case is that of so-called "direct democracy" in its different forms (from "workers' councils" or "self-government" to "multitudes"). Political theorists and activists who today advocate such an approach, fighting for local self-organization against state power and representative democracy, as a rule hold to the utopian idea of a radical revolutionary rupture through which direct-democratic self-organization will encompass the entire social body. Typical here is Hardt and Negri's *Multitude*: after describing multiple forms of resistance to Empire, the book ends with a messianic note pointing towards the great Rupture, the moment of Decision when the movement of multitudes will be transubstantiated into the sudden birth of a new world: "After this long season of violence and contradictions, global civil war, corruption of imperial bio-power, and infinite toil of the bio-political multitudes, the extraordinary accumulations of grievances and reform proposals must at some point be transformed by a strong event, a radical insurrectional demand."[35] However, at this point, where one would expect some theoretical determination of this rupture, what we get is again a withdrawal into philosophy: "A philosophical book like this, however, is not the place for us to evaluate whether the time for revolutionary political decision is imminent."[36] Hardt and Negri here make an all too hasty leap: of course one cannot ask them for a detailed empirical description of the Decision, of the passage to the globalized "absolute democracy," to the multitude that will rule itself; but what if their justified refusal to engage in pseudo-concrete futuristic predictions masks an inherent notional deadlock or impossibility? That is to say, what one can and should expect is some description of the notional structure of this qualitative jump, of the passage from the multitudes *resisting* the One of sovereign Power to the multitudes annihilating state power and directly becoming the global structuring principle of society. Leaving the notional structure of this passage in a darkness elucidated only by vague homologies and examples from resistance movements only raises the suspicion that this direct, self-transparent rule of everyone over everyone, this democracy *tout court*, will coincide with its opposite. This is why such generalization is properly *utopian*: it cannot see its own structural impossibility, how it can only thrive within a field dominated by what it fights against.

To better grasp this notion of the non-All, let us turn to a wonderful dialectical joke in Lubitch's *Ninotchka*: the hero visits a cafeteria and orders coffee without cream; the waiter replies: "Sorry, but we've run out of cream. Can I bring you coffee without milk?"[37] In both cases, the customer gets straight coffee, but this One-coffee is each time accompanied by a different negation, first

35 Michael Hardt and Antonio Negri, *Multitude*, New York: The Penguin Press 2004, p. 358.

36 Ibid, p. 357.

37 I owe this reference to Alenka Zupančič.

coffee-with-no-cream, then coffee-with-no-milk.[38] What we encounter here is the logic of differentiality where the lack itself functions as a positive feature—the paradox also rendered nicely by an old Yugoslav joke about Montenegrins (people from Montenegro were stigmatized as lazy in ex-Yugoslavia): why does a Montenegrin guy, when going to sleep, put two glasses, one full and one empty, at the side of his bed? Because he is too lazy to think in advance whether he will be thirsty during the night. The point of this joke is that the absence itself has to be positively registered: it is not enough to have a full glass of water, since, if the Montenegrin is not thirsty, he will simply ignore it—this negative fact itself has to be registered, the no-need-for-water has to be materialized in the void of the empty glass. A political equivalent can be found in a well-known joke from socialist-era Poland. A customer enters a store and asks: "You probably don't have butter, or do you?" The answer: "Sorry, but we're the store that doesn't have toilet paper; the one across the street is the one that doesn't have butter!" Or consider contemporary Brazil where, during a carnival, people from all classes will dance together in the street, momentarily forgetting their race and class differences—but it is obviously not the same if a jobless worker joins the dance, forgetting his worries about how to take care of his family, or if a rich banker lets himself go and feels good about being one with the people, forgetting that he has just refused a loan to the poor worker. They are both the same on the street, but the worker is dancing without milk, while the banker is dancing without cream.

We should supplement this structure of the un-said that accompanies what is said, of the negation which reverberates in what is asserted, with the symmetrical version of getting more than you asked for—in the terms of our joke, of getting coffee with milk when one asked only for a black coffee. Is not this ideological mechanism structurally the same as the relationship between played and unplayed notes in Schumann's "Humoresque"? The point is that the way ideology cheats is not so much by directly lying (telling us we are being served coffee while we are effectively being served tea), but by engendering the wrong un-said implication (telling us we are being served coffee without cream while we are effectively being served coffee without milk). We do not expect the public discourse of those in power to tell us everything, to disclose all their secret maneuvers; most of us accept that some things have to be done discreetly, in the shadows, but we also expect these things to be done for the common good. At the beginning of the Marx Brothers' *Go West* (1940), Groucho buys a ticket at the railway station counter and gives the clerk a bundle of dollar notes, nonchalantly remarking: "It's OK, you don't have to count it!" The clerk nonetheless carefully counts the money and indignantly replies: "But there is not enough money here!" To which Groucho responds: "I told you not to count it!" Did not

38 In a similar way, East Europeans in 1990 wanted not only democracy-without-communism, but also democracy-without-capitalism.

Dick Cheney treat us in a similar way when he said that, in the "war on terror," some things had to be done out of public view in order to get results? When we were shocked to discover the truth about mass killings, torture, etc., but also about Cheney promoting his own business interests (Halliburton), his reply was basically: "I told you things have to be done out of public view!"

Can the underlying logic of these jokes, however, really be reduced to differentiality? Is "coffee with no-milk" instead of "coffee with no-cream" a case of symbolic differentiality, of absence itself counting as a positive feature? In other words, in both cases, what we "really get" is exactly the same plain coffee, the difference residing only in the purely differential fact that the absence which defines this coffee is the absence of milk instead of the absence of cream, and, as we know from Lacan, there is no absence in the Real, things can be "present in the mode of absence" only in the symbolic space where something can be missing at its (symbolic) place.[39] What complicates the issue is the double negation at work in "coffee with no-milk": this coffee is not just "with no-milk" but "not with no-cream," and this second negation is not purely symbolic, even if it may appear that what is added is just a new differential opposition ("with no-cream" versus "not with no-cream"). It is "coffee with milk" which would have functioned differentially, as "coffee with no-cream," and, within this differential space, "coffee not with no-cream" is simply "coffee *with* cream." Is it then that we have to add another differential opposition, that of "coffee with X" versus "coffee without X"? Our thesis is that this last opposition is not symbolic or differential, since it concerns the *objet petit a*, the real of a *je ne sais quoi* which makes coffee an object of desire, that which is "in coffee more than coffee itself." Or, as Alenka Zupančič subtly reconstructed the waiter's reasoning:

> If [the customer] wants just straight coffee, he should have been indifferent towards what it is without. There is thus a desire at work in his explicit rejection of cream, and, as a good waiter, I should try to follow this desire, since, in this case, "coffee without cream" is in no way the same as "straight coffee." The solution is in the metonymy of lack, since desire itself is nothing but this metonymy. Let us then give him a coffee without milk.[40]

It may appear that "coffee without milk" instead of "coffee without cream" is a case of differentiality, not of the negation of the negation which generates the "minimal difference" of the *objet a*—or is it? A coffee "not without cream" is not a coffee *with* milk, but a coffee without *milk*, i.e., the negation of another

---

39 This is why, for Lacan, castration is symbolic: in the Real, nothing is missing in a woman's body, it is only for the gaze which expected to see a penis that its absence is experienced as such.

40 Alenka Zupančič, "Med dvema ne," *Problemi* 8–9 (2010).

supplement. There is a difference between "plain coffee" and "coffee not without cream" (i.e., "coffee without milk"): the second is still marked by a lack, but the place of the lack has shifted. Where is the *objet a* here? We have to ask a simple question: why do we add milk or cream to coffee? Because there is something missing in coffee alone, and we try to fill this void—in short, the series of supplements to coffee are attempts to fill in the non-identity of coffee with itself. What this means (among other things) is that there is no full self-identical "plain coffee," that every simple "just coffee" is already a "coffee without." And it is here that the *objet a* is located: coffee is in itself not One but a One plus something which is less than One and more than nothing. The structure is the same as that of *Kinder Surprise* chocolate eggs: after unwrapping the egg and cracking the shell open, one finds a small plastic toy inside. Is not this toy the *objet petit a* at its purest, a small object filling in the central void of our desire, the hidden treasure, *agalma*, at the center of the thing we desire? This material ("Real") void at the center, of course, stands for the structural ("formal") gap on account of which no product is "really *that*," no product lives up to the expectation it arouses. This reflexive logic of filling the void is at work even (and especially) when we are offered a product "with nothing added," standing for authentic quality, like "just plain best coffee, with no additives to ruin the taste": in this case, the object is not just directly itself, but is redoubled, functioning as its own supplement—it itself fills the void its mere fact creates, as in saying "this coffee is ... just simple coffee."

It is hard not to mention here another incident involving coffee from popular cinema, this time from the English working-class drama *Brassed Off*. The hero walks home a pretty young woman who, when they reach the entrance to her flat, asks him if he would like to come in for a coffee. To his answer—"There's a problem—I don't drink coffee"—she replies with a smile: "No problem—I don't have any..." The erotic power of her reply lies in how—again through a double negation—she makes an embarrassingly direct sexual invitation without ever mentioning sex: when she first invites the guy in for a coffee and then admits she has no coffee, she does not cancel her invitation, she just makes it clear that the coffee invitation was a stand-in or pretext, indifferent in itself, for the sexual invitation. Along the same lines, we can imagine a dialogue between the US and Europe in late 2002, as the invasion of Iraq was being prepared for: the US says to Europe: "Would you care to join us in the attack on Iraq to find the WMD?"; Europe replies: "But we have no facilities to search for the WMD!"; the Rumsfeld answer: "No problem, there are no WMD in Iraq." Is not the general formula of humanitarian interventions also similar?—"Let us intervene in country X to bring humanitarian help and alleviate the suffering taking place there!" "But our intervention will mostly just cause more suffering and death!" "No problem, this will give us a reason to intervene even more."

What does all this mean with regard to sexual difference? Sexual difference is not differential (in the precise sense of the differentiality of the signifier): when Lacan privileges the phallus, this does not mean that sexual difference is structured along the axis of its presence or absence—man has it, woman does not have it, where (following the basic rule of the differential system) the absence of a feature also counts as a positive feature, or, to paraphrase Sherlock Holmes: "Is there any other point about seeing your sister naked to which you would wish to draw my attention?" "To the curious thing I noticed between her legs." "There was nothing between her legs." "That was the curious thing." In this refusal of differentiality as the principle of sexual difference, Lacan moves beyond his own earlier position which was, precisely, a differential one: man and woman were opposed with regard to the couple being/having (man *has* the phallus, woman does not have it, she *is* it). Now, however, the phallic signifier is not the feature whose presence or absence distinguishes man and woman: in the formulae of sexuation, it is operative on both sides, masculine and feminine, and, in both cases, it works as the operator of the impossible relationship (non-relationship) between S and J, speaking subject and *jouissance*—the phallic signifier stands for the *jouissance* accessible to a speaking being, integrated into the symbolic order.[41] Consequently, in the same way that there is only one sex plus the not-All which resists it, there is only phallic *jouissance* plus an X which resists it, although, properly speaking, it does not exist, since "there is no *jouissance* which is not phallic."[42] This is why, when Lacan speaks of the mysteriously spectral "other *jouissance*," he treats it as something which does not exist and yet still works, functions, exerts a certain efficacy—a non-existing object with real properties. "Masculine" and "feminine" are two modes (each of them contradictory in its own way) of dealing with this impossible (non-)relationship between the symbolic order and *jouissance*. Or, insofar as the subject of the signifier ($) is the exception to the symbolic universality, and the *objet a* its objectal counterpoint, standing for the excess of enjoyment (surplus-enjoyment), Lacan's formula of fantasy ($-a) is yet another version of this same impossible non-relationship: the non-relationship between the two sides of the same coin (the empty place with no element filling it in and the excessive element without its place). Guy Le Gaufey is right to emphasize that, if we ignore this crucial point, then no matter how formalized and non-intuitive our propositions are we reduce Lacan's formulae of sexuation to being just another way of grounding, in a modern "scientific" manner, the oldest intuitions about the great cosmic polarity and eternal

41 The deadlock of the phallus is rendered superbly by Lacan in the ironic statement that the "phallus is the conscientious objector to the service we owe to the other sex" (quoted in François Balmès, *Dieu, le sexe et la vérité*, Ramonville Saint-Agne: Érès 2007, p. 129): phallic *jouissance* is masturbatory, it misses the Other (sex), reducing it to the *objet a*.

42 Jacques Lacan, *Le séminaire, Livre XX: Encore*, Paris: Seuil 1975, p. 97.

struggle of the sexes, with all its concomitant theses, including the normativity of sexual difference (the "proper" division of sexual roles, with regard to which one can dismiss divergences as perversions).[43]

In a purely differential relationship, each entity consists in its difference from its opposite: woman is not-man and man is not-woman. Lacan's complication with regard to sexual difference is that, while one may claim that "all (all elements of the human species) that is not-man is woman," the non-All of woman precludes us from saying that "all that is not-woman is man": there is something of not-woman which is not man; or, as Lacan put it succinctly: "since woman is 'non-all,' why should all that is not woman be man?"[44] The two sexes do not divide the human gender among themselves so that what is not one is the other: while this holds for the masculine side (what is not man is woman), it does not hold for the feminine side (all that is not woman is *not* man)—the consequence of this breach of symmetry is: "*exit* yin and yang and all those oppositions which, in different cultures, pretend to regulate the number of sexes."[45] Sexes are more than one and less than two: they cannot be counted as two, there is only one and something (or, rather, less than something but more than nothing) which eludes it. In other words, 1 + *a* precedes 1 + 1. Consequently, what, on the feminine side, contradicts the negative universal ("there is no x for which it holds that nonFx"), that is, the negative particular of "non-all are x Fx," is

> the affirmation of the "nothing" pursued by Lacan from the very beginning, this nothing which is neither that of Hegel nor that of Freud, [and which is] the very absence of the subject to whom one could attach a predicate. This affirmation is thus the affirmation of that which exists with regard to a function (of the predicate), without satisfying this function (possessing the predicate).[46]

In other words, since "there is no x for which it holds that nonFx," the x which makes the set non-All can only be this nothing itself, the "barred" subject ($). This is how we should read the impossible conjunction (the non-relationship) of $ and *a*: the subject is the void, the empty position, a subject without a predicate, while *a* is a predicate without its proper subject—something like "coffee without milk" (or, rather, coffee without caffeine).[47] This notion of the subject as "more

43 See Le Gaufey, *Le Pastout de Lacan*.

44 Jacques Lacan, seminar of May 10, 1972, in *Le séminaire, Livre XIX: ...ou pire*, Paris: Seuil 2011.

45 Le Gaufey, *Le Pastout de Lacan*, p. 41.

46 Ibid., pp. 142–3.

47 If the subject is inextricably linked with non-existence, if "the subject introduces the nothingness as such" (the subject is barred, a void, the "*néantisation*" [nothingification] of being, etc.), then does not Lacan's "Woman does not exist" point towards the privileged link between woman and subjectivity?

than one but less than two" accounts for why being alone and being solitary are not the same: one can be solitary without being alone insofar as one can still be in company with oneself, with the shadowy double of oneself. True loneliness occurs not when there are no others around me, but when I am deprived even of my shadow.

Each sex is not the negation of the other, but an obstacle to the other: not something whose identity is established through its difference to the other, but something whose identity is thwarted from within by the other. For such a (non-)relationship which eludes differentiality, Ernesto Laclau reserved the term "antagonism."[48] Antagonism is, at its most radical, not the opposition or incommensurability of the Two, but an effect or articulation of the inconsistency of the One, of its deferral with regard to itself. Sexual difference or antagonism is not, as the common wisdom would have it, about the irreconcilable struggle between the two sexes ("men are from Mars and women are from Venus")—for this cliché, each of the sexes has its full identity in itself, and the problem is that these two identities are "out of sync," not on the same wavelength. This position merely turns around the ideological topic of Man and Woman complementing each other: alone, they are truncated; only together do they form the One. We thus have the rightist deviation (the sexualized cosmology with its polarity of two "cosmic principles," *yin* and *yang*, etc., to which today's pop-cultural New Agers like Dan Brown are returning) and the leftist deviation (from Deleuze to Butler: the plurality of polymorphous perversion is secondarily restrained by the imposed Oedipal norm of sexual difference). And there should be no preference for either—both are worse.

---

48 Laclau's duality of difference and equivalence, however, remains caught in the logic of external opposition. What Laclau does not develop is the conceptual mediation of the two opposites, how the very logic of difference (differentiality: the identity of each element resides only in its difference towards all others) *immanently* leads to antagonism. Differentiality, in order to remain pure (i.e., to avoid reference to any kind of external support in the guise of some element which is not grounded in differences but sustains itself in its identity), has to include a marker of the difference between the field (of differences) itself and its outside, a "pure" difference. This "pure" difference, however, already has to function as antagonism, it is what curtails or thwarts the identity of each of the elements. This is why, as Laclau put it, external difference is always also internal difference: it is not only that the difference between the field itself and its outside has to be reflected into the field itself, preventing its closure, thwarting its fullness; it is also that the differential identity of every element is simultaneously constituted and thwarted by the differential network.

The antinomies of sexual difference

The antagonistic nature of sexual difference means that what appears as the obstacle to the sexual relationship is simultaneously its condition of possibility—here, "negation of the negation" means that in ridding ourselves of the obstacle we also lose that which it had thwarted. We now know that Emily Hale was T. S. Eliot's "lady of silences," the object of his discreet love attachment, in the long years of separation from his wife Vivienne: all this time, almost two decades, was spent waiting for the moment when Eliot would be free to marry her. However, here is what happened when, on January 23, 1947, Eliot was informed that Vivienne had died:

> He was shocked by his wife's death, but even more by its consequences. For now, unexpectedly, he was free to marry Emily Hale, which, for the last fifteen years, she and his family had believed was what he wanted. Yet at once he realized that he had no emotions or desires to share … "I have met myself as a middle-aged man," says the hero of Eliot's new play, *The Cocktail Party*, when he discovers, after his wife departs, that he has lost his wish to marry the shining, devoted Celia. The worst moment, he adds, is when you feel that you have lost the desire for all that was most desirable.[49]

The problem was that Vivienne remained Eliot's symptom throughout, the "knot" of his ambiguous libidinal investment: "The death of Vivienne meant the loss of Eliot's focus of torment,"[50] or, as Eliot himself put it through his hero in *The Cocktail Party*, a fictional account of this trauma: "I cannot live with her, but also cannot live without her." The unbearable core of the Vivienne-Thing was concentrated in her hysterical outbursts: Eliot never visited Vivienne in the asylum, because he feared "the nakedness of her emotional demands … the compelling power of her 'Welsh shriek.'"[51] Vivienne was like Rebecca versus Emily as the new Mrs. De Winter: "The whole oppression, the unreality / Of the role she had almost imposed upon me / With the obstinate, unconscious, sub-human strength / That some woman have." As such, she was the object-cause of Eliot's desire, that which made him desire Emily, or believe that he desired her—no wonder, then, that the moment she disappeared the desire for Emily disappeared with her. The conclusion to be drawn from Eliot's *imbroglio* is clear: there was no love in his relationship to either Vivienne or Emily, for, as Lacan pointed out, love supplements the impossibility of sexual relationship. It can do

49 Lyndall Gordon, *T .S. Eliot: An Imperfect Life*, New York: W. W. Norton & Company 2000, p. 394.
50 Ibid., p. 395.
51 Ibid.

this in different ways, one of which is for love to function as perversion: a perverse supplement which makes the Other exist through love, and in this sense a pervert is a "knight of love."[52] Historical forms of love are thus, from a clinical standpoint, forms of perversion (and Lacan complains here that psychoanalysis did not invent any new perversions). In clear contrast, the late Lacan affirms love as a contingent encounter between two subjects, of their unconsciousnesses, subtracted from narcissism—in this authentic love, sexual relationship "*cesse de ne pas s'écrire*." Here we are beyond pure and impure, love for the Other and self-love, disinterested and interested: "Love is nothing more than a saying [*un dire*] as event."[53]

The standard notion of love in psychoanalysis is reductionist: there is no pure love, love is just "sublimated" sexual lust. Until his late teaching, Lacan also insisted on the narcissistic character of love: in loving an Other, I love myself in the Other; even if the Other is more to me than myself, even if I am ready to sacrifice myself for the Other, what I love in the Other is my idealized perfected Ego, my Supreme Good—but still *my* Good. The surprise here is that Lacan inverts the usual opposition of love versus desire as ethics versus pathological lust: he locates the ethical dimension not in love but in desire—ethics is for him the ethics of desire, of the fidelity to desire, of not compromising on one's desire.[54]

Furthermore, the late Lacan surprisingly reasserts the possibility of another, authentic or pure love of the Other, of the Other as such, not my imaginary other. He refers here to medieval and early modern theology (Fénélon) which distinguished between "physical" love and pure "ecstatic" love. In the first (developed by Aristotle and Aquinas), one can only love another if he is my good, so we love God as our supreme Good. In the second, the loving subject enacts a complete self-erasure, a complete dedication to the Other in its alterity, without return, without benefice, whose exemplary case is mystical self-erasure. Here Lacan engages in an extreme theological speculation, imagining an impossible situation: "the peak of the love for God should have been to tell him 'if this is thy will, condemn me,' that is to say, the exact opposite of the aspiration to the supreme good."[55] Even if there is no mercy from God, even if God were to damn

52 See Balmès, *Dieu, le sexe et la vérité*, p. 161.

53 Jacques Lacan, seminar of December 18, 1973, in *Le séminaire, Livre XXI: Les non-dupes errent* (unpublished).

54 In the hermeneutics of suspicion of love, Lacan goes much further than an ordinary denunciation of secret profit in selfless love—even if my sacrifice for the Other is pure, it is a sacrifice done in order to avoid or conceal the Other's castration, the lack in the Other. The surprising example here is the Stalinist show trial, in which the accused is called on to confess their guilt to save the purity of the Party.

55 Jacques Lacan, *Lacan in Italia, 1953–1978*, Milan: La Salamandra 1978, p. 98.

me completely to external suffering, my love for Him is so great that I would still fully love him. This would be love, if love is to have *le moindre sens*. François Balmès here asks the right question: where is God in all this, why theology? As he perceptively notes, pure love must be distinguished from pure desire: the latter implies the murder of its object, it is a desire purified of all pathological objects, as desire for the void or lack itself, while pure love needs a radical Other to refer to.[56] This is why the radical Other (as one of the names of the divine) is a necessary correlate of pure love.

This leads Lacan to address the complex interaction between love and sexuality, culminating in the canonical thesis according to which love supplements the impossibility of sexual relationship. The starting point is *il n'y a pas de rapport sexuel*. In outlining this discordance, Lacan refers to Freud: there are no representations of sexual difference; all we have is the active/passive opposition, but even this fails—and what this means is that the only support of sexual difference is, for *both* sexes, masquerade. Masquerade has to be opposed here to parade in the animal kingdom: in the latter, males parade in order to be accepted as sexual partners by the females, while in masquerade, it is the woman who is masked. This reversal signals the passage from imaginary to symbolic: for the feminine masquerade to work, the big Other has to be present, since sexual difference is Real, but a Real immanent to the symbolic.

In sexuality, everything hinges on the Otherness of the other sex: masculine and feminine are not simply opposed as others of each other (woman as the other of man and vice versa), since the masculine "phallic" position is the Same "in itself," and the feminine position the Other sex "in itself." We are dealing here with a refined Hegelian self-relating of opposites: the relationship of otherness (each is related to its other) is reflected back into the terms, so that one of the terms (the masculine) stands for the Same and the other for the Other. If *the* Woman were to exist, she would be the Other of the Other, the guarantee of its completeness and consistency.[57]

A similar self-relating pertains to the status of sexuality itself. It is a commonplace that, for psychoanalysis, sexuality is what one defends oneself against (through repression, etc.); however, sexuality is simultaneously, at a more radical level, itself a defense—against what? Against the traumatic truth that "there is no Other."[58] Since the first figure of the Other is the mother, "there is no big Other" first means that the "mother is castrated"—sexuality (in the ordinary sense of sexual relations with another subject, a partner, where the couple forms

56 Balmès, *Dieu, le sexe et la vérité*, pp. 186–7.

57 The big Other is ambiguous: there is the Other as radical Other, the ultimate addressee, the other Subject "beyond the wall of language," *and* the Between itself, the medium of the interaction between the subject and its other.

58 Balmès, *Dieu, le sexe et la vérité*, p. 101.

a complementary Whole) is a defense against the fact that the radical partner (Other) does not exist at all.

Back to Freud's legendary example of the patient who told him: "I do not know who this woman in my dream is, but I am sure of one thing, that it is not my mother!" As Alenka Zupančič has pointed out, the underlying paradox is that the patient's emphatic "This is not my mother!" means the exact opposite *at two different levels*. First, there is the obvious level of denial: in the patient's unconscious, the figure is, of course, his mother, and denial is the price the patient has to pay for bringing this maternal figure to consciousness. There is, however, another level at which "This is not my mother!" asserts the existence of the Mother: the Mother, the impossible/Real incestuous object of desire, fully exists in its inaccessible In-itself, and "This is not my mother!" just gives voice to the disappointment, signaling an experience of *ce n'est pas ça*, of "This miserable figure cannot be that real Mother!"[59] No object we find in reality is *that*, so the subject can only glide from one to another object. But is this metonymy of desire the last word? Here enter the drive and its sublimation in love: the object of love is a miracle of coincidence; in it, an ordinary object (person) is elevated to the level of the Thing, so that here, the subject can fully say, "This is *that*!" or "You are *you*!" where this tautology announces the miracle of the fragile coincidence of an ordinary object with the absolute Thing. All this is missed by the contemporary patient whose answer to Freud's question would be: "Whoever this woman in my dream is, I am sure she has something to do with my mother!"—this open admission is so depressing since it is sustained by a radical de-sublimation: mother is just mother, so what? We can also see in what sense de-sublimation coincides with full and successful repression: the mother can be openly mentioned, because the properly incestuous dimension is totally erased.

Negation thus operates at two levels here: first, there is the simple *Verneinung* of "This is not my mother!"; then, there is the gap between the mother as an object in reality and the Mother as the impossible/Real object of desire. This difference can be marked through the two opposed versions of truth as *adequatio*: the first level concerns the simple common-sense notion of truth as *adequatio* of our notion (statement) to reality (a statement is true if what it claims is confirmed by reality); the second level concerns truth as *adequatio* of a thing to its own notion (an actual state is a "true" state if it meets certain conditions). Is this second gap between mother as an object in reality and the Real-impossible Mother (in short, the "symbolic castration," the loss of the incestuous object, the "primordial repression") then the primordial form of negation? In other words, does the origin of negativity lie in the fact that, if that woman is or is not the mother, the Mother is always lost?

59 Zupančič, "Med dvema ne."

This brings us to two paradoxical conclusions nicely formulated by Balmès: "sexuality is constantly sustained by actively denying its essential condition of possibility"; castration is "what renders possible sexuality as a relation to the Other, and also what renders it impossible."[60]

How, then, can we conceptualize the sexual act with regard to the fact that *il n'y a pas de rapport sexuel*? The philosophy of dialectical materialism teaches us to reject simultaneously both the rightist and the leftist deviations; in this case, the rightist deviation, in its conservative-Catholic guise, claims that the sexual act is in itself an act of animal copulation, and that it needs to be supplemented by gentle kisses and whispers which give it a more civilized spiritual coating; while the leftist deviation preaches our total immersion in the sexual act—the two lovers should dissolve their separate identities and lose themselves in the intensity of copulation. In rejecting both of these deviations, dialectical materialism begins with the axiom of de-centering: the sex organs involved in copulation function as "organs without bodies," organs invested with libidinal intensity which are experienced as minimally separated from the subjects' bodies—it is not the subjects themselves who copulate but their organs "out there." The subject can never directly identify with these organs, it cannot fully assume them as "its own": the very focus of its sexual activity at its most intense is "ex-timate" with regard to it. This means that even (or precisely) in the most intense sexual activity, the participating subject is reduced to the role of a helpless, passive observer of its own activity, to a gaze fascinated by what is taking place—and it is this coincidence of the most intense activity with a helplessly fascinated passivity which constitutes the subjective attitude of the subject involved in a sexual act.

There is more to this passivity than may at first appear. In *De anima* (27:5), Tertullian provides a delightful description of the sexual act, orgasm included. In the traditional Christian manner, he first endorses the act itself, rejecting it only when it is excessive—the difficulty here, of course, is that with regard to human sexuality proper it is formally impossible to distinguish normal or modest sexual activity from its excessive eroticization. The explanation lies in the inherent reflexivity of sexualization discovered already by Freud: the protective rituals designed to keep excessive sexuality at bay become sexualized themselves, the prohibition of desire reverts into the desire of prohibition, and so on. One can thus imagine a couple reducing their sexual activity to a minimal level, depriving it of all excess, only to find that the minimalism itself becomes invested with an excessive sexual *jouissance* (along the lines of those partners who, to spice up their sex life, treat it as a disciplinary measure, dress up in uniforms, follow strict rules, etc.). Therein lies the obscenity of Tertullian's *de*

60 Balmès, *Dieu, le sexe et la vérité*, p. 102.

facto role: one can imagine a couple, tired of experimenting and orgies, deciding to "do it *à la* Tertullian" as a last desperate solution to make sex more exciting. There is no excessive sex because, the moment we enter the human universe, sex itself *is* an excess. Tertullian then goes on to describe how, in the sexual act,

> both the soul and the flesh discharge a duty together: the soul supplies desire, the flesh contributes the gratification of it; the soul furnishes the instigation, the flesh affords the realization. The entire man being excited by the one effort of both natures, his seminal substance is discharged, deriving its fluidity from the body, and its warmth from the soul. Now if the soul in Greek is a word which is synonymous with cold, how does it come to pass that the body grows cold after the soul has quitted it? Indeed (if I run the risk of offending modesty even, in my desire to prove the truth), I cannot help asking, whether we do not, in that very heat of extreme gratification when the generative fluid is ejected, feel that somewhat of our soul has gone from us? And do we not experience a faintness and prostration along with a dimness of sight? This, then, must be the soul-producing seed, which arises at once from the out-drip of the soul, just as that fluid is the body-producing seed which proceeds from the drainage of the flesh.[61]

However, what if we read the claim that, in orgasm, "somewhat of our soul has gone from us," not as a transferring of the soul from the father to the future newborn, but—ignoring insemination and focusing on the phenomenology of the act itself—as a *kenotic emptying of the subject's substantial content ("soul")*? What if, in the orgasm, the subject is momentarily deprived of the ballast of its "wealth of personality" and is reduced to the evanescent void of a pure subject witnessing its own disappearance?

Balmès systematizes this paradoxical nature of sexuality in a Kantian way, enumerating a series of "antinomies" of sexual reason:

> the *antinomy of sexual enjoyment*: *thesis*—sexual *jouissance* is everywhere, it colors all our pleasures; *antithesis*—sexual *jouissance* is not sexual.

The explanation of this antinomy resides in the overlapping of lack and excess: because it lacks its proper place, *jouissance* spreads everywhere. The two sides can be condensed in the tautology: "the sexual is defined by the failure to reach the sexual."[62]

---

61 Tertullian, "A Treatise on the Soul," trans. Peter Holmes, in *The Ante-Nicene Fathers*, Vol. 3, New York: Charles Scribner's Sons 1918, p. 208.

62 Balmès, *Dieu, le sexe et la vérité*, p. 105. What is the precise relationship between love and the excess of unnamable *jouissance*? Is it enough to say that love as the encounter of the Two transubstantiates sexuality from masturbatory pleasure into an Event? Does this

> the *antinomy of the two and the Other*: *thesis*—in the real of sex, there are two, and only two, sexes, man and woman; *antithesis*—from the moment we enter language, there is no second (other) sex.

Lacan insists here on "binary logic," on the Real of sexual difference, and qualifies the denial of the Real of sexual difference as the (idealist) denial of castration. Retroactively, this diagnosis takes on additional weight today, in relation to the rise of what Balmès ironically refers to as "*foucauldo-lacanisme*," the celebration of the multitude of "sexes," of sexual identities (e.g., Judith Butler's performative constructivism as an idealist denial of the Real of sexual difference). However, we should add that this duality of sexes is a strange one, since one of the two is missing; it is not the complementary duality of *yin* and *yang*, but a radically asymmetric duality in which the Same confronts the place of/as its own lack.

> the *antinomy of woman and Other*: *thesis*—woman is not the place of the Other; *antithesis*—woman is the radical Other.

This antinomy is generated by the fact that the symbolic Other as a place emerges with the erasure of the feminine Other Sex.

> the *antinomy of Other and body*: *thesis*—one only enjoys the Other; *antithesis*—there is no *jouissance* of the Other (objective genitive).

The explanation of this last antinomy is that enjoyment as Real has to refer to an Otherness; however, this Otherness is as such inaccessible, Real/impossible. The underlying matrix generating these antinomies is that, in the sexual relationship, *two* relationships overlap: the relationship between the two sexes (masculine, feminine), and the relationship between the subject and its (asymmetrical) Other. The Other Sex, embodied in the primordial Other (Mother), is evacuated, emptied of *jouissance*, excluded, and it is this "voidance" which creates the Other as the symbolic place, as the Between, the medium of intersubjective relations. This is the *Ur-Verdrängung*, the primordial metaphoric substitution: the Other Sex is replaced by the symbolic big Other. This means that there is sexuality (sexual tension between man and woman) precisely because the Woman as Other does not exist.[63]

---

not follow the logic of the All and its exception? So what about the abyss of the non-All of *jouissance*? Is not this opposition the same as that of the mathematical and dynamic antinomies in Kant? The dynamic antinomy is structurally secondary, it resolves the deadlock of the mathematical antinomy—so is it that, in a homologous way, love resolves the deadlock of *jouissance*?

63 This is why, as Lacan put it, Woman is one of the Names-of-the-Father (one of the

Balmès is justified in pointing out that the relationship here is ambiguous: is it that language (the symbolic Other) comes second, as a defense, a protective screen, against the Other Sex, or is it that the Other Sex is repressed with the entry of the symbolic big Other? In other words, is it that there is no sexual relationship because we dwell in language, or is it that language is a defense against the impossibility of the sexual relationship? The underlying paradox is that, in the tension between the Real of sexual difference and the symbolic, the symbolic order is an effect which rebels against its own cause, and, vice versa, language itself retroactively generates the heterogeneous Otherness which it represses or excludes. Here is Balmès's superb ironic conclusion: "It is thus 'in the sexual relationship' which is not a relationship and which is not sexual (which means the same thing) that the woman is the Other (neither of whom exists). Well, it's exactly like that."[64] While we should be careful not to confuse the different cases, the underlying model is nonetheless formally the same: an entity—woman, the Other, sexuality, the subject itself...—is rendered possible by its own impossibility; that is, in (the little bit of) its own positive existence, it as it were *materializes its own impossibility*. The status of the subject is thus immanently temporal: the subject is a virtual entity, it "is" not (in the present), it is a virtual X which always "will have been"—the pre-subjective thrust towards (signifying) representation (Lacan designates it with the triangle of the Greek "delta") fails, and the subject "is" this failure, emerging retroactively as the failure of its own representation.

What this paradoxical coincidence of opposites bears witness to is the antagonistic nature of the entity in question, antagonistic as opposed to differential. In the same way, the antagonistic inseparability of the two sexes does not mean that their relationship is differential in the symbolic sense, that each sex's identity is nothing but its difference with regard to the opposite sex: if this were the case, then the identity of each sex would be fully determined through its differential features. To arrive at the antagonism as Real, we must add a further turn of the screw: each sex does not supplement the other, but functions as the obstacle preventing the other from achieving its full identity. "Man" names that which prevents "woman" from fully realizing itself, and vice versa. In the class struggle, there is also "no class relationship": the "bourgeoisie" names the class which prevents the proletariat from fully becoming itself. Lacan's claim that sexual difference is "Real-impossible" is strictly synonymous with his claim that "there is no sexual relationship": sexual difference is not a fixed set of "static" symbolic oppositions and inclusions or exclusions (with heterosexual normativity relegating homosexuality and other "perversions" to a secondary role), but the name

---

names of the Divine): if *the* Woman were to exist, she would be the Other of the Other, the Subject which personifies, dominates, and regulates the very impersonal Between, the big Other as the anonymous symbolic Order.

64 Balmès, *Dieu, le sexe et la vérité*, p. 118.

of a deadlock, a trauma, an open question, something that *resists* every attempt at symbolization. Every translation of sexual difference into a set of symbolic oppositions is doomed to fail, and it is this very "impossibility" that opens up the terrain of the hegemonic struggle for what "sexual difference" will mean.

Why Lacan is not a nominalist

Sexual difference and class difference are thus both real in the very precise formal sense of being rooted in an antagonism: the difference paradoxically precedes the two terms whose difference it is. In a dense and unique passage from his 1971 *Seminar XVIII*, Lacan provides a precise definition of this logic of antagonism, including his identification with dialectical materialism, which comes as a surprise precisely because it is stated as a self-evident premise:

> If there is something I am, it is clear that I am not a nominalist. What I want to say is that my starting point is not that the name is something like a nameplate which attaches itself, just like that, onto the real. And one has to choose. If one is a nominalist, one has to renounce completely dialectical materialism, so that, all in all, I evidently reject the nominalist tradition which is effectively the only danger of idealism which can arise in a discourse like mine. The point is not to be a realist in the sense in which one was a realist in Medieval times, in the sense of the realism of the universals; the point is to emphasize that our discourse, our scientific discourse, can only find the real insofar as it depends on the function of the semblant.
>
> The articulation, and I mean the algebraic articulation, of the semblant—and because of this we are only dealing with letters—and its effects, this is the only apparatus which enables us to designate what is real. What is real is what opens up a hole in this semblant, in this articulated semblant which is the scientific discourse. The scientific discourse progresses without even worrying if it is a discourse of semblance or not. All that matters is that its network, its texture, its *lattice*, as one is used to say, makes the right holes appear at the right place. The only reference reached by its deductions is the impossible. This impossible is the real. In physics, we aim at something which is real with the help of the discursive apparatus which, in its crispness, encounters the limits of its consistency.[65]

As they say in *Inglourious Basterds*, the Führer himself could not have put it better—here we find *in nuce* the difference between Lacan's dialectical materialism and the "aleatory materialism" Althusser struggled to formulate in his last

65 Jacques Lacan, *Le séminaire, Livre XVIII: D'un discours qui ne serait pas du semblant*, Paris: Seuil 2006, p. 28. My thanks to Alenka Zupančič, who drew my attention to this passage.

writings, where he also claims that nominalism is the only consistent materialist position. But what kind of "realist" is Lacan? He defines his position as that of the "realism of *jouissance*," but here we should avoid the trap of elevating *jouissance* into some kind of substantial In-itself which resists being captured by symbolic semblants. For Lacan, *jouissance* is a weird substance with no substantial positivity: it is discernible only as the virtual cause of the cracks, distortions, and imbalances in the texture of symbolic semblants. That is to say, with regard to reality, Lacan agrees with Althusser's materialist nominalism of exceptions (or "clinamina"): what actually exists are only exceptions, they are all the *reality* there is. (This is the motif of historicist nominalism endlessly repeated in cultural studies: there is no Woman as such, there are just lesbians, working women, single mothers, and so on and so forth.) However, what nominalism does not see is the *Real* of a certain impossibility or antagonism which is the virtual cause generating multiple realities. In his book on modernity, Jameson deploys this Real in his concise critique of recently fashionable theories of "alternate modernities":

> How then can the ideologues of "modernity" in its current sense manage to distinguish their product—the information revolution, and globalized, free-market modernity—from the detestable older kind, without getting themselves involved in asking the kinds of serious political and economic, systemic questions that the concept of a postmodernity makes unavoidable? The answer is simple: you talk about "alternate" or "alternative" modernities. Everyone knows the formula by now: this means that there can be a modernity for everybody which is different from the standard or hegemonic Anglo-Saxon model. Whatever you dislike about the latter, including the subaltern position it leaves you in, can be effaced by the reassuring and "cultural" notion that you can fashion your own modernity differently, so that there can be a Latin-American kind, or an Indian kind or an African kind, and so forth ... But this is to overlook the other fundamental meaning of modernity which is that of a worldwide capitalism itself.[66]

The significance of this critique reaches far beyond the case of modernity—it concerns the fundamental limitation of nominalist historicizing. The recourse to the multitude ("there is no single modernity with a fixed essence, there are multiple modernities, each of them irreducible to the others...") is false not because it does not recognize a unique fixed "essence" of modernity, but because multiplication here functions as a disavowal of the antagonism that inheres in the notion of modernity as such: its falsity lies in the fact that it frees the universal notion of modernity of its antagonism, of the way it is embedded in the capitalist

66 Fredric Jameson, *A Singular Modernity*, London: Verso Books 2002, p. 12.

system, by relegating this aspect to just one of its historical subspecies.[67] Insofar as this inherent antagonism could be designated as a "castrative" dimension—and insofar as, according to Freud, the disavowal of castration is represented as the multiplication of phallus-representatives (a multitude of phalluses signals castration, the lack of the one)—it is easy to conceive such a multiplication of modernities as a form of fetishist disavowal.

Jameson's critique of the notion of alternate modernities thus provides a model for the properly *dialectical* relationship between the Universal and the Particular: the difference is not on the side of particular content (as the traditional *differentia specifica*), but on the side of the Universal. The Universal is not the encompassing container of the particular content, the peaceful medium or background for the conflict of particularities; the Universal "as such" is the site of an unbearable antagonism or self-contradiction, and (the multitude of) its particular species are ultimately nothing but so many attempts to obfuscate/reconcile/master this antagonism. In other words, the Universal names the site of a Problem-Deadlock, of a burning Question, and the Particulars are attempted but failed Answers to this Problem. For example, the concept of the State names a certain problem: how to contain the class antagonism of a society? All particular forms of the State are so many (failed) attempts to find a solution to this problem.

This is how we should read Lacan's statement that the point is not to be a realist in the medieval sense, but in the sense that our (scientific) discourse "can only find the real insofar as it depends on the function of the semblant": reality is a semblant, but not in the simple sense that it is a deceptive appearance hiding true Being—there is nothing, no true substantial real, behind the veil of phenomenal reality. Reality is a semblant in the sense that its structure already materializes a certain fantasy which obfuscates the Real of a social antagonism. This is why we "can only find the real insofar as it depends on the function of the semblant": by way of identifying the impossibilities, cracks, antagonisms which underlie and generate the inconsistent multiplicity of semblants.

Perhaps we can construct a triad here: (1) for Hegel, we have contradiction, inconsistency, as Real, but not in mathematics, only in concepts; (2) for modern science, we have the Real articulated in mathematical formulae, but not as inconsistent; (3) for Lacan, we have the Real residing in the impasse of mathematical formalization.

---

67 We should not forget that the first half of the twentieth century was marked by two big projects which perfectly fit this notion of "alternate modernity": fascism and communism. Was not the basic idea of fascism that of a modernity which would offer an alternative to the standard Anglo-Saxon liberal-capitalist one, which would save the core of capitalist modernity by casting away its "contingent" Jewish-individualist-profiteering distortion? And was not the rapid industrialization of the USSR in the late 1920s and 1930s not also an attempt at modernization different from the Western-capitalist version?

And exactly the same goes for *jouissance*: when Lacan talks about *jouissance féminine*, he always qualifies it—"if a thing like that were to exist (but it does not)"—thereby confirming its incommensurability with the order of (symbolic) existence.[68] *Jouissance féminine* does not exist, but *il y a de jouissance féminine*, "there is" feminine enjoyment. This *il y a*, like the German *es gibt* which plays such a key role in late Heidegger, is clearly opposed to existence (in English, the distinction gets blurred, since one cannot avoid the verb "to be" in translation). *Jouissance* is thus not a positive substance caught in the symbolic network, it is something that shines through only in the cracks and openings of the symbolic order—not because we, who dwell within that order, cannot regain it directly, but, more radically, because it is generated by the cracks and inconsistencies of the symbolic order itself.

We should be attentive here to the difference between the inexistence of *jouissance féminine* and the inexistence of a father who would fit its symbolic function. ("If there is no such father, it still remains true that the father is God, it is simply that this formula is confirmed only by the empty sector of the square.")[69] In the case of the father, we have a discrepancy between the symbolic function (of the Father) and the reality of individuals who never fit this function, while in the case of *jouissance féminine*, we have the Real of *jouissance* which eludes symbolization. In other words, in the first case, the gap is between reality and the symbolic, while in the second case, the gap is between the symbolic and the Real: miserable individuals called fathers exist, they just do not fit their symbolic function, which remains an "empty sector of the square"; but *jouissance féminine*, precisely, does not exist.

One standard definition of the Lacanian Real describes it as that which always returns to the same place, that which remains the same in all possible symbolic universes. This notion of the Real as a "hard core" that resists symbolization must be supplemented by its opposite: the Real is also a "pure appearance," that which exists only when we look upon reality from a certain perspective—the moment we shift our point of view, the object disappears. What both extremes exclude in the standard notion of reality as something which resists in its In-itself, but changes with regard to its properties: when we shift perspective, it appears different. However, these two opposed notions of reality can be thought together—if one bears in mind the crucial shift that takes place in Lacan's teaching with regard to the Real. From the 1960s onwards, the Real is no longer that which remains the same in all symbolic universes; with regard to the common notion of reality, the Real is *not* the underlying sameness which persists through the multitude of different points of view on an object. The Real is, on the contrary, *that which generates these differences*, the elusive "hard core"

68 Lacan, *Le séminaire, Livre XX: Encore*, p. 97.

69 Lacan, seminar of January 17, 1962, in *Le séminaire, Livre XI: L'identification.*

that the multiple points of view try (and fail) to recapture. This is why the Real "at its purest" is the "pure appearance": a difference which cannot be grounded in any real features of the object; a "pure" difference.

In *Mr. & Mrs. Smith*, Brad Pitt and Angelina Jolie play a bored married couple seeking advice from a therapist, while, unbeknownst to each other, they are both employed (with different agencies) as professional assassins (the plot, of course, takes off when each is given the assignment to kill the other). Here we encounter an interpretive dilemma: are Pitt and Jolie an everyday couple dreaming (fantasizing) about being top contract killers in order to liven up their marriage, or, vice versa, are they professional killers fantasizing about living the life of an ordinary married couple? (There is then a link with Hitchcock's film of the same title: both are "comedies of remarriage.") When Karl Kraus, who knew Trotsky from his stay in Vienna before the First World War, heard that the latter had saved the October Revolution by organizing the Red Army, he snapped back: "Who would have expected of Herr Bronstein from Café Central to do that!" Here again we have the same dilemma: was it Trotsky, the great revolutionary, who, as part of his underground work, had to spend time in Café Central in Vienna; or was it the gentle and loquacious Herr Bronstein from Café Central who later became the great revolutionary? Both situations are variations on Chuang-Tzu's famous story about how, on waking after dreaming that he was a butterfly, he was not sure whether he was Chuang-Tzu dreaming he was a butterfly or a butterfly dreaming he was Chuang-Tzu. Ideologists of multiple shifting identities like to quote this passage, but, as a rule, they stop short and leave out the key insight that follows: "However, there must be some sort of difference between Chuang-Tzu and a butterfly!" This gap is the site of the Real: the Real is not the "true reality" to which we awaken (if we ever do), but the very gap that separates one dream from another.

On a closer look, however, we can immediately see that there is a further step to be taken here, since the relationship of the two opposites is not symmetrical. True, "bourgeoisie" names the class which prevents the proletariat from fully becoming itself, but it is not true that the proletariat prevents the bourgeoisie from fully becoming itself. True, the masculine subject prevents the feminine subject from fully becoming itself, but the reverse is not true. This means that each sex is not simply One-in-itself and Other-of-the-Other: the relationship between One and Other is not purely formal and as such applied to each of the two sexes, but is reflected in the very quality of the two sexes—the masculine sex is "in itself" One, and the feminine "in itself" (i.e., not only for its Other, but with regard to itself) is "the other sex" (as Simone de Beauvoir put it). So there is only one sex which is itself, the One, and the other sex is neither another One nor some kind of all-embracing substantial Otherness within which we all dwell (like the primordial Mother). The same goes for class struggle: we do not simply have two classes; there is—as Marx himself put it—only one class "as such," the bourgeoisie; classes prior to the bourgeoisie (feudal lords, clergy, etc.) are not yet classes in the full sense of the term, their class identity is covered up by other hierarchical determinations (castes, estates...); after the bourgeoisie, there is the proletariat, which is a non-class in the guise of a class and, as such, the Other not only for the bourgeoisie but in and for itself.

How then to define woman if not as simply non-man, man's symmetrical or complementary counterpart? The Kantian notion of "infinite or indefinite judgment" as opposed to negative judgment can again be of some help here: the positive judgment "the soul is mortal" can be negated in two ways, when a predicate is denied to the subject ("the soul is not mortal") and when a non-predicate is affirmed ("the soul is non-mortal"). In exactly the same way, we should not say that woman is not man, but that woman *is non-man*—in Hegelese, woman is not only the negation of man, but the negation of the negation, opening up a third space of non-non-man which not only does not bring us back to man but leaves behind the entire field of man and its opposite. And, again, in exactly the same way, the proletariat is not the class opposite of the bourgeoisie, it is non-bourgeoisie, which means non-non-bourgeoisie. We thus have not two classes, but one—the bourgeoisie—and its negation of the negation, a non-non-class, a weird class which can only win by abolishing itself as class and thereby doing away with all classes. The proletariat is the living, existing paradox of a class which is a non-class—or, as Rammstein put it in their *Ohne dich*: "*ohne dich kann ich nicht sein, ohne dich / mit dir bin ich auch allein, ohne dich*" (without you I cannot be, without you / with you I am also alone, without you); in short, even when I am with you, I am "alone with you." The proletariat is alone even when it is with the bourgeoisie, related to it.

But is this Other (the Other which is Other with regard to itself) radically outside the order of the One, like the mythical *jouissance féminine*? Can it have only a spectral presence, having effects but without properly existing? This, precisely, is the last trap to be avoided: no, the Other which is not-not-One is even more "here" than the One—women are here, workers are here. What then is their status? Let us go by way of a more general ontological thesis: we get from 1 to 2 because 1 is not fully 1: the emergence of 2 is an attempt by 1 to catch its own excess through its own reduplication. In other words, in the passage from 1 to 2, the split implicit in 1 is explicated. However, this series of 1s—1 + 1 + 1 +...—never reaches the Two of radical Otherness, the Other which cannot be reduced to another One. How to reach this Otherness? There are two potential traps here: (1) evading the impasse of radical Otherness by positing an original multiplicity which is only secondarily constrained by binary logic; (2) elevating Otherness, in a Levinasian or some other way, into a substantial force or site which dominates me ("there is an Other in me, something stronger, a Force which speaks through me," even when this Other is called the "Unconscious"). Lacan avoids this trap by formulating the antinomy of the Other (as elaborated by Balmès):

> *Thesis—There is the Other*: the Unconscious is the speech of the Other, desire is desire of the Other, the Other is the place of Truth presupposed or implied even (or especially) when we are lying; and so on.
>
> *Antithesis—There is no Other*: the Other is barred, inconsistent, lacking; the goal of the analysis is to bring the subject to assume the Other's inexistence; and so forth.[70]

To clarify this, we should first note that both thesis and antithesis can be read in (at least) three different ways. Following the triad of ISR, the Other (which exists) can be the imaginary Other (the ego's mirror-image), the symbolic Other (the anonymous symbolic order, the place of truth), and the real Other (the abyss of the Other-Thing, of the subject qua Neighbor). "There is no Other" can be read as: a lack or hole in the Other (a missing signifier, the exception on which the Other is grounded); the inconsistency of the Other (the Other as non-All, antagonistic, and which as such cannot be totalized); or the simple assertion of the virtual character of the big Other (the symbolic order does not exist as part of reality, it is an ideal structure which regulates our activity in social reality).[71]

The resolution of this "antinomy" is provided by the redoubled formula: *there is no Other of the Other*, the Other is the Other with regard to itself. What this means is that the de-centering of the subject in the Other is in itself redoubled: true, the subject is de-centered, its truth is not deep in itself but "out there," in the symbolic order in whose web it is caught and whose effect it ultimately is. However, this symbolic Other in which the subject is constitutively alienated is not a full substantial field, but is separated from itself, articulated around an inherent point of impossibility, around what Lacan designated as its ex-timate core. Lacan's name for this ex-timate core which de-centers the de-centered subject's Other itself is, of course, the *objet a*, surplus-enjoyment, the object-cause of desire. This paradoxical object functions as a kind of bug or glitch in the

---

70 See Balmès, *Dieu, le sexe et la vérité*.

71 As Bruce Fink pointed out, we find in Lacan two types of negative judgments: the negation of existence ("*la Femme n'existe pas*") and the more outright negation ("*il n'y a pas de l'Autre de l'Autre*"). These two negations are not to be confused: while Woman does not exist, there definitely are women. What the negation of existence denies is the full ontic status of an entity (the existence of a particular entity guaranteed or constituted by its limit), while "there is no such thing as..." is an outright denial. The couple of One and Other should be read along these lines: there is no big Other, but "*Y a d'l'Un*," there is something of the One.

big Other, as an immanent obstacle to its full actualization, and the subject is only a correlative to this glitch: without the glitch, there would have been no subject, the Other would have been a complete, smoothly running order. The paradox is thus that the very glitch which makes the Other incomplete, inconsistent, lacking, and so on, is precisely what makes the Other Other, irreducible to another One.

Negation of the negation: Lacan versus Hegel?

How does this Lacanian negation of the negation—in its two main versions: the redoubled negation which generates the excess of the non-All, and the move from alienation to separation—relate to the Hegelian negation of the negation? Is the Hegelian version strong enough to contain (account for) the Lacanian version? Lacan repeatedly insists that his "negation of the negation," in contrast to Hegel's, does not result in a return to any kind of positivity, no matter how sublated or mediated that positivity might be. In *Vertigo*, Scottie reaches the end when he discovers that Madeleine was a fake from the very beginning, "no longer (not) without Madeleine," which, again, does not mean that he is *with* Madeleine, but that he has lost the loss itself, the very point of reference which circumscribed the place of the loss structuring his desire. In a way, he loses desire itself, its object-cause. This move is still Hegelian, for Hegel can well think the negation of the negation as a radical loss. The question is thus not "Does the Hegelian negation of the negation erase the loss in a return to full unity?" but rather: "Can Hegel think the additional fourth phase in which the self-relating movement of the negation of the negation itself engenders a particular tic, a singular excessive-repetitive gesture (like Julie's suicidal explosion of passion at the end of *La nouvelle Heloise*, or Sygne's tic at the end of Claudel's *L'Otage*)?"

As we have already seen, the Lacanian negation of the negation is located on the feminine side of the "formulae of sexuation," in the notion of the non-All: there is nothing which is not a fact of discourse; however, this non-not-discourse does not mean that all is discourse, but, precisely, that not-All is discourse—what is outside is not a positive something but the *objet a*, more than nothing but not something, not One.[72] Alternatively: there is no subject which is not

72 What Freud called a "partial object" is also more than nothing and less than One: One is a Body, a partial object is its lack or excess; i.e., it is not only a separated part of a Whole (body), it is *partial with regard to itself*—this is what Democritus did not see when he conceived atoms as Ones which can be counted, and the void as external to them, as the empty space surrounding them: as Hegel put it, one should internalize the void, conceiving it as the very core of the identity of the One—only in this way does movement become immanent to atoms.

castrated, but this does not mean that all subjects are castrated (the non-castrated remainder is, of course, the *objet a*). The Real that we touch upon here, in this double negation, can be linked to Kantian infinite judgment, the affirmation of a non-predicate: "he is undead" does not simply mean that he is alive, but that he is alive as not dead, as a living dead. "He is undead" means that he is not-not-dead.[73] In the same way, the Freudian Unconscious is like the undead: it is not simply not-conscious but non-not-conscious, and, in this double negation, a *no* not only persists, but is even redoubled: undead remains not-dead *and* not-alive. Is not the *objet a* in the same way a non-not-object and, in *this* sense, an object which embodies the void?

This double negation can also have the structure of a choice which, while not forced, is rendered indifferent since, whatever our decision, the result will be the same. Such was allegedly the case in Vietnam where, after the defeat of the South, Northern propagandists picked up young people on the streets and forced them to watch a long documentary propaganda film. After the screening, the viewers were asked if they liked the film. If they answered no, they were told that obviously they did not really understand it and so would have to watch it again; if they answered yes, they were told: "Good, since you like it so much, you can now watch it again!" Yes and no amount to the same thing, which, at a more basic level, amounts to a "no" (the boredom involved in seeing the film again). Similar (but not the same) is the legendary answer of a Hearst newspaper editor to Hearst's inquiry as to why he did not want to take a long-deserved holiday: "I'm afraid that if I go, there will be chaos, everything will fall apart—but I'm even more afraid that, if I go, things will just go on as normal without me, proving that I am not really needed!" A certain negative choice (no holiday, seeing the film again) is supported by both yes and no; there is, however, an asymmetry in the answers, which comes out clearly if we imagine the dialogue as a succession of two answers: first, the reaction is the obvious (negative) one (I did not like the film; I am afraid everything will fall apart if I take a holiday); then, when this reaction fails to produce the desired outcome, the opposite (positive) reason is given (I liked the film; everything will be fine without me), which fails even more miserably. No wonder that the Hearst editor's answer can be reformulated as a dialogue along the lines of the Rabinovitch joke: "Why don't you take a holiday, you deserve it!"; "I don't want to, for two reasons. First, I'm afraid that everything will fall apart here if I take a holiday..."; "But you are totally wrong, things will just go on as normal when you're not here!" "That is my second reason."

---

73 This real of the double negation is nonetheless not the same as the Kantian sublime, where the Real is touched through the failure of phenomenal representation: the undead-real is not sublime, but obscene.

This Lacanian matrix of the "negation of the negation" is clearly discernible in Leo Strauss's notion of the need for a philosopher to employ "noble lies," to resort to myth, to narratives *ad captum vulgi*. The problem is that Strauss does not draw all the consequences from the ambiguity of this stance, torn as he is between the idea that wise philosophers know the truth but judge it inappropriate for the common people, who cannot bear it (it would undermine the very fundamentals of their morality, which needs the "noble lie" of a personal God who punishes sins and rewards good deeds), and the idea that the core of truth is inaccessible to conceptual thought as such, which is why philosophers themselves have to resort to myths and other forms of fabulation to fill in the structural gaps in their knowledge. Strauss is, of course, aware of the ambiguity of the status of a secret: a secret is not only what the teacher knows but refrains from divulging to the non-initiated—a secret is also a secret for the teacher himself, something that he cannot fully penetrate and articulate in conceptual terms. Consequently, a philosopher uses parabolic and enigmatic speech for two reasons: in order to conceal the true core of his teaching from the common people, who are not ready for it, and because the use of such speech is the only way to describe the highest philosophical insights.[74]

No wonder, then, that Strauss answers in a properly Hegelian way the common-sense reproach according to which, when we are offered an esoteric explanation of a work which is already in itself esoteric (as with, say, Maimonides's reading of the Bible), the explanation will be twice as esoteric and, consequently, twice as difficult to understand as the esoteric work itself:

> thanks to Maimonides, the secret teaching is accessible to us in two different versions: in the original Biblical version, and in the derivative version of [Maimonides's] *Guide*. Each version by itself might be wholly incomprehensible; but we may become able to decipher both by using the light which one sheds on the other. Our position resembles then that of an archeologist confronted with an inscription in an unknown language, who subsequently discovers another inscription reproducing the translation of that text into another unknown language ... [Maimonides] wrote the *Guide* according to the rules which he was wont to follow in reading the Bible. Therefore, if we wish to understand the *Guide*, we must read it according to the rules which Maimonides applies in that work to the explanation of the Bible.[75]

The redoubling of the problem thus paradoxically generates its own solution. One should bear in mind here that when Strauss emphasized the difference between exoteric and esoteric teaching, he conceived this opposition in a way

74 Leo Strauss, *Persecution and the Art of Writing*, Chicago: University of Chicago Press 1988, p. 57.
75 Ibid., pp. 60–1.

almost exactly opposite to today's New Age defenders of esoteric wisdom. The content of New Age wisdom is some spiritual higher reality accessible only to the initiated few, while common mortals see around them only vulgar reality; for Strauss, on the contrary, and in a properly dialectical way, such narratives of spiritual mystery are the very model of fables concocted *ad captum vulgi*. Is this not confirmed by the success of the recent wave of religious thrillers epitomized by Dan Brown's *The Da Vinci Code*? These works are perhaps the best indicator of the contemporary ideological shift: the hero is in search of an old manuscript which will reveal some shattering secret that threatens to undermine the very foundations of (institutionalized) Christianity; a "criminal" edge is provided by the desperate and ruthless attempts of the Church (or some hard-line faction within it) to suppress the document. The secret as a rule focuses on the "repressed" feminine dimension of the divine: Christ was married to Mary Magdalene; the Grail is actually the female body, etc. The paradox assumed here is that it is *only* through the "monotheistic" suspension of the feminine signifier, of the polarity of masculine and feminine, that the space emerges for what we broadly refer to as "feminism" proper, for the rise of feminine subjectivity (which ultimately coincides with subjectivity as such). For Strauss, by contrast, the unbearable esoteric secret is the fact that there is no God or immortal soul, no divine justice, that there is only this terrestrial world which has no deeper meaning and carries no guarantee of a happy outcome.

When Strauss deploys the inherent paradox of a theology which proceeds *ad captum vulgi*, he thus provides a textbook case of the Hegelian negation of the negation.[76] In the first step, Strauss, following Spinoza, asserts that, in the Bible, God speaks in the language of ordinary people, adapting his speech to vulgar prejudices (presenting himself as a supreme person, a wise lawgiver who performs miracles, utters prophecies, and dispenses mercy)—in short, he tells stories which mobilize the powers of human imagination. However, in the second step, the question necessarily pops up: is not the idea of a God as a supreme Person who employs ruses, displays mercy and rage, and so on, in itself a common idea which only can occur when one speaks "with a view to the capacity of the vulgar"?

Another example: Badiou uses the term "inaesthetics" (*inesthétique*) to refer to "a relation of philosophy to art that, maintaining that art is itself a producer of truths, makes no claim to turn art into an object for philosophy. Against aesthetic speculation, inaesthetics describes the strictly intraphilosophical effects produced by the independent existence of some works of art."[77] Badiou's opposition to philosophical aesthetics is thus double: (1) art is not

76 Ibid., pp. 178–9.

77 Alain Badiou, *Handbook of Inaesthetics*, Palo Alto: Stanford University Press 2005, p. xii.

opposed to thinking, art generates its own truth, which is why philosophy does not preside over art, explicating in conceptual terms the truth that art stages in pre-conceptual modes of representation (but it also does not elevate art into a privileged medium of truth); (2) philosophy does not deploy a universal theory of art, it describes the intra-philosophical effects of *some* works of art. Nevertheless, we should note that this distance from aesthetics is inherent to it, that the term "inaesthetics" functions like a predicate in an infinite judgment, as a negation which remains within the negated field—"inaesthetics" is non-non-aesthetics (just as "inhuman" is non-non-human, non-human within the field of the human).

Where then is the non-All in the relationship between necessity and contingency? Is it that necessity is universal and contingency its constitutive exception—everything is necessary except necessity itself, the fact of which is contingent, and so on; or vice versa—everything is contingent except contingency itself, the fact of which is necessary, etc.? A first hint is given by Le Gaufey, who ingeniously links this grounding of universality in the exception of its enunciation to the (in)famous cry of a compulsive neurotic: "Anything but that!"—expressing his readiness to give away everything but that which really matters ("Take it all, just not this book!" etc.): "'Anything but that!' the cry, if there is one, of a man confronted with castration, assumes here [in the case of 'all men are mortal'] the form of a 'everyone, but not me,' which asserts itself as the *sine qua non* of the enunciation of an 'all.'"[78] The difference between the two is that the exception which grounds universality is contingent (a contingency of enunciation grounding the universal necessity), while the compulsive neurotic's exception is necessary: the one thing he is not ready to give is necessary, everything else is contingent. This means that contingency as exception is primordial, and that the reversal of roles (necessity as exception) is its compulsive-neurotic inversion. This conclusion imposes itself the moment we formulate all four positions that follow from each of these two opposed starting points: (1) everything is necessary; there is something which is not necessary; there is nothing which is not necessary; not-all things are necessary; (2) everything is contingent; there is something which is not contingent; there is nothing which is not contingent; not-all things are contingent. The true foundation of dialectical materialism is not the necessity of contingency, but the contingency of necessity. In other words, while the second position opts for a secret invisible necessity beneath the surface of contingency (the big compulsive topic), the first position asserts contingency as the abyssal ground of necessity itself.

In a brilliant move, Le Gaufey applies this logic of universality and its constitutive exception to the relationship between psychoanalytic theory and clinical

78 Le Gaufey, *Le Pastout de Lacan*, p. 145.

practice. In the standard theoretical view, particular cases are used to verify (or falsify) a general concept—say, we analyze a concrete case of paranoia and see if it fits our general notion (e.g., paranoia is the result of displaced homosexual attachment, etc.). Le Gaufey, on the contrary, reads concrete cases as constitutive exceptions: each case "rebels" against its universality, it never simply illustrates it. However, Le Gaufey here all too naïvely endorses the opposition between conceptual realists and empirical nominalists: "For the first, the conceptual architecture first articulates the order of the world. For the second, it misses it at first, and it is from this failure that the object shines forth, is grounded in existence."[79] For a Hegelian, this is literally true—more literally than intended by Le Gaufey: it is not only that the object eludes our conceptual grasp, it is that the "object" in the strict sense emerges as the result of (is generated by) the failure of our conceptual grasp. This is why Le Gaufey also unwittingly speaks the truth when he writes: "*The feature displayed by the object, the situation or the individual, and which allows us to subsume it under a concept, is actually not of the same nature as the feature present in the concept itself.*"[80] What this means, read literally, is that the "truth" of the discord between the individual case and its universal concept is the inherent discord within the concept itself: the feature in question redoubles itself into the universal feature and the same feature in its particular (over)determination.

It is because of this nominalist-empiricist (mis)reading of the logic of exception that Le Gaufey misses the opposite aspect of the Freudian relationship between theory and practice, the obverse of the excess of praxis: psychoanalytic theory is not merely the theory of psychoanalytic practice, but, simultaneously, the theory of the ultimate failure of this (its own) practice, a theoretical account of why the very conditions which gave birth to psychoanalysis render it "impossible" as a profession—theory here relates to the impossible-Real core of the practice.[81] It is this ultimate failure of the practice that renders its theory necessary: theory is not simply external to practice, confronting practice as the immense field of reality; the opening of the very gap between theory and practice, the exemption (subtraction) of theory from practice, is in itself a practical act, maybe the most radical one.

We can thus articulate the relationship between theory and practice as a square of the formulae of sexuation: on the left (masculine) side: all cases are subsumed under a universal concept of clinical theory / there exists at least one case which is not subsumed under any universal concept; on the right (feminine) side: there is no case which is not subsumed under a universal concept /

79 Ibid., p. 122.

80 Ibid., p. 121.

81 Another parallel with Marxism, which is also a theory of revolutionary practice and an account of the failure of revolutionary attempts.

not-all cases are subsumed under a universal concept. The feminine side (there is nothing outside theory, inconsistency is immanent to theory, an effect of its non-All character) is here the "truth" of the masculine side (theory is universal, but undermined by factual exceptions).

The Lacanian negation of the negation also enables us to see why the logic of carnivalesque suspension is limited to traditional hierarchical societies: with the full deployment of capitalism, it is "normal" life itself which, in a way, is today carnivalized, with its constant self-revolutionizing, with its reversals, crises, and reinventions. How, then, are we to revolutionize an order whose very principle is one of constant self-revolutionizing? This is the problem of the negation of the negation: how to negate capitalism without returning to some form of premodern stability (or, even worse, to some kind of "synthesis" between change and stability, a more stable and organic capitalism known as fascism...). Here, again, not-not-capitalism is not a premodern order (or any combination between modernity and tradition, this eternal fascist temptation which is today re-emerging as the Confucian "capitalism with Asian values"), but also not the overcoming of capitalism the way Marx conceived it, which involved a certain version of the Hegelian *Aufhebung*, a version of throwing out the dirty bath water (capitalist exploitation) and keeping the healthy baby (unleashed human productivity). Therein resides the properly utopian misunderstanding of *Aufhebung*: to distinguish in the phenomenon both its healthy core and the unfortunate particular conditions which prevent the full actualization of this core, and then to get rid of those conditions in order to enable the core to fully actualize its potential. Capitalism is thus *aufgehoben*, sublated, in communism: negated but maintained, since its essential core is raised to a higher level. What such an approach blinds us to is the fact that the obstacle to the full deployment of the essence is simultaneously its condition of possibility, so that when we remove the false envelope of the particular conditions, we lose the core itself. Here, more than anywhere, the true task is not to throw away the dirty water and keep the baby, but to throw away the allegedly healthy baby (and the dirty water will disappear by—take care of—itself).

Recall the paradox of the notion of reflexivity as "*the movement whereby what has been used to generate a system becomes, through a change in perspective, part of the system it generates.*"[82] As a rule, this reflexive appearance of the generating movement within the generated system, in the guise of what Hegel called the "oppositional determination," takes the form of the opposite: within the material sphere, Spirit appears in the guise of the most inert moment (crane, as in "the Spirit is a bone," the formless black stone in Mecca); in the later stage of a revolutionary process, when the Revolution starts to devour its own children,

82 N. Katherine Hayles, *How We Became Post-Human*, Chicago: Chicago University Press 1999, p. 8.

the political agents who effectively set the process in motion are relegated to the role of being its main obstacle, as waverers or outright traitors who are not ready to follow the revolutionary logic to its conclusion. Along the same lines, once the socio-symbolic order is fully established, the very dimension which introduced the "transcendent" attitude that defines a human being, namely *sexuality*, the uniquely human "undead" sexual passion, appears as its very opposite, as the main *obstacle* to the elevation of a human being to pure spirituality, as that which ties him or her down to the inertia of bodily existence. For this reason, the end of sexuality represented by the much-vaunted "post-human" self-cloning entity soon expected to emerge, far from opening up the way to a pure spirituality, will simultaneously signal the end of what is traditionally designated as the uniquely human capacity for spiritual transcendence. For all the celebration of the new "enhanced" possibilities for sexual life that Virtual Reality has to offer, nothing can conceal the fact that, once cloning supplements sexual difference, the game is effectively over.[83]

"There *is* a non-relationship"

So, to conclude, one can propose a "unified theory" of the formulae of sexuation and the formulae of four discourses: the masculine axis consists of the master's discourse and the university discourse (university as universality and the master as its constitutive exception), and the feminine axis of the hysterical discourse and the analyst's discourse (no exception and non-All). We then have the following series of equations:

S_1 = Master = exception S_2 = University = universality
$ = Hysteria = no-exception *a* = Analyst = non-All

83 And, incidentally, with all the focus on the new experiences of pleasure that lie ahead with the development of Virtual Reality, neuronal implants, etc., what about new "enhanced" possibilities of *torture*? Do not biogenetics and Virtual Reality combined open up new and unheard-of horizons for extending our ability to endure pain (by widening our sensory capacity to sustain pain, by inventing new forms of inflicting it)? Perhaps the ultimate Sadean figure of the "undead" victim of torture, who can bear endless pain without recourse to the escape into death, may also become a reality? Perhaps, in a decade or two, the most horrifying cases of torture (say, what was done to the Chief-of-Staff of the Dominican Army after the failed coup in which the dictator Trujillo was killed—sewing his eyes together so that he was not able to see his torturers, and then for four months slowly cutting off parts of his body in the most painful ways possible, like using blunt scissors to detach his genitals) will look like naïve children's games.

We can see here how, in order to correlate the two squares, we have to turn one 90 degrees in relation to the other: with regard to the four discourses, the line that separates masculine from feminine runs horizontally; that is, it is the upper couple which is masculine and the lower one which is feminine.[84] The hysterical subjective position allows for no exception, no x which is not-Fx (a hysteric provokes its master, endlessly questioning him: show me your exception), while the analyst asserts the non-All—not as the exception-to-All of a Master-Signifier, but in the guise of *a* which stands for the gap/inconsistency.[85] In other words, the masculine universal is positive/affirmative (all x are Fx), while the feminine universal is negative (no x which is not-Fx)—no one should be left out; this is why the masculine universal relies on a positive exception, while the feminine universal undermines the All from within, in the guise of its inconsistency.

This theory nonetheless leaves some questions unanswered. First, do the two versions of the universal (universality with exception; non-All with no exception) cover the entire span of possibilities? Is it not that the very logic of "singular universality," of the symptomatic "part of no-part" which stands directly for universality, fits neither of the two versions? Second, and linked to the first, Lacan struggled for years with the passage from "there is no (sexual) relationship" to "there is a non-relationship": he was repeatedly trying "to *give body* to the difference, to isolate the non-relationship as an indispensable ingredient of the constitution of the subject."[86]

Frege drew attention to the ambiguity of the notion of indeterminacy: "We should, of course, talk about 'indeterminacy,' but 'indeterminate' is not a qualitative epithet of 'number,' it is rather an adverb modifying 'indicate.' One doesn't say that x designates an indeterminate number, it indicates in an indeterminate way numbers."[87] There is an underlying shift at work here: from indicating in

84 And, insofar as, with regard to the Kantian sublime, the masculine position is dynamic and the feminine position mathematical, the formulae of sexuation also allow us to formalize the two modes of the sublime: the dynamic sublime focuses on the Master-Signifier as the intensity of the excessive force dominating the series, while the feminine sublime exposes itself to the endless series which cannot be totalized.

85 A typical hysterical position is that of a poet confronted with the theorist: he complains that the theorist reduces his art to an illustration of abstract theory, but at the same time challenges the theorist to go on and produce a theory which will effectively hold.

86 Le Gaufey, *Le Pastout de Lacan*, p. 151. There is also a non-relationship between the partial object and the body/organism to which it belongs: the partial object is not harmoniously inserted into the Whole of a body, it rebels against "its" body and acts on its own. However, this non-relationship is not simply homologous to the non-relationship between the two sexes—one can even say that the excess of the partial object with regard to the body comes first, i.e., that it is what causes the non-relationship between the two (sexed) bodies.

87 Gottlob Frege, *Écrits logiques et philosophiques*, Paris: Seuil 1973, p. 163.

an indeterminate way numbers to designating an indeterminate number (here, "indeterminate" *is* a qualitative epithet of a number)—or, to put it in a somewhat simplified way, a shift from designating a broad field of numbers (each of them determinate) which can occupy the place of x, to a single number which is immediately indeterminate. This direct "reification" of indeterminacy, where the indeterminacy as such (as the lack of determination) becomes directly the determination of an object, is also at work in the *objet a*, an object which is the lack (of the object) positivized.

When Lacan opposes the One, he targets two of its modalities, the imaginary One (of the specular fusion into One-ness) and the symbolic One (which is reductive, concerning the unary feature—*le trait unaire*—to which an object is reduced in its symbolic registration; this one is the One of differential articulation, not of fusion). The problem is: is there also a One of the Real? Is this role played by the *Y a d'l'Un* mentioned in *Encore*, which is a One prior to the differential articulation of the big Other, a non-delimitated but nonetheless particular One, a One which is neither qualitatively not quantitatively determined, a "there is something of the One" designating a minimal contraction, condensation, of the libidinal flow into a *sinthome*?

Lacan's *il n'y a pas de l'Autre* is strictly correlative to his *Y a d'l'Un*, "there is something of the One": insofar as the One of *Y a d'l'Un* is an "indivisible remainder" which makes the sexual relationship inexistent, *Y a d'l'Un* is also strictly correlative to *il n'y a pas de rapport sexuel*: it is the very object-obstacle to this rapport. The One of *Y a d'l'Un* is not primarily the mystical all-encompassing One of the infamous "oceanic feeling" derided by Freud, but a "little piece of the real," the excremental remainder which disturbs the harmony of the Two. Clarifying this crucial distinction, Le Gaufey draws our attention to a subtle passage in late Lacan from "*il n'y a pas de rapport sexuel*" to "*il y a du non-rapport (sexuel)*," a shift which precisely fits Kant's distinction between negative judgment (the negation of a predicate) and infinite judgment (the affirmation of a non-predicate). "There is no sexual relationship" can still be read as a variation on the old motif of the eternal conflict between the sexes. "There is a non-relationship" implies something much more radical: the positivization of this impossibility of the sexual relationship in a paradoxical "trans-finite" object which overlaps with its own lack or which is in excess with regard to itself. This means that masculine and feminine are not simply two out-of-sync entities, but that sexual difference in a way precedes the two sexes (the difference of which it is), so that the two sexes somehow come (logically) later, they react to, endeavor to resolve or symbolize, the deadlock of the Difference, and this deadlock is materialized in the pseudo-object called the *objet a*. This is why we should not say of the *objet a* simply that it is not sexual: it is un-sexual in exactly the same sense in which vampires are undead: the "undead" are neither alive nor dead but the monstrous living dead, and, in the same way, the *objet a* is neither sexual nor non-sexual but "sexually asexual," a monstrosity which does not fit the coordinates of either of the two sexes but is still sexual. As Lacan pointed out, what is at stake here is nothing less than a change in the "principle of all principles," from the ontological principle of non-contradiction to the principle that there is no sexual relationship.

It is easy to see how this passage from "there is no relationship" to "there *is* a non-relationship" evokes the Kantian passage from negative to infinite judgment: "he is not dead" is not the same as "he is undead," just as "there is no relationship" is not the same as "there is a non-relationship." The importance of this passage, with regard to sexual difference, is that, if we stop at "there is no sexual relationship" as our ultimate horizon, we remain in the traditional space of the eternal struggle between the two sexes. Even Jacques-Alain Miller sometimes sounds like this—when, for example, he reads "there is no sexual relationship" along the lines of "male with regard to female is not like a key which fits its lock," as a simple assertion of disharmony in contrast to harmony. Once we pass to "there *is* a non-relationship," even this kind of Heraclitean "unity/harmony in conflict" is left behind, since masculine and feminine are no longer symmetrical opposite poles: one of them (feminine) contains its own negation and thus breaks out of the confines of the opposition—not-woman is not man, but the abyss of not-woman *within* the feminine, as the undead remain within the domain of the dead (as the living dead).

François Wahl once made a critical remark, directed at Badiou, that "the argument that enjoins us to deduce the existence of non-belonging from the negation of belonging merely reiterates the ontological argument"—maybe, but is this not the only version of the ontological argument that a materialist can endorse?[88] The situation is strictly homologous to that of relationship: if there is no sexual relationship, there has to be an impossible object which gives body to a non-relationship (the asexual *objet a*); if there is no class relationship, there has to be a social agent which embodies this non-relationship, class struggle as such (the "part of no-part" of the social body, its "organ without a body"). This reversal of "there is no relationship" into "there is a non-relationship," this notion of a paradoxical object in which negativity itself acquires positive existence, is crucial: without it, we remain at the abstract level of the "eternal struggle of two opposed principles."

The passage from "*il n'y a pas de rapport sexuel*" to "*il y a du non-rapport (sexuel)*" is also homologous to the passage in Hegel from determinate reflection

88 As paraphrased in Ray Brassier, *Nihil Unbound: Enlightenment and Extinction*, London: Palgrave Macmillan 2007, p. 104, citing François Wahl, "Présentation, Représentation, Apparaître," in *Alain Badiou: Penser le multiple*, ed. Charles Ramond, Paris: L'Harmattan 2002, pp. 169–87.

to reflexive determination—or indeed to the passage in Marxism from materialist dialectics to dialectical materialism. The shift we are dealing with here is the key dialectical shift—the one most difficult to grasp for a "negative dialectics" in love with explosions of negativity, with all imaginable forms of "resistance" and "subversion," but unable to overcome its own parasitizing on the preceding positive order—from the wild dance of the liberation from the (oppressive) System to (what the German Idealists called) the System of Liberty. Two examples from revolutionary politics should suffice here: it is easy to become enamored of the multitude of free-thinkers who blossomed in the pre-revolutionary France of the late eighteenth century, from libertarians debating in the salons, enjoying the paradoxes of their own inconsistencies, to the pathetic artists amusing those in power with their own protests against power; it is much more difficult to fully endorse the reversal of this unrest in the harsh new Order of the Revolutionary Terror. In a homologous way, it is easy to enjoy the creative unrest of the years immediately following the October Revolution, with suprematists, futurists, constructivists, and so on, competing for primacy in revolutionary fervor; it is much more difficult to recognize in the horrors of the forced collectivization of the late 1920s an attempt to translate this revolutionary fervor into a new positive social order.

We should also not confuse the series of Lacan's "*il n'y a pas...*" (*de l'Autre*) with the series of "*n'existe pas*": "*n'existe pas*" denies the full symbolic existence of the negated object (already for Hegel, existence is not being, but being as the appearing of an underlying symbolic-notional essence), while "*il n'y a pas*" is more radical, it denies the very pre-essential nomadic being of specters and other pre-ontological entities. In short, *la Femme n'existe pas, mais il y a des femmes*. The same goes for God and the unconscious: God does not exist, but "there are gods" who haunt us; the unconscious does not exist as a full ontological entity (Jung thought it did exist), but it insists in haunting us—which is why Lacan said that the true formula of atheism is "God is the unconscious."[89]

The reason Lacan, in his later teaching, turned to the theme of knots was precisely in order to think the non-relationship as embodied in a paradoxical element (which would vaguely fit the singular universal, the "part of no-part").[90] Here enters the Borromean knot, consisting of three circles intertwined in such a way that no two are directly connected but are held together only through the third, so that if we cut the third knot, the other two will also be disconnected—in short, there is no relationship between any two circles. What is this third circle? The *objet a*? The *sinthome*? The symbolic order itself? Here Lacan, at the

89 Incidentally, this non-existence of God has nothing to do with Levinas's and Marion's "God beyond being."

90 As we have already seen, *den*, Democritus's name for the atom, is arguably the most appropriate name for a non-relationship.

very end of his teaching, reached a deadlock to which, in an authentically tragic mode, he openly confessed:

> The metaphor of the Borromean knot is, in its most simple state, inadequate. It abuses the metaphor, because there really is no thing which supports the imaginary, the symbolic, and the real. What is essential in what I am saying is that there is no sexual relationship. That there is no sexual relationship because there is an imaginary, a symbolic, and a real, this is what I did not dare to say. But I nonetheless said it. It is evident that I was wrong, but I simply let myself slide into it. This is disturbing, it is even more than annoying. It is even more annoying that it is not justified. This is how things look to me today, and this is what I confess to you. All right![91]

Two things should be noted here. First, retroactively, one can see where the obvious mistake lay: the Borromean knot works as a metaphor only if we think the three circles as simultaneous, intertwined on the same surface. (The only way to save this model would be to add a fourth element holding the three together, which Lacan did with his notion of the *sinthome* holding together the ISR triad.) Second, why was Lacan, by his own confession, wrong to say that there is no sexual relationship because there is an imaginary, a symbolic, and a Real? Because the three are not given simultaneously as a triad—they rather function like the Kierkegaardian triad of Aesthetic-Ethical-Religious, where the choice is always between two terms, an either/or; in other words, the three terms do not operate at the same ontological level, so that we encounter a certain minimal temporality: first the antagonism between the Aesthetic and the Ethical; then, with the passage to the Ethical, the antagonism *repeats* itself in the (new) guise of the jump from the Ethical to the Religious. One can thus even say that, in a weird "negation of the negation," the Religious is the return of the Aesthetic within the domain of the Ethical: the Religious is non-non-Aesthetic.[92] Similarly, in Lacan's triad of imaginary-symbolic-Real, or in Freud's of ego-superego-Id, when we focus on one term, the other two get condensed into one (under the hegemony of one of them). If we focus on the imaginary, the Real and the symbolic get contracted into the imaginary's opposite under the domination of the symbolic; if we focus on R, I and S get contracted under the domination of S.[93]

---

91 Jacques Lacan, seminar of January 9, 1979, in *Le séminaire, Livre XXVI: La topologie et le temps* (unpublished).

92 One can even sexualize this shift: the aesthetic-ethical axis (the overcoming of the aesthetic attitude through ethical engagement) is masculine, while the ethical-religious axis (the religious suspension of the ethical) is feminine.

93 Therein resides the shift in Lacan's work announced by his *Seminar VII* on the ethics of psychoanalysis: the shift from the axis I–S to the axis S–R.

What Lacan is struggling with here is how to formulate or formalize an impossible/Real object which keeps the two sexes apart and, simultaneously, is the only thing, a third thing, which indirectly connects the two. Insofar as this object is an obstacle to the identity of each sex, this means that every sex is grounded by its immanent impossibility. The inadequacy of the Borromean metaphor is that it makes it appear as if, when the third circle is cut off, the two other circles (the two sexes) simply wander off, each going its own way—as if the two sexes have some kind of consistency outside of their constitutive difference. How can we think this dependence of the two sexes outside differentiality?

> In short, the non-relationship—which had the ambition to affirm the absence of relationship—loses its support. There is no "thing" to support such a ... concept ... To conclude, the non-relationship did not find its object, and remains an affirmation which can only be related to its enunciation.[94]

But is then every object which gives body to non-relationship a fetish? Are we dealing here with something homologous to the structure of anti-Semitism: the two non-related circles are the two classes, capitalists and proletarians, and their non-relationship exists in the figure of the Jew? This (falsely) radical formulation brings us to a "dynamic" position which presupposes a non-relationship as an unfathomable elusive "absolute difference" already betrayed by any object which tries to positivize "there is no relationship" into "there is (embodied in this object) a non-relationship," like the *objet a* which poses as the obstacle to the direct relationship between the sexes. We can see what is wrong here if we pursue further this homology of sexual difference and class antagonism. The axiomatic basis of communist politics is not simply the dualist "class struggle," but, more precisely, the Third moment as the subtraction from the Two of hegemonic politics. That is to say, the hegemonic ideological field imposes on us a plane of (ideological) visibility with its own "principal contradiction" (today, the opposition between market-freedom-democracy and fundamentalism-terrorism-totalitarianism—"Islamo-Fascism," etc.), and the first thing we must do is reject (subtract from) this opposition, recognize it as a false opposition destined to obfuscate the true line of division. Lacan's formula for this redoubling is 1 + 1 + a: the "official" antagonism (the Two) is always supplemented by an "indivisible remainder" which indicates its foreclosed dimension. In other words, the *true* antagonism is always reflexive, it is the antagonism between the "official" antagonism and that which is foreclosed by it (this is why, in Lacan's mathematics, 1 + 1 = 3). Today, again, the true antagonism is not between liberal

94 Le Gaufey, *Le Pastout de Lacan*, pp. 166, 168.

multiculturalism and fundamentalism, but between the very field of their opposition and the excluded Third (radical emancipatory politics).

This is why Lacan's formula of "1 + 1 + a" is best exemplified by the class struggle: the two classes plus the excess of the "Jew," the *objet a*, the supplement to the antagonistic couple. The function of this supplementary element is double: it is a fetishistic disavowal of the class antagonism, yet precisely as such, it stands for this antagonism, forever preventing "class peace." In other words, if we had just the two classes, just 1 + 1 without the supplement, we would not have a "pure" class antagonism but, on the contrary, class peace: two classes complementing each other in a harmonious Whole. The paradox is thus that it is the very element which blurs or displaces the "purity" of the class struggle that serves as its "prime mover." Critics of Marxism who point out that there are never only two classes opposed in social life thus miss the point: it is precisely because there are never just two classes opposed that there is class struggle. We never have a pure confrontation of the two antagonistic classes, there are always third elements which displace the struggle, and these third elements are not just a "complication" of the class struggle, they *are* the class struggle. Without them, we would not have class struggle proper, but a simple differential relationship of the two opposed classes: class struggle is precisely the struggle for hegemony, for the appropriation of these third elements.

Here is the final sentence from the Wikipedia description of the film *Super 8*: "The movie ends with the star ship blasting off towards the creature's home planet while Joe and Alice hold hands." The couple is created when the Thing which served as the ambiguous obstacle disappears—ambiguous, because it was nonetheless needed to bring the couple together in the first place. This is what *il n'y a pas de rapport sexuel* means "in practice": the direct relationship is impossible, a third object serving as obstacle is needed to establish a link. Lars von Trier's *Melancholia* stages an interesting reversal of this classic formula of an object-Thing (an asteroid, aliens) which serves as the enabling obstacle to the production of the couple: at the film's end, the Thing (a planet on a collision course with Earth) does not withdraw; it hits Earth, destroying all life, and the film deals with the different ways the main characters deal with the impending catastrophe (from suicide to cynical acceptance).

This allows us also to approach in a new way Badiou's concept of the "point" as the point of decision, as the moment at which the complexity of a situation is "filtered" through a binary disposition and thus reduced to a simple choice: all things considered, are we *against* or *for* (Should we attack or retreat? Support that proclamation or oppose it?). With regard to the Third moment as the subtraction from the Two of hegemonic politics, we should always bear in mind that one basic operation of hegemonic ideology is to *enforce a false point*, to impose on us a false choice—as in today's "war on terror," when anyone who tries to draw attention to the complexity and ambiguity of the situation is sooner or later interrupted by an impatient voice saying: "OK, enough of this muddle—we are engaged in a difficult struggle in which the fate of the free world is at stake, so please, make it clear, where do you really stand: do you support freedom and democracy or not?"[95] The obverse of this imposition of a false choice is, of course, the blurring of the true line of division—here Nazism, with its designation of the Jewish enemy as an agent of the "plutocratic-Bolshevik plot," remains unsurpassed. In this designation, the mechanism is almost laid bare: the true opposition ("plutocrats" versus "Bolsheviks," i.e., capitalists versus proletarians) is literally obliterated, blurred into One, and therein lies the function of the name "Jew"—to serve as the operator of this obliteration. The first task of emancipatory politics is therefore to distinguish between "false" and "true" points, "false" and "true" choices, to bring back the third element whose obliteration sustains the false choice—just as, today, the false choice of "liberal democracy or Islamo-Fascism" is sustained by the obliteration of radical secular emancipatory politics.

We should be clear, then, in rejecting the dangerous motto "my enemy's enemy is my friend," which may lead us in particular into discerning a "progressive" anti-imperialist potential in fundamentalist Islamist movements. The ideological universe of organizations like Hezbollah is based on a blurring of the differences between capitalist neo-imperialism and secular progressive emancipation: within Hezbollah's ideological space, women's emancipation, gay rights, etc., are *nothing but* the "decadent" moral aspect of Western imperialism. We can see clearly here how the bourgeoisie functions in the masculine way, and the proletariat in the feminine: for the bourgeoisie, the field of the political is a closed dual relationship where the enemy of my enemy is my friend, for which they are now paying a heavy price—today's enemies, Muslim fundamentalists, were yesterday enemies of the (common) enemy (Soviet communism); for the proletariat as non-All, the field is not closed in this binary fashion—my enemy's enemy is not my friend (no alliance with religious fundamentalists), but, on the other hand, to be non-non-bourgeois is not to be bourgeois again, but our (the proletariat's) prospective ally.

---

95 One can also imagine a humanitarian version of such pseudo-ethical blackmail: "OK, enough of this muddle about neo-colonialism, the responsibility of the West, and so on—do you want to do something to really help the millions suffering in Africa, or do you just want to use them to score points in your ideologico-political struggle?"

Part IV

THE CIGARETTE AFTER

CHAPTER 12

The Foursome of Terror, Anxiety, Courage … and Enthusiasm

My ongoing debate with Badiou could be read as a series of variations on the motif of how to redeem Hegel, how to reclaim him for the contemporary universe of radical contingency. In terms of the most elementary ontological coordinates, my difference with Badiou is threefold, with regard to the triad Being/World/Event. At the level of being, the multiplicity of multiples has to be supplemented by the "barred One," the Void as the impossibility of the One becoming One. At the level of appearance, the world has to be conceived of as language-bound: each world is sustained by a Master-Signifier (the true reference of what Badiou calls a "point"). At the level of the Event, the "negativity" of anxiety and the (death) drive has to be posited as prior to the affirmative enthusiasm for the Event, as its condition of possibility.

What is missing in Badiou is an ontology of the Event. That is to say, when Badiou posits the Truth-Event as the exception to the order of Being (all there is are bodies and languages, with the exception of Truths), he adds that, as a materialist, he of course presumes that an Event is just a "torsion of being," that it exists only in the sum of its consequences, its inscriptions into the order of Being. In order to conceptualize the mode of existence of the Event, we thus need an ontology of virtual (non-)being, of a virtual X present only in its effects, or, even, retroactively generated by its own effects.

Being/World/Event

It is easy to imagine Badiou's rejoinder to my first thesis: is not the notion of a multiplicity of "worlds" (transcendental structures) set against the background of the barred One yet another case of post-philosophical metaphysics? Metaphysics because it provides no space for (mathematics as) general ontology which, for Badiou, guarantees that we remain within materialism? And does not this lack of a general ontology which defines the common texture of being also make it impossible to account for universal Truths, Truths which reach across single worlds (such as, in art, the plays of Aeschylus and Sophocles which, although embedded in the Ancient Greek world, continue to speak to us)? The key point here is how, precisely, we are to conceive the multiplicity of worlds.

Let me begin by defending Badiou against a critical point, recently made by Peter Hallward, which concerns the very ontological fundamentals of Badiou's philosophical edifice, the relationship between Being and beings:

> The problem is that Badiou assumes but does not account for the status of the middle and mediating term—the status of *beings*. Neither Badiou's ontology nor his logic seem to provide any clear place for ordinary ontic reality. What appears in our various Parisian worlds, clearly, are not instances of pure being or multiplicity, but people. Depending on the transcendental configuration of their world, these people can then appear or exist as tranquil workers, patriotic heroes or rebellious insurgents, but in each case the transcendental appears to take the elementary ontic status of its inhabitants for granted. Between the being of a pure multiplicity and an appearing as docile or insurgent lies an abyss without mediation. The space that in other philosophies might be filled by an account of material actualization or emergent self-realization (or any number of alternatives) is one that Badiou, so far, prefers to consign to contingency. If the transcendental of a world determines the ways in which its objects may appear, Badiou seems to presume a meta-transcendental register which simply *gives* a world the ontic raw material of its objects ...[1]

The gist of Hallward's argument is clear: the ontological structure of a purely formal mathematical multiplicity is not enough to provide (account for) the "raw material," the ontic density of beings, of positive entities (material objects) caught up in a world, organized through its transcendental frame. Convincing as it appears, this argument nonetheless imputes to Badiou's notion of the "transcendental" a perspectival status: it only works if, in a traditional Kantian way, we conceive the transcendental as the network that structures our perspective on noumenal reality. If, however, we follow Badiou and conceive the World—the transcendental structuring principle—as strictly immanent to ontic reality, then we have to conclude that beings, in their material density and with their wealth of properties, exist *always* and *only* as part of a World and its determinate situation. Beings are not neutral "raw stuff" caught up in one and then another transcendental network—the only neutral "stuff" outside every situation is mathematical multiplicity. There is another important consequence to be drawn from this absolute immanence of the transcendental: we should totally reject any notion of the symptomal point of a situation as an effect of the resistance of the inconsistent multiplicity of ontic reality to getting caught in the grid of transcendental consistency. The point of inconsistency, of the "symptomal torsion" of a situation, is generated by its immanent transcendental structure.

---

1 Peter Hallward, "Order and Event: On Badiou's *Logics of Worlds*," *New Left Review* 53 (September–October 2008), p. 118.

Here we can discern the key lesson of Hegelian idealism for today's materialism: the basic premise of materialism is not the existence of some obscure impenetrable material density or thick "matter" which indicates that "everything is not just thought," just notional determinations, that there is something "really out there" irreducible to notional determinations. For a materialism which has absorbed the lesson of Hegel, "reality out there" (the real-in-itself) really *is* "dematerialized," an "abstract" interplay of purely formal interrelations in which "matter (in its thickness) disappears." Far from indicating a radical externality resisting the subject, the thickness of objectivity resisting the subject's grasp is precisely the *subjective* moment, the most elementary "reifying" illusion of subjectivity, what the subject *adds* to the real-in-itself. This brings us to another key lesson of Hegel: whenever we are dealing with the tension between our (subjective) notional determinations and the stuff "out there" which resists our grasp, this tension is by definition secondary, an effect or reifying (mis)perception of what is originally an inner imbalance or antagonism in the texture of notions themselves. Therein lies Hegel's basic "idealist" wager: every tension between notional determinations and reality can be reduced to an immanent tension of notional determinations. So where is the "materialism" here? In the fact that these tensions or antagonisms are constitutive and irreducible, that we can never arrive at a "pure" and fully actualized notional structure.

There is nonetheless a problem with Badiou's elevation of mathematics into a model of the sciences: no modern science can be reduced to mathematical formalism, since it always includes also a minimum of empirical testing and measurement which introduce the aspect of the contingency of the Real—no one knows in advance what the measurements will show. This element is missing in mathematics where the contingency is limited to the selection or positing of the axioms with which the theoretician begins, while all that follows are the rational consequences of the axioms. Even such an "abstract" science like quantum physics, in which the dense positive materiality is dissolved into the pure virtuality of quantum waves, has to expose itself to measurement.

Is the conclusion then that, for this very reason, mathematics is not a science, but a philosophical discipline, the only true universal ontology? Or, on the contrary, that in order to pass from mathematics to ontology proper, one needs a minimum of contingency able to disrupt or surprise the necessity involved in generating formulae from axioms? Insofar as mathematics is the pure ontology of being, we approach here the most sensitive and obscure part of Badiou's philosophical "system," the transition from being to appearing. Although the professed task of Badiou's *Logics of Worlds* is to answer the question of how a world (of appearing) emerges from the pure multiplicity of being, he does not (even pretend to) really answer this question—he merely posits this transition, namely the emergence of a world, as a fact, and then goes on to describe the transcendental structure of a world. From time to time, however, he risks a formulation which borders on Gnostic *Schwärmerei*, as in the following passage:

> A kind of push, which is essentially topological, makes it that the multiple is not satisfied by being what it is since, as appearing, it is *there* that it has to be what it is. But what does this "being-there" mean, this being which comes to be insofar as it appears? It is not possible to separate an extension from what dwells in it, or a world from the objects which compose it.[2]

Note how Badiou here claims the exact opposite of Heidegger: the whole point of Heidegger's "ontological difference" as the difference between appearing entities and the horizon-world of appearing is that one can and should separate a world from the objects which compose it—ontological difference *is* this separation. The problem here is *the* problem: not that of how we pass from appearances to true being, but the opposite, the truly hard one—how we pass from being to appearing, how and why does being start to appear to itself? In other words, the problem is one of locality, of a focal point always presupposed in a "world."

In his *Human Touch*, Michael Frayn noted the radical relativity of our notion of the universe: when we talk about the micro-dimensions of quantum physics, so small as to be unimaginable, or about the vastness of the universe, so large that we are an imperceptible speck within it, we always presuppose our gaze, our "normal" measure of greatness: quantum waves are small, the universe is large, with regard to our standards. The lesson is that *every* notion of "objective reality" is bound to a subjective point. How, then, do we pass from the totally "flat" and incommensurable or de-focalized Real to a focused World, to a field constituted through a transcendental measure? Heidegger refuses this problem as, precisely, metaphysical: for him, the horizon of appearing is the ultimate horizon, there is nothing beyond it, only the abyssal play of *Ereignis*, and if we try to reach beyond, we become involved in a nonsensical endeavor to deduce the very ontological horizon of ontic reality from this reality.

Ray Brassier is thus right to insist on Badiou's "failure to clarify the connection between ontological inconsistency and ontical consistency," that is, the passage from Being to a World.[3] We should add only (but not only) a terminological clarification: the consistency of a world is not merely ontic, it is transcendental-ontological, for a world is the unity of the ontic and the ontological-transcendental horizon, it is the ontic multiplicity given within a certain ontological horizon, while being-in-itself is purely ontic, ontic without an ontological horizon, given without givenness. (This is why its science is mathematics, while worlds hinge on a logic, on an onto-logic.)

---

2 Alain Badiou, *Second manifeste pour la philosophie*, Paris: Fayard 2009, p. 39.

3 Ray Brassier, *Nihil Unbound: Enlightenment and Extinction*, London: Palgrave Macmillan 2007, p. 111.

In the history of philosophy, the most consistent answer to this question (in a certain sense one could say the *only* true answer) was provided by the German Idealists, especially Schelling and Hegel. In his *Weltalter* manuscripts, Schelling outlined the birth of *logos* (the articulated World) out of the pre-ontological antagonism of drives, while Hegel, in his *Logic*, tries to demonstrate how "appearing" (correlative to Essence) emerges out of the immanent inconsistencies ("contradictions") of Being. In spite of the insurmountable differences between Schelling and Hegel, the two share a key feature: they try to account for the emergence of appearing with reference to some kind of tension or antagonism or contradiction in the preceding order of being. This route, however, is excluded a priori by Badiou, since his axiom is that "being as being is absolutely homogeneous: a mathematically thinkable pure multiplicity."[4] This is why all Badiou can do is offer obscure hints about "a kind of push" of being towards appearing which belongs more to the Schopenhauerian Gnostic notion of how the abyssal Ground of Being harbors an obscure inexplicable will to appear.[5] Badiou touches upon the same problem when he explains the "fundamental principle of materialism":

> "Every atom of appearing is real." This axiom indicates that, at the atomic level (which means: when we are dealing with only one element of the multiple which appears), we can identify the atom of appearing and a real element of the multiple in question (in the ontological sense: this element "belongs" to it). We enter here the deepest considerations of the link between ontology and logic, between being and appearing. To adopt the principle of materialism means to admit that, at a minimal point of appearing, there is a kind of "fusion" with the being which appears. An atom of appearing is in a way "prescribed" by a real element of the multiple.[6]

But is not this notion of a "fusion" between appearing and being a pseudo-solution along the lines of Descartes's pineal gland? Is it not the case that, once we are within a world, there is no externality with regard to it since everything is focalized with regard to its transcendental structure? How, then, can we break out of the prison-house of a world? This brings us to our second critical remark: Badiou does not really account for how Truths can reach across different worlds. How can we combine this trans-worldly character of Truth with his emphatic claim that every Truth is localized, the Truth *of* a certain situation within a World? The key axiom of Badiou's "logics of worlds" concerns the concept of the

4 Badiou, *Second manifeste pour la philosophie*, pp. 39–40.

5 Not without irony, one can compare such speculative formulations to the similar propositions about the deeper unity of the sensual and the noumenal found in Kant's posthumously published manuscripts.

6 Badiou, *Second manifeste pour la philosophie*, pp. 66–7.

"inexistent" of a world: "*If a multiplicity appears in a world, one element of this multiplicity and only one is an inexistent of this world.*"[7] A "non-existent" is an element which is part of a world but participates in it with the minimal degree of intensity; that is, the transcendental structure of this world renders it "invisible": "The thing is in the world, but its appearing in the world is the destruction of its identity."[8] The classical example is, of course, Marx's notion of the proletariat which belongs to the existing society but within its horizon is invisible in its specific function. Such an inexistent is, of course, the "evental site" of a world: when the Event occurs, the inexistent passes from minimal to maximal existence, or, to quote the well-known line from the "Internationale": "We were nothing, we shall be all." As Badiou makes clear, this inexistence is not ontological (at the level of being, workers are massively present in capitalist society), but phenomenological: they are here, but invisible in their specific mode of existence. The philosophical question here is: why, exactly, does every world contain a "non-existent"? Its necessity

> depends on the axiom of materialism, according to which every atom is real. Perhaps we should see in this dependence a dialectical statement: if the world is regulated at the level of the One, or at the atomic level, by a materialist prescription of the type appearing = being, then *negation is [exists], in the form of an element hit by inexistence.*[9]

In short, precisely because of the gap between being (irreducible multiplicity) and appearing (the domain of atoms-Ones), the unity (overlapping) of being and appearing (existence) can only appear within the (transcendental) space of appearance in a negative way, in the guise of an inexistent, a One which is (from within the transcendental frame that regulates appearing) not-One, an atom which, while part of the world of appearing, is not properly covered by it, participates minimally in it. This inexistent is the point of symptomal torsion of a world: it functions as a "universal singular," a singular element which directly participates in the universal (belongs to its world), but lacks a determinate place in it. At the formal level of the logic of the signifier, this inexistent is the empty "signifier without a signified," the zero-signifier which, deprived of all determinate meaning, stands only for the presence of meaning as such, in contrast to its absence, to non-meaning: its meaning is tautological, it means only that things have meaning, without saying what this meaning is. Lévi-Strauss, who first theorized this empty signifier, also grounded its necessity in the gap between the irreducible multiplicity of the Real and the always-limited network of signifiers

7 Ibid., p. 72.
8 Ibid., p. 77.
9 Ibid., p. 74.

(Ones) which try to capture this excess of the Real.[10] Or, to refer to Marx's analysis of the commodity-form, it is as if, over and above lions, tigers, worms, fishes, and other particular species of animals, there exists animal as such, a direct embodiment of the genus. What the transcendental field of a world obfuscates is that this "inexistent" which has no place within its world simultaneously stands for the universality of its world: within the horizon of a world, the "inexistent" appears simply as a dispersed multiplicity of obscure marginal elements.

How, then, does an Event change a world whose Truth it enacts? Here enters the notion of subtraction: it is the concept of subtraction which resolves the open question of Badiou's *Being and Event*, which is that of the link or intersection between being and Event. How do we avoid the reproach that an Event is a proto-religious miracle which intervenes from some transcendent Beyond into the order of being? At its most elementary, subtraction is precisely the way an Event inscribes itself into being, it is the subtractive movement which opens up the space for the Event within the order of being. We should also note how, in contrast to Badiou's "affirmationist" insistence on the positivity of an Event, subtraction designates a negative move, a withdrawal, the reduction to a minimum (to the "minimal difference"). What Badiou calls "subtraction" is thus another name, his name, for *negativity in its affirmative dimension*, for a negativity which is not just a destructive gesture, but gives, opens up a new dimension. No wonder, then, that Badiou's "subtraction" functions like Hegel's *Aufhebung*: it contains three different layers of meaning: (1) to withdraw, disconnect; (2) to reduce the complexity of a situation to its minimal difference; (3) to destroy the existing order. As in Hegel, the solution is not to differentiate the three meanings (eventually proposing a specific term for each of them), but to grasp subtraction as the unity of its three dimensions: we should withdraw from our immersion in a situation in such a way that this withdrawal renders visible the "minimal difference" sustaining its multiplicity and thereby causes its disintegration, in the same way that removing a card from a house of cards causes the collapse of the entire edifice.

Badiou grounds this solution in three premises: (1) The multiple which localizes the evental mutation should already be there in the world, it should appear in it; that is, the mutation should not occur as the effect of a transcendental intervention of some miraculous Outside. (2) The transcendental of the world in question should not be modified in its internal rules, for we remain in the same world. (3) The "inexistent" multiple somehow supplements the functioning of the transcendental rules, so that the mutation should concern the relationship between the multiple and the transcendental of its world. His solution is thus that "*there is a local mutation in the appearing when a multiple falls itself under*

10 The underlying and correct implication is that there is One only at the level of the signifier: in the Real, there is no One—except for obscurantists.

the measure of the identities which authorizes the comparison between its elements. Or when the support-of-being of the appearing appears locally."[11] What happens here is that a multiple "is counted under its own law of appearance": "We call 'site' a multiple which appears in a new way, insofar as it falls under the general measure of the degrees of identity which prescribe its own appearing element by element. Let us say that *a site makes (itself) appear itself*."[12] This can happen precisely because the site is a "universal singular": since the inexistent does not have a particular content (its content is reduced to a minimum), one cannot just endow it with a greater intensity of appearing (like the fascists who want the proper role of work to be recognized in the social organism); at this symptomal point, a local mutation is only possible if the very universal "support-of-being of the appearing appears locally." When proletarians no longer appear as obscure background entities, but as a direct embodiment of the universal, an evental mutation occurs: in their singular being, the universality (of their world) as such is momentarily visible.[13]

The question to be raised here is this: why should an Event not designate a modification of the very internal rules of the transcendental of a world? Why do we not actually pass from one to another world? Is it not that, for a non-existent to change into a being with the maximum intensity of existence, the very rules which measure the intensity of being have to change? If proletarians are to count

---

11 Ibid., p. 91.

12 Ibid., p. 93.

13 How, then, does the Badiouian Event stand with regard to formulae of sexuation? Some Lacanian feminist critics claim that the exceptional status of the Event with regard to ordinary "human-animal" life, its status as the exception to universality, compels us to locate it on the male side of the formulae—and, indeed, is not this logic of exception to universality confirmed by Badiou's own formulations, such as when he says: "*There is nothing but bodies and languages* ...," to which materialist dialectics adds "*...with the exception of truths*" (Alain Badiou, *Logiques des mondes*, Paris: Seuil 2006, p. 9)? Furthermore, does not the heroic-phallic connotation of the fidelity to an Event (the idea of "enforcing" the truth) also bear witness to its masculine nature? There is nonetheless a key feature which renders such a reading problematic, convincing as it may appear: on the male side of Lacan's formulae of sexuation, the exception is the exception to universality (all but x are ...) which, as such, grounds this universality, while in the case of the Badiouian Truth-Event, the evental Truth *is* universal; i.e., here, exception does not ground universality (with regard to which it is an exception), the exception (an evental Truth) *is* universality. Or, to put it in another way, universality is here singular, it is what Hegel called a universality "for itself," a universality posited as such in a singular point. Or, to put yet another way, universality is here not the outcome of a neutral view to which we gain access after elevating ourselves above particular or partial engaged positions; universality is, on the contrary, something which is accessible only to an engaged subjective position. The supreme case here is the Marxian proletariat which stands for the exception, the "part of no-part," of the social body, and is precisely as such the "universal class."

as "being-human as such," does not the very measure of what counts as "being-human" have to be modified? In other words, is it not that an inexistent which is the point of symptomal torsion of a world can only be made fully existent if we pass into another world?

This brings us to the very complex and ambiguous relationship between inconsistency and truth in Badiou's thought. As Hallward has pointed out, for Badiou, "inconsistency is a category of truth, rather than knowledge or experience": reality is, at its most elementary ontological level, an inconsistent multiplicity that no One can totalize into a consistent unity.[14] Of course, reality always appears to us within a determinate situation, as a particular world whose consistency is regulated by its transcendental features. But, as Badiou puts it:

> A truth is this minimal consistency (a part, an immanence without concept) which indicates in the situation the inconsistency that makes its being ... Since the groundless ground of what is presented is inconsistency, a truth will be that which, from within the presented and as a *part* of the presented, brings forth the inconsistency upon which, ultimately, the consistency of presentation depends.[15]

Here is how Hallward deploys the consequences of this notion of truth as inconsistency:

> Perhaps the two most important general notions that underlie this philosophy of truth are *fidelity* and *inconsistency*. However varied the circumstances of its production, a truth always involves a fidelity to inconsistency. The semantic tension between these terms is only apparent. Fidelity: a principled commitment, variously maintained, to the infinite and universalizable implications of a disruptive event.[16] Inconsistency: the presumption, variously occasioned, that such disruption touches on the very being of being. Inconsistency is the ontological basis, so to speak, of a determined wager on the infinitely revolutionary orientation and destiny of thought. Fidelity is the subjective discipline required to sustain this destiny and thus to affirm an "immortality" that Badiou readily associates with the legacy of Saint Paul and Pascal. Inconsistency is what there is and fidelity is a response to what happens, but it is only by being faithful to the consequences of what happens that we can think the truth of what there is. In every case, "the truth of the situation is its inconsistency," and "a truth does not draw its support from consistency but from inconsistency."[17]

---

14 Hallward, "Order and Event," p. 100.

15 Alain Badiou, *Manifeste pour la philosophie*, Paris: Seuil 1989, pp. 90, 88.

16 Is not Badiou's notion of fidelity to an Event as the highest (the only true) freedom a variation on the old Protestant motto that obedience is the highest form of freedom?

17 Hallward, "Order and Event," pp. 98–9.

The term "inconsistency" is used here in two senses that are not clearly distinguished. First, there is inconsistency as the "true ontological foundation of any multiple-being," namely "a multiple-deployment that no unity can gather"—inconsistency is here the starting point, the zero-level of pure presence, that which is subsequently counted-as-one, organized into a world, that which subsequently appears within a given transcendental horizon. Then, there is inconsistency as the symptomal knot of a world, the excess which cannot be accounted for in its terms. (Exactly the same ambiguity characterizes the Lacanian Real.)

A bit of clumsy elementary reasoning may be useful here: if inconsistency is "what there is" and fidelity is fidelity to inconsistency, does this then mean that the Badiouian fidelity to a Truth-Event is ultimately a fidelity to what there is? Is a Truth-Event then only the intervention of the inconsistent multiplicity into a consistent situation, the index of how every totalizing representation of the inconsistent multiplicity fails to capture it fully? If this is the case, then we are back in the standard post-Hegelian universe of the productivity of a life-process which is always in excess over its re-presentations, so that re-presentations (situations, Worlds, totalizations) are like temporary envelopes which can be discarded when the productive force of presence overgrows them. At this level, inconsistency as the symptomal point of a situation is simply an index of the failure of this situation, an index of the need to drop it. We can even accommodate at this level Badiou's notion of the symptomal point as "nothing (the element without place) which becomes all": the symptomal point is the element within a situation which counts for nothing within its (transcendental) coordinates; through the evental revolution, this nothing (the "part of no-part") becomes All, the basic structuring principle of a new situation (like the proletariat before and after the revolution). However, considered in this way, the Event is only a passage from one to another World, a founding of a new World, a "World in becoming"—the whole process can be grasped in the terms of an opposition between the inconsistent multiplicity of Being and the consistency of a World as a form of appearance of multiplicity.

This couple is, however, clearly not "strong enough" to provide the coordinates for Badiou's notion of a Truth-Event: a Truth-Event is not only the "revenge" of the inconsistency upon a consistent situation; fidelity to a Truth-Event is a work of imposing a new order onto the multiplicity of Being, for Truth is a "project" which is enforced upon the unnamable of a situation. In a way, Truth is itself even more forcefully imposing than a World: there is no pre-established harmony between Being and Event, for the enforcing of a Truth onto the multiple reality in no way "expresses" the "inner truth" of reality itself.

Truth, inconsistency, and the symptomal point

There is thus a potential tension between truth as fidelity to inconsistency and Truth as enforcing a project upon being; that is to say, the key dilemma is whether it is sufficient to define an Event as the intrusion of the inconsistency into a consistent situation, as the return of its repressed in the guise of a symptomal torsion, of an excessive element which formally belongs to a situation but lacks a proper place in it (Rancière's "part of no-part"). Is it not the case that such points of symptomal torsion are not yet Events themselves but only what Badiou calls "evental sites," possible places where an Event can occur?

If, however, Truth is an Order enforced or imposed on the multiplicity of being, then the question arises: how does Truth differ from a World? Can Truth become a World?[18] To put it bluntly: does an Event, like every situation (or World), also have (or, rather, generate) its point of symptomal torsion, so that a Truth-Event is merely the passage between one and another World? The answer, of course, is no. The Truth enforced upon a situation is of a radically different nature to a World. Again, to put it bluntly: a World is historical, a transcendental-historical organization of a sphere of Being, while—as Badiou repeatedly emphasizes in his unabashedly Platonic way—Truth is eternal, in enforcing it one enforces onto reality an eternal Idea. We are thus dealing with two radically different levels: a World is a formation of human finitude, "hermeneutic" (a horizon of meaning); the evental Truth is eternal, the trans-historical persistence of an eternal Idea which continues to haunt us "in all possible worlds."

As the Idea "only exists in its power to make an object come 'in truth,' and thus to sustain that there is universal, it is not itself presentable, since it *is* the presentation-to-the-true. In a word: there is no Idea of Idea. By the way, one can name this absence 'Truth.'"[19] Truth thus always relies on a "there is no metalanguage": it occurs when we cannot step back and adopt a reflexive distance, when the only (impossible) step back would have been into the horizon itself. The sign of an Idea is that we "cannot go further back": we have reached the limit, the only thing behind an object is the void of its presentation. For example, a work of art is a Truth-Event when it cannot be dissolved further into its positive (social, politico-ideological, aesthetic) historical conditions, when there is more in its pure appearing than in the complex conditions that sustain it, so that we can only admire its appearance as such.

Both World and Truth-Event are modes of appearing: a World consists of the transcendental coordinates of appearing, while a Truth-Event (or an immortal

---

18 The ambiguity here—that while for Badiou an Event is the point of inconsistency and subversion of a World, he ends up calling for a new World against capitalist atonal worldlessness—is symptomal of this subterranean link between World and Truth-Event.

19 Badiou, *Second manifeste pour la philosophie*, p. 112.

Idea) is something that, rather than appearing, "shines through," trans-pires in reality. The status of the World is hermeneutic, it provides the horizon of meaning that determines our experience of reality, while the status of the Idea is Real, it is a virtual-immovable X whose traces are discernible in reality. In other words, the universality of a World is always "false" in the Marxist critico-ideological sense: every World is based upon an exclusion or "repression" which can be detected through its points of symptomal torsion, while the universality of Truth is unconditional, for it is not based upon a constitutive exception, it does not generate its point of symptomal torsion.

Badiou takes this claim literally: at the beginning of his *Logics of Worlds*, he takes the example of a horse as an object of visual art and attempts to demonstrate how two historical extremes—the famous Lascaux cave-drawings of a horse and Picasso's horses—both render the same "eternal Idea" of a horse. Much more important examples in this context are the great Events of modern emancipatory politics: the French Revolution, the October Revolution, the Chinese Cultural Revolution. In all these cases, Badiou staunchly opposes (what he perceives as) the "Hegelian" reading which interprets the final failure of these Events as the result of their immanent limitations, so that the failure of the Event is its "truth": due to the immanent limitations of its egalitarian project, the French Revolution had to end in the triumph of the bourgeois market, as the "truth" of the enthusiastic dreams which had inspired the revolutionaries; likewise, the October Revolution had to end in Stalinism; the Cultural Revolution had to end in the recent triumph of capitalism in China. In each case, the interpretive method is the same, that of a "symptomal reading" which sees in what appeared to the engaged participants as the failure or betrayal of their project the realization of the very truth of that project. The disappointed revolutionaries are thus dismissed as hysterical "beautiful souls" who refuse to recognize in the catastrophe they deplore the outcome and "truth" of their own acts. It is easy to discern in this the motif of the Cunning of Reason: the revolutionaries were the instruments of historical Necessity, mere tools employed in the realization of something they themselves despised.

For Badiou, on the contrary, the failure of a revolution simply indicates the exhaustion of a sequence: it does not in any way reveal its truth, its fateful limitations. Take the Cultural Revolution, which can be read at two different levels. If we read it as a part of historical reality (being), we can easily submit it to a "dialectical" analysis in which the final outcome of a historical process is taken to reveal its "truth": the ultimate failure of the Cultural Revolution bears witness to the inherent inconsistency of the very project (or "notion"), it is the explication-deployment-actualization of that inconsistency (in the same way that, for Marx, the vulgar reality of capitalist profit-seeking was the "truth" of the noble Jacobin revolutionary heroism). If, however, we analyze it as an Event, as an enactment of the eternal Idea of egalitarian Justice, then the ultimate outcome of the Cultural Revolution, its catastrophic failure and reversal into savage capitalist expansion, does not exhaust the Real of the Cultural Revolution: its eternal Idea survives its defeat in socio-historical reality, it continues to lead the spectral life of a failed utopia which will haunt future generations, patiently awaiting its next resurrection.

There is a basic philosophical dilemma underlying this alternative: it may seem that the only consistent Hegelian standpoint is one which measures the notion by the success or failure of its actualization, so that, from the perspective of the total mediation of essence by its appearance, any transcendence of the Idea over its actualization is discredited. The consequence is that, if we insist on the eternal Idea which survives its historical defeat, then this necessarily entails—in Hegelese—a regression from the level of the Notion as the fully actualized unity of essence and appearance to the level of the Essence supposed to transcend its appearing. But is this actually the case? One can also claim that the excess of the utopian Idea does not contradict the total mediation of the Idea and its appearing: the basic Hegelian insight according to which the failure of reality to fully actualize an Idea is simultaneously the failure (limitation) of this Idea itself continues to hold. The gap that separates the Idea from its actualization signals a gap within this Idea itself—but in what, precisely, does this gap consist?

The ambiguity of Lacan's motif "Kant avec Sade" may be of some help here, but only if we reverse the commonplace reading according to which Sadean perversion is the "truth" of Kant, more "radical" than Kant, that it draws out the consequences Kant himself did not have the courage to confront. It is not in this sense that Sade is the truth of Kant; on the contrary, Sadean perversion emerges as a result of the Kantian compromise, of Kant's avoidance of the consequences of his breakthrough. Sade is the *symptom* of Kant: while it is true that Kant retreated from drawing all the consequences of his ethical revolution, the space for the figure of Sade is opened up by this compromise, by Kant's unwillingness to go to the end, to maintain full fidelity to his philosophical breakthrough. Far from being simply and directly "the truth of Kant," Sade is the symptom of how Kant betrayed the truth of his own discovery—the obscene Sadean *jouisseur* is a stigma bearing witness to Kant's ethical compromise; the apparent "radicality" of this figure (the willingness of the Sadean hero to go all the way in his Will-to-Enjoy) is a mask for its exact opposite. In other words, the true horror is not the Sadean orgy, but the real core of the Kantian ethic itself—to paraphrase Brecht yet again, what is the miserable Evil of a Sadean group orgy in comparison with the "diabolical Evil" that pertains to a pure ethical act? *Mutatis mutandis*, the same goes for the relationship between the Cultural Revolution and contemporary Chinese capitalism as its "truth": this outcome is also a sign that Mao retreated from drawing all the consequences of the Revolution, for the space for the triumph of capitalism was opened up by this compromise, by Mao's unwillingness to go to the end, to maintain his fidelity to the Idea.

The "symptom" functions here in a different way from the "symptomal point" of a situation: while, in the second case, the "symptom" indicates the failure or falsity of the situation as such and is thereby its "truth," in the first case, the "symptom" indicates not the failure of the Idea as such, but rather the failure of the subject's fidelity to the Idea. In the second case, the symptom is "the truth of ...," while in the first case it bears witness to the fact that the subject "compromised (gave way with regard to) his desire." Consider another "symptom": Richard Wagner's anti-Semitism. The predominant critical Cultural Studies reading of Wagner interprets his anti-Semitism as the "truth" of his project, as the key which enables us to identify what is false even in Wagner's most sublime visions and musical achievements. But one can also read it as an indication of Wagner's inconsistency, of his infidelity to his own project, and show how the very narrative and musical texture of his work undermines it.[20]

The question is not which of these two logics of the symptom is the right one—it depends on what type of universality or totality we are dealing with. In the case of capitalism, the Marxist view that crises, wars, and other "deviant" phenomena are its "truth" fully holds. Democracy is a more ambiguous case—exemplary here is the legendary study of the "authoritarian personality" in which Adorno participated. The features of the "authoritarian personality" are clearly opposed to the standard figure of the "open" democratic personality, and the underlying dilemma is whether these two types of personality are opposed in a struggle, so that we should fight for one against the other, or whether the "authoritarian" personality is in fact the symptomal "truth" of the "democratic" personality. Along these lines, the shift from Adorno to Habermas apropos modernity can itself be formulated in these terms: at the heart of Adorno's and Horkheimer's "dialectic of enlightenment" is the idea that phenomena such as fascism are "symptoms" of modernity, its necessary consequence (which is why, as Horkheimer memorably put it, those who do not want to talk critically about capitalism should also keep silent about fascism). For Habermas, by contrast, they are "symptoms" or indicators of the fact that modernity remains an "unfinished project," that it has not yet deployed all its potential.

Does this logic of the Idea as an "unfinished project" not commit us to Derrida's notion of a gap between the spectral Idea that continues to haunt historical reality and the Idea in its positive form, as a determinate program to be realized? Every determinate form of the Idea, every translation of the Idea into a positive program, betrays the messianic Promise at its spectral core. We are thus

20 For example, the central figure of his entire work, the hero condemned to the obscene immortality of an endless wandering and seeking redemption in death, is clearly a figure of the Wandering Jew.

back in pseudo-Kantian Levinasian territory, where eternal Truth is conceived as a regulative Idea which is forever "to come," which never arrives in its full actuality. But is this the only solution?

There is no human animal

There is a different way to read the "eternality" of the Idea. Recall that, for Hegel, the "resolution" of a contradiction does not entail the abolition of difference, but its full admission. It took even Lacan a long time to reach this insight. Throughout his development, Lacan was looking for a "quilting point," a link that would hold together or at least mediate between S (the symbolic semblance) and J (the Real of *jouissance*). The main solution is to elevate the phallus into the signifier of the lack of a signifier which, as the signifier of castration, holds the place of *jouissance* within the symbolic order; then, there is the *objet a* itself as the surplus-enjoyment generated by the loss of *jouissance*, which is the obverse of the entry into the symbolic order, as *jouissance* located not on the side of the real *jouissance* but, paradoxically, on the side of the symbolic. In "Lituraterre," he finally drops this search for the symbolic pineal gland (which for Descartes marked the bodily point at which body and soul interact) and endorses the Hegelian solution: *it is the gap itself that forever separates S and J, which holds them together*, since this gap is constitutive of both of them: the symbolic arises through the gap that separates it from full *jouissance*, and this *jouissance* itself is a specter produced by the gaps and holes in the symbolic. To designate this interdependence, Lacan introduces the term *littorale*, standing for the letter in its "coast-like" dimension and thereby "figuring that one domain [which] in its entirety makes for the other a frontier, because of their being foreign to each other, to the extent of not falling into a reciprocal relation. Is the edge of the hole in knowledge not what it traces?"[21] So when Lacan says that "between knowledge and jouissance, there is a *littoral*," we should hear in this the evocation of *jouis-sense* (enjoy-meant), of a letter reduced to a *sinthome*, a signifying formula of enjoyment.[22] Therein resides late Lacan's final "Hegelian" insight: the convergence of the two incompatible dimensions (the Real and the symbolic) is sustained by their very divergence, for difference is constitutive of what it differentiates. Or, to put it in more formal terms: it is the very intersection between the two fields which constitutes them.

It is along these lines that, in his reading of Saint Paul, Badiou offer a perceptive interpretation of the subjective passage from the Law to love. In both cases,

21 Jacques Lacan, "Lituraterre," *Autres écrits*, Paris: Seuil 2001, p. 14.

22 Ibid., p. 16.

we are dealing with division, with a "divided subject"; however, the modality of the division is thoroughly different. The subject of the Law is "decentered" in the sense that it is caught up in the self-destructive, vicious cycle of sin and the Law in which one pole engenders its opposite. Paul gave an unsurpassable description of this entanglement in *Romans* 7:

> We know that the law is spiritual; but I am carnal, sold into slavery to sin. What I do, I do not understand. For I do not do what I want, but I do what I hate. Now if I do what I do not want, I concur that the law is good. So now it is no longer I who do it, but sin that dwells in me. For I know that good does not dwell in me, that is, in my flesh. The willing is ready at hand, but doing the good is not. For I do not do the good I want, but I do the evil I do not want. Now if I do what I do not want, it is no longer I who do it, but sin that dwells in me. So, then, I discover the principle that when I want to do right, evil is at hand. For I take delight in the law of God, in my inner self, but I see in my members another principle at war with the law of my mind, taking me captive to the law of sin that dwells in my members. Miserable one that I am!

It is thus not that I am merely torn between two opposites, the Law and sin; the problem is that I cannot even clearly distinguish them: I want to follow the Law, but I end up in sin. This vicious cycle is (not so much overcome as) broken out of in the experience of love, more precisely: in the experience of the radical gap that separates love from the Law. Therein lies the radical difference between the couple Law/sin and the couple Law/love. The gap that separates Law and sin is not a real difference: their truth is their mutual implication or confusion—the Law generates sin and feeds upon it, one cannot ever draw a clear line of separation between the two. It is only with the couple Law/love that we attain real difference: these two moments are radically separated, they are not "mediated," one is not the form of appearance of its opposite. In other words, the difference between the two couples is not substantial, but purely formal: we are dealing with the same content in its two modalities. In its indistinction or mediation, the couple is that of Law/sin; in the radical distinction of the two, it is Law/love. It is therefore wrong to ask the question "Are we then forever condemned to the split between the Law and love? What about the synthesis between the Law and love?" The split between the Law and sin is of a radically different nature than the split between the Law and love: instead of a vicious cycle of mutual reinforcement, we have a clear distinction of two different domains. Once we become fully aware of the dimension of love in its radical difference from the Law, love has in a way already won, since this difference is visible only when one already dwells in love, from the standpoint of love. In this precise sense, there is no need for a further "synthesis" between Law and love: paradoxically, their "synthesis" is already the very experience of their radical split. In the same way, for Chesterton, the book of Job "saved [the Jews] from an enormous collapse and decay":

> Here in this book the question is really asked whether God invariably punishes vice with terrestrial punishment and rewards virtue with terrestrial prosperity. If the Jews had answered that question wrongly they might have lost all their after influence in human history. They might have sunk even down to the level of modern well-educated society. For when once people have begun to believe that prosperity is the reward of virtue, their next calamity is obvious. If prosperity is regarded as the reward of virtue it will be regarded as the symptom of virtue. Men will leave off the heavy task of making good men successful. They will adopt the easier task of making out successful men good.[23]

No synthesis is needed here: the experience of the radical gap between prosperity and virtue is already the victory of virtue. It is along these lines that we should oppose the "eternal Idea" as the inaccessible Goal to the "eternal Idea" as a *principle of division*—or, as Badiou put it: "The idea is that which allows a division."[24] In relation to a confusing and "complex" situation, an Idea renders its contours clear, allowing us to draw a line of division with reference to the antagonism which underlies the situation. The "eternity" of the Idea does not rely on the "spurious infinity" of an endless approach to an impossible goal; the "eternity" of an Idea is the eternity of division. It is this feature which makes the Idea non-All ("feminine" in the terms of Lacan's formulae of sexuation): the Idea compels us to divide without any pre-existing encompassing unity—more precisely (and paradoxically), every unity is here a form of division.

The Kantian "regulative Idea" is on the side of desire with its forever elusive object-cause: with every object, the desiring subject experiences a "*ce n'est pas ça*" (this is not *that*—not what I really want), every positive determinate object falls short of the elusive spectral "X" after which desire runs. With the Idea as the principle of division, by contrast, we are on the side of the drive: the "eternity" of the Idea is nothing other than the repetitive insistence of the drive. However, in the terms of the triad of Being/World/Event, this solution only works if we add to it another term, a name for the terrifying void called by some mystics the "night of the world," the reign of the pure death drive. If an individual belongs to the order of being, if a human (being) is located in a world, and if a subject has its place within the order of an Event, a neighbor always evokes the abyss of the "night of the world." Our hypothesis is that it is only with reference to this abyss that one can answer the question "How can an Event explode in the midst of

23 G. K. Chesterton, "Introduction," in *The Book of Job*, London: Cecil Palmer & Hayward 1916, p. xxvi.

24 Badiou, seminar on Plato, December 5, 2007.

Being? How must the domain of Being be structured so that an Event is possible within it?" Badiou—as a materialist—is aware of the idealist danger that lurks in the assertion of their radical heterogeneity, of the irreducibility of the Event to the order of Being:

> We must point out that in what concerns its material the event is not a miracle. What I mean is that what composes an event is always extracted from a situation, always related back to a singular multiplicity, to its state, to the language that is connected to it, etc. In fact, so as not to succumb to an obscurantist theory of creation *ex nihilo*, we must accept that an event is nothing but a part of a given situation, nothing but a *fragment of being*.[25]

However, here we should go further than Badiou himself is prepared to: there is no Beyond of Being which inscribes itself into the order of Being—there is nothing but the order of Being. Recall again the paradox of Einstein's general theory of relativity, in which matter does not curve space but is an effect of space's curvature: an Event does not curve the space of Being through its inscription into it—on the contrary, an Event is *nothing but* this curvature of the space of Being. "All there is" is the interstice, the non-self-coincidence of Being, the ontological non-closure of the order of Being.[26] The difference between the Event and Being is the difference on account of which the "same" series of real occurrences, which, in the eyes of a neutral observer, are simply part of ordinary reality, are in the eyes of an engaged participant inscriptions of the fidelity to an Event. For example, the "same" occurrences (say, battles on the streets of St. Petersburg), which to a neutral historian are just violent twists and turns in Russian history, are, for an engaged revolutionary, aspects of the epochal Event of the October Revolution.

But, again, how are we to grasp the thesis that "an event is nothing but a part of a given situation, nothing but a *fragment of being*"? Why, if it is a part of the situation, is it then irreducible to this situation, why cannot it be causally "deduced" from it? The underlying philosophical choice is here once again: Kant or Hegel, Kantian transcendental finitude or Hegelian speculative infinity. From the Kantian viewpoint, an Event appears as irreducible to its situation (to the order of Being) on account of the radical finitude of the subject who is "touched by the grace" of an Event and engaged in it. Here enters Badiou's distinction between the multiplicity of Being and a particular World (a situation, a mode

25 Alain Badiou, *Theoretical Writings*, London: Continuum 2004, p. 43.

26 Which is why one should ask the key question: is there a Being without an Event, simply external to it, or is *every* order of Being the disavowal-obliteration of a founding Event, a "perverse" *je sais bien, mais quand meme* ..., a reduction-reinscription of the Event into the causal order of Being?

of Appearance of Being), a distinction which basically corresponds to Kant's distinction between In-itself and For-us. As Meillassoux has demonstrated, the only In-itself admissible within our scientific modern universe is the In-itself of a radically contingent mathematicized multiplicity, and there are no Events at the level of the multiplicity of Being—any talk about Events at the level of Being would take us back to the premodern notion of Sense as immanent to reality. But then, again, the very difference of Event and Being hinges on the finitude of our subjectivity: ultimately, it is simply that, on account of our finitude, we cannot adopt a neutral view of the infinity of Being, a view which would enable us to locate the Event as a "fragment of being" in the totality of being.[27] The only alternative to this Kantian perspective is a Hegelian one: one can and should fully assert creation *ex nihilo* in a materialist (non-obscurantist) way if one asserts the non-All (ontological incompleteness) of reality. From this standpoint, an Event is irreducible to the order of Being (or to a situation with regard to which it is Event); it is also In-itself *not* just a "fragment of being," not because it is grounded in some "higher" spiritual reality, but because it emerges out of the void in the order of being. It is to this void that suture refers.

The only solution here is to admit that the couple Being/Event is not exhaustive, that there must be a third level. Insofar as an Event is a distortion or twist of Being, is it not possible to think this distortion *independently of* (or as prior to) the Event, so that the "Event" ultimately names a minimal "fetishization" of the immanent distortion of the texture of Being into its virtual object-cause? And is not the Freudo-Lacanian name for this distortion the *drive*, the death drive? Badiou distinguishes man qua mortal "human animal" from the "inhuman" subject as the agent of a truth-procedure: as an animal endowed with intelligence and able to develop instruments to reach its goals, man pursues happiness and pleasure, worries about death, and so on; but only as a subject faithful to a Truth-Event does man truly rise above animality. How, then, does the Freudian unconscious fit into this duality of the human animal and the subject (defined by its relation to the Truth-Event)? Badiou himself proposed a clear-cut solution:

> the formal operations of incorporation into the place of the Other and of the splitting of the subject constitute under the name of the unconscious the substructure of the human animal, and not the occurrence—no matter how rare—of the process of a truth that a subjectivated body treats point by point.[28]

---

27 Consequently, insofar as the Event is the intrusion of infinity into our lives, and insofar as the distinction between Being and Event is only operative from the standpoint of our finitude, it seems that Jean-Luc Nancy is right in his claim that Badiou's "infinity" is a name for its exact opposite, for human finitude: the "Event" is the infinite the way it appears within the horizon of finitude.

28 Alain Badiou, *Logiques des mondes*, Paris: Seuil 2006, pp. 502–3, as translated in

But this solution should be rejected: there is no way to account for the Freudian Unconscious in terms of what Badiou calls the "human animal," a living being bent on survival, a being whose life follows "pathological" interests (in the Kantian sense): the "human animal" leads a life regulated by the pleasure principle, a life unperturbed by the shocking intrusion of a Real which introduces a point of fixation that persists "beyond the pleasure principle." What distinguishes humans from animals (the "human animal" included) is not consciousness—one can easily concede that animals do have some kind of self-awareness—but the un-conscious: animals do not have the Unconscious. One should thus say that the Unconscious, or, rather, the domain of the "death drive," this distortion or destabilization of animal instinctual life, is what renders a life capable of transforming itself into a subject of Truth: only a living being with an Unconscious can become the receptacle of a Truth-Event.

The problem with Badiou's dualism is thus that it ignores Freud's basic lesson: there is no "human animal," a human being is from its birth (and even before) torn away from its animal constraints, its instincts are "denaturalized," caught up in the circularity of the (death) drive, functioning "beyond the pleasure principle," marked by the stigma of what Eric Santner called "undeadness" or the excess of life. This is why there is no place for the "death drive" in Badiou's theory, for that "distortion" of human animality which precedes the fidelity to an Event. It is not only the "miracle" of a traumatic encounter with an Event which detaches a human subject from its animality: its libido is already in itself detached.[29] No wonder, then, that Badiou has such problems with the notion of the (death) drive that he regularly dismisses it as a morbid obsession, and so forth.[30]

The standard criticism of Badiou concerns the miraculous divine-like emergence of the Event which, as if from nowhere, intervenes into the complacent

Bruno Bosteels, "Force of Nonlaw: Alain Badiou's Theory of Justice," *Cardozo Law Review* 29 (April 2008), p. 1919.

29 Taking a step further, we can even venture that there is no animal *tout court*, if by "animal" we mean a living being fully fitted to its environment: the lesson of Darwinism is that every harmonious balance in the exchange between an organism and its environment is temporary and fragile, that it can explode at any moment; such a notion of animality as a balance disturbed by human hubris is a fantasy.

30 Badiou's reluctance to address the death drive should be contrasted to some of the more orthodox Freudian contributors to *Cahiers pour l'Analyse* (in particular Serge Leclaire and André Green), who remained skeptical about the *Cahiers'* apparent push towards uncompromising formalization and emphasized the drive as the element which resists formalization. We should note here that these authors were also critical of Lacan and, especially, of Miller: what the late Lacan and Miller tried to do was precisely to radically formalize (de-biologize) the drive, reading it as a purely formal "twist" or repetitive torsion of the signifying order.

order of Being: is not such a notion of the Event a remainder of religious thought, apparent whenever Badiou himself talks about "grace" and the "miracle" of the Event? Such criticism accepts the order of Being with its "animal life" as given, and then goes on to locate the difference between materialism and idealism in the question "Can we 'materialistically' generate the Event out of the order of Being, or do we proceed like 'idealists' and conceive it as an external intervention into the order of Being?" In both cases, the "finite" order of Being is accepted as a positive fact; the question is only whether this order can generate the "infinite" Event out of itself. The properly Hegelian move here is to problematize the shared premise itself. In other words, Hegel's criticism of all attempts to prove the existence of God out of the structure of the finite natural world (we cannot explain its teleology without a higher rational entity, and so on) is that they "dogmatically" accept our ordinary finite reality as an unproblematic fact, and then go on to demonstrate the existence of God from this premise—in this way, their very procedure undermines their thesis (asserting the origin of finite reality in God): God comes second, becomes dependent on what should depend on Him. In contrast to this common-sense reliance on the fact of finite reality, truly dialectical thought starts by problematizing the full actuality of finite reality itself: does *this* reality fully exist, or is it just a self-sublating chimera?[31]

So, returning to the criticism of Badiou's notion of the Event as "religious," as a miracle which disturbs the finite life of the human animal, we should answer with a question: does this "human animal" really exist, or is it just a myth—and an *idealist* myth, for that matter? In other words, the basic idealist strategy is to reduce nature (bodily reality) to a primitive level which obviously excludes "higher" capacities and thereby create some space for the external intervention of a "higher" spiritual dimension. Kant is exemplary here: according to him, if one finds oneself shipwrecked along with another survivor, and the largest piece of flotsam around will support only a single person, then moral considerations are no longer valid—there is no moral law preventing me from fighting to death with the other survivor to secure the raft; I can do so with moral impunity. It is here that, perhaps, one encounters the limit of Kantian ethics: what about someone who willingly sacrifices himself to give the other person a chance to survive—and, furthermore, is ready to do so for no pathological reason? Since there is no moral law commanding him to do so, does this mean that such an act has no ethical status? Does not this strange exception demonstrate that ruthless egotism, a commitment to personal survival and gain, is the silent "pathological" presupposition of Kantian ethics—that is, that the Kantian ethical edifice

31 It is at this level that Hegel also locates the difference between ancient and modern skepticism: the greatness of ancient skepticism was to doubt the existence of "obvious" finite material reality, while modern empiricist skepticism doubts the existence of anything beyond this reality.

can only sustain itself by silently presupposing a "pathological" image of man as a ruthless utilitarian egotist? (In exactly the same way, the Kantian political edifice, built on the notion of ideal legal power, can only maintain itself by silently presupposing a "pathological" image of the subjects of this power as "a race of devils.")

Is not Badiou also all too Kantian with his opposition of "mere animal life" and the miracle of Event? The properly dialectical-materialist solution here is not, of course, the direct spiritualization of nature in the mode of Romantic *Naturphilosophie*, but an immanent de-naturalization of nature. We should thus, for purely conceptual reasons, expand the opposition of human animal and subject[32] into four basic existential positions: the *individual* (what Badiou calls the "human animal," the ordinary human being oriented by utilitarian motives and engaged in "servicing the goods"); the *human* (the individual aware of the precariousness and mortality of its position); the *subject* (a human being that overcomes its subordination to the "pleasure principle" by way of a heroic fidelity to a Truth-Event); the *neighbor* (not the Levinasian version, which is closer to the second position, but the Freudo-Lacanian one, the abyssal inhuman *Ding* whose proximity causes anxiety). A Greimasian semiotic square imposes itself here, with the two axes of human versus inhuman and positivity versus negativity: the *individual* is a positively attuned human (living an ordinary life), in contrast to the negatively attuned *human* (aware of the precariousness and mortality of its condition); the *subject* is a positively attuned agent engaged in an over-human truth-process, in contrast to the *neighbor* attuned to the negative stance of anxiety. Different figures can be located along these lines—for example, Christ is a "human subject," combining precarious mortality with a fidelity to Truth.

32 In his afterword to Peter Hallward's collection *Think Again*, Badiou approvingly quotes Lin Biao: "The essence of revisionism is the fear of death" (Peter Hallward, ed., *Think Again: Alain Badiou and the Future of Philosophy*, London: Continuum 2004, p. 257). This existential radicalization of the political opposition between orthodoxy and revisionism throws new light on the old '68 motto "the personal is political": here, the political becomes personal, the ultimate root of political revisionism is located in the intimate experience of the fear of death. Badiou's version of it would be that, since "revisionism" is, at its most basic, the failure to subjectivize oneself, to assume fidelity to a Truth-Event, being a revisionist means remaining within the survivalist horizon of the "human animal." There is, however, an ambiguity that clings to Lin Biao's statement: it can be read as saying that the root of political revisionism lies in human nature which makes us fear death; but it can also be read as saying that, since there is no unchangeable human nature, our very intimate fear of death is already politically overdetermined, for it arises in an individualist and egotistical society with little sense of communal solidarity, which is why, in a communist society, people would no longer fear death.

Badiou against Levinas

Leszek Kolakowski once wrote that man can be a moral being only insofar as he is weak, limited, fragile, and with a "broken heart"—this is the liberal core of Levinas's thought, a core to which Butler also subscribes when she focuses on the fragile symbolic status of a human subject, caught in the abyss of decentered symbolic representation, and whose very identity hinges on an external, inconsistent network. It is this precarious status of subjectivity which functions as the zero-level of all ethics: the absolute call, the injunction, emanating from the vulnerable neighbor's face. To be an ethical subject means to experience oneself, in one's singularity, as the addressee of that unconditional call, as responsible and responding to it even when one chooses to ignore it.[33]

The first thing to note here is the basic asymmetry of the situation: the other's face makes an unconditional demand on us; we did not ask for it, and we are not allowed to refuse it. (And, of course, what Levinas means by "the face" is not directly the physical face: a face can also be a mask for the face, there is no direct representation of the face.) This demand is the Real which cannot be captured by any words; it marks the limit of language, every translation of it into language already distorts it. It is not simply external to discourse—it is its inner limit, as the encounter with the other which opens up the space for discourse, since there can be no discourse without the other. It is the *real* of a violent encounter that (as Badiou would put it) throws me out of my existence as a human animal.[34] And Butler is fully justified in emphasizing that this ethical injunction, at its most basic level, is a reaction to the quasi-automatic reaction to get rid of the other-neighbor, to kill him (this urge can easily be accounted for in Freudo-Lacanian terms as the basic reaction to the encounter with the intrusive Neighbor-Thing):

> If the first impulse towards the other's vulnerability is the desire to kill, the ethical injunction is precisely to militate against that first impulse. In psychoanalytic terms, that would mean marshalling the desire to kill in the service of an internal desire to kill one's own aggression and sense of priority. The result would probably be neurotic, but it may be that psychoanalysis meets a limit here. For Levinas, it is the ethical itself that gets one out of the circuitry of bad conscience, the logic by which the prohibition against aggression becomes the internal conduit for aggression itself.

---

33 See Judith Butler, *Precarious Life*, London: Verso Books 2006. From a Christian perspective, we should go to the end here: if man is created in God's image, the becoming-man-of-God means that the same goes for God: in Christ, God becomes a fragile absolute, precarious, vulnerable, and impotent.

34 The irony here is that, with Butler, the encounter with the Other in its precariousness and fragility (finitude, mortality) has exactly the same structure as the Badiouian encounter of the Event which opens up the dimension of immortality or eternity.

> Aggression is then turned back upon oneself in the form of super-egoic cruelty. If the ethical moves us beyond bad conscience, it is because bad conscience is, after all, only a negative version of narcissism, and so still a form of narcissism. The face of the Other comes to me from outside, and interrupts the narcissistic circuit.[35]

Something is terribly wrong here: psychoanalysis is first limited to the economy of narcissistic-egotistic aggression and its superegoic reversal, and from that, of course, the inevitable conclusion follows—that the proper dimension of the ethical lies outside the scope of psychoanalysis, that "psychoanalysis meets a limit here," that it can read the ethical only as the neurotic-masochistic reversal of narcissistic aggression. But for Freud and Lacan (as was convincingly elaborated by Jean Laplanche), the traumatic encounter with the Other as a desiring which "interrupts the narcissistic circuit" is precisely the basic experience constitutive of desiring subjectivity—which is why, for Lacan, desire is a "desire of the Other." Thus Lacan's "ethics of psychoanalysis" stands for his attempt to demonstrate that there is an ethical dimension discovered in the psychoanalytic experience, a dimension which has nothing whatsoever to do with any kind of reduction of the "higher" ethical sphere to "lower" neurotic libidinal vicissitudes. Lacan's option involves neither the aggressive thrust to annihilate the Other-Neighbor-Thing, nor its reversal into accepting the Other as the source of an unconditional ethical injunction. But why not?

We should note that, in Levinas's account, it is not me who experiences myself as precarious, but the Other who addresses me. This is why, in my very asymmetric subordination to the Other's call, in my unconditional responsibility, in my being taken hostage by the Other, I assume supremacy over the Other. Do we not encounter this wounded-precarious Other almost daily, in advertisements for charity which bombard us with images of starving or disfigured children crying in agony? Far from undermining the hegemonic ideology, such adverts are one of its exemplary manifestations. Butler shows how the face itself can function as an instrument of dehumanization, like the faces of evil fundamentalists or despots (bin Laden, Saddam Hussein), and how the power regime also decides which faces we are allowed to see as worthy of grief and mourning and which not—it was pictures of children burning from napalm that generated ethical outrage in the US public over Vietnam. Today, the very fragility of the suffering Other is part of the humanitarian ideological offensive.

What must be added to the precariousness and vulnerability of the ethical subject is the notion of absolute fidelity, the reference to an absolute point of infinity, in accordance with Pascal's well-known thought that man is a tiny speck of dust in the universe, but at the same time infinite spirit. Fragility alone does

35 Butler, *Precarious Life*, pp. 137–8.

not account for ethics—the gaze of a tortured or wounded animal does not in itself make it an ethical subject. The two minimal components of the ethical subject are its precarious vulnerability *and* its fidelity to an "immortal Truth" (a principle for which, in clear and sometimes ridiculous contrast to its vulnerability and limitations, the subject is ready to put everything at stake)—it is only this presence of an "immortal Truth" that makes human vulnerability different from that of a wounded animal. Furthermore, to these two, we should also add the "demonic" immortality whose Freudian name is the (death) drive, the very core of the Neighbor-Thing.[36]

But, again, cannot this fidelity be understood precisely as a fidelity to the call of the vulnerable Other in all its precariousness? The answer is not that the ethical agent should also experience his or her own fragility—the temptation to be resisted here is the ethical *domestication* of the neighbor, or what Levinas effectively did with his notion of the neighbor as the abyssal point from which the call of ethical responsibility emanates. Levinas deploys the notion of the subject as constituted by its recognition of an unconditional ethical Call engendered by the experience of injustices and wrongs: the subject emerges as a reaction to the traumatic encounter with the helpless suffering Other (the Neighbor). This is why it is constitutively decentered, not autonomous, but split by the ethical Call, a subject defined by the experience of an internalized demand that it can never meet, a demand that exceeds it. The paradox constitutive of the subject is thus that the demand that the subject cannot meet is what makes the subject, so that the subject is constitutively divided, its autonomy "always usurped by the heteronomous experience of the other's demand": "my relation to the other is not some benign benevolence, compassionate care or respect for the other's autonomy, but is the obsessive experience of a responsibility that persecutes me with its sheer weight. I am the other's hostage."[37] My elementary situation is thus that of an eternal struggle against myself: I am forever split between egotistic rootedness in a particular familiar world around which my life gravitates, and the unconditional call of responsibility for the Other: "The I which arises in enjoyment as a separate being having apart in itself the centre around which its existence gravitates, is confirmed in its singularity by purging itself of this gravitation, and purges itself interminably."[38] Levinas likes to quote Dostoyevsky here: "We are all responsible for everything and guilty in front of everyone, but

36 This is why, in psychoanalytic treatment, there is no face-to-face, neither the analyst nor his analysand sees the other's face: only in this way can the dimension of the Neighbor-Thing emerge.

37 Simon Critchley, *Infinitely Demanding*, London: Verso Books 2007, p. 10.

38 Emmanuel Levinas, *Totality and Infinity*, The Hague: Martinus Nijhoff 1979, p. 44. Would not this version of what Badiou calls "pitiless censorship of oneself" make the heart of every Stalinist lover of purges leap with joy?

I am that more than all others." The underlying cruelty is that of the superego, of course.

What is the superego? In a Motel One, close to Alexanderplatz in Berlin, the do-not-disturb signs read: "I am enjoying my Motel One room … please don't disturb!" Not only is this message obscene insofar as it compels the hotel guest who wants peace and quiet to declare that he is enjoying his room, the deeper obscenity resides in the fact that his desire not to be disturbed is implicitly characterized as a desire to enjoy himself in peace (and not, for example, to sleep or to work).

Recall the strange fact, regularly evoked by Primo Levi and other Holocaust survivors, about how their intimate reaction to their survival was marked by a deep split: consciously, they were fully aware that their survival was the result of a meaningless accident, that they were not in any way guilty for it, that the only guilty perpetrators were their Nazi torturers. At the same time, they were (more than merely) haunted by an "irrational" feeling of guilt, as if they had survived at the expense of others and were thus somehow responsible for their deaths—as is well known, this unbearable feeling of guilt drove many of them to suicide. This displays the agency of the superego at its purest: as the obscene agency which manipulates us into a spiraling movement of self-destruction. The function of the superego is precisely to obfuscate the cause of the terror constitutive of our being-human, the inhuman core of being-human, the dimension of what the German Idealists called negativity and Freud called the death drive. Far from being the traumatic hard core of the Real from which sublimations protect us, the superego is itself a mask screening off the Real. For Levinas, the traumatic intrusion of the radically heterogeneous Real Thing which decenters the subject is *identical with* the ethical Call of the Good, while, for Lacan, on the contrary, it is the primordial "evil Thing," something that can never be sublated into a version of the Good, something which forever remains a disturbing cut. Therein lies the revenge of Evil for our domestication of the Neighbor as the source of the ethical call: the "repressed Evil" returns in the guise of the superego's distortion of the ethical call itself.

But there is a further question to be raised here: is the opposition between fellow-man and Neighbor the ultimate horizon of our experience of others? It is clear that for Levinas the "face" is not the name for my fellow-man with whom I can empathize, who is "like me," my *semblant*, but the name for a radical facelessness, for the Real of the abyss of an Otherness whose intrusion destabilizes every homeostatic exchange with others. However, does not the very fact that Levinas can use the term "face" to designate its opposite, the faceless abyss of the other, point to the link between the two, to the fact that they belong to the same field? Is not the faceless abyss of the Neighbor a faceless Beyond engendered by the face itself, the face's inherent overcoming, like the terrifying image (vortex, maelstrom, Medusa's head, Irma's throat ...) which is too strong for our eyes, which closes down the very dimension of what can be seen? Insofar as, for Lacan, the face functions as an imaginary lure, the Real of the faceless Neighbor is the imaginary Real; the question is thus whether there is another, symbolic, Real. What emerges if, in a vague homology, we push the symbolic as far as the same self-canceling into which the face is pushed to give rise to the faceless abyss of the Neighbor? What would be the status of the human individual as a symbolic Real? What emerges at this point is the subject, the Cartesian *cogito* which, according to Lacan, is none other than the subject of the unconscious. No wonder that Lacan refers to this subject as an "answer of the real": it emerges when the symbolic is pushed to the limit of its impossibility, of its immanent Real. This subject is totally de-substantialized; coinciding with its own failure-to-be, it is a mere cut, a gap, in the order of being.

If the axis fellow-man/Neighbor remains our ultimate horizon, we have to abandon the dimension of universality: the Neighbor is a singular abyss which resists universality. But is it then the case that the non-universalizable Neighbor is the ultimate horizon of our ethico-political activity? Is the highest norm the injunction to respect the neighbor's Otherness? No wonder Levinas is so popular today among leftist-multiculturalist liberals who improvise endlessly on the motif of impossible universality—every universality is exclusive, it imposes a particular standard as universal. The question to be posed here is whether every ethical universality is really based on the exclusion of the abyss of the Neighbor, or whether there is a universality which does *not* exclude the Neighbor. The answer is: yes, the universality grounded in the "part of no-part," the singular universality exemplified in those who lack a determined place in the social totality, who are "out of place" in it and as such directly stand for the universal dimension.

From terror to enthusiasm

While the Neighbor is non-universalizable, the Subject *is* universal(izable). This universality is no longer a universality founded on an exception, it is the universality of a gap, a cut: not the underlying universal feature shared by all particulars, but the cut of an impossibility which runs through them all. Reading Badiou retroactively from this standpoint, we can discern how he does already offer an implicit reply to this question (how a distortion at the level of Being, of its animal life, opens up the space for an Event) in his early masterpiece *The Theory of Subject* (1982), where he deploys his own four fundamental concepts —the four fundamental subjective-affective attitudes towards the Real. He opposes two couples: the Sophoclean couple of terror and anxiety (Creon's terror, Antigone's anxiety), and the Aeschylean couple of courage and justice (Orestes's courage, Athena's justice). On the grounds of internal consistency, I proposed to replace justice with enthusiasm, for the reasons I shall now outline.

Often cited is the chorus from *Antigone* about man being the most "demonic" of all creatures, as a being of excess, a being that violates all proper measure. However, it is crucial to bear in mind the exact location of these lines: the chorus intervenes immediately after it becomes known that somebody (it is not yet known who) has defied Creon's order and performed the funeral ritual on Polynices's body. It is *this* act which is perceived as a "demonic" excessive act, and not Creon's prohibition—Antigone is far from being the place-holder of moderation, of respect for proper limits, against Creon's sacrilegious hubris. This is what makes problematic Badiou's reading of Creon as the figure who stands for "the law's inner excess over itself, laid bare in superegoic fury":

> "Creon" is the name of the superego: the deregulated law—destroyed and, by its own native essence, returned as an excess over the place that it prescribes. "Antigone" is the name of anxiety, that is, the principle of the infinity of the real which is unplaceable in the regulated finitude of the place. From this point of view, Antigone and Creon, although antagonists in the play, accomplish the same process, the formation of the Sophoclean tragic subject.[39]

Bosteels, who recently took over this reading, specifies this dimension of the Law as that of the violence registered by the tautology "the law is the law":

> This element of excess and destruction is what Badiou calls the nonlaw in the law, which as such lies revealed in the ferocity of the superego injunction, reduced to a pure *You must*, or to redundancies of the type *The law is the law*: "The nonlaw is what manifests itself as the affirmative of the law; for this reason the superego can be simultaneously the index of the law and of its destruction." Through the notion of the superego, the law itself in other words paradoxically lays bare its potential for subversion from within.[40]

However, is it not that, in the central confrontation between Antigone and Creon, it is the former who stands for the tautology "the law is the law," while Creon is a pragmatic *Realpolitiker* who gives reasons for his prohibition of Polynices's funeral (the interests of the polis are superior to the individual grievances, Polynices's funeral would trigger a new civil war which might lead to the

---

39 Alain Badiou, *Théorie du sujet*, Paris: Seuil 1982, p. 179, as translated in Bosteels, "Force of Nonlaw," p. 1909.

40 Bosteels, "Force of Nonlaw," p. 1910.

destruction of Thebes)? Antigone's only answer to all this is a repeated variation on "I insist! I stick to my rule!"

As we have said, Badiou supplements the "Sophoclean" couple anxiety-superego (Antigone-Creon) with the "Aeschylean" couple of courage and justice (Orestes-Athena): while the Sophoclean universe remains caught in the cycle of violence and revenge, Aeschylus opens up the possibility of a *new* law which will break the cycle. However, Badiou insists that all four are necessary constituents of a Truth-Event: "The courage of the scission of the laws, the anxiety of an opaque persecution, the superego of the blood-thirsty Erinyes, and finally justice according to the consistency of the new—four concepts to articulate the subject."[41] The actuality of Aeschylus is attested by *The Suppliants*, a play which tackles the problem of how to deal with those seeking refuge from tyranny. The "suppliants" are the fifty daughters of Danaus; they arrive at Argos fleeing the fifty sons of King Aegyptus (of Egypt), who wish to marry them. The king of Argos is reluctant to accept them, fearing the wrath of Aegyptus and war with Egypt; however, the popular assembly of the city overrules him and the suppliants are given shelter. What the people display here is courage (risking war with Egypt) and a sense of justice (protecting the "suppliants" from their brutal fate).

Badiou proposes his own tetrad of the "four fundamental concepts of the Truth-Event," his own version of Lacan's "four fundamental concepts of psychoanalysis"; Bosteels also notes that, in *Logiques des mondes*, Badiou returns to this tetrad, with a small but significant change: the "superego" is replaced by "terror" as a necessary constituent of every Truth-Event—in politics as well as in other domains, no truth happens without some form of terror: "None of that which overcomes the finitude in the human animal, subordinating it to the eternity of the True by its incorporation to a subject in becoming, has ever been able to occur without anxiety, courage and justice. But no more, as a general rule, without terror."[42] There are many deeply relevant insights in this tetrad, from the assertion of the inevitable role of terror in emancipatory politics to the crucial distinction between heroism and justice:

41 Badiou, *Théorie du sujet*, p. 176, as translated in Bosteels, "Force of Nonlaw," p. 1913. Badiou sometimes proposes "justice" as the Master-Signifier that should replace all-too-heavily ideologically invested notions like "freedom" or "democracy"—but do we not encounter the same problem with justice? Plato (Badiou's main reference) determines justice as the state in which every particular determination occupies its proper place within its totality, within the global social order. Is this not the corporatist anti-egalitarian motto *par excellence*? A lot of additional explanation is thus needed if "justice" is to be elevated into the Master-Signifier of radical emancipatory politics.

42 Badiou, *Logiques des mondes*, p. 99, as translated in Bosteels, "Force of Nonlaw," p. 1915.

> If heroism is the subjective figure of facing up to the impossible, then courage is the virtue of endurance in the impossible. Courage is not the point itself, it is holding on to the point. What demands courage is holding on, in a different duration from the one imposed by the law of the world.[43]

Heroism without courage is limited to a momentary pathetic suicidal gesture followed by the conformist "sobriety" of returning to the common sense of everyday Life: the truly difficult thing is to persist courageously in fidelity to the Event. Furthermore, Badiou's tetrad allows for a very pertinent diagnosis of our contemporary predicament: "I believe that this subjective figure, whose dialectic is built on anxiety and the superego, always prevails in times of decadence and disarray, both in history and in life."[44] Or, to quote Bosteels's perspicuous paraphrase:

> the Sophoclean dominant of our times can be seen as a symptom of the fact that once courage and justice are dismissed as so many illusions of dogmatic voluntarism, what we are left with are precisely only the twin dispositions of anxiety and terror, that is to say, an excessive dimension of the real as too-much that at the same time exposes the fragility and precariousness of the law qua nonlaw.[45]

The problem which persists here is double. First, is "justice" really a term which belongs to the same series of "emotional" responses to the encounter of a Truth? Does locating it in this series not "subjectivize" it too much? A possible alternative candidate would have been *enthusiasm* (which, already in Kant, designates a subjective elevation which bears witness to the encounter with a noumenal Real). In other words, insofar as anxiety and courage form a pair of opposites, do not terror and enthusiasm form another symmetrical couple? In the same way that courage can only emerge against the background of anxiety (the courage to accomplish an act which is not covered by the "big Other"), enthusiasm can only emerge against the background of terror, as its immanent reversal.[46] As is well known, Freud claimed that anxiety is the only affect which does not cheat—so what about enthusiasm? Does not enthusiasm as a rule cheat? Do we not find all around us false enthusiasms? Here we should recall that enthusiasm can only emerge against the background of terror: it is this background which as it were

43 Alain Badiou, *The Meaning of Sarkozy*, London: Verso Books 2008, pp. 72–3.

44 Badiou, *Théorie du sujet*, p. 180, as translated in Bosteels, "Force of Nonlaw," p. 1920.

45 Bosteels, "Force of Nonlaw," p. 1920.

46 As, once again, was already clear to Kant, for whom the terror at our utter impotence in face of the unleashed violence of some natural power turns into enthusiasm when we become aware of how not even the mightiest natural violence can threaten our autonomy as free moral agents.

guarantees its authenticity, locates it into the relation to the Real, and distinguishes it from the false enthusiasm.

Second, can "terror" really be conceived as replacing the "superego"? It is true that, according to the vague notion of "totalitarian terror," the state does not function as a constrained legal power, but as an unconstrained exercise of a superego agency which makes you all the more guilty the more you are innocent. However, to put it in somewhat simplified terms, not only is terror, for Badiou, an unavoidable aspect of the subjective relating to a Truth; he also goes to the (political) end and insists that terror is present in all radical emancipatory politics, ironically referring to his own politics as the "search for a good terror." So it is not only that the experience of terror is always part of the attitude of the subject awed by the intrusion of a Truth that derails its daily life—recall Heiner Müller's famous motto: "*the first appearance of the new is the dread*." Much more radically, terror is a legitimate part of every radical democratic politics: its ruthless exercise of popular justice cannot but appear as terror. And it is absolutely crucial to distinguish this emancipatory terror in both its aspects, the subjective experience as well as the exercise of power, from the superego-excesses of legal power, the excess of non-law at the very heart of the law. Whatever Creon stands for, opportunistic *Realpolitik* or the superego-excess of legal power, he definitely does not stand for emancipatory terror.

Correcting Badiou, we should thus propose a new—third—series of the "four fundamental concepts of emancipatory politics": anxiety, courage, terror, enthusiasm. Heidegger already developed in detail this point about anxiety: when the very basis of our existence is shattered by terror, when a mere ontic fear changes into anxiety, when we are confronted with the ontological Void of our being, we are violently torn out of what Badiou calls our utilitarian-hedonistic "animal life" (and what Heidegger calls our engaged being-in-the-world). Although such an "out-of-joint" experience of radical dislocation is not yet an Event, it is its necessary precondition: only a dislocated subject, a subject torn out of its life world, can recognize itself as the addressee of an Event and courageously commit itself to a fidelity to its Truth.

There is, however, a difference with Badiou to be drawn out here: while for him the experience of anxiety, of out-of-jointness, of negativity in general, is a precondition of the Event—its retroactive negative shadow, as it were—we must confer on it a "stronger," more autonomous role. Negativity (whose Freudian name is the "death drive") is the primordial ontological fact: for a human being, there is no "animal life" prior to it, for a human being is constitutively "out-of-joint." Every "normality" is a secondary *normalization* of the primordial dislocation that is the "death drive," and it is only through the terrorizing experience of the utter vacuity of every positive order of "normality" that a space is opened up for an Event.

This, then, is the ultimate difference between Badiou and Lacan: Badiou's starting point is an affirmative project and the fidelity to it; while, for Lacan, the primordial fact is that of negativity (ontologically, of the impossibility of the One being One), and the fidelity to a Truth-Event is secondary, a possibility whose space is opened up by negativity.

This key intermediary notion of anxiety also enables us to resolve an inconsistency in Badiou's notion of an Event: if an Event is self-referential in the sense that it includes its own nomination (there is an Event only for the subjects engaged in it, who "believe in it"; there is no Event for a neutral observer), how is it that Badiou can distinguish different modes of subjectivity which are simultaneously modalities of how the subject relates to the Event (echoing Kant's thesis that the conditions of our experience of the object are simultaneously the conditions of the object itself)? We should thus drop the notion that truth, as opposed to knowledge, is something that only an engaged gaze, the gaze of a subject who "believes in it," can see. In his *Logiques des mondes*, Badiou himself corrected his thesis that there is a Truth-Event only for those who recognize themselves in it: while a Truth is always the truth of a particular historical situation, it affects the *entire* situation. Badiou elaborates four possible responses to an Event: the faithful subject; the reactive subject; the obscure subject; and resurrection. Perhaps this list should be complicated a little, so that there are six responses in all; for example:

The responses to the Freud-Event are: (1) fidelity (Lacan); (2) reactive normalization, re-integration into the predominant field (ego-psychology, "dynamic psychotherapy"); (3) outright denial (cognitivism); (4) obscurantist mystification in a pseudo-Event (Jung); (5) total enforcement (Reich, Freudo-Marxism); (6) resurrection of Freud's "eternal" message in the various "returns to Freud."

The responses to a love-Event are: (1) fidelity; (2) normalization, re-integration (marriage); (3) outright rejection of the evental status (libertinage, the transformation of the Event into sexual adventure); (4) thorough rejection of sexual love (abstinence); (5) obscurantist suicidal passion *à la* Tristan; (6) resurrected love (re-encounter).

The responses to the Marxism-Event are: (1) fidelity (communism, Leninism); (2) reactive re-integration (social democracy); (3) outright denial of the evental status (liberalism, Furet); (4) catastrophic total counter-attack in the guise of a pseudo-Event (fascism); (5) total enforcement of the Event, which ends up in an "obscure disaster" (Stalinism, the Khmer Rouge); (6) renewal of Marxism (Lenin, Trotsky, Mao …).

So how do (1) and (6) coexist (in figures like Lenin or Lacan)? This brings us to a further hypothesis: an Event is necessarily missed the first time—true fidelity is only possible in the form of resurrection, as a defense against "revisionism": Freud did not see the full significance of his discovery, it was only Lacan's "return to Freud" that allowed us to get to its core; or, as Stanley Cavell put it apropos Hollywood comedies of re-marriage, the only true marriage is the second marriage (to the same person).[47]

When Badiou describes the interaction of the different subjective types which define a historical sequence (faithful, reactive, obscure), he emphasizes how "*contrary to what Hegelian dialectics and dogmatized Marxism claim, the historical present doesn't coincide with the present of the body of truth.*"[48] In every historical present, the "body of truth" coexists and interacts with those who react to the Truth-Event by trying to reinscribe it into the field of pre-evental processes, and those who struggle to destroy the body of truth (as, in politics, communists, liberal democrats, fascists), while for Hegelians and vulgar Marxists, every historical epoch is under the sign of one single (hegemonic) notion. However, does not the Marxist notion of the "non-synchronicity of the synchronous" (Ernst Bloch), of the coexistence within the same epoch of segments which belong to different stages, indicate the very same interaction? This is precisely the point of the Marxist concept of "articulation": of how, with the rise of the new, the old gets re-functionalized and assumes a different role in the new totality (recall how the Catholic Church reinvented itself in each new phase of modernity). Furthermore, contrary to misleading appearances, does not Hegel's notion of "totality" also aim at the same complex articulation?

But back to Badiou: if an Event exists only for those engaged within it, how can we sustain the notion of a subjectivity which denies (or ignores) the Event? Does denying it imply that the Event already in some sense exists for the denying subject? My hypothesis is that anxiety here plays the crucial role. An Event always occurs within a world, within its transcendental coordinates, and its emergence affects the *entirety* of that world: no one can really ignore it—for example, the post-Evental liberal who tries to prove that there was no Event, that the October Revolution was just a quirk of Russian history, is not the same as the pre-Evental liberal, since he is already mediated by the Event, reacting to it. It is one thing not to know something, another thing to act as if one does not know it. The Event in its first emergence causes anxiety, since by definition it shatters the transcendental coordinates of a world. It is this anxiety which affects everyone, all subjects of a world, and denying or ignoring the

47 Is it then possible to imagine the attitude of the fetishistic split towards an Event: "I know very well that there was no Event, just the ordinary run of things, but, perhaps unfortunately, nonetheless ... (I believe) there *was* one"?

48 Badiou, *Second manifeste pour la philosophie*, p. 121.

Event, trying to reintegrate it into the coordinates of the (old) world, etc., are reactions triggered by this anxiety, reactive ways of coping with the Event's traumatic impact. (Social democracy, liberal ignorance, and fascism are reactions to the anxiety caused by a communist event.) But only an authentic subjective fidelity to the Event succeeds in "converting" anxiety into enthusiasm (almost in the Freudian sense of converting affects): it displays the courage to confront or accept the Event in its full traumatic impact, and to transform this anxiety into the enthusiasm of emancipatory struggle. In this precise sense, anxiety is the necessary background of enthusiasm: there is no enthusiasm without anxiety, enthusiasm does not begin in itself, it is formally the result of the conversion of anxiety. This is also why Badiou is justified in designating regressive reactions to the Event as modes of subjectivity: the emergence of subjectivity is not limited to the enthusiastic endorsement of the Event, but to anxiety, and anxiety as the first reaction to the Event is universal, it affects the entire field of the world shattered by an Event.

The reference to anxiety also enables us to formulate the inner limit to each of the post-Evental truth-procedures which follow the triad of True-Beautiful-Good: Science concerns the True, Art the Beautiful, and Politics the Good. The fourth procedure, Love, does not operate at the same level: it is more "fundamental" and "universal" than the others.[49] The structure is therefore not that of the four, but of 3 + 1—a feature perhaps not emphasized enough by Badiou (although, apropos sexual difference, he does remark that women tend to approach all [other] truth-procedures through love). Not only psychoanalysis, philosophy and religion also belong to love (the very term "philosophy" means *love* of wisdom)—is love, then, Badiou's "Asiatic mode of production," the category into which he throws all truth-procedures which don't fit the other three modes (from psychoanalysis to theology), as well as the underlying structuring principle of the entire field?[50]

In each truth-domain, anxiety signals the encounter with a *minimal difference* which hinders the absolute reduction or purification, that is, which is simultaneously the condition of possibility and the condition of impossibility (the immanent limit) of the domain in question: in science, *ontological difference*, which prevents the scientistic reduction of the object of

49 Within the domain of art itself, this triad is reflected as the triad of epic (the True), lyric (the Beautiful), and drama (the Good).

50 Badiou is here ambiguous in denying religion any Truth status in a materialist way. The mystery remains: how then can a religious text (Paul) have been the first to establish the very formal matrix of a Truth-Event? One can even go further and, following Badiou, link this triad to the three grand theories of the twentieth century: Marxism is epic (privileging literature), psychoanalysis dramatic (privileging theater), and (Heideggerian) phenomenology lyric (privileging poetry).

knowledge to a positive entity (as in cognitivist brain sciences); in politics, *class difference*, which prevents the political project from fulfilling itself in a new non-antagonistic "harmonious society"; in love, *sexual difference*, which stands for the impossibility of the sexual relationship; and, in art, the minimal gap between art and daily life which condemns to failure all modernist attempts to unite the two. Each time the difference persists; however, each time, the point is not to "respect the limit" but to push through to the end in order to encounter the minimal difference: to push through the cognitivist reduction of man to a brain machine to discover the "negativity" of the death drive; to push through the modernist unification of art and life to discover the "minimal difference" between the two dimensions (Malevich, Duchamp); to push through love to confront the limit of sexual difference; likewise, one must push through a revolutionary process to the end in order to confront the insurmountable antagonism.

Badiou wrote recently of "the real as such, the real of 'there is no,' the real as the impossibility of a relationship, or, let us risk the philosopheme, pure being as unbound multiplicity. Or the void."[51] He poses here a problematic sign of equality between the Lacanian Real and his own real, ignoring the key difference: the Lacanian Real is not simply a void of unbound multiplicity, what is missing here is precisely the "there is no" which, for Lacan, is not only a "there is no relationship" between unbound elements of a multiplicity, but the extreme of an antagonism which inextricably binds together the antagonism's two aspects. "There is no sexual relationship" does not mean that there is a multiplicity of unbound or unrelated sexual positions, i.e., that there is no common measure between the masculine and the feminine positions; sexual difference is rather "impossible" because it is, in a sense, prior to both positions: masculine and feminine are the two ways to symbolize the deadlock of sexual difference. This misunderstanding has crucial consequences for how Badiou formulates the core of Lacan's antiphilosophy, his basic reproach to philosophy, summarized by Badiou in the following:

> Philosophy is a subversion of three by the two. Philosophy refuses to accept that the three is irreducibly originary, that it cannot be reduced to the two. This is, I think, the reason for the continuous and complex controversy between Lacan and Hegel, since Hegel proposes a position of the three which is necessarily engendered by the two. Which two? The two of contradiction. It is with regard to this position that Hegel is for Lacan the most philosophical of philosophers.[52]

51 Alain Badiou and Barbara Cassin, *Il n'y a pas de rapport sexuel*, Paris: Fayard 2010, p. 117.
52 Ibid., pp. 124–5.

One is tempted to invert this reproach: it is philosophy which passes all too quickly from the One to the Three, refusing to think the Two as the inherent impossibility of the One. The primordial (pre-philosophical, mythical) form of the Two is that of the cosmic sexualized polarity (light and darkness, *yin* and *yang*, etc.). With philosophy, this polarity is reduced to the One (*logos*, the higher principle) generating the totality of being out of itself; this is why philosophy endeavors to contain the lower element, to reduce it to a moment in the self-deployment of the higher element.[53] Does the answer then lie in a "materialist" reversal which generates the higher element out of the lower (*logos* from the interaction of bodies, the One from the multiple—as in ancient Greek atomism which conceives everything as the result of the interaction of atoms in the void)?

It is here that we encounter the unprecedented originality of Hegel. On a first approach (according to the official *doxa*), Hegel's thought is the ultimate example of the One overcoming its self-division through the Three (the "synthesis" by means of which the One re-appropriates its alienated Otherness). It is thus true that "Hegel proposes a position of the three which is necessarily engendered by the two"; however, it is precisely through this engendering that Hegel affirms a Two which is no longer the pre-philosophical mythical Two, the Two of a symmetrical polarity, but the Two of the non-coincidence of the One with itself. This is why, when (against the phantom of "Slovene readings" of a Kantian Lacan) Badiou asserts Lacan's anti-Kantianism, he misrecognizes the Hegelian nature of Lacan's distance towards Kant. Here is how Badiou answers the key question "How does Lacan escape Kantianism?":

> if the real is subtracted from knowing, we enter the critical speech which tells us that the real (the in-itself) is unknowable, and which limits knowledge to phenomena. Finally, reality would be the phenomenal donation of things, and the real its point of inaccessibility to which one simply relates through the act, i.e., to which one has a practical relationship. There is a prescriptive, not a cognitive, relationship towards the real. The real gives itself in practical reason, in the categorical imperative, and not in theoretical reason which structures phenomena. There are readings of Lacan and of Kant, Slovene readings (Žižek, Zupančič, Riha, Sumic ...) which go in this direction, and which are very forceful. As far as I am concerned, I think that Lacan avoids the critical trap, and that he is in no way Kantian. His gesture is not to propose that the real is unknowable, or that it is knowable. Lacan's thesis asserts

53 And the eternal Gnostic search for the "secret teachings" of the great philosophical masters always tries to unearth traces of pre-philosophical mythic dualism: in the case of Plato, say, his "secret teaching" is supposed to posit matter (*chora*, the "receptable") as a positive counter-force to Ideas—in an exact parallel to the search for the "secret teaching" of Christ which supposedly reinscribes pagan sexual difference into the divine sphere, reintroducing into it the feminine moment.

> the exteriority of the real to the antinomy of knowing and ignoring. The real as such does not rely on the alternate categories of knowing and ignoring. It relies on what Lacan tries to invent under the name of "demonstrating."[54]

For Lacan, the Real can only be demonstrated through formal logic, not in a direct way, but negatively, through a deadlock of logical formalization: the Real can only be discerned in the guise of a gap, an antagonism. The primordial status of the Real is that of an obstacle, the absent cause of a failure, a cause which has no positive ontological consistency in itself but is present only through and in its effects. To put it succinctly: one tries to formalize the Real, one fails, and the Real *is* this failure. This is why, in the Lacanian Real, opposites coincide: the Real is simultaneously what cannot be symbolized *and* the very obstacle which prevents this symbolization. And this coincidence, the coincidence of a Thing with the very obstacle which prevents our access to it, in other words this overlapping of epistemological failure and ontological impossibility, is profoundly Hegelian.

Badiou and antiphilosophy

How does this difference between Badiou and Lacan affect Badiou's delimitation of antiphilosophy? The basic motif of antiphilosophy is the assertion of a pure presence (the Real Life of society for Marx, Existence for Kierkegaard, Will for Schopenhauer and Nietzsche, etc.) irreducible to and excessive with regard to the network of philosophical concepts or representations. The surprise is that Badiou, who coined this critical term, retains a strange solidarity with antiphilosophers on account of his unproblematic reliance on the couple "presence and representation." The great theme of post-Hegelian antiphilosophy is the excess of the pre-conceptual productivity of Presence over its representation: representation is reduced to the "mirror of representation," which reflects in a distorted way its productive ground:

> Post-Hegelian philosophy (or, if one prefers, antiphilosophy) started off with this fundamental claim: symbolic representations which were traditionally considered as access to the truth and to the real of Being do in fact alienate us from Being and deform it (or our perception of it). And classical philosophy (or "metaphysics") was suddenly recognised as the queen of this representative misrepresentation.
>
> Indeed, if one were to name one central issue that distinguishes the rise of modern thought, it is perhaps none other than precisely the issue of representation (and the question of One and/or Multiple is part of this issue), its profound interrogation, and the whole consequent turn against (the logic of) representation. This

54 Badiou and Cassin, *Il n'y a pas de rapport sexuel*, pp. 128–9.

> is perhaps most perceptible in (modern) art which frontally attacked the notion of art as representation … In politics, this also was a central issue: who represents the people and how they can be properly represented? Why are some represented and some not? And what if the very idea of representation is the source of society's evils and its alienation? The realm of politics is especially interesting in this respect since the introduction of a "representative" system coincided with the very questioning of its pertinence. Something similar took place in respect to the generic procedure of love: a simultaneous demand that love be properly represented by the institution of marriage (the new imperative that one should marry out of love), and a massive "observation" that this is in fact impossible, i.e. that marriage can never truly represent the real of love.[55]

In so-called "post-structuralism," the relation between the two terms is inverted: presence itself is denounced as the illusory result of a dispersed productive process defined as anti-presence, as a process of self-differing, and so on; however, the encompassing framework remains that of production versus representation, of a productive process occluded by/in the false transparency of its representation. With regard to Badiou, the problem is how to relate the couple of presence and representation to the triad of Being/World/Event—more precisely, insofar as Being names the presence of inconsistent multiplicity and World its representation, its organization into a consistent situation regulated by its immanent transcendentals—how to conceive the Event with regard to the couple of presence and representation.

Where, then, does the flaw in Badiou's account reside? Badiou reacted to the "obscure disaster" of the fall of the socialist regimes—and, more generally, to the exhaustion of the revolutionary event of the twentieth century—by taking a step from history to ontology: it is important to note how it was only after this "obscure disaster" that Badiou started to play with the double meaning of the term "state" (*état*)—the "state of things" and State as the apparatus of social power. The danger of this move is that, by establishing a direct link, a short-circuit, as it were, between a particular historical form of social organization and a basic ontological feature of the universe, it (implicitly, at least) ontologizes or eternalizes the state as a form of political organization: (the political) state becomes something we should resist, subtract ourselves from, act at a distance from, but simultaneously something which can never be abolished (save in utopian dreams). Is not this step from history to ontology, from the State qua political apparatus to the state qua state of things, this short-circuit wherein State = state, an elementary ideological operation? This overblown notion of the State, which effectively tends to overlap with the state (of things) in the broadest sense,

55 Alenka Zupančič, "The Fifth Condition," in Hallward, ed., *Think Again: Alain Badiou and the Future of Philosophy*, pp. 197–8.

is effectively Badiou's symptom; along these lines, at a conference on communism in London in March 2009, Judith Balso claimed that opinions themselves are part of the State. The notion of the State has to be over-expanded in this way precisely because the autonomy of "civil society" with regard to the State is ignored, so the "State" has to cover the entire economic sphere, as well as the sphere of "private" opinions.

As a consequence of this short-circuit, Badiou gets caught in the typical Kantian ambiguity apropos the question of whether abandoning the form of Party-State, subtracting oneself from State, acting in the interstices of State, is an a priori necessity of radical emancipatory politics as such, or just the expression of a certain (our) historical moment, that of the global defeat of radical politics? In other words, when Badiou interprets the failure of the Cultural Revolution as the exhaustion of the "Leninist" Party-State revolutionary paradigm, does he mean that this paradigm was appropriate for its period (the twentieth century) and is no longer appropriate for our period, or does he mean that our historical moment has the privilege of giving us an insight into a universal feature of radical emancipatory politics which was obfuscated in previous epochs (which is why the "Leninist" paradigm ended up in a dismal failure, in an "obscure disaster")? Badiou is ambiguous here: sometimes he implies that we are dealing with a succession of historical epochs, and sometimes (say, when he talks about the end of History, of global politics, even conceiving it as the last consequence of the "death of God," and emphasizes that politics should be a local intervention into a local situation) that we are dealing with an a priori necessity.

To put it another way, the problem with state-representation is not that it contaminates or mystifies the presence of the productive Real, but quite the opposite: it constitutes this presence (or, rather, its illusion). The state (apparatus) does not contaminate (or act as a parasite upon) the "apolitical" spheres of the economy, of private life, of sexuality, etc., rather it constitutes them as apolitical or pre-political—the ultimate task of state apparatuses is to depoliticize these spheres, to regulate their apolitical status by means of coercive and ideological apparatuses. This is why, in a properly Marxist perspective, the ill-famed "withering away of the State" does not aim at a de-politicization of society, but (in its first step, at least) at its radical and thorough "politicization": one does not "abolish the state" by getting rid of its excess in a transparent-harmonious self-organization of society, but by "abolishing" the specter of apolitical spheres, by demonstrating how "there is nothing which is not political," up to and including people's most intimate dreams. No wonder, then, that in accordance with his reliance on the couple presence and representation, Badiou exempts—as a malicious afterthought, one is tempted to say "subtracts" —the economy (the sphere of "servicing the goods," of production-exchange-distribution) from the domain of Truth. Does this exemption not also imply that the economy is a sphere of productive presence prior to its (political) representation? Badiou thereby effectively accepts the depoliticization of the economy as a fact, not as an effect of ideological censorship; that is, he ignores the fundamental Marxist insight that the economy is always a *political* economy.

"Idealism" and "metaphysics" are names for the illusion that the circle of representation can close in upon itself, wiping out all traces of its de-centered production process. Antiphilosophy here develops its own version of the logic of "suture," conceiving it as the mode in which the exterior is inscribed in the interior, thus "suturing" the field, producing the effect of self-enclosure with no need for an exterior, effacing the traces of its own production. Traces of the production process, its gaps, its mechanisms, are obliterated, so that the product can appear as a naturalized organic whole (likewise with identification, which is not simply full emotional immersion in the quasi-reality of a story, but a much more complex split process). Suture is thus somewhat like the basic matrix of Alistair Maclean's adventure thrillers from the 1950s and 1960s (*Guns of Navarone, Polar Station Zebra, Where Eagles Dare*): a group of dedicated commandos on a dangerous mission all of a sudden discover that there must be an enemy agent among them, i.e., that their Otherness (the Enemy) is inscribed *within* their set.

Much more crucial, however, is the obverse aspect: not only "no interior without exterior," but also "no exterior without interior." Therein lies the lesson of Kant's transcendental idealism: in order to appear as a consistent Whole, external reality has to be "sutured" by a subjective element, an artificial supplement that must be added to it in order to generate the effect of reality, like the painted background that confers on a scene the illusory effect of "reality." This, for Lacan, is the *objet petit a*: the subjective element constitutive of objective-external reality.

The matrix of an external site of production that inscribes itself into the domain of illusions it generates thus has to be supplemented: by itself, it simply cannot account for the emergence of the *subject*. According to standard (cinematic) suture theory, the "subject" is the illusory stand-in, *within* the domain of the constituted or generated, for its absent cause, for its production process: the "subject" is the imaginary agent which, while dwelling inside the space of the constituted phenomena, is (mis)perceived as their generator. This, however, is not what the Lacanian "barred subject" is about: the latter can be conceptualized only if we take into account how the very externality of the generative process ex-sists only insofar as the stand-in of the constituted domain is present in it.

When, in Prokofiev's ballet *Romeo and Juliet*, Romeo finds Juliet dead, his dance expresses his desperate effort to resuscitate her—here, the action in a sense takes place at two levels, not only at the level of what the dance evokes, but also at the level of the dance itself. The fact that the dancing Romeo drags around Juliet's corpse, suspended like a beached squid, can also be read as his desperate effort to return her immobile body to the state of *dance* itself, to restore its capacity to magically sublate the inertia of gravity and freely float in the air—his dance is thus in a way a reflexive dance, a dance aimed at the very (dis)ability of his partner to dance. The designated external content (Romeo's lament for Juliet) is sustained by the self-reference to the form itself.

The notion of reflexivity might be of some help here.[56] To put it succinctly, "suture" means that external difference is always also internal, that the external limitation of a field of phenomena always reflects itself within this field, as its inherent impossibility to fully become itself. To take the elementary example of sexual difference: in a patriarchal society, the external limit or opposition that divides women from men also functions as the inherent obstacle preventing women from fully realizing their potential. We can see how, in this precise sense, suture is the exact opposite of the illusory self-enclosed totality that successfully erases the decentered traces of its production process: suture means precisely that such self-enclosure is a priori impossible, that the excluded externality always leaves its traces within—or, to put it in standard Freudian terms, that there is no repression (from the scene of phenomenal self-experience) without the return of the repressed.

This is what Lacan aims at in his persistent references to *torus* and other variations of Möbius-band-like structures in which the relationship between inside and outside is inverted: if we want to grasp the minimal structure of subjectivity, the clear-cut opposition between inner subjective experience and outer objective reality is not sufficient—there is an excess on both sides. On the one hand, we should accept the lesson of Kant's transcendental idealism: out of the confused multitude of impressions, "objective reality" emerges through the intervention of the subject's transcendental act. In other words, Kant does not deny the distinction between the multitude of subjective impressions and objective reality; his point is merely that this very distinction results from the intervention of a subjective gesture of transcendental constitution. In a homologous way, Lacan's "Master-Signifier" is the "subjective" signifying feature which sustains the "objective" symbolic structure itself: if we abstract this subjective excess from the objective symbolic order, the very objectivity of that order disintegrates. Suture is thus not a secondary short-circuit of the two levels—it comes

56 The term "reflection" had two main uses in twentieth-century epistemology. On the one hand, there is "reflection" in the Hegelian dialectical sense: the bending of the subject's gaze onto itself, the inclusion of the process of knowing itself into the known object; on the other hand, there is the infamous dialectical-materialist "theory of reflection": the notion of our knowledge as the—always imperfect—subjective reflection/mirroring of the "objective" reality existing independently of us. The point is not just to dismiss the second use as vulgar, but to grasp the passage from the second to the first use as a movement inherent in the very concept of reflection.

first, it logically *precedes* the two levels that overlap in it, as the subjective gesture of suturing that constitutes (what appears to us as) objective reality.

Lacan's claim that the "imaginary" number (the square root of -1) is the "meaning of the phallus," its signified, is often invoked as an outstanding example his intellectual imposture—so what does he mean by it? The paradox of the square root of -1 is that it is an "impossible" number whose value can never be positivized, but which nonetheless "functions." What does this have to do with the phallus? Precisely insofar as it is the signifier of the impossible fullness of meaning, the phallus is a "signifier without a signified"—the "minus 1," the supplementary feature which sticks out from the series of "normal" signifiers, the element in which excess and lack coincide. The impossible fullness at the level of meaning (of the signified) is sustained by the void (the castrating dimension) at the level of the signifier—we encounter the "meaning of the phallus" when, apropos some notion, we enthusiastically sense that "this is *it*, the true thing, the true meaning," although we are never able to explicate *what*, precisely, this meaning *is*. For example, in a political discourse, the Master-Signifier "Our Nation" functions as this kind of empty signifier standing for the impossible fullness of meaning; its meaning is "imaginary" in the sense that its content is impossible to positivize—if you ask a member of the Nation to define of what his National identity consists, his ultimate answer will be, "I cannot explain, you must feel it, it is *it*, what our lives are really about."

We can now see how Lacan's definition of the signifier as that which "represents the subject for another signifier," in its convoluted self-referential form (*explanandum* resurges in *explanans*), relies on a very precise rehabilitation of the centrality of representation—not representation as the secondary mirror of a primordial productive process, but representation as something reflexively inscribed into the very represented dimension of the productive process. This means that the gap, the self-referentially convoluted twist, is operative already in the "productive presence" itself. To put it in classical Marxist terms, it is not enough to demonstrate how politico-ideological struggles are a theater of shadows reflecting the "true reality" of the economic process; one should supplement this with a demonstration of how the politico-ideological struggle is inscribed into the very heart of the economic process. This is what Marx called "class struggle," and it is why he speaks of "*political* economy." (One of the names for this strange "ideology" at the very heart of the economic process, for the "illusion" which sustains reality itself, is "commodity fetishism.")

Furthermore, this means we must dispense with the standard notion of the One (in all its different guises, right up to the Master-Signifier) as a secondary "totalization" of a primordially dispersed and inconsistent field of productivity. To express the paradox in its most radical form: it is the One itself which introduces inconsistency proper—without the One, there would have been just flat, indifferent multiplicity. The "One" is originally *the* signifier of (self-) division, the ultimate supplement or excess: by way of re-marking the pre-existing real, the One divides it from itself, introduces its non-coincidence with itself. Consequently, to radicalize things even further, the Lacanian One as the Master-Signifier is, *stricto sensu, the signifier of its own impossibility.* Lacan makes this clear when he emphasizes how every One, every Master-Signifier, is simultaneously S(A), a signifier of the lack of/in the Other, of its inconsistency. So it is not only that there is the Other because the One can never fully coincide with itself—there is One (Lacan's *Y a d'l'Un*) because the Other is "barred," lacking, inconsistent:

> Lacan's S_1, the (in)famous "master signifier" or "phallic signifier" is, paradoxically, the only way to write that "One is not" and that what "is" is the void that constitutes the original disjunction in the midst of every count-for-one. The count-for-one is always already two. S_1 is the matheme of what one can describe as "the One is not." It writes that "the One is not" by presenting the very thing that prevents it from being One. This is what S_1 says: the One is not; yet what is is not a pure multiple, but two. This is perhaps Lacan's crucial insight: if there is something on which one could lean in order to leave the "ontology of the One" behind, this something is not simply the multiple, but a Two.[57]

Everything hinges on this crucial point: deconstructionist or historicist "democratically materialist" antiphilosophy extols multiplicity and abhors "binary logic," seeing in the Two just a mirror-like redoubling of the One (this is why antiphilosophers like to criticize Hegel's succession of multiplicity, opposition, and contradiction, from the beginning of his "logic of essence," as an exemplary case of the gradual subordination of the multiple to the One); materialist dialectics knows that multiplicity without the Two is just a multiplicity of Ones, the monotonous night of a plurality in which all cows are black. What the antiphilosophical extolling of multiplicity misses is the non-coincidence of the One with itself, the non-coincidence which makes the One the very form of appearance of its opposite: it is not only that the complexity of its situation undermines every One—much more radically, it is the very one-ness of the One which redoubles it, functioning as an excess over the simple one. The function of void is crucial here: what explodes every One from within is not a complexity which subverts its unity, but the fact that a void is a part of every One: the signifier-One, the signifier which unifies or totalizes a multiplicity, is the point of the inscription into this multiplicity of its own void. Or, in terms of the Deleuzian "minimal difference" (a purely virtual difference which registers the distance

57 Zupančič, "The Fifth Condition," p. 199.

of a thing from itself, without reference to any of its real properties), an actual identity is always sustained by a virtual minimal difference.

The same point can be made with regard to the shift in the status of the "excess": in the standard space of antiphilosophy, "excess" names the excess of productive presence over its representation, that X which eludes the totalization-through-representation. But once we acknowledge the gap in the space of productive presence itself, the excess becomes *the excess of representation itself which always already supplements productive presence.* A simple political reference will make this point clear: the Master (a king or leader) at the center of a social body, the One who totalizes it, is simultaneously the excess imposed on it from outside. The whole struggle of the power-center against the marginal excesses threatening its stability can never obfuscate the fact, visible once we accomplish a parallax shift of our view, that the original excess is that of the central One itself—as Lacan would have put it, the One is always already ex-timate with regard to what it unifies. The One totalizes the field it unifies by "condensing" in itself the very excess that threatens the field. We encounter here the same self-relating move of redoubled negation as in the case of the law as universalized crime (or property as a form of theft): we pass from the excess with regard to the field of representation (the excess of that which eludes representation) to the excess of representation itself, that is, to the representation itself as an excess with regard to what it represents.

Italo Calvino's "A King Listens" focuses on the sense of hearing: in an anonymous kingdom, the royal palace becomes a giant ear and the king, obsessed and paralyzed by fears of rebellion, tries to hear every tiny sound that reverberates through the palace: servants' footsteps, whispers and conversations, fanfare trumpets at ceremonies, the sounds of the city on the outskirts of the palace, riots, etc.[58] He cannot see the source of the sounds but is obsessed by interpreting their meaning and the destiny they predict. This state of interpretive paranoia only seems to come to a halt when he hears something that completely enchants him: through the window the wind carries the singing voice of a woman, a voice of pure beauty, unique and irreplaceable. For the king it is the sound of freedom; he steps out of the palace into the open space and mingles with the crowd. The first thing to bear in mind here is that this king is not a traditional monarch, but a modern totalitarian tyrant: the traditional king does not care about his environment, he arrogantly ignores it and leaves worrying about plots to his ministers; it is the modern Leader who is obsessed by plots—"to rule is to interpret" is a perfect formula of Stalinism, *the* system of an endless paranoid hermeneutics. So when the king is seduced by the pure feminine voice of immediate life-pleasure, this is obviously (although, unfortunately, not for Calvino himself) a fantasy—

58 Italo Calvino, "A King Listens," in *Under the Jaguar Sun*, London: Vintage 1993.

precisely the fantasy of breaking out of the closed circle of representations and rejoining the pure outside, that which needs no interpretation but merely gives body to the voice which enjoys its own exercise. What is missing here is the way the innocent externality of the voice is itself already reflexively marked by the mirror of interpretive representations—which is why one can imagine an alternative ending to the story: when the king exits the palace, following the voice, he is immediately arrested—the feminine voice was a trick used by the plotters to lure the king out of the safety of the palace. One can be sure that, after a thorough police interrogation, the woman would have sung a different song.

The same insight can also be formulated in the terms of the set-theoretical axiomatic: a set B is considered to be part of set A (its subset) if all the elements of B also belong to A, and, as is generally known, the number of elements of B is always larger than the number of elements of A—every A has more subsets (parts) than elements. Let us say that A is composed of three elements, a, b, and c; the corresponding number in B comprises all possible combinations of a, b, and c (a alone, b alone, c alone, a + b, a + c, b + c), plus a + b + c (since a set is by definition a part of itself), plus the empty set which is always a part of every set—altogether eight subsets. Cantor generalized this axiom, applying it also to infinite sets, which gives rise to the proliferation of infinities. Perhaps this abstract axiom provides the principle for why a complete mapping of the genome of a human organism in no way entails that we will be able to master the way this organism functions: the mapping gives only the elements of the set, saying nothing about the much larger number of its subsets (which come closer to determining how the genes effectively determine the organism). This excess of subsets over elements justifies Meillassoux in designating the proliferation of infinities as the "Cantorian non-All"—where the term "non-All" should be taken in its strict Lacanian sense.[59]

This brings us back to antiphilosophy, to the post-Hegelian cut in the history of philosophy. What happened "after Hegel" was not simply that the One of re-presentation was no longer able to totalize the multiplicity of present reality, but something much more precise. The One (of the Master-Signifier) lost its ability to "condense" (or, in Freudian terms of libidinal investment, to "bind") the excess, to (re-)mark it, to effectively function as its stand-in, its place-holder; so the excess became "unbound," a threat to the representative system in all its guises, from the rabble in politics to "free sex" in personal relations—something which was either to be feared and controlled or celebrated as the site of freedom and resistance:

59 Quentin Meillassoux, *After Finitude*, London: Continuum 2008, p. 127.

> a spectre of excess starts haunting the society, in its different spheres; and its "spectral" form is in no way insignificant. The Master's discourse (or, if one prefers, the authority of the One) is a social bond in which this excessive element is, if one may say so, in the "ideal" place, in the service of the hegemonic power of the One, which reigns by *assuming* the very excessiveness of excess. What happens with the destitution of this bond is, so to speak, that the ghost of excess escapes from the bottle. The process could be said to have started with the French revolution, to have reached its full extent in the nineteenth century, and continued through a part of twentieth century. The nineteenth century in particular was deeply haunted by this excessive element in all possible forms, from conceptual to phantasmagoric ... all serious thinkers sought to think at a maximal proximity to, if not in a direct confrontation with, this excess. A "tarrying with the excess" thus became the most prominent figure of thought. Utopias, designed to eliminate social and other injustice, mostly proposed to achieve this by eliminating this very excess. To a certain extent, even Marx was tempted by the possibility of eliminating, once and for all, the excessive, disharmonious element of society—the element in which he himself recognised its truth, its real and its symptom.[60]

The critical reference to Marx is crucial here—precisely as Marxists, on behalf of our fidelity to Marx's work, we should be clear on his fundamental mistake: he rightly perceived how capitalism unleashed the breathtaking dynamo of self-enhancing productivity—see his fascinated descriptions of how, in capitalism, "all things solid melt into air," of how capitalism is the greatest revolutionizer in the entire history of humanity; on the other hand, he also clearly perceived how this capitalist dynamic is propelled by its own inner obstacle or antagonism—the ultimate limit of capitalism is Capital itself, its incessant development and revolutionizing of its own material conditions is ultimately nothing but a desperate flight forward to escape its own debilitating inherent contradiction. On the basis of these insights, Marx's fundamental mistake was to conclude that a new social order (communism) was possible, an order that would not only maintain but even raise to a higher degree and release the full potential of that self-propelling spiral of productivity which, in capitalism, on account of its inherent obstacle ("contradiction"), is again and again thwarted by socially destructive economic crises. In short, what Marx overlooked was that this inherent obstacle or antagonism as the "condition of impossibility" of the full deployment of the productive forces is simultaneously its "condition of possibility": if we abolish the obstacle, we do not get the fully unleashed drive to productivity, but lose precisely this productivity itself—remove the obstacle, and the very potential it thwarted dissipates. Therein resides Lacan's fundamental reproach to Marx, which focuses on the ambiguous overlapping between surplus-value and surplus-enjoyment.

60 Zupančič, "The Fifth Condition," p. 196.

As we have just seen, Badiou's own position is ambiguous here: although he (rightly) endeavors to defend philosophy against the post-philosophical "passion of the real," he remains all too indebted to the post-philosophical *topos* of representation as the mystifying mirror of the productive real, of the re-presentative meta-structure as the site of the "counting-as-One" of the inconsistent multiplicity of presence:

> The problem of representation as meta-structure, and the consequent imperative to restrain oneself from representation or to pull oneself away from the "state," is something that belongs to another ontology than the ontology of the pure multiple, of infinity and of contingency. For in an infinite contingent universe there is no necessity for the "counting the count itself" to be situated on a meta-level. It can very well be situated on the same level as the counting itself, only separated from it by an irreducible interval (and it is this interval that Lacan calls the Real). Moreover, this is precisely *what makes* a situation "infinite." What makes it infinite is not the exclusion of any operation of representation (which would "want" to count it for one and thus to close it upon itself), but its inclusion. What makes the "presentation" infinite is precisely that it already *includes* representation.[61]

This brings us back to Hegel's uniqueness: the Hegelian "actual infinity" is the infinity generated by the self-relating of a totality, by the short-circuit which makes a totality an element of itself (or, rather, which makes a genus its own species), which makes re-presentation part of presence itself—and the Hegelian Real is nothing but this purely formal convoluted structure. In philosophical terms, this passage from the anti-philosophical substantial Real to the purely formal Real qua the immanent gap in the order of representations can again be located in the passage from Kant to Hegel. No wonder Schopenhauer, the key figure in nineteenth-century philosophy, claimed to be simply extending Kant in his interpretation of the Will as the Kantian noumenal Thing: the unknowable Thing which escapes our cognitive grasp and is accessible only at the level of practical reason is the first figure of the post-philosophical Real. What happens in Hegel is that the Real is thoroughly de-substantialized: it is not the transcendent X which resists symbolic representations, but the immanent gap, rupture, inconsistency, the "curvature" of the space of representations itself.

As such, Hegel's thought stands for the moment of passage between philosophy as the Master's discourse, the philosophy of the One that totalizes the multiplicity, and antiphilosophy which insists on the Real as that which escapes the grasp of the One. On the one hand, he clearly breaks with the metaphysical logic of counting-for-One; on the other hand, he refuses to admit any excess

61 Ibid., p. 200.

external to the field of notional representations. For Hegel, totalization-in-One always fails, the One is always already in excess with regard to itself, is itself the subversion of what it purports to achieve, and it is this tension internal to the One, this Two-ness which makes the One One and simultaneously dislocates it, which is the motor of the "dialectical process." In other words, Hegel effectively asserts that there is no Real external to the network of notional representations (which is why he is regularly misread as an "absolute idealist"). However, the Real does not disappear here in the global self-relating play of symbolic representations; it returns with a vengeance as the immanent gap, the obstacle, on account of which representations can never totalize themselves, on account of which they are "non-All."[62]

It is crucial not to confuse this Hegelian overcoming of the couple presence/representation in the "true infinity" of speculative self-relating with the standard deconstructionist move of demonstrating how the fullness of presence is "always already" corroded from within by the gap in re-presentation, and so on. As we have seen, the difference between the two positions is condensed in the different status each gives to the subject: for deconstruction, the subject is the self-identity to be deconstructed, while from a Hegelian perspective, the subject *is* the name for the reflexive gap in the substance. Furthermore, we should also not confuse the antiphilosophical "excess" which escapes re-presentation with the traditional philosophico-theological motif of the divine Absolute beyond the order of (representable) beings, "*epekeina tes ousias*" (Plato). The notion of a divine Absolute beyond representation is a constant from Plato's supreme Good to the Neoplatonist One; Orthodox Christianity tries to close this gap between the divine excess and the space of representation with its unique notion of the icon (the presence of the divine in its image). For the Orthodox Christians, the fact that the immaterial God took flesh in the form of Jesus Christ makes it possible to depict the Son of God in human form: since Christ himself is an icon of God, the Incarnation cancels the Old Testament prescriptions against making images. Not only is Christ the "image of the invisible God" (Colossians 1:15), people are also "made in God's image" and can therefore be considered living icons. To avoid the charge of idolatry, the Orthodox theologians emphasized that when a

62 As we saw in Chapter 1, at the very outset of philosophy, Plato also approached this non-All of the field of logos in his *Parmenides*—this is why the latter occupies a unique position between early and late Plato: a gap becomes visible here which Plato desperately tries to fill in his late dialogues. *Parmenides* is a proto-version of Hegel's logic, truly readable only retroactively, i.e., from the standpoint of Hegel's logic. Its eight (or nine) hypotheses are the first version of the complete (*and* non-All: complete in the sense of "no exception") set of categories, and, as in Hegel's logic, it is meaningless to ask which hypothesis is "true"—only the conclusion (nothing exists ...) is "true," which throws us back into the entire movement.

person venerates an image, the intention is to honor the person depicted, not the substance of the icon. As St. Basil the Great said: "If I point to a statue of Caesar and ask you 'Who is that?', your answer would properly be, 'It is Caesar.' When you say such you do not mean that the stone itself is Caesar, but rather, the name and honor you ascribe to the statue passes over to the original, the archetype, Caesar himself." This is also why, in the Eastern Orthodox tradition, only flat or bas relief images are used: the sensual quality of three-dimensional statues is taken to glorify the human aspect of the flesh rather than the divine nature of the spirit. The highest form of icon is "*acheiropoieta*" (not-made-by-hand), an icon that has allegedly come into existence miraculously, not made by a human painter, but the result of a mysterious emanation from the depicted object itself, and so seen as especially authoritative as to the true appearance of the subject.

An icon thus points beyond itself to the divine presence that dwells within it—exactly contrary to the antiphilosophical notion of an excess which functions as a rupture destabilizing the harmonious continuity of a representative image. In other words, the "excess" in an icon is that of divine transcendence, of the "invisible" spirit that reverberates in or through what we see, while the antiphilosophical "excess" is an excess of immanence over transcendence, like the "stains" in the early modernist paintings of van Gogh or Munch, the over-present blotches of heavy color (the yellow sky in van Gogh, blue-green water or grass in Munch) whose dense non-transparency draws attention to itself and thus disrupts the smooth passage of the eye towards the represented content.

The same ambiguity holds for Deleuze who, between *The Logic of Sense* and *Anti-Oedipus*, "regresses" to the logic of productive presence and its re-presentation.[63] This logic, which clearly dominates the entire notional apparatus of *Anti-Oedipus* with its opposition of molecular and molar, of production and its theatre of representation, can be discerned in the radically changed status of one of Deleuze's key concepts, that of the "pseudo-cause." Since *Anti-Oedipus* is a study of capitalism, no wonder that the supreme example it gives of a "pseudo-cause" is Capital itself; Deleuze refers here to the well-known section in the first volume of Marx's *Capital* dealing with the passage from money to capital. With this passage, money-as-substance becomes money-as-subject, the "abstract" universality of money (as universal equivalent of all commodities) becomes the "concrete" universality of a self-mediating or self-engendering movement. In this way, the endless self-propelling circulation of capital reaches the level of Hegelian "true infinity": every relation to external otherness is subsumed into a "private relation with itself." From this viewpoint, the "materialist reversal of Hegel" involves breaking this self-enclosed circle of self-mediation and admitting a radical Otherness, not engendered by capital itself, as the source of profit:

63 For an outstanding description of this "regression," see Peter Klepec, "On Deleuze's Conception of Quasi-Cause," *Filozofski Vestnik*, Vol. 29, No. 1 (2008), pp. 25–40.

the "decentered" labor force and its exploitation. In this precise sense, capital is a "pseudo-cause": it appears to function as a self-engendering totality, as its own cause, but this appearance only obfuscates its decentered "absent cause," the labor which produces surplus-value. This is why Deleuze praises the British empiricists for insisting upon external causality, or, rather, the externality of relations between things with regard to these things themselves—against the German Idealist tradition of internal causality, of the development of a thing as an expression or deployment of its inner potential, or, in Hegelian terms, the development from In-itself to For-itself. For Deleuze, on the contrary, there is no continuity between In-itself and For-itself—and this is also the basic insight of his interpretation of Hitchcock's films. In a typical Hitchcockian plot, the hero's life is all of a sudden perturbed when, as a result of some contingent change in external circumstances, his social identity is radically changed (at the beginning of *North by Northwest*, for example, Thornhill, an ordinary publicity manager, is mistakenly identified as the—in reality non-existent—secret agent George Kaplan).

Are things really as simple and clear as this, however? This Deleuzian formula only works if we remain within the field of the opposition between presence and re-presentation: only then does the "pseudo-cause" appear as the point of "suture" of the field of re-presentation, as the imaginary Cause which completes the self-sufficient circularity of the sphere of re-presentation and thus obfuscates its decentered real causes. This use of "pseudo-cause" displaces and obfuscates Deleuze's original use of the concept—the notion of "pseudo-cause" was introduced as an answer to a precise problem in his ontology of the virtual: how to combine the unambiguous affirmation of the Virtual as the site of production which generates constituted reality with the no less unambiguous statement that "the virtual is produced out of the actual":

> Multiplicities should not be conceived as possessing the capacity to actively interact with one another through these series. Deleuze thinks about them as endowed with only a mere capacity to be affected, since they are, in his words, "impassive entities —impassive results." The neutrality or sterility of multiplicities may be explained in the following way. Although their divergent universality makes them independent of any particular mechanism (the same multiplicity may be actualized by several causal mechanisms) *they do depend on the empirical fact that some causal mechanism or another actually exists* ... they are not transcendent but immanent entities ... Deleuze views multiplicities as *incorporeal effects of corporeal causes*, that is, as historical results of actual causes possessing no causal powers of their own. On the other hand, as he writes, "to the extent that they differ in nature from these causes, they enter, with one another, into relations of *quasi-causality*. Together they enter into a relation with a *quasi-cause* which is itself incorporeal and assures them a very

> special independence" ... Unlike actual capacities, which are always capacities to affect and be affected, virtual affects are sharply divided into a pure capacity to be affected (displayed by impassible multiplicities) and a *pure capacity to affect*.[64]

The concept of a quasi-cause is what prevents a regression into simple reductionism: it designates the pure agency of transcendental causality. Take Deleuze's own example from his *Cinema 2: The Time-Image*: the emergence of cinematic neorealism. One can, of course, explain neorealism in terms of a set of historical circumstances (the trauma of World War II, etc.). However, there is here an excess in the emergence of the New: neorealism is an Event which cannot simply be reduced to its material or historical causes, and the "quasi-cause" is the cause of this excess, the cause of that which makes an Event (an emergence of the New) irreducible to its historical circumstances. One can also say that the quasi-cause is a second-level cause, the meta-cause of the very excess of the effect over its (corporeal) causes. This is how what Deleuze says about being affected should be understood: insofar as the incorporeal Event is a pure affect (an impassive-neutral-sterile result), and insofar as the New (a new Event, an Event of/as the New) can only emerge if the chain of its corporeal causes is not complete, *we must postulate, over and above the network of corporeal causes, a pure, transcendental, capacity to affect*. This is also why Lacan so much appreciated *The Logic of Sense*: is not the Deleuzian quasi-cause the exact equivalent of Lacan's *objet petit a*, this pure, immaterial, spectral entity which serves as the object-cause of desire?

We should be very precise here in order not to miss the point: Deleuze is not affirming a simple psycho-physical dualism *à la* someone like John Searle; he is not offering two different "descriptions" of the same event. It is not that the same process (say, a speech act) can be described in a strictly naturalistic way, as a neuronal and bodily process embedded in its actual causality, and also "from within," at the level of meaning, where the causality ("I answered your question because I understood it") is a pseudo-causality. In such an approach, the material-corporeal causality remains complete, while the basic premise of Deleuze's ontology is precisely that corporeal causality is *not* complete: in the emergence of the New, something occurs which *cannot* be properly described at the level of corporeal causes and effects. The quasi-cause is not an illusory theater of shadows, like that of the child who thinks he is magically making a toy move, unaware of the mechanical causality which actually does the work—on the contrary, the quasi-cause *fills in the gap of corporeal causality*. In this strict sense, and insofar as the Event is the Sense-Event, the quasi-cause is non-sense as inherent to Sense: if a statement could be reduced to its sense, it would fall

64 Manuel DeLanda, *Intensive Science and Virtual Philosophy*, London: Continuum 2002, p. 75.

into reality—the relationship between Sense and its designated reality would simply be that of objects in the world. Non-sense is that which maintains the autonomy of the level of sense, of its surface flow of pure becoming, with regard to the designated reality ("referent").

Does this not bring us back to the unfortunate "phallic signifier" as the "pure" signifier without a signified? Is not the Lacanian phallus precisely the point of non-sense that sustains the flow of sense? As such, the phallus is the "transcendental signifier"—the non-sense within the field of sense—which distributes and regulates the series of Sense. Its "transcendental" status means that there is nothing "substantial" about it: the phallus is the semblance par excellence. What the phallus "causes" is the gap that separates the surface-event from bodily density: it is the "pseudo-cause" that sustains the autonomy of the field of Sense with regard to its true, effective, bodily cause. We might recall here Adorno's observation that the notion of transcendental constitution is the result of a kind of perspectival inversion: what the subject (mis)perceives as his constitutive power is actually his impotence, his incapacity to reach beyond the imposed limitations of his horizon. The transcendental constitutive power is a pseudo-power representing the flipside of the subject's blindness to the true bodily causes. The phallus qua cause is the pure semblance of a cause.

There is no structure without the "phallic" moment as the crossing-point of the two series (of signifier and signified), as the point of the short-circuit at which—as Lacan puts it in a very precise way—"the signifier falls into the signified." The point of non-sense within the field of Sense is the point at which the signifier's cause is inscribed into the field of Sense. Without this short-circuit, the signifier's structure would act as an external bodily cause and would thus be unable to produce the effect of Sense. On that account, the two series always contain a paradoxical entity that is "doubly inscribed" (that is simultaneously surplus and lack): a surplus of the signifier over the signified (the empty signifier without a signified) and the lack of the signified (the point of non-sense within the field of Sense).[65]

The "pseudo-cause" is thus not a "mere quasi-cause," an "illusory cause" in contrast to "real" causes—rather, it *gives body to (fills in) the gap in the order of real causes (and not only the gap in the order of re-presentation).* This is what complicates the simplistic notion of "suture" as the place-holder for the absent production process within the order of re-presentations. Along these lines, Badiou proposes to situate the couple Sartre-Althusser along the axis of the Cause versus causality: while Althusser conceived the field of history as determined by a complex asubjective structural causality, Sartre opposed this reduction and focused on Causes in the sense of points of reference which motivate political

65 I dealt in detail with this topic in my *Organs without Bodies: On Deleuze and Consequences*, London: Routledge 2003.

subjects (like "the Cause of the people"). Lacan also insists on a Cause as opposed to causality, although in a sense very different from that of Sartrean subjective engagement: for him, a Cause is that which interrupts the regular exercise of causality, that which is ex-centric with regard to the causal chain.[66] In this sense, the ultimate Cause for Lacan is the *objet petit a*, the object-cause of desire, or even, behind and beneath it, the Cause-Thing (*la Cause-Chose*) itself. With regard to the chain of causality, this Cause is, again, a pseudo-Cause.

To return to the Marxist reference to Hegel: no wonder that—from Marx himself through Lukács to the Frankfurt School—this reference is profoundly ambiguous, oscillating between two extremes: (1) the notion of Hegel's logic as the speculative-mystified articulation of the "logic of Capital" (Capital is the actual Substance-Subject, the historical Absolute which posits its own presuppositions and thus engenders itself); and (2) the notion of Hegel's logic as the idealist-mystified logic of the revolutionary process of emancipation.[67] We find this ambiguity already in Marx himself, who, in the above-quoted passage from *Capital*, presents capital as a Hegelian self-generating "concrete universality," while, in the famous fragment on the pre-capitalist modes of production from the *Grundrisse*, he conceives the entire historical process in Hegelian terms as a gradual emergence of an alienated subjectivity which, through the communist revolution, will unite itself with its substantial presuppositions.[68]

From his early writings (the once famous "Economic and Philosophical Manuscripts" of 1844), Marx succumbs to the (Feuerbachian) temptation of formulating "alienation" and class society in terms of a mirror-reversal of the "proper" relation of causality: in capitalism, the subject is enslaved to its own product, "dead labor" (capital) rules over "living labor" (the workers' productivity), the predicate becomes the subject of its own true subject, the effect becomes the cause of its own cause. What if, however, this "capitalist reversal" (the effect retroactively subsumes its cause, the process that generates capital appears as its own subordinated moment) is grounded in a more fundamental "reversal" constitutive of subjectivity as such? What if subjectivity *is* an effect which retroactively posits its cause, a "predicate reversed into subject"? With regard to the topic of productive presence and its re-presentation, this means that there is

66 To take a Freudian example: normally our speech is determined by linguistic, psychological, etc., causalities; but when a slip of the tongue occurs which conveys an unconscious message, some ex-centric cause has interrupted the smooth flow of causality.

67 As for example in Lukács's *History and Class Consciousness*: the proletariat is the actual Subject of history destined to appropriate the alienated historical Substance through the revolutionary act—which is why Lukács has to elevate Kantian transcendental formalism into the ideal expression of capitalist social reality, so that Hegel already appears as its mystified overcoming.

68 For a more detailed development of this point, see Interlude 3.

no subject-of-presence which precedes representation: the subject is as such an effect of representation (which is why Lacan rehabilitates representation in his very definition of the signifier as that which "represents the subject for another signifier"). The dialectical reversal is thus more complex than it may appear: at its most radical, it is not only the reversal of a predicate (the reason against becoming the reason for), but the shift of the predicate itself into the position of subject.

CHAPTER 13

The Foursome of Struggle, Historicity, Will ... and *Gelassenheit*

Why Lacan is not a Heideggerian

The main philosophical proponent of the critique of subjectivity is Heidegger, one of Lacan's main references, at least in the 1950s. For this reason, it is crucial to clarify how Lacan gradually moves from accepting Heidegger's critique of the Cartesian *cogito* as another version of the Freudian "decentering" of the subject to the paradoxical and counter-intuitive embracing of the *cogito* as the subject of the unconscious.

Lacan's starting point is Freud's notion of a primordial *Bejahung*, affirmation, as opposed to *Verwerfung* (usually [mis]translated as "foreclosure"): he reads *Bejahung* as primordial symbolization, against the background of Heidegger's notion of the essence of language as disclosure of being. However, things quickly get complicated here. As we saw earlier, in Freud there are four main forms, four versions, of "*Ver-*": *Verwerfung* (foreclosure/rejection), *Verdrängung* (repression), *Verneinung* (denial), *Verleugnung* (disavowal). In *Verwerfung*, the content is thrown out of the symbolic, de-symbolized, so that it can only return in the Real (in the guise of hallucinations). In *Verdrängung*, the content remains within the symbolic but is inaccessible to consciousness, relegated to the Other Scene, returning in the guise of symptoms. In *Verneinung*, the content is admitted into consciousness, but marked by a denial. In *Verleugnung*, it is admitted a positive form, but under the condition of *Isolierung*—its symbolic impact is suspended, it is not really integrated into the subject's symbolic universe. Take the signifier "mother": if it is foreclosed or rejected, it simply has no place in the subject's symbolic universe; if it is repressed, it forms the hidden reference of symptoms; if it is denied, we get the by now familiar form "Whoever that woman in my dream is, she is not my mother!"; if it is disavowed, the subject talks calmly about his mother, conceding everything ("Yes, of course this woman is my mother!"), but remains unaffected by the impact of this admission. It is easy to see how the violence of exclusion gradually diminishes here: from radical ejection, through repression (where the repressed returns within the symbolic) and denial (where the denied content is admitted into consciousness) to disavowal, where the subject can openly, without denial, talk about it.

All four forms already presuppose that the symbolic order is in place, since they deal with how some content relates to it; consequently, a more radical, "transcendental" question must be raised here, that of the negativity which founds the symbolic order itself. Is what Freud called *Ur-Verdrängung* (primordial repression) a candidate for this role? Primordial repression is not a repression of some content *into* the unconscious, but a repression constitutive *of* the unconscious, the gesture which creates the very space of the unconscious, the gap between the system cs/pcs and the unconscious. Here we must proceed very carefully: this primordial separation of the I from the unconscious, which generates all the standard anti-Cartesian variations ("I am not where I think," etc.), should not be conceived only as the separation of the I from the unconscious Substance, so that I perceive the core of my being outside myself, out of my grasp. The Hegelian lesson of Lacan is that de-centering is always redoubled: when the subject finds itself de-centered, deprived of the core of its being, this means that the Other, the de-centered site of the subject's being, is also in its turn de-centered, truncated, deprived of the unfathomable X that would guarantee its consistency. In other words, when the subject is de-centered, the core of its being is not the natural Substance, but the "big Other," the "second nature," the virtual symbolic order which is itself constructed around a lack. The gap that separates the subject from the big Other is thus simultaneously the gap in the heart of the Other itself. This overlapping of the two lacks is what makes it so hard to formulate the ambiguous relation between *Ausstossung* (the expulsion of the Real which is constitutive of the emergence of the symbolic order) and *Verwerfung* (the "foreclosure" of a signifier from the symbolic into the Real) in Freud and Lacan—sometimes they are identified and sometimes distinguished. François Balmès makes the appropriate observation:

> If *Ausstossung* is what we say it is, it is radically different from *Verwerfung*: far from being the mechanism proper to psychosis, it would be the opening of the field of the Other as such. In a sense, it would not be the rejection of the symbolic, but itself symbolization. We should not think here psychosis and hallucination, but the subject as such. Clinically, this corresponds to the fact that foreclosure doesn't prevent psychotics from dwelling in language.[1]

This conclusion is the result of a series of precise questions. The fact is that psychotics can speak, that, in some sense, they do dwell in language: "foreclosure" does not mean their exclusion from language, but the exclusion or suspension of the symbolic efficacy of a key signifier within their symbolic universe—if a signifier is excluded, then one must already be in the signifying order. Insofar as, for Freud and Lacan, *Verwerfung* is correlative to *Bejahung* (the "affirmation," the primordial gesture of subjectively assuming one's place in the symbolic

1 François Balmès, *Ce que Lacan dit de l'être*, Paris: Presses Universitaires de France 1999, p. 72.

universe), Balmès's solution is to distinguish between this *Bejahung* and an even more originary (or "primary") symbolization of the Real, the quasi-mythical zero-level of direct contact between the symbolic and the Real which coincides with the moment of their differentiation, the process of the rise of the symbolic, of the emergence of the primary battery of signifiers, whose obverse (negative) is the expulsion of the pre-symbolic Real. When the Wolfman, at the age of one, observed his parents' *coitus a tergo*, it left in his mind a memory trace: it was symbolized, but it was just retained as a libidinally neutral trace. Only after three more years or so—after Wolfman's sexual fantasies had been awakened and he had become intrigued by where children come from—was this trace *bejaht*, properly historicized, activated in his personal narrative as a way of locating himself in the universe of meaning. Psychotics accomplish the first step, they inhabit the symbolic order; what they are unable to do is to subjectively or performatively engage in language, to "historicize" their subjective process—in short, to accomplish the *Bejahung*.

As Balmès perceptively noted, it is for this reason that the lack occurs at a different level in psychosis: psychotics continue to dwell in the dense symbolic space of the primordial "full" (maternal) big Other, they do not assume symbolic castration in the proper sense of a loss which is in itself liberating, giving, "productive," opening up the space for things to appear in their (meaningful) being; for them, a loss can only be purely *privative*, a question of something being taken from them.

In a risky interpretive move, Lacan links this "primary" symbolization—which is accessible to psychotics and which precedes the subjective engagement they lack—to Heidegger's distinction between the originary dimension of language as the disclosure of Being and the dimension of speech as the bearer of (subjective) significations or as a means of intersubjective recognition. At this originary level of naming as showing (*Sagen* as *Zeigen*), the difference between signification and reference falls away, a word which names a thing does not "mean" it, it constitutes or discloses it in its Being, it opens up the space of its existence. This level is the level of appearing as such, not appearance as opposed to reality beneath it, but "pure" appearing which "is" entirely in its appearing, behind which there is nothing. In his seminar on psychoses, Lacan provides a nice description of such pure appearing and of the concomitant, properly metaphysical temptation to reduce it to its ground, to its hidden causes:

> The rainbow, *it is just that* [*c'est cela*]. And this *it is just that* implies that we will engage ourselves to our last breath to learn what is hidden behind it, what is the cause to which we can reduce it. Note how what from the very beginning characterizes the rainbow and the meteor—and everybody knows this, since it is for this reason that we call it a meteor—is precisely that there is nothing hidden behind. It is

> entirely in this appearance. What makes it persist for us, to the point that we never cease to ask questions about it, consists solely in the originary *it is just that*, that is to say, in the nomination as such of the rainbow. There is nothing else but this name.[2]

This inherent reflexive moment of "declaration" (the fact that every communication of a content always simultaneously "declares itself" as such) is what Heidegger identified as the "as such" that specifies the properly human dimension: an animal perceives a stone, but it does not perceive this stone "as such." This is the "reflexivity" of the signifier: every utterance not only transmits some content, but, simultaneously, *determines how the subject relates to this content* (in terms of German Idealism, determines that every consciousness is always already self-consciousness). To put it in Heidegger's terms, the psychotic is not *welt-los*, deprived of the world: he already dwells in the opening of Being.

This reading, however, as is often the case with Lacan, is accompanied by its (asymmetrical, true) opposite: by a reading which attributes to psychotics access to a "higher" level of symbolization and deprives them of the "lower" basic level. Insofar as Lacan reads the Freudian distinction between "representations of things" (*Sach-Vorstellungen*) and "representations of words" (*Wort-Vorstellungen*) as internal to the symbolic order—as the distinction between primordial symbolization, the establishment of the originary unconscious's battery of signifiers ("memory-traces," in the language of the early, pre-psychoanalytic, Freud), and secondary symbolization, the conscious/preconscious system of language—this furnishes him with a paradoxical definition of the psychotic's predicament: a psychotic is not one who regresses to a more "primitive" level of representations-of-things, who "treats words as things," as is commonly said; he is, on the contrary, someone who precisely disposes of representations-of-words without representations-of-things.[3] In other words, a psychotic can use language in a normal manner, but what he lacks is the unconscious background which gives the words we use their libidinal resonance, their specific subjective weight and color. Without this background, psychoanalytic interpretation is powerless, inoperative: "In psychosis, truth is without effect, which doesn't prevent the psychotic from saying it better than anyone else."[4] This is also one way to understand Lacan's misleadingly "eccentric" claim that normality is a species of psychosis: our "normal" common-sense definition of language is that it is an artificial secondary system of signs we use to transfer pre-existing information, and so on—what this definition ignores is the underlying level of subjective engagement, the position of enunciation; the paradox of the psychotic is that he is the only one who fully fits this definition, that is,

2 Jacques Lacan, *Le séminaire, Livre III: Les psychoses*, Paris: Seuil 1981, p. 358.

3 Balmès, *Ce que Lacan dit de l'être*, p. 91.

4 François Balmès, *Dieu, le sexe et la vérité*, Ramonville Saint-Agne: Érès 2007, p. 53.

who effectively uses language as a neutral secondary instrument which does not concern the speaker's very being:

> certain signifiers do not pass into the unconscious writing, and this is the case with the paternal signifier in psychosis. This does not preclude their presence at the preconscious level—as we can see in the case of the signifiers which we call foreclosed in psychosis and which are at the subject's disposal in his language.[5]

This oscillation seems to indicate that there is something wrong with the solution of distinguishing the two levels, the level of primary symbolization and the level of *Bejahung/Verwerfung*. (Solutions which rely on simply distinguishing between different levels are a priori suspicious.) What it loses is the basic paradox of the symbolic as *the two at the same*: ultimately, the expulsion of the Real from the symbolic and the rejection of a signifier overlap; that is, in the case of the symbolic Other, external and internal limitations coincide, the symbolic order can only emerge as delimited from the Real if it is delimited from itself, missing or excluding a central part of itself, not identical with itself. There is thus no *Ausstossung* without a *Verwerfung*—the price the symbolic has to pay in order to delimit itself from the Real is its own being-truncated. This is what Lacan is aiming at with his formula that there is no big Other, no Other of Other—and, as the late Lacan knew very well, this implies that, at a certain most basic level, we are all psychotics. However, we should be more precise here: the signifier which is foreclosed is not simply a missing one, one that is lacking, but rather a signifier that itself stands for the barred A, for the lack of signifier, for the incompleteness-inconsistency of the symbolic field. The psychotic's problem, then, is not that he dwells in a truncated symbolic order (Other), but, on the contrary, that he dwells in a "complete" Other, an Other which lacks the inscription of its lack.

There is thus no need to posit two phases, first the symbolization, the rise of the primary battery of signifiers through the expulsion of the Real, then the exclusion of a signifier: the two processes are one and the same, and psychosis comes afterwards, in a second stage, when—if—the signifier which stands for the very incompleteness or inconsistency of the Other, which registers this incompleteness, is foreclosed. This two-faced primordial *Ausstossung* has to be distinguished from the violent defensive measure of ejecting (what is experienced as) a foreign intruder, up to and including the infamous call *Juden raus!*, the ejection which reappears in all its brutality in today's hyper-reflexive society.

The Hegelian lesson of the global reflexivization-mediatization of our lives—that this process generates its own brutal immediacy—was best captured

5 Ibid., p. 81.

by Etienne Balibar's notion of excessive, non-functional cruelty as a feature of contemporary life, a cruelty whose figures range from "fundamentalist" racist and/or religious slaughter to "senseless" outbursts of violence performed by adolescents upon the homeless in our megalopolises, a violence one is tempted to call Id-Evil, a violence grounded in no utilitarian or ideological reasons. All the talk about foreigners stealing our jobs from us or about the threat they represent to our Western values should not deceive us: on closer examination, it soon becomes clear that this talk provides a rather superficial secondary rationalization. The explanation we ultimately get from a skinhead is that it makes him feel good to beat up foreigners because their presence disturbs him. What we encounter here is indeed Id-Evil, Evil structured and motivated by the most elementary imbalance in the relationship between the Ego and *jouissance*, by the tension between pleasure and the foreign body of *jouissance* at the very heart of it. Id-Evil thus stages the most elementary "short-circuit" in the relationship of the subject to the primordially missing object-cause of his desire: what "bothers" us in the "other" (Jew, Japanese, African, Turk) is that he appears to entertain a privileged relationship to the object—the other either possesses the object-treasure, having snatched it away from us (which is why we do not have it), or he poses a threat to our possession of the object. Here we can again employ the Hegelian "infinite judgment," asserting the speculative identity of these "useless" and "excessive" outbursts of violent immediacy, which display nothing but a pure and naked ("non-sublimated") hatred of Otherness, with the global reflexivization of society. Perhaps the ultimate example of this coincidence is the fate of psychoanalytic interpretation. Today, the formations of the unconscious (from dreams to hysterical symptoms) have definitely lost their innocence and are thoroughly reflexivized: the "free associations" of a typical educated analysand consist for the most part of attempts to provide a psychoanalytic explanation of their disturbances, so that one is quite justified in saying that we have not only Jungian, Kleinian, Lacanian ... interpretations of the symptoms, but symptoms themselves which are Jungian, Kleinian, Lacanian ... that is, whose reality involves an implicit reference to some psychoanalytic theory. The unfortunate result of this global reflexivization of interpretation (everything becomes interpretation, the unconscious interprets itself) is that the analyst's interpretation itself loses its performative "symbolic efficacy," leaving the symptom intact in the immediacy of its idiotic *jouissance*.

In what precise sense, then, does that which is foreclosed from the symbolic return in the Real? Consider verbal hallucinations: their content is massively symbolic, and they are, at the level of their ordinary meaning, fully understood by the (psychotic) subject, so, again, in what sense do they belong to the Real? Two interconnected features make them Real: isolation and certitude. They are foreclosed in the precise sense that they do not "exist" for the subject: they ex-sist, persist, and impose themselves outside the symbolic texture. They are isolated from their symbolic context, which is by definition one of trust and supposition, the context in which every presence arises against the background of its possible absence, every certitude is accompanied by a possible doubt, and in which one ultimately has to rely on a basic wager to trust the symbolic order. In religion proper, one does not know God, but one risks trusting in him, believing in him. A psychotic, on the contrary, proceeds like the Slovene punk group Laibach who, when asked during an interview about their relation to God, answered with reference to the "In God we trust" printed on every dollar note: "Like you Americans, we believe that God exists, but, unlike you, we do not trust Him." Or, as Balmès puts it succinctly, it is not that psychotics believe *in* the voices they hear, they simply believe *them*.[6] This is why psychotics have an absolute certitude about the voices they hear: they do not trust them, of course, they take them as evil voices which want to hurt them; but they simply know that the voices are real—this absolute certitude itself make them real.

Hegel versus Heidegger

"It is time to talk about the late Hegel. If there is something which is little known, it is the last period of Hegel's thought in Berlin."[7] Far from confirming Hegel's philosophy as a conservative (or, at least, conformist) *Staatsphilosoph*, it was during his last years in Berlin that Hegel, after a long effort, provided the definitive formulation of his key insights. This point should be insisted upon especially in response to one standard critique of Hegel, first formulated by the "young Hegelians," concerning the so-called contradiction between Hegel's dialectical method and his system: while the method approaches reality in its dynamic development, discerning in every determinate form the seeds of its own destruction and self-overcoming, the system endeavors to render the totality of being as an achieved order in which no further development is in view.[8] In the twentieth-century interpretations of Hegel developed under Heidegger's influence, this contradiction between the "logical" and the "historical" acquires

6 Ibid., p. 66.

7 Jean-Marie Lardic, in G. W. F. Hegel, *Leçons sur les preuves de l'existence de Dieu*, Paris: Aubier 1994, p. 9.

8 How are method and system related in Hegel's thought? According to the standard Marxist *doxa*, there is a contradiction between the two: Hegel's system is conservative, while his dialectical method is revolutionary, so we should liberate the method from the constraints of the system. What this naïve opposition misses is the identity of the two, somewhat like the strange fate about Stanislavsky's theatrical teaching, which in Russia was known as his "system," and later in the US, where it became very influential (in the Actor's Studio, etc.), as his "method."

a more radical underpinning: what they try to outline is a more fundamental ontological frame which is simultaneously both the source of Hegel's dialectical systematizing and what the latter betrays. The historical dimension is here not simply the fact of the unending evolution of all life forms, nor the philosophical opposition between the young Hegel who tries to grasp the historical antagonisms of social life and the old Hegel who compulsively steam-rollers all content with his dialectical machine, but rather the inherent tension between Hegel's systematic drive of notional self-mediation/sublation and a more original ontological project which, following Heidegger, Alexandre Koyré describes as the historicity of the human condition oriented towards the future.[9]

The root of what Hegel calls "negativity" is (our awareness of) the future: the future is what is not (yet), the power of negativity is ultimately identical to the power of time itself, this force which corrodes every firm identity. The proper temporality of a human being is thus not that of linear time, but that of engaged existence: a man projects his future and then actualizes it by way of a detour through past resources. This "existential" root of negativity is, according to Koyré, obfuscated by Hegel's system, which abolishes the primacy of the future and presents its entire content as the past "sublated" in its logical form—the standpoint adopted here is not that of engaged subjectivity, but that of Absolute Knowing. A similar critique of Hegel was deployed by Alexandre Kojève and Jean Hyppolite: what they all try to formulate is a tension or antagonism at the very core of Hegel's thought which remains unthought by Hegel—not for accidental reasons, but necessarily, which is why, precisely, *this antagonism cannot be dialecticized*, resolved or "sublated" through dialectical mediation. What all these philosophers offer is thus a critical "schizology" of Hegel.[10]

It is not difficult to recognize in this vision of the future-oriented temporality of the engaged subject the traces of Heidegger's assertion of finitude as the unsurpassable predicament of being-human: it is our radical finitude which exposes us to the opening of the future, to the horizon of what is to come, for transcendence and finitude are two sides of the same coin. No wonder, then, that it was Heidegger himself who proposed the most elaborate version of this critical reading of Hegel. Not the Heidegger of *Sein und Zeit*, but the later Heidegger, who tries to decipher the unthought dimension in Hegel through a close reading of the notion of the "experience" (*Erfahrung*) of consciousness in the *Phenomenology of Spirit*. Heidegger reads Hegel's famous critique of Kantian skepticism (we can only get to know the Absolute if the Absolute already wants to be *bei uns*, with us) through his own interpretation of *parousia* as the epochal disclosure of being: *parousia* is the way the Absolute (Hegel's name for the Truth

---

9 See Alexandre Koyré, "Hegel à Iena," in *Études d'histoire de la pensée philosophique*, Paris: Gallimard 1971.

10 I rely here on Catherine Malabou, *La chambre du milieu*, Paris: Hermann 2009.

of Being) is always already disclosed to us prior to any active effort on our part, that is, the way this disclosure of the Absolute grounds and directs our very effort to grasp it—or, as the mystics and theologians say, "you would not be searching for me if you had not already found me." Here is the passage—including the key claim that the Absolute itself "wishes to be beside us," with us, present to us, to disclose itself to us—which Heidegger reads as Hegel's own formulation of the old Greek notion of *parousia*:

> If the Absolute were only to be brought on the whole nearer to us by [our] agency, without any change being wrought in it, like a bird caught by a limestick, it would certainly scorn a trick of that sort, if it were not in its very nature, and did it not wish to be, beside us from the start.[11]

Rather than dismissing this claim as evidence of how Hegel remains a prisoner of the "metaphysics of presence," we should draw attention, first, to the fact that Heidegger himself offers a further variation on this same topic with his notion of *Dasein* as *das Da des Seins*, the "there" of Being itself, which means that Being itself "needs" man as its only "there," and that, in this sense, in spite of its withdrawal, it also "wants to be with us." Furthermore, this "wish to be with us" is more enigmatic and complex than it may appear—it can be conceived, again, along the lines of Kafka's parable "Before the Law," when the man from the country finally learns that the Door was there only for him and that now, upon his death, it will be closed. All the mystery of withdrawal, of the inaccessibility of what the Door concealed, was thus there only for the Man, destined to fascinate his gaze—the Door's reticence was a lure destined to obfuscate the fact that the Door "wished to be with the man." In other words, the trick of the Door was the same as that in the competition between Zeuxis and Parrhasius: the Door was like the painting of a curtain on the wall, there to create the illusion that it concealed some secret.

Why then, according to Heidegger, is Hegel unable to see the proper dimension of *parousia*? This brings us to Heidegger's next reproach: that Hegel's notion of negativity lacks a phenomenal dimension (fails to describe the experience in which negativity would appear as such), that Hegel never systematically exemplifies or makes appear the difference between rejection, negation, nothing, "is not," etc.[12] Hegelian dialectics just presupposes the occultation of its own phenomenologico-ontological foundation; the name of this occultation is, of course, subjectivity: Hegel always already subordinates negativity to the subject's

11 G. W. F. Hegel, *Phenomenology of Mind*, second rev. ed., trans. J. B. Baillie, Mineola: Dover 2003, p. 74.

12 Martin Heidegger, *Gesamtausgabe, Vol. 68: Hegel*, Frankfurt: Vittorio Klostermann 1993, p. 37.

"work of the negative," to the conceptual mediation or sublation of all phenomenal content. In this way, negativity is reduced to a secondary moment in the subject's work of self-mediation. This blindness to its own foundation is not secondary, but the enabling feature of Hegel's metaphysics of subjectivity: the dialectical *logos* can only function against the background of a pre-subjective *Absage*, renunciation or saying-no.

There is nonetheless a privileged phenomenal mode in which negativity can be experienced: pain. The path of experience is the path of the painful realization that there is a gap between "natural" and transcendental consciousness, between "for the consciousness itself" and "for us": the subject is violently deprived of the "natural" foundation of its being, its entire world collapses, and this process is repeated until it reaches Absolute Knowing. When he speaks about "transcendental pain" as the fundamental *Stimmung* of Hegel's thought, Heidegger is following a line which begins in Kant's *Critique of Practical Reason*, where Kant describes pain as the only "a priori" emotion, the emotion of my pathological ego being humiliated by the injunction of the moral law.[13] (Lacan sees in this transcendental privilege of pain the link between Kant and Sade.)

What Heidegger misses in his description of Hegelian "experience" as the path of *Verzweiflung* is the proper nature of the abyss it involves: it is not only natural consciousness which is shattered when it has to confront death, but also the transcendental background or frame as the measure of what the natural consciousness experiences as its inadequacy and failure—as Hegel put it, if what we thought to be true fails the measure of truth, this measure itself has to be abandoned. This is why Heidegger misses the vertiginous abyss of the dialectical process: there is no standard of truth that natural consciousness is gradually approaching through painful experience, for this very standard is itself caught up in the process, and thus undermined again and again.

This is also why Heidegger's criticism regarding Hegel's "machination" misses the point. According to Heidegger, the Hegelian process of experience moves at two levels, that of lived experience (*Erlebnis*) and that of conceptual machination (*Machenschaft*): at the level of lived experience, consciousness sees its world collapse and a new figure of the world appear, and experiences this passage as a pure leap with no logical bridge uniting the two positions. "For us," however, the dialectical analysis makes visible how the new world emerged as the "determinate negation" of the old one, as the necessary outcome of its crisis. Authentic lived experience, the opening to the New, is thus revealed as being underpinned by notional work: what the subject experiences as the inexplicable rise of a new world is actually the result of its own conceptual work taking place behind its back and can thus ultimately be read as having been produced by the

13 Ibid., p. 103.

subject's own conceptual machination. Here there is no experience of genuine otherness, the subject encounters only the results of its own (conceptual) work. But this reproach only holds if we ignore how both sides, the phenomenal "for itself" of the natural consciousness and the "for us" of the subterranean conceptual work, are caught up in the groundless, vertiginous abyss of a repeated loss. The "transcendental pain" is not only the pain the natural consciousness experiences, the pain of being separated from its truth; it is also the painful awareness that this truth itself is non-All, inconsistent.

Which brings us back to Heidegger's claim that Hegel fails to include the phenomenal experience of negativity: what if negativity names precisely the gap in the order of phenomenality, something which does *not* (and can never) appear? Not because it is a transcendental gesture which by definition eludes the phenomenal level, but because it is the paradoxical, difficult-to-think negativity which cannot be subsumed under any agent (experiential or not)—what Hegel calls "self-relating negativity," a negativity which precedes all positive grounding and whose negative gesture of withdrawal opens up the space for all positivity.

The torture-house of language

At this point, we can even invert Heidegger's critique of Hegel and claim that it is Heidegger himself who is unable to think this "transcendental pain"—and that he misses the path to thinking it precisely because he dispenses all too early with the term "the subject" in order to think the (inhuman) core of being-human. What, then, is the dimension of pain overlooked by Heidegger?

In his "Critique of Violence," Walter Benjamin raises the question: "Is any non-violent resolution of conflict possible?"[14] His answer is that it is possible in "relationships among private persons," in courtesy, sympathy, and trust: "there is a sphere of human agreement that is non-violent to the extent that it is wholly inaccessible to violence: the proper sphere of 'understanding,' language."[15] This thesis belongs to the mainstream tradition in which language or the symbolic order are conceived as a medium of reconciliation and mediation, of peaceful co-existence, as opposed to a violent medium of immediate and raw confrontation.[16]

14 Walter Benjamin, "Critique of Violence," in *Selected Writings*, Cambridge: Harvard University Press 1996, p. 243.

15 Ibid., p. 245.

16 An idea propagated by Habermas (see Jürgen Habermas, *The Theory of Communicative Action*, Vols. 1 and 2, New York: Beacon Press 1985), but also not alien to a certain Lacan (see Jacques Lacan, "The Function and Field of Speech and Language in Psychoanalysis," in *Écrits: The First Complete Edition in English*, trans. Bruce Fink, New York: W. W. Norton & Company 2006).

In language, rather than acting violently towards one another, we are meant to debate, to exchange words, and such an exchange, even when it is aggressive, presupposes a minimum recognition of the other.

What if, however, humans exceed animals in their capacity for violence precisely *because* they can speak? There are many violent features of language thematized by philosophers and sociologists from Heidegger to Bourdieu. There is nevertheless at least one violent aspect of language which is absent in Heidegger, and which is the focus of Lacan's theory of the symbolic order. Throughout his work, Lacan varies Heidegger's motif of language as the house of being: language is not man's creation and instrument, it is man who "dwells" in language: "Psychoanalysis should be the science of language inhabited by the subject."[17] Lacan's "paranoid" twist, his additional Freudian turn of the screw, comes with his characterization of this house as a *torture-house*: "In the light of the Freudian experience, man is a subject caught in and tortured by language."[18]

The military dictatorship in Argentina from 1976 to 1983 invented a grammatical peculiarity, a new passive use of active verbs: when thousands of leftist political activists and intellectuals disappeared, never to be seen again, tortured and killed by the military, who denied any knowledge of their fate, they were referred to as "disappeared," where the verb was used not in the simple sense that they had disappeared, but in an active transitive sense: they "were disappeared" (by the military secret services). In the Stalinist regime, a similar irregular inflexion affected the verb "to step down": when it was publicly announced that a high-up member of the nomenklatura had stepped down from his post (for health reasons, as a rule), and everyone knew it was really because he had lost out in the struggle between different cliques, people said he "had been stepped down"—again, an act normally attributed to the affected person (he steps down, he disappears) is reinterpreted as the result of the non-transparent activity of another agent (the secret police disappeared him, the majority in the nomenklatura stepped him down). And should we not read in exactly the same way Lacan's thesis that a human being does not speak but is spoken? The point is not that it is "spoken about," the topic of speech of other humans, but that, when (it appears that) it speaks, it "is spoken," in the same way that the unfortunate communist functionary was "stepped down." What this homology reveals is the status of language, of the "big Other," as the torture-house of the subject.

We usually take a subject's speech with all its inconsistencies as an expression of his or her inner turmoil, ambiguous emotions, and so forth; this holds even for a literary work of art: the task of a psychoanalytic reading is supposed to be to unearth the inner psychic turbulence which found its coded expression in the work of art. But something is missing in this classical account: speech

17 Lacan, *Le séminaire, Livre III: Les psychoses*, p. 276.

18 Ibid.

does not only register or express traumatic psychic life; the entry into speech is in itself a traumatic fact ("symbolic castration"). This means that we should include in the list of traumas that speech tries to cope with the traumatic impact of speech itself. The relationship between psychic turmoil and its expression in speech should thus also be reversed: speech does not simply express or articulate psychic troubles; at a certain key point, psychic turmoil itself is a reaction to the trauma of dwelling in the "torture-house of language."

The "prison-house of language" (the title of Fredric Jameson's early book on structuralism), is thus also a torture-house: all the psychopathological phenomena described by Freud, from conversion-symptoms inscribed into the body up to complete psychotic breakdowns, are scars of this permanent torture, so many signs of an original and irremediable gap between the subject and language, so many signs that man can never be at home in his own home. This is what Heidegger ignores, this dark side of our dwelling in language, and this is why there can be no place for the Real of *jouissance* in Heidegger's edifice, since the torturing aspect of language concerns primarily the vicissitudes of the libido. It is also why, in order to get the truth to speak, it is not enough to suspend the subject's active intervention and let language itself speak—as Elfriede Jelinek put it with extraordinary clarity: "Language should be tortured to tell the truth." Language must be twisted, denaturalized, extended, condensed, cut and reunited, made to work against itself. Language as the "big Other" is not an agent of wisdom to whose message we should attune ourselves, but a medium of cruel indifference and stupidity. The most elementary form of torturing one's language is called poetry—think of what a complex form like a sonnet does to language: it forces the free flow of speech into a Procrustean bed of fixed forms of rhythm and rhyme.

But what about Heidegger's procedure of listening to the soundless word of language itself, of bringing out the truth that already dwells within it? No wonder that the late Heidegger's thinking is poetic—can one imagine a torture more violent than what he does in, say, his famous reading of Parmenides's proposition "thinking-speaking and being are the same"? To extract the intended truth from it, he has to refer to the literal meaning of words (*legein* as gathering), to counter-intuitively displace the accent and scansion of the sentence, to translate single terms in a strongly interpretative descriptive way, and so on. From this perspective, late Wittgensteinian "ordinary language philosophy"—which sees itself as a kind of medical cure, correcting the erroneous use of ordinary language which gives rise to "philosophical problems"—wants to eliminate precisely this "torturing" of language which would force it to deliver the truth (recall Rudolph Carnap's famous critique of Heidegger from the late 1920s, which claimed that the latter's ratiocinations were based on the misuse of "nothing" as a substantive).

Does the same not apply to cinema? Does not cinema also force its visual material to tell the truth through torture? First, there was Eisenstein's "montage of attractions," the mother of all cinematic torture: a violent cutting of continuous shots into fragments which are then re-united in a thoroughly artificial way, a no less violent reduction of the whole body or scene to close-ups of "partial objects" which float around in the cinematic space, cut off from the organic Whole to which they belong. Then there is Tarkovsky, Eisenstein's great enemy, who replaced the frantic Eisensteinian montage with its opposite, a stretching-out of time, a kind of cinematic equivalent of the "rack," the classic torture machine designed to stretch the victim's limbs. We can thus characterize Tarkovsky's polemic against Eisenstein as a dispute between two professional torturers over the relative merits of different devices.

This is also the ultimate reason why, against Heidegger's historicization of the subject as the agent of technological mastery in the modern age, against his replacement of the "subject" with *Dasein* as the name for the essence of being-human, Lacan stuck to the problematic term "the subject." When Lacan implies that Heidegger misses a crucial dimension of subjectivity, his point is not the silly humanist argument that Heidegger excessively "passivizes" man, turning him into an instrument of the revelation of Being and thus ignoring human creativity, and so forth. The point is, on the contrary, that Heidegger misses the properly traumatic impact of the very "passivity" of our being caught up in language, the tension between the human animal and language; there is a "subject" because the human animal does not "fit" language, the Lacanian "subject" is the tortured, mutilated subject.

Althusserians strongly insist on the constitutive double meaning of the term "subject": as the active transcendental agent, creator of (its) reality, and as the passive agent submitted (subjected) to a legal state order (*sujet de l'état*)—or, to give it a more general Lacanian twist, subjected to the big Other. Here, however, Lacan adds a much more radical dimension of passivity: as he puts it in his seminar on the ethics of psychoanalysis, the subject is "that [part-aspect of] the real which suffers from the signifier [*ce que du réel pâtit du signifiant*]"—the most elementary dimension of the subject is not activity, but passivity, enduring something. Here is how Lacan locates rituals of initiation which make a violent cut into the body, mutilating it:

> The rituals of initiation assume the form of the changing of form of these desires, of conferring on them in this way a function through which the subject's being identifies itself or announces itself as such, through which the subject, if one can put it this way, fully becomes a man, but also a woman. The *mutilation* serves here to orientate desire, enabling it to assume precisely this function of index, of something which is realized and which can only articulate itself, express itself, in a *symbolic*

> *beyond*, a beyond which is the one we today call being, a realization of being in the subject.[19]

The gap that separates Lacan from Heidegger is here clearly discernible precisely on account of their proximity, of the fact that, in order to designate the symbolic function at its most elementary, Lacan still uses Heidegger's term "being": in a human being, desires lose their mooring in biology, they are operative only insofar as they are inscribed within the horizon of Being which is sustained by language. However, in order for this transposition from the immediate biological reality of the body to the symbolic space of language to take place, it has to leave a mark of torture on the body in the form of its mutilation. It is thus not enough to say that "the Word became flesh": what we must add is that, in order for the Word to inscribe itself into flesh, a part of that flesh—the proverbial Shylockian pound—has to be sacrificed. Since there is no pre-established harmony between the Word and flesh, it is only through such a sacrifice that the flesh becomes receptive for the Word.

This brings us, finally, to the topic of *jouissance*. Philippe Lacoue-Labarthe located very precisely the gap that separates Lacan's interpretation of *Antigone* from Heidegger's (to which Lacan otherwise abundantly refers): what is totally missing in Heidegger is not only the dimension of the Real of *jouissance*, but, above all, the dimension of the "between-two-deaths" (the symbolic and the Real) which designates Antigone's subjective position after she is excommunicated from the polis by Creon. In an exact symmetry with her brother Polynices, who is dead in reality but denied the symbolic death, the rituals of burial, Antigone finds herself dead symbolically, excluded from the symbolic community, while biologically and subjectively still alive. In Agamben's terms, Antigone finds herself reduced to "bare life," to a position of *homo sacer*, whose exemplary case in the twentieth century is that of the inmates of the concentration camps. The stakes of this Heideggerian omission are thus very high, since they concern the ethico-political crux of the twentieth century, the "totalitarian" catastrophe in its extreme deployment. The omission is thus quite consistent with Heidegger's inability to resist the Nazi temptation:

> the "between-two-deaths" is the hell which our century realized or still promises to realize, and it is to this that Lacan replies and to which he wants to make psychoanalysis responsible. Did he not say that politics is the "hole" of metaphysics? The scene with Heidegger—and there is one—is in its entirety located here.[20]

---

19 Jacques Lacan, seminar of May 20, 1959, in *Le séminaire, Livre VI: Le désir et son interpretation* (unpublished).

20 Philippe Lacoue-Labarthe, "De l'éthique: à propos d'Antigone," in *Lacan avec les philosophes*, Paris: Albin Michel 1991, p. 28.

This also accounts for the disturbing ambiguity of Heidegger's description of death in extermination camps as no longer authentic death, involving the individual's assumption of its own death as the possibility of its highest impossibility, but just another anonymous industrial-technological process—people do not really "die" in the camps, they are just industrially exterminated. Heidegger thus obscenely suggests that the victims murdered in the camps somehow did not die "authentically," thereby translating their utter suffering into subjective "non-authenticity." The question he fails to raise is precisely how *they* subjectivized (related to) their predicament. Their death was indeed an industrial process of extermination for their executioners, *but not for themselves*.

Balmès here makes an acute observation: it is as if Lacan's implicit clinical reproach to Heidegger's existential analytic of *Dasein* as "being-towards-death" is that it is appropriate only for neurotics and fails to account for psychotics.[21] A psychotic subject occupies an existential position for which there is no place in Heidegger's mapping, the position of someone who in a certain sense "survives his own death." Psychotics no longer fit Heidegger's description of *Dasein*'s engaged existence, their life no longer involves freely engaging in a futural project against the background of assuming one's past; their life is beyond "care" (*Sorge*), their being is no longer directed "towards death."

This excess of *jouissance* that resists symbolization (logos) is the reason why, in the final two decades of his teaching, Lacan (sometimes almost pathetically) insists that he considers himself an antiphilosopher, someone who rebels against philosophy: philosophy is onto-logy, its basic premise is—as Parmenides, the first philosopher, had already put it—"thinking and being are the same," there is a mutual accord between thinking (logos as reason or speech) and being. Up to and including Heidegger, the Being philosophy had in mind was always the being whose house was language, the being sustained by language, the being whose horizon was opened by language; or, as Wittgenstein put it: the limits of my language are the limits of my world. Against this onto-logical premise of philosophy, Lacan focuses on the Real of *jouissance* as something which, though far from being simply external to language (it is rather "ex-timate" with regard to it), resists symbolization, remains a foreign kernel within it, appearing as a rupture, cut, gap, inconsistency, or impossibility:

> I challenge any philosopher to account now for the relation that there is between the emergence of the signifier and the way *jouissance* relates to being ... No philosophy, I say, meets us here today. The wretched aborted freaks of philosophy which we drag behind us from the beginning of the last [nineteenth] century as habits that are falling apart, are nothing but a way of dancing around rather than confronting this question, which is the only question about truth and which is called, and named by

21 Balmès, *Ce que Lacan dit de l'être*, p. 73.

> Freud, the death drive, the primordial masochism of *jouissance* ... All philosophical speech escapes and withdraws here.[22]

It is in this sense that Lacan describes his position as the "realism of *jouissance*." The "natural" enemy of this realism is, of course, Hegel's "panlogism," dismissed by Lacan as the climax of ontology, of philosophical logic (the self-deployment of logos) as the total explanation of being, through which being loses its opacity and becomes totally transparent. But, as we have seen, things with Hegel are not so simple. Following Lacan's own formulae of sexuation, is not the obverse of Hegel's basic thesis, "there is nothing which is not logos," the assertion of a non-All—"not-all is logos," or logos is not-all, since it is corroded and truncated from within by antagonisms and ruptures, and never fully itself?

Perhaps Lacan was somehow obscurely aware of all this, as implied in the above-quoted passage by the curious and unexpected limitation of his brutal dismissal of philosophy to the "wretched aborted freaks of philosophy which we drag behind us from the beginning of the last century," that is, to *post*-Hegelian thought. In other words, the more obvious thing to say would have been that it is precisely post-Hegelian thought which breaks with onto-logy, asserting the primacy of a trans-logical Will or Life—in the anti-logos (antiphilosophy) that runs from late Schelling through Schopenhauer to Nietzsche. It is as if Lacan had here learned Heidegger's lesson: Marx's formula "being determines consciousness" is not radical enough—all the talk about the actual life of engaged subjectivity as opposed to "mere speculative thought" remains trapped within the confines of ontology, because (as Heidegger demonstrated) being can only arise through logos. The difference with Heidegger is that Lacan, instead of accepting this accord (sameness) between Being and logos, tries to move beyond it, to a dimension of the Real indicated by the impossible juncture between the subject and *jouissance*. No wonder, then, that with regard to anxiety Lacan prefers Kierkegaard to Heidegger: he perceives Kierkegaard as the anti-Hegel for whom the paradox of Christian faith signals a radical break with the Ancient Greek ontology (in contrast to Heidegger's reduction of Christianity to a moment in the process of the decline of that ontology in medieval metaphysics). Faith is an existential leap into what (from an ontological viewpoint) can only appear as madness, a crazy decision unwarranted by any reason—Kierkegaard's God is really "beyond Being," a God of the Real, not the God of philosophers. Which is why, again, Lacan would accept Heidegger's famous statement, from the 1920s, when he abandoned the Catholic Church, that religion is a mortal enemy of philosophy—but he would see this as all the more reason to stick to the core of the Real inherent in the religious experience.

---

22 Jacques Lacan, seminar of June 8, 1966, in *Le séminaire, Livre XIII: L'objet de la psychanalyse* (unpublished).

The Lacanian "subject" names a gap in the symbolic, its status is Real—this is why, as Balmès pointed out in his crucial seminar on the logic of the fantasy (1966–7), after more than a decade of struggling with Heidegger, Lacan accomplishes his paradoxical and (for someone who adheres to Heidegger's notion of modern philosophy) totally unexpected move from Heidegger back to Descartes, to the Cartesian *cogito*. There really is a paradox here: Lacan first accepts Heidegger's point that the Cartesian *cogito*, which grounds modern science and its mathematicized universe, heralds the highest forgetting of Being; but for Lacan, the Real of *jouissance* is precisely external to Being, so that what was for Heidegger the argument *against* the *cogito* becomes for Lacan the argument *for* it—the Real of *jouissance* can only be approached when we exit the domain of being. This is why, for Lacan, not only is the *cogito* not to be reduced to the self-transparency of pure thought, but, paradoxically, the *cogito is* the subject of the unconscious—a gap or cut in the order of Being in which the Real of *jouissance* breaks through.

Of course, this *cogito* is the *cogito* "in becoming," not yet the *res cogitans*, the thinking substance which fully participates in Being and in the logos. In the seminar on the logic of fantasy, Lacan reads the truth of Descartes's *cogito ergo sum* more radically than in his earlier seminars, where he played endlessly on variations of "subverting" the subject. He began with decentering being in relation to thought—"I am not where I think," the core of my being ("*Kern unseres Wesens*") is not in my (self-)consciousness; however, he quickly became aware that such a reading only paves the way for the irrationalist *Lebensphilosophie* topic of Life deeper than mere thinking or language, which runs counter to Lacan's basic thesis that the Freudian unconscious is "structured like a language," that is, is thoroughly "rational" or discursive. So he moved on to a much more refined "I think where I am not," which decenters thinking with regard to my Being, the awareness of my full presence: the Unconscious is a purely virtual (in-existing, insisting) Other Place of a thought which escapes my being. Then, there is a different punctuation: "I think: 'therefore I am'"—my Being devalued to an illusion generated by my thought and so on. What all these versions share is their accent on the gap that separates *cogito* from *sum*, thought from being—Lacan's aim was to undermine the illusion of their overlap by pointing to a fissure in the apparent homogeneity of thinking-being. It was only towards the end of his teaching that he asserted their overlap—a negative one, for sure. In other words, Lacan finally grasps the most radical zero-point of the Cartesian *cogito* as the point of the negative intersection between being and thinking: the vanishing point at which I don't think *and* I am not. I *am not*: I am not a substance, a thing, an entity, I am reduced to a void in the order of being, to a gap, a *béance*.[23]

23 Recall how, for Lacan, the discourse of science presupposes the foreclosure of the subject—to put it in naïve terms, in it, the subject is reduced to zero: a scientific

I *do not think*: here, again, Lacan paradoxically accepts Heidegger's thesis that (modern mathematized) science "does not think"—but for him, this precisely means that it breaks out of the frame of onto-logy, of thinking as logos correlative to Being. As pure *cogito*, I do not think, I am reduced to "pure (form of) thought" which coincides with its opposite, that is, which has no content and is as such non-thinking. The tautology of thinking is self-canceling in the same way as is the tautology of being, which is why, for Lacan, the "I am that which I am" announced by the burning bush to Moses on Mount Sinai indicates a God beyond Being, God as Real.[24]

The importance of this Lacanian assertion of the *cogito* is that, with regard to the couple language-world, it assures a point external to it, a minimal point of singular universality which is literally world-less, trans-historical. This means we are condemned to our world, to the hermeneutic horizon of our finitude, or, as Gadamer put it, to the impenetrable background of historical "prejudices" which predetermine the field of what we can see and understand. Every world is sustained by language, and every "spoken" language sustains a world—this is what Heidegger was aiming at with his thesis on language as the "house of being"—is this not effectively our spontaneous ideology? There is an endlessly differentiated, complex reality which we, the individuals and communities embedded within it, always experience from the particular, finite perspective of our historical world. What democratic materialism furiously rejects is the notion that there can be an infinite universal Truth which cuts across this multitude of worlds—in politics, this supposedly entails a "totalitarianism" which imposes its truth as universal. This is why we are told to reject, for example, the Jacobins, who imposed onto the manifold nature of French society their universal notions of equality and other truths, and thus necessarily ended in terror. So there is another version of the democratic-materialist axiom: "All that takes place in today's society is a consequence of the dynamic of postmodern globalization, or of the (conservative-nostalgic, fundamentalist, old leftist, nationalist, religious ...) reactions and resistances to it"—to which materialist dialectics adds its proviso: "with the exception of the radical-emancipatory (communist) politics of truth."

Of course, the only way for us to articulate this truth is within language—by way of torturing language. As Hegel already knew, when we think, we think in

---

proposition should be valid for anyone who repeats the same experiment. The moment we have to include the subject's position of enunciation, we are no longer in science, but in a discourse of wisdom or initiation.

24 Balmès, *Ce que Lacan dit de l'être*, pp. 211–13. Here we can also establish a link with Meillassoux's version of speculative materialism: the scientific mathematized Real is outside the transcendental correlation of logos and being. See Quentin Meillassoux, *After Finitude*, London: Continuum 2008.

language against language. This brings us back to Benjamin: could we not apply his distinction between mythic violence and divine violence to the two modes of violence we were dealing with? The violence of language to which Heidegger refers is "mythic violence": it is a *sprach-bildende Gewalt*, a language-forming violence, to paraphrase Benjamin's definition of mythic violence as *staats-bildend*—the force of *mythos* as primordial narrativization or symbolization, or, to put it in Badiou's terms, the violent imposition of the transcendental coordinates of a World onto the multiplicity of Being. The violence of thinking (and of poetry, if we understand it differently from Heidegger) is, on the contrary, a case of what Benjamin calls "divine violence," it is *sprach-zerstoerend*, a language-destroying twisting of language that enables the trans-symbolic Real of a Truth to transpire in it. The rehabilitation of Descartes is thus only a first step: it should be followed with a rehabilitation of Plato.

Furthermore, the answer to Benjamin's question with which we began is not simply negative. There *is* a "language" which is outside violence, but Benjamin looks for it in the wrong place. It is not the language of peaceful communication among subjects, but the language of pure mathematics, this joyful study of multiplicities. Should we still call it language? Lacan's answer was no: he played with terms like "matheme" or "writing."

An alternative Heidegger

This excess of the *cogito* over its historicization also enables us to approach in a new way the ambiguous status of Evil in Heidegger. In his seminar on Schelling's "Treatise on Freedom," Heidegger has to admit a dimension of radical Evil which cannot be historicized, that is, reduced to the nihilism of modern technology. It is to the merit of Bret Davis that he has analyzed in detail this deadlock in Heidegger's thought.

The period between *Being and Time* and the Nietzsche seminars of the late 1930s was Heidegger's most productive period of research when, having accepted the ultimate failure of his original project, he began looking for a new beginning. Presenting the conclusion of this search in the Nietzsche seminars, Heidegger established his "grand narrative" of the history of the West as the history of the oblivion of Being, and it was only at this point that he historicized Will as the defining feature of modern subjectivity and its violent nihilism.[25] It is against this background that accounts of Heidegger's engagement with Nazism are usually given, an engagement most palpable in "On the Essence and Concept

25 In his *Ereignis* seminar of 1937, which is usually taken as the beginning of his "mature" late thought, Heidegger still speaks of the "will to *Ereignis*," an expression unthinkable a couple of years later.

of Nature, History, and State," Heidegger's seminar of the winter semester of 1933–4, in which he was still captivated by the nihilist decisionism of the Will.

The starting point (axiom, even) for our reading is that a certain dimension which opened up another potential path was lost in the elaboration of what one is tempted to call late Heideggerian orthodoxy. It is thus important to return to Heidegger's texts between *Being and Time* and the Nietzsche seminars and treat them not just as transitional works, but as containing a potential which became invisible with the establishment of the orthodoxy. True, in some sense, these texts remain Heidegger's "lowest point," more or less coinciding with his Nazi involvement. Our thesis, however, is that these same texts open up possibilities which point in an entirely different direction, towards a radical emancipatory politics. Although not pursued by Heidegger himself, these possibilities haunt his texts of the 1930s as an ominous spectral shadow.

In the US presidential elections of 2000, Al Gore, who it was generally thought would win, unexpectedly lost to George W. Bush (as a result of the electoral debacle in Florida). In the years following, Gore often ironically referred to himself as "the guy who was once the future US president"—a case of the future logged into the past, of something that was to-come but which unfortunately did not come. In the same way, the Heidegger of the mid-1930s "was a future communist": his involvement with the Nazis was not a simple mistake, but rather a "right step in the wrong direction," for Heidegger cannot be simply dismissed as a German *volkisch*-reactionary.[26]

Let us then take a closer look at "On the Essence and Concept of Nature, History, and State."[27] Heidegger's starting point involves an immediate transposition of the ontological difference between an entity (*Seiendes*) and its Being (*Sein*) onto the relationship between a people and its state: the state is "a way of Being and a kind of Being of the people. The people is the entity whose Being is the state." This gesture may appear problematic from within Heidegger's own field: is the state really a name for the Being of a people, for the ontological horizon of how a meaning of Being is disclosed to a people? Is the state not rather a set of ontic institutions and practices? If the state is the Being of a people, then "it is after all impossible to consider the people without a state—the entity without its Being, in a certain sense." Does this mean that those peoples

26 Even at the superficial political level, we now know that Heidegger followed the student revolt of the late 1960s with great sympathy, greeted Willy Brandt's electoral victory enthusiastically, and, after World War II, more or less consistently voted for the Social Democrats.

27 The quotes that follow are from the manuscript of this seminar from 1933/1934. See Martin Heidegger, "Über Wesen und Begriff von Natur, Geschichte und Staat," in *Heidegger-Jahrbuch, Vol. 4: Heidegger und der Nationalsozialismus I*, Freiburg: Karl Alber 2010.

which do not have a state are excluded from the history of Being? It is interesting to note here how, in contrast to the usual perception of him as an advocate of provincial life, Heidegger clearly opposes homeland to fatherland:

> The homeland is not to be confused with the fatherland. We can speak of the state only when to groundedness is added the will to expansion, or generally speaking, interaction. A homeland is something I have on the basis of my birth. There are quite particular relations between me and it in the sense of nature, in the sense of natural forces. Homeland expresses itself in groundedness and being bound to the earth. But nature works on the human being, grounds him, only when nature belongs as an environment, so to speak, to the people whose member that human being is. The homeland becomes the way of Being of a people only when the homeland becomes expansive, when it interacts with the outside—when it becomes a state. For this reason, peoples or their subgroups who do not step out beyond their connection to the homeland into their authentic way of Being—into the state—are in constant danger of losing their peoplehood and perishing. This is also the great problem of those Germans who live outside the borders of the Reich: they do have a German homeland, but they do not belong to the state of the Germans, the Reich, so they are deprived of their authentic way of Being.

Remember that these lines were delivered in 1934—do they not imply that the way to resolve this "great problem" is to *annex* to the Reich the homeland of those Germans living outside the German state, and thus to enable them to fully participate in their "authentic way of Being" (i.e., what Hitler actually did a couple of years later)? Heidegger continues with his analysis: what happens to a people (*Volk*) when it decides to form a state? "We should further inquire into what we understand by 'people,' since, in the French Revolution, the answer was also: the people." (Note the negative tone: we should inquire further, since it is sure that we do not mean "people" in the sense of the French Revolution.) In the "decision for a state," a people determines itself by way of deciding for a certain kind of state, or, to paraphrase the well-known proverb: tell me what kind of a state a people has, and I will tell you what kind of people it is. Humans have consciousness; they not only interact with things like animals, they care about them, knowingly relate to them. Members of a people thus know and care about their state, they will it. For a people, their state is not just an instrument of their welfare, but a thing that matters, a thing they love and are ready to sacrifice themselves for, an object of their *eros*. The constitution of a state is not just a matter of rational consideration and negotiation, of a social contract which regulates the welfare of individuals, but a commitment to a vision of shared life.

If, then, the people is the entity which is in the mode and way of the state, we should further specify the question: "What kind of shape or imprint does the people make on the state, and the state on the people?" Heidegger rejects the first answer, the shape of an organism, as missing the specifically human dimension; the same holds for the general answer: "order," since any objects, books, stones, can also be arranged in an order. "However, what does provide an appropriate answer is order in the sense of domination, rank, leadership and following [*Herrschaft, Rang, Führung und Gefolgschaft*]. What remains open here is: who dominates?" In its authentic mode, the relationship of domination and following is grounded in a common will, in a commitment to a shared goal: "Only where the leader and those led by him are brought together in one destiny [*Schicksal*] and struggle for the realization of one idea, does a true order grow." Where this shared commitment which grounds the readiness to fight is lacking, domination turns into exploitation and order is enforced, externally imposed upon the people. This is what happens in the modern liberal epoch: the state order is reduced to an abstract notion of order, the state becomes Hobbes's Leviathan imposed on the people as the agent of absolute sovereignty which, instead of expressing the deepest will of the people, monopolizes all violence and acts as the force of law constraining the will of individuals. Only after domination is reduced to sovereignty does the French Revolution become possible, in which sovereign power is transferred to the opposite pole of the social order, to the people: "The essence of the French Revolution can be properly understood and explained only from the principle of sovereignty in absolutism, as its counter-phenomenon."

In Germany itself, the living unity of the state and the people began to disintegrate with Bismarck:

> We have heard that a people, in addition to needing a leader, also needs a tradition that is carried on by a political nobility. The Second Reich fell prey to an irreparable collapse after Bismarck's death, and not only because Bismarck failed to create this political nobility. He was also incapable of regarding the proletariat as a phenomenon that was justified in itself, and to lead it back into the state by reaching out to it with understanding.

To the obvious counter-argument that, in Bismarck's Germany, the Junkers continued to play a much larger public role than in other European states and, furthermore, that Bismarck precisely did "reach out" to the proletariat with the first elements of a welfare state (social insurance, etc.), Heidegger would have probably answered that Bismarck's Germany was a modern authoritarian-bureaucratic state *par excellence*. In absolutism as well as in liberal democracy, the unity of will between the leader and the people is thus lost: the state moves between the two extremes, sovereign absolute power experienced by the people as an external authority, and the service or instrument of civil society, fulfilling tasks necessary for the smooth running of social life in which individuals follow their own interests. In both cases, the authentic expression of the people's will by their leader is unthinkable:

> The question of the consciousness of the will of the community is a problem in all democracies, a problem which can only become fertile when the will of the leader and the will of the people are recognized in their essential character. Our task today is to direct the basic relationship of our communal being towards this actuality of people and leader, where the two are one in actuality, since they cannot be separated.

What is there to add to these lines, spoken in 1934, to explain why Heidegger endorsed the Nazi takeover? Do we not have here a rather simplistic conservative-authoritarian vision which is not even very original, since it fits perfectly the standard coordinates of the conservative-national reaction to the Weimar republic? Indeed, the only open question here seems to be where, precisely, we should locate Heidegger on the spectrum delineated by the two extremes of committed Nazism and political naïveté: was Heidegger (as Emmanuel Faye claims) a fully fledged Nazi, did he directly "introduce Nazism into philosophy," or was he simply politically naïve, becoming caught up in a political game with no direct links to his thought? I propose to follow a different line: neither to assert a direct link between Heidegger's thought and Nazism, nor to emphasize the gap that divides them (that is, to sacrifice Heidegger as a naïve or corrupt person in order to save the purity of his thought), but to transpose this gap into the heart of his thought itself, to demonstrate how the space for the Nazi engagement was opened up by the immanent failure or inconsistency of his thought, by the jumps and passages which are "illegitimate" in terms of this thought itself. In any serious philosophical analysis, external critique has to be grounded in immanent critique: hence we must show how Heidegger's external failure (his Nazi involvement) reflects the fact that he fell short as measured by his own aims and standards.

From will to drive

Such an immanent critique of Heidegger has a long history, beginning with the early Habermas's attempt to think "Heidegger against Heidegger." There are many other pertinent readings along these lines—suffice it to mention Jean-Luc Nancy's observation that, already in *Being and Time*, Heidegger strangely leaves out the analytic of *Mit-Sein* as a dimension constitutive of *Dasein*. Our starting point will be a different one, focusing on a feature that cannot but strike the reader of Heidegger's texts of the 1930s, and especially of the seminar "On the

Essence and Concept of Nature, History, and State": the preponderance of the topic of the *Will.* The homeland and the fatherland differ in that only the latter implies the state, while the former is a mere "province," a distinction which relies on the fact that "province" stands for a passive rootedness in a particular soil and set of customs, while the state implies an active will to expansion and confrontation with neighboring peoples. The province thus lacks political will proper, in contrast to the state, which is grounded in political will. Heidegger's (in)famous short text from 1934, "Why Do I Stay in the Provinces?" (in which he explains his refusal to accept a university post in Berlin with reference to a rather ridiculous figure of the "subject supposed to know," a simple farmer who, after Heidegger asked him for advice, responded only with a shake of his head) thus takes on an unexpected prophetic dimension, pointing towards Heidegger's later advocacy of the province as the site of authentic being over the state as the domain of will to power and domination.

How, then, should we interpret this strange persistence of the Will which continues to haunt Heidegger not only through the 1930s, but even later, when its overcoming becomes the very focus of his thought? In his detailed study on this topic, Bret Davis proposes a twofold reading of this persistence: first, as a sign of "*Gelassenheit* as an unfinished project," an indication that Heidegger did not succeed in thoroughly "deconstructing" the Will, so that it is up to us, who continue in his path, to accomplish the job and draw all the consequences from *Gelassenheit*; second, as necessitating a distinction "between (1) what Heidegger calls 'the will' of subjectivity, a fundamental (dis)attunement that has risen up and prevailed in a particular epochal history of metaphysics, and (2) what we have (interpretively supplementing Heidegger) called 'ur-willing,' a non-historical dissonant excess which haunts the proper essence of non-willing."[28] Recall how, in his reading of the fragment of Anaximander on order and disorder, Heidegger considers the possibility that an entity

> may even insist [*bestehen*] upon its while solely to remain more present, in the sense of perduring [*Bestaendigen*].That which lingers persists [*beharrt*] in its presencing. In this way it extricates itself from its transitory while. It strikes the wilful pose of persistence, no longer concerning itself with whatever else is present. It stiffens—as if this were the only way to linger—and aims solely for continuance and subsistence.[29]

28 Bret W. Davis, *Heidegger and the Will: On the Way to Gelassenheit*, Evanston: Northwestern University Press 2007, p. 303.

29 As quoted in ibid., pp. 286–7; translation from Martin Heidegger, "The Anaximander Fragment," in *Early Greek Thinking*, trans. David Farrell Krell and Frank A. Capuzzi, New York: Harper & Row 1984, p. 42.

Davis's thesis is that this "rebellious whiling" refers to a non-historical ur-willing, a willing which is not limited to the epoch of modern subjectivity and its will to power.[30] But one should here raise a more fundamental question: is the Will the proper name for the "stuckness" which derails the natural flow? Is the not Freudian drive (the death drive) a much more appropriate name? The standard philosophical critique of the Freudian drive is that it is another version of the post-Hegelian "Will" first developed by the late Schelling and Schopenhauer and which reached its highest formulation in Nietzsche. Is this the case, however?

A reference to the use of sound in film might be of some help here. Recall the remarkable scene at the beginning of Sergio Leone's *Once Upon a Time in America*, in which we see a phone ringing loudly, but when a hand picks up the receiver, the ringing goes on—as if the musical life force of the sound is too strong to be contained by reality and persists beyond its limitations. Or recall a similar scene from David Lynch's *Mulholland Drive*, in which a performer sings Roy Orbison's "Crying" on stage, but when she collapses unconscious, the song goes on. Therein resides the difference between the Schopenhauerian Will and the Freudian (death) drive: while the Will is the substance of life, its productive presence, in excess over its representations or images, the drive is *a persistence which goes on even when the Will disappears or is suspended*: the insistence which persists even when it is deprived of its living support, the appearance which persists even when it is deprived of its substance. One has to be very precise here in order not to miss Lacan's point (and thereby confuse desire and drive): the drive is not an infinite longing for the Thing which gets fixated onto a partial object—the "drive" *is* this fixation itself in which resides the "death" dimension of every drive. The drive is not a universal thrust (towards the incestuous Thing) which brakes and is then broken up, it *is* this brake itself, a brake on instinct, its "stuckness," as Eric Santner would say.[31] The elementary matrix of the drive is not one of transcending all particular objects towards the void of the Thing (which is then accessible only in its metonymic stand-in), but that of our libido getting "stuck" on a particular object, condemned to circulate around it forever.

In trying to designate the excess of the drive, its too-muchness, one often resorts to the term "animality": what Deleuze called the "becoming-animal" (*le devenir-animal*) of a human being, rendered in an exemplary way in some of Kafka's stories. The paradox here is that one uses the term "animality" for the fundamental movement of overcoming animality itself, the working over of animal instincts—the drive is not instinct but its "denaturalization." There

30 For a closer analysis of the vicissitudes of the Will in Heidegger's development, see Chapter 3 of Slavoj Žižek, *In Defense of Lost Causes*, London: Verso Books 2008.

31 See Eric Santner, *On the Psychotheology of Everyday Life*, Chicago: University of Chicago Press 2001.

is, however, a deeper logic to this paradox: from within the established human universe of meaning, its own founding gesture is invisible, indiscernible from its opposite, so that it has to appear as its opposite. This, in simple terms, is the basic difference between psychoanalysis and Christianity: while both agree that the life of the "human animal" is disrupted by the violent intrusion of a properly meta-physical "immortal" dimension, psychoanalysis identifies this dimension as that of (specifically [in]human) sexuality, of the "undead" drive as opposed to the animal instinct, while Christianity sees in sexuality the very force which drags humans towards animality and prevents their access to immortality. Such is the unbearable "news" of psychoanalysis: not its emphasis on the role of sexuality as such, but its rendering visible the "meta-physical" dimension of human sexuality. The paradox of Christianity is that, in order to uphold its edifice, it has to violently suppress this meta-physical dimension of sexuality, to reduce it to animality. In other words, this violent de-spiritualization of the key dimension of being-human is the "truth" of the Christian elevation of human spirituality. Unfortunately, Hegel does the same in his theory of marriage—as does Heidegger too.

The standard idealist question "Is there (eternal) life after death?" should be countered by the materialist question: "Is there life before death?" This is the question Wolf Biermann asked in one of his songs—what bothers a materialist is: am I really alive here and now, or am I just vegetating, as a mere human animal bent on survival? When am I really alive? Precisely when I enact the "undead" drive in me, the "too-much-ness" of life. And I reach this point when I no longer act directly, but when "it" (*es*)—whose Christian name is the Holy Spirit—acts through me. At this point, I reach the Absolute.

The next, and crucial, step is to see how this "stuckness" is not just a consequence of our human deficiency or finitude, of our inability to grasp pure Being from our partial perspective (if it were, then the solution would lie in a kind of Oriental self-effacement, an immersion in the primordial Void); rather, this "stuckness" bears witness to a strife at the very heart of Being itself. Deeply pertinent here is Gregory Fried's reading of Heidegger's entire opus through the interpretive lense of his reference to Heraclitus's *polemos* (struggle—in German, *Krieg*, *Kampf*, or, predominantly in Heidegger, *Auseinandersetzung*) from the latter's famous fragment 53: "War is both father of all and king of all: it reveals the gods on the one hand and humans on the other, makes slaves on the one hand, the free on the other."[32] It is not only that the stable identity of each entity is temporary, that they all sooner or later disappear, disintegrate, return to the primordial chaos; their (temporary) identity itself emerges through struggle, for stable identity is something that must be gained through an ordeal—even "class

32 See Gregory Fried, *Heidegger's Polemos: From Being to Politics*, New Haven: Yale University Press 2000.

struggle" is already present here, in the guise of the war which "makes slaves on the one hand, the free on the other."

There is, however, a further step to be taken with regard to *polemos*: it is easy to posit struggle as "father of all" and then elevate this struggle itself into a higher harmony, in the sense that Being becomes the hidden concord of the struggling poles, like a cosmic music in which the opposites harmoniously echo each other. So, to put it bluntly, is this strife part of the Harmony itself, or is it a more radical discord, one which derails the very Harmony of Being? As Davis perceptively notes, Heidegger is ambiguous here, oscillating between the radically open "strife" of Being and its reinscription into the teleological reversal of Danger into Saving in which, as Jean-Luc Nancy put it, "'discord' is at best what makes 'unity appear'":[33]

> Is being a fugue into which all dissonance is in the end necessarily harmonized? Or does evil haunt the gift of being as its non-sublatable dissonant excess? If the former idea pulls Heidegger's thought back towards the systematicity of idealism, the latter suggestion draws him into the uncharted region of thinking the essential negativity and finitude of being itself.[34]

Note how the same reproach that Heidegger directed at Schelling recoils back onto Heidegger himself: for Heidegger, Schelling was unable to "inextricably inscribe non-sublatable negativity and finitude into the abyssal heart of being itself,"[35] that is, to accept that the *Unwesen* of evil

> is no longer that of either an inessential or dialectically necessary alienation from an original plenum; it is an originary dissonant excess of the essencing of being itself. The ambivalent occurrence of being in its essential finitude entails the ineradicable possibility of evil.[36]

This option raises an even more vertiginous series of questions: What if there is *stricto sensu* no world, no disclosure of being, prior to this "stuckness"? What if there is no *Gelassenheit* which is disturbed by the excess of willing? What if it is this very excess or stuckness which opens up the space for *Gelassenheit*? The primordial fact is then not the fugue of Being (or the inner peace of *Gelassenheit*), which is later disturbed or perverted by the rise of ur-willing; the primordial fact is this ur-willing itself, its disturbance of the "natural" fugue. Put another way:

---

33 Jean-Luc Nancy, *The Experience of Freedom*, trans. Bridget McDonald, Palo Alto: Stanford University Press 1993, pp. 131–2.

34 Davis, *Heidegger and the Will*, p. 294.

35 Ibid., p. 291.

36 Ibid.

in order for a human being to withdraw from full immersion in its environment into the inner peace of *Gelassenheit*, this immersion has first to be broken by way of the excessive "stuckness" of the drive. Davis talks frequently about the "residue" of the will—an expression which cannot but remind us of Schelling's "indivisible remainder" of the Real which cannot be dissolved or resolved in its ideal or notional mediation. The conclusion to be drawn from this is that we must reverse the entire perspective and perceive the "residue" itself as constitutive of the very positive order it smears, perceive the will not just as an irreducible obstacle, but as a positive condition of *Gelassenheit*.

Heidegger's relation to Schelling is crucial here: his two consecutive readings of the latter's treatise on freedom play the same symptomal role as do his two consecutive readings of the chorus from *Antigone*—in both cases, the second reading is a "regression," failing to resolve the creative tension of the first. According to Heidegger, the uniqueness of Schelling was to try to elaborate a "system of freedom" as a "metaphysics of evil": for Schelling, freedom is not abstract idealist freedom, freedom of the unconstrained deployment of Reason, but the concrete freedom of a living human being caught up in the tension between Good and Evil, and the possibility of such utterly contingent actual Evil cannot be justified in the terms of the systematicity of the Absolute. What Schelling was not ready to do was fully endorse the abyss of freedom by abandoning the idealist-systematic frame and accepting human finitude and temporality as our unsurpassable horizon.

But what if it is precisely this idealist-systematic frame of the Absolute which enables Schelling to make his most radical step, that of grounding human freedom in the *Verrücktheit* (madness/inversion) of the Absolute itself? The moment we abandon the frame of the Absolute and enter the space of post-Hegelian finitude—where, as the story goes, we are dealing "not with abstractions, embodied notions, but with concrete living individuals, their pain and struggles"—the fundamental Schellingian question "How is the Absolute to be structured in order to render human freedom thinkable?" becomes meaningless. In Lacanese, within this horizon of finitude, only alienation (of humanity from itself, from its potential, etc.) is thinkable, not separation (of the Absolute from itself). In Christian terms, only the overcoming of God's estrangement from man is thinkable, not the kenosis of God himself, his self-emptying and Incarnation. Schelling himself struggled with the radicality of his conclusion:

> it is entirely correct to say dialectically that good and evil are the same thing, only seen from different aspects, or evil in itself, i.e., viewed in the root of its identity, is the good; just as, on the other hand, the good, viewed in its division or non-identity, is evil ... there is only one principle for everything; it is one and the same essence ... that rules with the will of love and the good and with the will of wrath and evil ...

> Evil, however, is not an essence but a dissonant excess [*Unwesen*] which has reality only in opposition, but not in itself. And for this very reason absolute identity, the spirit of love, is prior to evil, because evil can appear only in opposition to it.[37]

But we should correct Schelling here: evil is ontologically prior to good because "evil" is the primordial dissonance or excess in the natural order of being, the "stuckness" or derailment of the natural run of things, and "good" is the secondary (re)integration of this excess. It is *Unwesen* which creates the space for the appearance of a *Wesen*, or, in Hegelese: Good is self-sublated (universalized) Evil. So why was Heidegger not ready to go to the end here? What lurks behind here is, of course, the figure of Hölderlin. Both Hölderlin and Heidegger deploy the same apocalyptic-eschatological logic in which history culminates in total danger and devastation: in order to gain salvation, one must first pass through the greatest danger.[38] Of course, Heidegger's emphasis is on how this logic must be distinguished from the Hegelian "negation of the negation." But how does Heidegger distinguish his own notion of the "strife" at the heart of Being from the German Idealist notion of the negativity at the heart of the Absolute? One distinguishing feature is that, in German Idealism, negativity is a subordinate moment in the movement of the Idea's self-mediation, in the game that the Absolute plays with itself, merely giving its opposite-other enough rope to hang itself. In Hegel, according to Davis,

> Spirit reaches out to—or indeed posits out of itself—the other than itself only to cunningly bring this other back into its original sameness. Spirit needs this reincorporation of the other even at the risk of alienating itself from itself, sacrificing its initial solitary immediacy for the sake of the incorporative transformation of all otherness into a mediated and thus self-consciously self-identical totality.[39]

In spite of his breakthrough to the very edge of metaphysics, Schelling remains caught in the same trap: his definition of human freedom as the freedom for good and evil indicates a shift from the systematic Idealist self-development of

37 F. W. J. Schelling, "Philosophical Investigations into the Essence of Human Freedom and Related Matters," trans. Priscilla Hayden-Roy, in Ernst Behler, ed., *Philosophy of German Idealism*, London: Continuum 1987, pp. 270–1, 278–9.

38 Peter Koslowski proposed a variation of Fichte's famous thesis that the kind of philosophy one upholds depends on the kind of man one is: the kind of philosopher one is depends on the kind of theory of original sin (the Fall) one upholds. Does not the same hold today? For ecologists, the "original sin" is the Cartesian domination over a nature reduced to mechanical object; for Marxists, the Fall is the rise of class society; for Heideggerians, the Fall is the forgetting of the truth of Being, etc.

39 Davis, *Heidegger and the Will*, p. 171.

the Absolute to the radical existential openness of the actual finite human being. The status of this freedom, however, remains profoundly ambiguous:

> Does God's love let the ground operate for the sake of the most far-reaching revelation of his unconditional subjectivity—a self-revelation of absolute mastery that would require so much as the submission of "free slaves"? Or does this love intimate a letting-be that lets go of the will to closure of the system of the Absolute, of the very will to unconditional subjectivity itself?[40]

Ultimately, as Davis notes, Schelling opts for the second version:

> The will of love "lets the ground operate" in independence; it allows the insurgence of the will of the ground in order that, by ultimately subordinating this rebellious will of darkness to the order of light, it may manifest its own omnipotence. God lets man freely become the inverse god, so that the dissonance of evil may in the end serve as a foil for the sake of the revelation of the superior harmony of divine love.[41]

Because of this limitation, "Schelling's bold attempt to think a 'system of freedom' as a 'metaphysics of evil' in the end falls back into a 'systematicity' of the Absolute. Evil is required and justified for the sake of the revelation of the omnipotence of the divine will of love."[42] In contrast to Hegel and Schelling, so the argument goes, Heidegger's "strife" is not the cunning game of Being's self-mediation, but a genuinely "open" game in which nothing guarantees the outcome, since the strife is primordial and constitutive and there is no "reconciliation" that would abolish it. But is this scheme adequate? With regard to Hegel, it misses the key aspect of the dialectical process, the trans-substantiation which marks the dialectical reversal: the "sameness" to which the process returns after alienation is not "substantially the same" as the initial sameness, it is another Sameness which totalizes the dispersed moments. This is why alienation or negation is irreducible: what happens in the "negation of the negation" is the accomplishment of negation; in it, the immediate starting point is definitively lost. So there is no single Absolute Subject to cunningly play the game of self-alienation with itself—this subject emerges, is constituted, *through* alienation. Insofar as the starting point is the immediacy of nature, Spirit "returns to itself" in internalizing-itself from the externality of nature, and it *constitutes* itself through this "return to itself." Or, to put it in the traditional terms of Good versus Evil, the Hegelian Good is not the Absolute that mediates or sublates Evil, it is Evil itself which gets universalized and thus reappears as Good. Hegel's

40 Ibid., p. 120.
41 Ibid., p. 110.
42 Ibid., pp. 115–16.

vision here is even more radical than that of the "open" strife of Good and Evil: for him, this strife is inherent to Evil, it *is* Evil, and Good names merely the partial and fragile self-sublations of Evil.

THE NON-HISTORICAL CORE OF HISTORICITY

What we confront here is the problem of historicity at its most radical: a historicity which goes "all the way down" and cannot be reduced to the deployment or revelation in history of a non-historical Absolute. In a way, the true *Kehre* from *Sein und Zeit* to the late Heidegger is the shift from ahistorical formal-transcendental analysis to radical historicity.[43] To put it in (the not quite appropriate) terms of German Idealism, Heidegger's achievement is to elaborate a radically historicized transcendentalism: Heideggerian historicity is the historicity of transcendental horizons themselves, of the different modes of the disclosure of being, with no agent regulating the process—historicity happens as an *es gibt* (*il y a*), the radically contingent abyss of a world-game.[44]

This radical historicity reaches its definitive formulation with the shift from Being to *Ereignis*, which thoroughly undermines the idea of Being as a kind of super-subject of history, sending its messages or epochs to man. *Ereignis* means that Being is *nothing but* the *chiaroscuro* of these messages, *nothing but* the way it relates to man. Man is finite, and *Ereignis* also: the very structure of finitude, the play of Clearing or Concealment with nothing behind it. "It" is just the impersonal it, a "there is." There is an un-historical dimension at work here, but what is un-historical is the very formal structure of historicity itself.[45]

43 Attentive interpreters have noticed the multiplicity of meanings of Heidegger's *Kehre*; the three main ones are: (1) the shift in Heidegger's thought from Being to *Ereignis*; (2) the shift in the world-history of Being from technology to *Ereignis*; (3) the strife in *Ereignis* itself between it and its *Unwesen*, *Ent-Eignis*.

44 This is also why there is no place for the Lacanian Real in Heidegger's thought. The most concise definition of the Real is that it is a *given without givenness*: it is just given, with no possibility of accounting for its being-given by any agency of giving, even if it be the impersonal "*es gibt / il y a*," without a phenomenological horizon opening the space for it to appear. It is the impossible point of the ontic without the ontological.

45 Is not Heidegger's notion of epochal historicity a kind of reversal of the Kantian relationship between the transcendental a priori and the multiplicity of the matter unified by the transcendental frame? While in Kant, the transcendental frame is the universal trans-historical moment and the ontic the empirical multiplicity of changeable matter, in Heidegger, it is the transcendental frame (the disclosure of being) which is historical, changing with the epochs, and the ontic (the "Earth") which is the trans-historical "stuff" disclosed in different historical modes of its appearing. We can thus have the same "reality" which appears differently, which is differently disclosed, to people living in different historical periods.

It is this emphasis on radical historicity that forever separates Heidegger from so-called Oriental thought: in spite of the similarity of *Gelassenheit* to nirvana and so on, the attainment of the zero-level of nirvana is meaningless within the horizon of Heidegger's thought—it would mean something like doing away with all shadows of concealment.[46] Like Kafka's man from the country who learns that the Door is there for him only, *Dasein* has to experience how Being needs us, how our strife with Being is Being's strife with itself.

What Heidegger calls *Ereignis* is the event-arrival of Truth, of a new "hermeneutic" horizon within which beings appear as what they are—Being *is*, for Heidegger, the "Sense of Being." Heidegger's ontological difference is the difference between beings and their non-ontic horizon of meaning. Some readers interpret ontological difference in terms of essence versus existence—as the difference between *what* things are and the mere fact *that* they are—and point out that metaphysics overlooks this difference when it subordinates being to some essential entity (Idea, God, Subject, Will ...). But, as Heidegger makes clear in his "Letter on Humanism," such a Sartrean reversal which asserts the priority of existence over essence (recall Sartre's disturbing description of the inertia of senseless existence in his *Nausea*) remains within the confines of metaphysics. For Heidegger, the point of ontological difference is precisely that to draw such a line of separation between mere existence and its horizon of sense is impossible: radical historicity means that being is always already disclosed in a horizon of meaning, never as pure neutral being. So when Badiou writes that "a poem is not a guardian of being, as Heidegger thought, but the *exposition* in language of the resources of appearing," he is, from the Heideggerian standpoint, constructing a false and meaningless opposition: what Heidegger calls "Being" *is* the "truth of Being," the specific disclosure of a world as the horizon of appearing.[47] We can measure here the distance that separates Heidegger's notion of ontological difference from Badiou's:

> We know that Heidegger linked the destiny of metaphysics to the misunderstanding of the ontological difference which is thought as the difference between being and entities. If one interprets entities as the "there" of being, or as the worldly localization

---

46 When Heidegger speaks of the "concealment of concealment itself" or the "oblivion of oblivion," this should not be reduced to a double movement of first forgetting Being in our immersion in beings and then forgetting this forgetting itself: forgetting *is* always also a forgetting of forgetting itself, otherwise it is not forgetting at all—in this sense, as Heidegger put it, it is not only that Being withdraws itself, but Being is *nothing but* its own withdrawal. (Furthermore, concealment is a concealment of concealment in a much more literal way: what is concealed is not Being in its purity but the fact that concealment is part of Being itself.)

47 Alain Badiou, *Second manifeste pour la philosophie*, Paris: Fayard 2009, p. 39.

> of a pure multiple, or as the appearing of the multiple-being—which is in any case possible—one can say that what Heidegger calls ontological difference concerns the immanent gap between mathematics and logics. In order to follow Heidegger, it would thus be appropriate to call "metaphysics" every orientation of a thought which confounds under the same Idea mathematics and logics.[48]

A brief note of explanation: for Badiou, mathematics is the only true ontology, the science of Being as such, in itself, which consists of pure multiplicities of multiplicities against the background of a Void, while a logic is always the logic of a world, the immanent structure of the transcendental coordinates of a certain mode of appearing of entities. For Badiou, the multiplicity of worlds is irreducible, and there is no higher unifying matrix that would allow us to deduce one from the other, or to mediate them into a higher totality—therein resides the fateful limitation of Hegel's logic.

There is no place in Heidegger for such a notion of ontological difference: Heidegger's ontological difference is the difference between appearing entities and the ontological horizon of their appearing, and, from this perspective, entities outside their appearing are a pre-ontological X whose status is totally ambiguous and non-thematized.

A closer analysis reveals how the radical historicity embraced by the late Heidegger resolves a deadlock which had haunted the analysis of *Dasein* in *Sein und Zeit*, in which two couples echo each other without fully overlapping. First, there is the opposition between *Zuhanden* and *Vorhanden*, between being engaged in the world and adopting towards it the attitude of a disengaged observer, which is an ontologically secondary mode (we assume theoretical distance when things malfunction, when our engagement meets an obstacle). Then, we have the opposition between authentic *Dasein* and its *Verfallenheit* into "*das Man*," between choosing one's project through assuming one's mortality, and non-authentic obedience to the anonymous "this is what one does." How, exactly, are these two couples related? Obviously, they form a kind of semiotic square whose terms are disposed along the two axes of authentic versus inauthentic and engagement-in-the-world versus withdrawal-from-the-world: there are two modes of engagement, authentic being-in-the-world and inauthentic "das Man," and there are two modes of withdrawal, the authentic assumption of one's mortality through anxiety and the inauthentic distance of the subject towards objectivized "reality." The catch is, of course, that the two inauthentic modes overlap (partially, at least): inauthentic engagement involves technological manipulation in which subject stands opposed to "external reality."

Heidegger sometimes hints at a link between "das Man" and the reduction of things to *vorhandene* objects of theory; this, however, implies the standard

48 Ibid., p. 51.

doubtful presupposition that our most common *Verfallenheit* into "das Man" is structured by the metaphysical categories—almost a kind of the Hegelian infinite judgment, a coincidence of opposites: here, of the most vulgar and superficial following the predominant trend of what "one" is supposed to do and think, and of the high speculative and metaphysical efforts of the greatest Western thinkers from Plato to Hegel. The most succinct definition of modern technology is precisely that it paradoxically unites *Verfallenheit*, immersion in worldly affairs, the will to dominate, with theoretical distance: objects of technology are not *Zuhanden*, they are *Vorhanden*, technological Reason is theoretical, not practical.

The first task of *Sein und Zeit* is to provide a phenomenological description of the "immediacy of everyday *Dasein*," not yet contaminated by the traditional metaphysical categorical apparatus: where metaphysics talks about objects endowed with properties, a phenomenology of everyday life sees things which are always already ready-to-use, part of our engagement, components of a meaningful world-structure; where metaphysics talks about a subject who relates to the world, or is opposed to objects in the world, phenomenology sees a human being always already in the world, engaged with things, and so on. The idea here is that traditional metaphysics (which is to be "de(con)structed" by phenomenology) is a kind of secondary screen, an imposed network covering up the true structure of everyday life. The task is thus to dispense with the metaphysical prejudices and describe phenomena the way they are in themselves; however, since our predominant philosophical attitude is already deeply infected by metaphysics, such a pure phenomenological description is the most difficult task, requiring the hard work of ridding ourselves of traditional metaphysics. Heidegger thus searches for the conceptual apparatus that would sustain such a description in different sources, from Paulinian early Christianity to Aristotelian *phronesis*.

Heidegger's own life offers an ironic comment on this tension between the immediacy of everyday life and its metaphysical misreading: it seems that, in his final years at least, he returned to Catholicism, since he left instructions that he should be buried as a Catholic, with a Church funeral. So while in his philosophy he theorized the immediacy of pre-metaphysical life, in his everyday life he ultimately remained faithful to Christianity, which, in his theory, he had dismissed as the result of the Roman misreading of the original Greek disclosure of Being, as the key step in onto-theological forgetting of Being, and as a metaphysical-ontological screen obfuscating the immediacy of life. It is thus as if the terms had changed places: Heidegger's immediate life was metaphysically structured, while his theory opened up the structure of the immediacy of everyday life.

As we have seen, in the period that immediately followed *Sein und Zeit*, having reached an impasse in the project as planned, Heidegger for a couple of years searched desperately for a philosophical reference point that would enable him to re-found the project. Of greatest interest here are his two attempts to "repeat" Kant: in *Kant and the Problem of Metaphysics*, he referred to the transcendental imagination as the key to understanding the primordial temporalization of Being, while in 1930, he briefly explored the potential of the *Critique of Practical Reason*, interpreting the categorical imperative as "*the fundamental law of a finite pure willing.*"[49] The unique act of authentic decision, the choice of a project defining one's life—assumed when one reaches the border of death as the ultimate (im)possibility of a human life—is now interpreted in the Kantian terms of the subject's autonomy and self-legislating freedom, as the act of pure will which unilaterally determines the law of practical reason.

Heidegger was well aware that Kant would reject such a (re)formulation, since, from the standpoint of his universalist rationalism, it smacks too much of voluntaristic self-will: the pure practical will does not arbitrarily create its own law, it discovers it as the a priori transcendental structure of every ethical activity. For Heidegger, of course, it is Kant who remains within the confines of rationalist-universalist metaphysics, unable to think the finitude of human being. Davis, as one might expect, raises the suspicion that Heidegger's subordination of ethical will to a decisionism of historical contingency paved the way for Heidegger's Nazi engagement.

However, we need to be very precise here: the Kantian ethics of the autonomy of the will is not a "cognitive" ethics, an ethics of recognizing and following the moral Law which is already given. Heidegger is basically right in his reading of Kant: in an ethical act, I do not just follow my duty, I decide what my duty is. But it is precisely for *this* reason that Kant totally rejects any form of sacrificial "deferred willing," of deferring one's will to the will of the State or of a Leader: moral autonomy means precisely that I have to stand fully behind my duty, that I can never assume the perverse position of being the instrument of the Other's Will. The problem with Heidegger here is that, paradoxically, he is not "subjectivist-decisionist" enough: his early "decisionism" is all too much the obverse of responding to—following—a pre-ordained Destiny. Radical "subjectivism" (the insistence on the decision—and the responsibility for it—being absolutely mine) and universalism are not opposed, they are two aspects of the same position of singular universality; what both are opposed to is the particular historical Destiny of a community (a people). *This* is where the possibility of following Hitler arises: when we recognize in him not the voice of universal Reason, but the voice of a concrete historical Destiny of the German nation.

The great shift that occurs in Heidegger's thinking from the 1930s onwards lies in the radical historicization of this opposition: traditional metaphysics is no longer a false screen covering up the structure of everyday life, but the

49 Martin Heidegger, *The Essence of Human Freedom: An Introduction to Philosophy*, trans. Ted Sadler, London: Continuum 2005, p. 193.

elaboration of the epochal, historically specific, fundamental "attunement" which provides the structure for our lives. All great metaphysics ultimately *is* a phenomenological ontology of the historical "immediacy of everyday *Dasein*": Aristotle provided the ontology that structured the everyday experience of Greek citizens; the philosophy of modern subjectivity provides the structure of willing, domination, and "inner experience," which is the structure of our daily lives in modern dynamic capitalist societies. Stepping out of metaphysics is thus no longer just a matter of seeing through the obfuscating network and perceiving the true nature of everyday life, but a matter of historical change in the fundamental attunement of everyday life itself. The turn in philosophy from traditional metaphysics to post-metaphysical phenomenology is part of the world-historical turn (*Kehre*) in Being itself.

The naïve question to be asked here is this: how are figures like Meister Eckhart, Angelus Silesius, and Hölderlin possible, how are their intimations of a non-metaphysical dimension (of *Gelassenheit*, of *ohne Warum*, of the essence of poetry) possible in the space of such radicalized historicity? Do they not suggest "the possibility of a non-historical excess to the history of metaphysics, an excess which both critically calls into question the seamless rule of its epochs and affirmatively suggests the possibility of participating in a transition to an other beginning beyond the closure of metaphysics in the technological will to will"?[50] The same should be asked apropos everyday life: in our epoch of technology, is our daily life today fully determined by the epochal disclosure of *Gestell*, or is there something in our daily mores—encountering a work of art, wondering at beauty, a simple immersion in some activity—which resists technology? Heidegger seems to oscillate between the notion that such distantiations are always already included in technology (such as tourism, artistic consumption, etc., which allow us to recharge and then return with more energy to the technological universe) and the opposite idea that—since technology is not reducible to machines and so on, but is a way that Being is disclosed to us—one can continue to use technology at a distance, without being caught up in *Gestell* and reducing entities to material for technological manipulation:

> We can use technical devices, and yet with proper use also keep ourselves so free of them, that we may let go of them at any time ... let them alone as something which does not affect our most inner and proper being ... We let technical devices enter our daily life, and at the same time leave them outside ... I would call this comportment toward technology which expresses "yes" at the same time as "no," by an old word: releasement [*Gelassenheit*] toward things.[51]

50 Davis, *Heidegger and the Will*, p. 145.

51 Martin Heidegger, *Discourse on Thinking*, trans. John M. Anderson and E. Hans Freund, New York: Harper & Row 1966, p. 54.

Here we encounter Heidegger at his worst, perfectly fitting the "cool" postmodern attitude. The greatest Oriental wisdom is supposed to reside in the ability not to simply withdraw from the world, but to participate in its affairs with an inner distance, to "do it without doing it," without being really engaged in it. Ironically, this version of *Gelassenheit* finds its equivalent in today's expression "cool"—a "cool" person does everything with an air of indifference or inner distance.

From *Gelassenheit* to class struggle

The same tension between historicity and the a-historical dimension is at work also in the opposite of the Will, in *Gelassenheit*. *Gelassenheit* is not merely the name for man's non-historical proper attitude towards Being, it is also the name for the specific attunement that will follow the reign of technology; the Will is not only the name for the epoch of modern subjectivity, but also the name for an eternal temptation, possibility of *Unwesen*, that is part of the humanity of man. More precisely, *Gelassenheit* works at three levels of temporality: it is always already here as constitutive of being-human; it is to come as the predominant attitude with the other beginning after the Turn; it is here and now as a possibility that each of us can actualize in our attitude and behavior, thus preparing the way for the other beginning.[52] How are we to resolve the ambiguity of Heidegger's attempt to go through metaphysics: is the goal to reach its hidden beginnings, or to move beyond it to a radically new beginning, the "other beginning" which leaves behind the entire history of metaphysics? Note that a homologous ambiguity is at work in Derrida, who often varies the motif that the end of the "age of the sign" is discernible on the horizon; although this age will perhaps never pass, we will never leave it behind: today, the metaphysics of presence has reached closure, but still we will never be able to step out of it. The entire deadlock of "deconstruction" is condensed in this strange temporality of the endlessly postponed (deferred) consummation of the end of metaphysics, as if we are condemned to dwell endlessly in the limbo of the time of the end of (metaphysical) time. This, perhaps more than democracy, is the true Derridean "to-come" (*à venir*): always to come, never fully here.[53] There are basically only

52 Even the words Heidegger uses to describe the outlines of the "new beginning" often rely on hidden homologies with metaphysics: *das Geviert*—the Four-Fold of earth, sky, humans, and gods—is his version of the Aristotelian four causes: earth is the material cause, sky (the Apollonian form) the formal cause, humans as agents the efficient cause, and the gods the final cause.

53 Derrida strictly opposes his "to-come ..." to the Kantian regulative Idea: the to-come implies an unconditional urgency to act now and is, as such, the very opposite of adopting a gradual approach to an inaccessible Ideal. However, there are two counter-points to be

two ways to resolve this deadlock. Either the exit out of metaphysics is in itself a wrong (metaphysical) notion, so that this dwelling in the end of time is the only non-metaphysical position available; or one *defines metaphysics itself as the desire to exit a field of containment*, so that, paradoxically, the only way to truly exit metaphysics is to renounce this desire, to fully endorse one's containment. How then are we to get out of this impasse? A reference to Kierkegaard is pertinent here: the New is Repetition, one can only retrieve the first Beginning by way of a new one which brings out the lost potential of the first.

If this is the case, however, what happens with radical historicity—radical in the sense that Being is *nothing but* the events of the epochal history of being, that there is no substantial Being behind this that only partially discloses itself in the game of disclosure or withdrawal?

> Being itself is "finite" or "historical" in the sense that it "is" only as the temporal events of revealing/concealing. The history of being is, on the one hand, the continuity of an increasing withdrawal of being (and the corresponding rise of the will), and yet, on the other hand, being is nothing but this (dis)continuous movement of revealing/concealing, granting-in-withdrawal.[54]

Shall we say then that history is nothing but the epochal deployment of the strife/"negativity" in Being itself? That the modern Will to power is nothing but a historical actualization of a potential that dwells in the non-historical structure of Being itself?

> The non-historical must be seen as inseparably interwoven with the historical, rather than as independently set over against it. In fact, it is only when we fall into historicism (in the sense of historical relativism) that any suggestion of the non-historical can only be heard as a failure to think historicity.[55] Heidegger's *radical* thinking of historicity, on the other hand, demands that we also think its relation to the non-historical. However, the non-historical ... "is" only in and through its historical determinations.[56]

---

made here. First, this urgency is there already in Kant, who should not be set up as a straw man. Second, Derrida necessarily oscillates here between this urgency of acting in the moment and the gap that separates each act (as a contingent intervention) from the spectral idea of Justice.

54 Davis, *Heidegger and the Will*, p. 266.

55 Take historicism at its most radical: today's anti-essentialist discourse theories (Butler, Laclau) which account for every "stable" formation, up to and including our sexual identities and nature itself, as an effect of contingent articulations—the ensuing vision of history is that of a flat, ahistorical, "eternal present" in which the game of re-articulation goes on and on.

56 Davis, *Heidegger and the Will*, p. 208.

The conclusion to be drawn is clear: if being is nothing but the movement of its revealing or disclosure, then the "forgetting of being" is also and above all self-relating, the forgetting or withdrawal of this historical play of revealing and withdrawal itself. And if we take this into account, then "the other beginning would not be a complete eradication of the problem of willing, but rather a vigilant opening to it, a watchful recognition of the finitude of our selves caught between this problem of willing and the possibility of non-willing."[57]

We should note here the invocation of vigilance, which occurs a couple of times in Davis's book, such as on page 280 ("would the other beginning be a time where non-willing, or at least decisive or incisive moments thereof, would be made possible precisely through a vigilant openness to a certain never-finally-eradicable problem of 'willing'?"), on page 282, and again on page 286: "The other beginning would, in that case, not only entail an attunement to the harmonious play of ek-sistence/in-sistence, but also a vigilant recognition of the impulse to persistence, an impulse which, when left unchecked, would pull one back towards wilful subjectivity." But the term "vigilance" is extremely problematic here: not only is "vigilance" a willing attitude par excellence, so that we arrive at the pragmatic paradox of "willingly watch over our willingness"; more radically even, if what is concealed in the withdrawal of being is ultimately the very game of revealing or concealing, then is not the "vigilant" attitude of watching over forgetfulness *the very source of the problem* (in the same way that the absolute striving towards the Good is the very source of Evil)?

To avoid such paradoxes, we have to make a choice: either we take the "impulse to persistence" as a kind of eternal temptation of the human mind akin to Kantian "radical evil" as the tendency to "fall" inscribed into the very human condition, or we fully assert this "fall" (the "rebellious whiling" which throws out of joint the flow of reality) as the grounding gesture of being-human. With regard to politics, this changes everything. The first change concerns the status of the *polemos* constitutive of politics. Does not Heidegger's idea that the order implied by the state is the order of domination and servitude strangely recall the classical Marxist notion of the state as strictly linked to the division of society into classes? So when Heidegger, in his reading of Heraclitus's fragment 53, insists on how the "struggle meant here is originary struggle, for it allows those who struggle to originate as such in the first place," is not class struggle, within the political, the name of this struggle constitutive of those who struggle, and not just a conflict between pre-existing social agents?[58] Recall here the lesson of Louis Althusser: "class struggle" paradoxically *precedes* classes as determinate

57 Ibid., p. 279.

58 Martin Heidegger, *Introduction to Metaphysics*, trans. Gregory Fried and Richard Polt, New Haven: Yale University Press 2000, p. 65.

social groups, for every class position and determination is already an effect of the "class struggle." (This is why "class struggle" is another name for the fact that "society does not exist"—it does not exist as a positive order of entities.) In other words, we should always bear in mind that, for a true Marxist, "classes" are *not* categories of positive social reality, parts of the social body, but categories of the Real of a political struggle which cuts across the entire social body, preventing its "totalization."

However, Heidegger ignores such a reading of the *polemos* as the struggle between those who dominate and those who serve them: if the homeland "becomes the way of Being of a people only when the homeland becomes *expansive*, when it *interacts with the outside*—when it becomes a state," then it is clear that the *polemos* is primarily the strife with the *external* enemy. No wonder that, when Heidegger elaborates the essence of the political, he sympathetically compares his notion of the political with two other notions: Bismarck's idea of politics as the art of the possible (not just opportunistic strategic calculation, but the leader's ability to grasp the "essential possibility" offered by a historical constellation and to mobilize the people for it), and Carl Schmitt's idea of the antagonistic friend/enemy relationship—that is, the tension with the *external* enemy—as the defining feature of the political.

The paradox is that (as in the case of sexual difference) Heidegger ignores the properly ontological status of class struggle as a strife or antagonism which cannot be reduced to an ontic conflict, since it overdetermines the horizon of appearance of all ontic social entities. It is class struggle (social antagonism), not the state, which is the mode of Being of a people—the state is there to obfuscate this antagonism. Such a radicalized notion of the *polemos* as class struggle brings us to the second change, closely linked with the first: another way to approach the "question of the consciousness of the will of the community" as "a problem in all democracies." Heidegger's idea of political commitment involves the unity of a people and the leader who mobilizes them in a shared struggle against an (external) enemy, bringing them all together ("accepting" even the proletariat). If, however, we take class struggle as the *polemos* constitutive of political life, then the problem of the common political will appears in a radically different way: how to build the collective will of the oppressed in the class struggle, the emancipatory will which takes the class *polemos* to its extreme. (And was this will not at work already in Ancient Greek democracy, was it not operative at the very core of the Athenian *polis*?) This collective will is the crucial component of communism, which

> seeks to enable the conversion of work into will. Communism aims to complete the transition, via the struggle of collective self-emancipation, from a suffered necessity to autonomous self-determination. It is the deliberate effort, on a world-historical

> scale, to universalize the material conditions under which free voluntary action might prevail over involuntary labour or passivity. Or rather: communism is the project through which voluntary action seeks to universalize the conditions for voluntary action.[59]

Exemplary cases of such activity can be found in

> people like Robespierre, Toussaint L'Ouverture or John Brown: confronted with an indefensible institution like slavery, when the opportunity arose they resolved to work immediately and by all available means for its elimination. Che Guevara and Paulo Freire would do the same in the face of imperialism and oppression. Today Dr. Paul Farmer and his "Partners in Health," in Haiti, Chile and elsewhere, adopt a somewhat similar approach when confronted by indefensible inequalities in the global provision of healthcare. In each case the basic logic is as simple as could be: an idea, like the idea of communism, or equality, or justice, commands that we should strive to realize it without compromises or delay, before the means of such realization have been recognized as feasible or legitimate, or even "possible." It is the deliberate striving towards realization itself that will convert the impossible into the possible, and explode the parameters of the feasible.[60]

Such collective activity realizes the "actuality of people and leader, where the two are one actuality, since they cannot be separated." Along these lines, Badiou recently proposed a rehabilitation of the revolutionary communist "cult of personality": the real of a Truth-Event is inscribed into the space of symbolic fiction through a proper name (of a leader)—Lenin, Stalin, Mao, Che Guevara.[61] Far from signaling the corruption of a revolutionary process, the celebration of the leader's proper name is immanent to that process: to put it in somewhat crude terms, without the mobilizing role of a proper name, the political movement remains caught in the positive order of Being rendered by the conceptual categories—it is only through the intervention of a proper name that the dimension of "demanding the impossible," of changing the very contours of what appears as possible, arises.

What if this "essential possibility" of communism, ignored by Heidegger himself, and not Heidegger's continuing hidden fidelity to fascism, is the truth of his ill-famed doubts about democracy in his posthumously published *Der*

---

59 Peter Hallward, "Communism of the Intellect, Communism of the Will," in Costas Douzinas and Slavoj Žižek, eds., *The Idea of Communism*, London: Verso Books 2010, p. 117.

60 Ibid., p. 112.

61 See Alain Badiou, "The Idea of Communism," in Douzinas and Žižek, eds., *The Idea of Communism*.

Spiegel interview: "How can a political system accommodate itself to the technological age, and which political system would this be? I have no answer to this question. I am not convinced that it is democracy."[62] How are we to read this statement? The obvious reading would be that, for Heidegger, a more adequate political response to the technological age than liberal democracy is probably some kind of "totalitarian" socio-political mobilization in the Nazi or Soviet style; the no less obvious counter-argument to such a position is that it ignores how liberal-democratic freedom and individualist hedonism mobilize individuals much more effectively, turning them into workaholics:

> One can wonder as to whether Heidegger was right to suggest, as he did in the *Der Spiegel* interview, that democracy is perhaps not the most adequate response to technology. With the collapse of fascism and of soviet communism, the liberal model has proven to be the most effective and powerful vehicle of the global spread of technology, which has become increasingly indistinguishable from the forces of Capital.[63]

But it would also be easy to reply that the rise of so-called "capitalism with Asian values" in the last decade unexpectedly justifies Heidegger's doubt—this is what is so unsettling about contemporary China: the suspicion that its authoritarian capitalism is not merely a remainder of our past, a repetition of the process of capitalist accumulation which in Europe took place from the sixteenth century to the eighteenth, but a sign of the future. What if it signals that democracy, as we understand it, is no longer a condition and driving force of economic development, but rather its obstacle?

Nevertheless, we can take the risk of reading Heidegger's statement on democracy in a different way: the problem he is struggling with is not simply that of determining which political order best *fits* the global spread of modern technology; it is, rather, whether anything can be done, at the level of political activity, to *counter* the danger to being-human that lurks in modern technology. It never entered Heidegger's mind to propose—say, in a liberal mode—that the failure of his Nazi engagement was merely the failure of a certain kind of engagement which conferred on the political the task of carrying out "a project of onto-destinal significance," so that the lesson of this failure was simply that we should endorse a more *modest* political engagement. Therein lies the limitation of what one may call "liberal Heideggerianism" (from Hubert Dreyfus to John Caputo): from the failure of Heidegger's political engagement, they

62 Martin Heidegger, "Only a God Can Save Us: *Der Spiegel*'s interview with Martin Heidegger," in Richard Wolin, ed., *The Heidegger Controversy: A Critical Reader*, Cambridge, MA: MIT Press 1993, p. 104.

63 Miguel de Beistegui, *Heidegger and the Political*, London: Routledge 1998, p. 116.

draw the conclusion that we should renounce any such engagement with destinal ontological pretensions and engage in a modest, "merely ontic," pragmatic politics, leaving destinal questions to poets and thinkers.

The answer of traditional Heideggerians to the reading proposed here would be, of course, that, in advocating a communist radicalization of Heidegger's politics, we are falling into the worst trap of the modern subjectivist decisionism of the Will, replacing one (fascist) totalitarianism with its Left mirror-image—which is in a way even worse, since, in its "internationalism," it endeavors to erase the last traces of "provincial" homeland, to render people literally rootless (a feature it shares with capitalist neoliberalism). This, however, is not where the core of the problem lies; it rather concerns the sphere of capitalist economic life: crazy, tasteless even, as it may sound, the problem with Hitler was that *he was "not violent enough,"* his violence was not "essential" enough. Hitler did *not* really act, all his actions were fundamentally *reactions*, for he acted so that nothing would really change, staging a gigantic spectacle of pseudo-Revolution so that the capitalist order would survive. Hannah Arendt was right when (implicitly against Heidegger) she pointed out that fascism, although a reaction to bourgeois banality, remains its inherent negation, remains trapped within the horizon of bourgeois society: the true problem of Nazism is not that it "went too far" in its subjectivist-nihilist hubris of exercising total power, but that it did *not* go far enough, that its violence was an impotent acting-out which, ultimately, remained in the service of the very order it despised. Hitler's grand gestures of contempt for bourgeois self-complacency and so on were ultimately in the service of enabling this complacency to survive: far from effectively disturbing the much-despised "decadent" bourgeois order, far from awakening the Germans from their immersion in its complacency, Nazism was a dream which enabled them to carry on.

The fact remains that, as we have tried to indicate apropos the status of the *polemos* and collective will, Heidegger does not follow his own logic to the end when he endorses the fascist compromise. To employ again a familiar metaphor: fascism wants to throw out the dirty bath water (the liberal-democratic individualism that comes with capitalism) and keep the baby (capitalist relations of production), and the way it tries to do this is, again, to throw out the dirty water (the radical *polemos* which cuts across the entire social body) and keep the baby (the corporatist unity of the people). But what should be done is the exact opposite: to throw out both babies (capitalist relations as well as their corporatist pacification) and keep the dirty water of radical struggle. The paradox is thus that, in order to save Heidegger from Nazism, we need *more* will and struggle and *less Gelassenheit*.[64]

64 Against Davis's sympathies for Zen Buddhism, one should bear in mind that Japanese militarism perfectly suited Zen warriors who killed with *Gelassenheit*.

This, then, is our true choice when we read Heidegger's "pro-Nazi" seminars from 1933–4: do we engage in sanctimonious criticism and gloat in the *Besserwisserei* of our later historical position, or do we focus on the missed potential in these seminars, raising the difficult question of how to resuscitate them in an era when, after the great failure of the twentieth-century communist project, the problems to which communism tried to find an answer (radical social conflicts, collective will) are still with us?

CHAPTER 14

The Ontology of Quantum Physics

Is not what Badiou calls the Event, at its most basic, the very rise of representation or appearing out of the flat stupidity of being? So that the Event proper (the Truth-Event in Badiou's sense) is the For-itself of the In-itself of appearing? Insofar as appearing is always appearing for a thought (for a thinking subject), we can go further and say that the rise of a thought as such is an Event—as Badiou likes to say, thought as such is communist.

The key question is thus: how is thought possible in a universe of matter, how can it arise out of matter? Like thought, the subject (Self) is also immaterial: its One-ness, its self-identity, is not reducible to its material support. I am precisely *not* my body: the Self can only arise against the background of the death of its substantial being, of what it is "objectively." So, again, how can one explain the rise of subjectivity out of the "incomplete" ontology, how are these two dimensions (the abyss/void of subjectivity, the incompleteness of reality) to be thought together? We should apply here something like a weak anthropic principle: how should the Real be structured so that it allows for the emergence of subjectivity (in its autonomous efficacy, not as a mere "user's illusion")?

This confronts us with a hard choice: is the void of subjectivity a particular domain ("region") of the "universal" incompleteness / void of reality, or is that incompleteness already in itself a mode of subjectivity, such that subjectivity is always already part of the Absolute, and reality is not even thinkable without subjectivity (as in Heidegger, where there is no *Sein* without *Da-Sein* as its locality)? It is at this precise point that Ray Brassier criticizes me for choosing the second, "transcendental," option, unable as I am to think the Void of Being as such without subjectivity; from my standpoint, however, Brassier is here following Meillassoux, who pays a fateful price for his suspension of the transcendental dimension—the price of a regression to a "naïve" ontology of spheres or levels in the style of Nicolai Hartmann: material reality, life, thought. This is a move which is to be avoided at all costs.

The ontological problem

The first step in resolving this deadlock is to invert the standard "realist" notion of an ontologically fully constituted reality which exists "out there independently of our mind" and is then only imperfectly "reflected" in human cognition—the lesson of Kant's transcendental idealism should be fully absorbed here: it is the subjective act of transcendental synthesis which transforms the chaotic array of sensual impressions into "objective reality." Shamelessly ignoring the objection that we are confounding ontological and empirical levels, here we must invoke quantum physics: it is the collapse of the quantum waves in the act of perception which fixes quantum oscillations into a single objective reality. And, furthermore, this point must be universalized: every figure of reality is rooted in a determinate standpoint. Even at a level closer to us, we know how different "reality" appears to a frog or a bird, starting with the different tapestry of colors: each living being perceives (and interacts with) its own "reality." And one should push this insight to the extreme of Cartesian doubt: the very notion of greatness should be relativized. How do we know that our Milky Way is not just a speck of dust in another universe? Why, when we think about aliens, do we always accept that, though they may be smaller or larger than us, they nonetheless live in a world which is proportionally of the same order of greatness as ours? Perhaps aliens are already here, but just so large or so small that we do not even notice each other. Remember that thought itself exists only for beings which think, but also only for beings of a physical grandeur comparable to ours: if we were to observe ourselves from too close (or too far), there would be no meaning or thought discernible in our acts, and our brain would be just a tiny (or gigantic) piece of living matter.[1]

It is against this background that one can make out the contours of what can perhaps only be designated by the oxymoron "transcendental materialism" (proposed by Adrian Johnston): all reality is transcendentally constituted, "correlative" to a subjective position, and, to push this through to the end, the way out of this "correlationist" circle is not to try to directly reach the In-itself, but to inscribe this transcendental correlation *into the Thing itself*. The path to the In-itself leads through the subjective gap, since the gap between For-us and In-itself is immanent to the In-itself: appearance is itself "objective," therein resides the truth of the realist problem of "How can we pass from appearance For-us to reality In-itself?"

---

1 It is true that, if we accept the hypothesis of the Big Bang, we can nonetheless formulate an immanent measure or limit of grandeur to the universe, namely that there is, in this case, a zero-point of measurement (the singularity of the beginning) as well as the All (of the finite universe), so that the imagined observer cannot jump along an infinite scale of grandeur. However, what about *many* Big Bangs following each other?

It may appear that the basic defining feature of materialism is a common-sense trust in the reality of the external world—we do not live in the fancies of our imagination, caught up in its web, there is a rich and full-blooded world open to us out there. But this is the premise any serious form of dialectical materialism has to do away with: there is no "objective" reality, every reality is already transcendentally constituted. "Reality" is not the transcendent hard core that eludes our grasp, accessible to us only in a distorted perspectival approach; it is rather the very gap that separates different perspectival approaches. The "Real" is not the inaccessible X, it is the very cause or obstacle that distorts our view on reality, that prevents our direct access to it. The real difficulty is to think the subjective perspective as inscribed in "reality" itself.

It is true that, at the most elementary level of the natural sciences, epistemological shifts and ruptures should not be directly grounded in ontological shifts or ruptures in the Thing itself—not every epistemological limitation is an indication of ontological incompleteness. The epistemological passage from classical physics to the theory of relativity did not mean that this shift in our knowledge was correlated to a shift in nature itself, that in Newton's times nature itself was Newtonian and that its laws mysteriously changed with the arrival of Einstein—at this level, clearly, it was our knowledge of nature that changed, not nature itself. But this is not the whole story: there *is* nonetheless a level at which the epistemological break of modern physics is to be correlated to an ontological shift—the level not of knowledge, but of truth as the subjective position from which knowledge is generated. What is totally lacking in Meillassoux is the dimension of truth in its opposition to knowledge: truth as that self-reflective "engaged" or "practical" knowledge which is validated not through its *adequatio rei* but through the way it relates to the subject's position of enunciation (a statement which is factually "true" can be "existentially" a lie). This is the dimension Meillassoux ignores in his critical account of the Transcendental: since, for him, there is no truth outside knowledge, the Transcendental is dismissed as a deceptive lure.

Is it not possible to define Hegel's (idealist) premise as the claim that all knowledge can be ultimately generated from truth? Hegel tries to overcome Kantian "formalism"—the irreducible gap that separates the transcendental form from its heterogeneous contingent content—by deploying their total "mediation," that is, by reducing objective knowledge to a reified or naturalized form-of-appearance of the dialectical truth. The standard scientific argument is that there is a limit to this procedure. Let us take science at its most "subjective," in quantum physics, which (in its Copenhagen interpretation, at least) effectively claims that the cognition of an object creates (or, at least, transforms) it: the measurement itself, through the collapse of the wave function, makes the empirical reality as we know it appear. It would nonetheless be wrong to claim that the great revolutions in the history of physics (the rise of Newtonian physics, of relativity theory, and of quantum physics) or of biology (Karl Linné's systematization, Darwin's evolutionism, etc.) are simultaneously (dialectically mediated by) the transformation of its object, in the same way that, for Georg Lukács, the proletariat's acquiring of self-consciousness (becoming aware of its historical mission) changes its object (through this awareness, the proletariat in its social reality turns into a revolutionary subject). The most we can say with regard to the natural sciences is that, as Lukács put it, nature itself is a historical category, that our basic understanding of what counts as "nature" changes with the great historical breaks: in the absolutist seventeenth century, nature appeared as a hierarchical system of species and subspecies; in the dynamic nineteenth century, characterized by capitalist competition, nature appears as the site of the evolutionary struggle for survival (it is well known that Darwin came up with his theory by transposing Malthus's insights onto nature); in the twentieth century, nature was as a rule perceived through the lenses of systems theory; and it is already a commonplace to draw a parallel between the shift to the auto-poetic, self-organizing dynamic of natural processes in recent decades and the passage to new forms of the capitalist dynamic following the decline of the centralized welfare state.

However, it would be a far and fateful step to conclude from such historical mediations of our notion of nature that, in the course of fundamental historical changes, nature itself also changes: when Einstein's theory replaced Newton's, no one would have claimed that this reflected or registered a homologous change in its object of cognition, in nature itself. What Einstein did was offer a deeper and more adequate scientific theory of nature. Nature did not become ontologically indeterminate with the rise of quantum physics; the discovery of the "principle of uncertainty" means that it always was like that, and no matter how strongly "historically mediated" these scientific discoveries are, they refer to some reality external to the historical process. To a transcendental philosopher, it is clearly too easy to apply here the well-known distinction between the conditions of discovery for a certain scientific theory and the conditions of its validity (although capitalist competition was a necessary historical condition for Darwin's discovery, this does not mean that it also conditions the truth-value of the theory of evolution): the ontological claims of a scientific theory are stronger, being ultimately incompatible with their historicist or transcendental relativization. To claim that modern physics is part of the male-dominated culture of domination and exploitation is one thing, but to say that its basic underlying premises are formed in advance by this culture is definitely saying too much. And, as Meillassoux has pointed out, the classic transcendental claim that the validity of every "objective" natural science is constrained by the a priori horizon which constitutes its domain, i.e., that its theories are valid and meaningful only within this horizon, also goes too far.

The difficult problem is how to think the relationship between scientific knowledge and historical truth if neither of them can be reduced to the other. Perhaps the solution is nonetheless provided by Hegel. Hegel will appear to be deducing or generating all knowledge from the self-relating truth-process only if we conceive his system as a closed circle of necessary deductions; the moment we fully take into account the radical retroactivity of the dialectical process, "deduction" itself becomes a retroactive ordering of a contingent process. Take, for example, the impossibility of reconciling relativity theory and quantum physics in a consistent Theory of Everything: there is no way to resolve the tension between the two by means of an "immanent" dialectical reflection in which the problem itself becomes its own solution. All we can do is wait for a contingent scientific breakthrough—only then will it be possible to retroactively reconstruct the logic of the process.

As we have seen, the price Meillassoux pays for excluding the complex of Truth-Event-Subject is the return of a naïve ontology of levels: physical reality, life, mind. The transcendental dimension of transcendental materialism prevents this regression to naïve ontology: what if we discover that this hierarchy is false? That, for instance, dolphins think better than we do? Only transcendental materialism can provide a materialist reading of the simple fact (noted by the "Christian materialist" Peter van Inwagen, in one unexpected encounter of contemporary philosophy with Hegel) that ordinary objects like chairs, computers, etc., simply *do not exist*: for example, a chair is not actually, for itself, a chair—all we have is a collection of "simples" (more elementary objects "arranged chair-wise"); so, although a chair functions as a chair, it is composed of a multitude of parts (wood, nails, fabric ...) which are, in themselves, totally indifferent to this arrangement; there is, *stricto sensu*, no "whole" of which the nail is here a part. Only with organisms do we have a Whole. Here, the unity is minimally "for itself"; parts really interact.[2] As was noted already by Lynn Margulis, the elementary form of life, a cell, is characterized precisely by such a minimum of self-relating, a minimum exclusively through which the limit between Inside and Outside that characterizes an organism can emerge. And, as Hegel put it, thought is only a further development of this For-itself.

In biology, for instance, we have at the level of reality only bodily interaction. "Life proper" emerges at the minimally "ideal" level, as an immaterial event which provides the form of unity of the living body which allows it to "remain the same" throughout the incessant change of its material components. The basic problem of evolutionary cognitivism—that of the emergence of this ideal life-pattern—is none other than the old metaphysical enigma of the relationship between chaos and order, between the Multiple and the One, between parts and

2 Peter van Inwagen, *Material Beings*, Ithaca: Cornell University Press 1990.

their whole. How can we get "order for free," that is, how can order emerge out of initial disorder? How can we account for a whole that is more than the mere sum of its parts? How can a One with a distinct self-identity emerge out of the interaction of its multiple constituents? A series of contemporary researchers, from Margulis to Francisco Varela, have contended that the true problem is not how an organism and its environment interact or connect, but, rather, the opposite: how does a distinct self-identical organism emerge out of its environment? How does a cell form the membrane which separates its inside from its outside? The true problem is thus not how an organism adapts to its environment, but how it is that there is something, a distinct entity, which must adapt itself in the first place. And it is here, at this crucial point, that today's biological language starts to resemble, quite uncannily, the language of Hegel.

This relationship between the empirical and the transcendental-historical gets further complicated with the fact that, over the last few decades, technological progress in experimental physics has opened up a new domain, that of "experimental metaphysics," unthinkable in the classical scientific universe: "questions previously thought to be a matter solely for philosophical debate have been brought into the orbit of empirical inquiry."[3] What were until now merely topics for "thought experiments" are gradually becoming the topics of actual laboratory experiments—exemplary here is the famous Einstein-Rosen-Podolsky double-slit experiment, first just imagined, then actually performed by Alain Aspect. The properly "metaphysical" propositions tested are the ontological status of contingency, the locality-condition of causality, the status of reality independent of our observation of it (or some other form of interaction with it), and so on. Nonetheless, we should be careful here not to overestimate the philosophical consequences of this "experimental metaphysics": the very possibility of "empirically testing" so-called metaphysical (basic ontological and epistemological) propositions bears witness to a radical break which cannot be accounted for in empirical terms.

This is where Stephen Hawking goes wrong when, at the very beginning of his bestseller *The Grand Design*, he triumphantly proclaims that "philosophy is dead."[4] With the latest advances in quantum physics and cosmology (M-theory), he claims, so-called experimental metaphysics has reached its apogee. Upon a closer look, of course, we soon discover that we are not quite there yet—almost, but not quite. Furthermore, it would be easy to reject this claim by demonstrating the continuing pertinence of philosophy for Hawking himself (not to mention the fact that his own book is definitely not science, but a very

3 Karen Barad, *Meeting the Universe Halfway: Quantum Physics and the Entanglement of Matter and Meaning*, Durham: Duke University Press 2007, p. 35.

4 Stephen Hawking and Leonard Mlodinow, *The Grand Design*, New York: Bantam 2010, p. 5.

problematic popular generalization): Hawking relies on a series of methodological and ontological presuppositions which he takes for granted. Only two pages after making the claim that philosophy is dead, he describes his own approach as "model-dependent realism," based on "the idea that our brains interpret the input from our sensory organs by making a model of the world. When such a model is successful at explaining events, we tend to attribute to it ... the quality of reality"; however, "if two models (or theories) accurately predict the same events, one cannot be said to be more real than the other; rather, we are free to use whichever model is most convenient."[5] If ever there was a philosophical (epistemological) position, this is one (and a rather vulgar one at that). Not to mention the further fact that this "model-dependent realism" is simply too weak to do the job assigned to it by Hawking, that of providing the epistemological frame for interpreting the well-known paradoxes of quantum physics, their incompatibility with common-sense ontology. However, in spite of all these problematic features, we should admit that quantum physics and cosmology do have philosophical implications, and that they do confront philosophy with a challenge.[6]

Similar here is the position of Nicholas Fearn, whose "symptom" is discernible already from the Contents list of his book: the longest chapter ("Postmodernism and Pragmatism") is an umbrella chapter covering everything that is excluded by the horizon of the book, by its choice of what philosophy is.[7] The duality in the chapter title is significant: "postmodernism" as the outside and "pragmatism" (mainly Rorty) as the inscription of this outside within the field of analytical-cognitive thought. The book's abiding theme is the gradual transposition of philosophical problems into scientific ones—philosophy, caught in insoluble dilemmas, reaches maturity when it cancels or overcomes itself by posing its problems in scientific terms. General ontology thus becomes quantum physics *cum* theory of relativity; epistemology the cognitive account of our acquisition of knowledge; ethics the evolutionist inquiry into the rise of moral norms and their adaptive function. This is how Fearn elegantly accounts for the fact that, in some philosophical disciplines, approaches out of tune with current scientific thinking tend to proliferate: this is "what one would expect in a field that has been vacated by philosophy's regular armies and left to partisans who refuse to accept defeat."[8] In short, once the problem is fully transposed into

---

5 Ibid., p. 7.

6 Furthermore, one cannot help noticing that, as to the positive content of Hawking's Theory of Everything, it bears an unmistakable resemblance to dialectical materialism, or is at least fully compatible with a reasonable version of dialectical materialism.

7 See Nicholas Fearn, *Philosophy: The Latest Answers to the Oldest Questions*, London: Atlantic Books 2005.

8 Ibid., p. 37.

terms which in principle make its scientific solution possible, there is no more work for philosophers to do on it. The serious ones among them will move elsewhere, while those who remain are simply partisans of the old positions resisting the inevitable defeat—and, paradoxically, their very predominance (i.e., the absence of "serious" philosophers) is another sign of that defeat. Fearn's example is that of the problem of free will versus natural determinism: the fact that most philosophers today who work in this field are incompatibilists simply signals that compatibilists have already won the battle with their naturalistic account of how (what we mean by) freedom can be united with determinism, so "they have better things to do than reoccupy secured ground."[9]

How are we to escape from this impasse? Adrian Johnston is right to emphasize the *engaged* character of Badiou's philosophy, its readiness to take risks by engaging itself on behalf of particular scientific, political, and artistic achievements: Badiou's thought is not a distanced reflection, it courageously "jumps into the world" and links its fate to the fate of a scientific discovery, political project, love encounter, and so on. This readiness of a philosopher to involve himself with an impure, contingent, historical "pathological" stain is what Badiou is aiming at when he speaks about science, art, politics, and love as the four "conditions" of philosophy, and it is in this sense that one should also read Lenin's statement that, with every great scientific discovery, the definition of materialism changes radically. Today, *the* scientific discovery which needs philosophical rethinking is quantum physics—how are we to interpret its ontological implications whilst avoiding the double trap of superficial pragmatic empiricism and obscurantist idealism ("mind creates reality")? Lenin's *Materialism and Empirio-Criticism* has to be thoroughly rewritten—firstly by abandoning the aforementioned naïve notion of fully constituted material reality as the sole true reality outside our minds. This notion of material reality as "all" relies on the overlooked exception of its transcendental constitution. The minimal definition of materialism hinges on the admission of a *gap between what Schelling called Existence and the Ground of Existence*: prior to fully existent reality, there is a chaotic non-All proto-reality, a pre-ontological, virtual fluctuation of a not yet fully constituted real. This pre-ontological real is what Badiou calls pure multiplicity, in contrast to the level of appearances, which is the level of reality constituted by the transcendental horizon of a world. This is why, in a strange reversal of the standard distribution of predicates, contemporary idealism insists on corporeality, on the unfathomable density and inertia of matter, while materialism is more and more "abstract," reducing reality to a process rendered in mathematical formulae and formal permutations of elements.[10]

9 Ibid., p. 36.

10 No wonder the greatest poet of the material inertia in cinema, Andrei Tarkovsky, is simultaneously one of the great cinematic "spiritualists." More broadly, do not the three

Franz Brentano, from whom Husserl took the notion of intentionality, proposed the concept of *teleiosis* in order to resolve Zeno's paradox of movement (at any determinate moment, a flying arrow occupies a certain point in space, so when does it move?); *teleiosis* stands for the virtual orientation of an actual point. Take two arrows at a certain point in time, one of them at rest, the other flying: although each of them occupies a determinate point in space, they do not occupy it in the same way, because their respective *teleiosis* is different—the *teleiosis* of the first arrow is zero, while the *teleiosis* of the second one is positive (its strength depending on the velocity of its movement) and with a given direction. This potentiality of movement is part of the actuality of an object: if we want to describe an object in its full reality, we have to include its *teleiosis*. Do we not encounter something strictly homologous in differential calculus? The primary motivation for the study of so-called differentiation was the tangential line problem: how to find, for a given curve, the slope of the straight line that is tangential to the curve at a given point? When we try to determine the slope of a line that "touches" a given curve at a given point, are we not trying to determine the spatial direction of that point, its *teleiosis*? No wonder that, in his Great Logic, in the section on "Quantum," Hegel spends dozens of pages discussing differential calculus, rejecting precisely the notion, usually attributed to him, that the *mathematical* infinite "is called the *relative* infinite, while the ordinary *metaphysical* infinite—by which is understood the abstract, spurious infinite—is called absolute":

> in point of fact it is this metaphysical infinite which is merely relative, because the negation which it expresses is opposed to a limit only in such a manner that this limit *persists* outside it and is not sublated by it; the mathematical infinite, on the contrary, has within itself truly sublated the finite limit because the beyond of the latter is united with it.[11]

The ordinary metaphysical notion of the infinite conceives it as an Absolute which persists in itself beyond the finite: the limit which separates it from the finite is external to it, for the negation of the finite is not part of the identity of the Absolute. In the case of the mathematical infinite, on the contrary, the infinite is not something outside the series of finite numbers, but the infinity of this

---

aspects of the Lacanian Real fit the three aspects of materialism? First, the "imaginary" Real: the proverbial grain of dust, the material "indivisible remainder" which cannot be sublated in the symbolic process. Then, the "symbolic" Real: scientific letters and formulae which render the structure of material reality. Finally, the "real" Real: the cut of pure difference, of the inconsistency of structure.

11 G. W. F. Hegel, *Hegel's Science of Logic*, trans. A. V. Miller, Atlantic Highlands: Humanities Press International 1989, p. 249.

very series. The limit that separates the infinite from the finite is immanent to the finite—one can even say that the mathematical infinite is nothing but this limit. In differential calculus, this limit as such is autonomized, rendered independent: when we calculate the slope of the straight line that is tangential to the curve at a given point, we effectively calculate the slope (spatial direction) of a given point of the curve, the spatial direction of something whose spatial length is reduced to the infinitely small, to zero. This means that, in the result of differential calculus, we have a quantitative relationship between two terms (a straight line and a curve) whose quantity is reduced to zero (a point), that is, we have a quantitative relationship which remains after the quantity of the two relata is abolished; but when we subtract the quantity of an entity, what remains is its quality, so the paradox of differential calculus is that the quantitative relationship expressed in its result functions as a quality: "the so-called infinitesimals express the vanishing of the sides of the ratio as quanta, and what remains is their quantitative relation solely as qualitatively determined."[12]

And since, for Hegel, time is the sublation (negation of the negation) of space, we can also say that *teleiosis* is the inscription of time into space in the sense of space-time, of time as another (fourth) dimension of space: *teleiosis* supplements the three dimensions which determine the spatial position of an object with the virtual and temporal dimension of its spatial movement. A purely spatial definition which immobilizes its object produces a non-actual abstraction, not a full reality; the unfinished (ontologically incomplete) character of reality which compels us to include the virtuality of *teleiosis* in the definition of an object is thus not its limitation, but a positive condition of its actual existence. The same holds also for large historical objects: the definition of a nation should include its past and future, its memories and illusions. To paraphrase an old critic of Renan, a nation is a group of people united by a mistaken view about the past, a hatred of their present neighbors, and dangerous illusions about their future. (For example, today's Slovenes are united by myths about a Slovene kingdom in the eighth century, their hatred of [at this moment] the Croats, and the illusion that they are on their way to becoming the next Switzerland.) Each historical form is a totality which encompasses not only its retroactively posited past, but also its own future, a future which is by definition never realized: it is the immanent future of this present, so that, when the present form disintegrates, it undermines also its past and its future.[13] This is also how we should understand diffraction in relation to the blurred edges of an object: not in the common-sense manner which tells us that, upon a closer look, its lines of demarcation are

12 Ibid., p. 269.

13 Along these lines, we can perhaps conceive the wave function in quantum physics as the *teleiosis* of an object deprived of the object's actuality, as the direction of a point without its reality.

imprecise, but in the sense that the virtuality of an object's future movements are part of that object's reality.

We can see from this example that, if for no other reason, Lenin's gesture should be repeated in the context of denouncing spiritualist appropriations of quantum physics. For example, there is no direct link or even a sign of equation between (human) freedom and quantum indeterminacy: simple intuition tells us that if an occurrence depends on pure chance, if there is no causality in which to ground it, this in no way makes it an act of freedom. Freedom is not the absence of causality, it occurs not when there is no causality, but when my free will is the cause of an event or decision—when something happens not without cause, but because I wanted it to happen. On the opposite side, Dennett proceeds all too quickly in naturalizing freedom, that is, in equating it with inner necessity, with the deployment of an inner potential: an organism is "free" when no external obstacles prevent it from realizing its inner inclinations—again, simple intuition tells us that this is not what we mean by freedom.

To avoid succumbing to similar speculations about how, according to quantum physics, mind creates reality and so on, the first thing to keep in mind is that the propositions of quantum physics only function within a complex apparatus of mathematical formalization: if one directly confronts its paradoxical implications (synchronicity, time running backwards, etc.) with our common-sensical ontology, ignoring the apparatus of mathematical formalization, the way is then open for New Age mysticism. The second thing to bear in mind, however, is that the quantum universe is not mathematical in the sense of involving the immanent development of the consequences of initial axioms, but rather thoroughly scientific in the sense of relying on measurements and thereby exposing itself to the contingency of empirical content. This is why scientific common sense (what Althusser called the "spontaneous ideology of scientists") dismisses questions about the ontological implications of quantum physics as irrelevant to science:

> It is a common view among many of today's physicists that quantum mechanics provides us with no picture of "reality" at all! The formalism of quantum mechanics, on this view, is to be taken as just that: a mathematical formalism. This formalism, as many quantum physicists would argue, tells us essentially nothing about an actual quantum reality of the world, but merely allows us to compute probabilities for alternative realities that might occur.[14]

14 Roger Penrose, *The Road to Reality: A Complete Guide to the Laws of the Universe*, London: Vintage Books 2004, p. 782.

There is a moment of truth in this dismissal: translating quantum phenomena into a larger context to impress the public is wrong and misleading—in our reality, objects do not occupy two places at once, and so on. However, the ontological question persists, even if it remains unanswered: what is the ontological status of the phenomena covered by quantum formulae? While obviously not part of our daily reality, they must have a status which cannot be reduced to the scientists' imagination or discursive constructs.

The so-called Copenhagen interpretation of quantum mechanics, associated with Bohr, gave rise to a plethora of other interpretations which tried to resolve what was seen as its deadlock. These included the collapse of the wave function by consciousness or by gravity; the idea that the wave function never collapses, since all possibilities are actualized in different worlds; the non-local hidden variables theory which restores determinism; decoherence, which accounts for the collapse by way of the interaction of the object with its randomly fluctuating environment, and so on. All these attempts should be read following the model of diffraction: as attempts to "re-normalize" the traumatic ontological shock of quantum physics. To quote Anton Zeilinger: "The search for interpretations different from the Copenhagen interpretation very often is motivated by trying to evade its radical consequences, that is, an act of cognitive repression on the part of the proposers."[15] Formulated by Evelyn Fox Keller, this notion of "cognitive repression" refers to the "unwillingness to let go of the basic tenets of classical physics: the objectivity and knowability of nature."[16] Can we not also apply here the notion of diffraction? Does not the Copenhagen interpretation work as a kind of obstacle, a point of impossibility, causing epistemological diffraction, that is, giving rise to a multiplicity of conflicting interpretations attempting to "renormalize" its excess, to re-inscribe it into the traditional epistemological and ontological space?

There are major debates about the exact moment of the collapse of the wave function; the three main positions fit perfectly the Lacanian triad of Real/symbolic/imaginary: the real of measurement (when the result is registered by the measuring machine, establishing contact between quantum micro-reality and ordinary macro-reality), the imaginary of perception (when the result is perceived by a consciousness), and the symbolic inscription (when the result is inscribed into the language shared by the community of researchers). Does this debate not signal a kind of ontological inconsistency in quantum physics? The latter accounts for the collapse of the wave function (and thus for the emergence of "ordinary" reality) in terms of the act of perception or registration (a single reality emerges through the act of measurement), but it then explains (or, rather, describes) this measurement in terms of the ordinary reality that only emerges

15 Quoted from Barad, *Meeting the Universe Halfway*, p. 287.

16 Quoted from ibid.

through it (the measuring machine is hit by electrons, etc.), and this obviously involves a *circulus vitiosus*. One consistent solution here is an explicitly theological one: the only way to account for the reality of the universe as such is to posit a point of observation external to it, which can only be something like a God's eye.

There is, however, another way to think this paradox. When Jacques-Alain Miller emphasizes the immanence of the *percipiens* to the *perceptum* as Lacan's crucial move in the theory of the field of vision, would it be legitimate to link this to quantum physics, which also asserts the immanence of the observer to the observed? There are, of course, differences that stand out: in quantum physics, the observer is not immanent to the observed in the sense of being inscribed into it, but in the more elementary sense of its act of observation being constitutive of the observed. Furthermore, this observer is not the Lacanian subject (of desire), but the subject of science, the subject for whom reality is "flat," for whom there is no blind spot in reality from which the object returns the gaze. In other words, one should bear in mind that Lacan's notion of the immanence of the *percipiens* to the *perceptum* refers to perception sustained by desire: the point in the perceived picture from which the object returns the gaze is the "impossible" point at which the object-cause of desire is located. It is the objectal counterpoint to the subject's desire, what attracts me "in you more than yourself," and is as such only perceivable, indeed only ex-sists, for a perception sustained by desire.

Quantum physics clearly has weird ontological consequences. The origin of this weirdness is the duality of (extended) wave and (compact) particle which arose out of an enigma noted by de Broglie when he tried to conceive the electron as a particle: "If an electron in a hydrogen atom were a compact particle, how could it possibly 'know' the size of an orbit in order to follow only those orbits allowed by Bohr's by-now famous formula?"[17] Bohr's solution to the ontological status of complementarity (wave or particle) is that

> the microscopic system, the atom, [does not exist] in and of itself. We must always include in our discussion—implicitly at least—the different macroscopic experimental apparatuses used to display each of the two complementary aspects. All is then fine, because it is ultimately only the classical behavior of such apparatus that we report ... although physicists talk of atoms and other microscopic entities as if they were actual physical things, they are really only concepts we use to describe the behavior of our measuring instruments.[18]

It is crucial that this description be given in the plain language used to talk about everyday external reality—consequently, it is tempting to apply here the early

17 Bruce Rosenblum and Fred Kuttner, *Quantum Enigma: Physics Encounters Consciousness*, London: Gerald Duckworth 2007, p. 66.
18 As summarized in ibid., pp. 108–9.

Althusserian distinction between the "real object" and the "object of knowledge": the only real objects we are dealing with in quantum physics are the objects of ordinary reality; the entire quantum sphere has no ontological status proper, it is merely an "object of knowledge," a conceptual construct whose function is to provide the formulae to explain the behavior of measuring objects which are part of ordinary reality. It is thus strictly nonsensical to speak about quantum processes as constituting an autonomous sphere of being: in reality, there are no objects which can be in two places simultaneously, etc., "all there is" ontologically is our ordinary reality, what is "beyond" are only mathematical formulae which give a certain credibility to what our instruments measure, not any kind of insight into "what Nature is trying to tell us."[19] Our experience of everyday reality thus remains the phenomenological background and foundation of quantum theory.

The temptation to be resisted here is that of interpreting the way quantum physics undermines our common notion of reality existing independently of our perception as a sign of some "deeper meaning," of another, more "spiritual" reality—even John Wheeler, himself no stranger to a "spiritualist" reading of quantum physics, has clearly pointed out that "'consciousness' has nothing whatsoever to do with the quantum process. We are dealing with an event that makes itself known by an irreversible act of amplification, by an indelible record, an act of registration … [Meaning] is a separate part of the story, important but not to be confused with 'quantum phenomena.'"[20]

Although Bohr avoids this trap, his limit betrays his lack of the properly philosophical transcendental reflection, discernible in the fundamental ontological inconsistency of his account of how what we perceive as ordinary "external reality" emerges only through the collapse of the wave function in the act of measuring: if ordinary empirical reality constitutes itself through measuring, how do we account for the measuring apparatuses themselves which are part of this same empirical reality? Are we not dealing here with a *petitio principii*, that is, is not the *explanandum* part of the *explanans*?

Knowledge in the Real

A fact rarely noticed is that the propositions of quantum physics which defy our common-sense view of material reality strangely echo another domain, that of language, of the symbolic order—it is as if quantum processes are closer to the universe of language than anything one finds in "nature," as if, in the quantum universe, the human spirit encounters itself outside itself, in the guise of its

19 Ibid., p. 164.
20 Quoted in ibid., p. 165.

uncanny "natural" double. Take Lacan's characterization of the "hard sciences" as dealing with what he calls *savoir dans le réel* (knowledge in the real): it is as if there is a knowledge of the laws of nature directly inscribed into the Real of natural objects and processes—a stone, for instance, "knows" what laws of gravity to obey when it falls. In another example of the scientific "knowledge in the real," Ernest Rutherford queried how a particle knows where to go when it jumps from one "rail" to another around the atom's core—rails that do not exist as material objects but are purely ideal trajectories. It may seem that therein lies the difference between nature and history: in human history, "laws" are norms which can be forgotten or disobeyed.

At its most daring, quantum physics does seem to allow for the paradox of the proverbial cartoon cat suspended in mid-air, of the momentary suspension or "forgetting" of knowledge in the real. Imagine you have to take a flight on day X to collect a newly inherited fortune which must be picked up the next day but do not have enough money to buy the ticket. Then you discover that the airline's accounting system is set up so that if you wire the ticket payment within 24 hours of arriving at your destination, no one will ever know it was not paid for prior to departure. In a homologous way,

> the energy a particle has can wildly fluctuate so long as this fluctuation is over a short enough time scale. So, just as the accounting system of the airline "allows" you to "borrow" the money for a plane ticket provided you pay it back quickly enough, quantum mechanics allows a particle to "borrow" energy so long as it can relinquish it within a time frame determined by Heisenberg's uncertainty principle ... But quantum mechanics forces us to take the analogy one important step further. Imagine someone who is a compulsive borrower and goes from friend to friend asking for money ... Borrow and return, borrow and return—over and over again with unflagging intensity he takes in money only to give it back in short order ... a similar frantic shifting back and forth of energy and momentum is occurring perpetually in the universe of microscopic distance and time intervals.[21]

This is how, even in an empty region of space, a particle emerges out of Nothing, "borrowing" its energy from the future and paying for it (with its annihilation) before the system notices what it has done. The whole network can function like this, in a rhythm of borrowing and annihilation, one borrowing from the other, displacing the debt onto the other, postponing the payment—it is really as if the subparticle domain is playing Wall-Street-style games with futures. What this presupposes is a minimal gap between things in their immediate brute reality and the registration of this reality in some medium (of the big Other): one can

21 Brian Greene, *The Elegant Universe*, New York: W. W. Norton & Company 1999, pp. 116–19.

cheat insofar as the second moment (registration) is delayed with regard to the first. What makes quantum physics so strange is that one can cheat "in reality," with one's being. In other words, the "spookiness" of quantum physics is not its radical heterogeneity with regard to our common sense, but, rather, its uncanny resemblance to what we consider specifically human—here, indeed, one is tempted to say that quantum physics "deconstructs" the standard binary opposition of nature and culture. Let us go quickly through the list of these features:[22]

(1) Within the symbolic order, possibility as such possesses an actuality of its own; that is, it produces real effects—for example, the father's authority is fundamentally virtual, a threat of violence. In a similar way, in the quantum universe, the actual trajectory of a particle can only be explained if one takes into account all of its possible trajectories within its wave function. In both cases, the actualization does not simply abolish the previous panoply of possibilities: what might have happened continues to echo in what actually happens as its virtual background.

(2) Both in the symbolic universe and in the quantum universe, we encounter what Lacan calls "knowledge in the real": if, in the famous double-slit experiment, we observe an electron's trajectory in order to discover through which of the two slits it will pass, the electron will behave as a particle; if we do not observe it, it will display the properties of a wave—as if the electron somehow knew whether it was being observed or not. Is such behavior not limited to the symbolic universe in which our "taking ourselves to be X" makes us act like X?

(3) When quantum physicists try to explain the collapse of the wave function, they resort again and again to the metaphor of language: this collapse occurs when a quantum event "leaves a trace" in the observation apparatus, when it is "registered" in some way. We obtain here a relationship of externality—an event becomes fully itself, it realizes itself, only when its external surroundings "take note" of it—which echoes the process of symbolic realization in which an event fully actualizes itself only through its symbolic registration, its inscription into a symbolic network, which is external to it.

(4) Furthermore, there is a temporal dimension to this externality of registration: a minimum of time always elapses between a quantum event and its registration, and this minimal delay opens up the space for a kind of ontological cheating with virtual particles (an electron can create a proton and thereby violate the principle of constant energy, on condition that it reabsorbs it quickly enough,

22 I rely here on the third chapter ("Quantum Physics with Lacan") of my *Indivisible Remainder*, London: Verso Books 1996.

before its environment "takes note" of the discrepancy). This delay also opens the way for temporal retroactivity: the present registration decides what must have happened—for example, if, in the double-slit experiment, an electron is observed, it will not only (now) behave as a particle, its past will also retroactively become ("will have been") that of a particle, in a homology with the symbolic universe in which a present radical intervention (the rise of a new Master-Signifier) can retroactively rewrite the (meaning of the) entire past.[23] Perhaps, then, insofar as retroactivity is a crucial feature of the Hegelian dialectics, and insofar as retroactivity is only thinkable in an "open" ontology of not yet fully constituted reality, the reference to Hegel can be of some help in bringing out the ontological consequences of quantum physics.

How far should we go with this parallel? Is it just an approximate metaphor? Does it bear witness to the fact that our entire comprehension of reality is already over determined by the symbolic order, so that even our grasp of natural reality is always already "structured like a language"? Or should we risk a step further and claim that there is something which strangely recalls (or points towards) symbolic structures already present in "physical" reality itself? If we do draw that conclusion, then the entire "spontaneous philosophical ideology" of the gap that separates nature from culture (a form of ideology often clearly discernible in Lacan himself) has to be abandoned. According to this "spontaneous ideology," nature stands for the primacy of actuality over potentiality, its domain is the domain of the pure positivity of being where there are no lacks (gaps) in the strict symbolic sense; if, however, we take the ontological consequences of quantum physics seriously, then we have to suppose that the symbolic order pre-exists in a "wild" natural form, albeit in what Schelling would have called a lower potency. We thus have to posit a kind of ontological triad of quantum proto-reality (the pre-ontological quantum oscillations), ordinary physical reality, and the "immaterial" virtual level of Sense-Events. How are these three aspects related?

The basic feature of symbolic reality is its ontological incompleteness, its "non-All": it has no immanent consistency, it is a multiplicity of "floating signifiers" which can only be stabilized through the intervention of a Master-Signifier—in clear contrast, so it seems, to natural reality, which is what it is, without any symbolic intervention. But is this so? Is not the key ontological consequence of quantum physics that quantum proto-reality also needs a homologous "quilting point" (here called the collapse of the wave function) to stabilize itself into the ordinary reality of everyday objects and temporal processes? We thus encounter here also the (temporal) gap between the inconsistent

23 To cite Borges, with the emergence of Kafka, Poe and Dostoyevsky are no longer what they were, for, from the standpoint of Kafka, we can see in them dimensions which were not previously there.

proto-reality and the decentered agency of its registration which constitutes it as full reality: here too, reality is not fully itself, but decentered with regard to itself; it becomes itself retroactively, through its registration. In philosophy, this gap is prefigured in Schelling's distinction between Existence and the Ground of Existence, between reality and proto-reality. Let us backtrack here: in what does Schelling's philosophical revolution consist? According to the standard academic *doxa*, Schelling broke out of the idealist closure of the Notion's self-mediation by way of asserting a more balanced bi-polarity of the Ideal and the Real: "negative philosophy" (the analysis of the notional essence) must be supplemented by "positive philosophy," which deals with the positive order of existence. In nature as well as in human history, the ideal rational order can only thrive against the background of the impenetrable Ground of "irrational" drives and passions. The climax of philosophical development, the standpoint of the Absolute, is thus not the "sublation" (*Aufhebung*) of all reality in its ideal Notion, but the neutral medium of the two dimensions—the Absolute is ideal-real. Such a reading, however, obfuscates Schelling's true breakthrough, his distinction, first introduced in his essay on human freedom from 1807, between (logical) Existence and the impenetrable Ground of Existence, the Real of pre-logical drives.[24] This proto-ontological domain of drives is not simply "nature," but the spectral domain of the not yet fully constituted reality. Schelling's opposition of the proto-ontological Real of drives (the Ground of Being) and ontologically fully constituted Being itself (which, of course, is "sexed" as the opposition of the Feminine and the Masculine) thus radically displaces the standard philosophical couples of Nature and Spirit, the Real and the Ideal, Existence and Essence, etc. The real Ground of Existence is impenetrable, dense, inert, yet at the same time spectral, "irreal," ontologically not fully constituted, while Existence is ideal, yet at the same time, in contrast to the Ground, fully "real," fully existent.

The theological implications of this gap between proto-reality and its full constitution through symbolic registration are of special interest: insofar as "God" is the agent who creates things by observing them, quantum indeterminacy compels us to posit a God who is *omnipotent, but not omniscient*: "If God collapses the wave functions of large things to reality by His observation, quantum experiments indicate that He is not observing the small."[25] The ontological cheating with virtual particles is a way to cheat God himself, the ultimate agency taking note of everything that goes on; in other words, God himself does not control the quantum processes, and therein resides the atheist lesson of quantum physics. Einstein was right with his famous claim "God doesn't

24 See F. W. J. Schelling, "Philosophical Investigations into the Essence of Human Freedom and Related Matters," trans. Priscilla Hayden-Roy, in Ernst Behler, ed., *Philosophy of German Idealism*, London: Continuum 1987.

25 Rosenblum and Kuttner, *Quantum Enigma*, p. 171.

cheat"—what he forgot to add is that he himself can be cheated. Insofar as the materialist thesis is that "God is unconscious" (God doesn't know), quantum physics is effectively materialist: there are micro-processes (quantum oscillations) not registered by the system.

Let us recapitulate the quantum measurement paradox. In the double-slit experiment, when particles are sent through the slits one by one, they nevertheless—if they are not observed—form the pattern of a wave. Since the wave-pattern presupposes the interaction of particles, and since, in this experiment, each particle travels alone, with what does it interact? Does it inhabit a synchronous atemporal space where it can interact with past and future? Or does it interact *with itself*? This brings us to the notion of superposition: the particle interacts with itself, so that it simultaneously takes all possible paths, which are "superimposed" on one another. Does this not evoke Nietzsche's idea of the "shortest shadow," the moment when an object is not accompanied by another, but by its own shadow—or, rather, in which the object is not an actual One, but merely a composite of its multiple shadows, of more-than-nothings or less-than-zeroes? The enigma of the double-slit experiment is thus triple:

(1) Even if we shoot the electrons individually, one after the other, they will, if we do not measure their path, form a wave pattern—but how can they? With what does each individual electron interact? (With itself.)

(2) Even if we measure (or not) the path after the electrons have already passed through the slits, the pattern still depends on our measurement—but how can it, when the measurement takes place after the passage through the slit? It seems as though we can retroactively change the past.

(3) Even if we do not enact measurement at all, the mere fact that the measurement apparatus (and, with it, the possibility of measurement) is there makes the electron behave as a particle—but how can it, when it was in no way affected by the measurement apparatus?

There are, again, two deviant approaches to this enigma: the spiritualist one (the [observer's] mind creates reality, the universe has to be observed by God in order to exist), and over-hasty naturalization (the collapse of the wave function needs no observer in the sense of a consciousness, observing stands for simple registration by the environment, so everything in nature is "observed" all the time by the environment with which it interacts). The basic enigma is the following: insofar as the result of our measurement depends on our free choice of what to measure, the only way to avoid the implication that our observation creates reality is either to deny our free will or to adopt a Malebranchean solution ("the world conspires to correlate our free choices with the physical situations we then observe").[26]

The eternal naïve-realist question "How does objective reality look without me, independently of me?" is a pseudo-problem, since it relies on a violent abstraction from the very reality it attempts to grasp: "objective reality" as a mathematicized set of relations is "for us" the result of a long process of conceptual abstraction. This does not devalue the result, making it simply dependent on our "subjective standpoint," but it does involve a paradox: *"objective reality" (the way we construct it through science) is a Real which cannot be experienced as reality.* In its effort to grasp reality "independently of me," mathematicized science erases "me" from reality, ignoring (not the transcendental way I constitute reality, but) the way I am *part of* this reality. The true question is therefore how I (as the site where reality appears to itself) emerge in "objective reality" (or, more pointedly, how can a universe of meaning arise in the meaningless Real). As materialists, we should take into account two criteria that an adequate answer should meet: (1) the answer should be genuinely materialist, with no spiritualist cheating; (2) we should accept that the ordinary mechanistic-materialist notion of "objective reality" will not do the job. It is here that quantum physics enters the stage: the paradoxes of the double-slit experiment clearly demonstrate that the proto-real domain of quantum waves and particles is obviously not reducible to our standard notion of "external reality," its properties do not fit our notion of material objects and processes which take place "out there"; however, the domain of quantum waves and particles is no less obviously a meaningless Real.

Here we must take into account the subtle difference between Heisenberg's uncertainty principle and Bohr's complementarity, the difference between merely epistemological and fully ontological incompleteness: while Heisenberg's point is that we cannot establish the simultaneous position and momentum of a particle because the very act of measurement intervenes in the measured constellation and disturbs its coordinates, Bohr's point is a much stronger one concerning the very nature of reality itself—particles in themselves do not have a determinate position and momentum, thus we should abandon the standard notion of "objective reality" populated by things equipped with a fully determined set of properties.

For Heidegger, ontological difference is ultimately grounded in our finitude: what Heidegger calls the Event (*Ereignis*) is the ultimate abyss out of which Being reveals itself to us in a multitude of historically destined horizons, and Being discloses or withdraws itself because not all beings open to us. To put it bluntly, there is a difference between worldly entities and the horizon of their

26 Ibid., p. 170.

disclosure *because* entities disclose themselves to us within a horizon which is always rooted in our finitude. Here, however, we should repeat the move from Kant to Hegel: Heidegger never confounds the ontological disclosure of entities with their ontic production—for him, the idea of humans as the Being-There of the disclosure of Being does not mean that entities exist only for humans, not independently of them. If all of humanity were to be wiped out, entities would still be there as they were prior to the emergence of man, they would just not ex-sist in the full ontological sense of appearing within a horizon of Being. But what if we transpose ontological difference (the difference between entities and "nothingness" of the ontological horizon of their disclosure) into the Thing-in-itself, and (re)conceive it as the ontological incompleteness of reality (as quantum physics implies)? What if we posit that "Things-in-themselves" emerge against the background of the Void or Nothingness, the way this Void is conceived in quantum physics, as not just a negative void, but the portent of all possible reality? This is the only truly consistent "transcendental materialism" which is possible after the Kantian transcendental idealism. For a true dialectician, the ultimate mystery is not "Why is there something rather than nothing?" but "Why is there nothing rather than something?": how is it that, the more we analyze reality, the more we find a void?

What this amounts to is that ontological difference should not be limited to the finitude of human beings to whom entities appear within the (historically) given horizon of a world, that is, against the background of withdrawal, in the inextricable mixture of disclosure and veil. This structure of reality as "non-All" is to be taken in fully ontological terms: it is not that, within our finite horizon, the In-itself of reality always appears against the background of its withdrawal and concealment; reality is "in itself" non-All. In other words, the structure of disclosure or concealment, the fact that things always emerge out of their background Void truncated, never fully ontologically constituted, is that of reality itself, not only of our finite perception of it. Therein, perhaps, lies the ultimate philosophical consequence of quantum physics: that what its most brilliant and daring experiments demonstrate is not that the description of reality it offers is incomplete, but that reality itself is ontologically "incomplete," indeterminate—the lack that we take as an effect of our limited knowledge of reality is part of reality itself. In a properly Hegelian way, then, it is our very epistemological limitation which locates us in the Real: what appears as the limitation of our knowledge is the feature of reality itself, its "non-All."

Again, what this means is that the move from Kant to Hegel should be repeated apropos Heidegger: Heidegger's history of Being is ultimately a historically radicalized version of Kantian transcendentalism. For Heidegger, the history of Being is the history of epochal disclosures of the Sense of Being destined to man; as such, this history is the ultimate limit of what we can know—every knowledge of ours already presupposes and moves within a historically given disclosure of Being, the abyssal play of these disclosures which just "happen" is as far as we can go. The ontological implication of quantum physics is not that we can go further and penetrate reality in itself, but that the limitation posited by Heidegger belongs to the In-itself itself. Is this not the underlying implication of the quantum concept of Nothingness (Void) as pregnant with a multiplicity of entities which can emerge out of it, that is, "out of nothing"? Reality-in-itself is Nothingness, the Void, and out of this Void, partial, not yet fully constituted constellations of reality appear; these constellations are never "all," they are always ontologically truncated, as if visible (and existing) only from a certain limited perspective. There is only a multiplicity of truncated universes: from the standpoint of the All, there is nothing but the Void. Or, to risk a simplified formulation: "objectively" there is nothing, since all determinate universes exist only from a limited perspective.

The clearest answer to *the* enigma "What happened before the Big Bang, that singular point at which all physical laws are suspended?" is therefore: *nothing*. For Paul Davies, a partisan of this view, the Big Bang is the absolute beginning of time—it did not happen in time, it created time itself, so the question "What happened before?" is as meaningless as the question "What is farther north than the North Pole?" If this were not the case, then everything that takes place now would be the infinitely repeatable copy of something that has already happened. According to the standard "theological" reading, the punctual infinite density of matter at the point of singularity which is the Big Bang stands for the absolute Beginning, the unfathomable point of creation at which God directly intervened and created the universe. The Big Bang is thus a kind of umbilical cord directly linking the material universe to a transcendent dimension. Such an expanding universe is finite in time and space, yet without limits because of the curvature of space. There are, however, problems with this standard view. According to some measurements, there are traces of matter older than the extrapolated moment of the Big Bang in our universe. The solution could be that our universe is like a mirror-hall whose visual echoing makes the space appear larger than it is. Because of such echoing, when the same signal from another galaxy reaches us via two different paths, it appears to us that we are dealing with two different galaxies (or that the same galaxy is simultaneously at two distant places).

Nick Bostrom has proposed a more radical solution for such inconsistencies: our universe is a sophisticated computer simulation, a kind of virtual reality programmed by a civilization incomparably more developed than ours. The program is so perfect that it makes it possible for us, as simulated beings, to experience emotions and the illusion of freedom. From time to time, however, there are glitches in the system, the system violates its own rules (or, perhaps, applies "cheat-codes"), and we experience the effects as "miracles" or UFOs.[27] This version basically reads as a secularized theological scenario, with the difference that our creator is not a supernatural being but just another, much more developed, natural species. So, if we know (or presume) that our universe is "simulated," has been willfully created by higher beings, how then can we discern their traces and/or read their motives? Do they want us to remain totally immersed in the simulated environment? If yes, is this because they are testing us, epistemologically or ethically?[28] Were we created for fun, as a work of art, as part of a scientific experiment, or for some other reason? (Recall many novels and films, from Heinlein's *Strange Profession of Jonathan Hoag* to *The Truman Show*, *The Thirteenth Floor*, and *The Matrix*.) Can we imagine living in a simulated world without a creator's intention?

What this solution does is transpose the gap between our phenomenal universe and its noumenal Beyond into that universe itself, redoubling it into two universes: our phenomenal universe is virtualized, reduced to a simulation by agents operating in another, much more developed, "true" universe. The next logical step is to multiply the phenomenal universes themselves, without invoking a quasi-divine privileged universe. Along these lines, Neil Turok and Paul Steinhardt proposed a new version of the multiple-worlds theory, according to which our four-dimensional reality (the three dimensions of space plus time) stands in relation to true reality the way a two-dimensional surface stands in relation to our three-dimensional reality: there are more dimension(s) and parallel universes, we just cannot perceive them. According to this model, the Big Bang resulted from a crash (collapse) between two such parallel universes: such a crash does not create time, it just resets the clock of a universe.

The next logical step after that is to transpose this multiplicity into a temporal succession within the same universe. Along these lines, Martin Bojowald replaced the Big Bang with the Big Bounce: the time-space continuum from time to time tears apart; the ensuing collapse brings about a new Big Bang, in which the density of quantum forces causes a kind of "amnesia" of the universe—all information about what went on before the Big Bang is erased, thus with every new Big Bang the universe wipes out its past and starts again *ex nihilo*.

Finally, there is the Stephen Hawking hypothesis of "irrational time" (in the sense of irrational numbers), which dispenses with the very notion of the Big Bang: the curvature of time means that, like space, time has no limit, although it

---

27 Nick Bostrom, "Playthings of a Higher Mind," *Times Higher Education Supplement*, May 16, 2003. Also known as "The Simulation Argument: Why the Probability that You Are Living in a Matrix is Quite High."

28 Recall how Kant thought that our ignorance of noumenal reality is a condition for our being able to act ethically: if we were to know Things in themselves, we would act like automata.

is finite (curved into itself). The idea of the Big Bang results from applying to the universe the logic of a single linear time and thus extrapolating to a zero-point, where in truth there is merely an endless circular movement.

Do not these five versions form a complete series of possible variations? Are we not dealing here with a systematic series of hypotheses like the set of the relations between the One and the Being deployed and analyzed by Plato in the second part of his *Parmenides*? Perhaps contemporary cosmology needs such a "Hegelian" conceptual systematization of the underlying matrix that generates the multitude of actually existing theories. Does this take us back to the ancient Oriental wisdom according to which all things are just ephemeral fragments which emerge out of the primordial Void and will inevitably return back to it? Not at all: the key difference is that, in the case of Oriental wisdom, the primordial Void stands for eternal peace, which serves as the neutral abyss or ground of the struggle between the opposite poles, while from the Hegelian standpoint, the Void names the extreme tension, antagonism, or impossibility which generates the multiplicity of determinate entities. There is multiplicity because the One is in itself barred, out-of-joint with regard to itself. This brings us on to another consequence of this weird ontology of the thwarted (or barred) One: the two aspects of a parallax gap (wave and particle, say) are never symmetrical, for the primordial gap is between (curtailed) something and nothing, and the complementarity between the two aspects of the gap function so that we have first the gap between nothing (void) and something, and only then, in a (logically) second time, a second "something" that fills in the Void, so that we get a parallax gap between two somethings. For example, in Lacan's formulae of sexuation, the feminine formulae (or mathematical antinomies) have a (logical) priority; it is only in the second moment that the dynamic antinomies enter as attempts to resolve the deadlock of the mathematical antinomies.

One can venture that the same holds for the antinomy (complementarity) between waves and particles. In our spontaneous scientific ontology, we take chaotic waves and fluidity to be more elementary than firmly outlined and delimited objects: reason (or some other force of determination) imposes on the chaotic fluidity clear forms which, upon closer inspection, reveal themselves to be blurred, affected by the chaos of matter (no physically drawn triangle is really a triangle). It is against this spontaneous image that the radical nature of quantum physics should be measured: its ontology is the exact opposite, for in it, continuous fluidity is a feature of the higher level, while, when we approach reality in its microscopic dimension, we discover that it is actually constituted of discrete parts (quanta). One should not underestimate the denaturalizing effect of this reversal: the universe all of a sudden becomes something artificially composed from building blocks—it is as if, getting too close to a person, we discover that they are not a "real," organic person but are composed of tiny Lego bricks.

In our common-sense view (and in ordinary reality), on the contrary, the particle has precedence over the wave. For example, in a desert, sand dunes moved by the wind function like waves, but the idea is that, had we much greater knowledge than we actually possess, we would be able to reduce this wave behavior to particles: even the largest sand dune is ultimately just a composite of small grains. To treat the movement of sand like a wave is thus a gross functional simplification.[29] The common-sense ontology that underlies this view is that every wave-movement must be a movement of something, of things which materially exist and are moved: waves do not properly exist, they are a property or event which happens *to* something that exists. The quantum revolution here not only posits the original irreducible duality of waves and particles; within this duality, it (more or less openly) privileges the wave: for example, it proposes a shift from understanding waves as interactions between particles to understanding particles as nodal points in the interaction of waves. For quantum physics, waves thus cannot be reduced to a property of (or something that happens to) particles. This is also why Bohr claims that quantum physics deals with (measures) phenomena, not things which "stand behind" phenomena as their substantial support: the entire traditional problem of distinguishing between properties which belong to "Things-in-themselves" and properties which merely "appear" to belong to things because of our perceptive apparatus is thus undermined: this distinction between primary and secondary properties no longer makes sense, because the way a thing "appears," the way it is "for the other," is inscribed into it "in-itself." To add insult to injury, the very appearance of "things" as things, as substantial entities, is the result of the collapse of the wave function through perception, so that the common-sense relationship is again turned around: the notion of "objective" things is subjective, dependent on perception, while wave-oscillations precede perception and are thus more "objective."

The key task is then to interpret this incompleteness without abandoning the notion of the Real, that is, to avoid the subjectivist reading of the fact that the act of measurement itself co-constitutes what it measures. Heisenberg's version of indeterminacy (the "uncertainty principle") still leaves enough room not only to save the notion of an objective reality independent of the observer (if out of the observer's reach), but even to determine it, to get to know it as it is in itself: if the inaccessibility of the In-itself is due only to its distortion by the measuring apparatus, is it not then possible to determine the effect on the observed object of the measuring procedure and then, by subtracting this effect from the result, get the measured object the way it is in itself (or the way it was, prior to measurement)? For example, if I know that my counting a sum of money will add twenty units to it, and the result of my counting is 120 units, then I know that, prior to

29 Although a mystery remains here, the proverbial mystery of the additional grain of sand which makes out of individual grains a heap proper (functioning like a wave).

my counting, the sum was 100 units. Bohr argues against this possibility: for a priori reasons, one cannot determine the effect of the measurement interaction on the measured object. For example, if we measure the position or momentum of an electron by firing a photon at it,

> it is not possible to determine the effect of the photon on the particle (electron), since we would need to determine the photon's position and momentum simultaneously, which is physically impossible given that the measurements of position and momentum require mutually exclusive apparatuses for their respective determination. Therefore we arrive at Bohr's conclusion: *observation is only possible on the condition that the effect of the measurement is indeterminable.* Now, the fact that the measurement interaction is indeterminable is crucial because it means that we can't subtract the effect of the measurement and thereby deduce the properties that the particle (is presumed to have) had before the measurement.[30]

One cannot but notice the similarity of Bohr's reasoning here to the very first paragraphs of the "Introduction" to Hegel's *Phenomenology of Spirit*, where he describes the absurd consequences of the standard representationalist approach according to which knowledge is "the instrument by which to take possession of the Absolute, or the means through which to get a sight of it":

> if knowledge is the instrument by which to get possession of absolute Reality, the suggestion immediately occurs that the application of an instrument to anything does *not* leave it as it is for itself, but rather entails in the process, and has in view, a moulding and alteration of it. Or, again, if knowledge is not an instrument which we actively employ, but a kind of passive medium through which the light of the truth reaches us, then here, too, we do not receive it as it is in itself, but as it is through and in this medium. In either case we employ a means which immediately brings about the very opposite of its own end; or, rather, the absurdity lies in making use of any means at all. It seems indeed open to us to find in the knowledge of the way in which the *instrument* operates, a remedy for this parlous state; for thereby it becomes possible to remove from the result the part which, in our idea of the Absolute received through that instrument, belongs to the instrument, and thus to get the truth in its purity. But this improvement would, as a matter of fact, only bring us back to the point where we were before. If we take away again from a definitely formed thing that which the instrument has done in the shaping of it, then the thing (in this case the Absolute) stands before us once more just as it was previous to all this trouble, which, as we now see, was superfluous. If the Absolute were only to be brought on the whole nearer to us by this agency, without any change being wrought in it, like a

30 Barad, *Meeting the Universe Halfway*, p. 113.

> bird caught by a limestick, it would certainly scorn a trick of that sort, if it were not in its very nature, and did it not wish to be, beside us from the start. For a trick is what knowledge in such a case would be, since by all its busy toil and trouble it gives itself the air of doing something quite different from bringing about a relation that is merely immediate, and so a waste of time to establish. Or, again, if the examination of knowledge, which we represent as a medium, makes us acquainted with the law of its refraction, it is likewise useless to eliminate this examination from the result.[31]

Although Hegel's context is totally different from that of Bohr (if nothing else, Hegel was writing about the philosophical knowledge of the Absolute, while Bohr was struggling with the epistemological implications of measuring atomic particles), the underlying line of argumentation is strictly homologous: they both reject a position which first posits a gap between the knowing subject and the object-to-be-known, and then deals with the (self-created) problem of how to bridge this gap. In other words, they both combine false modesty (we are just finite subjects confronting an opaque transcendent reality) with the arrogance of invoking a meta-language (the subject can somehow step outside of its own limitations to compare its limited perspective with reality in itself). And the solution of both is basically the same: to include the subject in the "self-movement" of the object-to-be-known. The Hegelian name for this inclusion is reflexivity.[32] How does this work in quantum physics?

Agential realism

Here enters the "agential realism" deployed by Karen Barad: "According to agential realism, knowing, thinking, measuring, theorizing, and observing are

31 G. W. F. Hegel, *The Phenomenology of Mind*, Vol. 1, trans. J. B. Baillie, New York: MacMillan 1910, pp. 73–5.

32 Barad rejects the notion of reflexivity as a tool for conceiving the inclusion of the observer in the observed content, with the argument that "reflexivity is founded on representationalism": "Reflexivity takes for granted the idea that representations reflect (social or natural) reality. That is, reflexivity is based on the belief that practices of representing have no effect on the objects of investigation and that we have a kind of access to representations that we don't have to the objects themselves. Reflexivity, like reflection, still holds the world at a distance" (*Meeting the Universe Halfway*, p. 87). But this notion simply misses the core of Hegelian reflexivity, which is the inclusion of the act of reflection in the object itself: for Hegel, the distance between the object and its reflection is not external (i.e., the object is in itself, the reflection is how it appears to the observing subject), but is inscribed into the object itself as its innermost constituent—the object becomes what it is through its reflection. The exteriority implied by the notion of reflexivity is precisely what Barad calls an "exteriority within."

subjective material practices of intra-acting within and as part of the world."[33] Agential realism leaves behind the standard modern topic of the subject confronted with "objective reality," the topic which opens up the usual epistemological dilemmas ("can the subject reach independent reality, or is it caught in the circle of its subjective representations?"): its basic ontological unit is the *phenomenon* in which both sides are irreducibly and inextricably entangled: phenomena display "the ontological inseparability of objects and apparatuses."[34] But the fact that we do not produce our knowledge from afar, observing reality from a distant, objective, non-entangled position, does not mean that we should renounce objectivity as such, that all our knowledge is subjective: such a reading still presupposes a representational distance between our subjective view-from-outside and the things themselves. How, then, are we to think the objectivity (also in the sense of universality) of our knowledge?

Bohr, whose reflections Barad tries to systematize here, emphasizes that such an account does not imply subjectivist relativism: objectivity is maintained, but it no longer means that the result of the observation tells us something about the reality of the observed object prior to the act of measurement; rather, it means that whenever we repeat the same act of measurement under the same conditions (the same entanglement of object and apparatus), we will obtain the same result, so that there is no reference to a particular observer. The subjectivist or idealist reading of quantum physics ("the mind creates reality, there is no reality independent of our minds") is thus patently false: the true implication of quantum physics is the opposite, compelling us to conceive how our knowing of reality is included in reality itself.

The lesson of Bohr is thus not that reality is subjective, but that we—the observing subjects—are part of the reality we observe. This is not a question of spiritualism, but of knowledge itself being grounded in material practices. In short, the implicit lesson of Bohr's reflections amounts to a *materialist* critique of the naïve-realist epistemology and ontology of Lenin's *Materialism and Empirio-Criticism* with its notion of knowledge as an (always imperfect) "reflection" of the objective reality existing independently of us. This naïve materialism treats reality-in-itself in two contradictory ways: (1) as infinitely *richer* than our knowledge and perception of it (we can only approach asymptotically the infinite wealth of reality); (2) as much *poorer* than our experience and perception of it: reality is stripped of all "secondary properties" (colors, tastes, and so on), so that all that remains are the abstract mathematical forms of its basic elements. This paradoxical oscillation between the opposites is the price naïve materialism pays for its abstract procedure.

---

33 Barad, *Meeting the Universe Halfway*, p. 90.

34 Ibid., p. 128.

Bohr reveals the idealist presupposition of such a position: if reality is "out there," and we are endlessly approaching it, then—implicitly, at least—we, the observers, are not part of this reality, but stand somewhere outside of it.[35] Within the entangled unity of a phenomenon, there is no a priori unambiguous way to distinguish between the agency of observation and the observed object: every such division hinges on a contingent agential cut within the unity of a phenomenon, a cut which is not just a "subjective" mental decision, but is "constructed, agentially enacted, materially conditioned":[36]

> *The boundary between the "object of observation" and the "agencies of observation" is indeterminate in the sense of the absence of a specific physical arrangement of the apparatus.* What constitutes the object of observation and what constitutes the agencies of observation are determinable only on the condition that the measurement apparatus is specified. *The apparatus enacts a cut delineating the object from the agencies of observation.* Clearly, then, as we have noted, *observations do not refer to properties of observation-independent objects (since they don't preexist as such).*[37]

Within the same phenomenon, different cuts are possible, each of them isolating a different aspect of the phenomenon as the observed object. Take the case of using a stick to find one's way around a dark room: we can treat the stick as a measuring apparatus, as a prolongation of our hand, as a tool enabling us to "measure" (recognize) the contours of the room; or, complementarily, if we already know the contours of the room very well, we can treat the stick itself as the object to be measured (when it touches a wall which we know to be a certain distance from where we stand, we can determine the length of the stick; if we hit the top of a table in front of us, we can estimate the plasticity of the stick; etc.). In a homologous way, in the double-slit experiment, we can use the slits as an instrument to measure the flow of particles, or we can use the flow of particles as an instrument to measure the property of the slits—what we cannot do is directly measure the apparatus of measurement itself; to do this, we would need to enact a different agential cut by means of which both the measuring agency and the measured object both become part of a new object: "the measurement interaction can be accounted for only if the measuring device is itself treated as an object."[38] In other words, "a 'measuring instrument' cannot characterize

35 And the spiritualist misreading of quantum physics ("the observer creates reality") merely opposes to this vulgar abstract materialism a no less vulgar idealism: here, it is not the object but the subject which is exempted from the concrete reality of a phenomenon and presupposed as the abstract source of reality.

36 Barad, *Meeting the Universe Halfway*, p. 115.

37 Ibid., p. 114.

38 Ibid.

(i.e., be used to measure) itself," it cannot measure its own entanglement with the measured object, since each measurement relies on a contingent cut within a phenomenon, a cut by means of which a part of the phenomenon is measured by another of its parts.[39] This means that measurements (and, consequently, our knowledge) are always local, drawing a line of separation which makes a part of the phenomenon describable in "classical" (non-quantum) terms; as such, measurements are part of the global quantum reality which encompasses the world of classically described objects and processes as its subordinate moment. This insight has important consequences for cosmology:

> there simply is no outside to the universe for the measuring agencies to go to in order to measure the universe as a whole ... since there is no outside to the universe, there is no way to describe the entire system, so that description always occurs from within: *only one part of the world can be made intelligible to itself at a time, because the other part of the world has to be the part that it makes a difference to.*[40]

It may appear easy to oppose idealism and materialism here: the idealist position proposes God as the outside observer who can comprehend and "measure" the entire universe, while for the materialist position there is no outside, every observer remains within the world. In Lacanese, the idealist position is "masculine," it totalizes the universe through the observer as the point of exception, while materialism is "feminine"; that is, it asserts the "non-All" of every measurement.[41] However, it would be too easy to simply privilege the "feminine" non-All and to reduce the "masculine" totalization-through-exception to a secondary illusion—here, more than ever, we should insist on (sexual) difference itself as

39 Ibid., p. 347.

40 Ibid., pp. 350–1.

41 Another inscription of the opposition between idealism and materialism in cosmology occurs in the ongoing debate about the Big Bang: no wonder the Catholic Church has for decades now supported Big Bang theory, reading it as the moment of God's direct intervention, the singular point at which universal laws of nature are suspended. The materialist answer to Big Bang theory is the cyclical theory of the universe, which reads the Big Bang not as the zero-point of the inexplicable absolute beginning, but as the moment of passage from one universe to another, a passage which can also be accounted for by the laws of nature. The idea (relying on string theory—and the problems with string theory signal the potential weakness of this approach) is that there are more than the usual four dimensions in the universe (three spatial dimensions plus time): there is (at least) another spatial dimension which maintains an infinitesimal but still operational distance between our world (a "brane": a multi-dimensional membrane) and its double; at the end of a cosmic cycle, the two branes collapse into each other, the distance separating them is canceled, and this collapse engenders the explosion of a new world. See Rosenblum and Kuttner, *Quantum Enigma.*

the primary fact, as the impossible Real with regard to which both positions, "masculine" and "feminine," appear as secondary, as two attempts to resolve its deadlock.

What this means with regard to the philosophical consequences of quantum physics and cosmology is that one cannot simply locate the "agential cut" which generates the classical universe within the quantum non-All, thereby reducing the classical reality to a phenomenon within the quantum universe, for quantum reality is not simply the encompassing unity including its "opposite," classical reality. Here also, we must be attentive to the frame within which quantum reality appears to us: the encompassing frame itself is in a way already part of the enframed content. In other words, what we are effectively dealing with is classical reality, no matter how blurred it is: the wave functions and all other quanta are ultimately something we reconstruct as the cause of the measurements we observe and register in strictly classical terms. What we encounter here is the paradox elaborated by Louis Dumont as constitutive of hierarchy: the "higher" ontological order has to appear within the perspective of the "lower" order as subordinated to the latter, as its effect—in this case, quantum reality which is ontologically "higher" (causing and encompassing classical reality) has to appear, within this reality, as something subordinated to it and grounded in it. And it is not enough to dismiss this reversal as merely epistemological ("while quantum reality is the true reality which causes classical reality, relations are reversed in our process of knowledge")—here again we should transpose the epistemological reversal back into ontology and ask the key question: why is this reversal necessary for the ontological sphere itself?[42]

The answer is that we have to presuppose a more radical Cut which already traverses the non-All. The structure of sexual difference is already that of diffraction: the difference itself precedes the two entities between which it differentiates; in other words, it works like the diffractive obstacle, so that both sexual positions, masculine and feminine, must be conceived as reactions to the obstacle or deadlock, as two ways of coping with it. The reason Barad does not take into account this more radical ontological cut lies in her implicit naturalism. Fully versed in Butler's and Foucault's discourse theories, Barad emphasizes how the apparatuses which provide the frame for agential cuts are not just material, in the immediate sense of being part of nature, but are also socially conditioned, always reliant on a complex network of social and ideological practices. Her critical point against Butler, Foucault, and other historicist discourse-theorists is that, although they critically reject the Cartesian humanist position, they continue to privilege the human standpoint: their historicism limits history to human history, to the complex network of discursive practices and formations

42 This is homologous to the question of hierarchy: why can the higher order retain its priority only if it appears within the lower order as subordinated to it?

which determine the horizon of intelligibility. The gap between (human) history and nature persists in their work, offering only yet another version of the standard anti-naturalist motif of nature as a historically conditioned discursive category: what counts as "natural" ultimately depends on historical discursive processes. Barad here risks a fateful step further into a full "naturalization" of the very notion of discourse: rejecting "humanist remains" in Bohr's epistemology (his identification of the "observer" with human subject), her agential realist account argues that

> intelligibility is an ontological performance of the world in its ongoing articulation. It is not a human-dependent characteristic, but a feature of the world in its differential becoming ... Knowing entails specific practices through which the world is differentially articulated and accounted for. In some instances, "nonhumans" (even beings without brains) emerge as partaking in the world's active engagement in practices of knowing.[43]

Barad's radical ontological conclusion is thus that "matter and meaning are mutually articulated":[44] "Discursive practices are the material conditions for making meaning. In my posthumanist account, meaning is not a human-based notion; rather, meaning is an ongoing performance of the world in its differential intelligibility."[45] She mentions a primitive, brainless deep-sea organism whose entire surface mirrors light changes and triggers an escape motion when these changes are read as dangerous—an example of the mutual articulation of meaning and matter. But Barad's conclusion nonetheless works all too smoothly: true, it liquidates the last "humanist remains"—that is, it removes the final vestiges of what Meillassoux calls "transcendental correlationism" (the axiom that every object or part of reality emerges as the objective correlate of a "positing" subject)—but the price it pays is that of *ontologizing correlation itself* by locating meaning directly in nature, in the guise of the unity of apparatuses and objects.

The problem here is the implied *continuity* of the line leading from the natural correlation between organism and its environment to the structure of meaning proper to the symbolic order. In nature, differences make differences: there are agential cuts which establish a difference between the series of "causes" and the series of "effects," an organism measures its environment and reacts accordingly; nonetheless, what is missing is a short-circuit between the two series of differences, a mark belonging to the series of "effects" which retroactively inscribes itself into the series of "causes." Deleuze's name for this paradoxical mark is "dark precursor," a term he introduces in *Difference and*

43 Barad, *Meeting the Universe Halfway*, p. 149.

44 Ibid., p. 152.

45 Ibid., p. 335.

Repetition: "Thunderbolts explode between different intensities, but they are preceded by an imperceptible dark precursor [*précurseur sombre*], which determines their path in advance, but in reverse, as though intagliated."[46] As such, the dark precursor is the signifier of a meta-difference:

> given two heterogeneous series, two series of differences, the precursor plays the part of the differenciator of these differences. In this manner, by virtue of its own power, it puts them into immediate relation to one another: it is the in-itself of difference or the "differently different"—in other words, difference in the second degree, the self-different which relates different to different by itself. Because the path it traces is invisible and becomes visible only in reverse, to the extent that it is traveled over and covered by the phenomenon it induces within the system, it has no place other than that from which it is "missing," no identity other than that which it lacks: it is precisely the object = x, the one which is "lacking in its place" as it lacks its own identity.[47]

Or, as Ian Buchanan puts it concisely: "Dark precursors are those moments in a text which must be read in reverse if we are not to mistake effects for causes."[48] In *The Logic of Sense*, Deleuze develops this concept with direct reference to the Lacanian notion of the "pure signifier": there has to be a short-circuit between the two series, that of the signifier and that of the signified, in order for the effect-of-sense to take place. This short-circuit is what Lacan calls the "quilting point," the direct inscription of the signifier into the order of the signified in the guise of an "empty" signifier without signified. This signifier represents the (signifying) cause within the order of its effects, thus subverting the (mis)perceived "natural" order within which the signifier appears as the effect or expression of the signified. This is why the correspondence between the two series of differences that we find in nature is not yet meaning—or, if it is, it is merely a pure denotative signal, the registering of a correspondence between two sets of differences, but not yet *sense*. Meaning has to be distinguished from sense: Deleuze demonstrated how sense can only arise against the background of nonsense, since sense is by definition the making sense of a nonsense.

Take, once again, the example of anti-Semitism: it enacts a correspondence between a series of features of social life (financial corruption, sexual depravity, media manipulation, etc.) and a series of homologous hypothetic features of the "Jewish character" (Jews are corrupt, sexually depraved, they control

46 Gilles Deleuze, *Difference and Repetition*, trans. Paul Patton, London: Continuum 2001, p. 119.

47 Ibid., pp. 119–20.

48 Ian Buchanan, *Deleuzism: A Metacommentary*, Durham: Duke University Press 2000, p. 5.

and manipulate our media ...) in order establish the conclusion that Jews are the ultimate cause of these disturbing features of our society. This conclusion is, however, supported by a much more complex intellectual process. First, there is a reversal at the level of causality: if someone claims that "the Jews are degenerate, exploitative, and manipulative," this does not yet make him an anti-Semite; the true anti-Semite will add: "This guy is degenerate, exploitative, and manipulative, *because he is a Jew*." We are not dealing here with a simple circularity, for the underlying logic is not: "He is degenerate because he is a Jew, and Jews are degenerate." Something more takes place here: in this reversal, an excess, a mysterious *je ne sais quoi*, is generated, the underlying logic of which is: "there is some mysterious ingredient in Jews, an essence of being-Jewish, which causes them to be degenerate, etc." A *pseudo-cause* is thus introduced, as the mysterious ingredient which makes a Jew a Jew; a "deeper sense" emerges, things all of a sudden become clear, everything makes sense, because the Jew is identified as the source of all our troubles. This sense is, of course, itself sustained by non-sense, by the nonsensical short-circuit of the inclusion of the name of an object among its properties. And this additional reversal which "makes sense" is what is missing in Barad's claim that we find meaning already in pre-human nature, in the way natural organisms interact (or, rather, intra-act) with their environment. In other words, although in her critique of "essentialism" Barad emphasizes again and again the importance of differences and differentiating, what she leaves out of consideration is ultimately *difference itself*, the self-relating "pure" difference which precedes the terms it differentiates.

Here we arrive at the crux of the problem: the aim of our critique of Barad's conclusions is not to propose a new version of the classical gap that separates humans from animals by claiming that the short-circuit which "makes sense" out of nonsense is specifically human. The insight that, in quantum mechanics, we encounter in nature (in, as it were, a lower power/potency) a weird proto-version of what we usually perceive as the specifically human symbolic dimension should be maintained; our thesis is that a proto-version of the differential short-circuit ignored by Barad *can* be found at work in the quantum field. To establish this, we must first repeat the fundamental Hegelian reversal: the problem is not "how can we pass from the classical universe to the universe of quantum waves?" but exactly the opposite—"why and how does the quantum universe itself immanently require the collapse of the wave function, its 'decoherence' into the classical universe?" Why and how is the collapse inherent to the quantum universe? In other words, it is not only that there is no classical reality which is not sustained by fuzzy quantum fluctuations; it is also that there is no quantum universe which is not always already hooked onto some bit of classical reality. The problem of the collapse of the wave function in the act of measurement is that it has to be formulated in classical, not quantum, terms—this is why

> the collapse of the wave function occupies an anomalous position within quantum mechanics. It is *required* by the fact that observations occur, but it is not predicted by quantum theory. It is *an additional postulate, which must be made in order that quantum mechanics be consistent.*[49]

Note the precise formulation: a measurement formulated in the terms of classical reality is necessary for quantum mechanics itself to be consistent, it is an addition of the classic reality which "sutures" the quantum field. There have been multiple attempts to resolve this anomaly. First, there is the dualist position: we are dealing with two different levels of reality, classical "macro"-reality obeying ordinary laws, and "micro"-reality obeying quantum laws; then, there is the more extreme position according to which all there is is classical reality, and the quantum sphere is just a rational construct or presupposition designed to account for measurements formulated in classical terms. For Barad, reality is also one, but it is the one of entangled phenomena which obey quantum laws: it is only *within* a phenomenon, as part of the *intra*-action of its components (to talk about "interaction" already concedes too much to classical ontology, since it implies that separated parts somehow interact), that a cut is enacted and the object is fixed as observed. The cut isolates the object as the "cause" and the mark in the measuring apparatus as the "effect," so that a change or difference in the object is entangled with a change or difference in the apparatus—but this cut is *inherent* to a phenomenon.

The key notion here is that of the unity of the entire phenomenon which encompasses the object and the apparatus; this is why, when, in the double-slit experiment, the path of each particle is measured and the interference pattern disappears, we should avoid any mystique about how particles somehow "know" whether they are being observed or not and behave accordingly. But we should also not read this fact as the result of an empirical disturbance of particles by the process of measurement (it is not that a wave changes into a collection of particles when it is disturbed by photons measuring its path). What changes is the entire phenomenal *dispositif* which enacts a different agential cut, one which allows measuring:

> *all that is required to degrade the interference pattern is the possibility of distinguishing paths* ... what matters is "contextuality"—the condition of possibility of

49 George Greenstein and Arthur G. Zajonc, *The Quantum Challenge: Modern Research on the Foundations of Quantum Mechanics*, Sudbury, MA: Jones and Bartlett 1997, p. 187; as quoted in Barad, *Meeting the Universe Halfway*, p. 285 (emphases added).

> definition—rather than the actual measurement itself. Since it has been confirmed experimentally that the interference pattern disappears without any which-path measurement having actually been performed—but *just by the mere possibility of distinguishing paths*—these findings offer a clear challenge to any explanation of the destruction of the interference pattern that relies on a mechanical disturbance as its causal mechanism.[50]

Note the occurrence of the transcendental term "condition of possibility": the apparatuses play a kind of transcendental role, structuring the field of intelligibility of a phenomenon. This is why a mere possibility of measuring suffices: the interference pattern disappears with the mere possibility of distinguishing paths, even in the absence of any empirical measurement, not because individual particles somehow "know" their path is observed, but because the possibility of measuring is transcendentally constitutive of their field of intelligibility. This is also how one can account for the even more perplexing case of the delayed measurement which seems to be able to "change the past":

> not only is it possible to restore the interference pattern by erasing the which-path information ... but we can decide whether or not to erase the which-path information after the atom has passed through the slits and registered its mark on some screen ... if the experimenter can decide whether or not an interference pattern will result by deciding whether or not to erase the which path information long after each atom has already hit the careen then it seems the experimenter has control over the past. How can this be?[51]

Again, the key is provided by the unity of the phenomenon, by the "ontological priority of phenomena over objects": the paradox only arises if we isolate particles as autonomous "objects" which magically change their behavior once they "know" they are (or even: will be) observed:

> If one focuses on abstract individual entities the result is an utter mystery, we cannot account for the seemingly impossible behavior of the atoms. It's not that the experimenter changes a past that had already been present or that atoms fall into line with a new future simply by erasing information. The point is that the past was never simply there to begin with and the future is not simply what will unfold; the "past" and the "future" are iteratively reworked and enfolded ... There is no spooky-action-at-a-distance coordination between individual particles separated in space or individual events separated in time. Space and time are phenomenal, that is, they are

50 Barad, *Meeting the Universe Halfway*, pp. 305–6.
51 Ibid., pp. 311–12.

> intra-actively produced in the making of phenomena; neither space nor time exist as determinate givens outside of phenomena.[52]

In short, each phenomenon encompasses its own "past" and "future" which are created once the coordinates of this phenomenon are set by an agential cut. What this means is that each phenomenon already involves an agential cut, already involves the collapse of the (local) wave function. Each phenomenon thus gives body to a *specific difference*: to a cut which opposes an agent and an object. The background of this plurality of phenomena—the In-itself, to put it in Kantian terms—is the void or vacuum, pure quantum potentiality: every phenomenon breaks the balance of the vacuum. If it is already difficult to imagine the emergence out of nothing of a little piece of reality, how can the entire universe emerge *ex nihilo*? Quantum physics here offers a beautiful and properly dialectical solution: of course no single object within a given universe can emerge out of nothing, but the entire universe can do so, and for a very precise reason: "One requirement any law of nature must satisfy is that it dictates that the energy of an isolated body surrounded by empty space is positive, which means that one has to do work to assemble the body"; otherwise,

> there would be no reason that bodies could not appear anywhere and everywhere. Empty space would therefore be unstable ... If the total energy of the universe must always remain zero, and it costs energy to create a body, how can a whole universe be created out of nothing? That is why there must be a law like gravity ... Because gravity shapes space and time, it allows space-time to be locally stable but globally unstable. On the scale of the entire universe, the positive energy of the matter can be balanced by the negative gravitational energy, and so there is no restriction on the creation of whole universes. Because there is a law like gravity, the universe can and will create itself from nothing.[53]

The dialectical beauty of this argument is that it inverts the standard idea of a universe which is locally unstable but globally stable, as in the old conservative saw that something must change so that everything remains the same: the stability and harmony of the Whole is the very harmony of the continuous struggle between its parts. What quantum physics proposes is, on the contrary, global instability as the basis of local stability: entities within a universe have to obey stable rules, they are part of a causal chain, but what is contingent is the very totality of this chain. Does this mean, however, that at this level of the pure potentiality of the Void, there are no differences? No: there is *pure difference* in the guise of the gap between two vacuums, the topic of the Higgs field. Let us

52 Ibid., p. 315.
53 Hawking and Mlodinow, *The Grand Design*, pp. 179–80.

approach the paradox of the Higgs field via, once again, a parallel with the status of the "Nation" in our socio-political imaginary.

What is a "Nation" to which we "belong" if not one of the names for the Freudo-Lacanian "Thing": the unnamable X, the black hole of the symbolic universe which can never be defined by a set of positive properties, but can only be signaled by tautological pseudo-explanations like "It is just what it is, you have to be a German (or …) to know what it means"? It is not in front of us, its members, but behind us, as the impenetrable background of our collective existence. Think of the art of choosing which queue to join: any precise definable strategy will turn out to be counterproductive if it is followed by too many participants (like the well-known example of most drivers taking a detour through a side-road because the main road is expected to be clogged up, with the result that the side-road gets congested and the main road is free of traffic). If, however, the opposite strategy of randomly choosing any queue is followed by almost all participants, a predictable pattern will emerge which, again, will enable those following a strategy that takes this pattern into account to choose the fastest line. There are nonetheless some people who regularly *do* choose the faster queue—how do they do it? The true art is to find a balance between these two extremes: adopting a limited strategy which takes into account the short-term fluctuations and imbalances before every strategy becomes fully self-destructive. Something similar goes on with naming the X of one's Nation-Thing: both fully consistent strategies (either acting as if one can define a Nation-Thing with a set of properties—the equivalent of a definable strategy of choosing a queue, or just insisting that the Nation-Thing is an unfathomable tautology—the equivalent of choosing the queue randomly) are self-destructive, so that all that one can do is apply the "poetic" approach of picking out fleeting particular features which somehow give a particular spin to the empty Nation-Thing, while remaining ever so particular, that is, without imposing themselves as universal properties of all (or even the majority of) the members of a Nation—say, in the case of the English, drinking warm beer, playing cricket, fox hunting, and so forth.

Hanif Kureishi was once telling me about his new novel, which had a different narrative to his earlier books. I ironically asked him: "But the hero is nonetheless an immigrant with a Pakistani father who is a failed writer …" He replied: "What's the problem? Don't we all have Pakistani fathers who are failed writers?" He was right—and this is what Hegel meant by singularity elevated into universality: the pathological twist that Kureishi identified in his father is part of *every* father; there is no normal father, everybody's father is a figure who failed to live up to his expectations and thus left to his son the task of settling his symbolic debts. In this sense, Kureishi's "Pakistani failed writer" is a universal singular, a singular standing in for universality. This is what hegemony is about, this short-circuit between the universal and its paradigmatic case (in the precise Kuhnian sense of the term): it is not enough to say that Kureishi's own case is one in a series of cases exemplifying the universal fact that being a father is yet another "impossible profession"—one should take a step further and claim that, precisely, we all have Pakistani fathers who are failed writers. In other words, let us imagine being-a-father as a universal ideal which all empirical fathers endeavor to approach but ultimately fail to reach: this means that the true universality is not that of the ideal being-a-father, but that of failure itself. The "Pakistani failed writer" is Kureishi's name for the Father-Thing, giving it a specific spin—it is poets who are the original spin-doctors. Therein also resides the art of "naming" a Nation-Thing: to invent or name such specific "spins" which give a flavor of the Nation-Thing while maintaining a proper distance towards it, thereby respecting its unnamability. Such is the art, or one of them, of the poets.

The parallel with modern cosmology reveals more than one might expect here. Insofar as the Nation-Thing functions as a kind of semiotic "black hole," we should bring into play the notion of the "event horizon." In general relativity, the event horizon designates a boundary in space-time: the area surrounding the black hole, beyond which events cannot affect an outside observer. Light emitted from inside the horizon can never reach the observer, so that anything that passes through the horizon from the observer's side is never seen again. Where is the equivalent of a poetic nomination of the Nation-Thing? Perhaps in so-called "Hawking radiation," a thermal radiation predicted by Stephen Hawking in 1975 to be emitted by black holes: quantum effects allow black holes to emit black body radiation from just beyond the event-horizon; this radiation does not come directly from the black hole itself, but is the result of virtual particles being boosted by the black hole's gravitation into becoming real particles: vacuum fluctuations cause a particle-antiparticle pair to appear close to the event-horizon of a black hole; one of the pair falls into the black hole whilst the other escapes, and to an outside observer it would appear that the black hole has just emitted a particle. Are not poetic nominations of a Thing something like this? To an outside observer (reader), it appears that the Nation-Thing itself has emitted this nomination. One is tempted to go even further with this parallel and include in it the "Higgs boson," a hypothetical elementary particle which is the quantum of the Higgs field, a paradoxical field which acquires a non-zero value in empty space. This is why the Higgs boson is also called the "God particle": it is a "something" of which the "nothing" itself is made, literally the "stuff of nothing." So too the Freudian Thing: the stuff of nothing.

The two vacuums

The Higgs field undermines the standard New Age appropriations of the quantum Void as the Nothing-All, a pure potentiality at the abyssal origin of all things, the Plotinian formless Over-One in which all determinate Ones disappear. The "Higgs field" controls whether forces and particles behave differently or not: when it is "switched on" (operative), symmetries are broken between elementary particles, and their complex pattern of differences emerges; when it is "switched off" (inoperative), forces and particles are indistinguishable from one another, the system is in a state of vacuum—this is why particle scientists search so desperately for the (hypothetical, for the time being) Higgs Particle, sometimes referring to it as the "god particle." This particle is the equivalent of what Lacan calls the *objet petit a*, the object-cause of desire, namely the cause disturbing the symmetry of a vacuum, the X which breaks the symmetry and introduces differences—in short, nothing less than the cause of the passage from nothing (the vacuum, the void of pure potentialities) to something (actual different particles and forces). How is this miraculous particle even thinkable in a materialist way? How can we avoid here the obscurantist idea of a mystical cause of all objects?[54]

The materialist solution is very precise, and it concerns the key paradox of the Higgs field: as with every field, Higgs is characterized by its energy density and by its strength—however, "it is energetically favorable for the Higgs field to be switched on and for the symmetries between particles and forces to be broken."[55] In short, when we have the pure vacuum (with the Higgs field switched off), the Higgs field still has to spend some energy—nothing comes for free; it is not the zero-point at which the universe is just "resting in itself" in total release—the nothing has to be sustained by an investment of energy. In other words, energetically, it costs something to maintain the nothing (the void of the pure vacuum). Maybe some theosophical traditions are on the right track here, such as the Talmudic idea that, prior to creating something, God had to create nothing, to withdraw, to clear the space for creation. This paradox compels us to introduce a distinction between two vacuums: first, there is the "false" vacuum in which the Higgs field is switched off, i.e., there is pure symmetry with no differentiated particles or forces; this vacuum is "false" because it can only be sustained by a certain amount of energy expenditure. Then, there is the "true" vacuum in which, although the Higgs field is switched on and the symmetry

54 All theosophical speculations focus on this point: at the very beginning (or, more precisely, *before* the beginning), there is nothing, the void of pure potentiality, the will which wants nothing, the divine abyss prior to God, and this void is then inexplicably disturbed or lost.

55 Paul J. Steinhardt and Neil Turok, *Endless Universe: Beyond the Big Bang*, London: Phoenix 2008, p. 82.

broken, i.e., there is a certain differentiation of particles and forces, the amount of energy spent is zero. In other words, energetically, the Higgs field is in a state of inactivity, of absolute repose.[56] At the beginning, there is the false vacuum; this vacuum is disturbed and the symmetry is broken because, as with every energetic system, the Higgs field tends towards the minimization of its energy expenditure. This is why "there is something and not nothing": because, energetically, *something is cheaper than nothing.* We are here back at the notion of *den* in Democritus: a "something cheaper than nothing," a weird pre-ontological "something" which is less than nothing.

It is thus crucial to distinguish between the two Nothings: the Nothing of the pre-ontological *den*, of "less-than-nothings," and the Nothing posited as such, as direct negation—in order for Something to emerge, the pre-ontological Nothing has to be negated, has to be posited as a direct/explicit emptiness, and it is only within this emptiness that Something can emerge, that there can be "Something instead of Nothing." The first act of creation is thus the emptying of the space, the creating of Nothing (in Freudian terms, the death drive and creative sublimation are intricately linked).

Is not the Epicurean notion of the *clinamen* the first philosophical model of this structure of the double vacuum, of the idea that an entity only is insofar as it "comes too late" with regard to itself, to its own identity? In contrast to Democritus, who claimed that atoms fall straight down in empty space, Epicurus attributed to them the spontaneous tendency to deviate from their straight paths. This is why, in Lacanese, one could say that the passage from Democritus to Epicurus is the passage from the One to the surplus-object: Democritus's atoms are "ones," while Epicurus's atoms are surplus-objects—no wonder that Marx's theoretical path begins with his doctoral thesis on the difference between the philosophies of Democritus and Epicurus.

Perhaps this gives us a minimal definition of materialism: the irreducible distance between the two vacuums. And this is why even Buddhism remains "idealist": there, the two vacuums become confused in the notion of nirvana. Even Freud did not quite grasp this clearly, sometimes confounding the death drive with the "nirvana principle," thereby missing the core of his notion of the death drive as the "undead" obscene immortality of a repetition which insists beyond life and death. Nirvana as the return to a pre-organic peace is a "false" vacuum, since it "costs more" (in terms of energy expenditure) than the circular movement of the drive.[57]

---

56 Ibid., p. 92.

57 Within the domain of the drive, the same gap appears in the guise of the difference between the drive's *goal* and *aim*, as elaborated by Lacan: the drive's goal—to reach its object—is "false," it masks its "true" aim, which is to reproduce its own circular movement by way of repeatedly missing its object. If the fantasized unity with the object brought

We encounter a homologous structure also on the market: when Tim Hartford talks about "the men who knew the value of nothing,"[58] we should complicate the formula by drawing a parallel with Stephen Jay Gould's famous essay on the relationship between the price and size of Hershey chocolate bars. Comparing price and size changes from 1949 through 1979, Gould discovered how the company gradually reduced the size of the bars, then made them larger (though not as large as they were originally) and raised the price ... then they started to reduce the size again. If we take this process to its logical conclusion, at some point which could be exactly calculated, the company would be selling a package with nothing in it, and this nothing would have a price which could be precisely determined.[59] The Lacanian *objet a* is precisely this something which sustains the nothing, the "price of nothing," in exactly the same way in which a certain energy is needed to sustain the vacuum. The common-sense reaction to all this would be that surely we can only talk about "less than nothing" in a symbolic space where, for example, my bank balance might be minus $15,000. In reality, there is by definition nothing that is "less than nothing." But is this really the case? Quantum physics undermines precisely this elementary ontological presupposition.

There is nonetheless a way in which authentic Buddhism is aware of this paradox. To take an example from popular culture: when, in the remake of *The Karate Kid* (2010), the young American boy protests to his Chinese kung fu teacher, "How can I win my fight if I only stand still?" the teacher replies: "Being still is not the same as doing nothing." We can understand this proposition against the background of the well-known (but no less adequate) cliché about a wise ruler who knows how to play one subordinate off against another, so that their plots neutralize each other—a simple example of how the Whole of the kingdom is at peace while the parts fight each other. In contrast to this "doing nothing" of the Whole sustained by the frantic activity of the parts, "standing still," as a sudden interruption of movement, disturbs the peace of

---

the full/impossible incestuous *jouissance*, the drive's repeated missing of its object does not simply compel us to be satisfied with a lesser enjoyment, but generates a surplus-enjoyment of its own, the *plus-de-jouir*. The paradox of the death drive is thus strictly homologous to that of the Higgs field: from the standpoint of the libidinal economy, it is "cheaper" for the system to repeatedly traverse the circle of the drive than to stay at absolute rest.

58 See Tim Hartford, *The Undercover Economist*, London: Abacus 2007, p. 77–8.

59 See Stephen Jay Gould, "Phyletic Size Decrease in Hershey Bars," in *Hen's Teeth and Horses' Toes*, New York: W. W. Norton & Company 1994. This is the profit: the price of nothing we pay when we buy something from a capitalist. The capitalist economy counts with the price of nothing, it involves the reference to a virtual Zero which has a precise price.

the harmonious functioning (the circular movement) of the Whole.[60] Do we not have here, once again, a homologous duality of vacuums: the vacuum of "standing still" and the vacuum of "doing nothing"? In a kind of repetition of the paradox of the Higgs field, in order to effectively "do nothing," one should not "stand still," but be active in a certain way, since, if one is really inactive, if one just stands still, this immobility causes havoc and chaos.[61]

If we want to describe the minimal ontological coordinates of the universe, it is thus not enough simply to posit the endless multiplicity of phenomena against the background of the vacuum or void as their universality: the vacuum itself is always already split between the "false" and the "true" vacuum, a split which originally or constitutively disturbs it. Or, to risk an anachronistic Hegelian formulation: it is thanks to this split in the vacuum itself that the "substance is always already subject." Here it is crucial to distinguish between the subject and the agent: the agent is a particular entity embedded in the context of a phenomenon, the entity whose contours are constituted through a particular agential cut and in contrast to the object which emerges through the same cut; the subject, on the contrary, is a void which is not determined by its context but disentangled from it, or, rather, is the very gesture of such a disentanglement. In other words, the opposition of agent and object is the result of the agential cut; but when the "object" is the vacuum itself, it is supplemented by the *pure* difference which "is" subject. The shift from specific to pure difference is thus the same as the shift from agent to subject. And, insofar as the subject is for Hegel not only the name for a cut, but also the name for the emergence of appearance, is not so-called de-coherence, the collapse of the wave function which makes ordinary reality appear, also the name for a cut, a break, in the entanglement of quantum fluctuations? Why does Barad not make this point?

---

60 In Tolstoy's *War and Peace*, the opposition between Napoleon and Kutuzov is one between active passivity and passive activity: Napoleon is frantically active, moving and attacking all the time, but this very activity is fundamentally passive—he passively follows his fate which pushes him into activity, a victim of historical forces he does not understand. Marshall Kutuzov, his Russian military counterpart, is passive in his acts—withdrawing, just persisting—yet his passivity is sustained by an active will to endure and win.

61 There is a personality type which exemplifies the catastrophic consequences of "doing nothing": the subject who just stands still, doing and noticing nothing wrong, while causing catastrophes all around him. According to Ray Monk, Bertrand Russell was such a type, sitting still at the center of his family network and enjoying life, while suicides multiplied around him. Here we can invoke a common experience: when one is over-excited, attempting to calm oneself down by ceasing all activity usually fails since it is counter-productive—it demands a lot of effort to abstain from activity in such a state. It is much more effective to pursue some minimal meaningless activity, like rhythmically pulling or squeezing one's fingers—such automatic activity brings much more calm than does complete inactivity.

Barad offers many variations on the motif that "details matter": in every experimental set-up, one must be very attentive to material details which can lead to enormous differences in the final result (the "butterfly effect"); in other words, the experiment can never be reduced to its abstract-ideal coordinates. However, is not the opposite fact much more interesting, namely, that the same global form persists through all the variations of the details? What should surprise us is that this ideal form exerts its own efficacy, that it generates the same material effects, so that we can almost always safely ignore the material details—like the form of a wave which remains the same in a sand storm, although the grains of sand which constitute it are never the same. Perhaps this efficacy of the abstraction (the abstract form) is the basis of idealism: its status is not merely epistemological, but also ontological, for the tension between the abstract notion of an object and the details of its material existence is part of the object itself. Barad is right to commend Bohr for transposing the merely epistemological "uncertainty" of measurement into the ontological incompleteness of the (measured) object itself, but she fails to make the same move apropos ideality: what if all the "bad" features she enumerates ("essentialist" notions of identity, and so on) are also not only a result of the observer's epistemological mistake, but, as it were, the result of a "mistake" inscribed into reality itself? To put it another way, Barad proposes a list of features opposing ("good") diffraction and ("bad") reflection: diffraction pattern versus mirror image, differences versus sameness, relationalities versus mimesis, performativity versus representationalism, entangled ontology versus separate entities, intra-action versus interaction of separate entities, phenomena versus things, attending to detailed patterns and fine-grained features versus reifying simplification, the entanglement of subject and object within a phenomenon versus the fixed opposition between the two, complex network versus binary oppositions, etc. But is not this very opposition between diffraction and reflection (or between performativity and representation) itself a rude binary opposition between truth and illusion?[62]

Closely linked to this critical point is another: Barad also repeatedly claims that meaning is not an ideal entity, but a material practice embedded in

62 We should make the same move apropos the opposition of *performative* and *constative*: for decades, we have heard how language is an activity, not a medium of representation which denotes an independent state of things but a life-practice which "does things," which constitutes new relations in the world—has the time not come to ask the obverse question? How can a practice which is fully embedded in a life world start to function in a representative way, subtracting itself from its life-world entanglement, adopting a distanced position of observation and denotation? Hegel praised this "miracle" as the infinite power of Understanding, which can separate—or, at least, treat as separated—what in real life belongs together.

apparatuses, and so forth. But how are we then to account for its ideal status, illusory as it may be? Concepts may be always and constitutively embedded in material practices, but they are not *only* this. The problem is not to locate concepts in material practice, but to explain how material practices can generate the ideal entity we experience as a concept. In a similar way, Barad repeatedly deploys the motif of the Cartesian subject as the external agent of disentangled observation, to be replaced by agential entanglement: we are part of the observed reality, the cut between subject and object is contingently enacted, and so on. But the true problem is to explain how this "false" appearance of a disentangled subject can emerge in the first place: can it really be accounted for in the terms of the agential cut within the entanglement of a phenomenon? Is it not that we have to presuppose a more radical trans-phenomenal cut as a kind of transcendental a priori that makes intra-active agential cuts possible?

Here, perhaps, a more radical reading of diffraction is needed: the very notion of diffraction has to be diffracted. As Barad notes, "diffraction has to do with the way waves combine when they overlap and the apparent bending and spreading of waves that occurs when waves encounter an obstruction."[63] Diffraction itself is thus diffracted into combining and splitting, into overlapping and spreading. This duality does not refer to two consecutive phases of a process, like a wave which, upon encountering an obstruction, splits into two waves which then, meeting up again on the other side of the obstacle, interfere. Rather, the duality refers to two aspects of one and the same process: diffraction is a splitting which generates what it splits into two, for there is no unity preceding the split. In other words, we should conceive diffraction not as a liberating *dehiscence* of the One, but as the very movement of the constitution of the One, as the disunity, the gap, which gives birth to the One. Thus radicalized, diffraction is revealed as another name for parallax, the shift of perspective needed to produce the effect of the depth of the Real, as if an object acquires the impenetrable density of the Real only when its reality reveals itself to be inconsistent: the observed X is real only insofar as it is the impossible point at which two incompatible realities overlap—now it is a wave, but if we measure it differently, it is a particle.

This means that the two vacuums are also not symmetrical: we are not dealing with a polarity, but with the displaced One, a One which is, as it were, retarded with regard to itself, always already "fallen," its symmetry always already broken.[64] The "pure" vacuum always reveals itself as "false," drawn towards the balance of a "true" vacuum which already involves a minimum of activity and disturbance. It is crucial that this tension between the two vacuums be maintained: the "false vacuum" cannot simply be dismissed as a mere illusion, leaving

63 Barad, *Meeting the Universe Halfway*, p. 74.

64 Perhaps Derrida was aiming at something similar with his notion of *différance*.

only the "true" vacuum, so that the only true peace is that of incessant activity, of balanced circular motion—the "true" vacuum itself remains forever a traumatic disturbance.

Complementarity in quantum physics (wave or particle) excludes any dialectical relationship, there is no mediation between the parallax gap that separates the two aspects—is this gap the non-dialectical ground of negativity? The old metaphysical problem of how to name the nameless abyss pops up here in the context of how to name the primordial gap: contradiction, antagonism, symbolic castration, parallax, diffraction, complementarity ... up to *difference*. As Jameson hinted, perhaps one should leave this gap nameless, but what we should not abstain from is at least an interim outline of the ontology implied by such a universe.

Recall the example of the revolutionary lovers living in a permanent state of emergency, totally dedicated to the Cause, ready to sacrifice all personal sexual fulfillment for it, but simultaneously totally dedicated to each other: the radical *disjunction* between sexual passion and social-revolutionary activity is fully recognized here, for the two dimensions are accepted as totally heterogeneous, each irreducible to the other, and it is this very acceptance of the gap which makes the relationship non-antagonistic. This example can serve as a model for the properly dialectical reconciliation: the two dimensions are not mediated or united in a higher "synthesis," they are merely accepted in their incommensurability. This is why the insurmountable parallax gap, the confrontation of two closely linked perspectives between which no neutral common ground is possible, is *not* a Kantian revenge over Hegel, that is, yet another name for a fundamental *antinomy* which can never be dialectically mediated or sublated. Hegelian reconciliation is a reconciliation with the irreducibility of the antinomy, and it is in this way that the antinomy loses its antagonistic character.

Y'a de den

So where does all this leave us with regard to Hegel? We all know the famous opening lines of "Burnt Norton," the first of T. S. Eliot's *Four Quartets*:

> Time present and time past
> Are both perhaps present in time future,
> And time future contained in time past.
> If all time is eternally present
> All time is unredeemable.

There is a parody on these lines (admired by Eliot himself) which, by merely changing or adding a word here and there, transforms them into a pure and simple banality, in the style of "Yesterday I was a day younger than today, and tomorrow I will be a day older ..." Does not something homologous occur in the predominant reception of Hegel's thought? What we get is an endlessly repeated series of banalities: Hegel's thought as the ultimate expression, to the point of madness even, of metaphysical onto-teleology; the dialectical process as a closed circle in which things "become what they are," in which nothing really new can emerge; the elevation of the Concept into a monster whose self-movement engenders all of reality; the a priori confidence that all negativity, splits, antagonisms, are "reconciled" in the final sublation, and so on and so forth. Here, we need only introduce a little displacement, and the entire image of a grand metaphysical process turns into a freakish monstrosity. Yes, things "become what they are," but *literally*: in a contingent and open process, they become what, *retroactively*, it appears that they always already were. Yes, antagonism is "reconciled," but not in the sense that it magically disappears—what Hegel calls "reconciliation" is, at its most basic, a reconciliation with the antagonism. Yes, in the course of a dialectical process, its ground (starting point) is retroactively posited by its result, but this retroactive positing never closes in a full circle, a discontinuity always persists between a ground and what the ground grounds, and so on.

The ultimate "Hegelian" banality concerns the fact, emphasized by Lebrun, that, whatever the radical contingency of the process, Hegel holds out the promise that, at the end, *we can always tell a story about the process*. What the critics of Hegel usually question is the happy ending: the assurance that every negativity will be sublated in a higher unity. This questioning, however, relies on a false presupposition: the idea that the story Hegel is telling is the arch-ideological story of the primordial Fall, the story of how One divides into Two, of how original innocence is disturbed by division or alienation, and so on. Then, of course, the reproach is that once the original unity is lost it can never be regained. But is this really the story Hegel is telling? Let us approach this key question through a detour.

When we speak about myths in psychoanalysis, we are effectively speaking about *one* myth, the Oedipus myth—all other Freudian myths (the myth of the primordial father, Freud's version of the Moses myth) are variations on it, although necessary ones. However, with the Hamlet narrative, things get complicated. The standard, pre-Lacanian, "naïve" psychoanalytic reading of course focuses on Hamlet's incestuous desire for his mother. Hamlet's shock at his father's death is thus explained in terms of the traumatic impact the fulfillment of an unconscious violent desire (in this case, for the father to die) has on the subject; the specter of the dead father who appears to Hamlet is the projection of his own guilt with regard to his death-wish; his hatred of Claudius is an effect of narcissistic rivalry—Claudius, instead of Hamlet himself, got his mother; his disgust for Ophelia and womankind in general expresses his revulsion at sex in its suffocating incestuous modality, which arises with the lack of the paternal prohibition or sanction. So, according to this standard reading, Hamlet as a modernized version of Oedipus bears witness to the strengthening of the Oedipal prohibition of incest in the passage from Antiquity to Modernity: in the case of Oedipus, we are still dealing with incest, while in *Hamlet*, the incestuous wish is repressed and displaced. And it seems that the very diagnosis of Hamlet as an obsessional neurotic points in this direction: in contrast to hysteria which is found throughout all (at least Western) history, obsessional neurosis is a distinctly modern phenomenon.

While one should not underestimate the strength of this robust, even heroic, Freudian reading of Hamlet as a modernized version of the Oedipus myth, the problem is how to harmonize it with the fact that, although—in the Goethean lineage—Hamlet may appear a model of the modern (introverted, brooding, indecisive) intellectual, the myth of Hamlet is older than that of Oedipus. The kernel of the Hamlet narrative (the son avenges his father against the father's evil brother who murdered him and took over his throne; the son survives the illegitimate rule of his uncle by playing the fool and making "crazy" but truthful remarks) is a universal myth found everywhere, from old Nordic cultures through Ancient Egypt up to Iran and Polynesia. The expected chronological order is thus reversed: what appears to be the original mythical story comes second, preceded by its more "corrupted," ironic, mediated copy. This paradox of (what is experienced as) repetition (a distorted copy) preceding the "pure" original is what defines *historicity proper* in contrast to the ideological (hi)story of a Fall: history proper begins when our vision of the past is no longer colored by our (negative) experience of the present, when we are able to perceive the past as an epoch regulated by forms of social organization which radically differ from the present ones. Fredric Jameson has pointed out that the original topic of a narrative, the narrative "as such," is the narrative of a Fall, of how things went wrong, of how the old harmony was destroyed (in the case of Hamlet, how the evil uncle overthrew the good father-king). This narrative is the elementary form of ideology, and as such the key step in the critique of ideology should be to invert it—which brings us back to Hegel: the story he is telling in his account of a dialectical process is not the story of how an original organic unity alienates itself from itself, but the story of how this organic unity never existed in the first place, of how its status is by definition that of a retroactive fantasy—the Fall itself generates the mirage of what it is the Fall from.

The same paradox holds for belief: viewing the present as an era of cynical non-belief, we tend to imagine the past as a time when people "really believed"—but was there ever an era when people "really believed"? As Robert Pfaller demonstrated in his *Illusionen der Anderen*,[65] the direct belief in a truth which is subjectively fully assumed ("Here I stand!") is a modern phenomenon, in contrast to traditional beliefs-at-a-distance, such as underpin conventions of politeness or other rituals. Premodern societies did not believe directly, but at a distance, which explains the misreading inherent in, for example, the Enlightenment critique of "primitive" myths—faced with a notion such as a tribe having originated from a fish or a bird, the critics first take it as a literal belief, then reject it as naïve and "fetishistic." They thereby impose their own notion of belief on the "primitivized" Other.[66] Pfaller is right to emphasize how, today, we believe more than ever: the most skeptical attitude, that of deconstruction, relies on the figure of an Other who "really believes." The postmodern need for the permanent use of devices of ironic distantiation (quotation marks, etc.) betrays the underlying fear that, without these devices, belief would be direct and immediate—it is as if saying "I love you" instead of the ironic "As the poets would say, 'I love you,'" would entail a directly assumed belief that I love you, as if a certain distance is not operative already in the statement "I love you." We can see how the idea of an earlier age of naïve belief also follows the logic of the Fall: what it obfuscates is the fact that such belief is a retroactive fantasy generated by the cynical present. In reality, people never "really believed": in premodern times, belief was not "literal," it included a distance which was lost with the passage to modernity.

So, to conclude, let us recapitulate not only this chapter, but the focal point of the entire book, by taking as a starting point Ray Brassier's question: "*How does thought think the death of thinking?*"[67] To really think the end of the universe (not only the extinction of the human race, but the end of the universe itself predicted by quantum cosmology), we have to grasp this end as "something that *has already happened*,"[68] and to think our present from this impossible standpoint. The very last words of Brassier's book define philosophy at its most radical as

---

65 See Robert Pfaller, *Die Illusionen der anderen: Über das Lustprinzip in der Kultur*, Frankfurt: Suhrkamp 2002.

66 One commonplace about philosophers today is that their very analysis of the hypocrisy of the dominant system betrays their naïveté: why are they still shocked to see people inconsistently violate their professed values when it suits their interests? Do they really expect people to be consistent and principled? He we should defend authentic philosophers: what surprises them is the exact *opposite* feature—not that people do not "really believe" and act upon their professed principles, but that *people who profess their cynicism and radical pragmatic opportunism secretly believe much more than they are ready to admit*, even if they transpose these beliefs onto (non-existent) "others."

67 Ray Brassier, *Nihil Unbound: Enlightenment and Extinction*, London: Palgrave Macmillan 2007, p. 223.

68 Ibid.

"the organon of extinction"[69]—the attempt to think being from the standpoint of extinction means to think externality without thinking, without (the implicit presence of) the mind. But there is something wrong, some key dimension is blurred, when we formulate the problem in this way: it is easy to think the universe prior to the emergence of humanity, there are hundreds of popularizing books written about the Big Bang, the evolution of life on Earth, and so on. The true problem lies elsewhere and is only indicated by the transcendental retort "How can we be sure that the scientific view of pre-human objective reality is not already constituted by a transcendental horizon?": the true problem is how can I think *myself* as if I am already dead or, more precisely, extinct? Certainly not through any kind of mystical immersion in a primordial abyss, but, paradoxically, through a radical dis-embodying, through depriving myself of all "pathological" features of my finitude—and *this* is the *cogito*, this zero-point of the disembodied gaze which sustains "objective" science. This dis-embodied X which may think itself as part of the object, as already dead, this "undead" X is the subject, so that the problem is not how to think the In-itself without mind, but how to think the "objectal" status of this zero-point of thinking itself. This forever-elusive objectal counterpart of the subject, the "fossil" which "is" the subject, is what Lacan calls the *objet a*, and it is this paradoxical object which is the only true In-itself.

Ultimately, the alternative we are dealing with here is between two versions of the death drive: either Brassier's reading of Freud (as an heroic step beyond the Nietzschean will-to-life into fully assuming the will-to-know as the will-to-nothingess, the will to reach the In-itself by way of thinking the end of thinking), or Lacan's reading of Freud (the death drive as the undead compulsion-to-repeat). Brassier's Freudian option repeats Freud's confusion between the death drive and the nirvana principle, reading the former as a striving for the return of the organic to the inorganic or of matter itself to the primordial void, while Lacan conceives the death drive as a disturbance of any void, as the insistence of a pre-ontological X on account of which "it moves." The ultimate ontological choice is thus not the choice between nothing and something, but between nothing (extinction) and less than nothing (*eppur si muove*).

In a way, the difference between Brassier's position and the Lacano-Hegelian position can be summed up by a simple replacement: Brassier refers to Freud's triple de-centering or humiliation of man's narcissism—Copernicus, Darwin, psychoanalysis—but he replaces psychoanalysis with cognitivism.[70] The latter fully naturalizes our mind, reducing it to a phenomenon arising naturally out of evolution—but perhaps Brassier proceeds too fast here: while cognitivism de-centers the human mind from outside, treating it as an effect of objective natural

69 Ibid., p. 239.

70 Ibid., p. 40.

mechanisms, only psychoanalysis de-centers it *from within*, revealing how the human mind involves not only objective neuronal processes but also "subjective" processes of thinking which are inaccessible to it.

Referring to François Laruelle, Brassier defines materialism in terms of the Marxist-sounding notion of "determination in the last instance," which should be opposed to the similar notion of overdetermination: "determination-in-the-last-instance is the causality which renders it universally possible for any object X to determine its own 'real' cognition, but only in the last instance."[71] Overdetermination is transcendental; that is, the point of transcendentalism is that a subject can never fully "objectivize" itself, reduce itself to a part of "objective reality" in front of it, since such a reality is always already transcendentally constituted by subjectivity: no matter to what extent I succeed in accounting for myself as a phenomenon within the "great chain of being," as an effect determined by a network of natural (or supernatural) causes, this causal image is always already overdetermined by the transcendental horizon which structures my approach to reality. To this transcendental overdetermination, Brassier opposes the naturalist determination in the last instance: a serious materialist can only assume that every subjective horizon within which reality appears, every subjective constitution or mediation of reality, has to be ultimately determined by its place within objective reality, has to be conceived as part of the all-encompassing natural process. The contrast is clear here: overdetermination does not stand for the way an all-encompassing Whole determines the interplay of its parts, but, on the contrary, for the way a part of the whole emerges as a self-relating One which overdetermines the network of its relations with others. In this precise sense, the elementary form of overdetermination is *life*: a living being is part of the world, but it relates to its environment as a function of its self-relating (to take the simplest example: an organism relates to food because it needs it). Overdetermination is a name for this paradoxical reversal by means of which a moment subsumes under itself the whole out of which it grew (or, in Hegelese, posits its presuppositions).

Such a relationship between overdetermination and determination in the last instance is antagonistic, since the former makes any direct conceptualization of the latter impossible. At the level of temporality, the structure of overdetermination is that of retroactivity, of an effect which retroactively posits (overdetermines) the very causes by which it is determined in the last instance, and the reduction of overdetermination to determination in the last instance means that we have succeeded in retroactively transposing causality back into the linear causal network. Why, then, does (symbolic-retroactive) overdetermination emerge at all? Is its status ultimately that of an illusion, albeit

71 François Laurelle, *Introduction au non-marxisme*, Paris: PUF, p. 48; as quoted in Brassier, *Nihil Unbound*, p. 138.

a spontaneous and necessary one? The only way to avoid this conclusion is to break the linear determinist chain and assert the ontological openness of reality: overdetermination is not illusory insofar as it retroactively fills in the gaps in the chain of causality.[72]

Does not Brassier himself admit this complication when—again, following Laruelle—he concedes that thought can touch the Real only through the overlapping of two foreclosures?

> [I]dealism is not circumvented by subtracting intellectual intuition from the reality to which it provides access, but by short-circuiting the transcendental difference between thinking and being so that what is foreclosed to thought in the object coincides (albeit non-synthetically) with what is foreclosed to the object in thought.[73]

This formula is very precise: "what is foreclosed to thought in the object" (the *transcendent* In-itself of the object inaccessible to thought) overlaps with "what is foreclosed to the object in thought" (the *immanence* of the subject excluded from the realm of objectivity). This overlapping of the two "foreclosures" (not to be confused with Lacan's *forclusion*) repeats the basic Hegelo-Lacanian move: the very distance which separates us from the In-itself is immanent to the In-itself, makes us (the subject) an unaccountable/"impossible" gap or cut within the In-itself. Insofar as, for Lacan, "what is foreclosed to thought in the object" is the "impossible" *objet a*, and "what is foreclosed to the object in thought" is $, the void of the barred subject itself, this overlapping brings us back to Lacan's formula $-*a*.

No wonder, then, that we can approach the Real only via a (proto-Hegelian) detour through error: "Thinking needs to be *occasioned* by objectifying transcendence in order for it to be able to assume the real as its unobjectifiable cause-of-the-last-instance … Thus determination-in-the-last-instance requires objectifying transcendence even as it modifies it."[74] In other words, *la vérité surgit de la méprise*: the process of knowing has to be triggered by a transcendent object, in order to cancel this erroneous transcendence in the second step. How, then, can we touch the Real in thinking?

---

72 The terminological reference to Marx is not as arbitrary as it may appear: in Marxist terms, the relationship between determination in the last instance and overdetermination is that between the economy and politics: the economy determines in the last instance, while politics (political class struggle) overdetermines the entire process. One cannot reduce overdetermination to determination in the last instance—this would be the same as reducing political class struggle to a secondary effect of economic processes. Again, the duality between determination in the last instance and overdetermination should be conceived as that of a parallax split.

73 Brassier, *Nihil Unbound*, p. 139.

74 Ibid., p. 140.

> To think oneself in accordance with a real which is without essence does not mean to think oneself to be this rather than that; a human being rather than a thing. To think oneself according to an inconsistent real which punctures nothingness itself means to think oneself as identical with a last-instance which is devoid of even the minimal consistency of the void. The real is less than nothing—which is certainly not to equate it with the impossible (Lacan).[75]

The only thing to drop from this (sympathetic) summary of Laruelle's position is the final qualification: the Lacanian Real-impossible is precisely such a "given without givenness," without a phenomenological horizon opening the space for it to appear, the impossible point of the ontic without the ontological. The key question here is whether this impossibility applies only to us (and as such is epistemological, concerning the fact that it is impossible for us, as finite humans, to relate to reality outside of an ontological horizon), or whether it is inherent to the Real In-itself.

In a way, Brassier is right to reject the identity of the inconsistent (ics) real with the Lacanian Real-impossible: for Lacan, there is an impossibility inscribed into the very core of the Real. To return to Democritus: *den* is the name of the pre-ontological ics multiplicity of less-than-Ones (and thereby less-than-Nothings), which is the only dialectical-materialist candidate for the In-itself. The question is: is this ics multiplicity sufficient as a (pre-)ontological starting point? When Badiou says that there is no One, it all hinges on how this negation is to be understood: is it simply the assertion of pure multiplicity, or is it asserting that the negation of the One is the immanent negative feature of that pure multiplicity itself? In the terms of the joke quoted in Chapter 10, is the ics multiplicity just plain coffee or *coffee without ... (x)*? The Lacano-Hegelian axiom is that *the impossibility of the One is the immanent negative feature of the ics multiplicity*: there is an ics multiplicity because there is no One, because the One is in itself blocked, impossible.[76]

What, then, is the "Thing-in-itself" from a dialectical-materialist standpoint? The best way to answer this question is, again, to oppose dialectical materialism to Buddhism: in Buddhism, the In-itself is the void, nothing, and ordinary reality is a play of appearances. The question ultimately unanswered here is how we get from nothing to something. How do illusory appearances arise out of the void? The dialectical-materialist answer is: only if this something is *less* than nothing, the pre-ontological proto-reality of *den*. From within this proto-reality, our ordinary reality appears through the emergence of a subject which constitutes "objective reality": every positive reality of Ones is already phenomenal, transcendentally constituted, "correlated" to a subject—in

75 Ibid., p. 137.

76 Note how "the One is not" brings us back to the hypotheses of Plato's *Parmenides*.

Badiou's terms, every reality is that of a world defined by its transcendental coordinates.

How, then, do we pass from the In-itself of proto-reality to transcendentally constituted reality proper? Laruelle is right to point out that the In-itself is not "outside," as an external Real independent of the transcendental field: in the couple subject and object, the In-itself is on the side of the subject, since *there are (transcendentally constituted) objects (of "external reality") because there is a split subject.* This constitutive split of the subject (which precedes the split between subject and object) is the split between the void that "is" the subject ($) and the impossible-Real objectal counterpart of the subject, the purely virtual *objet a.* What we call "external reality" (as a consistent field of positively existing objects) arises through subtraction, that is, when something is subtracted from it—and this something is the *objet a.* The correlation between subject and object (objective reality) is thus sustained by the correlation between this same subject and its objectal correlate, the impossible-Real *objet a,* and this second correlation is of a totally different kind: it is a kind of negative correlation, an impossible link, a non-relationship, between two moments which can never meet within the same space (like subject and object), not because they are too far away, but because they are one and the same entity on the two sides of a Möbius band. This impossible-Real virtual object is not external to the symbolic, but its immanent impediment, what makes the symbolic space curved; more precisely, it "is" nothing but this curvature of the symbolic space.

What this means, in effect, is that *there is no ontology of the Real*: the very field of ontology, of the positive order of Being, emerges through the subtraction of the Real. The order of Being and the Real are mutually exclusive: the Real is the immanent blockage or impediment of the order of Being, what makes the order of Being inconsistent. This is why, at the level of ontology, transcendental correlationism is right: every "reality," every positive order of Being, is ontological, correlative to *logos,* transcendentally constituted through the symbolic order—"language is the house of being," as Heidegger put it.

But do we not get caught in a contradictory redoubling here: the Real is a gap in the order of Being (reality) *and* a gap in the symbolic order? The reason there is no contradiction is that "reality" *is* transcendentally constituted by the symbolic order, so that "the limits of my language are the limits of my world" (Wittgenstein). In the common transcendental view, there is some kind of Real-in-itself (like the Kantian *Ding an sich*) which is then formed or "constituted" into reality by the subject; due to the subject's finitude, we cannot totalize reality, reality is irreducibly inconsistent, "antinomic," and so forth—we cannot gain access to the Real, which remains transcendent. The gap or inconsistency thus concerns only our symbolically constituted reality, not the Real in itself. Lacan here takes a step strictly homologous to the move from Kant to Hegel with regard to antinomies and the Thing-in-itself: the Real is not the external In-itself that eludes the symbolic grasp, that the symbolic can only encircle in an inconsistent and antinomic way; the Real is *nothing but* the gap or antagonism that thwarts the symbolic from within—the symbolic touches the Real in a totally immanent way. We are thus led back to the key paradox of the Real: it is not simply the inaccessible In-itself, it is simultaneously the Thing-in-itself and the obstacle which prevents our access to the Thing-in-itself. Therein lies already the basic reflexive move of Christianity, as well as of the Hegelian dialectic: in Christianity, the very gap that separates a believer from God is what ensures his identity with God, since, in the figure of the abandoned Christ on the Cross, God is separated from himself; in Hegel, an epistemological obstacle becomes an ontological feature of the Thing itself (contradiction is not only an index of the imperfection of our knowledge, the limitation of our knowledge brings us in contact with the [limitation of the] Thing itself).

The Real is thus an effect of the symbolic, not in the sense of performativity, of the "symbolic construction of reality," but in the totally different sense of a kind of ontological "collateral damage" of symbolic operations: the process of symbolization is inherently thwarted, doomed to fail, and the Real *is* this immanent failure of the symbolic. The circular temporality of the process of symbolization is crucial here: the Real is the effect of the failure of the symbolic to reach (not the In-itself, but) *itself*, to fully realize itself, but this failure occurs because the symbolic is thwarted in itself. It is in this sense that, for Lacan, the subject itself is an "answer of the Real": a subject wants to say something, it fails, and this failure *is* the subject—a "subject of the signifier" is literally the result of the failure to become itself. In this sense, also, within the symbolic space, the effect is *a reaction against its cause*, while the cause is a retroactive effect of its cause: the subject produces signifiers which fail, and the subject qua Real is the effect of this failure.

But does this mean that we end up in a kind of idealism of the symbolic—what we experience as "reality" is symbolically constructed, and even the Real which eludes the grasp of the symbolic is a result of the immanent failure of the symbolic? No, because *it is through this very failure to be itself that the symbolic touches the Real.* In contrast to transcendentalism, Lacan agrees that we have access to the In-itself: Lacan is not a discourse-idealist who claims that we are forever caught in the web of symbolic practices, unable to reach the In-itself. However, we do not touch the Real by way of breaking out of the "prison-house of language" and gaining access to the external transcendent referent—every external referent ("fully existing positive reality") is already transcendentally constituted. We touch the Real-in-itself in our very failure to touch it, since the Real *is*, at its most radical, the gap, the "minimal difference," that separates the One from itself.

It is therefore not enough to say that, while things exist out there in their meaningless reality, language performatively adds meaning to them: the symbolic transcendentally constitutes reality in a much stronger ontological sense, in its being itself. The true question is how this performativity (the "magic" of "doing things with words") is possible. It is not simply that the ultimate failure of symbolic performativity produces the excess of the Real as the immanent obstacle to the process of symbolization; this obstacle, the gap or antagonism that hinders the symbolic process from within, is the condition of performativity:

> it is because being is always also a form of antagonism/distortion that these [performative] operations are effective. This is what makes "performativity" possible to begin with, what makes it ontologically (and not only logically) effective. If the symbolic is productive of being, and not only of the ways (and norms) of being, it is because of what prevents being to be *qua* being, because of its inherent contradiction, which is precisely not symbolic, but real.[77]

In short, the symbolic can be productive of being only insofar as the order of being is in itself thwarted, incomplete, marked by an immanent gap or antagonism.

This brings us back to the properly Lacanian notion of sexuality as the immanent limit of ontology. One has to oppose here sexuality and animal sex (copulation): animal sex is not "sexual" in the precise sense of human sexuality.[78] Human sexuality is not defined by its bodily content; it is a formal feature, a distortion or protraction of the space-and-time which can affect any activity, even those which have nothing to do with sexuality. How does an activity that is in itself definitely asexual acquire sexual connotations? It is "sexualized" when it fails to achieve its asexual goal and gets caught up in a vicious cycle of futile repetition. We enter sexuality when an activity or gesture that "officially" serves some instrumental goal becomes an end-in-itself, when we start to enjoy the very "dysfunctional" repetition of this gesture and thereby suspend its purposefulness. For example: I meet a friend and we shake hands, but instead of letting go after the first shake, I continue to hold his hand and squeeze it rhythmically—with this simple non-functional protraction, I generate an obscene sexual undertone. It is in this sense that "sexuality (as the real) is not some being that exists *beyond* the symbolic, it 'exists' solely as the *curving of the symbolic space that takes place because of the additional something produced with the signifying gesture*."[79] In other words, sexuality as Real is not external to the symbolic field,

---

77 Alenka Zupančič, "Sexual Difference and Ontology" (unpublished manuscript).
78 It is in this sense that we should read those theologians who claim that Adam and Eve did copulate while in the Garden of Eden, but did so as a simple instrumental activity, like sowing seeds in a field, without any underlying sexual tension.
79 Zupančič, "Sexual Difference and Ontology."

it is its immanent curvature or distortion, it occurs because the symbolic field is blocked by an inherent impossibility.

And this brings us back finally to the triad of the premodern sexualized view of cosmos, modern desexualized ontology, and Lacan's re-assertion of sexuality in its ontological dimension *within* the modern desexualized universe, as its inherent limitation: "De-sexualization of ontology (its no longer being conceived as a combinatory of two, 'masculine' and 'feminine', principles) coincides with the sexual appearing as the real/disruptive point of being."[80] Desexualized modern ontology attempts to describe a flat, neutral (neutered) order of being (the anonymous multiplicity of subatomic particles or forces), but in order to do so, it has to ignore the inconsistency or incompleteness of the order of being, the immanent impossibility which thwarts every ontology. Every field of ontology, even at its most radical (like the mathematical ontology of Badiou), has to subtract the impossible/Real (the curved space of sexuation) from the order of being.

80 Ibid.

Conclusion: The Political Suspension of the Ethical

What the inexistence of the big Other signals is that every ethical and/or moral edifice has to be grounded in an abyssal act which is, in the most radical sense imaginable, *political*. Politics is the very space in which, without any external guarantee, ethical decisions are made and negotiated. The idea that one can ground politics in ethics, or that politics is ultimately a strategic effort to realize prior ethical positions, is a version of the illusion of the "big Other." From the question "Which ethics fits psychoanalysis?" we should therefore pass to the question "Which politics fits psychoanalysis?"

With regard to politics, Freud's ultimate position is the same as Lacan's: psychoanalysis does not provide new positive political programs for action; its ultimate achievement, the "bottom line" of analysis, is to have discerned the contours of a "negativity," a disruptive force, which poses a threat to every stable collective link. Since a political act intervenes in a state of things, simultaneously creating instability and trying to establish a new positive order, one can say that psychoanalysis confronts us with the zero-level of politics, a pre-political "transcendental" condition of possibility of politics, a gap which opens up the space for the political act to intervene in, a gap which is saturated by the political effort to impose a new order. In Lacanian terms, psychoanalysis confronts us with the zero-level at which "nothing is taking place but the place itself," while politics proper intervenes in this place with a new Master-Signifier, imposing fidelity on it, legitimizing us in "enforcing" on reality the project sustained by this Master-Signifier.

Consequently, one can say that, with regard to the gap or antagonism which defines the human condition, the relationship between psychoanalysis and politics is that of a parallax split, of a missed encounter between a "not yet" and a "too late": psychoanalysis opens up the gap before the act, while politics already sutures the gap, introducing a new consistency, imposing a new Master-Signifier.[1] But does every politics, every political act, necessarily involve a self-blinding cover-up of the gap? What if there is no pure experience of the gap, what if every version of the gap is already viewed from the standpoint of a

1 See Mladen Dolar, *Oficirji, služkinje in dimnikarji*, Ljubljana: Analecta 2010. In literature, the corresponding couple is perhaps that of Sophocles versus Aeschylus: the tragic deadlock versus a new order, terror versus a new harmony.

certain political engagement? So there is a conservative-tragic celebration of the gap (we are ultimately doomed to fail, heroic acts can only temporarily postpone the final fall, the most we can do is fall in an authentic way), a liberal pragmatic assertion of the gap (democracy admits the imperfection of our societies, there is no final solution to our woes, just a more or less successful pragmatic tinkering), and the radical-leftist eternalization of struggle (Mao: "class struggle will go on forever"). Each of these positions can also be formulated in terms of its own specific denial of the antagonism: the conservative organic harmony, the liberal balancing of conflicts through the translation of antagonism into agonistic competition, the leftist post-revolutionary paradise-to-come.

But, again, are these three versions of the gap equal? Is not the leftist version to be privileged, insofar as it is the only one to conceive the gap not only as struggle but as an immanent antagonism or discord constitutive of the social dimension itself? This means that here, too, we should posit the coincidence of opposites: the gap is visible "as such" only from the standpoint of extreme leftist engagement. Is this parallax gap, this extreme coincidence of opposites (pure form and the contingent material excess which gives body to it, wave and particle in quantum physics, universality and full partisan engagement, etc., up to and including fidelity to a universal Cause and intimate love), the dead-point of the "dialectic in suspense" (as Benjamin put it), a case of pure "contradiction" (or, rather, antinomy) which no dialectical mediation or reconciliation can overcome? The parallax gap is, on the contrary, *the very form of the "reconciliation" of opposites*: one simply has to recognize the gap. Universality is "reconciled" with partisan political engagement in the guise of the engagement which stands for universality (then proletarian emancipatory engagement); pure form is "reconciled" with its content in the guise of the formless excess of content which stands for form as such; or, in Hegel's political vision, the universal Rational State is "reconciled" with particular content in the guise of the Monarch, whose legitimization is simultaneously purely symbolic (his title) and "irrational" (biological: his birth alone justifies his being a monarch).

We should reject here the common-sense view according to which, by dispelling all mystifications and illusions, psychoanalysis makes us aware of what we truly are, what we really want, and thus leaves us at the threshold of a truly free decision no longer dependent on self-delusion. Lacan himself seems to endorse this view when he claims that "if, perhaps, the analysis makes us ready for the moral action, it ultimately leaves us at its door": "the ethical limits of the analysis coincide with the limits of its praxis. This praxis is only a prelude to a moral action as such."[2] However, does not Lacan outline here a kind of *political suspension of the ethical*? Once we become aware of the radical contingency of

2 Jacques Lacan, *Le séminaire, Livre VII: L'éthique de la psychanalyse*, Paris: Seuil 1986, p. 30.

our acts, the moral act in its opposition to the political becomes impossible, since every act involves a decision grounded only in itself, a decision which is, as such and in the most elementary sense, political. Freud himself is here too hasty: he opposes artificial crowds (the church, the army) and "regressive" primary crowds, like a wild mob engaged in passionate collective violence (lynching, pogroms). Furthermore, from his liberal perspective, the reactionary lynch mob and the leftist revolutionary crowd are treated as libidinally identical, involving the same unleashing of the destructive or unbinding death drive.[3] It appears as though, for Freud, the "regressive" primary crowd, exemplarily operative in the destructive violence of a mob, is the zero-level of the unbinding of a social link, the social "death drive" at its purest.

The theological implications of this violence are unexpectedly far-reaching: what if the ultimate addressee of the biblical commandment "Do not kill" is God (Jehovah) himself, and we fragile humans are his neighbors exposed to divine rage? How often, in the Old Testament, do we encounter God as a dark stranger who brutally intrudes into human lives and sows destruction? When Levinas wrote that our first reaction to a neighbor is to kill him, was he not implying that this originally refers to God's relationship to humans, so that the commandment "Do not kill" is an appeal to God to control his rage? Insofar as the Jewish solution is a dead God, a God who survives only in the "dead letter" of the sacred book, of the Law to be interpreted, what dies with the death of God is precisely the God of the Real, of destructive fury and revenge. That often stated claim—God died in Auschwitz—thus has to be inverted: God came alive in Auschwitz. Recall the story from the Talmud about two rabbis debating a theological point: the one losing the debate calls upon God himself to intervene and decide the issue, but when God duly arrives, the other rabbi tells him that since his work of creation is already accomplished, he now has nothing to say and should leave, which God then does. It is as if, in Auschwitz, God came back, with catastrophic consequences. The true horror does not occur when we are abandoned by God, but when God gets too close to us.

---

3 Freud's voting preferences (in a letter, he reported that, as a rule, he did not vote—the exception occurred only when there was a liberal candidate in his district) are thus not just a private matter, they are grounded in his theory. The limits of Freudian liberal neutrality became clear in 1934, when Dolfuss took over in Austria, imposing a corporate state, and armed conflicts exploded in Vienna suburbs (especially around *Karl Marx Hof*, a big workers housing project which was the pride of Social Democracy). The scene was not without its surreal aspects: in central Vienna, life in the famous cafés went on as normal (with Dolfuss presenting himself as defender of this normality), while a mile or so away, soldiers were bombarding workers' blocks. In this situation, the psychoanalytic association issued a directive prohibiting its members from taking sides in the conflict—effectively siding with Dolfuss and making its own small contribution to the Nazi takeover four years later.

We should add to this Freudian position at least three points. First, Freud fails to clearly distinguish between the church-model and the army-model of the artificial crowd: while the "church" stands for the hierarchical social order which tries to maintain peace and equilibrium by making necessary compromises, the "army" stands for an egalitarian collective defined not by its internal hierarchy but by its opposition to an enemy which is out to destroy it—radical emancipatory movements are always modeled on the army, not the church, and millenarian churches are really structured like armies. Second, "regressive" primary crowds do not come first, they are not the "natural" foundation for the rise of "artificial" crowds: they come *afterwards*, as a kind of obscene supplement that sustains the "artificial" crowd, thus relating to the latter like the superego to the symbolic Law. While the symbolic Law demands obedience, the superego provides the obscene enjoyment which attaches us to the Law. Last but not least, is the wild mob really the zero-level of the unbinding of a social link? Is it not rather a panicky *reaction* to the gap or inconsistency that cuts across a social edifice? The violence of the mob is by definition directed at the object (mis)perceived as the external cause of the gap (the Jews, exemplarily), as if the destruction of that object will abolish the gap.

So, again, what are the political consequences of asserting this gap? There are three basic options. First, there is the liberal option essentially advocated by Freud himself: the gap means that we should not fully identify with any positive political project, but retain a minimal distance towards them all, since politics is as such the domain of the Master-Signifier and of symbolic and/or imaginary identifications. Then, there is the conservative option: against the eternal threat of destructive "negativity," it is all the more necessary to impose onto social life a strict order based on a Master-Signifier. Finally, there is a Trotskyist-Deleuzian leftist version: true radical politics is a matter of "permanent revolution," of persisting in permanent self-revolutionizing, without allowing this flux to stabilize itself into a new positive order. With Lacan and politics, it is thus the same as with Hegel: there are three main interpretations, the conservative (emphasizing the symbolic authority as a *sine qua non* of the social order), the leftist (using Lacan for the critique of patriarchal ideology and practice), and the cynically permissive liberal version (to each his or her own *jouissance*). This liberal interpretation participates in the short-circuit between ontology and politics typical of postmodern thought: radical leftist politics is rejected as "metaphysical," as imposing on social life a universal metaphysical vision, as striving for a totally self-transparent and regulated society, and, since life resists the constraints of any such ideological straight-jacket, this politics necessarily ends in totalitarian terror. Such a political stance is very comfortable: while legitimizing a pragmatic politics without risks, it is able to present its cynical liberalism as the most radical-critical position.

So which of these three options is the correct one? The first should be rejected as taking the easy way out, claiming that the question itself is wrong: there is no "true" or "correct" version, the choice is undecidable, open. But, again, which of the three is the correct option? The answer is, of course, the fourth. In other words, as we have already seen, we should reject the presupposition shared by all three. In a properly Hegelian way, the distinction between the zero-level of the empty place and its filling-up with a positive project must be rejected as false: the zero-level is never "there," it can be experienced only retroactively, as the pre-supposition of a new political intervention, of imposing a new order. The question is thus the Hegelian one of a positive order whose positivity gives body to the negativity by accomplishing it.

For the earlier Lacan, both the ethics of symbolic realization and the ethics of confronting the Real Thing call for the heroic stance of pushing things to the limit in order to leave behind our everyday *Verfallenheit*, our fallen existence (one must "subjectivize one's own death" by casting off the wealth of imaginary identifications, thereby attaining the limit-position of a pure subject without an ego; one must violently transgress the very limit of the symbolic order, heroically confronting the dangerous Beyond of the Real Thing). Renouncing this radicalism, the later Lacan re-conceives psychoanalytic treatment in a much more modest way: "one does not need to learn all of the truth. A little bit is sufficient."[4] Here the very idea of psychoanalysis as a radical "limit experience" is rejected: "One should not push an analysis too far. When the patient thinks he is happy to live, it is enough."[5] How far we are here from Antigone's heroic attempt to attain the "pure desire" by entering the prohibited domain of *ate*! Psychoanalytic treatment is now no longer a radical transformation of subjectivity, but a local patching-up which does not even leave any long-term traces. (Along these lines, Lacan draws attention to the neglected fact that, when Freud met the Rat-man again, years after his treatment, the latter had totally forgotten about his analysis.) This more modest approach was fully articulated in Jacques-Alain Miller's reading which focuses on late Lacan: in his last seminars, Lacan leaves behind the notion of "traversing the fantasy" as the concluding moment of the psychoanalytic process; in its place he introduces the opposite gesture of accepting the ultimate non-analyzable obstacle called the *sinthome*. If the symptom is a formation of the unconscious to be dissolved through interpretation, the *sinthome* is the "indivisible remainder" which resists interpretation and interpretive dissolution, a minimal figure or node which condenses the subject's unique mode of enjoyment. The goal of analysis is thus reformulated as "identification with the symptom": instead of dissolving his unique *sinthome*, the subject should become aware of it and learn how to use it,

4 Jacques Lacan, "Radiophonie," in *Autres écrits*, Paris: Seuil 2001, p. 442.

5 Jacques Lacan, "Conférences aux USA," *Scilicet* 6/7 (1976), p. 15.

how to deal with it, instead of allowing the *sinthome* to determine him behind his back:

> The analytic experience enables us to re-appropriate our desire. In the best case, one can thus hope to arrive at "wanting what one desires" and "desiring what one wants." If the experience is brought to its conclusion, it allows us to identify ourselves with our "incurable": not only to find oneself in it, but to make use of it.[6]

Through this identification, the opposition of meaning and enjoyment is also overcome in their "synthesis," that of *jouis-sens* (enjoy-meant, enjoying the sense): the subject is not reduced to an idiotic autistic enjoyment, s/he continues to speak, but his/her talk now functions as a play with semblances, as an empty blah-blah-blah which generates enjoyment. This would be Lacan's version of *eppur si muove*: even after we have seen through imaginary and symbolic semblances, the game goes on in the guise of the circulation of *jouis-sens*, the subject is not dissolved in the abyss of the Real.

Relying on this new notion of the final moment of the analytic process, Miller deploys a simplified version of the "critique of instrumental reason," establishing a link between democratic culture and racism: our era privileges the universalizing scientific rationality which admits only mathematically quantified statements whose truth-value does not depend on an idiosyncratic subjective position; in this sense, both universalism and egalitarian-democratic passion are the results of the hegemony of the scientific discourse. But if we extend the validity of scientific reason into the social field, the results are dangerous: universalizing passion pushes us to search for a universal mode of enjoyment that will be best for all, so those who resist it are disqualified as "barbarians": "Due to the progress of science, racism has thus a bright future. The more refined discriminations provided by science we have, the more segregation in society we get."[7] This is why psychoanalysis is under such attack today: it focuses on the uniqueness of each subject's mode of enjoyment, a uniqueness which resists scientific universalization as well as democratic egalitarianism: "Democratic leveling may be very nice, but it doesn't replace the eroticism of exception."[8]

One has to concede that Miller has fearlessly spelt out the political implications of this insistence on the uniqueness of the subject's mode of enjoyment: psychoanalysis "reveals social ideals in their nature of semblances, and we can add, of semblances with regard to a real which is the real of enjoyment. This is

---

6 Nicolas Fleury, *Le réel insensé: Introduction à la pensée de Jacques-Alain Miller*, Paris: Germina 2010, p. 136.

7 Ibid., p. 98.

8 Jacques-Alain Miller, "La psychanalyse, la cité, les communautés," *La cause freudienne* 68 (February 2008), p. 118.

the cynical position, which resides in saying that enjoyment is *the only thing that is true*."[9] What this means is that a psychoanalyst

> occupies the position of an ironist who takes care not to intervene into the political field. He acts so that semblances remain at their places while making sure that the subjects under his care do not take them as *real* ... one should somehow bring oneself to remain *taken in by them* (fooled by them). Lacan could say that "those who are not taken in err": if one doesn't act as if semblances are real, if one doesn't leave their efficacy undisturbed, things take a turn for the worse. Those who think that all signs of power are mere semblances and rely on the arbitrariness of the discourse of the master are the bad boys: they are even more alienated.[10]

In relation to politics then, a psychoanalyst thus "doesn't propose projects, he cannot propose them, he can only mock the projects of others, which limits the scope of his statements. The ironist has no great design, he waits for the other to speak first and then brings about his fall as fast as possible ... Let us say this is political wisdom, nothing more."[11] The axiom of this "wisdom" is that

> one should protect the semblances of power for the good reason that one should be able to continue to *enjoy*. The point is not to attach oneself to the semblances of the existing power, but to consider them necessary. "This defines a cynicism in the mode of Voltaire who let it be understood that God is our invention which is necessary to maintain people in a proper decorum." Society is kept together only by semblances, "which means: there is no society without repression, without identification, and above all without routine. Routine is essential."[12]

The result is thus a kind of cynical liberal conservatism: in order to maintain stability, one has to respect and follow routines established by a choice which is

> always arbitrary and authoritarian. "There is no progressivism which holds," but rather a particular kind of hedonism called "liberalism of enjoyment." One has to maintain intact the routine of the *cité*, its laws and traditions, and accept that a kind of obscurantism is necessary in order to maintain social order. "There are questions one shouldn't ask. If you turn the social turtle on its back, you will never succeed in turning it back onto its paws."[13]

9 Ibid., p. 109.

10 Fleury, *Le réel insensé*, pp. 93–4.

11 Miller, "La psychanalyse, la cité, les communautés," pp. 109–10.

12 Fleury, *Le réel insensé*, p. 95 (quotations from Miller).

13 Ibid., p. 96 (quotations from Miller).

Against Miller's cynical-hedonist idea of a subject who, while admitting the necessity of symbolic semblances (ideals, Master-Signifiers, without which any society would fall apart), relates to them at a distance, aware that they are semblances and that the only Real is that of bodily *jouissance*, we should emphasize that such a stance of "enjoy and let others enjoy" would be possible only in a new communist order which has opened up the field for authentic idiosyncrasies:

> a Utopia of misfits and oddballs, in which the constraints for uniformization and conformity have been removed, and human beings grow wild like plants in a state of nature ... no longer fettered by the constraints of a now oppressive sociality, [they] blossom into the neurotics, compulsives, obsessives, paranoids and schizophrenics, whom our society considers sick but who, in a world of true freedom, may make up the flora and fauna of "human nature" itself.[14]

As we have seen, Miller is of course critical of the standardization of enjoyment demanded by the market to sell commodities, but his objection remains at the level of standard cultural critique; moreover, he ignores the specific socio-symbolic conditions for such a thriving of idiosyncrasies. As was noted long ago, capitalism is marked by a contradiction between ideological individualism (the interpellation of individuals as subjects free to follow their unique desires) and the leveling pressures of the market, imposing standardized modes of enjoyment as a condition of the commodification of mass consumption (while we are encouraged to indulge in our idiosyncrasies, the media bombard us with ideals and paradigms of *how* to do this). Communism is in this sense not a further leveled down "socialization" which curtails individual idiosyncrasies, but a social reconstruction which creates the space for their free deployment. Traces of this are found even in literary and Hollywood utopias of a social space subtracted from commodification, from the houses in which a group of eccentrics dwell in some of Dickens's novels, to the crazy large family house in Frank Capra's *You Can't Take It with You* whose inhabitants include Essie Carmichael (who makes candy as a hobby and dreams of being a ballerina), Paul Sycamore (a tinkerer who manufactures fireworks in the basement), Mr. DePina (who visited to speak to Paul eight years previously and has never left), Ed Carmichael (an amateur printer who prints anything that sounds good to him, including dinner menus for his family and little quotes that he places in the boxes of Essie's candy), and Boris Kolenkhov (a Russian very concerned with world politics; he is opinionated and often loudly declares that something "stinks").

At a more theoretical level, we should problematize Miller's (and, maybe, if one accepts his reading, the late Lacan's) rather crude nominalist opposition between the singularity of the Real of *jouissance* and the envelope of symbolic

14 Fredric Jameson, *The Seeds of Time*, New York: Columbia University Press 1994, p. 99.

semblances. What gets lost here is the great insight of Lacan's *Seminar XX (Encore)*: that the status of *jouissance* itself is in a way that of a redoubled semblance, a semblance within semblance. *Jouissance* does not exist in itself, it simply insists as a remainder or product of the symbolic process, of its immanent inconsistencies and antagonisms; in other words, symbolic semblances are not semblances with regard to some firm substantial Real-in-itself, this Real is (as Lacan himself formulated it) discernible only through impasses of symbolization.

From this perspective, an entirely different reading of Lacan's *les non-dupes errent* imposes itself. If we follow Miller's reading based on the opposition between symbolic semblances and the Real of enjoyment, *les non-dupes errent* amounts the cynical old saw that, although our values, ideals, rules, etc., are just semblances, we should not undermine them but act as if they were real in order to prevent the social fabric from disintegrating. But from a properly Lacanian standpoint, *les non-dupes errent* means almost the exact opposite: the true illusion consists not in taking symbolic semblances as real, but in substantializing the Real itself, in taking the Real as a substantial In-itself and reducing the symbolic to a mere texture of semblances. In other words, those who err are precisely those cynics who dismiss the symbolic texture as a mere semblance and are blind to its efficacy, to the way the symbolic affects the Real, to the way we can intervene into the Real through the symbolic. Ideology does not reside primarily in taking seriously the network of symbolic semblances which encircle the hard core of *jouissance*; at a more fundamental level, ideology is the cynical dismissal of these semblances as "mere semblances" with regard to the Real of *jouissance*.

We should push on to the end here and also apply this logic to the topic of the primordial crime which founds every power—Joseph de Maistre is among those who clearly formulated this highest anti-Enlightenment axiom: "There are mysterious laws which it is not good to reveal, which should be covered by a religious silence and revered as a *mystery*."[15] And he makes it clear which mystery in particular he has in mind: the mystery of the sacrifice, of the efficacy of the sacrifice—how is it that the infinitely good God demands blood sacrifices, that these sacrifices can also be achieved by substitution (sacrificing animals instead of human culprits), and that the most effective sacrifice is the one in which the innocent voluntarily offers to spill his blood for the guilty? No wonder de Maistre's booklet is strangely prescient of René Girard and his motif of "things which are hidden from the beginning of the world." Here, however, we should resist the false fascination: what the law ultimately hides is that *there is nothing to hide*, that there is no terrifying mystery sustaining it (even if the mystery is that

15 Joseph de Maistre, *Éclaircissement sur les sacrifices*, Paris: L'Herne 2009, p. 7: "Il existe des mystérieuses lois qu'il n'est pas bon de divulguer, qu'il faut couvrir d'un silence religieux et revérer comme un mystère."

of a horrible founding crime or some other form of radical Evil), that the law is grounded only in its own tautology.

The most radical critical analysis of the "mystery of sacrifice" as a fundamental ideological category is in fact provided by Jean-Pierre Dupuy. Although the "official" topic of Dupuy's *The Mark of the Sacred* is the link between sacrifice and the sacred, its true focus is the ultimate mystery of the so-called human or social sciences, that of the origins of what Lacan calls the "big Other," what Hegel called "externalization" (*Entäusserung*), what Marx called "alienation," and—why not?—what Friedrich von Hayek called "self-transcendence": how, out of the interaction of individuals, can the appearance of an "objective order" arrive which cannot be reduced to that interaction, but is experienced by the individuals involved as a substantial agency which determines their lives?[16] It is all too easy to "unmask" such a "substance," to show, by means of a phenomenological genesis, how it gradually becomes "reified" and sedimented: the problem is that the presupposition of such a spectral or virtual substance is in a way co-substantial with being-human—those who are unable to relate to it as such, those who directly subjectivize it, are called psychotics.

Dupuy's great theoretical breakthrough is to link this emergence of the "big Other" to the complex logic of the sacrifice constitutive of the dimension of the sacred, that is, to the rise of the distinction between the sacred and the profane: through the sacrifice, the big Other, the transcendent agency which sets limits to our activity, is sustained. The third link in this chain is hierarchy: the ultimate function of sacrifice is to legitimize and enact a hierarchical order (which works only if it is supported by some figure of the transcendent big Other). It is here that the first properly *dialectical* twist in Dupuy's line of argumentation occurs: relying on Louis Dumont's *Homo Hierarchicus*, he explains how hierarchy implies not only a hierarchical order, but also its immanent loop or reversal: true, the social space is divided into higher and lower hierarchical levels, but *within the lower level, the lower is higher than the higher.*[17] An example is provided by the relationship between Church and State in Christianity: in principle, of course, the Church is above the State; however, as thinkers from Augustine to Hegel made clear, *within the secular order of the State, the State is above the Church* (in other words the Church *as a social institution* should be subordinated to the State)—if it is not, if the Church wants directly to rule also as a secular power, then it becomes unavoidably corrupted from within, reducing itself to just another secular power using its religious teaching as the ideology to justify its secular rule.[18]

16 Jean-Pierre Dupuy, *La marque du sacré*, Paris: Carnets Nord 2008.

17 Louis Dumont, *Homo Hierarchicus*, New Delhi: Oxford University Press 1988.

18 As Dumont demonstrated, long before Christianity, this paradoxical reversal is clearly discernible in the ancient Indian Veda, the first fully elaborated ideology of hierarchy:

Dupuy's next, even more crucial move is to formulate this twist in the logic of hierarchy in terms of the negative self-relationship between the universal and the particular, between the All and its parts, that is, of a process in the course of which the universal encounters itself among its species in the guise of its "oppositional determination." To return to our example: the Church is the encompassing unity of all human lives, standing for its highest authority and conferring on all its parts their proper place in the great hierarchical order of the universe; however, it encounters itself as a subordinate element of the terrestrial State power which is in principle subordinated to it: the Church as a social institution is protected by and has to obey the laws of the State. Insofar as the higher and the lower also relate here as the Good and the Evil (the good divine domain versus the terrestrial sphere of power struggles, egotistical interests, the search for pleasure, etc.), one can also say that, through this loop or twist immanent to hierarchy, the "higher" Good dominates, controls, and uses the "lower" Evil, even if it may appear, superficially (to a gaze constrained by the terrestrial perspective), that religion with its pretense to occupying a "higher" place is just an ideological legitimization of "lower" interests (for example, that the Church ultimately just legitimizes socially hierarchical relations), that religion secretly pulls the strings as the hidden power which allows and mobilizes Evil for the larger Good. One is almost tempted to use the term "overdetermination" here: although it is the secular power which immediately plays the determining role, this role is itself overdetermined by the religious/sacred All.[19] How are we to read this complex self-relating entwinement of the "higher" and the "lower"? There are two main alternatives, which perfectly fit the opposition between idealism and materialism:

(1) The traditional theological (pseudo-)Hegelian matrix of containing the *pharmakon*: the higher all-embracing All allows the lower Evil, but contains it, making it serve the higher goal. There are many figures of this matrix: the (pseudo-)Hegelian "Cunning of Reason" (Reason is the unity of itself and particular egotistical passions, mobilizing the latter to achieve its secret goal of universal rationality); Marx's historical process in which violence serves progress; the "invisible hand" of the market which mobilizes individual egoism for the common good and so on.

(2) A more radical (and truly Hegelian) notion of Evil which distinguishes itself from itself by way of externalizing itself in a transcendent figure of the

---

the caste of preachers is in principle superior to the caste of warriors, but, within the actual power structure of the state, they are *de facto* subordinated to warriors.

19 Of course, for the partisan of the "critique of ideology," this very notion of religion secretly dominating and controlling social life is an ideological illusion par excellence.

Good. From this perspective, far from Evil being encompassed as a subordinated moment, the difference between Good and Evil is inherent to Evil, Good is nothing but universalized Evil, Evil is itself the unity of itself and Good. Evil controls or contains itself by generating a specter of transcendent Good; however, it can only do this by superseding its "ordinary" mode of Evil in an infinitized or absolutized Evil. This is why the self-containing of Evil through the positing of some transcendent power which limits it can always explode; this is why Hegel has to admit an excess of negativity which always threatens to disturb the rational order. All the talk about the "materialist reversal" of Hegel, about the tension between the "idealist" and the "materialist" Hegel, is pointless if it is not grounded in precisely this topic of the two opposed and conflicting ways of reading the negative self-relating of universality.

This self-reflected inversion of hierarchy is what distinguishes Reason from Understanding: while the ideal of Understanding is a simple and clearly articulated hierarchy, Reason supplements it with an inversion on account of which, as Dupuy puts it, within the lower level of a hierarchy, the lower stands higher than the higher. As we have seen, priests (or philosophers) stand higher than brutal secular power, but within the domain of power, they are subordinated to it—the gap that allows for this reversal is crucial for the functioning of power, which is why the Platonic dream of unifying the two aspects in the figure of the philosopher-king (realized only with Stalin) has to fail miserably.[20] The same point can also be put in the terms of the metaphor of Evil as a stain in the picture: if, in traditional teleology, Evil is a stain legitimized by the overall harmony, contributing to it, then, from a materialist standpoint, the Good itself is a self-organization or self-limitation of stains, the result of a limit, a "minimal difference," within the field of Evil. This is why moments of crisis are so dangerous—in them, the obscure obverse of the transcendent Good, the "dark side of God," the violence which sustains the very containment of violence, appears as such: "We believed that the good rules over the evil, its 'opposite,' but it appears now that it is rather the evil which rules over itself by assuming a distance towards itself, by positing itself outside itself; thus 'self-externalized,' the superior level appears as good."[21] Dupuy's point is that the sacred is, as to its content, the same as the terrible or Evil; their difference is purely formal or structural—what makes the sacred "sacred" is its exorbitant character, which makes it a limitation of "ordinary" evil. To see this, we should not only focus on religious prohibitions and obligations, but also bear in mind the rituals practiced by a religion, and the contradiction,

20 One could, of course, argue that the higher status of the priest is only an ideological illusion tolerated by warriors to legitimize their actual power, but this illusion is nonetheless necessary, a key feature of the charisma of power.

21 Dupuy, *La marque du sacré*, p. 13.

already noted by Hegel, between prohibitions and rituals: "Often, the ritual consists in staging the violation of … prohibitions and violations."[22] The sacred is nothing but our own violence, but "expelled, externalized, hypostasized."[23] The sacred sacrifice to the gods is the same as an act of murder—what makes it sacred is the fact that it limits or contains violence, including murder, in ordinary life. In those moments when the sacred falls into crisis, this distinction disintegrates: there is no sacred exception, a sacrifice is perceived as a simple murder—but this also means that there is nothing, no external limit, to contain our ordinary violence.

Therein resides the ethical dilemma Christianity tries to resolve: how to contain violence without sacrificial exception, without an external limit. Following René Girard, Dupuy demonstrates how Christianity stages the same sacrificial process, but with a crucially different cognitive spin: the story is not told by the collective staging the sacrifice, but by the victim, from the standpoint of the victim whose full innocence is thereby asserted. (The first step towards this reversal can already be discerned in the Book of Job, where the story is told from the perspective of the innocent victim of divine wrath.) Once the innocence of the sacrificial victim is *known*, the efficacy of the entire sacrificial mechanism of scapegoating is undermined: sacrifices (even of the magnitude of a holocaust) become hypocritical, inoperative, fake, but we also lose the containment of violence enacted by the sacrifice: "Concerning Christianity, it is not a morality but an epistemology: it says the truth about the sacred, and thereby deprives it of its creative power, for better or for worse. Humans alone decide on this."[24] Therein lies the world-historical rupture enacted by Christianity: *now we know*, and we can no longer pretend that we don't know. As we have seen, the impact of this knowledge one cannot get rid of once it has been gained is not only liberating, but deeply ambiguous: it also deprives society of the stabilizing role of scapegoating and thus opens up the space for a violence not contained by any mythic limit. This is how, in a truly perceptive insight, Dupuy reads the scandalous lines from Matthew: "Do not think that I came to bring peace on the earth; I did not come to bring peace, but a sword" (Matthew 10:34). And the same logic holds for international relations: far from making violent conflicts impossible, the abolition of sovereign states and the establishment of a single world state or power would rather open up the field for new forms of violence within the "world empire," with no sovereign state to set limits to it: "Far from guaranteeing eternal peace, the cosmopolitan ideal would rather be the favorable condition for limitless violence."[25]

---

22 Ibid., p. 143.

23 Ibid., p. 151.

24 Ibid., p. 161.

25 Monique Canto-Sperber, "Devons-nous désirer la paix perpétuelle?" in *Jean-Pierre*

The role of contingency is crucial here: once the efficacy of the transcendent Other is suspended and the process (of decision) has to be confronted in its contingency, the problem of the post-sacred world is that this contingency cannot be fully assumed, and so has to be sustained by what Lacan called *le peu du réel*, a little piece of the contingent Real which acts as *la réponse du réel*, the "answer of the Real." Hegel was deeply aware of this paradox when he opposed ancient democracy to modern monarchy: it was precisely because the ancient Greeks did not have a figure of pure subjectivity (a king) at the summit of their state edifice that they needed to resort to "superstitious" practices—such as looking for signs in the flight-paths of birds or in the entrails of animals—to guide the polis in making crucial decisions. It was clear to Hegel that the modern world cannot dispense with this contingent Real and organize social life only through choices and decisions based on "objective" qualifications (the illusion of what Lacan later called the discourse of the University): there is always some aspect of ritual involved in being invested with a title, even if the conferring of the title follows automatically from certain "objective" criteria having been met. A semantic analysis of, for example, what "passing one's exams with the highest grades" means, cannot be reduced to "proving that one has certain actual properties—knowledge, skills, etc."; to all this, a ritual must be added by means of which the results of the exam are proclaimed and the grade is conferred and acknowledged. As we saw earlier, there is always a minimal gap, a distance, between these two levels: even if I am absolutely sure that I have answered all the exam questions correctly, there *has* to be something contingent—a moment of surprise, the thrill of the unexpected—in the announcement of the results, which is why, when waiting for the announcement, we cannot ever fully escape the anxiety of expectation. Take political elections: even if the result is known in advance, its public proclamation is anticipated with excitement—indeed, to make something into Fate, contingency is needed. This is what, as a rule, critics of the widespread procedures of "evaluation" miss: what makes evaluation problematic is not the fact that it reduces unique subjects with a wealth of inner experience to a set of quantifiable properties, but that it tries to reduce the symbolic act of investiture (the investing of a subject with a title) to a procedure totally grounded in the knowledge and measurement of what the subject in question "really is."

Violence threatens to explode not when there is too much contingency in the social space, but when one tries to eliminate this contingency. Is it at this level that we should look for what one might call, in rather bland terms, the social function of hierarchy? Dupuy here makes yet another unexpected turn, conceiving hierarchy as one of the four procedures ("symbolic *dispositifs*") whose

---

Dupuy: Dans l'oeil du cyclone. Colloque de Cerisy, ed. Mark Anspach, Paris: Carnets Nord 2008, p. 157.

function it is to make the relationship of superiority non-humiliating for those subordinated: *hierarchy* itself;[26] *demystification*;[27] *contingency*;[28] and *complexity*.[29] Contrary to appearances, these mechanisms do not contest or threaten hierarchy, but make it palatable, since "what triggers the turmoil of envy is the idea that the other deserves his good luck and not the opposite idea which is the only one that can be openly expressed."[30] From this premise, Dupuy draws the conclusion that it would be a great mistake to think that a society which is just and which also perceives itself as just will thereby be free of all resentment—on the contrary, it is precisely in such a society that those who occupy inferior positions will only find an outlet for their hurt pride in violent outbursts of resentment.

The standard objection to utilitarianism is that it cannot really account for the full and unconditional ethical commitment to the Good: its ethics is only a kind of "pact of the wolves" in which individuals obey ethical rules insofar as this suits their interests. The truth is exactly the opposite: egotism or the concern for one's well-being is *not* opposed to the common Good, since altruistic norms can easily be deduced from egotistic concerns.[31] Individualism versus communitarianism, utilitarianism versus the assertion of universal norms, are *false* oppositions, since the two opposed options amount to the same in their results. Conservative (Catholic and other) critics who complain how, in today's hedonistic-egotistical society, true values have disappeared totally miss the point. The true opposite of egotistical self-love is not altruism, a concern for the common Good, but envy or *ressentiment*, which makes me act *against* my own interests: evil enters in when I prefer the misfortune of my neighbor to my own

26 An externally imposed order of social roles in clear contradistinction to the immanent higher or lower value of individuals—I thereby experience my lower social status as totally independent of my inherent value.

27 The critico-ideological procedure which demonstrates that relations of superiority or inferiority are not founded in meritocracy, but are the result of objective ideological and social struggles: my social status depends on objective social processes, not on my merits—as Dupuy puts it acerbically, social demystification "plays in our egalitarian, competitive and meritocratic societies the same role as hierarchy in traditional societies" (*La marque du sacré*, p. 208)—it enables us to avoid the painful conclusion that the other's superiority is the result of his merits and achievements.

28 The same mechanism, only without its social-critical edge: our position on the social scale depends on a natural and social lottery—lucky are those who are born with better dispositions and into rich families.

29 Superiority or inferiority depend on a complex social process which is independent of individuals' intentions or merits—for example, the invisible hand of the market can cause my failure and my neighbor's success, even if I worked much harder and was much more intelligent.

30 Dupuy, *La marque du sacré*, p. 211.

31 See the most famous example: Robert Axelrod, *The Evolution of Cooperation*, New York: Basic Books 1984.

fortune, so that I am ready to suffer myself just to make sure that my neighbor will suffer more. This excess of envy lies at the basis of Rousseau's well-known, but nonetheless not fully exploited, distinction between egotism, *amour-de-soi* (that love of the self which is natural), and *amour-propre*, the perverted preference of oneself to others in which a person focuses not on achieving a goal, but on destroying the obstacle to it:

> The primitive passions, which all directly tend towards our happiness, make us deal only with objects which relate to them, and whose principle is only amour-de-soi, are all in their essence lovable and tender; however, when, *diverted from their objects by obstacles, they are more occupied with the obstacle they try to get rid of, than with the object they try to reach,* they change their nature and become irascible and hateful. This is how amour-de-soi, which is a noble and absolute feeling, becomes amour-propre, that is to say, a relative feeling by means of which one compares oneself, a feeling which demands preferences, *whose enjoyment is purely negative and which does not strive to find satisfaction in our own well-being, but only in the misfortune of others.*[32]

An evil person is thus *not* an egotist, "thinking only about his own interests." A true egotist is too busy taking care of his own good to have time to cause misfortune to others. The primary vice of a bad person is precisely that he is more preoccupied with others than with himself. Rousseau is describing a precise libidinal mechanism: the inversion which generates the shift of the libidinal investment from the object to the obstacle itself.[33] Here is why egalitarianism itself should never be accepted at face value: the notion (and practice) of egalitarian justice, insofar as it is sustained by envy, relies on an inversion of the standard renunciation undertaken for the benefit of others: "I am ready to renounce it, so that others will (also) *not* (be able to) have it!" Far from being opposed to the spirit of sacrifice, Evil here emerges as the very spirit of sacrifice, a readiness to ignore one's own well-being—if, through my sacrifice, I can deprive the Other of his *enjoyment*.

True Evil thus makes us act *against* our own interests—or, to put it in Badiou's terms, what interrupts the life of the egotist-utilitarian "human animal" is not an encounter with the eternal Platonic Idea of the Good, but the encounter with a figure of Evil, and—as Lacan argued in his seminar on the ethics of psychoanalysis, "Good is a mask of Evil," the way for Evil to be re-normalized or domesticated. We should thus invert Badiou's notion of Evil as secondary with regard to the Good, as a betrayal of the fidelity to an Event, as a failure of Good:

32 Jean-Jacques Rousseau, *Rousseau, Judge of Jean-Jacques: Dialogues*, Hanover: Dartmouth College Press 1990, p. 63.

33 See Jean-Pierre Dupuy, *Petite métaphysique des tsunamis*, Paris: Seuil 2005, p. 68.

Evil comes first, in the guise of a brutal intrusion which disturbs the flow of our animal life.

Back to Dupuy: his limitation is clearly discernible in his rejection of class struggle as determined by this logic of envious violence: class struggle is for him the exemplary case of what Rousseau called perverted self-love, in which one cares more for the destruction of the enemy (which is perceived as the obstacle to my happiness) than for one's own happiness. Dupuy's only way out is to abandon the logic of victimhood and accept negotiations between all parties concerned, treated as equal in their dignity: "The transformation of the conflicts between social classes, between capital and labor, in the course of the twentieth century amply demonstrates that this path is not utopian. We progressively passed from the class struggle to social coordination, the rhetoric of victimhood was mostly replaced by wage negotiations. From now on, bosses and trade union organizations view each other as partners with interests which are simultaneously divergent and convergent."[34] But is this really the only possible conclusion from Dupuy's premises? Does not such a replacement of struggle by negotiation also rely on a magical disappearance of envy, which then stages a surprising comeback in the form of different fundamentalisms?

Furthermore, we stumble here upon another ambiguity: it is not that this absence of limits should be read in terms of the standard alternative "either humanity will find a way to set itself limits or it will perish from its own uncontained violence." If there is a lesson to be learned from the so-called "totalitarian" experience, it is that the temptation is exactly the opposite: the danger of imposing, in the absence of any divine limit, a *new* pseudo-limit, a fake transcendence on behalf of which I act (from Stalinism to religious fundamentalism). Even ecology functions as ideology the moment it is evoked as a new Limit: it has every chance of developing into the predominant form of the ideology of global capitalism, a new opium for the masses replacing the declining religion,[35] taking over the old latter's fundamental function, that of assuming an unquestionable authority which can impose limits. The lesson this ecology constantly hammers into us is our finitude: we are not Cartesian subjects extracted from reality, we are finite beings embedded in a bio-sphere which vastly exceeds our own horizons. In our exploitation of natural resources, we are borrowing from the future, and hence should treat the Earth with respect, as something ultimately Sacred, something that should not be unveiled totally, that should and will forever remain a Mystery, a power we should learn to trust, not dominate.

Against such temptations, one should insist that the *sine qua non* of a really radical ecology is the *public use of reason* (in the Kantian sense, as opposed to the "private use" constrained in advance by state and other institutions). According

34 Dupuy, *La marque du sacré*, p. 224.

35 I take this expression from Alain Badiou.

to an Associated Press report from May 19, 2011, the Chinese authorities have now admitted that the Three Gorges Dam, which created a 410-mile-long reservoir, the world's largest hydroelectric project, has caused a slew of urgent environmental, geological, and economic problems. They even now admit that filling the reservoir has increased the frequency of earthquakes. Among the main problems are widespread contamination of Yangtze tributaries and lakes with copper, zinc, lead, and ammonium. Furthermore, because the dam blocked the free flow of water on Yangtze, China's biggest watershed, it made the drought which hit China in the summer of 2011 much worse: crops withered and the low ebb along many rivers has affected hydroelectric plants, compounding widespread power shortages. Finally, much of China's industry and inland shipping depend on the Yangtze, but shipping is stalled at some points downstream from the dam because of the low water level. Although the authorities have now announced major plans to deal with the problems, it is clear that most of them were caused by official pressures which obstructed the "public use of reason": no one can now say "we didn't know," since the problems had all been predicted by independent scientists and civic groups.

But is not the Kantian couple of the public versus the private use of reason accompanied by what, in more contemporary terms, we could call the suspension of the symbolic efficacy (or performative power) of the public use of reason? Kant does not reject the standard formula of obedience "Don't think, obey!" with its direct "revolutionary" opposite "Don't just obey (follow what others are telling you), think (for yourself)!"; his formula is "Think and obey!" that is, think publicly (in the free use of reason) and obey privately (as part of the hierarchical machinery of power). In short, thinking freely does not legitimate my just doing anything—the most I can do when my "public use of reason" leads me to see the weaknesses and injustices of the existing order is to appeal to the ruler for reforms. One can go even a step further here and claim, with Chesterton, that the abstract-inconsistent freedom to think (and doubt) actively prevents actual freedom:

> We may say broadly that free thought is the best of all the safeguards against freedom. Managed in a modern style the emancipation of the slave's mind is the best way of preventing the emancipation of the slave. Teach him to worry about whether he wants to be free, and he will not free himself.[36]

But is the subtraction of thinking from acting, the suspension of its efficacy, really as clear and unequivocal as that? Is not Kant's secret strategy (intended or not) like the well-known trick employed in court battles, when a lawyer makes a statement in front of the jury which he knows the judge will find inadmissible

36 G. K. Chesterton, *Orthodoxy*, San Francisco: Ignatius Press 1995, p. 45.

and order the jury to "ignore"—which, of course, is impossible, since the damage has already been done. Is not the suspension of efficacy in the public use of reason also a subtraction which opens up a place for some new social practice? It is too easy to point out the obvious difference between the Kantian public use of reason and Marxist revolutionary class consciousness: the first is neutral or disengaged, the second is "partial" and fully engaged. However, the "proletarian position" can be defined precisely as that point at which the public use of reason becomes practical-effective in itself without regressing into the "privacy" of the private use of reason, since the position from which it is exercised is that of the "part of no-part" of the social body, its excess which directly stands for universality. What happens with the Stalinist reduction of the Marxist theory to the status of a servant of the Party-State is precisely the reduction of the public to the private use of reason.

It is fashionable, in some of today's neo-pagan "post-secular" circles, to affirm the dimension of the Sacred as a space in which every religion dwells but which is prior to religion (there can be the Sacred without religion, but not the other way round). (Sometimes, this priority of the Sacred is even given an anti-religious spin, as a way to remain agnostic while nonetheless engaged in deep spiritual experience.) Following Dupuy, we should reverse matters here: the radical break introduced by Christianity consists in the fact that it is the first religion *without* the sacred, a religion whose unique achievement is precisely to demystify the Sacred.

What practical stance follows from this paradox of religion without the sacred? There is a Jewish story about a Talmud specialist opposed to the death penalty who, embarrassed by the fact that the penalty was ordained by God himself, proposed a wonderfully practical solution: not to overturn the divine injunction directly, which would be blasphemous, but to treat it as God's slip of the tongue, his moment of madness, and invent a complex network of sub-regulations and conditions which, while leaving the possibility of the death penalty intact, ensure that it will never be actually realized.[37] The beauty of this procedure is that it inverts the standard procedure of prohibiting something in principle (like torture), but then slipping in enough qualifications ("except in specified extreme circumstances ...") to ensure that it can be done whenever one really wants to do it. It is thus either "In principle, yes, but in practice, never" or "In principle, no, but when exceptional circumstances demand it, yes." Note the asymmetry between the two cases: the prohibition is much stronger when one allows torture in principle—in the first case, the principled "yes" is *never* allowed to realize itself, while in the other case, the principled "no" is *exceptionally* allowed to realize itself. Insofar as the "God who enjoins us to kill" is one

37 I owe this data to Eric Santner.

of the names of the apocalyptic Thing, the strategy of the Talmud scholar is a way of practicing what Dupuy calls "enlightened catastrophism": one accepts the final catastrophe—the obscenity of people killing their neighbors in the name of justice—as inevitable, written into our destiny, and one engages in postponing it for as long as possible, hopefully indefinitely. Here is how, along these lines, Dupuy sums up Günther Anders's reflections apropos Hiroshima:

> On that day history became "obsolete." Humanity became able to destroy itself, and nothing can make it lose this "negative omnipotence," even a global disarmament or a total denuclearization of the world. *The apocalypse is inscribed as a destiny in our future, and the best we can do is delay its occurrence indefinitely.* We are in excess. On August 1945 we entered the era of the "freeze" and of the "second death" of all that existed: since the meaning of the past depends on future acts, the becoming-obsolete of the future, its programmed ending, does not mean that the past no longer has any meaning, it means that it never had any meaning.[38]

It is against this background that we should read the basic Paulinian notion of living in an "apocalyptic time," a "time at the end of time": the apocalyptic time is precisely the time of such an indefinite postponement, the time of freeze in-between two deaths: in some sense, we are already dead, since the catastrophe is already here, casting its shadow from the future—after Hiroshima, we can no longer play the simple humanist game of insisting that we have a choice ("It depends on us whether we follow the path of self-destruction or the path of gradual healing"); once such a catastrophe has happened, we lose the innocence of such a position, we can only (indefinitely, maybe) postpone its reoccurrence.[39] This is how, in yet another hermeneutic coup, Dupuy reads Christ's skeptical words against the prophets of doom:

> As he went out of the temple, one of his disciples said to him, "Teacher, see what kind of stones and what kind of buildings!" Jesus said to him, "Do you see these great buildings? There will not be left here one stone on another, which will not be thrown down." As he sat on the Mount of Olives opposite the temple, Peter, James, John, and Andrew asked him privately, "Tell us, when will these things be? What is the sign that these things are all about to be fulfilled?" Jesus, answering, began to tell them, "Be careful that no one leads you astray. For many will come in my name, saying, 'I am he!' and will lead many astray. When you hear of wars and rumors of

---

38 Dupuy, *La marque du sacré*, p. 240.

39 In a homologous way, the danger of nanotechnology is not only that scientists will create a monster which will start to develop out of (our) control: when we try to create a new life, it is precisely our aim to bring about an uncontrollable self-organizing and self-expanding entity (ibid., p. 43).

> wars, don't be troubled. For those must happen, but the end is not yet … Then if anyone tells you, 'Look, here is the Christ!' or, 'Look, there!' don't believe it. For there will arise false Christs and false prophets, and they will show signs and wonders, that they may lead astray, if possible, even the chosen ones. But you watch." (Mark 13:1–23)

These lines are tremendous in their unexpected wisdom: do they not exactly correspond to the stance of the above-mentioned Talmudic scholar? Their message is: yes, of course, there will be a catastrophe, but watch patiently, don't believe it, don't succumb to hasty extrapolations, don't indulge yourself in the properly perverse pleasure of thinking "This is it!" in all its diverse forms (global warming will drown us all in a decade; biogenetics will mean the end of being-human; we are approaching a society of total digital control; and so on and so forth). Far from luring us into such a self-destructive, perverse rapture, adopting the properly apocalyptic stance is—today more than ever—the only way to keep a cool head. What gives this need to maintain sobriety an additional sense of urgency is the contemporary predominance of a cynical ideology which seems to condemn every critique to practical irrelevance. The irrationality of capitalist rationalism, the counter-productivity of its accelerated productivism, are well known, having been analyzed in detail not only by the Frankfurt School authors and loners like Ivan Illich, but also by numerous critics in the great ideologico-critical wave which accompanied the upheavals of the 1960s. When the same topic is resuscitated today, in our cynical times, it is not just in order to return to the past, but rather to add a crucial reflexive twist:

> What is new and different today is precisely the fact that, thirty years later, we know that *the knowledge we already possessed* was in no way sufficient to make us change our behavior. This fact is not a minor detail, it constitutes a key element of the problem. In the 1960s and '70s, it was simpler to believe that another world was possible. This is why these years continue to inspire so much nostalgia. During this epoch, one could still imagine that warnings based on the present situation could influence the future in a positive way. Today, we know it, the future is not what it was.[40]

Therein lies the basic lesson of the failure of traditional *Ideologie-Kritik*: knowing is not enough, one can know what one is doing and still go ahead and do it. The reason is that such knowledge operates under the condition of its fetishistic disavowal: one knows, but one does not really believe what one knows. This insight led Dupuy to propose a radical solution: since one believes only

40 Mark Anspach, "Un philosophe entre Tantale et Jonas," in *Jean-Pierre Dupuy: Dans l'oeil du cyclone*, pp. 10–11.

when the catastrophe has really occurred (by which time it is too late to act), one must project oneself into the aftermath of the catastrophe, confer on the catastrophe the reality of something which has already taken place. We all know the tactical move of taking a step back in order to jump further ahead; Dupuy turns this procedure around: one has to jump ahead into the aftermath of the catastrophe in order to be able to step back from the brink.[41] In other words, we must assume the catastrophe as our destiny. In our ordinary lives, we pursue our individual goals and ignore the "destiny" in which we participate in this way: the catastrophic "fixed point" which appears as external destiny, although it is we ourselves who bring it about through our activity: "Destiny is here this exteriority which is not exterior, since the agents themselves project it out of their system: this is why it is appropriate to talk about auto-externalization or auto-transcendence."[42]

Giorgio Agamben's name (taken from Foucault) for what Dupuy calls "self-transcending of society" is the *dispositif*, and it is striking how Agamben also linked it to the topic of the sacred, although, in contrast to Dupuy, with an accent on profanation. Agamben pointed out the link between the Foucauldian *dispositif* and the young Hegel's notion of "positivity" as the substantial social order imposed on the subject and experienced by it as external fate, not as an organic part of itself. As such, the *dispositif* is the matrix of governability: it is "that in and through which a pure activity of governing without any foundation in being realizes itself. It is for this reason that *dispositifs* always have to imply a process of subjectivation. They have to produce their subject."[43] The ontological presupposition of such a notion of *dispositif* is "a general and massive partition of being into two large sets or classes: on the one hand, the living beings (or substances), on the other hand, the dispositifs within which the living beings never cease to be caught."[44]

There is a series of complex echoes between this notion of a *dispositif*, Althusser's notion of Ideological State Apparatuses and ideological interpellation, and Lacan's notion of the "big Other": Foucault, Althusser, and Lacan insist on the crucial ambiguity of the term the "subject" (as both free agent and as subject to power)—the subject qua free agent emerges through its subjection to the *dispositif*/ISA/"big Other." As Agamben points out, "desubjectivation" ("alienation") and subjectivation are thus the two sides of the same coin: it is the very desubjectivation of a living being, its subordination to a *dispositif*, which subjectivizes it. When Althusser claims that ideology interpellates individuals

41 Ibid., p. 19.

42 Dupuy, "De l'oeil du cyclone au point fixe endogène," in *Jean-Pierre Dupuy: Dans l'oeil du cyclone*, p. 313.

43 Giorgio Agamben, *Qu'est-ce qu'un dispositif?*, Paris: Payot & Rivages 2007, pp. 26–7.

44 Ibid., p. 30.

into subjects, "individuals" stand here for the living beings on which a *dispositif* of ISAs works, imposing on them a network of micro-practices, while the "subject" is *not* a category of living being, of substance, but the result of these living beings being caught in an ISA *dispositif* (or in a symbolic order).[45] Where Althusser falls short is in his disappointing and misplaced insistence on the "materiality" of the ISA: the primordial form of *dispositif*, the "big Other" of the symbolic institution, is precisely immaterial, a virtual order—as such, it is the correlative of the subject as distinct from the individual qua living being. Neither the subject nor the *dispositif* of the big Other are categories of substantial being. One can perfectly well translate these coordinates into Lacan's matrix of the discourse of the University: *homo sacer*, the subject reduced to bare life, is, in terms of Lacan's theory of discourses, the *objet a*, the "other" of the University discourse worked upon by the *dispositif* of knowledge. Can we then say that Agamben inverts Lacan: that, for him, it is the University discourse which is the truth of the Master's discourse? The "product" of the University discourse is $, the subject—the *dispositif* (the network of S_2, of knowledge) works on the bare life of the individual, engendering out of it the subject. Today, however, we are witnessing a radical change in the working of this mechanism—Agamben defines our contemporary post-political or bio-political era as a society in which multiple *dispositifs* desubjectivize individuals without producing a new subjectivity, without subjectivizing them:

> From here comes the eclipse of politics which supposed real subjects or identities (workers' movement, bourgeoisie, etc.) and the triumph of economy, that is to say, of the pure activity of governing which pursues only its own reproduction. The Right and the Left which today follow each other in managing power have thus very little to do with the political context from which the terms which designate them originate. Today these terms simply name the two poles (the one which targets without any scruples the desubjectivation and the one which wants to cover it up with the hypocritical mask of the good citizen of democracy) of the same machine of government.[46]

"Bio-politics" designates this constellation in which *dispositifs* no longer generate subjects ("interpellate individuals into subjects"), but merely administer and regulate individuals' bare life—in bio-politics, we are all potentially reduced to *homini sacri*.[47] The outcome of this reduction, however, involves an unexpected

---

45 In Deleuzian terms, living being is a substance, while the subject is an event.

46 Agamben, *Qu'est-ce qu'un dispositif?*, pp. 46–7.

47 Is every bio-politics necessarily bio-theo-politics, as Lorenzo Chiesa has suggested? Yes, but in a very precise sense: the notion of "bare life" can only emerge within the theological horizon, as the founding gesture of reducing all reality to "mere life," to which one then opposes the transcendent divine dimension. In this sense, "materialism"

twist—Agamben draws attention to the fact that the inoffensive desubjectivized citizen of post-industrial democracies, who in no way opposes the hegemonic *dispositifs* but zealously executes all their injunctions and is thus controlled by them even in the most intimate details of his or her life, is "nonetheless (and perhaps for this very reason) considered as a potential terrorist":[48] "In the eyes of the authority (and, perhaps, the authority is right in this), nothing resembles a terrorist more than an ordinary man."[49] The more the ordinary man is controlled by cameras, by digital scanning, by data collection, the more he appears as an inscrutable, un-governable X which subtracts itself from the *dispositifs* the more it obeys them with docility. It is not that it poses a threat to the machine of government by actively resisting it: its very passivity suspends the performative efficacy of the *dispositifs*, making their machine "run on empty," turning it into a self-parody which serves nothing. How can this happen? What is the exact status of this X? To eradicate the profound ambiguity of Agamben's account, we should apply here the Lacanian distinction between the subject ($) and subjectivation: the X that emerges when a *dispositif* totally desubjectivizes an individual is that of the subject itself, the unfathomable void that ontologically precedes subjectivization (the rise of the "inner life" of self-experience).

Agamben formulates the problem in terms of profanation: the notion of *dispositif* has its origin in theology, linked the Greek *oikonomia*, which, in early Christianity, related not to God in himself, but to God's relation to the world (of humans), to how God administers his kingdom. (In radical Hegelian theology, this distinction vanishes: God is *nothing but* the "economy" of his relating to the world.) A *dispositif* is thus always minimally sacred: when a living being is caught in a *dispositif*, it is by definition dis-appropriated. The practices by means of which it participates in and is regulated by a *dispositif* are separated from their "common use" by living beings: being caught in a *dispositif*, a living being serves the sacred big Other. This is where profanation comes in as a counter-strategy: "The problem of profanation of *dispositifs* (that is to say, of the restitution to the common use of what was caught in *dispositifs* and separated [from living beings] in them) is of the utmost urgency."[50]

But what if there is no such "common use" prior to *dispositifs*? What if the primordial function of *dispositifs* is precisely to organize and administer the "common use"? In this case, profanation is not the restitution of a common use, but, on the contrary, its *destitution*—in profanation, an ideological practice

---

effectively is a theological notion: it is what remains of theology after we subtract from it the divine. In contrast to this, the first gesture of a genuine materialism is not to deny the divine, but, on the contrary, to deny that there is such a thing as "mere (animal) life."

48 Agamben, *Qu'est-ce qu'un dispositif?*, p. 48.

49 Ibid., pp. 48–9.

50 Ibid., p. 50.

is de-contextualized, de-functionalized, made to run on empty. To put it yet another way, if the founding move that establishes a symbolic universe is the empty gesture, how is a gesture emptied? How is its content neutralized? Through repetition, which forms the very core of what Agamben calls profanation: in the opposition between the sacred and the secular, the profanation of the secular does not equal secularization; profanation puts the sacred text or practice into a different context, it subtracts it from its proper context and functioning. As such, profanation remains in the domain of non-utility, merely enacting a "perverted" non-utility. To profane a mass is to perform a black mass, not to study the mass as an object of the psychology of religion. In Kafka's *The Trial*, the weird extended debate between Joseph K. and the Priest about the Law is deeply profane—it is the Priest who, in his reading of the parable "Before the Law," is the true agent of profanation. One can even say that Kafka is the greatest profaner of the Jewish Law. Or, apropos the topic of Heidegger and sexuality: secularization would be to interpret Heidegger's style of writing as an alienated fetishization of language, profanation would be to render in this style phenomena like sexual practices that Heidegger would never have addressed. As such, profanation—not secularization—is the true materialist undermining of the Sacred: secularization always relies on its disavowed sacred foundation, which survives either as an exception or as a formal structure. Protestantism realizes this split between the Sacred and the secular at its most radical: it secularizes the material world, but keeps religion apart, and it introduces the formal religious principle into the capitalist economy itself.[51]

Here, however, we should perhaps supplement Agamben: the paradoxical precedence of transgression over what it violates allows us to throw a critical light on his concept of profanation. If we conceive profanation as a gesture of extraction from the proper life-world context and use, is not such an extraction also *the very definition of sacralization*? Take poetry: is it not "born" when a phrase or a group of words is "decontextualized" and becomes caught up in an autonomous process of repetitive insistence? When, instead of "come here," I say "come, come here," is this not the minimum of poeticization? There is thus a zero-level at which profanation cannot be distinguished from sacralization. So we have here again the same paradox of displaced classification that we find in Emile Benveniste's analysis of passive, active, and middle verbs. Just as, in Benveniste, the original opposition is not between passive and active, with the middle intervening as a third mediating or neutral moment, but between active and middle, so too here, the original opposition is between the secular-everyday-useful and the Profane, and the "Sacred" stands for a secondary shift or mystification of the Profane. The emergence of the human or symbolic universe lies in the minimum

51 *Mutatis mutandis*, the same goes for Stalinist communism—it is secularized, not profaned religion.

gesture of a "profanatory decontextualization" of a signal or gesture, and "sacralization" comes afterwards, as an attempt to gentrify, to domesticate, this excess, this rapturous impact of the profane. In Japanese, *bakku-shan* signifies "a girl who looks like she might be pretty when seen from behind, but isn't when seen from the front"—is not the relationship between profane and sacred something like this? A thing which appears (is experienced as) sacred when viewed from behind, from a proper distance, is effectively a profane excess. To paraphrase Rilke, the Sacred is the last veil that conceals the horror of the Profane. So what would the profanation of Christianity be? What if Christ himself—the comical aspect of the embodiment of God in a ridiculous mortal—already *is* the profanation of divinity? What if, in contrast to other religions which can be profaned only by men, in Christianity God profanes *himself*?

For this solution to work, we have to abandon the fundamentals of what one can only call Agamben's ideology: his elementary dualism of living beings and *dispositifs*. There are no living beings, human individuals (can) get caught in *dispositifs* precisely because they are not merely living beings, because their very life substance is derailed or distorted (the Freudian name of this distortion is, of course, the death drive). This is why the human being is not a "rational animal," not defined by a dimension or quality which adds itself to substantial animality: in order for such an addition to occur, a space for it, its possibility, has to be first opened up by a distortion of animality itself. The Lacanian name for this distortion or excess is the *objet a* (surplus-enjoyment), and, as Lacan convincingly demonstrated, even Hegel here falls short, missing this dimension of surplus-enjoyment in the struggle for recognition and its outcome.

According to the standard view (propagated by, among others, Kojève), what is at stake in the Hegelian struggle between the (future) master and servant is the separation of the subject from its body: through its readiness to sacrifice its biological body (life), the subject asserts the life of the spirit as higher and as independent of its biological life. This other (higher) dimension is embodied in language, which is, in a way, the negativity of death transposed into a new positive order: the word is the murderer of the thing it designates, it extracts the concept of the thing in its independence from the empirical thing. From the Freudian-Lacanian standpoint, however, such a description of the passage from the biological body to its symbolization, to the spiritual life of language, misses something crucial: namely, how the symbolization of the body retroactively generates a fantasmatic inexistent organ which stands for what is lost in the process of symbolization:

> This lamella, this organ, whose characteristic is not to exist, but which is nevertheless an organ ... is the libido. It is the libido, qua pure life instinct, that is to say, immortal life, irrepressible life, life that has need of no organ, simplified, indestructible life.

> It is precisely what is subtracted from the living being by virtue of the fact that it is subject to the cycle of sexed reproduction. And it is of this that all the forms of the *objet a* that can be enumerated are the representatives, the equivalents.[52]

A common motif of the phenomenological description of being human is that of embodied existence, of experiencing a body as one's own, as a lived body, not just as an object, a *res extensa*, in the world—the enigma of what it means not only to have a body, but to "be" (in) a living body. The twentieth century effected a double undermining of this immediate experience of the organic body: on the one hand, the biogenetic reduction of the body to a mechanism regulated by genetic codes and, in this sense, to an "artificial" mechanism; on the other hand, the fantasmatic body, a body structured according not to biology but to libidinal investments, which is the topic of psychoanalysis, from "partial objects" (autonomous organs without bodies, like an eye or a fist which survive on their own, as a perfect example of the drive—not the object of a drive, but the drive *as* an [impossible] object) to their mythical prototype, the *lamella*. In some of Francis Bacon's drawings, we find a (naked, usually) body accompanied by a formless form, weird, dark, and stain-like, which seems to grow out of it, barely attached to it, as a kind of uncanny protuberance which the body can never fully recuperate or reintegrate, and which thereby destabilizes beyond repair the organic Whole of the body—this is what Lacan aimed at with his notion of the *lamella* (or the *hommelette*).

This forever lost excess of pure or indestructible life is—in the guise of the *objet a*, the object-cause of desire—also what "eternalizes" human desire, making it infinitely plastic and unsatisfiable (in contrast to instinctual needs). It is therefore wrong to claim that, since the master does not work, he remains stuck at the natural level: what the servant's products satisfy are not merely the master's natural needs, but his needs transformed into an infinite desire for excessive luxuries displayed in competition with the luxuries of other masters—the servant brings the master rare delicacies, luxury furniture, expensive jewelry, and so on. This is why the master becomes the servant of his servant: he depends on the servant not for the satisfaction of his natural needs, but for the satisfaction of his highly cultivated artificial needs.

This excess is at work across the entire range of culture, from high art to the lowest consumerism. The standard formula of artistic minimalism is "less is more": if we abstain from adding any superficial ornament, if we go even further

---

52 Jacques Lacan, *The Four Fundamental Concepts of Psycho-Analysis*, New York: W. W. Norton & Company 1978, pp. 197–8. When Lacan talks of the body being subjected "to the cycle of sexed reproduction," he doesn't mean biological mating, but sexual difference as the impossible-Real of the symbolic order. In brutally direct terms: animals who reproduce through mating do not have a *lamella*.

and refuse to fill in the gaps or truncate what would have been the completed form of our product, this very loss will generate additional meaning and create a kind of depth. Surprisingly (or perhaps not), we find a similar logic of "more for less" in the consumerist universe of commodities, where "less" is the proverbial one cent subtracted from the full rounded price ($4.99, not $5), and "more" the no less proverbial surplus that we get for free, known to all buyers of toothpaste: the top quarter of the tube is often a different color, with large letters announcing: "1/3 more for free." The catch is, of course, that the "full" product which sets the standard for this is more or less fictional: we never get to see a toothpaste without the surplus priced at the full $5—a clear sign that the reality of this "more for less" is "less for more." From a Freudian perspective, it is easy to see how this paradox of "more for less" is grounded in the reflexive reversal of the renunciation of pleasure into a new source of pleasure. Lacan's formula for this reversal is a fraction of the small a (surplus-enjoyment) above minus phi (castration): an enjoyment generated by the very renunciation of enjoyment and, in this sense, a "less" which is "more."

This brings us to the crux of the debate between Judith Butler and Catherine Malabou over the relationship between Hegel and Foucault (recall that Agamben is an anti-Hegelian Foucauldian).[53] According to Foucault, Hegel assumes the total sublation (*Aufhebung*) of the body in its symbolization: the subject emerges through—and is equivalent to—its subjection (submission) to the symbolic order, its laws and regulations; that is, for Hegel, the free and autonomous subject *is* the subject integrated into the symbolic order. What Hegel does not see is how this process of symbolization, of submissive regulation, generates what it "represses" and regulates. Recall Foucault's thesis, developed in his *History of Sexuality*, about how the medical-pedagogical discourse disciplining sexuality produces the excess it tries to tame ("sex"), a process already begun in late antiquity when the detailed Christian descriptions of all possible sexual temptations retroactively generated what they tried to suppress. The proliferation of pleasures is thus the obverse of the power which regulates them: power itself generates resistance to itself, the excess it can never control—the reactions of a sexualized body to its subjection to disciplinary norms are unpredictable.

Foucault remains ambiguous here, shifting the accent (sometimes almost imperceptibly) between *Discipline and Punish* and the first volume of *History of Sexuality* and volumes two and three of the latter: while in both cases, power and resistance are intertwined and support each other, the earlier works put the accent on how resistance is appropriated in advance by power, so that power mechanisms dominate the entire field and we are the subjects of power precisely when we resist it; later, however, the accent shifts onto how power generates the

53 See Judith Butler and Catherine Malabou, *Sois mon corps: Une lecture contemporaine de la domination et de la servitude chez Hegel*, Paris: Bayard 2010.

excess of resistance which it can never control—far from manipulating resistance to itself, power thus becomes unable to control its own effects. What this oscillation betrays is that the entire field of the opposition between power and resistance is false and has to be abandoned—but how? Butler herself shows the way: as a good Hegelian, she adds a key reflexive turn which amounts to a kind of Hegelian response to Foucault: not only do the mechanisms of repression and regulation generate the excess they endeavor to repress; these mechanisms themselves become libidinally invested, generating a perverse source of surplus-enjoyment of their own. In short, the repression of a desire necessarily turns into a desire for repression, the renunciation of a pleasure turns into the pleasure of renunciation, the regulation of pleasures into a pleasure of regulation. This is what Foucault does not take into account: how, for example, the disciplinary practice of regulating pleasures itself gets infected by pleasure, as in obsessive or masochistic rituals. The true excess (of pleasure) is thus not the excess generated by disciplinary practices, but these practices themselves, which literally come in excess of what they regulate.[54]

No wonder that the standard political use of recognition as a key feature of Hegel's social thought is limited to liberal readings of Hegel—Jameson has already noted that the ongoing focus on mutual recognition in such readings "reveals yet a third Hegel, alongside the Marxist and the fascist one, namely a 'democratic' or Habermasian Hegel":[55] the ontologically and politically "deflated" Hegel, the Hegel who celebrates bourgeois law and order as the summit of human development.[56] Therein lies the common denominator of liberal readings of Hegel's political thought (and not only the political thought): reciprocal recognition is the ultimate goal and at the same time the minimal presupposition of subjectivity, the immanent condition of the very fact of self-consciousness—"I am recognized, therefore I am." I am a free subject only insofar I am recognized as free by other free subjects (subjects recognized by me as free). Perhaps, however, the time has come to problematize the central role played by this notion: it is

54 Sometimes Foucault does come close to this insight—in the first volume of his *History of Sexuality*, say, where he writes that we have at last invented "another pleasure: pleasure in the truth about pleasure, pleasure in getting to know, analyze, reveal pleasures" (Michel Foucault, *The History of Sexuality, Vol. 1: An Introduction*, trans. Robert Hurley, New York: Vintage 1990, p. 71). Such insights are, however, not developed into a systematic reflexivity of desire.

55 Fredric Jameson, *The Hegel Variations*, London: Verso Books 2010, p. 54.

56 The same goes for Lacan: there is a conservative Lacan who warns against the dissolution of the Name-of-the-Father, exemplified by Pierre Legendre's work and falsely targeted by Judith Butler; there is a liberal Lacan exemplified in recent years by Jacques-Alain Miller, who reads Lacan's analysis of the events of 1968 as a liberal critique of revolutionaries; and then there is the radical-revolutionary Lacan, from Copjec and Badiou to the Ljubljana school.

strictly correlative to the "deflationary" reading of Hegel as a philosopher who articulates the normative conditions of free life.[57]

Mutual recognition is, of course, the outcome of a long process which begins with the struggle to the death between the (future) master and servant. In this struggle, the tension between attachment and detachment (to/from one's body, or to/from material reality in general) repeats itself, but at a higher level, which brings about their dialectical unity: attachment itself becomes the form of appearance of its opposite. We thus need to break out of the false oscillation between attachment and detachment: detachment is primordial, constitutive of subjectivity, a subject never directly "is" its body; all one need add is that this very detachment (from the body) can only be enacted through an excessive attachment to an "organ without a body." The paradox is thus that the zero-level of negativity is not a negative gesture, but an excessive affirmation: by getting stuck on a partial object, by affirming it repetitively, the subject detaches itself from its body, enters into a negative relationship towards its body.

How do I signal to the other my detachment from my particular biological life? By unconditionally attaching myself to some totally trivial and indifferent little-bit-of-the-Real for which I am ready to put everything, including my life, at stake—the very worthlessness of the object for which I am ready to risk everything makes it clear that what is at stake is not it but myself, my freedom. It is against this background of the subject as actual infinity that we should read the well-known passage in which Hegel describes how, in experiencing the fear of

57 This "deflated" liberal Hegel of recognition is paradigmatically American (although one can argue that it was first outlined by Habermas, he was nevertheless already influenced by the American pragmatic tradition, e.g., G. H. Mead's notion of intersubjectivity based on the mutual identification of subjects, so that I can see myself through the eyes of the other). It is thus perhaps more than a historical curiosity that the first American Hegelian school was, at the origins of pragmatism, *the* American philosophical movement. It began in 1856 when Henry Conrad Brokmeyer, a Prussian immigrant, retreated deep into the Missouri woods with a gun, a dog, and a copy of Hegel's *Science of Logic*. Alone with this book over the next two years, Brokmeyer became convinced that Hegel's thought should be extended to include the US: Hegel was right that history has a direction which moves from east to west, but he lived too early to see the move from Europe to the US. History unfolds in the direction of a world-historical city, culminating in a flowering of freedom under a rational state. Even in the US itself, the spirit moves from the east to the west, towards the biggest American city west of the Mississippi: St. Louis. Brokmeyer applied to the US Hegel's notion of history progressing through conflicts: religion versus science, abolitionism versus slavery, up to St. Louis versus Chicago. After St. Louis was dwarfed by Chicago, the disappointed Brokmeyer moved further west—it was said, in the last years of his life, he conducted a Hegel-focused kindergarten class for the Creek Indians in their Oklahoma territory. But his influence persisted, reaching C. S. Peirce, the father of pragmatism. See Kerry Howley, "Hegel Hits the Frontier," *The Daily* (May 19, 2011).

death during his confrontation with the master, the servant gets a whiff of the infinite power of negativity; through this experience, he is forced to accept the worthlessness of his particular Self:

> For this consciousness was not in peril and fear for this element or that, nor for this or that moment of time, it was afraid for its entire being; it felt the fear of death, the sovereign master. It has been in that experience melted to its inmost soul, has trembled throughout its every fibre, and all that was fixed and steadfast has quaked within it. This complete perturbation of its entire substance, this absolute dissolution of all its stability into fluent continuity, is, however, the simple, ultimate nature of self-consciousness, absolute negativity, pure self-relating existence, which consequently is involved in this type of consciousness.[58]

The rather boring objection to the struggle to the death between the future master and the future servant is that Hegel cheats by silently ignoring the deadlock of the obvious radical solution: the two really do fight to the death, but since that result would bring the dialectical process to a halt, the struggle is not really fought without restraint, it presupposes a certain implicit symbolic pact that the result will not be death. In the days prior to the battle of Ilipa, one of the key battles of the Second Punic War in 206 BC, a strange ritual emerged between the two armies, the Carthaginians commanded by Hasdrubal, Hannibal's brother, and the Romans commanded by Scipio. One morning, after deploying their forces in a battle formation,

> the two armies stood and watched each other. For all their initial confidence, neither commander wished to push his men forward and force a battle. After some hours, with the sun beginning to set, Hasdrubal gave the order for his men to return to camp. Observing this, Scipio did the same.
>
> Over the following days this became almost a routine. At a late hour, which in itself suggested no great enthusiasm for battle, Hasdrubal led his army on to the edge of the plain. The Romans would then match the move, both armies deploying in the same formation as on the first day. Then the armies would stand and wait, until near the end of the day, first the Carthaginians and then the Romans returned to their respective camps.[59]

Only after several days of this did Scipio decided to provoke the battle. The only benefit of such posturing was a marginal moral one: Hasdrubal could claim that he laid down the challenge to the enemy each day, while Scipio could claim that

58 G. W. F. Hegel, *Phenomenology of Mind*, second rev. ed., trans. J. B. Baillie, Mineola: Dover 2003, p. 110.

59 Adrian Goldsworthy, *In the Name of Rome*, London: Orion Books 2004, pp. 69–70.

he only withdrew after the enemy did so. Such cases are a welcome reminder of how much of warfare involves not simply physical conflict but a complex symbolic ritual of posturing.

Butler proposes a strange and counter-intuitive (but strangely convincing) reading of this conclusive moment of the dialectic of master and servant: through the fear of death which shatters the foundations of his entire being, the servant assumes his finitude, he becomes aware of himself as a fragile, vulnerable being. What Butler fails to emphasize is the positive obverse of this fragile finitude: the negative force which threatens the individual and shakes the foundations of his life is not in itself the "ultimate nature of self-consciousness, absolute negativity, pure self-relating existence"; it is thus not external to the subject (like the figure of the master in front of him, threatening him from outside), but his very core, the very heart of his being. This is the way the awareness of one's finitude immediately reverts into the experience of one's true infinity, which is self-relating negativity.

This dimension of infinity is missing in Foucault, which is why Malabou is justified in her reproach to Foucault (and, implicitly, Butler) that the Foucauldian subject engaged in the "care of the self" remains caught in a closed loop of self-affection. Precisely insofar as it is aware of its fragile finitude and turned towards the future—that is, insofar as it is attached not to what it *is* but to the void or opening of what it may become, and therefore engaged in permanent self-criticism, the continuous "courageous" questioning of its given forms—the Foucauldian subject remains attached to itself, relating to its (self-)critical activity as the final point of reference. Such a stance remains at the level of the "abstract" opposition of subject and substance, asserting the predominance of the subject attached to itself in contrast to all objective content. More specifically, we should abandon the entire paradigm of "resistance to a *dispositif*": the idea that, while a *dispositif* determines the network of the Self's activity, it simultaneously opens up the space for the subject's "resistance," for its (partial and marginal) undermining and displacement of the *dispositif*. The task of emancipatory politics lies elsewhere: not in elaborating a proliferation of strategies for how to "resist" the predominant *dispositif* from marginal subjective positions, but in thinking about the modalities of a possible radical rupture in the predominant *dispositif* itself. In all the talk about "sites of resistance," we tend to forget that, difficult as it is to imagine today, from time to time the very *dispositifs* which we resist do actually change.

The debate between Butler and Malabou is nonetheless sustained by a shared premise according to which, "although there is no body which would be mine without the other's body, there is also no possible definitive dis-appropriation of my body, no more than a possible definitive appropriation of the other's body."[60]

60 Butler and Malabou, *Sois mon corps*, p. 8. The mechanism described by Butler as the disavowed injunction "Be my body!" (a Master orders me to be—to act as—his body,

Is this premise not confirmed by two recent Hollywood productions, each of which stages and tests the extreme of a subject completely passing over into another body, but with opposite results? In *Avatar*, the transfer succeeds and the hero successfully moves his soul from his own to his other (aboriginal) body, while in *Surrogates* (2009, based on the 2005–6 comic book series, directed by Jonathan Mostow), the humans rebel against their avatars and return to their proper bodies.

Avatar should be compared to films like *Who Framed Roger Rabbit?* or *The Matrix* in which the hero is caught between our ordinary reality and an imagined universe—of cartoons in *Roger Rabbit*, of digital reality in *The Matrix*, and of the digitally enhanced ordinary reality of the aboriginal planet in *Avatar*. What one should thus bear in mind is that, although *Avatar*'s narrative is supposed to take place in one and the same "real" reality, we are dealing—at the level of the underlying symbolic economy—with two realities: the ordinary world of imperialist colonialism and (not the miserable reality of exploited aboriginals, but) the fantasy-world of the aboriginals who live in an incestuous link with nature. The end of the film thus has to be read as a desperate solution in which the hero fully migrates from real reality into the fantasy-world—as if, in *The Matrix*, Neo were to decide to fully immerse himself again in the Matrix. A more immediate contrast to *Avatar* is *Surrogates*, set in 2017, when people live in near-total isolation, rarely leaving the safety and comfort of their homes, thanks to remotely controlled robotic bodies that serve as "surrogates," designed as better-looking versions of their human operators. Because people are safe all the time, and any damage done to a surrogate is not felt by its owner, it is a peaceful world free from fear, pain, and crime. Predictably, the story revolves around the alienation and lack of authenticity in this world: at the film's end, all the surrogates are disconnected and people are compelled to start using their own bodies again. The contrast between *Surrogates* and *Avatar* could not be more apparent.

This does not mean, however, that we should reject *Avatar* in favor of a more "authentic" and heroic acceptance of our ordinary reality as the only real world there is. Even if reality is "more real" than fantasy, it still needs fantasy to retain its consistency: if we subtract fantasy, the fantasmatic frame, from reality, reality

---

but in a disavowed way: I should pretend that I am not really that, but continue to be a free independent individual) seems to concern, much more than bodies, the modern relationship of domination in which the servant has to act as free and willingly accept the subordinated role: the modern master's order is that his servant pretend to be free rather than a servant. Take the role of the wife in a marriage in which patriarchal values continue to have a subterranean existence: the wife has to serve her husband, but in the context of a free and equal relationship; this is why the first act of rebellion is to openly proclaim one's servitude, to refuse to act as free where one is de facto not free. The effects of such refusal are shattering, since in modern conditions, servitude can only reproduce itself as disavowed.

itself loses its consistency and disintegrates. The lesson is thus that the very alternative of "either accept reality or choose fantasy" is a false one: what Lacan calls *la traversée du fantasme* has nothing to do with dispelling illusions and accepting reality the way it is. This is why, precisely when we are shown someone doing just that—renouncing all illusions and embracing miserable reality—we should focus on identifying the minimal fantasmatic contours of this reality. If we really want to change or escape from our social reality, the first thing to do is to change the fantasies tailored to make us fit this reality; because the hero of *Avatar* does not do this, his subjective position is what, apropos Sade, Lacan called *le dupe de son fantasme*.

How to escape or "negate" the constraints of the existing universe is thus not only a difficult empirical problem, but perhaps even more difficult to imagine or to conceptualize. In mid-April 2011, the media reported that the Chinese government had prohibited showing on TV and in cinemas films dealing with time travel and alternative histories, with the argument that such stories introduce frivolity into serious historical matters—even the fictional escape into an alternate reality is considered too dangerous. We in the West do not need such an explicit prohibition: as the disposition of what is considered possible and what impossible shows, ideology exerts sufficient material power to prevent alternative history narratives from being taken with a minimum of seriousness.

This material power becomes most palpable precisely where one would least expect it: in critical situations, when the hegemonic ideological narrative is being undermined. We live in such a situation today. According to Hegel, repetition plays a precise role in history: when something happens just once, it may be dismissed as a mere accident, as something that might have been avoided with a better handling of the situation; but when the same event repeats itself, this is a sign that we are dealing with a deeper historical necessity. When Napoleon lost for the first time in 1813, it looked like just bad luck; when he lost the second time at Waterloo, it was clear that his time was over. And does the same not hold for the ongoing financial crisis? When it first hit the markets in September 2008, it looked like an accident to be corrected through better regulation, and so on; now that signs of a repeated financial meltdown are gathering, it is clear that we are dealing with a structural necessity.

How does the hegemonic ideology prepare us to react to such a predicament? There is an anecdote (apocryphal, for sure) about an exchange of telegrams between German and Austrian army headquarters in the middle of the First World War: the Germans sent the message "Here, on our part of the front, the situation is serious, but not catastrophic," to which the Austrians replied "Here, the situation is catastrophic, but not serious." Is this not increasingly the way many of us, at least in the developed world, relate to our global predicament? We all know about the impending catastrophe, but somehow we cannot take it seriously. In psychoanalysis, this attitude is called a fetishistic split: I know very well, but … (I do not really believe it), and is a clear indication of the material force of ideology which makes us refuse what we see and know.[61]

So where does this split come from? Here is Ed Ayres's description: "We are being confronted by something so completely outside our collective experience that we don't really see it, even when the evidence is overwhelming. For us, that 'something' is a blitz of enormous biological and physical alterations in the world that has been sustaining us."[62] In order to cope with this threat, our collective ideology is mobilizing mechanisms of dissimulation and self-deception up to and including the direct will to ignorance: "a general pattern of behavior among threatened human societies is to become more blinkered, rather than more focused on the crisis, as they fall."[63] Catastrophic, but not serious …

While such a disavowal is clearly discernible in how the majority relates to ecological threats, we can discern the same mechanism in the predominant reaction to the prospect of a new financial collapse: it is difficult to really accept that the long period of post-World-War-II progress and stability in the developed Western world is approaching its end. What makes the situation especially volatile is the fact that the disavowal is supplemented by its opposite, excessive panicky reactions: in the fragile domain of financial speculations, rumors can inflate or destroy the value of companies—sometimes even whole economies—in a matter of days. Since the capitalist economy has to borrow from the future, accumulating debts which will never be fully repaid, trust is a fundamental ingredient of the system—but this trust is inherently paradoxical and "irrational": I trust that I can get access to my bank account at any time, but while this can hold

61 An exemplary case of the material power of ideology is *The Diagnostic and Statistical Manual of Mental Disorders* (DSM), published by the American Psychiatric Association. Its goal is to provide "a common language and standard criteria for the classification of mental disorders. It is used in the US and in varying degrees around the world, by clinicians, researchers, psychiatric drug regulation agencies, health insurance companies, pharmaceutical companies, and policy makers. There have been four revisions since it was first published in 1952, gradually including more mental disorders, although some have been removed and are no longer considered to be mental disorders, most notably homosexuality"; the next (fifth) edition, DSM-5, is due for publication in May 2013. (See the Wikipedia entry for "Diagnostic and Statistical Manual of Mental Disorders." I rely here on the critical analysis by Sarah Kamens.) The role of the DSM is crucial because hospitals, clinics, and insurance companies generally require a DSM diagnosis of all patients treated—and since the health-industrial complex in the US turns around twice as much money as the notorious military-industrial complex, one can imagine the far-reaching financial consequences of seemingly marginal changes in the DSM classifications.

62 Ed Ayres, *God's Last Offer: Negotiating for a Sustainable Future*, New York: Four Walls Eight Windows 1999, p. 6.

63 Ibid., p. 141.

for me individually, it cannot hold for the majority (if the majority effectively test the system and try to withdraw their money, the entire system will collapse). Crises are thus simultaneously disavowed and triggered out of nowhere, with no "real" causes. Can we even imagine, along these lines, the economic and social consequences of the collapse of the US dollar or the Euro?

The riots in the UK suburbs in 2011 were a zero-level reaction to this ongoing crisis—but why were the protesters pushed towards this kind of violence? Zygmunt Bauman was on the right track when he characterized the riots as acts of "defective and disqualified consumers": more than anything else, they were a consumerist carnival of destruction, a consumerist desire violently redirected when unable to realize itself in the "proper" way (by shopping). As such, they of course also contained a moment of genuine protest, a kind of ironic reply to the consumerist ideology with which we are bombarded in our daily lives: "You call on us to consume while simultaneously depriving us of the possibility to do it properly—so here we are doing it the only way open to us!" The riots thus in a way stage the truth of "post-ideological society," displaying in a painfully palpable form the material force of ideology. The problem with such riots is not their violence per se, but the fact that it is not truly self-assertive—in Nietzsche's terms, it is reactive, not active, impotent rage and despair masked as a display of force, envy masked as triumphant carnival.

The danger is that religion will fill in this void and restore meaning. That is to say, the riots need to be situated in the series they form with another type of violence perceived by the liberal majority today as a threat to our way of life: terrorist attacks and suicide bombings. In both instances, violence and counter-violence are caught up in a deadly vicious cycle, each generating the very forces it tries to combat. In both cases, we are dealing with blind *passages à l'acte*, where violence is an implicit admission of impotence. The difference is that, in contrast to the Paris *banlieue* or British riots which were a "zero-level" protest, violent outbursts which wanted nothing, terrorist attacks act on behalf of that *absolute* Meaning provided by religion. So how are we to pass from such violent reactions to a new reorganization of the totality of social life? To do this requires a strong body able to make quick decisions and realize them with the necessary harshness. Who can accomplish the next step? A new tetrad emerges here, the tetrad of *people-movement-party-leader.*

The people is still here, but no longer as the mythical sovereign Subject whose will is to be enacted. Hegel was right in his critique of the democratic power of the people: "the people" should be re-conceived as the passive background of the political process—the majority is always and by definition passive, there is no guarantee that it is right, and the most it can do is acknowledge and recognize itself in a project imposed by political agents. As such, the role of the people is ultimately a negative one: "free elections" (or a referendum) serve as a check on the party movements, as an impediment designed to prevent what Badiou calls the brutal and destructive "*forçage*" (enforcement) of the Truth onto the positive order of Being regulated by opinions. This is all that electoral democracy can do; the positive step into a new order is beyond its scope.

In contrast to any elevation of authentic ordinary people, we should insist on how the process of their transformation into political agents is irreducibly *violent*. John Carpenter's *They Live* (1988), a neglected masterpiece of the Hollywood Left, tells the story of John Nada (Spanish for "nothing"), a homeless laborer who finds work on a Los Angeles construction site but has no place to stay. One of the other workers, Frank Armitage, takes him to spend the night at a local shantytown. While being shown around that night, he notices some odd behavior at a small church across the street. Investigating the next day, he accidentally stumbles on several boxes full of sunglasses hidden in a secret compartment in a wall. When he later puts on a pair of the glasses for the first time, he notices that a publicity billboard now simply displays the word "OBEY," while another urges the viewer to "MARRY AND REPRODUCE." He also sees that paper money now bears the words "THIS IS YOUR GOD." What we get here is a beautifully naïve *mise-en-scène* of the critique of ideology: through the critico-ideological glasses, we directly see the Master-Signifier beneath the chain of knowledge—we learn to see dictatorship *in* democracy, and seeing it hurts. We learn in the film that wearing the critico-ideological glasses for too long gives the viewer a bad headache: it is very painful to be deprived of the ideological surplus-enjoyment. When Nada tries to convince Armitage to put the glasses on, his friend resists, and a long fight follows, worthy of *Fight Club* (another masterpiece of the Hollywood Left). It starts with Nada saying to Armitage: "I'm giving you a choice. Either put on these glasses or start eating that trash can." (The fight takes place among overturned trash bins.) The fight, which goes on for an unbearable eight minutes, with occasional pauses for an exchange of friendly smiles, is in itself totally "irrational"—why does Armitage not just agree to put the glasses on to satisfy his friend? The only explanation is that he *knows* his friend wants him to see something dangerous, to access a prohibited knowledge which will totally spoil the relative peace of his daily life. The violence staged here is a positive violence, a condition of liberation—the lesson is that our liberation from ideology is not a spontaneous act, an act of discovering our true Self. The key feature here is that to see the true nature of things, we need the glasses: it is not that we have to take off ideological glasses in order to see "reality as it is": we are "naturally" in ideology, our natural sight is ideological. How does a woman become a feminist subject? Only through renouncing the crumbs of enjoyment offered by the patriarchal discourse, from reliance on males for "protection" to the pleasures provided by male "gallantry" (paying the restaurant bill, opening doors, and so on).

When people try to "organize themselves" directly in movements, the most they can create is an egalitarian space for debate where speakers are chosen by lottery and everyone is given the same (short) time to speak, etc. But such protest movements prove inadequate the moment one has to act, to impose a new order—at this point, something like a *Party* is needed. Even in a radical protest movement, people *do not* know what they want, they demand a new Master to tell them. But if the people do not know, does the Party? Are we back at the standard topic of the Party possessing historical insight and leading the people?

It is Brecht who gives us a clue here. In what is for some the most problematic song of *The Measure Taken*, the celebration of the Party, he proposes something much more unique and precise than it may at first appear. It looks like Brecht is simply elevating the Party into the incarnation of Absolute Knowledge, an historical agent with complete and perfect insight into the historical situation, a "subject supposed to know" if there ever was one: "You have two eyes, but the Party has a thousand eyes!" However, a close reading of the song makes it clear that something different is going on: in their reprimand to the young communist, the chorus says that the Party does *not* know all, that the young communist may be *right* in his disagreement with the predominant Party line: "Show us the way which we should take, and we / shall follow it like you, but / do not take the right way without us. / Without us, this way is / the falsest one. / Do not separate yourself from us." This means that the authority of the Party is *not* that of determinate positive knowledge, but that of the *form* of knowledge, of a new type of knowledge linked to a collective political subject. The crucial point on which the chorus insists is simply that, if the young comrade thinks that he is right, he should fight for his position *within* the collective form of the Party, not outside it—to put it in a somewhat pathetic way, if he is right, then the Party needs him even more than its other members. What the Party demands is that one ground one's "I" in the "We" of the Party's collective identity: fight with us, fight for us, fight for your truth against the Party line, *just do not do it alone*, outside the Party.

Movements as agents of politicization are a phenomenon of "qualitative democracy": even in the mass protests in Tahrir Square in Cairo, the people who gathered there were always a minority—the reason they "stood for the people" hinged on their mobilizing role in the political dynamic. In a homologous way, the organizing role of a Party has nothing to do with its access to some privileged knowledge: a Party is not a figure of the Lacanian subject-supposed-to-know but an open field of knowledge in which "all possible mistakes" occur (Lenin). However, even this mobilizing role of movements and parties is not enough: the gap that separates the people themselves from organized forms of political agency has to be somehow overcome—but how? Not by the proximity of the people and these organized forms; something more is needed, and the paradox is that this "more" is a *Leader*, the unity of Party and people. We should not be afraid to draw all the consequences from this insight, endorsing the lesson of Hegel's justification of monarchy and ruthlessly slaughtering many liberal sacred cows on the way. The problem with the Stalinist leader was not an excessive "cult of personality," but quite the opposite: he was not enough of a Master but remained part of the bureaucratic-party Knowledge, the exemplary subject-supposed-to-know.

To take this step "beyond the possible" in *today's* constellation, we must shift the accent of our reading of Marx's *Capital* to "the fundamental structural centrality of unemployment in the text of *Capital* itself": "unemployment is structurally inseparable from the dynamic of accumulation and expansion which constitutes the very nature of capitalism as such."[64] In what is arguably the extreme point of the "unity of opposites" in the sphere of the economy, it is the very success of capitalism (higher productivity, etc.) which produces unemployment (renders more and more workers useless)—what should be a blessing (less hard labor needed) becomes a curse. The world market is thus, with regard to its immanent dynamic, "a space in which everyone has once been a productive laborer, and in which labor has everywhere begun to price itself out of the system."[65] That is to say, in the ongoing process of capitalist globalization, the category of the unemployed acquires a new quality beyond the classic notion of the "reserve army of labor": the category should now include "those massive populations around the world who have, as it were, 'dropped out of history,' who have been deliberately excluded from the modernizing projects of First World capitalism and written off as hopeless or terminal cases":[66] so-called "failed states" (Congo, Somalia), victims of famine or ecological disasters, trapped in pseudo-archaic "ethnic hatreds," objects of philanthropy and NGOs or (often the same people) of the "war on terror." The category of the unemployed should thus be expanded to encompass a wide range of the global population, from the temporary unemployed, through the no-longer employable and permanently unemployed, up to people living in slums and other types of ghettos (i.e., all those often dismissed by Marx himself as "lumpenproletarians"), and, finally, all those areas, populations or states excluded from the global capitalist process, like blank spaces in ancient maps. Does not this extension of the circle of the "unemployed" bring us back from Marx to Hegel: the "rabble" is back, emerging at the very core of emancipatory struggles? That is to say, such a re-categorization changes the entire "cognitive mapping" of the situation: what once lay in the inert background of History becomes a potential agent of emancipatory

64 Fredric Jameson, *Representing Capital*, London: Verso Books 2011, p. 149.

65 Fredric Jameson, *Valences of the Dialectic*, London: Verso Books 2009, pp. 580–1.

66 Jameson, *Representing Capital*, p. 149.

struggle. Recall Marx's dismissive characterization of the French peasants in his *Eighteenth Brumaire*:

> the great mass of the French nation is formed by the simple addition of homologous magnitudes, much as potatoes in a sack form a sack of potatoes ... Insofar as there is merely a local interconnection among these small-holding peasants, and the identity of their interests forms no community, no national bond, and no political organization among them, they do not constitute a class. They are therefore incapable of asserting their class interest in their own name, whether through a parliament or a convention. They cannot represent themselves, they must be represented.[67]

In the great twentieth-century revolutionary mobilizations of peasants (from China to Bolivia), these "sacks of potatoes" excluded from the historical process began actively to represent themselves. We should nonetheless add three qualifications to Jameson's deployment of this idea. First, the semiotic square proposed by Jameson—whose terms are (1) workers, (2) the reserve army of the (temporarily) unemployed, (3) the (permanently) unemployable, and (4) the "formerly employed" but now unemployable—needs to be corrected: would not a more appropriate fourth term be the *illegally employed*, from those working in black markets and slums up to and including different forms of slavery?[68] Second, Jameson fails to emphasize how those "excluded" are often nonetheless *included* in the world market. Take the case of today's Congo: beneath the façade of "primitive ethnic passions" exploding yet again in the African "heart of darkness," it is easy to make out the contours of global capitalism. After the fall of Mobutu, Congo no longer exists as a united state; its eastern part especially is now a multiplicity of territories ruled by local warlords each controlling their patch of land with an army which, as a rule, includes drugged children, and each with business links to a foreign company or corporation exploiting the (mostly) mining wealth in the region. This arrangement suits both partners: the corporations get the mining rights without taxes and so on, the warlords get money. The irony is that many of these minerals are used in high-tech products like laptops and cell phones—in short: forget about the savage customs of the local population, just subtract from the equation the technology companies and the whole system of ethnic warfare fuelled by ancient passions will fall apart.

Jameson's third category, the "permanently unemployable," should be supplemented by its opposite, which consists of those educated but with no chance of finding employment: a whole generation of students have almost no chance of finding a job corresponding to their qualifications, which leads to massive

67 Karl Marx, *The Eighteenth Brumaire of Louis Bonaparte*, trans. Saul K. Padover, Moscow: Progress Publishers 1934.
68 Jameson, *Valences of the Dialectic*, p. 580.

protests; and the worst way to resolve this gap is to directly subordinate education to the demands of the market—if for no other reason than that the market dynamic itself renders the education provided by universities "obsolete."

Jameson here makes a further (paradoxical, but thoroughly justified) step: he characterizes this new structural unemployment as a form of *exploitation*—the exploited are not only workers producing surplus-value appropriated by capital, they also include those structurally prevented from getting caught up in the capitalist vortex of exploited wage labor, including whole geographical zones and even nation states. How, then, are we to rethink the concept of exploitation? A radical change is needed here: in a properly dialectical twist, exploitation includes its own negation—the exploited are not only those who produce or "create," but also (and even more so) those who are condemned *not* to "create." This returns us for the last time to the structure of the Rabinovitch joke: "Why do you think you are exploited?" "For two reasons. First, when I work, the capitalist appropriates my surplus-value." "But you are now unemployed—no one is appropriating your surplus-value because you create none!" "This is the second reason …" Everything hinges here on the fact that the capitalist circuit not only needs workers, but also generates a "reserve army" of those who cannot find work: the latter are not simply outside the circulation of capital, they are actively produced as not-working by this circulation. Or, to refer again to the *Ninotchka* joke, they are not simply not-working, their not-working is their positive feature in the same way as "without milk" is the positive feature of "coffee without milk."

The importance of this accent on exploitation becomes clear when we oppose it to *domination*, the favored motif of different versions of the postmodern "micro-politics of power." In short, the theories of Foucault and Agamben are insufficient: all their detailed elaborations of the regulatory power mechanisms of domination, all the wealth of notions such as the excluded, bare life, *homo sacer*, etc., must be grounded in (or mediated by) the centrality of exploitation; without this reference to the economic, the fight against domination remains "an essentially moral or ethical one, which leads to punctual revolts and acts of resistance rather than to the transformation of the mode of production as such"[69]—the positive program of such ideologies of "power" is generally one of some type of "direct" democracy. The outcome of the emphasis on domination is a democratic program, while the outcome of the emphasis on exploitation is a communist program. There lies the limit of describing the horrors of the Third World in terms of the effects of domination: the goal becomes democracy and freedom. Even the reference to "imperialism" (instead of capitalism) functions as a case of how "an economic category can so easily modulate into a concept of power or domination"[70]—and the implication of this shift towards domination

69 Jameson, *Representing Capital*, p. 150.

70 Ibid., p. 151.

is, of course, the belief in another ("alternate") modernity in which capitalism will function in a "fairer" way, without domination.

What this notion of domination fails to register is that only in capitalism is exploitation "naturalized," inscribed into the functioning of the economy—it is not the result of extra-economic pressure and violence, and this is why, in capitalism, we have personal freedom and equality: there is no need for direct social domination, domination is already inscribed in the structure of the production process. This is also why the category of surplus-value is crucial here: Marx always emphasized that the exchange between worker and capitalist is "just" in the sense that workers (as a rule) get paid the full value of their labor-power as a commodity—there is no direct "exploitation" here; that is, it is not that workers "are not paid the full value of the commodity they are selling to the capitalists." So while in a market economy I remain *de facto* dependent, this dependency is nonetheless "civilized," realized in the form of a "free" market exchange between me and other persons instead of in the form of direct servitude or even physical coercion. It is easy to ridicule Ayn Rand, but there is a grain of truth in the famous "hymn to money" from her *Atlas Shrugged*: "Until and unless you discover that money is the root of all good, you ask for your own destruction. When money ceases to become the means by which men deal with one another, then men become the tools of other men. Blood, whips and guns or dollars. Take your choice—there is no other."[71] Did Marx not say something similar in his well-known formula of how, in the universe of commodities, "relations between people assume the guise of relations among things"? In the market economy, relations between people can appear as relations of mutually recognized freedom and equality: domination is no longer directly enacted and visible as such.

The liberal answer to domination is recognition (as we have seen, a favored topic among "liberal Hegelians"): recognition "becomes a stake in a multicultural settlement by which the various groups peaceably and electorally divide up the spoils."[72] The subjects of recognition are not classes (it is meaningless to demand the recognition of the proletariat as a collective subject—if anything, fascism does this, demanding the mutual recognition of classes). Subjects of recognition are those defined by race, gender, etc.—the politics of recognition remains within the bourgeois civil society framework, it is not yet class politics.[73]

The recurrent story of the contemporary Left is that of a leader or party elected with universal enthusiasm, promising a "new world" (Mandela, Lula, etc.)—but, then, sooner or later, usually after a couple of years, they confront the key dilemma: whether to dare to mess with the capitalist mechanism, or whether

71 Ayn Rand, *Atlas Shrugged*, London: Penguin Books 2007, p. 871.

72 Jameson, *Valences of the Dialectic*, p. 568.

73 Ibid.

to just "play the game." If one disturbs the mechanism, one will be very swiftly "punished" by market perturbations, economic chaos, and the rest.[74] So although it is true that anti-capitalism cannot be the direct goal of political action—in politics, one opposes concrete political agents and their actions, not an anonymous "system"—we should apply here the Lacanian distinction between goal and aim: anti-capitalism, if not the immediate goal of emancipatory politics, should be its ultimate aim, the horizon of all its activity. Is this not the lesson of Marx's notion of the "critique of *political* economy"? Although the sphere of the economy appears "apolitical," it is the secret point of reference and structuring principle of political struggles.

Returning to Rand, what is problematic is her underlying premise: that the only choice is between direct and indirect relations of domination and exploitation, with any alternative dismissed as utopian. However, as noted above, we should nonetheless recognize the moment of truth in Rand's otherwise ridiculously ideological claim: the great lesson of state socialism was indeed that an immediate abolition of private property and market-regulated exchange, in the absence of concrete forms of social regulation of the process of production, necessarily resuscitates direct relations of servitude and domination. Jameson himself falls short with regard to this point: focusing on how capitalist exploitation is compatible with democracy, how legal freedom can be the very form of exploitation, he ignores the sad lesson of the twentieth-century experience of the Left: if we merely abolish the market (including market exploitation) without replacing it with an adequate form of communist organization of production and exchange, domination returns with a vengeance, and with it direct exploitation.

When dealing with the topic of human rights, the critique of ideology tends to commit two (opposed) mistakes. The first is the obvious one: the symptomal point (excess, self-negation, antagonism) of a field is reduced to a mere accident, an empirical imperfection, rather than something that emerges necessarily. The notion of universal human rights *de facto* privileges a determinate set of particular cultural values (European individualism, etc.), which means that their universality is false. However, there is also the opposite mistake: the entire field is collapsed into its symptom—"bourgeois" freedom and equality are *directly and only* capitalist ideological masks for domination and exploitation, "universal human rights" are *directly and only* the means of justifying imperialist colonialist interventions, etc. While the first mistake is part of critico-ideological common sense, the second is usually neglected and as such all the more dangerous. The properly Marxist critical notion of "formal freedom" is much more refined: yes,

74 This is why it is all too simple to criticize Mandela for abandoning the socialist perspective after the end of apartheid: did he really have a choice? Was the move towards socialism a real option in that particular context?

"bourgeois freedom" is merely formal, but, as such, it is *the only form of appearance (or potential site) of actual freedom*. In short, if one prematurely abolishes "formal" freedom, one loses also (the potential of) actual freedom—or, to put it in more practical terms, in its very abstraction, formal freedom not only obfuscates actual unfreedom, it simultaneously opens up the space for the critical analysis of actual unfreedom.[75]

What further complicates the situation is that the rise of blank spaces in global capitalism is in itself also a proof that capitalism can no longer afford a universal civil order of freedom and democracy, that it increasingly requires exclusion and domination. The case of the Tiananmen crackdown in China is exemplary here: what was quashed by the brutal military intervention was not the prospect of a fast entry into the liberal-democratic capitalist order, but the genuinely utopian possibility of a more democratic *and* more just society: the explosion of brutal capitalism after 1990 went hand in hand with the reassertion of non-democratic Party rule. Recall the classical Marxist thesis on early modern England: it was in the bourgeoisie's own interest to leave the *political* power to the aristocracy and keep for itself the *economic* power. Maybe something homologous is going on in today's China: it was in the interest of the new capitalists to leave political power to the Communist Party.

How, then, are we to break out of the deadlock of post-political dehistoricization? What to do after the Occupy Wall Street movement, when the protests which started far away (Middle East, Greece, Spain, UK) reached the center, and are now reinforced and rolling out all around the world? What should be resisted at this stage is precisely a quick translation of the energy of the protest into a set of "concrete" pragmatic demands. The protests did create a vacuum—a vacuum in the field of hegemonic ideology, and time is needed to fill this vacuum in a proper way, since it is pregnant, an opening for the truly New. What we should always bear in mind is that any debate here and now necessarily remains a debate on the enemy's turf: time is needed to deploy the new content. All we say now can be taken (recuperated) from us—everything except our silence. This silence, this rejection of dialogue, of all forms of clinching, is our "terror," ominous and threatening as it should be.

Does this negative gesture of protesters not bring us back to Melville's *Bartleby*, to Bartleby's "I would prefer not to"? Bartleby says, "I would prefer

---

75 The legal career of Jacques Verges represents a clear case of this second mistake in practice. Having recognized the hypocrisy of the Western legal system (in 1945, having defeated fascism in the name of human freedoms and rights, the Western powers practiced brutal colonialist oppression in Algeria, Vietnam, etc.), Verges ended up defending those accused by the West of terrorism, from Klaus Barbie to Pol Pot. Although his goal is to unmask the hypocrisy of the Western liberal legal system, such a procedure is unable to propose any alternate system of justice.

not to" and *not* "I don't prefer (or care) to do it"—we are thereby back at Kant's distinction between negative and infinite judgment. In his refusal of the Master's order, Bartleby does not negate the predicate, he rather *affirms a non-predicate*: what he says is not that he *doesn't want to do it*; he says that *he prefers (wants) not to do it*. This is how we pass from the politics of "resistance," parasitical upon what it negates, to a politics which opens up a new space outside the hegemonic position *and* its negation.[76] In the terms of Occupy Wall Street, the protesters are not saying only that they would prefer not to participate in the dance of capital and its circulation, they would also "prefer not to" cast a critical vote (for "our" candidates) or engage in any form of "constructive dialogue." This is the gesture of subtraction at its purest, the reduction of all qualitative differences to a purely formal minimal difference which opens up the space for the New. There is a long road ahead, and soon we will have to address the truly difficult questions—not about what we do not want, but about what we *do* want. What form of social organization can replace the actually existing capitalism? What type of new leaders do we need? And what organs, including those of control and repression? The twentieth-century alternatives obviously did not work. While it is thrilling to enjoy the pleasures of "horizontal organization," of protesting crowds with their egalitarian solidarity and free open-ended debates, these debates will have to coalesce not only around some new Master-Signifiers, but also in concrete answers to the old Leninist question "What is to be done?" Reacting to the Paris protests of 1968, Lacan said: "What you aspire to as revolutionaries is a master. You will get one."[77] Although this diagnostic/prognostic should be rejected as a universal statement about every revolutionary upheaval, it contains a grain of truth: insofar as the protest remains at the level of a hysterical provocation of the Master, without a positive program for the new order to replace the old one, it effectively functions as a (disavowed, of course) call for a new Master.

Faced with the demands of the protesters, intellectuals are definitely not in the position of the subjects supposed to know: they cannot operationalize these demands, or translate them into proposals for precise and realistic measures. With the fall of twentieth-century communism, they forever forfeited the role of the vanguard which knows the laws of history and can guide the innocents along its path. The people, however, also do not have access to the requisite knowledge—the "people" as a new figure of the subject supposed to know is a myth of the Party which claims to act on its behalf, from Mao's guideline to "learn from the peasants" to Heidegger's aforementioned appeal to his old farmer friend in

76 For a more detailed elaboration of this "Bartleby-politics," see the last pages of my *The Parallax View*, Cambridge, MA: MIT Press 2006.

77 Jacques Lacan at Vincennes, December 3, 1969: "*Ce à quoi vous aspirez comme révolutionnaires, c'est à un Maître. Vous l'aurez.*"

his short text "Why Do I Stay in the Provinces?" from 1934, a month after he resigned as the dean of the Freiburg University:

> Recently I got a second invitation to teach at the University of Berlin. On that occasion I left Freiburg and withdrew to the cabin. I listened to what the mountains and the forest and the farmlands were saying, and I went to see an old friend of mine, a 75-year old farmer. He had read about the call to Berlin in the newspapers. What would he say? Slowly he fixed the sure gaze of his clear eyes on mine, and keeping his mouth tightly shut, he thoughtfully put his faithful hand on my shoulder. Ever so slightly he shook his head. That meant: absolutely no![78]

One can only imagine what the old farmer was really thinking—in all probability, he knew what answer Heidegger wanted from him and politely provided it. No wisdom of ordinary men will tell the protesters *warum bleiben wir in Wall Street*. There is no Subject who knows, and neither intellectuals nor ordinary people are that subject. Is this a deadlock then: a blind man leading the blind, or, more precisely, each of them assuming that the other is not blind? No, because their respective ignorance is not symmetrical: it is the people who have the answers, they just do not know the questions to which they have (or, rather, are) the answer. John Berger wrote about the "multitudes" of those who find themselves on the wrong side of the Wall (which divides those who are in from those who are out):

> The multitudes have answers to questions which have not yet been posed, and they have the capacity to outlive the walls. The questions are not yet asked because to do so requires words and concepts which ring true, and those currently being used to name events have been rendered meaningless: Democracy, Liberty, Productivity, etc. With new concepts the questions will soon be posed, for history involves precisely such a process of questioning. Soon? Within a generation.[79]

Claude Lévi-Strauss wrote that the prohibition of incest is not a question, an enigma, but an answer to a question that we do not know. We should treat the demands of the Wall Street protests in a similar way: intellectuals should not primarily take them as demands, questions, for which they should produce clear answers, programs about what to do. They are answers, and intellectuals should propose the questions to which they are answers. The situation is like

---

78 Martin Heidegger, "Why Do I Stay in the Provinces?" trans. Thomas Sheehan, in *Heidegger: The Man and the Thinker*, ed. Thomas Sheehan, Chicago: Precedent Publishing 1981, p. 29.

79 John Berger, "Afterword," in Andrey Platonov, *Soul and Other Stories*, New York: New York Review Books 2007, p. 317.

that in psychoanalysis, where the patient knows the answer (his symptoms are such answers) but does not know what they are the answers to, and the analyst has to formulate the questions. Only through such patient work will a program emerge.

Badiou has argued, in relation to Aristotle's principle of non-contradiction and the principle of the excluded middle, that there are three modes of negation.[80] Of the four logical possibilities, Badiou begins by dismissing the last one (negation which obeys neither principle) as "inconsistent," equivalent to the complete dissolution of all potency of negativity, so that three consistent forms remain, each of them fitting a certain logical framework: (1) negation obeys both principles—classical logic (Aristotle); (2) negation obeys the principle of contradiction, but not the excluded middle—intuitionist logic (Brouwer, Heyting); (3) negation obeys the excluded middle, but not the principle of contradiction—paraconsistent logic (the Brazilian school, da Costa). In classical logic, the negation of P excludes not only P itself, but any other possibility concerning the contents of the proposition P. In intuitionist logic, the negation of P excludes P itself, but not some other possibilities which are somewhere between P and non-P. In paraconsistent logic, the negation of P excludes that sort of space between P and non-P, but not P itself—P is not really suppressed by its negation (no wonder Badiou links this negation in which "P lies inside the negation of P" to Hegel's dialectic). For example, in the classical ethico-legal domain, someone is either guilty or innocent, with no zone in between; in the intuitionist space, we always have intermediate values, like "guilty with attenuating circumstances," "innocent because, while certainly guilty, there is insufficient proof," etc. In the paraconsistent space (not unfamiliar to certain theologies), one can be both at the same time, although there is no third option: my deep awareness of my guilt is the only proof I can have of my innocence, and so on.

As might be expected, Badiou's privileged example is that of revolution. The communist revolution is classical, a radical confrontation with no third option, either us or them: the poor worker who before the revolution appears as nothing in the political field, becomes the new hero of this field. In the intuitionist space of social-democratic reformism, the poor worker appears in the political field, but is in no way its new hero: the idea is to reach a compromise, to find a third way, to maintain capitalism, but with more social responsibility, and so forth. In the third case of paraconsistent space, we get a sort of undecidability between event and non-event: something happens, but, from the point of view of the world, everything is identical, so we have event and non-event simultaneously—a false event, a simulacrum, as in the fascist "revolution" which denounces "plutocratic exploitation" and maintains capitalism. As Badiou concludes: "The

80 See Alain Badiou, "The Three Negations," *Cardozo Law Review*, Vol. 29, No. 5 (April 2008), pp. 1877–83.

lesson is that, when the world is intuitionistic, a true change must be classical, and a false change paraconsistent."

But what if today's late-capitalist world is no longer intuitionistic? Is not "postmodern" capitalism an increasingly paraconsistent system in which, in a variety of modes, P is non-P: the order is its own transgression, capitalism can thrive under communist rule, and so on? Here, classical change no longer works, because the negation gets caught up in the game. The only remaining solution is thus to go with the fourth option (dismissed by Badiou, but which should be given a different reading). The first thing to remember is the radical asymmetry of the class struggle: the aim of the proletariat is not simply to negate (in whatever way) its enemy, the capitalists, but to negate (abolish) itself as a class. This is why we are dealing here with a "third way" (neither proletarian nor capitalist) which is not excluded, but also with a suspension of the principle of contradiction (it is the proletariat itself which strives to abolish itself, its condition).

What does this mean in terms of the libidinal economy? In a letter to Einstein, as well as in his *New Introductory Lectures to Psychoanalysis*, Freud proposed as a utopian solution for the deadlocks of humanity the "dictatorship of reason"—men should unite and together subordinate and master their irrational unconscious forces. The problem here, of course, lies with the very distinction between reason and the unconscious: on the one hand, the Freudian unconscious is "rational," discursive, having nothing to do with a reservoir of dark primitive instincts; on the other hand, reason is for Freud always close to "rationalization," to finding (false) reasons for a cause whose true nature is disavowed. The intersection between reason and drive is best signaled by the fact that Freud uses the same formulation for both: the voice of reason or of the drive is often silent, slow, but it persists forever. This intersection is our only hope.

The communist horizon is peopled by two millennia of failed radical-egalitarian rebellions from Spartacus onwards—yes, they were all lost causes, but, as G. K. Chesterton put it in his *What's Wrong with the World*, "the lost causes are exactly those which might have saved the world."[81]

81 G. K. Chesterton, *What's Wrong with the World*, London: Cassell 1910, p. 36.

Index